Eastern Europe

a Lonely Planet shoestring guide

David Stanley

Eastern Europe

3rd edition

Published by
  Lonely Planet Publications
  Head Office: PO Box 617, Hawthorn, Vic 3122, Australia
  Branches: 155 Filbert St, Suite 251, Oakland, CA 94607, USA
                10 Barley Mow Passage, Chiswick, London W4 4PH, UK
                71 bis rue de Cardinal Lemoine, 75005 Paris, France

Printed by
SNP Printing Pte Ltd., Singapore

Photographs by
Krzysztof Dydyński (KD), Steve Fallon (SF), Richard Nebeský (RN), Hungarian Tourist Board (HTB),
The Image Bank (TIM), International Photographic Library (IPL)

Front cover: High view of the old town square, Prague, the Czech Republic by David Hanson
(The Photo Library, Sydney)
Title page: Fishers' Bastion in the Castle District, Budapest, Hungary (Hungarian Tourist Board)

First Published
April 1989

This Edition
January 1995

**Although the authors and publisher have tried to make the information as
accurate as possible, they accept no responsibility for any loss, injury or
inconvenience sustained by any person using this book.**

National Library of Australia Cataloguing in Publication Data

Stanley, David
  Eastern Europe on a shoestring

  3rd ed.
  Includes index.
  ISBN 0 86442 246 6.

  1.Europe, Eastern – Description and travel – Guide-books.
  I. Title. (Series: Lonely Planet on a shoestring).

914.704

text & maps © Lonely Planet 1995
photos © photographers as indicated 1995
climate charts compiled from information supplied by Patrick J Tyson, © Patrick J Tyson, 1995

All rights reserved. No part of this publication may be reproduced, stored in a retrieval system or transmitted
in any form by any means, electronic, mechanical, photocopying, recording or otherwise, except brief extracts
for the purpose of review, without the written permission of the publisher and copyright owner.

David Stanley

A quarter century ago David Stanley's right thumb carried him out of Toronto, Canada, and on to a journey which has so far wound through 169 countries, including a three-year trip from Tokyo to Kabul. His travel guidebooks for the South Pacific, Micronesia and Eastern Europe opened those areas to budget travellers for the first time.

During the late 1960s Stanley got involved in Mexican culture by spending a year in several small towns near Guanajuato. Later he studied at the universities of Barcelona and Florence, before settling down to get an honours degree (with distinction) in Spanish literature from the University of Guelph, Canada. This landed him a job as a tour guide in Fidel Castro's Cuba and there Stanley developed an interest in 'socialist tourism'. Since then he's visited all the countries covered in this book many times.

Having had the rare opportunity to spend long periods in Eastern Europe researching this book in the years immediately before and after 1989, Stanley is a keen observer of the changes presently taking place. From his base in Amsterdam he makes frequent trips to Eastern Europe (jammed between journeys to the 85 countries worldwide he still hasn't visited). In travel writing Stanley has found a perfect outlet for his restless wanderlust. His zodiac sign is Virgo.

From the Author

The nationalities of those listed below are identified by the international automobile identification signs which follow their names:

A (Austria), AL (Albania), AUS (Australia), B (Belgium), BG (Bulgaria), CDN (Canada), ČR (Czech Republic), D (Germany), DK (Denmark), E (Spain), (GB) United Kingdom, H (Hungary), HR (Croatia), I (Italy), IL (Israel), IRL (Ireland), J (Japan), NL (Netherlands), NZ (New Zealand), PL (Poland), RO (Romania), S (Sweden), SF (Finland), SK (Slovakia), SLO (Slovenia), USA (United States of America), YU (Yugoslavia) and ZA (South Africa).

Special thanks to Sheldon Zelsman (CDN) for his thought-provoking observations

about Auschwitz, to Kristin Lister (D) and Jürgen Grotz (D) for a 25-page letter detailing their 80-day odyssey around the region, to Shirley Hudson (USA), Martin Fedorski (GB) and Chris & Kay Nellins (GB) for their extensive cycling notes, to Michael van Verk (NL) for six pages of precise information on Romania, to Mirjana Žilić (HR) of the Croatian National Tourism Office for convincing me to go back to Dubrovnik, to Tomaž Lovrenčič (SLO) for carefully checking all the Slovene spellings in that chapter, to Iztok Altbauer (SLO), Adrian Grigorescu (RO), Sandi Jejčič (SLO), Maria Krajnak/-Legulky (SK), Igor Nikolovski (USA), Lise Noemi (HR), Andrej Oštrbenk (SLO) and Nives Posavec (HR) for help in translating the vocabularies, to Jos Poelman of the Dutch STD Foundation, Box 9074, 3506 UK Utrecht (NL), for information on AIDS, to Musiques du Monde, Singel 281, Amsterdam (NL), for providing the dozens of CDs used to prepare the music sections and to Ria de Vos (NL) for her criticism, suggestions and support.

While out doing my field research I keep my identity to myself and of the dozens of Shoestring travellers I bumped into during my last six-month trip, the only one who connected me with this book was Russell Gripper of Concord West, Australia. For the record, no 'freebies' from hotels, restaurants, tour operators, airlines etc were solicited or received during the field research involved in the preparation of this book.

The following government officials and tourism workers took the trouble to reply to written enquiries from the author:

Fiona Anelay (GB), Lisa Arlt (USA), Gordon Bastin (GB), J H Beran (ČR), Mike Bugsgang (GB), Bonnie Jo Campbell (USA), N Dandolova (BG), Walter Danner (CDN), Gilbert Dingle (AUS), Alexander Duma (GB), Jana Erzetič (SLO), Jon Harbour (D), Attila Hetey (GB), Svilen Iliev (BG), George Janaček (ČR), Desanka Kocic (YU), Nena Komarica (HR), Rolf Kunze (D), Kathryn Kutrubes (USA), Silvija Letica (HR), John Lewis (CDN), Valerie Nagy (H), Rüdiger Pier (D), László Pordány (H), Prof Stjepan Puljiz (HR), Pavli Qesku (AL), Pavel Řehák (ČR), Alexandra Ruppeldtová (SK), Miroslav Sekel (SK), Jack Shulman (USA), Dan Sitaru (RO), Jože Stare (SLO), Tomas Stockel (SK), Robert Strauss (GB), András Szarvas (H), András Szilágyi (H), Vlado Tance (SLO), Hugo Verweij (NL), Jaroslava Votavová (ČR), Manuela Vulpe (RO), Bee Whilems (GB), Frank & Doreen Whitebrook (AUS), Ralph Wilczkowski (USA), Maria A Williamson (GB) and Callon Zukowski (ČR).

Thanks also to the many readers who wrote in with their suggestions and comments on the last edition. They are listed at the end of the book.

From the Publisher

This edition of *Eastern Europe* was edited in Melbourne, Australia by Frith Pike assisted by Sue Harvey and Ian Folletta.

Frith Pike and Sue Harvey with help from Adrienne Costanzo, Kristin Odijk and Ian Ward proofed the text.

The maps were drawn or updated by Marcel Gaston and Louise Keppie. Jane Hart designed the cover, and Marcel Gaston, the title page. Marcel was also responsible for layout.

Thanks to Glenn Beanland and Valerie Tellini for help with layout, to Dan Levin for creating the accented fonts and to Chris Lee Ack for his work with the fonts for the cartography.

Thanks also to Jim Jenkin who checked and keyed in the Cyrillic script and Richard Nebeský who helped proof the Czech Republic and Slovakia chapters.

Warning & Request

Things change – prices go up, schedules change, good places go bad and bad places go bankrupt – nothing stays the same. So if you find things better or worse, recently opened or long since closed, please write and tell us and help make the next edition better.

Your letters will be used to help update future editions and, where possible, important changes will also be included in a Stop Press section in reprints.

We greatly appreciate all information that is sent to us by travellers. Back at Lonely Planet we employ a hard-working readers' letters team to sort through the many letters we receive. The best ones will be rewarded with a free copy of the next edition or another Lonely Planet guide if you prefer. We give away lots of books, but, unfortunately, not every letter/postcard receives one.

Contents

Map Legend

BOUNDARIES

International Boundary
Provincial Boundary
Disputed Boundary

ROUTES

Freeway
Highway
Major Road
Unsealed Road or Track
City Road
City Street
Railway
Underground Railway
Tram
Walking Track
Ferry Route
Cable Car or Chairlift

AREA FEATURES

Park, Gardens
National Park
Forest
Built-Up Area
Pedestrian Mall
Market
Christian Cemetery
Non-Christian Cemetery
Beach or Desert

HYDROGRAPHIC FEATURES

Coastline
River, Creek
Intermittent River or Creek
Lake, Intermittent Lake
Canal
Swamp

SYMBOLS

✪ CAPITAL		National Capital
◉ Capital		Provincial Capital
CITY		Major City
● City		City
● Town		Town
● Village		Village
■		Hotel, Pension
▼		Restaurant
▼		Pub, Bar
✉	☎	Post Office, Telephone
❶	⑤	Tourist Information, Bank
●	P	Transport, Parking
🏛	⌂	Museum, Youth Hostel
⌖	▲	Caravan Park, Camping Ground
† ⊟ †		Church, Cathedral
⚚	✡	Mosque, Synagogue
⟂	⚕	Buddhist Temple, Hindu Temple

✚	★	Hospital, Police Station
✈	✝	Airport, Airfield
▱	✿	Swimming Pool, Gardens
❖	🐘	Shopping Centre, Zoo
←	A25	One Way Street, Route Number
	∴	Archaeological Site or Ruins
🛡	🏰	Castle, Stately Home or Palace
⚐	■	Monument, Tomb
◠	⌂	Cave, Hut or Chalet
▲	※	Mountain or Hill, Lookout
🛆	⊿	Lighthouse, Shipwreck
)(	⚲	Pass, Spring
		Ancient or City Wall
		Rapids, Waterfalls
		Cliff or Escarpment, Tunnel
		Railway Station
Ⓜ	Ⓤ	Underground Stations

Note: not all symbols displayed above appear in this book

Introduction

When the first edition of this book appeared in April 1989, Eastern Europe seemed solidly anchored behind the Iron Curtain. Seven months later the old regimes collapsed and in October 1990 East Germany ceased to exist. We scrambled to adapt the travelling information to the new realities and in December 1991 brought out a second edition. The following year Yugoslavia and Czechoslovakia split into seven states and once again much of the book has had to be rewritten. As this third edition goes into print most of the region seems stable enough, although a dreadful war is still raging in Bosnia-Hercegovina and unpredictable extremists are gaining ground in Russia.

We have received a letter from Mr László Pordány, the Ambassador of Hungary in Australia, urging us to stop calling the region Eastern Europe. According to Mr Pordány, 'Eastern Europe' is a misnomer which carries the stigma of over four decades of Soviet domination. He points out that prior to WW II the four northernmost countries (Poland, Czech Republic, Slovakia and Hungary) plus Austria, Germany and perhaps Switzerland, were part of a region traditionally known as Mitteleuropa, which translates into English rather poorly as 'central Europe'. Our problem lies in the fact that about half the book is devoted to the Balkan region which has never been considered part of Mitteleuropa.

Bad connotations aside, from the traveller's point of view the countries of 'Eastern Europe' still have a lot in common and basic things like restaurants, accommodation facilities, entertainment and public

13

Countries & Populations

Country	Area (sq km)	Capital	Country Population (Millions)	Capital Population
Albania	28,748	Tirana	3.0	250,000
Bosnia-Hercegovina	51,129	Sarajevo	5.0	500,000
Bulgaria	110,912	Sofia	9.0	1,250,000
Croatia	56,538	Zagreb	5.0	1,000,000
Czech Republic	78,864	Prague	10.0	1,500,000
Hungary	93,032	Budapest	10.0	2,000,000
Macedonia	25,713	Skopje	2.0	600,000
Poland	312,683	Warsaw	38.0	1,700,000
Romania	237,500	Bucharest	23.0	2,300,000
Slovakia	49,035	Bratislava	5.3	440,000
Slovenia	20,251	Ljubljana	2.0	330,000
Yugoslavia	102,173	Belgrade	11.0	1,500,000

transportation tend to work the same way throughout the region. In many cases, officialdom itself continues to reinforce the old divisions by requiring tourist visas of Australians, Canadians and New Zealanders (the British and US governments have been far more effective in having their citizens relieved of these annoying requirements). Canadians still need a visa for every country except Hungary and Slovenia, Australians for all but Slovenia and New Zealanders don't even get those small breaks.

Despite the bureaucratic hurdles, travelling in Eastern Europe is well worth the effort. From the Baltic to the Balkans a treasure-trove of history and natural beauty awaits you. Central Europe has been the source of much of our Western culture, especially in literature and music, and this volatile region has shaped world history. This century alone, both world wars began here and the 1989 democratic revolutions wrapped up the East-West Cold War. Apart from this legacy there are vast forests, rugged mountains, quiet lakes and mighty

rivers just waiting to be discovered. The many museums, churches and castles of Eastern Europe equal those of Western Europe in every respect, and prices in general are lower. You'll be amazed at the ease and convenience of travel.

All of the countries are fascinating in their diversity and to really understand the region you'll need to visit several of them. Don't spend all of your time in the capitals as you'll usually find it's much cheaper and less crowded in provincial towns. In this book we've converted all local prices into US dollars at the official bank rate in force at the time.

In some cases prices will have gone up but within individual chapters accommodation prices should remain relative to one another, so you'll soon be able to judge how much you'll need to spend. One thing is certain – travel in Eastern Europe will never be nicer than it is right now. The longer you put off your trip the larger the crowds of other Westerners will be and the more you'll have to pay. The time to go is now!

Facts about the Region

HISTORY

To put Eastern Europe's incredibly complex history into perspective it's useful to draw several lines across the map. The most important such line is the Danube River. The Danube formed the northern boundary of the Roman Empire for about 500 years, with an extension into Dacia (Romania) from 106 to 271 AD. When the empire was divided into eastern and western halves in 395, another line was drawn south from Aquincum (Budapest) to north Africa. Even today this line corresponds closely to the division between the Orthodox and Roman Catholic churches. The Western Roman Empire collapsed in 476 but Byzantium survived until the fall of Constantinople to the Turks in 1453.

The period of the migrating peoples changed the ethnic character of Eastern Europe. Long before Rome the Slavs had lived north of the Carpathian Mountains from the Vistula to the Dnieper rivers. To the west were the Celts and later the Germans. Beginning in the 6th century, the Slavic tribes moved south of the Carpathian Mountains and by the 9th century had occupied everything east of a line running from Berlin to the Adriatic. In the south they expanded as far as Greece. The Daco-Roman population of present Romania proved numerous enough to absorb the newcomers. In Albania the original Illyrian inhabitants also survived. The Slavs became peaceful farmers who lived in democratically governed communities.

In 896 the Magyars (Hungarians) swept in from the east and occupied the Danube Basin. Hungarian horsemen spread terror throughout Europe with raids as far as the Pyrenees but, after they were defeated by the Germans at Augsburg in 955, the tribes accepted Christianity, and on Christmas Day of the year 1000 Stephen (István) I was crowned king. The Hungarians carved out a great empire in central Europe which extended south to Belgrade and east across Transylvania. In 1018 they annexed Slovakia and in 1102 they acquired Croatia.

Around the millennium most of the peoples of Eastern Europe accepted Christianity. Feudal states began to form in Bohemia, Bulgaria, Croatia, Hungary, Lithuania, Poland and Serbia. After the Tatar invasion of 1241, many cities were fortified.

Saxon communities in Slovakia and Transylvania date from the 13th century when Germans were invited into Hungary and Poland to form a buffer against fresh Tatar attacks from the east. The continuous German *Drang nach Osten* (drive to the east) which began at this time was slowed by the defeat of the Teutonic Knights by a combined Polish-Lithuanian army at Grunwald in 1410. In 1701 Berlin became capital of Prussia and a renewed eastward expansion under Frederick the Great culminated in the complete partition of Poland by 1795. Only in 1945 was this process temporarily reversed.

Turkish expansion into Europe was made easier by rivalry between the Catholic (Austria, Hungary, Venice) and Orthodox (Bulgaria, Byzantium, Serbia) states. The defeat of Serbia at the Battle of Kosovo in 1389 opened the floodgates of the Balkans. The Hungarians managed to halt the Turkish advance temporarily at Belgrade in 1456, but in 1526 they were defeated at the Battle of Mohács. The Turks spread as far north as the southern foothills of the Carpathians, drawing another line across the map of Europe. In 1529 they unsuccessfully laid siege to Vienna and in 1532 were stopped again at Kőszeg. Hungary remained under Ottoman rule until the defeat of the second Turkish siege of Vienna in 1683. A combined Christian army liberated Buda in 1686 and by 1699 the Turks had been driven from all of Hungary.

After the fall of Hungary to the Turks, the Austrian Habsburg dynasty assumed the thrones of Hungary, Bohemia and Croatia. In

1620 the Catholic Habsburgs tightened their grip on Bohemia, and then expanded into Hungary and the Balkans in the wake of the declining Ottoman Empire. From 1703 to 1711 Hungarians led by the Transylvanian duke Ferenc Rákóczi II fought an unsuccessful war of independence against the Habsburgs. During the 18th and 19th centuries the Habsburgs controlled a vast empire from Prague to Belgrade and east into Transylvania. In 1867 Austria and Hungary agreed to share control of the region through a dual Austro-Hungarian monarchy.

Poland was wiped off the map of Europe by the partitions of 1722, 1793 and 1795. Prussia and Russia took most of Poland for themselves, with Austria receiving a small slice in the south. It's not hard to understand why the Poles sided with Napoleon whose entry into Eastern Europe in 1806 marked the beginning of the transition from feudal autocracy to modern, bourgeois capitalism. Napoleon's final defeat in 1815 allowed the Prussians and Habsburgs to reimpose their rule but in 1848 there were unsuccessful liberal-democratic revolutions throughout central Europe against the prevailing absolutism.

In the Balkans the uprisings and wars against Ottoman oppression continued into the 20th century. In 1876 the Bulgarians rose against the Turks, leading to the Russo-Turkish War of 1877 and Bulgarian autonomy in 1878. Bulgarian independence followed in 1908. Romania and Serbia declared complete independence from the Turks in 1878 and the Habsburgs occupied Bosnia-Hercegovina that same year, annexing it outright in 1908. Macedonia and Albania remained under Turkey until the First Balkan War (1912). After the Second Balkan War (1913), Serbia and Greece divided Macedonia between themselves. Bulgarian dissatisfaction with this result led to further fighting during both world wars.

In 1914 Habsburg and tsarist imperial ambitions clashed in the Balkans and all of Europe was drawn into a catastrophic war. By November 1918, war weariness led to the collapse of the autocracies in Russia, Austria-Hungary, Bulgaria and Germany as sailors mutinied and troops abandoned the fronts. The end of WW I saw the restoration of Poland and the creation of Czechoslovakia and Yugoslavia. Although the new borders were supposed to follow ethnic boundaries, Northern and Western Bohemia went to Czechoslovakia despite the largely German population. Similarly, the Hungarians of Slovakia, Transylvania and Vojvodina; the Albanians of Kosovo; and the Ukrainians of south-east Poland all became homogeneous majorities in foreign countries next to their motherland. This situation contributed to the outbreak of WW II.

After 1933 Eastern Europe suffered under constant Nazi aggression backed by threats and violence. In September 1938, Britain and France sold out Czechoslovakia at the Munich Conference, ending the possibility of any effective military resistance to the Nazis in the east. Bulgaria, Hungary and Romania soon fell in line behind Germany. Uncertain of Western backing after Munich, the Soviet Union signed a nonaggression pact with Germany on 23 August 1939 to buy time. When Poland resisted Hitler's demands it was promptly invaded, touching off WW II. Yugoslavia and the USSR had a similar fate in 1941.

Hitler's programme of military expansion led to the destruction of Germany. In February 1943 the German 6th Army capitulated at Stalingrad, and by May 1945 the Soviet army had captured Berlin. At the 1943 Teheran Conference, Churchill had proposed a second front from the Middle East through the Balkans to forestall a Soviet advance into Europe, but this was rejected and the 1944 Anglo-American landings were in France. At the Yalta Conference in February 1945, Churchill, Roosevelt and Stalin agreed on 'spheres of influence' in Europe. The Potsdam Conference of August 1945 divided Germany and Berlin into four occupation zones. The borders of Poland and the USSR moved west and those Germans who had not already fled East Prussia, Pomerania and Silesia were deported.

A Dubrovnik – past and future, Croatia, (Robert Everts – IPL)
B Zachariáše z Hradce, Telč, Czech Republic, (RN)
C Drawbridge and Barbican at Siklós Castle, Hungary, (SF)
D Thurzov Dom, Levoča, Slovakia, (RN)

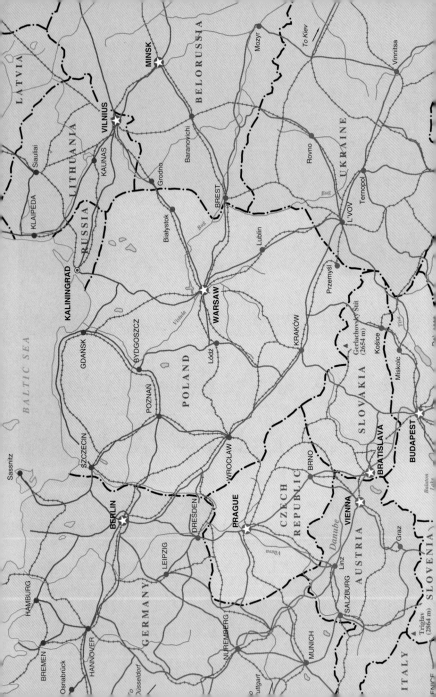

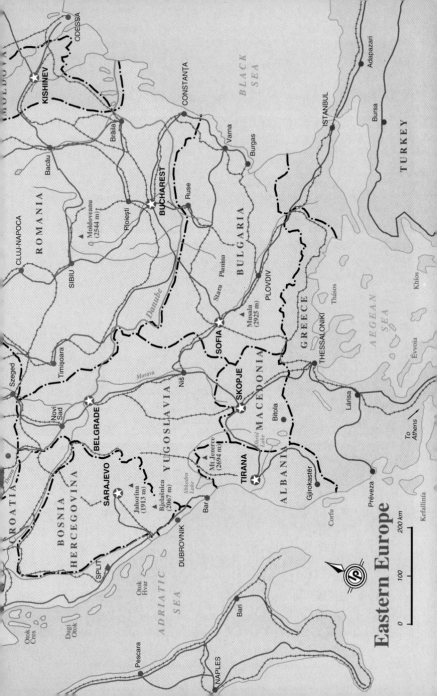

Eastern Europe

Top: Chain Bridge and the Royal Palace by night, Budapest, Hungary, (HTB)
Middle: Stone Bridge and river, Mostar, Bosnia Hercegovina, before it was shelled
into oblivion, (Jon Davison – TIM)
Bottom: The Old Town Square, Warsaw, Poland, (KD)

Post WW II

With the arrival of Soviet troops in Bulgaria, East Germany, Hungary and Romania, communist-led governments took over from Nazi or monarcho-fascist regimes. Communist partisans took control in Yugoslavia and Albania. Czechoslovakia continued as a democratic coalition until the Communist Party took full control during a political crisis in March 1948. The events in Czechoslovakia set off a chain reaction as the frustrated Western allies decided it was time to consolidate the areas under their control against further communist advances. In June 1948, a new currency linked to the US dollar was introduced into the three western sectors of Berlin, allegedly to facilitate postwar reconstruction.

This created a tremendous problem for communist officials in East Germany where nationalisation of the economy was not yet complete. Rather than face an uncontrollable black market which would have bled them white, the Soviet army closed the surface transit routes from West Germany to West Berlin a few days later. The air routes remained open and for 11 months the 'Berlin Airlift' supplied the western zones of the city. This crisis may be seen as the beginning of the 'Cold War'.

The lines were drawn even more clearly when NATO formed in April 1949. The Federal Republic of Germany was created in September, the German Democratic Republic in October. The Council for Mutual Economic Aid (Comecon), the dominant economic planning body in Eastern Europe until 1990, was also created in 1949. The Warsaw Pact was not signed until May 1955, when West Germany was admitted to NATO. Only after the 1975 Helsinki Conference on Security & Cooperation in Europe (CSCE), at which 35 governments accepted the status quo in Europe, did tensions begin to relax.

Between 1945 and 1989, the communist governments throughout Eastern Europe emphasised heavy industry, central planning and social justice. Agriculture was collectivised in all of the countries except Poland and Yugoslavia. Yet there were wide variations in approach and in later years Bulgaria, Czechoslovakia, East Germany and Hungary attained respectable levels of development, while the inhabitants of Poland, Romania and the USSR suffered prolonged hardship. Well before the 1989 communist breakdown, there were popular upheavals in East Germany (1953), Hungary (1956), Czechoslovakia (1968), Poland (1956, 1970, 1976, 1981) and Romania (1987), but these were suppressed by military force.

By the late 1980s the Soviet Union had fallen far behind the West in economic and technological development, and in practice had ceased to be a superpower. In effect, Soviet leader Mikhail Gorbachev abandoned the postwar system of 'spheres of influence' and adopted a policy of nonintervention towards Eastern Europe. Thus local communist governments could no longer count on Soviet military support to remain in power. The first crack in the Eastern bloc appeared in Poland in April 1989, when the communist regime agreed to legalise Solidarity and allow partially free elections. The Solidarity election victory in June 1989 and the appointment of non-communist Tadeusz Mazowiecki as prime minister in August were unprecedented events watched all across Eastern Europe.

Changes were also taking place in Hungary, which began dismantling its border controls with Austria in May 1989 and opened its borders in September. In October the Hungarian communists relinquished their monopoly on power.

Yet the event which really signalled the end of Eastern European communism was the crumbling of the Berlin Wall on 9 November 1989. East Germans had begun flowing to the West through Hungary at the rate of 5000 a week in the summer of 1989. When the Soviet Union failed to order Hungary to halt the flow, antigovernment demonstrations began in Leipzig in September and these grew until hardliner Erich Honecker was forced to resign as East Germany's leader on 9 October. After a demonstration in East Berlin on 5 November attended by one million people, the communists dramatically opened the Wall. On 1 July 1990 the two Germanys formed an economic union and on 3 October the country was formally reunited.

The fall of the Wall had sudden repercussions in Czechoslovakia where student demonstrations began on 17 November 1989 culminating in the resignation of the communist government 10 days later.

On 10 November 1989 hardliner Todor Zhivkov, who had headed the Bulgarian government for the previous 35 years, was sacked. Besides the opening of the Berlin Wall, the political event which captured world attention most dramatically was the violent overthrow of the Ceauşescu regime in Romania in December 1989, complete with the execution of Nicolai and Elena Ceauşescu by firing squad.

The final act was played out in the Soviet Union itself. After an abortive military coup by communist hardliners in August 1991, the three Baltic states quickly declared their independence and in December the USSR was transformed into a 'Commonwealth of Independent States' dominated by the Russian Federation.

These events seemed to demonstrate that state socialism had run its course. The booming prosperity of Western Europe made the collapse of uncompetitive Eastern Europe almost inevitable as economic paralysis led Eastern European consumers to revolt. The communist system had worked fine for rebuilding heavy industry after WW II, but technologically the region was falling far behind and being economically marginalised. Without the two essential ingredients of a modern society – parliamentary democracy and a market economy – further progress would have been difficult.

The fall of communism was also a result of the arms race. With their stable economies, strong national currencies and high rate of economic growth, Western countries were able to increase military expenditures and modernise their forces at a rate the communist countries could only match by curtailing consumer production. In his

December 1991 farewell address, Mikhail Gorbachev said:

This country was suffocating in the shackles of the bureaucratic command system. Doomed to cater to ideology, and suffer and carry the onerous burden of the arms race, it found itself at the breaking point ... the mad militarisation of the country crippled our economy, public attitudes and morals.

In February 1991 the Warsaw Pact was disbanded, yet NATO remained intact, and in 1993 it extended its influence eastward by offering the ex-Warsaw Pact countries a cooperative arrangement called 'Partnership for Peace' which included no security guarantees.

The crumbling of the totalitarian regimes gave rise to a resurgence of narrow nationalism right across the region, leading to the breakup of Czechoslovakia and Yugoslavia. In 1985 Serbian ideologues formulated the concept of a 'Greater Serbia' which was to assert its authority in post-Tito Yugoslavia. When Serbia unilaterally scrapped the autonomy of Kosovo Province in 1989 the other republics of Yugoslavia became alarmed and in 1990 non-communist governments were elected in Croatia and Slovenia. These republics declared their independence in 1991 leading to a civil war in Croatia which only ended with the arrival of United Nations peacekeepers. In 1992 the European Community (now called the European Union) bowed to German pressure and hastily recognised Croatia, Slovenia and Bosnia-Hercegovina, thereby contributing to the eruption of a new war as Serbia and later Croatia snatched territory from the elected Bosnian government. At the start of 1993 Czechoslovakia split peacefully into Slovakia and the Czech Republic.

Right across Eastern Europe, ethnic intolerance continues to be exploited by politicians short on economic solutions. Hungary is still haunted by the loss of two-thirds of its territory and half its population after WW I. The nationalist disease is manifested in the official rehabilitation of wartime fascist leaders such as Hungary's

Miklós Horthy, Romania's Ion Antonescu, Slovakia's Jozef Tiso and Croatia's Ante Pavelić. Poland's prewar dictator, Marshall Józef Piłsudski, is lionised by President Wałęsa. A clutch of pretenders are manoeuvring behind the scenes to reclaim the royal thrones of Albania, Bulgaria, Romania and Serbia.

It's now clear that the crowds which brought about the 1989 revolutions had an unrealistic idea of life in the West. Economic restructuring and the abrupt curtailing of trade within the former Soviet bloc have led to big drops in industrial output and gross domestic products, budget deficits, mass unemployment and declining living standards for large segments of the populations. Agricultural productivity has declined by 10% to 40% while corruption and crime have increased. In countries where the government attempted to solve these problems by printing money, high inflation has impoverished millions of people. Social benefits like guaranteed employment, nurseries, free education and medical care have been slashed, and the positions of women and national minorities made worse.

The frustration and disillusionment was expressed at the ballot box as the former communists were returned to power through free elections in Lithuania in 1992, Poland in 1993 and Ukraine and Hungary in 1994. In almost all of the other countries of Eastern Europe the former communists are the second-largest political party (in Romania and Yugoslavia the old communist establishments retained power by posing as nationalists). Yet today's socialists are quite a different breed from yesterday's communists and only the pace of economic change is in question.

Machiavelli's words in *The Prince*, sum up the Eastern European dilemma thus:

There is nothing more difficult to execute, nor more dubious of success, nor more dangerous to administer than to introduce a new order of things; for he who introduces it has all those who profit from the old order as his enemies, and he has only lukewarm allies in all those who might profit from the new.

That Gorbachev's efforts to democratise communism turned into a movement to dismantle it should not have come as such a surprise. Alexis de Tocqueville once wrote that the most dangerous time for a bad government is the moment when it attempts to reform itself. The irreversible changes of 1989 have set in motion a process of reform which will continue for many years.

For all its rhetoric, the Cold War was mostly a sham which produced profits in the West and stability in the East. Now that this phoney war has finally collapsed, new regional conflicts have erupted and these will be far more difficult to control than the predictable superpower confrontations of yesteryear. The big winner will probably be reunited Germany which has quickly moved in to fill the economic vacuum left by the USSR's demise. What has really ended is a long hangover from WW II. Eastern Europe is being remade and the opportunity to see the process in motion makes this an exciting area to visit.

GEOGRAPHY

The pivotal mountain range of central Europe is the Carpathian Mountains, which swing round from Romania into Slovakia. There's excellent hiking in this range, especially in Romania's Făgăraş Mountains and the Tatra Mountains of Slovakia and Poland. The Balkan Mountains are shared by Albania, Bosnia-Hercegovina, Bulgaria, Croatia, Greece, Macedonia and Yugoslavia. Musala Peak (2925 metres) in Bulgaria's Rila Massif is the highest in Eastern Europe. North-west of Ljubljana, Slovenia, are the Julian Alps.

One of the scenic highlights of Eastern Europe is the Dalmatian Coast of Croatia. Here the mountains dip into the Adriatic to form a broken coastline with countless islands of Grecian beauty. The best beaches in the region are those along the Black Sea in Bulgaria and Romania. The Baltic coast of Poland has a beauty all of its own. The most popular lake in Eastern Europe is Hungary's Balaton Lake.

Another great geographical feature of

Eastern Europe is the Danube River, the second-largest river in Europe after the Volga. Napoleon called the Danube the 'king of the rivers of Europe'. The 2850-km-long Danube flows through nine countries, past four capitals – 1075 km of this is in Romania. To see the Danube at its best, tour the Danube Bend in Hungary or Romania's Danube Delta. The greatest river north of the Carpathians is Poland's Vistula, which passes through Kraków, Warsaw and Toruń.

Taken together, the 12 countries covered in this book total an area of 1,166,650 sq km, a bit less than the Canadian province of Quebec. Poland and Romania are by far the largest countries, while Slovenia, Macedonia and Albania are the smallest.

PEOPLE

While Western Europe is dominated by five large nations, Eastern Europe is fragmented into over a dozen nationalities. The Slavs – by far the most numerous ethnic group in Eastern Europe – are divided into three distinct groups: the West Slavs (Czechs, Poles, Slovaks and Sorbs), the South Slavs (Bulgarians, Croats, Macedonians, Montenegrins, Serbs and Slovenes) and the East Slavs (Belorussians, Russians and Ukrainians). The Albanians, Gypsies, Hungarians and Romanians are non-Slavic groups.

Only the Czech Republic, Hungary, Poland and Slovenia have largely homogeneous populations. The largest minority groups are the Albanians of Yugoslavia and Macedonia; the Greeks of Albania; the Hungarians of Romania, Yugoslavia and Slovakia; the Serbs of Croatia and Bosnia-Hercegovina and the Turks of Bulgaria. The Bulgarians claim that the Macedonians are Bulgarians.

In the 14th century the Jews were expelled from most of Western Europe and many settled in Poland, Romania and Russia where they continued to speak a German dialect called Yiddish. Here they suffered a long persecution which was only attenuated by the Bolshevik Revolution in Russia and Western pressure for minority rights in Poland, Romania and elsewhere after WW I.

Before WW II Jews accounted for a third of the population of Warsaw but the Holocaust and subsequent migration to Israel decimated Jewish communities throughout Europe and today Hungary's 80,000-member Jewish community is the largest in Eastern Europe.

The Gypsies

The English term 'Gypsy' reflects an early belief that these people came from Egypt, though it is now known that they originated in northern India. Gypsies themselves refer to their community as Rom and their language as Romany. Their westward migration began before the 10th century, and by the 14th century some groups had reached the Balkans and soon after, Central Europe. A second wave of westward Gypsy migration began in 1855, after the Romanian Gypsies were freed from serfdom by the Moldavian prince Grigore Ghica. Half a million Gypsies died in Nazi death camps during WW II (an oft-forgotten fact).

About half of Europe's eight million Gypsies live in Eastern Europe, including some two million in Romania, 550,000 in Bulgaria, 250,000 in Hungary, 170,000 in Yugoslavia, 150,000 in Croatia, 115,000 in the Czech Republic, 80,000 in Slovakia, 45,000 in Macedonia, 15,000 in Poland and 10,000 in Albania. (Some of these figures are only estimates as Gypsies frequently fail to declare themselves as such at censuses.)

Without a homeland of their own and largely unrepresented in government, the Gypsies have suffered worsening living conditions, mass unemployment and official harassment since 1989. Statistically, Gypsy families are twice the size of non-Gypsy families, and are a form of collective social security common in the Third World. Unfortunately, the Gypsies are often subjected to blanket condemnation based on racial stereotypes by people who would be shocked if they heard other racial or religious groups referred to in the same terms.

ECONOMY

Until 1990 the economic activities of Eastern

Europe and the USSR were coordinated by the Council for Mutual Economic Aid (CMEA or Comecon), founded in 1949. The concept was that each country would specialise in producing whatever suited it best, though in practice the Soviet Union provided Eastern Europe with raw materials such as oil, natural gas, iron ore, cotton, timber and mineral ores, receiving manufactured goods like machinery, textiles and footwear in return.

Long-term contracts were intended to make economic planning easier, but the lack of competition and 40 years of trade focused on supplying the Soviet Union left Eastern Europe with outdated industries uncompetitive on world markets. Trade within the group was originally conducted in 'accounting roubles', but this proved unworkable as large debts piled up and in its final decade nearly all Comecon trade was done on a barter basis. The crash of the administrative command systems in 1989 made the 'coordination of economic plans' obsolete and in 1991 Comecon was formally dissolved. Since January 1991 all regional trade has been conducted in hard currency and, by 1992, 75% of Eastern European trade was with the West. For most of the countries Germany is the largest Western trading partner and Germany's *Osthandel* (eastern trade) goes back several decades, often predating diplomatic links.

Since 1989 two circles of development have emerged in Eastern Europe. The inner circle includes Poland, the Czech Republic, Slovakia, Hungary and Slovenia, all of which are on the fast track to closer ties with Western Europe. In February 1991 Poland, Hungary and what was then Czechoslovakia established the Visegrád group to coordinate policy towards international organisations such as the EC (now the EU), NATO, the IMF and the GATT. In December 1992 the Visegrád countries signed a free trade agreement which aims at economic integration by the year 2000, although agriculture is not covered by the agreement. Further south, the Alpen-Adria grouping facilitates cooperation between Bavaria, Austria, Hungary,

Croatia, Slovenia and adjacent regions of Italy. In Poland and Hungary private companies now account for 40% of overall production and in 1992 Poland became the first country in the region since 1989 to show a small increase in industrial production.

In contrast the Balkan states of Albania, Bulgaria, Croatia, Macedonia, Romania and Yugoslavia face a variety of problems, and their favourable position between the wealthy Middle East and Western Europe has yet to be exploited. Huge economic losses have resulted from the upheaval in ex-Yugoslavia and development is hampered by large military expenditures. The hundreds of planes and thousands of tanks absorb a much higher percentage of the gross national product of these countries than is the case in the West. Triple-digit inflation has become a way of life in Albania, Croatia, Romania and Yugoslavia.

European Union membership seems out of the question for even the relatively advanced Central European countries before the year 2000, and even in Hungary, Poland and the Czech Republic living standards won't approach those of the West for a decade or more. In 1989 and early 1990 there was talk of a 'new Marshall Plan' for Eastern Europe, but with West German attention diverted towards East Germany and the USA absorbed in the Gulf War, interest declined and Western aid and investment have been rather meagre. Certainly nothing compared to the equivalent of US$400 billion made available to Western Europe in the late 1940s under the Marshall Plan has been offered. Hungary has attracted the most Western investment, followed by the Czech Republic and Poland.

Purchasing power on the domestic markets remains low and economic recovery can only be generated by exports. Yet Western Europe has kept its doors closed to Eastern Europe's most exportable products, especially steel, chemicals, textiles and agricultural produce (which together comprise 40% of exports to the EU). In December 1991 Hungary, Poland and former Czechoslovakia signed 'Europe Agreements' with the European Community and in 1993 Bulgaria and Romania followed. These arrangements provide for free trade within 10 years. The Eastern countries can maintain tariffs on Western industrial goods for 10 years while Western tariffs on 'sensitive' Eastern imports may stay in place for five or six years. Sudden surges of imports can be restricted and Eastern agricultural exports may only increase by 10% a year. When Eastern European steel exports to the EC jumped sharply in 1992, the restrictions were quickly imposed. Farm lobbies in the West have fought tooth and nail against food imports from the East.

Yet since 1991 the European Union has had a trade surplus with virtually every Eastern European country and the Easterners have said repeatedly that all they want is the chance to profit from their lower production costs through free trade. As is too often the case in aid programmes, the Western loans and technical advice are mostly self-serving and do things for people instead of letting them do things for themselves. (A parallel exists in Bosnia-Hercegovina where Western relief supplies have tended to feed the combatants and keep the war going, while all requests from the elected Bosnian government to be allowed to purchase arms to defend itself have been denied.)

Eastern European environmental problems, especially acid rain from the burning of sulphurous brown coal, call for urgent attention. (A forest affected by acid rain is recognisable by the bent tops of the coniferous trees.) The region comprising Saxony in eastern Germany, Polish Silesia and northern Bohemia and Moravia in the Czech Republic – one of the most polluted areas in Europe – has been dubbed the 'triangle of death'. Raw sewage and untreated industrial wastes are dumped in major rivers like the Vistula and the Danube.

In 1992 there were six nuclear power plants with 24 reactors based on discredited Soviet technology in operation in Hungary, Bulgaria and former Czechoslovakia. Construction of further nuclear facilities has been halted in Poland, but the huge VVER-1000 reactor at Temelín in the Czech Republic has been completed despite Austrian objections that it is unsafe. The four-reactor VVER-440 plants at Kozloduj, Bulgaria, and Paks, Hungary, each supply nearly half the electricity of those countries. Kozloduj is considered the most dangerous nuclear power plant outside the former Soviet Union. Thus far Western governments have provided lots of advice on how to improve safety at these plants but little practical help.

The privatisation of state assets and foreign investment should spark an economic revival in the long run, but meanwhile the vast majority of workers earning the equivalent of from US$100 to US$200 a month are having difficulty making ends meet, and the huge apartment-block complexes of Eastern Europe may yet become havens for drug dealing and crime.

As the economies contract and excess workers become redundant, women were often the first to be laid off and the last to be hired. In Poland they account for 60% of the unemployed and even those with jobs earn an average of 25% less than men doing the same work. Government child care which was once free has been scrapped. Linked to this are campaigns to make abortion illegal and put women back in the home. Women returning from maternity leave no longer automatically get their jobs back. On the positive side, things like sanitary napkins, tampons, Western cosmetics and the latest fashions are now more readily available.

Many Eastern Europeans have sought fast personal solutions through emigration to Western Europe, especially from the poorer areas like Albania, Romania, ex-Yugoslavia and the former USSR. In 1989 some 1.3 million Easterners moved West – the greatest population shift since WW II – and it has been estimated that over the next decade another 10 million people will leave Eastern Europe and the former Soviet Union. The overriding aim of Western aid to the ex-communist states is to foster economic and political stability, thereby helping to avoid the unleashing of this flood of economic refugees and minimising the danger of extremist elements taking power in their homelands. Some of the parallels between Central Europe in the early 1930s and Eastern Europe in the 1990s are frightening.

RELIGION

Tempered by decades of official disfavour and occasional outright persecution, organised religion in the East is generally a more influential factor in both public and private lives than it is in the materialistic West. Catholicism is the main religion in the Czech Republic, Slovakia, Hungary, Poland, Croatia and Slovenia. There are large Protestant minorities in Hungary and Romania. Muslims constitute a majority in Albania and Bosnia-Hercegovina.

In 1054 the pope excommunicated the Church of Constantinople and all Orthodox churches which refused to accept papal infallibility. Nowadays the Orthodox faith is prevalent in Bulgaria, Romania, Macedonia and Yugoslavia with patriarchs in Belgrade, Bucharest and Sofia, and metropolitans in Prague and Warsaw. There have been many attempts to reunify the Orthodox and Roman Catholic churches. Orthodox churches that have accepted papal supremacy while retaining the Orthodox Eastern rite are known as Uniates or Greek Catholics.

On Sunday it's well worth taking the opportunity to attend the religious services of a faith unfamiliar to you (something you'd probably never think of doing at home). However, do try to have a little patience and see the service through to the end.

LANGUAGE

German is probably the best international language to know. It's widely understood by the older people in the Czech Republic and Hungary. It's also helpful along the Adriatic and Black Sea coasts, where German tourists prevail, and in Poland. If you know French, Italian or Spanish you won't understand spoken Romanian, but you'll pick up isolated words and the meaning of simple texts.

Russian was taught in the schools after 1945, but since 1989 English has been far more common and there's always someone

at major hotels and travel agencies who knows it. Many students and young professionals speak good English and are often happy to have the chance to talk to Western visitors. In the past French was widely taught in Bulgaria, Romania and Serbia.

It's always easier to make yourself understood if you write your message down using numbers instead of words. For instance, when buying tickets, write down the time according to the 24-hour clock and use a Roman numeral for the month when writing the date. If you want to know about reservations, write down a large capital 'R' with a box around it and a question mark. To ascertain a price, repeat the name of the local currency in a questioning way (złoty? forint? etc), offering a pen and paper on which your informant can write the answer. A surprising amount of information can be communicated in this way, if you're imaginative.

Twelve major languages are spoken in the countries covered in this book. Nine of these (Bulgarian, Croatian, Czech, Macedonian, Polish, Serbian, Slovak, Slovene and Sorbian) are Slavic languages. These languages are closely related in grammar and vocabulary and if you pick up a few words in one language you'll be surprised how the corresponding phrases in the others are almost identical. The other major languages you'll encounter are Albanian, Hungarian and Romanian.

In this book we provide basic vocabularies translated into most of these languages. For far more extensive coverage of Bulgarian, Czech, Hungarian, Polish and Romanian than is possible herein pick up Lonely Planet's *Eastern Europe Phrasebook*. Albanian, Croatian, Macedonian, Serbian and Slovene are covered in their *Mediterranean Europe Phrasebook*. These handy little books include pronunciation guides in addition to the standard translations.

The large number of languages in Eastern Europe can be confusing and using the wrong words in the wrong countries doesn't help. As you're travelling between two countries it would help to copy out the words for thank you, hello and goodbye from our vocabulary sections and repeat them over and over as you travel to prepare yourself for the change.

In 863 the Greek missionaries Sts Cyril and Methodius created the Cyrillic alphabet that is used in Bulgaria, Macedonia, Yugoslavia and the former Soviet Union. Cyrillic script was used in Romania until the mid-19th century. Cyril and Methodius worked among the Slavs of Great Moravia in the territory of the present Czech Republic and Slovakia. After their death their disciples were forced out of Great Moravia by a

German bishop and the Latin liturgy was reimposed. At Ohrid in what was then Bulgaria (present Macedonia) their disciple Clement founded the first Slavic university in 893. The Slavs have a tremendous respect for the Cyrillic alphabet which helped them resist cultural assimilation by dominant neighbours and renders their languages more precisely (notice how many accents must be used when a Slavic language is written in Latin characters). It only takes a few hours to learn this alphabet, so make the effort if you're visiting these countries.

Facts for the Visitor

PLANNING

When, How Much & How Long?

Spring (from April to mid-June) is the best time to visit Eastern Europe as the days are long, the weather good, the theatres open, off-season rates in effect and the locals not yet jaded by waves of summertime visitors. The only drawback is that school outings often occur during this period, and being crowded into a hostel or train with a bunch of noisy preteens is no fun. Summer (from mid-June to early September) is the ideal time for hiking and camping, the peak season for budget travellers and just about everyone else. September can be an excellent month with autumn colours on the trees, fruit and vegetables plentiful, low-season tariffs coming back into effect and the tourist masses returned home. You can still swim in the southern Adriatic in September, but in October the camping grounds close down and the days become shorter. From October to March it can be rather cold and dark with smog from coal-burning furnaces, though this is the peak theatre and concert season in the cities.

This book is designed for the independent budget traveller who intends to stay at economy hotels, youth hostels or in private rooms; take lunch at self-services and dinner at moderate full-service restaurants; go to a concert or disco a couple of nights a week; sightsee independently on foot or by public transport and travel 2nd class by train or bus. With a little care it should be possible to do all that on under US$30 a day in most of these countries. Two people travelling together can save about 35% on accommodation costs, and tent campers will spend even less.

To cover all of the areas described in this book you'll need at least three weeks each for Poland and Romania, two weeks each for Albania, Bulgaria, Croatia, the Czech Republic, Hungary, Slovakia and Yugoslavia, and a week apiece for Slovenia and Macedonia. Of course, not everyone has almost six months for holidays, so you'll have to pick and choose. Try to avoid hopping from capital to capital.

What to Bring

Bring an internal-frame backpack which converts into a canvas suitcase by zipping the straps into the back. Big external-frame backpacks are fine for mountain climbing but don't fit into coin lockers and are a real nuisance on public transport. A day pack or shoulder bag will also be required. A neck pouch or money belt worn under your clothing is the safest way to carry money and documents (never pack such things in your luggage). If you want to camp you'll need a tent and sleeping bag, otherwise forget the tent and you won't really need the sleeping bag either. Clothing which can be added in layers according to the climate is much better than a bulky coat.

Bring photos of your home, family, place of employment etc, as conversation pieces. Shaving cream, tampons and condoms may be of poor quality or unavailable in Eastern Europe and you should also bring your own toilet paper. A rubber sink plug and a pocket calculator with clock and alarm functions will come in handy, and a small pocket compass can prove invaluable in orienting yourself when you first arrive in a town. Campers especially should bring along insect repellent. A personal notebook in which to record tips from other travellers is always handy.

While there's no problem bringing in the type of personal effects most people travel with, be aware that antiques, books printed before 1945, crystal glass, gemstones, lottery tickets, philatelic stamps, precious metals (gold, silver, platinum), securities and valuable works of art must sometimes be declared in writing. To bring a video camera or personal computer into some countries, you may need the original purchase receipt.

Don't carry letters or parcels on behalf of third parties. Entry with banknotes of any Eastern European country may also be restricted. Throughout the region customs checks are pretty cursory these days and you probably won't even have to open your bags, just be aware of the restrictions.

Appearances & Conduct

Though high heels and ties won't be required, Eastern Europeans are more conservative dressers than North Americans. You'll usually be admitted to 1st-class restaurants, opera houses, concert halls, discos, hotel bars and the like even in jeans, but you'll feel more comfortable if you dress up a little. Shorts or miniskirts are not the best attire for visiting churches.

Although Eastern Europeans routinely shake hands, a man should wait for the woman to extend her hand first. In polite greetings use the person's title (Professor, Doctor etc) before the surname. People only address friends, relatives and those much younger than themselves by their first names.

If you're invited for dinner at a local home take flowers for the hostess (but not red roses which have romantic implications) and a bottle of wine or brandy for the host. As most people get up early to go to work, evening visits usually end by 11 pm. In most of Europe people hold the knife in the right hand, the fork in the left, and keep both hands above the table during the meal.

The Top 10

According to the author the 10 highlights of Eastern Europe are:

• Budapest, Hungary
• Dalmatian coast, Croatia
• Diocletian's Palace, Split, Croatia
• Dubrovnik city walls, Croatia
• Rila Mountains, Bulgaria
• Rynek Główny, Kraków, Poland
• Sighişoara, Romania
• High Tatra Mountains, Poland/Slovakia
• Veliko Târnovo, Bulgaria
• Zamość, Poland

The Bottom 10

The author rates these as the 10 worst attractions of the region:

• Banja Luka, Bosnia-Hercegovina
• Hunedoara steel mill, Romania
• Kozloduj nuclear power plant, Bulgaria
• McDonald's Restaurant, Warsaw, Poland
• metallurgical combine, Elbasan, Albania
• National Museum of History, Sofia, Bulgaria
• Postojna Caves, Slovenia
• Prague, Czech Republic, in the tourist season
• Siófok, Hungary
• U Fleků Beer Hall, Prague, Czech Republic

The World Heritage List

UNESCO keeps a list of 'cultural and natural treasures of the world's heritage' including these in Eastern Europe:

Albania
• Butrint ruins
Bulgaria
• Boyana Church near Sofia
• Ivanovo rock-hewn churches near Ruse
• Kazanlâk Thracian Tomb
• Madara Horseman
• Nesebâr (old city)
• Pirin National Park
• Rila Monastery
• Srebarna Nature Reserve
• Thracian Tomb of Svechtari
Croatia
• Dubrovnik (old city)
• Plitvice Lakes National Park
• Split (historic centre with Diocletian Palace)
Czech Republic
• Český Krumlov (historic centre)
• Prague (historic centre)
• Telč (historic centre)
Hungary
• Budapest (banks of the Danube with the district of Buda Castle)
• Hollókő (traditional village)
Macedonia
• Ohrid and its lake
Poland
• Auschwitz Concentration Camp
• Belovezhskaya Puscha
• Bialowieza National Park
• Kraków (historic centre)
• Warsaw (historic centre)
• Wieliczka salt mines near Kraków
• Zamość (old city)

Romania
- Biertan fortified church
- Bukovina painted churches
- Danube Delta
- Horezu Monastery

Slovakia
- Banská Štiavnica medieval mining centre
- Spišský hrad
- Vlkolinec folk village near Ružomberok

Slovenia
- Škocjan Caves

Yugoslavia
- Durmitor National Park
- Kotor and its gulf
- Stari Ras and Sopoćani
- Studenica Monastery

VISAS

Romania still requires a visa of everyone, but UK and US passport holders now have visa-free status in most other Eastern European countries. Australians require visas for every country except Slovenia. Canadians aren't much better off with a visa necessary everywhere except in Hungary and Slovenia. New Zealanders have to apply for a visa for every single country. Albania pretends that many nationals don't require a tourist visa but charges an 'entry tax' equivalent to the visa fee of everyone at the border.

Separate visas are required for the Czech Republic and Slovakia. Of the five former Yugoslav states, Slovenia has abolished visas for most Westerners (except New Zealanders), but most English speakers other than the British still need visas for Croatia, Macedonia and Yugoslavia. All three countries issue tourist visas free of charge. A Canadian passport is one of the worst to have in Eastern Europe as several countries such as the Czech Republic, Poland, Slovakia and Albania charge Canadians punitive US$50 visa fees in retaliation for the fees their nationals must pay to visit Canada (the CDN$50 tourist visa fee implemented by the Canadian Ministry of Immigration in April 1991 has led to a sharp devaluation in the value of the Canadian passport world-wide).

Visas are usually issued immediately by consulates in Eastern Europe, although Bulgarian and Polish consulates levy a 50% to 100% surcharge for prompt 'express visa service'. Otherwise Bulgarian consulates make you wait seven working days for your tourist visa. Bulgarian visas are also available at the border but at about double the usual price. Those nationals requiring a Czech Republic, Hungarian, Polish, Slovakian or Yugoslav visa are strongly advised to get it at a consulate and not to rely on it being available at the border (you could be kicked off the bus or train). Albanian, Croatian and Macedonian visas, on the other hand, are usually easily obtainable at the border and visiting one of their consulates is usually a waste of time as they aren't set up to issue visas and will just tell you to get it at the border. Romanian visas are available at both embassies and at the border for about the same price, but it's usually better to get your Romanian visa in advance.

Consulates are generally open weekday mornings (if there's both an embassy and a consulate, you want the consulate). Consulates in countries not next to the one you want to visit are far less crowded (for example, get your Polish visa in Bucharest, your Hungarian visa in Sofia or Warsaw, your Slovakian visa in Zagreb etc). Take your own pen with you and be sure to have a good supply of passport photos which actually look like you.

You can also apply for a visa from a consulate in your home country by registered mail, though this takes about two weeks unless you request 'express' service for an additional fee. First you must write for an application form enclosing a stamped, self-addressed envelope.

In the USA you can obtain your visas for an additional fee of US$32 per visa on top of the consular and mailing fees through Visa Services (☎ 202-387 0300 or 800-222 8472), 1519 Connecticut Ave North-West, Suite 300, Washington DC 20036. The same type of service is offered in Canada by the International Travel Document Service or 'Intervisa' (☎ 613-235 5580), 323 Somerset East, Ottawa, Ontario K1N 6W4. Intervisa publishes a visa manual which clearly states the current visa requirements of Canadian,

Visa Requirements					
Country	USA	Australia	NZ	UK	Canada
Albania (1) (2)	none	required	required	none	none
Bulgaria (3)	none	required	required	required	required
Croatia (2)	required	required	required	none	required
Czech Republic	none	required	required	none	required
Hungary	none	required	required	none	none
Macedonia (2)	required	required	required	none	required
Poland	none	required	required	none	required
Romania (2)	required	required	required	required	required
Slovakia	none	required	required	none	required
Slovenia (2)	none	none	required	none	none
Yugoslavia	required	required	required	required	required

(1) An 'entry tax' equivalent to a visa fee is collected from everyone at the border.
(2) Issued at the border for the usual price (if any)
(3) Issued at the border for double price

US and British nationals for 135 countries. The CDN$165 cost includes a one-year subscription for their monthly update and a 10% discount on their visa service charge (CDN$20 for tourist visas).

Visa fees (US$10 to US$50 per entry) must be paid in cash hard currency (no travellers' cheques). Most countries will issue double-entry visas upon request for double the normal fee. Visas may be used any time within three to six months from the date of issue and you're usually allowed to spend a month in a country.

Decide in advance if it's a tourist or transit visa you want. Transit visas are often cheaper and issued sooner, but it's usually not possible to extend a transit visa or change it to a tourist visa.

The visa form may instruct you to report to police within 48 hours of arrival. If you're staying at a hotel or other official accommodation (camping ground, youth hostel, private room arranged by a travel agency etc) this will be taken care of for you by the travel agency or the hotel or camping-ground reception. In Bulgaria reception staff at the hotel or camping ground will stamp the back of your 'statistical card' to prove that you were registered, and immigration will look at the stamps as you're leaving the country.

If too many nights are unaccounted for, you could have some explaining to do. If you're staying with friends or in a private room arranged on the street, you're supposed to register with the police. During the communist era these regulations were strictly enforced but things are pretty casual these days.

You're required to have your passport with you at all times and you'll have to show it when checking into hotels, changing travellers' cheques, leaving baggage at a left-luggage office etc. If you stay 30 days or less in a country you don't need to apply for an exit permit but if you're staying for a longer period ask about this at a tourist office. If you lose your passport or visa and are issued with a replacement, then you *do* have to apply to the police for an exit permit before you will be permitted to leave the country. The authority issuing your new passport will be able to advise you on the procedure.

For a visa extension, ask a tourist information office how to go about it. You'll probably have to report to the police in person. Office hours are short and the lines long, so don't leave it till the last minute. Try to avoid this inconvenience by asking for enough time when you collect your visa in the first place.

The chart shows which nationalities require visas in Eastern Europe.

Consulates in Greece

Greece is a major southern gateway to the region and most of the Eastern European consulates are in the suburb of Paleo Psihiko, north-east of central Athens. Get there on bus No 603 from Akadimias St. Paleo Psihiko has a confusing network of circular streets and the bus drivers don't speak English, so have someone write out the address you want in Greek. Get off at Psihiko Town Hall for the Bulgarian Consulate, 33 Stratigou Kalari St (open weekdays from 10 am to noon), and the Romanian Consulate, 7 Em Benaki St (open Monday and Wednesday from 4.30 to 6.30 pm; Tuesday, Thursday and Friday from 10 am to noon). Ask directions.

For the Hungarian Consulate, 16 Kalvou St (open weekdays from 9 am to noon), stay on bus No 603 to the corner of Diamandidou and Kalvou streets. The Slovak Consulate, 6 Georgiu Seferis St (open weekdays from 9 to 11 am), is near the Hungarian one; the Polish Consulate, 22 Chryssanthemon St (open weekdays from 8.30 to 11.30 am except Wednesday 11 am to 7 pm) is five blocks west of these.

The Yugoslav Consulate is at 106 Vassilissis Sofias (open weekdays from 8.30 to 11 am) between Paleo Psihiko and downtown Athens.

There is also a Bulgarian Consulate-General at Nikolau Manou 12, Thessaloniki.

The Former Soviet Union

Russia and Ukraine are still caught in the grip of post-communist bureaucrats who demand an invitation or hotel vouchers as a condition for visiting their countries. The hotel vouchers are intended to perpetuate state monopolies like Intourist and force you to stay in expensive government-owned hotels, thereby effectively eliminating private operators from the tourist accommodation business. As in China, it's sometimes possible to get around the regulations, but this takes persistence and a lot of ingenuity.

Some Ukrainian embassies are more pliable than others, so start checking early. When available, one-month Ukrainian visas are about US$50 at consulates, or US$30 with a seven-day wait. At the Ukrainian border all you'll get is a 72-hour transit visa for US$50.

The Russian Federation will only issue a tourist visa to those showing accommodation prepaid at US$50/90 single/double a night and up. Tourist visas may take from five to 10 working days to issue and cost about US$60 each (the exact amount varies according to nationality). Transit visas are usually obtainable the same day if you have through transportation tickets with reservations. At last report there were no border controls between Belorussia and Russia.

Visas for Moldova and the Baltic states are now being issued promptly and Lithuanian visas are also valid for Latvia and Estonia. For more information turn to the consulate listings in the Warsaw and Bucharest sections of this book.

The visa situation in these countries is changing fast and the only way to be sure is to go to a consulate and ask. Get there early in the day as the queues can be horrendous. For anyone wanting to visit the former Soviet Union on the cheap, Poland is the best gateway country as it has land borders with Russia, Lithuania, Belorussia and Ukraine, allowing you the chance to pick another country. Hungary is the worst gateway as the Ukrainian Embassy in Budapest is demanding and train fares from Hungary are high.

Western Embassies

A reciprocal agreement signed in 1986 between Australia and Canada extends consular services to nationals of the other country when only one of the two is represented. In Eastern Europe this benefits Australians who have the right to treat Canada's embassies in Bucharest and Prague as their own. Australia and Canada both have consulates or embassies in Belgrade, Budapest, Warsaw and Zagreb, but neither country is represented in Bratislava, Ljubljana, Skopje, Sofia and Tirana. In Bratislava, Ljubljana and Sofia, Canadians and Australians can request assistance at the British Embassy, something New Zealanders must do throughout Eastern Europe. The only countries where the UK doesn't have a consulate or embassy are Albania and Macedonia, although a British Chargé d'Affaires works out of the French Embassy in Tirana. In Skopje all English speakers must turn to the American Centar for emergency assistance and advice. The USA is represented everywhere.

DOCUMENTS

The only document you'll need is a passport that is valid for at least six months beyond your departure date. You can pick up most required visas upon arrival in Europe but have about 10 passport-size photos ready when you apply. For security, carry a photocopy of your passport identification page, driving licence, credit cards, purchase receipts for travellers' cheques, camera identification number, airline tickets, train pass etc, in a secure place separate from the originals and leave another copy at home.

A Hostelling International (HI) or Youth Hostel Association (YHA) membership card could save you money in several Eastern European countries. If you're a student bring along a current International Student Identity Card (ISIC) or purchase one at a student travel agency the first chance you get (proof of student status is required). Nonstudents under 26 years of age can obtain a Youth International Educational Exchange (YIEE) card from most offices issuing the ISIC and receive many of the same reductions. If you're a member of an automobile club, bring along your membership card (or a 'Card of Introduction') as this could entitle you to breakdown service, maps and legal advice from sister clubs in Eastern Europe at reduced rates.

MONEY

Deutschmarks (DM) and US dollars are the currencies of choice in Eastern Europe. Bring half your money in US dollars or Deutschmarks *in cash* and the rest in American Express travellers' cheques in a variety of denominations. It's worth having plenty of small-denomination banknotes as it's often difficult to make up change in hard currency. However, don't bring dollar banknotes with any writing or rubber stamp marks on them, or that are damaged or badly worn, as these will often be handed back.

Almost everywhere in Eastern Europe cash is preferred to travellers' cheques. Banks usually charge from 1% to 2% commission to change travellers' cheques (from 3% to 5% in Bulgaria and Romania) and they're open during limited hours. In this book we recommend the most efficient banks of each country. In Poland and Bulgaria you may have to search a long time to find a bank accepting travellers' cheques. As long as United Nations sanctions remain in effect against Yugoslavia, travellers' cheques cannot be cashed there (this doesn't apply to Croatia, Macedonia and Slovenia where cheques are fine).

Private exchange offices in Poland, Romania, Bulgaria, Slovenia and Albania change cash at excellent rates without commission. Not only are their rates a few per cent higher than those offered by the banks for travellers' cheques but they stay open much longer hours, occasionally even 24 hours a day. Take care in the Czech Republic, Slovakia and Hungary, however, as some private exchange offices deduct exorbitant commissions of up to 10%. Before signing a travellers' cheque or handing over any cash always check the commission and rate. Some exchange offices in Budapest and Prague employ trickery to cheat tourists by advertising high rates on large boards without specifying clearly that these are the selling rates. Other times you only get the advertised rate if you change large amounts such as US$2250, or perhaps a hidden commission is extra. Don't be taken in.

American Express and Thomas Cook offices cash their own travellers' cheques without commission but both give rates lower than banks. (A cheeky little sign posted at American Express offices reads: 'There's no reason for it: *it's just our policy*'.) If you're changing over US$20, you're often better off going to a bank and paying the standard 1% to 2% commission to change there (except in Prague where American Express and Thomas Cook pay good rates for travellers' cheques).

American Express now has full-service offices in Budapest, Prague, Warsaw, Moscow and St Petersburg, joining the well-established American Express facilities in Athens, Berlin and Vienna. Elsewhere American Express is represented by leading travel agencies and it's this level of service which has led us to recommend them above other companies. Thomas Cook is not at all as fast with refunds for lost cheques and other travellers' cheque companies may only be represented by some inefficient state bank. American Express offices will break large American Express travellers' cheques down into smaller denominations at no charge (don't believe them if they try to convince you that it's not in your best interests to do so).

Of course, the main advantage of travellers' cheques is that they're insured against loss or theft. Keep a running list of which cheques you've cashed in case the remaining cheques are stolen and you have to make a claim. To report stolen American Express travellers' cheques, ring 44-273-571 600 in England reverse charges from anywhere in Eastern Europe (if you can't call reverse charges, quickly give your number and ask them to call you right back). We've tried to give the addresses of American Express offices and representatives wherever they exist, and you can also go directly to them if one happens to be nearby. To report stolen Thomas Cook travellers' cheques, dial 44-733-502 995 or go to a Hertz Rent-a-Car office. Officially, you're required to report stolen or lost travellers' cheques to the issuing company with 24 hours to be entitled to a prompt refund.

Carrying large amounts of cash on your person is always risky, so you'll have to weigh the advantages of the greater convenience of cash against the greater security of cheques. If you decide to go with cash you'll probably have to bring it with you from home as banks and American Express offices in Eastern Europe charge from 6% to 15% commission to convert dollar travellers' cheques into dollars cash, if they will do it at all. Only in Poland and Slovenia is it possible to swap cheques for cash without losing a bundle.

You're going to need Western cash to pay for visas at consulates, and international transportation tickets must sometimes be paid in cash hard currency. Occasionally hotel bills and sightseeing tours must be paid directly in hard currency; some hotels and car rental agencies give discounts to those paying with cash US dollars or Deutschmarks. Banknotes of US$5 and US$10 can be used to pay for almost anything when you first arrive in a country and they're also handy should you temporarily run out of local currency.

As yet, none of the Eastern European currencies is freely convertible on world markets and it's usually difficult to change excess local currency back into dollars or marks before you leave. Only in Poland is currency trading really free with private exchange offices (kantors) changing cash back and forth without restrictions. Because local currency can't be changed back, you'll have to calculate carefully how much you really think you'll need and spend anything you have left over on something portable like chocolate bars just prior to departure. If you happen to run out on a weekend or in the evening you can often change money at the luxury hotels, but check the rate. Some of the countries have a standard official rate you receive wherever you change and travel agencies are sometimes faster and more efficient than the banks, though their commission is often higher.

Reader George Von der Muhll of Santa Cruz, California, sent us this:

In most countries we found that only one local bank could cash travellers' cheques, and then often at *poor* rates during limited hours. Regrettably, cash – greenback dollars – should not be treated as an emergency reserve but rather as the basic medium of exchange, to be supplemented on occasion by a reserve of travellers' cheques. Since, surprisingly, the same seems increasingly true in Germany and Austria (where local banks sometimes charge 10% commissions), travellers' cheques, despite the security they bring, look increasingly like an obsolete medium.

Black Market

The days when you could get five times the official rate for cash on the street in Poland and Romania are probably gone for good. A 'black market' exists whenever a government puts restrictions on free currency trading through regulations which prohibit banks and licensed foreign exchange dealers from changing the national currency into Western hard currency. A black market is eliminated overnight when a currency is made internally convertible, but as yet only Poland has had the political will to do this (some governments claim their currencies are convertible, but you soon discover otherwise when you try to change excess local currency back into dollars).

These days the most you'll get on the black market is 25% above the official rate and usually you're lucky to get 5% or 10%. Changing money on the street is extremely risky in the Czech Republic, Slovakia, Hungary, Romania and Bulgaria as many of the people offering to change are professional thieves with years of experience in cheating tourists. In Croatia, Yugoslavia, Macedonia and Albania, on the other hand, changing money on the street is routine with little or no danger involved.

If you decide to use the black market, hang onto your cash until you have the offered money in your hand, then count it one more time before putting it in your pocket. If during an exchange the marketeer takes the local currency back from you after you've counted it, break off contact immediately as a rip-off is definitely intended. In that circumstance, the money you have counted will disappear in a sleight-of-hand trick and you'll end up with a packet of newsprint, smaller bills or counterfeit bills produced on a colour photocopy machine. You only have to be ripped off once in this way to cancel all your earnings on four or five illegal exchanges.

Never change with two men together. If a second man appears while you're negotiating, split. Beware of anyone wearing a jogging suit as they're probably dressed that way to avoid suspicion as they run away. Don't be pressured into changing more than you originally intended. Thieves will always insist that you change a large amount – one way of recognising them. Know what the local currency looks like and don't be in a hurry. Black marketeers play on your greed and fear. These days the police are not interested, so if someone starts shouting that the police are coming (as a diversion) it means that you have just been ripped off. Beware of receiving obsolete Polish or Yugoslav currency.

The import and export of most Eastern European currencies is prohibited and customs officers will occasionally ask if you have any local currency as you're leaving, and anything worth over a couple of dollars may be confiscated. Customs checks are pretty lax these days and if you simply say you don't have any local currency (if asked) the officers probably won't pursue the matter. Keep in mind, however, that the Eastern European currencies are almost worthless outside the region and it's usually impossible to reconvert soft currency into hard currency. Only change what you need, and go on a spending spree on your last few days if there's anything left.

Tipping

Throughout Eastern Europe you tip by rounding up restaurant bills, taxi fares etc to the next even figure as you're paying. In some countries restaurants will already have added a service charge to your bill, so you needn't round it up much. Throughout the region 10% is quite sufficient if you feel you have been well attended. The waiters in any establishment which caters mostly to foreign tourists will expect such a tip. If you're dissatisfied with the food or service, or feel you have been overcharged, you can convey the message by paying the exact amount. If 'rounding up' means you're only giving honest waiters a couple of cents, add a few more coins to keep them happy. Never leave tips on restaurant tables as this is not the custom anywhere – the waiter will just assume you don't intend to tip and someone else may pocket the coins.

Restaurant cloakroom and public toilet attendants may expect a small tip unless a standard fee is posted. Coins worth the equivalent of US$0.10 in the empty plate on the counter should be do the trick. Unconventional tips such as Western banknotes will sometimes have more impact than their equivalent value in local currency but in general, do as you would at home, and don't over tip.

ELECTRICITY

In all of Eastern Europe the electric current is 220 V AC, 50 Hz. North American 120-V appliances will require a voltage converter and even then, 60-cycle electrical devices such as clocks and timers will not operate properly. Everywhere in Eastern Europe the electrical plugs are circular with two round prongs. Appliances with any other type of plug will need a plug adapter. The availability of electric outlets depends on the category of the accommodation.

POST & TELECOMMUNICATIONS

If you wish to receive mail you can have it sent care of poste restante (general delivery) or American Express. If you're using poste restante, tell your correspondents to put the number 1 after the city name to ensure that the letter goes to the main post office in that city. You should also have them underline your last name, as letters are often misfiled under first names. We provide the full addresses of poste restante offices in capital cities in the chapter introductions under the heading Receiving Mail. These offices seldom hold letters longer than one month (often just 15 days) and some, such as those in ex-Yugoslavia, charge a small fee for each letter picked up.

American Express offices and representatives will hold 'clients' mail' and telegrams which you can pick up at no charge provided you have an American Express credit card

(without the card you may be charged US$2 per letter). We also provide these addresses in the chapter introductions. American Express will forward mail for a flat fee of about US$5, but what they won't do is accept parcels, registered letters, notices for registered letters, answer telephone enquiries about mail or hold mail longer than 30 days. In general, they're safer and more efficient than poste restante.

Some Western consulates will hold letters (but not parcels) for their nationals, but you ought to check this at a passport office before leaving home as it varies from country to country. Pick up a current list of the addresses of your country's diplomatic missions while you're there. The US Embassy in Prague has written to us advising that any letters arriving in their mail room addressed to persons not on their staff will be returned to sender.

When deciding on your mail pick-up points, don't choose too many or you'll sacrifice the flexibility of being able to change your plans after arrival. Try to pick a central location you'll be transiting several times during office hours. A good plan is to provide your correspondents with a complete list of all possible addresses before you set out, then inform them which addresses to use as you're going along.

To send a parcel from Eastern Europe you sometimes have to take it (unwrapped) to a main post office. Parcels weighing over two kg must often be taken to a special customs post office. Have the paper, string and tape ready. They'll usually ask to see your passport and note the number on the form. If you don't have a return address within the country just put your name care of any large tourist hotel to satisfy them.

In some countries air mail isn't that much more expensive than surface mail, if so be sure to use it. Occasionally you'll have to pay duty in hard currency on souvenirs mailed from the country, but once a parcel is accepted it will probably reach its destination.

Postage is cheap in Poland, the Czech Republic, Slovakia, Romania and Bulgaria, so mail lots of postcards from these countries.

Telephone

Telephone service ranges from good in Hungary, Bulgaria and all the ex-Yugoslav states, to average in the Czech Republic, Slovakia and Albania, and poor in Poland and Romania. Throughout the region, telephone centres are generally in the same building as the main post office. Here you can often dial your own call from one of the booths inside an enclosed area, paying the cashier as you leave. Public telephones are almost always found at post offices and telephone cards are becoming increasingly popular everywhere except Romania and Albania.

Phone calls made from hotel rooms are subject to heavy surcharges. Ask your hotel receptionist if it's possible to call reverse charges which is usually much cheaper.

To place an international call you must dial your international access code (varies from country to country), the country code, the area or city code without the initial zero and the number. To make a domestic call to another city in the same country dial the area code with the initial zero and the number. Area codes for individual cities are provided in the chapter introductions. The regional country codes are 36 (Hungary), 40 (Romania), 42 (Czech Republic and Slovakia), 48 (Poland), 355 (Albania) and 359 (Bulgaria). Until recently all five ex-Yugoslav states used country code 38, but on 1 November 1993 this was changed to 381 (Yugoslavia), 385 (Croatia), 386 (Slovenia), 387 (Bosnia-Hercegovina) and 389 (Macedonia).

TIME

Most of the places covered in this book are on Central European Time (GMT/UTC plus one hour), the same time used from Spain to Poland. Romania, Bulgaria and Greece are on East European Time (GMT/UTC plus two hours). If it's 6 pm in Warsaw and Madrid, it will be 7 pm in Bucharest and Sofia, 8 pm in Moscow, 5 pm in London, noon in New York, 9 am in California and 3 am the next morning in Melbourne, Australia.

Daylight-saving time runs from April to September (clocks everywhere are turned an hour forward during these months). If you're travelling in Eastern Europe at this time, you'll get a bonus hour of daylight every afternoon! Just make sure you don't get caught out with timetables on the 'changeover' Sunday.

BOOKS
Background Reading

Eastern Europe and Communist Rule by J F Brown (Duke University Press, Durham, UK, 1988) is a readable political history of Eastern Europe's four decades of communism with special attention to the 1970s and 1980s. Published just prior to the collapse of communism, Brown's book presents a unique picture of a disappeared world unclouded by current revisionism. A more recent book by the same author is *Surge to Freedom: The End of Communist Rule in Eastern Europe*.

Lighting the Night: Revolution in Eastern Europe by William Echikson is a fast-moving account of the events of 1989 which puts things nicely in perspective – highly recommended. *Newsweek* correspondent Andrew Nagorski's *The Birth of Freedom* also captures the essence of post-1989 Eastern Europe. For a more scholarly account, see *Revolutions in Eastern Europe* edited by Roger East (Pinter Publishers, London, UK).

In *The Fall of Yugoslavia: The Third Balkans War* BBC correspondent Misha Glenny unravels the enigma of a conflict which has brought many of the moral premises of Western society into question. Christopher Cviic's *Remaking the Balkans* (Pinter Publishers, London, UK) provides concise background on current trends in Romania, Bulgaria, ex-Yugoslavia and Albania.

The June 1991 issue of *National Geographic* magazine has an excellent article on environmental problems in Eastern Europe.

Angus Fraser's *The Gypsies* (Blackwell,

UK, 1992) is a useful history of this people up to 1989.

The Central & East European Publishing Project (☎ 01865-31 0793), St Antony's College Annexe, Belsyre Court, 57 Woodstock Rd, Oxford OX2 6HQ, England, UK is a charitable foundation which assists Eastern European publishers and supports and promotes translation of works by Eastern European authors. Books in English published with the CEEPP's help include *Politics in Hungary* by János Kis, *The Days of the Consuls* by Ivo Andrić, *The Hour of Sand* by Ana Blandiana and *My Childhood at the Gate of Unrest* by Paul Goma.

Travel Books

Among the most intriguing travel books on Eastern Europe are *A Time of Gifts* (Penguin Books, 1979) and *Between the Woods and the Water* (Penguin Books, 1987) by Patrick Leigh Fermor. In December 1933 Fermor set out on a year-and-a-half walk from Holland to Turkey on a budget of £1 a week. The first volume covers the stretch from Rotterdam to the Danube, the second Hungary and Romania. Though the style of travel Fermor describes is possible today only in a few Third World countries where life remains simple, his books would make wonderful companions for anyone curious enough to retrace his steps.

In *Balkan Ghosts* Robert D Kaplan offers a contemporary traveller's view of a region torn by ethnic strife and economic upheaval. His book could well be read in tandem with Rebecca West's 1937 classic Balkan travelogue *Black Lamb and Grey Falcon*.

Brian Hall's enjoyable *Stealing from a Deep Place: Travels in South-Eastern Europe* details a bicycle trip through Hungary, Romania and Bulgaria prior to the fall of communism. Hall offers many insights, seen through the eyes of a budget traveller.

Guidebooks

Lonely Planet publishes 'travel survival kits' to many individual European countries and these provide far greater detail on much wider areas than is possible in 'on a shoestring' guides such as this. Even if you already have a shoestring guide, it's still worth picking up the travel survival kit if you'll be spending a long time in a particular area.

If you're the sort of person who travels with two guidebooks, however, you're probably better off having books from different publishers. In Eastern Europe 'brand X' is the series of country guides appearing under the name *The Rough Guide* in the UK and *The Real Guide* in the USA. Written in a lively contemporary style with lots of interesting background material, they're excellent.

The classic series of guidebooks to the individual Eastern European countries is *Nagel's Encyclopedia-Guides*, published in Switzerland (Nagel Publishers, 7 rue de l'Orangerie, CH-1211 Geneva 7, Switzerland) in English, French and German editions. Although these books provide good history and description, there's very little practical information and they're expensive and hard to find.

Jim Haynes takes quite a different approach in his *People to People* guides which provide the names and addresses of hundreds of individuals all across Eastern Europe who are interested in meeting foreign travellers, showing them around and even providing places to stay. These books, published by Canongate Press, Edinburgh, Scotland, UK and Zephyr Press, Boston, USA are a great help in making local contacts.

Schedules for the main Eastern European train and ferry routes are given in the monthly *Thomas Cook Continental Timetable*. Thomas Cook travel agencies often sell single copies, and you'll find yourself referring to the Eastern Europe pages constantly. At most large train stations in Germany you can pick up an *Auslandskursbuch* for only DM10 which provides railway timetables for all European countries plus Morocco.

Volume one of *Budget Accommodation* published by Hostelling International (HI), formerly known as the International Youth Hostel Federation (IYHF), lists official youth hostels in all of the Eastern European countries except Albania and Romania.

The Bartholomew *World Travel Map, Eastern Europe* (1:2,500,000) is very useful for getting an overview of the area (the author has had a copy on his desk ever since he first started work on this book in 1986). Indexed city maps can be purchased in large cities but keep in mind that maps published before 1991 will have obsolete street names.

Periodicals

Business Central Europe (25 St James's St, London SW1A 1HG, England, UK) is a monthly magazine put out by *The Economist*. At US$45 a year, it's good value. Also specialising in Eastern Europe is *Business Europa* (21 Gold St, Saffron Walden, Essex CB10 1EJ, England, UK), published every two months (US$30 a year to Europe, US$45 to North America).

For more detailed coverage of Poland, the Czech Republic, Slovakia and Hungary there's the *Central European Business Weekly* (Vinohradská 93, 12000 Prague 2, Czech Republic). To receive an airmailed copy each week for six months send US$87 if you live in Europe, US$115 elsewhere. It's also sold at major newsstands in all four countries.

One of the best sources of news about Romania, Bulgaria, ex-Yugoslavia and Albania is the weekly *Balkan News International* (4 Avevra St, Papagos, 15669 Athens, Greece). Airmailed annual subscriptions are DM400 in Europe, US$350 elsewhere. An annoying aspect of this paper is their use of the term FYROM (Former Yugoslav Republic of Macedonia) for Macedonia and their apologetic coverage of present Yugoslavia.

Both Budapest and Prague have excellent weekly newspapers in English and these are described in the respective chapters.

Recordings

One of the largest producers of compact discs of Eastern European music is Hannibal Records (Box 2401, London W2 5SF, England, UK and Box 667, Rocky Hill, NJ 08553, USA). Well known artists appearing on Hannibal include Trio Bulgarka, Muzsikás, Vujicsics, Ivo Papasov, Yanka Rupkina and Márta Sebestyén.

HEALTH

Eastern Europe is a fairly healthy place to travel around. The tap water is usually safe to drink although standards do vary, so it's always best to ask advice locally (especially in Poland and Romania). If you decide not to drink tap water, then you shouldn't use ice cubes either as even luxury hotels often make their ice from tap water. In these cases also avoid leafy vegetables which will have been washed in tap water, and take care with raw or undercooked eggs which can cause intestinal illnesses.

Air pollution is worst in winter when coal is universally used for heating, but heavy cigarette smoking is a more immediate nuisance and nonsmokers can expect to receive little or no consideration. Eastern Europeans are among the heaviest cigarette smokers in the world and the big US tobacco companies have moved in quickly to profit from this weakness.

No vaccinations are required unless you arrive directly from an infected area outside Europe. An injection of gamma globulin against infectious hepatitis A spread by contaminated food or water is probably the best shot to get, but wait until you're just about to leave as the protection period is only six months. Some authorities recommend vaccination against typhoid (also spread by food and water) but this would only be necessary if you planned a long stay and really intended to rough it.

In emergencies you should resort to the casualty ward of any large general hospital. Finding the right hospital can sometimes take time, so in cases of real urgency you should have someone call an ambulance. Hospital emergency departments in Eastern Europe can cope with most medical problems and the fees they ask are usually a lot less than a foreigner would pay in any Western country. Most hospital doctors are eager to practise their English and will be very helpful, though in many cases the facilities are overcrowded.

Private medical practice is still far less common here than it is in the West but if you do manage to find a private doctor able to communicate you'll receive faster, more personalised attention than you would at a hospital. Embassies, tourist information offices and receptionists in luxury hotels can often supply the name of an English-speaking doctor or dentist.

If your problem isn't so serious try asking for advice at a pharmacy (chemist). Locally produced drugs and medicines are inexpensive and there's often someone there who understands a little English, German or at least sign language. Drug stores also sell multivitamins (ask for the 'forte' variety), bottled medicinal water and even herbal tea. For diarrhoea get charcoal tablets (generic name: *carbo activatus)* such as Norit. Western brand names are expensive in the East, so bring along any medicines you cannot do without, including something for headaches, common colds and an upset stomach. Prescriptions must be expressed in generic terminology.

Health resorts and spas are common in Bulgaria, the Czech Republic, Slovakia, Hungary, Romania and ex-Yugoslavia, offering complete medical programmes for payment in hard currency. In Bratislava, Budapest and Prague there are special offices booking spa treatment from around US$80 a day including room and board. Hungary is especially famous for its hot springs which are accessible to everyone for a couple of dollars a visit, and massages and other health services are available at these. Less known but similar are the thermal baths of Bulgaria. In the Czech Republic and Slovakia such baths are usually reserved for patients under medical supervision.

Ms Femi Sobo of Newcastle upon Tyne, England, UK sent us this general advice:

Travelling takes a lot out of you and the body needs rest. I travelled to Warsaw, Gdańsk and Berlin in six days and by the time I got to Prague on the seventh day I was so tired that I was looking for somewhere to sit down by 10 am. If I had spent two nights in most places instead of only one I would not have been so exhausted and willing to cut my holiday by a week just to come home for a cup of tea and a comfortable bed.

Health Insurance

You'll have to pay for medical care but consultation fees and hospital bed charges are usually much lower than in Western countries. Special travel insurance policies only pay off if you have a really serious accident.

If you decide to buy travel insurance make sure it covers emergency medical evacuation to your home country and (if possible) baggage insurance. Such policies only cover charges above and beyond what your national health insurance will pay – if you're not covered at home such policies are usually invalid. Of course, the insurance companies will happily take your money and only bring up this crucial point if you have to make a claim. Some policies specifically exclude 'dangerous activities' such as skiing, motorcycling or mountaineering, which would make the insurance pretty useless if you intended to do such things. It's shameful the way some travel agents push worthless travel insurance just to get an extra commission. Read all the fine print and ask a lot of questions before buying the equivalent of a lottery ticket.

AIDS

In 1981 scientists in the USA and France first recognised the Acquired Immune Deficiency Syndrome (AIDS) which was later discovered to be caused by a virus called the Human Immuno-deficiency Virus (HIV). HIV breaks down the body's immunity to infections leading to full-blown AIDS. The virus can lie hidden in the body for many years without producing any obvious symptoms or before developing into the AIDS disease.

HIV lives in red blood cells and is present in the sexual fluids of humans. It's difficult to catch and is spread mostly through sexual intercourse, by needle or syringe sharing among intravenous drug users, in blood transfusions and during pregnancy. The HIV virus cannot be transmitted by shaking hands, kissing, cuddling, fondling, sneezing, cooking food or sharing eating or drinking utensils. HIV is not present in saliva, sweat, tears, urine or faeces; toilet seats, swimming pools or mosquito bites do not cause AIDS. Ostracising a known AIDS victim is not only immoral but it is also absurd.

Most blood banks now screen their products for HIV and you can protect yourself against dirty needles by only allowing an injection if you see the syringe taken out of a fresh unopened pack.

The best defence during sex is the proper use of a condom (it shouldn't fall off or 'leak'). Pack a supply of condoms with you when you leave for Eastern Europe as those sold locally may be of inferior quality. HIV is spread more often through anal than vaginal sex because the lining of the rectum is much weaker than that of the vagina and ordinary condoms sometimes tear when used in anal sex. During oral sex you must make sure you don't get any semen or menstrual blood in your mouth. A woman runs 10 times the risk of catching AIDS from a man than the other way around and the threat is always greater when another sexually transmitted disease (STD) is present.

By mid-1993 an estimated 14 million people worldwide were HIV carriers and hundreds of thousands had died of AIDS. In Eastern Europe only a few thousand people are as yet affected: in Romania as a result of blood transfusions, and in Poland due to drug abuse, while in Hungary HIV predominantly affects homosexuals, and in Croatia, mostly heterosexuals. Though the incidence of AIDS is still low in Eastern Europe compared to Western Europe or North America, its very existence calls for a basic change in human behaviour. No vaccine or drug exists which can prevent or cure AIDS and because the virus mutates frequently no remedy may ever be totally effective. Other STDs such as syphilis, gonorrhoea, chlamydia, hepatitis B and herpes are far more common than AIDS and can lead to serious complications such

as infertility, but at least they can usually be cured.

The euphoria of travel can make it easier to fall in love or have sex with a stranger, so travellers must be informed of these dangers. As a tourist you should always practice safe sex. You never know who is infected or even if you yourself have become infected. It's important to bring the subject up *before* you start to make love. The golden rule is safe sex or no sex.

An HIV infection can be detected through a blood test because the antibodies created by the body to fight off the virus can be seen under a microscope. It takes at least three weeks for the antibodies to be produced and in some cases as long as six months before they can be picked up during a screening test. If you think you may have run a risk you should discuss the appropriateness of a test with your doctor. It's always better to know if you are infected so as to be able to avoid infecting others, obtain early treatment of symptoms and make realistic plans. If you know someone with AIDS you should give them all the support you can (there is no danger in such contact unless blood is present).

DANGERS & ANNOYANCES

Avoid paying bribes to persons in official positions, such as police, border guards, train conductors, ticket inspectors etc. If corrupt cops want to hold you up because some obscure stamp is missing from your documentation or on another pretext, just let them and consider the experience an integral part of your trip. Don't worry at all if they take you to the police station for interrogation as you'll have a unique opportunity to observe the quality of justice in that country from the inside and higher officers will eventually let you go (assuming, of course, you haven't committed any real crime). If you do have to pay a fine or supplementary charge, insist on a proper receipt before turning over any money. In all of this, try to maintain your usual good humour as any threats from you will only make matters worse.

Never give money, sweets or pens to children on the street as this creates a real nuisance. In some countries you must beware of colourfully dressed female beggars (often with small children) who make a living out of hassling foreigners, but in general, Eastern Europe is relatively safer than Western Europe. Some locals will tell you how dangerous their city is and recount cases of muggings, break-ins etc. Mostly they're comparing the present situation to that before 1989 when the crime rate was almost zero and what street crime exists is often committed by people from the former Soviet Union. Other than the moneychanging rackets previously described and car theft, there's no systematic criminal activity directed at foreigners, though that's no reason to lower your guard. Look purposeful, keep alert and you'll be OK.

FILM & PHOTOGRAPHY

Automatic 35 mm cameras are popular because they're compact and you have only to aim and shoot. Some have a zoom capacity. Photojournalists usually carry a heavy single-lens reflex (SLR) camera but this exceeds the needs of most travellers. Bring at least five rolls of film (and spare batteries) with you, although Kodak film is becoming readily available. Slow ISO 100 film is fine in bright sunlight but ISO 200 film is better on cloudy days. Fast ISO 400 film is preferable for indoor photos with flash or to freeze movement – the film most likely to forgive underexposure or overexposure. Kodak Express one-hour colour film developing centres are popping up all across Eastern Europe, easily recognisable by their bright yellow signs. It's fun to be able to see your photos right away and it allows you to develop your technique.

Wayne J Andrews of Eastman Kodak offers the following suggestions for enhanced photography. Keep your photos simple with one main subject and an uncomplicated background. Get as close to your subjects as you can and lower or raise the camera to their level. Include people in the foreground of scenic shots to add interest and perspective. Watch for signs or banners

where you can photograph family and friends to introduce a story. Use your flash both indoors and outdoors but check the instructions for the maximum flash distance for your camera and film. Stand at an angle to shiny objects which might reflect the flash. On bright summer days the sun can cause unflattering shadows between 11 am and 3 pm. Panoramas come out best early or late in the day. Most of all, be creative. Look for interesting details and compose the photo before you push the trigger. Instead of taking a head-on photo of a group of people, step to one side and ask them to face you. The angle improves the photo. Photograph subjects coming towards you rather than passing by.

In most Eastern European countries it's prohibited to take pictures of anything that might be considered of strategic value, such as bridges, tunnels, harbours, docks, reservoirs, dams, train stations, airports, government buildings, radio or TV stations, power plants, factories, laboratories, mines, border crossings, military installations, local soldiers or police. Especially avoid taking photos of any of these from a bus or train as there will be lots of witnesses (and the photos will probably end up blurred anyway). Occasionally you'll see a funny little sign showing a crossed-out camera indicating that there's something of interest in the vicinity. These days local officials are a lot less paranoid about photography than they were, just use common sense when it comes to the above. And do have the courtesy to ask permission before taking close-up photos of people.

ACTIVITIES
Canoeing & Kayaking

Those with folding kayaks will want to launch them on the Krutynia River in Poland's Great Mazurian Lakes district or on the Danube, Rába and Tisza rivers in Hungary. Special canoeing tours are offered in both these countries, as well as in Croatia. One of the world's great kayaking adventures is the Tour International Danubien (TID) on the Danube River in July and

August (see the general Getting Around section for more information).

Cycling

For information on this activity or means of transport see the Bicycle section under Getting Around.

Hiking

There's excellent hiking in Eastern Europe with numerous well-marked trails through forests, mountains and the various national parks. Public transport will often take you to the trailheads, and chalets or mountain 'huts' provide shelter and perhaps a hot bowl of soup. In this book we include detailed information on hiking through the High Tatra Mountains of Poland and Slovakia, the Malá Fatra of Slovakia, the Bucegi and Făgăraş ranges in Romania's Carpathian Mountains, the Rila Mountains of Bulgaria and Slovenia's Julian Alps, but there are many other less well-known hiking areas. The best months for hiking are from June to September, especially late in August and early September when the snow and crowds will have melted.

Horse Riding

Though horse riding can be arranged in all the countries, it's best developed in Hungary and Poland. See the Activities sections in the Facts for the Visitor sections of those chapters.

Sailing & Yachting

Eastern Europe's most famous yachting area is the passage between the long rugged islands off Croatia's Dalmatian Coast. Yacht tours and rentals are available there, though you certainly won't be able to do this 'on a shoestring'. If your means are limited, the Great Mazurian Lakes of north-east Poland are a better choice as small groups can rent sailing boats by the day for very reasonable rates. Hungary's Balaton Lake is also popular among sailing enthusiasts.

Skiing

Eastern Europe's premier skiing areas are the High Tatra Mountains of Poland and Slovakia, the Romanian Carpathians near Braşov, Mt Vitosha and Borovets near Sofia, Bulgaria, and Slovenia's Julian Alps. The season runs from mid-December to March and serious skiers with limited time should look into an all-inclusive package tour. It's also possible to do it on your own for less if you don't mind competing for facilities with lots of locals. (If you go up a ski lift for purposes other than skiing, be sure to check what time it stops running or you could have problems getting back down.)

White-Water Rafting

This exciting activity is offered in summer on two of Eastern Europe's most scenic rivers: the Tara River in Montenegro and the Soča River in Slovenia. Rafting on the Dunajec River along the border of Poland and Slovakia is fun but it's not a whitewater experience.

Courses

Language Information on special summer language courses for foreigners are given in the Facts for the Visitor sections in the Bulgaria, Croatia, the Czech Republic, Hungary, Poland and Romania chapters. Embassies often have information on study possibilities in their countries. Summer schools in Eastern Europe run by Western universities tend to be much more expensive than local courses, though it may be easier to transfer credits.

It's also possible to arrange local language tutors for a reasonable amount. Check with schools teaching English to local residents or ask a tourist office for advice. If this is your intention, bring a good textbook and bilingual dictionary with you from home as books for teaching Eastern European languages to English speakers can be hard to find.

WORK

English teaching is a growth industry in Eastern Europe and probably the best avenue to explore if you don't have a lot of money. Though you should be able to find work teaching English, local wage levels average just US$100 to US$150 a month, so you won't get rich doing it. Some countries require an AIDS test as a condition for issuing a work permit.

INFORMATION OFFICES

The former official government tourism monopolies – Albturist (Albania), Balkantourist (Bulgaria), Čedok (Czech Republic), Ibusz (Hungary), the Oficiul Naţionál de Turism (Romania), Orbis (Poland) and Satur (Slovakia) – have branches in nearly every city and town within their own country and foreign offices throughout Europe. The addresses of some of the offices abroad are listed in the Facts for the Visitor section of each chapter. Bear in mind that these are commercial travel agencies which reserve hotel rooms, sell transportation tickets and sightseeing tours etc. In many cases they will also provide general tourist information, but with state subsidies gone, their main objective now is to make a profit and stay in business. Don't expect free service because no one is paying for them to provide it.

Some countries also have a student travel bureau, such as Almatur (Poland), the CKM (Czech Republic and Slovakia), Express (Hungary) and Orbita (Bulgaria). Their primary task is to organise excursions for youth groups within the country, but often they assist foreign youth as well by selling ISIC student cards and discounted international train tickets or by booking youth hostels.

Large cities often maintain municipal information offices which are excellent sources of free information on local attractions, theatres, events etc. In Hungary the Ministry of Tourism has established a unique network of Tourinform offices around the country.

Offices of the national airlines can provide current visa information about their own country and most maintain offices in all of the cities they serve. (Remember, however, that entry requirements by air may be different than those by land.) The companies to contact are Adria Airways (Slovenia), Albanian Airlines and Arbëria Airlines

(Albania), Balkan Airlines (Bulgaria), Czechoslovak Airlines (Czech Republic and Slovakia), Croatia Airlines (Croatia), JAT Yugoslav Airlines (Yugoslavia), LOT Polish Airlines (Poland), Malév Hungarian Airlines (Hungary), Palair (Macedonia) and TAROM (Romania). Airline offices often have free tourist brochures about their home country on the counter.

The national railway companies usually have a central ticket office in each major city within their respective countries. Go to these offices for tickets and reservations rather than struggling with the throng at the train station. The railway offices and some of the travel agencies are packed around mid-afternoon, so check the opening hours and go early.

Railway information counters in train stations aren't usually equipped to provide tourist information, and the clerks at the ticket windows will often refuse to give train times if you could have got them from the information counter. Tourist information offices are sometimes not the best sources of train or bus information, so double-check what they tell you. Always try to use the correct information office for the sort of thing you want to know.

Throughout this book we've tried to list the most effective information offices. The service at these varies, improving if you're both courteous and persistent. If it becomes obvious that an office is no more interested in helping you than you are in paying top dollar, leave quietly and make your own arrangements. Each chapter explains how this can be done.

ACCOMMODATION
Camping

The cheapest way to go is camping (US$2 to US$10 per person) and there are numerous camping grounds throughout the region. Most are large 'autocamps' intended mainly for motorists though they're often easily accessible on public transport and there's almost always space for backpackers with tents. Many camping grounds rent small on-site cabins or bungalows for double or triple the regular camping fee. In the most popular resorts all the bungalows may be full in July and August, but ask.

Quality varies from one country to the next. It's abysmal in Romania, unreliable in Bulgaria, crowded in Hungary and variable in Poland. Only coastal Croatia has nudist camping grounds (marked FKK) which are actually excellent places to stay because of their secluded locations. A camping carnet (available from your local automobile or camping club) gets you a 5% to 10% discount at some camping grounds and often serves as a guarantee so you don't have to leave your passport at reception.

The camping grounds may be open from April to October, May to September, or perhaps only June to August, depending on the category of the facility and demand. A few privatised camping grounds are now open year-round. Unlike at camping grounds in Western Europe, you may be allowed to build a campfire (though ask first). Freelance camping is often prohibited, so before you pitch your tent on a beach or in an open field observe what others are doing. If in doubt keep out of sight of the road – good policy regardless.

Hostels

Youth Hostels affiliated to Hostelling International (HI), or the International Youth Hostel Federation (IYHF) as it was previously called, are found in all of the countries except Albania and Romania. A youth hostel card is not essential to stay at most of the hostels, although you often get a small discount if you have one. If you don't have a valid YHA membership card you can buy an international guest card valid at hostels around the world.

The hostels in Poland are similar to those in Western Europe and easily used. Polish hostels tend to be extremely basic but they're inexpensive (US$3) and friendly. In the Czech Republic and Slovakia many hostels are actually fairly luxurious 'junior' hotels with double rooms often fully occupied by groups. Most of the Hungarian hostels are regular student dormitories only open to

travellers for six or seven weeks in midsummer. In Budapest and Prague a large number of privately-operated hostels have appeared in recent years, many open year-round. Yugoslavia used to have a large network of hostels but most are now being used to house war refugees. The hostels in Bulgaria are usually in rural or mountain areas.

Many Czech Republic, Slovakian and Hungarian cities have dormitories known as 'tourist hostels' which are not connected with Hostelling International and have no rules. (You'll find, for example, there are mixed dorms, no curfews, and that smoking and drinking are permitted in the rooms.) These places are intended for local visitors and you may have to be persistent to use them (US$2 to US$5 per person).

In July and August accommodation in vacant student dormitories is readily available in Poland, the Czech Republic, Slovakia, Hungary, Slovenia, Croatia and Macedonia. Beds in doubles and triples go for US$5 and up, and often you'll have the room to yourself. A student or youth hostel card is not required though occasionally it will get you a reduced rate. The student travel agencies mentioned above may have information about these.

Another low budget possibility is accommodation in workers' hostels which are similar to the above but open year-round. You'll find them in Poland, the Czech Republic, Slovakia and Hungary. Tourist offices often provide such addresses when you ask for the cheapest possible rooms and we list as many as we can in this book. The rooms are just as good as those in a cheap hotel and at about US$6 per person they're excellent value.

Private Rooms

In every Eastern European country, travel agencies arrange private-room accommodation in local homes. In Hungary you can get a private room almost anywhere but in the other countries only the main tourist centres have them. Some 1st-class rooms are like mini-apartments with cooking facilities and private bathrooms for the use of guests alone.

Prices vary from US$5 to US$20 per person but there's often a 30% to 50% surcharge if you stay less than three or four nights. In Hungary, the Czech Republic and Croatia increased taxation has made such rooms less attractive than they were but they're still good value and usually cheaper than a hotel.

Sometimes you'll be offered a *sobe* (private room) by a proprietor on the street for a lower price than the agencies charge. Along the Adriatic coast of Croatia this is a common practice. You can also knock on the doors of houses bearing sobe or zimmer frei signs and ask if they have a room for you. If the price asked is too high, try bargaining.

In large cities the rooms are often in high-rise complexes in distant suburbs, but public transport is good and the agency arranging the room should be able to sell you a detailed city map. You usually can't occupy the room until 5 pm, so leave your bag at the station. Besides having a place to stay, you'll get to experience a slice of local life.

Pensions

Since 1989, small private pensions have proliferated. Priced somewhere between hotels and private rooms, pensions usually have less than 10 rooms and the resident proprietors often make a good portion of their income from a small restaurant on the premises. You'll get a lot more personal attention than you would at a hotel at the cost of a wee bit of your privacy. If you arrive at night or on a weekend when the travel agencies assigning private rooms are closed, pensions are well worth a try, though they could be full. Call ahead to check prices and ask about reservations – German is almost always spoken, as is, increasingly, English.

Hotels

Standard high-rise tourist hotels exist in every city but in this book we've concentrated on the older two-star hotels. There are still quite a few 'grand hotels' around, overflowing with old-fashioned Victorian elegance. Hotels are usually graded as five-star (deluxe-category), four-star (A*

category), three-star (A category), two-star (B category), or one-star (C category).

Rooms at one and two-star hotels begin around US$15/25 single/double. Singles are sometimes hard to find. The cheapest rooms have a washbasin but shared bath which means you'll have to go down the corridor to use the toilet or shower. In some hotels the communal showers are kept locked and you're charged extra every time you get the key. Occasionally you can get a reduction on the room rate by asking for a room without breakfast.

By European standards, hotel accommodation is relatively inexpensive, except in Croatia, Yugoslavia and Macedonia where hotels are a lot more expensive than camping and private rooms. The Romanian Automobile Club has a special deal offering reduced rates at two and three-star hotels if you purchase 'hotel coupons' in advance (see the Facts for the Visitor section of that chapter).

Hotel pricing in much of Eastern Europe is still based on the old socialist slogan, 'from each according to his ability, to each according to his needs' and, except in Hungary and Poland, foreigners pay much more than locals for the same rooms at state-owned hotels. Because of this two-price system, hotels in the Czech Republic, for example, are 50% to 100% more expensive than a comparable hotel would be in Poland. This situation often explains why all those overpriced hotels were full.

Mountain Huts

In the mountain areas of Bulgaria, Slovakia, Poland, Romania and Slovenia there are mountain 'huts' or chalets offering dormitory accommodation (under US$10 per person) and basic meals to hikers. It's usually not possible to reserve a bed at a hut, although in Bulgaria the huts and the HI youth hostels are the same thing. Weather conditions will probably limit your use of the huts to summer, although some are open all year. Huts near roads or cable cars fill up fast, as do those in popular areas such as the Tatra Mountains. The huts are excellent places to meet Eastern European students.

Waiting Rooms & Trains

Other places to stay at a pinch are train-station waiting rooms. So long as you have a ticket this is no problem but always put your luggage in a coin locker or left-luggage office (cloakroom) before dozing off. In Romania the waiting rooms have nice padded seats.

Also compare the price of a hotel to that of a 2nd-class couchette or a 1st-class sleeper (US$3 to US$6) on an overnight train. Couchettes are very practical in Bulgaria, the Czech Republic, Slovakia, Poland, Romania and Yugoslavia, so use your creativity to figure something out. The catch is that it's sometimes hard to get a couchette or sleeper reservation, so don't leave it too late.

FOOD

The cheapest and fastest place to eat is at a self-service cafeteria *(buffet express)*. Set up by the communists to feed the masses, quite a few of these places still exist although they're fast disappearing from large cities. You usually pay at the end of the line, but sometimes (especially in Poland) you pay at the beginning of the line and get a ticket. Cashiers tend to be indulgent with tourists who can't speak the language, so just point at something acceptable that someone else is eating. Otherwise ask the person in line behind you what a certain dish is called. Some self-services offer genuine local dishes at surprisingly low prices and you can usually get a beer with the meal (but seldom in Poland).

Self-services tend to close around 7 pm weekdays, at 1 pm on Saturday and all day Sunday. For busy sightseers they're just the place for breakfast or lunch. Regular table-service restaurants have longer opening hours than the self-services. Hotel restaurants keep the longest hours, so try them if everything else is closed. The hotel restaurants of Bulgaria, Romania, the Czech Republic, Slovakia and Poland offer fine food properly served at very reasonable prices.

The communists opened many restaurants as a way of providing jobs and absorbing excess income not covered by goods in the marketplace. Often there wasn't enough food available to supply these establishments and whole categories listed on the menu would be unavailable. The serving staff kept out undesirables (that is, the general public) with a reservation requirement. In the privatisation process many such restaurants have proved uneconomic and disappeared though you still stumble across them.

It's worth trying the folkloric restaurants where regional cuisine is offered. These are known as *csárdas* in Hungary or *mehanas* in Bulgaria. In Slovakia and Hungary there are excellent wine restaurants *(vinárna* or *borozó)* and beer halls *(pivnice* or *söröző)*. Czech beer is about the best in the world and the wines of Bulgaria, Hungary, Romania, Slovakia, Slovenia and Croatia are excellent.

The latest craze in Eastern Europe is pizza and private pizzerias are popping up everywhere just as the proletarian self-services close down. Be aware, however, that many of these places serve cheap mass-produced pizza vaguely resembling cardboard with a topping of tomato sauce. Whenever you're entering a pizzeria in this part of the world note carefully what others are eating to avoid unappetising surprises. In cities with dishonest waiters, pizza is always a good choice as the price is more or less fixed – just watch the price of the drinks. Never order your drink until *after* you've decided on your meal.

Throughout Eastern Europe restaurant menus are translated into German and increasingly into English. In better restaurants you should always ask to see a menu to get an idea of the price range. If a menu with specific prices is not available, even only in the local language, seriously consider walking out, otherwise there's a good chance you'll be overcharged. Waiters who resist bringing you the menu probably intend to overcharge you. Enough places with proper menus do exist, so you can afford to be strict on this point.

Not everything on the menu will be available, so when the waiters return ask them to recommend something that is listed on it. If the waiter asks you if you want 'pommes frites' it probably means the vegetables are not included in the price of the main plate and you will be charged extra. As you order make a mental note of the maximum amount your bill could possibly be and if the waiter comes up with a much higher figure ask to see the menu again and check each item before producing any money (although restaurants with different sets of menus with varying prices are not unknown). On the other hand, if you're charged about what you expected, round your bill up by around 10% as a way of saying thanks.

Also beware of cafés and bars which don't have price lists posted on the wall as these are the most likely to overcharge you. The best solution is to stick your head in the door and if you don't see a price list, just look elsewhere as it's a real pain to have to ask the price of everything. If none of the local eating and drinking establishments post price lists or have menus, boycott them all and buy groceries in a local store which you can eat picnic-style on a park bench or at the beach.

You may have to share your table in Eastern European restaurants with whoever shows up, which could be a problem if you're a nonsmoker and your new companions smoke. Men dressed in shorts are not admitted to better restaurants and in winter everyone must check in their coat. After Western Europe you'll find the food cheap in Eastern Europe – there's no official double pricing as there is for hotel rooms, and a little extra money goes a long way here, so splash out now and then.

ENTERTAINMENT

If you enjoy music and theatre you can see first-rate performances at reasonable prices in Eastern Europe. Every large city has an opera house and a separate theatre for operettas and musicals. There will be a concert hall (*filharmonia*) plus dramatic, satirical and puppet theatres, and sometimes a permanent circus. Jazz clubs are found in the Czech Republic, Hungary and Poland.

Apart from the capitals many provincial towns such as Brno, Győr, Kraków, Pécs, Varna and Wrocław are important musical centres. Municipal information offices are your best source of information about cultural events. All performances are listed in the daily papers, and although you may not know the language, enough information will be comprehensible in the listings to enable you to locate the theatre and try for tickets.

There are theatrical ticket offices in Warsaw, Budapest and Prague, but you'll get better seats by going directly to the theatre box office (*kassa*) itself. If this fails try for a ticket at the door half an hour before showtime. In Prague many performances are sold out weeks in advance but scalpers and travel agencies usually have tickets available at premium prices.

Most theatres close for a six-week holiday during the summer (from mid-June to mid-September). Instead look for performances by visiting companies at open-air theatres or on public squares. Folklore programmes are often offered and there are summer festivals. Most Eastern European towns have a Cultural Centre which publishes a monthly list of regular events.

Cinemas are cheap, though since 1989, sex and violence have been standard fare. Check carefully whether the film is in the original language with subtitles or has been dubbed into the local language. Latecomers are not admitted and it's rude to walk out in the middle of a film. Smoking is not allowed in cinemas. Discos and nightclubs stay open late everywhere and they're good places to make local contacts and have a lot of fun.

THINGS TO BUY

Some Eastern European countries are still short of consumer goods and when something especially good comes on the market it sells out fast. Thus it's important to buy things when you see them! Books and records are good value, as are musical and scientific instruments. High-quality art books are produced in the Czech Republic, Hungary and Poland. Eyeglasses are often inexpensive, so get an extra pair if you know your prescription. If you want newspapers and magazines in English, go to the boutique in the most luxurious hotel in town.

When you enter a supermarket or certain sections at department stores, you must pick up a shopping basket at the entrance. Stores use this system as a means of controlling the number of people inside: if the baskets are all taken you must wait at the cash register until you can get one from somebody who's leaving. If you enter without a basket you'll have an unnecessary argument with the sales staff. Many grocery shops do not provide plastic bags in which to carry away your purchases, so bring your own or an empty day pack.

Goods purchased with local currency over a certain value may be subject to export tax. Customs officials get strict about this if it looks like you're trying to make a business of it by exporting too many of the same item. Otherwise they may just think you're an easy mark who might be willing to give them a tip to be done with them (insist on a receipt if you're forced to pay anything). Duty is charged on valuable articles like fur or leather coats, gold jewellery, antique watches and expensive-looking works of art. If you have such things with you on arrival in Eastern Europe ask if you need to declare them, though since 1989 things have become a lot more relaxed than they were.

Getting There & Away

AIR

Airfares to/from Eastern Europe are usually expensive so if you're coming from North America, Australia or New Zealand, your best bet is to buy the cheapest possible ticket to Western Europe and proceed from there by bus or train. Look for a discount ticket to London, Amsterdam, Vienna, Athens, Istanbul or anywhere in Germany. Vienna is a useful gateway as the Czech Republic, Slovakia, Hungary and Slovenia are all just hours away.

Emphasise that you want the cheapest possible fare whenever dealing with travel agencies or airlines, and compare prices at several offices before deciding. You may be able to save money by advancing or delaying your trip slightly to take advantage of a lower seasonal fare. Start enquiring well ahead as some low fares have advance purchase requirements. Some round-trip excursion fares with fixed dates are cheaper but there are big penalties for subsequent changes or cancellations.

Everything else being equal, you might take the airport tax into consideration when picking your destination. Airport departure taxes are collected in Albania (US$10), Croatia (US$8), Macedonia (US$13), Poland (US$10), Slovakia (US$2.50), Slovenia (US$14) and Yugoslavia (US$7), whereas Bulgaria, Romania, Hungary and the Czech Republic have no airport taxes on either domestic or international flights.

To/From North America

Icelandair flies from Baltimore, Fort Lauderdale, New York and Orlando to Amsterdam, Copenhagen, Glasgow, Hamburg, London, Luxembourg, Oslo, Salzburg and Stockholm via Reykjavík, with onward bus connections available in Luxembourg to Cologne, Düsseldorf and Stuttgart (bus reservations required, US$13). In the USA call Icelandair toll-free on 800-223 5500 to ask about off-season and 'last minute' one-way fares.

It's possible to get cheaper one-way fares to Europe from 'bucket shops' or 'consolidators' in New York City. These agencies purchase blocks of 'empty' seats from airlines at a fraction of their value and pass the savings on to you. For example, TFI Tours (☎ 212-736 1140 or 800-745 8000), 34 West 32nd St, 12th floor, New York, NY 10001-3898, promises 'daily departures with guaranteed reservations on scheduled airlines'. TFI has cheap flights to Bucharest, Budapest, Kraków, Prague, Sofia, Warsaw and Zagreb from cities right across the USA with a maximum stay of 10 months. The Sunday travel sections of the *Toronto Star, Boston Globe, Chicago Sun Times, Dallas Morning News, Los Angeles Times, San Francisco Chronicle, Miami Herald* and *New York Times* carry ads from many such companies.

If you're a student check both Council Travel (☎ 510-848 8604) and the Student Travel Network (☎ 800-777 0112), two competing chains of student-orientated travel agencies with offices in college towns right across the USA. In Canada they're called Travel CUTS (☎ 416-979 2406).

To/From Australia & New Zealand

Garuda Indonesia flies from Melbourne to Amsterdam, Frankfurt, London, Paris or Rome, but its flights tend to be disorganised. Malaysian Airlines will get you to Athens.

Lauda Air offers Adelaide-Sydney-Bangkok-Vienna (or London) flights. Stopovers in Bangkok are one week maximum but there are no other restrictions and Lauda uses modern aircraft with lots of legroom. The Lauda flight arrives in Vienna in the morning, allowing you to continue to Hungary or Slovakia on the same day.

Aeroflot is a couple of hundred dollars cheaper but it has old equipment, theoretical schedules, and there's a long delay changing planes in Moscow. However, Aeroflot will enable you to fly to Eastern Europe without going through Western Europe first, and depending on how you look at it, a stopover in Moscow could be an added bonus.

Call your local STA office to ask what they've got going to Europe. In New Zealand it's Student Travel (☎ 9-39 9723). They also sell tickets to non-students.

To/From the UK

Regular one-way air fares from Britain to Eastern Europe are expensive though tickets to Berlin are often cheaper than the train. If you're going to the Balkans compare the price of a cheap package tour booked on a 'last minute' basis as this may be no more than the flight alone. Check the London weeklies *Time Out* and *TNT* for ads from bucket shops offering cheap flights.

Campus Travel (☎ 0171-730 3402) with 31 offices in major towns around the UK sells an 'open jaw' return trip routing from London to Prague and from Thessaloniki to London which allows you to traverse the countries of your choice without having to return to your starting point. These tickets are available to anyone, with discounts for students and those aged under 26 years. The many STA offices (☎ 0171-937 9921) offer similar deals.

To/From Africa

Bucket shops in Nairobi, Kenya, sell cheap Egypt Air tickets to Athens with a free stop in Cairo. From Greece there are buses to Bulgaria and Albania, and trains to Macedonia. You can also fly Aeroflot from Nairobi to almost any Eastern European capital via Moscow for about the same price. Bucket shops like Prince Travel in the Nairobi Tower have these tickets but insist on confirmed reservations before putting down any money.

The Balkan Bulgarian Airlines office on Talaat Harb St in Cairo sells cheap tickets from many African cities to Europe via Sofia. For example, if you are in Egypt and want to visit Zimbabwe before flying to Europe you'd do well to buy all the required tickets before leaving Cairo.

To/From Asia

From South-East Asia the very cheapest fares to Western Europe are offered by the Eastern European carriers. Ironically, these fares usually don't apply if you wish to end up in Eastern Europe itself, though you can often get a free stopover, which amounts to the same thing. The Aeroflot route from Singapore or Bangkok via Moscow is particularly popular. On flights with Balkan Bulgarian Airlines, Czechoslovak Airlines (ČSA), LOT-Polish Airlines and TAROM Romanian Air Transport you'll transit an Eastern European capital.

TRAIN
International Tickets

All regular international train tickets are valid for two months and you may stop off as often as you wish. In Eastern Europe international train tickets are usually more easily purchased at a travel agency, rather than in the train station.

Railway fares to/from and within Western Europe are expensive, so only buy a ticket as far as your first possible stop within Eastern Europe. From Amsterdam a one-way 2nd-class train ticket will cost US$105 to Poznań (Poland), US$154 to Cheb (Czech Republic), US$207 to Budapest (Hungary) and US$196 to Ljubljana (Slovenia). Domestic tickets within a single Eastern European country are much cheaper. Also compare the price of international buses discussed under Land following.

A good deal to know about if you're coming from Belgium, Denmark, France, Luxembourg or the Netherlands is the 'Super-Sparpreis-Ticket' which allows a round trip anywhere in Germany within one month for DM170 return (an accompanying person pays half-price). This ticket can be purchased at any German railway station but it is not valid on Friday, Sunday and public holidays (unless you pay a DM50 supplement). Convenient border stations accessible on the 'Super-Sparpreis' are Görlitz (for Poland), Schirnding (for the Czech Republic), Passau or Simbach (for Slovakia and Hungary) and Salzburg (for Slovenia).

Unlimited stopovers along the direct route are allowed. Of course, you have to get to a German train station to begin, but even with the cost of additional tickets at each end it might still work out cheaper than a through ticket.

If you have an ISIC student card, you can get a discount on international train tickets between the Eastern European countries, so always show your card when buying such tickets, though you may have to go to a special student travel office. Foreign students usually cannot get discounts on domestic train tickets within a single country or to Western Europe.

Persons under the age of 26 years are eligible for Eurotrain or 'BIJ' discounts on international train tickets between Eastern and Western Europe (student card not required). For each country you transit you get a different discount on that portion of the through fare: Austria 40%, Belgium 40%, Britain 35%, Czech Republic 40%, Denmark 20%, France 30%, Greece 30%, Spain 15%, Holland 30%, Italy 25%, Poland 50%, Portugal 30%, Germany 25%, Switzerland 35%, and Sweden 25%. One-way tickets of this type are also valid for two months and stopovers are allowed. These tickets must be purchased from a travel agency specialising in youth or student travel, such as Almatur in Poland, CKM Student Travel in the Czech Republic and Slovakia, and Express in Hungary. Wasteels offices around Europe also have these tickets. In Britain contact Wasteels (☎ 0171-834 7066), 121 Wilton Road, London SW1V 1JZ, England.

A special 'Eastbound Explorer' ticket from London to Prague, Budapest and Kraków and back (valid for two months) is available to persons aged under 26 years at £206 from Campus Travel (☎ 0171-730 3402), 52 Grosvenor Gardens, London SW1W 0AG, England, UK or at any student travel office.

Many international trains in Eastern Europe require compulsory seat reservations which are a nuisance to make, then when you get on the train you find it almost empty. This is a hold-over from the communist era when paranoid officials tried to make it as difficult as possible for their citizens to travel abroad and it will probably take years for the Eastern European railways to get rid of all this unnecessary red tape.

Railway Passes

The Inter-Rail pass (sold only to European residents) is valid for unlimited 2nd-class train travel in all of Eastern Europe except Albania. Although not valid within the country of purchase, it does get you a 50% reduction on one return-trip journey to the border (except in Britain). Some national railways levy reservation fees and supplements for travel on express trains and these may also be required of Inter-Railers.

For those under the age of 26, Inter-Rail allows you to travel through 26 countries by train for one month for £249. A '26 plus' Inter-Rail pass for people aged 26 years and over includes 19 countries at £209 for 15 days or £269 for one month. The ferry from Brindisi, Italy, to Patras, Greece, and all trains in Eastern Europe (except Albania) are included, but the ticket is not valid in the UK or on the cross-channel ferries. Proof of six months' residence in the UK is required. Information is available from British Rail (☎ 0171-834 2345 or 0171-828 0892), International Rail Centre, Victoria Station, London SW1V 1JY, England, UK.

In 1989 Hungary became the first (and as yet, the only) Eastern European country to accept the Eurail pass, a railway pass valid in 17 countries sold to persons living outside Europe. Eurail passes also come in two varieties. Persons aged 26 years and over must purchase a pass valid for 1st-class travel at US$498 for 15 days, US$648 for 21 days, US$798 for one month, US$1096 for two months or US$1398 for three months. Those aged 25 years and under on the first day of travel can get a 2nd-class Eurail pass at US$398 for 15 days, US$578 for one month or US$768 for two months. Several slightly cheaper variations exist allowing travel only on certain days during a set period or for two or three people travelling together.

For Poland, Eurail will take you to Görlitz,

Germany, from whence you can simply walk across the border. Vienna, Austria, is a convenient gateway to the Czech Republic, Slovakia and Hungary with frequent bus, boat and rail connections to them all. If you begin or end your Eurail pass in Vienna, you won't have to count the days spent touring the Austrian capital. Eurail travellers will find Trieste, Italy, the best gateway to ex-Yugoslavia with 15 buses a day to nearby Koper in Slovenia.

The Eurail pass is of little use for touring Eastern Europe, however, as only Hungary is included and the alternative means of travel are much cheaper, so only buy one with the intention of using it mostly in Western Europe. But to be frank, this type of pass makes you rush to get your money's worth and you skip over the very cultures you came to experience. They're only worth considering if you're a city-hopping fanatic who wants to pack the maximum number of countries into the minimum number of days.

Instead, regular one-way international train tickets are much better value than Eurail passes as a way of getting around Western Europe. Such tickets allow unlimited stopovers anywhere along the way within two months, provided you stick to the direct route listed on the ticket. For example, for US$220 you can travel 2nd class from Budapest to Lisbon, Portugal, stopping at points along the way in Austria, northern Italy, southern France and central Spain for as long as you like, so long as you reach Lisbon within the two months. After visiting Portugal you could buy another one-way ticket to some other distant point along a different route and get another two-month trip for a price far lower than the cheapest Eurail pass.

A 'European East Pass' is available in North America at US$185 for five days' 1st-class travel in 15 days or US$299 for 10 days' travel in one month. It's valid only in Austria, the Czech Republic, Hungary, Poland and Slovakia and is a lot more expensive than paying as you go in those countries.

Trans-Siberian/Mongolian
Through trains link China to Moscow in five or six days with onward connections in Moscow to all Eastern European capitals. It used to be very cheap to travel from Budapest to Beijing on these trains, but in 1991 ticket prices in Hungary increased drastically on this route and you'll now pay at least US$500 one way in 2nd class. A better place to look for a ticket to China is Warsaw where prices are less than half those charged in Budapest. Westbound travel from China to Europe also costs only about US$250, so this is a good way of getting from Asia to Eastern Europe.

Westbound, wait till you get to Beijing to buy your ticket, as tickets sold in Western countries are much more expensive. The China International Travel Service (CITS) in Beijing and Shanghai books sleepers to Moscow, but not over a month nor less than five days in advance. Reservations between China and Moscow are tight in June, July and August and 10 days are required to arrange Russian and Mongolian transit visas in Beijing. You can't make your onward train reservation from Moscow to Eastern Europe until you get to Moscow.

If you plan to do this trip, pick up Robert Strauss' *Trans-Siberian Rail Guide* (Compass Publications, UK, and Hunter Publishing, USA) before leaving home.

LAND
To/From the UK
The cheapest way to go from London to Eastern Europe is by bus and with the opening of the Channel Tunnel in 1994 bus routes are sure to multiply. Regular long-distance bus routes now operate from London's Victoria Coach Terminal to Budapest (£95 single, £150 return), Prague (£65 single, £105 return) and Warsaw (£70 single, £110 return). You may have to change buses in Amsterdam, Brussels, Frankfurt or elsewhere, and German drivers often ask an extra DM 3 per piece of luggage. Still, a bus ticket from Britain to any Eastern European capital costs about half what you would have to pay on the train and discounts are available to those aged under 26 or over 59 years. Return tickets are valid for six months. Many ser-

vices are only weekly and advance reservations are advisable. Information is available from National Express (☎ 0171-730 0202). The names of other agencies booking tickets to/from Britain are included in the Getting There & Away sections of the respective chapters.

To/From Western Europe

Numerous railway lines link the two Europes, but again, buses are much cheaper than trains. If you're headed for anywhere in Poland, the Czech Republic, Slovakia, Hungary or Croatia, be sure to check schedules and prices at one of these agencies:

Austria
   Blaguss Reisen, Wiedner Hauptstrasse 15, Vienna (☎ 0222-50 1800)
Belgium
   Europabus, Place de Brouckere 50, Brussels (☎ 2-217 0025)
   Europabus, Van Stralenstraat 20, Antwerp (☎ 3-233 8663)
Denmark
   Thinggaard/Eurolines, Amagerbrogade 15, Copenhagen (☎ 31-575 744)
France
   Eurolines Paris, Gare Routiere Internationale Galliéni, Avenue du Général de Gaulle, 93170 Bagnolet, Paris (☎ 4972 5151)
   Eurolines, Centre d'échanges de Lyon-Perrache, niveau 1, Cour de Verdun, 69002 Lyon (☎ 7241 0909)
Germany
   Deutsche Touring GmbH, Am Romerhof 17, Frankfurt/Main (☎ 069-790 3234)
Ireland
   Bus Eireann, Busaras, Dublin (☎ 01-366 111)
Italy
   Eurolines, Piazza Castello, 1e etage, 20121 Milan (☎ 02-7200 4194)
   Lazzi Express, Via Tagliamento 27/r, Rome (☎ 06-884 0840)
Netherlands
   Budget Bus/Eurolines, Rokin 10, 1012 KR Amsterdam (☎ 020-627 5151)
   Eurolines, Conradstraat 20, 3013 AP Rotterdam (☎ 10-412 4444)
Portugal
   Eurolines/Intercentro, Rua Actor Taborda 33, Lisbon (☎ 1-571 745)
Spain
   Bus Station de Sants, C/Viriato, Barcelona (☎ 93-490 4000)

SAIA, Bus Station, Canarias 19, Madrid (☎ 91-530 7600)
Sweden
   Eurolines, Kyrkogatan 40, 41115 Gothenburg (Göteborg) (☎ 031-100240)
   Swebus, Vasagatan 12, Stockholm (☎ 08-234 810)
Switzerland
   Eurolines, Eggman/Frey Hauptstrasse 66, CH-4112 Bättwil (☎ 061-731 2174)

Also check the Getting There & Away section in the particular country chapters' introductions for more information. Commercial travel agencies throughout Europe often sell tickets for these buses or will know another agency which does. Otherwise just ask at the main international bus station wherever you happen to be. Price is the main advantage of these buses as they're less comfortable than the train and there's heavy cigarette smoking on some services (ask about this when booking).

Other Routes For the Czech Republic or Slovakia take a train from Linz, Austria, to České Budějovice; a bus from Vienna to Brno or Bratislava; or a train from Vienna to Bratislava or Břeclav. For Hungary there are buses from Vienna to Sopron and Budapest, as well as trains. In summer the Danube hydrofoil glides expensively from Vienna to Budapest (US$65 one way).

There are many ways to reach ex-Yugoslavia. Several railway lines converge on Ljubljana from Austria and Italy. The main line from Munich to Athens runs via Budapest and Belgrade. There are trains twice a day between Thessaloniki and Skopje.

From Greece to Bulgaria a bus will be half the price of the train. Travel agencies in Athens and Thessaloniki selling tickets are listed in the Getting There & Away section of the Bulgaria chapter. The main railway line from Istanbul to Belgrade passes through Sofia and there are also cheap buses from Istanbul to Bucharest.

SEA

There are ferries to Świnoujście and Gdańsk (Poland) from Copenhagen (Denmark),

Ystad (Sweden), Oxelösund (Sweden) and Helsinki (Finland). There are ferries from Corfu (Greece) to Saranda (Albania), as well as numerous lines across the Adriatic from Italy to Croatia.

The cheapest way to go from Sweden to the Czech Republic, Slovakia or Hungary is to take the ferry from Trelleborg to Sassnitz in Germany. In Sassnitz buy a train ticket across eastern Germany to Děčín (Czech Republic) where you'll be able to pick up a domestic ticket across the Czech Republic and Slovakia. Don't buy a through ticket in Sweden itself as this will be much more expensive.

PACKAGE TOURS

A package tour is worth considering only if your time is very limited or you have a special interest such as skiing, canoeing, sailing, horse riding, bicycling, spa treatment etc. Cruises down the Danube River are also available but they're very expensive. Most tour prices are for double occupancy, which means singles have to share a double room with a stranger of the same sex or pay a single supplement for a single room.

New Millennium Holidays (☎ 0121-711 2232), 20 High St, Solihull, West Midlands B91 3TB, England, UK runs inexpensive bus tours year-round from Britain to Poland, Hungary, Romania, the Czech Republic and Slovakia. Several trips are to spas such as Hévíz (Hungary), Baile Felix (Romania) and Trenčianske Teplice (Slovakia). Their packages vary from eight to 17 days, some combining two countries, with return travel from Ramsgate, accommodation with shared bath and half board included. If you enjoy group travel on a low budget, you ought to request their colour brochure.

Another British company highly experi-

enced in booking travel to Eastern Europe is Regent Holidays (☎ 0117-921 1711, fax 0117-925 4866), 15 John St, Bristol BS1 2HR, England, UK. The best company we know arranging travel to the former Soviet Union is Progressive Tours (☎ 0171-262 1676), 12 Porchester Place, Marble Arch, London W2 2BS, England, UK.

In Australia you can obtain a detailed brochure outlining dozens of up-market tours from the Eastern Europe Travel Bureau (☎ 02-262 1144), Suite 501, 75 King St, Sydney, NSW 2000. Their office in Victoria (☎ 03-600 0299) is at Suite 313, 343 Little Collins St, Melbourne, Vic 3000.

Goulash Tours (☎ 616-349 8817), Box 2972, Kalamazoo, MI 49003, USA, offers several bicycling tours of Eastern Europe each summer. Participants must bring their own bicycle and all equipment.

WARNING

This chapter is particularly vulnerable to change – prices for international travel are volatile, routes are introduced and cancelled, schedules change, special deals come and go, and rules and visa requirements are amended. Airlines and governments seem to take a perverse pleasure in making price structures and regulations as complicated as possible. You should check directly with the airline or travel agent to make sure you understand how a fare (and ticket you may buy) works. In addition, the travel industry is highly competitive and there are many lurks and perks. The upshot of this is that you should get opinions, quotes and advice from as many airlines and travel agents as possible before you part with your hard-earned cash. The details given in this chapter should be regarded as pointers and are not a substitute for careful, up-to-date research.

Getting Around

AIR

Considering the cheapness of bus and train travel within Eastern Europe, air travel is a real luxury. Domestic flights operate within Bulgaria, Croatia, Poland, Slovakia, Romania and Yugoslavia but fares are high, often because of a two-fare system with foreign tourists paying much more than nationals. However, there are no airport taxes on local flights within individual countries (other than a US$2 domestic airport tax in Yugoslavia). For domestic flights and prices see Getting Around in the chapter introductions.

BUS

Buses are slightly more expensive to travel on than trains. In most Eastern European countries buses complement the railways rather than duplicate their routes, but in the Czech Republic, Slovakia and Hungary you often have a choice of either bus or train. In these three countries you're better off taking buses for short trips and express trains for long journeys.

The ticketing system varies in each country, but to be safe always try to buy a ticket in advance at the station. If this is not possible you'll be told so. In the Czech Republic the ČSAD bus system is computerised. Hungary and Croatia also have good bus services. In Bulgaria private bus lines have appeared recently in competition with the trains. Occasionally you'll be charged extra for baggage (always in Croatia).

US traveller Sarah Slover, who travelled all over Hungary, the Czech Republic and Slovakia, sent us these comments:

My travels went very smoothly. I was on a *lot* of buses and trains and not a single one left late or broke down and I always got a seat, usually immediately. I enjoyed my trip and found travelling alone to be safe and easy. People definitely noticed I was foreign but didn't stare or make comments like they did in Latin America.

TRAIN

You'll probably do most of your travelling within Eastern Europe by train. All of the countries have well-developed railway networks similar to those of Western Europe and you'll have a choice between local trains which stop at every station, and express trains. Both have advantages. Travelling on local trains is often only half the cost of the express trains and they never have seat reservation requirements. Once you find a place to sit it's yours for the trip, and since passengers are constantly coming and going you eventually get a place even on a full train. First-class travel by local train costs about the same as 2nd class on an express and is quite comfortable, so long as you're in no hurry. First-class compartments have six seats, 2nd-class ones have eight seats.

If you choose an express be sure to get an express ticket and ask if seat reservations are compulsory. It's sometimes a hassle getting these tickets, so don't leave it too late. Express trains are often marked in red on posted timetables, local trains in black. The symbol 'R' with a box around it means reservations are mandatory while an 'R' without a box may only mean reservations are possible. The boards listing departures are usually yellow, and those for arrivals are white.

Tickets for express trains are best purchased at the central train ticket office a day before. On overnight trains always try to book a 2nd-class couchette or a 1st-class sleeper a few days in advance. Make sure your ticketing is all in order before you board the train. If you have to arrange a reservation, buy a ticket or upgrade a local ticket to an express one on a moving train, you'll pay a healthy supplement. As a comparison of costs, a 100-km 2nd-class ticket for the cheapest category of train will cost you US$0.65 in Romania, US$1 in the Czech Republic or Slovakia, US$2 in Poland or Croatia, US$3.25 in Hungary and US$3.75 in Slovenia.

It's best to sit in the middle or front carriages of trains as many stations are poorly marked, often with only one sign on the main building. If there's any doubt, write the name of your destination on a piece of paper and show it to the other passengers so they can let you know when to get off (or advise you if you've strayed onto the wrong train). Such a request from you can also break the ice and lead to interesting conversations.

Luggage

Almost every train station in Eastern Europe has a luggage room (left-luggage or cloakroom) where you can deposit your luggage as soon as you arrive. In Poland this can be expensive as you're charged 1% of the declared value of your luggage. Croatia and Hungary also charge a fairly high fee of nearly US$1 while cloakrooms are very cheap in the other countries. You usually pay the fee when you pick up your bag – handy if you're just arriving in a new country with no local currency. In main stations the left-luggage office is open around the clock.

Many train stations also have complicated coin lockers. You compose a four-digit number on the inside of the door, insert a coin and close the locker. To open it again you arrange the same number on the outside and with luck the door will open. Don't forget the number or the location of your locker!

CAR & MOTORBIKE

To drive a car into most Eastern European countries you'll need the car registration papers and liability insurance (the 'green card'), although a carnet is not required. If you don't have proper insurance it's sometimes possible to buy it at the border. If you're not the car owner, you must have notarised written permission to be in possession of the car (or have the car rental agreement). Details of the car, boat or other vehicle may be written into your passport. If you're driving a camper van or caravan, you may be asked to provide an inventory of the equipment carried inside. The vehicle must bear a country identification sticker.

Although not always required, you should bring an international driving licence.

Many cities don't allow private cars in the centre of town and finding parking space is difficult, so it's often best to find a place to stay at the edge of town and commute by public transport. Park in well-frequented areas, lock the car and consider removing the windshield wipers at night. If you have a new car, a steering-wheel lock may save it from being stolen.

According to World Health Organisation statistics, driving in Eastern Europe is five times more dangerous than it is in Western Europe. Driving at night can be especially hazardous as the roads are often narrow and winding, and horse-drawn vehicles, bicycles, pedestrians and even domestic animals may be encountered at any time. In case of an accident you're supposed to notify the police and file an insurance claim. Never sign any documents you cannot read – insist on a translation and sign that if it's acceptable. If your car has significant body damage from a previous accident, point this out to customs upon arrival and have it noted somewhere, as damaged vehicles are only allowed to leave the country with police permission.

Travel by private car often allows you to get off the beaten track and to avoid overpriced accommodation by simply moving on. With public transport prices going up fast, it could even work out cheaper if there are a few of you.

Fuel

Petrol coupons are sometimes required and you usually have to pay in hard currency and they are non-refundable. The regulations change frequently, so ask about this at any information office you find at the border.

Unleaded fuel (*Bleifrei* in German) is hard to find in Eastern Europe, so bring a 20-litre can in which to carry an extra supply, especially if your car is fitted with a catalytic converter, as this expensive component can be ruined by leaded fuel. Check your car's octane requirement: if it's a modern model designed for unleaded fuel but without a converter, it'll run quite happily on regular (sometimes called 'normal') 92/94 octane leaded. If in doubt, however, use only premium (super) fuel with an octane rating of around 98, particularly if your Western car is an older model. Don't use the 86 octane 'normal' which many of the locals use in their vehicles because it'll make your high-compression Western engine ping like mad. The tank opening of cars burning unleaded fuel may be too small for the type of fuel nozzle used with leaded fuel, so you'll need a funnel. Modern motorcycles are all set up for unleaded fuel but don't have catalytic converters, which means they'll have no trouble with 92/94 octane leaded; however, stick to 98 octane super on older models.

If you have to transit Austria to/from the region, be aware that Austrian petrol stations don't always accept credit cards and Austrian banks charge very high commissions to change money.

Road Rules

Standard international road signs are used throughout Eastern Europe. Everywhere you drive on the right side of the road and overtake on the left. Keep right except when overtaking, and use your turning signals for any change of lane and when pulling away from the kerb. You're not allowed to pass a whole line of cars whether they are moving or stopped. Speed limits are posted, and are generally 110 km/h on motorways (freeways), 80 km/h on the open road and 60 km/h in built-up areas. Motorcycles are usually limited to 90 km/h on motorways, and vehicles with trailers to 80 km/h. In towns you may only honk the horn to avoid an accident. The use of seat belts is mandatory and motorcyclists must wear a helmet. Children under 12 years and intoxicated passengers are not permitted in the front seat. Driving after drinking even the smallest amount of alcohol or beer is a serious offence.

Throughout Europe, when two roads of equal importance intersect, the vehicle coming from the right has the right of way. In many countries this also applies to cyclists, so take care. On roundabouts (traffic circles) vehicles already in the roundabout

have the right of way. Public transport vehicles pulling out from a stop also have right of way. Stay out of lanes marked 'bus' except when you're making a right-hand turn. Pedestrians have the right of way at marked crossings and whenever you're making a turn. In Europe it's prohibited to turn right against a red light even after coming to a stop.

It's usually illegal to stop or stand at the top of slopes, in front of pedestrian crossings, at bus or tram stops, on bridges or level crossings or within three metres of a car filling up at a petrol station. You must use a red reflector warning triangle when parking on a highway (in an emergency). If you don't use the triangle and another vehicle hits you from behind, you will be held responsible. You must use headlights when driving through heavy fog during the day.

Beware of trams (streetcars) as these have priority at crossroads and when turning right (provided they signal the turn). Don't pass a tram which is stopping to let off passengers until everyone is out and the tram doors have closed again (unless, of course, there's a safety island). Never pass a tram on the left or stop within one metre of tram tracks. A police officer who sees you blocking a tram route by waiting to turn left will flag you over. Traffic police administer fines on the spot (always ask for a receipt).

Car Rental

Car rentals in Eastern Europe are costly, varying from US$20 to US$38 a day plus US$0.20 to US$0.38 a km for the cheapest model. On a weekly basis, you'll pay anywhere from US$325 to US$550 with unlimited mileage. Collision Damage Waiver (CDW) insurance will be around US$10 per day and another US$12 a day must be paid for Loss Damage Waiver (LDW) insurance against car theft. A surcharge is often payable if you rent the car at a car rental counter in an airport or at a luxury hotel instead of at the company's regular business office. Additional drivers are about US$8 extra and taxes of up to 25% may not be included in the quoted prices. The most expensive countries in which to rent are Poland and Hungary.

The international chains best represented in Eastern Europe are Avis (in Poland, the Czech Republic, Hungary, Bulgaria, Croatia and Yugoslavia), Budget (in Poland, Hungary, Slovenia and Croatia), Europcar (in the Czech Republic, Slovakia, Hungary, Bulgaria and Croatia) and Hertz (in Poland, Slovakia, Hungary, Romania, Bulgaria, Slovenia and Croatia). Local companies not connected with any chain usually offer lower prices but when comparing rates beware of printed tariffs intended only for local residents which may be much lower than the prices foreigners are charged. If in doubt, ask. The chain companies often allow you to drop the car off at their locations in other cities at no additional charge.

If you're coming from North America, Australia or New Zealand, ask your airline if it has any special deals for rental cars in Europe, or check the ads in the weekend travel sections of major newspapers. You can often arrange something in advance for much less than you'd pay on the spot in Europe.

If renting from abroad, you must tell the agency exactly which countries you plan to visit so it can make sure the insurance is in order. Many German agencies refuse to allow their cars to be taken to Eastern Europe because of an increasing incidence of car theft. Hertz won't allow their any of vehicles to be taken to the former Soviet Union or ex-Yugoslavia (Slovenia excepted) and their luxury models are also banned from Bulgaria, Hungary, Poland and Romania.

In any case, it's better to resist the temptation to rent the most luxurious model, as it will stand out and could be a target for theft, vandalism or occasional harassment by traffic police. Finding unleaded fuel in Eastern Europe is problematic and petrol pumps of any kind are few and far between, so ask for a car that burns leaded fuel and is easy on fuel consumption.

Car Purchase

Since 1990, Eastern Europeans have flooded Western Europe on car-buying expeditions – a good indication that what's available back home isn't competitive.

BICYCLE

Cycling is a cheap, convenient, healthy, environmentally sound and, above all, *fun* way of getting around. This book was entirely researched on public transport and foot, so we'll let our readers on wheels take over.

Len Houwers of Levin, New Zealand, sent us this:

My girlfriend and I have been travelling through Europe and Asia for over a year now on pedal power: two mountain bikes, rear carrier packs, front handle-bar bag, sleeping bags and tent. Having spent five months cycling through Europe we can recommend the bike as a totally independent vehicle for travellers which allows you to get really close to the countryside and people, provided it stays dry and you're not in a hurry. We averaged about 400 km a week, which was four days cycling and three rest days to cover various city sights. At most hotels the reception allowed us to park our bikes in our room or they found a spare lockable room free of charge. International travel by train is a hassle as they usually separate you from your bike which gets sent ahead. To avoid this separation, travel to border towns by train, cross the border by bike, then catch another train on the other side.

Bruce Burger of Seattle, Washington, USA clarified this point:

It's fairly easy to take bikes on trains and on most trains you can choose from two methods. The official method is to take your bike to the baggage office in the train station after buying your ticket. They will put a tag on it and either take it from you or, occasionally, tell you to take it to the platform when the train arrives. In small stations without baggage offices, you do this at the ticket window. The unofficial method is just to take your bike to the baggage car of the train (the car with wide doors and no seats) and look for the conductor to take it from you. Make sure you state your destination clearly. Either way there will be a small charge depending on the length of the voyage. You should remove the panniers etc.

Jenny Visser and Mike Fee of Wellington, New Zealand, sent the following:

We cycled and camped through Slovakia, Poland, Hungary, Bulgaria and a little of Yugoslavia, covering approximately 4000 km in over eight weeks. We would like to point out just how ideal much of Eastern Europe is for cycling. Eastern European roads were of surprisingly good quality (although when they did deteriorate they were appalling) and they were nearly always quiet. This allowed us to relax and enjoy the cycling, a luxury not often available on busier northern and southern European roads. The negative side was the disgusting exhaust put out by all Eastern European vehicles, especially buses and trucks. Often we would be left gasping in a cloud of blue or black smoke as these vehicles lumbered along the road. We had thought that signposting outside the main centres might produce some difficulty for navigation, but again we were pleasantly surprised by its availability.

Martin Fedorski of Stockport, England, UK had this to report:

Eastern Europe is an excellent place to cycle. True, the roads are often in pretty dismal condition and in the towns you get choked by fumes, but to compensate there are miles and miles of quiet roads, many of them going through unexpectedly beautiful, interesting and sometimes grim places you would never see by any other means. The route I took went from Berlin to Karlovy Vary, Plzeň and Prague, then north-east and east along the Polish border to Kraków. From there I went south across the Tatra and Slovakia to Budapest, down the Danube and across the Great Plain to Arad, Romania, then via the Calafat/Vidin ferry to Sofia and Thessaloniki. The scenery in the Tatra and Slovakia was excellent – some of the best cycling I did on the trip – but the Hungarian Great Plain was dull and hot even with the towns spaced widely apart. In Romania even the European trunk roads were very quiet and fine for cycling down. Romania left the deepest impression on me. I have nothing but admiration for the way the people cope with the real day-to-day hardships they have to endure. I found it hard to believe it was Europe at all sometimes when I saw people working in the fields doing everything by hand or animal power. In Bulgaria I came down the Iskâr Valley from Gara Lakatnik to Novi Iskâr and the gorges, cliffs and caves were as spectacular as anything else I saw. On my trip, cycle shops would spring up unexpectedly here and there, however you would never know when to expect a shop so I'd recommend carrying as many spares as you can (or as few as you dare, depending on your experience).

Shirley Hudson of Mosier, Oregon, USA sent this:

Many bicycle parts are now readily available. Mountain bikes are very popular so 26-inch and even 24-inch tyres are available in every country. The Czech Republic probably has the highest quality bicycles, followed by Slovakia, Poland and Hungary. Bulgaria and especially Romania don't have much as yet, but mountain bikes are becoming popular there too. We saw 'long reach' derailleurs in Slovakia, the Czech Republic and Poland. Two British cyclists with very new bicycles said that the bikes in Eastern Europe don't have the latest technology but technology four years old in the West. My bicycle is eight years old so parts were no problem. Do take spare brake and derailleur cables, however, as they break in the most inconvenient places.

HITCHING

As long as public transport remains cheap, hitchhiking is more something for the adventure than the transport and in Albania, Romania and sometimes Poland drivers expect riders to pay the equivalent of a bus fare. In Romania traffic is light and probably not going far and everywhere you'll be up against small, full vehicles. Many of the big Western cars you see are driven by tourists who never stop. This said, just make yourself a small cardboard destination sign and give it a try. City buses will usually take you to the edge of town. Before hitchhiking on a motorway (freeway) make sure it's not prohibited. If you look like a Westerner your chances of getting a ride will be much better.

Women will find hitchhiking safer than in Western Europe, but standard precautions should be taken: never accept a ride with two men, don't let your pack be put in the boot (trunk), only sit next to a door you can open, ask the driver where he/she is going before you say where you're going etc. Don't hesitate to refuse a ride if you feel at all uncomfortable, and insist on being let out at the first sign of trouble. Best of all, try to find a travelling companion (although three people will almost never get a ride).

BOAT

A number of interesting boat trips are possible. One of the most unforgettable is the journey on the big Jadrolinija car ferry down the Dalmatian Coast of Croatia from Split to Dubrovnik. The best river trip is through the Danube Delta from Tulcea to Sulina. Other classic trips include the slow boats from

Budapest to Esztergom or across Balaton Lake in Hungary. In Poland some cities on the Vistula offer river trips in their vicinity, and excursion boats ply the Great Mazurian Lakes in north-east Poland. Several boat trips are possible from Gdańsk, Poland. Most services operate from April to October only, sometimes for shorter periods.

Canoe or Kayak

Every summer since 1955, up to 2500 people have paddled themselves down the Danube under the banner of the Tour International Danubien (TID). Only a few dozen actually do the entire trip from Ingolstadt in Germany to Silistra in Bulgaria – most join for a week or a month, or as long as they can manage. The concept originated among the canoeing federations of all the countries along the Danube except Romania and the former USSR. The clubs form a special committee, but as the tour begins in Germany, enrolments are done under the aegis of the German Canoe Federation (DKV). Each national federation takes its turn leading the trip as its borders are crossed.

This is not a race. The world's longest annual canoe cruise covers 2081 km in daily laps of about 45 km spread over almost two months. It's possible to sign up for only a portion of the trip, and boat and bus transfers to/from Germany are arranged. Participants sleep in camps beside the river and combine sightseeing with travel. It's an unforgettable experience and some do the trip year after year. Many lasting friendships have originated on the TID.

You must provide your own canoe or kayak and camping gear, as the German Canoe Federation does not rent sporting boats of any kind. The most popular craft on the TID are folding kayaks or *folbots*, among the best of which are those manufactured by Klepper in Germany and Nautiraid in France. A knowledge of German (the official language of the TID) is a help, although not obligatory. Prior experience in canoeing and camping is also a definite plus. Applications close on 31 March and the trip itself lasts from the last Saturday in June to the second Saturday in August each year. You may join at Ingolstadt, Linz, Vienna, Bratislava, Budapest or Vidin.

Due to the political situation in former Yugoslavia, that section of the Danube is now off limits to recreational paddlers and TID participants leave the water in Hungary and are ferried through Romania to Bulgaria by bus.

For more information on the TID, send a self-addressed, stamped envelope or an International Postal Reply Coupon to any of the following people:

Rolf Kunze, Deutscher Kanu-Verband,
  Friedrich-Breuer-Strasse 42, D-53225
  Bonn, Germany (☎/fax 0228-47 2040)
Walter Danner, Villa Maya, 29 Kawartha Dr, Aylmer,
  Quebec J0X 2G0, Canada (☎ 819-682 5041)
Frank & Doreen Whitebrook, 10 Ridgeland Close,
  Richmond Hill, Lismore, NSW 2480, Australia
  (☎ 066-24 2077)

LOCAL TRANSPORT

Though ticket prices have greatly increased in recent years public transport in Eastern Europe is still inexpensive and the low price has no effect whatsoever on the service, which is generally first rate. In most cities, buses and trams begin moving at 5 am or earlier and continue until around 10.30 or 11.30 pm. There are metro (subway or underground) lines in Bucharest, Budapest and Prague. The Warsaw metro has been under construction for years and is still not open.

For all forms of public transport you must usually buy tickets in advance at a kiosk or from a machine. Information windows in bus and train stations sometimes have tickets for local transport. Once aboard you validate your own ticket by using a punch machine positioned near the door. Watch how the locals do it. Different tickets are sometimes required for buses, electric trolley buses, trams and the metro, but at other times they're all the same. If all the kiosks selling tickets are closed, ask another passenger to sell you a ticket. With increasing prices it's now possible to buy tickets from the driver or a conductor on some services.

Tickets are seldom checked, but you'll be

fined if an inspector catches you without a valid ticket (a costly and embarrassing experience). Pleading ignorance will not get you off the hook. Although many people – both locals and tourists – ride 'black', this is stealing and contributes to declining service and increasing fares. We recommend that you play by the rules and always do your best to have a valid ticket.

Throughout this book we provide the numbers of trams and buses passing the different sights and facilities mentioned herein. In the case of the trams, we don't usually specify where you have to catch these services, especially when a place is served by several lines, as such instructions would be extensive and perhaps confusing. The text or map should give you an idea which way you have to go, so just go to a main tram stop and hopefully you'll find one of the trams listed. Local people often know where you can catch a particular tram or bus.

Albania

Until recently considered a closed communist country, Albania caught world attention in late 1990 as the last domino to tumble in Eastern Europe's sudden series of democratic revolutions. Yet the recent changes date back to 1985 and the death of Enver Hoxha, Albania's Marxist-Leninist leader since 1944. The statues of Stalin and Hoxha have toppled, and the non-communist opposition has been elevated to power, putting Albania at a crossroads.

Long considered fair prey by every imperialist power, Albania chose a curious form of isolation. Backwardness, blood vendettas and illiteracy were replaced by what some claimed was the purest form of communism. Right up until December 1990, monuments, factories, boulevards and towns were dedicated to the memory of Joseph Stalin. Although Hoxha's iron-fisted rule did save Albania from annexation by Yugoslavia after WW II, it's unlikely that you'll find many in Albania with much good to say about him today. On the contrary, most blame him for the country's present problems.

Politics aside, few European countries have the allure of the mysterious Republika e Shqipërisë, or 'Land of the Eagle', as the Albanians call it. Albania is Europe's last unknown, with enchanting classical ruins at Durrës, Apolonia and Butrint, the charming 'museum towns' of Gjirokastra and Berat, vibrant cities like Tirana, Shkodra, Korça and Durrës, colourful folklore and majestic landscapes of mountains, forests, lakes and the sea. You can see a great number of things in a pocket-sized area and the Albanians are extremely friendly and curious about their handful of visitors.

In the capital, Tirana, and the port of Durrës people are already quite used to seeing foreigners, but almost everywhere else you'll be an object of curiosity. Things have improved since the collapse of the old system in 1992 and the trains are back on the

rails, increasing numbers of private buses are plying the roads, private rooms are becoming more readily available in the towns, travel agencies are opening and all areas of the country are now accessible to travellers. As Albania opens to the world for the first time, short-term visitors have the chance to meet the people in a way that's almost impossible elsewhere in Europe.

Facts about the Country

HISTORY
In the 2nd millennium BC, the Illyrians, ancestors of today's Albanians, occupied the western Balkans. The Greeks arrived in the 7th century BC to establish self-governing colonies at Epidamnos (now Durrës), Apolonia and Butrint. They traded peacefully with the Illyrians, who formed tribal

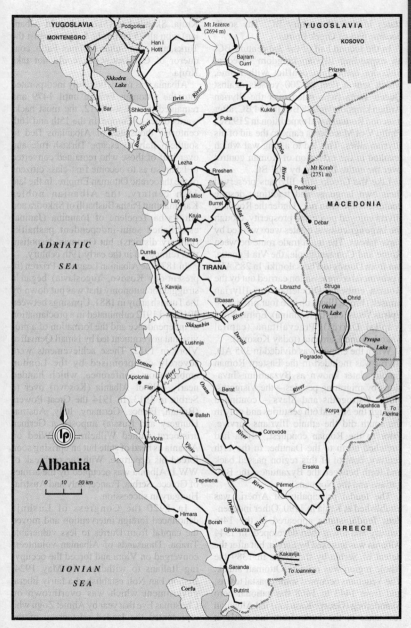

Albania

0   10   20 km

states in the 4th century BC. The south became part of Greek Epirus.

In the second half of the 3rd century BC, an expanding Illyrian kingdom based at Shkodra came into conflict with Rome, which sent a fleet of 200 vessels against Queen Teuta (who ruled over the Illyrian Ardian kingdom) in 228 BC. In 214 BC, after a second Roman naval expedition in 219 BC, Philip V of Macedonia came to the aid of his Illyrian allies. This led to a long war which resulted in the extension of Roman control over the entire Balkans by 167 BC.

Like the Greeks, the Illyrians preserved their own language and traditions despite centuries of Roman rule. Under the Romans, Illyria enjoyed peace and prosperity, though the large agricultural estates were worked by slave labour. The main trade route between Rome and Constantinople, the Via Egnatia, ran from Durrës to Thessaloniki. In 285 AD, a provincial reorganisation carried out by the Roman emperor Diocletian (an Illyrian himself) broke Illyria up into four provinces: Epirus Vetus (capital Ioannina), Epirus Nova (capital Durrës), Praevalitana (capital Shkodra) and Dardania (today Kosovo).

When the empire was divided in 395 AD, Illyria was included in the Eastern Roman Empire, later known as Byzantium. Invasions by migrating peoples – the Visigoths, Huns, Ostrogoths and Slavs – continued through the 5th and 6th centuries and only in the south did the ethnic Illyrians survive. Prior to the Roman conquest, Illyria had stretched north to the Danube. In the 11th century, control of this region passed back and forth between the Byzantines, the Bulgarians and the Normans.

The feudal principality of Arbëria was established at Kruja in 1190. Other independent feudal states appeared in the 14th century and towns then developed. In 1344 Albania was annexed by Serbia, but after the defeat of Serbia by the Turks in 1389 the whole region was open to Ottoman attack. The Venetians occupied some coastal towns, and from 1443 to 1468 the national hero Skanderbeg (George Kastrioti) led Albanian resistance to the Turks from his castle at Kruja. Skanderbeg (Skënderbeg in Albanian) won all 25 battles he fought against the Turks, and even Sultan Mehmet-Fatih, conqueror of Constantinople, could not take Kruja.

Albania was not definitively incorporated into the Ottoman Empire until 1479 and remained there until 1912, the most backward corner of Europe. In the 15th and 16th centuries thousands of Albanians fled to southern Italy to escape Turkish rule and over half of those who remained converted to Islam so as to become first-class citizens of the theocratic Ottoman Empire. In the late 18th century, the Albanian nobles Karamahmut Pasha Bushatlli of Shkodra and Ali Pasha Tepelena of Ioannina (Janina) established semi-independent pashaliks (military districts), but Ottoman despotism was reimposed in the early 19th century.

In 1878 the Albanian League at Prizren (in present-day Kosovo, Yugoslavia) began a struggle for autonomy that was put down by the Turkish army in 1881. Uprisings between 1910 and 1912 culminated in a proclamation of independence and the formation of a provisional government led by Ismail Qemali at Vlora in 1912. These achievements were severely compromised by the London ambassadors conference, which handed nearly half of Albania (Kosovo) over to Serbia in 1913. In 1914 the Great Powers (Britain, France, Germany, Italy, Austria-Hungary and Russia) imposed a German aristocrat named Wilhelm von Wied on Albania as head of state but an uprising soon forced his departure. With the outbreak of WW I, Albania was occupied by the armies of Greece, Serbia, France, Italy and Austria-Hungary in succession.

In 1920 the Congress of Lushnja denounced foreign intervention and moved the capital from Durrës to less vulnerable Tirana. Thousands of Albanian volunteers converged on Vlora and forced the occupying Italians to withdraw. In May 1924, Bishop Fan Noli established a fairly liberal government which was overthrown on Christmas Eve that year by Ahmet Zogu who represented the landed aristocracy of the lowlands and the tribal chieftains of the highlands. Zogu ruled with Italian support, declaring himself King Zog I in 1928, but his close collaboration with Italy backfired in April 1939 when Mussolini ordered an invasion of Albania. Zog fled to Britain and used gold looted from the Albanian treasury to rent a floor at London's Ritz Hotel.

On 8 November 1941 the Albanian Communist Party was founded with Enver Hoxha (pronounced Hodja) as first secretary, a position he held until his death in April 1985. The communists led the resistance to the Italians and, after 1943, to the Germans. A provisional government was formed at Berat in October 1944, and by 29 November the Albanian National Liberation Army had crushed the 'Balli Kombetar', a grouping of tribal quislings in the north, and pursued the last Nazi troops from the country. Albania was the only Eastern European country where the Soviet army was not involved in these operations. By tying down some 15 Nazi-fascist divisions this small country made an important contribution to the final outcome.

Post WW II

After the fighting died down, the National Liberation Front transformed itself into the Democratic Front, which won 92% of the vote in the December 1945 elections. In January 1946 the People's Republic of Albania was proclaimed, with Enver Hoxha as president. In February a programme of socialist construction was adopted and all large economic enterprises were nationalised. By 1952 seven years of elementary education had become mandatory (this was raised to eight years in 1963) and literacy was increased from just 15% before WW II to 75% today.

In October 1946 two British warships struck mines in the Corfu Channel, causing the loss of 44 lives. The British government blamed Albania and demanded £843,947 compensation. To back their claim they impounded 1574 kg of gold (now worth £10 million) which the fascists had stolen from

Albania. Albania has never accepted responsibility for the incident, nor has it agreed to pay damages. The stubborn British are still holding Albania's gold, despite agreeing in principle in 1992 to return it. It is now widely believed that Yugoslavia placed the mines. Good relations with Tito were always important to the British, whereas Albania was expendable.

In September 1948, Albania broke off relations with Yugoslavia, which had hoped to incorporate the country into the Yugoslav Federation. Instead, Albania allied itself with Stalin's USSR and put into effect a series of Soviet-style economic plans, the first a two-year plan, and then five-year plans beginning in 1951. In the early 1950s there were British-and US-backed landings in Albania by right-wing émigrés. One British attempt in 1949 was thwarted when Stalin passed to Hoxha a warning he had received from double agent Kim Philby.

Albania collaborated closely with the USSR until 1960, when a heavy-handed Khrushchev demanded a submarine base at Vlora. With the Soviet alliance becoming a liability, Albania broke diplomatic relations with the USSR in 1961 and reoriented itself towards the People's Republic of China.

From 1966 to 1967 Albania experienced a Chinese-style cultural revolution. Administrative workers were suddenly transferred to remote areas and younger cadres were placed in leading positions. The collectivisation of agriculture was completed and organised religion banned. Western literary works were withdrawn from circulation and a strong national culture firmly rooted in socialist ideals was carefully cultivated.

After the Soviet invasion of Czechoslovakia in 1968, Albania left the Warsaw Pact and began building concrete bunkers. Today, some 300,000 igloo-shaped bunkers and pillboxes with narrow gun slits are strung along all borders, both terrestrial and maritime, as well as the approaches to all towns. The highway from Durrës to Tirana is one bunker after another for 35 km. The amount of time and materials employed in creating these defences must have been tremendous and the bunkers still occupy much agricultural land today.

With the death of Mao Zedong in 1976 and the changes in China after 1978, Albania's unique relationship with China came to an end. In 1981 there was a power struggle within the Albanian Party of Labour (as the Communist Party had been called since November 1948) and former partisan hero and prime minister Mehmet Shehu 'committed suicide' after being accused of being a 'poliagent' (multiple spy).

Shehu had wanted to expand Albania's foreign contacts, an orientation which brought him into direct conflict with Hoxha. Until 1978 Albania had thrived on massive Yugoslav, Soviet and Chinese aid in succession, but building socialism alone without foreign loans or credit proved to be difficult. Because its exports didn't earn sufficient hard currency to pay for the import of essential equipment, technologically the country began to fall far behind.

Hoxha died after a long illness in April 1985 and his longtime associate Ramiz Alia assumed leadership of the 147,000-member Party of Labour. Aware of the economic decay caused by Albania's isolation, Alia began a liberalisation programme in 1986 and broadened Albania's ties with foreign countries. Travellers arriving in Albania at this time no longer had their guidebooks confiscated and their beards and long hair clipped by border barbers, and short skirts were allowed.

By early 1990 the collapse of communism in most of the rest of the region had created a sense of expectation in Albania and in June some 4500 Albanians took refuge in Western embassies in Tirana. After a brief confrontation these people were allowed to board ships to Brindisi, Italy, where they were granted political asylum.

After student demonstrations in December 1990, the government agreed to allow opposition parties and the Democratic Party led by heart surgeon Sali Berisha was formed. Further demonstrations won new concessions, including the promise of free elections and independent trade unions. The

government announced a reform programme and party hardliners were purged.

In early March 1991, as the election date approached, some 20,000 Albanians fled to Brindisi by ship, creating a crisis for the Italian government which had begun to view them as economic immigrants. Most were eventually allowed to stay. In the run-up to the 31 March 1991 elections, Alia won the support of the peasants by turning over state lands and granting them the right to sell their produce at markets. This manoeuvre netted the Party of Labour 169 seats in the 250-member People's Assembly which promptly re-elected Alia president for a five-year term.

In mid-May a general strike forced the renamed Socialist Party to form a coalition with the opposition Democrats in preparation for fresh elections the following year. As central economic planning collapsed, factories ceased production and the food distribution network broke down. In August another 15,000 young male Albanians attempted to take refuge in Italy, but this time they were met by Italian riot police and quickly deported. By late 1991 mass unemployment, rampant inflation and shortages of almost everything were throwing Albania into chaos and in December food riots began. Fearful of another refugee crisis, the European Community (now known as the European Union) stepped up economic aid and the Italian army established a large military base just south of Durrës, ostensibly to supervise EC food shipments.

The March 1992 elections brought 47 years of communist rule to an end as the Democratic Party took 92 of the 140 seats in a revamped parliament. After the resignation of Ramiz Alia, parliament elected Sali Berisha president in April. In their campaign, the Democrats promised that their victory would attract foreign investors and gain Western immigration quotas for Albanian workers and when these failed to materialise the socialists bounced back to win the municipal elections of July 1992.

In September 1992 Ramiz Alia was placed under house arrest after he wrote articles critical of the Democratic government for the socialist newspaper *24 Hours*, and in January 1993 the 73-year-old widow of Enver Hoxha, Nexhmije Hoxha, was sentenced to nine years imprisonment for allegedly misappropriating government funds between 1985 and 1990. In August 1993 the leader of the Socialist Party, Fatos Nano, was also arrested on trumped-up corruption charges. He was sentenced to 12 years imprisonment in April 1994. Persons once associated with the old regime are now being purged from the public service, their places taken by Democratic Party supporters (even though President Berisha and all the others are themselves former communists). In November 1993 Amnesty International issued a report condemning increasing human rights violations by the police against political opponents of the government. Meanwhile King Zog's son, a resident of South Africa, is manoeuvring for a return to Albania as King Leka I – an unlikely event.

In mid-1992 Albania signed a military agreement with Turkey, followed in December by Albania joining the Islamic Conference Association. This reorientation towards the Islamic world stems from practical security considerations. Greek politicians have made territorial claims to southern Albania (which they call Northern Epirus) and the alliance with Turkey is seen as a balance. In mid-1993 relations with Greece hit a new low following the deportation from Albania of a hardline Greek bishop who had attempted to organise the Greek minority in Albania for political ends. In retaliation, Athens ordered the expulsion of 20,000 of the 150,000 Albanian immigrants in Greece.

President Berisha has denounced Serbian oppression of the large Albanian majority in Kosovo and has repeatedly called for the deployment of United Nations peacekeeping troops in that area, warning that Albanians would react as a nation if Yugoslavia provoked a massacre of Albanians in Kosovo.

As yet, foreign investment in Albania has been meagre and the main source of government income is still the sale of European Union food aid. A 1993 law allows former owners to reclaim their property and this seems likely to discourage investment even more. The government has succeeded in reducing inflation from 240% in 1992 to 25% in 1993 by reducing the budget deficit. It could be another decade before conditions for the common people are greatly improved.

GEOGRAPHY

Albania's strategic position between Greece, Macedonia, Yugoslavia and Italy, just west of Bulgaria and Turkey, has been important throughout its history. Vlora watches over the narrow Strait of Otranto, which links the Adriatic Sea to the Ionian Sea. For decades Albania has acted as a barrier separating Greece from the rest of Europe. The Greek island of Corfu is only a few km from Saranda across the Ionian Sea.

Over three-quarters of this 28,748-sq-km country (a bit smaller than Belgium) consists of mountains and hills. There are three zones: a coastal plain, mountains and an interior plain. The coastal plain extends over 200 km from north to south and up to 50 km inland. The 2000-metre-high forested mountain spine that stretches along the entire length of Albania culminates at Mt Jezerce (2694 metres) in the north. Although Mt Jezerce is the highest mountain entirely within the country, Albania's highest peak is Mt Korab (2751 metres) on the border with Macedonia. The country is subject to destructive earthquakes, such as the one in 1979 which left 100,000 people homeless.

The longest river is the Drin River (285 km), which drains Ohrid Lake. In the north the Drin flows into the Buna, Albania's only navigable river, which connects shallow Shkodra Lake to the sea. Albania shares three large tectonic lakes with Yugoslavia, Macedonia and Greece: Shkodra, Ohrid and Prespa. Ohrid is the deepest lake in the Balkans (287 metres), while Prespa Lake, at 853 metres elevation, is one of the highest. The Ionian littoral, especially the 'Riviera of Flowers' from Vlora to Saranda, offers magnificent scenery. Forty per cent of the land is forested, and the many olive trees, citrus plantations and vineyards give Albania a true Mediterranean air.

ECONOMY

Albania stuck to strict Stalin-era central planning and wage and price controls longer than any other Eastern European country. Under communism two-thirds of the national income was directed towards consumption and social benefits, and the rest was used for capital investment. Industrial development was spread out, with factories in all regions. Unfortunately, much of the technology used is now thoroughly outdated and the goods produced are unable to compete on world markets. Between 1990 and 1992 industrial production fell 60%; huge investments will be required to turn the situation around.

The communist quest for higher production was carried out with little or no consideration for the environment and today's industrial wastelands are scenes of utter desolation far beyond anything else in Europe. You'll see ponds covered with a slick of oil leaking from a nearby oil well and large buildings with every window broken and the walls collapsing. Many Albanians treat their country like a giant garbage dump, the aluminum cans, cellophane candy wrappers and other debris of capitalism joining the tens of thousands of broken concrete bunkers and dozens of derelict factories left behind by communism. It's hard to believe this country will ever be cleaned up.

Albania is rich in natural resources such as crude oil, natural gas, coal, copper, iron, nickel and timber and is the world's third-largest producer of chrome, producing about 10% of the world's supply. The Central Mountains yield minerals such as copper in the north-east around Kukës, chromium farther south near the Drin River, and iron nickel closer to Ohrid Lake. The railway to Pogradec carries ore down to the steel mill at Elbasan – the major source of air and water pollution in central Albania. Textiles are made at Berat, Korça and Tirana.

Oil was discovered in Albania in 1917 and the country supplies all its own petroleum requirements. Fier's oil and gas have also enabled the production of chemical fertilisers. There are several huge hydroelectric dams on the Drin River in the north. Albania obtains 80% of its electricity from such dams and by 1970 electricity had reached every village in the country. From 1972 to 1990 Albania exported hydroelectricity to Yugoslavia and Greece. Both the steel mill and dams were built with Chinese technical assistance before 1978.

Under communist central planning Albania grew all its own food on collective farms, with surpluses available for export. About 20% of these farms were state farms run directly by the government, and the rest were cooperatives. The main crops were corn, cotton, potatoes, sugar beet, tobacco, vegetables and wheat. Lowland areas were collectivised in the 1950s, mountain areas during the 1967 Cultural Revolution.

Following the breakdown of authority in 1991, the peasants seized the cooperatives' lands, livestock and buildings and terminated deliveries to the state distribution network, leading to widespread food shortages. A high percentage of the farms are now being run on a subsistence basis with little surplus available to buy fertiliser and seed. Today, as ever, most fields are worked by hand.

Considering the country's small size, self-sufficiency was a real challenge, yet before 1990 Albania was one of the few countries in the world with no foreign debt (in 1976 a provision was included in its constitution forbidding any overseas loans). Now, however, the government has accumulated a US$1 billion foreign debt and must seek new loans just to cover interest on the existing loans.

With the public sector bankrupt, the government has been forced to increase drastically taxation on the private sector to make ends meet. Enver Hoxha's Sigurimi (secret police) has been replaced by the powerful tax-collecting Policia Financiare who drive expensive Italian vehicles and are almost a law unto themselves.

After the breaks with the USSR and

China, Albania's foreign trade had to be completely redirected, and until 1990 its main trading partners were Bulgaria, Czechoslovakia, Hungary, Italy and Yugoslavia, which purchased Albanian food products, asphalt, bitumen, chromium, crude oil and tobacco. Minerals, fuels and metals accounted for 47% of Albania's exports. Today Albania trades mostly with Italy and the USA. Now a new east-west trading route is taking shape from Turkey through Bulgaria, Macedonia and Albania to Italy. New highways and railways are already on the drawing boards and investments of US$2.5 billion are envisioned over the next 10 years.

POPULATION & PEOPLE

The Albanians are a hardy Mediterranean people, physically different from the more nordic Slavs. Although the Slavs and Greeks look down on the Albanians, the Albanians themselves have a sense of racial superiority based on their descent from the ancient Illyrians, who inhabited this region before the coming of the Romans. The country's name comes from the Albanoi, an ancient Illyrian tribe.

Over three million Albanians live in Albania and another two million suffer Serbian oppression in Kosovo (Greater Albania), in Yugoslavia, another Balkan tinderbox waiting to explode. A further 400,000 are in western Macedonia. Harsh economic conditions in Albania have unleashed successive waves of emigration: to Serbia in the 15th century, to Greece and Italy in the 16th century, to the USA in the 19th and 20th centuries and to Greece, Italy and Switzerland today. The Arbëreshi, longtime Albanian residents of 50 scattered villages in southern Italy, fled west in the 16th century to escape the Turks. As many as two million ethnic Albanians now live in Turkey itself, many of whom emigrated there from Serb-dominated Yugoslavia between 1912 and 1966. Since 1990 some 300,000 Albanians – 10% of the population – have migrated to Western Europe (especially Greece and Italy) to escape the economic hardships at home. Albania's largest source of income is

now remittances from Albanian workers abroad, in 1992 totalling US$400 million in cash, 21,000 used cars, 71,000 TV sets and 103,000 refrigerators.

Minorities inside Albania include 60,000 Greeks, 35,000 Romanians (known as Vlachs), 20,000 Macedonians and 10,000 Gypsies. Greek sources argue that Greeks are far more numerous than the official figure cited above, although such claims are often estimates based on factors such as the number of Greek Orthodox parishes in Albania before WW II and are thus inaccurate. The ethnic Greeks reside in southern Albania and they have often found themselves at the centre of political controversies. In 1975 the Albanian government implemented an assimilation programme to force Albanian Greeks to adopt 'acceptable' Albanian names and in late 1991 thousands fled from Albania to Greece. Greek nationalists have used the Greek minority as a pretext for territorial claims against Albania.

Albania is one of the most densely populated states of Europe, with 36% of the people living in urban areas (compared with only 15% before WW II). Under the communists birth control was forbidden (as part of the effort to make Albania self-sufficient by increasing the workforce); since WW II the population growth rate has been the highest in Europe (2.5% per annum), with the population doubling between 1923 and 1960 and again between 1960 and 1990. Part of this growth can be ascribed to an increase in life expectancy from 38 years in 1938 to 72.2 years today.

Albania is divided into 27 administrative districts *(rrethi)* and one municipality *(qytet)*. Tirana, the capital, is the largest city, with 250,000 inhabitants, followed by Durrës, Shkodra, Elbasan, Vlora, Korça, Fier and Berat. The apartment buildings which house a high percentage of the population may look decrepit on the outside but inside they're quite attractive. If you travel around the country much you'll most likely be invited to visit one.

The Shkumbin River forms a boundary between the Gheg cultural region of the north and the Tosk region in the south. The people in these regions still vary in dialect, musical culture and traditional dress (the Ghegs are also said to have larger noses). The communists worked hard to level regional differences by building an industrial complex in the Durrës-Tirana-Elbasan triangle, well away from the old tribal centres of Shkodra and Korça.

Traditional dress is still commonly seen in rural areas, especially on Sunday and holidays. The men wear an embroidered white shirt and knee trousers, the Ghegs with a white felt skullcap and the Tosks with a flat-topped white fez. Women's clothes are brighter than those of the men. Along with the standard white blouse with wide sleeves, women from Christian areas wear a red vest, and Muslim women have baggy pants tied at the ankles and a coloured headscarf. Older Muslim women wear a white scarf around the neck; white scarves may also be a sign of mourning.

ARTS

Literature

Prior to the adoption of a standardised orthography in 1909, very little literature was produced in Albania, though Albanians resident elsewhere in the Ottoman Empire or in Italy did write works. Among these was the noted poet Naim Frashëri (1846-1900), who lived in Istanbul and wrote in Greek. About the time of independence (1912), a group of romantic patriotic writers at Shkodra wrote epics and historical novels.

Perhaps the most interesting writer of the interwar period was Fan Noli (1880-1965). Educated as a priest in the USA, Fan Noli returned there to head the Albanian Orthodox Church in America after the Democratic government of Albania in which he served as premier was overthrown in 1924. Although many of his books are based on religious subjects, the introductions he wrote to his own translations of Cervantes, Ibsen, Omar Khayyám and Shakespeare established him as Albania's foremost literary critic.

Fan Noli's contemporary, the poet Migjeni (1911-38), focused on social issues until his early death from tuberculosis. In his 1936 poem, *Vargjet e lira* (Free Verse), Migjeni seeks to dispel the magic of the old myths and awaken the reader to present injustices.

Albania's best known contemporary writer is Ismail Kadare, born in 1935, whose 15 novels have been translated into 40 languages. Unfortunately the English editions are sometimes disappointing as they are translated from the French version rather than the Albanian original. *The Castle* (1970) describes the 15th century Turkish invasion of Albania, while *Chronicle in Stone* (1971) relates wartime experiences in Kadare's birthplace, Gjirokastra, as seen through the eyes of a boy. *Broken April* deals with the blood vendettas of the northern highlands before the 1939 Italian invasion. Among Kadare's other novels available in English are *The General of the Dead Army* (1963), *The Palace of Dreams* (1981) and *Doruntina*. Although Kadare lived in Tirana throughout the Hoxha years and even wrote a book, *The Great Winter* (1972), extolling Hoxha's defiance of Moscow, he sought political asylum in Paris in October 1990. His latest book, *Printemps Albanais* (Fayard, Paris, 1990), tells why.

Other notable Albanian writers whose books have appeared in English translations are Dritëro Agolli *(The Rise and Fall of Comrade Zylo)*, Teodore Laço and Naum Prifti. Now the publication of books in Albania has almost ceased due to a lack of paper.

Music

Polyphony, the blending of several independent vocal or instrumental parts, is a southern Albanian tradition that dates back to ancient Illyrian times. The peasant choirs perform in a variety of styles, and the songs, usually with epic-lyrical or historical themes, may be dramatic to the point of yodelling or slow and sober, with alternate male or female voices combining in harmonies of unexpected beauty. Instrumental polyphonic *kabas* are played by small Gypsy ensembles usually led by a clarinet. Improvisation gives way to dancing at colourful village weddings. One well-known group which often goes on tour outside Albania is the Lela Family of Përmet.

An outstanding recording of traditional Albanian music is the compact disc *Albania, Vocal and Instrumental Polyphony* (LDX 274 897) in the series 'Le Chant du Monde' (Musée de l'Homme, Paris).

The folk music of the Albanian-speaking villages founded five centuries ago in southern Italy has been popularised by Italian singer Silvana Licursi. Although Licursi sings in the Albanian language, her music bears a strong Italian imprint.

RELIGION

From 1967 to 1990 Albania was the only officially atheist state in the world. Public religious services were banned and many churches were converted to theatres or cinemas. In mid-1990 this situation was ended and in December of that year Nobel Prize-winner Mother Teresa of Calcutta, an ethnic Albanian from Macedonia, visited Albania and met President Alia. Traditionally, Albania has been 70% Sunni Muslim, 10% Roman Catholic (mostly in the north) and 17% Albanian Orthodox (mostly in the south). Albania is the only country in Europe with an Islamic majority. The spiritual vacuum left by the demise of communism is being filled by US evangelical imperialists who try to bring Jesus to the people and win converts from the other religions.

LANGUAGE

Albanian (Shqiptimi) is an Indo-European dialect of ancient Illyrian, with many Latin, Slavonic and (modern) Greek words. The two main dialects of Albanian diverged over the past thousand years. In 1909 a standardised form of the Gheg dialect of Elbasan was adopted as the official language, but since WW II a modified version of the Tosk dialect of southern Albania has been used. Outside the country, Albanians resident in former Yugoslavia speak Gheg, whereas those in Greece and Italy speak

Tosk. With practice you can sometimes differentiate between the dialects by listening for the nasalised vowels of Gheg. The Congress of Orthography at Tirana in 1972 established a unified written language based on the two dialects which is now universally accepted.

Until the break with the USSR in 1961, Russian was the most taught foreign language in Albania. Italian is the most useful foreign language to know in Albania, with English a strong second. Some of the older people will have learnt Italian in school before 1943; others have picked it up by watching Italian TV stations or through recent trips to Italy (as is the case with many of the young men).

Lonely Planet's *Mediterranean Europe Phrasebook* contains a helpful list of translated Albanian words and phrases. A complete 24-lesson Albanian language course with text and cassette tape is available for US$40 from Jack Shulman (☎ 718-633 0530), PO Box 912, Church Street Station, New York, NY 10008, USA.

Many Albanian place names have two forms because the definite article is a suffix. In this book we use the form most commonly used in English, but Tirana actually means *the* Tiranë. On signs at archaeological sites, *p.e. sonë* means BC, and *e sonë* means AD. Public toilets may be marked *burra* for men and *gra* for women or may simply show a man's or a woman's shoe or the figure of a man or woman. Albanians, like Bulgarians, shake their heads to say yes and nod to say no.

Pronunciation

Albanian is written phonetically and many words are easily pronounced by an English speaker as they are written. The Albanian *rr* is trilled and each vowel in a diphthong is pronounced. However, Albanian possesses certain sounds that are present in English but rendered differently. These include:

c	'ts'
ç	'ch'
dh	'th' as in 'this'

ALBANIA

gj	'gy' as in 'hogyard'
j	'y'
q	between 'ch' and 'ky', similar to the 'cu' in 'cure'
th	'th' as in 'thistle'
x	'dz'
xh	'dj'
zh	's' as in 'pleasure'

Greetings & Civilities

hello	tungjatjeta
goodbye	mirupafshim
good morning	mirëmengjes
good evening	mirëmbrëma
please	ju lutem
thank you	faleminderit
I am sorry/Forgive me.	Më falni.
yes	po
no	jo

Small Talk

I don't understand.	Nuk kuptoj.
Could you write it down?	A mund të ma shkruani?
What is it called?	Çfarë është kjo?
Where do you live?	Ku banoni?
What work do you do?	Ç'farë pune bëni?
I am a student.	Unë jam student.
I am very happy.	Jam shumë i lumtur. (male)
	Jam shumë e lumtur. (female)

Accommodation

youth hostel	bujtinë të rinjsh
camping ground	kamp
private room	dhomë private
How much is it?	Sa kushton?
Is that the price per person?	Është ky çmim për një njeri?
Is that the total price?	A është ky çmimi i plotë?
Are there any extra charges?	A ka ndonjë shtesë shpenzimesh?
Do I pay extra for showers?	A të paguaj për dushin?
Where is there a cheaper hotel?	Ku ka hotel më të lirë?

Should I make a reservation?	A më duhet t'a rezervoj?
single room	dhomë teke
double room	dhomë dyshe
It is very noisy.	Ka shumë zhurmë.
Where is the toilet?	Ku është banja?

Getting Around

What time does it leave?	Në ç'orë niset?
When is the first bus?	Kur niset autobusi i parë?
When is the last bus?	Kur vjen autobusi i fundit?
When is the next bus?	Kur niset autobusi tjetër?
That's too soon.	Shumë herët.
When is the next one after that?	Po tjetri mbas këtij kur niset?
How long does the trip take?	Sa zgjat udhëtimi?
arrival	mbritje
departure	nisje
timetable	orari
Where is the bus stop?	Ku është stacioni i autobusit?
Where is the train station?	Ku është stacioni i hekurudhës?
Where is the left-luggage room?	Ku është dhoma e bagazheve?

Around Town

Just a minute.	Një minutë, ju lutem.
Where is ...?	Ku është ...?
the bank	bankë
the post office	posta
the tourist information office	zyra e informacionit turistik
the museum	muzeu
Where are you going?	Ku po shkoni?
I am going to ...	Po shkoj në ...
Where is it?	Ku është?
I can't find it.	Nuk e gjej dot.
Is it far?	A është larg?
Please show me on the map.	Ju lutem ma tregoni në hartë.
left	majtas
right	djathtas

straight ahead	*drejt përpara*
I want ...	*Unë dua ...*
Do I need permission?	*A më duhet lejë?*

Entertainment

Where can I buy a ticket?	*Ku mund te blejë një biletë?*
I want to refund this ticket.	*Dua t'a kthej këtë biletë.*
Is this a good seat?	*A është vend i mirë ky?*
at the front	*në fillim*
ticket	*biletë*

Food

I do not eat meat.	*Unë nuk ha mish.*
self-service cafeteria	*kafeteri vetëshërbimi*
grocery store	*dyqan ushqimor*
fish	*peshk*
pork	*mish derri*
soup	*supë*
salad	*sallatë*
fresh vegetables	*zarzavate të freskëta*
milk	*qumësht*
bread	*bukë*
sugar	*sheqer*
ice cream	*akullore*
coffee	*kafe*
tea	*çaj*
mineral water	*ujë mineral*
beer	*birrë*
wine	*verë*
hot/cold	*nxehtë/ftohtë*

Shopping

Where can I buy one?	*Ku mund të blej një të tillë?*
How much does it cost?	*Sa kushton?*
That's (much) too expensive.	*Është shumë shtrënjtë.*
Is there a cheaper one?	*A ka më të lira?*

Time & Dates

today	*sot*
tonight	*sonte*
tomorrow	*nesër*

the day after tomorrow	*pasnesër*
What time does it open?	*Në çfarë ore hapet?*
What time does it close?	*Në ç'farë ore mbyllet?*
open	*hapur*
closed	*mbyllur*
in the morning	*në mëngjes*
in the evening	*në mbrëmje*
every day	*përditë*
At what time?	*Në ç'orë?*
when?	*kur?*

Monday	*E Hënë*
Tuesday	*E Martë*
Wednesday	*E Mërkurë*
Thursday	*E Ejte*
Friday	*E Premte*
Saturday	*E Shtunë*
Sunday	*E Diel*

January	*Janar*
February	*Shkurt*
March	*Mars*
April	*Prill*
May	*Maj*
June	*Qershor*
July	*Korrik*
August	*Gusht*
September	*Shtator*
October	*Tetor*
November	*Nëntor*
December	*Dhjetor*

Numbers

1	*Një*
2	*Dy*
3	*Tre*
4	*Katër*
5	*Pesë*
6	*Gjashtë*
7	*Shtatë*
8	*Tetë*
9	*Nëntë*
10	*Dhjetë*
11	*Njëmbëdhjetë*
12	*Dymbëdhjetë*
13	*Trembëdhjetë*
14	*Katërmbëdhjetë*

15	*Pesëmbëdhjetë*
16	*Gjashtëmbëdhjetë*
17	*Shtatëmbëdhjetë*
18	*Tetëmbëdhjetë*
19	*Nëntëmbëdhjetë*
20	*Njëzet*
21	*Njëzetenjë*
22	*Njëzetedy*
23	*Njëzetetre*
30	*Tridhjetë*
40	*Dyzet*
50	*Pesëdhjetë*
60	*Gjashtëdhjetë*
70	*Shtatëdhjetë*
80	*Tetëdhjetë*
90	*Nëntëdhjetë*
100	*Njëqind*
1000	*Njëmijë*
10,000	*Dhjetëmijë*
1,000,000	*Një milion*

Facts for the Visitor

VISAS & EMBASSIES

No visa is required by citizens of Austria, Bulgaria, Canada, Finland, Iceland, Norway, Sweden, Switzerland, Turkey, the USA and European Union countries. Travellers from other countries can obtain their Albanian visa at the border for a price equivalent to what an Albanian would pay for a tourist visa in those countries. Those who don't need a visa must still pay an 'entry tax' which again varies according to what Albanians are charged (Germans US$10, British US$40, Canadians US$50).

Upon payment of the 'entry tax' you'll be given a 'Permis de Circulation pour les Étrangers a Séjour Provisoire' (Travel Pass for Foreigners for a Temporary Stay). This three-page folder has several blank spaces which you're supposed to have stamped by the police in all of the provinces you visit. The document is not always rigorously checked when you turn it in at the border upon departure but a difficult official can ask for it at any time. How much longer this communist-era regulation will remain in

force is unknown but if you're given such a pass it's best to take it seriously.

Albanian Embassies

Albanian embassies are found in the following cities: Ankara, Athens, Beijing, Belgrade, Bonn, Brussels, Bucharest, Budapest, Cairo, Geneva, Havana, Istanbul, London, New York, Paris, Prague, Rome, Skopje, Sofia, Stockholm, Vienna, Warsaw and Washington.

France
    13 rue de la Pompe, Paris, France 75016
    (☎ 4553 5095)
UK
    6 Wilton Court, 59 Eccleston Square, London SW1V 1PH (☎ 0171-976 5295)
USA
    1150 18th St, Washington, DC 20036
    (☎ 202-249 2059)

MONEY

Albanian banknotes come in denominations of one, three, five, 10, 25, 50, 100, 500 and 1000 lekë. Coins under one lek have no value and people throw them away. Albania's huge, torn, dirty banknotes will strain your wallet. In 1964 the currency was revalued 10 times and prices are often still quoted at the old rate. Thus if people tell you that a ticket costs 1000 lekë, they may really mean 100 lekë, so take care not to pay 10 times more! Conversely, a taxi driver who quotes a fare of 1000 lekë may actually mean 1000 new lekë, so watch out. This situation can be very confusing.

In mid-1993, US$1 got you about 100 lekë. Everything can be paid for with lekë; you're often quoted prices in dollars but you can pay in lekë at the current rate. Although Albania is an inexpensive country for foreigners, for Albanians it's different as the average monthly wage is only 3000 lekë (US$30).

The private Banka e Kursimeve is usually the most efficient when it comes to changing travellers' cheques and they keep longer hours than the National Bank. Travellers' cheques in small denominations may also be used when paying bills at major hotels but cash is preferred everywhere. Some banks will change US dollar travellers' cheques into US dollars cash without commission. Credit cards are not accepted in Albania.

Every town has its free currency market which usually operates on the street in front of the main post office or state bank. Look for the men standing with a pocket calculator in hand. Such transactions are not dangerous and it all takes place quite openly, but make sure you count their money twice before tendering yours. The rate will be about the same as you would have got at the bank and the only advantages with changing money on the street are that you avoid the 1% commission, save time and don't have to worry about banking hours. Unlike the banks, the private moneychangers never run out of currency notes.

Deutschmarks are preferred in Yugoslavia but in Albania US dollars are the favourite foreign currency; you should bring along a supply of dollars in small bills as they can be used to bargain for everything from hotel rooms to curios and taxi rides. The import and export of Albanian currency is prohibited, but there's no reason to do either.

Tipping

You should round up restaurant bills slightly when paying. You're allowed to import a litre of alcohol duty-free and this will make an excellent gift for anyone who has been especially helpful. Don't bother bringing the permitted carton of duty-free cigarettes, however, as these are readily available from street vendors inside Albania. Instead, bring instant coffee, which is unavailable anywhere in the country. Albanian women appreciate Western cosmetics.

Some discretion should be used in tipping in order to avoid spoiling Albania. Tourists who hand out chewing gum or pens to children on the street are creating a serious nuisance. (Would they behave that way at home?)

CLIMATE & WHEN TO GO

Albania has a warm Mediterranean climate.

The summers are hot, clear and dry, and the winters, when 40% of the rain falls, are cool, cloudy and moist. In winter the high interior plateau can be very cold as continental air masses move in. Along the coast the climate is moderated by sea winds. Gjirokastra and Shkodra receive twice as much rain as Korça, with November, December and April being the wettest months. The sun shines longest from May to September and July is the warmest month, but even April and October are quite pleasant. The best month to visit is September, as it's still warm and fruit and vegetables are abundant. Winter is uncomfortable as most rooms are unheated and the tap water is ice-cold.

WHAT TO BRING

There's no need to bring food but you might bring water purification pills, a canteen or plastic water bottle, tea bags, toilet paper, tampons, condoms, paper napkins, soap, detergent, razor blades, a diarrhoea remedy, pens, writing paper, envelopes, spare batteries, camera film and any personal supplies you'll need. Most things are also available in Albanian shops.

SUGGESTED ITINERARIES

Depending on the length of your stay, you might want to see and do the following things in Albania:

Two days
    Visit Gjirokastra and Saranda/Butrint.
One week
    Visit Gjirokastra, Fier/Apolonia, Berat, Durrës, Tirana and Pogradec or Korça.
Two weeks
    Visit Gjirokastra, Fier/Apolonia, Berat, Durrës, Tirana, Kruja, Lezha, Shkodra and Kukës.
One month
    Visit every place included in this chapter.

TOURIST INFORMATION

There are no tourist information offices in Albania, but hotel receptionists will sometimes give you directions. You can now buy city maps of Tirana but in most other towns they're unobtainable. In addition, many streets lack signs and the buildings have no numbers! Some streets don't seem to have any name at all. Most of the towns are small enough that you can do without such things.

The Albania Society of Britain (☎ 0181-540 6824), 7 Nelson Road, London SW19 1HS, England, exists 'to promote contacts between Albania and Britain, to offer factual information concerning Albania and to foster cultural and social bonds between the two peoples'. The Society's quarterly journal *Albanian Life* carries a good range of interesting, readable articles, and membership (£8 in Britain, £12 overseas) includes a subscription.

In Australasia write to F G Clements, The Albania Society, PO Box 14074, Wellington, New Zealand.

In the USA, Jack Shulman (☎ 718-633 0530), PO Box 912, Church Street Station, New York, NY 10008, sells Albanian books, maps, videos, folk-music cassettes and English-Albanian language courses by mail order. Jack also carries English translations of Ismail Kadare's best novels.

In Germany you can contact the Deutsch-Albanische Freundschaftsgesellschaft eV (☎ /fax 040-511 1320), Bilser Strasse 9, D-22297 Hamburg, Germany, which publishes the quarterly magazine *Albanische Hefte*.

An excellent source of rare and out-of-print books on Albania is Eastern Books (☎ 0181-871 0880), 125a Astonville St, London SW18 5AQ, England, UK. Write for their 24-page catalogue of books about Albania. Also try Oxus Books (☎ 0181-870 3854), 121 Astonville St, London SW18 5AQ, England, UK.

BUSINESS HOURS & HOLIDAYS

Most shops open at 7 am and then close for a siesta from noon to 4 pm. They open again until 7 pm and some also open on Sunday. In summer the main shops stay open one hour later and private shops keep whatever hours they like. The state banks will change travellers' cheques from 7.30 to 11 am only.

Albanian museums don't seem to follow any pattern as far as opening hours go and museums in small towns may only open for a couple of hours a week. You may find them inexplicably closed during the posted hours or simply closed with no hours posted. Since state subsidies have been slashed, foreigners must pay US$1 to US$3 admission to major museums.

Public holidays include New Year's Day (1 January), Easter Monday (March/April), Labour Day (1 May), Independence & Liberation Day (28 November) and Christmas (25 December). Ramadan and Bajram, variable Muslim holidays, are also celebrated.

POST & TELECOMMUNICATIONS

Post

Postage is inexpensive and the service surprisingly reliable, but always use air mail. Ironically, sending an air-mail letter from Albania is half the price of sending a postcard – somebody seems to be taking the concept of 'tourist price' to its absurd extreme! There are no public mailboxes in Albania and you must hand in your letters at a post office in person. Leaving letters at hotel reception for mailing is unwise. Mail your parcels from the main post office in Tirana to reduce the amount of handling.

If you buy any books in Albania, be aware that all materials printed in Albania or in the Albanian language are confiscated by the Yugoslav border guards. Anyone leaving Albania through Montenegro or Kosovo should mail all Albanian publications home before leaving Tirana. Bring some padded envelopes or wrapping paper and string for the purpose. You shouldn't have any problems of this kind at the Macedonian or Greek borders.

Receiving Mail American Express cardholders can have their mail sent care of American Express/Ada Air, Rruga Kongresi i Përmetit 11, Tirana, Albania. Otherwise just use Poste Restante, Tirana, Albania. However, Albania is not a good country in which to receive mail as letters to Albania are often opened by people looking for money.

Telephone

Long-distance telephone calls made from main post offices are cheap, costing only US$1 a minute to Western Europe. You may be pleasantly surprised by how fast your calls go through but come early or late as these offices are often crowded around mid-afternoon.

Getting through to Albania (country code 355) takes persistence, and only Tirana (area code 42), Durrës (52), Elbasan (545) and Korça (824) have direct dialling; elsewhere you must go through an operator.

TIME

Albania is one hour ahead of GMT/UTC, which is the same as Yugoslavia, Macedonia and Italy, but one hour behind Greece. Albania goes on summer time at the end of March, when clocks are turned forward an hour. At the end of September, they're turned back an hour.

ELECTRICITY

The electric current is 220 V AC, 50 Hz, and plugs have two round pins.

WEIGHTS & MEASURES

Albania uses the metric system.

BOOKS & MAPS

One of the best travel guidebooks to Albania is *Nagel's Encyclopedia-Guide Albania* (Nagel Publishers, 5-7, Rue de l'Orangerie, 1211 Geneva 7, Switzerland), published in English and German editions in 1990. It's seldom found in bookshops, however, so consider ordering a copy through the mail well ahead. Nagel's provides no practical hotel or restaurant information but is good on historical background.

The first noteworthy post-communist (1994) travel guide to the country is the *Blue Guide Albania* by James Pettifer, available from A & C Black, Box 19, Huntingdon, Cambs PE19 3SF, England, UK.

High Albania by Edith Durham, first published in 1909 and recently reissued by Virago in the UK and Beacon Press in the USA, is an Englishwoman's account of the tribes of northern Albania based on seven years of travel in the area.

In *Albania, The Search for the Eagle's Song* (Brewin Books, Studley, Warwickshire, England, UK) June Emerson gives a picture of what it was like to visit Albania just before 1990. Untainted by hindsight, her book is an unwitting snapshot of a time that has vanished forever.

The Artful Albanian: The Memoirs of Enver Hoxha (Chatto & Windus, London, UK, 1986), edited by Jon Halliday, contains selected passages from the 3400 pages of Hoxha's six volumes of memoirs. Chapters like 'Decoding China' and 'Battling Khrushchev' will give you an insight into the mind of this controversial figure.

One of the best recent studies of Albanian history since 1912 is *Wounded Eagle: Albania's Fight for Survival* by Marko Milivojevic, published in August 1992 by The Institute for European Defence & Strategic Studies, 13-14 Golden Square, London W1R 3AG, England, UK.

Albania and the Albanians by Derek Hall (Pinter Publishers, London, England, UK) is a comprehensive political history of Albania published in 1994.

MEDIA

Some 18 newspapers are published in Tirana, up from seven in 1989. Many are sponsored by political parties, such as *Zëri i popullit* (The People's Voice), organ of the Socialist Party; *RD* (Democratic Renaissance), the Democratic Party's paper; *Alternativa*, the Social Democratic Party's paper; and *Republika*, the Republican Party's paper. The *Gazeta Shqiptare* is published in Albanian and Italian. *Drita* (Light), the weekly periodical of the League of Writers & Artists, features poetry in Albanian.

Freedom of the press is relative in Albania; a 1993 law makes the printing of 'false information' an offence punishable by a fine of up to US$8000. 'Insulting the high personalities of state' can lead to imprisonment. In early 1994 the British Broadcasting Corporation lost access to a medium-wave transmitter south of Tirana and BBC journalists began to be harassed by the secret police as a result of objective BBC reporting of the show trial of Fatos Nano, President Berisha's main political opponent. Local editors have been arrested for 'publishing official secrets'.

Try picking up Radio Tirana's daily broadcasts in English – to Europe at 10 pm GMT/UTC on 1395 medium wave and 9760 and 11,825 metres short wave, to Africa at 3.30 pm GMT/UTC on 7155 and 9760 metres short wave, and to North America at 1.30 and 2.30 am GMT/UTC on 9580 and 11,840 metres short wave.

FILM & PHOTOGRAPHY

Bring all the film you'll need. It's considered rude to take pictures of people without asking permission, but this will almost never be refused. If you promise to send prints of photos to local people, be sure to honour those promises. As a photographer you'll arouse a lot of friendly curiosity.

DANGERS & ANNOYANCES

Beware of pickpockets on crowded city buses and don't flash money around! Walking around the towns is safe during the day, even in small streets and among desolate apartment blocks, but at night you must beware of falling in deep potholes in the unlit streets and occasional gangs of youths. Be aware of theft generally but don't believe the horror stories you hear about Albania in Greece and elsewhere.

Take special care if accosted by colourfully dressed women and children begging, as they target foreigners and are very pushy. If you give them money once, they'll stick to you like glue whenever they see you again.

Corrupt police may attempt to extort money from you by claiming that something is wrong with your documentation or on another pretext. Strongly resist paying them anything without an official receipt. If they threaten to take you to the police station, just go along for the experience and see things through to the end. Always have your passport and Travel Pass with you.

The public toilets in Albania are among the worst you'll ever see.

HIGHLIGHTS
Museums & Galleries

The Onufri Museum in Berat Citadel houses real masterpieces of medieval icon painting. The National Museum of History in Tirana and the historical museum in Kruja Citadel are excellent. Tirana also has a good archaeological museum.

Castles & Historic Towns

Albania's two 'museum towns', Berat and Gjirokastra, both have remarkable citadels. The Tepelena Citadel on the road to Gjirokastra is also magnificent. Earthquakes, such as the one in 1979, have damaged many of the country's other historic towns, although Skanderbeg's Kruja Citadel has been carefully restored. The Rozafa Fortress at Shkodra is perhaps Albania's most evocative castle.

ACCOMMODATION

Most of the large tourist hotels are owned by the State Bureau for Tourism, Albturist. Prices average US$45/60 single/double for bed and breakfast, US$60 a day for a car and driver, US$30 a day for a guide and US$30 for airport transfers to Tirana or Durrës. Many Albturist hotels are in pretty bad shape, so it's always a good idea to check your room before checking in.

Since 1991 foreign visitors have been allowed to stay at any hotel which has a room, though there's often a lack of medium-priced places to stay – only tourist hotels and real dives. This book lists both the government-owned Albturist hotels and the lower-category hotels previously intended only for Albanians. Albanians generally pay US$2 to stay at the bottom-end places but foreigners are generally charged more, probably about US$5 per person. Prices often depend on how much they think you're willing to pay and bargaining is sometimes possible. The prices quoted in this book are only a guide and in places which have seldom accommodated foreigners you'll sometimes get the local price. Don't expect luxuries such as showers in these hotels and be grateful if there's any running water at all, much less in your room.

Almost every town of any size in Albania has a basic hotel and those in smaller places off the beaten tourist track are invariably cheaper than those in the cities covered in this book. You can often save money by stopping somewhere along the way for the night and catching an early bus on to your real destination the next morning.

In June 1992 the Albanian government established a US$10 per person per night tax on rooms in all tourist hotels, in addition to the 15% value-added tax. This forces hoteliers to charge foreigners far more than their rooms are worth or about 10 times what an Albanian would pay for the same accommodation. Not all hotels rigorously apply the taxes, although this could change.

Accommodation with Albanian families is usually less expensive and more interesting than staying at the tourist hotels and you'll receive many offers to stay. Several agencies in Tirana arrange private rooms but elsewhere you'll usually have to use your own initiative. People who go out of their way to be kind, inviting you home for meals or to stay, often expect you to reciprocate in future, perhaps by mailing them things or even helping someone in the family to immigrate to your country. If you know you'll never be able or willing to do such things, avoid taking up such offers.

There are no camping grounds but freelance camping is possible in emergencies. For security, camp out of sight of the road and never go off and leave your tent unattended. Don't camp in the same area more than one night, unless you have permission to camp next to someone's house and even then you risk losing things. Expect to arouse considerable curiosity.

FOOD
Lunch is the main meal of the day and in the evening restaurants close early, usually by 9 pm. Restaurants often have only a few dishes available. If there's a menu, check the prices, otherwise ask beforehand. Expect 15% tax to be added to your bill at any place with table service (which is never mentioned on the menu).

Since 1991 private restaurants have appeared but their prices have now increased to the point where they're rather expensive. The state-owned hotel restaurants are cheaper but the standards are low and they're also poor value. Everywhere beware of waiters who refuse to bring the menu, pad your bill with extras and 'forget' to bring your change. The many hamburger stands in the towns are a much better deal and cold Macedonian beer is available at prices lower than you'd pay in Skopje; just watch what you eat as standards of sanitation are often low.

Albanian cuisine, like that of Serbia, has been strongly influenced by Turkey. Grilled meats like *shishqebap* (shish kebab), *romstek* (minced meat patties) and *qofte* (meat balls) are served all across the Balkans. Some local dishes include *çomlek* (meat and onion stew), *fërges* (a rich beef stew), *rosto me salcë kosi* (roast beef with sour cream) and *tavë kosi* (mutton with yoghurt). Shkodra Lake carp and Ohrid Lake trout are the most common fish dishes. Try the ice cream *(akullore)*, which has a peculiar burnt taste.

DRINKS
Albanians take their coffee both as *kafe turke* (Turkish coffee) and *kafe ekspres* (espresso). Any tourist or resident expatriate will tell you not to drink the water, but Albanians do so all the time with no consequences. It all depends on what your stomach is acclimatised to. Avoid unbottled, ungased drinks as they may be questionable.

Albanian white wine is better than the vinegary red. Most of the beer consumed in Albania is imported from Macedonia or Greece. Raki (a clear brandy distilled from grapes) is taken as an apéritif. There's also cognac *(konjak)*, *uzo* (a colourless aniseed-flavoured liqueur like Greek ouzo) and various fruit liqueurs. *Fërnet* is a medicinal apéritif containing herbal essence, made at Korça.

Public bars and cafés patronised mostly by local men are very sociable and if you enter one for a drink with an Albanian always try to pay. Nine times out of ten your money will be refused and by having the opportunity to insist on paying your host will gain face in front of those present. The favourite Albanian drinking toast is *gëzuar!*

ENTERTAINMENT

Check the local theatre for performances. These are usually advertised on painted boards either in front of the theatre or on main streets. Ask someone to direct you to the venue if it's not clear. Soccer games take place at local stadiums on Saturday and Sunday afternoons. As a foreigner, you may need to ask someone to help you to obtain tickets.

THINGS TO BUY

Most of the hotels have tourist shops where you can buy Albanian handicrafts such as carpets; silk; items made from silver, copper and wood; embroidery; shoulder bags; handmade shoes; picture books; musical instruments; records and cassettes of folk music.

Getting There & Away

AIR

Rinas Airport is 23 km north-west of Tirana. There's a US$10 airport departure tax.

Ada Air arrives from Bari; Adria Airways from Ljubljana; Albanian Airlines from Rome, Zürich, Munich and Vienna; Alitalia from Rome; Arbëria Airlines from New York; Hemus Air from Sofia; Malév Hungarian Airlines from Budapest; Olympic Airlines from Athens and Ioannina; and Swissair from Zürich.

These expensive flights are used mostly by business people or Albanians resident abroad and are of little interest to budget travellers, who can come more cheaply and easily by road. An exception is Malév Hungarian Airline's service three times a week from Budapest to Tirana, which is good value at US$257 return and you avoid having to transit Yugoslavia. Adria Airways flights from Ljubljana are more expensive and their flight times highly inconvenient.

Unfortunately the Italian government requires airlines flying between Italy and Albania to charge unusually high fares, which makes Italy a poor gateway. For example, Tirana-Bari is US$286 one way, Tirana-Rome US$395 one way. It's no more expensive to fly further on Albanian Airlines (☎ /fax 42 857), a joint venture with Tyrolean Airlines of Austria, which has flights to Zürich (twice weekly, US$388 one way), Munich (three times a week, US$395 one way) and Vienna (three times a week, US$372 one way).

Before investing in any of the above compare the price of a cheap flight to Athens or Thessaloniki, from where Albania is easily accessible by local bus with a change of bus at the border.

LAND

Although Shkodra is linked to Podgorica, Yugoslavia by freight train, there's no passenger service.

The simplest way to get there by bus is from Greece. Nine Greek buses a day run from Ioannina, Greece, to the Albanian border at Kakavija (one hour, US$4). You must arrive at the border before 11 am to connect with the regular Albanian bus on to Tirana (242 km). In the other direction, the bus to Kakavija leaves Tirana at 3.30 am. Buy tickets from the Ardatrans kiosk behind the Palace of Culture (north side).

Alternatively, it's fairly easy to cover the 93 km from Korça to Florina, Greece, via Kapshtica (see the Korça section in this chapter for details). Unscheduled local buses from Tirana to Kakavija and Korça to Kapshtica leave throughout the day. To/from Athens you're better off going via Kakavija, to/from Thessaloniki via Kapshtica. (The cheapest hotel in Ioannina is the *Metropole* near the bus station at US$11/22 single/double.)

If you're Macedonia-bound, take a bus to Pogradec on the south side of Ohrid Lake and cross on foot via Sveti Naum, as described in the Pogradec section in this chapter. Mëmëdheu Tours in the yellow kiosk behind Hotel Tirana has a bus from Tirana to Skopje, Macedonia, daily at 9 am (129 km, 9½ hours, US$23). Arta Travel Agency in the next kiosk also has a daily bus to Skopje (US$20) and twice a week to Pristina, Yugoslavia (US$20).

A bus leaves Tirana for Sofia every Tuesday and Wednesday at 3 pm (505 km, US$30 plus US$4 tax). On Monday at noon there's a Turkish bus from Tirana to Istanbul (US$44 plus US$7 tax). Tickets are available from Albtransport, Rruga Congresi i Përmetit, Tirana.

Car & Motorbike

It is highly inadvisable to bring your own car to Albania for several reasons. Firstly, driving is hazardous because of the many narrow, rough-surfaced roads onto which cattle often wander. Pedestrians don't respect traffic rules either and can be seen strolling along, two or three abreast, oblivious to vehicles approaching from behind. Road signs are few and far between.

Secondly, some Albanian motorists are such irresponsible drivers that you'll be in actual physical danger. Albanian workers back home on visits from Western Europe often drive their flashy cars quite recklessly as a way of showing off.

Thirdly, vandalism of and theft from parked cars mean you'll have to keep a careful watch over the vehicle at all times and always park overnight in guarded parking lots or at police stations. If not, the kids will steal windscreen-wiper blades, radio antennas, name plates and anything else easily removed by day, and at night the big guys will help themselves to windshields, tyres, headlights etc.

Fourthly, corrupt police at roadblocks along the highways will see you as a means of supplementing their income and will care-fully go over your documents and vehicle until they find something wrong, which of course will be overlooked for a gratuity. The southern highway from Korça to Tepelena via Përmet is especially notorious for this.

Fifthly, petrol can be extremely difficult to find (unleaded fuel is unavailable). You'll often have to bribe filling-station attendants or truck drivers to get a kerosene-like sub-stance your car won't like at all.

The highway border crossings that follow are open to both motorists and persons on foot or bicycle.

To/From Yugoslavia You can cross at Han i Hotit (between Podgorica and Shkodra) and Morina (between Prizren and Kukës). For information about crossing at Morina see the Kukës section in this chapter and Prizren in the Yugoslavia chapter.

To/From Macedonia Cross at Tushemisht (near Sveti Naum, 29 km south of Ohrid), Qafa e Thanës (between Struga and Pogradec) and Maqellare (between Debar and Peshkopi). See the Pogradec section of this chapter for information about crossing at Tushemisht.

To/From Greece The border crossings are Kapshtica (between Florina and Korça) and Kakavija (between Ioannina and Gjirokastra).

SEA

The Italian company Adriatica di Navigazione offers ferry service to Durrës from Bari (220 km, nine hours), Ancona (550 km, 20 hours) and Trieste (750 km, 25 hours) several times a week. These routes are served by 1088-passenger, 272-vehicle ships of the *Palladio* class. The food aboard ship is good.

Deck fares are US$90 Bari-Durrës, US$130 Ancona-Durrës and US$140 Trieste-Durrës, and Pullman (airline-style) seats cost US$95 Bari-Durrës, US$140 Ancona-Durrës, US$160 Trieste-Durrës. Cabins for the Trieste-Durrës trip vary in price from US$175 for one bed in a four-bed inside cabin to US$300 for a single outside cabin. These are the high-season fares, applicable eastbound from July to mid-August, westbound from mid-August to mid-September. During other months it's about 25% cheaper. The cost of a return fare is double the one-way fare. Meals are not included and an Italian port tax of US$3 is charged on departures from Italy.

You must arrive at the port not less than two hours before departure; it's much better to be there three hours before as boarding is sometimes chaotic. This ferry arrives from Italy full of second-hand Italian or Swiss automobiles and southbound reservations for vehicles are required far in advance, though foot passengers should have no problem getting on.

In Trieste ferry tickets are available from Agenzia Marittima 'Agemar' (☎ 39-40 363737), Via Rossini 2, right on the old harbour five blocks from Trieste Railway Station. This booking office is closed from noon to 3 pm and on weekends. In Bari the agent is 'Agestea' (☎ 331555), Via Liside 4. In Ancona it's Maritime Agency Srl (☎ 204915), Via XXIX Settembre 2/0. In Albania tickets are sold at the harbour in Durrës.

Navigazione Aquila (☎ 085-906 4940; fax 085-906 4930) in Ortona, Italy (near Pescara), has a ferry service from Ortona to Durrës (450 km, 22 hours, US$88 for an airline seat, US$128 in a four-person cabin, US$178 for a single cabin). The Durrës agent is Italmar.

The fastest ferry connection between Bari and Durrës is the 315-passenger catamaran La Vikinga (3½ hours, US$119, students US$90). This high-speed vessel departs almost daily and travels at speeds of up to 90 km/h. The Bari agent is Morfimare (☎ 80-521 0022), Corso de Tullio 36/40.

The shortest and least expensive ferry trip to/from Italy is the Otranto-Vlora link (100 km, three a week, US$50). Tickets are available from Ellade Viaggi (☎ 0836-801 578; fax 0836-802 746), at the Maritime Station in Otranto, or Albania Travel & Tours (☎ 32 983) in Tirana. In Naples contact Linee

Lauro (☎ 081-551 3352), Piazza Municipio 88, 80133 Naples.

The Transeuropa ferry between Koper, Slovenia and Durrës runs three times a week (US$112 deck, US$142 in a four-bed cabin, US$172 in a two-bed cabin and US$227 single). They have a ticket office at the harbour in Durrës. In Koper contact Interagent (☎ 663 4193).

There are also three passenger ferries daily from Corfu, Greece to Saranda (two hours, US$32). In Corfu, contact the Sotiris Agency a couple of days in advance.

PACKAGE TOURS

Several companies offer package tours to Albania which include transport, accommodation, meals, admission fees and guides, but not visa fees, airport or arrival taxes, or alcohol with the meals. Single hotel rooms also cost extra. As always, group travel involves a trade-off of having everything arranged for you against your loss of control over the itinerary and the obligation to wait around for slower group members. The tours also isolate you from the everyday life of Albania.

The companies to contact are:

Regent Holidays, 15 John St, Bristol BS1 2HR, UK (☎ 0117-921 1711; fax 0117-925-4866)
Kutrubes Travel, 328 Tremont St, Boston, MA 02116 USA (☎ 617-426 5668)
Scope Reizen, Spoorstraat 41, NL-5931 PS Tegelen, The Netherlands (☎ 077-735 533)
Skanderbeg-Reisen GmbH, Postfach 102204, D-44722 Bochum, Germany (☎ 0234-308 686)
Egnatia Tours, Piaristengasse 60, A-1082 Vienna, Austria (☎ 0222-42 53 46)

Regent Holidays has a five-day bus tour to central Albania four times a year at £508, return flight from London included. Kutrubes Travel offers a 10-day bus tour of southern Albania every two weeks from May to October at US$2260, including air fare from Boston. Northern Albania is offered once in July and again in August (US$2367).

In 1994 Exodus (☎ 0181-673 0859), 9 Weir Rd, London SW12 OLT, England, UK, began to offer 15-day hiking tours to Albania between June and September. Their free brochure is quite informative.

Getting Around

BUS
Most Albanians travel around their country in private or state-owned buses. These run fairly frequently throughout the day between Tirana and Durrës (38 km) and the other towns north and south. Buses to Tirana depart from towns all around Albania at the crack of dawn. Tickets are sold by a conductor on board, and for foreigners the fares are low. Although old, the buses are usually comfortable enough, as the number of passengers is controlled by police.

TRAIN
Before 1948, Albania had no railways, but the communists built up a fairly comprehensive rail network based on the port of Durrës, with daily passenger trains leaving Tirana for Shkodra (98 km, 3½ hours), Fier (121 km, 4¼ hours), Ballsh (146 km), Vlora (155 km, 5½ hours) and Pogradec (189 km, seven hours). Seven trains a day make the 1½-hour, 36-km trip between Tirana and Durrës. In August 1986 a railway was completed from Shkodra to Podgorica, Yugoslavia, but this was for freight only.

The Albanian railways use mostly old Italian rolling stock seconded as a form of aid. There's still only one type of train ticket, so you can sit in 1st or 2nd class for the same price. Train fares are about a third cheaper than bus fares, but both are very cheap by European standards.

The trains are really only useful between Tirana and Durrës. All trains to southern Albania call at Durrës, a roundabout route that makes them much slower than the bus. To Shkodra the bus is also much faster. Still, travelling by train is an interesting way to see the country and meet the people. Many trains don't have any toilets.

BICYCLE
It's not advisable to attempt to tour Albania by bicycle. Not only are services few and far between, but you may be seen as a slow-moving target for thieves. Cases have been reported of foreigners in taxis being ambushed and robbed on lonely roads, and news of a foreign cyclist will travel far and wide. Due to this risk it's quite possible the Albanian authorities will be extremely reluctant to allow you to enter the country by bicycle, as they could conceivably be held responsible in case of a mishap, although entry by bicycle is not specifically forbidden. (This information is based on a letter from a British cyclist who spent one day in Albania before quickly returning to Greece after being warned that he was in danger.)

A German cyclist sent us this:

I had no problem crossing the border but my week in Albania was the hardest in eight months of cycling. As a single traveller I had always to be careful where I left my bicycle and whom I trusted. Of course, it's the same in any poor country but in Albania I felt very unsafe. For example, a drunk stopped me on the road and got angry because I didn't understand him. I was just lucky that a passing car stopped to help. Once I left my bicycle at a police station for three hours and when I returned I found that parts had been stolen. It's probably easier if there are two of you and you know a little Italian.

LOCAL TRANSPORT
Shared jitney taxis also run between cities. They usually cost about five times the bus fare per seat but for foreigners they're still relatively inexpensive. Ask locals what they think the fare should be and then bargain for something approaching that.

There are two types of taxis: the older private taxis, which are usually found around the market or at bus or train stations and accept lekë, and the shiny Mercedes tourist taxis parked beside Hotel Tirana which quote fares in US dollars. Always ask the price before getting in. Car rentals with or without a company driver are available in Tirana.

Hitchhiking is possible but with the buses so cheap, hitching will probably only be an emergency means of transport. You can get an indication of where a vehicle might be going from the letters on the licence plate: Berat (BR), Durrës (DR), Elbasan (EL), Fier (FR), Gjirokastra (GJ), Korça (KO), Kruja (KR), Lezha (LE), Pogradec (PG), Saranda (SR), Shkodra (SH), Tirana (TR), Vlora (VL).

Don't trust truck drivers who enthusiastically offer to give you a lift somewhere the following day as their plans could change and all the morning buses may have left before you find out about it. You can afford to be selective about the rides you accept as everyone will take you if they possibly can. Truck drivers usually refuse payment from foreigners for lifts (even if the Albanian passengers must pay). Never accept rides in cars containing three or more excited young men as they will drive wildly and do things which could get you into trouble.

City buses operate in Tirana, Durrës and Shkodra (pay the conductor). Watch your possessions on city buses.

Tirana

Tirana (Tiranë) is a pleasant city of 250,000 (compared with 30,000 before WW II), almost exactly midway between Rome and Istanbul. Mt Dajti (1612 metres) rises to the east. Founded by a Turkish pasha (military governor) in 1614, Tirana developed into a craft centre with a lively bazar. In 1920 the city was made capital of Albania and the bulky Italianate government buildings went up in the 1930s. Larger-than-life 'palaces of the people' blossomed around Skanderbeg Square and along Bulevardi Dëshmorët e Kombit (Martyrs of the Nation Blvd) during the communist era. You'll see Italian parks and a Turkish mosque, but the market area on the eastern side of Tirana is also worth exploring. The city is compact and can be visited on foot.

Orientation & Information

Money The State Bank of Albania (Banka e Shtetit Shqiptar) on Skanderbeg Square

(weekdays 8.30 am to noon) changes travellers' cheques for 1% commission.

A free currency market operates on the square directly in front of the State Bank. One of the men with a pocket calculator in hand will take you aside. A number of small kiosks here also change cash only for a similar rate.

Post & Telecommunications Poste restante in the main post office opens on weekdays from 7 am to 1 pm only.

The telephone centre is on Bulevardi Dëshmorët e Kombit opposite Hotel Arbëria and a little towards Skanderbeg Square. It's open 21 hours a day and calls go straight through. Tirana's telephone code is 42.

Foreign Embassies The American Embassy (☎ 32 875 or 32 222) is on Rruga Labinoti (weekdays 1 to 4 pm). Nationals of Australia, Canada and New Zealand can seek emergency assistance from the British Chargé d'Affaires presently based at the French Embassy (☎ 34 054) in Tirana.

The Yugoslav Embassy on Rruga Kongresi i Përmetit, entry from the rear of the building (weekdays 9 am to noon), is always crowded with Albanians, so get your visa elsewhere if possible.

On Rruga Skënderbeg (the street between Rruga Kongresi i Përmetit and Rruga Konferenca e Pezës blocked off with a big iron gate) are the embassies of Hungary (Monday and Wednesday 9 to 11 am only) and Bulgaria (Tuesday and Thursday noon to 1.30 pm only). The Macedonian Embassy is also on this street, provisionally located on the 2nd floor of the apartment building marked 'Ushqimore' near the Banka e Kursimeve kiosk.

Travel Agencies The American Express representative is Ada Air (☎ 33 214), Rruga Kongresi i Përmetit 11. They can't change travellers' cheques but are friendly and will answer general questions if they're not busy.

Albania Travel & Tours (☎ 32 983), Rruga Kongresi i Përmetit 102, sells tickets for the ferry from Vlora to Otranto, Italy (three a week, US$50), perhaps the cheapest way across the Adriatic. Skanderbeg Travel, a few blocks north-west up the same street, is also good about providing general information.

Many of the airline offices are adjacent on Rruga Kongresi i Përmetit just off Skanderbeg Square. Here you'll find Ada Air, Adria Airways, Arbëria Airlines, Albanian Airlines, Hemus Air and Malév Hungarian Airlines. Alitalia has an office on Skanderbeg Square behind the National Museum of History and Swissair is at Hotel Dajti. To reconfirm an Olympic Airways flight go to Albtransport on Rruga Kongresi i Përmetit.

Things to See

Most visits to Tirana begin on **Skanderbeg Square**, a great open space in the heart of the city. Beside the 15-storey Hotel Tirana (the tallest building in Albania), on the north side of the square, is the **National Museum of History** (1981), the largest and finest of its kind in Albania (open Tuesday to Saturday 9 am to noon and 5 to 7 pm, Friday and Sunday 9 am to 1 pm only, admission US$3). A huge mosaic mural entitled *Albania* covers one side of the museum building (the rooms describing the communist era are closed). Temporary exhibits are shown in the gallery on the side of the building facing Hotel Tirana (admission free).

To the east is another massive building, the **Palace of Culture**, which has a theatre, restaurant, cafés and art galleries. Construction of the palace began as a gift of the Soviet people in 1960 and was completed in 1966 after the 1961 Soviet-Albanian split. The entrance to the **National Library** is on the south side of the building. Opposite this is the cupola and minaret of the **Mosque of Ethem Bey** (1793), one of the most distinctive buildings in the city. Enter to see the beautifully painted dome. Tirana's **clock tower** (1830) stands beside the mosque.

On the west side of Skanderbeg Square is the State Bank of Albania, with the main post office behind it. The south side of the square is taken up by the massive yellow-and-red buildings of various government ministries. In the middle of the square is an equestrian statue (1968) of Skanderbeg himself looking straight up Bulevardi Dëshmorët e Kombit (formerly Bulevardi Stalin and Bulevardi Zog I before that), north towards the train station. A massive statue of Enver Hoxha stood on the high marble plinth between the National Museum of History and the State Bank for a couple of years.

Behind Skanderbeg's statue extends Bulevardi Dëshmorët e Kombit, leading directly south to the three arches of **Tirana University** (1957). As you stroll down this tree-lined boulevard, you'll see Tirana's **art gallery** (closed Monday), a one-time stronghold of socialist realism with a significant permanent collection that has been exhibited here since 1976. Nearby is the Italian-built **Hotel Dajti** which is worth entering.

Continue south on Bulevardi Dëshmorët e Kombit to the bridge over the Lana River. On the left just across the river are the sloping white-marble walls of the **former Enver Hoxha Museum** (1988), now an International Centre of Culture where conferences are sometimes held. The museum closed down at the start of 1991 and the brilliant red star was removed from the pyramid-shaped building's tip. Just beyond, on the right, is the four-storey former **Central Committee building** (1955) of the Party of Labour which now houses various ministries.

Follow Rruga Ismail Qemali, the street on the south side of the Central Committee building, a long block west to the **former residence of Enver Hoxha** on the northwest corner (ask). Formerly it was forbidden to walk along these streets, since many other party leaders lived in the surrounding mansions. When the area was first opened to the general public in 1991, great crowds of Albanians flocked here to see the style in which their 'proletarian' leaders lived.

On the left, farther south on Bulevardi Dëshmorët e Kombit, is the ultramodern **Palace of Congresses** (1986), next to which is the **Archaeological Museum** (open Monday to Saturday 7 am to 3 pm). There are no captions but a tour in English is

ALBANIA

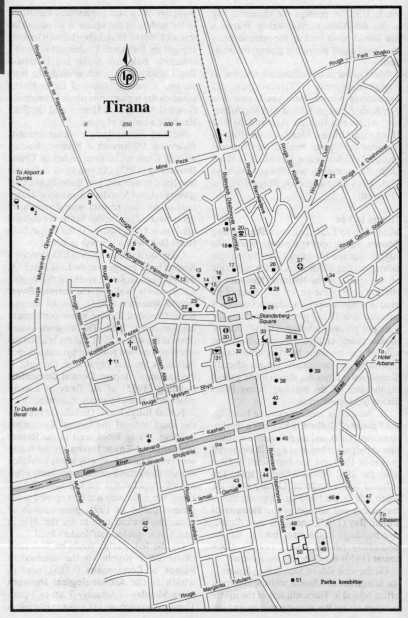

Tirana

0   250   500 m

PLACES TO STAY		8	Bulgarian Embassy	33	Mosque of Ethem
		9	Macedonian		Bey
6	Hotel Pensjone		Embassy	34	Market
19	Hotel Arbëria	10	Catholic Cathedral	36	Theatre
22	Hotel International	11	Orthodox Church	37	Guarded Parking
25	Hotel Tirana	12	Skanderbeg Travel	38	Art Gallery
26	Hotel Valbona	13	Albtransport	39	Parliament
35	Hotel Drini	15	Albania Travel &	41	Albania Today
40	Hotel Dajti		Tours		Exhibition
		17	Teatri i	42	Dinamo Bus
PLACES TO EAT			Estrades/Arena e		Station
			Cirkut	43	Former Residence
14	Restaurant Alba	18	Philatelic Bureau		of Enver Hoxha
16	Embeltore	20	Telephone Centre	44	Former Central
21	Arilta Restaurant	23	American		Committee Building
			Express/Ada Air	45	Former Enver
OTHER		24	National Museum of		Hoxha Museum
			History	46	Romanian Embassy
1	Northern Bus Station	27	Policlinic	47	American Embassy
2	Partizan Sports	28	Disko Club	48	Palace of
	Palace		Albania		Congresses
3	Buses to Kruja	29	Palace of Culture	49	Qemal Stafa
4	Train Station	30	State Bank of		Stadium
5	Yugoslavian		Albania	50	Archaeological
	Embassy	31	Main Post Office		Museum
7	Hungarian Embassy	32	Teatri i Kukallave	51	Tirana University

usually included in the US$2 admission price. Some 1800 selected objects from pre-historic times to the Middles Ages are on display and it's interesting to note how the simple artefacts of the Palaeolithic and Neolithic periods give way to the weapons and jewellery of the Copper and Bronze ages with evidence of social differentiation. Although Greek and Roman relics are well represented, evidence of the parallel Illyrian culture is present throughout, illustrating that the ancestors of the present Albanians inhabited these lands since time immemorial.

Behind the museum is **Qemal Stafa Stadium** (1946) where football matches are held every Saturday and Sunday afternoon, except during July and August. The boulevard terminates at the university, with the Faculty of Music on the right.

Beyond the university is **Parku kombëtar** (National Park), a large park with an open-air theatre (Teatri Veror) and an artificial lake. There's a superb view across the lake to the olive-coloured hills. Cross the dam retaining

the lake to **Tirana Zoo**. The excellent **botanical gardens** are just west of the zoo (ask directions). If you're keen, you can hire a rowing boat and paddle on the lake.

About five km south-east on Rruga Labinoti, which becomes the Elbasan Highway, is the **Martyrs' Cemetery** (Varrezat e dëshmorëve) where some 900 partisans who died during the War of National Liberation are buried. Large crowds once gathered here each year on 16 October, Enver Hoxha's birthday, since this is where he and other leading revolutionaries such as Gog Nushi, Qemal Stafa and Hysni Kapo were formerly interred. In May 1992 Hoxha's lead coffin was dug up and reburied in a common grave in a public cemetery on the other side of town. The hilltop setting with a beautiful view over the city and mountains is subdued, and a great white figure of Mother Albania (1972) stands watch. Nearby, on the opposite side of the highway, is the **former palace of King Zog**, now a government guesthouse.

West of Tirana's centre on Rruga

Konferenca e Pezës is the Catholic **Cathedral of St Anthony**, which served as the Rinia Cinema from 1967 to 1990. Many foreign embassies are situated along Rruga Skanderbeg just beyond the cathedral, but since the rush of refugees into these in 1991, access for Albanians is restricted.

Places to Stay

Private Rooms Staying in private rented apartments or with local families is no more expensive than patronising the tourist hotels and the accommodation is often better.

American Express/Ada Air, Rruga Kongresi i Përmetit 11, arranges private rooms at US$5 to US$50 per person (prices flexible).

Albania Travel & Tours, Rruga Kongresi i Përmetit 102 (Monday to Saturday 8 am to 2 pm and 4 to 8 pm), has private rooms at around US$10 per person plus US$1 for breakfast. They can also organise private rooms in Gjirokastra, Korça, Vlora and Durrës.

Skanderbeg Travel (☎ /fax 23946), Rruga Kongresi i Përmetit 5/11, a couple of blocks west of Albania Travel (weekdays 8.30 am to 1.30 pm and 4.30 to 7.30 pm), arranges private rooms at about US$10 for the room.

Hotels The main tourist hotel is the high-rise *Hotel Tirana* (☎ 34 447), erected in 1979 on Skanderbeg Square. The 168 rooms cost US$45/60 single/double with bath, US$60/80 with TV, fridge and minibar. Hotel Tirana was closed for renovations in 1994.

Right behind Hotel Tirana is the six-storey *Hotel Peza*, recently renovated by foreign interests. Room rates were unavailable at the time of going to press.

The 96 rooms at the six-storey *Hotel Arbëria* (☎ 42 813) on Bulevardi Dëshmorët e Kombit to the north of Skanderbeg Square cost US$23/35 single/double without bath or US$35/46 with bath. Check your room as some have broken windows and no running water, and the hotel is unheated in winter.

The five-storey, 71-room *Hotel Drini* (☎ 22 741), a block off the south-east corner

of Skanderbeg Square, is US$18 per person with bath. The rooms are filthy and there are no taps on the sinks. Worth trying is the six-storey *Hotel Arbana* on Bulevardi Shqiperia e Re, overlooking the Lana River. The 96 rooms with shared bath in this modern hotel are US$17 per person.

Foreign business people often stay at the imposing *Hotel Dajti* (☎ 33 327), erected in the 1930s by the Italians on Bulevardi Dëshmorët e Kombit. The 90 rooms with bath are US$50/90 for a single/double or US$105 for an apartment.

The rest of Tirana's hotels are in pretty bad shape. The least appealing hotel in Tirana is the *Hotel Valbona*, two blocks up Rruga Bajram Curri from Hotel Tirana. They're not at all used to having foreigners stay there and you'll need a bit of ingenuity to get in.

The very basic *Hotel International* (☎ 24 095), Rruga Kaja Karafili, an old yellow three-storey building on a backstreet just west of Skanderbeg Square, is popular among visitors from Egypt. There's no name on the building but it has a large 'restaurant' sign. Ask to see one of the 40 rooms, but bear in mind there's no shower in the building.

The *Hotel Pensjone* on Rruga Kongresi i Përmetit near the corner of Rruga Skenderbeg usually accepts Albanians only, but you can always try. It too has no shower on the premises. Don't even consider the Valbona, International or Pensjone if you're at all fussy about where you stay. Exactly how much you'll be charged at these three places is uncertain but the locals pay around US$2 per person.

Places to Eat

Most of the regular restaurants are over-priced. Tirana's first private restaurant is *Arilta*, Rruga Bajram Curri 178 (open daily 6 to 10 am, noon to 4 pm and 7 to 10 pm). It's is a trendy place and you may even spot the US ambassador at another table, of which there are only five, so drop by earlier to make reservations. Count on US$25 for dinner for two without wine.

Restaurant Alba, Rruga Kongresi i Përmetit next to Adria Airways, has an extensive, expensive menu and a pleasant spacious locale. A meal here costs the equivalent of a week's wages for an ordinary Albanian.

The Albturist restaurants in hotels such as the Arbëria now accept lekë and are a bit cheaper than most of the fancy private restaurants which have blossomed around Tirana recently. Their food is not exciting and the menu's sheer fantasy. *Hotel Tirana* sometimes serves a good breakfast.

In summer the *Bufe Restaurant Miqte*, right down beside the lake in Parku kombëtar, serves reasonable meals on its outdoor terrace.

The *Embeltore* in the north-west corner of Skanderbeg Square dishes out a good bowl of ice cream for a reasonable price.

Entertainment

As soon as you arrive, check the *Palace of Culture* on Skanderbeg Square for opera or ballet performances. Most events in Tirana are advertised on placards in front of this building. The ticket window opens at 5 pm and most performances begin at 7 pm.

You'll see variety shows in the *Teatri i Estades*, on the side of the older building facing the National Museum of History, or circus performances at the *Arena e Cirkut* facing Bulevardi Dëshmorët e Kombit (Saturday and Sunday at 11 am).

The *Teatri i Kukallave*, beside the State Bank on Skanderbeg Square, presents puppet shows for children on Sunday at 10 and 11 am all year round. During the school year there are also morning shows on certain weekdays (ask).

Pop concerts and sports events take place in the *Pallatin e Sportit Partizan* (Partizan Sports Palace, 1963), about two km from Skanderbeg Square on the road to Durrës.

Disko Club Albania, Rruga Bajram Curri near Hotel Tirana (daily 9 pm to 2 am), is hidden below street level under a parking lot. It's a little hard to find but spacious enough once you're down there.

Things to Buy

Tirana's public market, just north of the Sheshi Avni Rustemi roundabout several blocks east of the clock tower, is largest on Thursday and Sunday. A few shops here sell folkloric objects such as carved wooden trays, small boxes, wall hangings and bone necklaces.

The Philatelic Bureau (Filatelia), on Bulevardi Dëshmorët e Kombit, north-west of Hotel Tirana, charges 40 times the face value of the stamps but they're still not too expensive by Western standards and there is a good selection.

Newspapers in English are sold at Hotel Dajti.

Getting There & Away

Bus Both private and state-owned buses operate between Tirana and most towns. There's no real bus station in Tirana and venues change, so check for the latest departure points. Service to/from Durrës (38 km, US$0.40) is fairly frequent, leaving from the boulevard near the train station.

Buses to Berat (122 km), Elbasan (54 km), Fier (113 km), Gjirokastra (232 km), Kakavija, Korça (179 km), Lushnja (83 km), Pogradec (140 km), Saranda (289 km) and Vlora (147 km) leave from Dinamo Bus Station on the west side of Dinamo Stadium. At 6 am you can get buses to almost anywhere from here but they also leave when full throughout the day and as late as 5 pm you'll still find some to Berat, Elbasan, Fier and perhaps further.

Buses to Kruja (32 km) leave from Rruga Mine Peza on the north side of the traffic circle at the beginning of the highway to Durrës.

Buses to Lezha (69 km), Shkodra (116 km), Kukës (208 km) and points north leave from a station out on the Durrës highway just beyond the Partizan Sports Palace. Buses to Shkodra leave throughout the day but those to Kukës leave at 4 and 5 am only.

Train The train station is at the northern end of Bulevardi Dëshmorët e Kombit. Seven trains a day go to Durrës, a one-hour journey (36 km, US$0.50). Trains also depart for Ballsh (146 km, four hours, daily), Elbasan (four hours, three daily), Fier (121 km, 4¼ hours, daily), Pogradec (189 km, seven hours, twice daily), Shkodra (98 km, 3½ hours, twice daily) and Vlora (155 km, 5½ hours, daily).

Getting Around

To/From the Airport The bus to the airport leaves from in front of the Albtransport office, Rruga Kongresi i Përmetit (23 km, US$3, pay the driver). A tourist taxi from the airport to Tirana will cost US$30 for the car (or US$20 after bargaining).

Car & Motorbike There are two guarded parking lots, both charging US$3 a night. One is on Rruga Myslim Shyri, around the corner from the Hotel Dajti, and the other is directly behind the Hotel Tirana.

Car Rental American Express/Ada Air, Rruga Kongresi i Përmetit 11, rents cars at US$45 daily without a driver, US$50 daily with a driver/guide. As you may gather, they feel more comfortable with their own employee behind the wheel.

Taxi Local taxis park on the south side of the roundabout at the market. These will be much cheaper for excursions out into the countryside than the Mercedes taxis parked at Hotel Tirana, but the drivers don't speak English so take along someone to bargain and act as interpreter.

DURRËS

Unlike Tirana, Durrës (Durazzo in Italian) is an ancient city. In the year 627 BC the Greeks founded Epidamnos (Durrës) whose name the Romans changed to Dyrrhachium. It was the largest port on the eastern Adriatic and the start of the Via Egnatia (an extension of the Via Appia) to Constantinople. The famous Via Appia (Appian Way) to Rome began 150 km south-west of Durrës at Brindisi, Italy.

Durrës changed hands frequently before being taken in 1501 by the Turks, under whom the port dwindled into insignificance. A slow revival began in the 17th century and from 1914 to 1920 Durrës was the capital of

Albania. Landings here on 7 April 1939 by Mussolini's troops met fierce though brief resistance and those who fell are regarded as the first martyrs of the War of National Liberation.

Today, Roman ruins and Byzantine fortifications embellish this major industrial city and commercial port which lies 38 km west of Tirana. Durrës is Albania's second-largest city, with 85,000 inhabitants. On a bay southeast of the city are long sandy beaches where all of the tourist hotels are concentrated. In 1991 the city served as a staging point for desperate mobs attempting to escape by ship to Italy and there's now a heavy Italian military presence in the area. The car ferry from Italy lands here.

Information

Money The National Bank near the port (weekdays 8 to 11 am) changes travellers' cheques for a commission of US$1 per cheque. If you've just stepped off a ferry, this bank is half a block to the right as you leave the port.

The Banka e Kursimeve, halfway up the street from the port to the large mosque (Monday to Saturday 9 am to 2 pm), also changes travellers' cheques at US$1 per cheque.

Unofficial currency exchange is carried out on the street around the main post office in town.

Ferry Tickets Agjencia Detare Shteterore per Adriatica at the entrance to the port sells tickets for the car ferries to Trieste, Ancona and Bari. Shpresa Transeuropa (☎ 24 23) in a kiosk nearby handles the ferries between Durrës and Koper, Slovenia.

Italmar Shipping Agency (☎ 23 530) on the waterfront between the port entrance and the train station sells tickets for the weekly Navigazione Aquila ferry to Ortona, Italy.

The ticket office of the fast catamaran *La Vikinga* from Durrës to Bari is on the main street from the port to the mosque.

Some of the agencies require payment in Italian lira which you must purchase on the

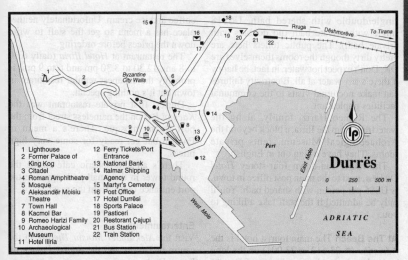

1 Lighthouse
2 Former Palace of
   King Kog
3 Citadel
4 Roman Amphitheatre
5 Mosque
6 Aleksandër Moisiu
   Theatre
7 Town Hall
8 Kacmol Bar
9 Romeo Harizi Family
10 Archaeological
   Museum
11 Hotel Iliria
12 Ferry Tickets/Port
   Entrance
13 National Bank
14 Italmar Shipping
   Agency
15 Martyr's Cemetery
16 Post Office
17 Hotel Durrësi
18 Sports Palace
19 Pasticeri
20 Restorant Çajupi
21 Bus Station
22 Train Station

Durrës

0   250   500 m

ADRIATIC
SEA

black market. If you have a valid ISIC student card always try for a student discount.

Things to See

A good place to begin your visit to Durrës is the **Archaeological Museum** (open 9 am to 1 pm, closed Monday, US$1 admission) which faces the waterfront promenade near the port. Its two rooms are small but each object is unique and there's a large sculpture garden outside. Behind the museum are the 6th century AD Byzantine **city walls**, built after the Visigoth invasion of 481 and supplemented by round Venetian towers in the 14th century.

The town's impressive **Roman amphitheatre**, built between the 1st and 2nd centuries AD, is on the hillside just inside the walls. Much of the amphitheatre has now been excavated and you can see a small built-in 10th century Byzantine church decorated with wall mosaics. Follow the road just inside the walls down towards the port and you'll find the **Sultan Fatih Mosque** (1502) and the **Moisiut Ekspozita e Kulturës Popullore** with ethnographic displays housed in the former home of actor

Alexander Moisi (1879-1935). It's open in the morning only.

The former **palace of King Ahmet Zog** is on the hill top west of the amphitheatre. In front of the palace is a statue of Skanderbeg and huge radar disks set up by the Italian army. The next hill beyond bears a **lighthouse** which affords a splendid view of Albanian coastal defenses, Durrës and the entire coast. The soldiers guarding the lighthouse will allow you to climb up for the view.

Later, as you're exploring the centre of the city, stop to see the **Roman baths** directly behind Aleksandër Moisiu Theatre on the central square. The large **mosque** on the square was erected with Egyptian aid in 1993, to replace one destroyed during the 1979 earthquake. At the western end of Rruga Dëshmorevë is the **Martyrs' Cemetery** guarded by half a dozen decrepit bunkers.

Places to Stay

In Town If you're arriving by ferry, look across the street to the left as you leave the port to see the three-storey *Hotel Iliria* (☎ 22 209). The 50 rooms here are US$12/17

single/double with shared bath, US$18 single with private bath (no doubles with private bath). The public toilets here are pretty dirty though the rooms themselves are OK. Don't expect hot water, in fact, be happy if there's any water at all. Electricity failures can make nocturnal visits to the communal facilities unpleasant.

The Romeo Harizi family, along the waterfront from the Iliria, a block beyond the Archaeological Museum, rents private rooms. They have a sign out in English.

The rather run-down four-storey *Hotel Durrësi*, next to the main post office in town, is US$5 per person with shared bath. You'll only be admitted if the staff take a liking to you.

At The Beach The main tourist hotel is the *Adriatiku* (☎ 23 612 or 23 001) on the long sandy beach five km south-east of Durrës. The 60 rooms in this appealing Stalin-era building are US$40/57 single/double with bath. At five stories it's the highest along the entire Albanian coast, a good indication of just how charmingly undeveloped tourism is here. The quality of the water lapping the Adriatiku's beach is somewhat less charming, so have a look before plunging in.

Next to the Adriatiku are the less expensive four-storey Durrësi, Apolonia, Butrinti and Kruja hotels, all charging about US$29/42 single/double with bath. At last report the Butrinti and Kruja were closed but the 128 rooms at *Hotel Durrësi* were available. Don't confuse this Durrësi with the other hotel of the same name in town. The four-storey *Hotel Apolonia* with 102 rooms facing the beach is similar to the Durrësi (at the beach).

One reader reported getting a room in a private villa near the beach just south-east of Hotel Adriatiku for US$10, so it pays to look around.

Places to Eat
Restorant Çajupi, west across the square from the train station, is a private restaurant which serves a rich bowl of beef soup. Just behind the Çajupi is the *Pasticeri*, with good

coffee and ice cream. Unfortunately neither place has a menu so get the staff to write down the prices before ordering.

The restaurant at *Hotel Iliria* (daily 6.30 to 8 am, 12.30 to 3.30 pm and 6 to 9 pm) is probably the cheapest regular restaurant in town but it's nothing special.

Durrës' first private restaurant was the *Kacmol Bar* on the nameless street from the port to the mosque. There's a menu in English but get ready for some very high prices.

There's an atmospheric café inside the round tower in the small park opposite the port entrance (entry from the rear).

Entertainment
Visit the *Aleksandër Moisiu Theatre* in the centre of Durrës and the *Sports Palace* on Rruga Dëshmorevë.

The *Judela Bar*, just up the street from the port to the mosque, has a special room where only women and couples are admitted from 6.30 to 10.30 pm.

Getting There & Away
Albania's 720-km railway network centres on Durrës. There are seven trains a day to Tirana (36 km, 1½ hours, US$0.50), two to Shkodra, one to Elbasan, two to Pogradec, one to Vlora and one to Ballsh. The station is beside the Tirana Highway, conveniently close to central Durrës. Tickets are sold at the 'Biletaria Trenit' office below the apartment building nearest the station or at a similar office below the next building. Buses to Tirana and elsewhere leave from in front of the train station and service is fairly frequent.

Ferries arrive in Durrës several times a week from Bari, Ortona, Ancona and Trieste in Italy. If boarding a ferry at Durrës allow plenty of time, as it can be a long, complicated nightmare, especially at night. One reader reported that his ferry left from a remote wharf past warehouses and across empty fields behind the train station, but that the locals were helpful when he asked directions.

Getting Around

There's a bus service on the main highway from the Adriatiku Hotel into Durrës. For the return journey, look for the bus near the main post office in Durrës. Pay the conductor.

Northern Albania

A visit to northern Albania usually includes only the coastal strip, but a journey into the interior is well worthwhile to see the marvellous scenery. Between Puka and Kukës the road winds up, down, over and around 60 km of spectacular mountains. Shkodra, the old Gheg capital near the lake of the same name, is a pleasant introduction to Albania for those arriving from Montenegro. South of here is Lezha and Skanderbeg's tomb. Kruja is 6.5 km off the main road but is often visited for its crucial historical importance to Albania and striking location 608 metres up on the side of a mountain.

KRUJA

In the 12th century, Kruja was already the capital of the Principality of Arberit, but this hilltop town attained its greatest fame between 1443 and 1468 when the national hero George Kastrioti(1405-68), also known as Skanderbeg, made Kruja his seat.

At a young age, George Kastrioti, son of an Albanian prince, was handed over as a hostage to the Turks, who converted him to Islam and gave him a military education at Edirne. There he became known as Iskander (after Alexander the Great) and Sultan Murat II promoted him to the rank of bey (governor), thus the name Skanderbeg. In 1443 the Turks suffered a defeat at the hands of the Hungarians at Niš, giving the nationally minded Skanderbeg the opportunity he had been waiting for to abandon Islam and the Ottoman army and rally his fellow Albanians against the Turks. Among the 13 Turkish invasions he subsequently repulsed was that led by Murat II himself in 1450. Pope Calixtus III named Skanderbeg 'captain general of the Holy See' and Venice formed an alliance with him. The Turks besieged Kruja four times and though beaten back in 1450, 1466 and 1467, they took control of Kruja in 1478 (after Skanderbeg's death) and Albanian resistance was suppressed.

Things to See

Set below towering mountains, the **citadel** that Skanderbeg defended still stands on an abrupt ridge above the modern town. In 1982 an excellent **historical museum** (open 9 am to 1 pm and 3 to 6 pm, Thursday 9 to 1 pm only, closed Monday, admission US$2) opened in the citadel. The saga of the Albanian struggle against the Ottoman Empire is richly told with models, maps and statuary. The museum was designed by Pranvera Hoxha, Enver's daughter, who attempted to portray Hoxha and Skanderbeg as parallel champions of Albanian independence. Like Hoxha, Skanderbeg was something of a social reformer who abolished the blood vendetta *(gjakmarrje)* but the feuds began afresh soon after his death.

In an old house opposite the main citadel museum is an **ethnographical museum** (open 9 am to 3 pm, Thursday 9 am to 1 pm and 3 to 6 pm, closed Wednesday). Hidden in the lower part of the citadel are the Teqja e Dollmës or **Bektashi tekke** (1773), place of worship of a mystical Islamic sect, and the 16th century **Turkish baths**, which are just below the tekke.

Between the citadel and the Skënderbeu Hotel is Kruja's 18th century **Turkish bazar**, which was later destroyed but has now been fully restored and made into a workplace for local artisans and craftspeople.

It's possible to climb to the top of the mountain above Kruja in an hour or so and it's even possible to hike back to Tirana along a path that begins near the citadel entrance.

Places to Stay & Eat

The four-storey *Hotel Skënderbeu* (☎ 529) is next to the equestrian statue of Skanderbeg near the terminus of the buses from Tirana. The 33 rooms are US$15/30 single/double without bath, US$30/50 with bath. A speciality of the hotel restaurant is a mixed plate with skallop (beef in sauce), kanellane (minced meat wrapped in pastry) and qofte (a long minced-meat patty).

A *Tourist Bar* in an old house above the citadel museum has a dining area downstairs full of rowdy local drunks and a much nicer café upstairs which offers drinks only.

Getting There & Away

It's possible to visit Kruja as a day trip from Tirana by local bus (32 km). If there's no bus direct to Kruja, get a bus to Fush-Kruja where you'll find many other buses to Kruja. For example, the Laç bus stops at Fush-Kruja. In the afternoon it will be much easier to get back to Tirana than it was to get there in the morning.

LEZHA

It was at Lezha (Alessio) in March 1444 that Skanderbeg succeeded in convincing the Albanian feudal lords to unite in a League of Lezha to resist the Turks. Skanderbeg died of fever here in 1468 and today his tomb may be visited among the ruins of the Franciscan **Church of St Nicholas**. Reproductions of his helmet and sword grace the gravestone and along the walls are 25 shields bearing the names and dates of battles he fought against the Turks.

Near the tomb beside the grey apartment blocks is the **Ethnographical Museum**, and on the hill top above is the medieval **Lezha Citadel**. Much of old Lezha was destroyed by an earthquake on 15 April 1979.

SHKODRA

Shkodra (also Shkodër and, in Italian, Scutari), the traditional centre of the Gheg cultural region in northern Albania, is one of the oldest cities in Europe. In 500 BC an Illyrian fortress already guarded the strategic crossing just west of the city where the Buna and Drin rivers meet and all traffic moving up the coast from Greece to Montenegro must pass. These rivers drain two of the Balkans' largest lakes: Shkodra, just to the north-west of the city, and Ohrid, far up the Drin River, beyond several massive hydro-electric dams. The route inland to Kosovo

also begins in Shkodra. North of Shkodra, line after line of cement bunkers point the way to the Han i Hotit border crossing into Montenegro (33 km). Tirana is 116 km south.

In the 3rd century BC, Queen Teuta's Illyrian kingdom was centred here. Despite wars with Rome in 228 and 219 BC, Shkodra was not taken by the Romans until 168 BC. Later the region passed to Byzantium before becoming the capital of the feudal realm of the Balshas in 1350. In 1396 the Venetians occupied Shkodra's Rozafa Fortress, which they held against Suleiman Pasha in 1473 but lost to Mehmet Pasha in 1479. The Turks lost 14,000 men in the first siege and 30,000 in the second.

As the Ottoman Empire declined in the late 18th century, Shkodra became the centre of a semi-independent pashalik, which led to a blossoming of commerce and crafts. In 1913, Montenegro attempted to annex Shkodra (it succeeded in taking Ulcinj), but this was not recognised by the international community and the town changed hands often during WW I. Badly damaged by the 1979 earthquake, Shkodra was subsequently repaired and now, with a population of 81,000, is Albania's fourth-largest city.

Orientation & Information

From the Migjenit Theatre on the Five Heroes Roundabout, Rruga Marin Barleti (formerly Bulevardi Stalin) runs south-east past the Hotel Rozafa and post office. The post office faces north-east up Bulevardi 13 Dhjetori, a delightful old street lit by antique lamps in the evening and lined with harmonious buildings, many of which are now shops where Albanian handicrafts are sold. The train station is at the far south-east end of Rruga Marin Barleti, 1.5 km from the centre of town, whereas buses leave from around Migjenit Theatre.

Money Two adjacent banks on Bulevardi 13 Dhjetori (weekdays 7 am to 1 pm) change travellers' cheques for 1% commission. Otherwise look for moneychangers along the street between these banks and the post office.

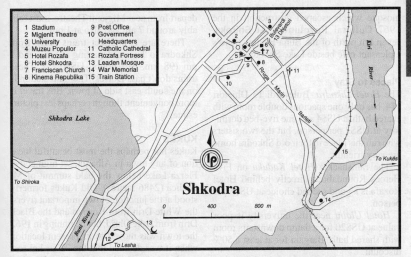

1 Stadium
2 Migjenit Theatre
3 University
4 Muzeu Popullor
5 Hotel Rozafa
6 Hotel Shkodra
7 Franciscan Church
8 Kinema Republika
9 Post Office
10 Government Headquarters
11 Catholic Cathedral
12 Rozafa Fortress
13 Leaden Mosque
14 War Memorial
15 Train Station

Shkodra

0   400   800 m

To Shiroka

To Lesha

To Kukës

Post & Telecommunications The post office on Rruga Marin Barleti, across the square from the Rozafa Hotel, is open Monday to Saturday from 7 am to 2 pm, Sunday 8 am to noon

The telephone centre here operates around the clock.

Things to See

The **Muzeu Popullor** in the eclectic palace (1860) of an English aristocrat opposite Hotel Rozafa contains recent paintings and historic photos upstairs, and an excellent archaeological collection downstairs.

Shkodra was always the most influential Catholic city of Albania, with a large cathedral and Jesuit and Franciscan monasteries, seminaries and religious libraries. From 1967 to 1990 the **Franciscan Church** on Rruga Ndre Mjeda off Bulevardi 13 Dhjetori was used as an auditorium known as the 'Pallati i Kulturës Vasil Shanto' but now it's a church once again. Just inside is a photo exhibit of Shkodra priests who died in communist prisons. Note especially the photos of Catholic poet Gjergj Fishta (1871-1940) formerly buried here but whose bones were dug up and thrown in the Drini River during the

Cultural Revolution. A few blocks south-east of here is the **Catholic cathedral** (1858), converted into a palace of sport by the communists and rededicated just in time for the papal visit in April 1993.

The Rozafa Fortress Two km south-west of Shkodra, near the southern end of Shkodra Lake, is the Rozafa Fortress, founded by the Illyrians in antiquity but rebuilt much later by the Venetians and Turks. Upon entering the second enclosure you pass a ruined church which was first converted into a mosque and then reach a restored stone palace. From the highest point there's a marvellous view on all sides.

The fortress derived its name from a woman named Rozafa, who was allegedly walled into the ramparts as an offering to the gods so that the construction would stand. The story goes that Rozafa asked that two holes be left in the stonework so that she could continue to suckle her baby. Nursing women still come to the fortress to smear their breasts with milky water taken from a spring here.

Below the fortress is the many-domed **Leaden Mosque** (1774), the only Shkodra mosque which escaped destruction in the 1967 Cultural Revolution. At **Shiroka**, seven km north of the Buna Bridge, there's a pleasant café beside Lake Shkodra.

Places to Stay

The *Hotel Shkodra*, Bulevardi 13 Dhjetori 114, has only one spacious double room with shared bath at US$4 and one five-bed dormitory at US$2 per person, but the two sisters who run this place in their old Shkodra home are very friendly.

The ramshackle *Hotel Kaduku* on Five Heroes Roundabout directly behind Hotel Rozafa is a good second choice at US$5 per person.

Hotel Ulqini near the university is poor value at US$20 for a damp downstairs room with shared bath. Bargain for at least a 50% discount.

The city's main tourist hotel where all tourists were required to stay until 1991 is the *Hotel Rozafa* (☎ 23 54), a nine-storey building on the Five Heroes Roundabout. Rooms are US$34 double without bath (no singles without bath), US$32/54 single/double with bath, breakfast included.

Places to Eat

The *Shkodra Restaurant*, Bulevardi 13 Dhjetori 158, serves basic Albanian dishes at very reasonable prices. A good breakfast place where you can consume Balkan burek and yoghurt standing up is the *Mengjezore*, Bulevardi 13 Dhjetori 170.

Shkodra's best private restaurant is the *Majagi Hebovija*, opposite the university residences a few blocks north-east of Hotel Rozafa.

Around sunset half the population of Shkodra go for a stroll along the lakeside promenade towards the Buna Bridge and there are several small restaurants where you can have fried fish, tomato salad and beer while observing the passing parade.

Getting There & Away

Buses to Tirana (frequent, 116 km, US$1) and Durrës (infrequent, 124 km, US$1.25)

depart from near Migjenit Theatre, most reliably around 7 am and also at 1 pm.

There are two direct trains daily from Shkodra to Tirana, departing at 5 am and 1 pm (98 km, 3½ hours, US$0.75). These trains don't pass Durrës. The train station is on the south-east side of town. Bus travel is more convenient, though perhaps less picturesque.

KUKËS

Kukës has perhaps the most beautiful location of any town in Albania, set high above Fierza Lake below the bald summit of Mt Gjalica (2486 metres). Old Kukës formerly stood at the junction of two important rivers, the White Drin from Kosovo and the Black Drin from Lake Ohrid, but beginning in 1962 the town was moved to its present location when it was decided that the 72-sq-km reservoir of the 'Light of the Party' hydroelectric dam would cover the old site. It's a pleasant place to get in tune with Albania if you've just arrived from Kosovo and a good stop on your way around the country.

Money Cash money changes hands among the trees at the market not far from the bus stop.

Places to Stay & Eat

Cheapest is the *Hotel Gjalica*, an unmarked three-storey building on the nameless main street in the centre of town opposite a place with a large yellow sign 'Fruta Perime'. A simple but adequate room with washbasin only and lumpy, smelly beds will be US$5 per person.

For a room with private bath the price jumps to US$20 per person at the four-storey *Hotel Drini* overlooking the lake on the same street as the post office.

One of Albania's finest hotels is the *Hotel Turizmi i Ri Kukës* (☎ 452), a five-storey cubist edifice on a peninsula jutting out into the lake, a five-minute walk from town. Rooms here are US$35 per person – better value than the Drini.

All three hotels have restaurants but forget the wretched one at the Gjalica. The terrace at the *Turizmi* is great for a drink and their restaurant is the best in town. A few basic places near the market serve lunch.

Getting There & Away
Several buses to Tirana (208 km, US$3) leave Kukës around 6 am. Getting to Shkodra (129 km, US$2) is problematic and if you can't find a direct bus it's best to take the Tirana bus to Puka (60 km) and look for an onward bus from there.

Occasional buses run the 17 km from Kukës to the Yugoslav border at Morina. The Albanian and Yugoslav border posts are adjacent and once across it should be fairly easy to cover the remaining 18 km to Prizren. Any Albanian books or newspapers will be confiscated by the Yugoslav border guards.

Southern Albania

The south of the country is rich in historical and natural beauty. Apolonia and Butrint are renowned classical ruins, and Berat and Gjirokastra are museum towns and strongholds of Tosk traditions. Korça is the cultural capital of the south, whereas Pogradec and Saranda, on Ohrid Lake and the Ionian Sea respectively, are undeveloped resort towns.

South-east of the industrialised Elbasan-Vlora plain, the land becomes extremely mountainous, with lovely valleys such as those of the Osum and Drino rivers where Berat and Gjirokastra are found. The 124 km of Ionian coast north from Saranda to Vlora are stunning, with 2000-metre mountains falling directly towards the sea and not a hotel in sight.

The 115-km road from Korça to Tepelena is one of the most scenic in Albania, with switchbacks up and down almost all the way. There are through buses from Korça to Gjirokastra and Saranda in the early morning; it's advisable not to stop in Erseka or Përmet but to go straight through as the behaviour of the young men in those towns leaves a lot to be desired. The local police also prey on foreign visitors and may decide to go through your documents until they find something warranting an appropriate tip. Luckily this is one of the few parts of Albania where this is so.

FIER & APOLONIA
Fier is a large town by the Gjanica River at a junction of road and rail routes, 89 km south of Durrës. Albania's oil industry is centred at Fier with a fertiliser plant, an oil refinery and a thermal power plant fuelled by natural gas. Fier has a pleasant riverside promenade.

Things to See
Near the post office is a **historical museum** with well-presented exhibits covering the district's long history.

By far the most interesting sight in the vicinity is the ruins of ancient **Apolonia** (Pojan), set on a hill top surrounded by impressive bunkers 12 km west of Fier. Apolonia was founded by Corinthian Greeks in 588 BC and quickly grew into an important city-state, minting its own currency. Under the Romans the city became a great cultural centre with a famous school of philosophy. Julius Caesar rewarded Apolonia with the title 'free city' for supporting him against Pompey the Great during a civil war in the 1st century BC and sent his nephew Octavius, the future Emperor Augustus, to complete his studies there. After a series of disasters, the population moved south to present-day Vlora (the ancient Avlon), and by the 5th century AD only a small village with a bishop remained at Apolonia.

Visitors first reach Fier's imposing 13th century Orthodox **Monastery of St Mary**. As well as the icons in the church, the capitals in the narthex and the Byzantine murals in the adjacent refectory are outstanding. The monastery now houses an extremely rich **archaeological museum** (admission US$1) with a large collection of ceramics and statuary from the site.

Only a small part of ancient Apolonia has as yet been uncovered. The first ruin to catch the eye is the roughly restored 2nd century AD **Bouleterion**, or Hall of the Agonothetes. In front of it is the 2nd century AD **Odeon** (a small theatre). To the west of this is a long, 3rd century BC **portico** with niches that once contained statues. Apolonia's **defensive walls** are nearby. The lower portion of these massive walls, which are four km long and up to 6.5 metres high, dates back to the 4th century BC.

Places to Stay & Eat

The *Hotel Fieri* (☎ 23 94) is a six-storey building by the river with 50 rooms with bath at US$22/40 single/double.

The *Hotel Apolonia* (☎ 21 11), a perfectly acceptable four-storey hotel across the street from the Fieri, has only rooms with shared bath and someone has given the management orders not to admit foreigners. This could change.

The *Bar Rugova*, a short walk north of the centre of town, has good ice cream and cold beer.

Getting There & Away

All buses between Tirana and Vlora or Gjirokastra pass this way and other buses run from Fier to Berat (42 km). There's also a daily train to/from Tirana (121 km, 4¼ hours).

Getting Around

There are village buses from Fier direct to Apolonia in the morning. You can also get there on the Seman bus but you'll have to walk four km from the junction to the ruins. In Fier the Seman bus leaves from a place called Zogu i Zi near the Historical Museum or from the train station.

VLORA

Vlora (Vlorë), the main port of southern Albania, sits on lovely Vlora Bay just across an 80-km strait from Otranto, Italy. Inexpensive ferries run between these towns three times a week, making this a useful gateway to/from southern Italy. This is probably the only real reason to come here as Vlora's own attractions don't warrant a special trip.

Money Moneychangers hang around the corner between Hotel Sazani and the post office. The Banka e Shtetit Shqiptar is a long block away if you have travellers' cheques and are there on a weekday morning.

Things to See

The **Archaeological Museum** is across the street from Hotel Sazani, and a house museum dedicated to the Laberia Patriotic Club (1908) is nearby.

In the park behind Hotel Sazani is a large stone **monument** commemorating the proclamation of an independent Albania at Vlora in 1912. A block south of this monument is the well-preserved **Murad Mosque** (1542). In 1480 and 1536 the Turks used Vlora as a base for unsuccessful invasions of Italy.

A **war cemetery** on the hillside directly opposite the 1912 monument overlooks the town and from there a road winds around to the **Liria Café** on a hill top with a sweeping view of the entire vicinity – a good place for a drink at sunset. A stone stairway descends directly back to town from the café.

You can take a bus from the 1912 monument down Vlora's main street to the south end of the **city beach** every half hour.

Places to Stay & Eat

The accommodation choices in Vlora are limited. The three-storey *Hotel Sazani* (☎ 31 52), near the post office and market in the centre of town, will start off asking US$10 per person for a basic room with shared bath, but try bargaining. The buffet at the Sazani serves reasonable meals (with beer).

There's also the more decrepit and perhaps cheaper *Hotel Kinezi* about two blocks east of the Sazani. Neither hotel has a shower.

The *Hotel Adriatik* (☎ 20 81), a three-storey building that looks rather like a factory near the bus station, is certainly not worth US$23/46 single/double without bath, US$40/80 with bath. It's several km from the nearest beach.

Getting There & Away

There are daily trains to Tirana (155 km, 5½ hours) and Durrës but buses are more frequent and convenient. Unfortunately no bus runs south along the 124-km Riviera of Flowers and the early morning bus to Saranda takes a roundabout 190-km route through Fier, Tepelena and Gjirokastra.

If you're interested in using the Linee Lauro ferry to Otranto, Italy (three times a week, 100 km, US$50), pick up tickets beforehand at Albania Travel & Tours in Tirana. The Otranto and Naples agents are listed in the chapter introduction. This is probably the cheapest way to cross the Adriatic.

SARANDA

Saranda (Sarandë) is a relatively uninteresting town on the Gulf of Saranda, between the mountains and the Ionian Sea, 61 km southwest of Gjirokastra. An early Christian monastery here dedicated to 40 saints (Santi Quaranta) gave Saranda its name. This southernmost harbour of Albania was once the ancient port of Onchesmos; today, Saranda's main attractions are its sunny climate and the nearby ruins of Butrint. Saranda's pebble beach is nothing special although the setting of the town is nice. Most of the inhabitants live in faceless apartment blocks. It's traditional for Albanians to spend their honeymoons in Saranda, perhaps to stare at the Greek island of Corfu, which is visible from the shore.

Things to See

Saranda's palm-fringed waterfront promenade is attractive but lacks the street life of nearby Greece. In the centre of town are some ancient ruins with a large mosaic covered with sand. A more reliable sight is the sun setting in the west behind Corfu.

Places to Stay

Until recently foreigners had to stay at the seven-storey *Hotel Butrinti* (☎ 417) overlooking the harbour just south of town. At US$30/40/50 single/double/triple with bath the Butrinti is reasonable value but beware of rooms without balconies as they are smaller but cost the same as the larger rooms with balconies. There's no beach here.

The *Camp e Punë Torëve Shtëpia Pushimi* is a large holiday camp for workers a km south along the bay from Hotel Butrinti. Foreigners pay US$18 per person here and the accommodation is fairly good (although the food is terrible).

You should also be able to find a place to stay by asking for a 'hotel privat'. One such place is the *Hotel Gjika Gjini* (☎ 413) on the hillside above town, reached via a series of steep lanes (you'll have to ask directions). Unfortunately the owner has an inflated idea of how much foreigners are willing to pay, but the price soon comes down with bargaining.

Getting There & Away

Buses to Saranda from both Tirana and Vlora follow an interior route via Gjirokastra; unfortunately there are no buses down the coast. Several buses to Gjirokastra (62 km) and Tirana (289 km) leave Saranda in the early morning. A bus to Butrint leaves Saranda around 8 am, returning at 2 pm.

Two Greek passenger ferries cross between Corfu and Saranda daily (US$32 one way). The boats depart from Corfu around 9.30 am, with the return ferry leaving Saranda at 1 pm Monday to Thursday and 4 pm Friday to Sunday. In Corfu contact Sotiris Agency (a few days in advance, if possible); in Saranda you buy your ticket on board. On weekends the ferry brings over tourists from Greece who are bused out to Butrint to see the ruins.

An Albanian boat, the *Harikla*, does the same trip in reverse, leaving Saranda for Corfu around 9 am and returning to Albania in the afternoon.

BUTRINT

The ancient ruins of Butrint, 18 km south of Saranda, are surprisingly extensive and interesting. Virgil claimed that the Trojans had founded Buthroton (Butrint), but no evidence of this has been found. Although the site had been inhabited long before, Greeks from Corfu settled on the hill in Butrint in the 6th century BC. Within a century Butrint had become a fortified trading city with an acropolis. The lower town began to develop in the 3rd century BC and many large stone buildings existed when the Romans took over in 167 BC. Butrint's prosperity continued throughout the Roman period and the Byzantines made it an ecclesiastical centre. Then the city declined; it was almost abandoned when Italian archaeologists arrived in 1927 and began carting off any relics of value to Italy until WW II interrupted their work. In recent years the Italian government has returned some important Butrint sculptures to Albania and these are now in Tirana's National Museum of History.

Things to See

The site (open daily 7 am to 2 pm) lies by a channel connecting salty Butrint Lake to the sea. A triangular **fortress** erected by warlord Ali Pasha Tepelena in the early 19th century watches over the modern vehicular ferry.

In the forest below the acropolis is Butrint's 3rd century BC **Greek theatre**, which was also in use during the Roman period. The small **public baths** with geometrical mosaics are nearby. Deeper in the forest is a wall covered with crisp Greek inscriptions, and a 6th century palaeo-Christian **baptistry** decorated with colourful mosaics of animals and birds which are covered by protective sand. Beyond a 6th century basilica stands a massive **Cyclopean wall** dating from the 4th century BC. Over one gate is a splendid relief of a lion killing a bull, symbolic of a protective force vanquishing assailants.

In a crenellated brick building on top of the acropolis is a **museum** (admission US$2) full of statuary from the site. There are good views from the terrace.

GJIROKASTRA

This strikingly picturesque museum town, midway between Fier and Ioannina, is like an Albanian eagle perched on the mountainside with a mighty citadel for its head. The fortress surveys the Drino Valley above the three-or four-storey tower houses clinging to the slopes. Both buildings and streets are made of the same white and black stone. For defence purposes during blood feuds, these unique stone-roofed houses *(kulla)* had no windows on the ground floor, which was used for storage, and the living quarters above were reached by an exterior stairway.

The town's Greek name, Argyrokastron, is said to refer to a Princess Argyro, who chose to throw herself from a tower rather than fall into the hands of enemies, though it's more likely to be derived from the Illyrian Argyres tribe which inhabited these parts.

Gjirokastra (also Gjirokastër) was well established by the 13th century, but the arrival of the Turks in 1417 brought on a decline. By the 17th century Gjirokastra was thriving again with a flourishing bazar where embroidery, felt, silk and the still-famous white cheese were traded. Ali Pasha Tepelena took the town in the early 19th century and strengthened the citadel. Today all new buildings must conform to a historical preservation plan.

Things to See

A list of all the museums of Gjirokastra with their opening times is posted in front of the Çayupi Hotel. Above the **Bazar Mosque** (1757) in the centre of town is the **Mëmëdheu ABC Monument**, commemorating the renaissance of Albanian education around the turn of the century, from which you get an excellent view of the town. (You may have to ask directions to find it.)

On the opposite side of the mosque is the 14th century **citadel** *(kalaja)*, now a Museum of Armaments (open daily, US$2) with a collection of old cannons and a two-seater US reconnaissance plane intercepted over Albania in 1957. During the 1920s the fortress was converted into a prison and the Nazis made full use of it during their stay in 1943-44. A National Folk Festival used to be held every five years in the open-air theatre beside the citadel but the last one was in 1988 and the tradition now seems to have been discontinued.

Enver Hoxha was born in 1908 in the winter room of his family home among the narrow cobbled streets of the Palorto quarter, up Rruga Bashkim Kosova beyond the

Gjimnazi Asim Zeneli. The original house burned down in 1916, but the building was reconstructed in 1966 as a **Museum of the National Liberation War** (US$1).

To see inside an authentic old Gjirokastra house erected in 1820 visit the **Ethnographic Museum** (closed Tuesday, US$1), just up the street from Enver Hoxha's house. The same staff have the keys to both museums but the admission tickets are separate. The guest room in this house, which originally belonged to the Skënduli family, has an original carved ceiling, decorated fireplace, furnishings, divans and carpets.

The 17th century **Turkish baths** *(hammam)* are below the Çayupi Hotel in the lower town, near the polyclinic, and the remnants of the **Mecate Mosque** are nearby. Gjirokastra also has a lively Sunday market.

Places to Stay

Foreigners are expected to stay at the overpriced *Çayupi Hotel* which is US$20/34 single/double without bath, US$46 double with bath.

Three cheaper hotels exist and although you'll arouse some curiosity by asking for them, they're always worth a try. The *Argjiro Hotel* is right next to the Çayupi, and across the street is the *Hotel Sapoti*. The decrepit *Hotel Zagoria* is a block behind the Sapoti.

A better bet is to ask around for a private room. A local school teacher named Drago will rent rooms at US$15 double including a goat cheese breakfast – if you can find him.

If possible, spend a night in Gjirokastra to allow yourself ample free time to wander around.

Getting There & Away

Gjirokastra is on the main bus route from Tirana to Kakavija and Saranda. Through buses stop on the main highway below Gjirokastra and only occasional city buses run up to the Çayupi Hotel below the citadel.

BERAT

Although not quite as enchanting as Gjirokastra, Berat deserves its status as Albania's second most important museum

town. Berat is sometimes called the 'city of a thousand windows' for the many openings in the white-plastered, red-roofed houses on terraces overlooking the Osum River. Along a ridge high above the gorge is a 14th century citadel that shelters small Orthodox churches. On the slope below this, all the way down to the river, is Mangalem, the old Muslim quarter. A seven-arched stone bridge (1780) leads to Gorica, the Christian quarter.

In the 3rd century BC an Illyrian fortress called Antipatria was built here on the site of an earlier settlement. The Byzantines strengthened the hill-top fortifications in the 5th and 6th centuries, as did the Bulgarians 400 years later. The Serbs renamed it Beligrad, or 'White City', which has become today's Berat. The Serbs occupied the citadel in 1345, but in 1450 the Ottoman Turks took Berat. The town revived in the 18th and 19th centuries as a Turkish crafts centre specialising in woodcarving. For a brief time in 1944, Berat was the capital of liberated Albania. Today, most of Albania's crude oil is extracted from wells just north-west of the city, but Berat itself is a textile town with a mill once known as 'Mao Zedong'.

Things to See

On the square in front of Hotel Tomori is a white hall where the National Liberation Council met from 20 to 23 October 1944 and formed a Provisional government of Albania, with Enver Hoxha as prime minister. Beyond this is the **Leaden Mosque** (built in 1555), named for the material covering its great dome. Under the communists the Leaden Mosque was turned into a museum of architecture, but it is now a mosque again.

Follow the busy street north towards the citadel from here and after a few blocks, behind the market building, you'll reach the **King's Mosque** (1512), formerly the Archaeological Museum. Inside is a fine wooden gallery for female worshippers and across the courtyard is the Alveti Tekke (1790), a smaller shrine where Islamic sects such as the Dervishes were once based.

By the nearby river is the Margarita

Tutulani Palace of Culture, a theatre worth checking for events. Beyond this is the **Bachelor's Mosque** (1827), now a folk-art museum (open Tuesday and Thursday only). A shop downstairs in this mosque sells cassettes of Albanian folk music.

Continue on towards the old stone bridge (1780) and you'll see the 14th century **Church of St Michael** high up on the hillside, below the citadel. In Mangalem, behind the Bachelor's Mosque, is the **Muzeu i Luftes** (closed Monday), which is worth seeing as much for its old Berati house as for its exhibits on the partisan struggle during WW II. Beyond the bank on the stone road leading up towards the citadel is the **Muzeu Etnografik** (open Wednesday and Friday only) in another fine old building.

After entering the **citadel** through its massive gate, continue straight ahead on the main street and ask anyone to direct you to the **Muzeu Onufri** (open daily 8.30 am to 4.30 pm, US$2. This museum and the Orthodox Cathedral of Our Lady (1797) are both within the monastery walls. The wooden iconostasis (1850) and pulpit in the cathedral are splendid. The museum has a large collection of icons, especially those of the famous mid-16th century artist after whom the museum is named. Onufri's paintings are more realistic, dramatic and colourful than those of his predecessors. Unfortunately, tourists have created a real nuisance around the Onufri Museum by giving sweets and pens to the children who hang out around there.

Other churches in the citadel include the 14th century **Church of the Holy Trinity** (*Shen Triadhes* in Albanian) on the west side near the walls. Its exterior is impressive but the frescoes inside are badly damaged. The 16th century **Church of the Evangelists** is most easily found by following the eastern citadel wall. At the south end of the citadel is a rustic **tavern** and battlements offering splendid views of Gorica and the modern city.

Places to Stay

The five-storey *Hotel Tomori* (☎ 602) is named after Mt Tomori (2416 metres), which overlooks Berat to the east. The hotel has no lift but the balcony-front views of the riverside park compensate for the climb. The 56 rooms go for US$15/20 single/double without bath or US$30/45 with bath.

Otherwise, you can stay at the three-storey *Hotel '10 Korriku'* which offers 30 rooms with shared bath at US$8 single or double. It's a couple of hundred metres east of the Leaden Mosque (ask).

Places to Eat

The *Shtëpia e Bardhë* (White House) Restaurant facing the river a little way west of the Bachelor's Mosque serves authentic Albanian food upstairs and has a good café downstairs. There's no sign but look for a white two-storey building with a balcony facing the river.

Getting There & Away

The bus station is next to the Leaden Mosque near Hotel Tomori. A bus from Tirana to Berat takes three hours, which is a little long for a day trip. Buses to Fier (47 km) and Tirana (122 km) are fairly frequent and some buses run from Berat direct to Gjirokastra (120 km).

ELBASAN

Elbasan, on the Shkumbin River, midway between Durrës and Pogradec and 54 km south-east of Tirana, has been prominent since 1974, when the Chinese built Albania's mammoth 'Steel of the Party' steel mill. There's also a cement factory and burgeoning pollution, though the old town retains a certain charm. With 83,000 inhabitants, Elbasan is Albania's third-largest city, having more than doubled in size since 1970.

The Romans founded Skampa (Elbasan) in the 1st century AD as a stopping point on the Via Egnatia. Stout stone walls with 26 towers were added in the 4th century to protect against invading barbarians and the Byzantines continued this trend, also making Skampa the seat of a bishopric. In 1466, Sultan Mohammed II rebuilt the walls as a check against Skanderbeg at Kruja and renamed the town El Basan ('The Fortress' in Turkish). Elbasan was an important trade and handicrafts centre throughout the Turkish period.

Elbasan can be visited as a day trip from Tirana and the drive across the mountains is spectacular. Ask someone to point out the Citadel of Petrela, which stands on a hill top above the Erzen River.

Things to See

In the centre of town is the Hotel Skampa beside the 17th century **Turkish baths**. Directly across the park on the other side of the hotel is Sejdini House, a typical 19th century Balkan building, now the **Ethnographical Museum**.

Opposite the hotel are the **city walls**, which were erected by the Turks and are still relatively intact on the south and west sides. Go through the **Bazar Gate** near the clock tower and follow a road directly north past the 15th century **King's Mosque** to **St Mary's Orthodox Church**, which has a fine stone arcade on each exterior side and a gilded pulpit and iconostasis inside. This church is usually locked to prevent theft but it's worth asking around for the person with the key (who will expect a tip). Visible from behind St Mary's is a large Catholic church (closed). On the west city wall is a museum dedicated to the partisan war.

Places to Stay & Eat

The eight-storey *Hotel Skampa* (☎ 26 61) has 112 rooms at US$17/30 single/double without bath or US$30/50 with bath.

On Rruga Qemal Stafa, two blocks east of Hotel Skampa, is the run-down *Hotel Adriatik* (☎ 26 62), an old three-storey, 18-room establishment with a basic restaurant. The staff are not accustomed to receiving foreigners but it's always worth a try.

Getting There & Away

All buses to/from Pogradec (86 km) pass through here but they arrive full. Getting a bus to Tirana is easier and there are also shared taxis from the parking lot next to the Skampa Hotel.

The train station is about five blocks from the Skampa and there are trains to Tirana and Durrës three times a day.

POGRADEC

Pogradec is a pleasant beach resort at the southern end of Ohrid Lake, 140 km southeast of Tirana. The 700-metre elevation gives the area a brisk, healthy climate and the scenery here is beautiful. Pogradec is much less developed than the Macedonian lake towns of Ohrid and Struga. The nearby border crossing at Sveti Naum makes this a natural gateway to/from Macedonia.

Places to Stay & Eat

The eight-storey *Guri i Kuq Hotel* (☎ 411) opposite the post office is named after the 'red-stone' mountain on the west side of the lake where nickel and chrome ore are extracted. Rooms are US$28/46 single/double with bath.

A much cheaper place to stay is the old, privately operated *Hotel Turizmi i Vjetar* on the beach about 200 yards west of the Guri i Kuq. Ohrid Lake trout *(koran)* is served in the *Bar Bufe Starova* downstairs in the Turizmi and the drinks menu is posted. Ask the Bufe staff about rooms.

On the square facing the modern theatre between these two is the ramshackle *Liqeni Hotel*.

Facing the lakeshore a km east of the centre is the *Shtepia e Pushimit te Ushterakëve* (☎ 348), a military officers' vacation resort where foreign tourists are accommodated at US$15 per person. The 60 rooms are only available from May to September but it's an interesting place to stay. Nearby is the *Shtepia e Pushimit Pogradec* (☎ 235), a vacation resort for Albanian workers which also rents rooms to foreigners.

Getting There & Away

The train station, with services to Tirana (189 km, seven hours) and Durrës twice a day, is near the mineral-processing factory, about four km from the Guri i Kuq Hotel. Buses also operate to Tirana (140 km), Korça (46 km) and other towns.

To/From Macedonia It's fairly easy to hitch the six km east from Pogradec to the Tushemisht border post with Macedonia. Halfway there is Drilon, a well-known touristic picnic spot, then the lakeside road goes through Tushemisht village and along the hillside to the border crossing. On the Macedonian side is the monastery of Sveti Naum where there is a bus and boat service to Ohrid (29 km), just below Macedonian customs (go down the hill at the end of the border fence). Tushemisht is a much better crossing for pedestrians and private cars than the Qafa e Thanës border crossing on the west side of the lake which is used mostly by trucks and other commercial vehicles.

KORÇA

Korça (Koritsa in Greek), the main city of the south-eastern interior, sits on a 869-metre-high plateau west of Florina, Greece, 39 km south of Ohrid Lake. Under the Turks, Korça was a major trading post and carpet-making town – it's still Albania's biggest carpet-and rug-producing centre. Although it is at the heart of a rich agricultural area, Korça saw hard times in the late 19th and early 20th centuries and became a centre of emigration from the country. Albanians abroad often regard Korça as home and quite a few still come back to retire here. Moneychangers work the street just west of Hotel Iliria.

Things to See

The **Muzeu Historik** is in the old two-storey building on Bulevardi Themistokli Gërmenji behind Hotel Iliria. Further up the boulevard on the left is the **Muzeu i Arsimit Kombëtar**, or Education Museum (open Tuesday, Thursday and Sunday only), housed in the first school to teach in the Albanian language (in 1887). Nearby at the top of the boulevard is the *National Warrior* statue (1932) by Odhise Paskali.

Plunge into the small streets behind this statue and veer left to find the former **Muzeu i Artet Mesjetar Shqiptar** (Museum of Albanian Medieval Art), once the most important of Korça's museums with several icons by Onufri. In a striking reversal of roles, Orthodox Albanians have recently taken over the modern museum building and turned it into a church to replace their original place of worship destroyed by the communists. Children in this area will run up to you asking for Bibles rather than money or pens!

Much of the old city centre was gouged out by urban renewal after devastating earthquakes in 1931 and 1960 which toppled the minarets and flattened the churches. Yet some of the colour of old Korça remains in the oriental-style **bazar area** west of Hotel Iliria. Delve into the crumbling cobbled streets lined with quaint old shops and swing south to the **Mirahorit Mosque** (1485), the oldest of its kind in Albania.

Places to Stay & Eat

The eight-storey *Hotel Iliria* (☎ 28 55) is US$19/22 single/double without bath, US$33/50 with bath.

Among Korça's hotels catering mostly to Albanians is the friendly *Hotel Pallas*, on the right just up Bulevardi Themistokli Gërmenji from Hotel Iliria. On the opposite side of the same building is the *Hotel Gramosi* (no sign – ask). *Hotel Borova* is on the square opposite the National Warrior statue. The prices asked of foreigners at these varies, but for Albanians it's about US$2.

Getting There & Away

There are buses to/from Tirana (179 km) via Elbasan. Korça is a gateway to Albania for anyone arriving from Florina, Greece, over the Kapshtica border crossing 28 km east. Buses to Kapshtica leave when full throughout the day from near Skanderbeg Stadium at the east end of Bulevardi Republike. From Kapshtica it's 65 km to Florina, a major Greek city with good connections to/from Thessaloniki.

Bosnia-Hercegovina

Bosnia-Hercegovina straddles the Dinaric Alps separating the Pannonian Plain from the Adriatic. Sandwiched between Croatia and Serbia, this mountainous country has been a meeting point of East and West for nearly two millennia. Here the realm of Orthodox Byzantium mingled with Catholic Rome, and the 15th century swell of Turkish power settled among the Slavs. This unique history created one of the most fascinating cultures in Europe, with a heterogeneous population of Croats, Serbs and Slavic converts to Islam.

In the 20th century Bosnia-Hercegovina has had more than its share of strife. Here WW I began when a Serbian nationalist assassinated an Austrian aristocrat, and much of the bitter partisan fighting of WW II took place in this region. After the war it looked like Bosnia-Hercegovina's varied peoples had learned to live together, and this third-largest republic of former Yugoslavia enjoyed 45 years of peace. All that ended in 1992 when Serbian super-nationalists shattered the country's social harmony with the active assistance of the federal army and hardline Serb officials in Belgrade.

In October 1991 Bosnia-Hercegovina declared its independence from former Yugoslavia but six months later Serbian extremists moved to set up a mini-state of their own following a pattern perfected in Croatia. The charming cities of Sarajevo and Mostar, and hundreds of smaller places, were soon caught in the crossfire and the glorious heritage of six centuries was reduced to rubble. The Bosnian atrocities have shocked the world and the final outcome is still undecided, though for the foreseeable future Bosnia-Hercegovina is unlikely to receive many tourists.

Facts about the Country

HISTORY

The ancient inhabitants of this region were

Illyrians, followed by the Romans who settled around the mineral springs at Ilidža near Sarajevo. When the Roman Empire was divided in 395 AD, the Drina River, today the border between Bosnia-Hercegovina and Serbia, became the line which divided the Western Roman Empire from Byzantium.

The Slavs arrived in the 7th century and in 960 the area became independent of Serbia. Beginning in the mid-12th century, the Hungarians exercised some control. The first Turkish raids came in 1383 and by 1463 Bosnia was a Turkish province with Sarajevo as capital. Hercegovina is named for Herceg (Duke) Stjepan Vukčic, who ruled the southern portion of the present republic from his mountaintop castle at Blagaj near Mostar until the Turkish conquest in 1468.

During the 400-year Turkish period, Bosnia-Hercegovina was completely assimilated and became the boundary between the Islamic and Christian worlds. Wars with Venice and Austria were frequent. After the

Bosnia-Hercegovina

Turkish conquest, a Christian heretic sect, the Bogomils, converted to Islam, and the region still forms a Muslim enclave deep within Christian Europe. Forty per cent of the local Slavic population is Sunni Muslim.

As Ottoman rule weakened in the 16th and 17th centuries, the Turks strengthened their hold on Bosnia-Hercegovina as an advance bulwark of their empire. The national revival movements of the mid-19th century led to a reawakening among the South Slavs, and in 1875-76 there were uprisings against the Turks in Bosnia and Bulgaria. In 1878 Turkey suffered a crushing defeat by Russia

in a war over Bulgaria and it was decided at the Congress of Berlin that Bosnia-Hercegovina would be occupied by Austria-Hungary. However the population desired autonomy and had to be brought under Habsburg rule by force.

Resentment that one foreign occupation had been replaced by another became more intense in 1908 when Austria annexed Bosnia-Hercegovina outright. The assassination of the Habsburg heir, Archduke Franz Ferdinand, by a Serbian nationalist at Sarajevo on 28 June 1914 (the 525th anniversary of the Battle of Kosovo), led Austria to declare war on Serbia. When Russia supported Serbia and Germany came to the aid of Austria, the world was soon at war.

After WW I, Bosnia-Hercegovina was annexed to royalist Serbia, then in 1941 to fascist Croatia, and during WW II this rugged area became a partisan stronghold. The foundations of postwar Yugoslavia were laid at Jajce in 1943, and after the war Bosnia-Hercegovina was granted republic status within Yugoslavia.

Recent History

In the republic's first free elections in November 1990, the communists were easily defeated by two nationalist parties representing the Serbian and Croatian communities and a predominantly Muslim party which favoured a multiethnic Bosnia-Hercegovina. The Croatian Democratic Community (HDZ) took 44 seats, the Serbian Democratic Party (SDS) 72 seats and the Party of Democratic Action (SDA) 86 seats. The SDA leader, Alija Izetbegović, who like Croatian president Franjo Tudjman had been a political prisoner during the communist era, became president.

The HDZ and SDA united politically against the Serbian nationalists and independence from Yugoslavia was declared on 15 October 1991, breaking an unwritten rule of Bosnian politics that each of the three nationalities would have a veto on important issues. To win international approval the Bosnian government held a referendum on independence in February 1992, and 99% of those casting ballots voted in favour. (Ethnic Serbs boycotted the vote.) At this the Serbian parliamentarians withdrew and set up a parliament of their own at Pale, 20 km east of Sarajevo.

Although Bosnia-Hercegovina's Muslim president went out of his way to guarantee Serbian rights and leaders of the Serbian, Croatian and Muslim communities initially agreed that the republic would be administratively divided into autonomous cantons, the Belgrade leadership made a bid for greater influence by inciting Serbian extremists to defend Bosnian Serbs from

'genocide'. On 6 April 1992 Bosnia-Hercegovina was duly recognised by the European Community (now called the European Union) and the USA, and in May it was admitted to the UN. This over-hasty recognition caused the decentralisation talks to break down.

The situation deteriorated quickly when Serbian snipers in the Holiday Inn Hotel opened fire on unarmed civilians demonstrating for peace in Sarajevo, killing over a dozen people. The first to die was a young student from Dubrovnik, Suada Dilberović, and the bridge on which she fell is now known as Suada Most. This provocation served as a signal for Serbian paramilitary formations to begin seizing territory with the full support of the 50,000 federal troops in Bosnia-Hercegovina, as had been done in Croatia.

Sarajevo came under siege by Serbian irregulars on 5 April 1992, after a large federal army barracks in the city was blockaded by the Bosnian government. Shelling by Serbian artillery positioned in the surrounding hills began on 2 May and by mid-June the historic centre of the city had been badly damaged. Though the federal troops were allowed to evacuate their barracks in early June, the siege of the city continued. The UN Security Council agreed in principle to send 1100 troops to Sarajevo to monitor the reopening of the city's airport to allow emergency relief flights and, after a dramatic six-hour visit by President Mitterrand of France on 28 June 1992, the airport was reopened and 1000 Canadian peacekeeping troops arrived a week later.

Meanwhile in April 1992 the Serbs had begun a systematic process of 'ethnic cleansing', brutally expelling the Muslim population from northern and eastern Bosnia to create a sanitised 300-km corridor between Serbian ethnic areas in the west and Serbia proper. A small village would be terrorised until its inhabitants fled to save their lives. The terrorists would then enter the village and loot and destroy the homes to prevent anyone from returning, and any elderly people who had refused to leave

BOSNIA

BOSNIA

would be massacred. The refugees became displaced persons with nowhere to go and the area was declared 'clean' for resettlement by Serbs. In August the grim conditions at Serb-run concentration camps were revealed and the world was stunned to learn that summary execution, torture, rape and mass deportation were being practised by the Serb side on a massive scale.

In August 1992 the UN Security Council authorised the use of force to deliver humanitarian relief supplies and in September another 6000 UN troops were sent to Bosnia-Hercegovina to protect aid shipments from the coast, joining the 1500 already deployed at Sarajevo airport. The impotence of these troops was dramatically displayed in January 1993 when the vice-premier of Bosnia-Hercegovina, Hakija Turajlić, was pulled out of a UN armoured personnel carrier at a Serbian checkpoint between the airport and Sarajevo and executed in front of French peacekeepers. The UN food aid did save tens of thousands from starvation.

By mid-1993 Serbian 'ethnic cleansing' was almost complete and in May 1993 the UN proposed setting up 'safe areas' for Muslims around Bihać, Goražde, Sarajevo, Srebrenica, Tuzla and Žepa. Some 60,000 Muslims had been trapped in Goražde since April 1992 and another 80,000 were surrounded at Srebrenica. In March 1993 the UN commander in Bosnia, Lieutenant-General Philippe Morillon, brought Srebrenica to world attention by refusing to leave the town until aid conveys were allowed in, but in April the town surrendered under UN auspices and 5000 civilians were evacuated by the UN. About the same time the USA began air drops of ready-to-eat meals to the Muslim enclaves in eastern Bosnia.

In September 1992 former Polish prime minister and UN envoy Tadeusz Mazowiecki had reported to the UN Human Rights Commission in Geneva that the Serbian side was responsible for most of the misdeeds committed in Bosnia-Hercegovina. Mazowiecki recommended war crimes trials for those responsible and in January 1993 US secretary of state Lawrence Eagleburger, a former US ambassador to Yugoslavia, named 10 Serbian leaders who warranted war-crimes prosecution, beginning with Serbian president Slobodan Milošević. In February 1993 the UN Security Council voted to set up a war crimes tribunal for ex-Yugoslavia and in May this was established at The Hague. In June 1994 the tribunal reported that in certain areas such as Prijedor the Serb leadership had planned acts of genocide as long as six months in advance and that there was no justification for the claim that all sides were equally guilty.

The Bosnian atrocities also led to calls for Western military intervention to separate the sides and impose a solution. In September 1991 the UN had declared a worldwide ban on arms sales to ex-Yugoslavia, but this was only effective against the poorly armed Bosnian government as the Serbs had inherited almost the entire arms stock of the federal army and the Croats were able to import vast quantities of surplus Warsaw Pact weapons via Hungary. The British and French opposed NATO military intervention out of fear that their peacekeeping troops in Bosnia might be endangered, and the Americans favoured leaving the Bosnian crisis to Europe. Only in February 1993 did the Security Council pass a motion allowing the peacekeepers to shoot back if fired upon.

In October 1992 the UN Security Council declared a 'no-fly' zone over Bosnia and, after this was simply ignored by the Serbs, threatened in December to shoot down any violators. In March 1993 the Security Council finally endorsed the use of force to police the no-fly zone and in mid-April NATO aircraft began patrolling the area. The Serb flights continued as before and none were challenged until a year later. By August 1993 the Bosnian Serbs were so sure Western nations would not intervene that when NATO threatened air strikes unless the siege of Sarajevo was lifted, Bosnian Serb leader Radovan Karadžić warned that if a single bomb hit a Serbian position it would mean all-out war, and NATO quickly backed down.

In May 1992 the UN had adopted wide-ranging economic sanctions against Serbia and Montenegro for fuelling the war and these were strengthened in April 1993. Though the sanctions forced Belgrade to present a low profile, they did little to ease the fighting in Bosnia. The elected Bosnian government repeatedly emphasised that it didn't want foreign ground troops to push back the Serb rebels, but only the right to purchase arms so they could do the job themselves.

In August 1992 a joint EC-UN conference on Bosnia was convened in London but it produced no results. Another peace conference was launched at Geneva in January 1993 with a proposal from the EC negotiator Lord Owen and the UN representative Cyrus Vance to divide Bosnia into 10 ethnically-based autonomous provinces. The Bosnian government initially rejected the Vance-Owen Plan because it rewarded 'ethnic cleansing', while the Serbs said no because it frustrated their principle aim of a 'Greater Serbia'. Only the Croats accepted the deal which they used as a pretext to consolidate their control of the areas assigned to them. In April Vance resigned in frustration from his position as UN mediator and his place was taken by Thorvald Stoltenberg of Norway.

In May 1993 the Bosnian Serbs rejected an 'improved' Vance-Owen Plan granting them a demilitarised corridor to Serbia. In response, newly elected US President Bill Clinton announced a 'lift and strike' policy to lift the arms embargo against the Muslims and strike at Serb artillery, but this proposal was quickly shelved when the British government refused to go along with it due to domestic political considerations. Clinton's brief dabble in Bosnian affairs only made matters worse by convincing the Serbs they had no longer to fear Western military intervention and could proceed to carve up the country with impunity.

In May 1993 Croatian president Franjo Tudjman made a bid for a 'Greater Croatia' by making a separate deal with the Bosnian Serbs to carve up Bosnia between themselves. Tudjman secretly sent regular Croatian troops to Bosnia and began cooperating with the Serbs militarily. Tudjman's cynical scheme hit a snag when the Croat forces were pushed back by the numerically superior Bosnian government army and the carnage in Bosnia spread.

After a February 1994 Serb mortar attack on a Sarajevo market which left 68 dead and 200 injured, NATO issued an ultimatum to the Bosnian Serbs to either withdraw their guns from the hills around the city within 10 days or face air strikes. After stalling for a week, the Serbs quickly began withdrawing their guns when Russia offered to send peacekeeping troops to Sarajevo, thereby freezing the front lines and making the partition of the city permanent.

The cessation of the Serb bombardment of Sarajevo in the face of impending NATO air strikes convinced the Americans that a more activist approach was necessary. On 28 February US fighters belatedly began enforcing the year-old no-fly zone over Bosnia by shooting down four Serb-controlled light attack aircraft (the first actual combat in NATO's 45-year history). In April NATO aircraft carried out their first air strikes against Bosnian Serb ground positions after the Serbs advanced on the UN 'protected area' around Goražde. The half-hearted NATO raids quickly ceased when a British plane was shot down.

Meanwhile at talks in Washington in March the USA pressured the Bosnian government to agree to join the Bosnian Croats in a federation which might perhaps be linked to Croatia in a confederation. Tudjman was presented with the choice of giving up his dream of a 'Greater Croatia' at Bosnian expense or facing UN economic sanctions. As we went to press, the Bosnian Serb side was still sticking to its guns.

Implications of the Bosnian Affair

By early 1994 some 170,000 people were dead or missing in Bosnia-Hercegovina, including thousands of children, and an estimated 20,000 Muslim women had been raped. Some 2,300,000 Muslims and Croats (half the population) had been forced to flee their homes under the most terrifying circumstances and the rest of the Muslim population was under siege. Some 30,500 UN peacekeeping troops were deployed in all of former Yugoslavia at an annual cost of US$1.2 billion.

Over one million people have left Bosnia-Hercegovina as war refugees. Germany, Austria, Switzerland and Hungary together accepted nearly half a million of them, but Britain has taken only 4500, France 2400 and the USA even fewer. Most Western countries have been extremely reluctant to admit any Bosnian refugees at all on the pretext that they should remain as close to Bosnia-Hercegovina as possible to facilitate their eventual return home, something which will probably be impossible.

To date Europe's first major attempt at international peacemaking has been a spectacular failure. Bosnian Serb leader Radovan Karadžić bought time for 'ethnic cleansing' to proceed by making many concessions and promises to Western negotiators, none of which were ever put into practice on the ground. Between April and August 1992 the Serbian forces grabbed 70% of Bosnia-Hercegovina for their third of the population and by late 1993 the Bosnian government was left with only 10%. Western leaders had declared that 'ethnic cleansing' and territorial gains by force would never be recognised internationally, but in the end they found it politically expedient to push for the creation of a small Bosnian protectorate in the area between Sarajevo, Zenica and Tuzla.

Croatia has taken advantage of the situation to occupy areas of south-western Bosnia-Hercegovina where they constitute a majority. (Most of the Serbs of that region were slaughtered by Croat fascists during WW II.) In June 1992 a 'Croatian Community of Herceg-Bosna' was set up at Mostar and in November heavy fighting erupted between Croats and Muslims after the presidents of Croatia and Yugoslavia cut a deal to partition Bosnia between themselves. Croatia has been careful to allow the Serbs to take the flak in the form of economic

sanctions and international condemnation while quietly carrying out the same sort of ethnic cleansing of Muslims as the Serbs though on a smaller scale. The Croat's deadly mini-siege of the Muslim quarter of Mostar received far less publicity than the siege of Sarajevo. In early 1994 some 5000 regular Croatian army troops were deployed in Bosnia-Hercegovina. This approach has weakened Croatia's case for the return of the Serb-occupied Krajina region to Croatia.

Germany has played a devious role in all of this by blocking sanctions against Croatia while standing back and letting others suffer the consequences. Germany bears considerable responsibility for the entire crisis in former Yugoslavia by pushing for early diplomatic recognition of the breakaway states in late 1991, thereby provoking the worst possible reaction from the Serbs.

There will be no winners in this senseless war. Even if the Bosnian Serbian 'statelet' achieves its goal of union in a Greater Serbia, the hatred will endure for generations and it will be a long time before an impoverished Serbia built on murder, torture, rape, robbery, intimidation and other atrocities will be accepted into an increasingly integrated Europe or regain any respect around the world.

GEOGRAPHY

Bosnia-Hercegovina is a mountainous 51,129-sq-km country on the west side of the Balkan Peninsula, almost cut off from the sea by Croatia. Most of the country's rivers flow north into the Sava and only the Neretva cuts south from Mostar through the Dinaric chain to Ploče (formerly called Kardeljevo) on the Adriatic. Bosnia-Hercegovina contains over 30 mountain peaks from 1700 to 2386 metres high.

POPULATION & PEOPLE

Bosnia-Hercegovina's population of around five million consists of 43% Muslim Slavs, 31% Orthodox Serbs and 17% Catholic Croats. After 1971 the Slavic 'Muslims' became a recognised nation within Yugoslavia, although Turk and Albanian Muslims were never counted in this group. Apart from those in Bosnia-Hercegovina, official 'Muslims' make up 13.4% of the population of Montenegro. In 1991 the largest cities were Sarajevo (525,980), Banja Luka (195,139), Zenica (145,577), Tuzla (131,861) and Mostar (126,067). By mid-1993 it was estimated that Sarajevo's population had been reduced to 300,000.

Before the current trouble started the population was incredibly mixed, with Croats concentrated in north-eastern Bosnia and western Hercegovina and many of the ethnic Serbs living in areas adjacent to Croatia in the north-west and west. 'Ethnic cleansing' has forced most of the Muslims out of areas separating the Bosnian Serbs from Serbia proper.

Serbs, Croats and Muslims are all South Slavs of the same ethnic stock. Physically the three peoples are indistinguishable and all speak the same language, which is called Croatian if written in Latin letters, Serbian if in Cyrillic (see the Croatian Language section in the Croatia chapter).

ARTS
Bosnia's best known writer is Ivo Andrić (1892-1975), winner of the 1961 Nobel Prize for Literature. His novels *Travnik Chronicle* and *The Bridge over the Drina*, both written during WW II, are fictional histories which deal with the intermingling of Islamic and Orthodox civilisations in the small Bosnian towns of Travnik and Višegrad.

Facts for the Visitor

VISAS
If you plan to visit the Serbian-controlled portions of Bosnia-Hercegovina from Yugoslavia, ask for a double-entry visa when you apply for your initial Yugoslavian tourist visa as you'll have to return the way you came. This is much less of a problem when entering from Croatia as Croatian visas are available at the border and the Croat officials are usually helpful to Westerners.

TELECOMMUNICATIONS
To call Bosnia-Hercegovina from Western Europe, dial the international access code (different from each country), 387 (the country code for Bosnia-Hercegovina), the area code (without the initial zero) and the number. Area codes include 070 (Jajce), 071 (Sarajevo), 078 (Banja Luka) and 088 (Mostar).

ACCOMMODATION
In the past you had a choice of hotels (rather expensive), private rooms and camping. There was a youth hostel on a hill near Sarajevo Railway Station. What is left of any of this today is uncertain.

FOOD
Bosnia's oriental background is savoured in its grilled meats, *bosanski lonac* (Bosnian stew of cabbage and meat), *baklava* (a Turkish sweet) and the ubiquitous *burek* (a layered cheese or meat pie).

Getting There & Away

LAND
At the time of going to press, communications were in chaos and Sarajevo was cut off from the outside world. In normal times trains from Zagreb and Belgrade followed a spectacular route down the Neretva River past Mostar to the Adriatic at Ploče. In April 1992 the line was blown up in two places. Many highway bridges have also been destroyed and the rival armies have set up roadblocks, thoroughly disrupting transport.

Access to the Croat-held portion of western Hercegovina is fairly easy with four buses a day from Split to Međugorje (156 km) and Mostar (179 km). You can also catch an overnight bus from Zagreb direct to Međugorje (see Getting There & Away in the Zagreb section).

For the Serb-held area, take one of the six daily trains from Šid (on the old main line between Belgrade and Zagreb) to Bijeljina (49 km), just inside Bosnia on the road to

BOSNIA

Tuzla. From Bijeljina buses run to Banja Luka. Alternatively, ask about buses direct to Bijeljina and Banja Luka at Belgrade Bus Station. While a visit to Međugorje is no problem, expect trouble if you attempt to go to Bijeljina. Obviously you'd need to have a good reason to want to enter the Serb-held areas and the Serbian authorities will want to know it.

Around the Country

SARAJEVO

Sarajevo, near the geographical centre of former Yugoslavia, is the capital of the Republic of Bosnia-Hercegovina. Sarajevo's 73 mosques by the Miljacka River in hilly, broken countryside, once gave Sarajevo the strongest Turkish flavour of any city in the Balkans. Apart from being the seat of the head of all of ex-Yugoslavia's Muslims, this large city had an Orthodox metropolitan and a Catholic archbishop.

From the mid-15th century until 1878 Turkish governors ruled Bosnia from Sarajevo. The name comes from *saraj*, Turkish for 'palace'. When the Turks finally withdrew, half a century of Austro-Hungarian domination began, culminating in the assassination of Archduke Franz Ferdinand and his wife, Sophie, by Serbian nationalists.

Until the 1992 fighting, Sarajevo was the most Oriental city in Europe, retaining the essence of its rich history in the mosques, markets and local colour of Baščaršija, the picturesque old Turkish bazar. The riverfront remained largely unchanged since that fateful day in 1914 when history was irrevocably altered here. Seventy years later in 1984 Sarajevo again attracted world attention by hosting the 14th Winter Olympic Games.

For hundreds of years Sarajevo was a place where Muslims, Serbs, Croats, Turks, Jews and others could peacefully coexist. According to the 1991 census, the 525,980 inhabitants were 49.3% Muslim, 29.9% Serb, 6.6% Croat and 14.2% 'other'. From

April 1992 until February 1994 the inhabitants' tradition of tolerance and the historic heritage of six centuries was pounded into rubble by Serbian artillery, leaving over 10,000 people dead and 60,000 wounded. Though a NATO ultimatum has ended the shelling, Serbian separatists have not abandoned their plans to carve up the city and at the time of going to press, Sarajevo's future was still unknown.

JAJCE

Jajce (pronounced 'Yitse' with a long 'i' as in white) is a medieval walled city of cobbled streets and old houses in hilly country on the main highway from Sarajevo to Zagreb. Prior to the 15th century Turkish conquest, Jajce was the seat of the Christian kings of Bosnia and for a short period in 1943 it was the capital of liberated Yugoslavia. Here the 142 delegates to the second session of the Antifascist Council for the National Liberation of Yugoslavia (AVNOJ) on 29 November 1943 proclaimed a constitution outlining the principles of a new federal Yugoslavia and Marshal Tito officially replaced King Peter II as Yugoslavia's legitimate leader. In October 1992 Serbian separatists brutally expelled 35,000 Muslims from this historic city where they had previously been the largest ethnic group.

BANJA LUKA

This important crossroads on the Vrbas River in north-western Bosnia-Hercegovina has the dubious distinction of being the military headquarters of the Serbian separatists. Banja Luka was never much of a tourist centre and in 1993 the local Serbs made sure it never would be by blowing up all 16 of the city's mosques, complementing the damage previously done by WW II bombings and a 1969 earthquake.

MOSTAR

A medium-sized city among the vineyards between Dubrovnik and Sarajevo, Mostar is the main centre of Hercegovina. Founded by the Turks in the 15th century at a strategic river crossing, **Kujundžiluk**, the old quarter, once greeted thousands of daily visitors from the coastal resorts who came in search of instant Islamic culture. In May 1993 Croat forces in the western part of the city began a 10-month siege of the Muslim quarter east of the Neretva River, which was treated to sporadic artillery fire by night, sniper fire by day. The Croats forcibly expelled thousands of Muslims from the west bank of the Neretva and slaughtered hundreds more, and all of the town's 16th and 17th century mosques were destroyed. In November Mostar's famous **Turkish Bridge**, which had arched 20 metres above the green waters of the Neretva since 1566, was smashed by Croat artillery. Only the renewed Muslim-Croat alliance brokered in Washington in March 1994 brought an end to this tragedy.

MEĐUGORJE

Međugorje is one of Europe's most remarkable sights. On 24 June 1981 six teenagers in this dirt-poor mountain village in the hills between Čitluk and Ljubuški, 23 km southwest of Mostar, saw a miraculous apparition of the Virgin Mary, and Međugorje's instant economic boom began. A decade later Međugorje was awash with tour buses, dutyfree shops, souvenir stands, car rental

offices, travel agencies, furnished apartments, restaurants, traffic jams and shiny Mercedes taxis. 'Religious tourism' was developed as if this were a beach resort and shops sold postcards of Christ and the Virgin.

Today the civil war has greatly reduced the number of packaged pilgrims, but it's still possible to enter this Croat-held area by bus from Split and most of the tourist facilities are intact. Check at the **parish church of St James** (1969) for the daily programme of masses, meetings, recitations, blessings and prayers. Major feasts include the anniversary of the first apparition (June 24), the Assumption of the Virgin (15 August) and the Nativity of the Virgin (8 September).

In the past, apparitions appeared on Monday and Friday on the side of Podbrdo, the Hill of Apparitions, and you had a good chance of seeing a miracle there. It's about an hour's walk to this rocky hill from St James. Ask if the visionaries still receive their daily messages from the Virgin and if audiences are possible with them. (It must be noted that the Catholic Church has not officially acknowledged the Međugorje apparitions, the first in Europe since those of Lourdes, France, in 1858 and Fatima, Portugal, in 1917.)

Bulgaria (България)

Bulgaria comes as a pleasant surprise. The landscape is green and lush, not dry and arid like in Greece, and because Bulgaria doesn't get nearly as many Western tourists as it deserves, those who do come are assured of a warm welcome. The Bulgarians are helpful and friendly without ever being intrusive. Bulgaria is safe, there's plenty to see and do, and prices are very reasonable. The Rila Mountains and the Black Sea coast are natural attractions of European stature. Transport, public services, food, museums, monuments, climate, beaches – everything is good. Even the Bulgarian custom of shaking the head to show agreement and nodding to say no is unique.

The Cyrillic script and Turkish mosques are constant reminders that Bulgaria has one foot firmly in the east. Bulgaria has been liberated by Russia twice (in 1877 and 1944) and this close historical relationship made Bulgaria one of the Soviet Union's most dependable allies. In many ways, Bulgaria still lives in the shadow of communism, as you'll note when you apply for your visa or arrive at the border and are handed a 'statistical card' that must be stamped at every place you stay. As before, foreigners are charged higher prices than Bulgarians and the Bulgarian leva is not convertible.

More ominously, the Socialist Party (formerly the Communist Party) is still the largest single political party and the current changes are borne grudgingly by many. The people running the big hotels, the beach complexes and Balkantourist are the same individuals who held those posts before 1989 and they continue to discourage individual tourism. Group travel is heavily promoted and officially favoured (packaged tourists require no visa) while independent travellers are confronted with a number of bureaucratic hurdles, including an expensive, difficult-to-obtain visa with a seven-day waiting period if you want to pay the normal price.

Things *are* becoming easier due to the

increasing number of small private hotels and private-room agencies, and many cheaper hotels and camping grounds once closed to foreigners are now available, but the Bulgarian government deserves no credit for these improvements which have come about largely as a result of pressure from below. Bulgaria still has a long way to go to get to Europe.

Facts about the Country

HISTORY

In antiquity, Bulgaria, the land of Orpheus and Spartacus, belonged to the Kingdom of Macedonia and the inhabitants were Thracians. By 46 BC, the Romans had conquered the whole peninsula, which they divided into Moesia Inferior, north of the Stara Planina (Balkan Mountains), and Thrace to the south. Slavic tribes arrived in

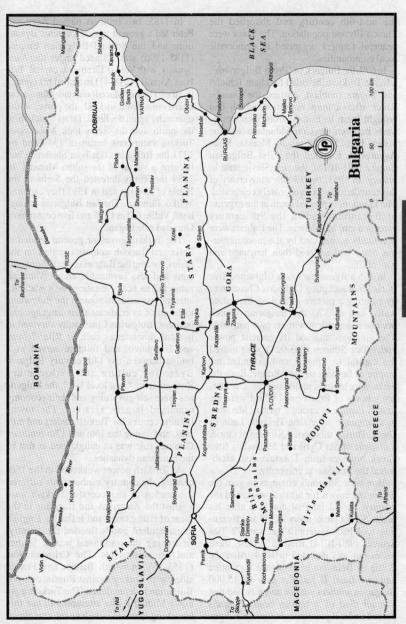

the mid-6th century and absorbed the Thraco-Illyrian population. The Slavs were peaceful farmers organised in democratic local communities.

In 679, the Bulgars, or 'Proto-Bulgarians', a fierce Turkic tribe ruled by khans (chiefs) and boyars (nobles), crossed the Danube River after a long migration which had brought them to Europe from their homelands between the Ural Mountains and the Volga. In 681 at Pliska in Moesia, Khan Asparoukh founded the First Bulgarian Empire (681-1018), the first Slavic state in history. In 1981, the 1300th anniversary of this foundation was passionately celebrated. The kingdom expanded south at the expense of Byzantium and in the 9th century extended into Macedonia. The Bulgars were eventually assimilated by the more numerous Slavs and adopted their language and way of life.

In 865 a Byzantine monk frightened Tsar Boris I into accepting Orthodox Christianity by painting a picture of hell on the palace walls, and in 870 the Bulgarian church became independent with its own patriarch. The kingdom attained its greatest power under Tsar Simeon (893-927), who moved the capital to Preslav and extended his empire as far west as the Adriatic. Even the Serbs were brought under his rule. The literary schools of Preslav and Ohrid were the first in Europe to create a written literature in a language other than Hebrew, Latin or Greek. During this period Kliment of Ohrid, a disciple of Sts Cyril and Methodius (two Greek brothers from Thessaloniki), established the first Slavic university.

However, Simeon's attempts to gain the Byzantine crown for himself weakened the country, as did internal conflicts after his death. Serbia broke away in 933 and Byzantium took back eastern Bulgaria in 972. Tsar Samuel (980-1014) tried to reverse these losses but was defeated in 1014. After the Battle of Belasitsa in 1014, the Byzantine emperor Basil II had the eyes of 15,000 Bulgarian soldiers put out and it is said that Samuel died of a broken heart. Bulgaria passed under Byzantine rule four years later.

In 1185, two brothers named Asen and Peter led a general uprising against Byzantium and the Second Bulgarian Empire (1185-1396) was founded under the Asen dynasty, with Veliko Târnovo as capital. Tsar Ivan Asen II (1218-41) extended his control to all of Thrace, Macedonia and Albania but after Ivan's death in 1241, the power of the monarchy again declined. Tatars struck from the north and the Serbs took Macedonia. Turkish incursions began in 1340 and by 1371 the Bulgarian tsar Ivan Shishman had become a vassal of the sultan Murad I. In 1389 the Turks defeated the Serbs at the Battle of Kosovo and in 1393 they captured Veliko Târnovo. The last Bulgarian stronghold, Vidin, fell in 1396 and five centuries of Ottoman rule began.

The Turkish governor general resided at Sofia and Turkish colonists settled on the plains, forcing the Bulgarians into the mountains and less favourable areas. Although subjected to heavy taxation, no systematic attempt was made to convert the Bulgarians to Islam or to eradicate their language and customs. Bulgarian Christianity survived in isolated monasteries such as Rila, Troyan and Bachkovo, and folklore served as a bridge between the 14th century Bulgaro-Byzantine culture and 19th century Romanticism. On a local level, the Bulgarians were self-governing and their economy remained largely agrarian. The towns became centres for Turkish traders and artisans, and during the 16th and 17th centuries Ottoman rule was as enlightened as that of the European dynasties.

As Turkish power weakened in the 18th century, the country's inhabitants suffered the burden of unsuccessful Turkish wars against the Austrians and Russians in the form of rising taxes and inflation. English manufactured goods flooded the country, destroying the traditional textile, leather and iron industries. The Crimean War (1853-56), in which Britain and France sided with Turkey against Russia, delayed Bulgarian independence. The Turkish governor Midhat Pasha attempted to use this breathing space to introduce reforms aimed at assimilating the Bulgarians, but it was too late.

In the early 19th century popular customs and folklore blossomed in the National Revival of Bulgarian culture *(vâzrazhdane)*. Schools were opened and books printed in the Bulgarian language for the first time. A struggle against Phanariote Greek domination of the Orthodox church began in 1860 when the supremacy of the Constantinople Patriarchate was rejected. Official Turkish recognition of an autonomous church in 1870 was a crucial step towards independence.

Underground leaders such as Hristo Botev, Lyuben Karavelov and Vasil Levski had been preparing a revolution for years when the revolt against the Turks broke out prematurely at Koprivshtitsa in April 1876. The Turks suppressed the uprising with unprecedented brutality, spreading tales of 'Bulgarian atrocities' throughout Europe. About 15,000 Bulgarians were massacred at Plovdiv and 58 villages destroyed. The story goes that Pazardzhik was saved by a daring clerk who moved one comma in an official order, turning 'burn the town, not spare it' into 'burn the town not, spare it' (which is slightly ungrammatical in English but not so in the original language).

These events led Serbia to declare war on Turkey, and in April 1877 it was joined by Russia and Romania. Decisive battles were fought at Pleven and Shipka. Russia suffered an appalling 200,000 casualties in the conflict. With the Russian army advancing to within 50 km of Istanbul, Turkey ceded 60% of the Balkan Peninsula to Bulgaria in the Treaty of San Stefano. The modern history of Bulgaria dates from this 1878 liberation.

Fearing the creation of a powerful Russian satellite in the Balkans, the Western powers reversed these gains at the Congress of Berlin which made southern Bulgaria an 'autonomous province', again nominally subject to the Turkish sultan, while Macedonia was to remain part of the Ottoman Empire. Northern Bulgaria adopted a liberal constitution in 1879, but this was suspended two years later by Prince Alexander of Battenberg, a German aristocrat whom the Bulgarians had elected as their prince. In 1885, southern Bulgaria (called 'Eastern Rumelia') was annexed to the new state, which had been created in 1878, and complete independence from Turkey was declared on 22 September 1908.

All three Balkan states – Bulgaria, Serbia and Greece – coveted Macedonia, which was still in Turkish hands, and the First Balkan War broke out in 1912. Turkey was quickly defeated but the three states could not agree on how to divide the spoils. On 29 June 1913 the Bulgarian army suddenly attacked its Serbian and Greek allies, probably on orders from the Bulgarian king Ferdinand (who ruled from 1908 to 1918). The Second Balkan War soon resulted in Bulgaria's defeat by these countries together with Romania. Macedonia was divided between Serbia and Greece while Romania took southern Dobruja from Bulgaria.

Bulgarian disenchantment with the loss of Macedonia, and the pro-German sympathies of the king, led Bulgaria to side with the Central Powers (Germany, Austria-Hungary and Turkey) against Serbia and Russia in WW I. There was widespread opposition to this policy within Bulgaria, and in September 1918 a mutiny among the troops led to the abdication of King Ferdinand and an armistice. Bulgaria lost additional territory to Greece and Serbia.

Elections in 1920 brought to office the antiwar leader Aleksander Stambolijski, whose government passed an agrarian reform bill dividing the large estates. However, there were serious problems with Macedonian refugees in Bulgaria and continuing terrorist activities within Macedonia itself. Stambolijski was killed during a right-wing coup in June 1923 and in September an armed uprising by agrarians and communists was suppressed. Thousands were killed in the ensuing reactionary terror. Georgi Dimitrov, the communist leader, managed a narrow escape to Russia.

An amnesty in 1926 restored a degree of normality to the country and the League of Nations provided financial aid to resettle the

BULGARIA

Macedonian refugees. The 1930s world economic crisis led to an authoritarian trend across Eastern Europe and in 1935 King Boris III took personal control of Bulgaria.

On 24 January 1937, Bulgaria signed a treaty of 'inviolable peace and sincere and perpetual friendship' with Yugoslavia. However, Bulgarian claims to Macedonia again led the country to side with Germany. In September 1940, Romania was forced to return southern Dobruja to Bulgaria on orders from Hitler and in 1941 Bulgaria joined the Nazi invasion of Yugoslavia. Fearing a popular uprising, however, King Boris rejected German demands to declare war on the USSR. In 1942, an underground Fatherland Front made up of all opposition groups including the communists was formed to resist the pro-German government. King Boris died mysteriously in August 1943 and a Council of Regency was set up to govern until his six-year-old son, Prince Simeon, came of age. The Front planned an armed uprising for 2 September 1944.

In August 1944, with the Soviet army advancing across Romania, Bulgaria declared itself neutral and disarmed the German troops present. The USSR insisted that Bulgaria declare war on Germany, whereupon Soviet soldiers entered Bulgaria unopposed and Fatherland Front partisans took Sofia on 9 September 1944 the monarchy was overthrown by the communists, led by Todor Zhivkov, in 1944. After this, the Bulgarian army fought alongside the Soviet army until the war's end.

Post WW II

After a referendum in 1946, Bulgaria was proclaimed a republic and on 27 October 1946 Georgi Dimitrov was elected prime minister. Peace treaties were signed in 1947 and all Soviet troops left the country. In 1954, all outstanding disputes with Greece were settled and in 1955 Bulgaria was admitted to the United Nations. In the 1980s, Bulgaria joined Greece in calls for a Balkan nuclear-free zone, but relations with Turkey remained strained.

Beginning in the late 1940s, industrialisation and the collectivisation of agriculture were carried out. Under Todor Zhivkov, Bulgaria's leader from 1954 to 1989, the country became one of the most prosperous in Eastern Europe. Within the framework of central planning, managers were allowed some flexibility and workers were given incentives to exceed their norms. Private-plot farming was allowed during the workers' spare time.

By late 1989, Gorbachev's *perestroika* was sending shock waves through Eastern Europe as veteran communists looked on uneasily. On 9 November 1989 the Berlin Wall fell and the next day an internal Communist Party coup put an end to the 35-year reign of 78-year-old Todor Zhivkov. Zhivkov was placed under house arrest 43 days later and in February 1991 he became the first ex-communist leader in Eastern Europe to stand trial for corruption during his period in office. In September 1992, Zhivkov was convicted of misusing state funds to finance flats and cars for 72 top officials and sentenced to seven years imprisonment. (Zhivkov claimed that such perks are a normal part of government and that he was being used as a scapegoat for Bulgaria's communist past.)

Free elections were planned for June 1990 and the Communist Party agreed to relinquish its monopoly on power and changed its name to the Bulgarian Socialist Party (BSP). A coalition of 16 different opposition groups founded the Union of Democratic Forces (UDF). The elections gave the BSP 211 parliamentary seats, the UDF 144 seats, the Movement for Rights and Freedoms (a party oriented towards the Turkish minority) 23 seats and the Agrarian Party 16 seats. A majority of city dwellers and the young voted for the opposition, whereas rural voters and older Bulgarians voted Socialist.

In mid-1990, the Socialist president Petar Mladenov was forced to resign after a controversy over his advocacy of the use of force against student demonstrators. On 1 August 1990, the socialist-dominated parliament elected Zhelyu Zhelev of the UDF to replace him in a compromise to quell tensions. During the June 1990 elections, the socialists had spoken out against 'shock therapy' reforms and advocated an easy transition to capitalism, but in October 1990, with the economy collapsing around them, they changed course and introduced a radical reform programme similar to that proposed by the opposition. This sparked nationwide strikes and demonstrations against threatened price hikes, and on 29 November 1990 Andrei Lukanov, the Socialist prime minister, resigned.

Lukanov was replaced by Dimiter Popov, an independent who formed a BSP/UDF coalition government to prepare for fresh elections. The October 1991 parliamentary elections were won by the UDF and Filip Dimitrov formed Bulgaria's first fully noncommunist government. President Zhelev was re-elected in January 1992. Then in October 1992, the UDF government was defeated in parliament by a coalition of ethnic Turkish members, UDF defectors and socialists, and an administration of technocrats was installed with Lyuben Berov as prime minister. With support for the UDF and socialists almost equally divided, the small Turkish party still holds the balance of power in parliament.

GEOGRAPHY

Bulgaria lies at the crossroads of Europe and Asia in the heart of the Balkan Peninsula. Covering 110,912 sq km, it's a bit smaller than the US state of Louisiana, yet an amazing variety of landforms are jammed into this relatively small area. From the high banks of the Danube, a windswept plain slopes up to the rounded summits of the Stara Planina. This east-west range runs right across the northern half of the country from the Black Sea to Yugoslavia. The Sredna Gora branch is separated from the main range by a fault that is followed by the railway from Sliven to Sofia. Some 70% of the world's rose oil, used in the manufacture of cosmetics and perfumes, comes from the Valley of Roses near Kazanlâk in this fault. Southern Bulgaria is even more mountain-

ous. Musala Peak (2925 metres) in the Rila Mountains south of Sofia is the highest mountain between the Alps and Transcaucasia and is almost equalled by Vihren Peak (2915 metres) in the Pirin Massif farther south. The Rila Mountains' sharply glaciated massifs with their bare rocky peaks, steep forested valleys and glacial lakes are the geographical core of the Balkans – a paradise for hikers. Besides the Rila Mountains, which are covered in this book, there's the Pirin National Park, just south of Bansko. Take a train from Pazardzhik to get there.

The Rodopi Mountains stretch west along the Greek border from Rila and Pirin, separating the Aegean Sea from the Thracian Plain of central Bulgaria. This plain opens on to the Black Sea coast with great bays and coastal lakes at Burgas and Varna. The long sandy beaches that lie all along this coast are among the finest in Europe.

Railways have been constructed along the great rivers of Bulgaria from Sofia: they follow the Iskâr River north-east towards the Danube, the Maritsa River south-east into Turkey and the Struma River south into Greece. About a third of Bulgaria is forested, with deciduous trees in the lowlands and conifers in the mountains.

ECONOMY

During the communist era, five-year plans were prepared and implemented by a Council of Ministers. Half the national budget was devoted to economic development, and industry grew from almost nothing until it contributed over half the gross national product. Growth continued through the 1970s, but the 1980s witnessed a slow-down due to technological shortcomings and economic inefficiencies. Attempts to introduce Hungarian-style, market-oriented reforms were half-hearted and in the last five years of communist rule Bulgaria rang up a US$12 billion foreign debt just to maintain living standards.

Bulgaria has always been primarily an agricultural country with two-thirds of the land devoted to growing cereals, including wheat, corn, barley, rye, oats and rice. Also important are industrial crops such as sunflowers, cotton, sugar beet and tobacco. Tobacco and cigarettes make up half of all agricultural exports and wine accounts for another 20%. Prior to WW II, agriculture suffered from the overdivision of the land, but by 1965, over one million small holdings had been consolidated into 920 collective and 165 state farms. On average, collective farms in Bulgaria were three times larger than those in Hungary and Romania and, despite a reduction of the agricultural workforce from 82% employment in 1948 to 39% in 1968, production was increased through the use of machinery, fertilisers and irrigation. The cooperatives are now in the process of being dismantled and the land returned to its former owners, leading to much disruption and confusion due to conflicting claims.

By 1970 the collectivisation of agriculture had led to a doubling of the percentage of Bulgarians living in urban areas, providing a basis for industrialisation. There are iron and steel works at Pernik and Kremikovci, on opposite sides of Sofia, a chemical plant at Dimitrovgrad produces fertilisers and a large petrochemical plant is at Burgas. Textile mills have been established in Plovdiv, Sliven and Sofia. Until recently, about 75% of Bulgaria's foreign trade was conducted with the Warsaw Pact countries with the USSR alone accounting for over half of the total. The quality of many of the products previously shipped to the USSR was low and orienting production to Western markets will be difficult, placing the future of Bulgaria's inefficient heavy industries in doubt.

There are oil refineries at Ruse and Burgas, and some oil and gas is produced north-east of Varna, but prior to 1990 Bulgaria obtained over 90% of its oil from the USSR at far below world prices. As deliveries from Russia dwindled, Bulgaria had hoped to switch to oil from Iraq (which owes Bulgaria US$1.2 billion) but the 1991 Gulf War prevented this. United Nations economic sanctions against Yugoslavia have cost Bulgaria hundreds of millions of dollars and no compensation has been paid by the EU or UN.

Brown coal found near Pernik is used by Bulgaria's iron industry, and lignite from open-pit mines at Dimitrovgrad is burned in dirty thermoelectric plants causing atmospheric pollution. Hydroelectric projects exist in the Rodopi Mountains, but 40% of Bulgaria's electricity comes from the Soviet-built nuclear plant at Kozloduj on the Danube.

Opened in 1974, Kozloduj is now rated as one of the world's 25 most dangerous nuclear facilities and in recent years minor accidents and safety scares have forced several partial shut downs, leading to power cuts across the country. Four of the six reactors at Kozloduj are of the pressurised-water VVER-440 type considered even less safe than the Chernobyl-style RBMK reactor. In 1993, panic-stricken Western governments allocated US$28 million to help improve safety at Kozloduj on the understanding that the four VVER-440 reactors would be shut down by the end of the decade. In 1990 public protests forced the Bulgarian government to halt construction of a second plant.

Bulgaria's internal political squabbles have retarded economic reform. Tax reform and new banking laws have been enacted, and foreigners are now allowed to own local businesses (agricultural land excluded), but foreign investment remains meagre and privatisation slow. Bulgaria's strategic location, skilled workforce and good infrastructure are big advantages but political instability, the large national debt, vested interests created by the old system and inexperience on the part of the reformers are slowing the way ahead. The International Monetary Fund has had to continually prod Bulgarian politicians to take action. Since 1989, the living standards of 90% of the population have been reduced. Only the fact that 75% of the people own their own residences has prevented widespread hardship. Unemployment stands at around 16%.

POPULATION & PEOPLE

About nine million people live in Bulgaria, 1,250,000 of them in the capital, Sofia. The other major cities are Plovdiv (375,000),

Varna (315,000), Burgas (205,000), Ruse (195,000), Stara Zagora (165,000) and Pleven (140,000). Dimitrovgrad and Pernik are major industrial centres. About 85% of the population comes from an Orthodox background and 13% are Sunni Muslims.

The Bulgarians, like the Serbs, are South Slavs. The largest national minorities are Turks (8.5%), Gypsies (2.6%) and Macedonians (2.5%). Ethnic Macedonians constitute a majority in the Pirin region south of Sofia. For most of this century a controversy has raged over whether the Macedonians are Bulgarians or a distinct ethnic group. Officially, Bulgaria recognises Macedonia as a country but does not recognise the Macedonians as a people. Activists attempting to politically organise the Macedonian minority in Bulgaria continue to suffer harassment by the Bulgarian authorities.

The 800,000 Turks live mostly in the north-east and in the eastern Rodopi foothills. Between 1912 and 1940 some 340,000 ethnic Turks left Bulgaria for Turkey, and after WW II another 200,000 left. In early 1985 the communists mounted a programme to forcibly assimilate the remaining Turkish inhabitants, all of whom were required to take Bulgarian names. The circumcision of male Muslim children was forbidden, separate Muslim cemeteries were abolished, many mosques were closed and Ramadan – the month of fasting – was attacked. Even the wearing of Turkish dress and speaking Turkish in public were banned. In early 1989, there were mass protests against these policies and, after a relaxation of passport laws, a further 350,000 Turkish Bulgarians left for Turkey (many have subsequently returned). With the fall of Todor Zhivkov in late 1989 the mosques reopened and in 1990 legislation was passed allowing the restoration of Muslim names. In 1991 optional instruction in Turkish resumed in public schools.

Some 250,000 Pomaks (Slavs who converted to Islam while Bulgaria was part of the Ottoman Empire) live in the Rodopi region south of Plovdiv. In the past, the Pomaks were subjected to the same assimilatory pressures as the Turks, with a particularly brutal name-changing campaign from 1971-73. Many Gypsies live in the Valley of Roses (especially around Sliven) and although the communists improved their living standards, the 550,000 Gypsies were denied the right to maintain their separate identity. Three-quarters of the Gypsies are Muslims.

At the outbreak of WW II, there were 50,000 Jews in Bulgaria and nearly all survived the war thanks to Bulgarian resistance to Nazi demands that they be deported to the death camps in Poland. Though the Bulgarian Jews were assembled in provincial labour camps and forced to wear the star of David, none were turned over to the Germans. After the war, most left for Israel and only about 5000 Jews live in Bulgaria today.

ARTS

After five centuries of Turkish rule, Bulgarian culture reappeared in the 19th century as writers and artists strove to reawaken national consciousness. Zahari Zograph (1810-53) painted magnificent frescoes in monasteries at Bachkovo, Preobrazhenski, Rila and Troyan, with scenes inspired by medieval Bulgarian art but more human than divine. In Orthodox churches, a high partition, called an iconostasis, separates the public and private areas. Zograph and his contemporaries painted sacred images known as icons on wooden panels to hang on these intricately carved walls.

It is sadly indicative of the troubled early history of the country that Bulgaria's three leading poets met violent deaths around the age of 30. The folk poetry of Hristo Botev (1848-76) features rebels who struggled for independence or noble outlaws who robbed from the rich and gave to the poor. *Borba* is a poetic condemnation of injustice, and *Mehanata* satirises café politicians. In 1876, Botev returned from exile in Romania and was killed in the anti-Ottoman uprising.

The symbolist Dimcho Debelyanov (1887-1916) expresses the purity of human feelings in his melodious lyric poetry. His poem *Orden* (1910) criticises the court of King Ferdinand. Despite this, Debelyanov volunteered for military service in WW I and was killed in action in Macedonia.

Geo Milev (1895-1925), who lost an eye in WW I, wrote poetry dealing with social themes. His epic poem *Septemvri* about the September 1923 agrarian revolution is the high point of Bulgarian expressionism. The authorities confiscated the volume in which the poem appeared and Milev was arrested and fined. After the trial Milev was kidnapped by the police and murdered.

The grand old man of Bulgarian literature is Ivan Vazov (1850-1921) whose novel *Under the Yoke* (1893) describes the 1876 uprising of the entire nation against the Turks. Vazov's *Epic of the Forgotten* is a cycle of poems to the heroes of the Bulgarian National Revival. His plays, written in the early 20th century, bring medieval Bulgarian history to life. Vazov was also a noted travel writer who never tired of writing stories about his country.

In his novel *The Iron Candlestick*, Dimitur Talev (1898-1966) went beyond socialist realism to portray the complexity of human nature against the background of Macedonia's struggle for liberation from the Ottoman Empire in the 19th century.

Music

Bulgaria's most common traditional folk instruments are the *gayda* (a goatskin bagpipe), the *tambura* (a four-stringed long-necked lute akin to the Greek bouzouki), the *gadulka* or rebec (a small pear-shaped fiddle), the *dayre* (tambourine), the *kaval* (a long, open flute), the *duduk* (a high-pitched flute), the *dvojanka* (double flute), the *ocarina* (a small ceramic flute), the *zurna* (a small, high-pitched horn), the *tarabuka* (vase drum) and the *teppan* (a large, cylindrical, double-headed drum). Bulgarian instrumental music bears a strong Turkish influence, especially in the use of the kaval, gadulka and gayda.

An ancient Greek myth ascribed a Thracian origin to Orpheus and the Muses.

Bulgarians today are still renowned singers and the country's Orthodox religious chants are the equivalent of classical music in the west. Bulgarian ecclesiastic music dating back to the 9th century played a key role in the 19th century Bulgarian National Revival. The songs, cantatas and oratorios convey the mysticism of chronicles, fables and legends and to hear Orthodox chants sung by a choir of up to a hundred is a moving experience. The old Bulgarian chants with their Church-Slavonic texts are sometimes performed during mass at churches such as Sofia's Aleksander Nevski Memorial Church.

Alongside the scholarly Byzantine traditions maintained in Orthodox church music is the Turkish influence evident in the spontaneous folk songs and dances of the villages. Through music the Bulgarians have always striven to maintain their unique cultural identity and this folk culture helped hold them together during five centuries of Ottoman rule. Many Bulgarian folk ballads describe the exploits of *hajduts* or brigands who struggled against the Turks. Love songs, working songs and *haydut* songs often employ the antiphonal, or responsive, technique in which one person or group echoes or answers another. The *horo* is a round dance accompanied by the penetrating sound of bagpipes.

Traditional Bulgarian village folk music contrasts with the highly arranged music of modern urban choirs such as the National Folk Ensemble 'Philip Kutev,' named for the pioneering composer/director who transformed Bulgarian village music into a sophisticated art form. In 1951 Kutev formed the first professional choir, the National Ensemble of Folk Songs and Dances, and during a remarkable career which only ended with his death in 1982 he composed nearly 500 of the adapted folk melodies his group performed.

Other groups of this kind include Blagoevgrad's 'Pirin' Ensemble, Pleven's Northern Ensemble and Plovdiv's 'Trakia' Ensemble. In recent years these choirs have attained great fame among Western European devotees of 'world music', especially after the release of the Le Mystere des Voix Bulgares recordings of the State Folk Ensemble by the Swiss producer Marcel Cellier (Disques Cellier, CH-1605 Chexbres, Switzerland).

The *Mystere* series presents an archaic peasant musical tradition which harks back to medieval times and even the 'mystery' of a pre-Christian culture. As in most peasant cultures, Bulgarian women were not given access to musical instruments so they performed the vocal parts. Bulgarian female choir singing is polyphonic and sudden upward leaps of the voice are characteristic. Trio Bulgarka, a group made up of the three former leaders of different sections of the State Folk Ensemble, are accomplished performers of the 'open-throat' singing technique. The Bisserov Sisters, also graduates of Kutev's national ensemble, sing the traditional songs of the Pirin Mountains.

The choirs were heavily subsidised during the communist era as a means of creating a 'national' culture, within certain limits. Carefully selected 'state music' was played during prime time over Sofia Radio and ethnic diversity or foreign influences were downplayed. Bagpipe orchestras of 20 or more players were also assembled by the communists.

Because this music was imposed from above it was often unpopular and since the fall of communism the emphasis has changed significantly. Sadly, with government subsidies gone and limited appeal inside Bulgaria, the music is being commercialised for a mass Western audience. Recent *Mystere* recordings include outside elements such as Turkish instrumental music, medieval French or Spanish court music and even Anglo-American pop, all of which would have been unthinkable before. Loznitsa, a new folk group made up of former members of the state folk ensembles, employs strumming tamburas and Gypsy-style fiddling in a desperate attempt to attune the music to Western ears. On the cover of their latest album they've traded their bright peasant costumes for T-shirts and jeans.

In 1974 Ivo Papasov formed a group with a distinctive music style somewhere between jazz, rock and folk, and Bulgarian wedding band or 'Stambolovo' music was born. Basically the music is traditional, but it employs modern instruments such as the electric guitar (instead of the tambura), clarinet (instead of the kaval), accordion and saxophone (instead of the gayda) and drum battery (instead of the teppan). The singing has deliberate vibratory effects that differ from the open-throated singing of the traditional female choirs. As with jazz there's much improvisation and at urban weddings the traditional circle dances are often supplemented by youths doing break dances before the band. Stambolovo music developed outside official channels, which feared that Gypsy and other foreign influences threatened to drown out the quieter national folk music.

LANGUAGE

For most Bulgarians, Russian is the second language. During the 1950s and 1960s French was the second most-taught foreign language after Russian and many middle-aged Bulgarians in the bureaucracy are tickled to show off their knowledge of it. Young people, tourism workers and business types are more likely to speak English. German tourists have been frequenting the Black Sea coast for years and their language is most widely known in that region.

The Cyrillic alphabet used in Bulgaria, the former USSR, Serbia and Macedonia dates back to the 9th century, when Sts Cyril and Methodius translated the Bible into Old Church Slavonic. As almost everything in Bulgaria is written in Cyrillic, it's essential to learn the alphabet. Several systems exist for transcribing Cyrillic into Latin script and in this book we've used the one illustrated herein, which is almost phonetic. The Cyrillic y is transcribed as u and pronounced as the u in lute, and the Cyrillic ъ is transcribed as â and pronounced as the u in but. The Cyrillic letter ь has no sound but softens the preceding consonant.

Some useful words to know are *ima* (there is), *nyama* (there isn't), *kolko struva* (how

The Cyrillic Alphabet – Bulgaria

Аа	a	Кк	k	Фф	f
Бб	b	Лл	l	Хх	h
Вв	v	Мм	m	Цц	ts
Гг	g	Нн	n	Чч	ch
Дд	d	Оо	o	Шш	sh
Ее	e	Пп	p	Щщ	sht
Жж	zh	Рр	r	Ъъ	â
Зз	z	Сс	s	Ьь	-
Ии	i	Тт	t	Юю	yu
Йй	y	Уу	u	Яя	ya

much), *dobar den* (good day), *dobre doshli* (welcome). *Dobre* (good) is a useful response in many situations. Public toilets are marked МЬЖЕ *mâzhe* for men, ЖЕНИ *zheni* for women. And keep in mind the Bulgarian idiosyncrasy of shaking the head to say 'yes' and nodding to say 'no'.

Lonely Planet's *Eastern Europe Phrasebook* has a much more extensive list of translated Bulgarian words and phrases. It takes a slightly different approach to that followed here by providing an Anglicised phonetic rendering instead of a standard transcription. The original Cyrillic spelling

is also given. If you'll be in Bulgaria longer than a few days it's useful to have this book with you.

Greetings & Civilities

hello
  zdraveyte
    здравейте
  zdrasti (colloquial)
    здрасти
goodbye
  dovizhdane
    довиждане
  chao
    чао (coll)
good morning
  dobro utro
    добро утро
good evening
  dobâr vecher
    добър вечер
please
  molya
    моля
thank you
  blagodarya
    благодаря
  mersi (coll)
    мерси
I am sorry (forgive me)
  sâzhalyavam (prostete)
    съжалявам (простете)
excuse me
  izvinete me
    извинете ме
yes
  da
    да
no
  ne
    не

Small Talk

I don't understand.
  Az ne razbiram.
    Аз не разбирам.
  Ne razbiram.(coll)
    Не разбирам.
Could you write it down?
  Mozhete li da go napishete?
    Можете ли да го напишете?

What is it called?
Kak se kazva tova?
Как се казва това?

Where do you live?
Vie kâde zhiveete?
Вие къде живеете?
Kâde zhiveete? (coll)
Къде живеете?

What work do you do?
Vie s kakvo se zanimavate?
Вие с какво се занимавате?
S kakvo se zanimavate? (coll)
С какво се занимавате?

I am a student.
Az sâm student (m)/*studentka* (f).
Аз съм студент/студентка.

I am very happy.
Az sâm mnogo shtastliv (m)/*shtastliva* (f).
Аз съм много щастлив/щастлива.
Mnogo se radvam. (coll)
Много се радвам.

Accommodation

youth hostel
mladezhki hotel (hizha/obshtezhitie)
младежки хотел (хижа/общежитие)

camping ground
myasto za lageruvane (myasto za kâmpinguvane)
място за лагеруване (място за къмпингуване)

private room
stoya v chastna kvartira
стоя в частна квартира

How much is it?
Kolko struva?
Колко струва?

Is that the price per person?
Tova tsenata na chovek li e?
Това цената на човек ли е?

Is that the total price?
Tova obshtata tsena li e?
Това общата цена ли е?

Are there any extra charges?
Tryabva li da se zaplashta dopâlnitelno za neshto?
Трябва ли да се заплаща допълнително за нещо?

Do I pay extra for showers?
Tryabva li da platya poveche za udobstvata?
Трябва ли да платя повече за удобствата?

Where is there a cheaper hotel?
Kâde moga da namerya po-evtin hotel?
Къде мога да намеря по-евтин отел?
Kâde ima po-evtin hotel? (coll)
Къде има по-евтин отел?

Should I make a reservation?
Tryabva li da napravya rezervatsiya?
Трябва ли да направя резервация?

single room
edinichna staya
единична стая

double room
dvoyna staya
двойна стая

It is very noisy.
Mnogo e shumno.
Много е шумно.

Where is the toilet?
Kâde e toaletnata?
Къде е тоалетната?

Getting Around

What time does it leave?
V kolko chasa trâgva?
В колко часа тръгва?

When is the first bus?
Koga e pârviyat avtobus?
Кога е първият автобус?

When is the last bus?
Koga e posledniyat avtobus?
Кога е последният автобус?

When is the next bus?
Koga e sledvashtiyat avtobus?
Кога е следващият автобус?

That's too soon.
Tova e dosta (tvârde) skoro.
Това е доста (твърде) скоро.

When is the next one after that?
Koga e po-sledvashtiyat avtobus?
Кога е по-следващият автобус?

How long does the trip take?
Kolko vreme se pâtuva do tam?
Колко време се пътува до там?

arrival
pristigane
пристигане
departure
zaminavane
заминаване
timetable
razpisanie
разписание
Where is the bus stop?
Kâde e avtobusnata spirka?
Къде е автобусната спирка?
Where is the train station?
Kâde e zhelezopâtnata gara?
Къде е железопътната гара?
Where is the left-luggage room?
Kâde e garderobât?
Къде е гардеробът?

Around Town

Just a minute.
Edin moment.
Един момент.
Where is ...?
Kâde e ...?
Къде е ...?
the bank
bankata
банката
the post office
poshtata
пощата
the tourist information office
byuroto za turisticheska informatsiya
бюрото за туристическа
информация
the museum
muzeya
музея
Where are you going?
Kâde otivate?
Къде отивате?
I am going to ...
Az otivam v ...
Аз отивам в ...
Where is it?
Kâde e tova?
Къде е това?

I can't find it.
Az ne moga da go namerya.
Аз не мога да го намеря.
Is it far?
Daleche li e?
Далече ли е?
Please show me on the map.
Molya pokazhete mi na kartata.
Моля покажете ми на картата.
left
lyavo
ляво
right
dyasno
дясно
straight ahead
napravo
направо
I want ...
Az iskam ...
Аз искам ...
Do I need permission?
Nuzhdaya li se ot razreshenie?
Нуждая ли се от разрешение?

Entertainment

Where can I buy a ticket?
Kâde moga da si kupya bilet?
Къде мога да си купя билет?
I want to refund this ticket.
Az iskam da vârna tozi bilet.
Аз искам да върна този билет.
Is this a good seat?
Dobro li e tova myasto?
Добро ли е това място?
at the front
otpred
отпред
ticket
bilet
билет

Food

I do not eat meat.
Az ne yam meso.
Аз не ям месо.
self-service cafeteria
zakusvalnya na samoobsluzhvane
закусвалня на самообслужване

grocery store
zarzavatchiynitsa
зарзаватчийница
fish
riba
риба
pork
svinsko meso
свинско месо
soup
supa
супа
salad
salata
салата
fresh vegetables
presni zelenchutsi
пресни зеленчуци
milk
mlyako
мляко
bread
hlyab
хляб
sugar
zahar
захар
ice cream
sladoled
сладолед
coffee
kafe
кафе
tea
chay
чай
mineral water
mineralna voda
минерална вода
beer
bira
бира
wine
vino
вино
hot/cold
goreshto/studeno
горещо/студено

Shopping
Where can I buy ...?
Kâde moga da kupya ...?
Къде мога да купя ...?
How much does it cost?
Kolko struva?
Колко струва?
That's (much) too expensive.
Tova e (mnogo) prekaleno skâpo.
Това е (много) прекалено скъпо.
Is there a cheaper one?
Ima li po-evtino?
Има ли по-евтино?
Can I pay with local currency?
Moga li da platya v levove?
Мога ли да платя в левове?

Time & Dates
today
dnes
днес
tonight
dovechera
довечера
tomorrow
utre
утре
the day after tomorrow
vdrugiden
вдругиден
What time does it open?
V kolko chasa otvarya?
В колко часа отваря?
What time does it close?
V kolko chasa zatvarya?
В колко часа затваря?
open
otvoreno
отворено
closed
zatvoreno
затворено
in the morning
sutrinta
сутринта
in the evening
vecherta
вечерта

BULGARIA

every day
 vseki den
  всеки ден
At what time?
 V kolko chasa?
  В колко часа?
when?
 koga?
  кога?

Monday
 ponedelnik
  понеделник
Tuesday
 vtornik
  вторник
Wednesday
 sryada
  сряда
Thursday
 chetvârtâk
  четвъртък
Friday
 petâk
  петък
Saturday
 sâbota
  събота
Sunday
 nedelya
  неделя

January
 yanuari
  януари
February
 fevruari
  февруари
March
 mart
  март
April
 april
  април
May
 may
  май
June
 yuni
  юни

July
 yuli
  юли
August
 avgust
  август
September
 septemvri
  септември
October
 oktomvri
  октомври
November
 noemvri
  ноември
December
 dekemvri
  декември

Numbers

1	*edno*
	едно
2	*dve*
	две
3	*tri*
	три
4	*chetiri*
	четири
5	*pet*
	пет
6	*shest*
	шест
7	*sedem*
	седем
8	*osem*
	осем
9	*devet*
	девет
10	*deset*
	десет
11	*edinayset*
	единайсет
12	*dvanayset*
	дванайсет
13	*trinayset*
	тринайсет
14	*chetirinayset*
	четиринайсет
15	*petnayset*
	петнайсет

16	*shestnayset*
	шестнайсет
17	*sedemnayset*
	седемнайсет
18	*osemnayset*
	осемнайсет
19	*devetnayset*
	деветнайсет
20	*dvayset*
	двайсет
21	*dvayset i edno*
	двайсет и едно
22	*dvayset i dve*
	двайсет и две
23	*dvayset i tri*
	двайсет и три
30	*triyset*
	трийсет
40	*chetirideset*
	четиридесет
50	*petdeset*
	петдесет
60	*sheyset*
	шейсет
70	*sedemdeset*
	седемдесет
80	*osemdeset*
	осемдесет
90	*devetdeset*
	деветдесет
100	*sto*
	сто
1000	*hilyada*
	хиляда
10,000	*deset hilyadi*
	десет хиляди
1,000,000	*edin milion*
	един милион

Facts for the Visitor

VISAS & EMBASSIES

Nationals of Austria and the USA are admitted without a visa but almost all other Western travellers do need visas. Unless you're willing to pay from 50% to 100% above the usual US$30 visa fee for on-the-spot service, Bulgarian consulates require seven working days to process tourist visa applications (a good indication of how slowly the Bulgarian bureaucracy works). Luckily they don't keep your passport while you're waiting and you only pay the fee when the visa is actually issued. Some consulates will issue three-month multiple entry visas (US$40). You can also get a Bulgarian visa at the border but this costs US$67 for a tourist visa, US$36 for a transit visa.

You must specify the number of days you wish to stay in Bulgaria to a maximum of 90 days. Put down the longest possible period you might stay there, to avoid the hassle of having to get an extension. You may use a tourist visa any time within three months of the date of issue. If you arrive on a package tour, you don't need to get a visa, an advantage the ex-communist bureaucrats hope will convince you to come with a group.

Thirty-hour transit visas (US$20) are usually issued at consulates on the spot but you must have an onward visa if one is required for the next country you're going to. Transit visas cannot be changed to tourist visas on arrival. If you're in transit, you're not supposed to stay at a hotel and some places won't accept you if they see a transit visa.

If you're one of the lucky ones who doesn't need a visa, tell the border guard that you want to stay 30 days as a tourist, otherwise they may automatically stamp your passport for only a five-day transit and you'll be slapped with a US$50 fine on departure if you stay longer. We've heard of Bulgarian officials who attempted to rip off departing passengers using the pretext that they only had a transit stamp, so take care.

Rubber Stamps

Everyone entering Bulgaria is given a 'statistical card' by immigration. The card must remain in the bearer's passport, and hotels, hostels, camping grounds and tourist offices arranging private accommodation stamp the back of it each night and write in the number of days you spent there. When you leave Bulgaria, immigration scrutinises the card to make sure that you have a stamp to account

BULGARIA

for every night spent in the country. If one or two nights are missing, it's generally no problem, but if too many nights are unaccounted for, the officials can levy an on-the-spot fine.

Avoid losing the card (US$20 fine) and check that people stamp it as they should. The purpose of the card is not to control your movements but simply to force you to stay in official accommodation where, it's hoped, you'll spend a lot of money. If you camp in the mountains, stay with friends or in a private room arranged on the street, you don't get a stamp and are liable for the fine. Of course, many Bulgarians are fed up with outlandish requirements of this kind and hotel receptions will often happily provide the missing stamps if you make your concerns known. Why the present administration chooses to perpetuate this communist-era bureaucratic control is a mystery, however it's best to take this small card seriously.

Bulgarian Embassies

For the addresses and opening hours of Bulgarian embassies in Belgrade, Bratislava, Bucharest, Budapest, Prague, Skopje, Tirana, Warsaw and Zagreb turn to those city sections in this book. Other Bulgarian embassies include the following:

Australia
    2/4 Carlotta Rd, Double Bay, NSW 2028
    (☎ 02-327 7592)
Canada
    325 Stewart St, Ottawa, Ontario K1N 6K5
    (☎ 613-789 3215)
    65 Overlea Blvd, Suite 406,
    Toronto, Ontario M4H 1P1 (☎ 416-696 2420)
Netherlands
    Duinrooseweg 9, 2597 KJ The Hague
    (☎ 70-354 0876)
UK
    187 Queen's Gate, London SW7 5HL
    (☎ 0171-584 9400)
USA
    1621 22nd St NW, Washington, DC 20008
    (☎ 202-483 5885)

MONEY

Bulgarian banknotes come in denominations

of one, two, five, 10, 20, 50, 100 and 200 leva. The old notes bearing the image of Georgi Dimitrov are being phased out though at last report they were still accepted. One lev (plural – leva) is divided into 100 stotinki and a variety of coins are used. In early 1991 the lev was allowed to float and price controls were removed leading to 79% inflation, but by mid-1992 the currency had stabilised. At last report the uniform exchange rate was US$1 = 27 leva.

There's no longer any compulsory exchange in Bulgaria and you may pay for almost everything directly in leva. Cash hard currency is easily changed in Bulgaria at numerous small exchange offices for no commission. Travellers' cheques, on the other hand, are a bit of a hassle as many banks refuse to change them and those that do give a lower rate than they pay for cash and from 3% to 5% commission is deducted. Hotel exchange counters also give low rates and deduct about 5% commission. For this reason you're well advised to bring cash to Bulgaria.

We can't recommend any single bank which consistently offers good service when changing travellers' cheques and if you're changing a lot it pays to compare the varying commission charges at the Tourist Sport Bank (or T Bank), the First Private Bank, the Electronic Bank, the First East International Bank, the Foreign Trade Bank and others. As long as the lev remains stable it's best to change enough money to tide you over for a week or more rather than wasting time searching for a bank every couple of days.

The lev is not a freely convertible currency and Bulgarian banks will not change excess leva back into dollars. You're supposed to be able to change back at the border provided you have official exchange receipts, but it would be unwise to bet much money on it. The first time you change money put the bank receipt in your money belt so you have it in case you need it and near the end of your visit change only what you're sure you can spend. It's still illegal to import and export Bulgarian currency.

Bulgarians are allowed to purchase

US$500 a year legally but foreign traders such as Turks, Macedonians and Albanians are unable to convert the leva they earn at street markets, hence the black market. You'll be offered up to 10% above the bank rate for cash on the street, but these transactions should be approached with extreme caution. You may be given counterfeit leva, short-changed or otherwise cheated, and the law won't be on your side. Some operators will try to give you Greek drachma, a unit of which is worth 10 times less than one lev. The old sleight of hand trick whereby the wad of bills is switched for a packet of paper at the last minute is also popular here.

Romanian currency cannot be changed in Bulgaria and banknotes issued before the 1962 monetary reform are worthless.

Costs

In April 1994 an 18% value added tax was introduced but you'll probably still find all forms of transport (including taxis), souvenirs, admissions, food and drink are cheap and consider Bulgaria an inexpensive country. Anything you can get for the same price as a Bulgarian will be cheap, but when there's a higher tourist price (such as there is for almost all accommodation) it can get expensive. Students often get half price on museum admissions. Compared to Romania, restaurant meals may be slightly more expensive but hotel rooms are generally cheaper.

CLIMATE & WHEN TO GO

Bulgaria has a temperate climate with cold, damp winters and hot, dry summers. The Rodopi Mountains form a barrier to the moderating Mediterranean influence of the Aegean, while the Danube Plains are open to the extremes of central Europe. Sofia has average daily temperatures above 15°C from May to September, above 11°C in April and October, above 5°C in March and November, and below freezing in December and January. The Black Sea moderates temperatures in the east of the country. Rainfall is highest in the mountains and in winter life is sometimes disrupted by heavy snowfalls.

SUGGESTED ITINERARIES

Depending on the length of your stay, you might want to see the following places in Bulgaria:

Two days
    Visit Sofia.
One week
    Visit Sofia, Veliko Târnovo and Varna.
Two weeks
    Visit Sofia, Rila Monastery, Koprivshtitsa, Hisarya, Veliko Târnovo, Madara, Varna and Burgas.
One month
    Visit most of the places included in this chapter.

TOURIST OFFICES

Balkantourist, the old government tourism monopoly, arranges accommodation, changes money, books sightseeing tours, and so on. In some towns Balkantourist now operates under a different name, such as Puldin Tours (Plovdiv), Mesembria Tourist (Nesebâr) or Dunav Tours (Ruse). Overseas they use the name Balkan Holidays. Staff at Balkan Holidays offices abroad are often evasive about answering questions regarding individual tourism and will try to convince you to sign up for one of their package tours. They're a good source of free brochures but don't believe everything they tell you.

Student travellers are catered for by the Orbita Youth Travel Agency, and 'Pirin', the travel bureau of the Bulgarian Tourist Union (though most Pirin offices around Bulgaria closed in 1992 due to lack of funds). 'Rila' railway ticket offices are found in the city centres. 'Shipka' is the travel agency of the Bulgarian Union of Motorists. Many smaller private travel agencies also exist.

Balkantourist Offices Abroad

Balkantourist offices outside Bulgaria include:

Netherlands
    Leidsestraat 43, 1017 NV Amsterdam
    (☎ 20-620 9400)

BULGARIA

UK
19 Conduit St, London W1R 9TD
(☎ 0171-491 4499)
USA
41 East 42nd St, Suite 508, New York, NY 10017
(☎ 212-573 5530)

BUSINESS HOURS & HOLIDAYS

Many shops close for lunch from 1 to 2 pm, but the exact times vary from place to place so you could find yourself locked out anytime between 11.45 am and 3.30 pm. Of course, street markets don't close for lunch. Some shops don't open until 9.30 am and many don't keep the posted times, so the most dependable shopping time is from 9.30 to 11.30 am. Some offices are closed from noon to 1 pm.

Public holidays include New Year (1 and 2 January), 1878 Liberation Day (3 March), Easter Monday (March/April), Labour Day (1 May), Cyrillic Alphabet Day (24 May) and Christmas (25 and 26 December). The Bulgarian Orthodox Easter falls at a different time to the Catholic Easter.

CULTURAL EVENTS

Bulgarians observe a number of traditional customs and folk festivals of interest. Trifon Zarezan on 14 February is the ancient festival of the wine growers. Vines are pruned and sprinkled with wine for a bounteous harvest. On 1 March Bulgarians give each other *martenitsi*, red-and-white tasselled threads worn for health and happiness at the coming of spring. Lazarouvane is a folk ritual associated with spring and youth. Students' Day is on 8 December. Koledouvane is the ritual singing of Christmas carols and takes place on 24 and 25 December.

At the Koprivshtitsa Folk Festival, which is held every four years (the next perhaps in August 1996), some 4000 finalists compete for awards in various fields. In Pernik at the National Festival of Koukeri and Sourvakari, held every other year in the second half of January (the next will be in 1995), thousands of participants perform ancient dances wearing traditional masks and costumes to drive away evil spirits and ask the good

spirits for fertility and a bounteous harvest. Annual folk festivals are held at Golden Sands during the second half of July, with Bulgarian groups participating, and at Burgas and Sunny Beach in August, with Bulgarian and foreign groups participating. The Festival of Roses is celebrated with folk songs and dances at Kazanlâk and Karlovo on the first Sunday in June.

The March Musical Days are held annually at Ruse, followed by the two-month Sofia Music Weeks International Festival of Contemporary Music beginning on 24 May. During the first week of June the Golden Orpheus International Pop Song Festival is held at Sunny Beach. Also in June is the International Ballroom Dancing Competition at Burgas. In July there's the Varna Summer Festival and the International Chamber Music Festival at Plovdiv. In October or November the Katya Popova Laureate Festival takes place at Pleven with concerts and recitals. A film festival is held in Sofia in November. The New Year Music Festival is held in Sofia's Palace of Culture.

The Plovdiv International Trade Fair is dedicated to consumer goods in May and industrial products in September.

POST & TELECOMMUNICATIONS

Postage for postcards and letters is low but find out the correct rates before leaving Sofia as provincial post offices quote varying rates.

Receiving Mail

Mail addressed c/o Poste Restante, Sofia 1000, Bulgaria, can be picked up at window No 8 (room to the right) in the main post office, ulitsa Vasil Levski at General Gurko (weekdays 8 am to 8 pm). Mail addressed to Sofia 1 is sent to a branch post office on Stambolijski bulevard.

American Express card holders can have their mail sent c/o Megatours, ulitsa Vasil Levski 1, 1000 Sofia, Bulgaria. (Balkantourist no longer represents American Express.) Megatours kindly allows you to sort your own mail.

Telephone

It's easy to telephone Western Europe from Bulgaria. International telephones are found in all large post offices and you simply enter a booth, dial 00 (Bulgaria's international access code), the country code, the city code and the number, and you're immediately connected. If you're calling a number inside Bulgaria itself dial only the city code with an initial 0 and the number. You pay the clerk as you leave. It's not possible to call North America or Australia in this way, however, as there's no automatic connection, and you must work through an operator, which is much more expensive. It's always a good way to unload excess leva on your last day in Bulgaria, though.

To call Bulgaria from abroad dial the international access code (varies from country to country), 359 (the country code for Bulgaria), the area code and the number. Important city codes include 2 (Sofia), 32 (Plovdiv), 52 (Varna and Golden Sands), 54 (Shumen), 56 (Burgas), 62 (Veliko Târnovo), 64 (Pleven), 82 (Ruse), 94 (Vidin), 291 (Bankya), 335 (Karlovo), 431 (Kazanlâk), 538 (Preslav), 554 (Nesebâr), 579 (Balchik), 670 (Troyan), 5514 (Sozopol), 995313 (Madara).

TIME

The time in Bulgaria is GMT/UTC plus two hours. From the end of March to the end of September, Bulgaria goes on summer time and clocks are turned forward an hour.

LAUNDRY

Coin-operated laundromats don't exist in Bulgaria but there are many dry cleaners (himichesko chistene) – ask your hotel receptionist or private room host for the nearest one. You'll be charged per piece for your laundry and it's best to allow them at least two days, although some places advertise two-hour service.

WEIGHTS & MEASURES

The electric current is 220 V AC, 50 Hz.

BOOKS & MAPS

No serious books about Bulgaria or translations of Bulgarian literature are available in English at Bulgarian bookshops.

By far the most complete travel guidebook to Bulgaria is *Nagel's Encyclopedia-Guide Bulgaria* (Nagel Publishers, Geneva). Perhaps the best of Nagel's Eastern European series, the 526 pages of the Bulgaria volume are packed with history and description. *The Rough Guide to Bulgaria* (Harrap Columbus, London) provides a lot more practical listings than Nagel's.

The Bulgarians from Pagan Times to the Ottoman Conquest by David Marshall Lang (Thames and Hudson, 1976) brings medieval Bulgaria to life. The maps, illustrations and lucid text make this book well worth checking out of your local library.

A Short History of Modern Bulgaria by R J Crampton (Cambridge University Press, 1987) is also useful if you want to read up before visiting. The book's last sentence is: 'The power of the Bulgarian Communist Party, however, is hardly likely to be challenged or to diminish.'

HEALTH

Visitors receive free medical attention in case of accident or emergency. Longer treatments must be paid for but the rates are reasonable. Prescribed medicines are inexpensive unless they're imported from the West.

There are 530 curative hot springs at 190 locations in Bulgaria, with a total daily output of 1.2 million cubic metres of mineral water. The springs of Bankya, Hisarya and Kyustendil have been known since antiquity. Other Bulgarian spas include Sandanski (23 km north of Kulata) and Velingrad.

DANGER & ANNOYANCES

There have been reports of travellers being drugged and robbed by seemingly friendly, English-speaking locals who invited them for a drink. As soon as the drug in your drink knocks you out, your valuables quickly disappear. This can happen in the middle of Sofia in broad daylight, so be on guard.

BULGARIA

ACTIVITIES

Skiing

Skiing is well developed in Bulgaria with the season running from December to April. Mt Vitosha, on the southern outskirts of Sofia, is the most accessible of Bulgaria's ski areas. International slalom and giant slalom competitions are held there in March. Bulgaria's largest ski resort is Borovets, 70 km south of Sofia, with the highest mountains in the Balkans as a backdrop. The 19 km of runs at Borovets are intended for advanced skiers and international competitions are often held there. Skiers on a package tours are often sent to Pamporovo, 84 km south of Plovdiv, which has 17 km of ski runs in all categories serviced by several lifts. The 3800-metre Snezhanka No 1 run is suitable for beginners and there are steep competition runs and nordic tracks as well. Bansko in the Pirin Mountains is Bulgaria's least commercialised ski resort.

Hiking

Mountain climbing is a feasible activity in Bulgaria and it doesn't take Edmund Hillary to scale Musala Peak (2925 metres) in the Rila Massif, the highest peak between the Alps and the Caucasus. Vihren Peak (2915 metres) in the Pirin Massif is almost as high and can be climbed from Bansko. The highest peak in the Stara Planina is Mt Botev (2376 metres), which you can climb via Troyan and Apriltsi. Those who appreciate less strenuous day hikes from the comfort of their lodgings will find possibilities at Koprivshtitsa, Madara, Rila and Veliko Târnovo.

Courses

Every August since 1977, Sts Cyril & Methodius University (fax 359-62-28 023), 5003 Veliko Târnovo, has run a one-month 'International Summer Seminar for Students in Bulgarian Language and Slavic Culture'. The US$500 cost includes tuition, accommodation, food and cultural activities. Beginner-level language classes are available and the course closes with a five-day group excursion to the Black Sea. Prominent academics and artists participate in the programme and it's a great opportunity to get involved if you're at all interested in Slavic studies. Applications close at the end of May, so write well in advance.

HIGHLIGHTS

Museums & Galleries

Many Bulgarian museums provide only Cyrillic captions and thus cannot be recommended. For example, the National Museum of History in Sofia would easily rate a mention here if the curators took their job seriously and, for example, posted English summaries in the rooms or prepared an English guidebook. As it is, everyone other than Bulgarians will find this outstanding collection little more than an assortment of shiny curios.

This used to be the case at the Foreign Art Gallery in Sofia, but new English labels affixed by the staff make quite a difference. Also in Sofia is the Ivan Vazov Museum for a peek into Bulgarian literature. The Etâr Ethnographic Village Museum and all of the house museums at Koprivshtitsa will delight lovers of traditional culture. The 1877 Panorama in Pleven brings a pivotal moment in Bulgarian history to life.

Castles

The Baba Vida Fortress in Vidin is the only intact medieval castle in Bulgaria. The Tsarevets Fortress in Veliko Târnovo was destroyed by the Turks but its historic significance emanates from its ruins. Even older are the ruined 9th century walls of the Inner City of Pliska and the Shumen Fortress, which are both of great historic importance to Bulgaria. Oldest of all and in much better shape are the 3rd century Roman walls of Hisarya.

Historic Towns

Of Bulgaria's historic towns, Nesebâr and Veliko Târnovo are survivors from the Middle Ages, and Koprivshtitsa and Plovdiv are representative of the 19th century Bulgarian National Revival. Melnik is one of many picturesque provincial villages.

ACCOMMODATION
Camping
The hard-to-find Balkantourist *Camping-plätze* map lists 103 camping grounds in Bulgaria. Although the map claims that many of them are open from May to October, you can only rely on them from June to early September. The opening dates for camping grounds listed in this book are also approximations. It's no use asking the people at Balkantourist about camping because they really don't know. Many privatised camping grounds are now open all year.

Camping fees are an average of US$3 per person a night. Most camping grounds rent small bungalows, but these are sometimes full, so bring a tent if you're on a low budget. Camping grounds along the coast tend to be crowded, whereas those in the interior usually have bungalows available that cost just slightly more than camping. One of Bulgaria's nicest camping grounds is at Madara. Camping outside the set camping grounds is prohibited.

Student Hotels
If you have a student card, the Orbita Youth Travel Agency, bulevard Hristo Botev 48, Sofia, may be able to book rooms for you in student hotels around the country. Once the reservations are made, you buy a voucher from Orbita to pay for the rooms at about US$10 per person a night. If you just show up at an Orbita hotel without a reservation, you will pay more, if the staff there accept you at all.

There are Orbita hotels in Rila village (about 22 km from the monastery), Batak (in the mountains south-west of Plovdiv), Lovech (between Troyan and Pleven), Veliko Târnovo, Shumen and Varna, as well as in the Kavarna and Primorsko resorts on the Black Sea. Some student hotels are open only in summer. Unfortunately, rooms in the Orbita Student Hotel in Sofia cost US$34 double and the Orbita Hotel in Varna is also very expensive.

Hostels
The HI handbook lists 52 youth hostels in

Bulgaria. The hostels come in two varieties. A *Turisticheski dom* or a *Turisticheska spalnya* is a fairly comfortable hotel or hostel with double rooms usually located in or near a town. A *hizha* is a mountain hut offering dormitory beds. Most of the Bulgarian hostels display the standard YHA symbol outside.

During the communist era it was essential to go first to Pirin, the travel bureau of the Bulgarian Tourist Union, to reserve a bed at a youth hostel, otherwise individuals were usually not admitted. Now such reservations are no longer required, which is lucky as most of the Pirin offices have closed since subsidies were withdrawn. Show your YHA membership card to the hostel clerks as soon as you arrive at a hostel so they'll know you're a member and give you a reduced rate. Hostels in Bulgaria are about US$4 with a YHA card, US$5 without, and they're open all day.

Private Rooms
Balkantourist claims to have 150,000 beds available in private houses and flats, 110,000 of them at the seaside. Along the Black Sea coast, private rooms are by far the cheapest and easiest way to go, but they're only available in the cities and towns as hotels have a monopoly at the resorts. There's sometimes a three-night minimum stay and people travelling alone often have to pay for double rooms. Always ask travel agencies about private rooms as your first accommodation preference.

Guesthouses
Since November 1989, privately owned hotels have appeared in Bulgaria and are the equivalent of guesthouses or pensions in other countries. All are fairly small with less than a dozen rooms and new ones are opening all the time. Prices are significantly higher than the private room rates. As yet, these places are concentrated in Sofia and along the Black Sea coast.

Hotels
Balkantourist used to enforce its monopoly

BULGARIA

over foreign tourism by preventing Western visitors from staying at cheap hotels that it did not own. As a result, you'd often be told that a hotel or dormitory was reserved for Bulgarians only, or they might just claim they were full. Now you can stay wherever you like though there are still different prices for Bulgarians and for foreigners.

Hotels are classified from one to five stars. The most expensive are called Interhotels, which can have anything from three to five stars. During July and August, most of the hotels along the Black Sea coast will be fully booked but private rooms will be available. Elsewhere rooms are usually always available and you can pay in leva. Very few of the hotels in Bulgaria have air-conditioning.

An unusual legacy of communism is the idea that you should share whatever you have, including your hotel room. Solo visitors are often quoted the price per bed in a double room, which you'd naturally assume is the price of a single. If in doubt, ask, otherwise you could be rudely awoken in the middle of the night by the arrival of your roommate!

FOOD

Food is inexpensive in Bulgaria and prices at the cheapest snack bar are only a third of those at a good hotel restaurant, so it's worth splashing out a little. If you have difficulty finding a restaurant to suit your fancy, just go to any up-market hotel and patronise its restaurant. Because the exchange rate is so good it's fairly cheap to eat there, even including a bottle of wine with the meal.

A folk-style tavern that serves traditional Bulgarian dishes is known as a *mehana*; these are often located in a basement and offer live music. Ask for the speciality at restaurants. Some waiters in Bulgaria overcharge foreigners slightly, so insist on seeing a menu with prices listed. They still expect the bill to be rounded up to the next round figure, however, and you can give a bit more if the service was efficient and honest. Tips should be given as you're paying, and not left on the table.

Restaurants sometimes charge extra for the garnishes (vegetables etc) that accompany the meals. Lunch is the main meal of the day.

Bulgarian Specialities

Popular Bulgarian dishes with a Turkish flavour include *kebabcheta* or *kebapche* (grilled meat rolls), *kavarma* (meat and vegetable casserole), *drob sarma* (chopped lamb liver baked with rice and eggs), *sarmi* (stuffed vine or cabbage leaves) and *kebab* (meat on a spit). To try several kinds of meats at one sitting, order a mixed grill *(meshana skara)*. *Topcheta supa* is a creamy soup with meatballs. *Plakiya* and *gyuvech* are rich fish and meat stews.

Vegetarians should watch for dishes based on cheese *(siren)*. *Sirene po shopski* is cheese, eggs and tomatoes baked in an earthenware pot. *Kashkaval pane* is breaded cheese. *Banitsa* is a baked cheese, spinach or boiled milk pastry like Bosnian *burek*, while *mekitsas* is a batter of eggs and yoghurt fried in oil. A *shopska* salad is made of fresh diced tomatoes, cucumbers, onions and peppers covered with grated white sheep's cheese – excellent. Bulgarian yoghurt is famous and *tarator* is a refreshing cold soup of yoghurt, diced cucumber and onions.

DRINKS

In Bulgaria, the production of wine is an ancient tradition dating back to the Empire of Thrace in the 9th century BC. Bulgaria today is one of the world's five leading exporters of wine, both red (Cabernet, Gamza, Mavrud, Melnik, Merlot, Otel, Pamid and Trakia) and white (Chardonnay, Euksinovgrad, Galatea, Misket, Riesling and Tamyanka).

Bulgarians swear by *slivova* or *rakiya* (plum brandy). Bulgaria's finest beers are Sagorka from Stara Zagora, Astika from Haskovo and Shumensko pivo from Shumen. Beware of their potency! All alcoholic drinks are cheap.

Bulgarian fruit juices (apricot, peach, plum) are exported all over Europe. Good quality Turkish and espresso coffee are available everywhere, often served with a sweet drink called *sok*. *Aryan* is a refreshing drink made from water and yoghurt which is sometimes available at bakeries.

Na zdrave! is 'cheers!' in Bulgarian.

ENTERTAINMENT

Go to the theatres, concert halls and ticket offices listed in this chapter to find out about events. If any of the festivals mentioned in the Cultural Events section coincide with your visit, ask staff at the local tourist office if they have a programme. Movies are shown in the original language with Bulgarian subtitles.

THINGS TO BUY

Typical souvenirs include embroidered dresses and blouses, linen, carpets, Valley of Roses perfume, pottery, leather goods, dolls in national costume, silver-filigree jewellery, recordings of folk music and wrought copper and iron. If you're bound for Romania, take along a few packs of BT cigarettes as gifts. You're allowed to take out up to US$20 of locally purchased souvenirs and articles for personal use. Beyond this, you could be charged an export tax of 100% or more.

Getting There & Away

AIR

Balkan Bulgarian Airlines has flights to Sofia from Algiers, Bahrain, Bangkok, Beirut, Cairo, Calcutta, Casablanca, Colombo, Doha, Dubai, Harare, Istanbul, Jakarta, Johannesburg, Karachi, Kuala Lumpur, Kuwait, Lagos, Larnaca, Malta, Muscat, New York, Singapore, Tel Aviv, Toronto, Tunis and many European cities. Bucket shops in Asia often sell Balkan Airlines tickets at cut rates, so ask around the budget travel agencies in Bangkok, Penang, Singapore etc.

Before buying a return air ticket from Western Europe or North America to Bulgaria, check the price of the cheapest package tour to the Black Sea resorts. This could be cheaper and you can just throw

away the hotel vouchers if you don't care to sit on the beach for two weeks. Specifically ask the price of a 'camping flight', which is always the cheapest deal.

Malév Hungarian Airlines, Stambolijski bulevard 26, Sofia, has very attractive youth fares for persons aged 25 years and under: US$55 one way to Budapest, US$160 to Amsterdam, US$175 to London. These tickets are valid only on Malév flights but many other destinations are available, so ask.

There's no airport departure tax in Bulgaria.

LAND
Bus

One of the easiest ways to get to Bulgaria is on the regular overnight bus service between Athens and Sofia (877 km, 15 hours, US$23 one way). A train ticket from Athens to Sofia costs US$52 one way. The customs check tends to be stricter on the train.

In Athens the Sofia bus departs from Omonia Square at 8 pm a couple of nights a week (usually Tuesday and Friday). Book with Economy Travel (☎ 363 8033), 18 El Venizelou St (in the arcade), or Mihail Tours (☎ 524 5762), 12 Ag Konstantinou St or 10 Omonia Square (upstairs).

Appia Tours (☎ 222 453), Mak Aminis 1, on the corner of Filippou St, Thessaloniki, has daily morning buses to Sofia (313 km, eight hours, US$15). Also try Constantinidis Travel (☎ 31 282 363) in Thessaloniki. Ask about student discounts. Cheap package bus tours to Bulgaria are available from the same agencies, eliminating the need to apply for a visa.

An increasing number of bus lines operate between Istanbul and Bulgaria, and their fares are also lower than what you'd pay on the train. These buses are listed under Getting There & Away in the city sections of this chapter. Bus travel to/from Skopje, Macedonia, and to/from Niš, Yugoslavia, is also very good.

Unfortunately, no buses operate between Romania and Bulgaria due to long delays at the border. There are lots of buses from Bucharest to Istanbul, however, and as these all pass through Bulgaria you could just get off after clearing Bulgarian customs. The low US$13 Bucharest-Istanbul fare makes this option well worth considering.

From mid-May to mid-October, Budget Bus (☎ 20-627 5151), Rokin 10, Amsterdam, has a twice weekly bus from Amsterdam to Sofia with a change at Frankfurt (37 hours, US$128 one way, US$242 return). Those aged 25 years and under receive a 10% discount.

Train

The main railway routes into Bulgaria are from Bucharest (Romania), Niš (Yugoslavia), Thessaloniki (Greece), and Edirne (Turkey). All these lines are served several times a day with through trains from Istanbul, Athens, Munich, Vienna, Berlin, Budapest, Belgrade, Warsaw, Kiev, Moscow, Vilnius and St Petersburg.

Train travel between Romania and Bulgaria is problematic because of occasional difficulties in purchasing tickets and the infrequency and inconvenience of the service, whereas the buses are much cheaper to/from Greece and Turkey. To/from Skopje, Macedonia, all train travel is via Niš, Yugoslavia, and a Yugoslav visa may be required (take a bus instead). Only to/from Yugoslavia is it as good to take the train.

To/From Romania Several long-distance trains originating in Russia or the Ukraine run between Romania and Bulgaria, but you're not allowed to take them (unless you offer a US$10 tip to the conductor). Between Bucharest and Sofia (545 km, 11 hours, US$11) or vice versa you may only use the unreserved overnight train. Southbound, this train passes Ruse and Pleven in the middle of the night; northbound it transits Pleven in the night and Ruse in the early morning. International train tickets are not sold at Ruse or Pleven train stations, so pick up an open ticket at a Rila office beforehand. This train is horrendously overcrowded and unless you want to stand jammed in the corridor all night, arrive at the station in Sofia or Bucharest very early.

To/From Yugoslavia & Beyond The *Meridian* express runs daily from Berlin-Lichtenberg to Sofia (1787 km) via Prague, Budapest, Novi Sad and Belgrade. Reservations are required if you're going north, but not if you're going south. Between Belgrade and Sofia (417 km, nine hours, US$16) the train travels overnight in both directions. Sofia to Budapest via Belgrade is US$34 (771 km, 16 hours).

The *Istanbul* express runs four days a week from Munich to Istanbul (2152 km) via Salzburg, Belgrade, Sofia and Kapikule. On this train, Sofia is 1501 km and 25 hours from Munich with a change of trains at Vienna. Reservations are required.

To/From Greece The overnight *Transbalkan* express links Sofia to Thessaloniki (372 km, nine hours, US$28) and Athens (882 km, 18 hours, US$52). If you're travelling from Sofia to Greece, don't take the train! Better to take one of the relatively hassle-free buses.

An unreserved day train runs between Plovdiv and Alexandroupolis (323 km, eight hours) in eastern Greece via Svilengrad.

To/From Turkey Beginning in 1885, the famous *Orient Express* route passed through Belgrade and Sofia on the way from Paris to Istanbul. Though this classic service no longer operates, the *Istanbul* and *Balkan* express trains still roll through Sofia and Plovdiv on their way south-east from central Europe to Istanbul. The *Istanbul* originates in Munich, the *Balkan* in Warsaw. Ask about compulsory reservations.

A train ticket from Sofia to Istanbul will cost around US$32 (636 km, 15 hours). Westbound, it's cheaper to buy a ticket only as far as the Turkish border town Kapikule and then pay the additional fare into Bulgaria on the train itself.

Train Tickets International train tickets should be purchased at Rila railway ticket offices. The Sofia Rila offices are crowded, so pick up your open international train ticket at a Rila office in some other Bulgarian city. Do so well ahead as Rila offices are only open on weekdays during business hours and such tickets are usually not sold at train stations (except in Sofia). Ask about seat reservations when you buy the ticket.

You pay for international train tickets in leva. Theoretically, student-card holders get a 30% discount on international train tickets between Eastern European countries. Ask about this at Orbita offices.

Car & Motorbike
When you enter Bulgaria by car you must state which border crossing you'll be using to leave the country and pay a road tax accordingly. If your plans change and you leave by a crossing with a higher tax you'll have to pay the difference, but there are no refunds if you leave via a shorter route.

Motorists in transit from Yugoslavia to Turkey can only use Kalotina and Kapitan-Andreevo and must follow the autoroute (US$10 toll) between Sofia and Plovdiv.

Here's a list of highway border crossings clockwise around Bulgaria, with the Bulgarian port of entry named.

To/From Turkey You may cross at Malko Târnovo (92 km south of Burgas) and Kapitan-Andreevo (20 km west of Edirne). To/from Greece you can cross at Kulata (127 km north of Thessaloniki) and Maritza Bridge near Svilengrad.

To/From Macedonia You can cross at Zlatarevo (37 km west of Kulata), Stanke Lisichkovo (26 km west of Blagoevgrad) and Gjueshevo (between Sofia and Skopje).

To/From Yugoslavia There are crossings at Strezimirovci (66 km west of Pernik), Kalotina (between Sofia and Niš), Vrâshka Chuka (45 km south-west of Vidin) and Bregovo (29 km north-west of Vidin).

To/From Romania You can cross at Vidin (opposite Calafat), Ruse (opposite Giurgiu), Silistra (opposite Călăraşi), Kardam (37 km north-east of Tolbuhin) and Durankulak (between Balchik and Mangalia). Expect

major delays entering/exiting Bulgaria by car to/from Romania. The waits are especially long on the Romanian side for southbound vehicles – be prepared to arrive at the Romanian border to find a line of cars a km long waiting to cross. Lines of trucks up to 10 km long have been reported!

Ferry
A regular car ferry crosses the Danube from Vidin to Calafat, Romania, hourly throughout the year (US$2 per person in hard currency). Bicycles are sometimes another US$2 each, sometimes free.

On Foot
You can avoid the hassle of getting an international train ticket by walking out of Bulgaria. One of the easiest ways to travel to/from Romania is on the regular ferry service between Vidin and Calafat, both of which are well connected to the rest of their respective countries by cheap local trains. See above and the Vidin and Calafat sections in this book for details.

On the Black Sea coast you can catch a bus to Durankulak, 62 km north-east of Balchik, then walk or hitchhike to the Romanian border, which is six km north. From there it's much easier to cover the last 10 km into Mangalia because bus No 14 runs from the Vama Veche border post to Mangalia 10 times a day (US$0.50).

For Turkey take a local train to Svilengrad; if you can't easily get an onward train ticket for the 39-km Svilengrad-Edirne hop, take a bus or taxi or hitchhike the 20 km from Svilengrad to Kapitan-Andreevo, the border post, and walk across (the train station is four km from the centre of Svilengrad and the border is two km beyond Kapitan-Andreevo village). Moneychangers and a Turkish *dolmuş* (minibus taxis) to Edirne (20 km, US$2.50) wait on the other side, and there are lots of buses from Edirne to Istanbul (247 km, US$5). It's also easy to enter Bulgaria this way.

Hitchhiking in Greece and Yugoslavia is pretty bad, so you're probably better off taking a bus (see the Bus section under

Getting There & Away). If you do decide to hitchhike to Greece, take a local train to Kulata, walk across and stick out your thumb.

PACKAGE TOURS

There are numerous all-inclusive tours to the Black Sea resorts. These are fairly cheap but you're tied to a beach hotel, and outside the peak season (from June to mid-September), facilities are limited. Though accommodation is included, these tours are often cheaper than a regular return plane ticket from northern Europe to Bulgaria. Another advantage of going in a tour group is that no visa is required. If you have to choose between Sunny Beach and Golden Sands for a beach package, pick Golden Sands – it is more attractive and better located. There are package ski holidays to Borovets and Mt Vitosha.

More imaginative than the beach holidays, but three times as expensive, are the tours featuring an eight-country cruise along the Danube from Ruse to Passau, Germany. There are also bus tours around the country, cycle tours, stays at luxury health resorts such as Sandanski, skiing at Borovets or Pamporovo, and so on. Balkantourist offices abroad will have details.

Getting Around

AIR

Balkan Airlines has five or six flights a day from Sofia to Varna and Burgas (US$65 one way). The expense of a domestic air ticket, however, may convince you that it's better to take the train.

Bus

Long-distance buses serve many points that are not directly connected by train. Take a bus to go from Sofia to Rila Monastery, from Pleven to Troyan, from Troyan to Plovdiv, from Burgas to Varna etc. Only as many tickets are sold as there are seats, so it's important to arrive at the bus station

(avtogara) early to make sure you get one. You usually buy the ticket at the office rather than from the driver. At way stations, tickets for long-distance buses can only be purchased after the bus arrives and the driver tells the ticket clerk how many seats are available. Long-distance buses generally leave in the very early morning.

Private buses now operate on long-distance routes in competition with the railways, especially from Sofia and Plovdiv to the Black Sea resorts. Overnight buses and all buses to the coast must be booked the day before as they are usually full.

TRAIN

The Bâlgarski Dârzhavni Zhelezitsi (BDZ), or Bulgarian State Railways, runs trains over 4278 km of track. The trains are classified as ekspresen (express), brzi (fast) or putnichki (slow). Trains from Sofia to Burgas go via either Karlovo or Plovdiv. Trains from Sofia to Varna go via either Karlovo or Gorna Oryahovitsa. All trains from Sofia to Ruse go via Pleven and Gorna Oryahovitsa. Service between Sofia and Plovdiv is fairly frequent. Sleepers and couchettes are available between Sofia and Burgas or Varna for a mere US$2 but you'll need to book well ahead to get one. Seat reservations are recommended on express trains to the Black Sea. Visit Rila offices for these bookings.

Gorna Oryahovitsa is a main railway junction in northern Bulgaria where trains from Sofia, Ruse, Varna and Stara Zagora meet. The branch line south from Gorna Oryahovitsa to Stara Zagora via Veliko Târnovo is the only north-south line across the centre of the country. Another branch line runs from Ruse to Varna, although buses (via Shumen) are faster and more frequent on this route. Bulgaria's most spectacular train ride is up the Iskâr Gorge from Sofia to Mezdra on the line to Vidin and Pleven. For rail buffs, it would even be worth doing it as a day trip.

Take care not to miss your station as stations are all poorly marked. Most have a sign in both Cyrillic and Latin script, but it's often badly placed. It's best to sit near the front of the train to be able to read the station names.

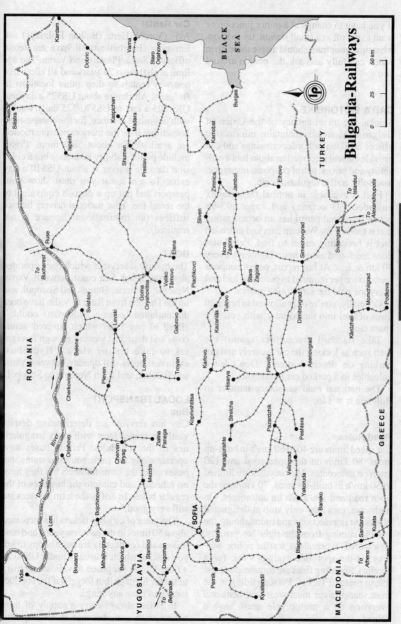

Bulgaria-Railways

BLACK SEA

50 km
25
0

BULGARIA

If you have to change at a minor junction or want to get off at a small station, try to know what time your train should arrive there, then watch carefully and ask the people around you.

CAR & MOTORBIKE

Shipka, the travel agency of the Union of Bulgarian Motorists, maintains information offices at all major border crossings and can provide current information about fuel availability and prices, petrol coupons, insurance, road tolls, traffic regulations etc.

Fuel is available in normal (86 octane), unleaded (93 octane) and super (93-98 octane). Normal petrol has an octane rating that is too low for Western cars and unleaded fuel is becoming easier to find. Petrol stations are found along main highways every 30 km or less. At last report, petrol coupons were no longer required to purchase fuel and everyone paid the same price in leva.

Officially, you're only allowed to bring 20 litres of fuel into the country with you in a spare tank.

Take standard precautions against car theft such as locking the car securely and not parking on deserted streets. Don't leave valuables in a parked car overnight.

The national road assistance number in Bulgaria is ☎ 146.

Road Rules

Car speed limits are 40 to 60 km/h in built-up areas, 80 km/h on the open road and 120 km/h on autoroutes. Motorcycles are limited to 50 km/h in built-up areas, 70 km/h on the open road and 100 km/h on autoroutes. On highways, cars may only stop at designated places. At intersections and roundabouts, the vehicle coming from the right has priority. Beware of overzealous traffic police who levy on-the-spot fines (always ask for a receipt). Speeding fines are routine along the transit route to Turkey. Persons riding in the front seat of a car must wear seat belts and everyone on a motorcycle must have a helmet.

Car Rental

Avis (Varco), Hertz (Balkan Holidays) and Europcar (Interbalkan) all have car rental offices in Sofia, Plovdiv and Varna. The age limit at all three is 21 years and all allow free one-way rentals to their other locations in Bulgaria. All charge about US$25 a day and US$0.25 a km, or US$70/325 daily/weekly with unlimited distance, for the cheapest car. Sometimes only the more expensive models are available for about 50% more. Prices include public liability insurance but a collision damage waiver is about US$10 a day extra. To rent a car you must show your passport and put up a deposit equivalent to the rental fee. Your national drivers licence suffices (an international licence is not required).

BOAT

The hydrofoil services which once operated along the Black Sea coast between Varna, Nesebâr, Pomorie, Burgas and Sozopol, and up the Danube from Ruse to Vidin have been discontinued because Bulgarians couldn't afford to pay fares which covered actual costs and there just weren't enough foreigners to take up the slack. 'Hydrobus' excursion boats still operate between Varna and Balchik, and from Nesebâr to Sozopol.

LOCAL TRANSPORT
Bus

City bus services are deteriorating despite vastly increased fares with many irregularities in the schedules. Private buses now operate along the same routes as municipal buses using the same numbers but they have no schedule and cut into the business of the regular buses. In Sofia, the tram services are still very good.

The price of city bus tickets has increased about 50 times in the past few years, and now drivers and conductors are quite happy to sell you a ticket which is usually under US$0.25 a ride. You're supposed to validate an extra ticket for luggage (but forget it if the conductor doesn't say anything).

In Sofia, always carry a supply of tram tickets with you, because if an inspector catches you without a ticket you're liable for a US$3 fine. Trams and trolley buses operate from 4 am to 1 am and buses operate until midnight. One and five-day transit passes are available in Sofia.

Taxi

Taxis are plentiful in Bulgaria and you can even flag them down on the street. They are most easily found in front of train stations but beware of those waiting at the luxury hotels. Taxi drivers in Bulgaria charge what the meter says and are not expensive. Always try to take a taxi with a meter that works, otherwise ask what the fare will be before-hand. The drivers don't usually charge you for the return journey, even if it's out of town. Fares are 50% higher from 10 pm to 5 am. Round up the meter fare to the next multiple of five or 10.

Sofia (София)

Sofia (Sofiya) sits on a 550-metre-high plateau in western Bulgaria at the foot of Mt Vitosha, just west of the Iskâr River. Its position at the very centre of the Balkan Peninsula, midway between the Adriatic and Black seas, made Sofia a crossroads of trans-European routes. The present city centre is attractive with large open areas paved with yellow bricks, tastefully rebuilt after WW II bombings. It's a remarkably clean, quiet city considering that much of Bulgaria's industry is concentrated here. If you can find reason-able accommodation, Sofia repays an unhurried stay.

History

Under various names, Sofia has a history that goes back thousands of years. The Thracian Serdi tribe settled here in the 7th century BC. In the 3rd century AD, the Romans built strong walls around Serdica (Sofia), their capital of Inner Dacia and an important stop-ping point on the Roman road from Naisus (present Niš, Yugoslavia) to Constantinople (Istanbul). After the Hun invasion of 441, the

town was rebuilt by the Byzantines. The Slavs gave Sredets (Sofia) a key role in the First Bulgarian Empire, then in 1018 the Byzantines retook Triaditsa (Sofia). At the end of the 12th century, the Bulgarians returned and Sredets became a major trading centre of the Second Bulgarian Empire.

The Turks captured Sofia in 1382 and made it the centre of the Rumelian beylerbeyship. The city declined during the feudal unrest of the 19th century, but with the establishment of the Third Bulgarian Empire in 1879, Sofia again became capital. Between 1879 and 1939, the population grew from 20,000 to 300,000. Today, 1,250,000 people live in Sofia. The Yugoslav border at Dimitrovgrad is only 55 km north-west of Sofia, and the city's off-centre location in Bulgaria is a reminder of the loss of Macedonia to Serbia and Greece in 1913.

Orientation

The central train station is on the north side of the city centre. On arrival at the station, go down into the underpass and walk right through to the far end. From there catch tram No 1 or 7 four stops to the centre of town. You can buy tram tickets in the underpass. The left-luggage office downstairs in the train station is open from 5.30 am to mid-night (you have to change money before you can use it). Sofia's bus stations do not have left-luggage offices.

From the station, bulevard Marija Luiza curves around and runs south through ploschtad Sveta Nedelya. Beyond the Holy Sunday Cathedral this thoroughfare becomes Vitosha bulevard (formerly Stalin bulevard), the fashionable avenue of modern Sofia. Many travel agencies and airline offices are found along Stambolijski bulevard, which runs west from the Holy Sunday Cathedral.

Largo opens east from ploschtad Sveta Nedelya and spills into ploschtad Batenberg. The former Georgi Dimitrov mausoleum on ploschtad Batenberg is the very heart of the city. Car Osvoboditel continues south-east as far as the Clement of Ohrid University, then

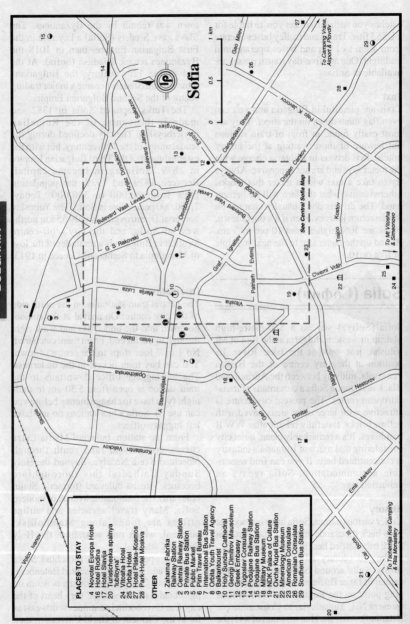

Sofia

runs on and out of the city as bulevard Carigradsko Shose.

Information

Tourist Offices There isn't any real tourist information office in Sofia (see Travel Agencies following).

Money The ultramodern, white-coloured Bulgarian Foreign Trade Bank across the street from the Sheraton Hotel is open weekdays from 8.20 am to 4.30 pm and changes travellers' cheques for a flat US$1 commission.

The First Private Bank, Sâborna 2a above Bulgarian Airlines behind the Sheraton (weekdays 9 am to 12.30 pm), changes US dollar travellers' cheques into US dollars cash for a flat US$10 commission for up to US$1000 – one of the only banks which will do this.

Non Stop Change, Buzludza 72, just west of the Palace of Culture, changes cash 24 hours a day at the usual rates.

Post & Telecommunications Sofia's main telephone centre is in a poorly marked building on ulitsa Stefan Karadza, an alley diagonally opposite the main post office, ulitsa Vasil Levski at General Gurko. It's open 24 hours and is rather chaotic.

The telephone centre in the shopping mall below the NDK Palace of Culture is smaller and only open weekdays from 7 am to 8 pm, Saturday from 7 am to 1 pm, but it's usually uncrowded and easy to use.

Sofia's telephone code is 02.

Western Consulates The British Embassy (☎ 885 361), bulevard Vasil Levski 38, east of the NDK Palace of Culture (Monday to Thursday 9 am to noon and 2 to 4 pm, Friday 9 am to noon), serves all Commonwealth nationals.

The US Embassy on Sofia's Central Park deals only with official business: all travel-related enquiries must be directed to the US Consulate (☎ 659 459), Kapitan Andreev 1, off bulevard Evlogi Georgiev (weekdays 9 am to 5 pm).

Eastern European Consulates The Slovak Consulate, bulevard Janko Sakazov 9, is open Monday, Wednesday and Friday from 10 to 11.30 am. A couple of blocks away is the Yugoslav Consulate, Veliko Târnovo 3, which opens weekdays from 9 am to noon. In this same area are the Albanian Consulate, Krakra 10 (Monday, Wednesday and Friday 10 am to noon), and the Croatian Consulate, Krakra 18 (weekdays 10 am to 2 pm).

The Hungarian Consulate, 6 Septemvri 57, behind the British Embassy, opens Monday, Tuesday, Thursday and Friday from 9 am to 10 am. The Polish Consulate, Khan Kroum 46 (open Monday to Wednesday and Friday from 9 am to 1 pm), is also behind the British Embassy (see the Central Sofia map).

The Romanian Consulate is on the east side of town, on the corner of Sipchenski Prohod and Sitnjakovo (take tram No 20 from bulevard Janka Sakazov). It opens Tuesday from 3 to 5 pm and Wednesday and Thursday from 10 am to noon. The consular section is in a separate pavilion around the back.

You shouldn't need a visa for Greece, but if you want to check join the throng at the Greek Consulate, Evlogi Georgiev 103. Check visa requirements for Turkey at the Turkish Embassy, bulevard Vasil Levski 80.

Travel Agencies The main Balkantourist office (☎ 877 233) that helps individual tourists is at Stambolijski bulevard 27 (open from 7 am to 9 pm). The people there reserve accommodation, change money and book sightseeing tours. They will also answer questions if they're not too busy.

The American Express representative is Megatours, ulitsa Vasil Levski 1, opposite the former Georgi Dimitrov Mausoleum.

For information (in Bulgarian) on hostels, go to the Pirin Travel Bureau (☎ 884 122) on Car Samuil, around the corner from Stambolijski bulevard 30 (weekdays 9 am to 5.30 pm). They can book hostel beds all around the country and sell Cyrillic hiking maps which mark all the mountain huts.

The Orbita Youth Travel Agency (☎ 800

102), bulevard Hristo Botev 48, sells ISIC student cards (US$4) and can book beds in student dormitories at US$5 per person for students, US$9 for non-students. The booking office is accessible through a poorly marked door inside Orbita's currency exchange office. Ask here about discounted student train tickets to other Eastern European countries.

The Tourist Information and Reservations office (☎ 883 114), Lavele 22 off Stambolijski bulevard, can book rooms at two-star hotels all around Bulgaria for about US$25/35 single/double with bath and breakfast (about 20% off the rate you'd pay if you just walked in and rented a room). In Sofia they offer the Hotel Slavia for this price.

For information on driving conditions in Bulgaria go to Shipka, the travel agency of the Union of Bulgarian Motorists (☎ 883 856), Lavele 18 just off Stambolijski bulevard. Shipka also books seats on international buses to Budapest (daily, US$32), Vienna (weekly, US$37), Munich (weekly, US$62), Berlin (four a week, US$56), Frankfurt (weekly, US$78), Amsterdam (weekly, US$100), Paris (weekly, US$97) and many other Western European cities.

Sport Tourist (☎ 832 613), bulevard Marija Luiza 79, sells bus tickets to Istanbul (daily, US$13); Amman, Jordan (daily, US$55); Munich (weekly, US$62) and many other cities in central and Western Europe.

The combined transportation ticket office in the lower level arcade at the NDK Palace of Culture sells domestic train tickets and books couchettes or sleepers to Varna and Burgas (only US$2 but fully booked well ahead). You can also purchase international tickets at this office. The clerk at the counter marked 'Eisenbahnfahrkarten für Auslandsreisen' can provide your international ticket and make any required seat or couchette reservations in the one operation. This office is crowded around mid-afternoon, so come early or late.

The main Rila office, ulitsa General Gurko 5 (open weekdays from 7 am to 7 pm), also sells international tickets. You must queue up for a ticket, queue up to pay, queue up to hand in the slip to get the ticket, then queue up again to make a reservation.

Adventure Travel The Odysseia-In Travel Agency (☎ 890 538, fax 659 167), on the side street behind Stambolijski bulevard 20, specialise in adventure travel. From June to August they run hiking tours through the Rila and Pirin mountains every two weeks for German and Dutch groups, and individuals who walk into their Sofia office are welcome to sign up. The price will be US$320 for one week, US$600 for two weeks, including transportation, accommodation, guides and horses to carry baggage, but not food (which can be purchased in the mountain huts where the groups stay). Odysseia-In also offers short two to three-day mountain treks, horse riding (US$10 per hour), fishing, paragliding and cave exploration. In winter, there are skiing holidays (US$620 for two weeks, equipment extra). They can also make advance bookings for private rooms in mountain areas at US$10 per person. If you need mountaineering or camping gear, or even a new backpack, they sell the best.

Bookshops The latest foreign newspapers in English can be purchased at the newsstand in the basement of the Sheraton Hotel.

Things to See
Sightseeing in Sofia is centred mostly around museums, although there are a number of old churches and mosques to visit. Begin with the largest: the neo-Byzantine **Aleksander Nevski Church** (1912), a memorial to the 200,000 Russian soldiers who died for Bulgaria's independence. In the crypt is a museum of icons (closed Tuesday). The 6th century basilica to the right across the square in front of the Aleksander Nevski Church is the **Church of St Sophia**, who gave her name to the city. By the church wall is the **Tomb of the Unknown Soldier**. The large white building behind the Aleksander Nevski Church contains the **Foreign Art Gallery** (closed Tuesday, free Sunday), with

an important collection of European paintings, as well as African, Japanese and Indian art.

The street that runs south from the Aleksander Nevski Church empties into ploschtad Narodno Sabranie where you'll find the **National Assembly** (1884) and an equestrian statue (1905) of Alexander II, the Russian tsar who freed Bulgaria from the Turks. Bulevard Car Osvoboditel runs west into ploschtad Batenberg, the heart of official Sofia. On the way, beyond the park, is **St Nicholas Russian Church** (1913) and then the **Natural Science Museum**, Car Osvoboditel 1 (closed Monday and Tuesday), with flora and fauna exhibits on four floors.

You'll then reach ploschtad Batenberg, which is dominated by the former **Georgi Dimitrov Mausoleum**. Dimitrov faced Hermann Goering at the Reichstag fire trail in 1933 and after spending the war years in the USSR was elected prime minister of Bulgaria in 1946. From his death in 1949 until mid-1990, when the wax-like body was cremated, the public was allowed to file reverently past the deified figure as an honour guard looked on. Today, the area around the graffiti-covered mausoleum is often used as a camping ground by political dissidents.

Opposite the mausoleum are the **National Art Gallery** (free Sunday, closed Monday) with Bulgarian paintings and the **Ethnographical Museum** (closed Monday and Tuesday), both housed in the former Royal Palace (1887). Before 1878, the residence of the Turkish governor occupied this same site. The park east of the mausoleum is dominated by the neoclassical **Ivan Vazov National Academic Theatre** (1907), designed by the Viennese architects Fellner and Hellmer.

Hidden behind the Bulgarian National Bank, at the western end of ploschtad Batenberg, are the nine lead-covered domes of the Buyuk Djami, or the Great Mosque (1496), now the **National Archaeological Museum** (closed Monday), which has an excellent collection of antique sculpture.

Facing Largo across the street from the Archaeological Museum is former **Party House** (1955), with the former Council of State on the north side of Largo and the former State Council on the south side, the most impressive Stalinist ensemble in Bulgaria. In August 1990 Party House was sacked by demonstrators, who burned part of the building and toppled the red star from the steeple. Traces of the fire are still clearly visible on the outside of the building, but the interior rotunda is untouched and presently used as a bazar. Upstairs is an impressive auditorium where church services take place on Sunday mornings. At other times the auditorium serves as a cinema and it's well worth buying a movie ticket just to get inside.

In the courtyard formed by the State Council and the Sheraton Hotel (1955) is an imposing 4th century Roman Rotunda that was converted into the **Church of St George** in the Middle Ages. On the dome inside are 11th to 14th century frescoes; outside, the ruins of Roman streets surround the church.

At the western end of Largo is a shopping mall below street level with the 14th century church of **St Petra Semerdjuska** and its frescoes (closed Sunday and Monday). The church was built at the beginning of the Turkish period, which explains its low profile and inconspicuous exterior. The **Banya Bashi Mosque** (1576), with its majestic minaret, is north of Largo, and nearby behind the supermarket (1911) is Sofia's **synagogue** (1909), which has a huge chandelier. Two blocks beyond the synagogue is the teeming public market along bulevard Stefan Stambolov.

South of Largo is **Holy Sunday Cathedral** (1863), restored after a 1924 bomb attempt here on King Boris III in which 124 people (including most of the cabinet) were killed. Beyond it on Vitosha bulevard is the **National Museum of History** (closed Monday, US$1) in the building of the former Palace of Justice (1936). This huge museum takes up two floors of an entire city block. Don't miss the 4th century BC Panagjurishte gold treasure in room No 3. Some of the exhibits appear to be copies, but it's hard to

BULGARIA

BULGARIA

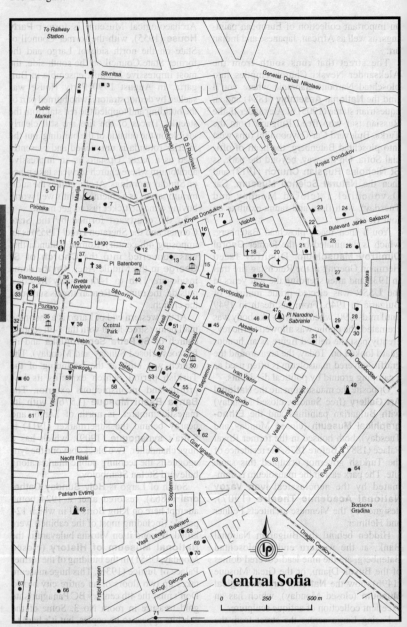

To Railway Station

Silivnitsa

General Danail Nikolaev

Public Market

Borisovski

G S Rakovski

Vasil Levski Bulevard

Knyaz Dondukov

Marija Luiza

Iskâr

Pirotska

Knyaz Dondukov

Vlabca

Bulevard Janko Sakazov

Largo

Pl Batenberg

Car Osvoboditel

Shipka

Krakra

Stamboliiski

Pl Sveta Nedelya

Sáborna

Pozitano

Central Park

Ulitsa Vasil Levski

Pl Narodno Sabranie

Aksakov

Car Osvoboditel

Alabin

Stefan

Denkoglu

G S Rakovski

Ivan Vazov

Karadza

General Gurko

Vitosha

6 Septemvri

Neofit Rilski

Graf Ignatiev

Vasil Levski Bulevard

Evlogi Georgiev

Borisova Gradina

Patriarh Evtimij

Dragan Cankov

6 Septemvri

Fritjof Nansen

Vasil Levski Bulevard

Evlogi Georgiev

Central Sofia

0   250   500 m

PLACES TO STAY

2	Edelweis Hotel/Sport Tourist	12	Former Party House	41	City Art Gallery
3	Sredna Gora Hotel	13	National Art Gallery & Ethnographical Museum	42	Former Georgi Dimitrov Mausoleum
4	Hotel Zdravec	14	Natural Science Museum	43	Ameican Express/ Megatour
8	Iskår Hotel	15	St Nicholas Russian Church	44	Sala Bulgaria
25	Serdika Hotel	17	National Academic Theatre for Opera & Ballet	46	Balkan Bulgarian Airlines
37	Sheraton Balkan Hotel			47	Monument to the Liberators
45	Slavinska Beseda Hotel	18	Church of St Sophia	48	National Assembly
57	Sevastopol Hotel	19	Patriarch's Palace	49	Soviet Army Monument
60	Hotel Baldjieva	20	Aleksander Nevski Church	50	Ivan Vazov Museum/Luciano

PLACES TO EAT

16	Pizzeria Venezia	21	Foreign Art Gallery	51	Ivan Vazov National Academic Theatre
32	Mishonex Restaurant	22	Vasil Levski Monument		
39	Vitosha Restaurant	23	Makedonski State Musical Theatre	52	Rila Railway Ticket Office
55	Budapest Restaurant	24	Slovak Consulate	53	Main Post Office & Telephone Centre
58	Ham Hum Self-Service	26	Albanian Consulate	54	Puppet Theatre
59	The King Restaurant	27	National Library	56	Satirical Theatre
61	Pizza Palace	28	Fine Art Sales Gallery	62	Saints Sedmotchislenitsi Church
		29	Clement of Ohrid University		

OTHER

		30	Croatian Embassy	63	Turkish Embassy
1	Lions Bridge	31	Disco Yalta	64	Vasil Levski Stadium
5	Synagogue	33	Balkantourist		
6	Banya Bashi Mosque	34	Shipka Travel Agency/Tourist Information & Reservations	65	1300th Anniversary Monument
7	Central Mineral Baths (Closed)			66	NDK Palace of Culture
9	Central Department Store	35	National Museum of History	67	Non Stop Change
10	St Petra Semerdjuska Church	36	Holy Sunday Cathedral	68	British Embassy
		38	Church of St George's Rotunda	69	Polish Consulate
11	Bulgarian Foreign Trade Bank	40	National Archaeological Museum	70	Hungarian Consulate
				71	American Consulate

tell since only Cyrillic labels are provided. Sadly, the lack of translated information makes much of the collection meaningless to foreigners. Beware of the museum closing an hour earlier than the posted time.

Vitosha, Sofia's most elegant boulevard, runs south from the Holy Sunday Cathedral to Sofia's modern **NDK Palace of Culture** (1981), often used for concerts and conferen-

ces. This ultramodern building was previously named after Lyudmila Zhivkov, minister of culture until her death in 1981 and daughter of Todor Zhivkov. Lyudmila was extremely popular in Bulgaria for her vigorous cultural nationalism. Visit the underground shopping arcade in front of the palace and take the elevator up to the roof for the view. On the square in front of the palace

BULGARIA

is the huge Monument to the 1300th Anniversary of Bulgaria.

Saints Sedmotchislenitsi Church, in what was originally the Black Mosque (1528), is on ulitsa Graf Ignatiev.

Mt Vitosha Mt Vitosha (2290 metres), the rounded mountain which looms just eight km south of Sofia, is a popular ski resort in winter and in summer the chair lift operates for the benefit of sightseers. If you have a little extra time, take a bus up Mt Vitosha to Hizha Aleko, where there's a chair lift approaching the summit. There are a number of hotels on the mountain, but they're geared for package tourism and have little to offer the individual visitor. Everything can be seen in a couple of hours and you'll get the best view of the city during the bus ride up the mountain. The Vitosha bus departs hourly from near the southern terminus of trams Nos 2 and 9.

Places to Stay
With the demise of communist-controlled tourism, it has become much easier to find a cheap place to stay in Sofia. Some hotel prices have come down, although foreigners still pay up to 10 times more than Bulgarians at the up-market hotels.

Camping *Camping Vrana* (☎ 781 213; open all year) is nine km out of the city on the Plovdiv Highway. From the central train station take bus No 213 out onto bulevard Carigradsko Shose, then change to bus No 5, 6 or 7, all of which pass the site. Alternatively, take tram No 20 south-east, then change to bus No 5 or 6. Camping costs US$4 per person plus US$3 per tent and bungalows are US$25 single or double. There's a restaurant on the premises – don't pitch your tent too close to it if you want to get any sleep.

Tschernija Kos Camping, 11 km southwest of Sofia on the main highway to Greece, offers camping and bungalows. From the city centre take tram No 5 to the end of the line, then bus No 58 or 59 till you see a huge white statue on the left-hand side of the road.

Though more difficult to reach on public transport than Camping Vrana, it's convenient if you're travelling to or from Rila Monastery. At last report, Tschernija Kos was in the process of being privatised and the new prices and conditions were still unknown. Both these camping grounds have plenty of space for campers.

Hostels *Turisticheska spalnya 'lubilcyna'*, also known as Hotel Tourist (☎ 204 991), Rizki Prochod 1 next to a Vietnamese refugee camp, offers beds in three, four and five-bed dorms at US$6.50 per person with a YHA card, US$8 without. The slot machines set the tone of this hostel. Even if your room is on the upper floor, make sure your window is securely locked before going out. Trams Nos 4 and 11 from the Ovcha Kupel Bus Station pass within a few blocks of the hostel and you get out amid a cluster of high-rise apartments (ask). Otherwise take bus No 77 from the train station to the last stop. This hostel is convenient if you want to catch the early bus to Rila Monastery as the Ovcha Kupel Bus Station is easily accessible by tram.

There are also several hostels on Mt Vitosha. *Hizha Aleko* is one (US$5 per person in an eight-bed dorm, US$7 per person in a five-bed dorm, US$10 per person in a double room). Staff at the Pirin Travel Bureau on Car Samuil, around the corner from Stambolijski bulevard 30, can make the necessary reservations for you.

Private Rooms The exchange and accommodation office on the upper level in the train station rents private rooms at US$8/10 single/double and also arranges rooms in student dormitories at US$5/8 (minimum three nights, student card required, available all year).

Balkantourist, Stambolijski bulevard 27 (Monday to Saturday until 9 pm, Sunday until 8 pm), books private rooms, but only after noon, when the rooms become available. A good room in the city centre will be around US$10/12 single/double.

Sport Tourist (☎ 831 473), bulevard

Marija Luiza 79 (weekdays 9 am to 5 pm), has private rooms at US$8 per person.

Markella Company (☎ 815 299), bulevard Marija Luiza 17, operates out of a kiosk at the back of the parking lot across the street from Central Department Store (weekdays 9.30 am to 7 pm, Saturday 9.30 am to 4 pm). Their only sign reads 'private lodgings – change' but their private room prices are lower than those at Balkantourist: US$8 double in the centre of town, US$6 in the suburbs (no singles). They also book a few small private hotels at Ovcha Kupel, west of the city centre at US$9 double.

Hotels The *Edelweiss Hotel* (☎ 835 431), bulevard Marija Luiza 79, and the *Sredna Gora Hotel* (☎ 835 311), bulevard Marija Luiza 60, are two old hotels on a noisy tram route between the train station and the centre of town. They only offer rooms with shared bath at US$8/12 single/double and of the two, the Edelweiss is slightly better, but both are only for hardy low-budget travellers who put price above all else. The Sredna Gora is very basic, has no hot water and is only worth trying as a last resort.

A step up is the better located *Sevastopol Hotel* (☎ 875 941), ulitsa Rakovski 116, on the corner of Graf Ignatiev, at US$11/15 single/double with shared bath. Ask for a room on the top floor to be further away from the noisy disco downstairs.

The *Hotel Baldjieva* (☎ 872 914), Car Asen 23, has one single room at US$17 and two doubles and one triple for US$27, all with shared bath. This pleasant, privately owned hotel is a good medium-priced choice in an excellent location but it's often full.

The four-storey *Hotel Slavia* (☎ 549 251), Sofijski Geroj 2 off bulevard Car Boris III, is Sofia's least expensive two-star hotel, with 66 rooms at US$30/42/58 single/double/triple with bath and breakfast. It's a little out of the way, a km south-west of Hotel Rodina, but trams Nos 5 and 19 rumble frequently to and from town and this neat modern hotel is just far enough away from the line that you aren't bothered by the noise.

East of the Centre Several small private hotels are in the Geo Milev district behind the expensive Hotel Pliska-Kosmos (tram No 20 to Kopernik). The largest is the *Hotel Rai-90* (☎ 729 690), Liditse 13, with eight rooms at US$18/25/36 single/double/triple with a bath shared between every two rooms. *Hotel Ganesha* (☎ 707 936), Anry Barbus 26 across the street, is charging US$15/25 single/double. The two-room *Hotel Praga* (☎ 727 461), Anry Barbus 35, is US$10 per person.

Places to Eat

With privatisation, all of Sofia's proletarian self-service cafeterias have closed and in their place a plethora of small private cafés and snack bars have appeared. There's now such a choice of better restaurants that you can afford to be choosy and insist on a menu with prices listed, preferably in English. If you're told no menu exists, walk out as some Sofia waiters unfairly overcharge foreigners.

Bottom End *Ham Hum*, Graf Ignatiev 12, has a small salad bar and offers a number of microwave dishes such as topcheta (meatball soup) and sarmi (stuffed cabbage leaves), plus draught beer. It's self-service but pleasant and inexpensive, and it's open 24 hours a day.

The *King Restaurant*, Denkoglu 38 just off Vitosha bulevard, has enough Arab-style gyros, burgers and sweets to feed Ali Baba and the 40 proverbial thieves.

For fresh grilled chicken it's *Mussi Fast Food*, Vitosha bulevard 59.

Middle The *Vitosha Restaurant*, downstairs from the arcade at Vitosha bulevard 1/3 opposite the National Museum of History, offers Bulgarian specialities such as sirene po shopski and kavarma v omlet. Specify that you want your beer cold (studeno) and coffee hot (goreshto), otherwise they'll both arrive at about the same temperature.

The *Mishonex Restaurant* (also known as the Erma Restaurant), ulitsa Alabin 25, behind the National Museum of History, may not present itself as specialising in national dishes but it serves a mixed grill which is hard to beat. Ask for the English menu translation (though prices are only found in the Bulgarian menu). Expect to be charged separately for each ingredient.

Restaurant Paradise, Pozitano 34 next to the circus, serves grilled meats with a Middle Eastern flavour and a generous shopska salad. They have a menu in English.

The *Pizza Palace*, Vitosha bulevard 34, bakes reasonable pizza and the menu is posted outside.

Pizzeria Venezia, Georgi Benkovski 12, a block from the National Opera, has the best pizza in Sofia (and maybe the best in Eastern Europe). It's cooked in their wood-fired oven after 6 pm (electric oven before 6 pm) and the price is right, so it's always jammed with locals – squeeze in where you can.

Despite the seedy neighbourhood *Restaurant Splendid*, Pirotska 7, lives up to its name in almost every way. Scrutinise the English menu posted outside and note the prices. At Splendid, linen tablecloths, candles, flawless service and excellent food will fit into even a backpacker's budget. Recommended.

Top End The *Cerveno Zname Restaurant* upstairs above Coop Café, Vitosha bulevard 16, may be Italian but it could end up being your favourite Sofia restaurant if you appreciate its many uses of cheese. A pianist plays as you dine. Reservations are recommended.

Cafés There are many pavement cafés along Vitosha bulevard and you can tell at a glance which ones offer the best deals by the number of local people sitting there. A great place for coffee and cakes is *Luciano*, Rakovski 135.

Entertainment

For an unforgettable evening of classical entertainment head for the *National Academic Theatre for Opera & Ballet* on ulitsa Vlabca, not far from the Aleksander Nevski Church. Tickets are sold inside and you should be able to get one.

For lighter fare, it's the *Makedonski State Musical Theatre* on bulevard Vasil Levski,

behind the Aleksander Nevski Church. You'll enjoy the operettas put on here, even if they are in Bulgarian – highly recommended. At both of these theatres, performances begin at 7 pm, with matinées on weekends.

The *Puppet Theatre*, ulitsa General Gurko 14, never fails to please. Performances here are usually on Saturday and Sunday at 11.30 am. Nearby is the *Satirical Theatre*, ulitsa Stefan Karadza 26. You won't understand a word of it, but the acting is superb. The *Ivan Vazov National Academic Theatre*, ulitsa Vasil Levski 5, presents classical theatre in Bulgarian.

A circus performs under the big tent in the square between Pozitano and Alabin streets, three blocks west of Vitosha bulevard (closed in summer).

Many concerts take place in the *Sala Bulgaria* at ulitsa Aksakov 3 and others are performed in the *NDK Palace of Culture*. In July and August, the Palace of Culture maintains a daily programme of events while Sofia's other theatres close for holidays. The ticket office at the Palace of Culture is accessible from the outside terrace through a separate entrance to the left of the main entrance (closes at 2 pm on Saturday).

A folklore show for tourists is put on nightly at 9 pm at the *Vodenicharski Mehani* (☎ 665 088) in Dragalevtsi, 13 km south of central Sofia (buses Nos 66 and 93). Typical Bulgarian food is served before the show. Getting back to Sofia is a problem as the buses will have stopped running by the time you come out and taxis are a rip-off here. Balkantourist (☎ 875 192), Vitosha bulevard 1, can provide a car and driver for the evening at US$35 for one person, US$45 for two, dinner and the show included.

Discos The disco in the basement of the *NDK Palace of Culture* cranks up nightly with the dancing beginning at 10.30 pm. Entry is from the lower arcade.

Others include *Anaconda Disco Dance*, Pirotska 5, which opens at 8 pm, the *Star Club* on ploschtad Vâzrazdane off Stambolijski bulevard, and *Disco Yalta*, Aksakov 31.

There's also a good disco in the *Sevastopol Hotel*, Rakovski 116, accessible from the hotel lobby (nightly from 10 pm).

Things to Buy

If you're in the market for an original painting or sculpture by a Bulgarian artist, go to the Fine Art Sales Gallery, Shipka 6. Don't miss the exhibitions on the upper floors. Ask about export regulations before making a major purchase. Better shops for Bulgarian consumers are along Vitosha bulevard and in the arcade below the NDK Palace of Culture.

The locals shop on the five floors of the Central Department Store (ZUM) on Largo. Lots of clothing is available – even leather coats and fur hats – or you can buy fancy knives, compact discs, postage stamps and souvenirs. A Kodak Express colour film developing centre is at the back of the ground floor. There's a supermarket in the basement and a self-service restaurant on the top floor.

Getting There & Away

Bus Places that you can reach more easily by bus than by train include Rila Monastery (120 km, three hours), Troyan (175 km) and Gabrovo (223 km). Direct services to the Rila Monastery and Melnik depart from the Ovcha Kupel Bus Station (trams No 5 or 19), and buses to Troyan and Gabrovo leave from the Podujane Bus Station near the Gerena Stadium, north-east of the centre (trolley bus No 2 or 3). Advance tickets for these buses are available at the ticket office in the arcade below the NDK Palace of Culture, but you must buy them at least one day beforehand.

A new bus station has appeared in front of the central train station with private buses to many places such as Varna, Burgas, Pleven, Veliko Târnovo, Shumen, Ruse and Sozopol, previously accessible from Sofia only by train. Tickets can be booked up to a week in advance at the kiosks on the side of the parking lot away from the train station and it's a good idea to do this a day or two before for the popular early morning or overnight buses. Buses to Istanbul leave from this station daily.

International Buses Buses depart from Sofia's International Bus Station, Damjan Gruev at 20 april, for Niš, Yugoslavia (twice daily except Sunday, 148 km, US$4), to Skopje, Macedonia (twice daily, 216 km, 6½ hours, US$10), to Ohrid, Macedonia (Sunday, 383 km, US$18), to Tirana, Albania (Friday and Sunday, 505 km, US$26), to Thessaloniki, Greece (daily, 313 km, US$15), to Athens, Greece (daily except Monday, 877 km, 12 to 15 hours, US$38), and to Istanbul (Tuesday and Sunday, 576 km, US$20). No buses operate to Romania due to bottlenecks at the border crossings.

For information about less expensive Greek tour buses to Thessaloniki and Athens, ask at the information desks in the Novotel Europa and Rodina hotels or talk to the Greek drivers outside. The Athens bus (US$23) departs from the Novotel Europa daily around noon. An Appia Tours bus goes to Thessaloniki (US$15) every afternoon, leaving from Hotel Rodina. Also check the bus information in the Getting There & Away section in this chapter.

Train All railway service in Bulgaria focuses on Sofia. There are international lines to Belgrade, Athens, Istanbul, Bucharest and beyond. For routes and fares consult the introductory Getting There & Away section of this chapter.

Important domestic express trains run to Ruse (via Pleven), to Varna (via Pleven or Karlovo) and to Burgas (via Karlovo or Plovdiv). For Veliko Târnovo change at Stara Zagora, Tulovo or Gorna Oryahovitsa. Plovdiv is only two hours from Sofia by express train. A local line east to Kazanlâk serves Koprivshtitsa, Karlovo (for Troyan) and Kazanlâk (for Shipka). Sleepers and couchettes are available to Burgas and Varna but they're usually fully booked.

Train Station Sofia's central train station can be a little confusing. In addition to the Cyrillic destination signs, the platforms *(peron)* are numbered in Roman numerals and the tracks *(kolovoz)* in Arabic numerals. Allow an extra 10 minutes to find your train,

BULGARIA

then ask several people to ensure that it really is the right one.

Domestic tickets are sold on the lower level, but same-day tickets to Vidin, Ruse, Varna and Burgas are sold upstairs. There are two Rila ticket offices downstairs opposite the regular ticket windows. The one closer to the middle of the hall sells sleepers within Bulgaria and international tickets. The one at the end sells advance tickets with seat reservations within Bulgaria. The left-luggage office is also on the lower level, as is the entrance to the tracks.

On the upper level is a tourist service currency exchange and accommodation office, theoretically open from 7 am to 10 pm. Near this tourist service office is an international ticket window that sells tickets for international trains only an hour prior to departure. The exchange offices on this level give a poor rate and deduct 2.5% commission or more, but they do keep long hours. On weekdays between 9.30 am to 4.30 pm, seek out the First Private Bank next to the restaurant on the upper mezzanine level which changes cash (but no travellers' cheques) without commission for the best rate you'll find in the station. You must pay a small fee to use the comfortable waiting room on the uppermost level.

Getting Around

To/From the Airport Vrazdebna Airport, 12 km east of Sofia, is accessible on city buses Nos 84 and 284 from the stop on bulevard Car Osvoboditel, opposite the university.

The main Balkan Bulgarian Airlines office is on ploschtad Narodno Sabranie, off Car Osvoboditel, with a branch office in the arcade below the NDK Palace of Culture.

Public Transport Sofia's public transport system is based on trams and is supplemented by buses and trolley buses. Tickets valid on all vehicles are sold at kiosks but these are poorly marked so get a good supply when you have a chance. Tram drivers also sell tickets. Inspectors often check tickets on trams serving the train station.

Public transit passes (*abonamentna karta*)

are available for one day (US$0.40) and five (US$1.60) days.

A 52-km, 48-station metro system is under construction in Sofia but it will probably be several years before the first line opens.

Car Rental For car rentals try Hertz Rent a Car (☎ 833 487), Vitosha bulevard 41, Avis (☎ 873 412), Car Kalojan 8 behind the Sheraton, and Europcar (☎ 835 049), Pozitano 8 also near the Sheraton. Hertz and Avis also have offices at the airport and Europcar is represented there by Interbalkan.

Taxi Government taxis have meters but private taxis don't and fares are per km based on the odometer reading. If there's no meter, check the price beforehand. You can flag taxis on the street and the drivers are usually honest, but make sure they understand your destination by naming a major landmark near it. Some drivers will take a roundabout route to justify a higher fare. Beware of taxis parked in front of luxury hotels.

Western Bulgaria

Western Bulgaria merges imperceptibly, with no natural boundaries, into Macedonia at the very heart of the Balkan Peninsula. Bulgaria's highest mountains are found in the Rila and Pirin massifs between Sofia and Greece. Medieval Bulgaria was ruled from towns in the north-east, but after independence in 1878, Sofia was chosen as the centrally located capital of 'Greater Bulgaria' (which included Macedonia).

The west has much to offer, from the excitement of Sofia to the thermal baths at Bankya and Sandanski, the history and natural beauty in the area around Rila and intact folklore in Pirin villages such as Bansko and Melnik. For travellers arriving from Western Europe, the west is the gateway to Bulgaria.

BANKYA (БАНКЯ)

A good place to escape the crowds is Bankya

spa, only 17 km west of Sofia. Few foreign tourists visit Bankya but it's popular among the Bulgarians, who fill the 40 sanatoriums and promenade through the well-kept parks. Unlike some Eastern European health resorts which are reserved for patients under medical supervision, everyone is welcome to bathe in these hot springs (36.5°C). When imbibed, the spa's mineral waters stimulate the digestive system.

Things to See & Do

Bankya's **mineral baths** are in the yellow semicircular building on one side of the park, a few blocks west of the train station. Men and women use facilities in separate wings of the building, and explanatory signs in French are posted. For US$1 you get a small, private cubicle with an individual bathing tub.

At last report, the large open-air bathing pool on the opposite side of the park was closed.

Places to Stay

The *'Zimmernachweis'* office, just across the small stream near the train station, arranges private rooms at US$3 per person; however, all the rooms could be taken if you arrive late in the day. There are lots of private hotel signs around town.

Getting There & Away

Local trains to the spa leave Sofia's Central Railway Station every hour from 5 am to midnight (19 km, 30 minutes). There's also a bus service.

THE RILA MOUNTAINS

The majestic Rila Mountains south of Sofia are *the* place to go hiking. Mountain hostels (hizhas) provide basic dormitory accommodation (about US$3 per person) and although many serve meals, sometimes all they have is soup so you had best bring food. The larger hostels provide linen, making a sleeping bag unnecessary. For current information on the hostels, enquire at the Pirin Travel Bureau, on Car Samuil, around the corner from Stambolijski bulevard 30, Sofia.

The classic trip is across the mountains from Complex Malyovitsa to Rila Monastery (Rilski Manastir), which can be done in one day, or in two days if you visit the Seven Lakes. A longer route to Rila Monastery begins at the ski resort of Borovets and includes a climb to the top of Musala Peak (2925 metres), the highest mountain in the Balkan Peninsula. You could also do both and make it a trip there and back in four or five days.

Samokov

Almost everyone on their way to Complex Malyovitsa or Borovets passes through Samokov on the Iskâr River, 62 km south-east of Sofia. The town sprang up as an iron-mining centre in the 14th century and later devoted itself to trade. The 19th century Samokov school of icon painting and wood-carving was famous. Just above the bus station is the beautiful **Bairakli Mosque** (1840) with a wooden dome decorated in the National Revival style.

Buses to Samokov leave frequently from the bus station below the overpass beyond Sofia's Park-Hotel Moskva (take trams Nos 14 and 19). There's an onward bus from Samokov to Complex Malyovitsa (27 km) approximately seven times a day (only three times a day in winter).

Complex Malyovitsa

This mountain resort (elevation 1750 metres) at the foot of the Rila Mountains is the site of the Central School of Alpinism and an ideal starting point for anyone wishing to hike over the mountains to Rila Monastery. The large wooden hotel operated by the Pirin Travel Bureau (make reservations at the Sofia office) offers rooms (US$11 per person) and 14-bed dormitories (US$6 per person) and there's a good restaurant. In winter the complex functions as a ski resort.

From Complex Malyovitsa you get a stunning view straight up the valley to the jagged double peak of Malyovitsa (2729 metres). You can hike to the peak from the complex in about four hours and a strong climber could make it right through to Rila Monas-

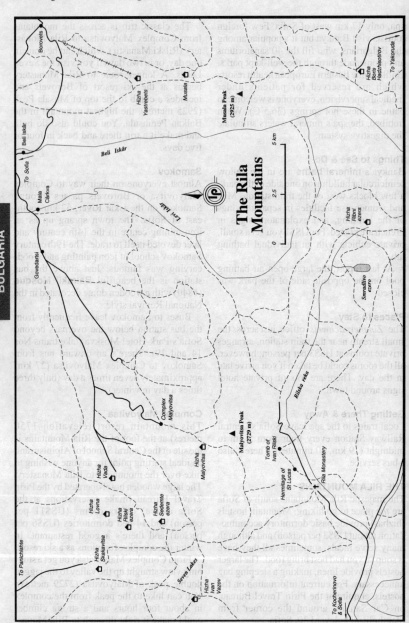

tery in a day. Try to buy the Rila hiking map in Sofia before coming, although maps are sometimes sold at the complex reception.

There are two buses a day from the bus station near Sofia's Park-Hotel Moskva direct to Complex Malyovitsa at 6 am and 2.30 pm. Buy tickets for the return bus trip at the hotel reception.

To Rila via Malyovitsa

About an hour's hike above Complex Malyovitsa is the *Hizha Malyovitsa* (2050 metres), where a dorm bed and bowl of soup are usually available (open all year). From Hizha Malyovitsa you can hike up to *Hizha Sedemte ezera* (no meals served, bring food) in about six hours. This hizha is right beside one of the legendary Seven Lakes on a mountain plateau at 2200 metres elevation. A notorious sun-worshipping cult was centred on these lakes beforeWW II. From Hizha Sedemte ezera you can hike down to Rila Monastery (elevation 1147 metres) in six hours.

To Rila via Borovets

From Sofia catch the bus to Samokov (as described in the Samokov section), where you'll find another bus every 30 minutes to Borovets (elevation 1300 metres, 72 km from Sofia). This popular ski resort founded by Prince Ferdinand in 1897 is up-market, so arrive early enough to make the stiff four-hour hike up to *Hizha Musala* (2389 metres) the same day. Check to see if the 4827-metre cable car (US$4) to *Hizha Yastrebets* (2363 metres) is operating from Borovets, as it saves you quite a climb. *Hotel Virginia* in Borovets is US$10 per person, breakfast included.

Musala Peak is only two hours beyond Hizha Musala. Carry on for another four hours to *Hizha Boris Hadzhisotirov* (2185 metres) beside Granchar Lake. There's a restaurant here and a road south to Yakoruda on the railway to Bansko. The next day it will take you five hours to reach *Hizha Ribni ezera* (2230 metres), between the Fish Lakes. The Smradlivo ezero (Stinking Lake), the largest lake in the Rila Mountains,

is only an hour from the hostel. Rila Monastery (1147 metres) is a four-hour walk from Hizha Ribni ezera.

RILA MONASTERY (РИЛСКИ МАНАСТИР)

Rila, Bulgaria's largest and most famous monastery, blends into a narrow valley 119 km south of Sofia, three hours away by bus. Rila was founded by Ivan Rilski in 927 as a colony of hermits, and in 1335 the monastery was moved three km to its present location. **Hrelyu's Tower**, the clock tower beside the church, is all that remains from this early period.

By the end of the 14th century, Rila Monastery had become a powerful feudal fief owning many villages. Plundered in the 15th century, Rila was restored in 1469 after the relics of Ivan Rilski were brought here from Veliko Târnovo in a nationwide patriotic procession. Under adverse conditions, Rila Monastery helped to keep Bulgarian culture alive during the long dark age of Turkish rule from the 15th to the 19th centuries. In 1833, a fire destroyed the monastery, but it was soon rebuilt on an even grander scale in the National Revival style.

Things to See & Do

The monastery's forbidding exterior contrasts dramatically with the warmth and cosiness of the striped arcades inside. Four levels of balconies surround the large, irregular courtyard and three **museums** occupy some of the 300 rooms. One museum contains the monastery's original charter (1378), signed and stamped by Tsar Ivan Shishman, and Brother Raphael's wooden cross bearing 1500 human figures, each the size of a grain of rice. There are excellent views of the surrounding mountains from the uppermost verandah. Don't miss the **kitchen** (1816) at courtyard level in the northern wing, with a 24-metre chimney cutting through all storeys by means of 10 rows of arches crowned by a small dome. Food was once prepared in huge cauldrons for the pilgrim masses.

The present magnificent **church** with its three great domes was built between 1834

BULGARIA

and 1837. The 1200 frescoes painted between 1840 and 1848 depict donors, Old Testament kings, apostles, angels, demons and martyrs, all with an extremely rich ornamentation of flowers, birds and stylised vines. The gilded iconostasis depicting 36 biblical scenes is a wonderful work by artists from Samokov and Bansko.

The monastery is open daily, but people wearing shorts are not admitted and backpacks must be left in a cloakroom outside. There's a fine view of the monastery from the cross on the hillside to the north-east.

A little over a km up the valley, beyond the turn-off to the camping ground, is the **Hermitage of St Lucas**, hidden in the trees on the left. From there a well-marked trail leads up through the forest to the **cave** where Ivan Rilski lived and is buried. According to a local legend, those able to pass through the hole in the roof of the cave have not sinned, and since it's easy to get through the legend is very popular.

Places to Stay & Eat
Rooms with attached bath (but no hot water) are available inside the monastery itself at US$10 per person. The reception is near the museum. There are several restaurants behind the monastery. Dorm accommodation (US$3) is available at the *Turisticheski Spalnia*, behind and above the old bakery (1866) near the snack bars. There's no shower here. *Camping Bor* is a km further up the valley beyond the monastery (open from June to September), and the three-star *Hotel Rilets* (US$20/24 single/double with bath) is nearby.

Getting There & Away
There's a small bus station on the west side of Rila Monastery. If you catch the early morning bus from Sofia, you can easily visit Rila on a day trip. Three buses a day depart from Sofia's Ovcha Kupel Bus Station (take trams No 5 and 19). The morning bus operates daily throughout the year. In winter, which lasts from October to March, the afternoon bus does the return trip from Rila to Sofia only from Friday to Sunday. Get tickets

to go from Sofia to Rila the day before at the booking office in the arcade below the NDK Palace of Culture in Sofia.

In summer, on Sunday and holidays, the return afternoon bus from Rila to Sofia may be sold out a day in advance, in which case ask about buses from Rila Monastery to Kocherinovo Railway Station, 29 km west on the railway line from Kulata to Sofia, or to Stanke Dimitrov on the road to Sofia.

Thrace

The Thrace of Greek and Roman antiquity was much larger than modern Thrace, only two-thirds of which lies within Bulgaria. The Maritsa River (which flows through Plovdiv) drains the region and flows south into the Aegean, forming the border between present-day Greek and Turkish Thrace. At Svilengrad, on the Maritsa, the three nations meet. Bulgaria's Thracian Plain is squeezed between the Sredna Gora and Rodopi mountain ranges and opens on to the Black Sea to the east.

Plovdiv is the capital of Bulgarian Thrace and has evocative vestiges of the Roman and Turkish periods. Hisarya, north of Plovdiv, has been a major spa since Roman times. Some of the finest monuments of the Bulgarian National Revival are found in the Bachkovo Monastery, Plovdiv and Koprivshtitsa.

KOPRIVSHTITSA (КОПРИВЩИЦА)
This picturesque village (elevation 1030 metres) in the Sredna Gora Mountains, 113 km east of Sofia, has been carefully preserved as an open-air museum of the Bulgarian National Revival. Legend tells of a beautiful young Bulgarian woman who obtained a *firman* (decree) from the Ottoman sultan that exempted the Koprivshtitsa villagers from paying tribute and allowed them to ride horses and carry arms. It is known for certain that the town was founded at the end of the 14th century by refugees fleeing the Turkish conquerors.

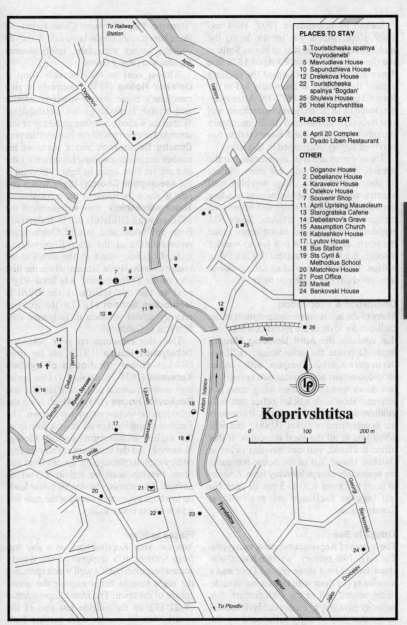

BULGARIA

Sacked by brigands in 1793, 1804 and 1809, Koprivshtitsa was rebuilt during the mid-19th century and was as big as Sofia at the time. It was here on 20 April 1876 that Todor Kableshkov proclaimed the uprising against the Turks that eventually led to the Russo-Turkish War of 1877-78. After independence in 1878, Bulgarian merchants and intellectuals abandoned their mountain retreats for the cities and Koprivshtitsa has survived largely unchanged to this day.

These events are well documented in the various house-museums, but even without its place in history the village would be well worth a visit for its cobbled streets winding between low-tiled red roofs and little stone bridges over trickling rivulets. Some 388 registered architectural monuments grace the town. Koprivshtitsa is a joy to wander through, but keep in mind that this is a living village. Try to avoid intruding and say *dobar den* (good day) to those you meet.

Orientation & Information

Many of the house-museums and most of the facilities for visitors are found near the park that contains the **April Uprising Mausoleum**. Opposite the mausoleum you'll see the modern April 20 Complex, with a coffee shop downstairs and a restaurant upstairs. A few doors west up the narrowing street is a souvenir shop with a ticket office that sells guidebooks, maps and postcards. It also sells the comprehensive ticket (US$1) that will admit you to all the local museums. If this office is closed, you can buy this ticket at Oslekov House. All of the house-museums are open daily except Monday from 7.30 am to noon and from 1.30 to 5 pm all year. No left-luggage facilities are available at Koprivshtitsa.

Things to See

The houses of Koprivshtitsa are of two types. The early 19th century 'wooden house' was characterised by a stone ground floor and a wooden upper floor with two rooms in each. In the second half of the 19th century, this austerity gave way to a more richly decorated house that was strongly influenced by the 'Baroque' Plovdiv house. Characteristic of these later houses are the large salons, carved ceilings, sunny verandahs, multicoloured façades and jutting eaves.

Almost next to the souvenir shop is **Oslekov House** (1856), formerly a rich merchant's home whose spacious interior and stylish furnishings are outstanding. Within the walled enclosure at the top of this street is a cemetery with the grave of the poet **Dimcho Debelyanov** and a statue of his mother anxiously awaiting his return ('I die and am yet born again in light.') Beyond is the **Assumption Church** (1817), which you pass to reach the house of the revolutionary **Todor Kableshkov**, now a museum of the 1876 uprising (all labels are in Bulgarian). Both this house and that of Oslekov are representative of the later Koprivshtitsa style. Continue south to the small stone bridge over the Byala Stream, where the first shot of the 1876 uprising was fired. Right next to the bus station is the **Cyril & Methodius School** (1837), the second primary school to teach in Bulgarian (the first was in Gabrovo).

The other museums on your ticket are **Debelyanov House** (1832), not far from Oslekov House; the **house of Lyuben Karavelov** (1834-79, ideologist of the uprising), now a museum portraying his life; and **Benkovski House** (1831), which is on the hillside in the south-eastern part of town. The Karavelov and Benkovski houses date from the earlier architectural period. Georgi Benkovski led the insurgent cavalry on legendary exploits through the Sredna Gora and Stara Planina until he fell in a Turkish ambush. The stairway beside his house leads up to a huge equestrian statue of the man and a view of the entire valley.

Places to Stay

You can visit Koprivshtitsa on a day trip from Sofia or as a stopover on the way to somewhere else, but it's well worth spending the night here to better capture the atmosphere of the town. The *Hotel Koprivshtitsa* (☎ 21 82), on the hillside just east of the centre, has 28 rooms with private bath

(US$10 per person) and two suites (US$24 double). There's no hot water (and sometimes no cold water either). Ask for a room overlooking the town.

There are no official private rooms in Koprivshtitsa but the hotel reception arranges accommodation in four lovely village houses. Each house has about five guest rooms with shared bath (US$10 per person) and there are two apartments with private shower (US$24 double). *Shuleva* and *Drehlekova* houses are next to the stairs leading up to the hotel. *Mavrudieva House*, a block behind the Karavelov museum, is a good choice for those seeking solitude. The most popular of the four is *Sapundzhieva House*, behind the bookshop in the centre of town, with four rooms and a two-room apartment with its own fireplace. Advance reservations can be made through the Tourist Information and Reservations office in Sofia, although the houses are seldom full.

If someone on the street offers you a private room it should cost about US$5 per person.

Youth hostellers could try the HI *Turisticheska spalnya 'Bogdan'*, Lyuben Karavelov 24 behind the market, though their gate is usually locked. The *Turisticheska spalnya 'Voyvodenets'*, behind the April 20 Complex, usually turns away foreigners who arrive without a reservation from the Balkan Tourist Association (Alabin 46, Sofia), though this could change.

Places to Eat

The restaurant upstairs in the April 20 Complex has a balcony overlooking the square. The *mehana* downstairs has no menu and their pricing is peculiar.

Just across the Topolnitza River from the April Uprising Mausoleum is the expensive *Dyado Liben Restaurant* (slow service) in another of the National Revival houses. It's closed Monday.

An increasing number of small private restaurants are opening around Koprivshtitsa (ask to see a menu with prices listed to avoid unpleasant surprises).

Getting There & Away

The train station is about 10 km from town, but connecting buses to Koprivshtitsa await every train (ticket from the driver). Train service to/from Sofia (99 km, 2½ hours) is every couple of hours. The morning express train from Sofia to Burgas via Karlovo will drop you here. If you're heading east from Koprivshtitsa, change trains at Karlovo for Hisarya, Plovdiv or Burgas, and change at Tulovo for Veliko Târnovo. (Between Koprivshtitsa and Klisura, just west of Koprivshtitsa on the line to Sofia, is a railway tunnel six km long.)

Going from Koprivshtitsa to Plovdiv is time-consuming as you must return to the railway line and change trains at Karlovo, as you can no longer connect through Strelcha or Panagjurishte by bus.

HISARYA (ИСАРЯ)

Even in antiquity, Hisarya, the Roman Augusta, was an important spa with fine marble baths, an aqueduct and paved streets. After the Gothic invasion of 251 AD, the Romans fortified their settlement with a strong city wall, and in the 5th and 6th centuries the town developed into an important episcopal centre with many churches. In the early Middle Ages, Toplitsa (as it was known under the Byzantines) continued to flourish, and later the Turks rebuilt the baths and renamed the town Hisar (fortress).

Hisarya's 22 hot springs spew forth 2800 litres of mineral water a minute at temperatures ranging from 27°C to 51°C. Bathing in these alkaline waters is said to ease digestive problems, and the Momina Banya (Maiden's Bath) mineral water bottled at Hisarya soothes the stomach and kidneys. Despite these attractions, this remarkable place is almost unknown to Western tourists. If you like spas, this is a great place to relax for a couple of days.

Orientation

The adjacent bus and train stations are just outside the north-west city walls. The left-luggage office in the train station opens from 7 am to noon and 1 to 6 pm but there's no left-luggage area at the bus station. Bulevard Ivan Vazov is the main north-south thoroughfare through the walled area passing the two cheaper hotels and the spa park. East across the ravine of Tekedere Stream are the expensive Augusta Hotel and the main mineral baths.

Post & Telecommunications Hisarya's telephone centre (daily 7 am to 9.30 pm) is right in front of the Archaeological Museum.

Things to See & Do

The rectangular **Roman wall**, which is 10 metres high and 2315 metres long, was completed in the 4th century AD and originally had 43 towers and four gates. Much of the area inside and around the walls is now a park with the ruins of various Early Christian basilicas and tombs, a small amphitheatre and mineral springs scattered among the modern constructions.

In the park below Hotel Balkan are three **public baths** called Toplitsa, Bistritsa and Svezhest, all open from 7.30 to 10.30 am and 1.30 to 6.30 pm daily. In front of these baths is a public fountain pouring forth unlimited quantities of mineral water to eager adherents of the drinking cure. People come from all over to fill empty bottles here, so bring along your canteen or cup for a free fill-up.

On the east side of town opposite the large modern theatre on bulevard General Gurko is the modern **Nova Momina Banya** bathhouse where you can wallow in warm mineral water (daily 7.30 am to 4.30 pm, Wednesday 7.30 to 11.30 am). Individual cabins and a large pool are available to the public. In the park below this is the older **Stara Momina Banya**, which remains open until 6.30 pm daily, and in front of Stara Momina is another fountain always crowded with people filling their containers with hot mineral water. A massage and thermal bath at the up-market **Hotel Augusta** 500 metres away will cost about US$7.

Between these two bath complexes is the **Archaeological Museum** which is open daily at ulitsa Stambolijski 8. On the side of the Poliklinika building opposite the

museum but facing the other direction is a large plastic map of Hisarya that is worth a look.

Places to Stay & Eat

There are at least two and perhaps three good, inexpensive places to stay within a 10-minute walk of the stations. The *Hotel Republika*, bulevard Ivan Vazov 30, is about US$10 double with shared bath. On the other side of the park, in front of the Republika, is the old *Hotel Balkan*, ulitsa Dimitâr Blagoev, which at last report was closed.

The *Slaveev Dol Camping Ground* (☎ 25 86) has a perfect location in the centre of town just above the public baths and park. Inexpensive bungalows are available, you may pitch a tent and they're open all year. There's a pleasant little snack bar here.

The *Gostilnitsa Yagoda Café* below the new four-storey building directly opposite the train station serves good, inexpensive meals. An office near this restaurant rents private rooms. There are many other reasonable bars and restaurants around town, which you'll discover for yourself on your strolls. The Hotel Balkan's terrace restaurant sometimes presents folk dancing.

Getting There & Away

About eight local trains a day link Hisarya to Plovdiv (50 km) with a change of trains at Dolna Mahala. Buses leaving Hisarya Bus Station include 10 to Karlovo (26 km), two to Kazanlâk (72 km), two to Veliko Târnovo (168 km), one to Ruse (271 km), two to Troyan (91 km), two to Pleven (162 km) and three to Plovdiv (41 km). Some of the long-distance buses are travelling to/from Plovdiv and tickets are only available after the bus arrives (ask).

PLOVDIV (ПЛОВДИВ)

Plovdiv, on the Upper Thracian Plain, is Bulgaria's second-largest city, occupying both banks of the Maritsa River. Two main communication corridors converge here: the route from Asia Minor to Europe, and the route from Central Asia to Greece via Ukraine. This strategic position accounts for

Plovdiv's pre-eminence, beginning in 341 BC when Philip II of Macedonia conquered Philipopolis (Plovdiv). The Romans left extensive remains in the city, which they called Trimontium, as did the Turks, who made Philibe (Plovdiv) the seat of the Bey of Roumelia; this was made up of Macedonia, Albania, Thrace and the autonomous province of Eastern Roumelia.

Yet it was the Bulgarian National Revival that gave Plovdiv's Three Hills the picturesque aspect that visitors appreciate today. The 19th century Plovdiv 'Baroque' house shares the dynamism and passion of historic Baroque but is uniquely Bulgarian. Arranged around the oval or square central salon are the drawing rooms and bedrooms of the family. The carved or painted ceiling and wall decorations are in excellent taste, as are the brightly painted façades. Many of these charming buildings, which were built by prosperous traders, are now open to the public as museums, galleries or restaurants and make a visit to Plovdiv well worthwhile.

Orientation

The train station is south-west of the old town. The left-luggage office (open 24 hours) faces the parking lot on the corner of the station building closest to the city centre. Cross the square in front of the station and take ulitsa Ivan Vazov on the right straight ahead into Central Square, a 10-minute walk away. Knjaz Alexandre, Plovdiv's pedestrian mall, runs north from this square, and you can reach the old town from here through the narrow streets to the right. The area north of the river is a grey, modern suburb devoid of interest.

Information

Puldin Tours, formerly Balkantourist, has three locations: 19 Noemvri Square opposite the Roman amphitheatre (☎ 231 924), Vâzrazhdane 60 (☎ 228 823) and bulevard Bulgaria 106 (☎ 555 120), near the fairground north of the river.

Money The National Bank, Krjaz Alexandre 13, deducts 15% commission on travellers'

cheques – a record for Eastern Europe! Also try the T-Bank on the side street next to Hotel Bulgaria. The hotels will change travellers' cheques but they give a poor rate and take 5% commission. It's best to change your money elsewhere.

Post & Telecommunications The telephone centre in the main post office on Central Square (rear of the building) is open from 6.30 am to 11 pm daily. Plovdiv's telephone code is 032.

Travel Agencies For international train tickets, couchettes and advance tickets on domestic railway lines, go to Byuro, Nezavisimost 29, next to the Citroën dealership (weekdays 8.30 am to 5 pm).

Laundry Same Day Cleaning on Vâzrazhdane opposite the fairground (weekdays 8 am to 6.30 pm) can do your laundry, but you'll pay per piece.

Things to See

Begin your sightseeing with the excavated remains of the **Roman Forum**, behind the modern post office on Central Square. Knjaz Alexandre, a bustling pedestrian mall, runs north from this square to the 15th century **Djoumaya Mosque**, also known as Friday Mosque, which is still used for Islamic religious services. Below ploschtad 19 Noemvri, in front of the mosque, is a section of the **Roman amphitheatre** (2nd century AD).

Continue straight ahead on the mall (now ulitsa Rajko Daskalov) and through an underpass to the **Imaret Mosque** (1445). Plovdiv's **Archaeological Museum** (closed Monday) is nearby on ploschtad Saedinenie, to the left. A copy of the 4th century BC gold treasure from Panagjurishte is on display (the original is now at the National Museum of History in Sofia). The monument in the square in front of the museum commemorates the 1885 union with Bulgaria of Eastern Roumelia (of which Plovdiv was the capital).

Return to the Djoumaya Mosque and go east on ulitsa Maksim Gorki into the old city,

BULGARIA

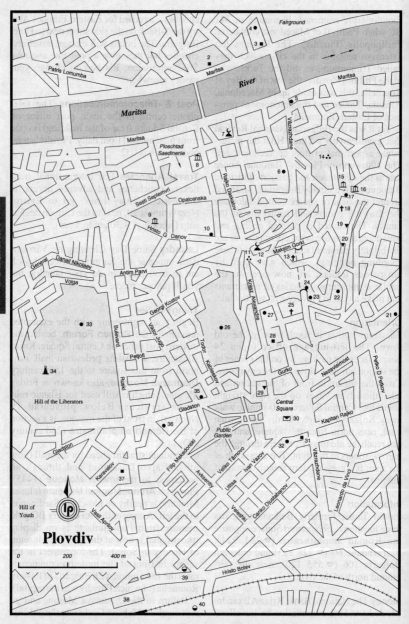

Plovdiv

0   200   400 m

PLACES TO STAY

1 Park Hotel St Petersburg
2 Hotel Novotel
3 Hotel Maritsa
28 Hotel Bulgaria
31 Hotel Trimontium
37 Leipzig Hotel

PLACES TO EAT

19 Alafrangite Restaurant
20 Restaurant Trakiyski Stan
29 Astika Restaurant

OTHER

4 Same Day Cleaning
5 Borledo Night Club
6 Puldin Tours
7 Imaret Mosque
8 Archaeological Museum
9 Natural History Museum
10 Puppet Theatre
11 Roman Amphitheatre
12 Djoumaya Mosque
13 Church of the Holy Virgin
14 Ruins of Eumolpias
15 Ethnographical Museum
16 National Revival Museum
17 Hisar Kapiya
18 Church of Constantin & Elena
21 Byuro Train Ticket Office
22 Lamartine House
23 Orbita Travel Agency
24 Roman Theatre
25 St Marina Church
26 Clock Tower
27 Art Gallery
30 Post Office
32 State Philharmonic
33 Open-Air Theatre
34 Monument to the Soviet Army
35 Art Gallery
36 Opera House
38 Railway Station
39 Main Bus Station
40 Rodopi Bus Station

which was named Trimontium (Three Hills) by the Romans. In recent years the **Church of Constantin & Elena** (1832) has been beautifully restored, and next to it is a very good icon gallery. In the National Revival mansion (1847) of the wealthy merchant Argir Koyumdjioglou, on ulitsa Doctor Tchomakov, just beyond the end of Maksim Gorki, is the **Ethnographical Museum** (closed Monday), which houses a collection of folk costumes. Up the street from this museum is a hilltop with the **ruins of Eumolpias**, a 2nd millennium BC Thracian settlement. There's a good view from the ruins.

The street beside the Ethnographical Museum leads down through **Hisar Kapiya**, the Roman eastern city gate, to Georgiadi House (1848), another fine example of Plovdiv Baroque, now the **National Revival Museum** (closed weekends).

To the south of this museum is a quaint, cobbled quarter, with colourful 19th century houses crowding the winding streets, so do a little exploring. At ulitsa Knyaz Ceretelev 19 is the Baroque house (1830) in which the French poet Alphonse de Lamartine stayed in 1833 during his *Voyage en Orient*.

Nearby to the west and directly above the southern entrance to a big highway tunnel is the 3000-seat **Roman theatre** (2nd century), now restored and once again in use at festival time. South west of the theatre is **St Marina Church** (1854) with a photogenic wooden tower and intricate iconostasis. From here it's only five minutes back to your starting point at the Roman Forum.

In summer, escape to the **public garden** off Central Square where you'll find a pond with rowing boats to rent.

Places to Stay

Camping *Camping Trakia* (☎ 551 360) is at the Gorski Kat Restaurant, about four km west of Plovdiv on the Sofia Highway. Take bus No 4, 18, 44 or 54 west on bulevard Bulgaria to the end of the line, then walk one km along the highway. Bus No 23 comes directly here hourly from the train station, at last report departing from the station 40 minutes after the hour and from the camping ground 15 minutes after the hour (check). The Gorski Kat Restaurant is good and there's a popular bar serving grilled meats at lunch time in the large auto service centre next to the camping ground. Camping Trakia

BULGARIA

was recently privatised and upgraded and the new charges for camping and bungalows were still unknown at press time. It's open all year.

Private Rooms Puldin Tours (locations given in the Information section) can arrange private room accommodation at US$8/10 single/double. During the Plovdiv Trade Fair (a couple of weeks in May and September) the price for these same rooms skyrockets to US$29/34 single/double (including breakfast)! If you don't want to pay that much, check carefully that your visit doesn't coincide with the fair (any Balkantourist office should have the exact dates).

The privately run Prima Vista Agency (☎ 272 778), General Gurko 6, just off Knjaz Alexandre, also arranges private rooms.

Hotels Plovdiv's two-star hotels are the 10-storey *Hotel Leipzig* (☎ 232 050), Ruski bulevard 70, four blocks from the train station (US$25/34 single/double), and the four-storey *Hotel Bulgaria* (☎ 226 798) in the centre of town (US$22/32 single/double), both including bath and breakfast. The *Novotel, Trimontium* and *Maritsa* hotels are much dearer.

The privately operated *Hotel Feniks* (☎ 224 729), Kapitan Rajko 79, five blocks east of Hotel Trimontium, has seven rooms in an apartment block for US$11/15 single/double with shared bath.

For information on accommodation in student dormitories or hostels, ask at the Orbita office on Vâzrazhdane near the south entrance to the highway tunnel. This office is very hard to find: it's on the 2nd floor of the high white house on the hillside almost in front of the tunnel, but you can't see their signs for the vegetation – look up.

Places to Eat

The *Astika Restaurant*, Knjaz Alexandre 50, is a cheap self-service cafeteria. The *Firebird Chinese Restaurant*, nearby in the Hotel Bulgaria, is quite reasonable and in summer you can dine outside in the courtyard.

The *Alafrangite Restaurant*, ulitsa Cyril

Nectariev 17, near the National Revival Museum in the old town, offers excellent Bulgarian meals on the outside patio or inside this typical 19th century edifice.

The *Starata Kashta*, adjacent to Alafrangite, and *Restaurant Trakiyski Stan*, Puldin 9, a block south of the Alafrangite (keep right), are similar and rather touristy, but nice. Folk music is often preformed at these three places, usually after 8 pm, so check them all before sitting down.

Entertainment

There's an office selling theatre tickets at ulitsa Knjaz Alexandre 49, but opera tickets are available from the opera itself. The *State Philharmonic* is next to Hotel Trimontium.

In summer there are folklore programmes in the courtyard of the *Trimontium Hotel* around 9 pm if a tour group is present (ask at the hotel reception in the late afternoon).

The *Borledo Night Club* on Vâzrazhdane near the river is a disco which opens around 10 pm nightly.

Getting There & Away

All trains between Istanbul and Belgrade pass through Plovdiv, and Sofia is only two hours away by frequent fast train (156 km). To get to Burgas (294 km) takes four hours with a few overnight trains. For Veliko Târnovo (234 km) you may have to change trains at Stara Zagora. There are 10 trains a day between Plovdiv and Karlovo (67 km, 1¼ hours) with connections for Hisarya.

For Turkey take a local train to Svilengrad (143 km, 2½ hours), a taxi to the border (14 km) and walk across. Otherwise, catch the overnight express train to Istanbul (480 km, 11 hours). For Greece take the unreserved day train to Alexandroupolis (323 km, eight hours). International tickets should be purchased in advance at the Byuro office mentioned under Travel Agency above.

Plovdiv has several bus stations. Buses to Troyan (124 km) leave from the Northern Bus Station at the north end of trolley bus lines Nos 2 and 3. Buses to Bachkovo Monastery (30 km), Pamporovo (83 km) and Smolyan (100 km) use the Rodopi Bus

Station, accessible through the tunnel under the tracks at the train station. Buses to Sofia (150 km), Burgas (272 km, five hours, US$4), Nesebâr (307 km), Sozopol (303 km) and Asenovgrad (19 km) depart from the main bus station near the train station. Bookings for private buses to the Black Sea must be made the day before. It's not as necessary to book buses to Sofia.

There's a bus to Istanbul every night from the Hotel Maritsa (420 km, 12 hours, US$15). Tickets are available from the hotel reception.

Getting Around

City bus tickets are sold by the conductor on board the bus.

Car Rental Hertz (☎ 552 849) and Europcar (☎ 551 963) have desks at the Hotel Novotel while Avis (☎ 455 242) is at the Hotel Maritsa.

BACHKOVO MONASTERY (БАЧКОВСКИ МАНАСТИР)

Thirty km south of Plovdiv, beside the highway up the Tschepelarska Valley, is the Bachkovo Monastery (Bachkovski Manastir), which was founded in 1083 by two Byzantine aristocrats, the brothers Gregory and Abasius Bakuriani. This is the largest monastery of its kind in Bulgaria after Rila. Sacked by the Turks in the 15th century, the monastery underwent major reconstruction 200 years later.

In the high courtyard are two churches: the smaller 12th century **Archangel Church**, painted in 1841 by Zahari Zograph, and the large **Church of the Assumption of Our Lady** (1604). On the northern side of the courtyard is a small **museum**, while one corner of the southern side is occupied by the former **refectory** (1606), with a marvellous painting of the genealogy of Jesus on the ceiling painted between 1623 and 1643.

Through the gate by the refectory is **St Nicholas Chapel** with a superb Last Judgment painted in 1840 by Zahari Zograph on the porch. Note the condemned Turks (without halos) on the right, and Zahari's

self-portrait (no beard) in the upper left corner.

Just below the monastery is a restaurant, camping ground and bungalows. To get there, take a bus from outside Plovdiv's main bus station to Asenovgrad (19 km) and then another bus on to Bachkovo. Direct buses to Bachkovo depart from Plovdiv's Rodopi Bus Station. If you have time, it's worth climbing up to the fortress ruins at Asenovgrad to enjoy the view of the tiny church perched at the edge of the abyss.

The Black Sea Coast

Every summer, Bulgaria's Black Sea beaches vie with those of neighbouring Romania to lure masses of sun seekers on holiday. Burgas and Varna take on a carnival atmosphere as camping grounds and hotels fill up, and small towns like Nesebâr and Sozopol become literally jammed with tourists. Fortunately, the hotel developments are concentrated in a few flashy resorts like Albena (38 hotels), Golden Sands (67 hotels), Druzhba (12 hotels) and Sunny Beach (112 hotels), all absolutely packed with Germans and Brits on package tours. The International Youth Centre at Primorsko is a programmed students' hang-out. But all along the 378-km coast it's fairly easy to escape the crowds and have a stretch of tideless golden beach to yourself.

The climate is warm and mild, and in winter the temperature rarely drops below freezing. Summer is the best time to visit. The average temperature is a warm 23°C but sea breezes keep it cool. Everything will be open, the restaurants will have their tables out on the street, the water will be warm and buses will carry you inexpensively along the coast. These days Eastern Europeans go west for their summer holidays whenever possible, so the buses are less crowded and rooms are much easier to find than they were a few years ago. In the off season, from mid-September to the end of May, even the big hotels slash staff and services drastically.

BULGARIA

Best of all, the Black Sea coast is cheap. This is one part of Bulgaria where you won't have to search far for a place to camp. If you don't have a tent, ask Balkantourist to assign you a private room. Bulgaria offers better beach facilities than Romania at lower prices but to stay at one of the big hotels you're better off on a package tour. However you do it, you'll have an exciting time and make lots of new friends.

GETTING AROUND
Unfortunately Bulgaria's Black Sea hydrofoil (*kometa*) service which once shuttled between Varna, Nesebâr, Burgas and Sozopol wasn't able to survive the transition to a market economy and in 1993 was suspended indefinitely. Still operating is a regular excursion boat known as a 'hydrobus', which runs from Varna to Golden Sands and Balchik daily from mid-June to mid-September, and another excursion boat operates between Nesebâr and Sozopol when groups have booked.

Though it's convenient to come from Sofia by train, travel up and down the coast is almost exclusively by bus. Six buses a day link Burgas and Varna (132 km, three hours), and many local buses make shorter trips north and south.

BURGAS (БУРГАС)
In the 17th century, fisher folk from Pomorie and Sozopol founded Burgas on a narrow spit between Burgasko Ezero and the sea. An ancient tower known as Pirgos gave the city its name. The town grew quickly after completion of the railway from Plovdiv in 1890 and the city's port was developed in 1903.

Smaller and less crowded than Varna, Burgas also has less to offer. The north side of the city is row after row of concrete apartments with a big oil refinery to the west. The old town by the port is still nice, however, and Burgas makes a convenient base from which to explore the towns up and down the coast. Once you have a good place to stay, it's a fairly relaxed town with an acceptable beach, good shopping and an abundance of restaurants. In summer, Burgas still gets its share of mosquitoes, but they're no longer malarial.

Orientation
The train station and the bus and marine terminals are all adjacent in the old town. The left-luggage office (daily 6 am to 11 pm) is next to the bus station, just outside the train station. Aleksandrovska, the pedestrian mall, runs north to the Soviet soldier monument on ploschtad Troikata. The beach is along the east side of the old town.

Information
There's a Balkantourist information office (open daily 8 am to 8 pm) opposite the train station. Orbita Student Travel (☎ 42 380) is at Filip Kutev 2a.

Money Balkantourist opposite the train station gives a good rate for cash but charges 8% commission to change a travellers' cheque.

The exchange counter at Balkan Airlines, Aleksandrovska 24, changes travellers' cheques for 3% commission.

The small exchange counter of the Pârva Chastna Banka, upstairs in the clothing store next to Golden Chris Kosmos Café on Bogoridi, across the street from Hotel Bulgaria, changes up to US$200 in travellers' cheques for a flat US$4 commission. They give a good rate and are open daily from 9 am to 8 pm.

Post & Telecommunications The post office on Car Petâr near the train station holds mail addressed c/o Poste Restante, 8000 Burgas, but to place an international telephone call you must go to the main post office on Ozvobozdenie (daily 7 am to 10 pm). Burgas' telephone code is 056.

Travel Agencies For all advance bus or train tickets go to the Rila office, Aleksandrovska 106 (weekdays 7 am to 7 pm, Saturday 8 am to 2 pm). Staff there can book couchettes to Sofia and you can also buy international train and bus tickets. If you want to take a bus to

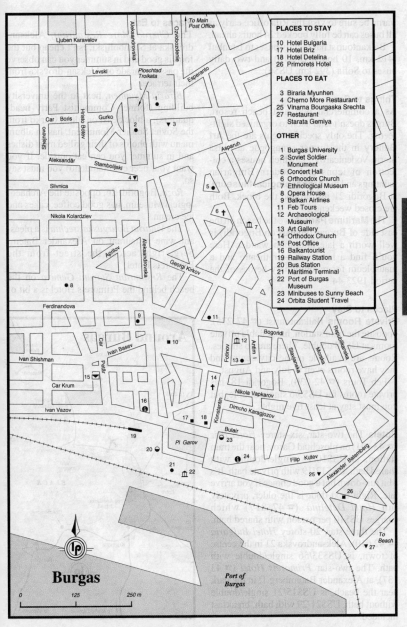

PLACES TO STAY

10 Hotel Bulgaria
17 Hotel Briz
18 Hotel Detelina
26 Primorets Hotel

PLACES TO EAT

3 Biraria Myunhen
4 Cherno More Restaurant
25 Vinarna Bourgaska Srechta
27 Restaurant
   Starata Gemiya

OTHER

1 Burgas University
2 Soviet Soldier
   Monument
5 Concert Hall
6 Orthodox Church
7 Ethnological Museum
8 Opera House
9 Balkan Airlines
11 Feb Tours
12 Archaeological
   Museum
13 Art Gallery
14 Orthodox Church
15 Post Office
16 Balkantourist
19 Railway Station
20 Bus Station
21 Maritime Terminal
22 Port of Burgas
   Museum
23 Minibuses to Sunny Beach
24 Orbita Student Travel

BULGARIA

Burgas

0   125   250 m

Port of
Burgas

Varna be sure to visit the Rila office early as all buses can be fully booked 24 hours ahead.

Balkantourist has nightly buses to Istanbul (412 km, 10 hours, US$18) and two daily buses to Sofia (392 km, US$6).

Things to See

As a commercial port and beach resort, Burgas doesn't lend itself to organised sightseeing. The only specific sights are the **Art Gallery** in the former synagogue at ulitsa Sterju Vodenicarov 22, which houses a collection of icons and modern Bulgarian paintings and the **Archaeological Museum**, at Bogoridi 21 just around the block. Both are closed weekends.

The **Maritime Park** above the beach on the east side of Burgas (go east on Bogoridi) is well worth a late afternoon wander. Here you'll find a large open-air theatre and a mausoleum for revolutionary heroes of the period 1923-44.

Places to Stay

Private Rooms Balkantourist (☎ 47 275), opposite the train station, has reliable private rooms at US$8 double. There are no singles. Rooms are available in the city centre and they have rooms even in July and August.

Feb Tours (☎ 42 030), Bogoridi 18, has private rooms for US$5/6 single/double, but you must stay at least five nights.

Hotels The two-star, six-storey *Hotel Briz* (☎ 43 191) on ploschtad Garov, near the train station, is US$10/15 single/double with shared bath, US$12/19 with private bath. It's a bit run-down but a good choice if you arrive late. Right next door is the older, privately run *Hotel Detelina* (☎ 47 817) which charges US$10 per person with shared bath.

The three-star, 20-storey *Hotel Bulgaria* (☎ 42 610), Aleksandrovska 21 in the centre of town, is US$33/56 single/double with bath. The two-star *Primorets Hotel* (☎ 43 137), at Alexander Batemberg 1, in the park near the beach, is US$15/21 single/double without bath, US$21/29 with bath, breakfast included.

Places to Eat

The *Cherno More Restaurant*, Aleksandrovska at Stambolijski, isn't cheap but the food is good and in summer you can observe the passing parade on Aleksan-drovska from their terrace.

Biraria Myunhen, next to the university building (former Communist Party headquarters), a block east on ulitsa Gurko from the Soviet Soldier Monument, has an album menu with photos of their grilled meat dishes and in summer you can eat outside. If you want your beer cold (studeno) you must say so.

Roza, Bogoridi 26, opposite the Archaeological Museum, has good coffee, cakes and ice cream.

The *Vinarna Bourgaska srechta* is a pleasant wine restaurant on Alexander Batemberg, right across the street from the Primorets Hotel.

The *Restaurant Starata Gemiya* on the beach behind the Primorets Hotel is a bit of

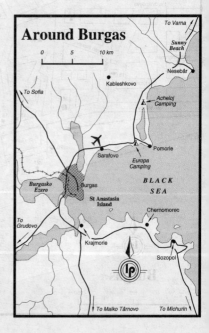

Around Burgas

0   5   10 km

To Varna

Sunny Beach

Nesebăr

Kableshkovo

Acheloj Camping

To Sofia

Pomorie

Sarafovo

Europa Camping

Burgasko Ezero

Burgas

BLACK SEA

St Anastasia Island

Chernomorec

To Grudovo

Krajmorie

Sozopol

To Malko Tărnovo   To Michurin

a tourist trap, but worth a look. It's actually a large wooden 'pirate' ship with a terrace where there's sometimes Bulgarian music and dancing (US$1 cover charge).

Entertainment

Sadly, the modern *Opera House* on Hristo Botev in the middle of town has fallen on hard times and part of the main entrance hall has been rented out as an automobile show-room! Check anyway for events.

At Antim I 26, just around the corner from the art gallery, is an open-air cinema with screenings at 9 pm nightly in summer.

In summer, countless cafés and bars mate-rialise among the trees of Maritime Park as large tents are set up and parasols are erected over tables placed along the walkways. Half of Burgas seems to be here and later there's disco dancing in some of the tents or at permanent structures like *Cocktail Bar Elite*. Ask around for this years' favourite club, or just follow the crowds.

Getting There & Away

Balkan Airlines has five flights a day from Sofia to Burgas for about US$65 one way. The Balkan Airlines office is at Aleksan-drovska 24. The airport is eight km north of town but bus No 15 from the bus station runs directly there every half-hour in the morning, hourly in the afternoon. The bus to Sunny Beach will also drop you at Sarafovo, a five-minute walk from the airport.

Express trains run between Sofia and Burgas seven times a day (470 km via Plovdiv or 450 km via Karlovo). Couchettes are available on the overnight Sofia trains but you must book well ahead. By express train, Plovdiv is 297 km and four hours from Burgas. For Veliko Târnovo change trains at Stara Zagora or Tulovo.

Bus service from between Burgas and Varna is six times daily (132 km, three hours). Frequent local buses run late into the night as far north as Sunny Beach. There are buses south to Sozopol every hour on the hour (tickets from a conductor).

SOZOPOL (СОЗОПОЛ)

Apollonia (Sozopol) was founded in 610 BC by Greeks from Miletus in Asia Minor. The settlement flourished as an independent trading state until sacked by the Romans in 72 BC, at which time the town's famous 13-metre-high bronze statue of Apollo was carted off to Rome as booty. Sozopol (which means 'town of salvation') never recovered from this calamity and remained a tiny fishing village until a revival in the early 19th century, when 150 houses were rebuilt in the traditional 'Black Sea' style.

Today, sturdy wooden dwellings built on lower floors made of stone choke the narrow cobbled streets of this picturesque little town as women below sell lace to visitors. On the west side of the peninsula, a Bulgarian naval base flanks the local fishing port and on the east side are two good beaches. A bustling tourist colony is blossoming to the south. Yet the entire Bulgarian coast south of Burgas is much less effected by high-rise resorts than Sunny Beach and Golden Sands, and the southernmost Black Sea beaches, furthest from the Danube, are cleaner.

Because of all this, Sozopol compares well with historic Nesebâr, its rival coastal town. Although the archaeological remains at Nesebâr are far more significant, Sozopol is more relaxed with an artistic community that migrates there every summer. It's nice to come for the arts festival during the first half of September, but Sozopol rates highly as an unstructured beach resort for the entire summer season from May to early October. It's one of the few beach resorts along the Bulgarian coast that really tries to cater for individual travellers.

Information

The telephone centre is in the post office in the middle of the old town (daily from 7 am to 9.30 pm). Sozopol's telephone code is 05514.

Things to See

Your best bet is just to wander around the old town, though there's an **Archaeological Museum** (captions in Bulgarian only) in the

BULGARIA

modern complex between the bus stop and the fishing harbour. The tiny 18th century **Church of the Virgin Mary**, almost hidden below street level at ulitsa Anaksimandâr 13, is worth a brief stop to see its wooden iconostasis.

You can hire one of the water taxis serving Zlatna Ribka Camping for an excursion to the **Ropotamo River** south of Sozopol at around US$17 for the boat. The trip takes about an hour each way and since up to 10 people can go for this price, it's worth getting a small group together.

Places to Stay

Camping *Zlatna Ribka Camping* is six km before Sozopol on the road from Burgas. No bungalows are available but there's plenty of camping space. The camping ground is at the southern end of the long beach you can see from Sozopol's harbour. In summer, small boats shuttle back and forth between Sozopol and Zlatna Ribka, leaving whenever there are 10 passengers waiting to go (US$0.25 per person or US$2.50 for a special trip). The water at Zlatna Ribka isn't as clear as that lapping the beaches south of Sozopol.

Private Rooms Some of the kiosks in the small market near the bus station (just back towards Burgas) change money and rent private rooms. They're only open from May to September.

Lotos Agency (☎ 429), Ropotamo 1 (daily from 8 am to 9 pm in summer only), has private rooms at US$7 per person with some singles available. In winter look for Lotos' president, Janny Bobchev (☎ 19 25), who lives nearby at Musala 7. He arranges private rooms all year. In summer, Lotos runs excursions up and down the coast.

Balkantourist, Ropotamo 28, on the beach south of the centre, has private rooms in the old town at US$6 per person (no singles).

Hotels The three-storey *Hotel Sozopol* (☎ 362) right next to the bus station is US$12 double with shared bath.

There are several small private hotels

(actually pensions) along Republikanska, the street running south towards the beach. Try the *Hotel Alfa Vita* (☎ 18 52) at No 9, *Hotel Radik* (☎ 17 06) at No 4 and *Hotel Konstant* (☎ 592) at No 8. All charge around US$12 double with shared bath (no singles). In midsummer all accommodation is tight.

Places to Eat

The *Perun Restaurant* overlooking the harbour just down from the Archaeological Museum is a nice place for a drink and the food is very reasonable.

The *Vinarska Izba* just south of the bus

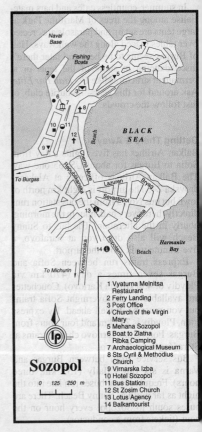

Sozopol

0   125   250 m

1 Vyaturna Melnitsa
   Restaurant
2 Ferry Landing
3 Post Office
4 Church of the Virgin
   Mary
5 Mehana Sozopol
6 Boat to Zlatna
   Ribka Camping
7 Archaeological Museum
8 Sts Cyril & Methodius
   Church
9 Virnarska Izba
10 Hotel Sozopol
11 Bus Station
12 St Zosim Church
13 Lotus Agency
14 Balkantourist

station has a patio where meals are served and after 10 pm there's dancing at their *Emanuela Night Club*.

The *Mehana Sozopol*, a large tavern on the main street leading into the old town, is fairly obvious and touristy but the outdoor terrace is nice. Local grilled meats are on offer.

The up-market *Vyaturna Melnitsa Restaurant*, below an old wooden lighthouse on Morski Skala, at the northern end of the old town, offers a bird's-eye view of a small island just off Sozopol from the restaurant terrace.

Getting There & Away

A crowded local bus travels to/from Burgas (34 km) hourly. There are only four buses a day south to Ahtopol and tickets are only sold after the arrival of the bus from Burgas.

SUNNY BEACH (СЛЪНУЕВ БРЯГ)

Sunny Beach, or Sonnenstrand (Slânchev Bryag), is Bulgaria's largest seaside resort, with 113 state-owned hotels (28,000 beds) stretching along a six-km sandy beach, 36 km north of Burgas. Sunny Beach caters especially to families with small children by providing playgrounds, children's pools, special menus, baby sitters and nurseries, and the gently sloping beach is safe for waders. Other attractions are sailing, windsurfing, tennis and horse riding, although everything along this package-tourist strip is overcrowded in summer and closed all winter.

Expect to be cheated at the restaurants in Sunny Beach and count your change carefully elsewhere – there are too many tourists around here. There are no left-luggage facilities at Sunny Beach.

Places to Stay

Camping There are two camping grounds at the northern end of the strip, both open from May to mid-October. *Camp Emona* by the beach is US$3 per person and US$3 per tent (no bungalows). It's absolutely jammed with tents.

The *Slantchev Briag Campground* (☎ 25 92), on the inland side of the main highway

a few hundred metres from Emona, has 180 small bungalows with shared bath at US$8 per person. Camping here is US$3 per person, US$3 per tent and US$1.25 per person tax. It's crowded and the facilities are only so-so, but there's lots of space (open from May to September). If you're alone this is probably the cheapest place to stay.

Hotels If you want to stay at one of the high-rise hotels in Sunny Beach, you'd do better to come on a package tour although the people at the Balkantourist accommodation office (☎ 23 46) near Hotel Kuban, in the centre of the complex, can arrange hotel rooms ranging from US$10 to US$20 per person. They don't have any private rooms – you must go to Nesebâr for that. Several two-star hotels, such as the *Pomorie* and *Diamant*, are open all year.

Getting There & Away

Buses to Burgas and Varna leave from the bus station about 250 metres south of Balkantourist, on the inland side of the main highway. Private minibuses also shuttle between Sunny Beach and Burgas for the same fare. Men standing near the bus stop will direct you to the next minibus – they're faster and more comfortable than the buses.

The Nesebâr-Sunny Beach bus stops right opposite Balkantourist.

A miniature road train runs from one end of the resort to the other every 15 minutes.

NESEBÂR (НЕСЕБЪР)

Nesebâr, the ancient Mesembria, was founded by Greek Chalcedonians on the site of an earlier Thracian settlement in 510 BC. Mesembria prospered through trade with the Thracians of the interior, declining after the Roman conquest in the 1st century BC. Under Byzantium, Mesembria regained its former importance and in the 5th and 6th centuries a number of imposing churches were erected, including the Metropolitan Church, the ruin of which you can still see. Byzantine nobles exiled here built more churches until the town had as many as 40.

Beginning in the 9th century, Nesebâr (the

BULGARIA

BULGARIA

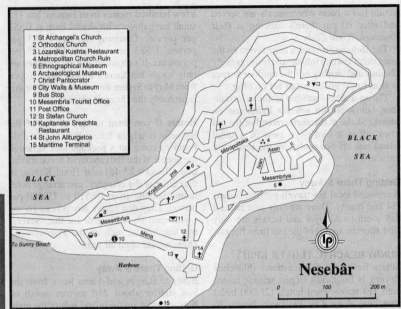

1 St Archangel's Church
2 Orthodox Church
3 Lozarska Kushta Restaurant
4 Metropolitan Church Ruin
5 Ethnographical Museum
6 Archaeological Museum
7 Christ Pantocrator
8 City Walls & Museum
9 Bus Stop
10 Mesembria Tourist Office
11 Post Office
12 St Stefan Church
13 Kapitanska Sreschta
   Restaurant
14 St John Aliturgetos
15 Maritime Terminal

BLACK
SEA

BLACK
SEA

To Sunny Beach

Harbour

Krabre zna

Mitropolitska

Ivan   Asen

Mesembriya

Mesembriya

Mena

Nesebâr

0   100   200 m

Slavic name now used) passed back and forth between Byzantium and Bulgaria many times but the town remained unscathed. Even the Turks left Nesebâr alone and allowed it to strengthen its fortifications to defend itself against Cossack pirates. Overshadowed by Varna, and later by Burgas, Nesebâr ceased to be an active trading town in the 18th century and today lives mostly from fishing and tourism.

The town sits on a small rocky peninsula connected to the mainland by a narrow isthmus. Remnants of the 2nd century city walls rise above the bus stop, and along the winding cobbled streets are picturesque stone and timber houses with wooden stairways and jutting 1st floors. Nesebâr is becoming highly commercialised with lots of twee little shops selling tourist junk at ludicrous prices. You even see restaurants advertising roast beef and Yorkshire pudding! In summer tourists from nearby Sunny Beach and vendors clog the narrow

streets of Nesebâr and you have to run a zigzag course to stay out of their way. The crowds do thin out in the eastern part of town, however.

Information

The telephone centre is in the post office in the middle of the old town (daily from 7.30 am to 10 pm). The telephone code is 0554.

Things to See

Scattered through the town are over a dozen medieval churches, most of them in ruins. Characteristic of the Nesebâr style are the horizontal strips of white stone and red brick offset by striped blind arches resting on vertical pilasters, the façades highlighted by ceramic discs and rosettes.

Of special interest is the 11th century **St Stefan Church** above the maritime terminal, almost completely covered inside with 16th century frescoes. The small but select collection of the **Archaeological Museum** is housed in the 10th century church of St John the Baptist. Ask about evening concerts held in the 6th century Metropolitan Church ruin.

Places to Stay

The Mesembria Tourist Office (☎ 28 55), formerly Balkantourist, between the bus stop and the harbour, has private rooms at US$17 double (no singles). It's OK to rent for one night. Many of the rooms are in the new town near the beach, just west across the isthmus.

The influx of tourists into Nesebâr is reflected in fast rising private room and restaurant prices, and it may now be possible to get a hotel room with private bath at Sunny Beach for only a few dollars more. Check hotel prices at Balkantourist in Sunny Beach before catching the bus to Nesebâr.

Nesebâr's only hotel, the *Mesembria*, is reserved for Balkan Holidays groups only from May to October. You may be allowed into their night club, however. Also try the *Nesebâr Resthouse* (☎ 60 35) in the same building as the post office.

Places to Eat

You'll find lots of places to eat and drink in Nesebâr. The *Kapitanska Srechta Restaurant*, an old sea captain's house that overlooks the harbour, has lots of atmosphere. It's rather touristy (the waiters are dressed in sailor suits) but at least you can get seafood here.

Farther off the beaten track is the *Lozarska Kushta Restaurant* near the east end of town, a typical Bulgarian tavern with local meat dishes.

Getting There & Away

Jam-packed buses run regularly between Nesebâr and Sunny Beach (10 km), where you change buses for Burgas or Varna.

Ask at the Mesembria Tourist Office about private buses direct to Plovdiv and Sofia, and book well ahead.

From mid-July to mid-September a 'hydrobus' makes a day trip to Sozopol, but only when a group has booked (ask at the maritime terminal and tourist office). Theo-

retically, it leaves Nesebâr daily at 9 am, departing from Sozopol at 4 pm.

VARNA (BAPHA)

Varna, Bulgaria's largest Black Sea port, has become the summer capital of Bulgaria. The city's history began in 585 BC when Miletian Greeks founded ancient Odessos. Varna flourished under the Romans. During the Middle Ages, Varna alternated between Byzantium and Bulgaria but remained prosperous. The Turks captured Varna in 1393 and made it a northern bastion of their empire. In 1444 the Polish-Hungarian king Vladislav III Jagiello was killed in battle here while leading a crusade against Ottoman expansion. After the Crimean War (1853-56) Turkey allowed its allies Britain and France to sell their products throughout the Ottoman Empire and Varna became a great trading centre. In 1866 the railway arrived from Ruse, providing a direct route from the Danube to the Black Sea. After WW II, much of Bulgaria's trade with the USSR passed through the port of Varna.

In recent years Varna has developed into an ideal resort with excellent beaches, parks, museums, historic sites, accommodation, restaurants, theatres and teeming pedestrian malls. The street signs are even in Latin as well as Cyrillic script! It's an attractive city on a bay hemmed in by hills that offer scenic views. Industrial installations like the big chemical plant at Devnya and the Shipbuilding Combine are well west of town. If you don't have time to visit more of the coast, come and see the sea at Varna.

Orientation

The bus and train stations are on opposite sides of the city, but buses Nos 1, 22 and 41 run between them. The maritime terminal is just south of the city centre, within walking distance from the train station. Everything north-east of the maritime terminal is beach and everything west of it is the commercial port. The left-luggage office at the train station is in a separate building across the street labelled 'Gepäckaufbewahrung' (open daily from 6 am to 10.30 pm). Access to the

BULGARIA

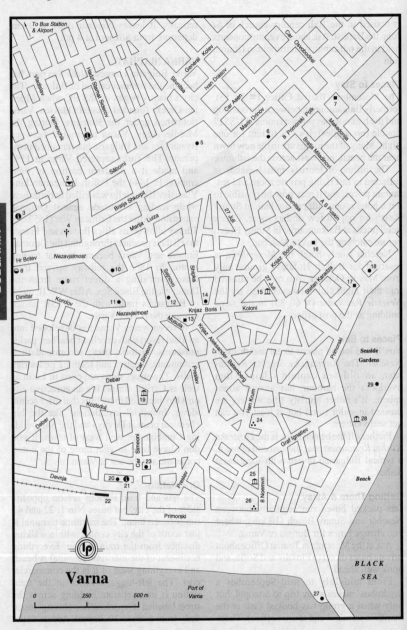

Varna

0   250   500 m

Port of
Varna

BLACK
SEA

PLACES TO STAY

7   Orbita Hotel
13   Musala Hotel/Balkantourist
16   Cherno More Hotel
17   Odesa Hotel

OTHER

1   Balkantourist
2   Main Post Office
3   Vectra Travel Agency
4   Assumption Cathedral
5   Museum of History & Art
6   Former Communist Headquarters
8   Buses to Beach Resorts
9   Dramatic Theatre
10   Court of Justice
11   Opera House
12   Puppet Theatre
14   Balkan Airlines
15   National Revival Museum
18   Festival & Congress Centre
19   Ethnographic Museum
20   Left-Luggage Office
21   Tourist Service George
22   Railway Station
23   Union of Bulgarian Motorists
24   Roman Thermae
25   City Historical Museum
26   Roman Baths
27   Maritime Terminal
28   Maritime Museum
29   Aquarium

left-luggage office at the bus station (daily from 6.30 am to 6.30 pm) is from the platform facing the buses near the men's toilet.

From the train station, walk north up ulitsa Car Simeoni and Gatchev into Nezavjsimost, the centre of town. A broad pedestrian mall, ulitsa Knjaz Boris I, runs east from here. North-west of Nezavjsimost is a major crossroads, where bulevard Vladislav Varnencik runs north-west to the bus station and the airport. The great Asparuh Bridge over the navigable channel between Varnensko Ezero and the Black Sea is just west of ploschtad Varnenska Komuna.

In summer, assorted pickpockets, sleight-of-hand moneychangers and snatch-and-run beggar children work the crowds along ulitsa Knjaz Boris I and Nezavjsimost. These people are not at all dangerous if you're aware they're there.

Information

Staff at Balkantourist, Musala 3, provide maps, information, rooms and international bus tickets.

The office of the Union of Bulgarian Motorists is at ulitsa Sofia 28, very near the train station.

Money Several banks are on ulitsa Knjas Boris I just off Nezavjsimost. The Electronic Bank (weekdays 9 am to 4 pm) charges US$3 per cheque to change travellers' cheques, while the First East International Bank (weekdays 9 am to 4 pm, Saturday 9 am to 1 pm) across the street charges 4% commission. The T Bank, a block down Knjas Boris I on the left (weekdays 9 am to 4 pm, Saturday 9 am to noon), charges US$2 plus 2% commission on any amount.

Post & Telecommunications You can place long-distance telephone calls at the main post office, Sâborni 36 (daily 7 am to 11 pm). Varna's telephone code is 052.

Travel Agencies The Rila office, Shipka 3, sells international train tickets.

Balkantourist, Musala 3, sells tickets for the daily private bus to Sofia (US$5 to Sofia or US$3 to Veliko Târnovo) and an overnight bus to Istanbul (US$22).

Public Toilet There are public toilets in the park across the street from the Musala Hotel.

Maps The stationary store next to the First East International Bank on ulitsa Knjaz Boris I sells a few good maps of Bulgaria and Cyrillic Pirin/Rila hiking maps.

Things to See

There are two sets of **Roman baths**. The newer baths are on Primorski, just above the port between the train station and the hydrofoil terminal. The upper floor of the **City Historical Museum** at ulitsa 8 Noemvri 3, next to these baths, gives an impression of

BULGARIA

Varna as a prewar seaside resort. Much more interesting are the other baths, the 2nd century **Roman Thermae** on ulitsa Han Krum, north from the City Museum and to the left. Besides the large, well-preserved baths, there's the beautiful **St Anastasius Orthodox Church** (built in 1602) within the compound.

Go east on ulitsa Graf Ignatiev from the Roman Thermae to the south-west end of the **Seaside Gardens**. This attractive park contains the **Maritime Museum** and, nearby, the **Aquarium** (1911). There's a good beach below the Seaside Gardens, but it's body-to-body in summer.

Walk through the gardens to the Odessa Hotel, then north-west on Slivnitsa to Varna's largest museum, the **Museum of History & Art** at ulitsa Marija Luiza 41. The ground floor of this neo-Renaissance former girls' high school is dedicated to archaeology. Unfortunately, few of the exhibits are captioned in anything other than Bulgarian but there's an excellent collection of icons.

West of this museum, ulitsa Marija Luiza cuts across Nezavjsimost where you'll find the **Assumption Cathedral** (1886), the town hall, the red-coloured Opera House (1921) and other sights.

Between this square and the train station is the **Ethnographic Museum**, ulitsa Panagjurishte 22, with a large collection of folk art and implements that was erected in 1860.

Many of Varna's museums and archaeological sites are open Tuesday to Sunday from 10 am to 5 pm.

Places to Stay
Camping The closest camping ground is *Panorama* at Golden Sands.

Private Rooms In the underpass leading to ulitsa Car Simeoni outside the train station is a Kvartirno Byuro kiosk (☎ 246 000) with private rooms at US$6 per person.

Tourist Service Office George (☎ 227 476), Car Simeoni 36, a half-block from the train station (the small exchange office on the left), has private rooms in the old town at

US$8/10 single/double. The office is open from 9 am to 9.30 pm in summer, 9 am to 6 pm in winter (closed Sunday), and the staff speak English.

Balkantourist (☎ 225 524), Musala 3 beside the Musala Hotel, rents private rooms at US$7/10 single/double. The Balkantourist private-room office at ulitsa General Kolev 5, just off Vladislav Varnencik, is less well known and thus slightly cheaper.

Vectra Travel Agency (☎ 228 205), Sâborni 48, near the cathedral (weekdays 8.30 am to 6.30 pm, Saturday 8.30 am to 1 pm), has private rooms at US$9/11 single/double.

Hotels The only cheap hotel right in town is the seedy, smelly *Hotel Musala* (☎ 223 925), Musala 3, off Nezavjsimost (US$9/18 single/double without bath or breakfast). If there are unoccupied beds in your room beware of the midnight knock on the door as the night clerk tries to fill them with whoever happens to show up. There's no shower in the building.

The *Orbita Hotel* (☎ 225 162), Car Osvoboditel 25, is overpriced at US$31/52 single/double with bath and breakfast yet it's packed all summer with Bulgarians and groups who get their rooms for a pittance – give it a miss.

Of Varna's luxury hotels, the three-star *Cherno More Hotel*, Slivnitsa 35, boasts the tallest building and the highest prices, but the two-star, four-storey *Odesa Hotel* (☎ 228 381), Slivnitsa 1, overlooking the Seaside Gardens, is closer to the beach (US$34/46 single/double with bath).

Privately owned hotels are springing up in Galata, 10 km south-east of Varna. One of the best is the five-room *Hotel Florina* (☎ 778 272), Chernomorska 16, run by English-speaking entrepreneur Nicolai Dimitrov. Rooms are US$8 per person with shared bath and meals are served. Bus No 17 runs to Galata every 20 minutes from 5 am to 10.30 pm from just outside Varna Railway Station. The Florina is worth considering if you want to be within easy commuting distance of Varna without having to stay in the city itself.

Places to Eat
Slivnitsa, between the Cherno More and Odesa hotels, is solidly lined with restaurants serving meals at the outdoor tables. Stroll along till you see someone eating a dish of something you fancy. Note especially the places with grilled meats and barbecued chicken.

The up-market *Bistro Rimski Termi*, right next to the City Historical Museum on 8 Noemvri, has a nice garden which is perfect for lunch in summer.

Entertainment
Both the *Opera House* and the *Dramatic Theatre* are on Nezavjsimost. The Varna Opera presents a regular series of operas all summer and the ticket office even has a programme printed in English (tickets US$6).

If you're in Varna between mid-June and mid-July, be sure to check the programme of the Varna Summer Festival, which features outstanding musical events. At this time you can enjoy opera and ballet in the open-air theatre in Seaside Gardens or Opera House, chamber music in St Anastasius Church, theatre in the Roman Thermae and concerts in the ultramodern *Festival & Congress Centre* (1986) on Slivnitsa, opposite the Odesa Hotel.

The *Orbi Dans Disco Club* below the Orbita Hotel is the place to be from 10 pm to 4 am.

Getting There & Away
Balkan Airlines has six flights a day from Sofia to Varna for about US$65 one way. Bus No 50 connects Varna Airport to town. The Balkan Airlines office is at Knjaz Boris I 15, on the corner of ulitsa Shipka.

Express trains go to Sofia (543 km via Pleven or 553 km via Karlovo) and couchettes are available on the overnight service (book well ahead). For Veliko Târnovo change trains at Gorna Oryahovitsa. Two trains a day go direct to Ruse (226 km, four

hours). The daily local train between Varna and Burgas takes five hours on a roundabout route (218 km).

Advance bus tickets can only be purchased at the bus station, bulevard Vladislav Varnencik 159, and to/from Burgas reservations are essential. Buses include six to Burgas (132 km, three hours), eight to Nesebâr (101 km), 10 to Balchik (46 km), eight to Kavarna (63 km), one to Durankulak (Romanian border, 107 km), six to Shumen (90 km) and one to Ruse (116 km). Southbound buses to Nesebâr, etc stop running at around 6 pm. There are no buses from here to Sofia or Veliko Târnovo. Ask about the bus to Constanta, Romania (151 km, twice a week, US$3).

Transportation to the beach resorts north of Varna is good, continuing late into the night. Bus No 99 runs to Camping Panorama at Golden Sands, 17 km north-east of Varna, from the south side of Hristo Botev, west of Assumption Cathedral. The bus to Albena also leaves from here (the last bus leaves around 6 pm). Purchase tickets in advance at the kiosk (small additional fee for luggage). Private minibuses also leave frequently from this stop, No 9 to Golden Sands and No 8 to Druzhba.

Car Rental
Avis (☎ 232 111) and Europcar (☎ 239 353) are both at the Cherno More Hotel. Avis and Hertz also have offices at the airport and Europcar is represented there by Interbalkan.

GOLDEN SANDS (ЗЛАТНИ ПЯСЪЦИ)
Golden Sands, or Goldstrand (Zlatni Pyasâtsi), is perhaps Bulgaria's most chic resort, the green wooded hills rising directly behind the four km of golden sands. Some 67 hotels (14,230 beds) are hidden among the trees and, aside from the beach life, Golden Sands offers all kinds of organised sports such as sailboarding, sailing, diving, water-skiing, archery, tennis and horse riding with qualified instructors available.

Other flashy resorts along this Bulgarian Riviera are Chalka, Druzhba and Albena, all of which feature high-rise hotels, jam-

BULGARIA

packed beaches and the sort of programmed holiday atmosphere that tourists on package holidays enjoy. All of these places, Golden Sands included, were built by the communists to accommodate large tour groups on pre-booked package tours and they're still not set up to receive individual travellers. Only expensive hotels are available, restaurant prices are high for those without meal vouchers and you're stuck in the middle of a sterile, tourist-oriented environment, isolated from everyday life, exactly as the socialist central planners intended.

The resorts do have fine beaches and the bus service from Varna is frequent and cheap, so, unless you love places like Waikiki, Miami or Surfers Paradise, the best plan by far is to get a private room in Varna or Balchik and commute to one of the resorts for a day in the sun.

Places to Stay

The Balkantourist accommodation service or *'nastanyavane'* (☎ 855 681), on the main highway near the polyclinic, just above Hotel Diana, books hotel rooms beginning at US$37/52 single/double with bath and breakfast. This office is open 24 hours in summer but rooms are only issued after noon (standard communist logic). The sign outside usually says 'no free beds'.

Camping Panorama (☎ 855 603) is by the highway at the northern end of Golden Sands, about a 10-minute walk from the beach. Bungalows are available at US$8/13 single/double. Buses Nos 53 and 99 from Varna stop there.

Private rooms are unavailable at Golden Sands.

Getting There & Away

Bus No 9 from Varna stops on the main highway, a 10-minute walk from the beach, though in summer small tourist trains run all around the resort.

ALBENA (АЛбЕНА)

Albena, another huge ex-communist holiday resort, seems to attract a younger clientele than Golden Sands, so it might be a better choice if you're into nightlife.

The Tourist Service office (☎ 21 52) opposite the bus station in Albena rents out hotel rooms beginning around US$26/30 single/double with bath but no breakfast. In summer, they're open 24 hours a day.

There's a camping ground near the entrance to the complex with bungalows for US$20/26 single/double.

BALCHIK (БАЛЧИК)

Balchik is a picturesque old town huddled below weathered white chalk bluffs, 47 km north-east of Varna. The Greek traders who settled here in the 5th century BC called the place 'Krunoi' for its springs and the Romans changed it to Dionysopolis in honour of the god of wine. From 1913 to 1940 Balchik and the rest of southern Dobruja belonged to Romania. It was here in 1931 that Queen Maria of Romania had an Oriental-style summer residence built overlooking the sea. It is said that the queen entertained many lovers in the building, and though it's easy to imagine such affairs in such a place, much of the romance has since worn off.

Balchik makes a good day trip from Varna, otherwise it's possible to arrange a stay and patronise the beach at nearby Albena.

Orientation & Information

Ulitsa Cherno More winds up from the port to the main bus station in the upper part of town, a 10-minute walk from the ferry wharf. The bus to Albena leaves from a small bus station near the port but buses to Varna depart from the main bus station.

Post & Telecommunications The post office is on ulitsa Ivan Vazov just off ulitsa Cherno More behind Hotel Balchik.

Balchik's telephone code is 0579.

Things to See

As you walk up ulitsa Cherno More from the port to the upper town you'll see a sign pointing the way to the **Icon Gallery** to the right, on the road which begins opposite the large bank. A block further up ulitsa Cherno

More is the local **Historical Museum** (closed weekends) on the left.

Queen Maria's villa is about two km west of the ferry wharf (follow the shore) and it's possible to enter whenever local artists exhibit their wares inside for sale. This villa and several other buildings are now included in Balchik's **botanical gardens**, which allegedly contain more than 600 varieties of Mediterranean plants and cacti. Unfortunately, they are poorly maintained, so don't come expecting a lot and you won't be disappointed.

Places to Stay & Eat

The one-star *Dionysopolis Hotel* (☎ 21 75), on ulitsa Primorski near the port, charges US$7/22 single/double (don't ask why – that's their price).

The small *Hotel Esperanza* (☎ 51 48), ulitsa Cherno More 16, is US$15 double. It's usually full but they'll find you a private room for a similar price. Ask at the bar below the hotel. The food in the Esperanza's restaurant is great.

The two-star *Hotel Balchik* (☎ 28 09), a modern three-storey hotel facing a park in the upper town just off ulitsa Cherno More, offers tidy rooms with bath at US$10/20 single/double – good value. Discounts are offered for stays of over three nights.

Restaurant Kavatsi facing the port offers good seafood.

Getting There & Away

From mid-June to mid-September a 'hydrobus' runs from Varna to Balchik daily, leaving Varna around 8.30 am and Balchik at 4.30 pm. The boat ride is a nice two-hour trip with an open deck where you can sit outside and enjoy the great views of the coast. This enjoyable Black Sea cruise costs US$4 from Varna to Balchik. Some services also call at Golden Sands.

It's fairly easy to make a round trip by returning to Varna on local buses with changes at Albena and Golden Sands. In summer local buses travel from Balchik to Albena (18 km) every 20 minutes, and bus No 2 from Albena to Golden Sands (16 km)

is also frequent. From Golden Sands, bus No 9 runs to Varna frequently.

Northern Bulgaria

Northern Bulgaria, between the Danube and the crest of the Stara Planina, corresponds to the ancient Roman province of Moesia Inferior. To the south was Roman Thrace and to the north, Dacia. Despite barbarian invasions in the 3rd century AD, Moesia remained part of the Eastern Roman Empire until the formation of Bulgaria in 681. Pliska and Preslav, historic capitals of the First Bulgarian Empire, and Veliko Târnovo, capital of the Second Bulgarian Empire, are all here. During the long Turkish period, Ruse and Vidin served as northern bastions of the Ottoman Empire. Much later, during the Bulgarian National Revival, the renowned monasteries at Preobrazhenski and Troyan were erected. During the Russo-Turkish War of 1877-78, the great battles of Pleven and Shipka waged here decided the fate of modern Bulgaria. All this makes northern Bulgaria a region of special interest for historians.

Coming or going from Romania, northern Bulgaria is the gateway. Many travellers cross the Friendship Bridge at Ruse, but the Calafat-Vidin ferry is a good alternative. There's also hiking in the Stara Planina. Northern Bulgaria is worth exploring.

MADARA (МАДАРА)

Madara, 18 km east of Shumen, is a convenient stopover between Varna and Ruse or Veliko Târnovo. From the train station, a wide stone stairway leads two km up towards the cliffs. Madara makes a convenient base for exploring the nearby capitals of the First Bulgarian Empire, Preslav and Pliska. There's plenty to see at Madara itself, so you could spend a couple of days here.

Things to See & Do

Archaeological remains dating from the 8th to 14th centuries can be seen below the cliffs

BULGARIA

of Madara. Higher up are some caves, but more famous is the **Madara horseman**, a relief of a mounted figure spearing a lion which symbolises victories of Khan Tervel over his enemies. It was carved in the early 8th century, 25 metres up on the rock face, and the adjacent Greek inscriptions date from the years 705 to 831.

North of the horseman, a regular stairway leads up to the top of 100-metre cliffs where there are fortifications from the First Bulgarian Empire, part of a defensive ring intended to protect the nearby capitals of Pliska and Preslav.

Places to Stay & Eat

Camping Madara (☎ 262), one of the nicest camp sites in Bulgaria, is a few hundred metres from the horseman. Open all year, it has 15 rustic cabins with shared bath (US$3 per person) and tent space (US$2 per person). The camping ground has a nice little restaurant of its own and there's a larger restaurant on the main road nearby. This peaceful site is a good place to come for a rest.

There's a youth hostel at Madara, the *Hizha 'Madarski Konnik'* (☎ 261), near the ticket office for the horseman. Beds are US$3.50 per person and reservations are not required for individuals. If the hostel is closed when you arrive ask at the café beside the entrance, which is operated by the same company. It's open all year.

Also check the two-star *Hotel Madara*, just 100 metres down the road to Shumen.

Getting There & Away

Madara is on the main railway line between Sofia and Varna via Pleven though not all express trains stop here. Every morning there are several trains to/from Varna (91 km, two hours).

Buses run from the archaeological area near the camping ground but there's only one bus a day to/from Shumen which at last report left Madara for Shumen at 1 pm, returning from Shumen to Madara at 4 pm. Trains pass about every three hours and if you don't wish to spend the night it's best to

plan a visit between two trains. There's no official left-luggage area at the train station but the staff may agree to keep your bags. Otherwise ask at the small bar in front of the station.

Five buses a day link Madara to the railway junction of Kaspichan (10 km), from where there are trains direct to Ruse and Varna. Buses also go to Novi Pasar and Pliska.

PLISKA (ПЛИСКА)

Pliska squats on a level plain 23 km northeast of Shumen and 12 km north of Madara. Founded by Khan Asparoukh in 681, Pliska was the capital of the First Bulgarian Empire in the 8th and 9th centuries. Though destroyed by the Byzantines in 811, Khan Omourtag rebuilt the town, which remained important even after the court moved to Preslav in 893.

There were three walled circuits at Pliska. The outermost fortification enclosed 23 sq km (including the present village) with an embankment and a ditch. The common people and soldiers lived in this Outer City. The Inner City, three km north of the village, had a 10-metre-high stone wall with guard towers. The rebuilt 9th century Eastern Gate gives access to the foundations of the **Big Palace** with its throne room, the ceremonial centre of the city. Just west was the Court Church, originally a pagan temple. This inner fortress also enclosed the **citadel**, clearly distinguished by its brick walls, where the khan used to reside. Underground passages led from the citadel to various points in the Inner City.

The **museum** at the site contains a model of the 9th century, three-naved **Great Basilica**, which has been partly rebuilt a km north of the main archaeological area. This great building, 100 metres long by 30 metres wide, is linked to the adoption of Christianity in Bulgaria in 865.

Getting There & Away

If you don't have your own vehicle, you will have trouble visiting Pliska as buses from Shumen come only every three hours and you still have to walk three km north to the ruins. There's no bus service to the ruins themselves and taxis are rare. Arriving by train is even worse, as the village of Pliska is six km north-west of Kaspichan, the nearest train station.

SHUMEN (ШУМЕН)

Shumen is a large city between Varna and Veliko Târnovo or Ruse, halfway from the Black Sea to the Danube. Both the Thracians and the Romans had settlements here, and, during the early Middle Ages, Shumen and nearby Preslav, Madara and Pliska became the birthplaces of medieval Bulgaria. Shumen was captured by the Turks in 1388. For the next five centuries, Chumla (Shumen) was an important market town with the largest mosque in Bulgaria. In the early 19th century, the Turks included it in their strategic quadrangle of fortified towns, along with Ruse, Silistra and Varna, as a defence against Russian advances.

Shumen is a transportation hub that you will pass through once or twice while touring this part of the country, and there are several things to see if you have time. The gigantic hilltop monument that overlooks Shumen was built in 1981 to commemorate 13 centuries of Bulgarian history on the 1300th anniversary of the founding of the First Bulgarian Empire.

Orientation & Information

The adjacent bus and train stations are on the east side of town. Follow bulevards Madara and Slavyanski west to the centre – a pleasant walk. The old Turkish town is to the west of Hotel Madara. The left-luggage office inside the train station is open 24 hours.

Post & Telecommunications There's a post office across the street from the bus station (the sign on the roof reads NOWA, which is POSTA in Cyrillic, of course). Shumen's telephone code is 054.

Travel Agencies Balkantourist, next to the Hotel Shumen, sells tickets for daily buses to Istanbul (US$20).

Things to See

A half-day visit to Shumen is best organised by taking bus No 10 from in front of the bus station west to the end of the line at the famous **brewery**. Shumensko pivo, the local beer, dates back to 1882 and the many prizes it has won are listed on the label. It has a nice bite. The wines of this region are also excellent.

From Kyoshkovete Park opposite the brewery hike, hitch, or take a taxi up to the **Shumen Fortress** (Shumenska Krepost), on the hilltop directly above. The walls and foundations of the 12th to 14th century medieval settlement have been rebuilt and the site museum contains artefacts found during the excavations, as well as maps and photos. There's a terrific view of Shumen from here.

In the western part of town below the fortress are a few scattered remnants of old Shumen that were not bulldozed for modern buildings. The **Tombul Mosque** (1744), visible from above, is the largest and most beautifully decorated in Bulgaria. The Turks built their mosque with stones torn from the ruins of earlier Bulgarian monuments. Beyond is the 16th century Turkish **covered market**.

Follow the pedestrian promenade back towards the stations. On the way you'll pass the **District Historical Museum**, bulevard Slavyanski, in the centre of the modern city. It has a large collection, but the captions are only in Bulgarian.

Places to Stay & Eat

Rather than looking for a room in Shumen, you're better off staying at Madara, if possible. Otherwise, Balkantourist (☎ 55 313) next to Hotel Shumen rents private rooms at US$5 per person, but they're closed weekends.

The rather run-down *Orbita Hotel* (☎ 56 374) in Kyoshkovete Park, beyond the brewery on the far west side of town, is US$5 for a double. The Orbita formerly catered mostly to Soviet tour groups and large photos of the old USSR still adorn the walls.

The three-star, seven-floor *Hotel Madara* (☎ 57 598) is expensive at US$29/33 for a single/double with bath. The communists began construction of a new shopping mall next to the Madara but the project has been abandoned, leaving a legacy of ugly half-finished buildings.

The old three-storey *Hotel Pliska* (☎ 55 277), on ploschtad Osvobozdanie above Restaurant Rigoletto in front of Hotel Madara, is US$10 for a double with shared bath.

Hotel Stariyagrad (☎ 55 376) up near the Shumen Fortress is US$8 per person.

The *Popsheitanovata Kushta Restaurant*, halfway between the Madara and Shumen hotels, serves traditional Bulgarian food in a quaint 19th century building.

Getting There & Away

Shumen is on the main line from Sofia to Varna via Pleven. For Veliko Târnovo change at Gorna Oryahovitsa. Madara is accessible by local train on the line to Kaspichan and Varna.

Three buses a day leave Shumen for Ruse (116 km). If their times aren't convenient, catch a bus to Razgrad (52 km, five daily) from which the service to Ruse is more frequent. Other buses leaving Shumen include three to Burgas (178 km), five to Varna (90 km), five to Pliska (23 km), four to Madara (18 km) and one every hour or more from platform No 1 to Preslav (20 km). Preslav is an easy connection, but the bus service to Pliska and Madara is infrequent and overcrowded.

PRESLAV (ПРЕСЛАВ)

Preslav, 20 km south-west of Shumen, was founded in the year 821 by Khan Omourtag. Khan Simeon moved his seat here from Pliska in 893 and Preslav remained capital of the First Bulgarian Empire until it was conquered by Byzantium in 971. A notable school of literature existed here and even after the court left for Veliko Târnovo, Preslav remained an important town. The Turks sacked Preslav in 1388 and hauled away its stones to construct mosques elsewhere.

The ruins of Veliki Preslav are two km south of the present town of Preslav. The five-sq-km outer city was protected by a high stone wall and contained churches, monasteries and the residences of the nobles. An inner wall encircled the 1.5-sq-km citadel with the royal palace at its centre. The most famous building was the **Round Gold Church**, built by Khan Simeon in 908 and partially restored in recent times. It derived its name from the dome, which was gilded on the outside and covered with mosaics inside.

The **archaeological museum** at the ruins contains architectural fragments and a model of the palace to help you visualise what it must have been like. Prize exhibits are a 10th century ceramic icon of St Theodore Stratilates from a nearby monastery and the 10th century silver goblet of Zhoupan Sivin.

The town of Preslav is easily accessible by local bus from Shumen. A good plan on arrival is to take a taxi out to the site museum and walk back. If you want to stay, there's the two-star *Hotel Preslav* (☎ 25 08) in the middle of town which also serves meals.

RUSE (РУСЕ)

Ruse, the largest Bulgarian port on the Danube, is a gateway to the country. Russian and Bulgarian riverboats stop here, as does the one overcrowded daily train to/from Bucharest. The double-decker highway/railway Friendship Bridge (1954), six km downstream, links Ruse to Giurgiu, Romania. This massive 2.8-km-long structure is the largest steel bridge in Europe; during high water the central section can be raised. The bridge's name is rather ironic as relations between Bulgaria and Romania are far from friendly and a chlorine and sodium plant across the river in Giurgiu delivers massive air pollution to Ruse.

Along the Bulgarian right bank of the Danube at Ruse are parks and promenades full of mementos of the two liberations (1878 and 1944). It's worth a stop if you've got the time.

History

A Roman fortress, Sexaginta Prista (60

PLACES TO STAY

3 Riga Hotel
12 Hotel Splendid
13 Hotel Balkan
17 Dounav Hotel
21 Hotel Helios

PLACES TO EAT

25 Restaurant Rila

OTHER

1 Transportation Museum
2 Soviet Army Monument
4 Baba Tonka Museum
5 Marine Terminal
6 Puppet Theatre
7 Rila Train Ticket Office
8 Dunav Tours
9 Concert Bureau
10 Pantheon
11 Post Office
14 Daytona Disco
15 Monument to Liberty
16 Former Party House

18 Opera House
19 First Private Bank
20 Historical Museum
22 Union of Bulgarian Motorists
23 Turkish Minaret
24 City Art Gallery
26 Bus Station
27 Railway Station

BULGARIA

Ruse

0   125   250 m

ships), was established here in 70 AD as part of the defensive Danubian Lines (the Roman defensive line along the south bank of the Danube River). Although strengthened by Emperor Justinian in the 6th century, the fort was finally obliterated during the 'barbarian' invasions of the 7th century.

The Slavs forsook the site and in the 9th century built the town of Cherven 30 km south on an easily defensible loop of the Cherni Lom River. Six churches, city walls and a citadel have been excavated at Cherven. The rock-hewn cave churches of Ivanovo, between Cherven and present-day Ruse, are another reminder of this period. After the Ottoman conquest in 1388, Cherven was abandoned.

The Turks rebuilt and strongly fortified Rouschouk (Ruse). The Russians captured the city in 1773 and 1811, but were forced to withdraw because of the Napoleonic attack on Moscow. In 1864, under the reforming Turkish *vali* (district governor) Midhat Pasha, founder of the Young Turks movement, Rouschouk was modernised and became capital of the Danubian Vilayet (including everything west to Niš, Yugoslavia). In 1866 a railway from Ruse to Varna linked the Danube directly to the Black Sea. The eclectic architecture of the city centre dates from the building boom which followed Ruse's liberation by Russian troops in 1878.

Orientation

The adjacent bus and train stations are on the south side of town. The left-luggage office at the train station is in the room marked 'café' in the rear left corner of the main station hall as you stand facing the tracks with your back to the front door. They're open 24 hours.

From the stations, walk or take a bus a km north up Borisova to ploschtad Svoboda, the centre of town. Among the 18 streets which meet on this square is Aleksandrovska, Ruse's pedestrian mall, which runs off in both directions.

Information

Try Dunav Tours, Rayko Daskalov 1, just off ploschtad Svoboda. There are also tourist desks in the Riga and Dounav hotels for information and currency exchange.

The Union of Bulgarian Motorists is at General Skobelev 45.

Money The First Private Bank, Aleksandrova 11 (weekdays 8.15 to 11.30 am and 1 to 3.30 pm, Saturday 8.30 am to 1.30 pm), will change up to US$1000 in travellers' cheques for a flat fee of US$7.50.

Post & Telecommunications The telephone centre in the main post office on ploschtad Svoboda is open daily from 7 am to 10 pm. Ruse's telephone code is 082.

Travel Agencies Tickets for the train to Bucharest are sold by Rila, Knyazheska 33 (weekdays 8 am to noon and 1 to 6 pm, Saturday 8 am to 1 pm). For some reason, a one-way 2nd-class ticket from Ruse to Bucharest is US$17 (compared with US$6 for Veliko Târnovo-Bucharest or US$11 Sofia-Bucharest at Rila offices in those cities). Reservations are not possible and you'll be very lucky to find a seat.

Things to See

Most of Ruse's monuments and museums are open from 9 am to noon and from 3 to 6 pm, daily except Monday. The **City Art Gallery** is at Borisova 45, between the train station and ploschtad Svoboda. The **Monument to Liberty**, created by the Italian sculptor Arnoldo Zocchi in 1908, dominates ploschtad Svoboda.

At the end of Petko D Petkov, east of the square, are the graves of Ruse's revolutionary heroes in the gold-domed **Pantheon** (1978). North-east of the Pantheon at the end of Saedinenie is the **Soviet Army Monument** (1949) with **Park na mladezta** (Youth Park) and the Danube beyond.

Railway buffs won't want to miss the **Transportation Museum**, by the Danube below Youth Park, in what was the first train station in Bulgaria (1866). It has a large collection of old equipment, including steam locomotive 148, the *Sultanie*, Bulgaria's first.

Proceed upstream along the Danube to the **Riga Hotel**, where there's an attractive terrace and promenade. The Panorama Bar (open from 6 pm to 1 am) on the 20th floor provides a sweeping view. Overlooking the Danube near this hotel is the **Baba Tonka Museum**, Pridunavski 6. Seven of Baba (Grannie) Tonka's children participated in the 1876 uprising against the Turks and one of them, Bilyana Raicheva, resided in what is now the museum building.

Places to Stay
Camping & Hostels The *Ribarska Koliba Campground* (☎ 224 068) is six km out of Ruse on the road to Sofia. It's US$3 per person to camp, US$7 for a two-person cabin or US$10 for a three-person caravan. There's a small bar by the gate of this pleasant wooded site above the Danube, which is open from May to mid-October. It's best to take a taxi from the train station (US$3) as buses Nos 6 and 16 from the centre of town to the camping ground are irregular and stop running at 9 pm.

A km beyond the camping ground is a HI youth hostel, the *Hizha Prista* (☎ 234 167), with dorm beds at US$4 per person with a YHA card, US$6 without a card. Reservations are not required and it's open all year round.

Private Rooms Dunav Tours (☎ 223 088), formerly Balkantourist, Rayko Daskalov 1, a block off ploschtad Svoboda towards Hotel Riga (closed weekends), has private rooms at US$8/9 single/double.

Hotels The *Hotel Balkan* (☎ 279 189), Aleksandrovska 26, is US$4 per person in neat clean rooms with washbasin but shared bath. The reception is in the bar upstairs.

The four-storey concrete *Hotel Helios* (☎ 225 661), ulitsa Nikolaevska 1, is also worth seeking out at US$5 per person.

The low-rise two-star *Dounav Hotel* (☎ 232 008), on ploschtad Svoboda (US$30/40 single/double with bath and breakfast), or the 16-storey three-star *Riga Hotel*, Pridunavski 22, overlooking the river, are both very expensive. The Dounav Hotel looks forbidding from the outside, but the rooms are large and comfortable.

Places to Eat
If you'd like to experience a genuine proletarian self-service cafeteria go to *Restaurant Rila*, ulitsa Borisova 49 (Monday to Thursday 6 am to 8.30 pm, Friday to Sunday 11 am to 7 pm). The top dish on the menu and a large beer shouldn't set you back more than a dollar – just point. Lots of lusty workers just sit in there and drink beer, though the bulk of the clientele are pensioners.

For elegant candle-lit dining to soft music try the *Ruse Restaurant*, Aleksandrovska 6. At the fancy *Panorama Restaurant* on the top floor of Hotel Riga (open 6 pm to 1 am) you get a knockout view of the Danube with your meal.

Near the Danube, down the hill from the Ribarska Koliba Campground, is the *Fisherman's Lodge* restaurant. Live music and an outdoor terrace make this a pleasant place on a summer's evening. Take a sunset stroll along the riverside before dinner.

Entertainment
Check the opera house just off ploschtad Svoboda and the puppet theatre at Knyazheska 9. The concert bureau, Aleksandrovska 61 on the corner of ploschtad Svoboda, will have information on the March Music Days Festival.

The flashy *Daytona Disco*, ulitsa Konstantin Irechek 5 (downstairs), is Ruse's top night spot (nightly from 10 pm).

Getting There & Away
Two trains a day go from Ruse to Varna (226 km, four hours), with others on this line stopping short at Kaspichan (142 km, three hours) near Madara. Express trains run to Sofia (404 km, seven hours) via Pleven, including one overnight train. For Veliko Târnovo (125 km, three hours) change trains at Gorna Oryahovitsa, although some local trains from Ruse go direct to Veliko Târnovo.

Express buses run to Silistra and Varna (each twice daily, 200 km), and also to Shumen (three times daily, 116 km, two hours). The camping ground and youth hostel are in a perfect location if you want to hitchhike to Veliko Târnovo, Pleven or Sofia.

To/From Romania Romania may as well be on the dark side of the moon as far as the people working at Ruse Railway Station are concerned. They don't sell tickets to Romania and the one daily train to Bucharest is not listed on their departures board. The information window in the station opens and closes when it likes and is generally rude and unhelpful (a good example of how things were in Bulgaria when the comrades ran the show). If 'information' is asked to answer questions about trains to Romania their customary contempt turns to open hostility. Trying to actually board the train to Bucharest (which at last report left Ruse at 6.45 am) is like a journey into the great unknown – no one will help you find the right platform and even when you see the train itself, you won't be sure it's real. Be prepared to stand packed in the corridor all the way to Bucharest. (For tickets to Romania see Travel Agencies above.)

For backpackers, a viable alternative to the mystery train is take bus No 12 from ulitsa Nikolaevska near the train station six km to the Friendship Bridge (Dunav Most) and hitch across the upper level (crossing on foot is prohibited). Cars pay US$20 toll to use the bridge and long delays for southbound vehicles are routine at Romanian customs. This chaos means there's no bus direct from Ruse to Romania.

GORNA ORYAHOVITSA (ГОРНА ОРЯХОВИЦА)

Despite the unpronounceable name, this important junction where the railway lines from Sofia to Varna and Ruse to Veliko Târnovo cross is a useful transit point. If you arrive by train from Sofia, Pleven, Ruse, Shumen or Varna you're better off getting out at Gorna Oryahovitsa and taking a bus to

Veliko Târnovo from there. Even if you're on a train from Ruse which is scheduled to continue to Veliko Târnovo and you've got a through ticket, stick your head out the window when you arrive at Gorna Oryahovitsa and note the departure time on the electric board as some trains are scheduled to sit there for up to two hours waiting for connections. This being the case, pick up your luggage, get off and go have a few drinks or a meal at a local restaurant. If you miss your onward train don't worry, as there are lots of buses from Gorna Oryahovitsa to Veliko Târnovo.

Bus No 10 from a street two blocks up from Gorna Oryahovitsa Railway Station runs to Veliko Târnovo every 20 minutes from 6 am to 9.30 pm. Minibuses parked directly in front of the station leave when full and are only slightly more expensive, but much faster. Both types of bus will drop you in the centre of Veliko Târnovo.

Places to Stay & Eat
The *Hotel Etoal* (☎ 57 212), near the bus No 10 stop, two blocks from Gorna Oryahovitsa Railway Station, has clean rooms with shared bath at US$4 per person. This new four-storey hotel is well worth considering if you're passing through late in the day and you might even decide to use it as a base. Arbanasi is only five km away on the private minibuses to Veliko Târnovo and when it's time to leave you'll be able to catch an early train.

If your train drops you at Gorna Oryahovitsa in the middle of the night it's no problem as there are several restaurants and bars around the station open 24 hours a day. There's even a disco directly below the station hall.

Restaurant Mimoza on the far side of the parking lot in front of Gorna Oryahovitsa Railway Station has good food and cold drinks.

VELIKO TÂRNOVO (ВЕЛИКО ТЪРНОВО)
Veliko Târnovo (Great Târnovo) is laced with history. The Yantra River winds through

a gorge in the centre of this 'city of tsars' and picturesque houses cling to the cliffs. Almost encircled by the river, the ruined Tsarevets Citadel recalls the Second Bulgarian Empire (1185-1393), when Veliko Târnovo was the capital. North-west, across the abyss, is the now overgrown Trapezitsa Hill, residence of the nobles and courtiers, while below in the valley the artisans' and merchants' quarter (Asenova) is marked by medieval churches. Renowned monasteries once stood on Sveta Gora Hill, where the university is today. The narrow streets of old Veliko Târnovo bear the imprint of the Bulgarian National Revival; the modern city spreads west. This is one town you won't want to miss.

History
Both the Thracians and Romans had settlements here and, in the 5th century AD, a Byzantine fortress was built on Tsarevets Hill by Emperor Justinian. The Slavs captured it in the 7th century and in 1185 the town was the main centre of the uprising against Byzantium led by the brothers Asen and Peter. With the foundation of the Second Bulgarian Empire in the 12th century, Veliko Târnovo became an imperial city, second only to Constantinople in this region. For the next two centuries, trade and culture flourished. The literary school founded here in 1350 by Theodosius of Târnovo attracted students from as far away as Serbia and Russia.

On 17 July 1393, Târnovgrad (Veliko Târnovo) fell to the Turks after a three-month siege. The fortress was destroyed. In the 19th century, Veliko Târnovo re-emerged as a crafts centre. Bulgarian culture gradually reasserted itself as part of the National Revival movement of the time and in 1877 the Russian general I V Gurko liberated the town. Today there is again a university at Veliko Târnovo. Nowhere else is the power of medieval Bulgaria experienced better.

Orientation
The train station is down by the river, far below the centre of town (catch buses Nos 4 and 13). Ulitsa Hristo Botev ends at a T-intersection with ulitsa Vasil Levski and the modern city to the left, and Nezavisimost and its continuation, ulitsa Stefan Stambolov, to the right.

The bus station is on Nikola Gabrovski, at the western edge of town (buses Nos 7, 10, 11 and 12). Many buses arriving in Veliko Târnovo stop near the market before going on to the bus station, so ask. Bus No 10 to/from Gorna Oryahovitsa begins at the bus station but passes through the middle of town.

The left-luggage office at the bus station is open from 7.30 to 11.30 am and 12.30 to 16.30 pm. At the train station, the left-luggage office is in a small building next to the main station. It's open 24 hours a day.

Information
Try Yantra Tours beside Hotel Etâr or the currency exchange counter or reception desk inside the Etâr itself.

Information on youth hostels may be available from the Pirin Travel Bureau, Stefan Stambolov 79 (upstairs in the old yellow building next to the youth hostel).

The Union of Bulgarian Motorists has a large service centre next to the Boljarski Stan Camping Ground on the Varna-Sofia highway west of town.

Money At last report no bank in Veliko Târnovo would change a travellers' cheque, though this could change. Even the usually ubiquitous private exchange offices are hard to find here, so it's best to plan on changing money elsewhere.

The currency exchange counters at Hotel Etâr and the nearby Interhotel Veliko Târnovo change travellers' cheques for a flat US$5 commission.

Post & Telecommunications The telephone centre in the main post office is open daily from 7 am to 10 pm. Veliko Târnovo's telephone code is 062.

Travel Agencies The Rila Railway Ticket Office, Nikola Gabrovski 42, halfway out to the main bus station (bus No 10), sells

BULGARIA

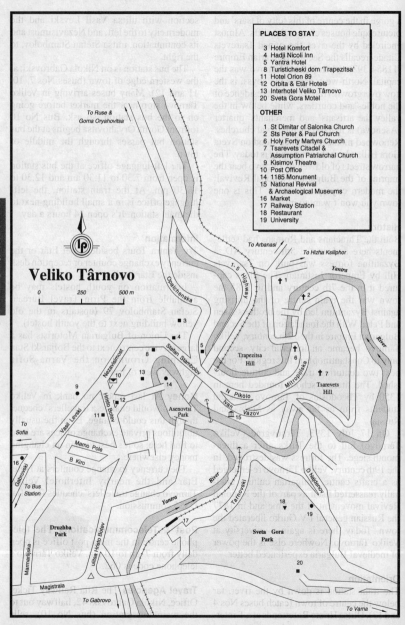

LP

Veliko Târnovo

0   250   500 m

PLACES TO STAY

3   Hotel Komfort
4   Hadji Nicoli Inn
5   Yantra Hotel
8   Turisticheski dom 'Trapezitsa'
11 Hotel Orion 89
12 Orbita & Etár Hotels
13 Interhotel Veliko Târnovo
20 Sveta Gora Motel

OTHER

1   St Dimitar of Salonika Church
2   Sts Peter & Paul Church
6   Holy Forty Martyrs Church
7   Tsarevets Citadel &
    Assumption Patriarchal Church
9   Kisimov Theatre
10 Post Office
14 1185 Monument
15 National Revival
    & Archaeological Museums
16 Market
17 Railway Station
18 Restaurant
19 University

To Ruse &
Gorna Oryahovitsa

To Arbanasi

To Hizha Ksilophor

1.5 Highway

Opalchenska

Yantra

Nezavisimost

Stefan Stambolov

Trapezitsa
Hill

Mitropolska

River

Tsarevets
Hill

N Pikolo

Ivan Vazov

Hristo Botev

Vasil Levski

Asenovtsi
Park

To
Sofia

Marno Pole

B Kiro

Gabrovski

To Bus
Station

Druzhba
Park

Marmardijska

Iulitsa Hristo Botev

Magistrala

To Gabrovo

River

Yantra

T Tárnovski

D Naidenov

Sveta Gora
Park

To Varna

advance train tickets and makes seat reservations for express trains. This is also a convenient, uncrowded place to pick up open international train tickets (US$6 to Bucharest).

Things to See

Opposite the Yantra Hotel on Stefan Stambolov you'll see a stairway leading up into Varusha, a colourful neighbourhood of picturesque streets. Go up and veer left, then go down stone-surfaced ulitsa G S Rakovski, where Bulgarian artisans keep small shops. At number 17 is the **Hadji Nicoli Inn** (1858), one of the best known National Revival buildings in Bulgaria. The street above ulitsa G S Rakovski is lined with quaint old houses and terminates at a church.

Return to the Yantra Hotel and walk east keeping right on Ivan Vazov until you reach the **Bulgarian National Revival Museum** (closed Tuesday and from November to March). The museum is in the old Turkish town hall (1872), the large blue building you see straight ahead. Notice the stone building with six arches beside this museum. The **Archaeological Museum** (closed Monday) is in the basement, down the stairway between the two buildings.

Follow the street on the left to the entrance to **Tsarevets Citadel** (daily, US$1), which was sacked and burned by the Turks in 1393. This vast fortress offers great views from the rebuilt **Assumption Patriarchal Church** at the top of the hill. Just below, to the north, are the foundations of the extensive **Royal Palace** on three terraces. Twenty-two successive kings ruled Bulgaria from this palace. Continue north to a bluff directly above the large factory. This was **Execution Rock**, from which traitors were pushed into the Yantra River. At the southern end of the fortress is the **Baldwin Tower** (rebuilt in 1932) where Baldwin I of Flanders, the deposed Latin emperor of Byzantium, was imprisoned and finally executed after his defeat in 1205.

From the entrance to Tsarevets Hill walk down the steep incline to the **Holy Forty Martyrs Church** by the river at the foot of the hill. The church was built by Tsar Ivan Asen II to commemorate his victory over the despot of Epirus, Teodor Komnin, at Klokotnitsa in 1230, as recorded on the Asen Column inside. Originally a royal mausoleum, Holy Forty Martyrs Church was converted into a mosque by the Turks. There are murals to be seen, but the church has been closed for restoration for many years.

Turn right (don't cross the river) and continue two blocks to the 13th century **Sts Peter & Paul Church** with frescoes. Walk back a little, then cross the big wooden bridge and continue right up through the village till you see a church enclosed by a high stone wall. This is **St Dimitâr of Salonika**, the town's oldest church. During the consecration of this church in 1185, the noblemen brothers Asen and Peter proclaimed an uprising against Byzantine rule. Later, St Dimitâr of Salonika was used for royal coronations. From here you can return to the city centre on bus No 7 or 11.

To Sveta Gora Another memorable walk begins at the Interhotel Veliko Târnovo (check out the photos hanging in the lobby). Cross the footbridge behind the hotel to reach **Asenovtsi Park**, which has an art gallery and a great monument to the re-establishment of the Bulgarian Empire by Asen I in 1185. From here you'll get the classic view of the city's tiers of rustic houses hanging above the Yantra Gorge.

After an eyeful, walk south-east towards **Sveta Gora Park** and climb the stairs to the restaurant you can see protruding through the trees, from where you'll get a sweeping view of the city and its surroundings. The founders of the Târnovo schools of literature and painting were active in the monasteries of Sveta Gora, which have since disappeared. Return the way you came or ask directions to the university, where you can get a bus.

Preobrazhenski Monastery A recommended side trip is Preobrazhenski (Transfiguration) Monastery, seven km north of Veliko Târnovo, on one of the two

BULGARIA

roads to Gorna Oryahovitsa. The location on a wooded hillside below the cliffs of the Yantra Gorge is lovely. The ruins of the 14th century monastery destroyed by the Turks are 500 metres south of the present monastery (rebuilt in 1825 with frescoes (1851) by Zahari Zograph and large icons (1864) by Stanislav Dospevski). Preobrazhenski Monastery suffered serious damage from falling rocks during a storm in 1991 and you might check to see if the church will be open before going out there.

Get there on bus No 10, which runs frequently between Veliko Târnovo and Gorna Oryahovitsa. From the stop it's a two-km climb to the monastery. The **Holy Trinity Monastery** (1847) is below the cliffs on the opposite side of the gorge from Preobrazhenski and is accessible only on foot (1½ hours).

Arbanasi In summer, another good side trip is to the village of Arbanasi, 10 km north-east of Veliko Târnovo. Originally founded by Albanians, Arbanasi grew rich after Sultan Süleyman I gave it to one of his sons-in-law in 1538 thus exempting the town from the Ottoman Empire's ruinous taxation.

A comprehensive ticket (US$1) sold at a kiosk near the bus stop in the centre of Arbanasi admits you to four buildings in the village. **Hadzhi Ilieba House** is a typical, two-storey Arbanasi house of the 16th century. **Konstantsalieva House** dates from the 17th century and is built like a fortress. The high stone walls topped by red tiles surrounding the property were intended to protect the womenfolk from prying Turkish eyes (every house in Arbanasi is surrounded by such walls). The highlight of this typical Bulgarian village is **Nativity Church**, the interior of which is completely covered with colourful frescoes painted between 1632 and 1649. Over 3500 figures are depicted in some 2000 scenes. The interior of **Archangel Church**, on the low hill behind the restaurant in the middle of the village, is also covered with marvellous paintings. There's much more to see along Arbanasi's winding lanes, but on Monday and from October to March, everything will be closed.

If you'd like to spend the night in the village, the *Journalists' Club* or 'Klub Pri Zhurnalista' (☎ 21 875) near Konstantsalieva House rents rooms in its typical Arbanasi dwelling at US$11 per person with shared facilities. The privately run *Hotel Constantin & Elena*, just down from Nativity Church, is similar.

The nine rooms at the five-star *Arbanasi Palace Hotel* (☎ 30 176) begin at US$120 double with breakfast. This building (1975) is popularly known as the former residence of communist boss Todor Zhivkov, though in fact Zhivkov seldom slept there and it was used mostly for state functions, seminars and conferences. Even if you're not up to laying out such big bucks, it's well worth visiting the 'palace' for its marvellous view of Veliko Târnovo.

Buses arrive from Veliko Târnovo Bus Station every couple of hours, or just take a taxi and catch a bus back. Most of the private minibuses shuttling between Gorna Oryahovitsa Railway Station and Veliko Târnovo use the old road which passes within one km of Arbanasi, and they're the easiest way of all to come.

Places to Stay
Camping *Boljarski Stan Camping Ground* (☎ 41 859) on the west edge of town has simple bungalows for US$4/6/9 single/double/triple and camping space at US$2.50 per person plus US$2.50 per tent. There's a good traditional restaurant at the entrance and they're open year round. Bus No 11 stops near the camping ground on its way from the centre of town to the bus station – get off at the beginning of the Sofia highway and look for a hole in the fence which leads straight to the restaurant.

Youth Hostels The new four-storey *Turisticheski dom 'Trapezitsa'* (☎ 22 061) has a great location right in the centre of town at Stefan Stambolov 79. Beds in two-bedded rooms with bath are US$5 per person with a YHA card, US$7 without a card.

Hostel-style accommodation is available all year at the recently privatised *Turisticheski dom 'Momina Krepost'* (also known as 'Hizha Ksiliphor'), in a lovely woodland setting north-east of Veliko Târnovo. Take bus No 7 or 11 east to the end of the line. Walk straight ahead beside the river for a bit to a factory, then turn left up the hill and continue for another two km to a café which rents out bungalows (US$10 double). The dormitory on the top floor of the main building is US$2 per person. You can also get there by taking a bus bound for Arbanasi to the access road, and then walk down to the hostel.

Private Rooms & Hotels *Hotel Orbita* (☎ 22 041), Hristo Botev 15, is US$4 per person – the reception is up at the top of the stairs. Across the street is the *Hotel Orion 89* (☎ 39 956), Hristo Botev 14, with rooms at US$10 per person.

The two-star, 14-floor *Hotel Etâr* (☎ 218 138), ulitsa Ivailo 1, is in the building directly behind the Hotel Orbita. Hotel rooms are US$8/16 single/double without bath, US$15/30 with private bath, and the hotel currency exchange counter organises private room accommodation at US$9 per person. They're closed on weekends. The Etâr's restaurant is good.

The three-star *Yantra Hotel* (☎ 20 391), Opalchenska on the corner of Stefan Stambolov, is US$26/44 single/double with bath but without breakfast. The rooms on the main floor are noisy when the band is playing in the restaurant. A small private hotel with a large red sign is at ulitsa Stefan Denchev 2 just a little west on Stefan Stambolov from the Yantra Hotel.

The *Hotel Komfort* (☎ 28 728), ulitsa Panayot Tipografov 5, in the picturesque Varusha district just above Hotel Yantra, is perhaps the nicest of Veliko Târnovo's small private hotels. The 12 rooms go for US$10 per person and those on the upper floors include a spectacular view of Tsarevets Hill.

Places to Eat
The fast food restaurant at Nezavisimost 17

probably has the best view available from any such establishment anywhere in Europe. The rear *Sala Panorama* is also great for just a coffee if hamburgers aren't your style. For a token fee you can use their toilets.

On the back terrace restaurant of the *Hotel Yantra* you can feast on the view of the river as much as the food. The service is fast and reliable, especially if you try to use a few words of Bulgarian. It is a little pricey.

The *Suhindoa 'White Bear' Restaurant*, Mamarchev 12, up the stairs from opposite the Yantra Hotel, serves typical Bulgarian specialities and there's even a menu in English. They're open from noon to midnight daily except Sunday.

There's a good market west on Vasil Levski, on the corner of Nikola Gabrovski. Stock up on fresh vegetables and fruit here. *Café Didy Snack Bar* at the entrance to the market serves a good lunch on weekdays.

Entertainment
Veliko Târnovo's best disco is above Cinema Poltava in the large modern complex next to the post office. A more up-market place with a sexy floorshow is the night club downstairs in the *Interhotel Veliko Târnovo* (nightly from 10 pm to 4 am).

Light & Sound In summer there's an incredible light-and-sound show at Tsarevets Citadel around 10 pm, with the whole of Tsarevets Hill lit in myriad colours. The show's only put on when groups are present and the receptionist at the Interhotel Veliko Târnovo only knows for sure if there'll be a show that night two hours in advance. He/she also sells tickets (US$7 per person) which grant you the honour of watching the show seated in one of the blue plastic chairs in the stand opposite the citadel ticket kiosk. Of course, you can see the show for free from many other parts of town, including the downstairs restaurant at the Yantra Hotel.

Getting There & Away
To get a train to Pleven, Sofia, Ruse or Varna, take bus No 10, which runs frequently, to Gorna Oryahovitsa Railway Station. Some

local trains from Dimitrovgrad direct to Ruse stop at Veliko Târnovo Railway Station. To go to/from Burgas or Plovdiv, change trains at Stara Zagora or Tulovo.

Buses to Plovdiv (197 km) run over Shipka Pass and four a day go to Sofia (247 km). Other buses from Veliko Târnovo include one to Kazanlâk (96 km), five to Sevlievo (56 km), two to Burgas (223 km) and five to Ruse (103 km). To reach Etâr, take the hourly bus to Gabrovo (49 km) and change there. No buses run to Troyan but the four buses to Lovech (104 km) all stop in Sevlievo for about 10 minutes, allowing you time to check if there's a connecting bus to Troyan. If there isn't, you can always get back on the Lovech bus and connect there.

Several luxury tourist coaches between Sofia and Varna pick up passengers outside Hotel Etâr, but tickets are only available from the driver if seats happen to be free. Times are posted in front of the Group Company office beside the hotel and at the hotel reception. Check the ticket prices carefully.

THE STARA PLANINA (СТАРА ПЛАНИНА)

A good slice of the Stara Planina (Balkan Mountains) can be seen on a loop from Veliko Târnovo to Pleven going via Gabrovo, Etâr, Shipka, Kazanlâk, Karlovo, Troyan and Lovech, or vice versa. You'll visit old monasteries, war memorials, quaint villages and the forested peaks themselves.

It's not possible to do all this in one day, so you'll have to spend a night or two somewhere. There are several camping grounds between Veliko Târnovo and Karlovo, all with bungalows for those without tents, and between Karlovo and Pleven you'll find youth hostels and inexpensive hotels. The accommodation situation in Kazanlâk is grim, so try to avoid staying there. Hisarya is a good alternative stopping point, though slightly off the main route.

It's a bit of an adventure to do this loop on public transport, but it calls for a hardy, rough-and-ready traveller willing to put up with occasional difficulties and delays. Quite a variety of attractions are packed into this little circuit.

ETÂR (ЕТЪР)

Take the hourly bus from Veliko Târnovo to Gabrovo (49 km), where you connect with the bus to Etâr (nine km). The turn-off from the main Gabrovo-Kazanlâk highway is at the *Ljubovo Campground* (open from mid-May to September), two km west of Etâr. Here you'll find cabins (US$8 double) as well as tent space, but no restaurant.

The **Etâr Ethnographic Village Museum** is open from Tuesday to Sunday from 8 am to 5 pm. You cansee Bulgarian craftspeople (bakers, cartwrights, cobblers, furriers, glass workers, hatters, jewellers, leather workers, millers, potters, smiths, weavers) practising their age-old trades in typical 18th and 19th century Gabrovo houses that were reconstructed here in the 1960s. Some of the workshops on the right bank of the stream running through the wooded site are powered by water. The items produced by craftspeople along the arts and crafts street on the left bank may be purchased. At the far end of the village is a small tavern where you can sample the local brew or have lunch. Coffee and traditional pastries are also served. This is one of Bulgaria's most appealing attractions.

To continue, return to Ljubovo on the Gabrovo bus and pick up one of the 12 daily Kazanlâk buses there. These buses are often crowded and it may be better to go back into Gabrovo and board the Kazanlâk bus at its starting point. You ought to check the times of this bus when you're in Garbrovo, before going to Etâr.

SHIPKA (ШИПКА)

At the top of 1306-metre **Shipka Pass** over the Stara Planina between Gabrovo and Shipka is a large monument (1934) commemorating the Russian troops and Bulgarian volunteers who, in August 1877, fought back numerous attacks by vastly superior Turkish forces intent on relieving the besieged Turks at Pleven. The *Stoletov Campground* (bungalows) is also up at the pass, but it gets cool at night. Near a huge circular memorial pavilion, 12 km east of the pass along a side road, is *Hizha 'Buzludzha'*, a good base for hikers.

Shipka is a quaint little village, 13 km beyond the pass. Poking through the trees above the village are the five golden, onion-shaped domes of a huge **votive church** (1902) built after the Russo-Turkish War (1877-78). The church bells were cast from spent cartridges from the battle and in the crypt lie the remains of the Russian solders who perished. You'll get a great view of the Valley of Roses from up there. From Shipka village bus No 6 runs hourly into Kazanlâk (12 km). Check to see if the hotel above the restaurant opposite the bus stop in Shipka has reopened.

KAZANLÂK (КАЗАНЛЪК)

Kazanlâk, an important stop on the railway line from Burgas to Sofia, is tucked between the Stara Planina and Sredna Gora mountains in the Valley of Roses. This is not a particularly attractive town, but it is a useful base for visiting nearby attractions. The Festival of Roses, held on the first Sunday in June, features carnivals and parades in Kazanlâk and Karlovo.

Orientation

The bus and train stations in Kazanlâk are adjacent. To attract the attention of the left-luggage staff in the train station, ring the bell on the wall between ticket windows Nos 3 and 4. From the stations, walk about three blocks north on bulevard Rozova Dolina to the Roza and Kazanlâk hotels.

Things to See & Do

The **Archaeological Museum** is two blocks north of Hotel Kazanlâk up ulitsa Iskâra. Many items found in the tombs and other ancient sites of this region are kept there, but the captions are only in Bulgarian. Ask the guards to open room No 25 downstairs if it happens to be closed.

In Tjulbeto Park, two km north-east of the stations, is a 4th century BC **Thracian tomb**

with delicate frescoes discovered during the construction of a bomb shelter in 1944. The original brick tomb has been scrupulously protected since then and cannot be visited, but a full-scale replica has been created nearby. Along the vaulted entry corridor, or *dromos*, is a double frieze with battle scenes. The burial chamber itself is 12 metres in diameter and covered by a beehive dome showing a funeral feast and chariot race. This unique example of Thracian painting is well worth seeing.

The Valley of Roses is the source of 70% of the world's supply of rose attar. The roses bloom from late May to early June and must be picked before sunrise when still wet with dew if the fragrance is to be preserved. Two thousand petals are required for a single gram of attar of roses. Some of the finest perfumes originate here. A **rose museum** is at the edge of town by the road to Shipka.

Places to Stay

The Shipka bus passes the *Kasanlaschka Rosa Campground* (open from May to mid-October) between Shipka and Kazanlâk. It's the highest category camping ground in this area and the most likely to have a bungalow (expensive) if you need it.

The tourist bureau on the 2nd floor in Hotel Kazanlâk (closed weekends) may have a private room for you, or then again, maybe they won't.

The two-star, 80-room *Hotel Roza* (☎ 24 605), at bulevard Rozova Dolina 1, four blocks up from the train station, and the 52-room *Hotel Zornitza* (☎ 22 384), just above the Thracian Tomb, a couple of km away, both charge US$24/36 for singles/doubles with private bath and US$2 per person for breakfast.

At last report the *Hotel Vesta*, ulitsa Navdar Voyvoda 3, directly behind the large white marble House of Culture, four blocks north of Hotel Roza, was closed for reconstruction. Check as they may have reopened by the time you get there and it will probably be a better deal than the overpriced Balkantourist hotels mentioned above.

Entertainment

Disko Star faces the market not far from an old Turkish minaret, a few blocks north-west of Hotel Roza.

Getting There & Away

Kazanlâk is on the main line from Burgas to Sofia via Karlovo. To/from Veliko Târnovo change at Tulovo or go by bus via Gabrovo, which is better. To go to Shipka (12 km) take bus No 6 (hourly) from a stop on the street a block west of the bus and train stations. Other buses from Kazanlâk include 12 to Gabrovo (47 km), four to Veliko Târnovo (96 km), four to Plovdiv (114 km) and two to Hisarya (72 km).

KARLOVO (КАРЛОВО)

Karlovo, in the Valley of Roses, 58 km north of Plovdiv, is a transportation hub you may pass through at one time or another. Trains and buses from here to Kazanlâk (56 km) and Plovdiv (67 km) are frequent. Ten buses a day cover the 26 km to/from Hisarya, but only two stop at Karlovo on their way between Plovdiv and Troyan via Hisarya.

If you have time to kill in Karlovo there's the **Vasil Levski Museum** up near the main square, though the town is not worth a special trip.

The privately run *Hotel Hemus* (☎ 45 97), ulitsa Vasil Levski 87, is right behind Karlovo Bus Station (US$4 per person). If it's full, ask the staff to recommend a similar place.

TROYAN (ТРОЯН)

Troyan, a small town by the Beli Osâm River, at the foot of 1525-metre Troyan Pass, is a base for visiting Troyan Monastery, 10 km east. There's a good choice of places to stay and an hourly bus from Troyan Bus Station runs right to the monastery door.

Orientation

The information-cum-left-luggage office in the bus station is open from 6.30 am to noon and 2 to 4.30 pm, but don't count on anyone being there at weekends. Troyan Railway Station is just above the bus station (though

you can't see it from the bus station – ask) and it has a left-luggage office theoretically open 24 hours a day. The train station is worth a visit anyway for the huge relief map of Bulgaria hanging on the wall of the ticket office.

Things to See

There's a good **Arts & Crafts Museum** in the main square if you have time to see it.

Troyan Monastery, founded in 1600 and Bulgaria's third-largest monastery, is famous as a centre of the Bulgarian National Revival. The church was rebuilt in 1835 and covered with frescoes by Zahari Zograph in 1849. Look for his self-portrait, paintbrush in hand, by one of the windows inside the church. The condemned in the *Last Judgment* on the church's exterior façade are Turks. Many of the frescoes inside the church are blackened by candle soot. Noted anti-Ottoman revolutionaries such as Georgi Benkovski and Vasil Levski found shelter in the monastery, and the room up on the monastery's 3rd floor where Levski was lodged is now a small museum. Folk art is sold at a nearby bazar.

Places to Stay

In Town There are three good places to stay in Troyan. The basic *Hotel Edelweiss*, ulitsa Rakovski 51, just north of Troyan Bus Station, is US$5/8 single/double with shared bath. For some strange reason the staff here may be reluctant to stamp your 'statistical card'. Just across the river from the Hotel Edelweiss is the two-star *Hotel Troyan* (☎ 24 323) with singles/doubles with private bath at US$9/12. Some rooms have balconies facing the river. The Troyan could certainly do with a facelift, but the price is right.

The friendly, welcoming HI youth hostel *Turisticheski dom 'Nikola Gaberski'* (☎ 26 017 or 26 117), on the hill just east of Troyan Bus Station, is open all year and offers comfortable double rooms at US$5 per person. Taking a taxi directly there from the bus station will cost under US$1. There's a stairway directly up to the hostel from town and, once you know the way, it's quite convenient. You don't need a YHA card to stay here although it might get you a small discount – recommended.

At the Monastery You can stay in nice little rooms with shared bath at a guesthouse inside Troyan Monastery (☎ 28 66) for US$8 per person – a rare treat well worth considering. The reception is to the right just inside the first gate.

In the unlikely event that they're full, there's also the small *Hotel Momina Sâlza* (☎ 25 03) above the post office across the street from the monastery and a little back towards Troyan town (US$7 per person). Several other places to stay with similar prices are in the neighbourhood, so you're sure to find something.

The restaurant across the street from the monastery is a good place to sample the local plum brandy *(slivova)* and they serve tasty meat dishes to a local crowd. Also try the 'Troyanska' dry sausage.

Near Troyan Hikers will like the *Hizha 'Zora'* (open in July and August only) at Apriltsi, 19 km east of Troyan Monastery, with a bus service from Troyan every two hours. The hostel manager doesn't speak English but is helpful. On Sunday food can be hard to find. Apriltsi is the base for climbing Mt Botev (2376 metres), the highest peak in the Stara Planina. *Hizha 'Pleven'* is up near the summit. A direct bus to Sofia leaves Apriltsi in the very early morning.

Getting There & Away
Troyan Railway Station is just above the bus station. There are five trains a day to Levski via Lovech. Four buses a day go from Troyan to Sofia (174 km), two to Karlovo (66 km), Hisarya (92 km) and Plovdiv (124 km, three hours), two to Pleven (70 km) and four to Sevlievo (45 km). No direct buses link Troyan to Veliko Târnovo. You must change buses in Sevlievo. Buses run almost hourly to Lovech (36 km), where you can connect for Pleven. (If you have time, the old Varosha quarter of Lovech, with its covered wooden bridge, is worth a look.)

To get to Troyan Monastery, look for the Cherni Osâm bus.

PLEVEN (ПЛЕВЕН)
Pleven, between Ruse and Sofia, 35 km south of the Danube, is best known as the site of a five-month battle in 1877 between the Turks, under Osman Pasha, and a Russo-Romanian army. An entire Turkish army of 11 pashas, 2000 officers and 37,000 men was encircled and captured in this decisive engagement. Apart from sites related to the battle, there are parks and an inviting city centre to see. Pleven doesn't receive many Western visitors, so you'll be assured of a warm welcome.

Orientation
Pleven's adjacent bus and train stations are on the north side of town. The left-luggage office (open 24 hours) at the train station is in a corner of the station building facing the parking lot. The left-luggage office inside the bus station is open from 7 am to 6 pm. From the stations, ulitsa Danail Popov runs south towards the centre, passing many large stores. Ploschtad Vâzrazhdane is the very heart of the city. Vasil Levski, a pleasant pedestrian street, curves back towards the stations from this spacious square.

Information
Pleventourist (Balkantourist) is at San Stefano 3, near the District Museum.

The business office of the Union of Bulgarian Motorists is at General Radeski 6a, a block from the main post office.

Money Pleven is a poor place to change money as the few banks and exchange offices give poor rates. Most banks won't take travellers' cheques, though you could try the large Obedinena Bâlgarska Banka, next to the Rostov Na Don Hotel (weekdays 8 to 11 am).

Post & Telecommunications The telephone centre is in the main post office next to the Town Hall and opposite the mauso-

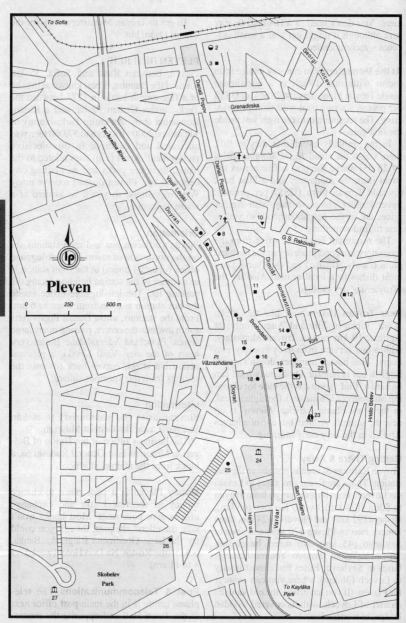

To Sofia

Georgi Kocev

Danail Popov

Grenadirska

Tuchenitsa River

Vasil Levski

Danail Popov

Doyran

G S Rakovski

Dimitâr Konstantinov

Pleven

0   250   500 m

Svoboda

Kiril

Pl
Vâzrazhdane

Doyran

Hristo Botev

Hemus

San Stefano

Vardar

Skobelev
Park

To Kayláka
Park

PLACES TO STAY

3   Hotel Pleven
11 Hotel Rostov na Don
12 Hotel Balkan

PLACES TO EAT

10 Restaurant Tsentral

OTHER

1   Railway Station
2   Bus Station
4   St Paraskeva Church
5   Orbita Student Travel
6   Railway Ticket Office
7   St Nicholas Church
8   Dramatic Theatre
9   National Revival Park
13 Monument to the Soviet Army
14 Puppet Theatre
15 City Art Gallery
16 The Common Grave
17 Former Party House
18 Concert Hall
19 Mausoleum
20 Town Hall
21 Post Office
22 Union of Bulgarian Motorists
23 Balkantourist/Pleventourist
24 District Historical Museum
25 Iliya Beshkov Art Gallery
26 Freedom Monument
27 1877 Panorama

leum (daily from 7 am to 10 pm). Pleven's telephone code is 064.

Travel Agencies Domestic and international train tickets are available at Rila, Zamenhov 2 (closed weekends). Across the street is Orbita Student Travel, Zamenhov 3.

Things to See

Begin your visit with a taxi ride to Pleven's most unique sight, the **1877 Panorama** on a hilltop above the city. Inside this large building (1977) is a fantastic 360° mural painting of the third assault on Pleven (11 September 1877). Another huge painting shows the final Turkish attempt (10 December 1877) to break out of their encirclement. Buy the brochure which explains the many details or request a guide who speaks a language you understand (no additional charge). Hand luggage must be left at the kiosk outside.

From the panorama, walk down the broad path east through **Skobelev Park**, veering to the left at the end. You'll see period artillery pieces, an ossuary and numerous monuments to the dead. In the centre of the monumental stairway leading back down to the city is a Freedom Monument and on the right at the bottom of the steps is the ultramodern **Iliya Beshkov Art Gallery** (1978), which is closed on Sunday. The **District Historical Museum** (closed Sunday and Monday), in the old yellow barracks (1888) across the street, has an impressive collection covering the entire history of Pleven and vicinity and includes theatrical and natural history exhibits.

Go through the park north of the museum towards the high white marble pillar marking the **Common Grave** of those who died in the struggle against fascism. This memorial faces the monumental fountain in the middle of ploschtad Vâzrazhdane, an attractive open space full of interest. In front of the fountain is the former Communist Party headquarters, and the **town hall** (1922), with its musical clock. Beside this is the **Mausoleum of Russian & Romanian Soldiers** (1907), a red-and-white striped building (closed Monday) commemorating the 31,000 Russian and 4500 Romanian soldiers who died in the Battle of Pleven. On the other side of the fountain, beyond the common grave, is the **City Art Gallery** (closed Sunday and Monday), with an extensive permanent collection of Bulgarian art in an Oriental-style building. The square merges north into ulitsa Vasil Levski at the **Monument to the Soviet Army** (1955).

Continue down this street to the **National Revival Park** on the right. This small park features old cannons and the house (closed Monday) where Osman Pasha surrendered his sword to Tsar Alexander II of Russia. Around the corner from the Dramatic Theatre is **St Nicholas Church** (1834),

BULGARIA

which was built below street level because at the time no church could be higher than a mosque. Now it's a good little museum of Bulgarian icons, in fact, it's half church, half museum, and in the early morning you'll see people lighting candles and praying before the captioned museum exhibits.

If you've still got some time, catch trolley bus No 3 or 7 from ulitsa Danail Popov to **Kaylâka Park**, four km south of the city at Mosta. This extensive park with very enjoyable walks between ponds and cliffs can keep you busy for hours.

Places to Stay
There isn't much of a selection of budget hotels at Pleven and the accommodation situation in Troyan is better, so try to plan your trip so you spend the night there.

Pleventourist, San Stefano 3 (closed weekends), grudgingly rents private rooms at US$11 a double.

A good choice is the '*Turisticheski dom*' *Hotel Turist* (☎ 34 352) near lovely Kaylâka Park, on a hill a few hundred metres from the Mosta trolley bus terminus (see Things to See above). As you enter the park from Mosta, look for a road along the left side of the park. This soon branches left and runs straight up to the hotel. It's US$6 per person with shared bath and show your YHA card for a possible discount. There's a restaurant upstairs.

At the other end of Kaylâka Park is the two-star *Kaylâka Hotel* (☎ 23 515). A hotel room will cost US$10/15 single/double with private facilities and there's a good restaurant on the terrace behind the hotel. To get there, take trolley bus No 3 or 7 from ulitsa Danail Popov to Mosta, then walk 25 minutes through the forest to the hotel. Bus No 4 from the train station runs right to the hotel, at last report leaving the station hourly on the half hour. The Kaylâka is soon to be privatised and renovated, so prices may go up.

Overlooking the bus station is the 12-storey, three-star *Hotel Pleven*. The 12-storey, two-star *Hotel Rostov Na Don* (☎ 23 892), in the centre of town, is

US$18/29 single/double with bath (breakfast extra).

Places to Eat
The egg breakfast at the café attached to the *Hotel Rostov Na Don* is a real treat.

One of Pleven's better restaurants is the *Tsentral* on ulitsa Dimitâr Konstantinov not far from St Nicholas Church (daily 11 am to 1 pm).

Pleven's most memorable meals are served at the *Peshterata Restaurant*, in a natural cave in Kaylâka Park between Mosta and the hotel. It caters to groups and in summer it can be hard for individuals to get seats, but there are several other good folk restaurants in the park.

Entertainment
Pleven's *Dramatic Theatre* is a fine old building (1869) on ulitsa Vasil Levski, and the *Concert Hall* stands on ploschtad Vâzrazhdane, beside the mausoleum. Also check the *puppet theatre* at ulitsa Dimiâtr Konstantinov 14, which is most likely to have a performance Sunday at 2 pm.

Theatre tickets are available from the Tickets Centre, Vasil Levski 149, which will have information on special events.

Getting There & Away
Trains to Sofia (194 km, four hours), Ruse (211 km, 2½ hours) and Varna (349 km, 5½ hours) are fairly frequent. (For two-thirds of its journey from Pleven to Sofia, the train follows the fantastic Iskâr Gorge.) For Vidin (287 km), change at Mezdra. For Veliko Târnovo, change at Gorna Oryahovitsa. You can pick up the single unreserved overnight train to Bucharest (319 km, eight hours) here in the middle of the night (but buy your open ticket beforehand at a Rila office). You won't get a seat.

For Troyan take a bus (twice daily, 70 km). If you don't catch the Troyan buses take the hourly bus to Lovech (35 km) and look for an onward bus or train to Troyan from there. The Troyan bus continues on to Karlovo, Hisarya and Plovdiv. In addition, there are two buses to Gabrovo (100 km) and another two to Vidin (226 km). The buses to Troyan, Hisarya, Plovdiv, Vidin or Gabrovo should be booked early at the station as they're sometimes full.

VIDIN (ВИДИН)

Vidin, the first major Bulgarian town on the Danube River below the famous Iron Gate, serves as a convenient entry or exit to/from Calafat, Romania, opposite. Actually, this is about the only reason to make the long trip up to Vidin.

History

On the site of the 3rd century BC Celtic settlement of Dunonia, the Romans built a fortress they called Bononia to control the Danube crossing here. Medieval Vidin was an important north-western bastion and trading centre of the Second Bulgarian Empire. In 1371, as Bulgaria wavered before the Ottoman onslaught, the king's son, Ivan Sratsimir, declared the region the independent Kingdom of Vidin with himself as ruler.

The fall of the city to the Turks in 1396 marked the completion of their conquest of Bulgaria. The Turks built an extensive city wall around Vidin, the various gates of which have survived to this day. By the 16th century, Vidin was the largest town in Bulgaria. As Turkish rule in turn weakened, a local pasha, Osman Pazvantoglu, declared his district independent of the sultan from 1792 to 1807. In 1878, Vidin was returned to Bulgaria by the Romanian army and in 1885 an attempt by Serbia to take the area was resisted.

Orientation

Central Vidin is very convenient, with the new riverboat terminal, train station and bus station all a block apart in the middle of town. The car ferry to/from Calafat is five km north. The left-luggage office in the train station is theoretically open 24 hours a day, but the staff take four long breaks, so note the posted shedule carefully.

Information

Try Balkantourist (☎ 24 976), General

Dondukov 7, or Orbita Student Travel at Tsar Simeon Veliki 6, just around the corner.

Money The receptionist at Hotel Bononiya changes travellers' cheques for 2% commission (no commission on cash).

The National Bank, at the back of the post-office building opposite the train station (weekdays 8 to 11 am), also charges 2% commission to change travellers' cheques, but tacks on a US$5 postage charge (no commission on cash). Their rate is a bit better than the hotel but worse than in Sofia, so only change the minimum.

Post & Telecommunications The telephone centre in the main post office opposite the train station is open daily from 7 am to 9.30 pm. Vidin's telephone code is 094.

Things to See

In the riverside park between the town centre and the fortress is the 18th century **Osman Pazvantoglu Mosque**, with a small religious library alongside. Nearby are the 17th century **Church of St Petka** and the 12th century **Church of St Panteleimon**. The former was partially sunk into the ground in deference to the mosque.

Vidin's main sight is the **Baba Vida Fortress** at the northern end of the park, overlooking the river. Baba Vida was built by the Bulgarians from the 10th to the 14th centuries on the ruined walls of 3rd century Roman Bononia. In the 17th century, the Turks rebuilt the fortress and today it's the best preserved medieval stone fortress in Bulgaria.

Places to Stay

Balkantourist (☎ 24 976), at General Dondukov 7 between the train station and Hotel Bononiya, has private rooms from US$5 per person.

The HI *Turisticheski dom 'Vidin'* (☎ 22 813), ulitsa Edelvays 3, just a few minutes' walk from the riverboat terminal in the centre of town, is no bargain at US$13 per person (or US$8 per person with a YHA card) with shared bath.

The six-storey, two-star *Hotel Bononiya* (☎ 23 031), facing a park near the river in the centre of town, is US$18/28 single/double with bath. The staff here are helpful.

Camping Nora (☎ 23 830) is just beyond the fairground, a couple of km west of town along ulitsa Ekzarh Yosif I. Bungalows are US$6 per person.

Getting There & Away

There are direct express trains between Vidin and Sofia (267 km, six hours). The overnight train between Sofia and Vidin has only 2nd-class carriages and no couchettes, but it's seldom overcrowded and you may even be able to stretch out across four seats. When boarding in Sofia be sure to get in a carriage labelled Vidin (and not Lom) as the train splits in half in the middle of the night.

There are two buses a day to Pleven (226 km).

The hydrofoil which formerly ran between Vidin and Ruse no longer operates. This makes the new Riverboat Terminal in the centre something of a white elephant as passenger boats no longer use it. Half the building is now an automobile showroom.

To/From Romania The Vidin-Calafat car ferry operates hourly all year from a landing five km north of Vidin. The crossing takes half an hour and you buy the ferry ticket on the boat. Only Bulgarians and Romanians may pay in leva or lei – foreigners must pay US$2 or DM3 in cash per person. Bicycles are either US$2 or free, depending on your luck. Take bus No 1 from beside the train station direct to the ferry. If you're arriving in Bulgaria, the bus stop for Vidin is about 500 metres down the road from customs. For pedestrians, the Vidin-Calafat crossing is a breeze since you can walk right past the endless line of trucks and shorter line of cars. If using this route, it's best to already have your Romanian or Bulgarian tourist visa and not plan to get it at the border. Turn to the Calafat section in the Romania chapter for more information.

Croatia

Croatia (Hrvatska) extends in an arc from the Danube River to Istria and south along the Adriatic coast to Dubrovnik. Roman Catholic since the 9th century, and under Hungary since 1102, Croatia only united with Orthodox Serbia in 1918. Croatia's centuries of resistance to Hungarian and Austrian domination were manifested in 1991 in its determined struggle for nationhood. Yet within Croatia itself, cultural differences remain between the Habsburg-influenced central European interior and the formerly Venetian Mediterranean coast.

The Croatian capital, Zagreb, is the country's cultural centre, and coastal Croatian towns like Poreč, Rovinj, Pula, Mali Lošinj, Krk, Rab, Zadar, Šibenik, Trogir, Split, Hvar, Korčula and Dubrovnik all have well-preserved historic centres with lots to see. Before 1991 the strikingly beautiful Mediterranean landscapes of this 56,538-sq-km country attracted nearly 10 million foreign visitors a year. Traditionally, tourism has been focused along the Adriatic coast where the combination of history, natural beauty, good climate, clear water and easy access are unsurpassed. There are numerous seaside resorts and the swimming is good. The atmosphere is relaxed – there are few rules about behaviour and few formalities. Since 1960 nudism has been promoted and Croatia is now *the* place to go in Europe to practise naturism.

When Yugoslavia split apart in 1991, 80% of the country's tourist resorts ended up in Croatia and only a few (such as Plitvice National Park) were cut off from the rest of Croatia. Istria and the lovely Adriatic islands were largely untouched by the fighting and remained peaceful and safe even during the dark days when Osijek, Vukovar and Dubrovnik were spread across the world's headlines. The bad publicity brought tourism almost to a standstill and although Istria and Krk are again popular, it will probably take years before the millions of annual visitors

return to Dalmatia. The lack of tourists means that south of Krk you'll have some beautiful places all to yourself.

Croatia at War

In mid-1991 heavy fighting erupted between Serbs and Croats in areas of Croatia bordering Bosnia-Hercegovina and Serbia. A year later the conflict spread to Bosnia-Hercegovina, with even more devastating results. Though Croatia has been relatively quiet since a UN-sponsored cease-fire took effect in January 1992, instability continues throughout the region.

For travellers Croatia can be divided into three areas. The first includes Zagreb, Istria and the islands of Lošinj, Cres, Krk and Rab, all of which are perfectly normal and quite safe to visit. Included in the second category are the Adriatic resorts right down to Dubrovnik. These are also safe and the coast is as enchanting as ever, though you must be prepared for inconveniences such as hotels being used as emergency housing for refugees, museums closed with the exhibits in storage for safekeeping, protective scaffolding covering monuments etc. The third area includes Plitvice and Krka national parks which are presently held by Serbian separatists and inaccessible from the rest of Croatia. The road and railway lines between Zagreb and Belgrade remain cut, and all travel between Croatia and Yugoslavia is via Hungary.

You might expect Croatia to be a depressing place because of the war, but this is not so. On the outside, life goes on seemingly unaffected by the nearby destruction. It's only when you talk to people that you learn the real price in the form of lowered living standards, disrupted lives, relatives in other areas killed or forced to flee their homes etc. Such insights bring you closer to the human component behind the headlines, which is what real travel is all about.

Facts about the Country

HISTORY

In 229 BC the Romans began their conquest of the indigenous Illyrians, establishing a colony at Salona (near Split) in Dalmatia. Emperor Augustus extended the empire and created the provinces of Illyricum (Dalmatia and Bosnia) and Pannonia (Croatia). In 285 AD, Emperor Diocletian decided to retire to his palace fortress in Split, today the greatest Roman ruin in Eastern Europe. When the empire was divided in 395, what is now Slovenia, Croatia and Bosnia-Hercegovina stayed with the Western Roman Empire, while present-day Serbia, Kosovo and Macedonia went to the Eastern Roman Empire, later known as the Byzantine Empire. Visigoth, Hun and Lombard invasions marked the fall of the Western Roman Empire in the 5th century.

Around the year 625, Slavic Croat tribes entered this region from present-day Poland and by 800 they had accepted Christianity. Under Frankish domination the Croats picked up the legacy of Roman civilisation, forming a kingdom under the Dalmatian duke Tomislav in 925. This prospered through the 11th century, but in 1101 Romanised Croatia united with Hungary to defend itself against the Orthodox Byzantine Empire. In 1242 a Tatar invasion devastated both Hungary and Croatia.

In the 14th century the Turks began pushing into the Balkans, defeating the Serbs in 1389 and the Hungarians in 1526. In 1527 Croatia turned to the Habsburgs of Austria for protection and remained under their control until 1918. The Adriatic coast was threatened but never conquered by the Turks, and, after the naval Battle of Lepanto in 1571, when Spanish and Venetian forces wiped out the Turkish fleet, this threat was much reduced. Venice occupied Istria and Dalmatia but the Republic of Dubrovnik maintained its independence. To form a buffer against the Turks, the Austrians invited Serbs to settle the 'Vojna Krajina' (military frontier) along the Bosnian border. The Serbs in the borderlands had an autonomous administration under Austrian control and these areas were not reincorporated into Croatia until 1881.

After Venice was shattered by Napoleonic France in 1797, the French occupied southern Croatia, entering Dubrovnik in 1808. Napoleon's merger of Dalmatia, Istria and Slovenia into the 'Illyrian provinces' in 1809 stimulated the concept of South Slav ('Yugoslav') unity. After Napoleon's defeat at Waterloo in 1815, Austria-Hungary moved in to pick up the pieces along the coast.

A revival of Croatian cultural and political life began in 1835. In 1848 a liberal democratic revolution led by Josip Jelačić was suppressed, but serfdom was abolished. An 1868 reform transferred Croatia from Austria to Hungary, united the territory with Hungarian Slavonia and granted a degree of internal autonomy. Dalmatia remained under Austria. During the decade before the outbreak of WW I, some 50,000 Croats emigrated to the USA.

With the defeat of the Austro-Hungarian

Croatia
(Hrvatska)

AUSTRIA

ITALY

SLOVENIA

Ljubljana

TRIESTE

Sava *River*

Čakovec

NAGYKANIZA

VARAŽDIN

Koprivnica

Đurđevac

ZAGREB

River

HUNGARY

Pécs

Barcs

Bjelovar

Virovitica

Drava *River*

D Miholjac

Beli Manastir

CROATIA

KARLOVAC

SISAK

Novska

Našice

OSIJEK

Umag

Poreč

Opatija Rijeka

Delnice

Pazin

Plomin

Crikvenica

Ogulin

Glina

Slavonska
Požega

Nova
Gradiška

Đakovo

Vukovar

Vinkovci

Rovinj

Krk

Slunj

Bosanska
Dubica

SLAVONSKI
BROD

Cres

Senj

Plitvice

Bosanski
Novi

Sava *River*

PULA

ISTRIA

Rab

Jablanac

BANJA LUKA

Bijeljina

Mali Lošinj

Pag

Karlobag

Starigrad
Paklenica

Obrovac

Jajce

ADRIATIC
SEA

ZADAR

Biograd

Knin

DALMATIA

SARAJEVO

Šibenik

Sinj

BOSNIA-
HERCEGOVINA

Trogir **Split**

Omiš

Imotski

Brač

Makarska

Mostar

Međugorje

Hvar

Ploče

0   50   100 km

Vela Luka

Korčula

YUGOSLAVIA

ITALY

Serbian Occupied Areas

Mljet

DUBROVNIK

Herceg-
Novi

CROATIA

empire in WW I, Croatia became part of the Kingdom of Serbs, Croats and Slovenes (called Yugoslavia after 1929) with a centralised government in Belgrade. This result was strongly resisted by Croatian nationalists who organised the Paris assassination of King Alexander I in 1934. In 1939 an administrative reorganisation granted Croatia some regional autonomy as the 'Banovina Hrvatska'. Italy had been promised the Adriatic coast as an incentive to join the war against Austria-Hungary in 1915 and it held much of northern Dalmatia from 1918 to 1943.

After the German invasion of Yugoslavia in March 1941, a puppet government dominated by the fascist Ustaša movement was set up in Croatia and Bosnia-Hercegovina under Ante Pavelić (who fled to Argentina after the war). At first the Ustaša tried to expel all Serbs from Croatia to Serbia, but when the Germans stopped this because of the problems it was causing, the Ustaša launched an extermination campaign which surpassed even that of the Nazis in scale, brutally murdering some 350,000 ethnic Serbs, Jews and Gypsies. The Ustaša program called for 'one-third of Serbs killed, one-third expelled and one-third converted to Catholicism'.

Not all Croats supported these policies, however. Marshal Tito was himself a Croat and tens of thousands of others fought bravely with his partisans. Massacres of Croats conducted by Serbian Četnik partisans in southern Croatia and Bosnia forced almost all antifascist Croats into the communist ranks, where they joined the numerous Serbs trying to defend themselves from the Ustaša. In all, about a million people died violently in a war which was fought mostly in Croatia and Bosnia-Hercegovina.

Recent History

Postwar Croatia was granted republic status within the Yugoslav Federation. Though the national capital remained in Belgrade, Tito chose Brijuni (Brioni) near Pula as his summer residence and spent six months a year there. During the 1960s Croatia and Slovenia moved far ahead of the southern republics economically, leading to demands for greater autonomy. This 'Croatian Spring' caused a backlash and purge of reformers in 1971 and increasing economic inertia due to a cumbersome system of 'self-management' of state enterprises by employees. After Tito died in 1980 the paralysis spread to government as the federal presidency began rotating annually among the republics.

In 1989 severe repression of the Albanian majority in Serbia's Kosovo province sparked renewed fears of Serbian hegemony and heralded the end of the Yugoslav Federation. With political changes sweeping Eastern Europe, many Croats felt the time had come to end more than four decades of communist rule and attain complete autonomy into the bargain. In the free elections of April 1990 Franjo Tudjman's Croatian Democratic Union (Hrvatska Demokratska Zajednica) easily defeated the old Communist Party. On 22 December 1990 a new Croatian constitution was promulgated, changing the status of Serbs in Croatia from that of a 'constituent nation' to a national minority.

The constitution's failure to guarantee minority rights stimulated the 600,000-strong ethnic Serbian community within Croatia to demand autonomy and continued protection by the Serbian-led Yugoslav army, and in early 1991 Serbian extremists within Croatia staged provocations designed to force federal military intervention. A May 1991 referendum (boycotted by the Serbs) produced a 93% vote in favour of independence, but when Croatia declared independence on 25 June 1991, the Serbian enclave of Krajina proclaimed its independence from Croatia.

Heavy fighting broke out in Krajina (the area around Knin north of Split), Baranja (the area north of the Drava River opposite Osijek) and Slavonia (the region west of the Danube). The 180,000-member, 2000-tank Yugoslav People's Army, dominated by Serbian communists, began to intervene on its own authority in support of Serbian irregulars under the pretext of halting ethnic violence. After European Community (EC) mediation, Croatia agreed to freeze its independence declaration for three months to avoid bloodshed.

In the three months following 25 June, a quarter of Croatia fell to Serbian militias and the federal army. After 13 July, when Yugoslav jets attacked Croat villages near Vukovar, the army stopped pretending to be a neutral arbitrator and joined openly in the war. In September the Croatian Government ordered a blockade of 32 federal military installations in the republic, lifting morale and gaining much-needed military equipment. The federal troops were only allowed to leave after laying down their weapons, and in Varaždin alone some 50 tanks and 60 armoured vehicles were taken. In response, the Yugoslav navy blockaded the Adriatic coast and laid siege to the strategic town of Vukovar on the Danube.

Meanwhile, long-range shelling of towns and villages by the federal army terrorised the inhabitants, and hundreds of thousands of people were forced to flee their homes, with 10,000 Croats banished from Ilok on the Danube alone. The many atrocities carried out by Serbian irregulars and Croatian paramilitary units have been carefully documented by the human rights group Helsinki Watch.

In early October 1991 the federal army and Montenegrin militia moved against Dubrovnik to protest against the ongoing blockade of their garrisons in Croatia, and on 7 October the presidential palace in Zagreb was rocketed by Yugoslav air-force jets in an unsuccessful assassination attempt against President Tudjman. As outrage spread over the siege of historic Dubrovnik, the EC ordered punitive sanctions against Serbia and Montenegro. On 19 November the heroic Croatian city of Vukovar finally fell when the army culminated a bloody three-month siege by concentrating 600 tanks and 30,000 soldiers there. During six months of fighting in Croatia 10,000 people died, hundreds of thousands fled and tens of thousands of homes were deliberately destroyed.

The EC's envoy, Lord Carrington, and other mediators cobbled together successive cease-fires which were soon broken. However, in early December the United Nations special envoy, Cyrus Vance, began more successful negotiations with Serbia over the deployment of a 14,000-member UN Protection Force (UNPROFOR) in the Serbian-held areas of Croatia. Beginning on 3 January 1992, a 15th cease-fire generally held. The federal army was allowed to withdraw from its bases inside Croatia without having to shamefully surrender its weapons and thus tensions diminished.

Meanwhile, Germany brought strong pressure to bear on its EC colleagues to recognise quickly the independence of Slovenia and Croatia, even though minority rights had not yet been guaranteed. When the three-month moratorium on independence expired on 8 October 1991, Croatia declared full independence. To fulfil a condition for EC recognition, in December the Croatian Parliament belatedly amended its constitution to protect minority and human rights, and in January 1992 the EC recognised Croatia. This was followed three months later by US recognition and in May 1992 Croatia was admitted to the United Nations.

The UN peace plan in Krajina was supposed to have led to the disarming of local Serb paramilitary formations, the repatriation of refugees and the return of the region to Croatia, but instead it only froze the existing situation and offered no permanent solution. The Srpska Krajina Republic proclaimed here on 19 December 1991 remains unrecognised.

In January 1993 the Croatian army suddenly launched an offensive in southern Krajina, pushing the Serbs back as much as 24 km in some areas and recapturing strategic points such as the site of the destroyed Maslenica bridge, Zemunik Airport near Zadar and the Perućac hydroelectric dam in the hills between Split and Bosnia-Hercegovina. The Krajina Serbs have vowed never to accept rule from Zagreb and in June 1993 they voted overwhelmingly to join the Bosnian Serbs (and eventually Greater Serbia). It would be unthinkable for any Croatian government to renounce sovereignty over the disputed areas and there will be no lasting peace in ex-Yugoslavia until this outstanding problem is settled.

GEOGRAPHY

At 56,538 sq km, Croatia is half the size of present-day Yugoslavia in area and population. The republic swings around like a boomerang from the Pannonian plains of Slavonia between the Sava, Drava and Danube rivers, across hilly central Croatia to the Istrian Peninsula, then south through Dalmatia along the rugged Adriatic coast.

The narrow Croatian coastal belt at the foot of the Dinaric Alps is only about 600 km long as the crow flies, but it's so indented that the actual length is 1778 km. If the 4012 km of coastline around the offshore islands is added to the total, the length becomes 5790 km. Most of the 'beaches' along this jagged coast consist of slabs of rock sprinkled with naturists – don't come expecting to find sand. Beach shoes are worth having along these rocky, urchin-infested shores. Officially there are no private beaches in Croatia, but you must pay to use 'managed' beaches.

Croatia's offshore islands are every bit as

beautiful as those in Greece. There are 1185 islands and islets along this tectonically submerged Adriatic coastline, 66 of them inhabited. The largest are Cres, Krk, Lošinj, Pag and Rab in the north; Dugi otok in the middle; and Brač, Hvar, Korčula, Mljet and Vis in the south. Most are elongated from north-west to south-east and barren with high mountains that drop right into the sea.

When the Yugoslav Federation collapsed, seven of its finest national parks ended up in Croatia. On the coastal islands are three national parks: Brijuni near Pula, Kornati near Zadar; and Mljet near Korčula. Krka National Park near Šibenik; and Plitvice National Park between Zagreb and Zadar feature a series of cascades. A coastal gorge can be seen at Paklenica National Park near Zadar. Mountainous Risnjak National Park near Delnice, east of Rijeka, is accessible, but Plitvice, Paklenica and Krka are closed. (The civil war in ex-Yugoslavia actually began at Plitvice on 31 March 1991 when Serbian Četniks took control of the park headquarters and began the systematic expulsion of 4000 Croats from the surrounding area. A Croatian policeman, Josip Jović, murdered at Plitvice by Serb gunmen that Easter Sunday, became the first casualty in this senseless war.)

ECONOMY

The former communist government of Yugoslavia emphasised heavy industry, especially in aluminium, chemicals, petroleum and shipbuilding. Today Croatia is the world's third-largest shipbuilder, with most of the output from the shipyards of Pula, Rijeka and Split intended for export. The chemical industry is centred at Krk, Rijeka, Split and Zagreb, machine-tool manufacture at Karlovac, Slavonski Brod and Zagreb, heavy electrical engineering at Zagreb and textiles at Zagreb and in north-west Croatia.

Eighty per cent of Croatia's petroleum comes from local oil wells – in fact most of the wells of ex-Yugoslavia were in Croatia, north and east of Zagreb. Fortunately these wells were outside the area of the recent war, though the refinery at Sisak burned down

after being hit by federal shells. In the past a third of Croatia's national income has come from tourism but in 1991 and 1992 Croatia received few visitors. By 1993, however, Germans, Austrians and some Italians had discovered that they could visit Istria and Krk without the slightest danger and these areas are again crowded. Almost no-one dared visit Dalmatia in 1993, though they easily could have.

The collectivisation of agriculture just after WW II failed and private farmers with small plots continue to work most of the land. The interior plains produce fruit, vegetables and grains (especially corn and wheat), while olives and grapes are cultivated along the coast.

Since independence Croatia has had to completely reorient its trade after the loss of markets in the southern regions of former Yugoslavia. In 1992, Italy, Germany and Slovenia together accounted for well over half of Croatia's imports and exports. Due to the war, the average wage is only US$125 a month, and a high percentage of the population is unemployed (16.9% in 1993), with the number due to increase sharply if troops are demobilised. The current policy of overvaluing the kuna penalises exporters while making imports cheap, a situation that will be difficult to sustain in the long term, especially with a war going on.

POPULATION & PEOPLE

Of Croatia's nearly five million inhabitants, 78% are Croats and 12% Serbs. Small communities of Slavic Muslims, Hungarians, Slovenes, Italians, Czechs and Albanians also exist. The Croats are mostly Roman Catholics; the Serbs, Orthodox Christians. Some 750,000 war refugees from Bosnia-Hercegovina and the Serb-held areas of Croatia now exist in precarious conditions in Croatia.

Another million Croats live in the other states of ex-Yugoslavia, especially Bosnia-Hercegovina, northern Vojvodina and around the Bay of Kotor in Montenegro. Some 2.3 million ethnic Croats live abroad, including almost 1.5 million in the USA,

270,000 in Germany, 240,000 in Australia, 150,000 in Canada and 150,000 in Argentina. Pittsburgh and Buenos Aires have the largest Croatian communities outside Europe. The largest cities in Croatia are Zagreb (one million), Split (300,000), Rijeka (225,000), Osijek (175,000) and Zadar (150,000).

Sadly, ethnic discrimination has been institutionalised in the Law of Citizenship passed by the Croatian Parliament in October 1991. It states that to become a citizen non-Croats (including Serbs born in Croatia) must demonstrate a knowledge of the Croatian language and Latin alphabet, and show an acceptance of Croatian culture. Dual citizenship is abolished and children from mixed marriages must declare themselves Croats to become citizens able to own property and obtain a work permit. State employees who refuse to take an oath of loyalty to Croatia are fired from their jobs.

ARTS

The work of sculptor Ivan Meštrović (1883-1962) is seen in town squares all around Croatia. Besides creating public monuments, Meštrović was responsible for designing imposing buildings such as the circular Croatian History Museum in Zagreb (presently closed). Both his sculpture and architecture display a powerful classical restraint he learned from Rodin. Meštrović's studio in Zagreb and his retirement home at Split have been made into galleries of his work.

Music

The folk music of the Croats bears many influences. The *kolo*, a lively Slavic round dance in which men and women alternate in the circle, is accompanied by Gypsy-style violinists or players of the *tambura*, a three- or five-string mandolin popular throughout Croatia. The measured guitar-playing or rhythmic accordions of Dalmatia have a gentle Italian air.

A recommended recording available locally on compact disc (DD-0030) is *Narodne Pjesme i Plesovi Sjeverne Hrvatske* (Northern Croatian Folk Songs & Dances)

by the Croatian folkloric ensemble 'Lado'. The 22 tracks on this album represent nine regions, with everything from haunting Balkan voices reminiscent of Bulgaria to lively Mediterranean dance rhythms.

LANGUAGE

As a result of history, tourism and the number of returned 'guest workers' from Germany, German is the most commonly spoken second language in Croatia. Many people in Istria understand Italian, and throughout Slovenia and Croatia, English is popular among the young.

Croatian is a South Slavic language, as are Serbian, Slovene, Macedonian and Bulgarian. Prior to 1991 both Croatian and Serbian were considered dialects of a single language known as Serbo-Croatian, a term rendered obsolete by events. As a result of civil war in former Yugoslavia, the local languages are being revised, so spellings and idioms may change. The most obvious difference, however, is that Serbian is written in Cyrillic script and Croatian in Roman script.

Geographical terms worth knowing are *aleja* (walkway), *cesta* (road), *donji* (lower), *gora* (hill), *grad* (town), *jezero* (lake), *krajina* (region), *luka* (harbour), *malo* (little, novo (new), *obala* (bank, shore), *otok* (island), *planina* (mountain), *polje* (valley), *prolaz* (strait), *put* (path), *rijeka* (river), *selo* (village), *šetalište* (way), *stanica* (station, stop), *stari* (old), *šuma* (forest), *sveti* (saint), *toplice* (spa), *trg* (square), *ulica* (street), *veliko* (big), *vrata* (pass), *vrh* (peak) and *zaljev* (bay).

Two words everyone should know are *ima* (there is) and *nema* (there isn't). If you make just a small effort to learn a few words, you'll distinguish yourself from the packaged tourists and be greatly appreciated by the local people.

Lonely Planet's *Mediterranean Europe Phrasebook* includes a useful chapter on the Serbian and Croatian languages with translations of key words and phrases from each appearing side by side, providing a clear comparison of the languages.

CROATIA

Pronunciation

The spelling of Serbian and Croatian is phonetically based: almost every word is written exactly as it is pronounced and every letter is pronounced. With regard to the position of stress, only one rule can be given: the last syllable of a word is never stressed. In most cases the accent falls on the first vowel in the word.

There are 30 letters in the Croatian alphabet. Many letters are pronounced as in English – the following are some specific pronunciations.

c	'ts' as in 'cats'
ć	'tch' as the 't' in 'future'
č	'tch' as in 'chop'
đ	'dj' as the 'di' in 'soldier'
dž	'j' as in 'just'
g	'g' as in 'got'
j	'y' as in 'young'
lj	'ly' as the 'li' in 'colliery'
nj	'ny' as in 'canyon'
š	'sh' as in 'hush'
ž	'zh' as the 's' in 'treasure'

The principal difference between Serbian and Croatian is in the pronunciation of the vowel **e** in certain words. A long **e** in Serbian becomes **ije** in Croatian (for example, *reka, rijeka*, 'river'), and a short **e** in Serbian becomes **je** in Croatian (for example, *pesma, pjesma*, 'song'). Sometimes, however, the vowel **e** is the same in both languages, as in *selo*, 'village'. There are also a number of variations in vocabulary.

Greetings & Civilities

hello	*bok*
good morning	*dobro jutro*
good evening	*dobro večer*
goodbye	*doviđenja*
please	*molim*
thank you	*hvala Vam*
excuse me/forgive me	*oprostite*
I am sorry.	*žao mi je*
yes	*da*
no	*ne*

Small Talk

I don't understand.	*Ne razumijem.*
Could you write it down?	*Možete li napisati?*
What is it called?	*Kako se zove?*
Where do you live?	*Gdje stanujete?*
What work do you do?	*Gdje ste zaposleni?*
I am a student.	*Ja sam student.*
I am very happy.	*Veoma sam sretan.*

Accommodation

youth hostel	*omladinsko odmaralište*
camping ground	*kamp*
private room	*privatna soba*
How much is it?	*Koliko košta?*
Is that the price per person?	*Je li to cijena po osobi?*
Is that the total price?	*Je li to ukupna cjena?*
Are there any extra charges?	*Ima li dodatnih troškove?*
Do I pay extra for showers?	*Da li se tuširanje posebno plaća?*
Where is there a cheaper hotel?	*Gdje ima jeftiniji hotel?*
Should I make a reservation?	*Trebam li napraviti rezervazciju?*
single room	*jednokrevetna soba*
double room	*dvokrevetna soba*
It is very noisy.	*Veoma je bučno.*
Where is the toilet?	*Gdje je WC?*

Getting Around

What time does it leave?	*Kada odlazi?*
When is the first bus?	*Kada ide prvi autobus?*
When is the last bus?	*Kada ide posljednji autobus?*
When is the next bus?	*Kada ide sljedeći autobus?*
That's too soon.	*To je prerano.*
When is the next one after that?	*Kada ide sljedeći nakon toga?*
How long does the trip take?	*Koliko dugo traje putovanje?*
arrival	*dolazak*
departure	*odlazak*

timetable	*vozni red*
Where is the bus stop?	*Gdje je autobusna postaja?*
Where is the train station?	*Gdje je željeznička postaja?*
Where is the left-luggage room?	*Gdje je garderoba?*

Around Town

Just a minute.	*Samo minuta.*
Where is ... ?	*Gdje je ...?*
the bank	*banka*
the post office	*pošta*
the tourist information office	*turistički informativni centar*
the museum	*muzej*
Where are you going?	*Kuda idete?*
I am going to ...	*Idem do ...*
Where is it?	*Gdje je?*
I can't find it.	*Ne mogu naći.*
Is it far?	*Je li daleko?*
Please show me on the map.	*Molim, pokažite mi na karti.*
left	*lijevo*
right	*desno*
straight ahead	*pravo*
I want ...	*Želim ...*
Do I need permission?	*Je li potrebna dozvola?*

Entertainment

Where can I buy a ticket?	*Gdje mogu kupiti kartu?*
Where can I refund this ticket?	*Gdje mogu vratiti ovu kartu?*
Is this a good seat?	*Je li to dobro mjesto?*
at the front	*naprijed*
ticket	*kartu*

Food

I do not eat meat.	*Ne jedem meso.*
self-service cafetaria	*restauracija sa samo-posluživanjem*
grocery store	*trgovina namirnica*
fish	*riba*
pork	*svinjetina*

soup	*juha*
salad	*salata*
fresh vegetables	*svježe povrće*
milk	*mlijeko*
bread	*kruh*
sugar	*šećer*
ice cream	*sladoled*
coffee	*kava*
tea	*čaj*
mineral water	*mineralna voda*
beer	*pivo*
wine	*vino*
hot/cold	*vruće/hladno*

Shopping

Where can I buy one?	*Gdje mogu kupiti jednu?*
How much does it cost?	*Koliko košta?*
That's too expensive.	*To je preskupo.*
Is there a cheaper one?	*Ima li jeftinije?*

Time & Dates

today	*danas*
tonight	*večeras*
tomorrow	*sutra*
the day after tomorrow	*prekosutra*
What time does it open?	*Kada se otvara?*
What time does it close?	*Kada se zatvara?*
open	*otvoreno*
closed	*zatvoreno*
in the morning	*ujutro*
in the evening	*navečer*
every day	*svaki dan*
At what time?	*U koliko sati?*
when?	*kada?*

Monday	*ponedjeljak*
Tuesday	*utorak*
Wednesday	*srijeda*
Thursday	*četvrtak*
Friday	*petak*
Saturday	*subota*
Sunday	*nedjelja*

January	*sječanj*
February	*veljača*
March	*ožujak*
April	*travanj*
May	*svibanj*
June	*lipanj*
July	*srpanj*
August	*kolovoz*
September	*rujan*
October	*listopad*
November	*studeni*
December	*prosinac*

Numbers

1	*jedan*
2	*dva*
3	*tri*
4	*četiri*
5	*pet*
6	*šest*
7	*sedam*
8	*osam*
9	*devet*
10	*deset*
11	*jedanaest*
12	*dvanaest*
13	*trinaest*
14	*četrnaest*
15	*petnaest*
16	*šesnaest*
17	*sedamnaest*
18	*osamnaest*
19	*devetneast*
20	*dvadeset*
21	*dvadeset jedan*
22	*dvadeset dva*
23	*dvadeset tri*
30	*trideset*
40	*četerdeset*
50	*pedeset*
60	*šezdeset*
70	*sedamdeset*
80	*osamdeset*
90	*devedeset*
100	*sto*
1000	*tisuća*
10,000	*deset tisuća*
1,000,000	*milion*

Facts for the Visitor

VISAS & EMBASSIES

Visitors from Australia, Canada, New Zealand and the USA require a visa to enter Croatia but visas are issued free of charge at Croatian consulates or at the border itself. United Kingdom nationals don't require a visa. Visas are valid for a maximum of three months with extensions possible.

While in Croatia, you're supposed to have your passport with you at all times. If you stay at a hotel or camping ground, the staff may keep your passport at the desk and give you a stamped card that serves the same purpose.

Many camping grounds in Croatia are happy to hold your camping carnet instead of the passport – you can't cash travellers' cheques without a passport.

Croatian Embassies

Croatian embassies and consulates around the world include the following:

Australia
  6 Bulwarra Close, O'Malley, Canberra, ACT 2606 (☎ 062-86 6988)
  9-24 Albert Rd, South Melbourne, Victoria 3205 (☎ 03-699 2633)
  379 Kent St, Level 4, Sydney, NSW 2000 (☎ 02-299 8899)
  78 Mill Point Rd, South Perth, WA 6151 (☎ 09-474 1620)
Canada
  116 Albert St, Suite 606, Ottawa, ON K1P 5G3 (☎ 613-230 7351)
  918 Dundas St E, Suite 302, Mississauga, ON L4Y 2B8 (☎ 416-277 1198)
New Zealand
  131 Lincoln Rd, Henderson, Box 83200, Edmonton, Auckland, New Zealand (☎ 09-836 5481)
UK
  18-21 Jermyn St, London SW1Y 6HP (☎ 0171-434 2946)
USA
  Congressional House 505, 236 Massachusetts Ave NE, Washington, DC 20002 (☎ 202-543 5580)

For the addresses of Croatian embassies in Bucharest, Budapest, Ljubljana, Prague and

Sofia, turn to the sections of this book relating to those cities.

MONEY

In January 1992, Croatia issued its own currency, the Croatian dinar (HRD) – banknotes which bore the portrait of astronomer Rudjer Bošković (1711-87). In the Serb-occupied areas Yugoslav dinars continued to be used.

In May 1994 the dinar was replaced by the *kuna* which takes it's name from the marten, a fox-like animal whose pelt served as a means of exchange in the Middle Ages. The new currency was originally going to be called the *kruna* (crown) but this was abandoned after protests that Croatia was reviving the currency of the wartime Ustaša regime.

In the past, inflation has been fierce (634% in 1992 and 1517% in 1993) but in October 1993 the Croatian government tightened the money supply and the dinar stabilised in preparation for the introduction of the kuna which is intended to be convertible on world markets.

You can easily verify if this is really so by asking if it's possible to convert excess kuna back into hard currency (governments in this part of the world often make misleading claims that their currencies are convertible, when in practice they are not).

There are numerous places to change money, all offering similar rates, so just ask at any travel agency for the location of the nearest. Banks and exchange offices keep long hours and both deduct a commission of 1.5% to change cash or travellers' cheques. Only change what you're sure you'll need because it's uncertain whether the kuna is really convertible back into hard currency. Visa credit cards are not accepted for cash advances in Croatia (American Express, MasterCard and Diners Club cards are said to be OK).

You're only allowed to import or export Croatian banknotes up to a value of around US$50 but there's no reason to do either. Hungarian currency is difficult to change in Croatia.

Black marketeers offer about 3% more than the official bank rate for cash on the street, with Deutschmarks (DM) being the preferred currency. These unofficial exchanges usually take place in main post offices or at train stations and are not dangerous. However, the small return makes the black market hardly worth seeking out and in practice you'll seldom be approached.

Costs

The government deliberately overvalues the kuna to obtain cheap foreign currency. Hotel prices are set in hard currency and thus are fairly constant, though you pay in Croatian kuna calculated at the daily official rate. Accommodation is expensive, partly because the rates are linked to hard currency, but more due to a two-price system in which foreigners pay several times more than locals for hotels, private rooms, camp sites etc. Transport, concert and theatre tickets are inexpensive because everyone pays the same price, and food is reasonably priced for Europe.

Average prices per person are US$7 to US$20 for a private room, US$3 to US$5 for a meal at a self-service and US$4 to US$6 for an average intercity bus fare. It's not that hard to do it on US$30 a day if you stay in hostels or private rooms and you'll pay less if you camp and self-cater, eating only things such as bread, cheese and canned fish or meat with yoghurt or wine (cooking facilities are seldom provided). A student card will get you half-price admission at some museums and galleries.

Your daily expenses will come way down if you can find a private room to use as a base for exploring nearby areas. Coastal towns which lend themselves to this include Rovinj, Mali Lošinj, Rab, Split, Korčula and Dubrovnik.

You'll get more of a feel for your surroundings if you spend four nights in a place, and using a town as a base allows you to make day trips without hassles over luggage or worrying about where you'll sleep. You will also escape the 30% to 50% surcharges on private rooms rented for under four nights.

CROATIA

If it still seems expensive, keep in mind that the average monthly income in Croatia is US$125, so it's much more difficult for the Croats. Most only manage to make ends meet because they still receive subsidised housing, health care, education etc, and many hold down two or three jobs. Relatives abroad send money home and country people grow much of their own food. Others have savings from the good years before 1991. Like people in the West, Croats buy consumer goods on credit and they're sharp dressers. It's difficult to understand how people manage to keep up appearances so well when the figures say their country is bankrupt.

Cheating The official dual pricing for accommodation has set a dangerous precedent. Some waiters in the main resorts now feel it's OK to exploit foreigners who may not understand the currency or prices, aren't regular customers and can't complain anyway. Check your bill in any establishment which caters mostly to tourists as they *habitually* overcharge. Avoid any eating or drinking place which doesn't have a menu with prices clearly stated. If the drinks aren't listed on the menu, they'll be about double what you'd expect. At coffee bars a standard trick is to serve foreigners their coffee in a larger cup for double the price. Point to a small cup if that's all you want. Even ice-cream sellers and bartenders will cheat you unless you check the price beforehand. Also beware of being short-changed. If you're sure you've been cheated, you can always ask for the *knjiga žalbe* (complaints book), though it's unlikely that private establishments will have one.

Tipping

If you're served fairly and well at a restaurant, you should round the bill up as you're paying. (Don't leave money on the table.) If a service charge has been added to the bill no tip is necessary. Bar bills and taxi fares can also be rounded up. Tour guides on day excursions expect to be tipped.

CLIMATE & WHEN TO GO

The climate varies from Mediterranean along the Adriatic coast to continental inland. The high coastal mountains help to shield the coast from the cold northerly winds, making for an early spring and late autumn. In spring and early summer a sea breeze called the *maestral* keeps the temperature down along the coast. Winter winds include the cold *bura* from the north and humid *široko* from the south.

The sunny coastal areas experience hot, dry summers and mild, rainy winters, while the interior regions are cold in winter and warm in summer. Because of a warm current flowing north up the Adriatic coast, sea temperatures never fall below 10°C in winter, and in August they go as high as 26°C. You can swim in the sea from mid-June until late September. The resorts south of Split are the warmest.

May is a nice month to travel along the Adriatic coast, with good weather and few tourists. June and September are also good but in July and August all Europe arrives and prices soar. September is perhaps the best month since it's not as hot as summer, though the sea remains warm, the crowds will have thinned out as children return to school, off-season accommodation rates will be in place and fruit such as figs and grapes will be abundant. In April and October it may be too cool for camping but the weather should still be fine along the coast, and private rooms will be plentiful and inexpensive.

SUGGESTED ITINERARIES

Depending on the length of your stay, you might want to see and do the following things:

Two days
  Visit Zagreb.
One week
  Visit Zagreb, Split and Dubrovnik.
Two weeks
  Visit Zagreb and all of Dalmatia.
One month
  Visit all areas covered in this chapter.

TOURIST OFFICES

Municipal tourist offices and any office

marked 'Turist Biro' will have free brochures and will be a good source of information on local events. These are found in Dubrovnik, Pula, Rijeka, Split and Zagreb. Most towns also have an office selling theatre and concert tickets.

Tourist information is also dispensed by commercial travel agencies such as Arenatourist, Atlas, Dalmacijaturist, Generalturist, Kompas, Croatia Express and Kvarner Express, which also arrange private rooms, sightseeing tours etc. Keep in mind that these are profit-making businesses, so don't be put off if you're asked to pay for a own plan etc. The agencies often sell local guidebooks which are excellent value if you'll be staying long in one place. Ask if they have the schedule for coastal ferries.

Croatian Tour Companies Abroad

The Croatian Ministry of Tourism has few offices abroad, but the tour companies listed here specialise in Croatia and will gladly mail you their brochures containing much information on the country:

Germany
Kroatische Zentrale für Tourismus, Karlsruher Strasse 18, D-60329 Frankfurt (☎ 069-252 045)
Netherlands
Phoenix Vakanties, Nieuwe Haven 133, 3116 AC Schiedam (☎ 010-473 4444)
UK
Phoenix Holidays, INA House, 210 Shepherds Bush Road, London W6 7NL (☎ 0171-371 1122)
USA
Atlas Ambassador of Dubrovnik, 60 East 42nd St, New York, NY 10165 (☎ 212-697 6767)

BUSINESS HOURS & HOLIDAYS

Banking hours are 7.30 am to 7 pm weekdays, 8 am to noon Saturdays. Many shops open from 8 am to 7 pm weekdays, 8 am to 2 pm Saturdays. Croats are early risers and by 7 am there will be lots of people on the street and many places will already be open.

The public holidays of Croatia are New Year's Day (1 January), Orthodox Christmas (6 and 7 January), Easter Monday (March/April), Labour Day (1 May), Statehood Day (30 May), Croatian National Uprising Day (22 June), Feast of the Assumption (15 August), All Saints' Day (1 November) and Christmas (25 and 26 December). Statehood Day marks the anniversary of the declaration of independence in 1991 while National Uprising Day commemorates the outbreak of resistance in 1941.

CULTURAL EVENTS

In July and August there are summer festivals in Dubrovnik, Opatija, Split and Zagreb. The many traditional annual events held around Croatia are included under Entertainment in the city and town descriptions.

POST & TELECOMMUNICATIONS
Receiving Mail

Mail sent to Poste Restante, 41000 Zagreb, Croatia, is held at the post office next to Zagreb Railway Station. A good coastal address to use is c/o Poste Restante, Main Post Office, 58101 Split, Croatia.

If you have an American Express card, you can have your mail addressed to Atlas Travel Agency, Trg Nikole Zrinjskog 17, 41000 Zagreb, Croatia, or Atlas Travel Agency, Trg Braće Radić, 58000 Split, Croatia.

Telephone

To call Croatia from abroad, dial your international access code, 385 (the country code for Croatia), the area code (without the initial zero) and the local number. Important area codes include 041 (Zagreb), 050 (Dubrovnik and Korčula), 051 (Opatija and Rijeka), 052 (Pula and Rovinj), 0531 (Poreč), 0532 (Krk, Mali Lošinj and Rab), 057 (Zadar) and 058 (Hvar, Split and Trogir).

To make a phone call from Croatia, go to the main post office – phone calls placed from hotel rooms are much more expensive. As there are no coins you'll need tokens or a telephone card to use public telephones. Phonecards come in three values: A, B and C. These can be purchased at any post office but different cities have different cards. A three-minute call from Croatia will be around US$5 to the UK or US$8 to the USA or Australia. The international access code is 99.

To place operator-assisted reverse-charge calls to Britain dial 99-38-0044. For reverse-charge calls to the USA dial 99-38-0041. The operators speak English.

TIME

Croatia is on Central European Time (GMT/UTC plus one hour). Daylight-saving time comes into effect at the end of March when clocks are turned forward an hour. At the end of September they're turned back an hour.

ELECTRICITY

Electricity is 220 V AC, 50 Hz. Croatia uses the standard European round-pronged plugs.

WEIGHTS & MEASURES

The metric system is used. Like other Continental Europeans, Croats indicate decimals with commas and thousands with points.

HEALTH

Everyone must pay to see a doctor at a public hospital (bolnica) or medical centre (dom zdravcja) but the charges are reasonable. Travel insurance would only pay off if you had a very serious accident and had to be hospitalised. The medical centres often have dentists on the staff, otherwise you can go to a private dental clinic (zubna ordinacija).

DANGERS & ANNOYANCES

Personal security and theft are not problems in Croatia, though women on their own may be harassed by local men in the coastal resorts. It's important to check all such approaches firmly. Women should stay within sight of other people and not go off sunbathing or hiking alone.

The police and military are well disciplined and it's highly unlikely you'll have any problems with them in any of the places covered in this chapter. Aggressive cigarette smoking is a bigger nuisance than war activity.

WORK

The Sunflower Centre for Grassroots Relie Work (fax 385-41-449 715), Maruševačka 8 41000 Zagreb, Croatia, accepts volunteers t do unpaid relief work among war refugees i Croatia year-round. Preference is given t applicants with experience working wit children – to social workers, teachers, psy chologists, nurses, artists, universit graduates, linguists and people with knowledge of a Slavic language.

The Croatian Heritage Foundatio organises summer 'task forces' of youn people from around the world who gather t assist in war reconstruction. For informatio call Mr Tomislav Stevenjać (☎ 02-736 3574 in Australia or Ms Sylvia Hrkač (☎ 416-60 6608) in the USA, or write to Hrvatsk matica iseljenika (fax 385-41-539 111), Tr Stjepana Radića 3, 41000 Zagreb, Croatia One US participant wrote, 'The experience had and the friends I made changed my life.

ACTIVITIES
Yachting

The long, rugged islands off Croatia's moun tainous coast all the way from Istria t Dubrovnik make this a yachting paradise anc the fine, deep channels with abundan anchorages and steady winds attract yachtie from around the world. Throughout the region there are quaint little ports where you can get provisions, and yachts can tie up righ in the middle of everything. Some 39 modern marinas dot the coast, 19 of them operated by the Adriatic Croatia International Club (ACI). Duty-free shops in the marinas sell beer by the case at bargain prices. In the Mediterranean only the Greek islands are comparable.

Those arriving with their own boat can check in or out at any of the following year-round ports: Umag, Poreč, Rovinj, Pula, Raša-Bršica, Mali Lošinj, Rijeka, Senj, Maslenica, Zadar, Šibenik, Split, Korčula, Ploče and Dubrovnik. In the summer season navigators can also use Novigrad, Sali, Primošten, Ravni Žakanj, Ubli and Komiža. Navigation permits are not required for unpowered boats and kayaks under three metres in length.

Yacht-charter brokers in North America and elsewhere arrange yacht rentals here, usually from Rovinj, Pula, Opatija and Split. You can either hire a 'bare boat' (no crew) for your party and set out on your own, or join a 'flotilla' of yachts sailing along a fixed route. If you plan to sail your own chartered yacht, you'll have to prove to the port captain that you're able. Crewed yacht charters are also available.

All charters are for a minimum of one week (Saturday evening to Saturday morning) and prices range from US$1350 to US$5375 a week, depending on the type of yacht, plus US$100 a day for the skipper. Of course, all food, drink and fuel are extra. Though certainly not for those 'on a shoestring', the per person price becomes affordable when split between a party of four to eight who were intending to go up-market anyway. The season runs from mid-May to September. Information is available from the Adriatic Croatia International Club (☎ 051-271 288, fax 051-271 824), M Tita 221, 51410 Opatija, Croatia.

Kayaking

There are countless possibilities for anyone carrying a folding sea kayak, especially among the Elafiti Islands (take the daily ferry from Dubrovnik to Lopud) and the Kornati Islands (take the daily ferry from Zadar to Sali). See Package Tours in the Getting There & Away section for information on sailing and kayaking tours.

Hiking

With much of the interior under Serbian control, the hiking possibilities in Croatia are reduced, though there are still good walks on some of the islands. To get a feel for the barren coastal mountains, climb Mt Ilija (961 metres) above Orebić, opposite Korčula.

Risnjak National Park at Crni Lug, 12 km west of Delnice between Zagreb and Rijeka, is a good (and safe) hiking area in summer. Buses run from Delnice to Crni Lug near the park entrance about three times a day, and there's a small park-operated hotel (☎ 051-836 133) at Crni Lug with rooms at US$20 per person with breakfast. (For accommodation at Delnice turn to the Rijeka section.) Because of the likelihood of heavy snowfalls, hiking is only advisable from late spring to early autumn. It's a nine-km, 2½-hour climb from the park entrance at Bijela Vodica to Veliki Risnjak (1528 metres). At last report, park admission was US$1.50.

Courses

The Croatian Heritage Foundation (Hrvatska matica iseljenika) runs a 'Summer School of Croatian Language & Culture' in Split and Zagreb during July and August (exact dates become known the preceding February). Though designed for people of Croatian descent living abroad, everyone is welcome. Aside from classroom instruction, cultural events and excursions are organised around Croatia.

Three 14-day 'Croaticum' programmes are offered at Supetar on Brač Island by the National University of Split, costing US$520 with tuition, full board, and excursions to Split, Trogir and other places included. Special 10-day folk-music and folk-dancing courses are also offered. Apply before 15 June with a deposit of US$100 to Narodno sveučilište/Ljetna škola, Dioklecijanova 7, 58000 Split, Croatia. The balance of the fee is payable upon arrival. The fax number is 385-58-44 825.

The Faculty of Arts of the University of Zagreb (founded in 1669) organises a more intensive, academically oriented four-week course, (US$360 school fees plus US$220 registration). Room and board (sharing a twin room) at a student dormitory is US$19 a day. Students sit for an exam at the end of the course and those who pass receive a certificate of merit. To enrol, you must send a deposit of US$100 by 1 June to Koordinator Ljetne škole, Hrvatska matica iseljenika, Trg Stjepana Radića 3, 41000 Zagreb, Croatia. The fax number is 385-41-539 111. Applications are also accepted by Professor Luka Budak (☎ 02-805 7054), Croatian Studies Department, Macquarie University,

CROATIA

Sydney, NSW 2109, Australia; Dr Vinko Grubišić (☎ 519-746 5243), Faculty of Arts, University of Waterloo, Waterloo, ON N2L 3G1, Canada; and Dr Joseph Conrad or Dr William March (☎ 913-864 4555), Department of Slavic Languages, University of Kansas, Lawrence, KS 66045, USA. Also ask about regular semester courses offered throughout the academic year.

These courses are an excellent way to learn about Croatian culture and meet a lot of interesting people, while providing a productive anchor for a Mediterranean holiday – highly recommended.

ACCOMMODATION

Along the coast, accommodation is priced according to three seasons which vary from place to place. Generally April, May and October are the cheapest months, June and September are medium, but in July and August count on paying at least 50% more. Prices for rooms in the interior regions are often constant all year. Add US$1 to US$2 per person per night 'residence tax' and a similar 'registration fee' to all official accommodation rates. Croats get a 65% discount, which explains why all the expensive hotels are full. Beware of the prices listed in official tourist brochures as these are often much lower than what is actually charged. Due to the political situation, accommodation is much cheaper in Dalmatia than in Kvarner or Istria.

This chapter provides the phone numbers of most accommodation facilities, so once you know your itinerary it pays to go to a post office, buy a telephone card and start calling around to check prices, availability etc. Most receptionists speak English.

Camping

Nearly 100 camping grounds are found along the Croatian coast. Most operate from mid-May to September only, although a few are open in April and October. In May and late September, call ahead to make sure that the camping ground really is open before beginning the long trek out. Don't go by the opening and closing dates you read in travel brochures or this book, as these are only approximate. Even local tourist offices can be wrong.

Many camping grounds are expensive for backpackers because the prices are set in dollars or Deutschmarks per person, and include the charge per tent, caravan, car, electric hook-up etc. This is fine for people with mobile homes who occupy a large area but bad news for those with only a small tent. If you don't have a vehicle, you're better off at camping grounds which have a much smaller fee per person and charge extra per tent, car, caravan, electric hook-up etc.

Germans are the largest users of Croatian camping grounds. Unfortunately, many of these are gigantic 'autocamps' with restaurants, shops and row upon row of caravans. Nudist camping grounds (marked FKK) are among the best because their secluded locations ensure peace and quiet. Freelance camping is officially prohibited.

Youth Hostels

The Croatian YHA (Ferijalni Savez Hrvatske), Trg hrvatskih velikana 13, 41000 Zagreb, operates summer youth hostels in Dubrovnik, Korčula, Pula, Punat, Šibenik and Zadar, and a year-round hostel at Zagreb. (There are plans to keep the Pula hostel open all year.) Bed and breakfast at these is around US$5 for YHA members, US$6 for non-members in the low season (May, June, September and October), or US$8 for members and US$9 for nonmembers in July and August. The Zagreb hostel has higher prices.

At last report, all of the youth hostels were partly occupied by war refugees and only those at Zagreb and Pula still accepted travellers. The Zadar and Šibenik hostels were damaged by shelling and won't reopen for some time. The Korčula hostel is closed because of a lack of guests and the Dubrovnik hostel has been taken over by the 'special police'.

Private Rooms

The best accommodation in Croatia is private rooms in local homes, the equivalent of small private guesthouses in other countries. Such rooms can be arranged by travel agencies but they add a lot of taxes and commission to your bill, so you'll almost always do better dealing directly with proprietors you meet on the street or by knocking on the doors of houses with *sobe* or *zimmer* signs. This way you avoid the residence tax and four-night minimum stay, but forgo the agency's quality control. The householder gets off without paying a large commission to the agency and 30% tax on the income. Hang around coastal bus stations and ferry terminals, luggage in hand, looking lost, and someone may find you.

If the price asked is too high, bargain. Be sure to clarify whether the price agreed upon is per person or for the room. At the agencies, singles are expensive and scarce, but on the street, sobe prices are usually per person, which favours the single traveller. Showers are always included. It often works out cheaper if you pay in cash Deutschmarks rather than kuna. Although renting an unofficial room is common practice along the Adriatic coast, be discreet, as technically you're breaking the law by not registering with the police. Don't brag to travel agencies about the low rate you got, for example.

If you stay less than four nights, the agencies add a 30% to 50% surcharge. Travel agencies classify the rooms according to categories I, II or III. If you want the cheapest room, ask for category III. In the resort areas many category I rooms have cooking facilities, and private apartments are available.

Some rooms are excellent, but at other times the landlord comes in every half-hour with only a brief knock on the door. Generally, what you pay for a private room won't be much more than camping or youth hostel charges. Also, staying in a private room is a way of meeting a local family. Unfortunately, private rooms are usually unavailable in interior towns, and very expensive in Zagreb.

Hotels

There are few cheap hotels in Croatia – prices generally begin around US$35

double, even in the off season. Still, if you're only staying one night and the private room agency is going to levy a 50% surcharge, you might consider getting a hotel room. In the off season when most rooms are empty you could try bargaining for a more realistic rate.

The staff at many of the state-run hotels have a couldn't-care-less attitude and just laugh at complaints. Maintenance isn't their concern and the level of service is often geared towards mass tours, not the individual, who has to pay a lot more.

Since 1991 many resort hotels along the Adriatic coast have been filled with refugees from the fighting in interior areas, but in all tourist areas there will be at least one hotel reserved for tourists.

FOOD

A restaurant *(restauracija)* or pub may also be called a *gostionica* and a café is a *kavana*. Self-service cafeterias are quick, easy and inexpensive, though the quality of the food varies. If the samples behind glass look cold or dried out, ask them to dish out a fresh plate for you. Better restaurants aren't that much more expensive if you choose carefully. In most of them the vegetables, salads and bread cost extra, and some deluxe restaurants add a 10% service charge (not mentioned on the menu). The fish dishes are often charged by weight, which makes it difficult to know how much a certain dish will cost. Ice-cream cones are priced by the scoop.

Restaurants in Croatia can be a hassle because they rarely post their menus outside, so to find out what they offer and the price range you have to walk in and ask to see the menu. Then if you don't like what you see, you must just walk back out and appear rude. Always check the menu, however, and if the price of the drinks or something else isn't listed, ask, otherwise you'll automatically be charged the 'tourist price'.

Breakfast is difficult in Croatia as all you can get easily is coffee. For eggs, toast and jam you'll have to go somewhere expensive, otherwise buy some bread, cheese and milk at a supermarket and picnic somewhere. Throughout ex-Yugoslavia the breakfast of the people is *burek*, a greasy layered pie made with meat *(mesa)* or cheese *(sira)* and cut on a huge metal tray.

A load of fruit and vegetables from the local market can make a healthy, cheap picnic lunch. There are plenty of supermarkets in Croatia – cheese, bread, wine and milk are readily available and fairly cheap. The person behind the meat counter at supermarkets will make a big cheese or bologna sandwich for you upon request and you only pay the regular price of the ingredients.

Regional Dishes

Italian pizza and pasta are a good option in Istria and Dalmatia, costing about half of what you'd pay in Western Europe. The Adriatic coast excels in seafood, including scampi, *prstaci* (shellfish) and Dalmatian *brodet* (mixed fish stewed with rice), all cooked in olive oil and served with boiled vegetables or *tartufe* (mushrooms) in Istria. In the Croatian interior, watch for *manistra od bobića* (beans and fresh maize soup) or *štrukle* (cottage cheese rolls). A Zagreb specialty is *štrukli* (boiled cheesecake).

DRINKS

It's customary to have a small glass of brandy before a meal and to accompany the food with one of Croatia's fine wines. Ask for the local regional wine. Croatia is also famous for its plum brandies *(šljivovica)*, herbal brandies *(travarica)*, cognacs *(vinjak)* and liqueurs such as *maraschino*, a cherry liqueur made in Zadar, or herbal *pelinkovac*. Italian-style espresso coffee (infused by a machine) is popular in Croatia.

Zagreb's Ožujsko beer *(pivo)* is very good but Karlovačko beer from Karlovac is better. You'll want to practise the word *živjeli!* (cheers!).

ENTERTAINMENT

Culture was heavily subsidised by the communists, and admission to operas, operettas and concerts is still reasonable. The main theatres offering musical programmes are listed herein, so note the location and drop by some time during the day to see what's on

and purchase tickets. In the interior cities, winter is the best time to enjoy the theatres and concert halls. The main season at the opera houses of Rijeka, Split and Zagreb runs from October to May. These close for holidays in summer and the cultural scene shifts to the many summer festivals. Ask municipal tourist offices about cultural events in their area.

Discos operate in summer in the coastal resorts and all year in the interior cities. If you're male, you'll find the local women aren't interested in meeting you; if you're female, you'll find the local men are too interested in meeting you, so it's always a good idea to go accompanied. It doesn't cost anything at all to participate in the early evening *korzo*, a casual promenade enjoyed by great crowds in the town centres.

Cinemas

The cheapest entertainment in Croatia is a movie at a *kino*. Admission fees are always low and the soundtracks are in the original language. American sex-and-violence films are the standard fare, however, and the last film of the day is usually hard-core pornography. Check the time on your ticket carefully, as admission is not allowed once the film has started.

THINGS TO BUY

Among the traditional handicraft products of Croatia are fine lace from the Dalmatian islands, handmade embroidery, woodcarvings, woollen and leather items, carpets, filigree jewellery, ceramics, national costumes and tapestries.

Getting There & Away

AIR

Croatia Airlines (☎ 041-451 244), ulica Teslina 5, Zagreb, has flights from Zagreb to Amsterdam, Berlin, Brussels, Budapest, Copenhagen, Düsseldorf, Frankfurt, Hamburg, London, Madrid, Manchester,

Moscow, Munich, Paris, Prague, Rome, Skopje, Stuttgart, Tirana, Vienna and Zürich.

A departure tax of US$8 is collected on international flights from Zagreb.

LAND

Bus

To/from Hungary you can catch a bus between Zagreb and Barcs five times a day (202 km, US$14) or twice daily to/from Nagykanizsa (176 km, US$9). From Barcs there are frequent trains to Pécs (67 km), then less frequent buses from Pécs to Szeged (188 km), where there are trains and buses to Subotica (47 km) in Vojvodina (Yugoslavia). Nagykanizsa is more convenient if you're travelling to/from Budapest. No buses run from Croatia to Serbia.

From Germany the buses of the Deutsche Touring GmbH are cheaper than the train. Buses to Croatia depart from Berlin, Cologne, Dortmund, Frankfurt/Main, Mannheim, Munich, Nuremberg and Stuttgart. Baggage is DM3 extra per piece. Service is usually only once or twice a week, but buses operate all year. Information is available at bus stations in the cities just mentioned.

Coming from the Netherlands, Budget Bus/Eurolines (☎ 020-627 5151), Rokin 10, Amsterdam, offers service twice a week all year to Zagreb (US$110 one way, US$175 return, 22 hours), Rijeka and Split (US$125 one way, US$190 return). Reductions are available for children under 13 but not for students or seniors. Europabus operates a similar weekly service all year from Antwerp (Belgium) to Zagreb. On all of the Dutch and Belgian services you must change buses at Munich, where you will be charged DM3 per piece for luggage, and an advance reservation is recommended (US$3). This is much cheaper than the train, which is US$196 one way 2nd class from Amsterdam to Ljubljana. One drawback is the heavy cigarette smoking aboard.

Train

Railway fares in Italy are relatively cheap, so if you can get across the Italian border from France or Switzerland, it won't cost an arm and a leg to take a train on to Trieste, where there are frequent bus connections to Croatia via Koper.

Intercity 296/297 goes overnight nightly from Munich to Zagreb (613 km, eight hours, US$61) via Salzburg and Ljubljana. Reservations are required southbound but not northbound. The *Eurocity Mimara* between Leipzig and Zagreb travels by day. The *Ljubljana* express from Vienna to Rijeka (615 km, eight hours), via Ljubljana, and the *Eurocity Croatia* from Vienna to Zagreb (472 km, 6½ hours, US$41) both travel via Maribor. Between Venice and Zagreb (US$26) there are the *Kras, Simplon* and *Venezia* express trains via Trieste and Ljubljana (seven hours). The *Simplon* conveys carriages originating in Geneva and Rome.

To go from Budapest to Zagreb via Siófok (412 km, 6½ hours, US$24) you have a choice of the *Agram, Adriatica, Drava* and *Maestral* express trains. A direct daily train links Zagreb to Pécs (267 km, five hours, US$16), leaving Pécs in the early morning and Zagreb in the afternoon. Since July 1991 no trains have linked Croatia directly with Serbia.

As well as the international express trains, there are unreserved local trains between Gyékényes, Hungary, and Koprivnica (15 km, 20 minutes, US$3) three times a day, with connections in Gyékényes to/from Nagykanizsa, Pécs and Kaposv r. Two unreserved trains a day travel between Varaždin and Nagykanizsa (72 km, 1½ hours, US$3).

Car & Motorbike

The main highway entry/exit points between Croatia and Hungary are Goričan (between Nagykanizsa and Varaždin), Gola (23 km east of Koprivnica), Terezino Polje (opposite Barcs) and Donji Miholjac (seven km south of Hark ny). There are 29 crossing points to/from Slovenia, too many to list here. We are uncertain of conditions at the 23 crossings into Bosnia-Hercegovina and the seven crossings into Yugoslavia are presently closed.

CROATIA

SEA

Ferry

In the past two companies have offered ferry service to Croatia. The Croatian Jadrolinija line served both Italy and Greece, and the Italian Adriatica Navigazione company specialised in service to/from Italy. At last report the Adriatica ferries weren't operating, although Jadrolinija has recommenced year-round service from Split to Ancona; the Dubrovnik to Bari ferry runs once or twice a week from June to September. International ferry services in general are still greatly reduced because of the high cost of war insurance, even though there is no longer any danger.

To/From Italy All year round there's a Jadrolinija ferry between Ancona and Split (13 hours, US$36) twice a week. Dubrovnik-Bari (eight hours, US$40) is weekly from June to September.

The Hellenic Mediterranean or Anek Lines (☎ 071-205 999; fax 071-54608) in Ancona has ferry service from Ancona to Split three times a week.

Navigazione Aquila (☎ 085-906 4940; fax 085-906 4930) in Ortona (near Pescara), has ferry service twice a week between Ortona and Split (US$35 deck).

Deck fares cost 25% to 50% higher in the peak season, which is from mid-July to mid-August eastbound, and from August to mid-September westbound. Italian port departure tax is US$4.

To/From Albania The Dalmacija Kvarner Line has a car ferry, the *Duje*, from Rijeka to Durrës twice a week all year round. One-way fares are US$100 deck, US$110 with an airline seat or US$140 per person in a two or three-bed cabin.

To/From Greece Jadrolinija used to run a ferry service from Igoumenitsa and Corfu in Greece to Dubrovnik and all the ports of call right up to Rijeka. At last report the ferry was operating only between Rijeka and Dubrovnik with service to Greece suspended.

If service is resumed and you buy a Jadrolinija ticket from Greece to Croatia always ask for a ticket to Split, which costs the same as Dubrovnik, Korčula or Hvar. The purser on board will stamp your ticket to permit free stopovers at intermediate points. After having the ticket so validated you can get off at any of the ports along the way and reboard a later service without having to buy another ticket. (Be sure to have the ticket stamped each time you want to get off.) With a ticket to Rijeka you can also get a free stop at Rab.

PACKAGE TOURS

Croatia's oldest tour company is Atlas Travel Agency, founded in Dubrovnik in 1923. Its 'adventure' tours feature bird-watching, canoeing, caving, cycling, diving, fishing, hiking, riding, sailing, sea kayaking and white-water rafting in both Croatia and Slovenia. The eight-day tours cost US$545 to US$888 all-inclusive and you join the group in Croatia, allowing you to combine the advantages of group and individual travel. These trips are the perfect way to be sure of being able to participate in these activities on a short visit. Travel agents in North America book through Atlas Ambassador of Dubrovnik (☎ 212-697 6767), 60 East 42nd St, New York, NY 10165.

Getting Around

AIR

Croatia Airlines has daily flights from Zagreb to Dubrovnik (US$85), Pula (US$60) and Split (US$78). Their twice-weekly flight to Skopje is very expensive at US$300 one way.

BUS

The bus service in Croatia is excellent. Fast express buses go everywhere, often many times a day, and they'll stop to pick up passengers at designated stops anywhere along their route. Buses charge about US$2 for each hour of travel and you can expect to cover about 40 km in that time. Luggage stowed in the baggage compartment under the bus is extra, costing around US$0.50 apiece, including insurance. If your bag is small you could carry it onto the bus, although the seats are often placed close together, making this impossible on crowded buses.

At large stations, bus tickets must be purchased at the office, not from drivers; try to book ahead to be sure of a seat. Lists of departures over the various windows at the bus stations tell you which one has tickets for your bus. Tickets for buses that arrive from somewhere else are usually purchased from the conductor. On Croatian bus schedules, *vozi svaki dan* means every day, *ne vozi nedjeljom ni praznikom* means not Sundays and public holidays.

Some buses travel overnight, getting you where you're going for what you'd have to pay for a room anyway. Don't expect to get much sleep, however, as the inside lights will be on and music will be blasting the whole night. Take care not to be left behind at meal or rest stops and beware of buses leaving 10 minutes early.

A Canadian reader sent us this:

I visited Hvar in 1990 and witnessed a scene which perhaps sheds some light on later events. About two dozen British tourists had lined up for the afternoon bus to Stari Grad. As the departure time approached, a large crowd of locals began pushing against the closed rear doors of the parked bus, ignoring the disapproving glares of the British in the queue at the front doors. About the time the bus was due to leave the driver strolled over, reached in the window and casually flipped a switch which opened all the doors at once. He then walked away. Only a couple of the indignant British managed to get aboard before all the seats were taken. The memory of those selfish, disorderly passengers and the couldn't-care-less attitude of the driver helped me understand what happened in the country a year later.

TRAIN

Because of the war, Croatian trains don't go any farther south than the lines running from Osijek to Zagreb via Koprivnica, and Zagreb to Rijeka via Karlovac. The railway line to Zadar, Šibenik and Split passes through Knin, a stronghold of Serbian separatists,

and service is likely to remain suspended for some time to come. No trains operate from Croatia to Serbia or Bosnia-Hercegovina.

Train trips you can still take easily in Croatia/Slovenia are Zagreb to Osijek (288 km, five hours), Koprivnica (92 km, 1½ hours, local), Varaždin (110 km, three hours, local), Ljubljana (160 km, three hours, local) and Rijeka (243 km, five hours, local). There's also Rijeka to Ljubljana (155 km, 2½ hours, local) and Pula to Ljubljana (258 km, five hours, local).

The train is about 15% cheaper than the bus and often more comfortable, if slower. Baggage is free. Local trains usually have only unreserved 2nd-class seats but they're rarely crowded. Reservations may be required on express trains. 'Executive' trains have only 1st-class seats and are 40% more expensive than local trains. No couchettes are available on any domestic services. Most train stations have left-luggage offices charging US$1 apiece (passport required).

On posted timetables in Croatia the word for arrivals is *dolazak*, and for departures it's *odlazak* or *polazak*. Other terms you may encounter include *poslovni* (executive train), *brzi* or *ubrazni* (fast train), *putnički* (local train), *rezerviranje mjesta obvezatno* (compulsory seat reservation), *presjedanje* (change of trains), *ne vozi nedjeljom i blagdanom* (no service Sundays and holidays) and *svakodnevno* (daily).

CAR & MOTORBIKE

Motorists will require their vehicle registration and the green insurance card to enter Croatia. Two-way amateur radios built into cars are no problem but must be reported at the border.

Both regular (86 octane) or premium (96 octane) grade petrol are available and some 200 service stations around Croatia now have lead-free fuel *(bezolovni)*. You have to pay tolls on the motorways around Zagreb, to use the Učka tunnel between Rijeka and Istria, and for the bridge to Krk Island.

The motorway from Zagreb to Belgrade and most interior roads into Serbia or Bosnia-Hercegovina (including that from

Zagreb to Zadar via Plitvice National Park) are closed. The road from Zagreb to Rijeka via Karlovac is open, however. The road from Karlovac to Senj is also open but it passes very close to the Serbian-controlled areas and foreign motorists may not be allowed to use it. (There's no problem for foreigners on buses.)

No motorways run along the coast, where the spectacular Adriatic highway from Italy to Albania hugs the steep slopes of the coastal range with abrupt drops to the sea and a curve a minute. You can drive as far south as Vitaljina, 56 km south-east of Dubrovnik.

The bridge at Maslenica on the main highway east of Zadar was destroyed by the federal army in November 1991, then held by Serbian separatists for over a year before being recaptured by the Croatian army during their surprise January 1993 offensive. A pontoon bridge has now been erected to replace the destroyed bridge but the area still comes under occasional shelling. For security reasons cars and buses travelling from Rijeka to Zadar presently go via an alternative route down Pag Island, crossing from Prizna on the mainland to Žigljen on Pag by ferry (operating 24 hours a day all year round). Another bridge connects the southern tip of Pag to the mainland near Zadar but this has been structurally weakened by the heavy traffic it was never intended to carry and heavy trucks must use the Maslenica pontoon bridge. The Pag bridge takes only one-way traffic at alternate times, but it's no problem at all for private cars.

Motorists can turn to the Hrvatski Autoklub (HAK) or Croatian Auto Club for help or advice. The addresses of local HAK offices are provided throughout this chapter and the nationwide HAK road assistance (*vučna služba*) number is ☎ 987.

Road Rules

Unless otherwise posted, the speed limits for cars and motorcycles are 60 km/h in built-up areas, 80 km/h on the open road, 100 km/h on main highways and 120 km/h on motorways. Police systematically fine motorists exceeding these limits. On any of Croatia's winding two-lane highways, it's illegal to pass long military convoys or a whole line of cars caught behind a slow-moving truck. Drive defensively, as local motorists lack discipline.

Car Rental

The large car rental chains represented in Croatia are Avis, Budget, Europcar and Hertz, with Europcar (offices in Rijeka, Split and Zagreb) being the cheapest and Hertz the most expensive. Avis and Hertz have offices at Zagreb and Split airports. Throughout Croatia, Avis is usually represented by Kvarner Express, Hertz by Kompas. Independent local companies are often less expensive than the international chains, but Avis, Budget and Hertz have the big advantage of offering one-way rentals which allow you to drop the car off at any of their stations in Croatia and Slovenia free of charge.

At all of the agencies the cheapest car is the Renault 4 and prices begin around US$20 a day plus US$0.20 per km (100 km minimum), or US$300 to US$350 a week with unlimited km. Third-party public liability insurance is included by law, but you are responsible for the first US$1500 to US$5000 damage done to the vehicle. Full collision insurance (CDW) is US$6 to US$8 a day extra (compulsory for those aged under 23) and theft insurance is another US$6 to US$8 a day. Add 20% tax to all charges. You may be able to get a reduced tax rate by paying in foreign currency or by credit card (ask).

The age limits vary from company to company. Hertz will rent to 18-years-olds who have had their licence for at least a year, but at Avis, Budget and Europcar you have to be 21. A cash deposit of US$200 to US$300 must be paid unless you're paying by credit card. Some local companies will give a 10% discount if you pay in cash rather than by credit card.

Sometimes you can get a lower car-rental rate by booking your car from abroad. Tour companies in Western Europe often have fly-drive packages which include a flight to Croatia and a car (two-person minimum).

HITCHING

The hitchhiking in Croatia is lousy. There are lots of little cars but they're usually full and the local motorists are not noted for their courtesy. Tourists never stop. Unfortunately, the image many Croats have of this activity is based on violent movies like *Hitch-hiker*.

BOAT

From March to mid-October big white and blue Jadrolinija car ferries *Ilirija, Istra, Liburnija* and *Slavija* operate almost daily along the Rijeka-Rab-Split-Hvar-Korčula-Dubrovnik coastal route. The most scenic section is Split to Dubrovnik, which all of the Jadrolinija ferries cover during the day. Rijeka to Split (13 hours) is usually an overnight trip in either direction. At last report the ferries weren't calling at Zadar because of the security situation.

The ferries are a lot more comfortable than the buses, though considerably more expensive. Deck fares out of Rijeka are US$16 to Rab, US$32 to Split or Hvar, US$44 to Korčula or Dubrovnik (slightly higher from mid-June to mid-September). Split to Dubrovnik is US$20. With a through ticket, you can stop over at any port for up to a week, provided you notify the purser beforehand and have your ticket validated. This is much cheaper than buying individual sector tickets. It's about 25% cheaper again to buy a through ticket from Rijeka to Dubrovnik at a travel agency outside Croatia. Cabins should be booked a week ahead but deck space is usually available on all sailings.

Deck passage on Jadrolinija is just that: reclining seats *(poltrone)* are about US$10 extra and four-berth cabins (if available) begin at US$30 per person. Cabins can be arranged at the reservation counter aboard ship, but advance bookings are recommended if you want to be sure of a place, and it's cheaper to buy your ticket at an agency. Deck space is fine for passages during daylight hours and when you can stretch out a sleeping bag on the upper deck in good weather, but if it's rainy you could end up sitting in the smoky cafeteria which stays open all night. During the crowded midsummer season, deck class can be unpleasant in wet weather.

Meals in the restaurants aboard Jadrolinija ships are about US$8 for lunch or dinner (drinks extra), and all the cafeteria offers is ham-and-cheese sandwiches for US$1. Coffee is cheap in the cafeteria but wine and spirits tend to be expensive. Breakfast in the restaurant is usually good value. It's best to bring some food and drink along with you.

Local Ferries

A ferry connection between Pula and Zadar (US$14) via Mali Lošinj operates three times a week from mid-June to September. Ferry service between Mali Lošinj and Zadar (US$8) is daily in summer.

Other local ferries connect the main offshore islands to the mainland. The most important of these are Brestova to Porozine on Cres Island (15 daily all year), Valbiska on Krk Island to Merag on Cres Island (nine daily all year), Baška on Krk Island to Lopar on Rab Island (two or three daily from June to September), Jablanac to Mišnjak on Rab Island (nine daily all year), Prizna to Žigljen on Pag Island (24 hours a day all year round), Zadar to Preko (eight daily all year), Split to Supetar on Brač Island (seven daily all year), Split to Stari Grad on Hvar Island (three daily all year), Drvenik to Sućuraj on Hvar Island (four daily all year), Split to Vela Luka on Korčula Island via Hvar (daily all year), Ploče to Trpanj (three daily all year), Orebić to Korčula Island (eight daily all year) and Dubrovnik to Polače on Mljet Island (six a week all year). In the off season service is greatly reduced, so check.

Taking a bicycle on these services incurs an extra fare. Some of the ferries operate only a couple of times a day, and once the vehicular capacity is reached, remaining motorists must wait for the next service. In summer the lines of waiting cars can be long, so it's important to arrive early. Foot passengers and cyclists should have no problem getting on.

Throughout Croatia, when asking about ferry times beware of ticket agents who give incomplete or misleading information about departures. Study the posted Croatian timetable carefully, *then* ask your questions.

Travel agencies such as Atlas Travel Agency run fast hydrofoils up and down the coast, especially between Rijeka and Split, with Rab and Hvar also served (Rijeka-Hvar is US$28, six hours). These services operate only once or twice a week and are advertised on placards outside the agencies.

Zagreb

Zagreb, an attractive city of over a million inhabitants, has been the capital of Croatia since 1557. Spread up from the Sava River, Zagreb sits on the southern slopes of Medvednica, the Zagreb uplands. Medieval Zagreb developed from the 11th to the 13th centuries in the twin towns of Kaptol and Gradec, Kaptol with St Stephen's Cathedral and Gradec centred on St Mark's Church. The clerics established themselves in Kaptol as early as 1094, whereas Gradec was the craftspeople's quarter.

Much of medieval Zagreb remains today, although the stately 19th century city between it and the train station is the present commercial centre. There are many fine parks, galleries and museums in both the upper and lower towns. Zagreb is also Croatia's main centre for primitive or naive art.

On the surface, Zagreb hardly appears to be the capital of a country at war. Affluent-looking consumers throng Ilica, and the clientele of the elegant cafés around Trg Jelačića is as sophisticated as ever. Fortunately, the city weathered the chaotic period which followed Yugoslavia's break-up without sustaining much damage. The people are well dressed and smiling, but most of Zagreb's museums are still closed, with the exhibits removed for safekeeping. Although the 'front' is only 50 km south of the city, wartime Zagreb functions quite normally and the biggest problem you'll encounter is finding a cheap place to stay.

Orientation

As you come out of the train station, you'll see a series of parks and pavilions directly in front of you and the twin Gothic towers of the cathedral in the distance. Trg Jelačića, beyond the north end of the parks, is the main city square. The bus station is one km east of the train station. Tram No 6 runs from the bus station to the train station and on up to Trg Jelačića.

The left-luggage offices in both the bus and train stations are open 24 hours a day. The price posted at left luggage in the bus station is *per hour* and it works out to US$3 a day, so be careful. At the train station you pay a fixed price of about US$1 per day.

Information

The tourist office (☎ 272 530), Trg Jelačića 11, is open weekdays from 8 am to 8 pm, weekends from 9 am to 6 pm. The quality of the information dispensed here varies according to who you talk with.

The Croatian Auto Club (HAK) has two travel offices in Zagreb: a smaller office at Draškovićeva ulica 46 (☎ 431 142) and a main information centre six blocks east at Derenčinova 20 (☎ 415 800).

Plitvice National Park has been closed since March 1991, but the park maintains an information office at Trg Tomislava 19 where you can find out about current access. They also have information on other national parks around Croatia.

Money The exchange offices at the bus and train stations change money at the bank rate with 1.5% commission. The exchange office in the train station (open 7 am to 9 pm) accepts travellers' cheques.

Post & Telecommunications Any poste restante mail is held (for one month) in the post office on the east side of the railway station. Zagreb is a good place to pick up mail, as the poste restante office here is open around the clock (except Sunday morning). Have your letters addressed to Poste Restante, 41000 Zagreb, Croatia.

This same post office is also the best place

to make long-distance telephone calls. Public telephones in Zagreb use tokens (*žeton*) or phonecards. Zagreb's telephone code is 041.

Foreign Embassies The British Embassy (☎ 339 147 or 334 245), 2nd floor, Astra Tower, Cibona Building, Savska cesta at Tratinska, is in the tall circular tower opposite the Technical Museum (weekdays 9 to 11 am). The US Embassy (☎ 444 800) is at Andrije Hebranga 2 (open weekdays 8 to 11.30 am). The governments of Australia and Canada have consular offices at Hotel Esplanade (☎ 435 666).

Also near the city centre are the Embassy of Bulgaria, Gajeva ulica 19 (weekdays 10 am to noon), and the Embassy of Slovakia, Prilaz Djure Deželića 10 (weekends 9 to 11 am). This is a convenient place to pick up a Slovak visa.

The Albanian Embassy operates out of the Mother Teresa Charitable Society, Preradovićeva 9 (weekdays 8.50 am to 3 pm), but they have little information.

The Embassy of Slovenia is at Savska cesta 41 at Avenida Vukovar, 9th floor (weekdays 9 am to noon).

The Czech Republic Embassy, Jurjevska 27a (weekdays 9 am to noon), is about two blocks north of Ilirski trg at the north end of Gradec. The Romanian Consulate, Becićeve stube 2, is farther up this way but hard to find, so start asking directions after you pass the Czech Embassy. The Polish Embassy, Krležin Gvozd 3, is on a hill west of Gradec.

The Hungarian Embassy, Cvjetno naselje 17b (open weekdays from 9 am to noon), is in the southern section of the city. Take tram No 4, 5, 14, 16 or 17 to Vjesnik and then ask, as it's also hard to find.

Travel Agencies Dali Travel, Trg hrvatskih velikana 13, the travel branch of the Croatian YHA, can provide information on HI youth hostels throughout Croatia and make advance bookings. They also sell ISIC student cards (US$6). It's open weekdays from 9 am to 3 pm.

The American Express representative is

Atlas Travel Agency (☎ 427 623), Trg Zrinjskoga 17, Zagreb 41000. It will hold clients' mail.

Bookshops Tehnička Knjiga, Masarykova ulica 17, has a number of excellent recent books in English on the war in Croatia and excellent (though expensive) maps.

Laundry In November 1991 Zagreb's first self-service laundrette, Perestrojka, opened at Gajeva 12 behind the Archaeological Museum. It is open Monday to Saturday from 7 am to 3 pm. To wash up to six kg costs US$2, plus US$1 to dry.

Emergency If you need to see a doctor, your best bet is the ultramodern Dom Zdravlja Centar (☎ 273 555), Runjaninova 4 near the Botanical Garden. It's open daily from 7 am to 8 pm and at last report the consultation fee was US$6.

The police office for foreigners is at Petrinjska 30.

Things to See
Kaptol Zagreb's colourful Dolac **vegetable market** is just up the steps from Trg Jelačića and north along Opatovina. It functions daily with especially large markets on Friday and Saturday. The twin neo-Gothic spires of **St Stephen's Cathedral** (1899) are nearby. Elements from the medieval cathedral on this site, destroyed by an earthquake in 1880, can be seen inside, including 13th century frescoes, Renaissance pews, marble altars and a Baroque pulpit. The Baroque **Archiepiscopal Palace** surrounds the cathedral, as do 16th century fortifications constructed when Zagreb was threatened by the Turks.

Gradec From ulica Radićeva 5 off Trg Jelačića a pedestrian walkway, stube Ivana Zakmardija, leads to the **Lotrščak Tower** and a funicular railway (1888) which connects the lower and upper towns. The tower may be climbed for a sweeping 360° view of the city (closed Sunday). To the right is Baroque **St Catherine's Church**, with Jezuitski trg beyond. The **Muzejski prostor**,

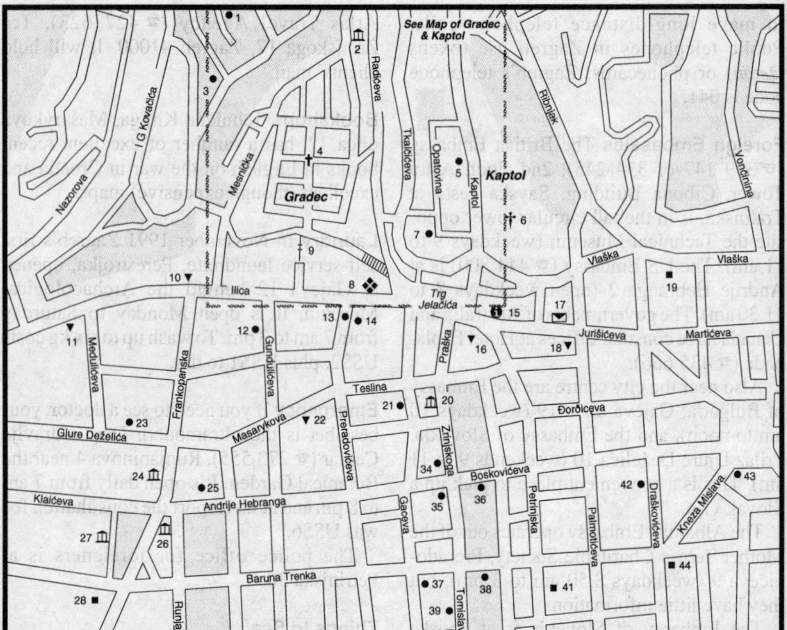
See Map of Gradec & Kaptol
Radićeva
G Kovačića
Mesnička
Nazorova
Gradec
Tkalčićeva
Opatovina
Kaptol
Ribnjak
Vončinina
Vlaška
Ilica
Trg Jelačića
Praška
Jurišićeva
Martićeva
Medulićeva
Frankopanska
Gundulićeva
Teslina
Preradovićeva
Masarykova
Gjure Deželića
Đorđićeva
Zrinjskoga
Boškovićeva
Petrinjska
Palmotićeva
Draškovićeva
Kneza Mislava
Klaićeva
Andrije Hebranga
Gajeva
Baruna Trenka
Runjaninova
Tomislava
Mihanovićeva
Botanical Garden
Savska cesta
Koturaška
Branimirova
To Bus Station
Miramarska
Paromlinska
Trnjanska cesta
Avenida Vukovar
Hrvatske Bratske Zajednice
To Airport
Slavonska
Zagreb
0
250
500 m

Jezuitski trg 4 (free admission on Monday), is Zagreb's premier exhibition hall where superb art shows are staged. Farther north and to the right is the 13th century **Stone Gate**, with a miraculous painting of the Virgin which escaped the devastating fire of 1731.

The colourful painted-tile roof of the Gothic **St Mark's Church** on Markov trg marks the centre of Gradec. Inside are works by Ivan Meštrović, Croatia's most famous modern sculptor. On the east side of St Mark's is the **Sabor** (1908), Croatia's National Assembly.

To the west of St Mark's is the 18th century **Banski Dvori Palace**, the presidential palace with guards in red ceremonial uniform before the door.

At Mletačka 8 nearby is the former **Meštrović Studio**, now a museum (closed Monday). Other museums in this area (all closed Monday) include the **Historical Museum of Croatia**, Matoševa 9, the **Gallery of Naive Art**, Ćirilometodska 3, and the **Natural History Museum**, Demetrova 1. More interesting is the recently renovated **City Museum**, Opatićka 20, with a scale model of old Gradec. Summaries in English and German are in each room of this museum which is housed in the former Convent of St Claire (1650).

The Lower Town Zagreb really is a city of museums. There are four on the parks between the train station and Trg Jelačića. The yellow pavilion (1897) across the park from the station presents changing contemporary art exhibitions. The second building north, also in the park, houses the **Strossmayer Gallery** of the Academy of Arts & Sciences with old master paintings (closed Monday). If the gallery's closed enter the

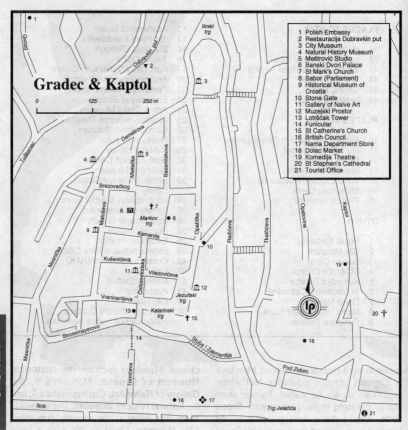

Gradec & Kaptol

0   125   250 m

1 Polish Embassy
2 Restauracija Dubravkin put
3 City Museum
4 Natural History Museum
5 Meštrović Studio
6 Banski Dvori Palace
7 St Mark's Church
8 Sabor (Parliament)
9 Historical Museum of Croatia
10 Stone Gate
11 Gallery of Naive Art
12 Muzejski Prostor
13 Lotršćak Tower
14 Funicular
15 St Catherine's Church
16 British Council
17 Nama Department Store
18 Dolac Market
19 Komedija Theatre
20 St Stephen's Cathedral
21 Tourist Office

CROATIA

interior courtyard anyway to see the Baška Slab (1102) from the island of Krk, one of the oldest inscriptions in the Croatian language.

The **Gallery of Modern Art** (closed Monday), adjacent at Andrije Hebranga 1, has a large collection of rather uninspiring paintings. The **Archaeological Museum** (closed Saturday), nearby at Trg Nikole Zrinjskog 19, displays prehistoric to medieval artefacts, as well as Egyptian mummies. There's a garden of Roman sculpture behind the museum. (At last report this museum was closed.)

West of the Centre The **Museum Mimara**, (open daily 10 am to 8 pm, Monday 2 to 8 pm only, US$2, free Monday) Rooseveltov trg 5, is one of the finest art galleries in Europe. Housed in a neo-Renaissance former school building (1883), this diverse collection shows the loving hand of Ante Topić Mimara, a private collector who donated over 3750 priceless objects to his native Zagreb, even though he spent much of his life in Salzburg, Austria. The Spanish, Italian and Dutch paintings are the highlight, but there are also large sections of glassware, sculpture and oriental art. (The permanent collection is presently in storage and only temporary exhibits may be seen.)

Nearby on Trg Maršala Tita is the neo-Baroque **Croatian National Theatre** (1895). Ivan Meštrović's *Fountain of Life* (1905) stands in front of the theatre. The **Ethnographic Museum**, Trg Mažuranića 14 (closed Monday), has a large collection of Croatian folk costumes with English explanations. South of here is the Art-Nouveau **National Library** (1907). The **Botanical Garden** on ulica Mihanovićeva (closed Monday, free admission) is attractive for the plants and landscaping as well as its restful corners.

Places to Stay

Camping There's a camping area beside the Pod starim hrastovima Restaurant at Sesvete, east of Zagreb. Take tram No 4, 7, 11 or 12 to Dubrava, then bus No 212 to Sesvete and get out at Varaždinska cesta. From the bus stop it's only an eight-minute walk north along the highway to the signposted camping ground. You may arrive to find the camping ground completely abandoned, in which case there'd probably be no problem pitching a tent for one night. Otherwise call the recently privatised restaurant at ☎ 201 656 and try to get information before heading out there.

Hostels Budget accommodation is in short supply in Zagreb, so an early arrival is recommended. The noisy 215-bed *Omladinski Hotel* (☎ 434 964) at Petrinjska 77 near the train station (open all year) is US$33 double without bath, US$45 with bath, plus US$0.75 per person tax (no singles). The six-bed dormitories here (US$11 per person) were occupied by war refugees from 1991 to early 1994, but at last report they were again available. The 10% YHA discount is only available to persons under 27 sleeping in the dormitory. You must check out by 9 am and can't occupy the room until 2 pm.

The *Studenthotel Cvjetno Naselje* (☎ 537 507) off Slavonska avenija in the southern section of the city charges US$28/39 for a single/double plus 10% tax, breakfast included. The rooms are good, each with private bath, and the staff are friendly. It's expensive because the 'higher ups' have decided foreigners can afford to pay a lot more than Croats. There's no student discount, although showing your ISIC and pleading poverty occasionally works. There's a self-service student restaurant here where a filling meal with a Coke will cost US$4. The Cvjetno Naselje is available to visitors from mid-July to the end of September only – the rest of the year it's a student dormitory. Take tram No 4, 5, 14, 16 or 17 south-west on Savska cesta to 'Vjesnik'. Opposite the stop is a tall building marked 'Vjesnik'. The student complex is just behind it. (Anyone needing a Hungarian visa should note that the Hungarian Embassy is only a few hundred metres from this hostel.)

In July and August make straight for the *Studentski dom Stjepan Radić*, Jarunska ulica 3, off Horvaćanska ulica in the southern part of the city near the Sava River (tram No 5 or 17). In the past rooms in this huge student complex have cost US$6 per person with a student card, US$13 per person without a card, although prices for foreigners have a way of going up with a bang in Zagreb, so be prepared.

Private Rooms Staza Agency (☎ 213 082), Heinzelova 3, off Kvaternikov trg in the eastern part of the city (tram No 4, 7, 11 or 12), has private rooms near their office or close to the bus station at US$19/29 single/double. Otherwise it's US$36 double in the centre of town. If you only stay one or two nights the price increases to US$25/38 single/double outside the centre (but still on tram lines) or US$46 double in the centre. Prices are high because almost half the money goes in taxes. Another half goes to the agency and your host only pockets a quarter of the money you pay! Staza's sign gives office hours of 9 am to 6 pm weekdays, 9 am to 1 pm Saturday, but the reliable English-speaking manager, Nadica Kratko, lives on the premises and says visitors can ring her doorbell anytime and she'll give them a room if she has one. Telephone reservations are not accepted. Nadica's standards are high and it's unlikely you'll have any complaints about your room.

Private rooms are also available from Di-prom Agency (☎ 523 617), Trnsko 25a, in Novi Zagreb south of the Sava River (tram No 7, 14 or 16 to Trnsko). Prices are US$25/38 for a single/double with a 30% surcharge if you stay only one night. Apartments are US$48 double and a US$1 per person per day tax is additional. Ninety per cent of their rooms are in high-rise apartment blocks in Novi Zagreb although they do have a few rooms in the city centre at the same price. Their office is in a school building and is only open weekdays from 7 am to 4 pm, Saturday 8 am to 1 pm.

Two buildings away from Di-prom is the Turističko Društvo Novi Zagreb (☎ 521 523), Trnsko 15e, which has private rooms in apartment buildings in this area at US$22/29 single/double, plus the US$1 tax, with a 30% surcharge for one-night stays, 20% extra for only two or three nights. Their office is theoretically open weekdays 8 am to 6 pm, Saturday 9 am to 1 pm.

If you're new to Croatia, don't be put off by these high prices. Along the coast, especially from Rab south, private rooms cost less than half as much.

Hotels There aren't any cheap hotels in Zagreb. Most of the older hotels have been renovated and the prices raised to B category. To make matters worse, United Nations personnel with fat expense allowances have flooded into Zagreb, exacerbating an already dismal accommodation situation. Even at the rip-off rates quoted below the snooty hotel clerks act as if they're doing you a favour giving you a room at all! If you can't arrange a morning arrival and afternoon departure to avoid spending the night in Zagreb, be prepared to bite the bullet and pay a lot more for a place to sleep than you would elsewhere in Croatia. The only easy escape is to book an overnight bus to Split or Dubrovnik.

The 110-room *Central Hotel* (☎ 425 777), Branimirova 3 opposite the train station, is US$46/62 single/double with bath and breakfast.

The six-storey *Hotel Astoria* (☎ 430 444), Petrinjska 71 near the Omladinski Hotel, has 130 rooms at US$54/77 single/double with private bath and breakfast.

The six-story *Hotel Jadran* (☎ 414 600), Vlaška 50 near the city centre, charges US$48/65 single/double with shower and breakfast.

If you're willing to spend that much consider splurging at the five-star *Hotel Esplanade* (☎ 435 666) next to the train station (US$138/168 single/double plus tax with bath and a buffet breakfast). This six-storey, 215-room hotel erected in 1924 is very elegant and there's a gambling casino right on the premises.

Places to Eat

Unlike accommodation, a good inexpensive meal is easily obtained in Zagreb. *Restaurant 'Jana' Samoposluga*, Petrinjska 79, a self-service cafeteria near the youth hostel, has pleasant décor but the food is unappetising. A better self-service is *Turist Express Restaurant*, Masarykova ulica 7 (weekdays until 9 pm, weekends until 4 pm).

The *Slavija Restaurant*, Jurišićeva 18 in the city centre, is an up-market lunch counter.

In summer the *Express Restaurant Četvrti Lovac*, Dezmanova 2 through the underpass marked 'Kino Sloboda', moves its tables out onto the street and dispenses pizza at reasonable prices. *Medulić*, Medulićeva 2 at Ilica, serves vegetarian food in the back dining room and the menu is in English.

For regional dishes and lots of local colour with your meal, dine in one of the outdoor restaurants up ulica Tkalčićeva from Trg Jelačića on summer evenings.

Cafés & Bars The *Rock Forum Café*, Gajeva ulica 13, occupies the rear sculpture garden of the Archaeological Museum and across the street is the *Hard Rock Café*, full of 1950s and 1960s memorabilia. Farther back in the passageway from Hard Rock is the *Art Café Thalia* which really tries to live up to its name. A couple of other cafés, art galleries and music shops share this lively complex at the corner of Teslina and Gajeva streets. If you're in Zagreb between October and May check out the *Boško Petrović Club* in the complex basement where there's jazz nightly.

Zagreb's most pretentious cafés are *Gradska Kavana* on Trg Jelačića and *Kazališna Kavana* on Trg Maršala Tita opposite the Croatian National Theatre.

Café Centar, Jurišićeva ulica 24, has great cakes and ice cream.

The *Pivnica Tomislav*, Trg Tomislava 18, facing the park in front of the train station, is a good local bar with inexpensive draught beer.

Entertainment

Zagreb is a happening city. Its theatres and concert halls present a great variety of programmes throughout the year. Many (but not all) are listed in the monthly brochure, *Zagreb events & performances*, which is usually available from the tourist office.

It's also worth making the rounds of the theatres in person to check the calendars. Tickets are usually available, even for the best shows. A small office marked 'Kazalište Komedija' (look for the posters) in the Blagasija Oktogon, a passage connecting Trg Petra Preradovića to Ilica near Trg Jelačića, also sells theatre tickets.

On odd years in April there's the Zagreb Biennial of Contemporary Music, since 1961 Croatia's most important musical event. Zagreb also hosts a festival of animated films every other year in June. Croatia's largest international fairs are the Zagreb spring (mid-April) and autumn (mid-September) grand trade fairs.

Theatre The neo-Baroque style *Croatian National Theatre*, at Trg Maršala Tita 15, was established in 1895. It offers opera and ballet performances and the box office is open Monday to Saturday from 10 am to 1 pm and 6 to 7.30 pm. You have a choice of orchestra *(parket)*, lodge *(lože)* or balcony *(balkon)* seats.

The *Komedija Theatre*, Kaptol 9 near the cathedral, stages operettas and musicals.

The ticket office of the *Vatroslav Lisinski Concert Hall*, just south of the train station, is open weekdays from 10 am to 1 pm and 5.30 to 7.30 pm, Saturday 10 am to 1 pm.

Concerts also take place at the *Academy of Music*, Gundulićeva 6a off Ilica.

There are performances at the *Puppet Theatre*, ulica Baruna Trenka 3, Saturday at 5 pm and Sunday at noon.

Discos Zagreb's most popular disco is *Saloon*, Tuškanac 1a (open after 9.30 pm daily except Monday). On weekends it's packed.

In the evening the cafés along Tkalčićeva north off Trg Jelačića buzz with activity as crowds spill out onto the street, drinks in hand. Farther up on Kozarska ulica the city's young people cluster shoulder to shoulder. Trg Petra Preradovića, Zagreb's flower market square, is also interesting.

Cinemas A notice board in the passage at Ilica 10 displays what's showing at all the cinemas of Zagreb (with addresses and times).

Spectator Sports Basketball is popular in Zagreb, and from October to April games take place at the *Cibona Centar*, Savska cesta 30 opposite the Technical Museum, usually on Saturday at 7.30 pm. Tickets are available at the door.

On Saturday afternoon soccer games are held at the *Maksimir Stadium*, Maksimirska 128 on the east side of Zagreb (tram No 4, 7, 11 or 12 to Bukovačka). If you arrive too early for the game, Zagreb's zoo is just across the street.

Things to Buy

Ilica is Zagreb's main shopping street. Get in touch with Croatian consumerism at the Nama department store on Ilica near Trg Jelačića. Some souvenirs are also sold here.

Folk-music compact discs are available from Fonoteca at Nama, Ilica 6, and Orfej, ulica Mirka Bogovića 1 (a block apart).

CROATIA

Rukotvorine, Ilica 52, has many appealing handicraft items, such as Croatian dolls, wall hangings, wooden objects, pottery, blankets and glassware.

The shops and grocery stores in the passage under the tracks beside the train station have long opening hours.

Getting There & Away

Bus Zagreb's big, modern bus station has a large, enclosed waiting room where you can stretch out while waiting for your bus (but there's no heating in winter). The signs posted in English at the station are reassuring, and the people at the information desk speak English too! Buy most international tickets at window Nos 2 and 3, tickets to Holland and Germany at window No 17, and change money (including travellers' cheques) at Croatia Tourist. The left-luggage office is open nonstop (take care – they charge *per hour*).

Buses depart from Zagreb for most of Croatia, Slovenia and places beyond. Buy an advance ticket at the station if you'll be travelling far.

The following domestic buses depart from Zagreb: Bled (200 km, four daily), Koper (253 km, five daily), Krk (229 km, daily), Ljubljana (135 km, 12 daily), Maribor (122 km, nine daily), Piran (273 km, daily), Poreč (264 km, four daily), Portorož (268 km, three daily, US$8), Pula (283 km, 10 daily), Rab (211 km, Friday only), Rijeka (173 km, 19 daily), Rovinj (278 km, five daily), Split (478 km, 22 daily), Varaždin (77 km, 23 daily), Mali Lošinj (298 km, daily) and Zadar (320 km, 14 daily). No buses operate to Serbia.

Croatia Express, Branimirova 1, opposite the train station, has a daily overnight bus from Zagreb to Dubrovnik (713 km, US$14). This bus leaves from in front of the train station. Another Croatia Express office at Trg Tomislava trg 17 sells tickets for an overnight bus to Međugorje in Bosnia-Hercegovina (13 hours, US$20).

To go to Hungary, there's Zagreb-Nagykanizsa (145 km, twice daily, US$9) or five daily Zagreb-Barcs buses (202 km,

US$14). Nagykanizsa is preferable if you're bound for Budapest or Balaton Lake, Barcs for Pécs or Yugoslavia.

Some other international buses worth knowing about are Zagreb to Vienna (371 km, daily at 9.30 pm, US$35), Munich (576 km, daily at 7 pm, US$50), Berlin (Tuesday, Saturday and Sunday, DM159, payment in Deutschmarks only), Amsterdam (twice a week, US$110) and Istanbul (twice weekly, US$91). Luggage is three Deutschmarks in cash per piece.

Train The *Maestral* express train departs from Zagreb for Budapest (412 km, seven hours, US$24) every morning. The *Adriatica* runs overnight. A ticket from Zagreb to Nagykanizsa, the first main junction inside Hungary, is US$10. Alternatively, take a train to Koprivnica or Varaždin and one of the two or three local trains into Hungary from there. A useful daily train runs between Zagreb and Pécs, Hungary (267 km, five hours, US$16), leaving Zagreb in the afternoon.

Zagreb is on both the Munich-Ljubljana and Vienna-Maribor main lines. There are trains twice a day between Munich and Zagreb (613 km, eight hours, US$61) via Salzburg. Three trains a day arrive from Venice (seven hours, US$26), one of them originating in Geneva and Rome.

There are five trains a day from Zagreb to Osijek (288 km, 4½ hours), 20 to Koprivnica (92 km, two hours), 11 to Varaždin (110 km, three hours), nine to Ljubljana (160 km, 2¼ hours), five to Rijeka (243 km, five hours) and two to Pula (418 km, 5½ hours). Reservations are required on some trains, so check. Beware of overcharging in the 1st-class ticket office (check the price beforehand at information).

In mid-1991 all rail, road and air traffic between Zagreb and Belgrade was cut, and to travel between the two cities it was necessary to do a loop through Hungary. This situation should change when the war is over and communications are normalised, so check for the latest information upon arrival. At last report no trains were running south

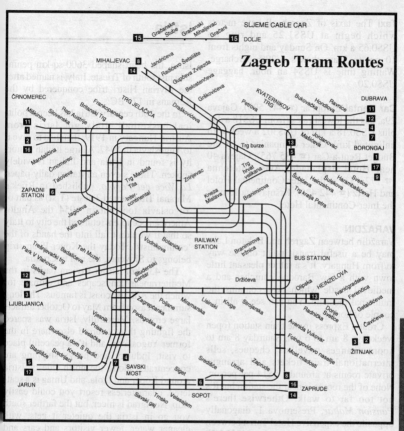

Zagreb Tram Routes

CROATIA

from Zagreb to Zadar or Split, as the line passed through areas held by Serbian separatists.

Getting Around

Public transport is based on an efficient but overcrowded network of trams, although the city centre is compact enough to make them unnecessary. Tram Nos 3 and 8 don't run on weekends. Buy tickets (US$0.65) at newspaper kiosks. You can use your ticket for transfers within 90 minutes but only in one direction.

A *dnevna karta* (day ticket) valid on all public transport until 4 am the next morning is available for US$1.75 at the Prodavaonica Karta ticket kiosk in the underground passage beside the train station. If they're closed the adjacent Vjesnik newsstand also has them (in fact, most Vjesnik or Tisak news outlets around Zagreb sell them). At the bus station the Tisak newsstand at the entrance to the platforms has day tickets.

To/From the Airport The Eurokont bus to Pleso Airport, 17 km south-east, leaves from the bus station every hour on the half-hour from 4.30 am to 7.30 pm and later if there are flights (US$2).

Taxi The taxis of Zagreb all have meters which begin at US$1.25 and ring up US$0.65 a km. On Sunday and nights from 10 pm to 5 am there's a 20% surcharge. Waiting time is US$4 an hour, baggage US$0.20.

Car Rental Europcar (☎ 447 500), Gajeva 29a, has the lowest rates (from US$18 a day plus US$0.18 a km or US$302 a week with unlimited km). Other companies to try are Budget Rent-a-Car (☎ 435 765), Gajeva 40 near Hotel Esplanade, Avis Autotehna (☎ 172 133) at the Inter-Continental Hotel and Hertz (☎ 442 423), Kršnjavoga 13 near the Inter-Continental Hotel.

VARAŽDIN

Varaždin between Zagreb and Balaton Lake may be a useful transit point on the way to/from Hungary. It's a rather pleasant little town with a few Baroque churches and a medieval castle which now contains the municipal museum. You can see it all in a couple of hours.

Croatia Express in the train station (open weekdays 8 am to 6 pm, Saturday 8 am to noon) changes travellers' cheques, sells international train tickets and arranges private rooms at around US$14 per person. None of the rooms is near the station but it's not too far to walk. Otherwise there's *Pansion Maltar*, Prešernova 1, diagonally opposite the expensive Hotel Turist between the train and bus stations, at US$25/38 single/double.

Train service from Zagreb to Varaždin (110 km) is every couple of hours and there are two unreserved local trains a day between Varaždin and Nagykanizsa, Hungary (72 km, US$3). Coming this way is cheaper than buying a through ticket to Hungary in Zagreb. The left-luggage office at the train station is open 24 hours a day.

Varaždin's bus and train stations are on opposite sides of town. There are 23 buses a day to Zagreb, eight to Maribor, four to Rijeka, three to Ljubljana, two each to Nagykaniza, Stuttgart and Munich and one to Vienna.

Istria

Istria, the heart-shaped 3600-sq-km peninsula just south of Trieste, Italy, is named after the Illyrian Histri tribe conquered by the Romans in 177 BC.

In the 20th century Istria has been a political basketball. Italy got Istria from Austria-Hungary in 1919, then had to give it to Yugoslavia in 1947. A large Italian minority is found in Istria and Italian is widely spoken. There's even an Italian daily paper, *La Voce del Popolo*, published in Rijeka. Marshal Tito wanted Trieste (Trst) as part of Yugoslavia too, but in 1954 the Anglo-American occupiers returned the city to Italy so that it wouldn't fall into the hands of the 'communists'. Today the Koper-Piran strip belongs to Slovenia, the rest to Croatia.

The 430-km Istrian Riviera basks in the Mediterranean landscapes and climate for which the Adriatic coast is famous. The long summer season from May to October attracts large crowds. Mercifully, Istria was spared the fighting that occurred elsewhere in the former Yugoslavia, and it's a peaceful place to visit. Industry and heavy shipping are concentrated along the north side of Istria around Koper and Izola, and Umag is a scattered, characterless resort you could easily skip. Novigrad is nicer, but the farther south you go in Istria the quieter it gets, with cleaner water, fewer visitors and cars and less industry. See Piran quickly, then move south to Rovinj, a perfect base from which to explore Poreč and Pula.

Getting There & Away

Koper and Rijeka are the main entry/exit points, with buses to most towns on Istria's west coast every couple of hours. Train service in Istria is limited, so plan on getting around by bus.

From April to September the Italian shipping company Adriatica Navigazion operates the fast motor vessel *Marcon* between Trieste and Istria, departing from Trieste five days a week at 8 am and return

CROATIA

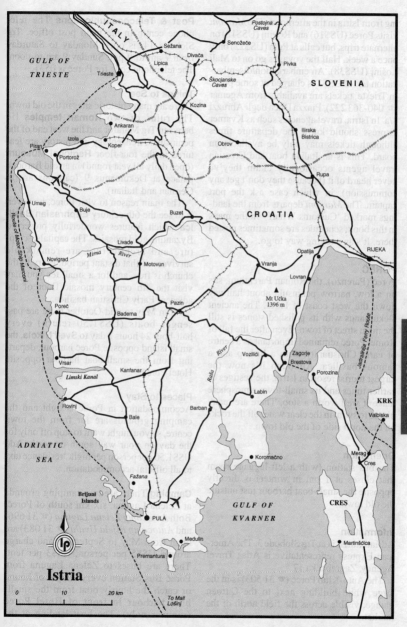

Istria

0   10   20 km

To Mali Lošinj

ing from Istria in the afternoon. The *Marconi* visits Poreč (US$16) and Rovinj (US$18) on alternate trips, but calls at Pula (US$22) only once a week. Half the voyages go on to Mali Lošinj (US$38). An embarkation/disembarkation tax of US$2 is charged at some ports. In Trieste, tickets are available from Agemar (☎ 040-363 222), Piazza Duca degli Abruzzi 1/a. In Istria, travel agencies such as Kvarner Express should know the departure times although tickets may only be available on board. This is an Italian boat and Croatian travel agents occasionally claim they've never heard of it (because they don't get any commission), in which case ask the port captain. The *Marconi* departs from the landings marked 'Customs Wharf' on the maps in this book; schedules are sometimes posted there. It's an exciting way to go.

POREČ

Poreč (Parenzo), the Roman Parentium, sits on a low, narrow peninsula about halfway down the west coast of Istria. The ancient Dekumanus with its polished stones is still the main street of town. Even after the fall of Rome, Poreč remained important as a centre of early Christianity, with a bishop and a famous basilica. Although it's now the largest tourist resort in Istria, the vestiges of earlier times and its small-town atmosphere make it well worth a stop. There are many places to swim in the clear water off the rocks on the north side of the old town.

Orientation

The bus station (with a left-luggage room that closes at 1 pm in winter) is directly opposite the small-boat harbour just outside the old town.

Information

Adriatikturist is at Trg Slobode 3. The American Express representative is Atlas Travel Agency, Zagrebačka 17.

The Auto-Klub Poreč (☎ 31 503) is in the large white building next to the Citroën garage, visible across the field north of the market.

Post & Telecommunications The telephone centre in the main post office, Trg Slobode 14, is open Monday to Saturday from 7 am to 9 pm, Sunday 9 am to noon. The telephone code for Poreč is 0531.

Things to See

There are many historic sites in the old town. The ruins of two **Roman temples** lie between Trg Marafor and the west end of the peninsula. Archaeology and history are featured in the four-floor **Regional Museum** (open daily all year round) in an old Baroque palace at Dekumanus 9 (captions are in German and Italian).

The main reason to visit Poreč, however, is to see the 6th century **Euphrasian Basilica** which features wonderfully preserved Byzantine gold mosaics. The capitals, sculpture and architecture are remarkable survivors of that distant period. Entry to the church is free, and for a small fee you may visit the 4th century mosaic floor of the adjacent Early Christian basilica.

From May to mid-October there are passenger boats (US$1.50 return) every half-hour 24 hours a day to **Sveti Nikola**, the small island opposite Poreč harbour, departing from the small-boat harbour opposite Hotel Poreč.

Places to Stay

Accommodation in Poreč is tight and the camping grounds are far from the town centre, so you might want to stop off only for the day on your way south or north. Add US$1.50 per person per night 'residence tax' to all official accommodation.

Camping There are two camping grounds at Zelena Laguna, six km south of Poreč. Both *Autocamp Zelena Laguna* (☎ 31 696) and *Autocamp Bijela Uvala* (☎ 31 083) are open from May to September and charge around US$5 per person, US$3 per tent. There are buses to Zelena Laguna from Poreč Bus Station every couple of hours, or catch the hourly boat from the small-boat harbour in front of Hotel Poreč (summer only). The boat landing at the

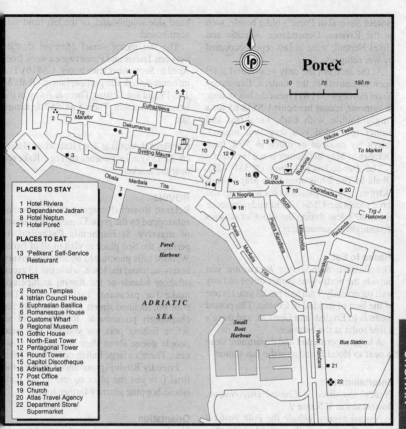

Poreč

0   75   150 m

PLACES TO STAY
1 Hotel Riviera
3 Depandance Jadran
8 Hotel Neptun
21 Hotel Poreč

PLACES TO EAT
13 'Peškera' Self-Service
   Restaurant

OTHER
2 Roman Temples
4 Istrian Council House
5 Euphrasian Basilica
6 Romanesque House
7 Customs Wharf
9 Regional Museum
10 Gothic House
11 North-East Tower
12 Pentagonal Tower
14 Round Tower
15 Capitol Discotheque
16 Adriatikturist
17 Post Office
18 Cinema
19 Church
20 Atlas Travel Agency
22 Department Store/
   Supermarket

ADRIATIC SEA

Poreč Harbour

Small Boat Harbour

To Market

Trg Slobode

A Negrija

Trg J Rakovca

Bus Station

CROATIA

Parentium Hotel is nearly two km from Autocamp Zelena Laguna, however, and even farther from Bijela Uvala. Ask if the boat will go on to Hotel Delfin, which is closer.

Private Rooms Adriatikturist (☎ 31 233), Trg Slobode 3 (and a second Adriatikturist office near the market), rents private rooms for US$12 per person. Kompas (☎ 32 339), Partizanska 2 beside the market, and Atlas Travel Agency, Zagrebačka 17, also have private rooms for similar prices.

If you only stay one to three nights there's

a 30% surcharge, and most agencies will not rent private rooms outside the main May to September tourist season, allegedly because the rooms aren't heated (in fact, with off-season rates in effect the owners and agencies just couldn't be bothered). Kompas is the only agency that may be willing to help you in the off season.

If none of the agencies in town is renting private rooms, walk south on Rade Končara and watch for houses with sobe or zimmer signs. Near Caffe Bar Janko down this way is Sun Tourist Service, Butorac 18, which rents private rooms all year round.

Hotels Several of Poreč's older hotels, such as the Riviera, Dependance Adriatic and Hotel Neptun, were at last report occupied by war refugees.

At the moment the only year-round hotel open to tourists is the modern, five-storey *Hotel Poreč* (☎ 351 811) near the bus station. In summer, rooms here cost US$38/65 for a single/double with bath, breakfast and dinner (provided you stay four nights). Prices are reduced as much as 50% from October to May but dinner is not included.

The *Depandance Jadran* (☎ 351 422), Obala M Tita 24, is open from May to mid-October only. Singles/doubles with bath and three meals are US$43/75 in midsummer or about 50% less during the shoulder seasons (four-night minimum stay).

Places to Eat

The *Peškera Self-Service Restaurant* just outside the north-west corner of the old city wall (open daily 9 am to 8 pm all year) is one of the best of its kind in Croatia. The posted menu is in English and German, and there's a free toilet at the entrance.

A large supermarket and department store is next to Hotel Poreč near the bus station.

Entertainment

Porečs' top disco is *Capitol Discotheque*, downstairs at V Nazor 9.

Annual events include the Folk Festival (June), the Inter Folk Fest (August), the Annual Art Exhibition (all summer until late August) and the Musical Summer (May to September). Ask about these at the tourist office as soon as you arrive.

Getting There & Away

The nearest train station is at Pazin, 30 km east (six buses daily from Poreč). Buses run twice a day to Portorož (54 km), Trieste (89 km) and Ljubljana (176 km), four times a day to Rovinj (38 km) and Zagreb (264 km), five times a day to Rijeka (80 km) and 12 times a day to Pula (56 km). Between Poreč and Rovinj the bus runs along the Lim Channel, a drowned valley. To see it, sit on the right-hand side southbound, or the left-hand side northbound.

The fast motor vessel *Marconi* shuttles between Trieste and Poreč twice a week from April to September (two hours, US$16). For information ask the port captain at Obala M Tita 17 and see Getting There & Away in the Istria introduction. There's a US$2 departure tax.

Car Rental Avis is at Trg J Rakovca 1; Hertz (☎ 32 113) is in a corner of Trg J Rakovca near the market.

ROVINJ

Relaxed Rovinj (Rovigno), its high peninsula topped by the great 57-metre-high tower of massive St Euphemia Cathedral, is perhaps the best place to visit in all of Istria. Wooded hills punctuated by low-rise luxury hotels surround the town, while the 13 green offshore islands of the Rovinj archipelago make for pleasant, varied views. The cobbled, inclined streets in the old town are charmingly picturesque. Rovinj is still an active fishing port, so you see the local people going about their day-to-day business. There's a large Italian community here.

Friendly Rovinj (pronounced without the final j) is just the place to rest up for your island-hopping journey farther south.

Orientation

The bus station is just south-east of the old town. Go down to the waterfront and follow it around to Trg Maršala Tita. The left-luggage office at the bus station opens daily from 5.15 am to 9 pm (ask at the ticket window).

Information

The tourist office is at Obala Pina Budicina 12, just off Trg Maršala Tita.

Motorists can turn to the Auto Moto Društva (HAK) next to the large parking lot on Obala Palih Boraca.

Phone calls can be made from the post office behind the bus station. The telephone code for Rovinj is 052.

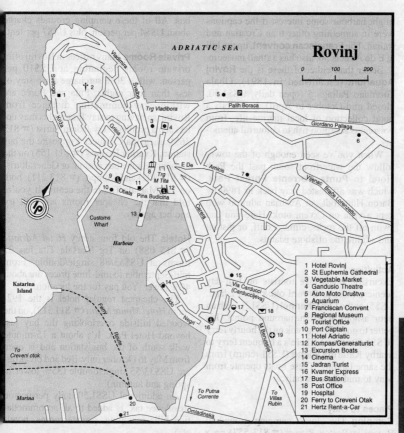

Rovinj

0   100   200

1 Hotel Rovinj
2 St Euphemia Cathedral
3 Vegetable Market
4 Gandusio Theatre
5 Auto Moto Društva
6 Aquarium
7 Franciscan Convent
8 Regional Museum
9 Tourist Office
10 Port Captain
11 Hotel Adriatic
12 Kompas/Generalturist
13 Excursion Boats
14 Cinema
15 Jadran Turist
16 Kvarner Express
17 Bus Station
18 Post Office
19 Hospital
20 Ferry to Creveni Otak
21 Hertz Rent-a-Car

Things to See

The only sight of Rovinj worth special attention is the **Cathedral of St Euphemia** (1736), which completely dominates the town from its hill-top location. This, the largest Baroque building in Istria, reflects the period during the 18th century when Rovinj was the most populous town in Istria, an important fishing centre and the bulwark of the Venetian fleet. Inside the cathedral, don't miss the tomb of St Euphemia (martyred in 304 AD) behind the right-hand altar. The saint's remains were brought here from Constantinople in 800. On the anniversary of her martyrdom (16 September) devotees congregate here. A copper statue of St Euphemia tops the cathedral's mighty tower.

Take a wander along the winding narrow backstreets below the cathedral, such as ulica Grisia, where local artists sell their work. Rovinj has developed into an important art centre, and each year in mid-August Rovinj's painters stage a big open-air art show in the town.

The **Regional Museum** on Trg Maršala Tita (closed Sunday and Monday) contains an unexciting collection of paintings and a few Etruscan artefacts found in Istria. These might harbour some interest if the captions were in something other than Croatian and Italian. The **Franciscan convent**, up the hill at E de Amicis 36, also has a small museum.

Better than either of these is the **Rovinj Aquarium** (established in 1891), Obala Giordano Paliaga 5 (open daily, US$1.50, closed mid-October to April). It exhibits a good collection of local marine life, from poisonous scorpion fish to colourful anemones.

When you've seen enough of the town, follow the waterfront south past the Park Hotel to **Punta Corrente Forest Park**, which was afforested way back in 1890 by Baron Hütterodt, an Austrian admiral who kept a villa on Crveni otok. Here you can swim off the rocks, climb a cliff, or just sit and admire the offshore islands.

Activities

Excursion boats take tourists on half-day scenic cruises to **Crveni okok** (Red Island, US$5) or the **Lim Channel** (US$12), with an hour ashore at the turnaround points. It's better to go to Crveni otok on the hourly ferry (US$1.50 return). There's a frequent ferry to nearby **Katarina Island** (US$1 return) from the same landing. These boats operate from May to mid-October only.

Places to Stay

Camping The closest camping ground to Rovinj is *Porton Biondi* (☎ 813 557) on a wooded hill two km north of the old town (open June to mid-September). If it's closed there's *FKK Monsena Camping* (☎ 813 535) three km farther north, a nudist camp open from May to September. Bungalows at Monsena are US$32/52 single/double from mid-July to August and about 25% less at other times (includes breakfast and dinner provided you stay three nights). Both of these are served by the Monsena bus, which terminates right in front of the reception of Monsena Camping.

Five km south-east of Rovinj is *Polari Camping* (☎ 813 441), open from May to early October. Get there on the Villas Rubin

bus. All of these camping grounds charge about US$4 per person, plus US$7 per tent.

Private Rooms Many offices in Rovinj offer private rooms beginning at US$10 per person, with a 30% surcharge for a stay of less than four nights. Pula and Poreč are within easy commuting distance from Rovinj, so having to stay four nights may not be such a problem. Try Jadran Turist (☎ 813 365), ulica Via Carducci 4 opposite the bus station; Kvarner Express (☎ 811 155) on the harbour near the bus station; or Generalturist (☎ 811 402) and Kompas (☎ 813 211), both on Trg Maršala Tita in the centre. If you're told that the cheaper rooms are full, try another agency.

Hotels The old four-storey *Hotel Adriatic* (☎ 815 088) on Trg Maršala Tita has 27 rooms at US$53/88 single/double. From mid-September to mid-June prices are about 40% lower. You pay for the location.

The cheapest regular hotel is the 192-room *Hotel Monte Mulin* (☎ 811 512), on the wooded hillside overlooking the bay just beyond Hotel Park. It's about a 15-minute walk south of the bus station and is open from May to October only. Bed and breakfast are US$33/55 single/double (35% lower in spring and autumn).

An additional US$1.50 daily per-person 'residence tax' is added to all accommodation bills (camping, private rooms, hotels etc).

Places to Eat

The many restaurants of Rovinj are all oriented towards the tourist market, so this may be the place to patronise the local grocery stores. One large supermarket is right next to Hotel Adriatic. There are several kiosks selling *burek* near the vegetable market, and the adjacent park or sea wall makes a perfect picnic site.

Entertainment

Check the *Gandusio Theatre* on Trg Valdibora where movies are shown most nights. The most popular disco is *Kotlić* on

Stjepan Radić at the edge of town on the way to Villas Rubin.

The city's annual events include the Rovinj-Pesaro Regata (early May), the Rovinj Fair (August) and the ACY Cup Match Yacht Race (September).

Getting There & Away
The closest train station is Kanfanar, 19 km away on the Pula-Divača line. There's a bus from Rovinj to Pula (34 km) every hour or so, nine a day to Poreč (38 km), five a day to Rijeka (84 km) and Zagreb (278 km), three a day to Koper (81 km), two a day to Ljubljana (190 km) and one a day to Split (509 km) and Dubrovnik (744 km).

From April to September the fast motor vessel *Marconi* glides between Rovinj and Trieste three times a week (two hours, US$18). Eurostar Travel on the harbour may have tickets, otherwise try asking the port captain on the opposite side of the same building.

Getting Around
Local buses run every two hours from the bus station, north to Monsena and south to Villas Rubin.

PULA
Pula (the ancient Polensium) is a large regional centre with some industry, a big naval base and a busy commercial harbour. The old town with its museums and well-preserved Roman ruins is certainly worth a visit and nearby are rocky wooded peninsulas overlooking the clear Adriatic waters, which may explain the many resort hotels and camping grounds concentrated there.

Orientation
The bus station (with a left-luggage office open from 5.30 am to 10 pm except for two half-hour breaks) is on ulica Mate Balote in the centre of town. One block south is Giardini, the central hub, while the harbour is just north of the bus station. The train station is near the water about one km north of town (with a left-luggage service from 9 am to 4 pm).

Information
The Tourist Association of Pula is at ulica Istarska 13 (weekdays 9 am to 1 pm). The American Express representative is Atlas Travel Agency (☎ 23 732), Petra Drapšina 1, Pula 52000. It will hold clients' mail.

Post & Telecommunications Long-distance telephone calls may be placed at the main post office on ulica Končara Rade (open till 8 pm daily). The telephone code for Pula is 052.

Travel Agencies Jadroagent (☎ 41 878), Obala maršala Tita 14, and the adjacent Kvarner Express office sell ferry tickets.

Via Tours on ulica Mate Balote next to the bus station sells express bus tickets to Zagreb and Trieste and train tickets to Munich and Vienna. Transimpex, Premanturska 6, also runs daily private buses from Pula to Zagreb (283 km, US$14) and Trieste (US$15).

Things to See
Pula's most imposing sight is the 1st century AD **Roman amphitheatre** (closed Sunday) overlooking the harbour north-east of the old town. At US$2.50 admission (students US$1.25) the amphitheatre is expensive, but you can see plenty for free from outside. Around the end of July a Croatian film festival is held in the amphitheatre, with an Italian film festival held a week later.

The **Archaeological Museum** (open daily in summer, closed weekends in winter, admission US$2, students US$1) is on the hill opposite the bus station. Even if you don't get into the museum be sure to visit the large sculpture garden around it, and the **Roman Theatre** behind. The garden is entered through 2nd century AD twin gates.

Along the street facing the bus station are **Roman walls** which mark the east boundary of old Pula. Follow these walls south and continue down Giardini to the **Triumphal Arch of Sergius** (27 BC). The street beyond the arch winds right around old Pula, changing names several times as it goes. Follow it to Trg Republike where you'll find the ancient **Temple of Augustus** and the **old**

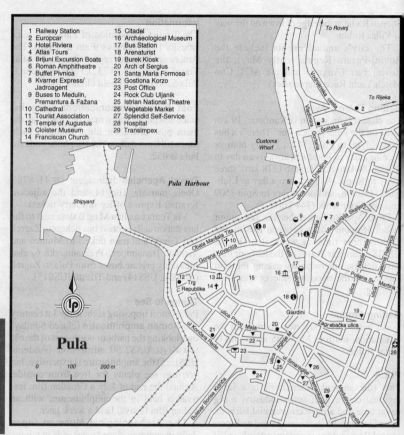

1 Railway Station
2 Europcar
3 Hotel Riviera
4 Atlas Tours
5 Brijuni Excursion Boats
6 Roman Amphitheatre
7 Buffet Pivnica
8 Kvarner Express/
   Jadroagent
9 Buses to Medulin,
   Premantura & Fažana
10 Cathedral
11 Tourist Association
12 Temple of Augustus
13 Cloister Museum
14 Franciscan Church
15 Citadel
16 Archaeological Museum
17 Bus Station
18 Arenaturist
19 Burek Kiosk
20 Arch of Sergius
21 Santa Maria Formosa
22 Gostiona Korzo
23 Post Office
24 Rock Club Uljanik
25 Istrian National Theatre
26 Vegetable Market
27 Splendid Self-Service
28 Hospital
29 Transimpex

To Rovinj
To Rijeka
Customs Wharf
Pula Harbour
Shipyard
Pula
0   100   200 m

town hall (1296). Above this square is the
Franciscan Church (1314), with a museum
in the cloister (entry from around the other
side) containing paintings, medieval frescoes, a Roman mosaic etc.

The **Museum of History** (open daily) is
in the 17th century Venetian citadel on a high
hill in the centre of the old town. The meagre
exhibits deal mostly with the maritime
history of Pula but the views of Pula from the
citadel walls are good.

Places to Stay

Camping The closest camping ground to

Pula is *Autocamp Stoja* (☎ 24 144; open
mid-April to mid-October) three km south-
west of the centre (take bus No 1 to the
terminus at Stoja). There's lots of space on
the shady promontory, with swimming possible off the rocks. The two restaurants at this
camping ground are good. There are more
camping grounds at **Medulin** and **Premantura**, coastal resorts south-east of Pula.

Hostels The *Ljetovalište Ferijalnog Saveza
Youth Hostel* (☎ 34 595), Zaljev Valsaline 4,
is three km south of central Pula in a great
location overlooking a clean pebble beach

open to the sea. Take the No 2 Verudela bus to the 'Piramida' stop and walk back to the first street, turn left and look for the sign. Beds are US$8 per person, and camping is allowed at the hostel (US$3). You can sit and sip cold beer on the hostel's terrace, where a rock band plays on some summer evenings, and also ask about Disco Piramida nearby. In the past the hostel has only been open from mid-April to mid-October but heating is being installed to allow them to stay open all year round. If the youth hostel is full and you have a tent, it's only a 10-minute walk from there to *Autocamp Ribarska Koliba* (☎ 22 966), open from mid-June to mid-September.

Private Rooms Arenaturist (☎ 34 355), Giardini 4 a block from the bus station, and Via Tours on ulica Mate Balote right next to the bus station, have private rooms all year round for US$10 per person, with an additional 30% surcharge if you stay less than four nights. Other offices offering similar rooms at similar rates in summer only are Brijuni Turist Biro (☎ 22 477), Ulica Istarska 3 beside the bus station, and Transimpex, Premanturska 6 near the main market. Transimpex is open on Saturday and Sunday mornings but the others are usually closed on weekends.

Hotels The cheapest hotel is the 112-room *Pension Ribarska Koliba* (☎ 22 966) near the camping ground of the same name, towards Verudela about three km south of Pula (No 2 Verudela bus). Singles/doubles with shared bath are US$20/33 (plus 25% in midsummer) but the place is often full with groups. The pension has a nice terrace overlooking a bay full of small boats. It's open from May to mid-October only.

Treat yourself to a little luxury at the B-category *Hotel Riviera* (☎ 41 166), Splitska ulica 1 overlooking the harbour. Comfortable rooms in this elegant old hotel erected in 1908 are US$28/47 single/double with shared bath, US$34/56 with private bath, breakfast included. From October to May prices are about 25% lower. Compare the

price of a room with half and full board as you check in.

Hotel Omir (☎ 22 019), Serdo Dobrića 6 just off Zagrebačka ulica near Giardini, is a private hotel with 11 rooms at US$38/63/76/90 single/double/triple/quad with bath and breakfast. If you're willing to pay that, you're better off at the Riviera.

Places to Eat

Splendid Self-Service, Narodni trg 5 opposite the vegetable market (open daily from 9.30 am to 9 pm), is easy since you see what you're getting and pay at the end of the line.

For grilled meats and local dishes such as goulash, smoked ham and squid risotto try *Gostiona Korzo*, ulica Prvog maja 34 (closed Sunday). Despite the plain exterior, it's a little expensive but manageable if you order carefully.

There are a couple of good burek and hamburger kiosks on the corner of Zagrebačka and Joakima Rakovca which are open from 7 am to 1 am.

The people at the cheese counter in *Puljanka Samoposluga* next to Kino Istra on Giardini will prepare healthy sandwiches while you wait and they're open Monday to Saturday from 6.30 am to 8 pm, Sunday 8 am to 6 pm.

Buffet Pivnica, in the back courtyard at Istarska 34 near the Roman amphitheatre (daily 8 am to 9 pm), is one of the least expensive places in Pula to get a draught beer, glass of wine or espresso coffee, and all prices are clearly listed. No food is available but there's a convenient free toilet.

Pula's most prestigious café is *Kavana Forum*, Trg Republike 8.

Entertainment

Posters around Pula announce live performances. *Rock Club Uljanik*, Jurja Dobrile 2, is great whenever something's on. You can dance there.

Two cinemas on Giardini are the Istra at No 13 and Giardini at No 2. Quality art films are shown at the Istrian National Theatre a couple of times a week.

Getting There & Away

Bus The 18 daily buses to Rijeka (110 km, 1½ hours) are sometimes crowded, especially the eight which continue on to Zagreb, so reserve a seat a day in advance if you can. Going from Pula to Rijeka, be sure to sit on the right-hand side of the bus for a stunning view of the Gulf of Kvarner.

Other buses from Pula include 20 a day to Rovinj (42 km), 12 to Poreč (56 km), eight to Zagreb (292 km), three to Zadar (333 km), two each to Postojna (161 km), Trieste (124 km) and Split (514 km) and one each to Portorož (90 km), Koper (104 km), Ljubljana (211 km) and Dubrovnik (749 km).

Train Ever since the days when Pula was the main port of the Austro-Hungarian empire, the railway line in Istria has run north towards Italy and Austria instead of east into what is now Croatia. Now that a new international border has been drawn across the line it's even more irrelevant and most local trains terminate at Buzet near the Slovenian border. However, two do go on to Divača (140 km) near Trieste, where you connect for Ljubljana.

One early morning train and one afternoon train run through to Zagreb (418 km) via Ljubljana but both services involve two sets of border controls and a new Croatian visa, so the only real reason to use the train would be to go to Ljubljana (258 km, four daily, US$11 local, US$14 express).

Boat For the ferry to Mali Lošinj (US$8 one way) and Zadar (US$14 one way), ask at Jadroagent or Kvarner Express on the harbour. The ferries leave on Monday, Tuesday and Friday from mid-June to September only.

Getting Around

There are only two city buses of interest to visitors, both of which stop at Giardini. Bus No 1 runs to the camping ground at Stoja, while bus No 2 to Verudela passes the youth hostel and Pension Ribarska Koliba. Frequencies vary from every 15 minutes to every 30 minutes with service from 6 am to 10.30 pm daily. Tokens (*kartice za autobus*) for both these are sold at newsstands for US$1.

BRIJUNI

The Brijuni (Brioni) island group consists of two main pine-covered islands and 12 islets off the coast of Istria just north-west of Pula. Each year from 1949 until his death in 1980, Marshal Tito spent six months at his summer residences on Brijuni in a style any Western capitalist would admire. Tito received 90 heads of state here, and at a meeting on Veliki Brijuni (the main island) in 1956 Tito, Nasser and Nehru laid the foundations of the non-aligned movement.

Tito had three palaces on Veliki Brijuni: Vila Jadranka, Bijela Vila and Vila Brionka. The famous 1956 Brijuni Declaration was signed in Bijela Vila, Tito's 'White House'. Tourists are driven past these three, but Tito's private retreat on the tiny islet of Vanga cannot be visited. In 1984 Brijuni was proclaimed a national park and some 680 species of plants grow on the islands, including many exotic subtropical species planted at Tito's request.

As you arrive, after a half-hour boat ride from Fažana on the mainland, you'll see Tito's two private yachts still tied up in the harbour, and four luxury hotels near the landing where his guests once stayed. The four-hour tour of Veliki Brijuni begins with a visit to **St German Church**, now a gallery of copies of medieval frescoes in Istrian churches. The **'Tito on Brijuni'** exhibit in another building includes large photos of Tito with film stars such as Gina Lollobrigida, Sophia Loren, Elizabeth Taylor and Richard Burton, all of whom visited Tito here.

Then you're driven around the island in a small train, past the palaces and through a **safari park**. The fenced area was Tito's private hunting ground, and the exotic animals presently there were given to Tito by world leaders. Deer wander wild across the island. You go past the ruins of a 1st century AD **Roman villa** without stopping, and then have a walk around an unexciting zoo.

owards the end of the tour you're herded uickly through the excellent **ethnographical museum** which has Croatian folk ostumes.

Getting There & Away

You may only visit Brijuni National Park with a group. Take a public bus from Pula to Fažana (eight km), then sign up for a tour (US$27) at the Brijuni Tourist Service office near the wharf. You must arrive at Fažana before noon to be sure of getting over that day.

Also check along the Pula waterfront for excursion boats to Brijuni. The five-hour boat trips from Pula to Brijuni may not actually visit the islands but only sail around them. Still, it makes a nice day out.

Gulf of Kvarner

The Gulf of Kvarner (Quarnero) stretches 100 km south from Rijeka between the Istrian Peninsula and the Croatian littoral. The many elongated islands are the peaks of a submerged branch of the Dinaric Alps, the range which follows the coast south all the way to Albania. Krk, Cres and Pag are among the largest islands in Croatia.

Rijeka, a bustling commercial port and communications hub at the north end of the gulf, is well connected to Italy and Austria by road and rail. The railway built from Budapest to Rijeka in 1845 gave Hungary its first direct outlet to the sea. Big crowds frequent nearby Opatija, a one-time bathing resort of the Habsburg elite, and Krk Island, now linked to the mainland by bridge. Historic Rab, the jewel of the Gulf of Kvarner, is much harder to reach; with some difficulty it can be used as a stepping stone on the way south.

RIJEKA

Rijeka, 126 km south of Ljubljana, is the sort of place you try to avoid but sometimes can't. Although the city does have a few saving graces, such as the pedestrian mall,

Korzo, and a colourful market, it seems to have lost its soul under a hail of WW II bombs. You don't have to dive far into the old town off Korzo to sense the confusion and decay. The belching industry, cars, shipyards, refineries, cranes and container ships jammed into the narrow coastal strip aren't beautiful. This largest of all Croatian ports does have a sort of crude energy, however, and if you like punishment Rijeka will give it to you.

Orientation

The bus station is on Trg Žabica below the Capuchin Church in the centre of town. If the left-luggage office in the bus station (open 5.30 am to 10.30 pm) is full, there's a larger *garderoba* (cloakroom) in the train station (open 24 hours), a seven-minute walk west on ulica Krešimirova. The Jadrolinija ferry wharf (no left-luggage) is just a few minutes east of the bus station.

Korzo runs east through the city centre towards the fast-moving Rječina River, once the border of Italy and Yugoslavia (the Italian and Croatian names of the city, Fiume and Rijeka, both mean river). Until 1918 Rijeka was the main port of Budapest and when Italy took Rijeka from Austria-Hungary in 1919, neighbouring Sušak was developed as a port by Yugoslavia. The cities merged when the whole area came under Yugoslav control after WW II.

Information

Try Kvarner Express, Trg P Togliattija 3 near the bus station, or the Turistički Savez Općine Rijeka (☎ 051-213 145) at Užarska 16 (2nd floor).

The Auto-Klub Rijeka (☎ 212 442), Dolac 11, assists motorists.

Money You can change money at Croatia Express on platform No 1 at the train station Monday to Saturday from 8 am to 9 pm, Sunday 9 am to 9 pm.

There's an exchange counter in the main post office opposite the old city tower on Korzo. If it's closed numerous individuals

CROATIA

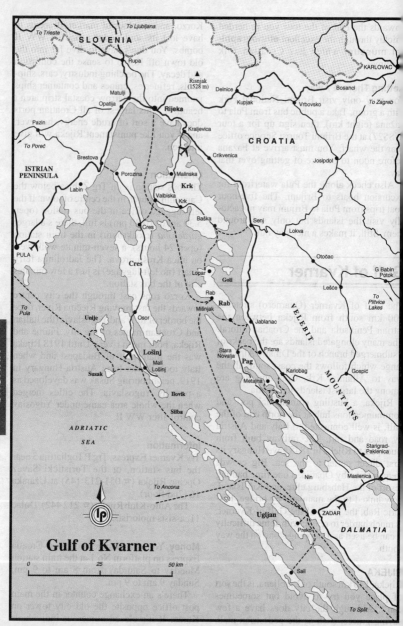

Gulf of Kvarner

hanging around here will offer to change cash at the usual bank rate.

Post & Telecommunications The telephone centre in the main post office on Korzo is open from 7 am to 9 pm daily. Rijeka's telephone code is 051.

Travel Agencies The American Express representative is Atlas Travel Agency (☎ 271 032) at Hotel Kvarner in nearby Opatija.

Croatia Express on platform No 1 at the train station sells international train tickets.

Jadroagent (☎ 211 276), at Trg Ivana Koblera 2, handles tickets to Durrës in Albania, aboard the car ferry *Duje*. They're a good source of information on all international ferry sailings from Croatia.

Newspapers Foreign newspapers are sold at Vjesnik, Korzo 26.

Things to See

The **Modern Art Gallery**, Dolac 1 (closed Sunday and Monday), is upstairs in the public library. The **Maritime Museum** and **National Revolution Museum** (both closed Sunday and Monday) are adjacent at Žrtava fašizma 18 above the city centre. Bullet holes in the side of the Maritime Museum, formerly the governor's palace (1893), attest to Rijeka's stormy history. Italian poet Gabriele d'Annunzio set up camp in the building after storming the city at the head of a couple of thousand volunteers in 1919, a provocation which led to the Italian border being moved east to the Rječina River.

If you have time, **Trsat Castle** (closed Monday), on a high ridge overlooking Rijeka and the canyon of the Rječina River, is worth a visit. Get there on bus No 1 from Fiumara in town or climb the 559 steps up from the arch beside the Rijeka Bank at the north end of Titov trg. In the Middle Ages the 13th century castle belonged to the Frankopan princes of Krk, but it was completely remodelled by the flamboyant Irish general Laval Nugent in the 19th century. There's also a Franciscan monastery (1453) at Trsat.

Places to Stay

Camping The closest camping ground is listed in the Opatija section.

Private Rooms In summer only, Kvarner Express (☎ 213 808), Trg P Togliattija 3, and Generalturist (☎ 212 900), F Supila 2, have private rooms for US$14/20 single/double, with a 30% discount if you stay four or more nights. Singles are seldom available and frequently all rooms are full.

Autotrans Turist Biro, Riva 20 just around the corner from the bus station (open Monday to Saturday from 7.30 am to 3 pm), has private rooms at US$14/22. Try them in the off season.

Landladies sometimes hang around the bus station in the evening looking for guests for their private rooms and this would be your best bet by far.

Hotels The 'cheapest' hotel is the 14-storey, C-category *Hotel Neboder* (☎ 217 355), Strossmajerova 1, a block beyond Hotel Kontinental. It's US$27/36 single/double without bath, US$33/43 with bath, breakfast included.

The imposing B-category *Hotel Kontinental* (☎ 216 477), A K Miošića 1, is US$42/55 single/double with private bath. The Kontinental was erected in 1888 and renovated in 1989, at which time prices doubled. Add US$1.50 tax per person per night to all official accommodation.

Delnice An alternative to staying in Rijeka is to go on to Delnice, 44 km east of Rijeka on the main road to Zagreb. The wooded countryside around Delnice is pleasant and Risnjak National Park is just 13 km northwest, but the immediate reason for coming is *Hotel Risnjak* (☎ 051-812 261), next to Delnice Bus Station and only about 200 metres from the train station. The 20 rooms with shower are US$14/25 single/double with breakfast and there's a large restaurant on the premises. It's seldom full.

Places to Eat

Restoran Index, ulica Krešimirova 18

CROATIA

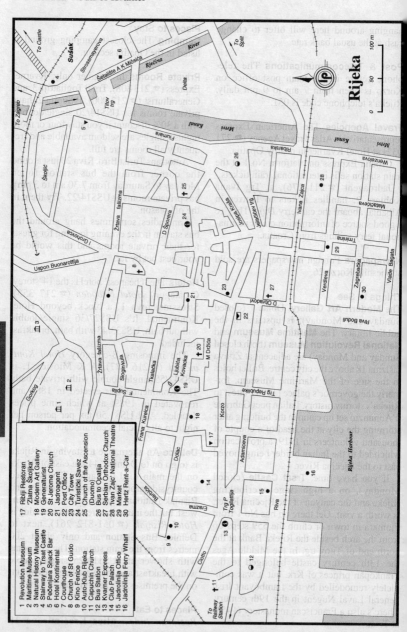

CROATIA

Rijeka

0   50   100 m

1   Revolution Museum
2   Maritime Museum
3   Natural History Museum
4   Stairway to Trsat Castle
5   Pečenjara Snack Bar
6   Hotel Kontinental
7   Courthouse
8   Church of St Guido
9   Kino Fenice
10 Auto-Klub Rijeka
11 Capuchin Church
12 Bus Station
13 Kvarner Express
14 Club Palach
15 Jadrolinija Office
16 Jadrolinija Ferry Wharf
17 Riblji Restoran
18 Zlatna Školjka
19 Modern Art Gallery
20 Generalturist
21 St Jerome Church
22 Jadroagent
23 Post Office
24 City Tower
25 Turistički Savez
26 Church of the Ascension
     (Duomo)
27 Serbian Orthodox Church
28 'Ivan Zajc' National Theatre
29 Market
30 Hertz Rent-a-Car

between the bus and train stations, has a good self-service section *(samoposluzi)*. The cashier may try to overcharge you so perhaps ask to have the price written on a piece of paper before getting your money out.

The up-market *Riblji Restoran 'Zlatna Školjka'*, in the passage at Korzo 34/36, specialises in seafoods.

A quick, stand-up snack bar is *Pečenjara*, Titov trg 6 across the river from Hotel Kontinental.

Entertainment

Performances at the *'Ivan Zajc' National Theatre* (1885) are mostly drama in Croatian, though opera and ballet are sometimes offered. The ticket office is open weekdays and Saturday mornings.

Special events take place at the Otvorena Scena Belveder in *Dom Sindikata 'Franco Belulović'*, Krešimirova 4, just past the level crossing as you go from the bus station to the train station. Cabaret Riječki performs here every Saturday at 9 pm.

Also check the *Hrvatski Kulturni Dom* (House of Croatian Culture), Strossmajerova 1, just up from Hotel Neboder.

Club Palach in the back alley accessible through a small passageway next to the Riječka Banka on Trg P Togliattija opens at 8 pm daily. It's a good, noncommercial place to drink and dance.

Rijeka's top disco is *Quorum Colors* near Preluk Autokamp between Rijeka and Opatija. In winter it's open Friday and Saturday from 9 pm to 4 am; in summer it opens nightly.

You've got your best chance of seeing a worthwhile film at Kino Fenice, Dolac 13.

Getting There & Away

Bus There are 12 buses a day between Rijeka and Krk (56 km, 1½ hours, US$4) using the huge Krk Bridge. The buses to Krk are overcrowded and a seat reservation in no way guarantees you a seat. Don't worry, the bus from Rijeka to Krk empties fairly fast so you won't be standing for long.

Other buses depart from Rijeka for Baška (76 km, six daily, US$5), Dubrovnik (639

km, two daily), Koper (86 km), Ljubljana (128 km, two daily, US$6), Mali Lošinj (122 km, four daily, US$7), Nova Gorica (132 km, daily), Poreč (91 km, five daily), Pula (110 km, 14 daily, 2½ hours, US$6), Rab (115 km, two daily), Rovinj (105 km, four daily), Split (404 km, seven daily), Trieste (70 km, four daily, US$6), Zadar (228 km) and Zagreb (173 km, 3½ hours, 16 daily).

Several international 'touring buses' leave from Rijeka Bus Station, all of them around 5 pm. There are buses four times a week to Mannheim and Dortmund (US$122); five times a week to Zürich (801 km, US$80) and Basel; six times a week to Frankfurt (US$91); and daily to Munich (571 km, US$50) and Stuttgart (786 km, US$74). The bus to Amsterdam (US$110) is weekly with a change of bus in Frankfurt. Luggage is DM3 per piece on all services (Deutschmarks in cash required). The cigarette smoke in these buses can be unpleasant.

Train Overnight trains leave Rijeka daily for Budapest (595 km, 11 hours, US$45), Munich, Salzburg (US$41) and Zagreb. Six trains a day run to Zagreb (243 km, five hours, US$5 local, US$9 express). Several of the seven daily services to Ljubljana (155 km, three hours, US$8) require a change of trains at the Slovenian border and again at Pivka or Postojna. The *poslovni* (executive) trains have only 1st-class seats and compulsory reservations.

Boat Jadrolinija (☎ 211 444), Riva 16, has tickets for the large coastal ferries between Rijeka and Dubrovnik from March to mid-October. The southbound ferries depart from Rijeka at 6 pm daily.

Fares are US$16 to Rab (three hours), US$32 to Split (13 hours) or Hvar (16 hours) and US$44 to Korčula (18 hours) or Dubrovnik (22 hours). Fares are slightly higher from mid-June to mid-August. Berths to Split are US$20 for one bed in a four-bed cabin, US$38 per person in a double or US$52 in a single. With a through ticket from Rijeka to Dubrovnik, you can have the purser validate your ticket for free stopovers at Rab,

CROATIA

Split, Hvar and Korčula – much cheaper than individual tickets. The ferry occasionally doesn't call at Rab if there's 'fog' (ie not enough passengers to drop off or pick up).

Since the Jadrolinija ferries travel between Rijeka and Split at night, you don't get to see a lot and it's probably better to go from Rijeka to Split by bus, allowing excellent views of the Adriatic coast. In contrast, the ferry trip from Split to Dubrovnik is highly recommended.

Car Rental ATR Rent a Car (☎ 37 544), Riva 20 near the bus station, has rental cars from US$50 a day including 100 km or US$85 with unlimited km. On a weekly basis it's US$400 with unlimited km. These prices are all-inclusive and they'll often give you a 10% discount in the off season. Also try Europcar (☎ 213 765), Pomerio 10a (a westward extension of Žrtava fašizma), and Hertz (☎ 39 900), Zagrebačka 21.

OPATIJA

Opatija, just a few km due west of Rijeka, was the fashionable seaside resort of the Austro-Hungarian empire until WW I. Many grand old hotels remain from this time, and the elegant waterfront promenade affords a fine view of the Gulf of Kvarner. The busy highway runs right along the coast and you get a passing glance of Opatija (the name means 'abbey') from the Pula bus. West of Opatija rises Mt Učka (1396 metres), the highest point on the Istrian Peninsula.

Information

The tourist office is at Maršala Tita 183.

Post & Telecommunications

The main post office, Eugena Kumičića 2, behind the market (tržnica), opens Monday to Saturday from 7 am to 8 pm, Sunday 9 am to noon. The telephone code for Opatija is 051.

Places to Stay

Preluk Autokamp (☎ 617 913), beside the busy highway between Rijeka and Opatija, is unreliably open from June to September.

City bus No 32 stops near this camping ground.

For private rooms, try the following places along Maršala Tita: Kvarner Express at No 177, Generalturist at No 178 and Kompas at No 170.

The cheapest hotel is the old three-storey Hotel Continental (☎ 271 511), Maršala Tita 169, where a room with bath and breakfast will be US$22/34 single/double. The cheaper rooms with shared bath are occupied by war refugees.

Getting There & Away

Bus No 32 from Jelačićev trg in Rijeka (13 km, US$1) runs right along the Opatija Riviera from Rijeka to Lovran every 20 minutes until late in the evening. There's no left-luggage facility at Opatija Bus Station which is on Trg Vladimira Gortana in the town centre.

KRK

Croatia's largest island, 409-sq-km Krk (Veglia), is barren and rocky with little vegetation. In 1980 Krk was joined to the mainland by the massive Krk Bridge, the largest concrete arch bridge in the world with a span of 390 metres. Since then, Krk has suffered from too rapid development – Rijeka Airport and some industry are at the north end of Krk, and big tourist hotels are in the middle and far south. Still, the main town (also called Krk) is rather picturesque and Baška has an impressive setting. You can easily stop at Krk town for a few hours of sightseeing, then catch a later bus to Baška and Krk's longest beach.

From the 12th to the 15th centuries, Krk and the surrounding region remained semi-independent under the Frankopan Dukes of Krk, an indigenous Croatian dynasty, at a time when much of the Adriatic was controlled by Venice. This history explains the various medieval sights in Krk town, the ducal seat.

Orientation & Information

The bus from Baška and Rijeka stops by the harbour, a few minutes' walk from the old

own of Krk. There's no left-luggage facility
at Krk Bus Station. Krk's telephone code is
☎532.

Things to See
The 14th century **Frankopan Castle** and
lovely 12th century Romanesque **cathedral**
are in the lower town near the harbour. In the
upper part of Krk are three old monastic
churches. The narrow streets of Krk are
worth exploring.

Places to Stay
Camping There are three camping grounds.
The closest is *Autocamp Ježevac* (☎ 221
081) on the coast, 10 minutes' walk south-
west of town. The rocky soil makes it nearly
impossible to use tent pegs, but there are lots
of stones to anchor your lines. There's good
shade and places to swim. *Camping Bor* is
on a hill inland from Ježevac, and *Camp
Politin FKK* (☎ 221 351) is a naturist camp
south-east of Krk just beyond the large resort
hotels.

Private Rooms Kvarner Express on the
harbour has private rooms for US$18 double
plus a 30% surcharge for less than four
nights. Similar rooms can be booked from a
tourist agency at the bus station and another
about a km back up the road to Rijeka at the
top of the hill.

Hostel From mid-June to September youth
hostel accommodation is available at the
Ljetovalište Ferialnog Saveza (☎ 854 037)
at Punat between Krk and Baška. All the
buses to Baška stop here.

Getting There & Away
About 13 buses a day ply between Rijeka and
Krk town (56 km, 1½ hours), of which seven
continue on to Baška (20 km, one hour). One
of the Rijeka buses is to/from Zagreb (229
km). To go from Krk to Lošinj change buses
at Malinska but check the times carefully as
the connection only works once or twice a
day.

BAŠKA
Baška at the south end of Krk Island, is a
popular resort with a two-km-long pebbly
beach set below a high ridge. The swimming
and scenery are better at Baška than at Krk
and the old town has a lot of charm. This is
a good base for hiking and the Chapel of
Sveti Ivan on the hillside above Baška offers
splendid views.

Orientation
The bus from Krk stops at the edge of the old
town between the beach and the harbour. To
reach the Lopar ferry, follow the street
closest to the water through the old town,
heading south-east for less than a km.

Places to Stay
Camping There are two camping possibilities. *Camping Zablce* (☎ 211 909), open
from May to September, is on the beach
visible south-west of the bus stop (look for
the rows of caravans). In heavy rain you risk
getting flooded here.

A better bet is *FKK Camp Bunculuka*
(☎ 211 806), open from May to September,
a naturist camping ground over the hill east
of the harbour (a 15-minute walk). It's quiet,
shady and conveniently close to town.

Private Rooms The people renting private
rooms at Baška don't like you to sleep alone
and single rooms are almost impossible to
find, either at the agencies or by knocking on
doors with *sobe* signs. Most people will also
refuse to rent you a room for one night and
just tell you to go to the hotel. They've got
enough German and Austrian motorists
screaming for rooms that they can afford to
be choosy.

All the agencies charge exactly the same
prices for private rooms and most have only
expensive 1st-category rooms with a few
2nd-category and no 3rd-category. Expect to
pay at least US$20 double (plus 30% if you
stay less than four nights). The tourist tax of
US$1 per person per day is extra.

The places to try are the tourist office,
Zvonimirova 114 just up the street from the
bus stop; Amplus Agency, next to the Riječka

CROATIA

Banka adjacent to the tourist office; and Kai Jadran and Kompas, both at the Hotel Corinthia nearby.

Hotels Small, basic rooms without private bath are available at the hotels *Velebit* and *Baška* right on the main beach for US$20/30 single/double, including breakfast (25% higher in midsummer, open June to mid-September only). Bookings must be made at the reception of the *Hotel Corinthia* (☎ 211 824) nearby where you'll take breakfast. You must insist on these rooms, as the Corinthia staff will try to steer you into much more expensive rooms in the main hotel.

Getting There & Away

The ferry from Baška to Lopar on Rab Island operates two or three times a day from June to mid-September (US$5). The rest of the year you could be forced to backtrack to Rijeka to get farther south.

RAB

Rab (Arbe) Island, near the centre of the Kvarner island group, is one of the most enticing in the Adriatic. The north-east side of Rab is barren and rocky, whereas the south-west side is fairly green with pine forests. High mountains protect Rab from the colder northern and eastern winds.

Medieval Rab town is built on a narrow peninsula pointing south which encloses a sheltered harbour. The old stone buildings climb from the harbour to a cliff overlooking the sea. For hundreds of years Rab was an outpost of Venice until the Austrians took over in the 19th century.

Even today you'll hear as much German as Croatian spoken on Rab and you'll find that transport, accommodation and food – virtually everything connected with a visit – is expensive. Even so, it's a convenient stepping stone between Krk and Zadar and one of the prettiest little towns on the Adriatic. Rab is also physically unaffected by the war, so you need have no worries about going there.

Orientation

The bus station is at the rear of the new commercial centre opposite the Merkur Department Store, a five-minute walk from the old town. The large Jadrolinija ferries tie up near the Riva Hotel in the old town.

Despite a sign at the bus station advertising a *garderoba* (left-luggage office), it's not operational because the station is only open limited hours.

Information

The Turist Biro is on Arba Municipium opposite the post office in the old town. Annual events to ask about here include the Rab Fair (25 to 27 July) and the Rab Music Evenings (June to September).

Post & Telecommunications Rab's post office is open Monday to Saturday from 7 am to 9 pm. Rab's telephone code is 0532.

Things to See

Four tall church towers rise above the red roofed mass of houses on Rab's high peninsula. If you follow Rade Končara north from the **Monastery of St Anthony** (1175) you soon reach the Romanesque **cathedral** alongside a pleasant terrace with a view overlooking the sea. Farther along, beyond a tall **Romanesque tower** and another convent, is a second terrace and **St Justine Church**, now a small museum of religious art. Just past the next chapel, look for a small gate giving access to a park with the foundations of Rab's oldest church and the fourth tower (which you can climb).

Rade Končara ends at the north city wall from which there's a splendid view of the town, harbour, sea and hill. The scene is especially beautiful just after sunset. North of the wall is the extensive **city park** with many shady walkways.

Places to Stay

Camping To sleep cheap, carry your tent south along the waterfront about 25 minutes to *Autocamp Padova* (☎ 771 355) at Banjol (US$3 per person, US$2 per tent). There's a wooded ridge by the camping ground where

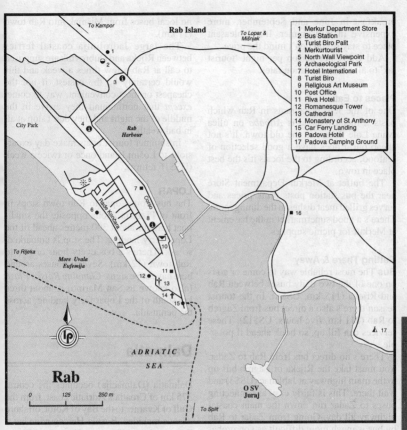

To Kampor

Rab Island

To Lopar & Mišnjak

City Park

Rab Harbour

Corso

Rade Končara

More Uvala Eufemija

To Rijeka

ADRIATIC SEA

Rab

0   125   250 m

O SV Juraj

To Split

1 Merkur Department Store
2 Bus Station
3 Turist Biro Palit
4 Merkurtourist
5 North Wall Viewpoint
6 Archaeological Park
7 Hotel International
8 Turist Biro
9 Religious Art Museum
10 Post Office
11 Riva Hotel
12 Romanesque Tower
13 Cathedral
14 Monastery of St Anthony
15 Car Ferry Landing
16 Padova Hotel
17 Padova Camping Ground

CROATIA

you can pitch a tent away from the noise and caravans. The beach is just below.

Private Rooms Several agencies rent private rooms, including Turist biro Palit (open April to October only) and Turist biro Kristofor, both on the corner near the bus station; Arbia Tours behind the bus station; Merkurtourist, next to the supermarket on the waterfront; and the Turist biro on Arba Municipium. The official tariff is US$15/23 single/double first category (private bath) in July and August (US$12/18 in June and Sep-

tember, US$11/15 the rest of the year), or US$10/14 single/double in third category in July and August (cheaper during other months). For stays of less than three nights there's a 30% surcharge. Some agencies forgo the single supplement, taxes and surcharges when things are slow.

You could be approached by women at the bus station offering private rooms.

Hotels The *Hotel International* (☎ 711 266), on Corso facing the harbour, has rooms at US$26/37 single/double with bath and breakfast in June and September, more expensive in midsummer. It's a pleasant place to stay if you don't mind the price.

Add US$1 per person per night 'tourist tax' to all accommodation rates.

Places to Eat

One of the few restaurants in Rab which posts a menu outside is *Alibaba* on ulica Ivana Lole Ribara in the old town. It's not cheap but it does have a good selection of seafood; according to the locals it's the best place in town.

The buffet at Merkur Department Store near the bus station posts drink prices and serves grilled meat dishes in the dining room. There's a good supermarket in the basement at Merkur for picnic supplies.

Getting There & Away

Bus The most reliable way to come or go is on one of the two daily buses between Rab and Rijeka (115 km, US$8). In the tourist season there's also a direct bus from Zagreb to Rab (211 km, five hours, US$12). These services can fill up, so book ahead if possible.

There's no direct bus from Rab to Zadar. You must take the Rijeka or Zagreb bus up to the main highway at Jablanac (US$3) and wait there. This is fairly easy as connecting buses to Zadar run down the main coastal highway all day. Going from Zadar to Rab by bus is much more difficult as you probably won't find a bus from Jablanac to Rab and may have to walk or hitchhike.

All the local travel agencies have bus and ferry schedules posted in their offices.

Boat The ferry from Baška on Krk Island to Lopar at the north end of Rab operates two or three times a day from June to mid-September only (US$5).

Unless you're on a through bus to/from Rijeka or Zagreb, the more frequent year-round ferry from Jablanac on the mainland to Mišnjak on Rab Island is problematic. Jablanac is four km off the main Rijeka-Split highway (downhill all the way) and there are

no local buses from Mišnjak into Rab town (11 km).

The large Jadrolinija coastal ferries between Rijeka and Dubrovnik are supposed to call at Rab a few times a week and this would certainly be the easiest, if not the cheapest or most convenient, way to come, *except* that northbound they arrive in the middle of the night and they don't stop at all in bad weather.

In summer tourist boats make day excursions to Lošinj Island once or twice a week (US$16 return).

LOPAR

The bus from Lopar to Rab town stops in front of Pizzeria Aloha opposite the small-boat harbour about 300 metres ahead of the Lopar ferry landing. The stop is unmarked, so ask. There's a bus every hour or two to Rab town (12 km). Several houses around here have sobe signs. *Camping Rajska Plaza* (also known as San Marino) is about three km south of the Lopar ferry landing, across the peninsula.

Dalmatia

Dalmatia (Dalmacija) occupies the central 375 km of Croatia's Adriatic coast, from the Gulf of Kvarner to the Bay of Kotor, offshore islands included. Bosnia-Hercegovina has a tiny opening to the sea at Neum near Ploče. The rugged Dinaric Alps form a 1500-metre-high barrier separating Dalmatia from Bosnia, with only two breaks: the Krka River canyon at Knin and the Neretva Valley at Mostar, both of which have railways. After the last Ice age, part of the coastal mountains were flooded, creating the same sort of long, high islands seen in the Gulf of Kvarner. The deep, protected passages between these islands are a paradise for sailors and cruisers.

Historical relics abound in towns like Zadar, Trogir, Split, Hvar, Korčula and Dubrovnik, framed by a striking natural beauty of barren slopes, green valleys and clear water. The ferry trip from Split to

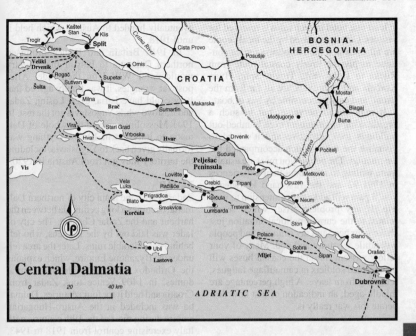

Central Dalmatia

0   20   40 km

ADRIATIC SEA

Dubrovnik is one of the classic journeys of Eastern Europe. The vineyards of Dalmatia supply half of Croatia's wine. A warm current flowing north up the coast keeps the climate mild – dry in summer, damp in winter. Dalmatia is noticeably warmer than Istria or the Gulf of Kvarner and it's possible to swim in the sea right up until the end of September. This is the Mediterranean at its best.

Dalmatia at War

Unfortunately Dalmatia has not been spared the violence of ex-Yugoslavia's ongoing civil war, and the historic centres of Zadar, Šibenik, Split and Dubrovnik suffered shelling in late 1991 and early 1992. In Split and Dubrovnik most of the damage has been repaired, but Zadar and Šibenik remain tense (although safe to visit). The coastal highway has stayed open throughout the conflict and dozens of buses now run from Zagreb and Rijeka to

Split and Dubrovnik every day without incident.

If you choose to visit Dalmatia you'll have to be prepared for a few small inconveniences, such as museums closed with the exhibits removed for safekeeping, monuments covered with protective scaffolding, water shortages, restaurants closed because of the absence of tourists, excursions cancelled, camping grounds used as camps by UN military forces and hotels full of refugees from Bosnia-Hercegovina. Also, you'll have to return the way you came, as it's impossible to continue overland through Bosnia-Hercegovina or Montenegro. At last report the Jadrolinija ferry from Split to Igoumenitsa, Greece, wasn't operating, though this could change.

On the positive side you'll have this beautiful area almost to yourself as most tourists don't stray beyond Istria and the Gulf of Kvarner. To attract business, prices here are much lower than they are farther north and at least one hotel in each town is reserved for visitors. Cafés patronised by the local people are all open and the Jadrolinija ferries continue to ply the lovely coastal route from Rijeka to Dubrovnik. Trogir, Split, Hvar, Korčula and Dubrovnik are all far from the 'front' and easily accessible by bus or boat.

It may sound perverse, but in such a breathtaking environment even bombed-out buildings look attractive and it's hard to visualise the terror which accompanied the destruction. The people you meet are usually quite willing to talk about their experiences in 1991-92 and the first-hand knowledge you'll gain will add a new dimension to your trip. If any problem arises which seems related to the current political situation just shake your head and say *situacija* and people will smile wistfully and nod. Many of your fellow passengers on the coastal buses will be unarmed soldiers in camouflage fatigues, returning from leave. A high percentage are middle-aged, an indication of just how desperate this war really is.

History
The Illyrians settled here around 1000 BC, followed in the 4th century BC by the Greeks, who established colonies at Korčula, Hvar and Salona. When Greek and Illyrian interests collided, the Romans intervened and after 74 years of wars they succeeded in subjugating the province of Dalmatia in 155 BC. Major Roman ruins are still seen in Zadar, Salona and Split. After the Western Roman Empire fell in the 5th century AD, the region became a battleground for barbarians, Byzantines and many other conquerors. The present inhabitants are descended from Slavic tribes which arrived in the 6th century.

Medieval Dalmatia was ruled at different times by Venice and Croatia. In 1409 Venice purchased Dalmatia from Louis of Naples, the Hungaro-Croatian king, and held it until Napoleon captured Venice itself in 1797. Most of the coastal towns still bear a deep Italian imprint, quite a contrast to the Turkish influence just a few dozen km inland. Through diplomatic deals Dalmatia was

eventually handed to Austria, which held it until 1918.

In 1915 Britain and France promised northern Dalmatia to Italy if that country would enter WW I on their side. After postwar wrangles, it was finally agreed that Italy could have Istria, Cres, Lošinj, Zadar and Lastovo while Yugoslavia got the rest. In 1941 Mussolini annexed the whole of Dalmatia to Italy but in 1947 everything was formally given back to Yugoslavia, including the territory Italy got from Austria in 1920.

ZADAR
Zadar (Zara), the main city of northern Dalmatia, occupies a long peninsula between the harbour and the Zadar Channel. The city of Iader was laid out by the Romans, who left behind considerable ruins. Later the area fell under the Byzantine Empire, which explains the Orthodox churches with their central domes. In 1409 Venice took Zadar from Croatia and held it for four centuries. Dalmatia was included in the Austro-Hungarian empire during most of the 19th century, with Italy exercising control from 1918 to 1943. Badly damaged by Anglo-American bombing raids in 1943-44, much of the city had to be rebuilt. Luckily, the original street plan was respected and an effort made to harmonise the new with what remained of old Zadar.

In November 1991, Zadar seemed to be reliving history as Yugoslav rockets ploughed into the old city, damaging the cathedral. For the next three months the city's inhabitants had to sleep on cots in their basements without running water, electricity or heating, unable to go out of their homes for fear of being hit. Ask any of the older people how much weight they lost during this dark time. This experience has embittered many residents and you may encounter some suspicion until people know who you are. Although Zadar was shelled indiscriminately from Serb positions in the surrounding countryside, the town sustained remarkably little damage, although some buildings are still pockmarked with bullet holes. The Serb gunners were pushed back

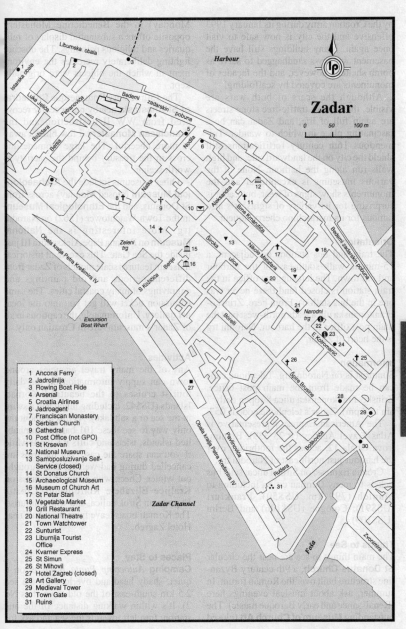

Zadar

0   50   100 m

1 Ancona Ferry
2 Jadrolinija
3 Rowing Boat Ride
4 Arsenal
5 Croatia Airlines
6 Jadroagent
7 Franciscan Monastery
8 Serbian Church
9 Cathedral
10 Post Office (not GPO)
11 St Krsevan
12 National Museum
13 Samoposluzivanje Self-
    Service (closed)
14 St Donatus Church
15 Archaeological Museum
16 Museum of Church Art
17 St Petar Stari
18 Vegetable Market
19 Grill Restaurant
20 National Theatre
21 Town Watchtower
22 Sunturist
23 Liburnija Tourist
    Office
24 Kvarner Express
25 St Simun
26 St Mihovil
27 Hotel Zagreb (closed)
28 Art Gallery
29 Medieval Tower
30 Town Gate
31 Ruins

Harbour

Zadar Channel

Excursion Boat Wharf

CROATIA

by the Croatian army during its January 1993 offensive and the city is now safe to visit once again. Many buildings still have the basement windows sandbagged to serve as bomb shelters, however, and the façades of monuments are covered by scaffolding.

Although the scars of both wars are visible, the narrow, traffic-free stone streets are again full of life, and Zadar can be a fascinating place in which to wander. Tremendous 16th century fortifications still shield the city on the landward side, and high walls run along the harbour. None of the various museums is exceptional and the monuments show signs of wear, but Zadar is surprising for its variety of sights. It's also famous for its maraschino cherry liqueur.

Orientation

The train and bus stations are adjacent, a 15-minute walk south-east of the harbour and old town. The left-luggage office in the train station is closed (and there never was one in the bus station). From here, Zrinsko-Frankopanska ulica leads north-west past the main post office to the harbour. Narodni trg is the heart of Zadar.

Information

Sunturist is on Narodni trg. Telephone calls can be made from the main post office, Zrinsko-Frankopanska ulica 8 (open daily 7 am to 8 pm). Zadar's telephone code is 057.

The American Express representative is Atlas Travel Agency (☎ 23 339), Branimirova Obala 12, across the footbridge over the harbour just north-east of Narodni trg.

Croatia Express, on Široka ulica, sells bus tickets to many German cities, including to Munich (799 km, US$50), Frankfurt (US$91), Cologne (US$106) and Berlin (US$109).

Things to See

The main things to see are near the circular St Donatus Church, a 9th century Byzantine structure built over the Roman forum. In summer, ask about musical evenings here (Renaissance and early Baroque music). The outstanding Museum of Church Art (closed Monday) in the Benedictine Monastery opposite offers a substantial display of reliquaries and religious paintings. The obscure lighting deliberately recreates the environment in which the objects were originally kept.

The 13th century Romanesque Cathedral of St Anastasia nearby never really recovered from WW II destruction and the Franciscan Monastery a few blocks away is more cheerful. The large Romanesque cross in the treasury behind the sacristy is worth seeing.

Other museums include the Archaeological Museum (closed Monday) across from St Donatus, and the Ethnological Museum in the Town Watchtower (1562) on Narodni trg. More interesting is the National Museum on Poljana Pape Aleksandra III just inside the Sea Gate. This excellent historical museum features scale models of Zadar from different periods and old paintings and engravings of many coastal cities. The same admission ticket will get you into the local art gallery. Unfortunately, the captions in all of Zadar's museums are in Croatian only.

Activities

Any of the many travel agencies around town can supply information on the daily tourist cruises to the beautiful Kornati Islands (US$42, including lunch and a swim in the sea or a salt lake). As this is about the only way to see these 101 barren, uninhabited islands, islets and cliffs it's worthwhile if you can spare the cash, but the trips are cancelled during bad weather and throughout winter. Check with Kvarner Express on Kraljice Elizabete Kotromanić, Croatia Express on Široka ulica, and with Sunturist. The Kornati boats leave from the wharf near Hotel Zagreb.

Places to Stay

Camping Autocamp Punta Bajlo is on a quiet, shady headland overlooking the sea 2.5 km south-east of the old town (bus No 2). It's within walking distance of the bus station: turn left towards the sea and ask for directions after a block or two. It could well be closed.

Hostels The 330-bed *Borik Youth Hostel* (☎ 443 145), Obala Kneza Trpimira 76, is near the beach on the coast a few km northwest. It's presently being used to house refugees and is closed.

Private Rooms Head for Narodni trg and the Sunturist office, or for Liburnija Tourist Office at Kraljice Elizabete Kotromanić 1 around the corner, both of which offer private rooms for US$10 per person, plus a 30% surcharge if you stay less than four nights.

With tourism down private rooms are a bit harder to find as the women who formerly looked for travellers at the bus station no longer bother. Just walk into the old town and ask around – many people know of someone who rents rooms to tourists. The political situation being what it is, landladies in Zadar are a little apprehensive about who they invite into their homes, but once you establish yourself as a Western tourist everything will be OK.

Hotel The B-category *Hotel Zagreb* on the promenade is being used for refugee housing.

The only hotel presently open is the expensive *Hotel Kolovare* (☎ 433 022), ulica Bože Peričića, 200 metres from the bus station. Those rooms not occupied by refugees are taken by the EU monitors and UN peacekeepers, though they usually have one or two left for the odd tourist at US$39/55 single/double.

Places to Eat
At last report the *Samoposluzivanje* self-service restaurant in the passage at Nikole Matafara 9 was being used as a military mess hall. This being the case, there's a large supermarket on Široka ulica around the corner where you can buy picnic supplies.

One of the only regular restaurants presently functioning is *Restaurant Basket*, on the corner of Obala Kralja Tomislava and

ulica Marka Marulića at the south-east end of the harbour. Around the corner on ulica Marka Marulića is *Disco Bar Forum*. The restaurant in the train station is also open.

For drinks, try *Bife Agava*, ulica Jurja Barakovića 6, a block towards the harbour from Narodni trg.

Entertainment
The National Theatre box office on Široka ulica has tickets to cultural programmes advertised on posters outside.

Major annual events include the town fair (July and August), the Dalmatian Song Festival (July and August), the Musical Evenings in St Donatus Church (August) and the Choral Festival (October).

Getting There & Away
Train & Bus The train service out of Zadar is suspended, as the line passes through Knin, the centre of an area controlled by Serbian separatists. Instead, catch a bus to Zagreb (320 km), Rijeka (228 km) or Split (158 km).

Boat At last report the Adriatica line (Adriatica Navigazione) ferries to/from Italy were not running and even the Jadrolinija coastal ferry from Rijeka to Dubrovnik had ceased to call at Zadar for security reasons. For current information on services to Italy, contact Jadroagent on ulica Natka Nodila just inside the city walls.

Jadrolinija (☎ 24 343), Liburnska obala 7 on the harbour, will know if the Jadrolinija ferry has returned; it has tickets for all local ferries. From June to September a daily afternoon ferry links Zadar to Mali Lošinj (US$8) and on Monday, Wednesday and Sunday to Pula (US$14).

On Thursday and Sunday there's a ferry to Zaglav on Dugi otok, a good day trip (on other days there's no connection to return to Zadar). Another Sunday cruise would be a ferry ride from Zadar to Silba and back with five stops at smaller islands (nine hours return), though there'll be no time to get off anywhere. The shortest ferry route is the rowing boat ride across the harbour from

CROATIA

TROGIR

Trogir (Trau), a lovely medieval town on the coast just 20 km west of Split, is well worth a stop if you're coming down from Zadar. A day trip to Trogir from Split can be easily combined with a visit to the Roman ruins of Salona. (See the section on Salona in this chapter.)

The old town of Trogir occupies a tiny island in the narrow channel between Čiovo Island and the mainland, just off the coastal highway. Many sights are seen on a 15-minute walk around this island. The nearest beach is four km west at the Medena Hotel.

Orientation

The heart of the old town is a few minutes' walk from the bus station. After crossing the small bridge near the station, go through the North Gate. Trogir's finest sights are around Narodni trg, slightly left and ahead.

There's no left-luggage office in Trogir Bus Station, so you'll end up toting your bags around town if you only visit the town as a stopover.

Information

The Turist Biro opposite the cathedral sells a map of the area. The telephone code for Trogir is 058.

Things to See

The glory of the three-naved Venetian **Cathedral of St Lovro** on Narodni trg is the Romanesque portal of Adam and Eve (1240) by Master Radovan, which you can admire for free any time. Enter the building through an obscure back door to see the perfect Renaissance Chapel of St Ivan, choir, pulpit, ciborium and treasury. You can even climb the cathedral tower for a delightful view. Also on Narodni trg are the **town hall**, with an excellent Gothic staircase, and the Renaissance loggia.

Places to Stay

Camping *Camping Rožac* is on Čiovo Island

(connected to Trogir by a bridge). It's a half-hour walk from Trogir Bus Station, or take the Okrug bus. *Medena Camping* (☎ 73 131) is just off the highway to Zadar about four km west of Trogir. *Seget Camping* is between Medina and Trogir. Check with the Turist Biro to make sure they're open before trekking out.

Private Rooms If you would like to stay at Trogir, the Turist Biro opposite the cathedral has private rooms for US$14/18 single/double, less 30% if you stay longer than four nights.

Getting There & Away

Southbound buses from Zadar (130 km) will drop you off here. Getting buses north from Trogir can be more difficult, as they often arrive full from Split.

City bus No 37 runs between Trogir and Split (28 km) every 20 minutes throughout the day, with a stop at Split Airport en route. If making a day trip to Trogir on bus No 37, also buy your ticket back to Split, as the ticket window at Trogir Bus Station is often closed. (Drivers also sell tickets if you're stuck.)

SPLIT

Split (Spalato), the largest Croatian city on the Adriatic coast, is the heart of Dalmatia. The old town is built around the harbour on the south side of a high peninsula sheltered from the open sea by many islands. Ferries to these islands are constantly coming and going. The entire west end of the peninsula is a vast wooded mountain park, while industry, shipyards, limestone quarries and the ugly commercial/military port are mercifully far enough away on the north side of the peninsula. The high coastal mountains set against the blue Adriatic provide a striking frame to the scene.

Split achieved fame when the Roman emperor Diocletian (245-313), noted for his persecution of early Christians, had his retirement palace built here from 295 to 305. After his death the great stone palace continued to be used as a retreat by Roman rulers.

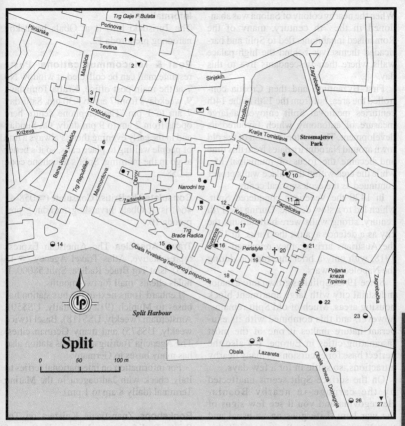

Split

0   50   100 m

Split Harbour

CROATIA

PLACES TO STAY	OTHER	17	Temple of Jupiter
		18	Basement Halls of
13 Central Hotel	1 Croatian National		Palace
16 Prenočište Slavija	Theatre	19	Vestibule
	4 Main Post Office	20	Cathedral
PLACES TO EAT	7 Fish Market	21	East Palace Gate
	8 Old Town Hall	22	Vegetable Market
2 Bastion Self-	9 Statue of	23	Bus No 17 to
Service Restau-	Gregorius of Nin		Camping Ground
rant	10 North Palace Gate	24	Airport Bus Stop
3 Pizzeria Galija	11 Town Museum	25	Adria Airlines
5 Burek Bar	12 West Palace Gate	26	Bus & Train
6 Ero Restaurant	14 Salona Bus Stop		Stations
	15 Turistički biro	27	Pizzeria Bakra

When the nearby colony of Salona was abandoned in the 7th century, many of the Romanised inhabitants fled to Split and barricaded themselves behind the high palace walls where their descendants live to this day.

First Byzantium and then Croatia controlled the area, but from the 12th to the 14th centuries medieval Split enjoyed a large measure of autonomy which favoured its development. The western portion of the old town around Narodni trg dates from this time and became the focus of municipal life, while the area within the palace walls proper continued as the ecclesiastical centre.

In 1420 the Venetians conquered Split, which led to a slow decline. During the 17th century, strong walls were built around the city as a defence against the Turks. In 1797 the Austrians arrived; they remained until 1918, with only a brief interruption during the Napoleonic wars.

Since 1945, Split has grown into a major industrial city with large apartment-block housing areas. Much of old Split remains, however, and this combined with its exuberant nature makes it one of the most fascinating cities in Europe. It's also the perfect base for excursions to many nearby attractions, so settle in for a few days.

On the surface Split seems unaffected by the carnage in nearby Bosnia-Hercegovina and you'll see few signs of the war here. Life goes on as usual and there's no reason at all not to visit this lovely Adriatic port. Be prepared, however, to find the doors of many of the museums mentioned under Things to See securely locked with no explanation posted.

Orientation

The bus, train and ferry terminals are adjacent on the east side of the harbour, a short walk from the old town. The *garderoba* (left-luggage) kiosk at the bus station is open from 6 am to 9 pm. The left-luggage office at the train station has closed. Obala hrvatskog narodnog preporoda, the waterfront promenade, is your best central reference point in Split.

Information

The Turistički biro is at Obala hrvatskog narodnog preporoda 12.

Post & Telecommunications Poste restante mail can be collected at window No 7 at the main post office, Kralja Tomislava 9, weekdays from 7 am to 7.30 pm, Saturday 7 am to 1 pm. The telephone centre here opens from 7 am to 9 pm daily. On Sunday and in the early evening there's always a line of people waiting to place calls, so it's better to go in the morning. Split's telephone code is 058.

Consulate The British Consulate (☎ 058-41 464) is at Obala hrvatskog narodnog preporoda 10.

Travel Agencies The American Express representative, Atlas Travel Agency (☎ 43 055), is at Trg Braće Radića, Split 58000. It holds clients' mail for two months.

Lenhard Tours next to the bus station has buses to Munich (912 km, daily, US$50), Amsterdam (weekly, US$118), Basel (twice weekly, US$75) and many German cities. The Agencija Touring at the bus station also has many buses to Germany.

For information on international ferries to Italy check with Jadroagent in the Marine Terminal (daily 8 am to 1 pm).

Bookshops Znanstvena Knjižara on Trg Braće Radića has a large selection of imported books in English but nothing in English by Croatian writers – only cheap adventure and romance.

The so-called International Book Shop, Obala hrvatskog narodnog preporoda 20, sells foreign newspapers (but few books).

Things to See

There's much more to see than can be mentioned here, so pick up a local guidebook if you're staying longer than a day or two. The old town is a vast open-air museum made all the more interesting by the everyday life still going on throughout.

Diocletian's Palace facing the harbour is

one of the most imposing extant Roman ruins anywhere. It was built as a strong rectangular fortress with walls 215 by 180 metres long and reinforced by towers. The imperial residence, temples and mausoleum were south of the main street connecting the east and west gates.

Enter through the central ground floor of the palace at Obala hrvatskog narodnog preporoda 22. On the left you'll see the excavated basement halls, which are empty but impressive. Continue through the passage to the **Peristyle**, a picturesque colonnaded square, with the neo-Romanesque cathedral tower rising above. The **vestibule**, an open dome above the ground-floor passageway at the south end of the Peristyle, is overpowering. A lane off the Peristyle opposite the cathedral leads to the **Temple of Jupiter**, now a baptistry.

On the east side of the Peristyle is the **cathedral**, originally Diocletian's mausoleum. The only reminder of Diocletian in the cathedral is a sculpture of his head in a circular stone wreath below the dome directly above the Baroque white-marble altar. The Romanesque wooden doors (1214) and stone pulpit are worth noting. You may climb the tower for a small fee.

The west palace gate opens onto medieval Narodni trg, dominated by the 15th century Venetian Gothic **old town hall**. Trg Braće Radića between Narodni trg and the harbour contains the surviving north tower of the 15th century Venetian garrison castle, which once extended to the water's edge. The east palace gate leads into the market area.

In the Middle Ages the nobility and rich merchants built residences within the old palace walls, one of which, the Papalic Palace, at Papalićeva (also known as Žarkova) ulica 5, is now the **town museum**. Go through the northern palace gate to see the powerful **statue** (1929) by Ivan Meštrović of the 10th century Slavic religious leader Gregorius of Nin, who fought for the right to say mass in Croatian.

Museums & Galleries Split's least known yet most interesting museum is the **Maritime Museum** (open 9 am to noon, closed Monday, free entry) in Gripe Fortress (1657) on a hill top east of the old town. The large exhibit of wartime maps, photos, artefacts and scale models is fascinating, but unfortunately all of the captions are in Croatian only.

Also worth the walk is the **Archaeological Museum**, Zrinjsko-Frankopanska 25, north of town (open mornings only, closed Monday). The best of this valuable collection, first assembled in 1820, is in the garden outside. The items in the showcases inside the museum building would be a lot more interesting if the captions were in something other than Croatian.

The other Split museums are west of the old town. The **Museum of Croatia** on Šetalište Ivana Meštrovića (closed Monday), looks impressive on the outside but inside the lack of captions legible to anyone other than Croats makes it hardly worth seeing. Some of the exhibits appear to be replicas, but it doesn't really matter since you don't know what you're looking at anyway!

A welcome contrast is encountered at the **Meštrović Gallery**, Šetalište Ivana Meštrovića 46 (presently closed). Here you will see a comprehensive, well-arranged collection of works by Ivan Meštrović, Croatia's premier modern sculptor, who built the gallery as a personal residence in 1931-39. Although Meštrović intended to retire here, he emigrated to the USA soon after WW II. Bus No 12 passes the gate infrequently. There are beaches on the south side of the peninsula below the gallery.

From the Meštrović Gallery it's possible to hike straight up **Marjan Hill**. Go up ulica Tonća Petrasova Marovića on the west side of the gallery and continue straight up the stairway to Put Meja ulica. Turn left and walk west to Put Meja 76. The trail begins on the west side of this building. Marjan Hill offers trails through the forest, viewpoints, old chapels and the local zoo.

Places to Stay
Camping The nearest camp site is at Trstenik, five km east near the beach (bus No 17 from the east side of the market).

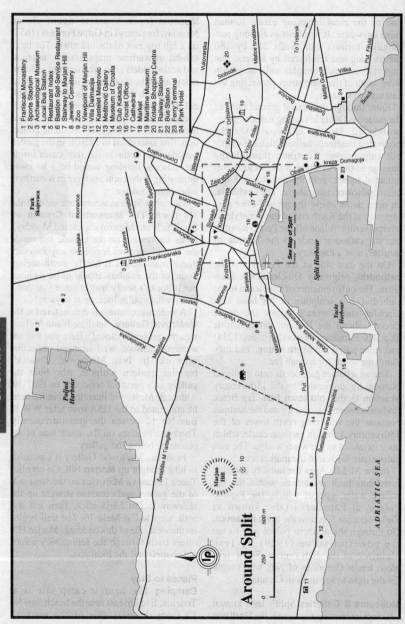

Around Split

1 Franciscan Monastery
2 Sports Stadium
3 Archaeological Museum
4 Local Bus Station
5 Restaurant Index
6 Bastion Self-Service Restaurant
7 Stairway to Marjan Hill
8 Jewish Cemetery
9 Zoo
10 Viewpoint of Marjan Hill
11 Villa Dalmacija
12 Kaštelet Meštrović
13 Meštrović Gallery
14 Museum of Croatia
15 Club Kakadu
16 Cathedral
17 Tourist Office
18 Market
19 Maritime Museum
20 Railway Station
21 Koteks Shopping Centre
22 Bus Station
23 Ferry Terminal
24 Park Hotel

ADRIATIC SEA

Marjan Hill

Split Harbour

See Map of Split

Poljud Harbour

Park Skojeraca

Yacht Harbour

500 m
250
0

Autocamp Trstenik (☎ 058-521 971), just beyond the last stop of bus No 17, on a cliff overlooking the sea, is shady with many pine trees and stairs leading down to the beach. From here a concrete path runs along the shore all the way back to Split (a 45-minute walk) past many swimming places, with several public showers.

Private Rooms The zimmer offered by women who look for clients around the bus station are the best budget accommodation in Split. Outside the peak summer season you can bargain over the price, but rooms tend to be rather basic and beyond the city centre. They typically cost around US$8 per person. Some sobe proprietors at the stations ask exorbitant prices, and you can often get an instant 50% reduction by saying it's too much and turning to leave. Try not to pay more for your room than you've paid elsewhere, or US$10 per person maximum (US$15 in midsummer).

Better, more convenient rooms are available from the Turistički biro, Obala hrvatskog narodnog preporoda 12. Prices begin at US$16/22 single/double, plus US$1 per person tax, less 30% if you stay four nights or more. Singles are seldom available here.

Hotels The 'cheapest' hotel is the ageing D-category *Central Hotel* (☎ 48 242), Narodni trg 1 opposite the old town hall, at US$26/40/49 single/double/triple with shared bath, breakfast included. A gambling casino operates here until 5 am.

Slightly better is the quieter 32-room *Prenočište Slavija* (☎ 47 053), Buvinova 3, at US$32/46/60 single/double/triple without bath, US$36/52/66 with bath, plus US$2 tax, breakfast included. Both of these are in the old town and open all year.

If you're willing to pay that, however, consider the B-category *Park Hotel* (☎ 058-515 411), Šetalište Baćvice 15 (US$63/77 single/double with private bath). This attractive 58-room resort hotel is a 10-minute walk from the old town, but closer to the bus and train stations and the beach.

Places to Eat
The cheapest place in town is *Restaurant Index*, a self-service student eatery at Svačićeva 8. Vegetarians should avoid this place. Better fare for only a little more is available at the *Bastion Self-Service*, Marmontova 9 (open daily). It's clean and inexpensive.

The *Burek Bar*, Domaldova 13, just down from the main post office, serves a good breakfast or lunch of burek and yoghurt for about a dollar. There are tables where you can sit.

Pizza, lasagna and draught beer are offered at *Pizzeria Bakra*, Radovanova 2, off ulica Sv Petra Starog just down from the vegetable market. It's patronised mostly by locals.

A more up-market pizza place is *Galija*, on Tončićeva (daily until 11 pm).

The *Koteks Shopping Centre*, a huge white complex 10 minutes' walk east of the old town beyond the Maritime Museum, is the largest of its kind in Dalmatia. It includes a supermarket, department store, boutiques, restaurants, bars, banks, post office, two bowling alleys, sports centre etc. If you want a slice of suburban Croatian life with your dinner, the *Pizzeria Koteks* upstairs in the centre has spaghetti, pizza and national meat dishes, plus draught beer. The menu is in Croatian only but it's a modern, friendly place. Many travellers stay in private rooms in this area.

Entertainment
In summer you'll probably find the best evening entertainment in the small streets of the old town, or along the waterfront promenade. During winter, opera and ballet are presented at the *Croatian National Theatre*, Trg Gaje Bulata. The best seats are about US$10 and tickets for the same night are usually available. This century-old theatre erected in 1891 was fully restored in 1979 in the original style; it's worth attending a performance for the architecture alone. At intermission, head upstairs to see the foyer.

The Split Summer Festival from mid-July to mid-August features opera, drama, ballet

CROATIA

and concerts on open-air stages. There's also the Feast of St Dujo (7 May) and the four-day Festival of Popular Music around the end of June. From June to September a variety of entertainment is presented in the old town in the evening.

Split's best known disco is *Club Kakadu* at the yacht harbour off Obala kneza Branimira (open daily from 10 pm until late).

Getting There & Away

Air Croatia Airlines has one-hour flights to/from Zagreb about four times a day (US$78).

Bus Advance bus tickets with seat reservations are recommended. There are through buses from the main bus station beside the harbour to Zadar (158 km, 25 daily), Zagreb (478 km, 22 daily), Rijeka (404 km, 12 daily), Ljubljana (532 km, two daily), Pula (514 km, two daily) and Rovinj (509 km, daily). To Bosnia-Hercegovina there are four daily buses from Split to Međugorje (156 km) and Mostar (179 km) despite the war. Croatia Express next to the bus station has a convenient overnight bus to Zagreb (US$14).

Bus No 37 to Solin, Split Airport and Trogir leaves from a local bus station on Domovinskog, one km north-east of the city centre. (See the map.)

To/From Dubrovnik The 10 daily buses between Split and Dubrovnik (235 km) pass through the small resort town of Neum which belongs to Bosnia-Hercegovina. Signs of the war are clearly visible here in the form of the burned and looted homes of Muslim 'departed residents', although the large tourist hotels are untouched. Today the Croatian flag flies over Neum, and Croatian police check the identity of bus passengers at checkpoints on both borders of the enclave (no problem).

Train In 1991 the railway line from Split to the interior was cut by ethnic fighting, and service was suspended. Trains still operate between Split and Šibenik (74 km).

Boat Jadrolinija (☎ 43 366) in the large Marine Terminal opposite the bus station handles services to Stari Grad on Hvar Island (US$9), operating three times a day all year round. The most useful local ferry is the daily service between Split and Ubli (Lastovo) which calls at Hvar (US$4) five times a week and at Vela Luka on Korčula Island (US$11) daily. This ferry departs from Vela Luka in the morning and Split in the afternoon; fares are half those charged for the same distance on the Rijeka-Dubrovnik line.

Jadrolinija also runs the big coastal ferries from Rijeka to Dubrovnik which stop at Rab, Zadar, Hvar and Korčula (from March to mid-October). The eight-hour southbound ferry trip to Dubrovnik is highly recommended. These ships usually leave Split at 8 am southbound and 7 pm northbound, but service is not always daily, so check the schedule at a travel agency beforehand. With a through ticket from Split to Dubrovnik (US$20) you can get free stops at Hvar and Korčula by having your ticket stamped by the purser before you disembark.

From June to September a Jadrolinija ferry runs between Split and Ancona, Italy, twice a week.

Getting Around

To/From the Airport The bus to Split Airport (US$2) leaves from Obala Lazareta 3, a five-minute walk from the train station. This bus departs 90 minutes before flight times. You can also get there on bus No 37, as described in Getting There & Away (two-zone ticket).

Bus Line up for city bus tickets at one of the very few kiosks around town which sell them, as newsstands don't have these tickets. For Trogir, buy a zone 3 ticket; Split Airport is zone 2; Solin and Trstenik are zone 1. Validate the ticket once aboard. Split bus tickets with an arrow at each end are good for two trips – you cancel one end at a time. You can also pay the driver, but that costs double. There's a US$10 fine if you're caught without a ticket.

Car Rental Compare prices at Cobra Rent-a-Car (☎ 42 889) and ST Rent-a-Car (☎ 44 344), adjacent at Obala Lazareta 3 in the centre. There's also Budget on Obala hrvatskog narodnog, Hertz (☎ 585 840), Obala kneza Branimira 1, and Europcar (☎ 523 099) at the Koteks Shopping Centre.

SALONA

The ruins of the ancient city of Salona (Solin), among the vineyards at the foot of the mountains just north-east of Split, are about the most interesting archaeological site in Croatia. Surrounded by noisy highways and industry today, Salona was the capital of the Roman province of Dalmatia from the time Julius Caesar elevated it to the status of colony. Salona held out against the barbarians and was only evacuated in 614 AD when the inhabitants fled to Split and neighbouring islands in the face of Avar and Slav attacks.

Things to See

A good place to begin your visit is at the large parking lot near the Snack Bar Salona. **Manastirine**, the fenced area behind the parking lot, was a burial place for early Christian martyrs prior to the legalisation of Christianity. Excavated remains of the subsequent cemetery and the 5th century basilica are highlights, although this area was outside the ancient city itself. Overlooking Manastirine is Tusculum, an archaeological museum with interesting sculpture embedded in the walls and in the garden. The Manastirine/Tusculum complex comprises an **archaeological reserve** open from 7 am to 2 pm.

A path bordered by cypresses leads south to the northern **city wall** of Salona. Notice the covered aqueduct along the inside base of the wall. The ruins you see in front of you as you stand on the wall were the Early Christian cult centre, including the three-aisled 5th century **cathedral** and small

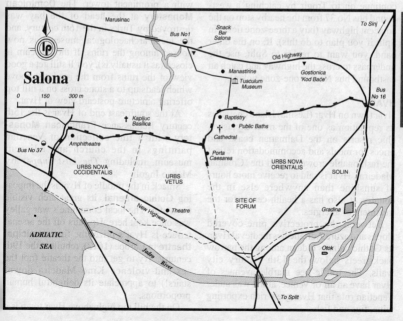

baptistry with inner columns. **Public baths** adjoin the cathedral on the east.

South-west is the 1st century east city gate, **Porta Caesarea**, later engulfed in the growth of Salona in all directions. Grooves in the stone road left by ancient chariots can still be seen at this gate.

Walk west along the city wall about 500 metres to **Kapljuc Basilica** on the right, another martyrs' burial place. At the west end of Salona is the huge 2nd century **amphitheatre**, only destroyed in the 17th century by the Venetians to prevent it from being used as a refuge by Turkish raiders.

Getting There & Away

The ruins are easily accessible on city bus No 1 direct to Snack Bar Salona every half-hour from opposite Trg Republike in Split. Bus No 16 will also bring you to Solin, but you have to get out where the Sinj Highway and city wall meet and then walk west along the old highway one km to the snack bar.

From the amphitheatre at Solin it's easy to continue on to Trogir by catching a west-bound bus No 37 from the nearby stop on the adjacent highway (buy a three-zone ticket in Split if you plan to do this). If, on the other hand, you want to return to Split, use the underpass to cross the highway and catch an eastbound bus No 37 (one-zone ticket).

HVAR

Hvar town on Hvar (Lesina) Island cherishes its reputation as one of the most exclusive, chic resorts on the Dalmatian coast, and prices for meals and accommodation reflect the fashionable crowd. Called the 'Croatian Madeira', Hvar is said to receive more hours of sunshine than anywhere else in the country. It also has a health centre for the treatment of allergies.

Between the protective pine-covered slopes and azure Adriatic lies medieval Hvar, its Gothic palaces hidden among the narrow backstreets below the 13th century city walls. The traffic-free marble avenues of Hvar have an air of Venice, and it was under Venetian rule that Hvar grew rich exporting wine, figs and fish.

Orientation

The big Jadrolinija ferries will drop you off right in the centre of old Hvar. The barge from Split calls at Stari Grad, 20 km east. The attendant at the public toilets beside the market adjoining the bus station holds luggage for US$1 apiece but they are only open during market hours, so check the closing time carefully.

Information

The Turist Biro is beside the Jadrolinija landing. Atlas Travel Agency facing the harbour represents American Express.

Post & Telecommunications Public telephones are available in the post office on the waterfront (Monday to Saturday 7 am to 9 pm). The telephone code for Hvar is 058.

Things to See

The full flavour of medieval Hvar is best savoured gently on the backstreets of the old town. At each end of town is a monastery with a prominent tower. The **Dominican Monastery** at the head of the bay was destroyed by Turks in the 16th century, and the local archaeological museum is now housed among the ruins. If the museum is closed (as it usually is), you'll still get a good view of the ruins from the road just above which leads up to a stone cross on a hill top offering a picture-postcard view of Hvar.

At the south-east end of Hvar is the 15th century Renaissance **Franciscan Monastery** with a fine collection of Venetian paintings in the church and adjacent museum, including *The Last Supper* by Matteo Ingoli.

Smack in the middle of Hvar is the imposing Gothic **arsenal**, its great arch visible from afar. The local commune's war galley was once kept here. Upstairs off the arsenal terrace is Hvar's prize, the first **municipal theatre** in Europe (1612), rebuilt in the 19th century. Try to get into the theatre (not the sex-and-violence Kino Madeira downstairs!) to appreciate its delightful human proportions.

On the hill top high above Hvar town is a

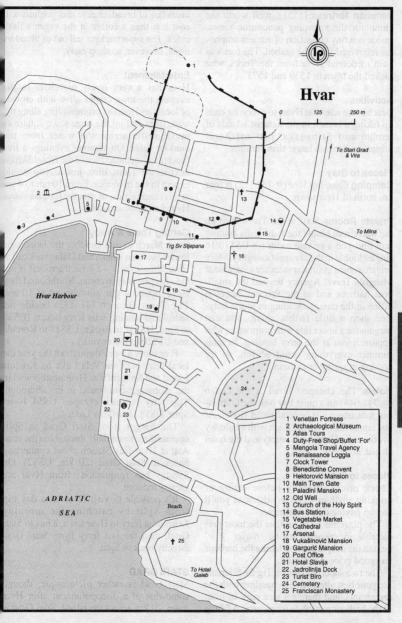

Hvar

0   125   250 m

To Stari Grad
& Vira

To Milna

Hvar Harbour

Trg Sv Stjepana

*ADRIATIC
SEA*

Beach

To Hotel
Galeb

1 Venetian Fortress
2 Archaeological Museum
3 Atlas Tours
4 Duty-Free Shop/Buffet 'For'
5 Mengola Travel Agency
6 Renaissance Loggia
7 Clock Tower
8 Benedictine Convent
9 Hektorović Mansion
10 Main Town Gate
11 Paladini Mansion
12 Old Well
13 Church of the Holy Spirit
14 Bus Station
15 Vegetable Market
16 Cathedral
17 Arsenal
18 Vukašinović Mansion
19 Gargurić Mansion
20 Post Office
21 Hotel Slavija
22 Jadrolinija Dock
23 Turist Biro
24 Cemetery
25 Franciscan Monastery

CROATIA

Venetian fortress (1551), well worth the climb for the sweeping panoramic views. Inside is a tiny collection of ancient amphoras recovered from the seabed. The fort was built to defend Hvar from the Turks, who sacked the town in 1539 and 1571.

Activities

Beaches are scarce at Hvar, so everyone ends up taking a launch to the naturist islands of Jerolim and Stipanska, just offshore. Stipanska is much larger than Jerolim.

Places to Stay

Camping *Camping Vira* (☎ 741 112) is four km north of Hvar town.

Private Rooms Staff at the Turist Biro on the waterfront beside the Jadrolinija landing will find you a private room for US$10/16 single/double in the cheapest category. More private rooms at similar rates are available at Mengola Travel Agency beyond the small-boat harbour and at the Privatni Smjestaj office in the passage leading in to the duty-free shop a little farther along. You can bargain for a lower rate with proprietors who approach you at the ferry landing. In mid-summer everything could be full, so try coming in spring or autumn.

Hotels The cheapest hotel is the *Galeb* (☎ 741 644) on a quiet bay past the Franciscan monastery just beyond Hotel Bodul. At last report the 30 rooms, each with a balcony overlooking Hvar, were empty and the hotel closed, so check.

Places to Eat

Check prices carefully before eating or drinking anything in Hvar, otherwise you'll end up paying double or triple.

The pizzerias of Hvar offer the most predictable inexpensive eating. *Buffet 'For'* next to the duty-free shop facing the harbour has good prices for drinks.

The two supermarkets on Trg Sv Stjepana are your best alternative to hassling with the restaurants, and there's a nice park in front of the harbour just made for picnics. A filling breakfast of bread, cheese and yoghurt will cost less than a coffee at the various flash cafés. The supermarkets sell out of bread by noon, however, so shop early.

Entertainment

Hvar has a very lively nightlife. In the evening the town comes alive with crowds of locals and tourists promenading along the waterfront and up the huge town square as music drifts across the water from the outdoor cafés. On summer evenings a live band plays on the terrace of the *Hotel Slavija* next to the Turist Biro, just as you would expect to see in Venice. From 10 pm to 4 am at this magical time of year the fortress above Hvar functions as a disco.

Getting There & Away

From March to mid-October the Jadrolinija ferries between Rijeka and Dubrovnik call at Hvar almost daily – by far the nicest if not the cheapest way to come. Northbound they leave around 4 pm, southbound at 10 am. The Turist Biro (☎ 741 132) beside the Jadrolinija landing sells ferry tickets (US$8 to Split, US$32 to Rijeka, US$17 to Korčula and US$20 to Dubrovnik).

Five times a week throughout the year the local ferry between Vela Luka on Korčula Island and Split calls at Hvar northbound in the morning, southbound in the afternoon. This ferry is much cheaper: US$4 Hvar-Split, US$6 Hvar-Vela Luka.

The barges from Stari Grad to Split operate three times daily throughout the year. Ask at Hvar Bus Station about connecting buses to Stari Grad (20 km, US$2). On Sunday bus frequencies from Hvar are greatly reduced.

It's possible to visit Hvar on a day trip from Split by catching the morning Jadrolinija ferry to Hvar town, a bus to Stari Grad, then the last ferry from Stari Grad directly back to Split.

STARI GRAD

Stari Grad is rather picturesque, though somewhat of a disappointment after Hvar town, 20 km across the island. Stari Grad is

CROATIA

on the site of an ancient beacon which once stood at the east end of the long inlet which bisects western Hvar. (Hvar gets its name from *Pharos*, Greek for lighthouse.) Stari Grad was the capital of the island until 1331 when the Venetians shifted the administration to Hvar. This explains the extensive medieval quarter you still see at Stari Grad. The palace of the Croat poet Petar Hektorović (1487-1572) is worth a visit to see the fish pond and garden.

Places to Stay

Kamp 'Jurjevac' (open from June to early September) is just off the harbour right in the centre of Stari Grad. There's no sign, so ask for directions.

Private-room proprietors are less likely to meet the buses and ferries here than in Hvar own and at last report there was no agency renting such rooms, so you'll just have to ask around.

Getting There & Away

Local ferries run from Split to Stari Grad (US$9) three times a day. The ferry landing at Stari Grad is about two km from town along a pleasant path by the pine-fringed bay. Buses also meet the ferries at Stari Grad.

There are three buses a day from Stari Grad to Hvar town (US$2 plus US$1 per piece of baggage).

KORČULA

The town of Korčula (Curzola) hugs a small, hilly peninsula jutting into the Adriatic Sea from Korčula Island. With its round defensive towers and compact cluster of red-roofed houses, Korčula is a typical medieval Dalmatian town. In contrast to Turkish cities like Mostar and Sarajevo, Korčula was controlled by Venice from the 14th to the 18th centuries. Venetian rule left its mark, especially on Cathedral Square. It's a peaceful little place (population 4000), the grey stone houses nestling between the deepgreen hills and gunmetal-blue sea with rustling palms all around.

Korčula is noticeably cheaper than Hvar and there's lots to see and do, so it's worth planning a relaxed four-night stay to avoid the 30% surcharge on private rooms. Day trips are possible to Orebić, Mljet, Lumbarda, Badija and Vela Luka.

Orientation

If you arrive on the big Jadrolinija car ferry it will drop you off below the walls of the old town of Korčula on Korčula Island. The passenger launch from Orebić is also convenient, terminating at the old harbour, but the barge from Orebić goes to Bon Repos in Dominče, several km south-east of the centre. There's no left-luggage office at the bus station.

Information

The Turist Biro is near the old town. Atlas Travel Agency is the local American Express representative.

Post & Telecommunications The post office (with public telephones) is rather hidden next to the stairs up to the old town. Korčula's telephone code is 050.

Things to See

Other than following the circuit of the former

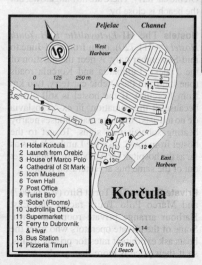

1 Hotel Korčula
2 Launch from Orebić
3 House of Marco Polo
4 Cathedral of St Mark
5 Icon Museum
6 Town Hall
7 Post Office
8 Turist Biro
9 'Sobe' (Rooms)
10 Jadrolinija Office
11 Supermarket
12 Ferry to Dubrovnik & Hvar
13 Bus Station
14 Pizzeria Timun

Korčula

Pelješac Channel

West Harbour

East Harbour

To The Beach

CROATIA

city walls or walking along the shore, sightseeing in Korčula centres on Cathedral Square. The Gothic **Cathedral of St Mark** features two paintings by Tintoretto (the *Three Saints* on the altar and the *Annunciation* to one side).

The **Treasury** in the 14th century Abbey Palace next to the cathedral is worth a look, and even better is the **Town Museum** in the 15th century Gabriellis Palace opposite. It's said that Marco Polo was born in Korčula in 1254; for a fee, you can climb the tower of the house that is supposed to have been his. There's also an **Icon Museum** in the old town. It isn't much of a museum, but visitors are let into the beautiful old Church of All Saints as a bonus.

Activities

In the high summer season ask about shuttle boats from Korčula to Badija Island, which features a 15th century Franciscan monastery (now a D-category hotel) and a naturist beach.

Places to Stay

Camping *Autocamp 'Kalac'* (☎ 711 182) is behind Hotel Bon Repos, not far from the Orebić car ferry. There are no bungalows, but the beach is close by.

Hostels The HI *Ljetovalište FSH Youth Hostel* (☎ 711 720), open from mid-June to mid-September only, is near the junction of the Trajekt, Lumbarda and Korčula roads (one km from the Orebić car ferry, two km from Korčula). If the hostel is still closed because of the 'situation' in ex-Yugoslavia (ie no tourists), there are many houses nearby bearing sobe/zimmer signs. To get to the hostel from town, take the Lumbarda bus as far as the hospital; for Autocamp 'Kalac', get out of the same bus at Hotel Bon Repos.

Private Rooms The Turist Biro (☎ 711 067) and Marco Polo Tours facing the East Harbour arrange private rooms in town. Some of the private operators who meet the boats ask exorbitant rates for private rooms, so if their price is more than you're accustomed to paying, check the agencies (which may charge a 30% supplement if you stay fewer than four nights).

There are numerous sobe and zimmer signs around town, so you could try knocking on doors. The houses on the road along the waterfront north-west from the old town are a good bet.

Hotels The B-category *Hotel Korčula* (☎ 711 078) facing Pelješac Channel on the edge of the old town is about US$32/54 single/double with breakfast (50% higher in July and August). The 22 rooms are often full.

Places to Eat

Restaurant Grill Planjak, between the supermarket and the Jadrolinija office in town, is good for chicken or steaks, national specialities like *raznjici*, *ćevapčići* and *pljeskavica*, and huge mugs of draught beer. You can also get morning coffee here.

The terrace at *Hotel Korčula* is a nice place for a coffee.

Entertainment

From May to September there's *moreška* sword dancing by the old town gate every Thursday evening at 9 pm (US$7 – tickets from the Turist Biro). *Cinema Liburna* is in the building marked 'kino' behind the Liburna Restaurant near the bus station.

Getting There & Away

Bus There's a daily bus service from Dubrovnik to Korčula (113 km, US$5). Twice a week there's a Zagreb-Korčula bus (US$22).

Six daily buses link Korčula town to Vela Luka (48 km, 1½ hours, US$1.50). Buses to Lumbarda run about hourly (seven km, US$0.35). No bus runs to Lumbarda on Sunday and service to Vela Luka is sharply reduced on weekends.

Ferry Getting to Korčula is easy since all the big Jadrolinija coastal ferries between Split and Dubrovnik tie up at the landing next to the old town. If it's too windy in the east harbour, this ferry lands at the west harbour in front of Hotel Korčula. If you didn't plan a stop here, your glimpse of Korčula from the railing will make you regret it. Car ferry tickets may be purchased at the Jadrolinija office (☎ 711 101) or the Turist Biro (same prices). Departures from Korčula are usually around noon in both directions.

Another approach is on the daily ferry from Split to Vela Luka at the west end of Korčula Island. Five times a week these services call at Hvar town en route. At US$6 from Vela Luka to Hvar or US$11 to Split this ferry is less than half the price of the large Jadrolinija coastal ferries which charge US$17 from Korčula to Hvar and US$21 to Split.

Between Orebić and Korčula instead of the barge-type car ferry which lands at Bon Repos a couple of km from town, look for the passenger launch (seven times a day year-round, 15 minutes, US$1 one way) which will drop you off at the Hotel Korčula right below the old town's towers. This is best if you're looking for a private room, but if you want to camp or stay at the youth hostel be sure to take the auto barge to Bon Repos in Dominče.

LUMBARDA

Just 15 minutes from Korčula town by bus, Lumbarda is a picturesque small settlement near the east end of Korčula Island. A good ocean beach (Plaza Pržina) is on the other side of the vineyards beyond the supermarket; the area around the lighthouse at the eastern tip of Korčula is a secret military installation closed to foreigners.

Staff at the Hotel Lumbarda reception arrange private rooms and there are a couple of camping grounds just up the road beside the hotel. 'Grk', a dry white wine originating in the vineyards around Lumbarda, is named after the Greek settlers who colonised Korkyra Melania (Korčula) in the 4th century BC.

VELA LUKA

Vela Luka at the west end of Korčula is the centre of the island's fishing industry

because of its large sheltered harbour. Tiny, wooded, button-shaped Ošjak Island in the bay just off Vela Luka is a national park. There isn't a lot to see at Vela Luka and no real beaches, so if you're arriving by ferry from Split or Hvar you might jump right on the waiting bus to Korčula town and look for a room there. Vela Luka does have the advantage of being a lot less touristy than Korčula.

Medicinal Baths

The Kalos Medical Centre (☎ 812 422) at Vela Luka uses medical mud (terapija blato) to treat rheumatism, and there's a heated saltwater swimming pool on the premises where underwater massage (podvodna masaža) is carried out. Regular massage and electrotherapy are also available, but all treatments must be prescribed by a physician. This is less of a problem than it sounds and the Kalos reception staff will help you make the arrangements. The mud bath (US$5) is only available weekday mornings until 10 am.

Places to Stay

The Turist Biro (☎ 82 042), open in summer only, arranges private rooms. It is beside the Jadran Hotel on the waterfront 100 metres from the ferry landing.

If the Turist Biro is closed your next best bet is the Pansion u Domaćinstva Barčot (☎ 812 014), ulica 62, directly behind the Jadran Hotel. This attractive 24-room guesthouse is open all year and prices are just a little above what you've been paying for private rooms. Some rooms on the 3rd floor have balconies.

Camping Mindel (☎ 812 494) is six km north-west of Vela Luka (no bus service).

Getting There & Away

The ferries from Split land at the west end of the harbour, and buses to Korčula town meet all arrivals. There's at least one boat a day from Vela Luka to Split (US$11), calling at Hvar (US$6) five times a week throughout the year. It leaves Vela Luka in the very early morning, so you might want to spend the

CROATIA

night here if you'll be catching one, although a bus from Korčula does connect.

OREBIĆ

Orebić, on the south coast of the Pelješac Peninsula between Korčula and Ploče, offers better beaches than those found at Korčula, 2.5 km across the water. The easy access by ferry from Korčula makes it the perfect place to go for the day, and a good alternative place to stay. All bus passengers to/from Dubrovnik or Zagreb will transit the town.

Things to See & Do

There's a good beach to the east of the port, two km along a peaceful waterfront road. A trail leads up from Hotel Bellevue to an old **Franciscan monastery** on a ridge high above the sea. The monastery is worth seeing and the view from above makes the climb worthwhile.

A more daring climb is to the top of **Mt Ilija** (961 metres), the bare grey massif that hangs above Orebić. The three-hour hike through thick vegetation begins on ulica Kralja Tomislava beside the cathedral near the port and is marked with red-and-white circles or red arrows. A second, more difficult route up Mt Ilija departs from the Franciscan monastery. The last half-hour is very steep and the final bit is a scramble over the rocks. The trail is safe and well marked, but avoid getting lost near the top as there's no rescue service. You'll get a sweeping view of the entire coast from up there.

Places to Stay & Eat

The helpful Turistički ured Orebić (☎ 713 014) next to the post office near the ferry landings (open April to September) rents private rooms and can provide a town map. If the tourist office is closed just walk around looking for *sobe* signs – you'll soon find something.

Autokamp Hauptstrand (☎ 713 399) is a pleasant 15-minute walk east along the shore from the port. It overlooks an excellent long beach. There are several other camping grounds near Orebić, but in the off season check first at the tourist office to make sure they're open.

If you arrive late in the afternoon on the bus from Dubrovnik it's probably better to spend the night in Orebić and take the morning ferry over to Korčula. In fact, Orebić would be well worth a couple of nights if you're a hiker or beach lover.

Getting There & Away

In Orebić the two ferry terminals and bus station are all adjacent. One bus leaves Orebić for Dubrovnik (113 km, US$5) in the morning and returns in the afternoon. Other buses run to Trpanj three times a day, to Lovište (16 km) twice a day. See Korčula for additional bus and ferry information.

MLJET ISLAND

Created in 1960, **Mljet National Park** occupies the western third of the green island of Mljet (Melita) between Korčula and Dubrovnik. The park centres around two saltwater lakes surrounded by pine-clad slopes. Most people visit on day trips from Korčula but it's also possible to come by regular ferry and spend a few days here. If you do, you'll have Mljet almost to yourself!

Orientation

The tour boats from Korčula arrive at Pomena wharf at Mljet's west end, where a good map of the island is posted. From Pomena it's a 15-minute walk to a jetty on Veliko jezero, the larger of the two lakes. Here the groups board a boat to a small lake islet where lunch is served at a 12th century **Benedictine monastery**, now a hotel.

Those who don't want to spend the rest of the afternoon swimming and sunbathing on the monastery island can catch an early boat back to the main island, allowing a couple of hours to walk along the lakeshore before catching the late-afternoon boat back to Korčula. There's a small landing opposite the monastery where the boat operator drops off passengers upon request. It's not possible to walk right around the larger lake as there's no bridge over the channel connecting the lakes to the sea.

CROATIA

Getting There & Away

Atlas Travel Agency (☎ 711 060) in Korčula offers a day trip to Mljet Island twice a week from mid-April to mid-October. The tour lasts from 8.30 am to 6 pm, and at US$20 per person, including the US$6 park entry fee, it's good value. The boat takes two hours to motor south-east from Korčula to Pomena. Lunch isn't included in the tour price and meals at the hotels on Mljet are very expensive, so it's best to bring a picnic.

You can also come on your own by taking the regular ferry from Dubrovnik to Polače on the north-west side of Mljet (daily except Sunday, US$4). There are private rooms on Mljet, and just east of Pomena is *Autokamp Sikjerica*. Mljet is a good island for cycling and the hotels rent bicycles.

Dubrovnik

Founded 1300 years ago by refugees from Epidaurus, Greece, medieval Dubrovnik (Ragusa) was the most important independent city-state on the Adriatic after Venice. Until the Napoleonic invasion of 1806, it remained an independent republic of merchants and sailors. Like Venice, Dubrovnik now survives mostly on tourism. Stari Grad, the perfectly preserved old town, is unique for its marble-paved squares, steep cobbled streets, tall houses, convents, churches, palaces, fountains and museums, all cut from the same light-coloured stone. The intact city walls keep motorists at bay, and the southerly position between Split and Albania makes for an agreeable climate and lush vegetation.

For those who watched the destruction of Dubrovnik on TV in late 1991, here's a bit of good news: the city is still there, as beautiful as ever, though many of the old stone buildings are now poked with bullet holes, which serve as reminders of the naval bombardments, artillery attacks and incendiary bombing during the eight-month siege by the federal army from October 1991 to May 1992. The cable car up 412-metre Srđ Mountain was destroyed. This brutal assault on a city which had been classed a world heritage treasure by UNESCO certainly marked a low point in the conflict.

Televised scenes of sunken ships and burning buildings scared away the tourist masses and the city is now suffering prolonged economic consequences in the form of no tourists, exacerbating the physical damage and the inconvenience of being cut off from its natural hinterland in Bosnia-Hercegovina and Montenegro. Yet much of the damage to Dubrovnik has already been repaired. The tenacious Croats were already out there patching up the holes just hours after the Serb bombs fell. Many buildings are still damaged but you don't see it as the shutters will be down and the windows closed. Most of the windows in town were broken but the only ones which haven't been repaired are those on the front of the Serbian church.

Though you won't find smoking ruins, at last report most of the palaces, churches and museums were closed (mostly due to a lack of visitors) and the façades of some were still covered with protective hoardings. But you can again walk around the city on the top of the wall and the streets are now refreshingly free of tourists. Restoration work on the historic monuments is well advanced and everything should be back to normal by the time you get there. Don't miss this highlight of Eastern Europe.

Orientation

The Jadrolinija ferry terminal and the bus station are a few hundred metres apart at Gruž, several km north-west of the old town. Left-luggage at the bus station is open from 5 am to 9 pm. The bus service into town is fairly frequent. The camping ground and most of the luxury tourist hotels are on the Lapad Peninsula, west of the bus station.

Information

The tourist information centre is on Placa, opposite the Franciscan monastery in the old town. The American Express representative is Atlas Travel Agency (☎ 442 222), Brsalje 17.

CROATIA

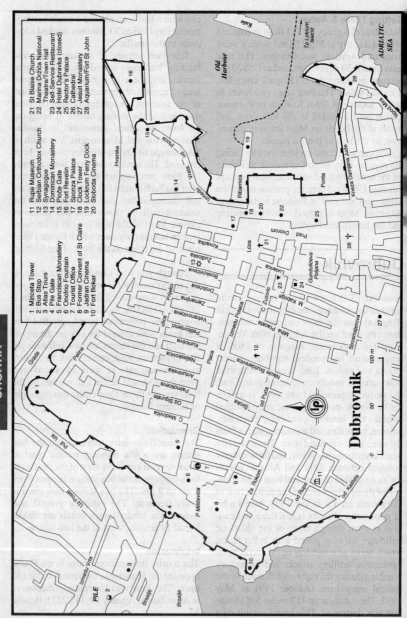

1	Minceta Tower	11	Rupe Museum	21	St Blaise Church
2	Bus Stop	12	Serbian Orthodox Church	22	Marina Držića National Theatre/Town Hall
3	Atlas Tours	13	Synagogue	23	Self-Service Restaurant
4	Pile Gate	14	Dominican Monastery	24	Hotel Dubravka (closed)
5	Franciscan Monastery	15	Ploče Gate	25	Rector's Palace
6	Onofrio Fountain	16	Fort Revelin	26	Cathedral
7	Tourist Office	17	Sponza Palace	27	Jesuit Monastery
8	Former Convent of St Claire	18	Clock Tower	28	Aquarium/Fort St John
9	Jadran Cinema	19	Lockrum Ferry Dock		
10	Fort Bokar	20	Sloboda Cinema		

ADRIATIC SEA

Old Harbour

To Lokrum Island

Kneza Damjana Jude

Ponta

Ribarnica

Hvarska

Placa

Kače

Pred Dvorom

Lučarica

Gundulićeva Poljana

Stjepana

Za Rokom

Siroka

od Puča

Nikole Božidarevića

Između Polača

Strossmajerova

Mira Pracata

C. Zuzoric

M Kaboge

Ljubica

Loža

Žudioska

Boškovićeva

Drobojeva

Zamanjina

Petilovrijenci

Kunićeva

Naljeskovica

Antuninska

Palmotičeva

Od Sigurate

Medovica

Kovačka

Prijeko

Vetranićeva

Ulica

Peline

Grada

Put Iza

Izmedu Vrta

Brsalje

Brsalje

Kaboge

Svetog Dominika

Frana Supila

Dubrovnik

PILE

CROATIA

0   50   100 m

Dubrovnik

Post & Telecommunications The main post office is at Ante Starčevića 2, a block up from Pile Gate (Monday to Saturday 7 am to 8 pm, Sunday 7 am to 2 pm). Place international telephone calls here. There's another post office/telephone centre at Lapad near Hotel Kompas. The telephone code for Dubrovnik is 050.

Things to See

You'll probably begin your visit at the city bus stop outside **Pile Gate**. As you enter the city, Placa, Dubrovnik's wonderful pedestrian promenade, extends before you all the way to the clock tower at the other end of town. Just inside Pile Gate is the huge **Onofrio Fountain** (1438) and the **Franciscan Monastery** with the third-oldest functioning pharmacy in Europe by the cloister (operating since 1391).

In front of the clock tower at the east end of Placa, you'll find the **Orlando Column** (1419) – a favourite meeting place. On opposite sides of Orlando are the 16th century **Sponza Palace** (now the State Archives) and **St Blaise's Church**, a lovely Italian Baroque building.

At the end of the broad street beside St Blaise is the Baroque **cathedral** and, between the two churches, the Gothic **Rector's Palace** (1441), now a museum with furnished rooms, Baroque paintings and historical exhibits. The elected rector was not permitted to leave the building during his one-month term without the permission of the Senate. The narrow street opposite this palace opens onto Gundulićeva Poljana, a bustling morning market. Up the stairway at the south end of the square is the imposing **Jesuit Monastery** (1725).

Return to the cathedral and take the narrow street in front to the **Aquarium** in Fort St John. Through an obscure entrance off the city walls, above the aquarium, is the **Maritime Museum**. If you're 'museumed out' you can safely give these two a miss.

By this time you'll be ready for a leisurely walk around the **city walls** themselves. Built between the 13th and 16th centuries and still intact today, these powerful walls are the finest in the world and Dubrovnik's main claim to fame. They enclose the entire city in a curtain of stone over two km long and up to 25 metres high, with two round towers, 14 square towers, two corner fortifications and a large fortress. The views over the town and sea are great, so make this walk the high point of your visit.

Whichever way you go, you'll notice the large **Dominican monastery** in the northeast corner of the city. Of all of Dubrovnik's religious museums, the one in the Dominican monastery is the largest and most worth paying to enter.

Dubrovnik has many other sights, such as the unmarked **synagogue** at ulica Žudioska 5 near the clock tower (10 am to noon daily except Sunday, donation). The uppermost streets of the old town below the north and south walls are pleasant to wander along.

To the Beach The closest beach to the old city is just beyond the 17th century **Lazareti** (former quarantine station) outside Ploče Gate. There are also 'managed' hotel beaches on the **Lapad Peninsula**, but you could be charged admission unless they think you're a guest.

A far better option is to take the ferry which shuttles six times a day from the small-boat harbour (May to October, US$1 return) to **Lokrum Island**, a national park with a rocky nudist (FKK) beach on its east side, a botanical garden and the ruins of a medieval Benedictine monastery.

A day trip can be made from Dubrovnik to the resort town of **Cavtat** just south-east. Bus No 10 runs often to Cavtat from Dubrovnik's bus station. Like Dubrovnik, Cavtat was founded by Greeks from Epidaurus and there are several churches, museums and historic monuments as well as beaches. Don't miss the memorial chapel to the Račič family by Ivan Mešstrović.

Places to Stay

Camping *Camping Solitude* (☎ 448 310) on the Lapad Peninsula (walk or catch bus No 6) may have reopened by the time you get there. All of the small caravans (mobile

CROATIA

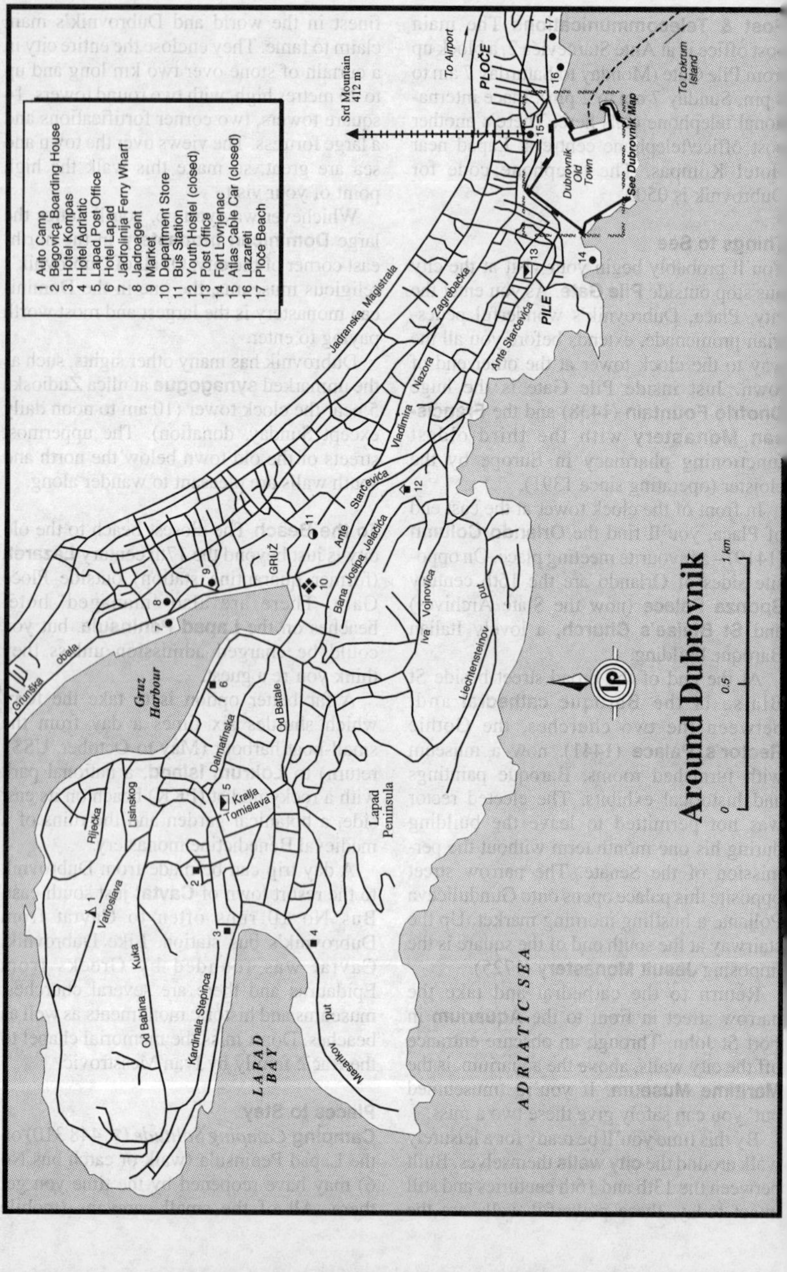

CROATIA

Around Dubrovnik

0   0.5   1 km

Legend

1 Auto Camp
2 Begovica Boarding House
3 Hotel Kompas
4 Hotel Adriatic
5 Lapad Post Office
6 Hotel Lapad
7 Jadrolinija Ferry Wharf
8 Jadroagent
9 Market
10 Department Store
11 Bus Station
12 Youth Hostel (closed)
13 Post Office
14 Fort Lovrijenac
15 Atlas Cable Car (closed)
16 Lazareti
17 Ploče Beach

Map labels: To Airport · PLOČE · To Lokrum Island · See Dubrovnik Map · Dubrovnik Old Town · PILE · Srd Mountain 412 m · Gruž Harbour · GRUŽ · Lapad Peninsula · LAPAD BAY · ADRIATIC SEA · Kralja Tomislava

Streets: Jadranska Magistrala · Zagrebačka · Ante Starčevića · Nazora · Vladimira · Iva Vojnovica · Liechtensteinov put · Bana Josipa Jelačića · Od Batale · Dalmatinska · Gruška obala · Rijeöka · Lisinskog · Vatroslava · Kuka · Od Babina · Kardinala Stepinca · Masarykov put · Mesarovo put

homes) previously available here were destroyed in 1991.

Hostels At last report the HI *youth hostel*, up Vinka Sagrestana from Bana Josipa Jelačića 17, was still occupied by members of the 'special police'.

Private Rooms The easiest way to find a place to stay is to accept the offer of a sobe from one of the women who will approach you at the ferry terminal. Their prices are lower than those charged by the room-finding agencies and are open to bargaining (from around US$10 per person). However, with tourism down, landladies no longer bother waiting at the bus station for the few arriving passengers. This will undoubtedly change.

Dalmacijaturist next to the Dubrovačka Bank opposite the port at Gruž arranges private rooms for about US$13/24 single/double. They may levy a 30% surcharge if you stay less than three nights. Also charging these prices are Atlas Travel Agency at the port and at Brsalje 17, outside Pile Gate next to the old town, and Kompas, Brsalje 10. The tourist office opposite the Franciscan monastery just through the gate is another place to try.

Hotels Dubrovnik's hotels are much more expensive than private rooms. The three hotels listed in previous editions of this book, the *Hotel Dubravka*, ulica od Puča 1 beside the vegetable market in the old town, the *Hotel Stadion* (☎ 411 449), right behind the bus station (same building), and the *Hotel Gruž*, Pionirska 4, directly above the Jadrolinija ferry landing, are presently occupied by refugees and closed, although this could change. (The Dubravka is in very bad shape.)

The bullet-scarred five-storey *Hotel Petka* (☎ 24 933), Obala Stjepana Radića 38, opposite the ferry landing, has 104 rooms at US$24/41 single/double with bath and breakfast. It's reliably open all year round.

A much nicer B-category place than this is the *Hotel Lapad* (☎ 25 755) on Lapadska

obala, an old hotel full of character facing the small-boat harbour. They have a swimming pool.

The *Begović Boarding House* (☎ 28 563), Primorska 17, a couple of blocks up from Lapad post office (bus No 6), has three rooms with shared bath at US$15/25 single/double and three small apartments for slightly more. There's a nice terrace out the back with a good view. Call ahead as they do fill at peak periods. They'll gladly pick you up at the port or bus station.

Places to Eat

The *Express Self-service Restaurant* on ulica Lućarica behind the Church of St Blaise is neither cheap nor good, and for just a little more you can get a much better meal at one of the expensive seafood restaurants along ulica Prijeko, a narrow street parallel to Placa. The restaurants at the far west end of the street are slightly cheaper. The cheapest way to fill your stomach in Dubrovnik is to buy the makings of a picnic at a local supermarket, such as the one in the department store near the bus station.

Konoba Primorka, Nikole Tesle 8 just west of the department store in Gruž, has a good selection of seafood and national dishes at medium prices. In summer you dine below the trees on a lamp-lit terrace.

At all Dubrovnik restaurants, beware of the price of the drinks, especially if they're not listed on the menu.

Entertainment

For entertainment, see a movie – they are cheaper than any of Dubrovnik's museums. The *Jadran Cinema* is just off Paska Miličevića near the tourist office.

Bakhos Disco is downstairs in the old Lazareti just outside the Ploče Gate.

The majestic 19th century *Marina Držića National Theatre* is on Pred Dvorum beside the Rector's Palace. Performances here are mostly drama in Croatian and it's closed all summer.

Ask at the tourist office about concerts and folk dancing. The Dubrovnik Summer Festival from mid-July to mid-August is a major

CROATIA

cultural event with over 100 performances at different venues in the old city. The Feast of St Blaise (3 February) and Carnival (February) are also celebrated.

Getting There & Away

Air Daily flights to/from Zagreb are operated by Croatia Airlines and a local carrier called Anić Airways. The fare should be US$85 one way but there are sometimes price wars, so compare. Anić also flies to Vienna (US$290). Kompas, Brsalje 10, sells tickets for all flights.

Bus Buses from Dubrovnik include one to Pula (749 km), three to Rijeka (639 km), eight to Zadar (393 km), nine to Split (235 km), three to Zagreb (713 km) and two to Orebić (113 km, US$5). To go to Korčula take one of the Orebić buses. During the busy summer season and on weekends, buses out of Dubrovnik can be crowded, so book a ticket well before the scheduled departure time.

The farthest south the buses from Dubrovnik now go is to Vitaljina, three times a day (56 km).

Boat The Jadrolinija coastal ferry north to Korčula (US$17), Hvar (US$20), Split (US$20) and Rijeka (US$44) is far more comfortable than the bus, if several times more expensive. Still, it's well worth the extra money. The ferry leaves at 10 am several times a week from March to mid-October. Buy a through ticket to your most distant destination, then have it stamped by the purser once aboard for free stopovers.

A local ferry leaves Dubrovnik for Polače on Mljet Island (four hours, US$4) at 1 pm daily except Sunday throughout the year.

Information on domestic ferries is available from Jadrolinija (☎ 23 068), Obala S Radića 40.

From June to September there's a weekly Jadrolinija car ferry from Dubrovnik to Bari, Italy (nine hours, US$40). In July and August fares are up to 25% higher. Tickets for international ferries are sold by Jadroagent, Obala S Radića 32 at the port.

At last report the Jadrolinija ferry service to Igoumenitsa, Greece, was suspended. Jadrolinija offices anywhere along the Croatian coast will know if it's running again.

Getting Around

To/From the Airport Čilipi International Airport is 24 km south-east of Dubrovnik. The Adria Airways and Croatia Airlines airport buses (US$1.50) leave from in front of Atlas Travel Agency, Brsalje 17, just outside Pile Gate, 1¾ hours before flight times.

Bus Pay your fare in exact change on city buses as you board – have small bills.

Car Rental Dubrovnik Rent-a-Car (☎ 21 983), Obala Stjepana Radića 29, near the port at Gruž, has cars with unlimited km from US$48 a day, tax and insurance included. Otherwise it's US$14 a day, plus US$0.14 a km (80-km minimum), plus US$6 CDW insurance, plus 20% tax.

Gulliver Rent-a-Car (☎ 27 888), Obala Stjepana Radića 31, charges about the same as Dubrovnik, but Hertz (☎ 23 779) at Hotel Kompas in Lapad is more expensive. At the first two you must be at least 21 years old, while Hertz will rent to people aged 18 and up. The biggest advantage of Hertz is that you can drop the car off at any of their offices around Croatia and Slovenia.

Czech Republic

Bohemia and Moravia together make up the Czech Republic, a Scotland-sized nation on the edge of the Germanic and Slavic worlds. It's one of Europe's most historic countries, full of fairytale castles, chateaux, manors and museums. The medieval cores of several dozen towns have been carefully preserved and there's so much to see that you could make repeated visits.

The Czech Republic is doubly inviting for its cultured, friendly people and excellent facilities. The transportation network is equalled only in Western Europe. Ninety per cent of English-speaking visitors limit themselves to Prague but the clever few who escape the hordes and high prices in the capital soon experience just how helpful the Czech people can be (almost everything outside Prague is still off the beaten tourist track).

Facts about the Country

HISTORY

In antiquity this area was inhabited by the Celts and was never part of the classical Roman Empire. The Celtic Boii tribe which inhabited the Bohemian basin gave the region its present name. Germanic tribes conquered the Celts in the 4th century AD, and between the 5th and 10th centuries the West Slavs settled here. From 830 to 907 the Slavic tribes united in the Great Moravian Empire and adopted Christianity. Cyril and Methodius, two Greek brothers from Thessaloniki, visited Great Moravia personally in 863 and invented the first Slavic alphabet here.

Towards the end of the 9th century, the Czechs seceded from the Great Moravian Empire and formed an independent state. In 995 the Czech lands were united under the native Přemysl dynasty as the principality of Bohemia. The Czech state then became a kingdom in the 12th century and reached its peak under Přemysl Otakar II from 1253 to 1278. Many towns were founded at this time.

The Přemysls died out in 1306 and, in 1310, John of Luxembourg gained the Bohemian throne through marriage and annexed the kingdom to the German empire. His son, Charles IV (depicted on the new 100 Kč banknote), became king of the Germans in 1346 and Holy Roman Emperor in 1355. Inclusion in this medieval empire led to a blossoming of trade and culture. The capital, Prague, was made an archbishopric in 1344 and in 1348 Charles University was founded. These kings were able to keep the feudal nobility in check, but under Wenceslas IV (1378-1419) the strength of the monarchy declined. The church became the largest landowner.

In 1415 the religious reformer Jan Hus, rector of Charles University, was burnt at the stake in Constance. His ideas inspired the nationalistic Hussite movement which swept

CZECH REPUBLIC

CZECH REPUBLIC

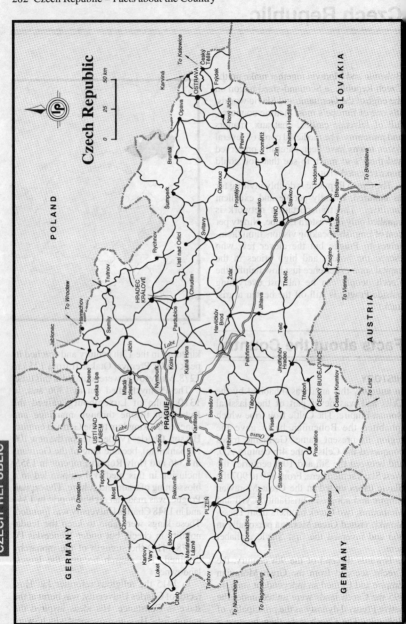

Czech Republic

0   25   50 km

POLAND

GERMANY

SLOVAKIA

AUSTRIA

To Wrocław
To Kraków
Český Těšín
Frýdek
Karviná
OSTRAVA
Opava
Nový Jičín
Bruntál
Přerov
Kroměříž
Zlín
Uherské Hradiště
Šumperk
Olomouc
Prostějov
Hodonín
Rychnov
Svitavy
Blansko
BRNO
Břeclav
To Bratislava
Jablonec
Trutnov
Žďár
Mikulov
Harrachov
Semily
HRADEC KRÁLOVÉ
Chrudim
Třebíč
Znojmo
Jičín
Pardubice
Havlíčkův Brod
Jihlava
To Vienna
Liberec
Česká Lípa
Mladá Boleslav
Labe
Kolín
Kutná Hora
Pelhřimov
Telč
Jindřichův Hradec
Děčín
Nymburk
ČESKÉ BUDĚJOVICE
Třeboň
Český Krumlov
To Dresden
ÚSTÍ NAD LABEM
Vltava
PRAGUE
Karlštejn
Labe
Kladno
Benešov
Tábor
To Linz
Teplice
Most
Kralupy
Příbram
Písek
Prachatice
Chomutov
Rakovník
Beroun
Rokycany
Strakonice
Karlovy Vary
Bečov
PLZEŇ
Klatovy
Domažlice
Otava
Loket
Mariánské Lázně
To Passau
Cheb
Tachov
To Nuremberg
To Regensburg
GERMANY

Bohemia from 1419 to 1434. After the defeat of the Hussites, the Jagiello dynasty occupied the Bohemian throne. Vladislav Jagiello merged the Bohemian and Hungarian states in 1490.

With the death of Ludovic Jagiello at the Battle of Mohács in 1526, the Austrian Habsburg dynasty ascended to the thrones of Bohemia and Hungary. Thus Bohemia, which was strongly affected by the Protestant Reformation, became subject to the Catholic Counter-Reformation backed by the Habsburgs. The Thirty Years' War, which devastated Europe from 1618 to 1648, began in Prague, and the defeat of the uprising of the Czech Estates at the Battle of White Mountain in 1620 marked the beginning of a long period of forced re-Catholicisation, Germanisation and oppression.

Yet, under the Habsburgs, Czech culture was never as totally suppressed as was Polish culture under the Russian tsars, for example, and during the early 19th century National Revival Movement the Czechs rediscovered their linguistic and cultural roots. Despite the defeat of the democratic revolution of 1848, the industrial revolution took firm hold here as a middle class emerged.

In 1914 Austro-Hungarian expansionism in the Balkans led to war, but no fighting took place in what is now the Czech Republic. Slovakia had been part of Hungary since the 11th century but on 28 October 1918 the Czechoslovak Republic, a common state of the Czechs and Slovaks, was proclaimed. The first president was Tomáš Garrigue Masaryk (who appears on the new 5000 Kč banknote), followed in 1935 by Eduard Beneš, who later headed a government-in-exile in London. Three-quarters of the Austro-Hungarian monarchy's industrial potential fell within Czechoslovakia, as did three million Germans.

After annexing Austria in the Anschluss of March 1938, Hitler turned his attention to Czechoslovakia. By the infamous Munich Pact of September 1938, Britain and France surrendered the border regions of Bohemia – the Sudetenland – to Nazi Germany, and in March 1939 the Germans occupied the rest of the country. The Czech lands were converted into the so-called 'Protectorate of Bohemia and Moravia' while Slovakia became a clero-fascist puppet state.

On 29 May 1942 the acting Nazi Reichs-Protector, Reinhard 'Hangman' Heydrich, was assassinated by two Czechs who had been parachuted in from London for the purpose. As a reprisal, the Nazis surrounded the peaceful village of Lidice, 25 km northwest of Prague, shot all the males and deported all the females to concentration camps. Czechs fought with the Allied forces on all fronts. After the German surrender in May 1945, the Soviet army occupied the country (West Bohemia was liberated by US troops). Unlike Germany and Poland which were devastated during WW II, Czechoslovakia was largely undamaged.

Post WW II

After liberation, a National Front was formed from the parties which had taken part in the antifascist struggle and in April 1945, even before the rest of the country had been freed, a meeting of the Front at Košice (Slovakia) laid down a programme for national reconstruction. A power struggle then developed between the socialists and those who favoured capitalism. After the Munich sellout, resentment against the West was rife and the strength of the Communist Party grew. In the Constituent National Assembly elections of May 1946, the communists won 38% of the votes and the Social Democrats 15.6%, forming a National Front majority. Communist Party chairman Klement Gottwald became prime minister.

In February 1948 the Social Democrats withdrew from the coalition in an attempt to overthrow Gottwald. Demonstrations and a general strike convinced President Beneš to accept the resignations of the 12 government ministers involved and appoint communist replacements. The new communist-led government then revised the constitution and voting system so that in fresh elections in May it received 86% of votes. Beneš resigned in June (and died in August) and, in July, Klement Gottwald became president.

In March 1948 the new government approved a land-reform bill limiting property ownership to 50 hectares and all businesses with over 50 employees were nationalised.

Soviet-style economic development continued through the 1950s and agriculture was reorganised on a large-scale collectivised basis. Gottwald died in 1953, after catching pneumonia at Stalin's funeral, and was succeeded by Antonín Zápotocký, and later by Antonín Novotný, who was president until March 1968.

In April 1968, the new first secretary of the Communist Party, Alexander Dubček, introduced liberalising reforms to create 'socialism with a human face'. Censorship ended, political prisoners were released and rapid decentralisation of the economy began. Dubček refused to bow to pressure from Moscow to withdraw the reforms, and this led to a political crisis.

On the night of 20 August 1968 the 'Prague Spring' came to an end as Czechoslovakia was occupied by 200,000 Soviet soldiers backed by token contingents from some of the other Warsaw Pact countries. The Czechs and Slovaks met the invaders with the same passive resistance they had previously applied to the Austro-Hungarians and Germans. The 'revisionists' were removed from office and conservative orthodoxy was re-established. One enduring reform of 1968 was the federative system, which established equal Czech and Slovak republics.

In 1969 the 'realist' Dr Gustáv Husák was elected first secretary and in 1975 president. Husák led Czechoslovakia through two decades of centralised socialist development which provided a reasonable standard of living. Yet opponents of the regime were marginalised and the population as a whole had to endure bureaucratic inconveniences, such as queuing for 30 hours to get an exit visa simply to travel abroad.

In 1977 the trial of the rock music group 'The Plastic People of the Universe' inspired the formation of the human rights group Charter 77. (The puritanical communist establishment saw in the nonconformism o the young musicians a threat to the statu quo, while those disenchanted with the regime viewed the trial as part of a pervasive assault on the human spirit.) Made up of a small assortment of Prague intellectuals Charter 77 functioned as an underground opposition throughout the 1980s.

By 1989 Gorbachev's *perestroika* wa sending shock waves through the region an the fall of the Berlin Wall on 9 November raised expectations that changes in Czecho slovakia were imminent. On Friday 17 November 1989 a student march up Prague's Národní ulice towards Wenceslas Squar (Václavské náměstí) was broken up by police.

The next Monday 250,000 people gath ered in Wenceslas Square to protest agains the violence used against the students. The protests widened with a general strike on 27 November 1989, culminating in the resigna tion of the Communist Party's Politburo. The 'Velvet Revolution' was over.

Civic Forum (Občanské Forum), ar umbrella organisation of opponents of the regime formed after the 17 November vio lence, was led by playwright-philosophe Václav Havel, Prague's best knowr 'dissident' and ex-political prisoner. Havel took over as the country's interim presiden by popular demand – in the free elections o June 1990, Civic Forum and its counterpar in Slovakia, Society against Violence, were successful. The Communist Party, which suffered a drop in membership from 1,700,000 in 1987 to 800,000 in 1990, still won 47 seats in the 300-seat Federal Parlia ment.

Recent History

With the strong central authority provided by the communists gone, old antagonisms between Slovakia and Prague re-emerged. The Federal Parliament tried to stabilise matters by approving a constitutional amendment in December 1990 which granted the Czech and Slovak republics greater autonomy in economic matters, with the Federal Government retaining control of defence and foreign affairs. Czechoslovakia officially changed its name to the Czech and Slovak Federative Republic (ČSFR), a federation of the Czech Republic (ČR) and the Slovak Republic (SR). Yet these moves failed to satisfy Slovak nationalists.

Meanwhile Civic Forum had split into two factions, the centrist Civic Movement made up of former dissidents such as foreign minister Jiří Dienstbier and president Václav Havel, and the Civic Democratic Party (ODS) led by right-wing technocrats like finance minister Václav Klaus. In Slovakia several separatist parties emerged.

To weaken the former communists and intimidate other left-wing political opponents, the ODS instigated a purge of former communist officials and alleged secret police informers in 1991, a process known as 'lustrace'. In January 1992 a law was passed banning former high-ranking communists from the public service for five years. Implementation of the law was placed in the hands of bureaucrats and the accused were to be presumed guilty until proven innocent. The 'dissemination of communist ideology' became a crime punishable by up to eight years in prison. These moves attracted the interest of international human rights groups.

The June 1992 elections sealed the fate of Czechoslovakia. Klaus' ODS took 48 seats in 150-seat Federal Parliament while 24 seats went to the Movement for a Democratic Slovakia (HZDS), a left-leaning Slovak nationalist party led by Vladimír Mečiar. The former communists came second in both republics with the Left Bloc (KSCM-LB) taking 19 seats in the Czech Republic and the Party of the Democratic Left (SDL') winning another 10 seats in Slovakia. Dienstbier's Civic Movement was wiped out.

The incompatibility of Klaus and Mečiar soon became apparent with the former pushing for shock-therapy economic reform while the latter wanted state intervention to save key industries in Slovakia. Mečiar's strident demands for Slovak sovereignty convinced Klaus and associates that Slovakia had become an obstacle on the road to fast economic reform. Calls from President Havel for a referendum on national unity were rejected by opportunistic politicians on both sides who only wanted to be masters of their own fiefs.

The defeat in July 1992 of President Havel's re-election bid by Slovak and former communist parliamentary deputies removed the last hope of compromise and Havel decided to step down early rather than preside over the country's dissolution. In August 1992 Klaus and Mečiar agreed that the Czechoslovak federation would cease to exist at the end of the year. In September 1992 Slovakia adopted a new constitution and in November 1992 the Federal Parliament voted itself out of existence. At midnight on 31 December 1992 a peaceful 'velvet divorce' freed both countries from what had become a non-functioning federation.

In January 1993 the Czech parliament elected Václav Havel president of the Czech Republic for a five-year term. Real power lies with parliament which can override the president's veto on most issues by a simple majority and prime minister Klaus has staked his political future on the success of rapid economic reform.

GEOGRAPHY

The Czech Republic is a landlocked country of 78,864 sq km squeezed between Germany, Austria, Slovakia and Poland. The Bohemian Massif is much older than the Carpathian Mountains and the broad, flat mountain ranges of the Czech Republic are quite different from the pronounced valleys, steep slopes, deep canyons and wild rivers of Slovakia. In general the mountains of Slovakia are higher and much more sharply defined than those of the Czech Republic.

Bohemia nestles between the Šumava Mountains along the Bavarian border, the Ore Mountains (Krušné Hory) along the eastern German border and the Giant Mountains (Krkonoše) along the Polish border east of Liberec. The Czech Republic's highest peak, Mt Sněžka (1602 metres), is in the Giant Mountains. The forests of northern

Bohemia have been devastated by acid rain resulting from the burning of poor quality brown coal at thermal power stations and in parts of the eastern Ore Mountains not a single tree has been left standing. Conifers in the Giant Mountains are stricken by airborne pollutants blown in from Polish Silesia.

The Czech Republic has been called 'the roof of Europe' because no rivers or streams flow into the country. The Morava River flows out of Moravia and enters the Danube just west of Bratislava. Bohemia's most famous river is the Vltava (Moldau in German), which originates near the Austrian border and flows north through Český Krumlov, České Budějovice and Prague. At Mělník it joins the Labe, which becomes the Elbe in Germany (where it passes Dresden and Hamburg on its way to the North Sea). The Baltic-bound Odra (Oder) River originates in the Czech Republic near Ostrava but soon enters Poland. Many rivers and streams are highly polluted due to inadequate sewage treatment and chemical fertiliser runoff.

The 120-sq-km Moravian Karst north of Brno features limestone caves, subterranean lakes and the Macocha Abyss, which is 138 metres deep.

ECONOMY

From 1948 to 1989 Czechoslovakia had a centrally planned economy with industry producing 70% of the national income. Cooperatives accounted for about three-quarters of agricultural land and state farms for the rest. The communists left behind a highly developed infrastructure, diversified production and low debt, but the country's industrial equipment was approaching obsolescence and there were many economic inefficiencies. Increased production was sought with scant regard for the environment and in recent years the price has been paid in terms of public health.

The industries and power plants of northern Bohemia and Moravia spew millions of tonnes of sulphur dioxide, nitrogen oxides and carbon monoxide into the atmosphere each year, creating one of Europe's most serious environmental disaster areas. The worst pollutant is sulphur dioxide created by burning lignite, a soft brown coal extracted from huge open-pit mines. In the towns the burning of coal for household heating creates choking smogs in winter and at certain times the sulphur dioxide levels in Prague are 20 times higher than official safety levels. Unfortunately this coal is one of the country's only existing energy sources and most of ex-Czechoslovakia's coal resources were in the Czech Republic. Nuclear generating stations are at Dukovany (between Znojmo and Brno) and Temelín (south-west of Tábor). The Austrian government has expressed fears that the Temelín plant is unsafe.

The largest industrial area is around Ostrava in North Moravia with coal mining, chemicals, a steel mill and car production. About 5000 rugged Tatra trucks a year are built at Kopřivnice near Ostrava. The main Škoda Works are at Plzeň but the Škoda car factory is at Mladá Boleslav, 54 km northeast of Prague, producing about 200,000 vehicles a year. Thanks to a partnership with Volkswagen, the quality of the Škoda automobile has been greatly enhanced in recent years.

In 1894 Tomáš Bat'a founded the Bata shoe factory at Zlín, east of Brno, which today produces over a quarter million pairs of shoes a week. The Bat'a family fled to Canada in 1938 and built a worldwide business and only in 1989 did they return to Czechoslovakia to begin anew. Half of the foreign investment in the Czech Republic has been by German companies. In 1992 the US firm Philip Morris bought a 65% share in the cigarette manufacturer Tabac.

Since 1991 privatisation has taken place in three stages. The first was the restitution to the original owners of some 100,000 small businesses and commercial properties confiscated by the communists. Then about 30,000 small retail outlets or service facilities throughout former Czechoslovakia were auctioned off to owner operators. This stage is now complete and the third and most difficult stage of privatising 1500 medium and large-sized companies in the Czech Republic is underway. Privatisation in the Czech Republic has been dogged by rumours of widespread corruption, such as former party officials skimming off the assets of firms and free-market advocates grabbing control of choice companies by dubious means.

Due to fears of foreign ownership, the paucity of domestic capital and a desire to involve large numbers of people in the process, the government devised a voucher privatisation scheme in which hundreds of millions of shares in 1200 state corporations arbitrarily valued at US$9 billion would be distributed to Czechs at giveaway prices. Every adult citizen was entitled to purchase 1000 voucher points for 1000 crowns (US$36). The points could be used to bid for shares in companies being privatised and many people assigned their points to investment funds which would act on their behalf.

The vouchers were issued during the winter of 1991-92 but implementation was delayed due to the separation of Slovakia. Finally, in May 1993 the government began distributing shares in 987 formerly state-owned firms purchased by 437 investment funds and millions of Czechs under voucher privatisation. Some 770 remaining companies were covered by a second round of voucher privatisation in late 1993. In April 1993 the Prague stock market opened and trading began in June 1993.

In early 1993 bankruptcy laws came into effect but these were relatively toothless and widespread bankruptcies (and mass unemployment) were postponed by allowing companies to pile up unrepayable debts. Budget deficits and inflation have been kept under control by fiscal restraint. In January 1991 most price controls were removed and prices jumped 49.2% during the first half of 1991 but in the second half of the year prices increased only 5%. Real wages declined 28% in 1991 and the gross domestic product fell 16% that year but unemployment was only 5%. The Czech Republic is the only country in Eastern Europe with free prices and near one-digit inflation. The average wage is about US$200 a month and the foreign debt stands at US$9 billion.

Tourism is booming with 83 million visitors to former Czechoslovakia in 1992. Germany was the biggest source of visitors, followed by Poland and Austria. Most are low-spending daytrippers: in 1992 the 60 million visitors to France spent US$119 billion while Czechoslovakia's 83 million spent just US$1.4 billion.

In 1988 53% of Czechoslovakia's exports went to the Warsaw Pact countries but in 1993 that area absorbed only 13% of Czech exports while 55% went west. The same trend appears in import statistics. The Czech Republic's largest trading partners by far in both the import and export categories are Germany, Slovakia, the former USSR and Austria in that order, with most of the trading in both directions in manufactured goods, machinery and transportation equipment. Iron and steel are the Czech Republic's biggest single export item (11% of the total in 1993) yet exports of Czech steel and cement to Western Europe are partly blocked by quotas and tariffs, and trade with Slovakia has dropped 50% since separation (Slovakia bought 20% of Czech exports in 1993).

POPULATION & PEOPLE

The Czech Republic is fairly homogeneous with 94% Czechs and 4% Slovaks. A small Polish minority lives in the borderlands near Ostrava. After WW II three million Sudeten Germans were evicted from Bohemia and only about 60,000 Germans remain today.

A majority of the people are Catholic and there's a saying that it took 40 years of Communism to make good Catholics of the Czechs! Religious tolerance is well established and the church makes little attempt to involve itself in politics. (What intolerance there is falls mainly upon the 115,000 Gypsies.)

There are 10,300,000 inhabitants. The major cities and their populations are Prague (1,500,000), Brno (391,000), Ostrava (331,000), Plzeň (175,000) and Olomouc (107,000).

CZECH REPUBLIC

ARTS

Czech culture has a long and distinguished history. Prague University, the oldest in Central Europe, was founded in 1348, about the time that the Gothic architect Petr Parléř was directing the construction of St Vitus Cathedral, Karlův most (Charles Bridge) and other illustrious works.

In the early 17th century, the region was torn by the Thirty Years' War, and the educational reformer Jan Ámos Comenius (1592-1670) was forced to flee Moravia. In exile Comenius (Komenský in Czech) produced a series of textbooks that were to be used throughout Europe for two centuries. His *The Visible World in Pictures*, featuring woodcuts made at Nuremberg, was the forerunner of today's illustrated schoolbook. (Comenius' portrait appears on the new 200 Kč banknote.)

The National Revival period of the early 19th century saw the re-emergence of the Czech language as a vehicle of culture. Late 19th century romanticism is exemplified in the historical novels of Alois Jirásek (1851-1930), whose works chronicled the entire history of the Czechs. His finest was *Temno* (Darkness) (1915), which dealt with the period of national decline. Karel Čapek, Karel (1890-1938) brought the Czech word *robot* (imitation human being) into international usage through a 1920 play featuring a human-like machine that almost manages to enslave humanity. Čapek's novel *The War with the Newts* (1936) was an allegory of the totalitarianism of the time.

Music

During the 17th century, when Bohemia and Moravia came under Austrian domination and German was the official language, Czech culture survived in folk music. Moravian folk orchestras are built around the *cymbalum*, a copper-stringed dulcimer of Middle Eastern origin which stands on four legs and is played by striking the strings with two mallets.

Bohemia's preeminent Baroque composer was Jan Dišmaš Zelenka (1679-1745) who spent much of his life in Vienna, Venice and especially Dresden where he was composer to the Saxon court. Though greatly esteemed by his contemporary Bach, Zelenka's works have become more widely known only during the past two decades. The symbolism and subtle expression of Zelenka's last masses are unique expressions of his introverted, restrained character.

The works of the Czech Republic's foremost composers, Bedřich Smetana (1824-84) and Antonín Dvořák (1841-1904), express the nostalgia, melancholy and joy – part of the Czech personality. In his operas Smetana used popular songs that display the innate peasant wisdom of the people to capture the nationalist sentiments of his time. Smetana's symphonic cycle *Má Vlast* (My Country) is a musical history of the country. Dvořák attracted world attention to Czech music through his use of native folk materials in works such as *Slavonic Dances* (1878).

The opera composer Leoš Janáček (1854-1928) shared Dvořák's intense interest in folk music and created an original national style by combining the scales and melodies of folk songs with the inflections of the Czech language. His best known works are *Jenufa* (1904) and *Příhody Lišky Bystroušky*, or The Cunning Little Vixen (1924). Janáček's *Christmas Mass* is often sung in Czech churches at Christmas.

Dance

Bohemia's greatest contribution to dance floors is the polka, a lively folk dance in which couples rapidly circle the floor in three-four time with three quick steps and a hop. Since its appearance in Paris in 1843, the form has been popular worldwide. Smetana used the polka in his opera *The Bartered Bride* (1866). In Moravia whirling couples dance the *vrtěná* while the *hošije* and *verbuňk* are vigorous male solo dances.

LANGUAGE

German is widely understood, especially in the western part of the republic. Under the communists everybody learned Russian at school but this now has been replaced by English.

Czech is a strange and convoluted language with a great aversion to the liberal use of vowels. Many words contain nothing that we could identify as a vowel. One famous tongue twister goes *strč prst skrz krk* which means 'stick your finger through your throat' and is pronounced just as it's spelt!

Czech and Slovak are closely related and mutually comprehensible West Slavic languages. In the 19th century Hussite Czech spelling was adopted to render other Slav languages such as Slovene and Croatian in Latin letters.

An English-Czech phrasebook will prove invaluable, but it can be hard to find one in the Czech Republic so consider taking Lonely Planet's *Eastern Europe Phrasebook* along with you. Some useful Czech words that are frequently used in this chapter are: *most* (bridge), *nábřeží* (embankment), *náměstí* (square), *nádraží* (station), *ostrov* (island), *třída* (avenue) and *ulice* (street). Men's toilets may be marked *páni* or *muži*, women's toilets *dámy* or *ženy*.

Pronunciation

Many Czech letters sound about the same as they do in English. An accent lengthens a vowel and the stress is always on the first syllable. It's a phonetic language, so if you follow the guidelines below you'll be understood. When consulting indexes on Czech maps, be aware that 'ch' comes after 'h'.

c	'ts'
č	'ch'
ch	'ch' as in 'loch'
ď	'd' as in 'duty'
ě	'ye'
j	'y' as in 'yet'
ň	'n' as the first 'n' in 'onion'
ř	'rzh'
š	'sh'
ť	't' as the first 't' in 'student'
ž	's' as in 'pleasure'

Greetings & Civilities

hello	*ahoj, dobrý den*
goodbye	*na shledanou*
good morning	*dobré jitro*
good evening	*dobrý večer*
please	*prosím*
thank you	*děkuji*
I am sorry./Forgive me.	*promiňte*
yes	*ano*
no	*ne*

Small Talk

I don't understand.	*nerozumím*
Could you write it down?	*Můžete to napsat?*
What is it called?	*Jak se to jmenuje?*
Where do you live?	*Kde bydlíte?*
What work do you do?	*Jakou práci děláte?*
I am a student.	*Jsem student.*
I am very happy.	*Jsem velmi šťastný.*

Accommodation

youth hostel	*mládežnická noclehárna*
camping ground	*kemping*
private room	*soukromý pokoj*
How much is it?	*Kolik to je?*
Is that the price per person?	*Je to cena za osobu?*
Is that the total price?	*Je to celková cena?*
Are there any extra charges?	*Jsou tu nějaké zvláštní poplatky?*
Do I pay extra for showers?	*Platí se zvlášť za sprchu?*
Where is there a cheaper hotel?	*Kde je levnější hotel?*
Should I make a reservation?	*Měl bych si zamluvit pokoj?*
single room	*jednolůžkový pokoj*
double room	*dvoulůžkový pokoj*
It is very noisy.	*Je velmi hlučný.*
Where is the toilet?	*Kde je záchod?*

Getting Around

What time does it leave?	*V kolik hodin to odjíždí?*
When is the first bus?	*Kdy jede první autobus?*

When is the last bus?	*Kdy jede poslední autobus?*
When is the next bus?	*Kdy jede příští autobus?*
That's too soon.	*To je příliš brzy.*
When is the next one after that?	*Kdy jede příští potomhle?*
How long does the trip take?	*Jak dlouho trvá cesta?*
arrival	*příjezdy*
departure	*odjezdy*
timetable	*jízdní řád*
Where is the bus stop?	*Kde je autobusová zastávka ?*
Where is the train station?	*Kde je nádraží?*
Where is the left-luggage room?	*Kde je úschovna zavazadel?*

Around Town

Just a minute.	*okamžik*
Where is...?	*Kde je...?*
the bank	*banka*
the post office	*pošta*
the tourist information office	*cestovní kancelář*
the museum	*muzeum*
Where are you going?	*Kam jdete?*
I am going to...	*Já jdu do...*
Where is it?	*Kde je to?*
I can't find it.	*Nemohu to najít.*
Is it far?	*Je to daleko?*
Please show me on the map.	*Prosím, ukažte mi to na mapě.*
left	*vlevo*
right	*vpravo*
straight ahead	*rovně*
I want ...	*Já chci ...*
Do I need permission?	*Potřebuji povolení?*

Entertainment

Where can I buy a ticket?	*Kde si mohu koupit lístek?*
I want to refund this ticket.	*Chci vrátit tento lístek.*
Is this a good seat?	*Je to dobré místo?*
at the front	*vpředu*

ticket	*lístek, vstupenka*

Food

I do not eat meat.	*Nejím maso.*
self-service cafeteria	*samoobslužná restaurace*
grocery store	*obchod potravin*
fish	*ryba*
pork	*vepřové*
soup	*polévka*
salad	*salát*
fresh vegetables	*čerstvá zelenina*
milk	*mléko*
bread	*chléb*
sugar	*cukr*
ice cream	*zmrzlina*
coffee	*káva*
tea	*čaj*
mineral water	*minerální voda*
beer	*pivo*
wine	*víno*
hot/cold	*horké/studené*

Shopping

Where can I buy one?	*Kde si mohu jeden koupit?*
How much does it cost?	*Kolik to stojí?*
That's (much) too expensive.	*To je příliž drahé.*
Is there a cheaper one?	*Je něco levnější?*

Time & Dates

today	*dnes*
tonight	*dnes večer*
tomorrow	*zítra*
the day after tomorrow	*pozítří*
What time does it open?	*Kdy se otevírá?*
What time does it close?	*Kdy se zavírá?*
open	*otevřeno*
closed	*zavřeno*
in the morning	*ráno*
in the evening	*večer*
every day	*každý den*
At what time?	*V kolik hodin?*
when?	*kdy?*

CZECH REPUBLIC

Monday	*pondělí*	
Tuesday	*úterý*	
Wednesday	*středa*	
Thursday	*čtvrtek*	
Friday	*pátek*	
Saturday	*sobota*	
Sunday	*neděle*	

January	*leden*	
February	*únor*	
March	*březen*	
April	*duben*	
May	*květen*	
June	*červen*	
July	*červenec*	
August	*srpen*	
September	*září*	
October	*říjen*	
November	*listopad*	
December	*prosinec*	

Numbers

1	*jeden*
2	*dva*
3	*tři*
4	*čtyři*
5	*pět*
6	*šest*
7	*sedm*
8	*osm*
9	*devět*
10	*deset*
11	*jedenáct*
12	*dvanáct*
13	*třináct*
14	*čtrnáct*
15	*patnáct*
16	*šestnáct*
17	*sedmnáct*
18	*osmnáct*
19	*devatenáct*
20	*dvacet*
21	*dvacet jedna*
22	*dvacet dva*
23	*dvacet tři*
30	*třicet*
40	*čtyřicet*
50	*padesát*
60	*šedesát*
70	*sedmdesát*

80	*osmdesát*
90	*devadesát*
100	*sto*
1000	*tisíc*
10,000	*deset tisíc*
1,000,000	*milión*

Facts for the Visitor

VISAS & EMBASSIES

Everyone requires a passport which won't expire within the following eight months. Americans require no visa for a stay of 30 days and British passport holders can stay six months without a visa. Citizens of Austria, Belgium, Denmark, Finland, France, Germany, Greece, Holland, Iceland, Ireland, Italy, Liechtenstein, Luxembourg, Monaco, Norway, Portugal, Spain, Sweden and Switzerland are allowed three months without a visa. Unfortunately citizens of Australia, Canada, Japan, New Zealand and most other non-European countries still do need a visa which should be obtained in advance at a consulate.

Visas are only available at three highway border crossings, one from Germany (Waidhaus/Rozvadov) and two from Austria (Wullowitz/Dolní Dvořiště and Klein Haugsdorf/Hatě), plus Prague Ruzyně Airport. Elsewhere you'll be refused entry if you need a visa and arrive without one. Visas are never issued on trains.

Czech tourist and transit visas are readily available at consulates throughout Europe at a cost of US$25 per entry (Canadians US$50). You will need two photos per entry (maximum two entries per visa). Don't get a transit visa which costs the same and cannot be changed to a tourist visa upon arrival. You'll be asked how many days you wish to stay in the Czech Republic, up to a maximum of 30 days, and this number will be written on your visa. You can use your visa at any time within six months of the date of issue.

There's a space for hotel stamps on the back of the visa form and although the old requirement of police registration is seldom enforced these days a difficult official can bring it up if he or she feels in the mood. Thus it's best to ask official places to stay such as hotels and camping grounds or travel agencies to stamp your visa form as you're checking in. That way you're covered for all eventualities.

Slovakian visas are not accepted at Czech border crossings and vice versa – if you want to visit both countries you must purchase two separate visas.

You can extend your stay at police stations inside the Czech Republic for about US$5. The offices handling these matters open for short hours and have long queues, so don't leave it till the last day. An easier way to solve this problem (provided you don't need a visa) is simply to leave the Czech Republic and return, in which case you'll have to make a point of asking the border guards to stamp your passport as you leave (they often don't bother).

Czech Embassies

In addition to the Czech Republic embassies in Belgrade, Bucharest, Budapest, Bratislava, Ljubljana, Warsaw and Zagreb listed elsewhere in this book, Czech embassies around the world include the following:

Australia
    38 Culgoa Circuit, O'Malley, Canberra, ACT 2606 (☎ 062-90 1386)
Canada
    50 Rideau Terrace, Ottawa, ON K1M 2A1 (☎ 613-749 1566)
Netherlands
    Paleisstr. 4, 2514 JA, The Hague (☎ 070-364 7638)
New Zealand
    12 Anne St, Wadestown, Wellington (☎ 472 3142)
UK
    26 Kensington Palace Gardens, London, W8 4QY (☎ 0171-727 4918)
USA
    3900 Spring of Freedom St NW, Washington, DC 20008 (☎ 202-363 6315)

MONEY

On 8 February 1993 the Czech and Slovakian currencies separated and within weeks the Slovakian crown was worth 10% less than the Czech crown. In September 1993 all banknotes issued by the former Czechoslovakian authorities were withdrawn from circulation in the Czech Republic and are now worthless. Don't accept any notes reading 'Korun Československých'. The old Czechoslovakian coins became invalid in November 1993.

The new banknotes come in denominations of 50, 100, 200, 500, 1000 and 5000 Czech crowns or 'Korun Českých' (Kč); coins are of 10, 20 and 50 haléřů (cents) and one, two, five, 10, 20 and 50 Kč. Always have a few small coins in your pocket for use in public toilets and for public transport machines.

Compulsory exchange has been abolished in the Czech Republic and everyone now receives the same standard bank rate. Since early 1991 the exchange rate has been fairly steady at about US$1 = 29 Kč with only about 11% annual inflation.

Changing money in the Czech Republic can be a hassle as many private exchange offices, especially in Prague, deduct exorbitant commissions (výlohy) of up to 10%. Some of these advertise higher rates on large boards but don't mention their sky-high commission – if in doubt, ask first.

Hotels charge 5% commission, Čedok travel agencies 3% and the banks take only 2% on better rates. The Komerční Banka is usually efficient about changing travellers' cheques for a standard US$2 commission and we list their branches throughout this chapter but even there you should always ask about the commission as it seems to vary from branch to branch. The American Express and Thomas Cook offices in Prague change their own travellers' cheques without commission but their rates are slightly lower than the banks.

The main drawbacks of the banks are their short opening hours and slowness. You'll sometimes have to spend up to an hour in line. Because of this, it's smart to change enough money to see you through the rest of your stay when you find somewhere offering good rates and charging a low commission.

Avoid getting caught without sufficient crowns on a weekend or public holiday when the banks are closed.

Some visitors dabble in the black market but they usually end up a little poorer and a little wiser because most of the people offering to change money on the street are professional thieves with years of experience in cheating tourists. They'll switch the bundle of banknotes after they've been counted for paper or small bills, or use some other trick, such as supplying Polish złoty notes instead of crown bills which are worth 700 times more! It's foolish to risk large amounts of cash with potential criminals, though it's less risky if you are propositioned by someone who can't run away, such as a waiter, taxi driver or hotel receptionist. Czechs are only allowed to legally purchase US$275 in hard currency a year, hence the black market.

However you change your money, once you have Czech currency you'll have to spend it, as it's difficult to change it back into hard currency despite misleading government claims that the crown is now a convertible currency. Most banks will only change crowns back into hard currency if you have a receipt to prove you originally changed with them. If you're going on to Poland and have crowns left over you can easily unload them at any Polish exchange office but you'll lose about 10%. Changing Czech currency in Germany and Hungary is difficult. The import or export of over 100 Kč is prohibited, so keep any crowns you may be carrying out of sight at the border.

Costs

Food, transportation and admission fees are fairly cheap, and it's mostly accommodation that makes this one of the most expensive countries in Eastern Europe. If you really want to travel on a low budget you'll have to spend a little more time looking for a cheap place to stay and/or be prepared to rough it. Get out of the capital and your costs will drop dramatically.

A disappointing side of the Czech concept of a 'free market economy' is the two-price system in which foreigners pay double the local price for many things. This may be official as it is at hotels, airline offices and some museums, or unofficial, such as when a waiter or taxi driver tries to pad your bill. A de facto tourist price for theatre tickets exists in Prague as most tickets are cornered by scalpers and travel agencies who resell them to foreigners at several times the original price. Sometimes simply questioning the price difference results in an 'error correction', but if it doesn't, you either pay the higher price or go elsewhere. Whenever you do get something for the local price (as is usually the case when buying beer or domestic train tickets) you'll find it very inexpensive.

There *are* public toilets throughout the Czech Republic and having to pay US$0.10 once or twice a day to use them won't break the budget.

In January 1993 all prices jumped 23% when a value added tax (VAT) was imposed (it's only 5% on food). This tax is included in the sticker price and not added at the cash register, so you won't feel it directly.

CLIMATE & WHEN TO GO

The climate is temperate with warm summers and cool, humid winters, and clearly defined spring and autumn seasons. Prague has average daily temperatures above 14°C from May to September, above 8°C in April and October, and below freezing in December and January. In winter dense fogs (or smogs) can set in anywhere.

SUGGESTED ITINERARIES

Depending on the length of your stay, you might want to see and do the following things in the Czech Republic:

Two days
    Visit České Budějovice and Český Krumlov.
One week
    Visit České Budějovice, Český Krumlov, Prague and Kutná Hora.
Two weeks
    Visit Prague, Kutná Hora, České Budějovice, Český Krumlov, Telč and Brno.

CZECH REPUBLIC

One month
  Visit all places mentioned in this chapter.

TOURIST OFFICES

There's a municipal information office in Prague called the Prague Information Service and the staff are very knowledgeable about sightseeing, food and entertainment. Receptionists in the expensive hotels are often helpful with information when they're not busy.

The former government tourism monopoly Čedok has numerous branch offices around the country which you can consult if you wish to change money, or want accommodation, travel or sightseeing arrangements made. It is, however, oriented towards the top end of the market. Čedok staff are sometimes willing to answer general questions although this is now a commercial travel agency and they're not paid to provide free information. The American Express office in Prague is in a similar position.

The Czech Republic's youth travel bureau is CKM Student Travel (Cestovní Kancelář Mládeže). Their offices in most cities are a better source of information on money-saving arrangements than Čedok and they also sell student cards.

Čedok Offices Abroad

Čedok offices in countries outside the Czech Republic include:

Netherlands
  Leidsestraat 4, 1017 PA Amsterdam
  (☎ 020-622 0101)
UK
  17-18 Old Bond St, London W1X 3DA
  (☎ 0171-629 6058)
USA
  10 East 40th St, Suite 1902, New York,
  NY 10016 (☎ 212-689 9720)

BUSINESS HOURS & HOLIDAYS

On weekdays shops open at around 8.30 am and close at 6 pm although some stay open until 7 pm on Thursday. Bakeries and grocery stores open earlier. Many small shops, particularly in country areas, close for a long lunch, and reopen by 3 pm at the latest.

Other shops are closed on Monday mornings. Almost everything closes at around noon on Saturday and is closed all day Sunday but hotel restaurants are open every day. Grocery stores also close at noon on Saturday and often you won't be let in the door after 11.30 am. Large supermarkets in department stores stay open until 2 pm on Saturday but the queues for shopping trolleys double in length. Some private grocery stores open on weekends but may sell out of milk and bread as these are only delivered on weekdays. Towns in the Czech Republic really die on the weekends as the locals retreat to their cottages in the countryside.

Most museums are closed on Monday and the day following a public holiday. Many gardens, castles and historic sites in the Czech Republic are closed from November to March and open on weekends only in April and October. In spring and autumn you may have to wait around for a group to form before being allowed in, so again, it's better to go on weekends. In winter, before making a long trip out to some attraction in the countryside, be sure to check that it's open. Staff at some isolated sights take an hour off for lunch, and ticket offices often close at 4 pm, even if the building itself is open until later. The main town museums stay open all year. Students usually get 50% off the entry price at museums, galleries, theatres, cinemas, fairs etc. Many churches remain closed except for services.

Public holidays include New Year's Day (1 January), Easter Monday (March/April), Labour Day (1 May), Liberation Day (8 May), Cyril and Methodius Day (5 July), Jan Hus Day (6 July), Republic Day (28 October) and Christmas (from 24 to 26 December). Republic Day commemorates 28 October 1918, when the independent Czechoslovak Republic was proclaimed. On New Year's Eve most restaurants and bars will either be rented out for private parties or closed (a situation repeated throughout much of Eastern Europe).

CULTURAL EVENTS

Since 1946 the Prague Spring International

Music Festival has taken place during the second half of May (most performances are sold out well ahead). In June there's a festival of brass band music at Kolín. In August the Frédéric Chopin Music Festival occurs in Mariánské Lázně. Karlovy Vary comes back with the Dvořák Autumn Music Festival in September. Prague's International Jazz Festival is held in October. Brno has a music festival in October.

Moravian folk-art traditions culminate in late June at the Strážnice Folk Festival between Brno and Bratislava. In mid-August the Chod Festival at Domažlice, 57 km south of Plzeň, affords a chance to witness the folk songs and dances of South and West Bohemia.

The Brno International Trade Fair of consumer goods takes place every spring. In August or September an agricultural exhibition is held in České Budějovice.

POST & TELECOMMUNICATIONS

Postage costs are much lower in the Czech Republic than in Hungary, so catch up on your postcard writing. Poland is also inexpensive but letters posted in Poland tend to move much more slowly than those mailed from the Czech Republic (two weeks to the USA). Always use airmail. Most post offices are open weekdays from 8 am to 7 pm.

To send parcels abroad, you will need to go to a post office with a customs section. Although the main post offices often don't have a customs section, staff there will be able to tell you which post office you should go to. These post offices are usually open from 8 am to 3 pm. Airmail is a little more than double surface mail for parcels. When sending books you'll have to be persistent to get the book rate (which does, in fact, exist).

Don't bother sending a parcel containing textiles. Although the post office may accept it (and your money) it will never leave the Czech Republic due to an archaic law which prohibits the export of textiles (even your own clothes) by post.

Receiving Mail

General delivery mail should be addressed c/o Poste Restante, Pošta 1, Jindřišská 14, 11000 Praha 1, Czech Republic.

American Express cardholders can receive mail addressed c/o American Express, Václavské náměstí 50, 11000 Praha 1, Czech Republic. American Express holds letters for 30 days, but parcels and registered mail will be returned to sender. This is a reliable place to receive mail.

Telephones

You can make international telephone calls at main post offices and, within Europe, they usually go through right away. Operator-assisted international telephone calls cost US$3 a minute to New Zealand, US$2 a minute to Australia, Canada, the USA and Japan, or US$1 a minute to most of Europe. All calls have a three-minute minimum. Check the rates with the clerk before placing your call and ask for a receipt.

Czech Telecom has installed lots of nice new blue card phones around the country and telephone cards (100-unit card US$4) are easily obtainable at newsstands and post offices. These phones still aren't connected to sufficient international lines so you may have to try a few times to get your call outside the country. Public telephones in post offices are more reliable than those on the street. The international access code is 00.

To call the Czech Republic from abroad, dial your international access code, 42 (the country code for the Czech Republic), the area code and the number. Important area codes include 2 (Prague), 5 (Brno), 17 (Karlovy Vary), 19 (Plzeň), 38 (České Budějovice), 66 (Telč), 165 (Mariánské Lázně), 166 (Cheb), 206 (Mělník), 321 (Kolín), 327 (Kutná Hora), 337 (Český Krumlov), 361 (Tábor), and 659 (Český Těšín). When dialling from within the Czech Republic you must add a 0 before the area code.

TIME

The time in the Czech Republic is GMT/UTC plus one hour. At the end of March the Czech Republic goes on summer time and clocks are set forward an hour. At the end of September they're turned back an hour.

WEIGHTS & MEASURES

The electric current is 220 V, 50 Hz AC. The metric system is used in the Czech Republic.

BOOKS

In *The Good Soldier Švejk*, satirist Jaroslav Hašek (1883-1923) pokes fun at the pettiness of the government and military service alike. In this Czech classic, a Prague dog-catcher is drafted into the Austrian army before WW I, and by carrying out stupid orders to the letter he succeeds in completely disrupting military life.

Nightfrost in Prague: the End of Humane Socialism by Zdeněk Mlynář (Karz Publishers, New York, 1980) is an inside political view of the events of 1968 by a former secretary of the Central Committee of the Communist Party of Czechoslovakia. Also interesting is *Hope Dies Last, The Autobiography of Alexander Dubček* (Kodansha America Inc, 114 5th Ave, New York, NY 10011).

Before 1989 the clandestine works of dissident authors were circulated in typewritten 'samizdat' editions of a few dozen carbon copies and the best were smuggled out and published abroad. For an anthology of these underground writings see *Goodbye samizdat!* edited by M Goetz-Stankiewicz (Northwestern University Press, Illinois, USA, 1993).

Ludvík Vaculík gives an insight into the mood of dissident Prague writers during the 1980s in his collection of chronicles, *A Cup of Coffee with My Interrogator* (Readers International, London, 1987), which has an introduction by Václav Havel.

The collection of papers entitled *Václav Havel or Living in Truth* (Meulenhoff, Amsterdam, 1986), edited by Jan Vladislav, includes Havel's famous 1978 essay 'The power of the powerless'. Havel describes the conformism of those who simply accepted the 'post-totalitarian system' by 'living within the lie'. In contrast, 'dissidents' who dared say, 'The emperor is naked!' endured

many difficulties but at least earned respect by 'living within the truth'. Michael Simmons' *The Reluctant President: A Political Life of Václav Havel* portrays this captivating figure well.

After the 1968 Soviet invasion, Czech novelist Milan Kundera saw his early works, *The Joke* and *Laughable Loves*, removed from library shelves; in 1975, he settled in France. In 1979, in response to publication of *The Book of Laughter and Forgetting*, which combines eroticism with political satire, the communist government revoked Kundera's Czech citizenship. His 1984 book, *The Unbearable Lightness of Being*, is about a brain surgeon who is reluctantly cast as a dissident after the 1968 Soviet invasion.

The Czech Republic's foremost resident writer is Ivan Klíma whose works were banned in Czechoslovakia from 1970 to 1989, though he continued to live and write there. Klíma novels such as *Love and Garbage* (1986) and *Waiting for Darkness, Waiting for Light* (1993) tackle the human dimension behind the contradictions of contemporary Czech life. *My Golden Trades* is a collection of stories about six individuals written before 1989 and recently translated into English.

Guidebooks

One of the most substantial guides is *Nagel's Encyclopedia-Guide Czechoslovakia* (Nagel Publishers, Geneva, 1985). Its 480 pages of detailed description and good maps cover the country exhaustively, though the practical information is simply tacked on at the end of the book in the form of lists.

Lonely Planet's *Czech & Slovak Republics – a travel survival kit* by John King and Richard Nebeský is a lot better when it comes to the nuts and bolts of travelling and there's also their *Prague city guide*. *Czechoslovakia: The Rough Guide* fits the area into a different framework.

MEDIA
Newspapers

The first issue of *Prognosis*, a fortnightly English-language newspaper, appeared in

March 1991. This high-quality publication carries a wide range of interesting local news and the eight-page 'Visitors' Guide' in every issue is an up-to-date guide to Prague. The restaurant and entertainment listings alone are worth the US$1 newsstand price. To subscribe, send a Visa card authorisation for US$42 (for 12 issues) to *Prognosis*, Africká 17, 160 00 Prague 6.

Also excellent is *The Prague Post*, a weekly business newspaper founded by a group of young US expatriates in October 1991. The *Post's* thick 'Culture' section contains all the practical visitor information you need. A 26-issue subscription costs US$75 inside Europe or US$90 outside Europe from Subscriptions Department, *The Prague Post*, Na poříčí 12, 115 30 Prague 1 (Visa cards accepted).

The *Prague News*, Truhlářská 16, 110 00 Prague 1, is an advertising-oriented tourist paper.

HEALTH

All health care is free to citizens of the Czech Republic. First aid is provided free to visitors in case of an accident. Otherwise, foreigners must pay a fee. British nationals receive free medical attention.

Thermal Baths

There are hundreds of curative mineral springs and dozens of health spas in the Czech Republic which use mineral waters, mud or peat. Most famous are the spas of West Bohemia (Františkovy Lázně, Karlovy Vary and Mariánské Lázně).

Unlike Hungary, where hot-spring waters are open to everyone, in the Czech Republic the spas are reserved for the medical treatment of patients. Yet all the spas have colonnades where you may join in the drinking cure', a social ritual that involves imbibing liberal quantities of warm spring water and then parading up and down to stimulate circulation. Admission is free but you need to bring your own cup.

Though the resorts are pleasant to visit, to receive medical treatment at a spa you must book in advance through Balnea (☎ 02-232

3767), Pařížská 11, 110 01 Prague 1. The recommended stay is 21 days though you can book for as few as three days. Daily prices begin at US$45/70 for a single/double in the cheapest category in the winter season, and rise to US$95/160 in the top category during the main summer season. Accompanying persons not taking a spa treatment get about a third off. From October to April prices are reduced. The price includes medical examination and care, spa curative treatment, room and board, and the spa tax. The clientele tends to be elderly. Čedok offices abroad will have full information about spa treatments.

ANNOYANCES

Confusingly, buildings on some streets have two sets of street numbers. In this case, the red number is the actual number while the blue number is the consecutive number though it's sometimes hard to tell which of the two is the one in your address. To make matters worse, the streets themselves are often poorly labelled and the recent name changes haven't helped at all. In case of problems, write the address down on a piece of paper and show it to a local.

Reader Anne Small of Tauranga, New Zealand, sent this:

At Prague Railway Station the need for a lavatory became urgent. A burly woman was sitting with the usual saucer between her huge elbows resting on the table. I was very tired having travelled all night from Poland and was confronted with my tenth new currency since leaving home and no had idea of the value of the money I placed in the saucer. I made only a step or two towards my place of relief when I was grabbed in a deathlock from behind, knocking my bags from my grip, and was frog-marched to the door, my head being belaboured at each step and my bag thrown after me! Two days later I was compelled to use that same place again and, taking no chances, I placed what seemed a huge sum in the saucer. I was able to go unmolested until later, when I tried to clean my teeth at the wash basin and was subjected to the same treatment again. I went to the accommodation office to complain and was told that the police were around the corner, which they weren't. I went down to the ground floor, bought a bottle of water and completed the teeth cleaning in front of the station, affording free amusement to the locals. A frightening experience for a seventy-two year old!

WORK

The Klub mladých cestovatelů or KMC
(☎ 02-235 6388), Karolíny Světlé 30,
Prague (metro: Národní třída), organises
international work camps from June to
August renovating historic buildings, doing
trail maintenance in national parks, teaching
English to children etc. You must sign up for
two or three weeks and there's no pay, but
room and board are provided. There's a
US$10 registration fee. Actually, you're sup-
posed to reserve months ahead through a
volunteer organisation in your home
country, but KMC often accepts individuals
who just show up at their Prague office when
they have space available on one of their
projects. It's possible the KMC office will
have moved by the time you get to Prague
but you should be able to track them down
with the help of the Prague Information
Service. The KMC camps are a great way to
do something useful on your trip while
making a lot of friends.

It's fairly easy to get jobs teaching English
but you'll be paid in crowns and they aren't
easily convertible or worth much. It's easier
to find a job in provincial centres than it is in
Prague and your living costs will be lower.
Be aware that companies employing foreigners without working and residence permits
face fines of US$8000 for the first offence
and US$32,000 for subsequent offences.
Obtaining these permits can take up to three
months. The laissez faire official attitudes
which immediately followed the Velvet Revolution are gradually disappearing.

ACTIVITIES
Hiking

Excellent day hikes are possible in the forests
around the West Bohemian spas, Karlovy
Vary and Mariánské Lázně. The Moravian
Karst area, north of Brno, is another easily
accessible hiking area.

Skiing

The Czech Republic's main ski resorts are
Špindlerův Mlýn and Pec pod Sněžkou in
Krkonoše National Park, north-west of
Svoboda nad Úpou along the Polish border.

The main season here is from January to
March.

Cycling

For information on bicycle rentals and suggested trips, see Activities in the Prague and
Český Krumlov sections of this chapter.

Canoeing & Yachting

For canoeing and yachting possibilities turn
to the Český Krumlov section of this chapter.

Golf

Mariánské Lázně has an 18-hole golf course.

Courses

The Institute of Linguistics & Professional
Training of Charles University (fax 42-2-
2422 9497), Jindřišká 29, 11000 Praha 1,
runs a three-week summer course for foreigners from mid-July to early August.
Participants have the choice of studying in
Prague (US$756 including accommodation)
or at Poděbrady, 50 km east (US$864 includ-
ing accommodation and all meals). Single
rooms are US$60 extra per month and group
excursions are additional.

Students at Poděbrady are able to use the
facilities of the local spa. The application
deadline is 15 June. No prior knowledge of
the Czech language is required and everyone
is welcome.

Charles University also offers regular 10-
month winter courses (from September to
June) for those interested in further study at
Czech universities or specialisation in Slavic
studies at a foreign university. (Students
wishing to have credits transferred to their
home university should obtain written
approval from the head of their department
before enrolling.)

The cost of tuition and materials is
US$1910 with 25 hours a week instruction,
US$2630 with 35 hours weekly. One can
also opt for one or two four-month semesters
at US$980 each (25 hours a week). Special
six-week language courses (US$380 tuition)
are available from time to time and individual tutors can be hired at US$8 an hour.
Participants are eligible for inexpensive

accommodation in student dormitories and in addition to Prague, one can study at Dobruška, Mariánské Lázně, Poděbrady, or Teplice.

HIGHLIGHTS
Historic Towns
The Czech Republic is a country of historic towns, and the five most authentic and picturesque are České Budějovice, Český Krumlov, Kutná Hora, Tábor and Telč (see the relevant sections later in this chapter).

Museums & Galleries
The Prague Jewish Museum in the former Prague ghetto is easily the largest and most authentic of its kind in Eastern Europe. Prague's finest art galleries are in the castle area, especially the collections of the National Gallery in the Šternberský Palace and the Basilica of St George. The 'panorama' in Brno's Technological Museum lets you see the world as it was in 1890. The beer museum in Plzeň sums up one of this country's noblest contributions to humanity.

Castles
Holy Roman emperor Charles IV's Karlštejn Castle looks like something out of Disneyland but it's genuine 14th century. Český Krumlov Castle has the same effect. Prague Castle is literally packed with art treasures. Brno's 17th century Špilberk Castle remains a symbol of Habsburg repression.

ACCOMMODATION
Camping
There are several hundred camping grounds in the Czech Republic, which are usually open from May to September. The camping grounds are primarily intended for motorists so you're often surrounded by noisy caravans and car campers. Those full of German cars with 'D' stickers on the back are invariably more expensive than those with mostly Czech cars, but all are reasonable. They're often accessible on public transport, but there's usually no hot water.

Most of these places have a small snack bar where beer is sold and many have small cabins for rent which are cheaper than a hotel room. Pitching your own tent in these camping grounds is definitely the least expensive form of accommodation. Freelance camping is prohibited.

Hostels
The Hostelling International handbook shows an impressive network of youth hostels in the Czech Republic, but when you actually try to use them, you often find that they're either full, closed or nonexistent. Some of the places listed in the handbook are rather luxurious 'Juniorhotels' with single and double rooms, especially those in Prague (always full), Karlovy Vary (presently closed) and Mariánské Lázně (a good bet).

In July and August many student dormitories become temporary youth hostels and in recent years a number of such dormitories in Prague have been converted into year-round Western-style hostels.

Hostelling is controlled by the Klub madých cestovatelů (KMC) or Club of Young Travellers (☎ 02-235 6388), Karolíny Světlé 30, Prague (metro: Národní třída), and CKM Student Travel, which has offices in all cities. To get into a hostel, it's sometimes best to go first to the CKM office and ask the staff there to make a reservation for you.

These offices keep very short business hours, sometimes only opening on weekday afternoons. If you go directly to the hostel itself, your chances vary. Occasionally CKM offices will agree to make advance bookings for you over the phone at hostels in other cities. A YHA/HI membership card is not usually required to stay at CKM youth hostels, though it will get you a reduced rate. An ISIC student card may also get you a discount, but only if you book direct (not through a CKM office).

There's another category of hostel not connected with the CKM. Tourist hostels (Turistické ubytovny) are intended for visitors from other Eastern European countries and provide very basic dormitory accommodation without the standards and controls associated with HI hostels (mixed dormitories, smoking in the room, no curfew etc). They're very cheap, but you'll have to be persuasive and persistent to stay in them. Ask about tourist hostels at Čedok offices and watch for the letters 'TU' on accommodation lists published in languages other than English.

Similarly the letters 'UH' refer to an *Ubytovací hostinec*, which is a pub or inn offering basic rooms without private facilities.

Private Rooms & Pensions

Private rooms are usually available, so ask for them at the Čedok offices in Brno, Karlovy Vary, Mariánské Lázně and Plzeň or at Pragotur in Prague. Some have a three-night minimum-stay requirement.

In Prague many private travel agencies now offer private rooms and, though their charges are higher than those of Čedok and Pragotur, the service is also better. This is the easiest way to find accommodation in Prague if you don't mind paying at least US$18/25 for a single/double a night.

Many small pensions (often just glorified private rooms) have appeared in South Bohemia in recent years offering more personalised service than the hotels at lower rates. Look for these and watch out for *privát zimmer frei* signs, announcing the availability of private rooms.

Hotels

The Czech Republic has a good network of hotels covering the entire country. In Prague the hotels are expensive, whereas hotels in smaller towns are usually cheaper and more likely to have rooms. Between 1990 and 1993 the value of the crown against the dollar remained fairly steady while hotel prices doubled and tripled. Czechs pay less than half as much as foreigners at hotels.

There are five categories of hotels: A* deluxe (five stars), A* (four stars), B* (three stars), B (two stars) and C (one star). The B-category hotels usually offer reasonable comfort for about US$15/25 a single/double with shared bath or US$25/35 with private

bath (50% higher in Prague). In small towns and villages, there are sometimes also C-category hotels, but renovations have upgraded most of them to B-category in the cities. In places well off the beaten track, the police may be able to help you find a place where you can stay when all else fails.

Many hotels will not rent rooms till 2 pm, so leave your luggage at the station. If you have a room with shared bath, you may have to pay US$2 extra to use the communal shower and search for the cleaning staff to get the key. Hotel receptionists usually sell soft drinks and beer for just slightly more than shop prices but these drinks are often kept under the counter, so ask.

FOOD

The cheapest places to eat at are the self-service restaurants *(samoobsluha)*. Sometimes these places have really tasty dishes like barbecued chicken or hot German sausage – just right for a quick cooked lunch between sights. Train stations often have good cheap restaurants or buffets but the cheapest meals are to be had in busy beer halls. If the place is crowded with locals, is noisy and looks chaotic, chances are it will have great lunch specials at low prices.

You'll rarely have trouble finding a place to eat, but when you do, try the dining room of any large hotel. Hotel restaurants in the Czech Republic are reasonable in hard-currency terms, though the atmosphere is often stuffy and formal. Check in your coat before entering or the waiter will send you back to do so. Pretentious service aside, these places will usually have menus in English or German with fish dishes available, and even vegetarians should be able to find something suitable. Hotel restaurants stay open later and don't close on weekends, and there's less likelihood of 'mistakes' on your bill than there might be at an independent tourist restaurant.

Lunches are generally bigger and cheaper than dinners in the less expensive places. Dinner is eaten early and latecomers may have little to choose from. Don't expect to be served at any restaurant if you arrive within

CZECH REPUBLIC

half an hour of closing time. It used to be rare for a restaurant to have everything listed on its menu but this has become less common with privatisation. Some waiters will tell tourists that all the cheaper dishes are finished to get them to order something more expensive.

Always check the posted menu before entering a restaurant to get an idea of the price range. If no menu is displayed inside or out, insist on seeing one before ordering. It doesn't matter if it's only in Czech (as is often the case). The main categories are *předkrmy* (hors d'oeuvres), *polévky* (soups), *studené jídlo* (cold dishes), *teplé jídlo* (warm dishes), *masitá jídla* (meat dishes), *ryby* (fish), *zelenina* (vegetables), *saláty* (salads), *ovoce* (fruit), *zákusky* (desserts) and *nápoje* (drinks). Anything that comes with *knedlíky* (dumplings) will be a hearty local meal.

The waiter may be able to translate the names of a few dishes, otherwise just take pot luck. If you simply let the waiter tell you what's available without seeing a price list, you'll be overcharged every time, so if the person serving refuses to show you a written menu, you should just get up and walk out. Some Prague restaurants, especially, are notorious for overcharging foreigners (see Places to Eat in the Prague section). Most beer halls have a system of marking everything you eat or drink on a small piece of paper which is left on your table and in such places you'll seldom have any problems.

Tipping is optional but if you were fairly served you should certainly round up the bill to the next 5 Kč (or to the next 10 Kč if the bill is over 100 Kč) as you're paying. Waiters at Prague restaurants accustomed to serving Americans will expect to be tipped more than this. Never leave coins worth less than 1 Kč as your only tip or you risk having them thrown back at you.

In Bohemia make frequent visits to the great little pastry shops (*kavárna* or *cukrárna*), which offer cakes, puddings and coffee as good as anything you'll find in neighbouring Austria at a fraction of the price.

Local Specialities

Czech cuisine is strong on sauces and gravies and weak on fresh vegetables. *Pražská šunka* (smoked Prague ham) is often taken as an hors d'oeuvre with Znojmo gherkins, followed by a thick soup, such as *bramborová polévka* (potato soup) and *zeleninová polévka* (vegetable soup). *Dršťková polévka* (tripe soup) is a treat not to be missed. The Czechs love meat dishes with *knedlíky* (flat circular dumplings) and/or sauerkraut. Carp *(kapr)* from the Bohemian fish ponds can be crumbed and fried or baked. Vegetarian dishes include *smažený sýr* (fried cheese) and *knedlíky s vejci* (scrambled eggs with dumplings). Czech fruit dumplings *(ovocné knedlíky)* come with melted butter or curd cheese and a whole fruit inside.

DRINKS

The Czech Republic is a beer drinker's paradise: where else could you get three or four big glasses of top quality Pilsner for under a dollar? You'll pay less than half the price you would in Poland and Czech beer halls *(pivnice)* put Munich to shame. The Czechs serve their draught beer with a high head of foam which makes for a rather flat brew, so you might want to order bottled beer and pour it yourself. However, the stuff on tap is dirt cheap and you're able to consume large quantities without upsetting your stomach because the gas has been removed.

One of the first words of Czech you'll learn is *pivo* (beer); alcohol-free beer is called *pito*. Bohemian beer is about the best in the world and the most famous brands are Budvar (the original Budweiser) and Plzeňský Prazdroj (the original Pilsner). South Moravia produces excellent wine, either red *(červené víno)* or white *(bílé víno)*. You can be sure of a good feed at a *vinárna* (wine restaurant).

Special things to try include Becherovka (an exquisite bittersweet Czech liqueur made at Karlovy Vary), *zubrovka* (vodka with herb extracts) and *slivovice* (plum brandy). Grog is rum with hot water and sugar – a great pick-me-up. *Limonáda* is a good nonalcoholic drink.

CZECH REPUBLIC

ENTERTAINMENT

Theatres and concert halls were heavily subsidised by the communists so admission prices are still well below those in Western Europe and the programmes are first-rate. In Prague, unfortunately, the best theatre tickets are cornered by scalpers and travel agencies who demand premium prices, but in smaller centres like Karlovy Vary, Plzeň, České Budějovice and Brno you can see top performances at minimal expense. Check the theatres listed early in the day. The Czech Republic is a conservative country when it comes to social customs and you are expected to dress up when going to the theatre. Most theatres are closed in summer.

Outside Prague, the nightlife is rather limited, though after 9 pm there's usually a band playing in the bar of the best hotel in town and on weekends a disco will be pumping up somewhere – ask. You must often contend with overbearing door attendants and contemptuous waiters. Movies are always very cheap and usually shown in the original language with local subtitles.

Spectator Sports

Ice hockey is the national sport, followed by soccer (football) and tennis. Among the best Czech hockey teams are Sparta (the Prague city club), the Dukla (military) club of Jihlava and the Poldi club of Kladno (near Prague), a factory club. Outstanding soccer teams include Sparta and Bohemians (Prague city clubs) and Baník from Ostrava (a factory club). Cross-country ski racing is popular in winter.

THINGS TO BUY

Good buys include china, Bohemian crystal, costume jewellery, garnets, fancy leather goods, special textiles, lace, embroidery, shoes, classical records, colour-photography books and souvenirs. The hardback, blank-page notebooks available at stationery shops in small towns (not Prague) make excellent journals.

Garnet jewellery has been a Bohemian speciality for over a century. The ancient Egyptians used this semiprecious gemstone as a kind of travel insurance that was guaranteed to protect the wearer from accidents

In most shops and supermarkets the number of people inside is controlled by shopping carts or baskets. You cannot enter without one, so pick one up at the door or stand in line and wait for someone to leave. You must even pick up a shopping basket when you enter a bookshop! Outside Prague the largest department store chain is Prior.

Before making any major purchases, be aware that goods worth over US$50 purchased in the Czech Republic may be subject to export duties as high as 300%. Typical souvenirs are supposed to be exempt but even then Czech customs officers have been known to levy excessive duties. Antiques and valuable-looking artworks are closely scrutinised.

Reader Judith L Nathanson of Andover, Massachusetts, sent us this:

We had an experience with a Czech border guard when we were taking the train from Prague back to Austria. The guard looked over a large poster, framed and wrapped up with lots of cardboard and bubblewrap, that we had bought in Prague and asked us how much it had cost. He then asked us how much Czech money we had with us, glanced cursorily in some little book and wrote some numbers on a piece of paper telling us that it was our 'duty' (it amounted to US$50). We had been quite deferential up to that point, but when we realised we were in the middle of a shakedown, we went directly into enraged English and told him that there was no way we were paying any duty to take goods *out* of a country. At that point he disappeared with our bill of sale and credit card slip (our only proof of purchase) and said something about talking to his superior, but he left the train and we never saw him (or our bill of sale) again. You might want to warn your readers about this kind of scam.

Getting There & Away

AIR

The national carrier, Czechoslovak Airlines (ČSA), flies to Prague from Abu Dhabi, Bahrain, Bangkok, Beirut, Cairo, Chicago, Damascus, Dubai, Istanbul, Kuwait, Larnaca, Montreal, New York, Sharjah, Sin gapore, Tel Aviv, Toronto, Tunis, and many European cities. Fare structures are complicated and variable, so in the USA telephone 300-223 2365 toll free for the latest information.

From Western Europe some return excursion flights are cheaper than a one-way ticket but they're nonrefundable once purchased and flight dates cannot be changed. All fares are seasonal, so check with your travel agent.

There's no airport departure tax on international flights leaving the Czech Republic.

LAND

Bus

There's a bus several times a day from Vienna (Mitte Busbahnhof) to Brno (129 km, three hours, US$8). Try to buy your ticket the day before.

From London, the Kingscourt Express (☎ 0181-769 9229), 35 Kingscourt Road, London SW16 1JA, and National Express (☎ 0121-456 1122), 4 Vicarde Road, Egbaston, Birmingham B15 3E9, have buses to Prague twice a week year-round (1277 km, 23 hours, £65 single, £105 return). Youth and senior citizen discounts are available. Returning to Britain, check the Prague departure point carefully.

Compare the price of a bus tour to Prague with New Millennium Holidays (☎ 0121-711 2232), 20 High St, Solihull, West Midlands B91 3TB, England, which will be about double a scheduled coach but bed and breakfast are included. Less expensive New Millennium tours to Brno also include dinner (offered year-round).

A bus operates between Paris and Prague 1066 km, 16½ hours, US$70 one-way, US$122 return) five times a week year-round. From April to September this bus is daily. In Paris tickets are available at the Eurolines Paris, Gare Routiere Internationale Galliéni (☎ 4972 5151), Ave du Général le Gaulle (metro: Galliéni). Ask about student discounts. For information on the weekly bus to Prague from Barcelona and Madrid contact Hospitalet de Llobregat ☎ 93-431 9511).

There's a Eurolines bus service twice a week throughout the year from Amsterdam to Prague (1133 km, 19 hours, US$75 one-way, US$125 return, with a 10% discount for those aged under 26 or over 59 years). From June to September this bus runs four times a week. This trip is rather tiring because it follows a roundabout route via Rotterdam, Antwerp and Brussels. In mid-1994 Eurolines began offering a special 'Capital Tripper' fare of US$150 for a circular trip from Amsterdam to Budapest, Prague and back to Amsterdam or vice versa (a Slovakian transit visa is required by some nationals). For tickets contact Budget Bus/Eurolines (☎ 020-627 5151), Rokin 10, Amsterdam, or Eurolines (☎ 2-217 0025), Place de Brouckere 50, Brussels.

From Denmark, DSB buses connect Copenhagen and Aalborg to Prague twice a week (13½ hours, US$75). Connections are available to/from Sweden and Norway. Any DSB travel agency in Denmark will have tickets. Numerous buses operate from Germany to Prague and information is easily obtained at German travel agencies and bus stations. Travelling by bus is almost always cheaper than by the train.

Some of the long-distance international buses you see advertised in bus stations around the Czech Republic are only for locals – foreigners are not accepted. Other times foreigners pay a higher fare than Czechs. Bus service to/from Western Europe is still much cheaper than the train. Turn to Travel Agencies in the Prague section for local offices selling tickets for these buses.

Train

The easiest (if not the cheapest) way to get from Western Europe to the Czech Republic is by train. Keep in mind that train fares within the Czech Republic are less expensive than tickets to/from Western Europe. When travelling between Western and Eastern Europe, pay as little of the Czech portion in hard currency as you can and use border towns such as Děčín, Cheb, Plzeň, České Budějovice and Břeclav as entry or exit points. In other words, buy tickets which terminate or begin in these towns.

Sample 2nd-class international train fares from Prague are US$13 to Budapest (616 km, nine hours), US$13 to Kraków, US$17 to Vienna (354 km, six hours), US$18 to Warsaw (740 km, 12 hours), US$27 to Nuremberg (371 km, six hours), US$28 to Berlin (377 km, 5½ hours) and US$37 to Belgrade (986 km, 15½ hours). (These fares are rather low and may soon be sharply increased.) From Amsterdam to Cheb is US$154 one-way in 2nd class.

In the Czech Republic you should purchase international train tickets in advance from Čedok, but do this somewhere other than Prague, as the Čedok office there is will most likely be 'mobbed'. All international tickets are valid for two months with unlimited stopovers. Students get a 25% discount on train tickets to other Eastern European countries. Inter-Rail passes (sold to European residents only) are accepted in the Czech Republic but Eurail is not.

Most of the major 'name trains' listed herein travel daily throughout the year and require compulsory seat reservations. First-class sleepers and 2nd-class couchettes are available on almost all of these trains. From mid-June to mid-September additional services are put on.

To/From Western Europe Prague is on the main line used by all direct trains from Berlin to Vienna and Budapest, so access from those cities is easy. The *Balt-Orient, Hungária, Meridian* and *Metropol* express trains all travel daily between Berlin-Lichtenberg and Prague, continuing on to Budapest. The morning *Vindobona* and afternoon *Neptun* also link Berlin to Prague.

The *Sanssouci, Smetana* and *Vindobona* express trains link Vienna to Prague via Tábor. It's also possible to travel north-west from Vienna on local 2nd-class trains by changing at Gmünd and České Velenice, the border points, twice a day. There are six trains from Vienna (Nordbahnhof or Süd) to Břeclav (146 km, 1½ hours, US$13). Twice a day there's a service between Linz, Austria, and České Budějovice (125 km, four hours, US$12). Three other connections between

Linz and České Budějovice involve a change of trains at Summerau and Horní Dvořiště. A daily train links Vienna (Franz Josefsbahnhof) to České Budějovice (219 km, 3½ hours), departing from Vienna in the early morning, České Budějovice in the late afternoon.

From western Germany you'll probably transit Nuremberg and Cheb. The *Západn* express train travels daily between Paris and Prague (1263 km, 18 hours) via Frankfurt/Main, Nuremberg and Cheb. Local railcars shuttle between Cheb and Schirnding, Germany, twice a day (13 km, 15 minutes). Trains from Zürich and Munich go via Furth im Wald and Plzeň. Three times a day there's an unreserved local train from Furth im Wald, Germany, to Domažlice (25 minutes). A lesser known route between Eastern Germany and the Czech Republic is Leipzig to Karlovy Vary (the *Karlex* express train, 240 km, five hours). Unreserved local trains from Bad Schandau, Germany, to Děčín (22 km, 30 minutes), and Zittau, Germany, to Liberec (27 km, one hour) operate every couple of hours.

To/From Eastern Europe All express trains running between Budapest and Berlin-Lichtenberg pass through Bratislava, Brno and Prague. Of these, the Eurocity *Hungária* is a day train, and the *Balt-Orient, Metropol* and *Pannónia* are night trains. Going south, the *Balt-Orient* runs during the day, the *Hungária* during the evening and the *Metropol* and *Pannónia* overnight. Southbound, the *Pannónia* express train is convenient as it begins in Prague, but northbound the *Pannónia* and the *Balt-Orient* often run late as they originate in Romania. Reservations are recommended. Many nationals require a separate Slovak visa to transit Slovakia on their way to Hungary.

Connections between Poland and Prague will go through either Wrocław or Katowice. The *Baltyk* travels to/from Gdynia via Wrocław, and the *Bohemia* runs between Warsaw and Prague via Wrocław, taking 12 hours. Take the *Silesia* if you want to go to/from Warsaw via Katowice to/from

Prague (11 hours). All of these trains avoid Slovakia.

Car & Motorbike

Some Czech border crossings may only be used by citizens of the neighbouring countries, but the crossings named below are open to everyone.

To/From Austria There are crossings at Mikulov (24 km west of Břeclav); Hatě (10 km south of Znojmo); Nová Bystřice (18 km south of Jindřichův Hradec); Halámky (south-east of České Budějovice); České Velenice (opposite Gmünd); Dolní Dvořiště (38 km south of České Budějovice); and Studánky (which is between Český Krumlov and Linz).

To/From Germany You can enter at Strážný (66 km north of Passau); Železná Ruda (81 km south of Plzeň); Folmava (between Regensburg and Plzeň); Rozvadov (between Nuremberg and Plzeň); Pomezí nad Ohří (eight km west of Cheb); Vojtanov (six km north of Františkovy Lázně); and Cínovec (48 km south of Dresden).

To/From Poland You can cross at Harrachov (between Liberec and Jelenia Góra); Náchod (43 km east of Kłodzko); Bohumín (12 km north of Ostrava); and Český Těšín (31 km east of Ostrava).

On Foot

If you want to avoid the hassle or expense of getting an international train ticket, consider walking across the border! To/from Poland, the easiest place to do this is at Český Těšín, which is on the opposite side of the Olše (Olza) River from Cieszyn, Poland. Both towns have good onward train or bus services, making this a viable option for the slightly adventurous traveller. (Turn to the end of this chapter for more information on Český Těšín.)

If you want to walk into Austria, a good place to do it is from Mikulov, an unspoiled Moravian town with a large chateau on one hill and a church on another. Mikulov is on

the railway line from Břeclav to Znojmo and the station is very close to the Austrian/Czech border point. From Brno, it's much faster to come by bus (50 km). You could easily cross on foot and then hitchhike the 77 km south to Vienna.

For information on crossing into Germany on foot turn to Getting There & Away in the Cheb section.

Getting Around

BUS

Within the Czech Republic, ČAD express buses are often faster and more convenient than the train. Buses are more expensive than trains, but, by European standards, both are cheap. Count on spending about US$1 for every hour of bus travel. You sometimes have to pay a small additional charge for checked luggage.

Because of numerous footnotes, posted bus timetables are almost impossible to read, so patronise information counters. Two crossed hammers as a footnote means the bus only operates on working days Monday to Friday. As more buses leave in the morning, it's better to get an early start. Many bus services don't operate on weekends – trains are more reliable at that time.

Since bus ticketing is computerised at main stations like Prague and Karlovy Vary, you can often book a seat ahead and be sure of a comfortable trip. At large stations, make sure you're in the right ticket line. Way stations are rarely computerised and you must just line up and pay the driver. Reservations can only be made in the originating station of the bus, and at peak periods you may have to stand part of the way if you don't have a reservation.

All over the Czech Republic, if you want to find a bus station or bus stop, write the letters ČAD on a piece of paper and show it to someone. If you want to find a train station, write ČD (which stands for Czech State Railways) on the paper.

Most bus and train stations have a left-luggage room *(úschovna)*. There's a 15-kg maximum-weight limit for left luggage but it's not always enforced. If you lose the receipt, you'll have to pay a fine to recover your bag.

Intercity and municipal bus service could deteriorate over the next few years as there's little new investment to modernise the aging fleets, and private companies will probably stick to the busiest and most profitable routes.

TRAIN

The Czech Railways or České Dráhy (ČD) provides clean, efficient train service to almost every part of the country. Railway lines tend to run south towards Austria, reflecting the region's political alignment in the late 19th century, when the tracks were first laid down. Although a line was built east from Prague to Kiev as early as the 1880s, only in 1955 was this main route to the Soviet border reopened as a modern double-track line – at a cost of a billion crowns.

Using the Czech railway system successfully involves a little ingenuity. Some trains operate only on certain days, but the footnotes on the posted timetables are incomprehensible. The clerks at the information counters seldom speak English (not even in major stations) so, to get a departure time, try writing down your destination and the date you wish to travel, then point to your watch and pray. Some railway information offices in the Czech Republic are computerised and will give you a printout in English with information about your train.

You must tell the ticket seller which type of train you want. On departure *(odjezdy)* notice boards in train stations the *druh vlaku* column indicates the category of each train: Ex (express – these are often international trains and stop at fewer stations than fast trains); R *(rychlík* – fast trains, for which you always pay a surcharge); Sp *(spěšný* – trains to mountain areas); and Os *(osobní* – ordinary trains).

The letter R inside a box or circle means that reservations are mandatory, while an R alone means that it's a fast train. Reservations are not possible on ordinary trains. In major cities, you usually have to make seat reservations *(rezervace míst)* at a different counter, so make sure you're standing in the right queue. A reservation costs only US$0.25, so make one whenever you can.

Express and rychlík trains are usually marked in red, and tickets for these often have a red strip across the middle. If you plan to travel on an express or rychlík train, make sure you get an express ticket, otherwise the conductor will levy a fine. Staff at ticket counters will happily sell you an invalid ticket and you'll have no recourse later. Most train tickets are valid for 48 hours, but check this when you buy your ticket. If you have to purchase a ticket or pay a supplement on the train for any reason, you'll have to pay extra charges to the conductor.

Train tickets are very reasonable at about US$1 for 100 km in 2nd class with a surcharge of US$1 for fast or intercity (IC) trains, US$2 extra for Eurocity (EC) trains. Always check to see if your train is an IC or EC and pay the surcharge in the station when buying your ticket, otherwise the conductor will charge you a supplement three times higher. First-class tickets cost 50% more than 2nd-class ones and nonsmoking compartments are available. Only express trains carry dining cars *(restaurační vůz)*.

In many stations, the complete timetable is posted on notice boards. Look at the map and find the connection you want, then look for the table with the corresponding number. Posted timetables usually give the platform *(nástupiště)* number. If you're going to be in the Czech Republic for any length of time, it's a good idea to purchase the complete railway timetable book, the *Jízdní řád*. It can be hard to find but you can usually get one at Nadas, Hybernská 5, Prague (Metro: náměstí Republiky). With this book your mobility will be vastly enhanced.

One way to save on hotel bills while getting around is by using overnight trains. Sleepers *(lůžko)* and couchettes *(lehátko)* are available from Košice to Bratislava, Brno, Děčín, Františkovy Lázně, Karlovy Vary, Liberec, Plzeň, Prague and vice versa. Book

CZECH REPUBLIC

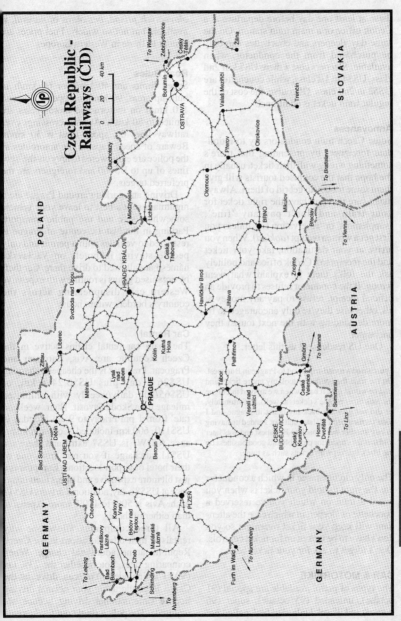

these at least one day before departure at a Čedok office or a main train station. On the same day sleepers and couchettes can only be purchased from the conductor, when available. Sleepers cost a mere US$3 in 2nd class, US$4 in 1st class, while couchettes are US$2 in 2nd class. Of course, the cost of the regular train ticket is additional.

Annoyances

Some Czech train conductors try to intimidate foreigners by pretending that there's something wrong with their ticket, usually in the hope that the confused tourists will give them some money to get rid of them. Always make sure that you have the right ticket for your train and don't pay any 'fine', 'supplement' or 'reservation fee' unless you first get a written receipt *(doklad)*. When you arrive at your destination, take your ticket and the receipt to a Čedok office and politely ask the folks there to explain what went wrong. If the conductor refuses to provide an official receipt, refuse to pay any money at all, otherwise they're only encouraged to be more demanding with the next tourist they encounter.

One US reader sent us this letter:

I purchased a round-trip ticket to Prague in Budapest. On the train the conductor took my entire ticket and said he would give it back when we arrived in Prague (he took other people's tickets as well). Unfortunately, he did *not* give me back my ticket in Prague and I didn't remember it till later that day. I ended up having to buy another ticket back to Budapest and was later told that the conductor probably did good business on the black market with tickets such as mine.

The only circumstance in which a conductor has the right to hold your ticket is when you board a train on which you've reserved a couchette or sleeper, in which case the attendant will keep your ticket overnight so you don't have to be woken up for ticket controls. Don't forget to ask for your ticket back.

CAR & MOTORBIKE

The types of petrol available are special (91 octane), unleaded (95 octane), super (96 octane) and diesel. Unleaded fuel, called *bez*

olovnatých přísad, *bez olova* or *natural*, is available but not so widely. Fuel prices are similar to those in Western Europe.

Road Rules

Speed limits are 40 km/h or 60 km/h in built-up areas, 90 km/h on open roads and 110 km/h on motorways; motorcycles are limited to 80 km/h. At level crossings over railway lines the speed limit is 30 km/h. Beware of speed traps on the autoroutes as the police are empowered to levy on-the-spot fines of up to US$60 and foreigners are the preferred targets.

Driving and parking around Prague are a nightmare so it's best to leave your vehicle somewhere safe and use public transport. Parking in the historic centre of Prague is restricted to vehicles with a permit and only people staying in hotels on Václavské náměstí are allowed to drive there. Car theft by organised gangs is routine with expensive Western cars disappearing across the country's borders within hours.

Car Rental

The main car rental chains active in the Czech Republic are Avis, Europcar and Pragocar. Pragocar is the cheapest, charging US$26 a day plus US$0.24 a km, or US$65/300 daily/weekly with unlimited mileage for a Škoda Favorit. Their 'weekend rate' from 1 pm Friday to 9 am Monday is US$110, 600 km included. Collision insurance (CDW) is US$7 extra and there's a US$11 surcharge if you rent from one of their hotel or airport locations. Europcar is a just bit more expensive and offers theft insurance at US$8 a day, additional drivers US$19 each. Avis is 50% to 100% more expensive than either of these.

All three companies allow one-way rentals to their other locations in the Czech Republic at no additional charge. When comparing rates, note whether the 23% tax (VAT) is included. You can drive in the Czech Republic using your normal driving licence (international driving licence not required). The police single out foreign cars or traffic fines, so try to get a Škoda when you rent a car.

BICYCLE

After a trip around the Czech Republic by bicycle, Richard Nebeský of Melbourne, Australia, had this to report:

The Czech Republic is small enough to be traversed on a bicycle. It is fairly safe for cyclists as most drivers will do their utmost to avoid them. Cyclists still should be careful as the roads are very narrow, potholed, and in towns the cobblestones and tram tracks can be a dangerous combination, especially when it has been raining. Theft is a problem especially in Prague, Brno and Plzeň, thus a good long chain and lock are a must.

Many locals use bicycles, so it's fairly easy to transport them on trains. First purchase your train ticket and then take it with your bicycle to the railway luggage office. There you fill out a card which will be attached to your bike; on the card you write your name, address, destination and departing station. You will be given a receipt that should include all the accessories that your bicycle has, such as lights and dynamo. You are not allowed to leave any luggage on the bicycle, and it is advisable to take off the pump and water bottles, as they could disappear along the way. The cost of transporting a bicycle is usually one-tenth of the train ticket. It is best to collect the bicycle from the goods carriage as soon as you arrive at your destination. You can also transport bicycles on most buses if they are not crowded and if the bus driver is willing.

LOCAL TRANSPORT

Buses and trams within cities operate from 4.30 am to 11.30 pm daily. In Prague some main bus and tram routes operate every 40 minutes all night. Tickets sold at newsstands must be validated once you're aboard as there are no conductors. Tickets are hard to find at night, on weekends and out in residential areas, so carry a good supply. Automats at Prague metro stations sell tickets which can be used on all forms of public transport in Prague.

Taxi

Taxis have meters and you pay what they show – just make sure the meter is switched on. Some Prague taxi drivers are highly experienced at overcharging tourists.

Prague

Prague (Praha in Czech) is like a history lesson come true. As you walk among the long stone palaces or across the Karlův most (Charles Bridge), with Smetana's Vltava flowing below and pointed towers all around, you'll feel as if history had stopped somewhere back in the 18th century. Goethe called Prague the prettiest gem in the stone crown of the world. A millennium earlier in 965 the Arab-Jewish merchant Ibrahim Ibn Jacob described Prague as a town of 'stone and lime'.

This story-book city in the centre of Bohemia experienced two architectural golden ages: a Gothic period under Holy Roman emperor Charles IV and then a Baroque period during the Habsburg Counter-Reformation. In the 18th century, Czech culture was suppressed, so it's not at all surprising that Prague's two greatest Baroque architects, Christopher and Kilian Dientzenhofer, were Germans.

Today Prague is a city of over a million inhabitants, the seat of government and leading centre of much of the country's intellectual and cultural life. Unlike Warsaw, Budapest and Berlin, which were major battlefields during WW II, Prague escaped almost unscathed and after the war, careful planning and preservation prevented haphazard modern development. Since 1989, however, central Prague has been swamped by unfettered capitalism as street vendors, cafés and restaurants take over pavements, streets and parks which were once public.

How you feel about Prague's current tourist glut may depend on where you're coming from. If you're arriving from London, Paris or Rome it may all seem quite

CZECH REPUBLIC

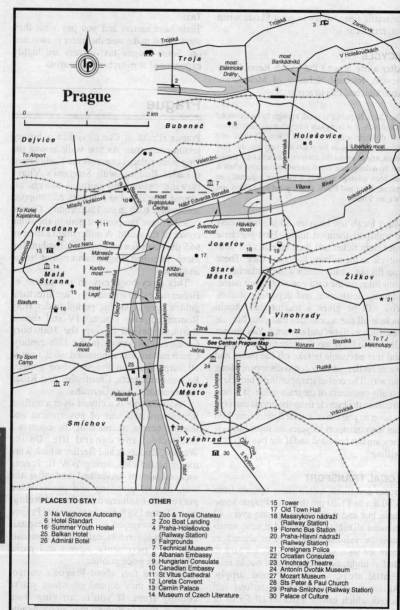

Prague

Troja

Bubeneč

Holešovice

Dejvice

To Airport

Hradčany

Malá Strana

Josefov

Staré Město

Žižkov

Vinohrady

Nové Město

Smíchov

Vyšehrad

See Central Prague Map

Vltava River

PLACES TO STAY	OTHER	15 Tower
3 Na Vlachovce Autocamp	1 Zoo & Troya Chateau	17 Old Town Hall
6 Hotel Standart	2 Zoo Boat Landing	18 Masarykovo nádraží
16 Summer Youth Hostel	4 Praha-Holešovice	(Railway Station)
25 Balkán Hotel	(Railway Station)	19 Florenc Bus Station
26 Admirál Botel	5 Fairgrounds	20 Praha-Hlavní nádraží
	7 Technical Museum	(Railway Station)
	8 Albanian Embassy	21 Foreigners Police
	9 Hungarian Consulate	22 Croatian Consulate
	10 Canadian Embassy	23 Vinohrady Theatre
	11 St Vitus Cathedral	24 Antonín Dvořák Museum
	12 Loreta Convent	27 Mozart Museum
	13 Černín Palace	28 Sts Peter & Paul Church
	14 Museum of Czech Literature	29 Praha-Smíchov (Railway Station)
		30 Palace of Culture

CZECH REPUBLIC

normal, but if you've been elsewhere in Eastern Europe for a while, you'll be in for a bit of a shock. As you're being jostled by the hawkers and golden hordes you may begin to feel that Prague has become a tacky tourist trap, but try to overcome those feelings and enjoy this great European art centre for all it's worth. Just take care not to make it your first and last stop in Bohemia.

Orientation

Almost exactly midway between Berlin and Vienna, Prague nestles in a picturesque valley, its high hills topped by castles and its river spanned by 17 bridges. This river, the Vltava (Moldau), swings through the centre of the city like a question mark, separating Malá Strana (Little Quarter), with the Baroque homes of the nobility, from Staré Město (Old Town), the early Gothic city centre. North of Malá Strana is Hradčany, the medieval castle district where royalty used to reside, while Nové Město (New Town) is a late Gothic extension of Staré Město to the south, almost as far as the old citadel, Vyšehrad. Only in 1784 did these four royal towns unite within a single system of fortifications.

Unforgettable features include Prague Castle, visible from almost everywhere in the city, and Václavské náměstí (Wenceslas Square), Prague's Champs Elysées, which points north-west to Staroměstské, the old town square. Between these two squares is Na příkopě, a busy pedestrian street where most of the information offices are found. Our maps of Prague are only for initial orientation – buy a detailed city map the first chance you get.

For information on facilities at Prague's various train and bus stations see Getting There & Away at the end of this section.

Information

There's a friendly tourist information kiosk in Hlavní nádraží Railway Station, right next to the metro entrance (weekdays 9 am to 7 pm, weekends 9 am to 6 pm).

The best place to pick up brochures and ask questions is at the Prague Information Service (PIS), Na příkopě 20 (metro: náměstí Republiky). Their monthly *Cultural Events* booklet in English is invaluable. They also sell city tours (US$15 for 2½ hours) and concert tickets (US$8 and up). Another PIS information centre is at Staroměstské náměstí 22, right opposite the clock on the old town hall.

Though actually a travel agency, Pragotur, U Obecního domu 2 (metro: náměstí Republiky), is usually helpful in providing general information when they're not too busy. They can also book tours, tickets and rooms for you at competitive rates.

Čedok, Na příkopě 18, also has an information counter.

If you want any information on motoring matters contact the Autoklub České Republiky (☎ 262 651), Opletalova 29, opposite Hlavní nádraží Railway Station. Nearby is Autoturist (☎ 773 455), Opletalova 21 (through the back courtyard).

Most newsstands have the English-language papers *Prognosis* and *The Prague Post* – without doubt, your best sources of the latest information on what's happening in Prague.

Money One of the best places in Prague to change travellers' cheques is the efficient American Express office (☎ 261 747) at Václavské náměstí 50 (weekdays 9 am to 6 pm, Saturday 9 am to noon). The three tellers provide fast service and no commission is charged on American Express travellers' cheques. There is a 1% commission on cheques from other companies (US$2 minimum) and 2% commission to change cash. They'll also change their own dollar travellers' cheques into dollars cash for 2% commission (US$2 minimum). Excess crowns can be changed back into dollars for 2%, but you must have an original exchange receipt issued by them. Their exchange rate is 1% lower than that offered by the banks but you still come out ahead, provided you have American Express cheques. Clients' mail is held here (see the chapter introduction for the address).

If you're carrying Thomas Cook

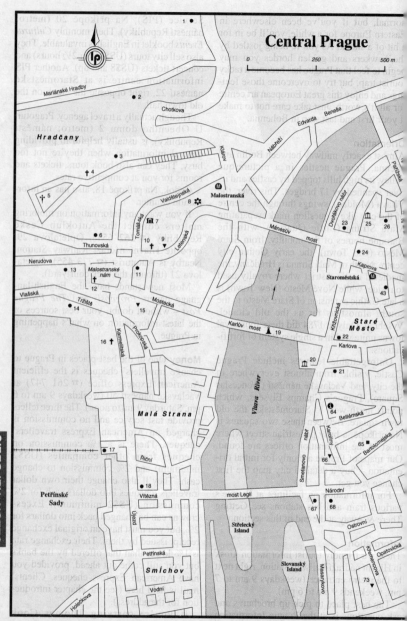

Central Prague

0   250   500 m

Marlánské Hradby

Hradčany

Chotkova

Edvarda Beneše

Nábřeží

Klárov

Valdštejnská

Ⓜ **Malostranská**

Tomášská

Letenská

Mánesův most

Dvořákovo nábř

Thunovská

Nerudova

Malostranské nám.

Malostranská

Kaprova

Staroměstská Ⓜ

Vlašská

Tržiště

Mostecká

Karmelitská

Karlův most

Prokopská

Vltava River

Křížovnická

Staré Město

Karlova

Malá Strana

Betlémská

Karoliny

Bartolomějská

Říční

Smetanovo nábř

Masarykovo

Úijezd

Vítězná

most Legií

Národní

Petřínské Sady

Střelecký Island

Ostrovní

Petřínská

Slovanský Island

Křemencova

Opatovická

Smíchov

Vodní

Holečkova

PLACES TO STAY

28 Inter-Continental Hotel
34 Merkur Hotel
53 Hybernia Hotel
61 Palace Hotel
65 Unitas Pension

PLACES TO EAT

9 U Svatého Tomáše Beer Hall
15 Vinárna Jadran
45 Club-Bar Quê Huong
49 Restaurace u Supa
66 Hostinec u Rotundy
72 Kotvy Garden Restaurant
73 U Fleků Beer Hall
75 Bufet Jídelna
76 Chicago & Indian Restaurants
77 Kavárna Luxor
83 Česká Hospoda V Krakovské

OTHER

1 Hungarian Consulate
2 Belveder Summer Palace
3 Golden Lane
4 Basilica of St George
5 St Vitus Cathedral
6 British Embassy
7 Wallenstein Palace
8 Wallenstein Gardens
10 St Thomas Church
11 Malostranská Beseda Theatre-Café
12 St Nicholas Church
13 Romanian Consulate
14 US Embassy
16 Church of Our Lady Victorious
17 Funicular Railway
18 Rock Club Borat
19 Statue of St John Nepomuk
20 Smetana Museum
21 Zábradlí Theatre
22 Clementinum
23 Dvořák Concert Hall
24 Bohemian Ventures Bookstore
25 Decorative Arts Museum
26 Old Jewish Cemetery
27 Staronová Synagogue
29 Čedok (Excursions Office)
30 Ron Boat Rentals
31 Convent of St Agnes
32 ČSA Office
33 Rock Club Bunkr
35 Municipal Museum
36 Florenc Bus Station
37 Bohemiatour
38 Kotva Department Store
39 St James Church
40 Týn Church
41 St Nicholas Church
42 Balnea
43 National Marionette Theatre
44 Old Town Hall
46 Carolinum
47 Former Klement Gottwald Museum
48 Tyl Theatre
50 Powder Gate
51 Nadas Bookstore
52 Masarykovo nádraží (Railway Station)
54 Universitas Tour
55 Prague Information Service
56 Čedok (train tickets)
57 Minor Children's Theatre
58 Pragocar
59 Autoklub České Republiky
60 CKM Student Travel Centre
62 Main Post Office
63 Disco Carioca
64 Klub mladých cestovatelů
67 National Theatre
68 Laterna Magika
69 Reduta Jazz Club
70 Máj Department Store
71 Dům Slovenské Kultůry
74 Varieté Praga
78 Praha-Hlavní nádraží (Railway Station)
79 Polish Consulate
80 American Express
81 State Opera
82 Parliament
84 National Museum
85 Agha RTU Jazz Centrum
86 Bulgarian Consulate
87 Stop City Accommodation

travellers' cheques you can cash them at a good rate without commission at Thomas Cook Travel Agency, Václavské náměstí 47 (weekdays 9 am to 7 pm, Saturday 9 am to 4 pm, Sunday 10 am to 5 pm). Other companies' travellers' cheques attract 2% commission.

The Česká Národní Banka/Komerčn Banka, Na příkopě 28 (weekdays 8 to 11.30 am and noon to 7 pm, Saturday 9 am to 2 pm), changes travellers' cheques for 2% commission (US$1 minimum). To conver dollar travellers' cheques into dollars cas they take 5%.

The Živnostenská Banka, Na příkopě 20 weekdays 8 am to 9.30 pm, Saturday 1.30 o 5.30 pm), also gives a good rate and charges 2% commission (minimum US$2). t's worth going in there just to admire the décor! There are always long queues at both these banks.

The Československá Obchodní Banka, Na příkopě 14 (weekdays 7.30 am to noon and 1 to 3.30 pm) has an automatic exchange machine under the staircase in the middle of he building which changes foreign banknotes at one of the best rates in town with only 1% commission and no minimum. Avoid the tellers in the bank's adjacent foreign exchange office who take 5% commission!

Pragotur, U Obecního domu 2, changes travellers' cheques at the regular bank rate for 4% commission and from April to December they're open on Sunday. Čedok, Na příkopě 18, charges only 3% commission but gives a slightly lower rate.

About eight exchange offices operate in Hlavní nádraží Railway Station charging anywhere from 4% to 9% commission. Some claim to charge only 1% but have already allowed for their commission by offering a lower rate. Ask if there's a minimum commission and only change enough to tide you over until you can get to American Express or a bank.

One of the biggest scams around Prague are the exorbitant commissions collected by he many small exchange offices in the train stations and along the tourist strips. For example, Exact Change charges 9.75% commission (US$3 minimum) and Chequepoint 10% commission (US$4 minimum). The precise amount of commission they take seems to vary, so be sure to ask first if you do business with these people. Also beware of tricky practices, such as posting the *selling* rates which are much higher than the *buying* rates they'll pay you, or advertising slightly higher rates without mentioning the high commission charges. (Incidentally, these high commissions are only for foreign tourists – Czechs pay a far lower commission to change money at these places.)

Persons offering to change money on the street are usually thieves. Especially beware of sleight-of-hand experts along Na příkopě and of pickpockets in restaurant queues. People who lean over to look at your menu are often more interested in your wallet. Pickpockets regularly work the crowd watching the Gothic horologe on the old town hall mark the hour. Recently the police have been cracking down on freelancers offering unofficial private rooms, pirate theatre tickets and black-market currency exchange, and you'll be propositioned a lot less than you would have been. Pickpockets and assorted other hustlers are also feeling the heat.

Post & Telecommunications The main post office, Jindřišská 14 (metro: Hlavní nádraží), is open 24 hours a day, but poste restante (window No 28) is only available weekdays from 7 am to 8 pm, Saturday 7 am to 1 pm. You can send parcels weighing up to two kg from windows No 14 to 17, buy telephone cards at window No 20 and get stamps at windows Nos 20 to 24. Information is at window No 30. Philatelic stamps are sold at windows No 38 and 39 (great for dressing up a bland letter or postcard). The telephone centre here is open from 7 am to 11 pm daily.

Parcels weighing over two kg and up to 15 kg maximum must be taken to Pošta 121 Celnice, Plzeňská 139 (metro to Anděl, then three stops west on tram No 4, 7 or 9). The parcel must be open for inspection and there are three forms to fill in. They're open Monday and Wednesday from 8.30 am to 6 pm, Tuesday, Thursday and Friday 8.30 am to 3 pm, and Saturday 8.30 am to 2 pm.

Prague's telephone code is 02.

Western Embassies Several of the foreign embassies are housed in magnificent Baroque palaces in Malá Strana, below the castle (metro: Malostranská).

The British Embassy (☎ 533 370), Thunovská 14, also serves New Zealanders.

A block over at Tržiště 15 is the American

Embassy (☎ 536 641). This embassy does not hold mail for tourists.

The Canadian Embassy (☎ 312 0251), Mickiewiczova 6 (metro: Hradčanská), provides full consular service to Australians.

Eastern Embassies The Hungarian Embassy, Badeniho 1 (open Monday, Tuesday, Wednesday and Friday from 9 am to noon; visas US$22 per entry), is near Hradčanská Metro Station.

A few blocks from Dejvická Metro Station are the Slovak Embassy, Pod hradbami 1 at Svatovítská (weekdays 8.30 am to noon), and the Embassy of Slovenia, Pod hradbami 15 (weekdays 9 am to noon).

Also accessible from Dejvická Metro Station are the Albanian Embassy, Pod kaštany 22 (Monday, Wednesday, Friday 9 am to noon), and the Russian Federation Embassy, Pod kaštany 16.

From Malostranská Metro Station you can reach the Romanian Embassy, Nerudova 5 (open Monday, Wednesday and Friday from 9 am to noon), and the Embassy of Yugoslavia, Mostecká 15 (open Monday, Wednesday and Friday from 9 am to noon).

On the other side of town near Muzeum Metro Station are the Polish Consulate, Václavské náměstí 49 (open weekdays from 9 am to 1 pm), and the Bulgarian Embassy, Krakovská 6 (open Monday, Tuesday, Thursday and Friday from 9 to 11 am).

The Croatian Embassy, Vinohradská 69 (weekdays 8 am to noon), is accessible from Jiřího z Poděbrad Metro Station.

Travel Agencies The CKM Student Travel Centre, Jindřišská 28 (metro: Hlavní nádraží), is helpful with information, sells ISIC student cards and makes reservations at youth hostels in Prague.

The travel office of the International Union of Students, Pařížská 25 (weekdays from 1 to 3 pm), also sells ISIC student identification cards (US$3).

Persons aged under 26 years can buy discounted Eurotrain railway tickets to Western Europe at the Wasteels office in Hlavní nádraží Railway Station or from CKM Student Travel, Žitná 11 (metro: Karlov náměstí). This CKM office also sells bus tickets to Western Europe.

Several offices around Prague sell bus tickets to Western European cities and these usually work out cheaper than the train (though they're less comfortable). The Čedok offices at Na příkopě 18 and Rytířsk 16 sell bus tickets to Amsterdam (US$79), Athens (US$90), Brussels (US$58), London (US$83) and Paris (US$79).

Bohemiatour, Zlatnická 7 (weekdays 8 am to 5 pm, Saturday 8 am to 4 pm), has international bus tickets to Amsterdam, Athens, Brussels, Cologne, Copenhagen, Frankfurt, Hamburg, London, Madrid, Marseilles, Milan, Munich, Paris, Rome, Sofia, Stockholm, Strasbourg, Vienna, Zagreb, Zürich and many other cities.

The Eurolines representative in Prague, ČAD Klíčov, Štěpánská 63 (top floor), has tickets for international buses to Amsterdam, Bordeaux, Brussels, Budapest, Frankfurt, London, Madrid, Münster, Paris, Stuttgart, Toulouse and Zagreb.

Travel Agency ČD in the arcade at Na příkopě 31 sells bus tickets to points all over Western Europe. The prices posted in the window are only for Czechs and foreign tourists can pay over 100% more for exactly the same ticket. For example, Prague to Zürich is US$35 for Czechs or US$75 for foreigners.

Čedok, Na příkopě 18, sells international train tickets but it can take hours to buy an international ticket at this Čedok office, so pick up your ticket in another town if at all possible. Another Čedok office nearby at Rytířská 16 has exactly the same tickets and is less crowded.

Balnea, Pařížská 11 (metro: Staroměstská), can arrange accommodation and treatment at Czech spas beginning at around US$45/70 single/double a night, all-inclusive (food, lodging, medical attention).

Laundry Laundry Kings, Dejvická 16 (metro: Hradčanská), is an US-style laundromat in Prague. It costs about US$4 to wash and dry six kg and takes about two hours. No reservations are accepted, just ask the attendants to put you on the waiting list as soon as you arrive. Laundry Kings sells detergent or you can bring your own. They also sell drinks and English-language newspapers. While your clothes are washing you can sit around in their lounge – a good place to meet other travellers as most of the clients are foreigners. There's also an interesting notice board here. Opening hours are weekdays from 6 am to 10 pm, weekends 8 am to 10 pm, but you must arrive by 8 pm.

Bookshops Knihy Melantrich, Na příkopě 3 (metro: Můstek), has a good selection of maps and local guidebooks. Prague's international bookshop is at Na příkopě 27. Nadas, Hybernská 5 (metro: náměstí Republiky), sells train timetables (*Jízdní řád*).

Bohemian Ventures, náměstí Jana Palacha 2 (Faculty of Philosophy building), has an excellent selection of paperbacks in English, including English translations of works by Czech authors (weekdays 9 am to 5 pm).

Československý Spisovatel, Národní 9 (metro: Národní třída), also has many books in English at slightly lower prices.

Vilímkovo Knihkupectví, Spálená 15 (metro: Národní třída), has detailed maps of many parts of the country.

The Ośrodek Kultury Polskiej, Jindřišská 3 (metro: Můstek), sells good maps of Polish cities.

The Geologické Knihy a Mapy, Malostranské náměstí 19 (metro: Malostranská), has geological tomes in English and detailed geological maps of every part of the country. These aren't designed for hiking, but may be useful if you're very interested in a certain area.

Visa Extensions To extend your visa or report a lost passport or visa go to the For-

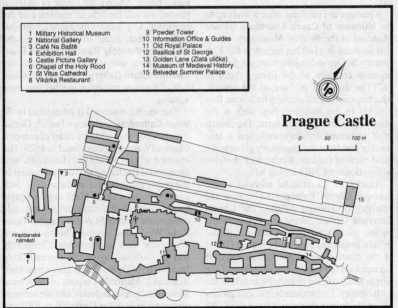

1 Military Historical Museum
2 National Gallery
3 Café Na Baště
4 Exhibition Hall
5 Castle Picture Gallery
6 Chapel of the Holy Rood
7 St Vitus Cathedral
8 Vikárka Restaurant
9 Powder Tower
10 Information Office & Guides
11 Old Royal Palace
12 Basilica of St George
13 Golden Lane (Zlatá ulička)
14 Museum of Medieval History
15 Belveder Summer Palace

Prague Castle

0   50   100 m

Hradčanské náměstí

eigners Police, Olšanská 2, about a 10-minute walk from Flora Metro Station (open Monday, Tuesday, Thursday 8 am to 3 pm, Wednesday 9 am to 5 pm, Friday 8 am to 2 pm). Visa extensions cost US$5.

Things to See

Hradčany Prague's finest churches and museums are found in Hradčany, the wonderful castle district stretching along a hilltop west of the river. Be aware that around midday it will be difficult to see many of the marvellous sights up there due to the hundreds of other people trying to do exactly the same thing as you at exactly the same moment. Early morning is the best time to visit and evening is even better (although all the museums will be closed).

The easiest way to organise a visit is to take the metro to Malostranská, then tram No 22 up the hill around to the back of Hradčany as far as the fourth stop, 'Památník Písemnictví'. From here Pohořelec and Loretánská streets slope down to the castle gate.

A passage at Pohořelec ulice 8 leads up to the **Museum of Czech Literature** (closed Monday) in the Strahov Monastery, which was founded in 1140 but rebuilt in the 17th century. Before visiting the museum, find the separate entrance to the library (built in 1679) to the right in front of the church, which opens for groups every half-hour. Buy a ticket in the museum, then wait at the library door for a group to form. The church itself is beautifully decorated, and a lane leading east from the monastery gives you a good view of the city. Return to Pohořelec and go down the hill keeping left.

Nearby on Loretánské náměstí is the Baroque **Černín Palace** (1687), now the Ministry of Foreign Affairs. The **Loreta Convent** (closed Monday), opposite the palace, shelters a fabulous treasure of diamonds, pearls and gold, and a replica (1631) of the Santa Casa in the Italian town of Loreto, said to be the Nazareth home of the Virgin Mary carried to Italy by angels in the 13th century. Unfortunately, the tour groups are so thick here that you'll have difficulty

getting near the most striking objects in the convent museum. Consider coming back in the afternoon when the multitudes have vanished.

Loretánská soon opens onto Hradčanské náměstí, with the main gate to Prague Castle at its eastern end. At Hradčanské náměstí 2 is the **Military Historical Museum**, which is open from May to October (closed Monday), housed in the Renaissance Schwarzenberg-Lobkowitz Palace (1563).

Just across the square at No 15 is the 18th-century Šternberský Palace which contains the **National Gallery**. This has the country's main collection of European paintings with whole rooms of Cranachs and Picassos. Luckily, the groups never have time to visit, so you can see it in relative peace. This and the many other branches of the National Gallery around Prague open Tuesday to Sunday from 10 am to 6 pm.

Prague Castle Prague Castle was founded in the 9th century, then rebuilt and extended many times. Always the centre of political power, it's still the official residence of the president. As you enter the castle compound under an arch dated 1614, you'll see the **Chapel of the Holy Rood** directly in front. On the north side of this courtyard is the **Castle Picture Gallery** with a good collection of Baroque paintings in what was once a stable.

The second courtyard is dominated by **St Vitus Cathedral**, a glorious French Gothic structure begun in 1344 by order of emperor Charles IV and only completed in 1929. The stained-glass windows, frescoes and tombstones (including that of the founder in the crypt) merit careful attention. The 14th century chapel with the black imperial eagle on the door on the cathedral's south side contains the tomb of St Wenceslas, the 'Good King Wenceslas' of the Christmas carol. Wenceslas' zeal in spreading Christianity and his submission to the German king Henry I led to his murder by his own brother, Boleslav I. Alarmed by reports of miracles at Wenceslas' grave, Boleslav had the remains reinterred in St Vitus Cathedral in 932, and

CZECH REPUBLIC

the saint's tomb soon became a great pilgrimage site. The small door beside the chapel windows leads to a chamber where the Bohemian crown jewels are kept; however, entry is not allowed. From Tuesday to Sunday you can climb the 287 steps of the cathedral tower for about a dollar.

On the south side of the cathedral is the entrance to the **Old Royal Palace** (closed Monday) with its huge Vladislav Hall, built between 1486 and 1502. A ramp to one side allowed mounted horsemen to ride into the hall and conduct jousts indoors. On 23 May 1618 two Catholic councillors were thrown from the window of an adjacent chamber by irate Protestant nobles, an act that touched off the Thirty Years' War, which devastated Europe from 1618 to 1648.

As you leave the palace, the **Basilica of St George** (1142), a remarkable Romanesque church, will be directly in front of you. In the Benedictine convent next to the church is the National Gallery's collection of Czech art from the Middle Ages to the 18th century (closed Monday).

Behind this gallery, follow the crowd into **Golden Lane** (Zlatá ulička), a 16th century tradesman's quarter of tiny houses built into the castle walls. The novelist Franz Kafka, who was born in Prague in 1883, lived and wrote in the tiny house at No 22.

On the right, just before the gate leading out of the castle, is **Lobkovický Palace** (closed Monday), Jirská 3, which houses a museum of medieval history containing replicas of the crown jewels. From the eastern end of the castle, a stairway leads back down towards Malostranská Metro Station.

Malá Strana From Malostranská Metro Station, follow Valdštejnská around to Valdštejnské náměstí, past many impressive palaces, especially the **Wallenstein Palace** (1630), now the Ministry of Culture, which fills the entire east side of the square. A famous figure in the Thirty Years' War, Albrecht Wallenstein started out on the Protestant side then went over to the Catholics and built this palace with the expropriated wealth of his former colleagues. In 1634 the

Habsburg emperor Ferdinand II learned that Wallenstein was about to switch sides once again and had him assassinated at Cheb. The palace gardens are accessible from May to September through a gate at Letenská ulice 10, a block away.

Continue south on Tomášská and round the corner to Letenská to reach **St Thomas Church**, a splendid Baroque edifice built in 1731. Behind Malostranské náměstí nearby is the formerly Jesuit **St Nicholas Church** (1755), the greatest Baroque building in Prague, its dome visible from afar. Malá Strana was built up in the 17th and 18th centuries, below the protective walls of Prague Castle, by the victorious Catholic clerics and nobility on the foundations of the Renaissance palaces of their Protestant predecessors.

After a wander around the square, follow the tram tracks south along Karmelitská. At Karmelitská 9, is the **Church of Our Lady Victorious** (1613) with the venerated wax Holy Infant of Prague (1628). Originally erected by Lutherans, this church was taken over by the Carmelite Order after the Catholic victory at the Battle of White Mountain (1620).

Backtrack a little and take narrow Prokopská ulice towards the river. You'll soon reach a beautiful square surrounded by fine Baroque palaces. Continue on the left on Lázeňská towards the massive stone towers of the **Church of Our Lady Below the Chain**.

To the left of the church, Lázeňská leads out to Mostecká with the **Karlův most** to the right. This enchanting bridge, built in 1357 and graced by 30 statues dating from the 18th century, was the only bridge in Prague until 1841. Take a leisurely stroll across it, but first climb the **tower** on the Malá Strana side for a great bird's-eye view. In the middle of the bridge is a bronze statue (1683) of St John Nepomuk who was thrown to his death in the river here in 1393 when he refused to tell King Wenceslas IV what the queen had confided to him at confession. Throughout the day, so many tourists and hawkers squeeze onto the bridge that you can hardly move. To feel the true romance of this bridge consider coming back in the very early morning or after midnight when the moon is full.

Across on the Staré Město side of the bridge is the 17th century **Clementinum**, once a Jesuit college but now the State Library, which has over three million volumes. After Prague Castle this is the largest historic building in the city. To the right and around at the end of Novotného lávka is the **Smetana Museum** (closed on Tuesday), in a former waterworks building beside the river. Ask to hear a recording of the composer's music. The view from the terrace in front of the museum is the best in Prague.

Staré Město Beside the Clementinum, narrow Karlova ulice leads east towards Staroměstské náměstí, Prague's old town square and still the heart of the city. Below the clock tower of the **old town hall** on the left is a Gothic horologe (1410) which entertains the throng with apostles, Christ, a skeleton and the cock every hour on the hour. Immediately after the show, a tour of the building, including the 15th century council chamber, begins inside. Do climb the tower for the view.

At the centre of Staroměstské náměstí is a **monument** to the religious reformer Jan Hus, erected in 1915 on the 500th anniversary of his death by fire at the stake. Facing one side of the square is the Baroque **St Nicholas Church**, designed by Kilian Dientzenhofer. More striking is the Gothic **Týn Church** (1365) with its twin steeples. The tomb of the 16th century Danish astronomer Tycho Brahe is in front of the main altar and the church is rich in artworks (open afternoons, closed Monday). In the past few years Staroměstské náměstí has been transformed from a quaint central European town square into a showplace for first world tourism and in summer it's really a circus.

From a corner of Staroměstské náměstí near the horologe, take Železná ulice southeast to the **Carolinum**, Železná 9, the oldest remaining part of Prague University, founded by Charles IV in 1348. Next to this

at Železná 11 is the neoclassical **Stavovské Theatre** (1783), where the premiere of Mozart's *Don Giovanni* took place on 29 October 1787 with the composer himself conducting.

Around the corner at Rytířská 29 is an ornate neo-Renaissance palace (1894), once the Klement Gottwald Museum and now a bank. From one corner of this building Na můstku leads into **Václavské náměstí**, Prague's fashionable boulevard (metro: Můstek). Stroll up the square past the majestic Art-Nouveau façades. If Staroměstské náměstí and Karlův most are centres of the tourist's Prague, Václavské náměstí is the city's focus for local residents and you'll see a lot more Czech people around here. At the upper end of Václavské náměstí stands an **equestrian statue** of the 10th century king Václav I or St Wenceslas, patron saint of Bohemia. In the 20th century, this vast square has often been the scene of public protests and just below the statue is a simple memorial with photos and flowers dedicated to those who resisted Soviet tanks here in 1968. Also here on 16 January 1969 a Czech student named Jan Palach publicly burned himself to protest the Soviet invasion. In 1989 demonstrators again gathered at this spot.

Looming above the south-eastern end of Václavské náměstí is the **National Museum** (metro: Muzeum) with ho-hum collections on prehistory, 19th and early 20th century history, mineralogy and a herd of stuffed animals. The captions are only in Czech and the neo-Renaissance museum building (1890) itself is as interesting as what's on display inside (closed Tuesday). The museum café is another saving grace.

Vyšehrad Take the metro to Vyšehrad where the **Palace of Culture** (1981) rises above a deep ravine crossed by the Nuselský Bridge (formerly known as the Klement Gottwald Bridge). During the communist era, unsmiling guards kept the public out of the palace unless they had business inside. Now the doors are wide open and you're free to explore at will.

From here the twin towers of the neo-Gothic **Sts Peter & Paul Church** are visible to the west. Walk towards them along Na Bučance and through the gates of the 17th century **Vyšehrad Citadel**, seat of the 11th century Přemysl princes of Bohemia. You pass the Romanesque **Rotunda of St Martin** before reaching **Slavín Cemetery**, right behind the Sts Peter & Paul Church. Many distinguished people are buried here, including the composers Smetana and Dvořák. The view of the Vltava Valley from the citadel battlements along the south side of the Vyšehrad ridge is superb.

Monday Specials In Prague on a Monday? Most museums and galleries will be closed, but the Prague Jewish Ghetto and the Mozart Museum stay open.

The **Prague Ghetto**, Pařížská 19 (metro: Staroměstská), includes a fascinating variety of monuments, now part of the **Prague Jewish Museum** (closed Saturday). The early Gothic Staronová Synagogue (1270) is one of the oldest in Europe. Tickets are sold in the museum across the lane from the synagogue, beside which is the pink Jewish Town Hall with its picturesque clock tower built in the 16th century. Follow the crowd down U Starého Hřbitova to the Klausen Synagogue (1694) and another section of the museum. You must cover your head to enter the synagogues and the staff will try to sell you an expensive cotton cap. If you don't want it, ask for a free paper cap (or bring a cap of your own).

The collections of the Prague Jewish Museum have a remarkable origin. In 1942 the Nazis brought the objects here from 153 Jewish communities in Bohemia and Moravia for a planned 'museum of an extinct people' to be opened once their extermination programme was completed! The interior of one of the buildings bears the names of 77,297 Czech Jews and the names of the camps where they perished. (On the list are the three sisters of Franz Kafka.)

Behind the Klausen Synagogue is the **Old Jewish Cemetery** with 12,000 tombstones – an evocative sight (separate ticket). The oldest grave is dated 1439, and, by 1787, when the cemetery ceased to be used, the area had became so crowded that burials were carried out one on top of the other as many as 12 layers deep!

If you're into music there's the **Mozart Museum** (open daily) in Villa Bertrámka, Mozartova 169 (metro: Anděl, then west on Plzeňská three blocks and left on Mozartova), where Mozart finished composing *Don Giovanni* in 1787. Czech film maker Miloš Forman's Oscar-winning movie *Amadeus* about the life of Mozart was shot mostly in Prague.

Nearby Palaces The early Baroque **Troya Chateau** (1685), north of the Vltava River, was recently reopened after many years of restoration work. The 17th century frescoes on the ceilings are now fresh and on the chateau walls hangs a fine collection of 19th century painting. This impressive red and white building, surrounded by formal gardens and built for Count Václav Vojtěch of Šternberg, is open from May to October only (closed Monday). On a wooded hillside next to the chateau is Prague's **zoo**, which is open daily. Get there on bus No 112 from Nádraží Holešovice Metro Station.

If the crowds in central Prague begin to get to you and you need a little peace, head for the **Hvězda Summer Palace** (closed Monday) which is in a large forest park west of the city. The Habsburgs built this Renaissance chateau in the 16th century as a summer residence and hunting lodge. The bloody final phase of the decisive Battle of White Mountain took place on the chateau grounds on 6 November 1620. The Catholic victory signified the reimposition of Habsburg rule on would-be Protestant Bohemia and the loss of national independence for exactly 300 years.

Today this place of national defeat functions as a **Museum of Czech Culture** especially dedicated to the novelist Alois Jirásek (ground floor) and the painter Mikoláš Aleš (upstairs). In the chateau basement is an exhibit on the battle. The name Hvězda means 'star' and the ground-floor stucco ceiling of this unique six-pointed building is one of the finest Renaissance artworks north of the Alps, yet the tour groups seldom visit. To get there, take the metro to Dejvická, then tram No 2 or 26 west to the end of the line. As you walk south on Libočka, you'll see the chateau's pointed roof rising out of the forest. Go under the train tracks and turn left. A stairway up into the forest is just beyond the large church.

Parks On a hot summer afternoon an easy escape from the throngs at the tourist sites is to take the funicular railway (one transit ticket) from Újezd up to the rose gardens of **Petřínské Sady**. From April to October you can climb an old iron tower (1891) here for one of the best views of Prague (US$1). A stairway behind the tower leads down into a series of picturesque lanes and back to Malostranské náměsti via Vlašská and Tržiště.

One Last Museum On your last afternoon in Prague, set aside a little time for the **Municipal Museum** (closed Monday), the large white neo-Renaissance building above Florenc Metro Station. Here you'll see maps and photos of the numerous monuments you've visited around town, plus interesting artefacts to put them in perspective. The museum sells a vast selection of postcards made from old photos of Prague. But the museum's crowning glory is a huge scale model of Prague created in 1834. Don't miss it!

Organised Tours Three times a day from April to October the Pražská Informační Služba, Panská 4 (metro: Můstek), organises 2½-hour bus tours of Prague with commentaries in English and German (US$15). The same office arranges personal guides for three-hour walking tours of the city at US$18 for one person, US$29 for two people or US$11 per person for three or more people (available year-round). Guides fluent in all major European languages are available.

Many private companies operating from kiosks along Na příkopě also offer city bus tours for similar prices. These are okay if your time is very short, though reader Anne Small of Tauranga, New Zealand, reported this:

I took a conducted tour of Prague Castle which turned out to be worse than the Vatican in July/August. It was the very worst tourist crush I have ever had. I saw very little because I had to use all of my energy saving my life. A ghastly experience. The guide was capable but was called upon to give the tour in four languages and only on the bus did I hear any of what she had to say. Your recommendation to visit the National Gallery was taken up and I found it a different world from the crush of the conducted tour spots.

The Čedok offices at Bílkova 6, near the Inter-Continental Hotel, at Na Příkopě 18 and at Rytířská 16 arrange bus excursions to historic sites in the environs, such as Karlštejn/Konopiště (US$49), Kutná Hora (US$41) and Karlovy Vary (US$49). Most, but not all, departures are only during the high season (from 15 May to 15 October). The tours are given in English, French and German only.

The Hotel Meran Tourist Office, Václavské náměstí 27, has a four-hour afternoon bus tour to Karlštejn for US$25 and a three-hour Prague city sightseeing tour from Monday to Saturday at 10 am and 1 pm for US$17.

Places to Stay
Camping The *University Sport Club Caravan Camp* (☎ 524 714) is Prague's easiest camping ground since it's right on Plzeňská, west of the city, next to tram lines Nos 4 and 9 (stop: Hotel Golf). They have four triple bungalows at US$15 for the unit but chances are you'll have to camp at US$4 per person and US$3 per tent.

If this camping ground is full walk three minutes back along Plzeňská towards Prague and you'll see a large sign pointing up the hill to the *Sport Camp* (☎ 520 218). Otherwise take tram No 4 or 9 from Anděl Metro Station to the Poštovka stop, then walk a km up the hill. Night tram No 58 passes hourly throughout the night. This site is less convenient if you're on foot as it's a stiff 10-minute climb from the tram stop but it's much larger, quieter and more likely to have space. It's also set on an incline so you may have to look around for a flat site and the airport flight path passes overhead. Camping is US$4 per person, plus US$3 per tent, and they have 60 small bungalows for US$11 double, US$15 triple or US$18 for four persons. The reception is open from 7 am to 9 pm daily. There's a poor restaurant on the premises. Both camping grounds are under the same management, so you can ask about one at the other, and they're open from April until the end of October.

Hostels The HI handbook lists the *CKM Juniorhotel* (☎ 299 941), at Žitná 12 (metro: Karlovo náměstí), as one of Prague's youth hostels, but you're invariably told it's full up with groups for the rest of the month. Trying to make an advance booking by mail is a waste of time and even if you do manage to get a room it will be US$47 double with bath and breakfast (no singles). Despite the listing in the HI handbook there are no discounts here for YHA/HI members.

The CKM Accommodation Service (☎ 205 446), Žitná 12 (open daily 9 am to 6 pm), upstairs in the Juniorhotel building (separate entrance), arranges beds in five-bedded rooms for about US$10 per person. Ask about the *Hotel VZ Praha* (☎ 291 118), Sokolská 33 on nearby Náměstí I P Pavlova, where CKM rents beds in triple rooms at US$11 per person with a YHA card, US$13 per person without a card (compared to US$54 double if you go to this hotel direct). This CKM office may agree to make reservations at Juniorhotels in other cities around the Czech Republic if you know your exact itinerary.

Also listed in the HI handbook is the *Hotel Standart* (☎ 806 751), Přístavní 1, a large six-storey hotel on a quiet street north of the centre. Rooms with shared bath are US$21/25/26 double/triple/quad or US$8 per bed in shared rooms if you have a YHA card. This is excellent value and you actually do have a chance of getting in. It's a 10-

minute walk from Nádraží Holešovice Railway/Metro Station: walk east on Vrbenského to Ortenovo náměstí, then right and south five short blocks on Osadní to the hotel.

If the Standart is full you could check *Pension Vltava*, Dělnická 35, just around the corner. A cheap stand-up buffet is at Dělnická 39.

The *Hotel Pražská Stavební Obnova* (☎ 427 810), Jemnická 4, a 15-minute walk or a five-minute bus ride from Kačerov Metro Station, offers beds in five-bed apartments at US$11 per person. This eight-storey complex is heavily patronised by groups on cheap bus tours from Germany, but individuals are welcome. The entrance is hard to find, hidden as it is in a corner between two eight-storey buildings, but just ask anyone for the 'PSO'. From Kačerov metro take bus No 106, 139 or 182 north to the second stop ('Na rolích'). There's no curfew.

The *Braník Youth Hostel* (☎ 462 641), Vrbova 1233, is a large 10-storey hostel on the south side of Prague. Bus No 197 from Anděl Metro Station and buses Nos 196, 198 and 199 from Smíchovské Nádraží Metro Station pass the hostel. It's US$10 per person, breakfast included, and a youth hostel card is not required.

Farther afield is the *TJ Dolní Měcholupy* (☎ 755 748) at the end of Pod Hřištěm, in a suburb about 10 km east of Prague. Take the metro to Skalka, and then bus No 228 or 229 to Dolnoměcholupská. Dorm beds cost US$7, breakfast is available, it's open all year and is often full. It's a good idea to have the CKM Student Travel Centre, Jindřišská 28 (metro: Hlavní nádraží), book a bed for you here before making the long trip out.

If it's getting late and you still don't have a bed, consider spending the night at the *Turistická Ubytovna TJ Sokol Karlín* (☎ 222 009) on Malého ulice, a five-minute walk from Florenc Bus Station (metro: Florenc). To get there, walk east along Křižíkova ulice past the Karlín Theatre and turn right on Pluku ulice just after the railway bridge. The hostel is just before the next railway bridge. The doors don't open until 6 pm and all you'll get is a dorm bed (US$6), but it sure beats the floor at the train station.

Student Dormitories The easiest place to arrange hostel accommodation on the spot is at the Strahov student dormitory complex opposite Spartakiádní Stadión west of the centre. Buses Nos 143, 149 and 217 run directly there from Dejvická Metro Station.

As you get off the bus you'll see 10 huge blocks of flats. All operate as separate hostels competing for your business and if you make the rounds of the various reception desks you should be able to find something. A bed in a double or triple room with shared bath will be around US$8 per person, otherwise it's US$4 per person in a five to 10-person dorm. A hostel or student card is not required (everyone is welcome). Though the capacity is huge, the whole complex does occasionally get booked out by groups.

In July and August every block will be accepting tourists, while in the off season only the *Estec Hostel* (Block No 5), *Juniorhostel* (Block No 7), *Hostel Spus* (block No 4) and the *Strahov Hostel* (block No 11) will be open. Noisy discos operate from 9 pm to 4 am downstairs in blocks Nos 1, 7 and 11, so those should be your last choices. The receptionist at *Hostel Spus* (☎ 557 498) is helpful and can book better rooms in a teachers' hostel elsewhere in the city at US$10 per person. The travel agencies in the train stations will book beds at Strahov, if you want to be sure of a place before coming but this will add a few dollars to your daily costs. There's a midnight curfew at most of the hostels. (We've received a complaint from a reader who had her backpack stolen from a locked room at Hostel Spus. Be suspicious if the desk clerk tells you it's necessary to change rooms at short notice and lock your bag to the furniture if you can.)

A similar place open from July to September only is *Kolej Kajetánka* (☎ 355 557), Radimova 12, Building 1. Take bus No 108 or 174 west from Hradčanská metro to 'Kajetánka' and look for two tall white towers. If the porter doesn't speak English go to the 'Ubytovací Kancelář' office inside the building. Kolej Kajetánka has 150 rooms at US$11/20 single/double.

Room-Finding Services AVE Limited (☎ 236 2560) at Hlavní nádraží and Holešovice train stations and at Ruzyně Airport rents a variety of private rooms, varying between rooms with shared bath in a distant suburb (from US$13/21 single/double) to rooms with bath in the city centre (from US$28/45 single/double). Private apartments in outer suburbs begin around US$32. AVE gives discounts for longer stays. They also know about hostel accommodation (US$16 per person in double rooms, breakfast included). The AVE branch at Hlavní nádraží is open from 6 am to 10 pm daily.

Vesta Tour at Hlavní nádraží Railway Station has private rooms on the metro line for US$15 per person and Agentura B & B at Nádraží Holešovice Railway Station has both hostel and private accommodations beginning at around US$10 per person.

Universitas Tour (☎ 223 550), Opletalova 32 near Hlavní nádraží Railway Station, arranges stays in university dormitories at US$9 per person in double and triple rooms. Pension accommodation is from US$11 per person. From mid-June to mid-September this office is open on weekends (business hours the rest of the year).

A good bet for a private room is Pragotur (☎ 231 7000), U Obecního domu 2 near the Powder Gate (metro: náměstí Republiky). The staff can arrange private rooms at US$18 per person near the centre, US$15 per person in outlying suburbs, plus a one-time US$2 commission. Pragotur also has hotel and dormitory space. They're open daily from April to December, Monday to Saturday in March, and weekdays only in January and February.

Top Tour (☎ 232 1077), Rybná 3, just a block down from Pragotur, is more expensive. First-category rooms (with private bath) are US$39/59 single/double and 2nd-category rooms (with shared bath) are US$24/39. Apartments are also available (US$66 double, US$95 for four people, US$120 for six people). Rooms are available in the city centre for an additional 10%, and the office is open daily all year until 7 pm.

Stop City Accommodation (☎ 257 840), Vinohradská 24, about six blocks from Hlavní nádraží Railway Station, arranges private rooms in the centre or on a metro line for US$13 to US$28 per person. They're open daily year-round from 11 am to 8 pm and the patient staff speaks perfect English.

You can also rent an unofficial private room from householders on the street looking for hard-currency guests. They'll ask about the same (US$18/35 single/double) as the agencies just listed – bargain if you think the price is too high and check the location on a good map before going. Be absolutely certain that you have understood the price correctly.

Libeň District A number of good places to stay exist in the Libeň district north of the centre. One of the strangest (and best) is *Na Vlachovce Autocamp* (☎ 841 290), Zenklova 217. Despite the name, there's no camping ground here. Instead you sleep in a small bungalow shaped like a Budvar beer keg (no joke!) for US$17 double. The kegs are 'uncorked' from April to October only. Get there on tram No 5, 17 or 25 from Nádraží Holešovice Metro Station to 'Ke Stírce' and walk straight through the folk restaurant here to the hotel reception in the back yard (if the restaurant is closed go around the block to the back gate).

A block from the Na Vlachovce is *Hotel Apollo Garni* (☎ 842 108), Kubišova 23, a modern four-storey hotel with rooms with bath at US$34/48 single/double, breakfast included. Across the street from the Apollo is *Pension Louda* (tariff unknown).

A better deal than these is the *Hotelový dům VS* (☎ 843 894), Střelničná 8, one stop further up the hill on the same trams (take tram No 17 or 25 from Nádraží Holešovice Metro Station to 'Střelničná'). The 60 rooms with shared bath in this new six-storey building are US$18/22 single/double, breakfast US$2 per person extra.

There's a year-round youth hostel in a small sports centre at *TJ Sokol Kobylisy*

Ubytovna (☎ 843 531), U školské zahrady 9, two blocks back behind Hotelový dům VS. The hostel reception is open from 5 pm to 9 pm only.

Hotels There are no longer any cheap hotels in Prague – prices at most of the older hotels in the city centre have increased 400% or more in the past few years. This is partly because foreigners are charged prices 50% to 100% higher than Czechs but it's mostly a result of privatisation and the onslaught on Prague by high-spending German and US tourists. Below we list a few survivors but they too could well have been fixed up and pushed out of sight by the time you get there, so you might consider calling ahead.

If you do find a satisfactory room, book for your entire stay in Prague, otherwise you risk having your stay cut short when you learn that your room has been assigned to someone else. Most Prague hotels charge US$2 extra for a shower if there's not one in the room.

Good for the money is the *Hotel Balkán* (☎ 540 777), Třída Svornosti 28, just two blocks from Anděl Metro Station. Rooms in this attractive old four-storey building are US$20/27 single/double without bath, US$32/37 with bath, breakfast included. The hotel also has a good restaurant and is just a block from the Vltava River.

The only budget hotel in the old town is *Unitas Pension* (☎ 232 7700), Bartolom-ějská 9 (metro: Národní třída). It has 40 dull rooms with shared bath at US$26/31 single/double and a generous breakfast is included. It's a pleasant place to stay but is often fully booked by noisy youth groups.

The five-storey, 65-room *Merkur Hotel* (☎ 231 6951), Těšnov 9, a five-minute walk from Florenc Bus Station, is US$29/47 single/double without bath, US$43/72 with bath, breakfast included. It's usually full of locals and groups who pay a lot less than this, but you can always try for laughs.

The functional six-storey *Hotel Hybernia* (☎ 220 4312), Hybernská 24 (metro: náměstí Republiky), right next to Masary-kova nádraží Railway Station, costs

US\$34/47/63 single/double/triple without bath, US\$63 double with bath, breakfast included. It has little to justify these prices other than location. (At last report the building was for sale, so the Hybernia may be gone before you get there.)

The tacky but friendly *Hotel Juventus* (☎ 255 151), Blanická 10 (metro: náměstí Míru), an older four-storey building, has only rooms with shared bath at US\$29/47 single/double, breakfast included. Because it's a bit off the beaten track it's more likely to have free rooms.

South of the Centre *Pension Pitaz* (☎ 430 441), Na Pankráci 58, a two-minute walk from Pražského povstání Metro Station, has rooms with bath at US\$29/36 single/double. This nondescript, six-storey concrete box is heavily booked by locals who pay much less than this.

Germans on cheap bus tours are the main guests at the *Hotel Zálesí* (☎ 472 1340), Pod višňovkou 21, on the southern side of the city. Get there on bus No 205 from Budějovická Metro Station or on bus No 121 or 196 from Kačerov Metro Station. It's a complex of several six-storey buildings offering rooms with a bath shared between two units at US\$20 double, US\$29 triple. Travel agencies such as CKM and those at Prague train stations book single beds in the double rooms for US\$14 (the hotel reception charges the full double rate to singles who book direct).

Further out on the same metro line is five-room *A V Pension Praha* (☎ 795 2929), Malebná 290, a four-minute walk from Chodov Metro Station. Bed and breakfast is US\$42/63 double/triple in winter or US\$58/89 in summer (no singles). The quality of the accommodation is high.

If a 20-minute metro ride doesn't deter you, consider the 23-storey *Hotel Kupa* (☎ 791 0323), Anežky Hodinové-Spurné 842, very close to Háje Metro Station. When you come out of the station look for the tallest building around. It's US\$28/38/44 single/double/triple, with each two rooms sharing a toilet and shower. The Kupa is

another favorite haunt of the cheap bus tour set and it should be treated only as a last resort.

Motels If you're arriving by car from Plzeň or Nuremberg and don't want to drive into town, consider the two-storey *Stop Motel* (☎ 525 648), Jeremiášova 974, near the exit from the motorway in Stodůlky west of the centre (bus No 164 or 184 from Nové Butovice Metro Station). Rooms with shared bath are about US\$13 per person and there's a restaurant on the premises.

Up-market Hotels The *Grand Hotel Europa* (☎ 262 748), Václavské náměstí 25 (metro: Můstek), is an Art-Nouveau extravaganza, brimming with old-world atmosphere for US\$41/60 single/double without bath and US\$64/85 single/double with bath, breakfast included. Considering the alternatives, this is good value.

Also in the big splurge category is the *Admirál Botel* (☎ 547 445), Hořejší nábřeží, about four blocks from Anděl Metro Station. This gigantic luxury barge permanently moored on the Vltava River has 84 double cabins at US\$60/75 single/double including breakfast. The four four-bed cabins go for US\$100 triple, US\$119 quad. Ask for a room facing the river.

Places to Eat

Tourism has had a heavy impact on the Prague restaurant scene. Cheaper restaurants have been privatised and gone up-market while many low-budget self-services have closed. Almost all the restaurants in the old town, the castle district, and along Václavské náměstí are now highly expensive, and if you're on a low budget it might be worth taking the metro to an outlying station and eating there.

Be aware that the serving staff in some Prague restaurants in the tourist centre shamelessly overcharge foreigners and about the only way to avoid this is to insist on seeing a menu (*jídelní lístek*), even a menu in Czech, to get an idea of the price range. Menus are often posted somewhere but if they're not, and the waiter refuses to show you one listing specific prices, just get up and walk out. By law, all Prague restaurants are required to have proper menus and a refusal to bring you one is a sure sign that a rip-off is intended.

When checking restaurant menus in Prague always have a glance at the price of the beer (*pivo*) as this varies a lot and can cancel your savings on lower meal prices. If the drink prices aren't listed expect them to be sky high (unless, of course, it's only a beer hall). At lunch time the waiter may bring you the more expensive dinner menu. Also beware of places with two menus, one for locals and another for tourists. If you don't get the same menu as is posted outside, just leave.

Even if you do check the menu price, the waiter may claim you were served a larger portion and try to charge you more than is listed. If in doubt, you could go to the extreme of writing down the individual price of each dish as you order, in full sight of the waiter. If you order from a Czech menu try to have some idea of what it is you're ordering, otherwise the waiter may bring you a different, cheaper dish but still charge the higher price of whatever it was you asked for (otherwise just order the cheapest dish). Extras like a side salad, bread and butter are charged extra, so if you're served something you didn't order and don't want, send it back. Many restaurants add a US$0.20 cover charge (*couvert*) to the bill and this is usually not mentioned on the menu. Most restaurants are closed by 9 pm and the service is often slow.

In this book we've tried to weed out the bad apples but we can't guarantee that you won't also be cheated at the restaurants listed herein. You take your choice and take your chances. However, if you're sure you were unfairly treated, let us hear about it and we'll consider dropping the offending establishment from the next edition. Several places have been taken out of this edition or had their listings changed solely on the basis of complaints from readers. (Seen from the other side, many Prague locals are pretty pissed off about the way their favourite haunts have been invaded and taken over by high-spending tourists, so if you stray into a place which is obviously a local hangout, be as polite and unobtrusive as possible.)

Self-Service About the cheapest self-service in the city centre is *Bufet Jídelna* below the high glass dome at the back of the arcade which you enter from Václavské náměstí 38. Cold beer is on tap (closed Sunday).

At *Bonal*, Václavské náměstí 57, right next to the King Wenceslas statue, you can get good coffee, croissants and sandwiches which you consume standing up.

Imbiss Krone, Václavské náměstí 21, offers tasty grilled chicken which you eat standing up. Study the English translation of the menu before you line up.

A more expensive self-service is on the 4th floor at Máj Department Store, Národní and Spálená (metro: Národní třída).

The *Delicatesse Buffet* at the Palace Hotel, opposite the main post office, near the corner of Jindřišská and Panská, has a self-service salad bar. There are tables to sit at.

Near Staroměstské náměstí, the self-service *Bistro* at Kaprova 14 isn't cheap, but you'll fill your stomach without breaking the bank. As always, the sharp, modern décor has a price.

Off Václavské náměstí You'll find the *Česhá Hospoda V Krakovské*, at Krakovská 20 (metro: Muzeum), just around the corner from American Express, offers good food, pleasant décor, fast friendly service and reasonable prices. Their menu in English, German and Italian includes a couple of vegetarian items and dark Braník beer is on tap.

If you're dying for a steak, it's *Americká Restaurant Chicago* in the basement at Štěpánská 63. This isn't just a crass US transplant but it represents the USA as the Czechs see it, which makes it fun. Next door is *Mayür Indický Snack Bar*, Štěpánská 65, with a dozen tasty choices for vegetarians. Don't confuse the snack bar with the more expensive Indian restaurant adjacent.

The rooftop *Rostov Restaurant*, Václavské náměstí 21 (entry from the side), is much less expensive than other similar places around here. The menu is posted downstairs in Czech. Take the lift up to the 7th floor. After 8 pm this locale becomes a disco.

The *Restaurace Na příkopě*, Na příkopě 17 (metro: Můstek), serves typical Czech and Jewish grilled beef at medium prices.

Bistro Slovanský Dům, Na příkopě 22, has a set three-course lunch *(denní menu)* costing about US$2, as advertised on a blackboard and the menu. You can eat in the dining room or on the terrace.

Off Staroměstské náměstí At Celetná 22 is *Restaurace u Supa*, a rather touristy place with a deep dark beer and meals.

One US reader wrote in recommending *Vinárna U Černého Slunce*, Kamzíková 9, in a tiny alley off Celetná between u Supa and the square, as a cosy, romantic (and very up-market) place to eat.

Also try *U Prince*, Staroměstské náměstí 28, near the old town hall. Beer prices on the terrace outside are higher than those charged inside and the menu is limited out there. Don't expect to find many bargain eateries in a tourist area like this.

The *Club-Bar Quê Huong*, Havelská 29, in the Vietnamese Cultural Centre near the Carolinum, is a good change of pace. It's open Monday to Saturday from 11 am to 8 pm and the menu is in English.

South of Staroměstské náměstí off Karlova is *Pivnice U Vejvodů*, Jilská 4, a tavern which an Austrian reader says is dark and inconspicuous but serves good food.

Off Národní třída For Slovak dishes, try the medium-priced garden restaurant at the *Dům Slovenské Kultúry*, Purkyňova 4, right beside Národní třída Metro Station.

U Fleků, Křemencova 11, is a German-style beer garden where you can sit at long communal tables in the back courtyard or in one of the front halls during bad weather. Waiters circulate periodically with mugs of the excellent dark 13° ale that is brewed in-house. Unfortunately in recent years U Fleků has deteriorated into something of a

tourist trap and the food and drink now cost about double what's charged at other beer halls around Prague, so you won't see many Czechs in there. Admission is collected when there's live music. (One reader wrote in to report that the haughty waiters at U Fleků didn't even want to serve him because they figured he wasn't going to spend a lot of money. Another urged us to warn travellers not to go there.)

If you don't like the atmosphere at U Fleků, check *Snack Bar Rytmus*, Křemencova 10, just across the street. Their inexpensive menu in English includes a few Chinese dishes and the waiters are friendly, though of course, there's not the setting of U Fleků.

The *U Kotvy Garden Restaurant*, Spálená 11, is similar to U Fleků but cheaper and thus more local.

Hostinec u Rotundy, Karolíny Světlé 17, is probably the cheapest pub in the old town (no meals are served).

Malá Strana *Grand Restaurant*, Karmelitská 20, has gone up-market and now posts its menu outside in English and German. It's good for grilled meats. Many slightly up-market tourist restaurants are on the side of Malostanské náměstí closest to Karlův most, including *Jo's Bar* at No 7 with Mexican food.

U Svatého Tomáše, Letenská 12 (metro: Malostranská), is a former beer hall which has evolved into a tourist restaurant. During the day the long tables down in the cellar will be full up with groups, so go out onto the back terrace (in summer) or up into the main dining room (in winter). At night head downstairs. The menu lists Bohemian specialties but the 12° Braník beer on tap has a better reputation than the food. (One reader commented: 'Nobody goes to U Svatého Tomáše except busloads of pitiful tourists who are dropped there by their guides and have no choice'.)

Hradčany Big mugs of draught beer and basic meals can be had at *U Černého Vola*,

Loretánské náměstí 1, just up from the Loreta Convent.

The up-market *Café Na Baště* (closed Monday), just inside Prague Castle to the left, serves decent meals but terrible coffee. The *Vikárka Restaurant* is right next to St Vitus Cathedral. At *Bonal* in a corner of Golden Lane you can get self-service coffee and croissants.

You'll see many other touristy restaurants up this way with prices as high as Hradčany itself. If you're on a tight budget have something filling to eat just before heading up this way.

Around Town *U Kalicha Restaurant*, Na bojišti 12 (metro: I P Pavlova), serves traditional Czech meals and big mugs of beer; it's open daily from 11 am to 3 pm and from 5 to 11 pm. Menus in English and German are available. This place featured in the novel *The Good Soldier Švejk* and it's a little expensive but still good for a splurge.

The *Snack Bar* on the ground floor in the Palace of Culture (metro: Vyšehrad) is fine for ice cream, a glass of wine or a pork chop and a beer (menu in English and German).

Restaurace Dejvická Sokolovna, Dejvická 2, just outside Hradčanská Metro Station, serves cheap pub lunches in the rear dining room. Be prepared to choose at random from the Czech menu.

Cafés The café of the *Grand Hotel Europa*, Václavské náměstí 25, is Prague's most elegant (but come before 3 pm when they start collecting a cover charge).

Kavárna Luxor, upstairs at Václavské náměstí 41, is less unpretentious but check the menu before ordering. From 9 pm to 4 am there's a disco here.

The Art-Deco *Kavárna Slávie*, at Národní 1 (metro: Národní třída), right opposite the National Theatre, has been a meeting place of the city's elite for decades.

Entertainment

Unfortunately, you'll only be able to enjoy Prague's many theatrical and musical offerings if you're prepared to spend a considerable amount of money. Official ticket prices are still low but all the best shows are sold out weeks ahead. Large blocks of tickets are reserved months in advance by travel agencies and most of the rest are snapped up by scalpers who resell them to foreigners for hard currency. When making the rounds of theatre box offices, look for the *vyprodáno* (sold out) notices before trying to figure out what's on.

The regular price for the best opera tickets is only about US$10 but you'll be forced to pay at least twice that for seats farther back. You'll probably be approached at the ticket office by a slightly nervous person with just the ticket you want, asking about three times the price printed on it. Sometimes the scalpers end up with more black tickets than they can resell, giving you the opportunity to bargain for a lower price at the door just before the performance. The travel agencies too often send someone to the theatre to sell excess or returned tickets just prior to the performance. Even the theatre ticket clerks themselves sometimes hold back choice tickets which they later sell under the counter at a premium to supplement their incomes.

If this situation annoys you, save your theatre-going until you get to Poland, Slovakia or Hungary where tickets to musical programmes of comparable quality go for about a third the price you'd pay in Prague. In Brno theatre tickets are also much more easily obtained for normal prices and the productions are equally as good.

Another good alternative to the expensive and/or frustrating theatres of Prague is to go to a movie. Cinema tickets are only US$1 and most films are shown in the original language with Czech subtitles. *Prognosis* and *The Prague Post* carry complete listings of what's on with times and cinema addresses.

Lots of organ concerts in old churches and recitals in historic buildings are put on for tourists and you'll see stacks of fliers advertising these in every tourist office or travel agency around Prague. Seats begin around US$8 but the programmes change from week to week so it's hard to give any specific recommendations.

Ticket Agencies A number of travel agencies specialise in selling theatre tickets for about the same price as the scalpers. The largest tourist ticket agency of this kind is the Hotel Meran Tourist Office, Václavské náměstí 27, a good place to begin as what's available is clearly displayed on a board behind the counter and the English-speaking staff is forthcoming with suggestions and advice. They often have tickets for the Laterna Magika (US$19), opera (US$19), National Theatre (US$21) and marionette theatre (US$14). Folklore shows by the Czech Song and Dance Ensemble are US$9. Also known as Bohemia Ticket International or simply BTI, this company has other offices at Na příkopě 16 and Karlova 8.

Even BTI may not have any tickets left for the National Theatre, State Opera, Stavovské Theatre and Laterna Magika, but you can make advance reservations through Bohemia Ticket International (☎ 231 2030; fax 231 2271), Salvátorská 6, Praha 1. Laterna Magika tickets should be ordered at least two months in advance.

Other main tourist ticket agencies include Čedok, Rytířská 16; American Express, Václavské náměstí 50; the Prague Information Service, Na příkopě 20; and Pragotur, Obecního domu 23. Čedok, Na příkopě 18, usually has tickets to the opera (US$14), marionette theatre (US$14), folklore show (US$9) and 'Bohemian Fantasy' (US$34 for the show only or US$50 with dinner). Čedok, Bílkova 6, sometimes has tickets for the State Opera (US$22) and other events, all for hard currency.

A ticket office for Czechs rather than tourists is Melantrich in the arcade at Václavské náměstí 38 and what they offer is advertised on posters. Don't expect them to speak English. Instead, just write down the date for which you need a ticket using a Roman numeral for the month and keep repeating the word 'music'. They often have tickets to rock concerts

Concert tickets are available from the FOK Symfonický Orchestr office on U Prašné brány right between the Powder Gate and Pragotur (metro: náměstí Republiky). They should have something (open weekdays 9 am to 5 pm).

Theatres Opera, ballet and classical drama (in Czech) are performed at the neo-Renaissance *National Theatre* (1883), Národní 2 (metro: Národní třída). Next door is the ultramodern *Laterna Magika* (1983), Národní 4, which offers a widely imitated combination of theatre, dance and film. Regular tickets, however, are usually sold out two months in advance.

Opera and ballet are also presented at the neo-Renaissance *State Opera* on Wilsonova (metro: Muzeum). The State Opera is much smaller than the National Theatre so you get better views from the balconies. Tickets are occasionally available and only opera and ballet are presented, so take anything you can get.

The neoclassical *Stavovské Theatre* (1783), Železná 11 (metro: Můstek), often presents opera, but be prepared to pay US$35 for a seat downstairs, US$15 for a place on an upper balcony. Headphones providing simultaneous translation into English are available for some Czech plays.

The ticket offices for the Laterna Magika and National Theatre (Národní Divadlo) are both just inside the Laterna Magika. The State Opera and Stavovské Theatre have their own ticket offices at the theatres, but all four are usually sold out weeks ahead. Evening performances begin at 7 pm, weekend matinees at 2 pm. Get there half an hour early and stand outside holding a small sign reading *hledám lístek* (I'm looking for a ticket) as someone may have an extra ticket for a companion who didn't show up which they'd be happy to unload at face value.

For operettas and musicals go to the *Karlín Theatre of Music*, Křižíkova 10, near Florenc Bus Station (metro: Florenc). Because it's a little out of the way and not as famous, tickets are often available – highly recommended. The ticket office is open

Monday to Saturday from 10 am to 1 pm and 2 to 6 pm.

A take-off of the Laterna Magika is the *Laterna Animata* in the Exhibition Grounds (metro: Holešovice) with a vertical film projected onto a parabolic stage. Tickets (US$22) are available at all the tourist ticket agencies. Several other theatres around town stage similar unspoken 'black theatre' or 'magic theatre' performances combining mime, film, dance, music or whatever. Admission to some is as low as US$8.

Plays in the Czech language by Václav Havel are often put on at the *Zábradlí Theatre*, Amenské náměstí 5 (metro: Staroměstská).

Concert Halls Prague's main concert venue is the neo-Renaissance *Dvořák Hall*, náměstí Jana Palacha (metro: Staroměstská), where the Prague Spring Music Festival is held in late May.

Prague's wonderful Art-Nouveau municipal concert hall, *Smetana Hall* or 'Obecního domu', náměstí Republiky 5, right next to the Powder Gate, is not used that often but when it is, tickets are available from FOK, which is around the corner, or at the box office inside, an hour before the performance.

Also check the *Palace of Culture* (metro: Vyšehrad) for events. Concerts are held there regularly and tickets are usually available at the box office.

Puppet Theatres The *Divadlo Minor*, Senovážné náměstí 28 (metro: náměstí Republiky), offers a mix of puppets and pantomime which is great fun, but sit in the back row if the place is full of school groups. Performances are at 9 am on weekdays and you can usually get a ticket (US$6) at the door just before the show.

A puppet theatre strictly for tourists is the so-called *National Marionette Theatre* or 'Říše loutek', Žatecká 1 (metro: Staroměstská). In midsummer there are evening performances twice daily, while in midwinter they're usually on Tuesday and Thursday.

Notices in the entrance hall tell what's on and tickets (US$13) are available at the door.

Jazz Clubs For jazz, try the *Reduta Jazz Club*, Národní 20 (metro: Národní třída). Founded in 1958, this is one of the oldest jazz clubs in Europe. It opens at 9 pm with music from 9.30 pm to midnight (US$3 cover charge). Tickets are sold after 3 pm on weekdays or after 5 pm on Saturday.

There's also the *Press Jazz Club*, upstairs at Pařížská 9 (open from 9 pm to 5 am nightly).

You can see and hear live jazz every night from 9 pm to midnight at the unpretentious *Agha RTA Jazz Centrum*, Krakovská 5 (metro: Muzeum).

Discos & Rock Clubs *Disco Carioca*, downstairs from the passage at Václavské náměstí 4 (metro: Můstek), is open from 9 pm to 5 am. Drinks cost normal prices. Nearby, out the back of the passage and to the left, is *Disco Barbara*, Jungmannovo náměstí 14 (daily 8 pm to 5 am).

Adjacent to the Reduta Jazz Club is the *Rock Cafe*, Národní 20, with a music shop selling punk T-shirts, skull & crossbones necklaces and rings etc. From 8 pm to 3 am there's hard rock music here (US$2 cover, normal drink prices). Wear black clothing if you can. *Club Exodus*, downstairs at Národní 25, offers disco dancing to a different style of music every night from 9 pm to 4 am. If you're looking for reggae or central African pop, try here.

One of Prague's best venues is *Rock Club Borát*, Újezd 18 at Vítězná (open from 8 pm daily except Monday) with a varied clientele. Also recommended is *Rock Club Bunkr*, Lodecká 2 (metro: Florenc), which attracts a younger crowd.

Rock Bar Uzi, Legerova 44, a block and a half south of I P Pavlova Metro Station, has disco dancing from 9 pm to 5 am (US$1 cover).

Malá Strana *Malostranská Beseda*, Malostranské náměstí 21 (metro: Malostranská), presents jazz, folk, country, rock music, rock

CZECH REPUBLIC

opera and so on nightly in their theatre-café. Most programmes begin at 8 pm.

Night Clubs The *Revue Alhambra Night Club* (open Tuesday to Sunday from 8.30 pm to 3 am) at the Ambassador Hotel, Václavské náměstí 5 (metro: Můstek), presents a Las Vegas-style floorshow nightly at 10.30 pm (US$18 per person minimum consumption and table charge). You can dance there before and after the show. Reservations should be made at the hotel reception.

A less touristy nightclub is the *Varieté Praha*, Vodičkova 30 just off Václavské náměstí, which has a two-hour floor show daily except Monday at 9.30 pm, then dancing from 11.30 pm to 2 am (US$9 cover charge for the best seats or US$5 near the back).

You'll see ads around town for the 'Bohemian Fantasy' extravaganza at *Palac Lucerna*, Štěpánská 61 off Václavské náměstí. This costs US$50 per person with dinner or US$34 per person for the show only (includes two drinks). It all happens four times a week from May to October and any theatrical ticket agency will have tickets.

Free Entertainment In the evening you can stroll along Na příkopě, where buskers play for the throng, or Václavské náměstí, where fast-food outlets, cinemas and night bars stay open till late. Můstek is thick with black-market hustlers after dark. The floodlit Staroměstské náměstí and the Karlův most are other magical attractions of nocturnal Prague.

Things to Buy
You'll find many interesting shops along Celetná, between Staroměstské náměstí and náměstí Republiky. The Kotva Department Store on náměstí Republiky is the largest in the country. There's also the Máj Department Store, Národní and Spálená (metro: Národní třída).

For Bohemian crystal check the two Sklo Glass shops in the Alfa Cinema Arcade, Václavské náměstí 28.

Getting There & Away

Air ČSA Czechoslovak Airlines (☎ 231 7395), Revoluční 25 (metro: náměstí Republiky), books daily flights from Prague to Bratislava (US$66), Poprad-Tatry (US$77) and Košice (US$87).

Bus Buses to Karlovy Vary (122 km), Brno (210 km, 2½ hours) and most other towns in the Czech Republic depart from the Florenc Bus Station, Křižíkova 4 (metro: Florenc). Seven express buses a day cover the 321 km from Florenc to Bratislava in 4½ hours (as compared to 5½ hours on the train). Reservations are recommended on all these services.

Most (but not all) international buses to Western Europe also arrive/depart Florenc Bus Station (for tickets, see Travel Agencies near the beginning of this section).

The left-luggage room at Florenc Bus Station is upstairs above the information office (daily 5 am to 11 pm).

Tickets Reservations at Prague's Florenc Bus Station are computerised. To obtain a ticket, first determine the departure time *(odjezdy)* of your bus by looking at the posted timetable beside platform No 1 or asking at the information counter. Then get in line at any of the ticket counters. Make sure that your bus isn't on the sold-out *(vyprodáno)* list on the TV screens here. If it is, pick another bus. The further ahead you book, the better your chances of getting the bus you want and reservations are possible 10 days in advance. Your bus ticket indicates the platform number *(stání)* and seat number *(sed)*. You may be charged extra for baggage. The coaches are quite comfortable (no standing) and fares are reasonable.

Tickets for private Cebus express buses to Karlovy Vary, Brno and some other points are not sold in the main station but at a kiosk on the pavement between the bus station and Florenc Metro Station.

Train Trains run from Berlin-Lichtenberg to Prague (386 km, seven hours) via Dresden every three or four hours. Several of the

CZECH REPUBLIC

rains arriving from Berlin continue on to Vienna. There's a service twice a day from Nuremberg (372 km, 6½ hours) via Cheb and twice daily from Linz, Austria (294 km, 5½ hours) via České Budějovice. Many rains arrive from Budapest (630 km, 10 hours) via Brno and Bratislava. From Poland you have the choice of arriving via Wrocław or Katowice. See Getting There & Away in the chapter introduction for more information.

From Praha-Holešovice and Hlavní nádraží, sleepers and couchettes are available on the nightly *Krušnohor* express train to Bratislava, Žilina, Poprad-Tatry and Košice. This is an excellent way to save one night's accommodation expenses while getting somewhere. A 1st-class sleeper from Prague to Bratislava will be US$11 including the ticket.

Train Stations Prague has four main train stations. International trains between Berlin and Budapest often stop at Praha-Holešovice Railway Station (metro: Nádraží Holešovice) on the north side of the city. Other important trains terminate at Praha-Hlavní nádraží (metro: Hlavní nádraží) or Masarykovo nádraží (metro: náměstí Republiky), both of which are close to the city centre. Some local trains to the south-west depart from Praha-Smíchov Railway Station (metro: Smíchovské nádraží).

Hlavní nádraží handles trains to Benešov (49 km, one hour), České Budějovice (169 km, 2½ hours), Cheb via Plzeň (220 km, four hours), Karlovy Vary via Chomutov (199 km, four hours), Košice (708 km, 10 hours), Mariánské Lázně (190 km, three hours), Plzeň (114 km, two hours) and Tábor (103 km, 1½ hours). Trains to Brno (257 km, 3½ hours) and Bratislava (398 km, 5½ hours) may leave from either Hlavní nádraží, Praha-Holešovice or Masarykovo nádraží. This is confusing, so carefully study the timetables posted in one of the stations to determine which one you'll be using, then confirm the time and station at the information counter or at Čedok. To go to Kutná

Hora (73 km, 1½ hours) you may use Praha-Holešovice or, more frequently, Masarykovo nádraží. Karlštejn trains always depart from Praha-Smíchov.

Hlavní nádraží is Prague's largest train station with several exchange offices and accommodation services upstairs, and a tourist-information booth downstairs. The self-service and full-service restaurants on the top floor are not exciting but they're better than the various fast-food outlets on the main floor. The 24-hour left-luggage office is in the basement, so drop your bags off upon arrival and stroll into town to look for a room or a meal (you pay the left-luggage fee when you pick the bags up). International tickets are sold at window No 26 upstairs while international couchettes and seat reservations are purchased at the office with yellow signs downstairs near the metro entrance. Couchettes to Slovakia (Bratislava and Košice) are sold at windows No 16 to 24 downstairs.

At Holešovice Station, window No 1 is for booking couchettes. There are currency exchange facilities in all these stations but high commissions are charged.

Getting Around
To/From the Airport Ruzyně Airport is 17 km west of the city centre. Every half-hour from 6 am to 6.30 pm daily an airport bus (under US$1) departs from the ČSA office, Revoluční 25 (metro: náměstí Republiky). Buy your ticket from the driver. There's a left-luggage office in this terminal open from 6 am to 6 pm. You can also reach the airport on city bus No 119 from Dejvická Metro Station (last bus at 11 pm).

Public Transport All public transport in Prague costs the same flat fare. Tickets (US$0.20) valid on trams, city buses and the metro are sold by automats at the entrance to all metro stations or at newspaper kiosks. Buy a good supply whenever you have the chance, then validate your ticket as you enter the vehicle or metro. For large luggage you must cancel one additional half-price ticket.

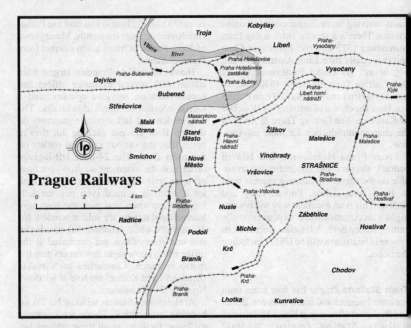

Prague Railways

Troja

Kobylisy

Libeň

Praha-Vysočany

Vltava River

Praha-Bubeneč

Dejvice

Praha-Holešovice

Praha-Holešovice zastávka

Praha-Bubny

Vysočany

Praha-Kyje

Bubeneč

Praha-Libeň horní nádraží

Střešovice

Masarykovo nádraží

Žižkov

Malá Strana

Staré Město

Praha-Hlavní nádraží

Malešice

Praha-Malešice

Smíchov

Nové Město

Vinohrady

STRAŠNICE

Vršovice

Praha-Strašnice

Praha-Hostivař

Praha-Smíchov

Praha-Vršovice

Nusle

Radlice

Michle

Zábĕhlice

Hostivař

Podolí

Krč

Braník

Praha-Krč

Chodov

Praha-Braník

Lhotka

Kunratice

0   2   4 km

Once validated, tickets are valid for 60 minutes. A cancelled ticket allows you to change from one metro line to another, but not from the metro to a tram or bus.

Being caught 'black' without a ticket entails a US$8 fine. Inspectors will often demand a higher fine from foreigners and pocket the difference, so insist on a receipt (*potvrzení*) before paying.

Tourist tickets (Turistická Jítová Jízdenka) valid on all forms of public transport are sold for periods of one (US$1), two (US$1.75), three (US$2.50), four (US$3) or five (US$3.50) days. These tickets are usually available at Pragotur, U Obecního domu 2, and Čedok, Na příkopě 18. One place where you can always get these passes is the Centrální Dispečink Městské Dopravy, Na bojišti 5 (metro: I P Pavlova), open weekdays from 6.30 to 6 pm, Saturday 7 am to 1 pm. Compare the price of a monthly pass (*měsíční jízdenka*) if you're staying over a week.

Pragotur, U Obecního domu 2, and Čedok, Na příkopě 18, sell a 'Prague Card' valid for three days use of the public transportation system and admission to 36 museums and sights for US$13. A booklet explaining exactly what you get comes with the card.

Underground The first line of the Prague Metro, built by the communists with Soviet assistance, opened on 9 May 1974. The metro operates from 5 am to midnight with three lines connecting all bus and train stations, as well as many tourist attractions. Don't get into the rear carriage, as station names are poorly displayed. In general, though, using the metro is easy and the recorded announcements are strangely reassuring.

Line A runs from the north-west side of the city at Dejvická to the east at Skalka; line B runs from the south-west at Nové Butovice to the north-east at Českomoravská; line C

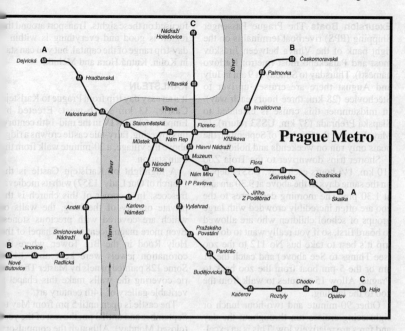

Prague Metro

uns from the north at Nádraží Holešovice to he south-east at Háje. Line A intersects line C at Muzeum; line B intersects line C at Florenc; line A intersects line B at Můstek.

A monitor at the end of the platforms tells ow long it has been since the last train went hrough. The way out is marked *výstup*.

After the metro closes down at midnight, lue-numbered night trams still rumble cross the city about every 40 minutes all ight. If you're planning a late evening find ut if one of these services passes anywhere ear where you're staying as taxis can be a ip-off late at night.

Car Rental Pragocar (☎ 222 324), Opletalova 33, is directly across the park in ront of Hlavní nádraží Railway Station. Europcar (☎ 231 3405), Pařížská 28, and Avis Rent-a-Car (☎ 231 7865), Elišky Krásnohorské 9, are both near the Inter-Continental Hotel (metro: Staroměstská). Budget has a desk inside the Inter-Continen-

tal itself. Most Čedok offices also rent cars at competitive rates. Avis, Budget, Hertz and Europcar all have offices at Ruzyně Airport but you'll be charged a US$11 surcharge if you use them.

If you're sure you want a car, you should book well in advance as they're often all taken in summer. Turn to Car Rental in the chapter introduction for sample rates.

Taxi Taxis are reasonable, but only if the meter is turned on. If the driver won't turn on the meter, clearly establish the price before you set out, otherwise you'll end up paying far more than normal. Only four passengers are allowed in a taxi.

Avoid taking taxis from Václavské náměstí or luxury hotels as these are much more expensive. If you feel you're being overcharged ask for a bill *(účet)* which the driver is obliged to provide.

Public transport is so good in Prague that taking a taxi is really a luxury.

CZECH REPUBLIC

Excursion Boats The Prague Passenger Shipping (PPS) riverboat terminal is on the right bank of the Vltava between Jiráskův most and Palackého most (metro: Karlovo náměstí). Thursday to Sunday at 9 am in July and August there are cruises upriver to Štěchovice (28 km, three hours each way). In midsummer this cruise is extended to Slapská Přehrada (37 km, US$3 return). In May, June and the first half of September, the boats only run on weekends and holidays.

Shorter trips downriver to the Troja Zoo (10 km, 1¼ hours each way, US$1) depart on the same days as the above at 9.30 am and at 1.30 pm. The morning departures to the zoo are often incredibly crowded with large groups of school children who are allowed to board first, so if you really want to do this trip it's best to take bus No 112 to the zoo (see Things to See above) and catch the 11 am or the 5 pm boat from the zoo back to Prague. Allow 15 minutes to walk from the zoo to the landing.

Other 90-minute and two-hour lunch or sightseeing cruises run throughout the day and fares are relatively low. This is an excellent alternative to signing up for an expensive bus tour to sights you can easily visit on your own.

The excursion boats of the Evropská Vodní Doprava (EVD) which leave from a landing behind the Inter-Continental Hotel are double or triple the price of the PPS boats.

You can row yourself up and down the Vltava in a boat rented from several places along the river (including Slovanský Island) for US$2 an hour.

Central Bohemia

Though dominated by Prague, Central Bohemia has much more to offer. Historic castles and chateaux rise out of the forests at Český Šternberk, Dobříš, Karlštejn, Kokořín, Konopiště, Křivoklát, Mělník, Žleby and elsewhere, while Kutná Hora is a lovely medieval town. Tourism is sharply focused on these sights. Transport around the region is good and everything is within day-trip range of the capital, but you can stay in Kolín, Kutná Hora and Mělník.

KARLŠTEJN

It's an easy day trip from Prague to Karlštejn Castle, 33 km south-west. Erected b Emperor Charles IV in the mid-14th century this towering, fairy-tale castle crowns a ridge above the village, a 20-minute walk from the train station.

A highlight of Karlštejn Castle is the Church of Our Lady (1357) with its medieval frescoes. In a corner of this church is the private oratory of the king, the walls of which are covered with precious stones Even more magnificent is the Chapel of the Holy Rood in the Big Tower, where the coronation jewels were kept until 1420 Some 128 painted panels by Master Theodoric covering the walls make this chapel a veritable gallery of 14th century art.

The castle is open until 5 pm from May to September and until 3 pm the rest of the year (closed Monday). Although the compulsory guided tours (US$4, students US$2) are usually in Czech, there are explanations in English posted in each room. More expensive tours in English are given five times a day. (Unfortunately, the most interesting parts of the castle have been closed for restoration for many years with no end in sight.

The Bohemian crystal shops around Karlštejn are less expensive than those in Prague.

Getting There & Away
Trains leave for Karlštejn about once an hour from Praha-Smíchov Railway Station (45 minutes).

KONOPIŠTĚ

Konopiště Castle, two km west of Benešov Railway Station, is 50 km south of Prague midway between Prague and Tábor. The castle dates back to the 14th century, but the Renaissance palace it shelters is from the 17th century. The whole complex overlooks a peaceful lake surrounded by a large forest

CZECH REPUBLIC

Archduke Franz Ferdinand d'Este, heir to the Austro-Hungarian throne, had Konopiště renovated in 1894 and added a large English park and rose garden. During six days of secret meetings here beginning on 11 June 1914, Archduke Ferdinand and Kaiser Wilhelm II of Germany tried to establish a common strategy for the impending world war. Ferdinand's huge collection of hunting trophies and weapons on display at the castle will shock animal rights activists. On 28 June 1914 the hunter, however, became the hunted and his assassination at Sarajevo touched off the very war the gentlemen had discussed. (In fairness it should be noted that Ferdinand was against military action.)

Konopiště Castle is open from April to October (closed Monday, admission US$2) but you must arrive by 2 pm if you want to see both the state chambers and the palace collections. The castle may only be visited with a boring Czech-speaking guide, so ask for the typed summary in English. Huge tour groups are led through the castle one after another.

Getting There & Away

Local trains leave Prague's Hlavní nádraží for Benešov (49 km, one hour) about once an hour. Most trains to/from Tábor (54 km, one hour) and České Budějovice (120 km, two hours) also stop here. There are occasional buses from Benešov Railway Station to the castle.

KUTNÁ HORA

In the 14th century, Kutná Hora, 66 km east of Prague, was the second-largest town in Bohemia after Prague. This was due to the rich veins of silver below the town itself and the silver *groschen* minted here was the hard currency of central Europe at the time. During the 16th century, Kutná Hora's boom burst and mining ceased in 1726, so the medieval townscape has come down to us basically unaltered.

If you're planning a day trip from Prague be aware that all of Kutná Hora's museums are closed on Monday and buses are irregular on weekends, so Tuesday to Friday are the best days to come. A better idea, however, is to make Kutná Hora a stopover on your way to/from Slovakia or Brno. There's ample low-budget accommodation and it's always much nicer to see things at a relaxed pace.

Orientation

The main train station is three km east of the centre whereas the bus station is more conveniently located just on the north-eastern edge of the old town.

The easiest way to visit Kutná Hora on a day trip is to arrive on the morning express train from Prague's Masarykovo nádraží, then take a 10-minute walk from Kutná Hora hlavni nadraží Railway Station to Sedlec to visit the ossuary (see the Things to See section that follows). From there it's another 15-minute walk or a five-minute bus ride to old Kutná Hora.

Things to See

At Sedlec, only a km from the train station on the way into town (turn right when you see a huge church), is a cemetery with a Gothic **ossuary** *(kostnice)* decorated with the bones of some 40,000 people. In 1870 František Rint, a local woodcarver, arranged the bones in the form of bells, a chandelier, monstrances and even the Schwarzenberg coat-of-arms – a truly macabre sight (US$1).

Continue two km south-west along Masarykova. As you enter the old town on Na Náměsti you'll see the Gothic **Church of Our Lady** on the left. Keep straight and turn left on Tylova which will take you up into Palackého náměstí, a quaint square created when the Gothic town hall was demolished after a fire in 1770.

From the upper end of Palackého náměstí a lane to the left leads directly to the tall tilting tower of the **St James Church** (1330), just past which is the Gothic Royal Mint, **Vlašský dvůr** or Italian Court, now occupied by city offices but still accessible through an entrance around the corner. Master craftsmen from Florence began stamping silver coins here in 1300.

From the front entrance to St James a series of cobbled, signposted streets slope

CZECH REPUBLIC

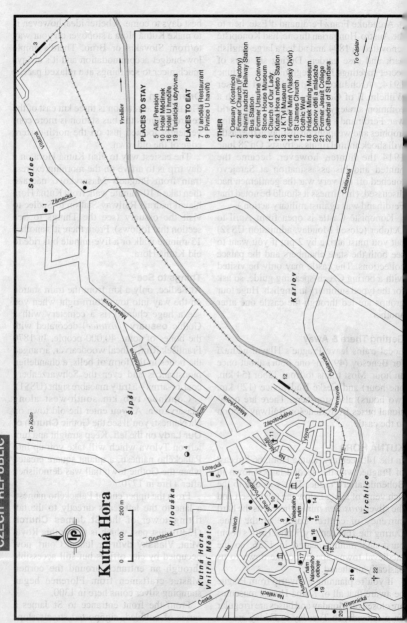

Kutná Hora

PLACES TO STAY

5 Alkr Pension
10 Hotel Mědínek
16 Hotel U hrnčíře
19 Turistická ubytovna

PLACES TO EAT

7 U anděla Restaurant
9 Pivnice U havířů

OTHER

1 Ossuary (Kostnice)
2 Former Church (Factory)
3 hlavní nadraží Railway Station
4 Bus Station
6 Former Ursuline Convent
8 Stone House Museum
11 Church of Our Lady
12 Kutná Hora město Station
13 J K Tyl Museum
14 Former Mint (Vlašský Dvůr)
15 St James Church
17 Gothic Well
18 Hrádek Mining Museum
20 Domov dětí a mládeže
21 Former Jesuit College
22 Cathedral of St Barbara

0   100   200 m

To Čáslav

Sedlec

Vrchlice

Vlašlice

Zámecká

Karlov

Masarykova

Čáslavská

To Kolín

Barborská

Šipší

Školní

Švermova

Lorecká

Zápotockého

Masarykova

Na valech

Tylova

Uhelný trh

UHLÍŘ z Nouře

Palackého nám

Vladislavova

Husova

Národního odboje

Kutná Hora
Vnitřní Město

Česká

Gruntecká

Hlouška

Kremnická

Vrchlice

down and up to the **Hrádek Mining Museum** (closed from November to March). This 15th century palace contains an exhibit on the mining that made Kutná Hora wealthy. Note especially the huge wooden device used in the Middle Ages to lift up to 1000 kg at a time from shafts that were 200 metres deep. This museum's main attraction, however, is the 45-minute guided tour through 500 metres of **medieval mine shafts** on one of the 20 levels below Kutná Hora. You don a white coat and helmet, and pick up a miner's lamp, but the tour (US$1.25) only begins when a group of at least five people gathers. This is usually no problem in midsummer or on weekends, but in early spring and late autumn you may have to wait around.

Just beyond the Hrádek is the 17th century former **Jesuit college** which has Baroque sculpture in front of it and a good view of the Vrchlice River Valley from the promenade. Nearby is Kutná Hora's greatest monument, the **Cathedral of St Barbara** (US$1), begun in 1388 by Petr Parléř, the architect of St Vitus Cathedral in Prague, and finished in 1547. The exquisite net vault above the central nave is supported by double flying buttresses in the French high-Gothic style.

From St Barbara retrace your steps past the Jesuit College and the Hrádek and keep straight on Barborská till it ends at Komenského náměstí. Turn left, then right, and right again down Husova two blocks till you see a Baroque **plague column** on the left. Walk up the street behind the column till you see an old building with a high triangular gable bearing figures of knights jousting, across the parking lot on the left. This is the **Stone House** (1485), Václavské náměstí 24, now the local historical museum.

Walk north-east down Václavské náměstí, which becomes Jiřího z Poděbrad, to the former **Ursuline convent** (1743) at No 13 on the left, which houses an exhibition of antiques. The bus station is straight ahead and down Lorecká to the left.

Places to Stay
Hostels Kutná Hora has no less than three hostels, all within a few minutes of each other.

A friendly, welcoming place to stay is the *U rytířů Hostel* (☎ 22 56), Rejskovo náměstí 123, just off Husova across the street from the large Gothic well in the middle of the road. The 20 rooms vary in price but average around US$7 per person. Most rooms are doubles with private bath.

Kutná Hora's official HI youth hostel is the *Domov dětí a mládeže*, conveniently located at Kremnická 8 just west of the old town. If it's closed or full, check out *Prifis Pension*, Kremnická 5, just across the street.

At a pinch you could also try the *Turistická ubytovna* (☎ 34 63), Smíškovo náměstí 56, a basic dormitory with a reception which opens only from 8 to 9 am and 5 to 6 pm.

Hotels The *Hotel Mědínek* (☎ 27 41), a modern four-storey hotel on Palackého náměstí, costs US$18/22 single/double without bath, US$29/43 with bath, breakfast included.

A better choice for a room in Kutná Hora is the *Hotel U hrnčíře* (☎ 21 13), Barborská 24, just down the street from the Hrádek. The five rooms in this quaint privately owned inn go for US$13 per person including breakfast, and they're often fully booked, so be sure to call ahead (the person answering the phone is more likely to speak German than English, an indication of who usually stays here). Even if you don't stay here, the U hrnčíře is an excellent place for a genteel lunch which is served in their garden in summer.

Alkr Pension, Lorecká 7, right near the bus station, has comfortable rooms with private bath and a small kitchenette costing US$15/18/29 single/double/triple.

Places to Eat
U anděla, náměstí Václavské 8, is a decent place to eat. In front of the plague column nearby is *Pivnice U havířů* (closed Monday), a local beer hall where inexpensive meals are served, with a more sedate *vinárna* at the back.

Getting There & Away

Kutná Hora is on the main railway line between Prague and Brno via Havlíčkův Brod although many express trains don't stop here (you may have to change at Kolín). Trains arrive from Prague's Masarykovo nádraží (73 km, 1½ hours) via Kolín every couple of hours.

The trains from Prague stop at Kutná Hora hlavní nádraží, about three km east of the centre. About 10 trains a day (on a branch line to Zruč nad Sázavou) link Kutná Hora hlavní nádraží to Kutná Hora město Station which is adjacent to the old town.

Weekdays there are about six express buses to Prague (70 km) but far fewer buses operate on weekends. If your timing doesn't coincide with a bus direct to Prague, take one to Kolín (12 km) where there are better connections to Prague. At Kutná Hora Bus Station, buses to Prague leave from stand No 6, to Kolín from stands Nos 2 and 10.

KOLÍN

Kolín on the Labe River is a friendly old town seldom visited by tourists. The Kmochův Festival of brass-band music is held here every June. The town centre is next to the river, a 15-minute walk from the adjacent bus and train stations.

It might be worth stopping here for a night if you're passing through on your way to/from Prague and it's a good base from which to visit Kutná Hora and Mělník.

Things to See

Kolín has a picturesque central square with a Baroque Marian column (1682) and fountain (1780) in the middle. A block away is the towering Gothic **St Bartholomew Church** begun by Petr Parléř. The **City Museum** (closed Monday) is next to this church.

Places to Stay & Eat

The *Hotel Savoy* (☎ 22 022), Rubešová 61 just off the central square, is US$13/17 single/double without bath, US$21 double with bath.

Two cheaper places are across the river

and a couple of blocks to the left (ask). The *Skautská Ubytovna 'Kalcovka'* (Scout's Hostel), off Za Baštou, a block back from Brankovická 25, has beds in double rooms at US$3 per person.

The *Turistická Ubytovna Zimní Stadión* (☎ 20 444), Brankovická 27, has triple rooms at US$13 (bus No 3 from the train station). There's a good restaurant at the Zimní Stadión, open daily until 10 pm.

Getting There & Away

Kolín is a major junction on the Prague-Košice main line, with frequent service to/from Prague (62 km, one hour). All trains to/from Moravia, Slovakia and Poland stop here. Another important line through Kolín is from Havlíčkův Brod to Děčín via Mělník. Buses run regularly from Kolín Bus Station to Kutná Hora, 12 km south by road.

MĚLNÍK

Central Bohemia is drained by the romantic Labe and Vltava rivers, which unite at Mělník, 32 km north of Prague, and flow north towards Germany, where they become the Elbe. It was Emperor Charles IV who introduced Burgundy vines to this fertile area in 1340. The finest Mělník wines are Ludmila, a red wine named after St Wenceslas' pious grandmother, and Chateau Mělník, a sparkling red wine.

On a bluff above the rivers is a Renaissance **chateau** (1554), now an art gallery and museum of viticulture (open from April to October, closed Monday). Both the chateau and the adjacent late Gothic **Peter & Paul Church** are near Mělník's picturesque central square, a 15-minute walk from the bus and train stations.

Places to Stay & Eat

The *Hotel Nádraží* (☎ 624 848), directly across the street from the train station, has large rooms with shared facilities at US$13/20 single/double. Their restaurant serves a tasty pork dish called *Srbské vepřové žebírko*.

The C-category *Hotel Zlatý Beránek* on Mělník's old town square has closed.

Getting There & Away

Direct trains go to Mělník from Kolín (71 km, 1½ hours) and Děčín (89 km, two hours), but services from Vysočany Railway station in Prague (50 km) involve a change at Všetaty, so you're better off coming by bus from Holešovice Metro Station in Prague (33 km, one hour).

In Prague, Praha-Vysočany Railway station is a 10-minute walk from Českomoravská Metro Station.

West Bohemia

Cheb and Plzeň are the western gateways to the Czech Republic. All trains from Western Germany pass this way and the stately old Habsburg spas, Karlovy Vary and Mariánské Lázně, are nearby. The proximity to Bavaria helps to explain the famous Pilsner beer which originated in Plzeň. South-west of Plzeň is Domažlice, centre of the Chod people, where folk festivals are held in August. In West Bohemia you can enjoy the charm of southern Germany at a fraction of the price.

KARLOVY VARY

Karlovy Vary (Karlsbad) is the largest and oldest of the Czech Republic's many spas. According to a local tradition, Emperor Charles IV discovered the hot springs by chance while hunting a stag. In 1358 he built a hunting lodge here and gave the town his name. Beginning in the 19th century, famous people such as Beethoven, Bismarck, Brahms, Chopin, Franz Josef I, Goethe, Liszt, Metternich, Paganini, Peter the Great, Schiller and Tolstoy came here to take the waters, and busts of a few of them grace the promenades. Karl Marx came to Karlovy Vary to take the cure in 1874, 1875 and 1876. Ludvík Moser began making glassware at Karlovy Vary in 1857 and today Bohemian crystal is prized around the world.

There are 12 hot springs at Karlovy Vary containing 40 chemical elements that are used in medical treatment of diseases of the digestive tract and metabolic disorders. If you have diarrhoea or constipation, this is the place to come. Mineral deposits from the springs form stone encrustations which are sold as souvenirs. Karlovy Vary's herbal Becherovka liqueur is known as the 13th spring.

Karlovy Vary still bears a definite Victorian air. The elegant colonnades and boulevards complement the many peaceful walks in the surrounding parks. The picturesque river valley winds between wooded hills, yet the spa offers all the facilities of a medium-sized town without the bother. After hustling around Prague this is a nice place to relax amidst charming scenery. It's hard not to like Karlovy Vary.

Orientation

Karlovy Vary has two train stations. Express trains from Prague and Cheb use Karlovy Vary horní nádraží, across the Ohře River, just north of the city. Trains to/from Mariánské Lázně stop at Karlovy Vary dolní nádraží, which is opposite the main ČAD bus station. The city bus station is in front of the market, three blocks east of dolní nádraží. T G Masaryka, the pedestrian mall in Karlovy Vary's city centre, runs east to the Teplá River. Upstream is the heart of the spa.

If you decide to walk from town to horní nádraží, you'll see a huge building labelled 'okresní úřad' directly in front of you as you cross the bridge. Go around behind this building and straight ahead until you see a signposted way on the left which leads through a tunnel and straight up to the station.

There's no left-luggage office at the bus station. Both train stations have left-luggage rooms but left luggage at horní nádraží is larger and more reliably open 24 hours a day.

Information

Čedok has two offices, one on the corner of Bechera and Moskevská, and another at Karla IV 1 closer to the spa.

There's an information office (open weekdays only) in a corner of the Vřídelní Colonnade. This office arranges spa treat-

CZECH REPUBLIC

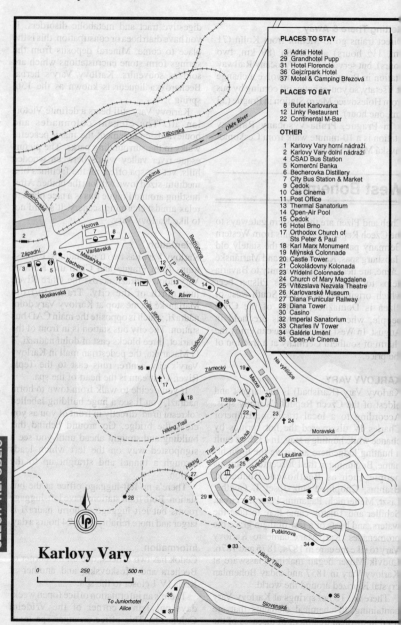

PLACES TO STAY

- 3 Adria Hotel
- 29 Grandhotel Pupp
- 31 Hotel Florencie
- 36 Gejzírpark Hotel
- 37 Motel & Camping Březová

PLACES TO EAT

- 8 Bufet Karlovarka
- 12 Linky Restaurant
- 22 Continental M-Bar

OTHER

- 1 Karlovy Vary horní nádraží
- 2 Karlovy Vary dolní nádraží
- 4 ČSAD Bus Station
- 5 Komerční Banka
- 6 Becherovka Distillery
- 7 City Bus Station & Market
- 9 Čedok
- 10 Čas Cinema
- 11 Post Office
- 13 Thermal Sanatorium
- 14 Open-Air Pool
- 15 Čedok
- 16 Hotel Brno
- 17 Orthodox Church of Sts Peter & Paul
- 18 Karl Marx Monument
- 19 Mlýnská Colonnade
- 20 Castle Tower
- 21 Čokoládovny Kolonáda
- 23 Vřídelní Colonnade
- 24 Church of Mary Magdalene
- 25 Vítězslava Nezvala Theatre
- 26 Karlovarské Museum
- 27 Diana Funicular Railway
- 28 Diana Tower
- 30 Casino
- 32 Imperial Sanatorium
- 33 Charles IV Tower
- 34 Galérie Umění
- 35 Open-Air Cinema

Karlovy Vary

0   250   500 m

To Juniorhotel Alice

CZECH REPUBLIC

ment for foreigners beginning at around US$70 per person a day including room and board.

Money The Komerční Banka, Bělehradká13 near the bus station, is open weekdays from 7.30 to 11.30 am and 1 to 4.30 pm.

Komerční Banka, Tržiště 11 next to Vřídelní Colonnade, opens weekdays from 8 am to noon and 1 to 4 pm.

Post & Telecommunications The telephone centre at the main post office, T G Masaryka 1, is open daily from 7.30 am to 8 pm. Karlovy Vary's telephone code is 017.

Things to See

As you follow the riverside promenade south from the stations, you'll pass the modern **Thermal Sanatorium** (1976) and the neo-classical **Mlýnská Colonnade** (1881), designed by Josef Žitek. Temporary exhibitions are held at Lázeňská 3 (once the Karl Marx Museum). On a nearby hill is the **old castle tower** (1608) on the site of Charles IV's 1358 hunting lodge. Today it's a restaurant. Down the hill from the castle is the **House of the Three Moors**, or Dagmar House, Tržiště 25, where Goethe stayed during his many visits to Karlovy Vary.

Opposite this building is a bridge which leads to the pulsing heart of Karlovy Vary, the Vřídlo or Sprundel Spring in the **Vřídelní Colonnade**. Here 2000 litres a minute of 72.2°C water shoot up 12 metres from a depth of 2500 metres. The colonnade, erected in 1975, was formerly named after the world's first astronaut, Yuri Gagarin, who visited the spa in 1961 and 1966. Throngs of Czech tourists, funny little cups in hand, pace up and down the colonnade, taking the drinking cure. Bring a cup of your own for some piping hot liquid refreshment and maybe it'll even do you some good.

Just above the Vřídelní Colonnade is the Baroque **Church of Mary Magdalene** (1736) designed by Kilian Dientzenhofer. Follow the Teplá River south-west past the **Vítězslava Nezvala Theatre** (1886) till you reach the **Karlovarské Museum** (closed Monday and Tuesday), Nová Louka 23, which has history and natural history displays on the local area.

Return to the Vřídelní Colonnade, cross the bridge again and follow the promenade west along the river towards the **Grandhotel Pupp**, a former meeting place of the European aristocracy. Just before the hotel you'll see Mariánská, an alley on the right leading to the bottom station of the **Diana Funicular Railway**, which ascends 166 metres to the top every 15 minutes from 10 am to 6 pm. Take a ride up to the **Diana Tower** for great views and pleasant walks through the forest. If the railway is closed, follow the network of footpaths that begins near this station. A café adjoins the Diana Tower.

Loket If you have an afternoon to spare, take a ČAD bus, which passes about every two hours, eight km south-west to Loket, where you'll find an impressive 13th century **castle** on the hilltop in the centre of town. A museum in the castle is dedicated to the china made in Loket since 1815. On the façade of the Hotel Bílý Kůň, in Loket's picturesque town square, is a plaque commemorating Goethe's seven visits. You might even consider staying at the *Bílý Kůň* (☎ 94 171) which also has a restaurant where you can get lunch.

You can walk back to Karlovy Vary from Loket in about three hours. Follow the blue-and-white trail down the left bank of the Ohře River, which flows between Cheb and Karlovy Vary, to the **Svatošské Rocks**. Here you cross the river on a footbridge and take the road to Doubí (served by Karlovy Vary city bus No 6). This riverside path down the forested valley is lovely.

Activities

Top off your sightseeing with a swim in the large **open-air thermal pool** *(bazén)* on the hill above the Thermal Sanatorium. Karlovy Vary's numerous sanatoriums are reserved for patients undergoing treatment prescribed by physicians – in fact, this is the only place which will let you in.

The bazén is open from 8 am to 9.30 pm

daily (from 9 am on Sunday), admission US$1 per hour. The bazén is closed every third Monday. There's also a sauna (reserved for women on Tuesday and Thursday, men on Monday and Wednesday, mixed other days), a solarium and a fitness club, all open daily. A board at the entrance explains it all in English.

Places to Stay

Private Rooms On weekends Karlovy Vary fills up with Germans on mini holidays and accommodation is tight. Čedok (☎ 22 294), on the corner of Bechera and Moskevská, will place you in a private home, but at US$27 double (no singles) they're greatly overpriced. Even then, the rooms are often full with Czechs who pay much less than you. A second Čedok office with private rooms is at Karla IV 1 and their rooms are sometimes cheaper.

W Private Travel Agency (☎ 27 768), náměstí Republiky 5 next to the bus station, has private rooms at US$10 to US$13 per person and they usually have something available.

Hotels The *Servis Pension Armabeton* (☎ 25 868), Sokolovská 72, is in an untouristed neighbourhood about a km west of horní nádraží Railway Station. It's US$17/23/26 double/triple/quad (no singles) with shared bath in this renovated 1902 building almost opposite the city brewery. There are several cheap bars and restaurants in the vicinity but it's on the opposite side of town from the spa.

If you're only staying for one night, a good bet is the *Adria Hotel* (☎ 23 765), Západní 1, opposite the ČAD bus station (US$18/27 single/double with bath). The C-category *Hotel Turist* (☎ 26 837), Bechera 18 near Čedok, is US$14 per person in double and triple rooms with shared bath (no singles). This place is run-down and not really worth the money.

Closer to the spa is the *Hotel Atlantic* (☎ 24 715), Tržiště 23 next to Vřídelní Colonnade, right in the middle of everything. It has a few bargain singles at US$25 including breakfast. Doubles are more expensive at US$57 without bath, US$69 with bath, breakfast included.

The *Hotel Wolker*, Tržiště 19 next to Hotel Atlantic, is cheap but to get a room you must go first to expensive Hotel Astoria, Vřídelní 23 opposite the Mlýnská Colonnade, where the snotty clerk will tell you the rooms at the Wolker aren't good enough for foreigners and it's full for the rest of the month. This situation could change.

The former state sanatoriums are being privatised and renovated for up-market (mostly German) tourism. For the time being you can get good deals on food and accommodation in these places – ask around. One such is the *Hotel Florencie* (☎ 24 160) Mariánskolázeňská 25, a five-storey Victorian hotel facing the casino. Rooms here are US$20/30 single/double without bath.

Karlovy Vary's premier address is the *Grandhotel Pupp* (☎ 209 111), Mírové náměstí 2, an imposing 358-room hotel founded in 1701 and operated from 1773 to 1945 and 1990 to the present by the Pupp family. A room here with bath and breakfast will set you back US$85 single, US$112 to US$125 double, or you can play the big shot for a lower price by dining at one of the hotel's pretentious restaurants.

Better value if you want to go up-market is the *Hotel Brno* (☎ 25 020), krále Jiřího 1, a four-storey villa on a hill overlooking the Russian Orthodox church and surrounding forests. Rooms without bath aren't cheap at US$25/42 single/double including breakfast, but they're spacious and well appointed. If the price doesn't bother you, it's a good choice.

South of Town There are two places to stay along Slovenská just south of the spa centre, which you can reach from the market on bus No 7 with the sign 'Březová'. The first place you come to is the friendly *Gejzírpark Hotel* (☎ 22 662) beside the public tennis courts, a new building with rooms at US$11 per person with shared bath. The hotel has free hot showers and, unlike those in many other hotels, they're not locked. You can use the 14 adjacent tennis courts at US$5 an hour –

ısk the hotel receptionist. The hotel restaurant is very slow but the food is good.

Not far from the Gejzírpark Hotel is *Motel Březová* (☎ 25 101), Slovenská 9, where motel rooms are US$25/26 double/triple (no singles) without bath or US$43 double with bath. The rooms are often fully booked by locals who pay much less. The camping ground here charges US$6 for one, US$9 for two. The location in a wooded valley near a stream is nice but it's often crowded with German and Austrian caravans. There's only enough hot water for the first two campers in the morning queue. The motel is open from April to October and camping is from May to September only.

Places to Eat

The *Drůbeží Grill* at Tržiště 31, just up the hill from the Vřídelní Colonnade, has tasty barbecued chicken and cold beer. Order rice (rýže) with your meal as the chips are rather greasy. Another great place for grilled chicken and beer is *Linky*, nábřeží Jana Palacha 2. At Drůbeží you pay a fixed price for a quarter or half chicken, while at Linky you pay by weight.

Restaurant Fortuna, Bechera 16, tries to be an US-style steak house.

Bars & Cafés

The best place for coffee, sinfully rich cakes and ice cream is the *Continental M-Bar*, Tržiště 27, near the Vřídelní Colonnade. Entry is through the Bohemia porcelain showroom. Upstairs from the showroom is a more spacious, more expensive café.

Café Elefant, Stará Louka 30, is perhaps Karlovy Vary's most popular non-hotel café.

A self-service beer bar called *Bistro Luisa* is near the lower station of the Diana Funicular Railway.

The *Bufet Karlovarská*, Horova 2, next to the city bus station, has cheap beer on tap.

Local Specialities

You can buy a box of the famous Lázeňské oplatky wafers at *Čokoládovny Kolonda*, Vřídelní 57 (next to Pošta No 3 post office).

Lovers of fine liqueurs will wish to stand outside the Becherova distillery at T G Masaryka 57 and look at the displays in the window or drop into the company store at No 53 to buy a bottle at a slightly reduced rate.

Entertainment

Karlovy Vary's main theatre is the *Divadlo Vítězslava Nezvala* on Divadlo náměstí, not far from the Vřídelní Colonnade, but it offers mostly drama in Czech. The main ticket office (*předprodej*) for the theatre is open Monday to Saturday from 1.30 to 6 pm. From mid-May to mid-September concerts are held in the colonnade daily except Monday.

Among the many cultural events are the Jazz Festival in March, the Dvořák Singing Contest in June, the International Magicians Meeting in July, the Dvořák Autumn Festival in September and the International Festival of Touristic Films in September.

Seeing a movie at *Čas Cinema*, T G Masaryka 3, is another option.

Getting There & Away

Bus There are direct trains to Prague, but it's faster and easier to take one of the hourly buses (122 km). Also take a bus between Karlovy Vary and Mariánské Lázně (47 km), as the train takes twice as long. To Cheb, however, the bus takes twice as long as a local train. The only way to go directly to Plzeň (83 km) and České Budějovice (220 km, five hours) is by bus. Seats on express buses can and should be reserved in advance by computer at the ČAD bus station (weekdays 6 am to 6 pm, Saturday 6 am to 1 pm).

Train The *Karlex* express train travels daily between Leipzig and Karlovy Vary (240 km, five hours) via Františkovy Lázně (reservations are recommended). To go to Nuremberg or beyond, you'll have to change at Cheb. Cheb (52 km, one hour) and Mariánské Lázně (53 km, two hours) are connected to Karlovy Vary by local trains. Couchettes and sleepers are available to/from Košice (897 km) on the *Krušnohor* express train.

Getting Around

Before boarding a city bus, buy some tickets from an automat (feed it small coins). A good service to know about is bus No 11, which runs hourly from horní nádraží Railway Station to the city bus station at the market, then on over the hills to Divadlo náměstí and the Vřídelní Colonnade. The more frequent city bus No 13 also runs to the market *tržnice* from horní nádraží.

Bus No 2 runs between the market and the Grandhotel Pupp (Lázně I) every half-hour or better from 6 am to 11 pm daily.

CHEB

This old medieval town on the Ohře River, near the western tip of the Czech Republic, is an easy day trip by train from Karlovy Vary or Mariánské Lázně. You can also visit Cheb as a stopover between Karlovy Vary and Mariánské Lázně as train service to both is good. Only a few km north of the Bavarian border, Cheb (formerly Eger) retains a strong German flavour.

Orientation & Information

The train station at the south-east end of třída Svobody is open all night, so you can wait there if you arrive or depart at an ungodly hour. The left-luggage office at the train station is open 24 hours a day.

Čedok is on the corner of Májová and třída Svobody.

The Cultural Information Office, náměstí krále Jiřího 33, sells theatre and concert tickets.

Money The Komerční Banka has an exchange window in the train station (open daily from 8 am to 1 pm and 2 to 6 pm). They change travellers' cheques for 2% commission (US$1 minimum) and give a good rate.

The main branch of the Komerční Banka is at Obrněné Brigády 20 (weekdays 7.30 to 11.30 am and 1 to 6 pm).

Post & Telecommunications The main post office is at náměstí krále Jiřího 38. Cheb's telephone code is 0166.

Things to See

Although the area around the train station is ugly, only a few minutes' away up třída Svobody is the picturesque town square, náměstí krále Jiřího. Burgher houses with sloping red-tile roofs surround the square and in the middle is **Špalíček**, a cluster of 16th century Gothic houses which were once Jewish shops. Behind these is the **Municipal Museum** (closed Monday) which has an excellent historical exhibition. The Thirty Years' War military commander Duke Albrecht Wallenstein was murdered in the building in 1634 and the museum devotes a room to him. Also on the square is the Baroque former new town hall (1728), now the **city art gallery**.

At the back of the Municipal Museum is **St Nicholas Church**, a massive Gothic structure with a sculpture-filled interior. Notice the portal (1270) and the Romanesque features, such as the twin towers. A few blocks away is **Cheb Castle** (open from April to October, closed Monday), erected in the 12th century by Friedrich I Barbarossa, leader of the Eastern crusades. The Black Tower dates from 1222 but the exterior fortifications were built in the 17th century. The 12th century Romanesque chapel in the castle is a rare sight in the Czech Republic.

Places to Stay

There are a number of small hotels in Cheb. The *Hotel Chebský Dvůr* (☎ 33 400), třída Svobody 93 near the bus station, is US$13 per person. The *Slávie Hotel* (☎ 33 216), třída Svobody 75, is US$14/23 single/double without bath, US$17/26 with bath. The friendly *Hradní Dvůr Hotel* (☎ 22 444), Dlouhá 12, costs US$11/22 single/double without bath, US$25 double with bath.

The *Hvězda Hotel* (☎ 22 549), náměstí krále Jiřího 4, is more expensive at US$18/27 single/double without bath, US$36 to US$58 double with bath, but it's pleasant, with some rooms overlooking the main square.

Private rooms from Čedok are US$15 a double (no singles).

CZECH REPUBLIC

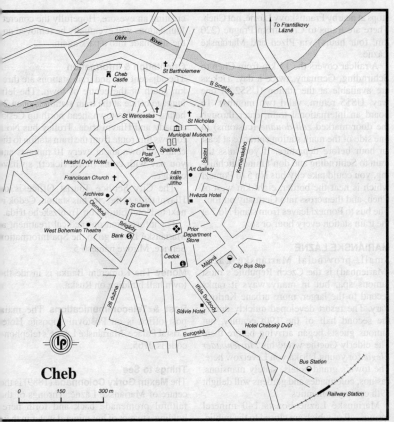

To Františkovy Lázně

Oke River

Cheb Castle

St Bartholemew

B Smetana

St Wenceslas

St Nicholas

Municipal Museum

Špaliček

Post Office

Hradní Dvůr Hotel

Franciscan Church

Art Gallery

nám krále Jiřího

Archives

St Clare

Hvězda Hotel

Obrněná

Brigády

West Bohemian Theatre

Bank

Prior Department Store

Čedok

City Bus Stop

Komenského

Školní

Mácova

28 dubna

Třída Svobody

Slávie Hotel

Europská

Hotel Chebský Dvůr

Bus Station

Railway Station

Cheb

0   150   300 m

CZECH REPUBLIC

The nearest camping grounds are at Dřenice (☎ 31 591) on Jesenice Lake, five km east of Cheb, and Lake Amerika, two km south-east of Františkovy Lázně. Both are open from mid-May to mid-September.

Places to Eat

Cheb's self-service is the *Restaurant Bohemia* at třída Svobody 18 near Čedok. The *Briga Mléčná Jídelna*, třída Svobody 74 beside the Slávie Hotel, is also fast and easy both are closed on Sunday.

There are a number of tourist restaurants around náměstí krále Jiřího, for example, the *Fortuna* at No 474 or *Kavarna Špaliček* at No 499.

The restaurant at the *Hradní Dvůr Hotel* is unpretentious and has Chebské pivo on tap. The *Hotel Chebský Dvůr* also has a very good restaurant.

Getting There & Away

Most trains arriving in the Czech Republic from Nuremberg (190 km, three hours) stop here, with express trains to/from Stuttgart (342 km, six hours), Frankfurt/Main (389 km, five hours) and Dortmund (728 km, eight hours) daily. The train from Leipzig stops at nearby Františkovy Lázně, not Cheb. There are trains to Cheb from Prague (220 km, four hours) via Plzeň and Mariánské Lázně.

A railcar covers the 13 km from Cheb to Schirnding, Germany, twice a day. Tickets are available at the station (US$2.50 one way, US$5 return, valid two months). To board an international train, enter through the door marked *zoll-douane* (customs) to one side of the main station entrance at least an hour before departure. If you miss the train to Schirnding and don't mind hitchhiking, you could take city bus No 5 to Pomezí which is near the border, eight km west of Cheb, and then cross into Germany on foot. The bus to Pomezí leaves from stand No 7 at the train station every hour or so.

MARIÁNSKÉ LÁZNĚ

Small, provincial Mariánské Lázně (Marienbad) is the Czech Republic's most famous spa, but in many ways it ranks second to the larger, more urbane Karlovy Vary. The resort developed quickly during the second half of the 19th century, but famous guests began arriving before then. The elderly Goethe wrote his *Marienbader Elegie* for young Ulrika von Levetzow here. The town's grand hotels, stately mansions, casinos, colonnades and gardens will delight 19th century romantics.

Mariánské Lázně boasts 140 mineral springs, all of which are closed to the public. Thirty-nine of these are used for treating diseases of the kidneys and of the urinary and respiratory tracts. The hillsides and open spaces around the massive Victorian bathhouses and hotels have been landscaped into parks with walks where overweight visitors can try to burn off some extra calories. The town's 628-metre elevation (compared with 447 metres elevation at Karlovy Vary) gives the spa a brisk climate which makes the pine-clad Bohemian hills to the north all the more inviting. You could even hike the green trail 35 km north to Loket in a very long day.

The communists began building a large hotel directly in front of the Maxim Gorky Colonnade and this has been left unfinished,

creating an eyesore. Hopefully the concrete foundations will eventually be removed and the site made into a park again.

Orientation & Information

The adjacent bus and train stations are three km south of the centre of town. The left luggage office at the train station is open 24 hours. To get to town, head north up Česky armády and Hlavní třída. Trolley bus No 7 follows this route from the train station to the centre of town about every 10 minutes and you pay with coins (not a ticket), so have change.

The City Service Tourist Office is on Hlavní třída at the city bus station. Čedok is next to Hotel Europa on Trebizskeho třída.

For information on medical treatment at Mariánské Lázně go to the Spa Information Service, Mírové náměstí 5.

Money The Komerční Banka is inside the town hall building on Ruská.

Post & Telecommunications The main post office is on Poštovní opposite Hotel Cristal Palace. Mariánské Lázně's telephone code is 0165.

Things to See

The **Maxim Gorky Colonnade** (1889) is the centre of Mariánské Lázně. Throngs of the faithful promenade back and forth here holding a teapot of hot mineral water in their hands as a sign of devotion to the drinking cure. At one end of the colonnade is the **Pavilion of the Cross Spring** (1818), and at the other is a new musical fountain which puts on free shows for the crowd on the stroke of every odd hour. The canned music (Muzak) is sometimes a little off key, but that's Marienbad.

A shop facing the Pavilion of the Cross, opposite the Maxim Gorky Colonnade, sells the delicious *Lázeňské oplatky*, a large circular wafer filled with sugar or chocolate. You can look through a side window to see them being made.

Above the Maxim Gorky Colonnade is the **Municipal Museum** (closed Monday) on

CZECH REPUBLIC

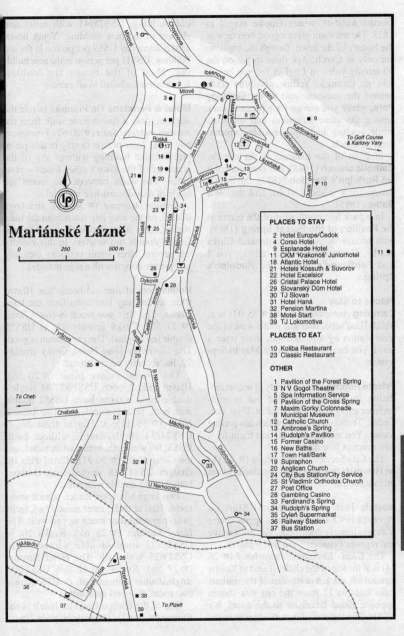

Mariánské Lázně

0   250   500 m

To Golf Course
& Karlovy Vary

To Cheb

To Plzeň

PLACES TO STAY

2 Hotel Europe/Čedok
4 Corso Hotel
9 Esplanade Hotel
11 CKM 'Krakonoš' Juniorhotel
18 Atlantic Hotel
21 Hotels Kossuth & Suvorov
22 Hotel Excelsior
26 Cristal Palace Hotel
29 Slovanský Dům Hotel
30 TJ Slovan
31 Hotel Haná
32 Pension Martina
38 Motel Start
39 TJ Lokomotiva

PLACES TO EAT

10 Koliba Restaurant
23 Classic Restaurant

OTHER

1 Pavilion of the Forest Spring
3 N V Gogol Theatre
5 Spa Information Service
6 Pavilion of the Cross Spring
7 Maxim Gorky Colonnade
12 Catholic Church
13 Ambrose's Spring
14 Rudolph's Pavilion
15 Former Casino
16 New Baths
17 Town Hall/Bank
19 Supraphon
20 Anglican Church
24 City Bus Station/City Service
25 St Vladimír Orthodox Church
27 Post Office
33 Gambling Casino
33 Ferdinand's Spring
34 Rudolph's Spring
35 Dyleň Supermarket
36 Railway Station
37 Bus Station

CZECH REPUBLIC

Goetha náměstí, where Goethe stayed in 1823. The museum gives a good overview of the history of the town, though the captions are only in Czech. Ask them to put on the 30-minute video in English for you before you go through. Yellow and-blue signs behind the museum lead to the **Geology Park**, where you can go for a pleasant walk among the stone structures and old trees while reading incomprehensible explanations in Czech.

In front of the museum is the circular **Catholic church** (1848), and just south of it are **Rudolph's Pavilion** (1823), the former casino (now a social club), and the **New Baths** (1895).

In a park just north-west of the centre is the **Pavilion of the Forest Spring** (1869), with bronze statues of Goethe and Ulrika nearby. Down towards the railway you'll find **Ferdinand's Spring** and **Rudolph's Spring**.

Places to Stay

Camping *Autocamp Luxor* (☎ 35 04) is at Velká Hled'sebe, four km south-west of the train station by a roundabout route (take a taxi if you can). It's open from May to September.

Private Rooms There's plenty of accommodation in Mariánské Lázně but in midsummer everything will be taken. If so, visit Čedok, Třebížského třída, which has private rooms. You must, however, rent them for a minimum of five days.

The City Service Tourist Office (☎ 42 18) on Hlavní třída at the city bus station also has private rooms.

Hostels Just south of Motel Start on Plzeňská is *TJ Lokomotiva*, a sports centre with inexpensive dorm beds. You must arrive and register between 5 pm and 9 pm.

The *CKM 'Krakonoš' Juniorhotel* (☎ 26 24) is at the top of the chairlift next to Koliba Restaurant, six km north-east of the stations (take bus No 12 from the city bus station opposite Hotel Excelsior to the door). It's US$16/25 single/double with shower in the

old building, US$28/41 with toilet and shower in the new building. Youth hostel card holders pay US$9 per person in the old building, US$11 per person in the new building. Most of the rooms are doubles. Breakfast is included in all rates.

Motel & Pensions On Plzeňská beside the stadium, only a five-minute walk from the stations, is *Motel Start* (☎ 20 62). Foreigners pay US$17 per person to stay in this plain, prefabricated building without any of the character of the town's other hotels – poor value. The walls between the rooms are made of a cardboard-like material.

Pension Martina (☎ 36 47), Jiráskova ulice 6, on the way into town from the train station, rents small flats with shared bath at US$18 double (no singles). In this vicinity are several other small pensions (actually just private rooms with a sign outside).

Hotels Lots of fine old hotels line Hlavní třída on the way into town from the train station. The first you reach is *Hotel Haná* (☎ 27 53), Český armády 48, at US$25 double (no singles). Their restaurant is good. The *Slovanský Dům Hotel*, Český armády 22, has recently been restored.

The *Cristal Palace Hotel* (☎ 20 56), Hlavní třída 2, costs US$19/37/48 single/double/triple without bath, US$52 double with bath, breakfast included. The *Atlantic Hotel* (☎ 59 11), at Hlavní třída 26, is US$24/34 single/double without bath, US$31/49 with bath, breakfast included, and the *Corso Hotel* (☎ 30 91), Hlavní třída 16, charges US$17/28 single/double without bath, US$45 double with bath.

Two large hotels on Ruská, a back street above Hlavní třída, cater mostly to Czechs (who pay a third as much as you will). The *Hotel Kossuth* (☎ 28 61), Ruská 20, is US$17/22 single/double without bath, US$19/25 with bath. The *Hotel Suvorov* (☎ 27 59), Ruská 18, is also US$17/22 single/double with bath or US$54 for a two-room, five-bed apartment.

One of the cheapest regular hotels is the *Europe* (☎ 20 63), Třebížského třída 2, with

CZECH REPUBLIC

rooms at US\$13/20/27 single/double/triple without bath, US\$20/31/40 with bath. In fact, everything about the Europa is slightly cheaper.

In midsummer, all hotel prices are significantly increased.

Places to Eat

The *Jalta Vinárna*, upstairs on Hlavní třída, next to Hotel Corso, serves good food.

The *Classic Restaurant*, Hlavní třída 50 next to the Excelsior Hotel, is good for a filling German-style breakfast of cold meats and cheeses. Their lunch and dinner menus have a special vegetarian section, plus assorted salads and reasonable meat dishes.

The *Zahradní Pivnice* is a German-style beer garden well hidden behind the Atlantic Hotel.

The *Koliba*, on ulice Dušíkova at the north-eastern edge of town, is an up-market, folk-style restaurant.

Entertainment

Check the *N V Gogol Theatre* (1868) for musical programmes. Many events are held at *Chopin Haus*, Hlavní třída 30.

The International Music Festival in May and July and the Chopin Festival in August are special events to ask about at Supraphon, Hlavní třída 30.

Discos The *American Night Club* in the Corso Hotel, Hlavní třída 16, is fine for the over 40s crowd, while the *Havana Club* in the Atlantic Hotel, Hlavní třída 26, is a bit better. The city youth, however, favour the *Cristal Club Disco* in the Cristal Palace Hotel, Hlavní třída 2, which is usually good fun for everyone.

Getting There & Away

There are direct buses between Mariánské Lázně and Karlovy Vary (47 km) which take half the time of the local train. If you'd like to stop off somewhere between the spas, choose Bečov nad Teplou, where you'll find a castle in a wooded valley.

Train services to Cheb (30 km, 30 minutes hours) and Plzeň (76 km, 1¼ hours) are

good. Most international express trains between Nuremberg and Prague stop at Mariánské Lázně.

PLZEŇ

The city of Plzeň (Pilsen), midway between Prague and Nuremberg, is the capital of West Bohemia. Located at the confluence of four rivers, this town was once an active medieval trading centre. An ironworks was founded at Plzeň in 1859, which Emil Škoda purchased 10 years later. The Škoda Engineering Works became a producer of high-quality armaments which attracted heavy bombing at the end of WW II. The rebuilt Škoda Works now produces machinery, locomotives and nuclear reactors.

Beer has been brewed at Plzeň for 700 years and the town is famous as the original home of Pilsner. The only genuine Pilsner trademark is Plzeňský Prazdroj, or Pilsner Urquell in its export variety. Although the emphasis is on industry, Plzeň has sights enough to keep you busy for a day. Devoted beer drinkers will not regret the pilgrimage.

Orientation

The main train station, Hlavní nádraží, is on the east side of town. The Central Autobus nádraží is west of the centre on Husova ulice, opposite the Škoda Works. Between these is the old town, which is centred around náměstí Republiky.

Tram No 2 goes from the train station to the centre of town and on to the bus station. The left-luggage office at the bus station is open weekdays from 7.30 am to 6.30 pm, Saturday 5 to 11 am, Sunday 2 to 7 pm. Left luggage at the train station is open 24 hours.

Information

Čedok is at Sedláčkova 12, just off náměstí Republiky.

Motorists in need of assistance can turn to the Autoklub Plzeň (☎ 220 736), Havlíčkova 6, or Autoturist (☎ 220 006), Sady Pětatřicátníků 3.

Money The Komerční Banka, just outside the main entrance to the train station, changes travellers' cheques for 2% commission (weekdays 7 am to 6.30 pm, Saturday 7 to 11.30 am).

Post & Telecommunications A 24-hour telephone centre is in the main post office at Solní 20. Plzeňv's telephone code is 019.

Things to See
The most convenient place to begin sightseeing is on náměstí Republiky, the old town square. Gothic **St Bartholomew Church** in the middle of the square has the highest tower in Bohemia (103 metres), climbable daily except Monday. Inside the soaring 13th century structure are a Gothic Madonna (1390) on the high altar and fine stained-glass windows. On the back of the outer side of the church is an iron grille. Touch the clean angel and make a wish. Outstanding among the many gabled buildings around the square is the Renaissance **town hall** (1558).

An old town house on the east side of the square contains the extensive **Ethnographical Museum** (closed Monday). Just south on Františkanská is the 14th century **Franciscan church**. Behind this church, around the block, is the **West Bohemian Museum**, with natural history exhibits and paintings (presently closed for renovations).

Beer Lovers Only Plzeň's most interesting sight by far is the **Museum of Beer Brewing** (closed Monday), Veleslavínova ulice 6, north-east of náměstí Republiky. Located in an authentic medieval malt house, the museum displays a fascinating collection of artefacts related to brewing. Ask for the explanatory text in English or German. If all that reading makes you thirsty, visit the *Pivnice na Parkánu*, which is right beside (or behind) the beer museum.

Just around the corner at Perlova 6 is an entrance to one section of the nine km of medieval **underground corridors** below Plzeň. These were originally built as refuges

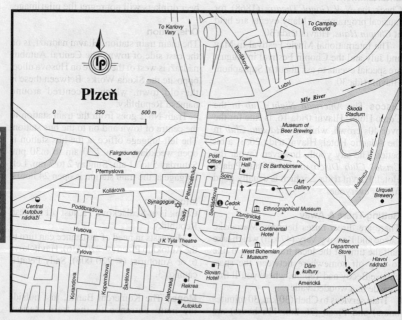

during sieges, hence the numerous wells. Some were later used to store kegs of beer. To enter you must wait for a group of at least five people to gather, then follow them on a boring Czech tour (ask for the text in English). The underground corridors are closed on Monday and Tuesday. The bottle shop at Perova 8 near the entrance to the corridors sells takeaway Pilsner Urquell if you get tired of waiting.

The famous **Urquell Brewery** is only a 10-minute walk from here, a little north of Hlavní nádraží. The twin-arched gate dated 1842-92, which appears on every genuine Pilsner label, is here. A tour of the brewing room and fermentation cellar is offered for individuals weekdays at 12.30 (US$1 including a film on the process). Groups are shown through the brewery throughout the day. Near the gate is the *Na spilce Restaurant* with inexpensive meals and brew (Monday to Saturday until 10 pm, Sunday until 9 pm). If you're a vegetarian look for the *sýry* section which lists cheese dishes. This is just the place for a glass of that 12-proof brew.

Places to Stay

Camping The two camping grounds (with bungalows) are at Bílá Hora, five km north of the city (bus No 20). Both are open from May to mid-September.

Hostels The *Sportovní klub učňů* (☎ 282 012) runs a year-round hostel *(ubytovna)* at Vejprnická ulice 56, about three km west of town but easily accessible on tram No 2 (direction Skvrňany) from the train or bus stations. Beds are US$8 per person and everyone is welcome. Ask CKM Student Travel, Dominikánská 1, about this hostel and other accommodation possibilities in student dormitories.

You can also stay at the university residence (☎ 223 049) at Bolevecká 30 just north of town at US$11 per person in double rooms. This 10-storey building can accommodate 500 people. Meals are served and it's open year-round. Get there on tram No 1 from the train station or centre of town. You don't have to be a student to stay there.

Čedok, Sedláčkova 12, books beds in this place.

Private Rooms Čedok, Sedláčkova 12, has private rooms for US$6/12 single/double. They don't mind if you only stay a night or two, but the rooms are often full.

Recrea (☎ 35 113), V Špice 6, has private rooms at US$13 per person including breakfast.

Petra Tour (☎ 35 765), Sedláčkova 28 behind the main post office, has private rooms beginning at US$13 per person. Their main advantage is that they're open from 9 am to 7 pm daily and they also change money.

Hotels & Pensions Hotel accommodation in Plzeň is expensive. The B-category *Slovan Hotel* (☎ 227 256), Smetanovy sady 1, a fine old hotel with a magnificent central stairway, is US$30/40/50 single/double/triple, breakfast included.

Also impressive is the *Continental Hotel* (☎ 723 5292), Zbrojnická 8, at US$37/55 single/double with shower, US$54/78 single/double with bathroom, buffet breakfast included. Ask about less expensive rooms without shower. Erected in 1929, the Continental is where you'll find Plzeň's gambling casino. (In 1992 photographer George Janeček from Salt Lake City, Utah, was able to recover the property his family had run until 1945.)

The modern seven-storey *Hotel Central* (☎ 226 757), náměstí Republiky, opposite St Bartholomew Church in the very centre of town, is overpriced at US$37/59 single/double with bath and breakfast.

Better value is *Pension Bárová* (☎ 36 652), Solní 8, in a renovated townhouse just off náměstí Republiky. The three attractive rooms with bath are US$19/32 single/double. *Pension Diaja*, Riegrova ulice 10 right behind Hotel Central, is similar (but with no tram noise).

Places to Eat

Finding a good cheap place to eat in Plzeň is

CZECH REPUBLIC

much easier than finding somewhere to sleep.

S & S Grill, Sedláčkova 7, half a block from Čedok, is a private place with attractive décor and great barbecued chicken priced by weight.

Fénix Bistro, náměstí Republiky 18, is an inexpensive self-service and *Jakko Grill Bar*, náměstí Republiky 14, is also good.

The *Restaurace Na spilce*, at the Urquell Brewery, serves inexpensive meals. The enormous fin-de-siecle restaurant in Hlavní nádraží is another good choice.

Entertainment

For entertainment, try the *J K Tyla Theatre* (1902) or the ultramodern *Dům kultury* beside the river. There's a disco in the basement at the *Continental Hotel*.

Getting There & Away

All international trains from Munich (330 km via Furth im Wald, 5½ hours) and Nuremberg (257 km via Cheb, four hours) stop at Plzeň. There are fast trains to České Budějovice (136 km, two hours), Cheb (106 km, two hours) and Prague (114 km, two hours). Train services to Mariánské Lázně (76 km, 1½ hours) are also good, but if you want to go to Karlovy Vary (83 km), take a bus. Buses also run to Mariánské Lázně, Prague and České Budějovice.

South Bohemia

South Bohemia is the most German-looking part of the Czech Republic. The many quaint little towns have a Bavarian or an Austrian flavour, enhanced by some 5000 medieval carp ponds in the surrounding countryside, many of them dating from the Middle Ages. On the Šumava ridge, south-west of Prachatice, is Mt Boubín (1362 metres) with its primeval forest of spruce, pine and beech trees. The Vltava River originates on this plateau.

After WW I, South Bohemia was given to Czechoslovakia on historical grounds, although over half of its population was

German and Hitler's claims to the area nearly touched off war in 1938. After WW II the Germans had to leave and the region became Czech, though Germanic touches linger in the hearty food and drink. Well off the beaten track, South Bohemia is overflowing with history.

ČESKÉ BUDĚJOVICE

České Budějovice (Budweis), the regional capital of South Bohemia, is a charming medieval city halfway between Plzeň and Vienna. Here the Vltava River meets the Malše and flows northwards to Prague. Founded in 1265, České Budějovice controlled the importation of salt and wine from Austria and was a Catholic stronghold in the 15th century. Nearby silver mines made the town rich in the 16th century. After a fire in 1641 much was rebuilt in the Baroque style. In 1832 the first horse-drawn railway on the continent arrived at České Budějovice from Linz, Austria, which is directly south.

High-quality Koh-i-Noor pencils are made here but the city is more famous as the original home of Budweiser beer (Budvar to the Czechs). České Budějovice is a perfect base for day trips to dozens of nearby attractions, so settle in for a couple of days. Picturesque little Bohemian towns within easy commuting distance include Český Krumlov, Jindřichův Hradec, Písek, Prachatice, Tábor and Třeboň.

Orientation & Information

It's a 10-minute walk west down Lannova třída from the adjacent bus and train stations to náměstí Přemysla Otakara II, the centre of town. There's a left-luggage office is at the bus station (weekdays 6.30 am to 6.30 pm, Saturday 6.30 am to 2 pm, Sunday 2 to 6 pm).

The tourist information office next to the town hall on náměstí Přemysla Otakara II sells maps of towns all around the Czech Republic and is good at answering questions.

The flashy Čedok office at náměstí Přemysla Otakara II 39, upstairs above the casino, is hard to find and the staff is only interested in selling travel services. CKM Student Travel, Karla IV 14, is similar.

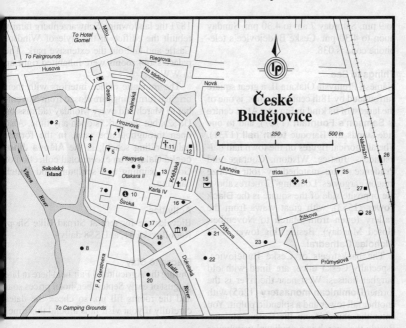

České Budějovice

PLACES TO STAY

12 Super Pension
13 Zvon Hotel
27 Grand Hotel

PLACES TO EAT

4 Masné Krámy
   Beer Hall
5 Cukárna U kláštera
25 Bufet Central

OTHER

1 Rabenstein Tower
2 Sports Stadium
3 Dominican
   Monastery
6 Bishop's
   Residence
7 Open-Air Theatre
8 Open-Air Theatre
9 Samson's
   Fountain
10 Čedok
11 St Nicholas
   Cathedral
14 St Anne's Church &
   Concert Hall
15 Post Office
16 CKM Student
   Travel
17 Jihočeské
   Theatre
18 Městský Dům
   kultury
19 Museum of South
   Bohemia
20 State Library
21 Dům kultury
22 Divadelní
   Sál DK
23 Jihočeský
   Autoklub
24 Prior Department
   Store
26 Railway
   Station
28 Bus Station

Motorists can turn to the Jihočeský Autoklub (☎ 36 177), Žižkova třída 13.

Money The Komerční Banka, Krajinská 19, next to Masné Krámy Beer Hall, changes travellers' cheques for 2% commission

(weekdays 7 am to 5 pm, Saturday 9 am to noon).

Post & Telecommunications The main post office, on Senovážné náměstí, has a telephone centre open weekdays from 6 am to 9 pm, Saturday 7 am to 4.30 pm, Sunday noon to 4.30 pm. České Budějovice's telephone code is 038.

Things to See

Náměstí Přemysla Otakara II, a great square surrounded by 18th century arches, is one of the largest of its kind in Europe. At its centre is **Samson's Fountain** (1727), and to one side stands the Baroque **town hall** (1731). The allegorical figures on the town hall balustrade – Justice, Wisdom, Courage and Prudence – are matched by four bronze dragon gargoyles. Looming 72 metres above the opposite side of the square is the **Black Tower** (1553), with great views from the gallery (open from March to November, closed Monday). Beside this tower is **St Nicholas Cathedral**.

The backstreets of České Budějovice, especially Česká ulice, are lined with old burgher houses. West near the river is the former **Dominican monastery** (1265) with another tall tower and a splendid pulpit. You enter the church from the Gothic cloister. Beside the church is a medieval warehouse where salt was kept until it could be sent down the Vltava to Prague. Stroll south along the riverside behind the warehouse, past the remaining sections of the 16th century walls. The **Museum of South Bohemia** (closed Monday) is just south of the old town.

To visit the **Budvar Brewery** you're supposed to make arrangements in advance by calling ☎ 24 027, extension 338. In fact, this brewery is in an industrial area several km north of the centre (bus No 2 or 6) and lacks the picturesque appearance of the Urquell Brewery in Plzeň. Although it could become easier to visit in future as tourism is developed, it's unlikely to ever become a big attraction.

Hluboká nad Vltavou One side trip not to miss takes in the neo-Gothic Tudor palace at Hluboká nad Vltavou (Frauenberg), 10 km north, which is easily accessible by bus. There used to be a castle here that was built in the 13th century, but between 1841 and 1871 the landowning Schwarzenberg family rebuilt the edifice in the style of Windsor Castle and laid out the extensive park. The palace's 144 rooms were inhabited right up to WW II.

The romantic palace interiors with their original furnishings are closed from November to March and every Monday (admission US$2), but the park is open any time. Also open throughout the year, in the former palace riding school, is the **Alšova Jihočeská Galerie**, an exceptional collection of Gothic painting and sculpture and Dutch painting.

Activities

Bicycles are for rent at Strnad Bike Shop, Rudolfovská 31, at US$8 daily.

Places to Stay

During the Agricultural Fair held here in late August or early September, hotel prices soar and the rooms fill up, so check the dates carefully if your visit falls around this time.

Camping Dlouhá Louka Autocamp (☎ 38 308), Stromovka 8, is a 20-minute walk south-west of town (bus No 6 from in front of Dům Kultury). Tent space is available here from May to September, and motel rooms (US$36 double with breakfast) are available all year. The showers are clean and the water hot, but beware of bar prices. The restaurant is said to be good.

The Stromovka Autocamp (☎ 53 402 or 28 877), just beyond Dlouhá Louka Autocamp, has three-person bungalows for US$12, four-person units for US$16 (open from April to October).

Hostels CKM Student Travel, Karla IV 14, arranges accommodation at the Škoda Ubytovna, a highrise hostel outside town, at US$10 per person in double rooms with bath. You must book and pay at the CKM office (weekdays 9 am to 5 pm). Also ask about the Branišovská student hostel (off Husova west of the centre), open in July and August only.

CZECH REPUBLIC

Private Rooms Čedok, náměstí Přemysla Otakara II 39, has private rooms at US$13 per person with breakfast, but not in the centre.

The best place to go for a private room is CTS Travel Service (☎ 25 061), upstairs at Krajinská 1 just off the main square. Rooms begin at US$7 per person, some of them in the old town, and the friendly, helpful staff will show you colour photos of the various possibilities. They can also book rooms in Český Krumlov and elsewhere in South Bohemia. They're open weekdays from 9 am to 6 pm, Saturday 9 am to 2 pm year-round, with extended hours from June to September (including Sunday from 9 am to 2 pm). You'd do well to check with them first.

Pensions Small private pensions around České Budějovice are a better deal than the hotels, but the quality varies, so you ought to ask to see the room before accepting it. Often a place will only have one or two rooms and will take in the sign as soon as they're rented, so you just have to walk around the old town looking. An example of this is *Pension Suchánek* (☎ 33 292), Česká 34, behind the Masné Krámy Beer Hall, which charges about US$25 double with bath.

Also check *Super Pension* (☎ 52 030), Mlýnská stoka 6, just off Kanovnická as you enter the old town. The owner doesn't live here, so you'll be lucky to find anyone to let you in.

Hotels The *Hotel Grand* (☎ 56 503), Nádražní 27 opposite the train station, is US$29/36 single/double with bath.

The *Zvon Hotel* (☎ 55 361), náměstí Přemysla Otakara II 28, is good value at US$20/30 single/double without bath, US$35/54 with bath, showers are US$2 extra. The Zvon has been expanded and upgraded in recent years.

Places to Eat

Try the local carp which is on many restaurant menus.

About the best place in town for a colourful meal is the *'Masné Krámy' beer hall* in the old meat market (1560), on the corner of Hroznová and 5 května. It's touristy but good.

A more locally oriented beer hall in this town of beer is *Restaurace Na Dvorku*, Kněžská 11 across from the Concert Hall. If Na Dvorku looks too raucous check out the more up-market *V Loubé*, Kněžská 15.

If Chinese cuisine is your fancy, try the *Čínska Restaurant*, Hroznova 18 near the Black Tower.

Bufet Central, Lannova třída 32, is a good place for a self-service breakfast on the way to the train station as they open at 6 am weekdays and 7 am Saturday (closed Sunday).

Cafés The *Cukrárna U kláštera*, Piaristická 18 just off the main square, is great for coffee and cakes (closed Sunday).

Café filharmonie in the concert hall, Kněžská at Karla IV, is perhaps České Budějovice's most elegant café.

Entertainment

České Budějovice has two cultural centres, both near the Museum of South Bohemia. The old *Městský Dům kultury* is by the river, and another *Dům kultury* is on the square behind the museum. You've a better chance of hearing music at the *Divadelní Sál DK* behind this newer Dům kultury.

The *Jihočeské Theatre*, by the river on ulice Dr Stejskala, presents mostly plays in Czech, but operas, operettas and concerts are also on their calendar, so check. *St Anne's Church*, Kněžská 6, functions as České Budějovice's concert hall.

There's a disco in the *Grand Hotel* across the street from the train station.

Getting There & Away

There are fast trains to Plzeň (136 km, two hours), Tábor (66 km, one hour), Prague (169 km, 2½ hours) and Jihlava (132 km, two hours). For shorter distances you're better off travelling by bus. The bus to Brno (182 km, four hours) travels via Telč (100 km, two hours).

Twice a day there's a train to/from Linz,

Austria (125 km, three hours, US$12). On three other occasions you can go to Linz with a change of trains at the border stations (Horní Dvořiště and Summerau). Connections with trains between Prague and Vienna are made at České Velenice, 50 km southeast of České Budějovice. One daily train runs directly to/from Vienna (Franz-Josefsbahnhof).

A bus to Vienna's Mitte Bahnhof (US$7) departs from České Budějovice Bus Station on Friday, and to Linz post office (US$3) via Český Krumlov on Wednesday and Saturday. In July and August this bus operates daily except Sunday and two buses go on to Salzburg. Pay the driver.

ČESKÝ KRUMLOV

Český Krumlov (Krumau), a small medieval town 25 km south of České Budějovice, is one of the most picturesque towns in Europe, its appearance almost unchanged since the 18th century. Built on an S-shaped bend of the Vltava River, the 13th century castle occupies a ridge along the left bank. The old town centre sits on the high tongue of land on the right bank. South-west are the Šumava Mountains, which separate Bohemia from Austria and Bavaria.

Český Krumlov's Gothic border castle, rebuilt into a huge Renaissance chateau by 16th century Italian architects, is second only to Prague Castle as a fortified Bohemian palace and citadel. The Renaissance lords of Rožmberk (Rosenberg) seated here possessed the largest landed estate in Bohemia, which passed to the Eggenbergs in 1622 and to the Schwarzenbergs in 1719. Though Český Krumlov is an easy day trip from České Budějovice, there are several places to stay should you care to linger.

Information

The Tourist Service, Zámek 57, sells maps from all over. Ask for local author and staff member Richard Franz who speaks good English and can answer any question about this region. Čedok is at Latrán 75.

Money The Komerční Banka, Latrán 20,

changes travellers' cheques for 2% commission (weekdays from 9 am to noon and 1 to 5 pm, Saturday 9 am to noon).

Post & Telecommunications You can make phone calls from the post office, Latrán 81, weekdays from 7 am to 6.30 pm, Saturday 7 am to 1 pm. Český Krumlov's telephone code is 0337.

Things to See

Get off the bus from České Budějovice at Český Krumlov Špičák, the first stop in town. Just above this stop is **Budějovická Gate** (1598), which leads directly into the old town. On the right, two blocks south, is the **castle** entrance. The oldest part of the castle is the lower section with its distinctive round tower, but it's the massive upper castle which contains the palace halls that are open to visitors. It is said that the castle is haunted by a white lady who appears from time to time to forecast doom.

Just across the high bridge behind the palace is the unique Rococo **chateau theatre** (1767). Behind this, a ramp to the right leads up to the former **riding school**, now a restaurant. Cherubs above the door offer the head and boots of a vanquished Turk. Above this are the Italian-style castle **gardens**. The **'Bellarie' summer pavilion** and a modern revolving open-air theatre are features of these gardens. The castle interiors are open from April to October only (visits are only conducted when a group forms), but you can walk through the courtyards and gardens almost any time.

On náměstí Svornosti across the river in the old town are the Gothic **town hall** and a Baroque plague column (1716). Just above the square is **St Vitus Church** (1439), a striking Gothic hall church. Nearby is the **Regional Museum** (closed Monday) with a surprisingly good collection housed in the old Jesuit seminary (1652). The scale model of Český Krumlov as it was in 1800 is a highlight. Continue in the same direction, turn left and you'll soon find the autobusové nádraží (bus station) and a bus back to České Budějovice. (You might ask directions as

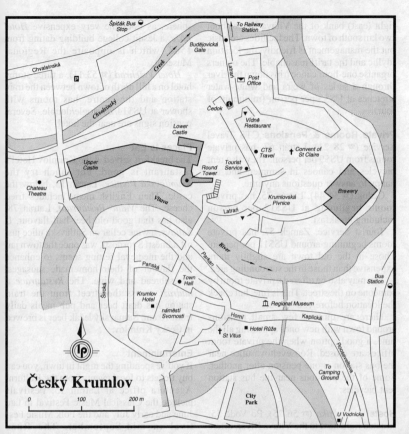

Český Krumlov

0   100   200 m

CZECH REPUBLIC

this bus station is not visible from the main road and is easy to miss.) There's a great view of town from near the bus station.

Activities
The Tourist Service (☎ 46 05), Zámek 57, knows about yachting possibilities on Upper Lipno Lake, south-west of Český Krumlov (about US$15 a day for three or four people). There are also canoe and rubber raft rentals in Vyšší Brod which allow you to paddle down the Vltava River 32 km to Český Krumlov in one day or all the way to České Budějovice in two days (US$22 a day).

Tourist Service just outside the castle gate can arrange all this.

Several places around town rent bicycles and it's a pleasant two-hour ride south-west to Lake Lipno, involving a climb then a drop to the lake and a great downhill on the way back. There's a nice casual café in Horní Planá on the north shore where you can get lunch. If the weather turns bad you can take your bike back to Český Krumlov from Horní Planá by train (six times a day).

Places to Stay
Camping The camping ground is on the

right (east) bank of the Vltava River about two km south of town. The facilities are basic but the management is friendly, the location idyllic and the tariff reasonable. The owners organise one-hour canoe trips down the river through a series of weirs and white-water stretches at US$5 per person (minimum of four).

Private Rooms & Pensions CTS Travel Service (☎ 28 21), Latrán 67, has private rooms from US$9 per person. They also rent bicycles and canoes in summer, and are happy to answer questions anytime.

Čedok (☎ 34 44), Latrán 75, has private rooms beginning at US$13 per person including breakfast.

Tourist Service, Zámek 57, has private rooms beginning around US$11 per person. Those in the old town are slightly more expensive than those in the surrounding area.

You may also be offered a private room by someone on the street. This is fine, but check the location before you set out.

There are quite a few small pensions around town with new ones appearing all the time, a good option when the private room offices are closed. Rooseveltova ulice near the bus station is one pension after another. Some of the pensions near the bus station rent bicycles.

Hostel *U Vodníka* (☎ 56 75), Po Vodě 55, situated right next to the Vltava River, offers accommodation in an eight-bunk dorm at US$5 per person, plus three double/triple rooms at US$16 for the room. Cooking facilities are available, there's a small English library and a nice garden out back. Walk south on Rooseveltova ulice and take the street on the right that leads down towards the river. The hostel is at the bottom of the hill on the right. Manager Callon Zukowski is a one-man Český Krumlov promoter with enough suggestions of local things to see and do to keep you busy for four or five days.

Hotels The *Krumlov Hotel* (☎ 22 55) on náměstí Svornosti (US$14/24 single/double without bath, US$20/40 with bath) has atmo-

sphere, as does the very expensive *Hotel Růže*, a Jesuit college building dating from 1588, which is opposite the Regional Museum.

Hotel Vyšehrad (☎ 53 11), a three-storey hotel on a hill north of town between the train station and the centre, has rooms with shower at US$14/20 single/double. Several pension signs are near the hotel.

Places to Eat
The breakfast served at the Krumlov Hotel's restaurant is good. For lunch try the *Krumlovská Pivnice*, Latrán 13, below the castle. Their English menu includes fried cheese. The *Vídně Restaurant*, Latrán 78, also has that good old beer-hall flavour. *U Šatlavy*, a wine cellar on Šatlavska ulice just off náměstí Svornosti, was once the town jail and the medieval setting seems to enhance the flavour of their homemade sausages, cheesebread and wine. The *Restaurace u nádraží* across the street from the train station has draft beer and pub meals daily from 10 am. Šumavský ležák beer is brewed in Český Krumlov.

Entertainment
If you're spending the night in town, you can buy tickets to local events from the Kulturní Agentura office at Latrán 15. Festivals include the Classical Music Festival in late June and early July and the Folk Music Festival in mid-September. The Růže (Five-Petaled Rose) Festival in mid-June includes three days of street performances, parades and medieval games.

Getting There & Away
The best way to come to Český Krumlov is by bus and the service from České Budějovice is quite frequent. Intervals between trains are greater and the station is several km north of town (though it's an easy downhill walk into town). For variety, you may wish to come by train and return by bus.

TÁBOR
In 1420 God's warriors, the Hussites, founded Tábor as a military bastion in defi-

ance of Catholic Europe. The town was organised according to the biblical precept that 'nothing is mine and nothing is yours, because the community is owned equally by everyone'. New arrivals threw all their worldly possessions into large casks at the marketplace and joined in communal work. This extreme nonconformism helped to give the word Bohemian the connotations we associate with it today.

Planned as a bulwark against Catholic reactionaries in České Budějovice and farther south, Tábor is a warren of narrow broken streets with protruding houses which were intended to weaken and shatter an enemy attack. Below ground, catacombs totalling 14 km provided a refuge for the defenders. This friendly old town, 100 km south of Prague, is well worth a brief stop.

Orientation & Information

From the train station walk west through the park between Hotel Bohemia and the bus station. Continue west down ulice 9 května until you reach a major intersection. Žižkovo náměstí, the old town square, is straight ahead on Palackého třída, a 15-minute walk from the stations. The left-luggage office at the bus station closes at 7 pm, so it's better to use the 24-hour facility at the train station.

Čedok is on třída 9 května next to the Palcát Hotel.

Money The Komerční Banka, on třída 9 května halfway into town from the stations, changes travellers' cheques weekdays from 7.30 am to 11.30 am and 1 pm to 4 pm.

Post & Telecommunications The post office/telephone centre is in the pink building on the opposite side of Žižkovo náměstí from the museum. Tábor's telephone code is 0361.

Things to See

A statue of the Hussite commander, Jan Žižka, graces Žižkovo náměstí, Tábor's main square. Žižka's military successes were due to the novel use of armoured wagons against crusading Catholic knights. Around

the square are the homes of rich burghers, spanning the period from late Gothic to Baroque. On the north side is the Gothic **Church of the Transfiguration of Our Lord on Mt Tábor** (built in 1440-1512) with Renaissance gables and a Baroque tower (1677).

The other imposing building on Žižkovo náměstí is the early Renaissance town hall (1521), now the **Museum of the Hussite Movement** (closed Monday), with the entrance to a visitable 650-metre stretch of the underground passages. You can visit the underground passages daily except Monday from April to October, but only when a group of 15 people forms. The passages, constructed in the 15th century as refuges during fires or times of war, were also used to store food and to mature lager.

The arch at Žižkovo náměstí 22, beside the old town hall, leads into Mariánská ulice and then Klokotská ulice, which runs south-west to the **Bechyně Gate**, now a small historical museum (closed Monday) which focuses on the life of the peasants. Kotnov Castle, founded here in the 12th century, was destroyed by fire in 1532; in the 17th century the ruins were made into a brewery which is still operating. The castle's remaining 15th century round tower may be climbed from the Bechyně Gate museum for a sweeping view of Tábor, the Lužnice River and the surrounding area.

Places to Stay

Private Rooms & Pensions Though you can easily visit Tábor as a stopover between Prague and České Budějovice, there are several places to stay. Čedok (☎ 22 235) on třída 9 května has private rooms at US$18 double (no singles).

The Inforcentrum (☎ 23 401), Křižíkovo náměstí 505, corner of třída 9 května near the entrance to the old town, has private rooms at US$5 to US$20 per person.

If you arrive at night or on a weekend when these offices are closed, walk into town looking for pension signs. One place advertising such rooms is at třída 9 května 569, not far from the stations.

CZECH REPUBLIC

Hotels Hotel accommodation is expensive. The old Hotel Slavia, opposite the adjacent bus and train stations, has been done up and renamed *Hotel Bohemia* (☎ 22 827), Husovo náměstí 591. Prices have been increased four times to US$42 single or double without bath, breakfast included. For a room with private bath you'll pay a rip-off US$50/100 single/double (about six times what it was just a couple of years ago).

The other hotels are on 9 května, between the stations and the town centre. You first come to the red-brick, neo-Gothic *Slovan Hotel* (☎ 23 435), ulice 9 května 678, which charges US$16/32 for single/double with shared bath (US$2 extra for a shower). Next is the modern *Palcát Hotel* (☎ 22 901), ulice 9 května 2471/2, a modern six-storey hotel where German tour groups always stay (US$37/57 single/double with shower and breakfast).

Places to Eat

A good place for a quick lunch is the *Pizza Restaurant*, Široká ulice 159, to the left off Palackého třída just before you reach Žižkovo náměstí.

A more pretentious choice would be the *Beseda Restaurant* next to the church on Žižkovo náměstí.

Entertainment

Tábor's two theatres, the *Městské Divadlo* and *Divadla Oskara Nedbala*, are next to one another on Palackého třída.

Getting There & Away

Tábor is on the main railway line between Prague and Vienna. The line from České Budějovice to Prague also passes through here. Local trains run to Pelhřimov.

To go from Tábor to Telč by train you must change at Horní Cerekev and Kostelec u Jihlavy, and although the connections are fairly good, the whole 107-km trip by local train takes three or four hours through unspoiled countryside. Otherwise take a bus to Jihlava (74 km) and another bus on to Telč (29 km) from there.

To go to Plzeň (113 km) or Brno (158 km) you're better off taking a bus. Eastbound buses to Jihlava and Brno leave only every couple of hours and the posted timetable bears numerous footnotes, so reconfirm your departure time at the information window.

Moravia

Moravia, the other historic land of the Czech Republic, is usually overlooked by tourists visiting Bohemia. This is an attraction in itself, but Moravia also has its own history and natural beauties, such as the karst area north of Brno. The theatres and art galleries of Brno, the capital, are excellent, and quaint towns like Kroměříž, Mikulov, Telč and Znojmo await discovery. The Moravian Gate between Břeclav and Ostrava is a natural corridor between Poland and the Danube basin. Heavy industry is concentrated in North Moravia, which is next to Polish Silesia, whereas fertile South Moravia produces excellent wines. Well placed in the geographical centre of the country, Moravia is a great place to explore.

TELČ

Telč (Teltsch) was founded in the 14th century by the feudal lords of Hradec as a fortified settlement with a castle separated from the town by a strong wall. The artificial ponds on each side of Telč provided security and a sure supply of fish. After a fire in 1530, Lord Zachariáš, then governor of Moravia, ordered the town and castle rebuilt in the Renaissance style by Italian masons. Profits from gold and silver mines allowed Lord and Lady Zachariáš to enjoy a regal lifestyle.

After the death of Zachariáš in 1589, building activity ceased and the complex you see today is largely as it was then. The main square of this loveliest of Czech towns is unmarred by modern constructions, and the fire hall at náměstí Zachariáše z Hradce 28 is poignant evidence of local concern to keep

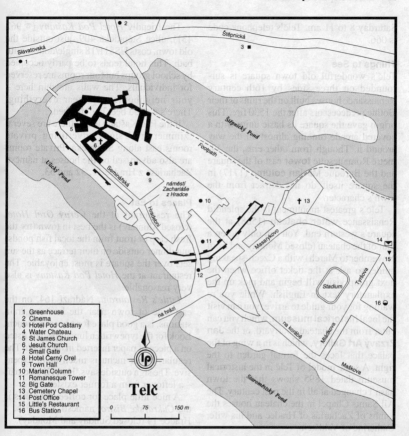

Key to map:

1 Greenhouse
2 Cinema
3 Hotel Pod Caštany
4 Water Chateau
5 St James Church
6 Jesuit Church
7 Small Gate
8 Hotel Černý Orel
9 Town Hall
10 Marian Column
11 Romanesque Tower
12 Big Gate
13 Cemetery Chapel
14 Post Office
15 Little's Restaurant
16 Bus Station

Telč

0   75   150 m

it that way. In 1992 Telč was added to UNESCO's 'world heritage' list. Surprisingly few visitors frequent the narrow, cobbled streets of the fairy-tale town of Telč.

Orientation & Information

The bus and train stations are a few hundred metres apart on the east side of town, a 10-minute walk along ulice Masarykova towards náměstí Zachariáše z Hradce, the old town square.

A left-luggage service is available at the train station 24 hours a day – ask the station-master.

There's an information office just inside the town hall.

Money The Česká Spořitelna, náměstí Zachariáše Hradce 21 (Monday and Wednesday 7.30 am to noon and 1 to 5.30 pm; Tuesday, Thursday and Friday 7.30 am to noon), changes travellers' cheques for 1% commission plus US$1 postage.

Post & Telecommunications The post office is on Staňkova, a block from the train station. The telephone section is open weekdays from 7.30 am to noon and 1 to 5.30 pm,

CZECH REPUBLIC

Saturday 8 to 11 am. Telč's telephone code is 066.

Things to See

Telč's wonderful old town square is surrounded on three sides by 16th century Renaissance houses built on the ruins of their Gothic predecessors after the 1530 fire. This origin gave the square its basic unity with a covered arcade running almost all the way around it. Though from other eras, the 49-metre Romanesque **tower** east of the square and the Baroque **Marian column** (1717) in the square itself do not detract from the town's character.

Telč's greatest monument is the splendid Renaissance **water chateau** (1568) at the square's western end. You can only go on a tour of the chateau (closed Monday and from November to March) with a Czech-speaking guide, so ask at the ticket office when the next group visit will begin and pick up the explanatory text in English. While you're waiting for your guide to arrive, you can visit the local **historical museum**, which you can enter from the chateau courtyard, or the **Jan Zrzavý Art Gallery**, which is in a wing of the palace that faces the formal garden to the right. A scale model of Telč in the historical museum dated 1895 shows that the town hasn't changed at all in the past century. The All Saints Chapel in the chateau houses the tombs of Zachariáš of Hradec and his wife, Catherine of Valdštejn.

The Baroque church (1655) of the former **Jesuit college** is next to the chateau; **St James Church** (1372) beyond is Gothic. Go through the gate beside St James Church to the large English-style park surrounding the duck ponds, which were once the town's defensive moat. You can go on restful walks along the ponds while enjoying gentle pastoral views of medieval towers.

Places to Stay

The *Černý Orel Hotel* (☎ 962 221), náměstí Zachariáše z Hradce 7, a quaint Baroque building, charges US$18/27 single/double with bath. Most rooms have a hot shower but the toilet is down the hall.

The friendly *Hotel Pod Kaštany* (☎ 962 431), ulice Štěpnická 409, just outside the old town, costs US$11/18 single/double with bath. This hotel tends to be partly occupied by school groups but four rooms are reserved for individuals. The walls are thin here – your neighbours will hear everything. There's a good beer bar attached.

If the Pod Kaštany is full there are several 'zimmer frei' signs advertising private rooms east along Štěpnická. Private rooms are also advertised on the houses at náměstí Zachariáše z Hradce 11, 32 and 53.

Places to Eat

The restaurant at the *Černý Orel Hotel* (closed Monday) is the best in town (try the fresh carp or trout from the local fish ponds) and dinner outside on their terrace as the sun sets over the square is most enjoyable. The restaurant at the *Hotel Pod Kaštany* is also very reasonable.

Little's Restaurant, Nádraží 164, on the east side of town near the bus and train stations, is a good place for a beer and lunch. Look for the typewritten lunch specials listed on a piece of paper inserted in the menu. The regular dinner menu is much more expensive. The sign outside says 'Hotel U Nádraží' – a leftover from a former existence.

A nice little place for coffee and cakes is the *Cukrářské Bistro*, náměstí Zachariáše z Hradce 14 (closed Sunday and Monday).

Getting There & Away

The railway line through Telč is pretty useless, as it dead ends at Slavonice on the Austrian border. Instead there are frequent buses from Telč to Jihlava (29 km). Buses travelling between České Budějovice and Brno stop at Telč about 10 times a day – about a 100-km, two-hour trip from Telč to either city at a cost of about US$2. Seven buses a day run to Prague (210 km, 2½ hours).

There's no information, ticket office or left-luggage area at the bus station. Tickets are sold by the drivers and timetables are posted.

BRNO

Halfway between Budapest and Prague, Brno (Brünn) has been the capital of Moravia since 1641 and its large fortress was an instrument of Habsburg domination. The botanist Gregor Mendel (1822-84) established the modern science of heredity through his studies of peas and bees carried out at the Augustinian monastery in Brno. After the Brno-Vienna railway was completed in 1839, Brno developed into a major industrial centre.

Brno has a rich cultural life and its compact centre holds a variety of fascinating sights. Most of central Brno is a pedestrian zone which makes browsing around a pleasure. Brno hasn't been overwhelmed by tourism the way Prague has and you're still treated like a normal person, even in the centre of town. Although you can visit Brno in a very busy day, stay longer and delve deeper. If you're a city slicker, you'll like Brno.

Orientation

Brno's main train station is at the southern edge of the old town centre. Opposite the train station is the beginning of Masarykova, a main thoroughfare which trams and pedestrians follow into the triangular náměstí Svobody, the centre of town. The bus station (autobusové nádraží) is 800 metres south of the train station, beyond the Prior Department Store. To get to the bus station, go through the pedestrian tunnel under the train tracks, then follow the crowd along the elevated walkway.

There are two 24-hour left-luggage offices in Brno Railway Station, one upstairs opposite the lockers, and another downstairs by the tunnel to the platforms (a good little map shop which also carries train timetables is just opposite the downstairs office). The left-luggage office at the bus station is open daily from 6.15 am to 10 pm.

Information

Čedok is at Divadelní 3. CKM Student Travel is at Česká 11.

The Kulturní a Informační Centrum in the old town hall, Radnická 8, has computers which can answer almost any question. They know about hotel and pension prices and will help you make reservations (open weekdays from 8 am to 6 pm, weekends 9 am to 5 pm).

Motorists can turn to the Autoklub České Republiky (☎ 4221 5030), Bašty 8, or Autoturist (☎ 4321 1913), Pekařská 24.

Money The Komerční Banka has an office inside the train station which changes travellers' cheques for 2% commission with a US$1 minimum (open Monday from 7 am to noon, Tuesday to Friday 7 am to noon and 1 pm to 6 pm, weekends 7 am to 1 pm).

There's also Non-Stop Exchange in the train station which in theory is open 24 hours a day but they take 5% commission on travellers' cheques and give a lower rate.

The Komerční Banka has another exchange office at náměstí Svobody 6 (open weekdays 7.30 am to 5.30 pm).

Post & Telecommunications The telephone centre in the post office at the western end of the train station is open 24 hours a day. Brno's telephone code is 05.

Consulates The Consulate General of the Russian Federation, Hlinky 146 opposite the fairgrounds, is open Monday, Wednesday and Friday from 9 am to 1 pm.

Travel Agencies České Dráhy Travel Agency next to the international ticket office in the train station sells bus tickets to Western Europe (US$75 to Amsterdam, US$81 to London).

Čedok, Divadelní 3, sells international bus and train tickets (but not domestic train tickets or couchettes).

The Taxatour office in the train station (look for YMCA sign on their door) arranges rides in private cars to Western European cities at favourable rates (Munich US$18, Stuttgart US$27, Bern US$33 etc).

Visa Extensions The foreigners police,

CZECH REPUBLIC

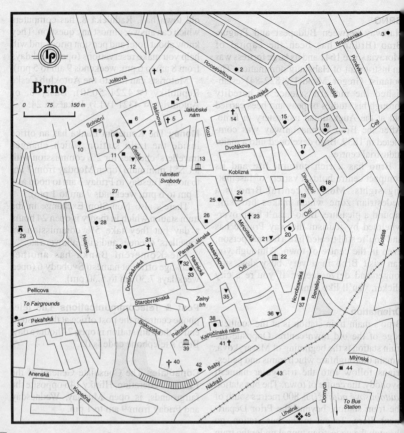

Brno

0   75   150 m

CZECH REPUBLIC

Kounicova 24, a northbound extension of Rašínova (Monday and Wednesday 8 am to noon and 1 to 4 pm, Tuesday 8 am to 1 pm, and Friday 7 to 11 am and noon to 3 pm), will have information about visa extensions. Also come here to report a lost passport or visa. Look for their separate entrance between the main police station and the post office.

Things to See

As you enter the city on Masarykova, turn left into Kapucínské náměstí to reach the

Capuchin monastery (1651). In the ventilated crypt (closed Monday) below the church are the intact mummies of monks and local aristocrats deposited here before 1784. At the western end of Kapucínské náměstí is the recently restored Dietrichstein Palace (1760), with the **South Moravian Museum** (closed Monday).

The street in front of the monastery soon leads into Zelný trh and its colourful **open-air market**. Carp used to be sold from the waters of the Baroque Parnassus Fountain (1695) at Christmas. The **Reduta Theatre**, also on Zelný trh, is where Mozart performed

PLACES TO STAY

4 Hotel U Jakuba
6 Hotel Avion
9 Slavia Hotel
11 Bulharský klub
19 Astoria Hotel
26 Europa Hotel
27 International Hotel
37 Grand Hotel
44 Metropol Hotel

PLACES TO EAT

7 Pivnice Pegas
12 Stopkova plzeňská
   pivnice/Sputnik
21 Baroko Vinárna
32 Vinárna U zlatého meče
35 Pizzera Sorento
36 Restaurace Gourmand

OTHER

1 St Thomas Church
2 Janáček Theatre
3 Radost Puppet Theatre

5 St James Church
8 CKM Student Travel
10 Beseda Concert Hall
13 Ethnographical Museum
14 Jesuit Church
15 Předprodej (Theatre Ticket Office)
16 City Art Gallery
17 Mahenovo Theatre
18 Čedok
20 Měnín Gate
22 Technological Museum
23 St John's Church
24 Main Post Office
25 Metro Night Club
28 Moravian Gallery of Applied Art
29 Špilberk Castle
30 New Town Hall
31 St Michael's Church
33 Old Town Hall
34 Autoturist
38 Reduta Theatre
39 South Moravian Museum
40 Cathedral of Sts Peter & Paul
41 Capuchin Monastery
42 Autoklub Česke Republiky
43 Main Railway Station
45 Prior Department Store

n 1767 and the operettas presented at the Reduta are still excellent.

On ulice Radnická, just off the northern side of Zelný trh, is Brno's 13th century **old town hall**, which has a splendid Gothic portal (1511) below the tower (which is well worth climbing for the small fee). Inside the passage behind the portal are a stuffed crocodile, or 'dragon', and a wheel, traditional symbols of the city. Legend tells how the dragon once terrorised wayfarers approaching the nearby Svratka River; the wheel was supposedly made by a cartwright in league with the devil.

Continue north and take a sharp left to **St Michael's Church** (1679) and the former Dominican convent. Facing the square on the far side of the church is the 16th century **new town hall** with its impressive courtyard, stairways and frescoes. Around the corner at ulice Husova 14 is the **Moravian Gallery of Applied Art** (closed Monday).

In the large park on the hill above this

gallery is the sinister silhouette of **Špilberk Castle**, founded in the 13th century and converted into a citadel and prison during the 17th century. Until 1855 opponents of the Habsburgs were held here, including the Italian poet Silvio Pellico and other members of the Carbonari (an Italian secret political society which fought for the unification of Italy). Sections of the castle and the castle museum are closed for restoration but you can visit the casemates (closed Monday). There's a good view from the ramparts.

From the park surrounding the castle go south on Husova one block to Šilingrovo náměstí on the left. There look for an unmarked street in the south-east corner of the square which leads directly towards an old five-storey green building; this is Biskupská ulice which will take you up Petrov Hill to neo-Gothic **Cathedral of Sts Peter & Paul**, which is hidden behind high buildings. The cathedral, rebuilt in the late 19th century on the site of an older basilica, occupies the site where the city's original castle stood. The Renaissance **bishop's palace** adjoins the cathedral. In 1645 the Swedish general Torstensson who was besieging Brno declared that he would leave if his troops hadn't captured the city by noon. At 11 am the Swedes were about to scale the walls when the cathedral bell keeper suddenly rang noon. True to his word, the general broke off the attack; since that day the cathedral bells have always rung noon at 11 am.

From Petrov Hill descend Petrská into Zelný trh and continue on ulice Orlí to the **Technological Museum** (closed Monday), another Brno curiosity. Buy a ticket for the Panorama, a rare apparatus installed here in 1890 which offers continuous showings of the wonders of the world in 3-D. The programme is changed every couple of weeks so there are lots of regular visitors. Nearby on ulice Minoritská is **St John's Church** (rebuilt in 1733) with fine altarpieces, an organ and painted ceilings.

On nearby náměstí Svobody is a striking plague column (1680). At ulice Kobližná 1 in a corner of the square is the **Ethnographical Museum** (closed Monday) which has Moravian folk costumes and implements. Just north is the parish church, **St James** (1473), with a soaring nave in the purest Gothic style. This is Brno's most powerful church. **St Thomas Church** and the former **Augustinian monastery**, now an art gallery (closed Monday), are just north of St James.

Also worth seeing is the **City Art Gallery** (Dům umění), Malinovského náměstí 2, beside the Mahenovo Theatre. Excellent art exhibitions are sometimes staged in this gallery (closed Monday, free Wednesday).

Slavkov u Brna On 2 December 1805 the famous 'Battle of the Three Emperors' took place in the open, rolling countryside between Brno and Slavkov u Brna (Austerlitz). Here Napoleon Bonaparte, a product of emerging bourgeois capitalism, defeated the combined armies of Emperor Franz I (Austria) and Tsar Alexander I (Russia), defenders of the aristocratic, feudal past. The battle was decided at Pracký Kopec, a hill 12 km west of Slavkov u Brna where a monument was erected in 1912. After the battle Napoleon spent four days concluding an armistice at the Baroque **chateau** (1705) in Slavkov u Brna.

Slavkov u Brna is 21 km east of Brno and is easily accessible by bus from Brno's autobusové nádraží (ask about times and platform numbers at the information counter). The chateau's historical exhibit on Napoleon's life is open Tuesday to Sunday from April to November. The decorated palace rooms and the gallery wing, which requires a separate ticket, are open daily from April to October. Unfortunately, Pracký Kopec is difficult to reach by public transport and hard to find.

Scenic Caves The caves, chasms and canyons of the Moravský Kras (Moravian Karst), 20 km north of Brno, have been created by the underground Punkva River. At Punkevní groups of 75 persons are admitted to the caves every 20 minutes. You walk one km through the deepest caves, admiring the stalactites and stalagmites, ending up at the foot of the Macocha Abyss. There you board a small boat for a 400-metre ride down the Punkva River out of the cave.

The visit to the Punkevní Caves takes 75 minutes (US$1.25 per person). The caves are open to the public all year, closing at 3 pm from April to September and at 1 pm from October to March. All tickets are usually sold out an hour before closing and in midsummer the trips will be fully booked for groups even earlier.

From Punkevní it's a 15-minute hike up to the top of the 138.7-metre-deep Macocha Abyss. Other caves to be visited in this area include Kateřinská, Balčárka and Sloupsko-Sošuvské. The Kateřinská Cave can be visited on a 30-minute tour (same hours as at Punkevní). Traces of prehistoric humans have been found in the caves.

To get there, take a train to Blansko, then walk over to the adjacent bus station. There's supposed to be a bus direct to the caves, leaving at 8 am and 11 am daily from May o September with connections back to Blansko in the afternoon, but it's automatically cancelled if there aren't at least 15 passengers. If this happens catch the Obůrka bus from stand No 12 at Blansko Bus Station to Nové Dvory, from which it's a pleasant 40-minute walk through the forest to Punkevní.

A so-called 'ecology train' carries motorists from the parking lot at Skalní Mlýn to the caves, but this service is of no use to anyone without a car because it's a 10-km walk along the highway from Blansko Railway Station to Skalní Mlýn. Buses listed on the board at the stop at Skalní Mlýn often don't show up, but it's not that hard to hitch back to Blansko.

It's also possible to take a bus from stand No 40 at Brno Bus Station to Jedovnice (29 km), departing every couple of hours. From Jedovnice follow the yellow hiking trail seven km to the Macocha Abyss via Kateřinská Cave.

The new, four-storey *Hotel Macocha* (☎ 0506 3203), Svitavská 35, right opposite the bus and train stations in Blansko, has 31 rooms at US$26 double with bath (no singles).

Places to Stay

The Czech Republic's most important international trade fairs take place in Brno in February, April, September and October. Before coming to Brno, check carefully that your visit does not coincide with one of these fairs, as hotel rates double at this time and all public facilities become very overcrowded. Fortunately, the hostel rates remain steady. In normal times, accommodation in Brno is good value compared to that in other Czech cities.

Camping *Autocamp Bobrava* (☎ 320 110) is just beyond Modřice, 12 km south of the city. Take tram No 2, 14 or 17 to the end of the line, then walk the remaining three km. Otherwise take a local train to Popovice Railway Station, 500 metres from the camping ground (get the times of returning trains before leaving Brno as no information is available at Popovice). Two-bed cabins are US$10, four-bed cabins US$15, while rooms in the motel are US$29 double. There's no hot water but the restaurant is good (open from May to September).

Hostels CKM Student Travel, Česká 11, knows of accommodation for students and youth hostellers in student dormitories, but these are only open during July and August.

The *Bulharský klub* (☎ 4221 1063), Skrytá 1, just around the corner from the CKM office, offers dorm beds at US$9 per person. This small pension in the centre of town is a good place to meet Eastern Europeans.

The *Ubytovna Teplárny a.s.* (☎ 571 919, extension 3500), Špitálka 11, off Cejl just east of the centre, offers comfortable triple rooms at US$3 per bed. This old four-storey building is opposite the factory with the huge pipe crossing the road. Walk east along Cejl to Cejl 52, then right on Radlas and right again on Špitálka.

South of the centre, the *Komárov Ubytovna* (☎ 339 341), Sladkého 13, rents beds in double rooms at US$8 per person. Take tram No 12 or 22 south to the end of the line, go through the underpass and follow Lužná ulice east three blocks, then right on Lomená. The hostel is the tall modern building about two blocks down on your left. Both Čedok and CKM will book beds in this place.

North of the centre, the student dormitory at *Koleje Purkyňovy* (☎ 740 888), Purkyňova 93, block C-2, rents beds (US$7) in double and triple rooms from mid-July until the end of August. Take tram No 13, 16 or 22 northbound and ask someone where to get off.

Year-round you can get a room at *Vysokoškolské Koleje* (☎ 759 533), Kolejní 2, block K-1, on the northern side of the city, for US$12 double (no singles). This large student complex is readily accessible by taking tram No 13, 16 or 22 north to the end of the line, then trolley bus No 53 right to the hostel.

Private Rooms Čedok, Divadelní 3,

arranges rooms in private homes for US$14 per person a night. Most private rooms are far from the centre but easily accessible on public transport. Čedok also arranges hostel accommodation at US$7 per person. These are always far from town.

Taxatour (☎ 4221 3348) in the train station arranges private rooms at US$15 per person in the centre, US$11 per person in the suburbs. It can also arrange accommodation in the *YMCA* on Hlinky ulice for US$8 per person.

Hotels The dumpy, old *Metropol Hotel* (☎ 337 112), Dornych 5 behind the train station, is overpriced at US$27/39 single/double without bath, US$33/55 with shower, breakfast included.

In the centre of town is the *Astoria Hotel* (☎ 4232 1302), Novobranská 3, a pleasant old five-storey hotel with rooms at US$19/25 single/double without bath, US$22/37 with bath, breakfast included.

The *Europa Hotel* (☎ 4221 6333), Jánská 1/3, is rather run-down and it's big advantage is location and price: US$18/26 single/double (no rooms with bath). Try for a room that doesn't face the tram line.

The modern *Hotel Avion* (☎ 4221 5016), Česká 20, is reasonable at US$16/26 single/double without bath, US$24/36 single/double with bath.

A step up in price is the friendly *Hotel U Jakuba* (☎ 4221 0795), Jakubské náměstí 6, at US$32/45 single/double with shower. The hotel restaurant is good. The U Jakuba is clean, well-managed and relatively free of tram noise.

The *Hotel Pegas* (☎ 4221 0104), Jakubská 4, is a recently renovated old building on a quiet street right in the centre of town. Rooms with bath and breakfast are US$32/50 single/double.

Places to Eat
Self-Service *Bufet Sputnik*, Česká 1/3, has grilled chicken, draught beer, coffee, and strawberry milkshakes! It's a great place to fill your stomach if you don't mind eating standing up.

Jídelna Samoobsluha U tří križat Minoritská 2 opposite St John's Church, is a self-service where you can at least sit down (closed weekends). There's a good local bee hall next door.

About the best ice-cream cones in town are dispensed by *Diana*, Česká 25, and there's a good takeaway pizza window nex door.

Another cheap stand-up buffet is in the train station and there's a good supermarke in the basement of Prior Department Store behind the station on the way to the bus station – perfect if you need to stock up on groceries for a long trip.

Restaurants One of the 10 top places to eat in Eastern Europe is *Pivnice Pegas*, Jakubská 4, an attractive new private restaurant with an extensive menu in English Their dark and light beer is brewed in two huge copper vats right on the premises and if you appreciate sizeable servings and hearty draught, you'll end up eating here more than once.

Stopkova plzeňská pivnice, Česká ulice 5 next to Sputnik, is a little more staid than Pegas but their menu (in German) is reasonable.

Pizzeria Sorento, Masarykovo 14, serves real pizza.

A good place to order a bottle of local wine with your meal is *Vinárna U zlatého meče*, Mečová 3.

For more elegant dining try the *Restaurace Gourmand*, Josefská 14 (downstairs), which specialises in French cuisine and local wines at prices which are fair for what you get (closed Sunday).

Entertainment
Except in midsummer when the artists are on holidays, Brno's theatres offer excellent performances. In Brno the tickets aren't all cornered by scalpers and profiteers as they are in Prague, but you are expected to dress up a bit.

Opera, operettas and ballet are performed at the modern *Janáček Theatre* (Janáčkovo divadlo), Sady osvobození. This large theatre which opened in 1966 is named after composer Leoš Janáček, who spent much of his life in Brno.

The nearby neo-Baroque *Mahenovo Theatre* (Mahenovo divadlo) (1882), a beautifully decorated old-style theatre designed by the famous Viennese theatrical architects Fellner and Hellmer, presents classical drama in Czech and operettas.

Do try to see an operetta at the historic *Reduta Theatre* (1734), Zelný trh 3. The singing and dancing are excellent and the programmes enjoyable even if you don't understand Czech.

For tickets to the Janáček, Mahenovo and Reduta theatres, go to Předprodej, Dvořákova 11, a small booking office behind the Mahenovo Theatre (open weekdays from 12.30 to 5.30 pm, and Saturday from 9 am to noon). The staff are usually helpful to foreign visitors.

Also check the *Beseda Concert Hall* next to the Slavia Hotel which has been closed for renovations for some time.

If you're around on Sunday, don't miss the *Radost Puppet Theatre*, Bratislavská 32, which puts on shows at 10 am and 2.30 pm (Sunday only). It's kids' stuff but great fun if you haven't enjoyed puppets for a while.

The Kulturní a Informační Centrum, Radnická 8, has tickets to rock and folk concerts at a variety of venues. Drop in to peruse their leaflets and posters early in your stay.

Discos *Metro Night Club*, Poštovská 6, opposite the main post office, opens at 9 pm daily except Sunday and Monday.

Crazy Night Disco, Veveří 32, is just three blocks north of the city centre. Northbound trams Nos 3, 10, 13, 14, 16, 21 and 22 all stop here. It's a sharp modern place which attracts a young local crowd (daily from 9 pm; US$2 cover).

Things to Buy

Forte Music Store, Minoritská 1, has a good selection of local compact discs and they don't mind playing things for you. A recommended CD usually in stock here is *The Most Beautiful Folk Songs of Moravia* (EDIT 41 0034-2 731).

Getting There & Away

Bus The bus to Vienna (Mitte Bahnhof) departs from platform No 20 at the bus station twice a day (127 km, US$8 one-way).

For shorter trips buses are faster and more efficient than the trains. A bus is better if you're going to Telč (96 km), Trenčín (134 km) or anywhere in South Bohemia.

Train All trains between Budapest and Berlin stop at Brno. If you're going to/from Vienna, change trains at Břeclav. To go to/from Košice, change trains at Přerov. Direct trains from Bratislava (141 km, two hours) and Prague (257 km, three hours) are frequent.

An overnight train with couchettes and sleepers runs between Brno and Košice. Reserve couchettes or sleepers at windows No 24 to 29 in the train station.

ČESKÝ TĚŠÍN

Český Těšín, a small northern Moravian town on the Olše River opposite Cieszyn, Poland, is a useful entry/exit point for those who enjoy the thrill of walking across borders while avoiding the hassle and expense of international train travel. Most of the people crossing the border here are Poles who come over with empty shopping carts and return home loaded down with cases of beer and alcohol.

Orientation

Two bridges, each with traffic in only one direction, link the towns; the Czech train station is about 500 metres from the bridges, the Polish station about a km away. Český Těšín Railway Station is much larger and more active than its counterpart on the Polish side. The left-luggage office is open 24 hours, except for three 30-minute breaks, and there's also a good self-service restaurant in the station.

For more information on Cieszyn turn to the Poland chapter of this book.

Money The Komerční Banka on the bridge

leading into the Czech Republic from Poland changes travellers' cheques for the usual 2% commission (weekdays 7.30 am to noon, Thursday 8.30 am to noon and 2 to 5 pm). All the other exchange offices you see around Český Těšín change only cash, charge a similar commission and give a lower rate. One such is Čedok, Hlavní třída 15.

Places to Stay & Eat

There are two reasonable hotels opposite the train station. The functional, three-storey *Hotel Slezský Dům* (☎ 57 141), Nádražní 10, is US$16/24 single/double with bath, while the imposing, five-storey *Hotel Piast* (☎ 55 651), Nádražní 18, is US$13 single without

bath, US$25 double with bath. This is better value than the hotels on the Polish side.

U Huberta, Hlavní třída 3, a block dead ahead from the bridge leading into the Czech Republic from Poland, is a great introduction to the country's beers halls and meals are served. Czech beer is much cheaper than Polish brew, so drink up.

Getting There & Away

Railway service from Český Těšín is good with eight trains a day to Prague (397 km, five hours), 25 to Žilina (69 km, two hours) and eight to Košice (311 km, 4½ hours). For Brno (209 km) change at Bohumín or Česká Třebová.

CZECH REPUBLIC

Hungary

Hungary has always been the gateway to Eastern Europe. Only a short hop from Vienna, this romantic land of Franz Liszt, Béla Bartók, Gypsy music and the blue Danube welcomes visitors. You'll be enchanted by Budapest, once a great imperial city, and Pécs, the warm heart of the south. The fine wines, fiery paprika, sweet violins, good theatre and colourful folklore conspire to extend your stay. The friendly Magyars are very inviting.

The booming Hungary of the 1990s comes as a surprise to English-speakers whose image of the country often dates back to the repression and bleak poverty of the 1950s. Today's prosperous modern cities bustling with well-dressed inhabitants are a far cry from the grey façades and the leaden-faced peasants queueing for bread in old newsreels. Here you can have all the glamour and excitement of Western Europe at prices you can still afford. It's just the place to kick off an Eastern European trip.

Facts about the Country

HISTORY

The Celts occupied Hungary in the final centuries BC but were conquered by the Romans in 10 AD. From the 1st to the 5th centuries all of Hungary west and south of the Danube (the area today known as Trans-danubia) was included in the Roman province of Pannonia. The Roman legion stationed at Aquincum (Budapest) guarded the north-eastern frontier of the Empire. The epicurean Romans planted the first vine-yards in Hungary and developed the thermal baths. In 408 the West Goths invaded the area, followed in 451 by Attila's Huns, then by the Lombards and Avars. From 795 Pannonia was part of the Carolingian empire.

In 896 seven Magyar tribes under Khan Árpád swept in from beyond the Volga River and occupied the Danube Basin. They terrorised Europe with raids as far as France and Italy until they converted to Roman Catholicism in the late 10th century. Hungary's first king and patron saint, Stephen I (Szent István), was crowned on Christmas Day in the year 1000, marking the foundation of the Hungarian state. After the Tatars sacked Hungary in 1241, many cities were fortified.

Feudal Hungary was a large and powerful state which included Transylvania (now in Romania), Slovakia and Croatia. The medieval capital shifted from Székesfehérvár to Esztergom, Buda and Visegrád. Hungary's Golden Bull (1222), enumerating the rights of the nobility, is just seven years younger than the Magna Carta and universities were founded in Pécs (1367) and Buda (1389).

In 1456 at Nándorfehérvár (present-day Belgrade) Hungarians under János Hunyadi stopped a Turkish advance into Hungary and under Hunyadi's son, Matthias Corvinus,

HUNGARY

Hungary

0   25   50 km

who ruled from 1458 to 1490, Hungary experienced a brief flowering of the Renaissance during a 'golden age'. Then in 1514 a peasant army that had assembled for a crusade against the Turks turned on the landowners. The serfs were eventually suppressed and their leader, György Dózsa, executed, but Hungary was seriously weakened. In 1526 the Hungarian army was defeated by the Turks at Mohács and by 1541 the Turks had occupied Buda.

For the next century the Kingdom of Hungary was reduced to a Habsburg-dominated buffer strip between Balaton Lake and Vienna with its seat at Pozsony (Bratislava). Continued Hungarian resistance to the Turks resulted in heroic battles at Kőszeg (1532), Eger (1552) and Szigetvár (1566). Though it was a Turkish vassal, the Principality of Transylvania was never fully integrated into the Ottoman Empire.

When the Turks were finally evicted in 1686 through the combined efforts of the Austrian and Polish armies, Hungary was subjected to Habsburg domination. From 1703 to 1711 Ferenc Rákóczi II, Prince of Transylvania, led the War of Independence against the Austrians, but the Hungarians were eventually overcome through force of numbers. During and after this war, the Habsburgs demolished any remaining medieval fortifications in order to deny their use to Hungarian rebels. Apart from the destruction, all the Turks left behind were a few bath houses in Buda and a couple of mosques in Pécs.

Hungary never fully recovered from these disasters. Most of the country's medieval monuments had been destroyed, and from the 18th century onwards Hungary had to be rebuilt almost from scratch.

The liberal-democratic revolution of 1848 led by Lajos Kossuth and the poet Sándor Petőfi against the Habsburgs demanded freedom for the serfs and independence. Although it was defeated in 1849, the uprising shook the oligarchy. In 1866 Austria was defeated by Bismarck's Prussia and the next year a compromise was struck between the Austrian capitalists and Hungarian landowners and a dual Austro-Hungarian monarchy formed. Although this partnership stimulated industrial development, it proved unfortunate in the long run because Hungary came to be viewed by its neighbours as a tool of Habsburg oppression. After WW I Hungary became independent from Austria, but the 1920 Trianon Treaty stripped the country of 68% of its territory and 58% of its population. These losses fuel resentment against neighbouring Romania, Slovakia and Yugoslavia to this day.

In August 1919, a 133-day socialist government led by Béla Kun was overthrown by counter-revolutionary elements and thousands were killed, imprisoned or forced to flee the country. In March 1920, Admiral Miklós Horthy established a reactionary regime which lasted 25 years. Before WW II Hungary was an agricultural country with a third of the farmland owned by a thousand magnates while two million peasants had no land at all.

In 1941 the Hungarians' desire to recover their country's 'lost territories' drew them into war alongside the Nazis. Towards the end of the war hundreds of thousands of Jews living outside the capital were deported to Auschwitz, though there wasn't time to round up all those in the Budapest ghetto and about half survived. When Horthy tried to make a separate peace with the Allies in October 1944, the occupying Germans ousted him and put the fascist Arrow Cross Party in power. In December 1944 a provisional government was established at Debrecen and by 4 April 1945 all of Hungary had been liberated by the Soviet army.

(Horthy died in exile in Portugal in 1957, but in 1993 he was reburied in Hungary with eight cabinet ministers in attendance and the prime minister himself expressing admiration for the man who had eagerly joined in all of Hitler's wars of aggression against Hungary's neighbours.)

Post WW II

After the war the communists divided the large estates among the peasantry and nationalised the means of production, folowing the Stalinist line of collectivised agriculture and heavy industry. In February 1956 Nikita Khrushchev denounced Stalin at a closed session of the 20th Party Congress in Moscow and in July, amid increasing expectations of wide-sweeping reform and democratisation, the hardline party leader Mátyás Rákosi was forced to resign.

On 23 October 1956 student demonstrators demanding the withdrawal of Soviet troops from Hungary were fired upon in front of the radio station in Budapest – a 20-metre-high statue of Stalin was pulled down during the demonstration. The next day Imre Nagy, a reform-minded communist, was made prime minister. Yet despite promises of improvements from the newly appointed officials, the disorders spread. On 28 October Nagy's government offered an amnesty to all those involved in the violence and promised to abolish the secret police (AVO) but the fighting intensified with some Hungarian military units going over to the rebels. Soviet troops, who had become directly involved in the conflict, began a slow withdrawal.

On 31 October hundreds of political prisoners were released and there were widespread revenge attacks on AVO agents with summary street executions by angry crowds. The same day Britain and France intervened militarily in Egypt in a dispute over the Suez Canal, diverting attention from Hungary. On 1 November Nagy announced that Hungary would leave the Warsaw Pact and become neutral. At this, the Soviet forces began to redeploy and on 4 November Soviet tanks moved into Budapest en masse, crushing the uprising with brute force. The fighting continued until 11 November resulting in 3000 Hungarians being killed and another 200,000 fleeing to neighbouring Austria. Nagy was arrested and deported to Romania where he was executed two years later, but most of the other prisoners were released from 1961 onwards. In 1989 Nagy was officially 'rehabilitated' and reburied in Budapest.

After the revolt, the Hungarian Socialist Workers' Party was reorganised and János

Kádár took over as president. In 1961 Kádár turned an old Stalinist slogan around to become, 'He who is not against us is with us', to symbolise the new social unity. After 1968 Hungary abandoned strict central economic planning and control for a limited market system based on incentives and efficiency. In a way Kádár was the grandfather of *perestroika* and the one who initiated the reform process in Eastern Europe. His innovative 'goulash communism' is discussed in the Economy section of this chapter.

In the 1970s and 1980s, Hungary balanced its free-wheeling economic programme with a foreign policy which consistently reflected that of the USSR. This was the exact opposite of neighbouring Romania, where an independent foreign policy was combined with orthodox 1950s internal central planning. By remaining a dependable Soviet ally during those years, Hungary was able to quietly lay the groundwork for the market economy of today.

In June 1987 Károly Grósz took over as premier and in May 1988, after Kádár retired, he became party secretary general. Under Grósz Hungary began moving towards full democracy, and beginning in January 1988 Hungarians were allowed to travel abroad freely. Change accelerated under the impetus of party reformers such as Imre Pozsgay and Rezső Nyers.

At a party congress in October 1989 the communists agreed to give up their monopoly on power, paving the way for free elections on 25 March 1990. The party's name was changed from the Hungarian Socialist Workers' Party to simply the Hungarian Socialist Party and a new programme advocating social democracy and a free-market economy was adopted. This was not enough to shake off the stigma of four decades of autocratic rule, however, and the 1990 elections were won by the centrist Hungarian Democratic Forum (MDF), which advocated a gradual transition towards capitalism. The right-wing Alliance of Free Democrats (SzDSz) which had called for much faster change came second and the Socialist Party trailed far behind. As

Gorbachev looked on, Hungary changed political systems with scarcely a murmur and the last Soviet troops left Hungary in June 1991.

In coalition with two smaller parties, Democratic Forum provided Hungary with sound government during its painful transition to a full market economy. These years saw Hungary's northern and southern neighbours split apart along ethnic lines. Prime minister József Antall did little to improve relations with Slovakia and Yugoslavia by claiming to be the 'emotional' and 'spiritual' prime minister of the large Hungarian minorities in those countries. In mid-1993 Democratic Forum was forced to expel István Csurka, a party vice president, after he made ultra-nationalistic statements which tarnished Hungary's image as a bastion of moderation and stability in a dangerous region. Antall died in December 1993 and was replaced by interior minister Péter Boross.

The economic changes of the past few years have resulted in declining living standards. In 1991 most state subsidies were removed leading to a severe recession exacerbated by the fiscal austerity necessary to reduce inflation and stimulate investment. This made life difficult for many Hungarians and in the May 1994 elections the Hungarian Socialist Party led by former communists won an absolute majority in parliament. This in no way implied a return to the past and Socialist leader Gyula Horn was quick to point out that it was his party which had initiated the whole reform process in the first place (as foreign minister in 1989 Horn played a key role in opening Hungary's border with Austria). All three main political parties advocate economic liberalisation and closer ties with the West but Hungarians have demonstrated that in future they want more consideration for the large majority which has yet to benefit from the changes.

GEOGRAPHY

Hungary (slightly bigger than Portugal) occupies the Carpathian Basin in the very centre of Eastern Europe and is not part of the Balkans. The 417-km Hungarian reach of the Danube River cuts through a southern extension of the Carpathian Mountains at the majestic Danube Bend north of Budapest. The Danube divides Hungary's 93,030 sq km in two: to the east is the Great Plain (Nagyalföld), to the west, Transdanubia (Dunántúl). The 579 km of the Hungarian portion of the Tisza River crosses the Great Plain about 100 km east of the Danube. The 'mountains' of Hungary are actually hills as they seldom exceed an elevation of 1000 metres (whereas mountains in Slovakia and Romania reach over 2000 metres). The highest peak is Kékes (1015 metres) in the Mátra Range north-east of Budapest.

Two-thirds of Hungary is less than 200 metres above sea level. The almost treeless Hungarian *puszta* (another name for the Great Plain) between the Danube and Romania is a harbinger of the steppes of Ukraine. Balaton Lake (covering 598 sq km) between the Danube and Austria reaches only 11.5 metres at its deepest point. The lake's average depth is three to four metres and the waters warm up quickly in summer. The over-use of nitrate fertilisers in agriculture has caused the groundwater beneath Hungary's low-lying plains to become contaminated with phosphates and in recent years the government has had to expend great efforts to protect Balaton Lake from pollution by fertiliser runoff and sewage.

There are five national parks. The two on the Great Plain, Hortobágy and Kiskunság, preserve the environment of the open puszta while Bükk National Park north of Eger protects the Bükk Mountains, Hungary's largest continuous mountain range. North again is Aggtelek National Park with the country's largest caves. Fertő-tó National Park is near Sopron.

ECONOMY

In a way Hungary was lucky not to have had the natural resources of Poland and Slovakia because without vast reserves of hard coal and iron ore the communists were never able to concentrate industrial development in heavy industry. The only metallic ore found here in significant quantities is bauxite of which Hungary is the largest European producer. After the 1956 political debacle, the emphasis shifted to light industry producing consumer goods.

Collectivised agriculture was introduced in Hungary between 1959 and 1961, and the country became a world leader in per capita grain and meat production. Hungary is self-sufficient in food, the main crops being barley, corn, potatoes, sugar beet and wheat. The collective farms have all been privatised but breaking them up into individual holdings has proved difficult.

Hungary was the first Eastern European country to move successfully towards an open marketplace; the economic reforms proposed by Mikhail Gorbachev in the late 1980s bore a distinct resemblance to those initiated by János Kádár two decades earlier. Kádár's 'New Economic Mechanism' combined central government planning with a market economy. Industrial plants and companies remained under state ownership but management was allowed wide discretionary power. The decentralised enterprises were required to compete and make a profit and those which consistently lost money had to declare bankruptcy. Foreign investment in joint ventures with state-owned firms was possible as early as 1972.

The competition resulted in an abundance of quality consumer goods with prices determined by actual costs or supply and demand rather than by state edicts. Numerous small, privately owned businesses such as bakeries, boutiques and restaurants had been functioning for years before 1990. Many Hungarians held after-hours jobs to supplement their incomes and taxation of this 'second economy' was an important source of government income. Yet despite providing this outlet for individual initiative, the communists restricted private enterprise to small family units cut off from credit and investment.

During the communist era two-thirds of Hungary's foreign trade was with the Soviet block and since the demise of the Moscow-based Council for Mutual Economic Assistance (Comecon) business has had to be reoriented towards the West. In 1990, 36% of Hungary's exports went to the European Community (now called the European Union). In 1991 it was 47% and in 1992 it grew to 52%. In 1992 the European Free Trade Association (EFTA) countries accounted for another 20% of exports. Hungary became an associate member of the European Union in 1991 with full membership envisioned by 2000, giving the country 10 years to prepare for unobstructed competition with the West.

In 1988 Hungary became the first Eastern European country to institute income tax and in June 1990 the Budapest Stock Exchange reopened after a hiatus of 42 years, Eastern Europe's first since the Stalin era. The stock market has not lived up to expectations due to the low return on stocks compared to other forms of investment and the turnover in government bonds on the exchange is 10 times the volume in stocks.

By mid-1994 Hungary had received US$7 billion in foreign investment, more than the rest of Eastern Europe combined. The USA has provided 40% of the investment, with Austria, Germany and France providing about 15% each. General Electric purchased the light-bulb manufacturer Tungsram in 1990 and General Motors, Suzuki, Audi and Ford have all set up automotive manufacturing plants in Hungary. Blue chips like the travel agency Ibusz, Danubius Hotels and Pick Salami have privatised in part by selling shares on the stock exchange, while Malév Hungarian Airlines has entered into a partnership with Italy's Alitalia. The private sector now accounts for almost 60% of the gross national product.

Yet despite all the investment, the Hungarian economy continues to contract, causing hardship and 13% unemployment. Tungsram has had to cut its workforce from 17,500 in 1990 to 10,400 in 1993 just to break even and the bus manufacturer Ikarus, which until 1989 produced 10% of all buses exported worldwide, has been forced to lay off thousands of employees to stay afloat.

Privatisation has proceeded slowly. In the

three years following its founding in 1990, the State Property Agency only managed to sell off 20% of state-owned properties. Hungary has a US$24 billion hard-currency debt to Western creditors, the highest per capita debt in Eastern Europe, which absorbs 35% of export income. In 1993 inflation was running at 23% with a budget deficit of US$2 billion (7% of the gross domestic product).

Hungary is the fifth most visited country in the world with over 22 million 'tourists' a year, about half of them from former Yugoslavia and Romania.

Hungary gets 48% of its electricity from four Soviet-built VVER-213 440-megawatt nuclear reactors at Paks on the Danube River and much of the rest comes from generators powered by burning dirty brown coal.

The average wage in Hungary is US$350 a month, the second-highest in Eastern Europe (after Slovenia).

There's a joke making the rounds in Budapest which illustrates what Hungarians expect from the current economic reforms. As two Budapesters are walking across the Chain Bridge they notice the Hungarian prime minister below walking on the waters of the Danube.

'A miracle!' cries the first.

'Nonsense,' retorts the second, 'he just can't swim'.

POPULATION & PEOPLE

Neither a Slavic nor a Germanic people, the Finno-Ugrian Hungarians were the last major ethnic group to arrive in Europe during the period of the great migrations. Some 10.3 million Hungarians live within their country, another five million abroad. The 1.7 million Hungarians in Transylvania constitute the second largest national minority in Europe (after the Albanians of Yugoslavia) and large numbers of Hungarians live in Slovakia, Yugoslavia, Ukraine, the USA and Canada. Minorities within Hungary include Germans (1.6%), Slovaks (1.1%), South Slavs (0.3%) and Romanians (0.2%). The quarter of a million Hungarian Gypsies live mostly in the northeastern corner of the country.

Religion-wise, 67.5% of the population is Catholic, 20% Calvinist and 5% Lutheran. Before WW II Hungary had 700,000 Jewish residents but now there are only about 80,000 (the largest Jewish community in Eastern Europe). Two-thirds of the people live in cities, over two million of them in Budapest. The next largest cities are Debrecen (215,000), Miskolc (195,000), Szeged (180,000), Pécs (170,000) and Győr (130,000). Hungary has the world's highest rates of suicide (48.4 per 100,000 men, 14.6 per 100,000 women) and abortion. Yet Hungary also has more poets per head than any country in Europe; 99% of the population is literate.

ARTS

Although the Renaissance flourished briefly in this region during the late 15th century, Hungary was isolated from the mainstream of European cultural development during the century and a half of Turkish rule which began in the mid-15th century. Then came domination by the Austrian Habsburgs until 1918 and, more recently, external interference from Nazi Germany and the USSR. Against this background, it's not surprising that Hungarian writers have struggled against oppression.

Hungary's greatest poet, Sándor Petőfi (1823-49), castigated both the privileges of the nobility and the plight of the common people. His poem *Talpra magyar* (Rise, Hungarian) became the anthem of the 1848 revolution in which he actively fought and died. Petőfi used the simple style of Hungarian folk songs to express subtle feelings and ideals.

An early colleague of Petőfi, novelist Mór Jókai (1825-1904), wrote historical works like *The Golden Age of Transylvania* (1852) and *Turkish World in Hungary* (1853) which are still widely read. The visual equivalent of Jókai's writings are the realist paintings depicting village life by the artist Mihály Munkácsy (1844-1900).

Hungary's finest 20th century lyric poet, Endre Ady (1877-1919), attacked the narrow materialism of the Hungary of his time provoking a storm of indignation from right-wing nationalists. Later Ady went on to describe the pain and suffering of war. The work of novelist Zsigmond Móricz (1879-1942) portrays the human conflicts of provincial life, and the work of poet Attila József (1905-37) expresses the torments faced by individuals in the technological age.

Hungary's best known contemporary writer is the novelist György Konrád (1933-) whose family only escaped deportation to Auschwitz because someone sent them to Austria by mistake. Konrád's *A Feast in the Garden* (1985) is an almost autobiographical account of the fate of the Jewish community in the small eastern Hungarian town where he grew up.

Perhaps the finest Hungarian novel of recent years is *The Book of Memories* (1985) which journalist Péter Nádas (1942-) laboured over for 11 years. This massive, complex work explores the lives of three main characters from the turn of the century, the 1950s and the 1970s.

Music

Hungarian folk music is played on the bagpipes, hurdy-gurdy, bombard, *tambur* (lute), flute and *cymbalum*. In times gone by, villages which were too poor to buy an organ often used the bagpipe during church services. The cymbalum, a zither or dulcimer with strings that are struck, gave origin to the piano. The *taragot*, a single-reed oboe of Hungarian origin, has a haunting sound not unlike that of a soprano saxophone.

The famous Hungarian pianist and composer Franz Liszt (Liszt Ferenc in Hungarian) (1811-86) was fascinated by the music of the Gypsies and even wrote a book on the subject. His *Hungarian Rhapsodies* pulse with the wild rhythms of Hungarian Gypsy music.

Opera composer Ferenc Erkel (1810-93) attempted to transform Italian opera into a Hungarian operatic style through the use of the *verbunkos*, a Gypsy dance based on Western European dance music. In his opera *Hunyadi László* (1844), Erkel utilised the *csárdás*, the national dance of Hungary,

which begins slowly but soon picks up as the couples whirl to syncopated rhythms. Erkel's 1861 opera *Bánk bán* captured the fiery nationalism of his time by portraying a 13th century revolt against the queen's hated foreign court.

Both Liszt and Erkel incorrectly assumed that what they heard the Gypsy musicians of their time playing was Gypsy music, when in fact it was mostly adapted Hungarian folk music and nostalgic ballads written by 19th century Hungarian nobles. Operetta composer Imre Kálmán (1882-1953) combined Liszt's Gypsy music with the Viennese waltz. Béla Bartók (1881-1945) and his colleague Zoltán Kodály (1882-1967) went beyond this urban 'Gypsy music' to collect genuine Hungarian folk music in remote villages and both integrated these folk songs and melodies into their own compositions.

Today folk music has largely disappeared in Hungarian villages as the lives of the peasants have been irrevocably changed. In Transylvania, however, folk music has survived as the Hungarian minority there seeks to preserve its identity by clinging to its traditional folk culture. The revival of folk music in Hungary in the 1970s drew inspiration from Transylvania and a journey there became *de rigueur* for all aspiring Hungarian folk musicians who later played at *táncház* (dance houses). The album *Blues for Transylvania* by Hungary's top folk group, Muzsikás, includes songs about conditions in Romania and the insecure position of the Hungarians living there.

Muzsikás' sound is appealing to Western ears because of the unique combination of traditional Hungarian instruments (bagpipe, buzuki, cymbalum, *duduk*, hurdy-gurdy, *kobsa*, shawm, tambur, Turkish horn), Western folk instruments (guitar, jews-harp, recorder) and classical instruments (cello, viola, violin, bass). Vocalist Márta Sebestyén's rich, earthy voice combines well with the group's lively folk rhythms.

Though Sebestyén's regular group is Muzsikás, she sings with many others including the Vujicsics Ensemble (pronounced voichich), which performs the

spirited folk music of the Serbian and Croatian minorities living in southern Hungary.
The skilfully arranged music of this professional group achieves its typical Balkan
sound through the use of traditional instruments such as the tambur, *tapan* (a big drum
hit at both ends with a stick), *okarina*
(ceramic flute), bagpipes and *zurna* (flute),
as well as the accordion, double-bass and
violin.

Though Hungarian Gypsies are not a
homogeneous ethnic group, their folk music
is of a unified style. The original Gypsy
musical tradition was mainly vocal and
lively stick dances and slow lyrical songs
relating the vicissitudes of life were accompanied only by snapping fingers, tapping pot
lids, water cans or spoons – other musical
instruments were not used. In the late 1960s
young Gypsies began using the guitar as part
of the Hungarian folk revival of the time. The
best known contemporary Gypsy group,
Kalyi Jag ('Black Fire'), sings mostly in
Romany and uses household utensils alongside the double bass, oral bass, guitar and
percussion.

Traditional Yiddish music is less known
than Gypsy music but is of similar origin
having once been closely associated with
Central European folk music. Until WW I
'klezmer' dance bands were led by the violin
and cymbalum, but the influence of Yiddish
theatre and the first wax recordings inspired
a switch to the clarinet which predominates
today. In 1990 the Klezmer Band of Budapest was formed to revive this happy mix of
jazz and the big band sound.

LANGUAGE

The Hungarians speak Magyar, a language
only they understand. Of the languages of
Europe only Finnish and Estonian are
related. Though many older Hungarians
understand German, this is one country
where it's unusual to meet someone on the
street who understands English. As usual, if
you have trouble making yourself understood, try writing down what you want to
say. Travel agency personnel usually do
speak English.

Some useful words to learn are: *utca*
(street), *körút* (boulevard), *út* (road), *tér*
(square), *útja* (avenue), *sétány* (promenade)
and *híd* (bridge). Public toilets (WC) are
marked *nôi* for women, *férfi* for men.
Hungarians put surnames before given
names. Lonely Planet's *Eastern Europe
Phrasebook* contains 72 pages of useful
words and expressions in Hungarian.

The longest word in the Hungarian language (meaning something like 'for your
unprofanability') is megszentségtelenithet-
etlenségeskedéseitekért.

Pronunciation

The Hungarian alphabet has 40 letters or
combinations of letters. In addition the
Roman letters 'q', 'w', 'x' and 'y' are used
in foreign words. Hungarian words are pronounced as they're written, with each letter
pronounced separately; there are no silent
letters or diphthongs. An acute accent lengthens an unaccented vowel, and a double acute
accent lengthens a vowel with a dieresis (for
example, ű is a long version of ü). A plural
is indicated by a final 'k' rather than an 's'.
Nem indicates a negative. The stress is
always on the first syllable.

c	'ts' as in 'hats'
cs	'ch' as in 'chair'
dz	'ds' as in 'roads'
dzs	'j' as in 'jump'
gy	'd' as in 'duty'
j	'y' as in 'yet'
ly	'y' as in 'yet'
ny	'n' as in 'onion'
s	'sh' as in 'shoe'
sz	's' as in 'see'
ty	't' as the first 't' in 'student'
zs	's' as in 'usual'

Greetings & Civilities

hello	*jó napot kivánok (formal)*
hello	*szia (informal)*
goodbye	*viszontlátásra*
goodbye	*viszlát (informal)*
good morning	*jó reggelt*
good evening	*jó estét*

please	*kérem*
thank you	*köszönöm*
thank you	*köszi (informal)*
I am sorry./Forgive me.	*Bocsánat.*
excuse me	*elnézést*
yes	*igen*
no	*nem*

Small Talk

I don't understand.	*Nem értem.*
Could you write it down?	*Kérem, írja le?*
What is it called?	*Hogy hívják?*
Where do you live?	*Hol lakik ön?*
What work do you do?	*Mi a foglalkozása?*
I am a student.	*Diák vagyok.*
I am very happy.	*Nagyon boldog vagyok.*

Accommodation

youth hostel	*ifjúsági szálló*
camping ground	*kemping*
private room	*fizetővendégszoba*
How much is it?	*Mibe kerül?*
Is that the price per person?	*Ez az ára személyenként?*
Is that the total price?	*Ez a teljes ár?*
Are there any extra charges?	*Kell ezért plusszt fizetnem?*
Do I pay extra for showers?	*Kell fizetni külön a fürdőszóbáért?*
Where is there a cheaper hotel?	*Hol van egy olcsóbb szálloda?*
Should I make a reservation?	*Szükséges a helyfoglalás?*
single room	*egyágyas szoba*
double room	*kétágyas szoba*
It is very noisy.	*Nagyon zajos.*
Where is the toilet?	*Hol van a mosdó?*

Getting Around

What time does it leave?	*Mikor indul?*
When is the first bus?	*Mikor indul az első autóbusz?*
When is the last bus?	*Mikor van az utolsó autóbusz?*
When is the next bus?	*Mikor indul a következő autóbusz?*
That's too soon.	*Az túl korai.*
When is the next one after that?	*Mikor van a következő azután?*
How long does the trip take?	*Mennyi ideig tart a kirándulás?*
arrival	*érkezés*
departure	*indulás*
timetable	*menetrend*
Where is the bus stop?	*Hol van az autóbuszmegálló?*
Where is the train station?	*Hol van a pályaudvar?*
Where is the left-luggage room?	*Hol van a csomagmegőrző?*

Around Town

Just a minute.	*Rögtön.*
Where is ...?	*Hol van ...?*
the bank	*bank*
the post office	*posta*
the tourist information office	*túrista információs iroda*
the museum	*múzeum*
Where are you going?	*Hová megy?*
I am going to ...	*Megyek ...*
Where is it?	*Hol van ez?*
I can't find it.	*Nem találom.*
Is it far?	*Messze van?*
Please show me on the map.	*Kérem, mutassa meg a térképen.*
left	*bal*
right	*jobb*
straight ahead	*előre*
I want ...	*Akarok ...*
Do I need permission?	*Szükségem van engedélyre?*

Entertainment

Where can I buy a ticket?	*Hol vehetek jegyet?*

I want to refund this ticket.	*Vissza akarom váltani ezt a jegyet.*
Is this a good seat?	*Ez jó hely?*
at the front	*elöl*
ticket	*jegyet*

Food

I do not eat meat.	*Nem eszem húst.*
self-service cafeteria	*önkiszolgáló étterem*
grocery store	*élelmiszerbolt*
fish	*hal*
pork	*disznó*
soup	*leves*
salad	*saláta*
fresh vegetables	*friss zöldség*
milk	*tej*
bread	*kenyér*
sugar	*cukor*
ice cream	*fagylalt*
coffee	*kávé*
tea	*tea*
mineral water	*ásványvíz*
beer	*sör*
wine	*bor*
hot/cold	*meleg/hideg*

Shopping

Where can I buy one?	*Hol vehetem meg ezt?*
How much does it cost?	*Mennyibe kerül?*
That's (much) too expensive.	*Az túl drága.*
Is there a cheaper one?	*Van ennél olcsóbb?*

Time & Dates

today	*ma*
tonight	*ma este*
tomorrow	*holnap*
the day after tomorrow	*holnap után*
What time does it open?	*Mikor nyit?*
What time does it close?	*Mikor zár?*

open	*nyitva*
closed	*zárva*
in the morning	*reggel*
in the evening	*este*
every day	*naponta*
At what time?	*Mikor?*
when?	*Hányadikán?*

Monday	*hétfő*
Tuesday	*kedd*
Wednesday	*szerda*
Thursday	*csütörtök*
Friday	*péntek*
Saturday	*szombat*
Sunday	*vasárnap*

January	*január*
February	*február*
March	*március*
April	*április*
May	*május*
June	*június*
July	*július*
August	*augusztus*
September	*szeptember*
October	*október*
November	*november*
December	*december*

Numbers

1	*egy*
2	*kettő*
3	*három*
4	*négy*
5	*öt*
6	*hat*
7	*hét*
8	*nyolc*
9	*kilenc*
10	*tíz*
11	*tizenegy*
12	*tizenkettő*
13	*tizenhárom*
14	*tizennégy*
15	*tizenöt*
16	*tizenhat*
17	*tizenhét*
18	*tizennyolc*
19	*tizenkilenc*

20	húsz
21	huszonegy
22	huszonkettö
23	huszonhárom
30	harminc
40	negyven
50	ötven
60	hatvan
70	hetven
80	nyolcvan
90	kilencven
100	száz
1000	ezer
10,000	tir ezer
1,000,000	millió

Facts for the Visitor

VISAS & EMBASSIES

Everyone entering Hungary must have a valid passport and in some cases also a visa. Nationals of the USA, Canada and most European countries do not require visas to visit Hungary. Citizens of Australia, Japan and New Zealand still require visas. If you hold a passport from one of these countries, check current visa requirements at a consulate or any Malév Hungarian Airlines office.

Visas are issued on the spot at Hungarian consulates upon receipt of between US$20 and US$25 and two photos. A double-entry tourist visa costs between US$30 and US$40 and you must have four photos. (If you know you'll be visiting Hungary twice, get a double-entry visa to avoid having to apply again somewhere else.) Some consulates charge US$5 extra for express service (10 minutes as opposed to 24 hours). Be sure to get a tourist rather than a transit visa. A tourist visa allows a stay of up to 90 days and can be used any time within three or six months. Visas are extended at local police stations for about US$10 (bring proof that you are staying in registered accommodation). A transit visa is only good for a stay of 48 hours, cannot be extended and costs the same price. On a transit visa you must enter and leave through different border crossings

and must have a visa for the next country you visit. Visas are issued at highway border crossings and the airport for US$40 but this usually involves a wait of an hour or more. Visas are never issued on trains.

A notice on the visa form instructs you to report to police within 48 hours of arrival. If you're staying in a private room arranged by a Hungarian travel agency, or at a hotel or camping ground, this formality will be taken care of for you. The agency or hotel will stamp your visa form and write in the nights you stayed with them. If you're staying with friends, you're supposed to report to the police in person. Upon departure from Hungary, an immigration officer will scrutinise the stamps and if too many nights are unaccounted for, you'll have some explaining to do. Your visa serves as an exit permit and you can leave Hungary any time within the 90-day validity period. Those not needing a visa only have to register with the police and get a stamp if they stay longer than 30 days.

Hungarian Embassies

In addition to the Hungarian embassies in Belgrade, Bucharest, Bratislava, Ljubljana, Prague, Sofia, Tirana, Warsaw and Zagreb listed elsewhere in this book, Hungarian embassies around the world include the following:

Australia
> 17 Beale Crescent, Deakin, ACT 2600
> (☎ 062-82 3226)
> Suite 405, Edgecliffe Centre, 203-233 New South Head Road, Edgecliffe, NSW 2027
> (☎ 02-328 7859)

Canada
> 7 Delaware Ave, Ottawa, ON K2P OZ2
> (☎ 613-232 1711)
> 1200 McGill College St, Suite 2040, Montreal, PQ H3G 4G7 (☎ 514-393 3302)
> 102 Bloor St West, Suite 1005, Toronto, ON M5S 1M8 (☎ 416-923 8981)

Netherlands
> Hogeweg 14, 2585 JD, The Hague
> (☎ 070-350 0404)

UK
> 35b Eaton Place, London, SW1X 8BY, England,
> (☎ 0171-235 2664)

USA
> 3910 Shoemaker St NW, Washington, DC 20008
> (☎ 202-362 6730)
> 11766 Wilshire Boulevard, Suite 410, Los
> Angeles, CA (☎ 310-473 9344)
> 227 East 52nd St, New York, NY 10022
> (☎ 212-752 0661)

MONEY

Unlike the situation in many other Eastern European countries, in Hungary travellers' cheques are a good way to carry money. You will need at least some cash hard currency in small bills to pay for visas and certain international transportation tickets, and on weekends and holidays cash is much better than travellers' cheques.

Travel agencies like Ibusz charge 1% commission to change money but they may not accept travellers' cheques. Post offices are poor places to change money as they usually accept only cash and give a lousy rate. The Orszagos Takarékpenztár or OPT Bank (National Savings & Commercial Bank) offers good rates and charges no commission on travellers' cheques, though not all OPT branches deal in hard currency. We list the most convenient OTP Bank branches throughout this chapter. Be aware that the foreign exchange counter in banks often closes before the rest of the bank, so go at least an hour before the closing times listed herein.

Several flashy foreign exchange outlets have established themselves in Hungary. They advertise excellent rates without commission, but *only on exchanges over US$2250*, otherwise you get a rate 10% lower. This distinction is only mentioned in tiny letters at the bottom of their large exchange-rate boards, sometimes in Hungarian. At other times they'll loudly announce 'no commission' then pay a rate 10% lower than the banks or advertise their higher selling rate instead of the buying rate they'll pay you. You may want to take advantage of their long hours and fast service to change a few dollars upon arrival, to tide you over until you can get to an Ibusz office or a bank, but never change large amounts with them. Whenever changing money somewhere other than at a bank be sure to check both the rate and the commission before producing any funds.

Only change as much as you intend to spend, as changing excess forints back into hard currency is difficult. Some Ibusz and National Bank branches will do it but only up to half the amount you changed originally (US$100 maximum), provided this is verified by receipts bearing your passport number, and they will deduct 7% commission. Don't leave it until the last moment to change money back because if you have to take forints out of the country you'll only get about 60% of their value at banks abroad. To convert US dollar travellers' cheques into dollars cash also costs 7% commission.

For cash advances on Diners Club, Master Card and Visa credit cards contact an Ibusz Bank (US$100 minimum). For American Express, go to the American Express office (☎ 251 0010) in Budapest.

Officially you're only allowed to import or export 1000 forints in notes not larger than 500 forints. Upon departure you could deposit Hungarian currency exceeding 1000 forints with customs against a receipt allowing you to pick it up at a savings bank on your next visit, less a 3% service charge. Banks in Vienna sell Hungarian currency at a nice discount.

The black-market rate for cash (never travellers' cheques) is about 25% higher than the official bank rate. Take care, however, as most of the people offering to change money on the street in Budapest are thieves. They will try to switch the counted money for a packet of cut paper, small bills or worthless Yugoslav banknotes at the last minute. If the person takes the money back from you after you have counted it, this is definitely his intention. These operators usually work in pairs. The second man will appear just as you're completing the transaction to cover the escape of the first by distracting you, perhaps by asking if you want to change more money with him. Anyone who tries to pay you with 50 or 100 forint notes or offers more than 25% above the official rate is almost certainly a thief. There is much less risk in dealing with someone who can't run away such as a waiter, taxi driver, landlord or vendor at a street market.

With any luck, by the time you read this Hungary will have finally made its currency fully convertible, ending this fun and games.

Currency

At last report US$1 = 100 forint (Ft). The Hungarian forint is divided into 100 fillér. There are both old and new coins of one, two, five, 10, 20 and 200 Ft; old coins of 10, 20 and 50 fillér also exist (the old coins work better in vending machines and public telephones). Banknotes come in denominations of 50, 100, 500, 1000 and 5000 Ft.

Hungarian notes must be the most picturesque in Eastern Europe. The 50 Ft note bears the likeness of the 18th century independence leader Ferenc Rákóczi II on the front and has mounted horsemen on the back. The 100 Ft note depicts the 19th century revolutionary Lajos Kossuth and a horse cart, and for 500 Ft you get the poet Endre Ady and a nice view of Budapest. The 1000 Ft note features the composer Béla Bartók and a mother nursing a baby. The 5000 Ft note has Count István Széchenyi on the front and his mansion at Nagycenk on the back.

Costs

In 1993 Hungary experienced 23% inflation. However, you should still be able to get by on US$25 a day by staying in private rooms, eating in unpretentious restaurants and travelling 2nd class by train. Two or more people travelling together or those camping and eating only at self-services can spend less.

Hungary is still reasonable because it doesn't discriminate against Western tourists with a two or three-price system, as is the case in most other Eastern European countries. What you pay for a hotel room will be about the same as a Hungarian would pay. The 25% value added tax (VAT) will have already been included in any price you're quoted.

Tipping

Hungarians routinely tip doctors, dentists, waiters, hairdressers and taxi drivers about 10%. In restaurants do this directly as you pay by rounding up the bill – don't wait to leave money on the table. If you feel you've been overcharged, you can make your point by paying exactly the amount asked and not a forint more.

CLIMATE & WHEN TO GO

Hungary has a temperate continental climate with Mediterranean and Atlantic influences. The winters can be cold, cloudy and humid, the summers warm. May, June and November are the rainiest months, although more rain falls in the west than in the east. Of the 2054 hours of sunshine a year at Budapest, 1526 occur in the period from April to September. July is the hottest month and January the coldest. The average annual temperature is 10°C.

SUGGESTED ITINERARIES

Depending on the length of your stay, you might want to see and do the following things in Hungary:

Two days
    Visit Budapest.
One week
    Visit Budapest, the Danube Bend and one or two of Győr, Kőszeg, Pécs, Kecskemét, Szeged or Eger depending on your next destination.
Two weeks
    Visit Budapest, the Danube Bend, Győr, Kőszeg, Hévíz, the north shore of Balaton Lake and one of Sopron, Pécs, Szeged or Eger depending on your next destination.
One month
    Visit all the places included in this chapter.

TOURIST OFFICES

The Hungarian Tourist Board, a branch of the Ministry of Industry & Trade, has established a chain of tourist information offices called Tourinform in many parts of Hungary and these are excellent places to ask general questions and pick up brochures.

If your query is about private accommodation, international train transportation or changing money, you should turn to a commercial travel agency, of which every Hungarian town has several. Ibusz is the largest travel company with over a hundred offices in Hungary plus representatives overseas (see the following list). Other national travel agencies with offices around the country include Cooptourist and Volántourist. Regional travel agencies in provincial centres (Dunatours, Balatontourist, Mecsek Tourist etc) are often more familiar with their own local area. The English-speaking staff in these offices are usually very courteous but keep in mind that they aren't paid to provide free information (although they often will if they have time).

The travel agency Express used to serve the youth and student market exclusively, but they now sell package tours more generally. They issue the ISIC student card (US$3) and sell reduced train tickets to students and all persons under the age of 26. Some Express offices also know about accommodation in student dormitories in July and August.

Ibusz Offices Abroad

Ibusz offices in countries outside Hungary include:

Netherlands
    Pampuslaan 1, 1382 JM Weesp
    (☎ 02940-30351)
UK
    Danube Travel, 6 Conduit St, London W1R 9TG
    (☎ 0171-493 0263)
USA
    One Parker Plaza, 4th floor, Fort Lee, NJ 07024
    (☎ 201-592 8585)

Tourist Literature

One publication to get hold of is the monthly *Programme in Ungarn/in Hungary* which lists concerts, opera and ballet performances, musicals, puppet shows, circuses, sporting events, exhibitions, museums and many other events and attractions not only in Budapest but around the country. Also useful are the *Hotel* and *Camping* brochures published annually by the Ministry of Tourism. These list all the official accommodation establishments which replied to their questionnaire. The hotels are categorised according to the star system, so you have an idea of how much each should charge. These free publications are often available at the Ibusz offices abroad, at the Malév Hungarian Airlines' offices and inside Hungary itself at luxury hotels and tourist offices. Otherwise go to Tourinform, Sütő utca 2, Budapest (metro: Deák tér), which will have all three.

BUSINESS HOURS & HOLIDAYS

Grocery stores open weekdays from 7 am to 7 pm, department stores from 10 am to 6 pm. Most shops stay open until 8 pm on Thursday but on Saturday close at 1 pm. Post offices open on weekdays from 8 am to 6 pm, and on Saturday from 8 am to 2 pm. In Hungarian the word for 'open' is *nyitva* and that for 'closed' is *zárva*.

Most museums are closed on Monday and the days following public holidays (and a few also on Tuesday). Museum admission fees have doubled and tripled in the last few years though most are still under US$1. Students get into most museums for half-price. Many museums are free one day a week but the exact day varies from place to place and from year to year.

The public holidays are New Year's Day (1 January), Day of the 1848 Revolution (15 March), Easter Monday (March/April), Labour Day (1 May), Whit Monday (May/June), St Stephen's Day (20 August), Republic Day (23 October) and Christmas (25 and 26 December).

CULTURAL EVENTS

Among Hungary's most outstanding annual events are the Budapest Spring Festival (held in the last third of March), Hortobágy Equestrian Days (late June), Sopron Early Music Days (mid-June to mid-July), Pécs Summer Theatre Festival (June and July), Szentendre Summer Festival (July), Kőszeg Street Theatre Festival (July), Szombathely Bartók Festival (July), Debrecen Jazz Days (July), Szeged Open-Air Festival (mid-July to mid-August), Horse Festival at Szilvásvárad (early September), Eger 'Agria' Folk Dance Meeting and Wine Harvest Days (September), Budapest Arts Weeks (September) and Budapest Contemporary Music Festival (September).

On the first Sunday in June there's a Folk Art Fair in Győr. St Stephen's Day (20 August) is celebrated with sporting events, parades and fireworks. On the same day there's a Floral Festival in Debrecen and a Bridge Fair in nearby Hortobágy. Formula 1 car races are held in August at the Hungaroring near Mogyoród, just north-east of Budapest.

The Budapest Spring Fair held in the second half of May features industrial products and the Autumn Fair in the middle of September focuses on consumer goods. Every March there's a Touristic Exhibition at Budapest's Hungexpo Fair Centre. In 1996 Vienna and Budapest will cohost a World's Fair with the theme 'Bridges to the Future' celebrating the links between Austria and Hungary, past and present. Twelve million visitors are expected to attend the six-month event marking the 1100th anniversary of the Magyar conquest of Hungary.

POST & TELECOMMUNICATIONS
Receiving Mail
Mail sent c/o Poste Restante, GPO, H-1364 Budapest 4, Hungary, is held at the main post office, Petőfi Sándor utca 13, but they send letters back after only 15 days, so take care.

American Express cardmembers can have their mail sent c/o American Express, Deák Ferenc utca 10, H-1052 Budapest, Hungary. Mail is held there for 30 days.

Telephone
You can make international calls on the old red coin phones though the new blue coin phones are much better, displaying the amount deposited and number dialled on a small screen. To call Western Europe is US$0.75 a minute, North America US$1.75 a minute and Australia US$2 a minute (there are no special times with reduced rates for international calls). If you use a coin phone have lots of old 10 and 20 Ft coins ready. The new coins either don't register or are counted as a lower denomination. Magnetic telephone cards can be used for international and local calls at card phones all around

Hungary. The cards come in values of US$2.75 or US$6.75.

For overseas calls, dial the international access code 00, the two-digit country code, the city or area code and the local number. For domestic calls within Hungary, dial the inland access code 06, the city or area code and the local number.

You can also get straight through to an operator based in your home country by dialling the 'Country Direct' number from a public phone (charges are reversed and your coin will be returned). These are:

Australia Direct	(☎ 00-800 06111)
Britain Direct (BT)	(☎ 00-800 04411)
Britain (Mercury)	(☎ 00-800 04412)
Canada Direct	(☎ 00-800 01211)
New Zealand Direct	(☎ 00-800 06411)
USA Direct (AT&T)	(☎ 00-800 01111)
USA MCI	(☎ 00-800 01411)
USA Sprint Express	(☎ 00-800 01877)

To call Hungary from abroad dial the international access code, 36 (the country code for Hungary), the area code and the number. Important area codes include 1 (Budapest), 22 (Székesfehérvár), 26 (Szentendre and Visegrád), 33 (Esztergom), 34 (Komárom), 36 (Eger and Szilvásvárad), 46 (Miskolc), 48 (Aggtelek), 52 (Debrecen), 62 (Szeged), 72 (Pécs and Siklós), 76 (Kecskemét), 83 (Keszthely), 84 (Siófok), 86 (Balatonfüred and Tihany), 87 (Badacsony), 94 (Kőszeg and Szombathely), 96 (Győr) and 99 (Sopron and Fertőd).

As telephone calls are easily made from booths on the street we don't generally list the sort of special telephone centres included in other chapters. If you have any problem finding a reliable public telephone simply go to any post office and you'll have a choice of several phones.

TIME
Time in Hungary is GMT/UTC plus one hour. The clock is put an hour forward at the end of March and an hour back at the end of September. As in German, in Hungarian 1/2 8 means 7.30 and not 8.30 (quite a few

English speakers arrive at appointments an hour late because of this distinction).

WEIGHTS & MEASURES
The electric current is 220 V, 50 Hz AC.

BOOKS & MAPS
Books are good value in Hungary and many titles are available in English. While visiting Budapest be sure to pick up an indexed city map at a bookstore.

The *Magyarország Autóatlasza* (Cartographia, Budapest) contains twenty-three 1:360,000 road maps of Hungary plus small street maps of almost every village and town in the country. The complete index makes this a valuable reference for motorists or anyone spending much time in the country. Cartographia also publishes a yellow *Budapest Guide* with 38 maps of the city, a street index and descriptive information in English.

You won't find a better guidebook than Lonely Planet's *Hungary, a travel survival kit* by Steve Fallon; *Hungary: The Rough Guide* by Dan Richardson is also excellent. Hungarian bookstores should have *Budapest, A Critical Guide* by Andras Torok – highly recommended.

Hungary by Paul Ignotus (Ernest Benn, London, 1972) is a good history of the country which is often available at libraries. Ignotus presents the country's history in a very personal way by constantly referring to Hungarian literature.

A History of Modern Hungary by Jörg K Hoensch (Longman, London, 1988) covers the period from 1867 to 1986 in a balanced way. Reg Gadney's *Cry Hungary! Uprising 1956* (Weidenfeld & Nicolson, London, 1986) is an illustrated chronicle of the 13-day revolt. Nigel Swain's *Hungary: The Rise and Fall of Feasible Socialism* (Verso Publishers, London and New York) focuses on the events of 1989.

In his amusing little book *Do It Yourself, Hungary's Hidden Economy* (Pluto Press, London, 1981), János Kenedi describes the machinations he employed to build himself a house outside Budapest. Kenedi's gentle exposé of the foibles of human nature provides a delightful glimpse of everyday life as it was in communist Hungary.

MEDIA
Several English-language weekly newspapers are published in Budapest. The *Daily News* (Box 3, H-1426 Budapest) has been around since 1967, although it's only a weekly now. Even during the communist era the *Daily News* established a reputation for its candid, informative reporting – one of the first papers of the former-communist bloc to do so.

Budapest Week (Nagy Diófa utca 7, H-1072 Budapest) contains an 'About Town' section with a detailed calender of events, plus a complete listing of films in English showing at Budapest cinemas.

The Budapest Sun (Dózsa György út 84/a II, H-1068 Budapest) includes a 'Style' insert which is a complete travel guide to the city with up-to-date information on restaurants and clubs, plus another extensive weekly calender. A six-month subscription is US$70 in Europe or US$85 elsewhere (payment by Visa card accepted). Both the *Week* and the *Sun* also provide an interesting mix of local news and are well worth picking up.

The *Budapest Business Journal* is aimed at business people working in Budapest.

Two English-language magazines are *The Hungarian Quarterly* (Box 3, Budapest H-1426) and the *Hungarian Digest*.

FILM & PHOTOGRAPHY
All the major brands of film are readily available and you can have your film developed in one hour at a dozen locations in Budapest, including Kodak Express on Váci utca near Vörösmarty tér.

HEALTH
If you have a medical problem go to the county hospital (*megyei kórház*) in county seats or the town hospital (*városi kórház*) in smaller centres and ask for the outpatients clinic (*rendelő intézet*). Hospitals also contain dental clinics.

First aid *(elsősegély)* attention in the case of an accident is free, but an examination *(orvosi vizsgálat)* by a doctor will be around US$15, an X-ray US$10. First aid and ambulance service are free if your life is in danger or permanent bodily damage can result. Prescription drugs and all locally made medicines are inexpensive. A bilateral agreement between Britain and Hungary allows for free medical treatment for citizens of one country in the other.

Rather than trying to find your way in a large hospital where few people speak English, however, it's often simpler to go directly to a private general practitioner *(orvosi rendelő)*. Their offices usually display a red cross outside. Fees are still lower than in the West.

Thermal Baths

There are 154 thermal baths in Hungary, most of them open to the public. The Romans first developed the baths of Budapest, and the Turks and Habsburgs followed suit. The thermal lake at Hévíz is probably Hungary's most impressive spa, though public thermal pools at Budapest, Eger, Győr, Gyula, Harkány and Komárom are also covered in this book.

In Budapest, Danubius Travels (☎ 117 3652) beneath the elevated car park on Szervita tér can provide information about medical programmes at the spas and make reservations on the spot. For example, a stay at the Thermál Hotel in Hévíz begins at around US$522/812 single/double a week, including half-pension, medical examination, massage, sauna, use of thermal baths, fitness room etc. From mid-October to March prices are 25% lower.

WORK

Budapest is already saturated with English teachers but it's still possible to get teaching jobs in provincial centres. Don't expect to save up a lot of money for travelling this way; instead look upon it as a good excuse to spend a bit of time in one place getting to know about Hungary. To obtain a work permit you'll need copies of your birth cer-

tificate and school transcript or academic record officially translated into Hungarian (at US$10 a page). An AIDS test is also mandatory (free for ISIC student card holders, otherwise about US$25). Your prospective employer must write a letter in Hungarian explaining why they are hiring you and not a Hungarian. Language schools often advertise in the English-language newspapers and making the rounds should produce leads. Your embassy may also have suggestions where you could apply.

ACTIVITIES

Water sports are concentrated around Balaton Lake, especially sailboarding at Balatonszemes and Killiántelep, and sailing at Balatonalmádi and Balatonboglár. Sailing boats and sailboards can be hired at many points around the lake. Motorboats are banned on the lake, so water-skiing is only possible at the FICC Rally Campground, Balatonfüred, where skiers are towed around a course by a moving cable.

Canoeing

There are many possibilities for canoeing or kayaking on the rivers of Hungary. The journey down the Danube from Rajka to Mohács (386 km) is fairly obvious but there are smaller, less congested waterways. For example, you can go down the 205 km of the Rába River from Szentgotthárd (on the Austrian border) to Győr. From Csenger near the far-eastern tip of Hungary, you can paddle down the Szamos and Tisza rivers to Szeged (570 km). A shorter trip would be from Gyula or Békés to Szeged (210 km) via the Koros and Tisza rivers. All of these places have train stations, making it easy to come and go, and there are many other possibilities.

Cycling

The possibilities for cyclists are many. The slopes of northern Hungary can be challenging, whereas Transdanubia is much gentler and the Great Plain monotonously flat (and in summer, hot). When planning your route, be aware that cycling is forbidden on motorways and main highways with a single-digit

HUNGARY

route number. Cycling is allowed on highways with two-digit numbers, although three-digit highways are preferable, as traffic is much lighter there. Bicycle touring is becoming very popular among Hungarians, which makes it all the nicer.

The following train stations rent bicycles at US$3 for one day, US$4 for two days or US$5 for three days: Balatonaliga, Balatonalmádi, Balatonföldvár, Balatonfüred, Balatonlelle, Balatonmáriafürdő, Balatonszemes, Keszthely, Kőszeg, Lébény-Mosonszentmiklós,Mosonmagyaróvár, Nagymaros, Nagymaros-Visegrád, Öttevény, Siófok, Szántód-Kőröshegy, Szécsény, Zamárdi and Zánka-Köveskál.

The Magyar Természetbarát Szövetség (Hungarian Nature-Lovers' Federation), Bajscy-Zsilinszky út 31, 2nd floor, Suite 3, Budapest, sells a useful cycling atlas entitled *Hungary by Bicycle* for US$3.

Hiking
Though Hungary doesn't have high mountains, you can enjoy good hiking in the forests around Aggtelek, Visegrád and Badacsony. North of Eger are the Bükk Mountains and south of Kecskemét the Bugac puszta, both national parks with marked hiking trails. Before you go there, pick up detailed hiking maps in Budapest as these are not always available locally.

Horse Riding
The Hungarians have a passion for horses that goes back over 1000 years and the sandy puszta seems almost made for horse riding. To get in some horse riding yourself, contact Pegazus Tours (☎ 117 1644), Ferenciek tere 5, H-1053 Budapest. The staff speak English. Pegazus works with several ranches and can make advance reservations for rooms (about US$50/75 single/double with half-board in midsummer, less in the off season) and horses (US$10 an hour). Ask about the Sarlóspuszta Riding Centre at Tatárszentgyorgy between Budapest and Kecskemét (closed from November to February), one of Hungary's finest.

Going through Pegazus is the only sure

way to arrange some riding because if you simply show up at a ranch in summer you may be told it's fully booked. It's cheaper however, to ask staff at provincial tourist offices about riding possibilities in their area and then try to get them to call ahead to make reservations. Few of the ranches are on bus or train routes, however, so unless you have your own transport be prepared for some long taxi rides. Turn to the Bugac and Szilvásvárad entries in this chapter for more information on horse riding.

Courses
Each July and August, Debrecen University organises a summer school course on the 'Hungarian Language and Culture'. There are two-week, 60-hour and four-week, 120-hour courses. A programme of related events such as films, musical evenings, folk dancing and sightseeing accompanies the courses. Tuition, excursions and a tram pass are US$225 for two weeks or US$450 for four weeks, plus US$50 registration for either. Course materials are another US$50 to US$100. Accommodation in a three-bedded room with full board is US$125 for each two-week period. Applications close on 15 May. For advanced students, there's an 80-hour winter course (apply before 15 December). For more information, contact the Debreceni Nyári Egyetem (☎ /fax 52-329 117), Egyetem tér 1, H-4010 Debrecen, Hungary.

HIGHLIGHTS
Museums & Galleries
Budapest's Museum of Fine Arts shelters a huge collection of old master paintings. The Museum of Contemporary History in Budapest Castle mounts informative exhibitions on recent issues. Two galleries of note dedicated to individual Hungarian artists are the Kovács Margit Museum in Szentendre and the Csontváry Museum in Pécs.

Castles
Hungary's most famous castles are those which resisted being overwhelmed by Turkish armies: Eger, Kőszeg, Siklós and

Szigetvár. Though in ruins, Visegrád Citadel symbolises the power of medieval Hungary.

Among Hungary's finest palaces are the Esterházy Palace at Fertőd, the Festetics Palace at Keszthely and the Széchenyi Mansion at Nagycenk.

Historic Towns

Many of Hungary's historic towns, including Eger, Győr, Sopron, Székesfehérvár and Veszprém, were rebuilt in the Baroque style during the 18th century. Kőszeg is one of the few towns which retains a strong medieval flavour, and Szentendre on the Danube has a Balkan air. The greatest monuments of the Turkish period are in Pécs.

ACCOMMODATION
Camping

Hungary has from 140 to 150 camping grounds and these are the cheapest places to stay. Small, private camping grounds accommodating as few as six tents are usually preferable to the large, noisy, 'official' camping grounds. Prices vary from US$4 to US$12 for two adults at one, two and three-star camp sites. The sites around Balaton Lake are more expensive and an additional US$0.75 per person 'resort tax' is levied in some areas. Some sites on the Great Plain have poor drainage.

Most camping grounds open from mid-May to mid-September and rent small bungalows (from US$7) to visitors without tents. In midsummer the bungalows may all be taken, so it pays to check with the local tourist office before making the trip. Members of the International Camping & Caravanning Club (FICC) and holders of student cards usually get a 10% discount, although this varies. Freelance camping is prohibited.

Youth Hostels & Student Dormitories

Despite the 23 hostels listed in the HI handbook, a YHA (Youth Hostels Association) card doesn't get you very far in Hungary. Excepting those in Budapest, most of the hostels are in places well off the beaten track

which you're unlikely to visit unless you go there specifically because there is a hostel. The only year-round youth hostels are in Budapest.

Hostel beds cost about US$7 in Budapest and a bit less elsewhere. A YHA card is not required although you occasionally get 10% off with one. Some hostels give an additional 25% discount if you show a student card. Camping is not allowed. There's no age limit at the hostels, they remain open all day and are often good places to meet other travellers.

In July and August Hungary's cheapest rooms are available in vacant student dormitories where beds in double, triple and quadruple rooms begin around US$5 per person. There's no need to show a student or hostel card, and it usually won't get you any discount. Express offices can generally tell you which dormitories to try and they'll sometimes call ahead to reserve your bed. Most dorms will admit you without the mediation of Express, however, though it often seems to be at the discretion of the person holding the keys.

Tourist Hostels

There's another class of accommodation which is similar to Western youth hostels but not included in the HI handbook. A tourist hostel (turistaszálló) offers beds in separate dormitories for men and women. There are no rules (for example, there are no curfews, smoking and drinking are allowed in the rooms). Tourist hostels are found in many cities and most stay open all year. The overnight fee will be around US$3 and in winter you'll probably have a whole room to yourself.

Private Rooms

Private accommodation used to be the cheapest way to go in Hungary but high government taxation, agency commissions and inflation have caused private room prices to double and sometimes triple in recent years while hotel rates have remained more stable, making private rooms less of the good deal they once were. In many cases you can now get a room at a cheap hotel for close to what you'd pay to occupy the spare room in someone's flat. Rooms in student dormitories, youth hostels and bungalows at camping grounds are now often cheaper than private rooms.

Expect to pay from US$6 to US$15 single, US$10 to US$30 double depending on whether the room is 1st, 2nd or 3rd class. Private rooms at Balaton Lake are slightly more expensive. Single rooms are often hard to come by and you'll usually have to pay a 20% supplement if you stay only two or three nights.

Private rooms are assigned by travel agencies which take your money and give you a voucher bearing the address. The offices usually close at 4 pm on weekdays and 1 pm on Saturday, so you must arrive early. (Longer hours are common in summer.) If the first room you're offered seems too expensive, ask if they have a cheaper one. There are usually several agencies offering private rooms, so ask around if the price is higher than usual or the location inconvenient. The rooms only become available after 5 pm, so leave your bags at the station.

If you decide to take a private room, you'll share a house or flat with a Hungarian family. The toilet facilities are usually communal but otherwise you can close your door and enjoy as much privacy as you please. All 1st and some 2nd and 3rd-class rooms have shared kitchen facilities. In Budapest you may have to take a room far from the centre of town, but public transport is good and cheap.

In Budapest private individuals at the train stations or on the street in front of Ibusz offices may offer you an unofficial private room (*szoba*). The prices these individuals ask are often higher than those asked at the agencies and you will have nowhere to complain in case of problems. Sometimes these people misrepresent the location or quality of their rooms to convince you to go with them. In resort areas watch for houses labelled *szobá kiado* or *zimmer frei*, advertising the availability of private rooms.

Pensions

Small, privately owned pensions are popular with German-speaking visitors who like the personalised service and homy atmosphere. Most pensions have less than seven rooms and the restaurant that goes with them is their real moneymaker. Always ask to see the room first and ask if there is another if you're not completely satisfied as the rooms can vary considerably. Prices are about twice what you'd pay for a comparable private room (from US$25 double) but you can go straight there without wasting time at a travel agency and waiting until 5 pm. You'll find pensions in main tourist areas like the Danube Bend, Balaton Lake, Sopron, and so on.

Hotels

Hungarian hotel rooms are usually more expensive than private rooms, but they are cheap by international standards (from US$12 single, US$15 double). A hotel may be the answer if you're only staying one night or if you arrive too late to get a private room. Two-star hotels usually have rooms with a private bathroom, whereas at one-star hotels the bathroom is usually down the hall.

If you want to be sure of finding accommodation in another Hungarian city, have a travel agency (such as Ibusz, Express, Cooptourist, Dunatours, Volántourist) reserve a hotel room for you. The staff will need a couple of days' notice, and in addition to the regular room rate you must pay the telex charges and a 10% commission. Still, if you're there in the busy summer season, it may be worth it.

FOOD

Hungary has a tasty national cuisine all of its own. Many dishes are seasoned with paprika, a red spice made from a sweet variety of red pepper which appears on restaurant tables beside the salt and pepper. Although paprika originated in Central America, the peasants of Szeged have been growing it since the early 18th century and it's now as important to Hungarian cuisine as the tomato is to Italian cuisine.

Hungarian goulash (gulyás) is a thick beef soup cooked with onions and potatoes. What we think of as goulash is here called pörkölt, meat stewed with onions and paprika. If sour cream is added to pörkölt it becomes paprikás. Pork is the most common meat dish. Cabbage is an important vegetable in Hungary, either stuffed in the Turkish fashion (töltött káposzta) or made into a thick cabbage soup (káposzta leves) that is popular among late diners. Other delicacies include goose-liver sandwiches and paprika chicken (paprikás csirke) served with tiny dumplings.

Fisherman's soup (halászlé) is a rich mixture of several kinds of boiled fish, tomatoes, green peppers and paprika. It's a full meal in itself. Balaton Lake pike (süllő) is generally served breaded and grilled.

Noodles with cottage cheese and tiny cubes of crisp fried bacon (túrós csusza) go well with fish dishes. Hungarian cream cheese (körözött) is a mixture of sheep cheese, paprika and caraway seeds. Strudel (rétes) is a typical layered pastry filled with apple, cherry, cabbage, curd or cheese. Look out for lángos, a huge Hungarian doughnut eaten with garlic salt, cheese and yoghurt.

Some dishes for vegetarians to request are rántott sajt (fried cheese), rántott gomba (fried mushrooms), gomba leves (mushroom soup), gyümöles leves (fruit soup), sajtos kenyer (sliced bread with melted cheese) and túrós csusza (cottage cheese crepes). Bab leves (bean soup) sometimes contains meat. Pancakes (palacsinta) may be made with cheese (sajt), mushrooms (gomba), nuts (dió) or poppy seeds (mák).

Of the two large supermarket chains, ABC and Csemege Julius Meinl, the latter is a bit more up-market and sometimes they sell take-away salads in plastic containers. Healthy brown bread is made from four to six different grains and is sprinkled with sesame, sunflower seeds and rolled oats. You can also find kifli, individual crescent rolls made from reform dough.

Restaurants

Hungarian restaurants (étterem or vendéglő) are relatively inexpensive. Meal prices begin around US$2 in a self-service restaurant, US$3 in a local restaurant and US$6 in a tourist restaurant. Lunch is the main meal of the day. Some restaurants offer a set lunch or 'menu' on weekdays and this is usually good value. It consists of soup, a side salad, a main course and occasionally a dessert.

Restaurant menus are often translated into German and sometimes into English. The main categories are levesek (soups), saláták (salads), előételek (appetisers), sajtok (cheeses), készéelek (ready-to-serve meals which are just heated up), frissensültek (freshly prepared meals), halételek (fish), szárnyasok (poultry), tészták (desserts) – useful to know if you have to choose blindly from a Hungarian menu. If you're in a bit of a hurry, order something from the készéelek section and not a frissensültek dish which may take 20 minutes to prepare.

If garnishes (köretek) such as rice, pommes frites, burgonya (boiled potatoes) etc are individually listed in a separate section of the menu it probably means they're not included with the main plate and will cost extra, though the waiter should indicate this by asking which ones you want and not just add them to your order.

Occasionally, a sharp waiter will bring you a side salad or something else you didn't order with the intention of inflating your bill. If you don't really want it, just say nem ezt rendeltem! (I didn't order that!) and send it back. At other times you'll be charged extra for some dish you never got or a special brand of imported beer when all you wanted was ordinary Hungarian draught beer. If you ask for a pohár (glass) or a korsó (half-litre mug) by name and don't just say 'beer' they're less likely to try this trick. If the prices of the drinks aren't listed on the menu they'll be higher than you expect.

Always insist on seeing a menu with prices listed to get an idea how much your meal will cost and if you're sure a waiter is deliberately overcharging but it's only by 10% to 15%, just pay the exact amount without a tip and try not to let it spoil your meal. Some places add a 10% service charge to the bill which also makes tipping unnecessary. Honest, attentive waiters, on the other hand, deserve their 10% (tip as you pay). Mini rip-offs by waiters are routine at Budapest restaurants.

Many tourist restaurants feature Gypsy music after 6 pm and the musicians are accustomed to receiving tips. Give them 100 Ft and they'll move to the next table. At better restaurants it's obligatory to check in your coat (US$0.10).

A *csárda* is a traditional inn or tavern offering spicy fare and fiery wine. *Borozó* denotes a wine cellar, *söröző* a pub offering draught beer (*csapolt sör*) and sometimes meals. A *bisztró* is an inexpensive restaurant that is often self-service (*önkiszolgáló*). *Büfés* are the cheapest places, although you may have to eat standing at a counter. Pastries, cakes and coffee are served at a *cukrászda*, while an *eszpresszó* is a café. A *bár* is a nightclub with music and dancing.

The Hungarian fast-food chains which sprang up in the 1980s are to be avoided for their dry, tasteless fare served on plastic plates. If there's anything worse than the US fast-food outlets it's City Grill, Dixie Chicken, Chips & Chicken and Paprika Aranybárány. In Hungary the ice cream is worth lining up for.

DRINKS
Hungarian wines match the cuisine admirably and the best wines have a Hungarian flag around the top of the bottle. The finest are those produced in the volcanic soils of Badacsony, Eger, Sopron and Tokaj. Southern Hungary (Pécs, Villány and Szekszárd) is also noted. One of the best Hungarian red wines is Egri Bikavér, and Tokaji Aszú is a very sweet golden-white wine of an almost liqueur consistency. Louis XIV of France called Tokaji Aszú 'the king of wines and wine of kings'. Medoc Noir is a strong, sweet red dessert wine. Others to watch for are Tihany Cabernet, Villány Pinot Noir, Soproni Kékfrankos, Badacsony Kéknyelű, Csopak Riesling and Móri Ezerjó (white). You can pick up a bottle of any of these at a local supermarket.

Also try the apricot, cherry or plum brandy (*pálinka*) which is to the Hungarians what schnapps is to the Germans. A shot before breakfast or dinner is in order. Mecseki and Hubertus are two Hungarian liqueurs.

Unicum, a semi-bitter herbal liqueur produced from 40 medicinal plants according to a secret recipe, has been the national drink of Hungary since 1790. Austrian emperor Joseph II christened the liqueur when he exclaimed '*Das ist ein Unikum!*' ('This drink is unique!'). Unicum comes in a round bottle and bears the brand name Zwack. It's not cheap: a 700-ml bottle costs US$12.

Though tourist restaurants often stock only Austrian beer as a way of justifying their high prices, Hungary does produce quality beer, one of the best of which is Dreher, brewed at Budapest. Many excellent German beers such as Kaiser are produced in Hungary under licence.

ENTERTAINMENT
Hungary is a paradise for culture vultures. In Budapest there are several musical events to choose from each evening and the best opera tickets seldom cost over US$10. Under the communists, culture was heavily subsidised by the state and many of the benefits remain. Unlike in Prague, tickets *are* available at normal prices and the friendly Hungarians usually go out of their way to help foreign visitors get seats. Besides the traditional opera, operetta and concerts, there are rock and jazz concerts, folk dancing, pantomime, planetarium presentations, movies, discos, floor shows and circuses to keep you smiling.

Excellent performances can also be seen in provincial towns such as Eger, Győr, Kecskemét, Pécs, Szeged, Székesfehérvár and Szombathely, all of which have fine modern theatres. Information about events is readily available at tourist offices. Some useful words to remember are *színház* (theatre), *pénztár* (ticket office) and *elkelt* (sold out).

In mid-June most theatres close for summer holidays, reopening in late September or October. Summer programmes especially designed for tourists, including operas, operettas and concerts, are twice as expensive as the programmes for regular subscribers in winter. On the other hand, there are many summer festivals from late June to mid-August, though the period from mid-August to late September is culturally dead.

Going to the movies in Hungary can be hit or miss as the programmes advertised outside may be coming attractions or even what's showing in some other cinema across town. To avoid unwelcome surprises, write down in Hungarian the name of the film you think you're going to see with a large question mark after it and show it to the ticket seller before you pay. Also be aware that many foreign films are dubbed into Hungarian, so again, try asking the ticket seller if the film is dubbed (*szinkronizált* or *magyarul beszélő*), or only has Hungarian subtitles (*feliratos*) and retains the original soundtrack. If you and the clerk are unable to communicate, just wait at the ticket window until another patron comes along who either speaks a little English or is willing to try to understand.

On the positive side, admission prices are extremely low in comparison with those in the West. The *Budapest Week* and the *Budapest Sun* provide comprehensive listings of what's on at Budapest's many cinemas with times, addresses and plot descriptions, but elsewhere around the country you're on your own. Unfortunately films by noted Hungarian directors like István Gaál, Miklós Jancsó, Zsolt Kezdi-Kovács, Károly Makk, Pál Sándor and István Szabó are likely to be in Hungarian with no subtitles (see them at a good art cinema at home).

THINGS TO BUY
Hungarian shops are as well-stocked as those in the West and the quality of the products is high. Food, alcohol, books and folk-music recordings are affordable and there is an excellent selection. Traditional products include folk-art embroidery and ceramics, wool carpets and wall hangings, bone lace, wooden toys, dolls, and Herend, Kalocsa or Zsolnay porcelain. If you might be interested in buying a painting, read Things to See in the Kecskemét section of this chapter.

Throughout Hungary, a Polish market is called a *Lengyel piac* though the vendors are as likely to be Ukrainians or Russians as Poles these days. These flea market-style events often occur in an open field near the edge of town and the locals usually know where.

In theory, visitors are only allowed to export US$50 worth of goods without receipts and not in commercial quantities. In practice, it's unlikely that you'll be asked to open your bags at the border. You can sometimes get a 25% discount from small private shops and street vendors if you offer to pay in cash hard currency, though you'll need small bills.

Getting There & Away

AIR
Malév Hungarian Airlines has direct flights to Budapest from Amsterdam, Athens, Beirut, Berlin, Brussels, Bucharest, Cairo, Cologne, Copenhagen, Damascus, Dresden, Frankfurt, Helsinki, Istanbul, Kaunas, Kiev, Larnaca, Leipzig, London, Madrid, Milan, Moscow, Munich, New York, Nuremberg, Paris, Prague, Rome, St Petersburg, Sofia, Stockholm, Stuttgart, Tel Aviv, Thessaloniki, Tirana, Trieste, Tunis, Vienna, Vilnius, Warsaw, Zagreb and Zürich.

Until recently Budapest's Ferihegy Airport handled all international flights but a new airport intended to receive tourist charters is under construction at Sármellék near Keszthely at the west end of Balaton Lake. There are no domestic flights in Hungary and there is no airport departure tax.

Malév has no student discounts on flights originating in Hungary but there is a youth fare available to persons aged 24 years or younger which is about 20% cheaper than the lowest discounted fare available to other passengers. It's available on one-way flights

HUNGARY

from Budapest: Amsterdam US$130, London US$190, New York US$385 high season, US$290 low season. Youth tickets to points in Europe can only be purchased one week in advance, to North America only three days in advance.

LAND

Budapest is well connected to all surrounding countries by road, rail, river and air. Trains arrive in Budapest from every neighbouring capital and in summer there's a hydrofoil service between Vienna and Budapest. Other major entry points by train are Sopron (from Vienna, Austria), Szombathely (from Graz, Austria), Pécs (from Zagreb, Croatia), Szeged (from Subotica, Yugoslavia), Miskolc (from Košice, Slovakia) and Sátoraljaújhely (from Slovenské Nové Mesto, Slovakia). By road there's bus service to/from all neighbouring countries, often the cheapest way to go. In Budapest, buses to/from Western Europe use the Erzsébet tér Bus Station while those serving Eastern Europe are from the Népstadion Bus Station.

Bus

To/From Western Europe There's a Eurolines bus service twice a week throughout the year from Rotterdam to Budapest via Amsterdam, Düsseldorf and Frankfurt/Main (1615 km, 24 hours, US$100 one way, US$162 return, with a 10% discount for those under 26 or over 59 years of age). From mid-June to mid-September the Amsterdam bus runs three times a week. Alternating services are operated by Dutch and Hungarian drivers. If you're a nonsmoker be sure to book the Hungarian bus as the Dutch drivers smoke continually and don't mind passengers following their example (whereas the Hungarian drivers don't allow smoking on their buses). Eurolines offers a special US$150 'Capital Tripper' fare to Amsterdam-Budapest-Prague-Amsterdam or vice versa. (A Slovak transit visa is required by some nationals.) The run from Amsterdam to Budapest is through Austria, so Czech and Slovak visas are not required. In Amsterdam

tickets are sold by Budget Bus/Eurolines (☎ 020-627 5151), Rokin 10. In Budapest you can buy them at the Erzsébet tér Bus Station. In summer this bus is often full, so try to book ahead.

A similar service from Brussels to Budapest (1395 km, 20 hours, US$95 one way, US$157 return) also operates twice a week from June to September. Ask for information from the Europabus office (☎ 2-217 0025), Place de Brouckere 50, Brussels 1000.

Other international buses departing from Budapest's Erzsébet tér Bus Station include those to Florence (weekly, 1025 km, 17½ hours, US$62), Hamburg (two a week, 1215 km, 17 hours, US$79), Milan (two a week, 1080 km, 17 hours, US$65), Munich (three a week, 701 km, 10 hours, US$58), Paris (weekly, 1525 km, 23 hours, US$81), Prague (twice weekly, US$21), Rijeka (twice weekly, US$40), Rome (weekly, 1310 km, 22 hours, US$77) and Pula (weekly, US$40). It's best to reserve seats on these long-distance buses a few days in advance, especially in summer.

From June to September buses run between Budapest and London twice a week (1770 km, 29 hours, US$125 one way, US$200 return – half the price of a train ticket. In London check with National Express (☎ 0171-730 0202) at the Victoria Coach Station. In Paris enquire about Hungary-bound buses at the Gare Routiere Internationale Galliéni (☎ 4972 5151), Avenue du Général de Gaulle (metro: Galliéni).

A cheaper bus between London and Budapest is operated by Attila Tours (☎ /fax 0171-372 0470), Suite 318, 36a Kilburn High Rd, London NW6 5UA, departing from each end every Saturday morning (£60/100 one way/return). Smoking is not allowed on these buses. In Budapest, tickets are available from Attila Tours (☎ /fax 209 0923), Suite 307, Karolina út 65 (tram No 49 from Deák tér to a railway bridge).

Also consider a low-cost bus tour with New Millennium Holidays (☎ 0121-711 2232), 20 High St, Solihull, West Midlands B91 3TB, England, UK. They have all-inclusive departures year-round to Alsópáhok near Keszthely.

To/From Austria Three buses travel daily between Vienna's Autobusbahnhof Mitte and Budapest's Erzsébet tér Bus Station, departing from Vienna at 7 am and 5 and 7 pm and from Budapest at 7 am, noon and 5 pm daily (254 km, US$23 one way, US$34 return). Smoking is not allowed on these buses. In Budapest you can make enquiries at the Erzsébet tér Bus Station and in Vienna at Blaguss Reisen (☎ 0222-50 1800), Wiedner Hauptstrasse 15, or at Autobusbahnhof Wien-Mitte.

To/From Romania The cheapest and easiest way by far to go from Hungary to Romania is by bus from Budapest's Népstadion Bus Station, Hungária körút 48-52 (metro: Népstadion). There are buses to Oradea/Nagyvárad (daily, 260 km, six hours, US$10), Arad (six a week, 276 km, seven hours, US$12), Timişoara/Temesvár (weekly, 327 km, eight hours, US$14), Cluj-Napoca/Kolozsvár (daily, 413 km, 9½ hours, US$19) and Brasov/Brassó (six a week, 790 km, 17½ hours, US$31). A return ticket is about 50% more than a one-way ticket.

The international ticket window at Népstadion Bus Station is open weekdays from 5.30 am to 6 pm, Saturday 5.30 am to 4 pm. On Sunday try paying the driver. The clerks at Népstadion speak no English, so study the posted timetables and then write down what you want. In this section the Hungarian names of the Romanian cities in question are provided as these are the ones you'll see written on the timetables. Tickets are easily purchased with forint – forget the train on these routes! Be aware, however, that there can be long delays at highway border crossings into Romania, though it's worse westbound than eastbound.

You'll also find daily buses from Szeged to Arad (106 km, US$5) and Timişoara (157 km).

To/From Slovakia & Poland The bus from Budapest to Bratislava/Pozsony (200 km,

US$9) runs only once a week (currently on Friday). More useful are the buses to Tatranská Lomnica/Tatralomnic (twice a week, 311 km, seven hours, US$13) and Zakopane (twice a week, US$15), on opposite sides of the Tatra Mountains, a route poorly served by train. The buses to Zakopane go via either Trstená (344 km, eight hours) or Łysa Polana (364 km, nine hours). All these leave from Népstadion Bus Station in Budapest.

To/From Former Yugoslavia & Turkey Other useful international buses from Népstadion Bus Station include those to Subotica/Szabatka, Yugoslavia (daily, 216 km, US$9) and Istanbul, Turkey (five a week, 1375 km, 25 hours, US$50). Tickets to Istanbul must be purchased with cash dollars and Romanian and Bulgarian transit visas are required. From Harkány, 22 km south of Pécs, you can catch a bus to Belgrade (US$19) three times a day.

You'll find frequent buses to Croatia and Slovenia from towns along the border, such as those from Pécs to Osijek (twice daily, 82 km, US$7), Barcs to Zagreb (five a day, 202 km, US$14), Nagykanizsa to Zagreb (twice daily, 176 km, US$9) and Lenti to Ljubljana (twice weekly, 235 km, five hours, US$12). With the border between Yugoslavia and Croatia closed, people from former Yugoslavia are forced to transit Hungary with bus changes in these towns.

Train
International railway fares from Hungary to other Eastern European countries are now from 10 to 15 times higher than they were in 1989. For instance, the 1989 edition of this book quoted a 1st-class fare of US$10 from Budapest to Berlin. Now you'll pay US$85 to cover the same distance in 2nd class. Similarly, from Budapest to Prague now costs US$55 in 2nd class, one way, compared with only US$6 in 1st class previously. Fares to Romania have also jumped spectacularly, making it essential to break your journey in border towns like Oradea or Arad if you're really serious about saving money.

HUNGARY

This is more of a problem if you buy your ticket in Hungary as tickets from Romania to Hungary are much cheaper: from Budapest to Bucharest is US$84 whereas from Bucharest to Budapest is US$31. This could change.

Other sample one-way 2nd-class train fares from Budapest are US$40 to Arad, US$27 to Belgrade, US$23 to Bratislava, US$85 to Bucharest, US$22 to Košice, US$39 to Kraków, US$26 to Oradea, US$29 to Vienna, US$55 to Warsaw and US$30 to Zagreb. Bulgaria-bound, a ticket from Budapest to Sofia via Belgrade is US$54 but via Bucharest it's US$117! Before investing in a train ticket to any of these places, check the price of a bus along the same route. Train tickets to Western Europe have always been highly expensive. For example, from Budapest to Amsterdam is US$207 one way in 2nd class.

You can usually pay for international train tickets with Hungarian forint if you have an exchange receipt bearing your passport number. Otherwise hard currency in cash may be required (this seems to vary). The student travel agency Express has Eurotrain fares to Western Europe for persons aged under 26 years and 50% reductions to Eastern Europe for ISIC student card holders (no student discounts to Western Europe). Inter-Rail passes (available only to European residents) are accepted in Hungary.

Hungarian students get a 33% discount on train journeys wholly within Hungary and it's sometimes possible to get such reduced tickets at Ibusz offices and train stations. If you do get such a reduction, the conductor will probably insist that you pay the 33% on the train and fine you US$3 for trying to use an invalid ticket. We've heard from several readers who had this experience.

Eurail passes are accepted in Hungary but it's almost impossible to use the train enough inside the country to get your per diem Eurail cost out of it. A good plan is to finish or begin your Eurail pass here, thus saving on high international fares to Western Europe while not having to count your days in Hungary. MÁV Hungarian Railways, Andrássy út 34,

Budapest, can sell you a Eurail pass but at prices even higher than those charged outside Europe (see Getting There & Away in the main introduction to this book).

If you want to make a long trip across Western Europe, a much better deal than the Eurail pass is a regular one-way 2nd-class ticket. International train tickets are valid for two months and unlimited stopovers are allowed. For instance, if you pay US$220 to travel from Budapest to Lisbon you can have a leisurely two-month trip stopping in Vienna, Venice, Milan, Nice and Salamanca or anywhere else along that direct route you'd care to visit without any additional train costs. It costs US$300 to go via Vienna, Salzburg, Munich, Paris and Salamanca. After seeing Portugal you could buy another one-way ticket to some other remote corner of Europe and have a different two-month trip.

Unless otherwise stated, all of the 'name trains' listed following operate daily throughout the year and reservations are usually required. Second-class couchettes and 1st-class sleepers are almost always available. Though most of these trains have dining cars they're expensive, so take along some food and drink. Trains which originate in Hungary are less likely to be delayed than those transiting the country. Local unreserved trains are cheaper and easier if you just want to get across the border.

To/From Western Europe From Vienna, there are eight express trains a day to Budapest-Keleti via Hegyeshalom (270 km, three hours). These include the *Liszt Ferenc* from Dortmund (1365 km, 15 hours) via Nuremberg, the *Orient-Expressz* from Paris (1662 km, 21 hours) via Munich and the *Wiener Walzer* from Basel (1219 km, 15 hours) via Innsbruck, all via Vienna Westbahnhof. The Eurocity *Lehár* arrives at Budapest-Déli from Vienna Südbahnhof. In Vienna ask about special half-price return tickets between Vienna and Budapest on the *Lehár*. Seat reservations are not required on these trains but they're highly recommended unless you want to stand.

Several unreserved local trains travel between Vienna-Südbahnhof and Sopron (84 km, 1½ hours, US$10) via Wiener Neustadt or Ebenfurth. Sometimes you must change trains in these towns. One local train runs between Graz, Austria, and Szombathely (146 km, four hours) though there are six other trains if you change at Szentgotthárd, the Hungarian border station.

To/From Prague & Berlin From Prague to Budapest (616 km, nine hours) there's the *Pannónia* express train. From Berlin-Lichtenberg (993 km, 15 hours) to Budapest via Prague and Bratislava there are the daily *Hungária* and *Metropol* express trains which terminate in Hungary. The *Balt-Orient* and *Meridian* express trains also travel to Budapest from Berlin-Lichtenberg, Prague and Bratislava, continuing on to Romania or Bulgaria.

To/From Slovakia & Poland The *Báthory* express train runs daily from Warsaw to Budapest (837 km, 13 hours) via Katowice and Trenčín. The *Polonia* express train travels between Warsaw and Budapest via Žilina and Banská Bystrica. From western Poland there's the *Bem* express train to Budapest from Szczecin, Poznań and Wrocław via Trenčín. The *Varsovia* express train arrives from Gdynia/Gdańsk. These trains transit the Czech Republic as well as Slovakia, so beware of taking them if you require a Czech visa as the Czech border guards will put you off the train. Instead catch the *Cracovia* express train from Kraków to Budapest (599 km, 12 hours) via Košice and Miskolc which crosses eastern Slovakia.

The *Rákóczi* express train also runs from Košice to Budapest (270 km, 4½ hours) with an extension to/from Poprad-Tatry in summer. The two local trains a day between Košice and Miskolc (88 km, three hours) require no reservations. Otherwise, there are six unreserved local trains a day from Sátoraljaújhely, Hungary, to Slovenské Nové Mesto, Slovakia. These connect with trains to/from Miskolc on the Hungarian side and to/from Košice on the Slovak side.

To/From Romania & Bulgaria From Bucharest to Budapest (874 km, 15 hours) the *Balt-Orient, Dacia* and *Pannónia* express trains all travel via Arad. The *Karpaty* express train passes Arad, Szolnok, Miskolc and Košice on its way to Warsaw. The *Ovidius* express train runs from Constanţa to Budapest (1068 km, 17½ hours). Via Oradea, there's the *Claudiopolis* from Cluj-Napoca to Budapest (402 km, 7½ hours) and the *Corona* from Braşov to Budapest (1002 km, 14 hours).

Two local Hungarian trains a day also run between Oradea and Budapest-Nyugati (249 km, five hours, US$26 eastbound, US$18 westbound) and these are useful as no reservations are required. At last report their departure times were 6.05 am and 3.00 pm from Budapest-Nyugati and 7.27 am and 3.27 pm from Oradea. If coming from Romania, buy your open ticket from Oradea to Budapest at a CFR train ticket office well ahead (but not in Bucharest), as such tickets are not sold at Oradea Railway Station.

To/From Former Yugoslavia From Budapest to Croatia there are the *Adriatica, Agram, Drava* and *Maestral* express trains to Zagreb (394 km, seven hours) via Siófok. None of these are very convenient as they all put you in expensive Zagreb at odd hours. The *Drava* at least gets there in the early afternoon and conveys carriages to/from Ljubljana (500 km, 7½ hours) and Rome (25 hours).

A useful daily service connects Pécs directly to Zagreb (267 km, five hours, US$16), departing from Pécs in the early morning, Zagreb in the afternoon. Local trains run between Gyékényes and Koprivnica (15 km, 20 minutes, US$3) three times a day and between Nagykanizsa and Varaždin (72 km, 1½ hours) twice daily. None of these trains require reservations.

Yugoslavia-bound, you can take the *Avala, Beograd, Balkán, Hellas* and *Meridian* express trains from Budapest to Belgrade

(354 km, six hours) via Subotica. The *Meridian* continues to Sofia (771 km, 15 hours) via Belgrade. Local unreserved trains shuttle between Szeged and Subotica (45 km, 1½ hours, US$2) three times a day.

To/From Moscow & China In the past, Star Tours (☎ 113 7062), József körút 45, Budapest, has sold tickets for the Trans-Siberian Railway, charging US$160/200 in 2nd/1st class from Budapest to Moscow (2110 km, two days) and US$350/440 from Moscow to Beijing (7865 km, five days). Payment in cash hard currency is required. In normal times they can make reservations for the Moscow-Beijing portion and you should be able to arrange everything in a week to 10 days.

Once you have your train ticket and reservations you can apply for a Chinese tourist visa (allow three days for processing), then a Russian transit visa (US$60) which you may be able to get in one day. If time is short, ask for the Russian train via Manchuria which eliminates the need for a Mongolian transit visa (another three days' processing). Three-day Ukrainian transit visas are usually available at the border for US$50.

If you want to stop in Moscow for a few days Star Tours can make the necessary reservations at US$60/70 single/double a night and up, payable in advance in cash. All transportation and hotel bookings must be confirmed before you can begin visa hunting. With Russia in political and economic chaos, it's often impossible for agencies like Star Tours to book any train travel to China at all, so it's much better to plan on doing the Trans-Siberian trip westbound rather than eastbound (in other words, beginning in China itself).

Ibusz sells regular 2nd-class train tickets from Budapest to Kiev for US$102, to Moscow for US$136, but they cannot sell tickets to China. (In 1989 a 1st-class ticket from Budapest to Beijing with a sleeper was only US$90 total.)

Car & Motorbike

Some highway border crossings are only open to citizens of Hungary, Slovakia, Romania, Croatia and Yugoslavia but the crossings mentioned here (listed clockwise around the country) are open to everyone. In each case the name of the Hungarian border post is provided.

To/From Slovakia The border crossings are at Rajka (16 km south-east of Bratislava), Vámosszabadi (13 km north of Győr), Komárom (opposite Komárno), Parassapuszta (80 km north of Budapest via Vác), Balassagyarmat, Somoskőújfalu (just north of Salgótarján), Bánréve (45 km north-west of Miskolc), Tornyosnémeti (21 km south of Košice) and Sátoraljaújhely (opposite Slovenské Nové Mesto).

To/From Ukraine You may cross at Záhony (opposite Cop).

To/From Romania You have a choice of Csengersima (11 km north-west of Satu Mare), Ártánd (14 km north-west of Oradea), Gyula (66 km north of Arad) and Nagylak (between Szeged and Arad).

To/From Former Yugoslavia There are border crossings at Roszke (between Szeged and Subotica), Tompa (11 km north-west of Subotica) and Hercegszántó (32 km south of Baja).

To/from Croatia there's Drávaszabolcs (eight km south of Harkány), Barcs (right on the Dráva River), Berzence (23 km west of Koprivnica) and Letenye (between Nagykanizsa and Varaždin).

To/from Slovenia there's Rédics (eight km south-west of Lenti) and Bajánsenye (west of Zalaegerszeg).

To/From Austria You can cross at Rábafüzes (five km north of Szentgotthárd), Bucsu (13 km west of Szombathely), Kőszeg, Kópháza (just south of Sopron), Sopron (61 km south of Vienna) and Hegyeshalom (70 km south-west of Vienna).

On Foot

If you want to avoid the hassle or expense of

getting an international train ticket, you can easily walk across the Danube bridge on the Hungarian/Slovak border at Komárom/Komárno, 100 km south-east of Bratislava. See the Komárom section in this chapter for details.

To/from Romania, the easiest place to cross on foot is Nagylak/Nădlac between Szeged and Arad. There are nine unreserved local trains a day from Szeged to Nagylak (47 km, 1¼ hours) near the border. After crossing into Romania you must walk or take a taxi six km to Nădlac, where you'll find four local trains a day to Arad (52 km, 1½ hours). See the Szeged section of this chapter for more information.

Slovenia-bound, take a train from Budapest to Zalaegerszeg (252 km via Tapolca, four hours by express train), then one of eight daily trains from Zalaegerszeg to Rédics (49 km, 1¼ hours) which is only two km from the main highway border crossing into Slovenia. From the border it's an interesting five-km downhill walk through Lendava to Lendava Bus Station where you'll have a choice of six daily buses to Ljubljana (204 km) and many more to Maribor (92 km).

RIVER
Hydrofoil
Hydrofoil service on the Danube from Budapest to Vienna operates daily from April to mid-October, twice daily from May to mid-September (282 km, 5½ hours). Fares are high at US$68 one way, US$100 return, but ISIC student card holders get a 20% discount and children aged 15 years and under get a 50% discount. Eurail pass holders also pay 50%. Taking along a bicycle costs US$9 each way.

Bring along something to eat and drink and arrive early to get a good seat. The fare is supposed to include lunch but a favourite trick of the crew is to announce after departure that there wasn't time to load the food and then hand out small refunds. A short while later they're back selling sandwiches and drinks, but for a higher price.

In Vienna tickets are available from the Mahart Agency (☎ 1-505 5644 or 505 3844),

Karlsplatz 2/8, A-1010 Vienna. In Budapest tickets are sold at the hydrofoil terminal on the river between the Erzsébet (Elizabeth) and Szabadság bridges or at Ibusz, Károly körút 3.

Getting Around

BUS
Hungary's bright yellow Volán buses are a good alternative to the trains and bus fares are only about 15% more expensive than comparable 2nd-class train fares (expect to pay around US$1.50 an hour or US$3.75 per 100 km). Taking buses is essential for crossing the southern part of the country, for instance, from Szombathely to Keszthely, Kaposvár, Pécs and Szeged. For short trips in the Danube Bend or Balaton Lake areas, buses are recommended. If you have a front seat, you'll see more from the bus than you would from the train, though you may be a little cramped. Seats on Volán buses are spaced far enough apart for you to be able to fit your pack between your knees, however. Tickets are usually available from the driver, but ask at the station to be sure. There are sometimes queues for intercity buses so it's wise to arrive at the bus stop early.

Bus timetables are clearly posted at stations and stops. Some footnotes you could see include *naponta* (daily), *hétköznap* (weekdays), *munkanapokon* (on workdays), *munkaszüneti napok kivételével naponta* (daily except holidays), *szabadnap kivételével naponta* (daily except Saturday), *szabad és munkaszüneti napokon* (on Saturday and holidays), *munkaszuneti napokan* (on holidays), *iskolai napokan* (on school days) and *szabadnap* (on Saturday).

TRAIN
The MÁV (Magyar Államvasutak) operates comfortable, reliable and not overcrowded railway services on 7769 km of track. Second-class train fares in Hungary are US$1.50 for 50 km, US$3.25 for 100 km, US$6.50 for 200 km or US$11.75 for 500

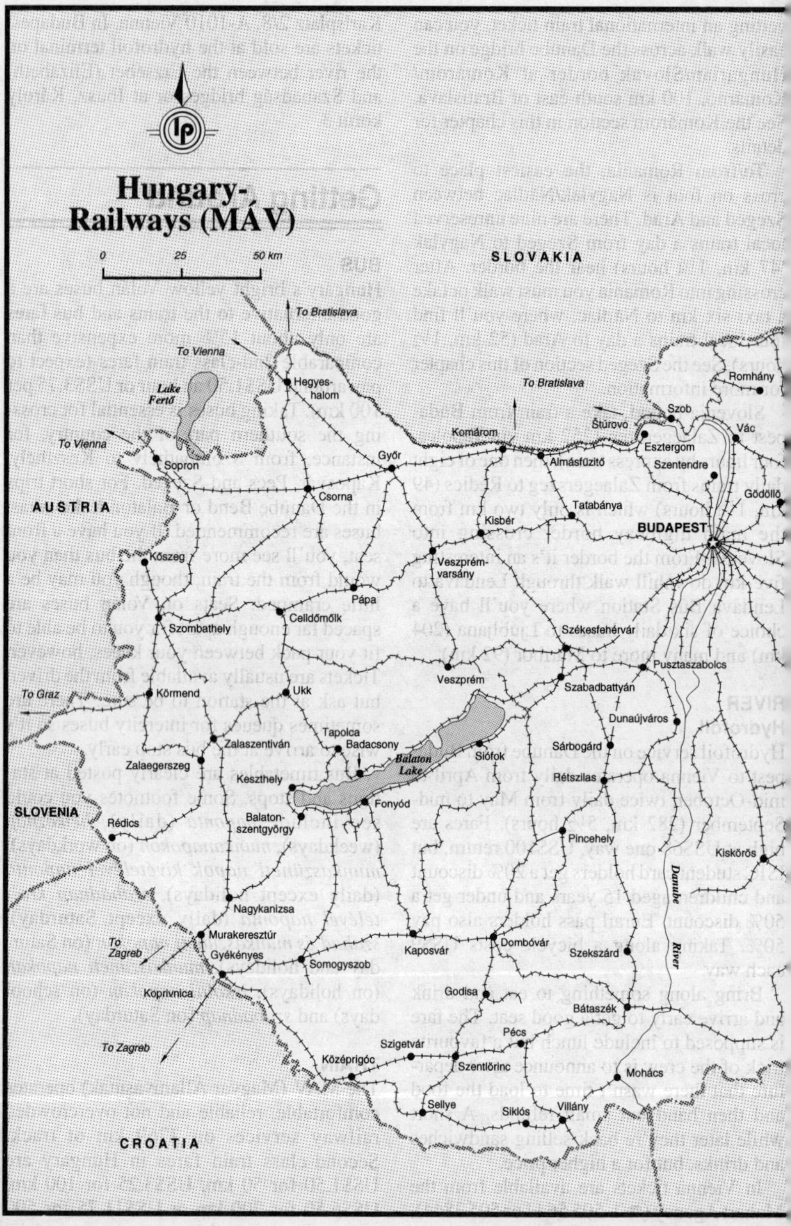

Hungary-
Railways (MÁV)

0   25   50 km

km. First class is 50% more but there's no price difference for express or local train tickets. You must watch out for express trains with compulsory seat reservations indicated on the timetables by an 'R' in a box. Seat reservations for these cost US$0.35 in the station or US$3.50 from the conductor. If you buy your ticket on the train rather than in the station, there's an additional US$2.50 surcharge.

An unlimited travel pass for all trains in Hungary is available at US$44/65 2nd/1st class for seven days, US$65/98 for 10 days. Reservation charges are additional, and since reservations are required on many express trains, this expensive pass doesn't give you the flexibility you might expect. It would only pay for itself if you stayed in Budapest and made a return trip to the farthest corners of the country every day.

If you'll be using trains extensively, you can buy a complete Hungarian timetable (*menetrend*) with an explanation of the symbols in a number of languages, including English, for US$3.50. In all Hungarian train stations a yellow board indicates departures (*indul*) and a white board arrivals (*érkezik*). Express trains are indicated in red, local trains in black. In some stations, large black and-white schedules are plastered all over walls. To locate the table you need, first find the posted railway map of the country, which indexes the route numbers at the top of the schedules.

All train stations have left-luggage offices, many of which stay open 24 hours a day. You often have to go and pay the fee (US$0.70) at another office (*pénztár*). A few large bus stations also have luggage rooms, but they generally close by 6 pm.

Routes

Most railway lines converge on Budapest. Some typical journeys with distances and travelling times by express train are Budapest to Győr (138 km, two hours), Sopron (210 km, three hours), Szombathely (236 km, 3½ hours), Pécs (229 km, three hours), Kecskemét (106 km, 1½ hours), Szeged (191 km, 2½ hours) and Miskolc (182 km,

two hours). Some shorter trips by local train are Budapest to Székesfehérvár (67 km, one hour), Veszprém (112 km, two hours) and Siófok (115 km, two hours).

CAR & MOTORBIKE

The available fuels are 86 octane (normal), 92 octane (super), 98 octane (extra), 95 octane (Eurosuper unleaded) and diesel. A map indicating where unleaded fuel (*olommentes uzemanyag*) can be purchased should be posted at all filling stations. Stations selling unleaded petrol often display a white sign with a blue border on which a green and black petrol pump appears. Some station attendants try to make foreigners pay for fuel in hard currency but this is not compulsory and petrol coupons have been abolished. In the past fuel has been readily available. You're not allowed to enter Hungary with extra fuel in a spare tank.

The 24-hour all-Hungary number for road assistance is ☎ 088. The breakdown service for foreigners provided by the Magyar Autóklub is at ☎ 115 1220 (answered in English 24 hours a day).

Road Rules

Speed limits for cars are 60 km/h in built-up areas, 80 km/h on main roads, 100 km/h on highways and 120 km/h on motorways. For motorbikes the speed limit is the same as for cars except in built-up areas where the limit is 50 km/h. The beginning of a built-up area is indicated by a white rectangular sign bearing the town or village's name. At the end of the built-up area there's another such sign with a red diagonal line through the name. A green flashing light at intersections is the equivalent of a yellow warning light in other countries. Traffic is restricted in central Budapest and parking fees at garages in the city centre are high, so use public transport.

Car Rental

The Budapest addresses of Avis, Budget, EuroDollar, Europcar, Hertz and a few local car rental companies are listed under Getting Around in the Budapest section of this chapter.

To rent a car from Avis and Hertz is very expensive, beginning at US$38 plus US$0.38 a km, or US$118 a day with unlimited mileage for the cheapest car. Collision damage waiver (CDW) insurance is US$10 a day and theft insurance will cost another US$4 daily. If you pick up your car at Budapest airport a US$15 surcharge (or 7%) will be added to your bill and additional drivers are another US$15. Add 25% tax to all these charges.

EuroDollar has cheaper Lada vehicles at US$20 a day and US$0.20 a km, or US$55 daily with unlimited mileage, plus US$8 CDW and 25% tax. On a weekly basis the unlimited-km rate is US$39 daily, or you can pay US$106 plus tax for a 'weekend' from noon Friday to 9 am Monday (considered three days when calculating daily insurance charges etc). Europcar is similar at US$24 a day plus US$0.24 a km or US$82/490/117 a day/week/weekend with unlimited mileage for a Lada 1300 (tax included). Local companies like Inka Rent-a-Car and Volántourist are cheaper again. Budapest Rent-a-Car has attractive unlimited mileage weekly rates beginning at US$300, including tax.

You must usually be 21 years old (18 at Hertz) and have a 'registered address in Hungary' (your hotel etc). If you don't have a credit card you'll need to leave a cash deposit of at least US$300, if they deign to rent to you at all. Avis and Hertz will allow you to take their cars outside Hungary (except to ex-Yugoslavia, Ukraine or Romania) but there are steep delivery charges on one-way rentals. Don't forget to allow for petrol, parking charges and traffic fines when calculating your costs.

BOAT

In summer there are regular passenger boats on Balaton Lake and the Danube River (from Budapest to Esztergom). Full details on these are given in the relevant sections in this chapter.

LOCAL TRANSPORT

Less than 10% of Hungarians own cars so public transport is well developed, with efficient city bus and trolleybus services in all towns. Budapest, Debrecen, Miskolc and Szeged also have trams (streetcars). In Budapest there's a metro (underground) system and a suburban railway known as the HÉV, which is the equivalent of the S-Bahn in Germany. You must purchase tickets for all these at newsstands or ticket windows beforehand and cancel them once aboard.

Taxi

Taxi stands are found at bus or train stations, markets and large hotels, otherwise you can flag them down on the street. At night the sign on the roof of the vehicle will be lit up when the taxi is free. Not all taxi meters run at the same rates and the flashy Mercedes taxis are much more expensive than the little Ladas. In Budapest, some drivers demand payment in hard currency from foreigners after the metro stops running.

Budapest

Hungary's capital, Budapest, straddles a curve of the Danube River where Transdanubia meets the Great Plain. One Hungarian in five lives here and Debrecen, the next largest Hungarian city, is only a tenth of the size of Budapest. More romantic than Warsaw, more easy-going than Prague, Budapest is the Paris of Eastern Europe. This gentle metropolis gets just as many visitors as Prague but it somehow manages to absorb them better and you won't experience tourist gridlock here the way you will in many Western European capitals. Finding an inexpensive place to stay in Budapest is much easier than it is in Prague.

The Romans built the town of Aquincum here and you can see their aqueduct and amphitheatres just north of Óbuda. Layer upon layer of history blankets Buda's castle district, and Pest's Váci utca is the city's equivalent to Bond St (London) for its fine shops and fashionable clientele. Add to this a big city park brimming with attractions, a chair lift and cog-wheel railway in the nearby

Buda Hills, riverboats plying upriver to the scenic Danube Bend, and hot thermal baths in authentic Turkish bathhouses and you have Budapest.

The city has many fascinating aspects. Eastern Europeans come here to make money or get a taste of the West, while we Westerners revel in the nightlife, theatres, museums, restaurants and cafés. It's hard to get enough of Budapest. As the river descends from the Black Forest to the Black Sea, few cities are more striking than this 'Queen of the Danube'. Stay for a week or two, and when you leave there'll be one more person in love with Budapest.

Orientation

Budapest is 249 km south-east of Vienna, exactly halfway between Sofia and Berlin. The Danube is Budapest's main street, dividing historic Buda from commercial Pest (in Vienna the river is several km north-east of the centre). All eight bridges which cross the Danube at Budapest were destroyed in the war and later rebuilt. Most visitors will arrive at one of the three main train stations, Keleti (east), Nyugati (west) and Déli (south), all on the metro lines which converge at Deák tér on the northern edge of the city centre's shopping area. For information on left-luggage facilities at these stations see Train Stations under Getting There & Away following.

From Deák tér, Andrássy út (Budapest's Broadway because of its many theatres) runs north-east to City Park, while Károly körút, Múzeum körút and Vamház körút swing around to the Szabadság híd (bridge) and Gellért Hill. Important crossroads in the city are Baross tér before Keleti Railway Station, Blaha Lujza tér where Rákóczi út meets Erzsébet körút, and Moszkva tér just north of Déli Railway Station and Castle Hill. Óbuda is at the western end of the Árpád híd north of Buda, and Aquincum is north of the Árpád híd.

Information

Your best source of general information about Budapest and Hungary is Tourinform

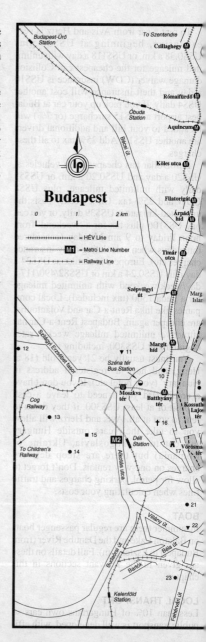

Budapest

0   1   2 km

++++++++++++ = HÉV Line

[M1] = Metro Line Number

············· = Railway Line

- Budapest-Úrö Station
- To Szentendre
- Csillaghegy Ⓜ
- Rómaifürdő Ⓜ
- Óbuda Station
- Aquincum Ⓜ
- Bécsi út
- Köles utca Ⓜ
- Filatorigát Ⓜ
- Árpád híd Ⓜ
- Timár utca Ⓜ
- Szépvölgyi út
- Marg Islar
- Szilágyi Erzsébet fasor
- Margit híd
- 12
- 11
- Szená tér Bus Station
- 10
- Ⓤ Moszkva tér
- Batthyány tér
- Kossuth Lajos tér
- Cog Railway
- 13
- † 16
- 15
- [M2] Déli Station
- To Children's Railway
- 14
- Vörösmart tér
- 17
- Alkotás utca
- Villány út
- 21
- 22
- Villány út
- Béla út
- Bartók
- 23
- Kelenföld Station
- Fehérvári út

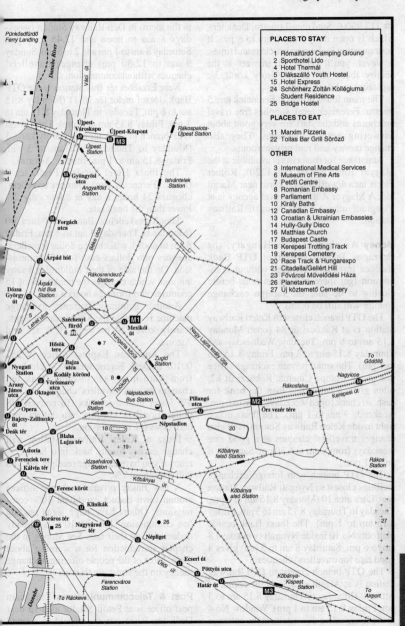

PLACES TO STAY

1 Rómaifürdő Camping Ground
2 Sporthotel Lido
4 Hotel Thermál
5 Diákszálló Youth Hostel
15 Hotel Express
24 Schönherz Zoltán Kollégiuma
   Student Residence
25 Bridge Hostel

PLACES TO EAT

11 Marxim Pizzeria
22 Tollas Bar Grill Söröző

OTHER

3 International Medical Services
6 Museum of Fine Arts
7 Petőfi Centre
8 Romanian Embassy
9 Parliament
10 Király Baths
12 Canadian Embassy
13 Croatian & Ukrainian Embassies
14 Hully-Gully Disco
16 Matthias Church
17 Budapest Castle
18 Kerepesi Trotting Track
19 Kerepesi Cemetery
20 Race Track & Hungarexpo
21 Citadella/Gellért Hill
23 Fővárosi Művelődési Háza
26 Planetarium
27 Új köztemető Cemetery

(☎ 117 9800), Sütő utca 2 (metro: Deák tér), which is open daily from 8 am to 8 pm. If your question is about train tickets and times, however, you'll get better answers at the nearby Ibusz offices at Károly körút 3/c (upstairs) or Károly körút 21.

The main Ibusz office, at Ferenciek tere 5 (metro: Ferenciek tere), supplies free travel brochures and the staff are very good about answering general questions. They also change money and rent private rooms.

Assistance for motorists is available at the Magyar Autóklub (☎ 115 1220), Rómer Flóris utca 4/a off Margit körút near Margit híd. A Magyar Autóklub travel agency is at Visegrádi utca 17 near Nyugati Railway Station.

Money As elsewhere in Hungary, the Orszagos Takarékpenztár or OTP Bank changes travellers' cheques without commission (get there at least an hour before closing to be sure the foreign exchange counter will still be open).

The OTP branch closest to Keleti Railway Station is at Rákóczi út 84 (open Monday 8.15 am to 6 pm, Tuesday, Wednesday and Thursday 8.15 am to 3 pm, Friday 8.15 am to 1 pm). The small private exchange office just inside Europa Cinema, Rákóczi út 82, often gives a better rate than the bank for cash, so check (open weekdays 9 am to 6 pm, weekends 9 am to 1 pm). The Ibusz office right inside Keleti Railway Station itself also changes travellers' cheques at a good rate weekdays from 8 am to 6.30 pm, Saturday 8 am to 1 pm.

The OTP branch with foreign exchange facilities closest to Nyugati Railway Station is at Tátra utca 10 (Monday 8.15 am to 6 pm, Tuesday to Thursday 8.15 am to 3 pm, Friday 8.15 am to 1 pm). The Ibusz Bank beside platform No 10 inside Nyugati (weekdays 8 am to 6 pm, Saturday 8 am to 3 pm) gives a good rate for travellers' cheques.

The OTP branch closest to Déli Railway Station is at Alagút utca 3, on the corner of Attila út (Monday to Thursday 8.15 am to 3 pm, Friday 8.15 am to 1 pm). Window No 4 in the Ibusz office downstairs at the entrance to the metro in Déli Railway Station (weekdays 8 am to noon and 12.45 to 6 pm, Saturday 8 am to 1 pm and 2 to 3 pm, Sunday 9 am to 12.30 pm) changes travellers' cheques without commission.

Near Erzsébet tér Bus Station is the OTP Bank, József nádor tér 10-11 (Monday 8.15 am to 6 pm, Tuesday to Thursday 8.15 am to 3 pm, Friday 8.15 am to 1 pm). The closest OTP branch to Deák tér is at Károly körút 1 (Monday to Thursday 8.15 am to 3 pm, Friday 8.15 am to 1 pm) (metro: Astoria).

The Ibusz Hotel Service, Petőfi tér 3 (metro: Ferenciek tere), changes travellers' cheques 24 hours a day at a rate only 2% lower than the bank rate.

The Kereskedelmi Bank, Váci utca 40 (Monday to Thursday 8 am to 1 pm, Friday 8 am to noon), will change dollar travellers' cheques into dollars cash for 3% commission. On the side of their building is a zany automat which changes the banknotes of 15 countries into forint 24 hours a day.

Another automatic currency exchange machine is outside the Kereskedelmi Bank, Károly kőrút 20 between Deák tér and Astoria.

The American Express office (☎ 251 0010) at Deák Ferenc utca 10, a block up from Vörösmarty tér towards Deák tér, changes its own travellers' cheques at a rate 3% lower than the banks. To convert US dollar travellers' cheques into dollars cash here costs 6% commission.

Ibusz at Keleti Railway Station will change excess forints back into hard currency if you have exchange receipts, but you will lose about 7%.

A few flashy private exchange offices around town deduct exorbitant 10% commissions. Others have huge signs reading 'no commission' but the 10% is already deducted from their rate. See Money in the chapter introduction for a warning about them. Most of the people offering to change money on the street are thieves.

Post & Telecommunications The main post office is at Petőfi Sándor utca 13 near Deák tér. Poste restante is held in a small office beside the post office boxes here (open weekdays from 8 am to 8 pm). You can mail parcels from a room on the opposite side of the main counters from poste restante and they sell boxes of varying sizes. The post office at Teréz körút 51-53 next to Nyugati Railway Station is open 24 hours.

The best place to make international telephone calls is at the telephone exchange, upstairs at Petőfi Sándor utca 17 (open Monday to Saturday from 8 am to 8 pm, Sunday 9 am to 3 pm). Ask the clerks on duty for the area code, then use the card phones against the wall. Calls go through immediately.

Budapest's telephone code is 1.

Western Consulates & Embassies The UK Embassy (☎ 118 2888), which also serves New Zealanders, is at Harmincad utca 6 just off Vörösmarty tér (Monday to Thursday 9 am to 12.30 pm and 2 to 4.30 pm, Friday 9 am to 12.30 pm).

The US Embassy (☎ 112 6450) is a few blocks north at Szabadság tér 12 (metro: Kossuth tér). Its hours are not posted.

The Australian Embassy (☎ 153 4233), Dózsa György út 90 (Monday to Thursday 8 am to 4.30 pm, Friday 8 am to 1.25 pm), is next to the Yugoslav Consulate (metro: Hősök tér).

The Canadian Consulate (☎ 176 7711 or 176 7686), Zugligeti út 51-53, is below the Buda Hills (take bus No 22 or 158 from Moszkva tér Metro Station). It's open weekdays from 9 am to noon and 2 to 4 pm.

Eastern European Consulates Budapest is a good place to pick up visas for other Eastern European countries. On your visa hunt take along a good supply of passport-size photos and US dollars in small bills, as forint and travellers' cheques are not accepted for visa fees. Some consulates won't accept Deutschmarks or US$100 notes.

Many of the consulates are on or near Andrássy út, for example, the Yugoslavian Consulate, Dózsa György út 92/a on Hősök tér, opposite the Műcsarnok Art Gallery (weekdays 10 am to 1 pm).

The Slovenian Consulate, Lendvay utca 23, is also near Hősök tér (Monday, Wednesday and Thursday 9 am to noon).

In this same area are the Polish Consulate, Bajza utca 15 (open weekdays from 9 am to 1 pm), and the Albanian Consulate, Bajza utca 26 (Monday and Thursday 10 am to 1 pm).

The Bulgarian Consulate at Andrássy út 115 (open Monday, Tuesday, Thursday and Friday from 9 am to 1 pm) is also near Hősök tér. Visa applications are only accepted until noon but for US$44 you'll get your tourist visa then and there.

All three of the above are near Bajza utca Metro Station. The Czech Consulate, Szegfű utca 4 (weekdays 8.30 am to 1 pm) (metro: Kodály körönd), is two blocks away.

The Romanian Consulate, Thököly út 72 (Monday, Tuesday and Wednesday from 8.30 am to 12.30 pm and Friday from 8.30 to 11.30 am) is south-east of City Park (bus No 7 north-east from Keleti Railway Station. The entrance is off Izsó utca around the corner. The guard opens the gate every so often to collect passports in which you are asked to insert the required fee (about US$35) in cash US dollars only. After about half an hour he'll reappear with your passport and visa.

The Consulate of Croatia, Nógrádi utca 28b (weekdays 9 am to 2 pm), is up in the Buda Hills. Take bus No 21 from Moszkva tér Metro up Istenhegyi utca till you see the ABC supermarket on your left. The consulate is often crowded with people from ex-Yugoslavia arranging complicated documentation, so rather than wait in line for hours on end, make your presence known to the receptionist behind the glass door and you'll have your free visa in five minutes.

Down the hill is the Ukrainian Consulate, Nógrádi utca 8 (Monday, Tuesday, Wednesday and Friday 9 am to noon). One-month visas here are US$50 but an invitation or hotel vouchers are required.

The Consulate of Slovakia is very inconveniently located at Gervey utca 44 at Balázs

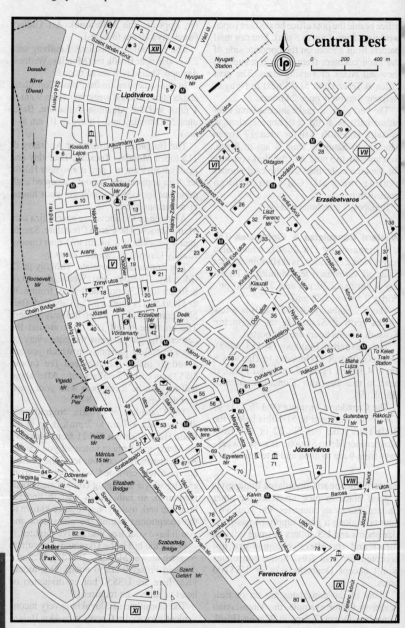

Central Pest

0   200   400 m

Danube
River
(Duna)

Lipótváros

Erzsébetváros

VI

VII

Oktagon

Andrássy út

Nyugati
Station

Nyugati
tér

Szent István körút

XII

Kossuth
Lajos
tér

Szabadság
tér

Alkotmány utca

Nádor utca

Arany János utca

V

Zrínyi utca

Roosevelt
tér

Chain Bridge

I

Döbrentei

Attila
utca

Hegyalja
út

Döbrentei
tér

Vigadó
tér

Ferry
Pier

Belgrád
rakpart

Belváros

József
Attila
utca

Vörösmarty
tér

Erzsébet
tér

Deák
tér

Károly körút

Petőfi
tér

Március
15 tér

Szabadsajtó út

Petőfi Sándor utca

Váci utca

Ferenciek
tere

Egyetem
tér

Kalvin
tér

Elizabeth
Bridge

Szent Gellért rakpart

Jubilee
Park

XI

Szabadság
Bridge

Szabadság
tér

Fővám
tér

Szent
Gellért tér

Podmaniczky utca

Váci út

Bajcsy-Zsilinszky út

Nagymező utca

Teréz körút

Liszt
Ferenc
tér

Paulay Ede utca

Király utca

Klauzál
tér

Dob utca

Wesselényi

Dohány utca

Rákóczi út

Akácfa utca

Erzsébet körút

Nyár utca

Blaha
Lujza
tér

To Keleti
Train
Station

Józsefváros

Gutenberg
tér

Rákóczi
tér

VIII

Baross

József körút

Üllői út

Rádáy utca

IX

Ferenc körút

Ferencváros

Vámház körút

Múzeum krt

Magyar utca

Váci utca

To Keleti
Train
Station

PLACES TO STAY

27	Medosz Hotel
39	Forum Hotel
40	Atrium Hyatt Hotel
43	Duna Marriott Hotel
60	Astoria Hotel
66	Metropol Hotel
69	Ottó & Viktor's Hostel (Summer Only)
80	Strawberry Hostel (Summer Only)
81	Gellért Hotel

PLACES TO EAT

2	La Pampa Restaurant
9	Semiramis (Arab Restaurant)
14	Karcsi Ételbár
18	Duna Palota
19	Kisharang Étkezde
20	Number One Espresso
24	Morrison's Bar
30	Bohémtanya Vendéglő
33	No 1 Falafel Faloda
35	Salom Restaurant
52	Bölcs Bagoly Önkiszolgáló Étterem
65	Café New York
68	Vegetárium Restaurant
70	Alföldi Kisvendéglo
76	Stop Étterem
78	Kaltenberg Söröző

OTHER

1	OTP Bank
3	Vígszínház (Comedy Theatre)
4	Autóklub Travel Agency
5	Panoráma Travel
6	Parliament
7	Cooptourist
8	Ethnographical Museum
10	Express (Train Tickets)
11	Express (Youth Hostel Bookings)
12	Soviet Army Memorial
13	American Embassy
15	Volántourist
16	Academy of Sciences
17	Budapest Tourist
21	St Stephen's Basilica
22	Dunatours
23	Központi Jegyiroda (Ticket Office)
25	State Opera House
26	Fővárosi Operett Színház
28	Puppet Theatre
29	Czech Republic Embassy
31	Arany János Theatre
32	MÁV Hungarian Railways Office
34	Academy of Music
36	Madách Theatre
37	Szabadidőközpont (Almássy Cultural Centre)
38	National Theatre
41	OTP Bank
42	Erzsébet tér Bus Station
44	Pesti Vigadó
45	Jegyiroda Országos Filharmonia
46	American Express
47	Tourinform
48	Ibusz 24-Hour Office
49	Main Post Office
50	Merlin Jazz Club
51	Inner-City Parish Church
53	International Bookstore
54	Ibusz (Private Rooms)
55	Town Hall
56	Express (Main Office)
57	Kereskedelmi Bank
58	Ibusz (Train Tickets)
59	Jewish Museum
61	OTP Bank
62	Patyolat Laundromat
63	Map Store
64	Maxim Variete Night Club
67	Kereskedelmi Bank
71	National Museum
72	Kenguru Ride Service
73	Tilos Á Kávéház
74	Star Tours
75	Hydrofoil Terminal
77	Old Pest Market Hall
79	Museum of Applied Arts
82	Citadella
83	Rudas Baths
84	Rác Baths

utca (weekdays 8.30 am to 1 pm) in a remote eastern suburb. Take bus No 7 east from Keleti Railway Station to the end of the line, then walk four blocks north-west on Nagy Lajos király útja to Gervey utca, turn right and continue another three blocks up to the consulate. This location is so poor it's hard to believe they'll stay there for long, so you might check the address with Tourinform

before making the long trip out. Otherwise call them at ☎ 251 7973. They charge Australians US$20, Canadians US$45.

Trans-Siberian Consulates If you decide to take the Trans-Siberian Railway east from Budapest to China or Japan, you'll need a Russian transit visa. The Russian Consulate, Andrássy út 104 (open Monday, Wednesday

HUNGARY

and Friday from 10 am to 1 pm), takes a week or more to issue tourist visas (transit visas are quicker). You must have confirmed transportation reservations right through the Russian Federation, plus accommodation vouchers for each night to be spent in a Russian city.

The Chinese Embassy, Benczúr utca 17 – entry from Bajza utca (Monday, Wednesday and Friday from 2.30 to 5 pm), is only a block from the Russian Consulate. You must get your Chinese visa first.

If you take the Chinese train from Moscow to Beijing, you'll also need to visit the Mongolian Embassy in the Buda Hills at Bogár utca 14/c (bus No 11 from Batthyány tér Metro to the Bayer Hungaria building on Törökvész út). (The Russian train to Beijing doesn't pass through Mongolia.)

Travel Agencies The MÁV Hungarian Railways office, Andrássy út 35 (metro: Opera), has international train tickets and can make advance seat reservations for domestic express trains at the same price you'd pay at the station.

Skip the queue at MÁV by going to Ibusz, upstairs at Károly körút 3/c (metro: Astoria or Deák tér), which sells the same tickets and can also make seat reservations. Another Ibusz office at Károly körút 21 also has international train tickets and information. Ibusz sells international tickets for the same prices charged at the train stations and they're more likely to speak English and be helpful.

Express (☎ 111 6418), Zoltán utca 10 (metro: Kossuth tér), open Monday to Thursday from 8.30 am to 4.30 pm, Friday from 8.30 am to 3 pm, sells Eurotrain tickets with a 30% discount on fares to Western Europe to persons under the age of 26. Express also has student fares with reductions of 25% to 50% on rail travel to other Eastern European countries. Another Express office at Semmelweis utca 4 (metro: Astoria) and Wasteels next to track No 9 at Keleti Railway Station also sells these tickets. You must have an ISIC card to get the student fare (no student fares are available on domestic tickets).

Keep in mind that all international train tickets must be paid for in cash hard currency unless you have an exchange receipt.

Express, Semmelweis utca 4, and the Express office at Keleti Railway Station sell the ISIC student card (US$3) but you must provide two photos and proof that you really are a student.

Panoráma Travel, Nyugati tér 7 (metro: Nyugati), has a bus to Munich four times a week (US$34). Other Panoráma buses run less frequently to Padua (US$35), Paris (US$64), Rimini (US$39), Stuttgart (US$55) and Zürich (US$66).

Kenguru (☎ 138 2019), Kőtfaragó utca 15 (Monday to Saturday 8 am to 6 pm) (metro: Blaha Lujza tér), arranges paid rides in private cars to many Western European cities. You pay the agency's fee plus a contribution to fuel costs. Sample charges are US$53 to Athens, US$36 to Berlin, US$62 to Amsterdam or Brussels, US$66 to Paris and US$73 to London. It's more pleasant than a long bus ride if you connect with the right driver. Enquiries from car drivers looking for paying passengers are most welcome here.

Jade Tours Imperial (☎ 112 8671) at Nyugati Railway Station (opposite Ibusz) offers organised sightseeing tours of Budapest and day trips to Balaton Lake and the Great Plain.

The Chosen Tours (☎ 166 5165) offers morning and afternoon tours focusing on Budapest's Jewish heritage daily except Saturday from mid-April to October. The 2½-hour ghetto walking tour (US$10) includes a stop at a kosher pastry shop while the 3½-hour bus tour (US$20) shows you the city through Jewish eyes. For Jews of Hungarian descent, The Chosen organises genealogical research and cemetery visits. The easiest way to make contact is by calling the number provided above (English is spoken).

Laundry Patyolat, Rákóczi út 8 (weekdays 7 am to 7 pm, Saturday 7 am to 1 pm) (metro: Astoria), is a self-service laundromat where you can wash up to five kg for US$3, plus another US$1 to dry. Laundry soap is supplied. Patience and the assistance of the women working here are required.

Another self-service laundromat is Mosoda, József nádor tér 9 (metro: Vörösmarty tér) (Monday, Wednesday and Friday 7 am to 3 pm, Tuesday and Thursday 11 am to 7 pm). This one has the advantage of a nice park opposite where you can sit and wait.

Bookshops Bestsellers, Október 6 utca 11 (metro: Arany János), specialises in books and magazines in English. Their slogan is, 'If we don't have it, we can order it'.

For general reading material in English, try the Antikvárium, Ferenciek tere 3 (metro: Ferenciek tere). Two better second-hand bookstores are at Múzeum körút 15 and 35 near the National Museum (metro: Kálvin tér).

The International Bookstore, Váci utca 32 (metro: Ferenciek tere), has travel guidebooks and maps, plus Hungarian and foreign art books. You can buy Lonely Planet titles there.

In the arcade at Petőfi Sándor utca 2 is a bookshop which stocks maps of cities all across Europe. The newsstand at Petőfi Sándor utca 17 has English newspapers.

There's a self-service map shop at Nyár utca 1 (metro: Blaha Lujza tér). Another map shop with different maps is at Bajcsy-Zsilinszky út 37 (metro: Arany János utca).

Emergency International Medical Services (☎ 129 8423), Váci út 202 (metro to Újpest-Városkapu, then walk about three blocks south), is a private medical clinic open 24 hours a day. On the outside this place looks like a factory with two stone statues of workers standing watch. General examinations cost around US$28 from 8 am to 8 pm or US$39 from 8 pm to 8 am. Home visits are US$55. Common X-rays average US$16. The British Embassy refers people here and English is spoken.

A dental clinic specialising in treating foreigners is Dental Express (☎ 142 4257), Városligeti fasor 32 (metro: Bajza tér), open weekdays from 9 am to 7 pm.

If you need to register with the police or want to report a lost passport or visa, go to the foreigners' police at Andrássy út 12 (metro: Opera). It's open on Monday from 8.30 am to noon and 2 to 5 pm, Tuesday, Wednesday and Friday from 8.30 am to noon and Thursday from 2 to 5 pm. Ask about visa extensions here. English is spoken. To report accidents, crime or theft (for insurance purposes) you must go to the main police station at Deák Ferenc utca 16-18 near Deák tér (daily 8 am to midnight). Bring along a translator if you can.

Things to See

Buda Most of Budapest's medieval vestiges are in Castle Hill (Várhegy), the castle district of Buda. The easiest way to get there is to take the metro to Moszkva tér, cross the bridge above the square and continue straight up Várfok utca to Várhegy's **Vienna Gate**. A minibus marked 'Budavari Sikló' follows this same route from the bridge, shuttling every few minutes from Moszkva tér to Budapest Castle.

Get off at the stop just after the Vienna Gate. Once through the gate, take a sharp right on Petermann biró utca past the National Archives to Kapisztrán tér. The **Magdalen Tower** is all that's left of a Gothic church destroyed in the last war. The white neoclassical building facing the square is the **Museum of Military History** (free Saturday), which you enter from the ramparts side straight ahead.

Walk south-east along Tóth Árpád sétány, the ramparts promenade, enjoying the views of the Buda Hills. The long black-and-white building below you is Budapest's Déli Railway Station. Halfway along the ramparts you'll catch a glimpse of the neo-Gothic tower of **Matthias Church** up Szentháromság utca. The church (rebuilt in 1896) has a colourful tiled roof outside, colourful murals inside and a museum which you enter through the crypt.

Franz Liszt wrote the *Hungarian Coronation Mass* for the 1867 coronation here of the Austrian king Franz Josef and his wife Elizabeth as king and queen of Hungary. Organ concerts are held in the church on Sunday at 7 pm every couple of weeks throughout the year. Behind the Matthias Church is an equestrian statue of St Stephen (977-1038), Hungary's first king, and alongside the statue is the **Fisherman's Bastion**, a late 19th century structure which offers great views of the parliament building and the Danube River.

From the **plague column** (1713) in front of Matthias Church, Tárnok utca runs southeast to the gate of the **Palace of Buda Castle**. The palace enjoyed its greatest splendour under King Matthias in the second half of the 15th century. Since then it has been destroyed and rebuilt three times, the last after WW II. Today the palace contains two important museums. The **National Gallery** (free Saturday) has a huge collection of Hungarian works of art from Gothic to contemporary. The historical paintings by Mihály Munkácsy are worth noting. The **Historical Museum** (closed Tuesday, free Wednesday) shelters objects discovered during the recent reconstruction of the palace, plus a good overall display on Budapest through the ages.

From the castle terrace take the **funicular railway** (US$1) or walk down to the vehicular tunnel under Castle Hill at the Buda end of the **Chain Bridge** (Lánchíd), which was opened in 1849 and was the first bridge to be built across the Hungarian section of the Danube. In the park in front of the lower funicular station is the **Zero Kilometre Stone** for all highway distances in Hungary.

Go through the small pedestrian tunnel under the end of the Chain Bridge and take tram No 19 south along the right bank of the Danube. Get off at Móricz Zsigmond körtér, the second stop beyond the Gellért Hotel (1918). Walk back a little, round the corner to the left and board bus No 27 at Villányi út 5. This bus will take you right up to the Citadella on Gellért Hill.

A commanding fortress, the **Citadella** (now a hotel) was built by the Austrians in 1854 to control the rebellious Hungarians. The **Statue of Liberty** at the southern end of the Citadella commemorates the Soviet sol-

diers who died to liberate Hungary in 1945. The bronze soldier statue was pulled down during the 1956 uprising but replaced a year later. You'll see your most memorable views of Budapest and the Danube from this hill. At night with the city all lit up below you the views are rather spectacular. You can easily walk down from the Citadella to the Gellért Hotel.

Pest Industrialisation allowed Budapest to develop rapidly during the late 19th century and one of the nicest places to get a feeling for this period is **City Park**, north-east of the centre. Take the metro to Széchenyi Fürdő. This line, the oldest underground railway on the continent, opened in 1896. You'll come out of the station right in the middle of the park beside the **Municipal Baths** (1913), behind which are an **amusement park**, the **Grand Circus** and the **zoo** (closed on Monday in winter).

Cross the busy boulevard to the south-east and you'll come to **Vajdahunyad Castle** (1896), a fascinating hotchpotch of replicas of actual buildings, many of them in what is now Romania. The **Agricultural Museum** (free on Tuesday) is housed in the castle (there's also a snack bar inside).

City Park's dominant feature is **Hősök tér** with a great monument erected in 1896 for the millennium of the Magyar conquest of Hungary. The Tomb of the Unknown Soldier is also here. On the south-east side of the square is the **Műcsarnok Art Gallery**, the most prestigious in the city, where important contemporary art shows are held (presently closed for reconstruction). On the other side of the square is the **Museum of Fine Arts** (1895), one of the richest of its kind in Europe (free Saturday). Here you'll see Hungary's major collection of foreign art, with prints and ancient sculpture on the ground floor, and European paintings on the 1st floor. The collection of Spanish paintings is one of the best outside Madrid.

From Hősök tér stately Andrássy út runs straight into the heart of Pest. To save yourself a long walk, take the metro to Opera. The **State Opera House** was built in the Italian neo-Renaissance style in 1884 and the tours (US$3) at 3 and 4 pm are worth taking, especially if you can't catch a performance. Many of the other great buildings along this section of Andrássy út also date from this time.

Proceed south-west on this fashionable avenue and round the corner onto Bajcsy-Zsilinszky út. You'll see the 96-metre-high neo-Renaissance dome of **St Stephen's Basilica** (1905) looming before you. The right hand of King St Stephen, founder of the Hungarian state, is kept in the chapel at the rear of the church, behind the altar. The ticket office just inside the basilica is charging admission to the treasury, not to the basilica itself. From July to September organ concerts are held here every Monday at 7 pm (US$8).

Cross the square in front of the basilica and continue straight ahead for a block on Zrínyi utca, then right on Október 6 utca. Proceed straight ahead onto Szabadság tér with the National Bank (1905) to the right and the Television Company (also 1905) to the left. At the end of the square in front of the US Embassy is the **Soviet Army Memorial** (1945).

As you look up Vécsey utca from the memorial you see the great neo-Gothic silhouette of the **parliament building** (1904) on Kossuth Lajos tér. The exterior is impressive but individual tourists are not allowed inside.

The **Ethnographic Museum** (1896) also faces Kossuth Lajos tér. The Hungarian ethnographical collection here is fully captioned in English.

There's a metro station on the south side of Kossuth Lajos tér and for a good long view of the parliament building, take the metro for one stop to Batthyány tér, where you'll also find a large public market hall and some old churches. Note the very deep tunnel as the line dives under the Danube at this point. Built by the communists with Soviet assistance, this metro line opened in 1973.

Óbuda & Aquincum In 1872 three towns – Buda, Pest and Óbuda – united to form Buda-pest as the Austro-Hungarian emperor Franz Josef sought to create a rival to Napoleon III's Paris. Óbuda is most easily reached by taking the HÉV suburban railway from Batthyány tér Metro Station to Árpád híd mh. The **Vásárely Museum** greets you right outside the HÉV station. Go round the corner onto Szentlélek tér, which takes you to Fő tér, the beautifully restored centre of old Óbuda. **Óbuda Town Hall** is at Fő tér 3, but the most interesting building is the Baroque **Zichy Mansion** (1752), Fő tér 1. At the back of the courtyard is an art gallery and the unique **Kassák Museum**, a tiny three-room exhibition with some real gems of early 20th century avant-garde art.

Return to the HÉV and take a train three stops farther north to Aquincum vm. Aquincum was the key military garrison of the Roman province of Pannonia. A **Roman aqueduct** used to pass this way from a spring in the nearby park and remains have been preserved in the median strip of the modern highway alongside the HÉV railway line. The 2nd century civilian **amphitheatre** is right beside the station. A few hundred metres away is a large excavated area and the **Aquincum Museum** (open from May to October, closed Monday). Don't miss the ancient musical organ with bronze pipes.

From Aquincum you have a choice of returning to Budapest or taking the HÉV on to Szentendre (see the Szentendre section). You can use regular yellow metro tickets as far as Békásmegyar on the HÉV, but to go to Szentendre you have to buy a special ticket which is checked by a conductor.

Other Museums Two museums in central Pest are worthy of special attention. The twin-towered synagogue (1859) on Dohány utca, the largest functioning synagogue in Europe and second largest in the world, contains the **Jewish Museum** (closed Saturday and from mid-October to mid-April). Sabbath services in the synagogue are on Friday evening and Saturday morning. The former Jewish ghetto extends behind this synagogue between Dohány, Kertész and Király streets, an area worth exploring. At

HUNGARY

the turn of the century a fifth of the population of Budapest was Jewish.

The **National Museum**, Múzeum körút 14-16 (metro: Kálvin tér), has Hungary's main collection of historical relics in a large neoclassical building (1847). Begin with the section on the ground floor, behind the cloakroom on the right, which covers the period up to the Magyar conquest. Behind the cloakroom on the left is the coronation regalia. These precious relics fell into the hands of the US troops in Germany in 1945 and were only restored to Hungary in 1978. Upstairs is a continuation of Hungarian history. The top floor contains a large natural history exhibit with dioramas to show the fauna in natural settings.

Most Budapest museums are closed on Monday and some are free on Saturday.

The Buda Hills If you have children with you, the Buda Hills are the place to take them. The variety of transportation opportunities makes visiting fun. Begin with a ride on the **cog railway** (fogaskerekű), which has been winding through pleasant wooded suburbs into the Buda Hills since 1874. The lower terminus of the cog railway is on Szilágyi Erzsébet fasor, opposite the circular high-rise Hotel Budapest and within walking distance from Moszkva tér Metro Station. The fare is one yellow metro ticket (daily, all year).

Near the upper terminus of the cog railway is Széchenyi-hegy Station of the **Pioneer Railway**, a 12-km scenic route opened in 1950, which operates hourly year-round daily except Monday (US$0.50). If Széchenyi-hegy Station looks closed, go in and knock on the ticket window – it may actually be open! Except for the engineer, this line is staffed mostly by children in order to interest them in transportation careers. Catch a train to János-hegy Station and walk up through the forest to the lookout tower on János-hegy (529 metres) with its 360° view. The **János-hegy chair lift** or *libegö* (operates daily, all year from 9.30 am to 4 pm, US$0.75) will take you down to Zugligeti út

where you can catch bus No 158 back to Moszkva tér Metro Station.

If instead of getting out at János-hegy you stay on the Pioneer Railway to Hűvösvölgy Station, the northern terminus, you can catch tram No 56 back to Moszkva tér.

Margaret Island When your head begins to spin from all the sights, take a walk from one end to the other of Margaret Island (Margit sziget). Bus No 26 from beside Nyugati Railway Station covers the island or you can get there on trams No 4 or 6, which stop halfway across the unusual three-way bridge leading to Margaret Island. As you stroll among the trees and statues, you'll come across the ruins of two medieval monasteries, a small zoo, a rose garden, an open-air theatre, swimming pools, cafés and a pseudo-Japanese garden with hot spring pools (beside the Hotel Thermál). The island is such a relaxing, restful place you'll feel as if you're ages away from the busy city.

Cemeteries Budapest's most offbeat sight is **Kerepesi Cemetery** on Fiumei út near Keleti Railway Station. Beginning a century ago, it was the final resting place of Hungary's wealthiest and most prominent inhabitants. The evocative sculptured monuments scattered among the trees give Kerepesi Cemetery a unique, almost classical air which will enchant the wanderer. The most notable personages built themselves huge mausoleums which now stand alongside memorials to communists of yesteryear. Half the streets in Hungary are named after people buried here.

The graves of communists who died during the 1956 uprising are in the circular enclosure on the left side of the main avenue straight ahead from the entrance. The tombs of more recent communist leaders, János Kádár (1912-89) among them, are a block or two over to the right. All are marked only by their name, the dates of their birth and death and a gold (previously red) star. Farther back are the 19th century mausoleums, including that of Ferenc Deák (1803-76), the politician who engineered the 1867 Austro-Hungarian 'compromise'.

In 1989 Imre Nagy (1896-1958), the man most closely associated with the 1956 revolution, was reburied in **Új köztemető**, Budapest's huge municipal cemetery on the far eastern side of town. Access to the municipal cemetery from Kerepesi Cemetery is fairly easy. As you leave Kerepesi, turn left on Fiumei út and walk south-east along the cemetery wall to the next tram stop (not the one near the cemetery entrance). Take tram No 28 south-east to the end of the line right at Új köztemető's gate. When you want to return to town, take bus No 95 from the cemetery gate direct to Keleti Railway Station or bus No 68 south-west to Kőbánya-Kispest metro.

Nagy and many other prominent figures from 1956, plus approximately 2000 people liquidated between 1945 and 1956, lie in *parcelláz* 300 and 301 in the far north-east of the cemetery, a 30-minute walk from the entrance. The communists used this site to dump the bodies of executed 'traitors' in mass graves precisely because it was so remote. A map of the Új köztemető stands near the gate and the way is clearly signposted. At peak periods you can take a microbus marked *'temetójarat'* around the cemetery or hire a taxi at the gate. The site has become a *de rigueur* pilgrimage point for those interested in 1956.

Places to Stay

Camping The largest camping ground in Budapest is *Rómaifürdő* (☎ 168 6260), Szentendrei út 189, with space for 2500 guests, in a shady park north of the city. To get there take the HÉV suburban railway from Batthyány tér Metro Station to Rómaifürdő vm Station, which is within sight of the camping ground. The facility is open all year so it's up to you to decide if it's warm enough for camping. Cabins are available from mid-April to mid-October at US$11 double in 3rd category, US$17 double in 2nd category. They have 43 cabins in total, but they're often full. Use of the

adjacent swimming pool, with lots of green grass on which to stretch out, is included, and nearby are a disco and several places to eat.

Up in the Buda Hills is *Hárshegy Camping* (☎ 115 1482) (open from Easter to mid-October), Hárshegyi út 7. Take bus No 22 from Moszkva tér Metro Station and watch for the signs on the right. Camping here costs US$3 per person, plus US$3 per tent. The 70 3rd-category duplex cabins without bath are US$13 single or double, US$19 triple. There are also six 2nd-category rooms with bath at US$36 single or double and 10 1st-category bungalows with bath at US$39 single or double.

A somewhat more convenient camping ground for those without their own transport is *Zugligeti Niche Camping* (☎ 156 8641), Zugligeti út 101, at the bottom station of the Buda Hills chair lift (take bus No 158 from Moszkva tér Metro Station to the end of the line). It's US$8 for two people to camp on one of the small hillside terraces. In addition, there's one on-site caravan at US$15 double, one bungalow at US$17 for two or three people and two rooms at US$22 double or US$33 for four persons. Their reception and buffet are in a couple of old Budapest trams parked at the entrance. Zugligeti Niche is open from April to mid-November and the friendly staff speak English.

Youth Hostels The Express office (☎ 131 7777) booking youth hostel beds is at Szabadság tér 16, a block from Kossuth tér Metro Station (Monday to Thursday until 4 pm, Friday until 2 pm). The main Express office at Semmelweis utca 4 (metro: Astoria) also has information during business hours, though they don't make bookings. You can also go directly to the hostels. Youth hostel or student cards are not required at any of the hostels, although they'll sometimes get you a 10% discount and they're accepted as identification (eliminating the need to leave your passport at the reception). The two Express offices and all the hostels listed in this section are open year-round.

The *Bridge Hostel* (☎ 215 7604), Soroksári út 12, off Boráros tér, is a modern seven-storey building facing the Danube. A bed in a three-bedded room is US$6 and doubles with shared bath are US$12. They have a total of 180 beds so there should be something available. Get there on tram No 4 from Ferenc körút Metro Station to the last stop before the Danube, or just walk.

A popular 23-bed crash pad on the southeast side of the city is *Back Pack Guest House* (☎ 185 5089), Takács Menyhért utca 33. A place in a seven-bed dorm is US$5, in a five-bed dorm US$6, plus US$0.75 for linen (first night only) and US$1.25 for a filling breakfast. Double rooms are available in winter only. There's a kitchen, laundry, lockers, TV lounge and no curfew, but it's cramped (and very sociable). After a day of exploring Budapest everyone sits outside on the front steps and tries to decide where to go that night over a few beers. Worldwise managers Attila and Krisztina are super friendly and helpful (their docile red setter Alex is only friendly). Watch out, this place is a trap: if you like the backpackers scene you may find it hard to leave. Access is relatively easy on bus No 7 or 7a (black number) from Keleti Railway Station or Ferenciek tere Metro (get out right after the bus goes under a railway bridge and look for small green signs or ask).

Hotel Express (☎ 175 2528), Beethoven utca 7/9, several blocks south-west of Déli Railway Station (take tram No 59 for two stops), is US$19 single or double, US$23 triple with shared bath. The toilet and shower are down the hall and breakfast costs extra. There's a 10% discount for YHA card-holders.

One of Budapest's nicest yet least known places to stay is the *Youth Centre of Csilebérc* (☎ 156 5772), Konkoly Thege utca 21 in the Buda Hills. This huge complex is the former Pioneer Camp and it's in a quiet, wooded location. Both the official Hungarian Youth Hostel Association and the American School are based here. Csilebérc offers a 36-room youth hostel *(turistaszálló)* at US$11/14 single/double (20% discount with a YHA card but not on singles), eight four-bed bun-galows with private bath at US$33, and camping at US$1.25 per person plus US$1.25 per tent (or US$2 per person if you sleep in one of their fixed dormitory tents). All of the above and the many sporting facilities are available year-round and easily accessible on bus No 21 (red number) from Moszkva tér Metro to the end of the line, then bus No 90 to the first stop after the railway tracks (or a 10-minute downhill walk). The complex reception *(központ)* is open 24 hours a day. The restaurant is inexpensive but closes at 8 pm.

Summer-Only Hostels In July and August private entrepreneurs rent vacant student dormitories from the government and turn them into youth hostels which they do their best to fill in order to make a profit. Competition is fierce and there are several rival hostel operators, so you can afford to shop around a bit. Beds average US$7 per person. Most of these hostels are open only in summer, so from September to June make sure a place is actually open before going far out of your way. Ask at Ibusz, Express or Tourinform, or call the hostel the night before. Functioning hostels always have receptionists who speak English, so if you get a monolingual Hungarian something's wrong. More Than Ways (see following) is the largest year-round operation, but their hostels are also the most crowded – great places to meet people.

In July and August backpackers are often approached at Keleti and Nyugati train stations by representatives from the different hostels offering free minibus rides to their hostels. This is fine but if you want a double room get a firm commitment that one is available that night, otherwise you could be stuck in a dormitory for days on end waiting for one to become available. The hostels rarely have single rooms, even if these are advertised in their brochures.

The most central youth hostel is *Ottó & Viktor's* (☎ 267 0311), Papnövelde utca 4-6, in the Apáczai Kollégiuma building just off Egyetem tér, a few minutes walk from Ferenciek tere or Astoria metro stations. Ottó and Viktor offer two, four and six-bedded rooms from late June to August only.

From late June to early September Széchenyi István Szakkollégium, Ráday utca 43-45, becomes *Strawberry Youth Hostel* (☎ 138 4766) with 60 rooms at US$9 per person in doubles, US$8 per person in triples, US$7 per person in quads. Nearby at Kinizsi utca 2-6 is another modern six-storey student residence which functions in exactly the same way, but opens and closes a little earlier. These places are within walking distance from Ferenc körút Metro Station and are a good bet in summer.

Most of the hostels belonging to the University of Technology are west of Ferenc körút Metro Station and in July and August it should be easy to find a bed here (though most function as regular student dormitories the rest of the year and are closed to travellers). One of the largest is the *Schönherz Zoltán Kollégiuma* (☎ 166 5422), Irinyi József utca 42 (tram No 4 from Ferenc körút Metro Station to the second stop west of the Danube). In July and August only this 22-storey skyscraper offers youth hostel beds at US$6 per person with a disco on the premises.

Other summertime hostels in the large student residential area near Schönherz Zoltán Kollégiuma are *Kármán Tódor Kollégium* (☎ 181 2313), Irinyi József utca 9-11, *Martos* (☎ 181 2171), Sztoczek József utca 7 (doubles here are US$14), *Vásárhelyi* (☎ 185 2216), Kruspér utca 2-4 opposite Martos, *Rózsa Ferenc/Epitesz Kollégium* (☎ 166 6677), Bercsényi utca 28-30, and *Baross Gábor Kollégium/Landler* (☎ 185 1444), Bartók Béla út 17. These have mostly rooms with two to four beds.

If you're arriving in Budapest on a train from southern or western Hungary (or Vienna) which stops at Kelenföld Railway Station, jump off there and go through the underpass to the white 14-storey residence of *Komját Aladár Kollégium* (☎ 166 5355), Rimaszombati út 2. In July and August they offer rooms with two, three and four beds.

The city centre is easily accessible from here on bus No 7 (red number).

More Than Ways The best news in years on the Budapest low-budget scene is the More Than Ways University Youth Hostels chain which operates eight youth hostels around Budapest in July and August. Towards the end of August seven of the hostels close and revert to their former lives as student dormitories but one hostel stays open year-round.

More Than Ways has its headquarters at the *Diakszálló Youth Hostel* (☎ 129 8644), Dózsa György út 152, a two-minute walk from Dózsa György út Metro Station. Although this 140-bed hostel is usually the most crowded (hordes of Western backpackers), they offer a free minibus transfer from there to any of their other hostels which still have beds available, so this is probably the best place to go first. The Diákszálló charges US$8/12 single/double or US$6 per person in dormitories of eight or 12 beds. The singles and doubles are almost always full in summer (but often available in winter).

Donáti Youth Hostel (☎ 201 1971), Donáti utca 46, a five-minute walk from Batthyány tér Metro Station, has only 72 dormitory beds but it's open only in summer.

All the More Than Ways hostels are open 24 hours a day and you can check in any time, but you must depart by 9 am or pay for another night. There's no curfew and a YHA card is not required (the signs at the hostel entrances stating that a student or hostel card are required are only there to keep out undesirables). The More Than Ways hostels can be noisy and a little chaotic at times but they're fine if you only want a cheap place to crash and meet other travellers.

Private Rooms Reasonable value for accommodation in Budapest are the private rooms assigned by local travel agencies. They generally cost US$11/17 single/double or more plus US$1 to US$2 tax, with a 20% supplement if you stay less than four nights. To get a single or a room in the centre of town, you may have to try several offices. There are lots of rooms available and even in

July and August you'll be able to find something. You'll probably need to buy an indexed city map to find your room.

Following is a list of various agencies, beginning with those closest to the transportation terminals. Most are open only during normal business hours so if you arrive late or on a weekend, try the Ibusz Accommodation Centre at Petőfi tér 3 (metro: Ferenciek tere) which never closes. If you arrive at Keleti Railway Station between 11.10 pm and 4.30 am when the metro isn't running, catch night bus No 78 from outside the nearby Grand Hotel to Erzébet hid. The centre's prices are higher than those of the following agencies, however, so only go there when the others are closed. Individuals on the street outside this Ibusz office will offer you an unofficial private room, but their prices are higher than those asked inside and there is no quality control.

You may also be offered a private room by entrepreneurs at the railway stations. These vary considerably and cases of travellers being promised an idyllic room in the centre of town, only to be taken to a dreary, cramped flat in some distant suburb are not unknown. Yet several readers report getting excellent rooms right on the metro from people outside the Ibusz office at Keleti Railway Station. You really have to use your own judgment here.

Near Keleti Railway Station The Ibusz office in Keleti Railway Station (open daily) has private rooms at US$9/11 single/double but there are few singles. Express opposite Ibusz also has private rooms.

Budapest Tourist at Baross tér 3, just beyond the overpass on the opposite side of the square from Keleti Railway Station, also arranges private rooms and changes money.

Near Nyugati Railway Station Ibusz at Nyugati Railway Station arranges private rooms. Also try Cooptourist and Budapest Tourist in the underground concourse at the entrance to the metro below Nyugati Railway Station. More rooms are for rent at Panoráma Travel, Nyugati tér 7, on the opposite side of the square from the station, and Volántourist, Teréz körút 38, also quite near Nyugati. A second Cooptourist office is in the opposite direction at Kossuth Lajos tér 13 near Parliament (metro: Kossuth tér).

Near Erzsébet tér Bus Station Dunatours at Bajcsy-Zsilinszky út 17 behind St Stephen's Basilica has reasonable rooms. To-Ma Tour, Október 6 utca 22, is expensive at US$17/20 single/double in the centre.

One of the largest offices in the city offering private rooms is Budapest Tourist, Roosevelt tér 5 (open until 6 pm on weekdays and Saturday mornings).

Near the Hydrofoil Terminal Some of Budapest's least expensive private rooms are available from Ibusz, Ferenciek tere 5 (metro: Ferenciek tere). They're open Saturday until 1 pm. The Ibusz 24-hour Accommodation Centre at Petőfi tér 3 is also within walking distance from both the hydrofoil and the bus station.

Near Déli Railway Station At Déli Railway Station private rooms are arranged by Ibusz, at the entrance to the metro, or Budapest Tourist, in the mall in front of the station. Also try Cooptourist, Attila út 107, directly across the park in front of Déli Railway Station.

Cheaper Hotels A hotel room will cost a bit more than a private room, though management doesn't mind if you stay only one night. There are no cheap hotels right in the city centre but the *Domnik Motel* (☎ 122 7655), Cházár András utca 3, directly behind a large church on Thököly út, is just two stops northeast of Keleti Railway Station on bus No 7 (black number). The 36 rooms with shared bath are US$18/22 single/double, breakfast included. This friendly pension is a convenient place to stay for a few nights.

The *Hotel Flandria* (☎ 129 6689), Szegedi út 27, is easily accessible on trams No 12 and 14 from Lehel tér Metro Station. Rooms with shared bath in this five-storey tourist hotel cost US$18/25 single/double including breakfast. They cater mostly to foreign groups.

One of the best deals in town if there are a few of you is the *Poscher Hotel* (☎ 149 0321), Kerekes utca 12-20, two blocks away from the Flandria. Also known as the Munkásszálloda Góliát, this huge 11-storey block accommodates workers as well as tourists. A room with four beds will cost US$11 for the room whether you're alone or in a gang of four. The atmosphere in the Poscher can be a little rough-and-ready at times – recommended for those who want to experience proletarian Budapest. There's a cheap self-service restaurant on the premises and check out *Club Viking* nearby at Kerekes utca 6.

If you've always dreamed of staying in a castle on the Danube you'll like the *Citadella Hotel* (☎ 166 5794) in the Citadel above Hotel Gellért (for public transport see Things to See above). The 11 twin rooms go for US$25/27 single/double without bath, US$28/36 with a leaky shower, and there are also 58 beds in 10-bed dormitories *(turistas-zallas)* at US$6 per person. The dorms are usually booked by groups a week ahead so try calling well in advance for a reservation.

Several inexpensive places are accessible on the HÉV suburban railway line to Szentendre from Batthyány tér Metro Station. The first is the one-star *Hotel Polo* (☎ 250 0192), Mozaik utca 1-3 near the Filatorigat HÉV Station. You can't see the hotel from the station, but it's beside a service station, behind a long, white building which runs along the east side of the tracks. Doubles with shared bath are US$21, while the one room with private bath is US$32 (no singles). It's a new hotel built in 1987 and is in the same building as the local Volkswagen dealer.

Upriver beside the Danube is the *Sporthotel Lidó* (☎ 188 6865), Nánási út 67, a 10-minute walk from Rómaifürdő HÉV Station. Singles/doubles are available all year at US$17/26 with shared bath, breakfast included. Show your YHA card here for a 10% discount. The Sporthotel Lidó has a sauna, solarium, fitness room and tennis courts which are available to guests, and from May to September there's a ferry service from the embankment behind the hotel to Budapest.

The *Hotel Touring* (☎ 180 1595), Pünkösdfürdő utca 38, at the north-west end of Budapest, is an 11-storey workers' residence which has 65 rooms with shared bath reserved for tourists at US$19/20/25/30 single/double/triple/quad including breakfast – good value for small groups. It's a 10-minute walk from Békásmegyar HÉV Station (ask directions from the station). A regular Budapest transit ticket will take you here.

More Expensive Hotels The old *Park Hotel* (☎ 113 5619), Baross tér 10, directly across from Keleti Railway Station, is US$31/41 single/double without bath, US$37/50 with shower (often full). The *Metropol Hotel* (☎ 142 1171), Rákóczi út 58 near Keleti (metro: Blaha Lujza tér), has singles/doubles at US$35/45 without bath, US$42/57 with bath.

A much better medium-priced hotel than these is the *Medosz Hotel* (☎ 153 1700), Jókai tér 9 in the theatre district. The 11 singles are US$31, the 53 doubles US$45, all with private bath and an excellent breakfast. There's no sign outside, so look for the modern 10-storey building marked 'háza' beside the 'Kolibri szinház' (metro: Oktogon).

Büro Panzió (☎ 115 1898), Dékán utca 3 at Retek utca, just a block off the north side of Moszkva tér, looks basic from the outside but the rooms (which cost US$38/48/60 single/double/triple with bath and breakfast) are comfortable and even luxurious (each with TV). Only a one-minute walk from the metro, this colourful place would be an excellent choice for the business traveller (fax, telex and photocopying on the premises) or anyone interested in value for money.

Places to Eat
Bottom End One of the few remaining self-service restaurants in Budapest is *Bölcs Bagoly Önkiszolgáló Étterem*, Váci utca 33

HUNGARY

(metro: Ferenciek tere) (weekdays 11.30 am to 3 pm). It's always crowded with local office workers who appreciate a cheap lunch.

The *Városház Snack*, Városház utca 16, opposite the town hall at the back exit of the main post office, serves good food at reasonable prices. At lunch time the place will be jammed with local office workers (weekdays 11 am to 7 pm).

The self-service *Önkiszolgáló Étterem* at Arany János utca 7, is open weekdays from 11.30 am to 4 pm only.

Another self-service place *Önkiszolgáló Étterem* is on the top floor of Skála Department Store directly opposite Nyugati Railway Station, accessible from the exterior terrace (open weekdays noon to 3 pm only).

One of the healthiest and least expensive places to eat in Budapest is *No 1 Falafel Faloda*, Paulay Ede utca 53 (metro: Opera or Oktogon).

It's strictly vegetarian and you pay a fixed price to stuff a piece of pitta bread or fill a plastic container yourself from the great assortment of salad bar options. There's also a large selection of teas and a place to sit down in the loft. The bright, modern décor attracts a sharp young crowd (open weekdays from 10 am to 8 pm only).

The clean and attractive *Saláta Bár*, in a corner of the Grand Hotel Hungária, on Baross tér facing the overpass across the square from Keleti Railway Station, has fresh salad although you have to eat standing up. The attendant fills your plate so just ask for 10 dkg (100 grams) of three or four things you fancy. Because this place is connected to a top hotel the food is very good.

Look for the *lángos* (doughnut) stand in the circular open-air courtyard outside Keleti Railway Station, on the far left as you go from the station to the metro entrance. This may be the best bargain in Budapest (closed Sunday).

Cheap German-style sausage and beer are consumed standing up at *Gasztró Hús Hentesáru*, Margít körút 2, right opposite the first stop of trams Nos 4 and 6 on the west side of the Margaret Bridge (Monday 7 am to 6 pm, Tuesday to Friday 6 am to 7 pm,

Saturday 6.30 am to 1 pm). Other Hús Hentesáru meat markets around Budapest offer the same sort of thing.

Central Pest The varied selection of regular restaurants listed following appear in geographical order across central Pest from north to south. Mexican food and other Latin American dishes are offered at *La Pampa*, Pannónia utca 7 off Szent István körút, behind the Vígszínház (metro: Nyugati tér).

Real Arab food is served at *Semiramis*, Alkotmány utca 20 near Nyugati Railway Station (there is additional seating upstairs). It's rather hidden halfway down the block.

The friendly *Karcsi Ételbár*, Jókai utca 20, a block back from Teréz körút four blocks from Nyugati Railway Station, serves very reasonable Hungarian meals and the menu posted outside also lists drinks! It doesn't serve lunch on weekends.

Kisharang Étkezde, Október 6 utca 17 (weekdays from 11 am to 8 pm, weekends 11.30 am to 3.30 pm), has excellent local fare at very reasonable prices. The menu is only in Hungarian and no English is spoken but just point at something on another table – the place is always crowded. Recommended. Next door is an excellent ice-cream place, if you still have room.

Dine in style at the restaurant upstairs in the *Duna Palota*, Zrínyi utca 5 (daily noon to 11 pm). This elegant palace erected in 1894 was formerly a military officers club. Complete food and drink menus are posted outside and prices are reasonable for a place like this.

The *Bohémtanya Vendéglő*, Paulay Ede utca 6 between Deák tér and the State Opera (metro: Bajcsy-Zsilinszky út), is an unpretentious but OK eatery that serves large portions. You may have to wait a while for a table. The menu is in English and German.

Morrison's Bar, Révay utca 25 next to the State Opera, serves meals although it's more of a drinking place.

There are two unpretentious kosher restaurants in what was the Jewish ghetto, north-east of Károly körút (metro: Astoria).

The *Hanna Restaurant*, Dob utca 35 (open weekdays from 11.30 am to 4 pm only), is part of an active Jewish community centre occupying buildings which survived the war. A block or two away at Klauzál tér 2 is the more commercial *Salom Restaurant*.

The *Astoria Hotel*, Kossuth Lajos utca 19 (metro: Astoria), puts on a good self-service buffet breakfast (US$4) every morning from 7 to 10 am in the turn-of-the-century dining room.

Vegetarium, Cukor utca 3 just off Ferenciek tere (noon to 10 pm daily), is a full-service vegetarian restaurant with a comprehensive English menu which includes some macrobiotic items. It's not cheap but most readers report they enjoyed the friendly service, good food and smoke-free atmosphere. After 7 pm an acoustic guitarist sets the mellow scene (there's a music list on each table, allowing you to make requests). Look for Vegetarium's big red apple logo.

Cabar, Iranyi utca 25, around the corner from Vegetarium (metro: Ferenciek tere), has Israeli-style sawarma and felafel which you eat standing up. There's a self-service salad bar – you'll be charged by the weight of the food you select. On the corner near Cabar is a good ice-cream place called *Gelato*.

Abelino Pizzeria, Duna utca 6 (down a side street from Ferenciek tere), has reasonable oven-baked pizza and draught beer. The service here is good (closed Sunday and holidays).

Typical Hungarian meals are served at the *Alföldi Kisvendéglo*, Kecskeméti utca 4 (metro: Kálvin tér). The menu lists different prices for small portions (*zóna adag*) and large portions (*adag*). The waiters sometimes serve foreigners who order large portions small portions, then charge for large portions, so you might be better off ordering a small portion in the first place. Got it?

Stop Étterem, Váci utca 86 at Fővám tér (metro: Kálvin tér), offers a good variety of fish, venison, pork, veal and poultry, plus four vegetarian selections. Prices are reasonable, the menu is in English, colour photos of many of the dishes are in the window and it's open almost 24 hours a day.

Kaltenberg Söröző, Kinizsi utca 30-36 (metro: Ferenc körút), combines substantial Hungarian meals, a German menu and the feel of one of the better US chain restaurants like Sizzlers. It's a reliable, medium-priced choice.

If you're not discouraged by the prospect of spending up to US$50 per person for dinner, *Gundel*, next to the zoo directly behind the Museum of Fine Art (metro: Széchenyi Fürdő), is probably Budapest's finest restaurant with a tradition dating back to 1894. It's not afraid to post the menu outside with prices (open daily from noon to 4 pm and 7 pm to midnight).

Castle District Expensive restaurants popular among tourists abound in the castle district, but weekdays from 11.30 am to 2 pm a self-service called simply the *Önkiszolgáló Étterem* functions inside the college at Országház utca 30. Take the elevator up to the 3rd floor.

A slightly better self-service (*önkiszolgáló étterem*) is above Fortuna Spaten, directly across the street from the Hilton Hotel on Fortuna utca, also open weekdays from 11 am to 2.30 pm.

The rather expensive *Régi Országház*, Országház utca 17, combines good wine with a medieval atmosphere.

Below Castle Hill A good little restaurant with regular table service inside the *Buda Concert Hall*, Corvin tér 8 (metro: Batthyány tér), directly below the Fisherman's Bastion on Castle Hill, serves lunch on weekdays from 7 am to 4 pm. It's worth the slight detour as the tourists up on the hill don't know this place.

The *Tabáni Kakas Restaurant*, Attila út 27, is a slightly up-market, old-style Hungarian restaurant.

Hearty Hungarian meals are served at *Söröző a Szent Jupáthoz*, Retek utca 16 a block north of Moszkva tér. The menu is posted outside in English and it's open 24 hours a day.

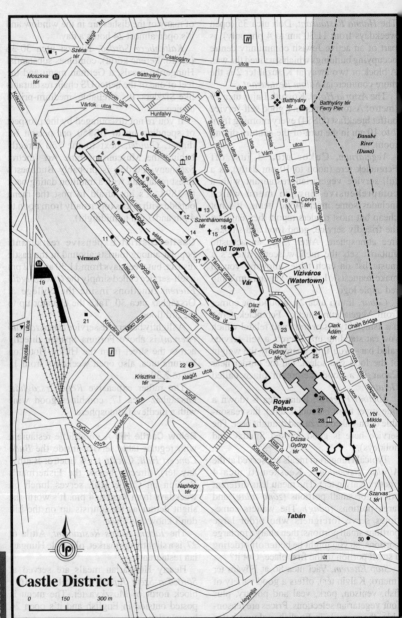

Castle District

0   150   300 m

PLACES TO STAY

1 Büro Panzió/Söröző a Szent Jupáthoz
2 Donáti Youth Hostel (Summer Only)
13 Hilton Hotel
21 Buda Penta Hotel

PLACES TO EAT

8 Önkiszolgáló Étterem
9 Régi Országház Restaurant
12 Fortuna Self-Service Restaurant (Upstairs)
14 Ruszwurm Café
20 Pizzeria Il Treno
29 Tabáni Kakas Restaurant

OTHER

3 Supermarket
4 Museum of Military History
5 National Archives
6 Vienna Gate
7 Magdalen Tower
10 Music History Museum
11 Cooptourist
15 Matthias Church
16 Fisherman's Bastion
17 Golden Eagle Pharmacy
18 Buda Concert Hall
19 Déli Train Station
22 OTP Bank
23 Várszinház (Castle Theatre)
24 Tram No 16
25 Funicular Railway
26 National Gallery
27 National Library
28 Historical Museum
30 Rác Baths

The *Marxim Pizzeria*, Kisrókus utca 23, a five-minute walk from Moszkva tér Metro daily until 1 am), is popular among workers from the surrounding factories who appreciate the Gulag Pizza, not to mention the Lenin and Anarchism varieties. Mementos of the Stalin years hang from the walls and you can drown all your uncertainties in cheap Belgian beer.

Pizzeria Il Treno, Alkotás utca 15, serves real hand-tossed pizza in its upbeat location across the street from Déli Railway Station. Only a barbarian would want to put tomato sauce on the pizza here! The food is reasonable but drinks are priced on the high side. The self-service salad bar makes this place a good choice for vegetarians. *Banya-Tanya Vendéglő*, half a block up from Il Treno, is a good local place.

Yet another choice is *La Prima Pizzeria*, Margit körút 3 opposite the stop of tram Nos 4 and 6 on the west side of the Danube. They bake good pizza and, on weekdays from noon to 3 pm, offer a set three-course meal *(gyermek menü)*. There's also a self-service salad bar.

On your way to the Citadella you might stop for lunch at the *Tollas Bar Grill Söröző*, Móricz Zsigmond körtér 4, which offers grilled chicken and draught beer. Next door is a *Cukrászda* where you can get great cakes and ice cream. These places are right at the point where you change from tram No 19 to bus No 27, as described in the Things to See section above.

Óbuda A number of up-market restaurants are around Fő tér, Óbuda (HÉV suburban railway from Batthyány tér Metro to Árpád híd mh). The *Postakocsi Restaurant*, Fő tér 2, is one; *Sipos Halászkert*, Szentlelek tér 8, founded in 1930 by Károly Sipos, is another (try the fish soup). In the evening there will be Gypsy music at both places and you'll certainly break the budget if you eat at either. Menus are posted outside.

Even if you aren't prepared to pay the sort of prices listed on those restaurant menus, Fő tér is still fine for a romantic stroll at night and there's a good little bar, the *Kis Dreher Söröző*, on Harrer Pál utca just off Fő tér.

Cafés Like Vienna, Budapest is famous for its cafés and the most famous of the famous is the *Gerbeaud Cukrászda*, on the west side of Vörösmarty tér, a fashionable meeting place of the city's elite since 1870. In recent years it has become pretentious and overpriced.

If anything, *Cukrászda Művész*, Andrássy út 29, almost opposite the opera, is more elegant than Gerbeaud and has a better selection of cakes at lower prices.

HUNGARY

Cheaper yet is *Perity mestercukrászat*, Andrássy út 37, with unbelievably rich desserts, great ice cream and drinks with prices clearly displayed (for a change).

The *Café New York*, Erzsébet körút 11 (metro: Blaha Lujza tér), has been a Budapest institution since 1895. The elegant turn-of-the-century décor glitters around the literati who still meet there. At least one visit must be made to the Café New York!

Number One Espresso, Sas utca 9 off Erzsébet tér (metro: Deák tér), is a good local pub with draught beer but no food (closed on Sunday).

A great place for cheap stand-up coffee and cakes is the *Jégbüfé*, Ferenciek tere 10 next to Ibusz (metro: Ferenciek tere). Write down the name of whatever it is you want and pay the cashier who will give you a voucher.

Up in the castle district, the perfect place for coffee and cakes is the crowded *Ruszwurm Café*, Szentháromság utca 7 near Matthias Church.

Beware of cafés in the centre that don't display the price of coffee – it will be double or triple what it costs everywhere else in the city. The places along Váci utca especially are becoming a rip-off.

Markets The old Pest market hall (presently closed for renovations) is on Fovam tér (metro: Kálvin tér). A large open-air street market (open Sunday) unfolds behind the large church above Lehel tér Metro Station.

A large supermarket (open Monday, Tuesday, Thursday and Friday from 6 am to 8 pm, Wednesday and Saturday from 7 am to 4.30 pm, Sunday from 7 am to 1 pm) is in the old market hall on the south side of Batthyány tér near the metro station. Stock up.

Entertainment

Opera & Operetta You should pay at least one visit to the *State Opera House* (1884), Andrássy út 22 (metro: Opera), to see the frescoes and incredibly rich gilded decoration in the Italian Renaissance style. The box office is on the left-hand side of the building behind the tour office (closed on Saturday and Monday). Tickets are more expensive for Friday and Saturday night.

Budapest has a second opera house, the modern *Erkel Színház* at Köztársaság tér 30 near Keleti Railway Station. Tickets are sold just inside the main doors (Tuesday to Saturday 11 am to 7 pm, Sunday 10 am to 1 pm and 4 to 7 pm).

Operettas are presented at the *Fővárosi Operett Színház*, Nagy-mező utca 17, a block from the State Opera House. Tickets are sold inside and it's worth checking here in summer as there are often programmes.

Musicals are performed at the *Madách Theatre*, Eszsébet körút 31/33 (metro: Blaha Lujza tér). The Madách presents an interesting mix of rock operas, musicals and straight drama in Hungarian – it's worth checking.

Concerts A monthly *Koncert Kalendarium* lists all concerts in Budapest that month and most nights you'll have two or three to choose from. The motto of the Budapest Spring Festival in late March is '10 days, 100 venues, 1000 events' and you'll have a good selection of musical events each night. Budapest's main concert hall is the *Pest Vigadó*, Vigadó tér 2 (metro: Vörösmarty tér). Other concerts are held at the *Academy of Music*, Király utca 64, on the corner of Liszt Ferenc tér (metro: Oktogon).

Circus The *Grand Circus*, Állatkerti körút 7 (metro: Széchenyi Fürdő), has performances on Saturday and Sunday at 10 am; Wednesday, Thursday, Friday and Saturday at 3 pm and Wednesday, Friday, Saturday and Sunday at 7 pm (closed in summer). Although the matinées are occasionally booked out by school groups, there's almost always space in the evening. Advance tickets are sold at the circus itself (US$3).

Planetarium & Puppets Budapest's *Planetarium* (metro: Népliget) features exciting laser light shows to the accompaniment of rock music. There are usually shows held from Monday to Saturday at 7.30 and 9 pm

You can purchase tickets (US$4) at the door or from any Budapest ticket agency.

The *Puppet Theatre*, Andrássy út 69 (metro: Vörösmarty utca), presents afternoon shows designed for children and evening programmes for adults. There's a special adult performance on Monday at 6 pm. The shows are generally held at 3 pm on weekdays and at 11 am and 4 pm on weekends. It's closed all summer.

Tánchaz Authentic participatory folk-music workshops (*tánchaz* or 'dance house') are held once or twice a week at the *Sazbadidő-központ* (☎ 122 9870), Almássy tér 6, a couple of blocks from Blaha Lujza tér Metro Station. The famous Gypsy group Kalyi Jag sometimes plays here, and there are Greek, Bulgarian and Israeli dance workshops quite regularly.

From mid-September to the end of June the well-known Hungarian folk group Muzsikás runs a workshop at the *Fővárosi Művelődési Háza*, Fehérvári út 47, every Tuesday from 7 to 11 pm (admission US$0.75). On Wednesday during these same months there's a Balkan dance workshop here (admission US$1). Get there on tram No 4 from Ferenc körút Metro Station, southwest to the end of the line at Fehérvári út.

Most people come to the *tánchaz* evenings to learn the folk dances that go with the music (and of course you can dance too). These workshops have nothing to do with tourism and are a great opportunity to hear musicians practising and get involved in a local scene at next to no expense. You become part of the programme instead of merely watching others perform.

The Tánchaz Festival of Folk & Popular Music unfolds at the Népstadion on a Saturday evening during the last third of each March as part of the Budapest Spring Festival.

Youth Scene The youth scene revolves around the *Petőfi Centre* (Fővárosi Ifjúsági Szabadidő Központ) in City Park (metro: Széchenyi Fürdő) where concerts by well-known international rock and blues groups are held a couple of times a month. It's great if you get tickets as the hall is small enough for you to really get close to the performers. The *tánchaz* evenings here give you the opportunity to learn folk dancing. Ask about Greek dancing (*görög tánchaz*) as this attracts oodles of young people who form massive circles and dance to the lively Greek folk music. Fan clubs dedicated to The Cure, Madonna, Metalica, Guns N' Roses, New Kids on the Block, Michael Jackson and others meet regularly in the centre and these are more fun than they sound. Those present spend the evening dancing to the music of their favourite stars in a small club room with subdued lighting and a bar, and videos are occasionally shown. Ask for the monthly Petőfi Centre programme at the information counter. The centre is easily accessible on trolleybus No 74 from in front of the synagogue on Dohány utca.

Blues, Jazz & Rock Clubs The *Merlin Jazz Club*, Gerlóczy utca 4, around the corner from Károly körút 28 (metro: Deák tér), has live music nightly from 10 pm.

From Tuesday to Saturday nights the *Made Inn Club*, Andrássy út 112 (metro: Bajza utca), presents live Latin American music, acoustic, pop or blues in a gentile setting. Thursday is a big night here (open daily 8 pm to 5 am).

Kávéház Tilos az Á, Mikszáth Kálmán tér 2, off Baross utca (metro: Kálvan tér), presents live blues or rock-and-roll groups from Thursday to Saturday nights and sometimes also on Wednesday. Some of the best music in Budapest is heard here. A block away at Krúdy Gyula utca 6 is *The Blues Pub* where you can also hear jazz.

Discos One of Budapest's top discos is *Globe* in City Park, across the street from the Municipal Baths (metro: Széchenyi Fürdő). Globe has a large modern dance floor – just the place to head when you start getting bored with the action at the nearby Petőfi Centre. It's open Friday, Saturday and Sunday from 9 pm to 4 am year-round (admission US$3).

Another very popular disco is *Hully-Gully*, Apor Vilmos tér 9, in the Buda Hills (tram No 59 five stops from Moszkva tér). The laser lighting, go-go girls and fair prices attract large crowds – almost nobody goes into *Randevu* next door. Hully-Gully is open daily from 9 pm to 5 am and the dress is informal.

Fortuna, Hess András tér 4, directly across the street from the Hilton Hotel in the castle district, functions as a disco after 10 pm from Thursday to Saturday during the school year. It's always packed with trendy Budapest youth and the music is good but they're selective about who they let in (try showing your ISIC).

Nightclubs Budapest's swankiest nightclub is *Maxim Variete* in the Emke Hotel, Akácfa utca 3 (metro: Blaha Lujza tér). The club's chorus line consists of 12 scantily dressed Maxim girls, and magicians, acrobats, singers and dancers, appearing in a Las Vegas-style extravaganza. Performances are at 10 pm and midnight daily (US$11 cover charge).

You'll find more of the same at the *Moulin Rouge Cabaret* (☎ 112 4492) beside the Fővárosi Operett Színház (metro: Opera). The cabaret also functions as a disco and occasional rock concerts are held here too.

Summertime Entertainment From mid-June to mid-September most of the regular theatres will be closed for holidays. Among the programmes put on for tourists at this time is a special operetta staged at the *Arany János Theatre*, Paulay Ede utca 35 (metro: Opera). Tickets are US$11 to US$28.

Every Monday, Friday and Saturday from May to mid-October at 8.30 pm, the Folklór Centrum presents a programme of Hungarian dancing accompanied by a Gypsy orchestra at the *Fővárosi Művelődési Háza* (☎ 181 1360), Fehérvári út 47 (for public transport see Táncház above). This performance is one of the best of its kind in Budapest.

Also in summer, the 40 dancers of the Hungarian State Folk Ensemble perform at the *Buda Concert Hall* (☎ 201 5928), Corvin

tér 8 (metro: Batthyány tér). The 1½-hour programmes begin at 7 pm every Tuesday, Wednesday and Thursday from April to October (but not in June). Both shows cost US$7 admission.

Every Wednesday at 8 pm year-round you can see Hungarian folk dancing at the stately *Duna Palota*, Zrínyi utca 5 just off Roosevelt tér in central Pest (US$6).

Ticket Agencies The busiest theatrical ticket agency is the Központi Jegyiroda, Andrássy út 18 (metro: Opera). They have tickets there to numerous theatres and events, although the best are gone a couple of days in advance.

For concert tickets try Jegyiroda Országos Filharmonia, Vörösmarty tér 1 (metro: Vörösmarty tér). Check out the zany elevator next to this office.

Music Mix, Váci utca 33 (metro: Ferenciek tere), has tickets to special events such as rock spectaculars, appearances by foreign superstars etc. Tickets here begin around US$20.

As you pursue your quest for tickets, you'll sometimes be told that everything is sold out. You usually get better seats by going directly to the theatre box office than you would by dealing with a ticket agency. Theatre tickets cost anywhere from US$2 to US$20.

Horse Races It should come as no surprise that the descendants of the nomadic Magyar tribes love horse racing. Races are held at the *Kerepesi Trotting Track*, Kerepesi út 9 near Keleti Railway Station (bus No 95 or trolley-bus No 80), throughout the year, beginning at 2 pm on Saturday (12 races) and 4 pm on Wednesday (10 races). Admission is US$0.50 and there's a large section where food and drinks are sold.

From mid-March to November regular horse races are held at the *Galopp Loversenypálya Race Track* on Albertirsai út, next to Hungarexpo, every Sunday beginning at 2 pm. From May to September horse races are also held here on Thursday, beginning at 4 pm. Each session lasts for about four hours (10 races). You can see the track and smell the horses from Pillangó utca Metro Station but the entrance is a 15-minute walk away (as you leave the station turn left, then left again onto Albertirsai út). It's great fun to observe this authentic local scene even if you aren't a gambler.

Thermal Baths Budapest is a major spa centre with numerous bathing establishments that are open to the public. Here the Danube follows the geological fault separating the Buda Hills from the Great Plain and over 40 million litres of warm mineral water gush forth daily from 123 thermal springs.

Begin your bathhouse tour with the *Gellért Baths* (enter through the side entrance of the eclectic hotel of the same name below Gellért Hill). Built in 1918, the thermal pools there maintain a constant temperature of 44°C and a large outdoor pool is open in summer. A price list two metres long is posted in English and German beside the ticket booth (entry costs US$3.50 for three hours, a tub bath for two people US$6, a cubicle US$1.50, a 30-minute massage US$4 etc). You must wear a bathing cap (supplied) in the swimming pool. Men and women are separated in the communal baths and if you're a couple paying extra for a two-person tub bath make sure you'll be allowed in together! Therapeutical services such as traction cure, ultrasonic, inhalation and short-wave treatments are available. Everything except the swimming pool is closed in the afternoon on weekends.

There are two famous bathing establishments near the Buda end of Erzsébet híd (Elizabeth Bridge). The *Rudas Baths* beside the river were built by the Turks in 1566 and retain a strong Islamic flavour. The Rudas Baths are open daily for men only (closed on Saturday afternoon and Sunday). Women should make for the *Rác Baths* at the foot of the hill, on the opposite side of the bridge. The Rác Baths are reserved for women on Monday, Wednesday and Friday and for men on Tuesday, Thursday and Saturday. Admission is US$1.25 at both these. Unlike the Gellért Baths which are accustomed to receiving tourists, all the posted information at the Rudas and Rác baths is in Hungarian. The resulting confusion is partly compensated for by their lower prices, so be persistent.

Everyone passing this way should seek out the *ivocsarnok*, or well room (closed weekends), which is below the bridge, within sight of the Rudas Baths. Here you can indulge in the drinking cure for a few coins. Pay the cashier who will give you a ticket which entitles you to a big mug of hot radioactive water.

The *Király Baths*, Fő utca 84 (metro: Batthyány tér), are genuine Turkish baths erected in 1570. Like at the Rác Baths there are alternate days for males (Monday, Wednesday and Friday) and females (Tuesday, Thursday and Saturday).

If you would rather bathe in ultramodern surroundings, try the *Hotel Thermál* on Margaret Island. The baths there are open to the public daily from 7 am to 8 pm, admission US$7. This includes the use of the three hot thermal pools and the sauna. A massage costs US$12. If you didn't bring your own bathing suit you'll have to buy one for US$12 (no rentals). This is Budapest's most luxurious bathing establishment by far.

The *Municipal Baths* right outside Széchenyi Fürdő Metro Station in City Park are US$1.25 admission for the whole day. A bathing cap must be worn in the swimming pool. These baths are less touristy than some of the others, yet large enough so that you won't stand out.

The easiest way to get to the baths is to take the metro to Batthyány tér, then tram No 19 south to Rácz, Rudas and Gellért, or walk north to Király. To go to Hotel Thermál, take bus No 26 from Nyugati Railway Station. There are lockers where you can leave your valuables. Some bath houses require you to wear a bathing suit while others do not. Have one with you and go with the tide. Most of the public baths hire out bathing suits and towels if you don't have your own. Unfortunately the baths are sometimes frequented by people whose interests go beyond getting clean, and friendly conversation should be approached with caution. Budapest's ornate public bathhouses are highly recommended.

Things to Buy

Before you do any shopping for handicrafts at street markets, have a look in the Folkart Centrum, Váci utca 14 (metro: Ferenciek tere), a large government store where prices are clearly marked. When you know what you want and are familiar with the prices, you'll be in a better position to bargain with street vendors.

Hanglemezek on the Danube side of Vörösmarty tér has compact discs of Hungarian folk music, including a few by Kalyi Jag and Muzsikás, amid all the tourist Gypsy music.

The Rózsa Gallery, Szentháromság utca 13 in the castle district (closed Monday), sells paintings by well-known Hungarian naive artists such as Kapolyi Makai Hedvig (born in 1940). Prices begin around US$300.

The philatelic shop at Szabad-Sajtó út 6 next to the John Bull Pub just off Ferenciek tere, sells cheap packets of Hungarian stamps.

In the far back corner of the Pest Market on Fovam tér (metro: Kálvin tér), past the strings of paprika and garlic, are a couple of stands where vendors sell genuine Hungarian folk costumes, dolls, painted eggs, embroidered tablecloths etc. You can also get *lángos* (big flat Hungarian doughnuts) or hot sausages here. (This market is presently closed.)

Getting There & Away

Bus There are three important bus stations in Budapest. For buses to Western Europe and most points west of the Danube, try the Erzsébet tér Bus Station (metro: Deák tér). There's a left-luggage office inside the Erzsébet tér Bus Station which is open daily from 6 am to 6 pm.

Some buses for Eastern Europe and places east of the Danube depart from the Népstadion Bus Station, Hungária körút 48-52 (metro: Népstadion). Left luggage at Népstadion is in the office marked 'csomagmegőrző' below the stairway opposite platform No 6 (daily 6 am to 6 pm). Rin the bell.

Buses to the Danube Bend, including Esztergom and Visegrád, leave from the bu station next to Árpád híd Metro Station. Fo details of international bus and train service see the general Getting There & Awa section in this chapter.

Train Budapest has three main train stations all connected by metro. Keleti Railwa Station (east) receives trains from Vienn Westbahnhof, Bucharest (via Arad), Bel grade, Poland, Košice, and norther Hungary.

Services from Bucharest (via Oradea), th Great Plain and the Danube Bend arrive a Nyugati Railway Station (west), also on th left bank of the Danube. Trains from Bratislava and Prague (via Štúrovo o Komárom) may use either Keleti or Nyugati

Trains from Vienna Südbahnhof, Zagreb Ljubljana, Pécs, Balaton Lake and wester Transdanubia generally use Déli Railwa Station (south) on the Buda side of the city There are exceptions to the above, howeve so be sure to check carefully which statio you'll be using.

If you arrive in Budapest on a specia summer train that continues through t another destination (Berlin to Bulgaria, fo example), beware of missing the stop as th trains often don't go in to a main station stopping instead at Köbánya-Kispest.

Train Stations When Keleti Railwa Station opened in 1884 it was the mos modern station in central Europe. Keleti ha somewhat better facilities than Nyugati. Th domestic ticket windows are down the stair way from the end of tracks Nos 7 and 8. The international ticket office (with Hungarian speaking staff) is in the main station hall nex to track No 6 (allow one hour to purchase ticket there in summer). The English-speak ing staff at the nearby Ibusz office in Kelet sell the same international tickets and thei queue is often shorter. The left-luggage office is also accessible from track No (open 24 hours).

Nyugati Railway Station is a historic iron structure built in 1877 by the engineer Alexandre Gustave Eiffel of Paris. The ticket offices are in the main hall next to track No 13. The left-luggage office at Nyugati is near Ibusz on platform No 10 (open 24 hours). A 24-hour supermarket operates inside Nyugati.

At Déli Railway Station, both the international and domestic ticket windows are upstairs at the end of the platforms. The left-luggage office is on the outer side of the building, downstairs next to the taxi rank and behind Mister Minit (daily 4 am to midnight).

For currency exchange facilities in and around the stations see Money above. Don't take your eyes off your luggage for even a few seconds in any of these stations.

Getting Around

To/From the Airport There are two terminals several km apart at Budapest Ferihegy Airport, 16 km south-east of the centre. Malév Hungarian Airlines, Air France and Lufthansa flights use the new Ferihegy No 2 terminal, while most other airlines fly out of the older Ferihegy No 1 terminal. Airport minibuses depart from the Erzsébet tér Bus Station every half-hour from 6 am to 9 pm (40 minutes, US$2.50) – buy your ticket from the driver. You can also get to Ferihegy Airport by taking the metro to Kőbánya-Kispest, then bus No 93 (red number) which stops at both terminals. Bus No 93 (black number) stops at Ferihegy No 1 only.

The Air Traffic and Airport Administration (LRI) operates a special eight-seater minibus which will take you between Terminal 1 and any address in Budapest for US$6 per person. This is much better than hassling with a taxi and is very convenient if you know exactly where you want to go upon arrival, though it's not the fastest way as each person is individually dropped off at their door. If you use this service to go to the airport allow an extra hour at least as they will drive around picking up other passengers. Ask for the LRI Airport Passenger Service in the Arrivals Hall or call ☎ 157 8555 to be picked up.

Flight information at the airport is ☎ 157 2122.

Public Transport Budapest has three underground metro lines intersecting at Deák tér: line M1, the 'yellow' line from Vörösmarty tér to Mexikoi út; line M2, the 'red' line from Déli to Örs Vezér tér; and line M3, the 'blue' line from Újpest-Központ to Köbánya-Kispest. A possible source of confusion on M2 is that one stop is called Vörösmarty tér and another is Vörösmarty utca. The HÉV suburban railway, which runs north from Batthyány tér Metro Station, is in effect a fourth metro line.

Unlike in Prague and Bucharest where you can change from one metro line to another without paying again, in Budapest you must cancel (use) another ticket if you change trains at Deák tér. There's also a very extensive network of tram, trolleybus and bus services. On certain bus lines the same numbered bus may have a black or a red number. In this case, the red-numbered bus is the express which makes limited stops. An invaluable transit map detailing all services is available at metro ticket booths.

To use public transport you must buy tickets at a kiosk, newsstand or metro entrance. Yellow tickets valid on the metro, trams, trolleybuses, regular buses and HÉV (as far as the city limits) cost US$0.30 each. You must validate your ticket once aboard. You may carry two pieces of luggage without paying an extra fare. Teams of ticket inspectors are sometimes waiting at the top of the escalators at metro exits (no escape possible). Never ride without a ticket on the HÉV as tickets are always checked there. The metro operates from 4.30 am till just after 11 pm. Certain tram and bus lines operate throughout the night. After 8 pm you must board buses through the front doors and show your ticket or transit pass (a sensible security precaution).

Transit Passes A day ticket for all trams, buses, trolleybuses, HÉV and metro lines

HUNGARY

costs US$2.25. You must specify the day you wish to use the pass and it's good only from midnight to midnight, so buy one the day before. Three days costs US$4.50 (no photo required).

To buy transit passes (bérletek) for longer periods you must supply one passport-size photo and write the serial number of your photo card (US$0.75 extra) onto the pass. A seven-day pass (hetibérlet) costs US$6, 14 days (kétheti bérlet) is US$8 and one month (havibérlet) is US$13. The monthly pass is valid up to the fifth day of the following month. These prices are for transit passes valid on the entire system, including buses. A pass without buses included is a dollar or two cheaper.

Transit passes can only be purchased at a few main metro stations. At Keleti Railway Station transit passes can be purchased at the Pénztár in the circular open-air courtyard at the entrance to the metro. At Nyugati Railway Station look for the Bérletpénztár down the stairs opposite the end of platform No 1. At Deák tér transit passes are sold in the underground passageway beneath Károly körút, at the ticket window beside the Transportation Museum. Transit passes are not sold at Déli Railway Station and you must go to Moszkva tér Metro Station.

Taxi Taxis aren't cheap and, considering the excellent public transportation network, they're a real extravagance. We've heard from several readers who were grossly overcharged by taxi drivers in Budapest, so taking a taxi in this city should be approached with caution. Not all taxi metres are set at the same rates and some are much more expensive than others. The shiny Western taxis with no name on the door and only a removable taxi sign on the roof are the most likely to cheat you. Instead try to use the smaller, older taxis with the company name painted on the doors. Reliable companies include City Taxi, 6 X 6, Fötaxi, Yellow Pages and Volántaxi. The rip-off taxis tend to park mostly at places frequented by tourists while the company taxis wait at markets and outlying metro stations where they're more likely to get Hungarian passengers. If you feel you are being grossly overcharged, insist on a receipt (számla) before paying then tell Tourinform or your hotel what happened. Better still, just avoid using taxis altogether.

Boats to the Danube Bend Mahart riverboats operate on the Danube between Budapest and Visegrád three times a day from mid-May to early September. One service continues on to Esztergom. In April, early May and late September the boat runs to Visegrád and Esztergom on weekends and holidays only. Some boats go via Szentendre, others via Vác, making it possible to do a round trip on different arms of the Danube. The Szentendre route is the more scenic.

In Budapest the boats leave from below Vigadó tér (metro: Vörösmarty tér) on the left bank. Ask at the yellow ticket office (☎ 118 1223) on the riverside below the Duna Marriott Hotel. They all stop first near Batthyány tér Metro Station.

This five-hour scenic cruise is highly recommended for a running view of Budapest and the river. There's an open deck upstairs where you can sit; the fare for the full one-way trip is only US$2 (bicycles US$1.25).

In addition to the regular cruises described above, from June to early September Mahart runs a hydrofoil nonstop between Budapest and Esztergom (68 km, 1½ hours, US$6 one way) on weekends and holidays only, departing from Budapest in the morning and Esztergom in the afternoon. You'll see mostly foreign tourists on the hydrofoils – the locals (and occasional noisy school groups!) prefer to take the slower, cheaper boats.

Sightseeing Cruises From May to September there are two-hour Mahart cruises (US$3) on the Danube daily at noon and 7 pm. In April the lunch-time cruise operates on weekends and holidays only. You can buy your ticket and board the boat at the yellow ticket office by the river at Vigadó tér below the Duna Marriott Hotel (metro: Vörösmarty tér). Other more expensive cruises such as the 'Legenda' cruises (US$12) are heavily promoted, but try to find the much cheaper Mahart boat. The night lights of the city rising to the castle, parliament and the Citadella make the evening trip far more attractive than the afternoon cruises, and the timing doesn't conflict with the rest of your sightseeing. The views of Budapest are great.

Local Ferries From May to September BKV passenger ferries run every hour from 9 am to 7 pm between Boráros tér, beside Petőfi híd (Petőfi Bridge), and Pünkösofürdő, with 10 stops along the way. Buy tickets (US$1) once aboard. The ferry stop closest to the castle district is Batthyány tér, and Petőfi tér is not far from Vörösmarty tér, a convenient place to pick up the boat on the Pest side.

The ticket clerk at the Petőfi tér landing may try to convince you to sign up for the one-hour cruise (US$6) instead of taking the regular passenger ferry *(vonaljárat)*, but just study the posted timetable and insist on what you want. Rómaifürdő is a good place to get off the ferry as it's easy to return to Budapest on the HÉV from there.

Car Rental The main Avis office (☎ 118 4685) is at the multi-level parking facility at Szervita tér 8 (metro: Deák tér). Hertz (☎ 117 7533) is at Aranykéz utca 4-8, off Váci utca, a block from Vörösmarty tér. Also in the centre is Inka Rent-a-Car (☎ 117 2150), Bajcsy-Zsilinszky út 16 (metro: Deák tér), and Budapest Rent-a-Car (☎ 117 2129), Roosevelt tér 5 off Zrínyi utca.

Within walking distance from Ferenc körút Metro Station are Coop-Car/EuroDollar (☎ 113-1466), Ferenc körút 43, Europcar (☎ 113 1492), Üllői út 62, and Volántourist Rent-a-Car (☎ 133 4783), Vaskapu utca 16. Budget Rent-a-Car (☎ 155 0482) has an office upstairs in the Buda Penta Hotel on Krisztina körút next to Déli Railway Station. Avis, Budapest, Budget and Hertz also have offices at both airport terminals while Europcar is at Ferihegy No 1 only. If you use an airport office you will be charged a special service surcharge of US$15 or 7% of the bill. Ask about other hidden extras such as collision insurance, theft insurance, 25% tax etc, which can add up to almost as much as the basic charge. Avis, Budget and Hertz are much more expensive than local companies like Budapest, Inka and Volántourist. Euro-Dollar and Europcar are medium-priced. See Getting Around in the chapter introduction for more information.

The Danube Bend

Between Vienna and Budapest, the Danube breaks through the Pilis and Börzsöny mountains in a sharp S-bend. Here medieval kings once ruled Hungary from majestic palaces overlooking the river at Esztergom and Visegrád. East of Visegrád, the river divides into two branches, with Szentendre and Vác facing different arms. Today the historic monuments, easy access, good facilities and forest trails combine to put this scenic area at the top of any visitor's list. This is the perfect place to come on a Danube River cruise.

GETTING THERE & AWAY

You can reach the Danube Bend from Budapest by rail, road, and river. The HÉV suburban railway runs to Szentendre, and Nagymaros and Esztergom are served by local trains from Budapest's Nyugati Railway Station. Szentendre, Visegrád and Esztergom are accessible by bus from Budapest's Árpád híd Bus Station. All of these services are fairly frequent and in summer Mahart riverboats stop at most of the places described in this section.

SZENTENDRE

A trip to Szentendre (St Andrew), 20 km north of Budapest on an arm of the Danube, should not be missed. In the late 17th century Serbian merchants fleeing the Turks settled here, bringing a Balkan influence. Although most of them returned home in the 19th century, the Serbian appearance remained. In

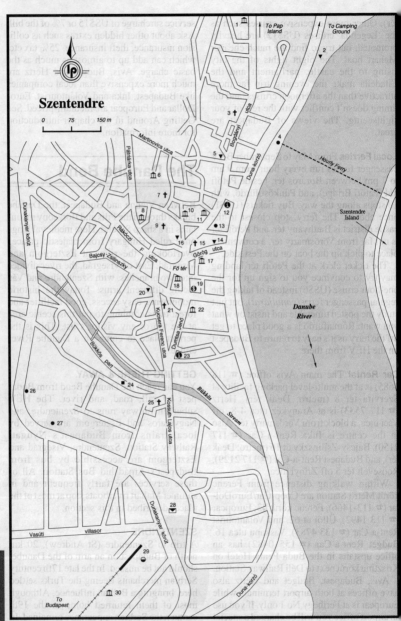

Szentendre

0   75   150 m

Danube
River

PLACES TO STAY

24 Bükkös Panzió

PLACES TO EAT

2   Wiking Restaurant
5   Bárczy Fogadó
14 Surányi István Cukrászda
16 Angyal Borozó
20 Rab-Ráby Vendéglő

OTHER

1   Kerényi Museum
3   Preobraženska Church
4   Ferry to Szentendre Island
6   Serbian Art Museum
7   Belgrade Church
8   Czóbel Béla Museum
9   Catholic Parish Church
10 Vajda Lajos Museum
11 Amos-Anna Museum
12 Ibusz
13 Dunatours
15 Blagovesztenska Greek Orthodox Church
17 Kováks Margit Museum
18 Kmetty Museum
19 OTP Bank
21 Sts Peter & Paul Church
22 Barcsay Collection
23 Tourinform
25 Požarevačka Church
26 Magyar Autóklub Service Facility
27 Roman Sculpture Garden
28 Post Office
29 HÉV Railway & Bus Stations
30 Transportation Museum

the early years of this century, Szentendre became a favourite of painters and sculptors, and the artists' colony is still alive and thriving today with numerous galleries exhibiting local artists' work.

In recent years Szentendre has become Hungary's main tourist centre and you'll see all the latest fashions displayed in front of the thousand and one boutiques and on the trendy tourists parading up and down the streets. The façades of many of the houses are obscured by clothing and embroidery hung up for sale and café tables extend far out onto the pavement with postcard racks

marking territory. Nevertheless, a stroll through the winding streets between the city's exotic Orthodox churches, or along the Danube embankment, is still a most enjoyable experience.

Orientation & Information

From the Szentendre HÉV station, it's only a short walk up Kossuth Lajos utca to Fő tér, the centre of the old town. The Danube embankment (Duna-korzó) is a block east of this square. The riverboat terminal and camping ground are a couple of km farther north. There's no left-luggage office at Szentendre HÉV/bus station but there is a transportation museum, however.

Tourinform, Dumtsa Jenő utca 22, has brochures and information on other parts of Hungary, as well as Szentendre. It distributes free brochures in English which describe the sights of Szentendre in far more detail than is possible here.

The Magyar Autóklub has a small service facility in the public parking lot on Dunakanyar körút.

Money Beware of the tricky exchange offices on Fő tér which advertise no commission but give a rate 10% lower than the bank unless you change at least US$2250 (the small notices advising you of this are in Hungarian!).

Instead, patronise the OTP Bank, Dumtsa Jenő utca 6, just off Fő tér (Monday 8 am to 3 pm, Tuesday to Thursday 8 am to 2 pm, Friday 8 am to 12.30 pm).

If the OTP Bank is closed, head for Ibusz, Bogdányi utca 1, which is open longer hours and gives a rate only about 2% lower than the bank for travellers' cheques.

Things to See

Begin with Fő tér, which on July evenings becomes a stage for theatrical performances. Most of the buildings around the square date from the 18th century, as does the plague column (1763) in the centre and also (in one corner) the **Blagovesztenska Greek Orthodox Church** (1752).

In an alley off the east side of Fő tér is the

Kovács Margit Museum at Vastagh György utca 1. It's the most delightful gallery in Szentendre and admission costs US$0.75. Margit Kovács (1902-77) based her decorative ceramic objects on Hungarian folk-art traditions, creating a style all of her own. Also be sure to see the **Ferenczy Museum**, Fő tér 6 beside the Greek Church, which displays the artwork of the Ferenczy clan, pioneers of the Szentendre artists' colony.

Narrow lanes lead up from Fő tér to the Catholic **parish church** (rebuilt in 1710) from where you get splendid views of the town. On Saturday and Sunday in July and August a large folk market is held here. The **Czóbel Béla Museum** is opposite the church. Just north is the tall red tower of **Belgrade Church** (1756), the finest of the Serbian churches. Beside the church is a museum of Serbian religious art.

Other art galleries worth seeing are the **Amos-Anna Museum**, Bogdányi utca 10, the **Kerényi Museum**, Ady Endre utca 6 on the way to Pap Island, and the **Barcsay Collection**, Dumsta Jenő utca 10 near Fő tér.

The **Ethnographic Open-air Museum** which is large and includes reconstructed farmhouses from around the country is about four km north-west of Szentendre. Buses from stand No 8 at the bus station run there only every couple of hours, but a minibus shuttle from the Tourinform office on Dumtsa Jenő utca will take you directly there almost whenever you want to go for US$1.25 return.

All of the museums are closed on Monday and a couple also on Tuesday. From November to March the open-air museum is closed and several other museums are only open on Friday, Saturday and Sunday.

Activities

In summer Ibusz rents bicycles at US$9 a day (shorter periods negotiable). Take the hourly ferry across to Szentendre Island and you'll have km of uncrowded cycling ahead of you.

The Wiking Restaurant on Duna-korzó just north of the centre rents jet skis at US$80 an hour.

Places to Stay

Camping *Aquatours Camping* (☎ 311 106), Ady Endre út 9-11, near the ferry landing just a short walk north of the centre, is a relaxing, quiet place to camp (US$2 per person, plus US$2 per tent) and they also have two single rooms (US$9) and four double rooms (US$14), all with toilet and shower, plus one four-bed house with toilet and kitchen (US$31). Ask the manager about canoe rentals (midsummer only). Aquatours is open from May to September.

Two km north of Szentendre near the Danube riverboat landing is *Pap-Sziget Camping* (☎ 310 697) run by Dunatours on Pap Island, just across the bridge from the Danubius Hotel bus stop. Camping is US$8 for two persons with tent and they also have 14 bungalows with bath at US$20 single or double, US$28 triple. The 20 motel rooms with shared bath are US$11 single or double, US$15 triple. All charges are plus US$1 tax per person per night, although the first night is free. Reception is open from 8 am to 4 pm only and you must check out by 10 am or you'll have to pay for another night. The overnight fee includes admission to the swimming pool next door and other facilities include a small supermarket, snack bar and restaurant. There's a disco here on weekends (ask about this when checking in and pitch your tent accordingly). This camping ground is open from May to September.

Private Rooms You can easily see Szentendre on a day trip from Budapest but the town also makes a good base from which to explore the Danube Bend. Dunatours (Idegenforgalmi Hivatal), Bogdányi utca 1, and Ibusz, Bogdányi utca 11, arrange private rooms. At US$15 double (no singles), Dunatours is about a dollar cheaper than Ibusz and in summer Dunatours is open weekends from 10 am to 6 pm.

Camping *Aquatours Camping* (☎ 311 106), Ady Endre út 9-11, near the ferry landing just a short walk north of the centre, is a relaxing, quiet place to camp (US$2 per person, plus US$2 per tent) and they also have two single rooms (US$9) and four double rooms (US$14), all with toilet and shower, plus one four-bed house with toilet and kitchen (US$31). Ask the manager about canoe rentals (midsummer only). Aquatours is open from May to September.

Two km north of Szentendre near the Danube riverboat landing is *Pap-Sziget Camping* (☎ 310 697) run by Dunatours on Pap Island, just across the bridge from the Danubius Hotel bus stop. Camping is US$8 for two persons with tent and they also have 14 bungalows with bath at US$20 single or double, US$28 triple. The 20 motel rooms with shared bath are US$11 single or double, US$15 triple. All charges are plus US$1 tax per person per night, although the first night is free. Reception is open from 8 am to 4 pm only and you must check out by 10 am or you'll have to pay for another night. The overnight fee includes admission to the swimming pool next door and other facilities include a small supermarket, snack bar and restaurant. There's a disco here on weekends (ask about this when checking in and pitch your tent accordingly). This camping ground is open from May to September.

Pensions & Hotels There are several small pensions around town but all are quite expensive. The cheapest is the *Mini Hotel Apollo* (☎ 310 909), Méhész utca 3, off Dunakanyar körút on the north side of town, with six rooms at US$15/17 single/double. It's open year-round.

The 10-room *Hotel Fenyes* (☎ 311 882), Ady Endre utca 26, north of the centre, is US$15 single or double, US$22 triple with shared bath, and you can also camp in their garden. It's a good backup choice if the camping grounds are full or closed (open year-round). Next door is the more expensive *Danubius Hotel*.

Places to Eat

An ABC supermarket is next to the HÉV station if you want to give Szentendre's touristy restaurants a miss and have a riverside picnic.

Dixie Chicken, Dumtsa Jenő utca 16, is

your standard greasy fast-food joint but they do have a salad bar and frozen yogurt, and you can sit in the back courtyard.

The *Régimódi Restaurant*, on Futó utca just down from the Kovács Margit Museum, occupies an old Szentendre house. *Angyal Borozó*, Alkotmány utca 4, posts an English menu outside. The *Bárczy Fogadó*, an old inn at Bogdányi utca 30, is more expensive.

Since 1974 Szentendre's best coffee, desserts and ice cream have been consumed standing up at *Surányi István Cukrászda*, Görög utca 4 (closed Monday and Tuesday). Hungarians flock here as it's one of the few places in town that charges normal prices.

Check to see if the lángos stall is open. These hot Hungarian doughnuts are one of the best deals in Szentendre but in winter the stall is only open on weekends. The stall is halfway up Váralja Lépcsö, a tiny alley between Fő tér 8 and 9 (closed Monday).

Getting There & Away

Access to Szentendre couldn't be easier. Take the HÉV from Budapest's Batthyány tér Metro Station to the end of the line (21 km, 40 minutes). There are several trains an hour. If you have a Budapest transit pass show it to the clerk when buying your HÉV ticket to/from Szentendre and you'll get a discount.

Buses from Budapest's Árpád híd Bus Station also run to Szentendre frequently. Onward service to Visegrád and Esztergom is good.

From mid-May to early September, Mahart riverboats between Budapest and Visegrád stop at Szentendre three times daily. In April, early May and late September the boat only operates once a day on weekends and holidays. The landing (*hajóállomás*) is near Pap Island, a km north of the centre.

VISEGRÁD

Visegrád is superbly situated on a horseshoe bend of the Danube, between the Pilis and Börzsöny mountains. For hundreds of years the river was the border of the Roman Empire. After Tatar invasions in the 13th

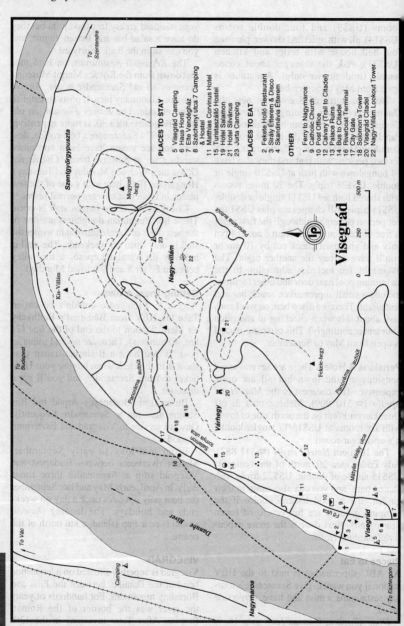

century, the Hungarian kings built a mighty citadel on a hill top with a wall running down to a lower castle near the river. In the 14th century a royal palace was built on the flood plain at the foot of the hills and the Angevin court moved here in 1323. For nearly two centuries Hungarian kings and queens alternated between Visegrád and Buda. The reign of the Renaissance monarch Matthias Corvinus in the 15th century was the period of greatest glory for Visegrád.

The destruction of Visegrád came with the Turks and later in 1702 when the Habsburgs blew up the citadel to prevent Hungarian independence fighters from using it as a base. All trace of the palace was lost until 1934 when archaeologists following descriptions in literary sources uncovered the ruins that you can visit today.

Things to See & Do

You can visit the **palace ruins** at Fő utca 27 daily except Monday throughout the year from 9 am to 4 pm. Some of the highlights are a red-marble fountain bearing the coat of arms of King Matthias in the Gothic courtyard and, on an upper terrace, a copy of the lion wall fountain, which is covered in winter. The original fountains are kept in the museum at **Solomon's Tower**, which is next on the list of sights to visit. The tower is on a low hill above the Danube, a few hundred metres from the palace ruins. This was part of a lower castle that was intended to control river traffic. The 13th century walls are up to eight metres thick! The tower museum is only open from May to October, daily except Monday, but visitors can enjoy the exterior any time.

Visegrád Citadel (1259) is on a high hill directly above Solomon's Tower, and is accessible on hiking trails (it is signposted as 'Fellegvár'). A local bus runs up to the citadel *(vár)* from the side street in front of the King Matthias monument near the Danube riverboat wharf about seven times a day. You can also hike up to the citadel in 40 minutes along a marked trail behind the Catholic church in town. Restoration work on the three defensive levels of the citadel

will continue for many years, but the view of the Danube Bend from the walls is well worth the climb. On another hill nearby is the **Nagy-Villám Lookout Tower** which offers another fabulous view.

Near Visegrád An excellent half-day hike from **Dömös** is the climb to the village of Dobogókő via the Rám-szakadék Gorge, which takes about three hours. There are sweeping views of the river and mountains through openings in the forest along the way. From Dobogókő you can catch a bus to Esztergom or Pomáz va HÉV station, but it's an easy downhill walk back to Dömös via Kortvelyes or Lukács-arok for a circle trip. These trails through the **Pilis Nature Reserve** are clearly marked, and in early summer you will find raspberries along the way.

Alternatively, you can take a small ferry across the Danube from Dömös to Dömösi átkéles, then climb to the caves that are visible on the hillside and hike back into the hills behind Nagymaros. The 1:40,000 *A Pilis* topographical map outlines the many hiking possibilities in this area (pick up a copy at a Budapest bookstore before coming).

The Nagymaros Barrage In 1977 the communist governments of Hungary and Czechoslovakia signed an agreement on the largest civil-engineering project in Europe. Two barrages across the Danube, one at Gabčíkovo in Slovakia west of Komárno and another at Nagymaros just upstream from Visegrád, would generate electricity, provide water for irrigation and improve navigation on the Danube. The Czechoslovakians began work on Gabčíkovo in earnest but Hungary was forced to withdraw from the US$5.8 billion scheme in 1981 due to a lack of funds. In 1985, however, construction began at Nagymaros after energy-hungry Austria offered to pay 70% of the US$3 billion cost of the Hungarian dam in exchange for 1.2 billion kilowatts of electricity over 20 years.

In May 1989 construction was suspended at Nagymaros after unprecedented public demonstrations in Budapest led by environmentalists who claimed that reduced water levels below the dams could contaminate the water supplies of millions of Hungarians and reduce the number of fish in the river by 50%, while flooding 122 sq km of forest and ruining one of Hungary's top tourist attractions, all to provide cheap electricity for Vienna! In 1990 Hungary was forced to pay US$250 million in compensation to the Austrian construction companies involved and in May 1992 Hungary unilaterally annulled the 1977 treaty.

Former Czechoslovakia completed the Gabčíkovo barrage on its own and a diversion canal was built through Slovak territory just north of the Danube to provide water for the 720-megawatt power plant. In October 1992 the Danube was partially blocked at Čunovo near Bratislava to rechannel water into the lateral canal and navigational channel, and all shipping on the Danube is now routed through the locks at Gabčíkovo. Water from the Slovak project re-enters the original Danube riverbed at Palkovičovo and the 60 km between Čunovo and Palkovičovo now carries only a fraction of its previous load. The shallow stretch between Štúrovo and Nagymaros remains impassible for large vessels when water levels on the Danube are low.

The affair seriously damaged Hungary's relations with Czechoslovakia's successor state, Slovakia, and both countries have asked the International Court of Justice in The Hague to rule on the matter. Slovakia has condemned Hungary's violation of its treaty obligations while Hungary has objected to Slovakia's expropriation of international waters. Lately, Hungary has dropped its insistence that Gabčíkovo must be closed and the dispute now centres on how much water should be allowed to flow down the original Danube which marks the international boundary between the countries.

This whole controversy comes back to modern society's insatiable thirst for energy. Coal and nuclear-powered generators aren't very attractive either, and the problems created by acid rain and nuclear wastes are just as serious as the potential ecological consequences of a barrage at Nagymaros. Perhaps an idyllically beautiful yet threatened spot like Visegrád is just the place to sit and ponder these problems.

Places to Stay

Hostels & Camping There are two tourist hostels (turistaszálló) at Visegrád. One is at Salamon tornya utca 5 near the Danube riverboat landing, but the nicest is perhaps the one at Széchenyi utca 7 near the centre of the village. It's beside a small stream, back behind the church with the green tower, and you are also allowed to camp. Dorm beds are US$4 per person, while camping is US$1.25 per person plus US$2.25 per tent. This quiet, uncrowded site should be the first place you check, but both it and the hostel at Salamon tornya utca 5 are closed from October to April.

Motorists may prefer Visegrád Camping (☎ 328 102), by the highway just south of the Nagymaros ferry. Camping space is US$2 per person, US$1 per tent, plus US$0.75 per person tax, but no bungalows are available (open May to September).

Private Rooms Many houses along Fő utca have signs advertising 'zimmer frei' ('room available'). One such is Haus Honti, Fő utca 66 next to a picturesque little stream. Also try the house at Fő utca 107 across the street.

Nearby at Fő utca 117 is the Elte Vendégház (☎ 328 165), a four-storey hotel with nine double rooms and 24 triples at US$9 per person (higher in July and August). It closes in winter.

Fanny Travel Agency, Fő utca 46 next to Skandinávia Étterem, has expensive private rooms.

Places to Eat

Skandinávia Étterem, Fő utca 48, has reasonable daily specials listed on a menu outside.

The Fekete Holló (closed Monday), a fish restaurant opposite the Nagymaros ferry on the Visegrád side, is touristy, so you're better off crossing the river to the Maros Vendéglő (closed Monday but open all year), near the

Nagymaros ferry wharf on the Nagymaros side. The food is good, prices are moderate and in summer you can dine on a terrace overlooking the river. Check the ferry times carefully if you want to return late to Visegrád.

Getting There & Away

Buses between Budapest's Árpád híd Bus Station and Esztergom sometimes go via Visegrád but bus service is more frequent from stands Nos 1 and 2 at the Szentendre HÉV station. In summer some buses from the HÉV go all the way up to Nagy-Villám, so ask.

From mid-May to early September Mahart riverboats ply between Budapest and Visegrád three times a day. Twice daily there's service to Esztergom. In April, early May and late September the boat only operates on weekends and holidays.

Hourly ferries cross the Danube to Nagymaros. Don't panic if the large car ferry closes down early for the night as a smaller passenger launch usually takes its place. The Nagymaros-Visegrád ferry operates all year except when the Danube freezes over, but service is also suspended when fog descends, a common occurrence in winter. From Nagymaros Railway Station, just inland from the ferry wharf, there are trains to Budapest-Nyugati about every hour (51 km, one hour).

ESZTERGOM

Esztergom, opposite Štúrovo in Slovakia, at the western entrance to the Danube Bend, is one of Hungary's most historic cities. The 2nd century Roman emperor-to-be Marcus Aurelius wrote his famous *Meditations* while he was camped here. Stephen I, founder of the Hungarian state, was born and crowned at Esztergom, which was capital of Hungary from the 10th to the 13th centuries. After the Tatar invasion of 1241, the king and court moved to Buda but Esztergom remained the ecclesiastical centre of Hungary, as it is today. Originally the clerics lived by the riverbank and royalty, on the hill top above. When the king departed, the arch-

bishop moved up and occupied the palace, maintaining Esztergom's prominence. In 1543 the Turks ravaged the town and much had to be rebuilt in the 18th and 19th centuries.

Orientation & Information

The train station is at the southern edge of town, a 10-minute walk south of the bus station. From the train station walk north on Baross Gábor út, then along Ady Endre utca to Simor János utca and the bus station. The ticket clerk at the train station holds luggage (open 24 hours) but no left-luggage service is available at the bus station.

The three information offices are Komturist, Lőrincz utca 6; Gran Tours, Széchenyi tér 25; and Express (☎ 313 113), Széchenyi tér 7.

The Magyar Autóklub (☎ 311 908), Schweidel utca 5, is south of the centre near the train station.

Money The OTP Bank on Bajcsy-Zsilinszky utca in the centre of town (open Monday from 8 am to 3.30 pm, Tuesday to Thursday 8 am to 2.30 pm and Friday 8 am to 12.30 pm) changes travellers' cheques.

Things to See

The bus station is a couple of blocks southeast of Széchenyi tér, the medieval market place, where the **town hall** (1773) is found. A block south is the **Inner City Parish Church** (1757), near a branch of the Danube that is lined by delightful little houseboats. Cross the footbridge to Primas Island and follow Gózhajó utca directly across to the riverboat landing on the main Danube channel.

Nearby stand the ruins of the **Mária Valéria Bridge**, the only bridge across the Danube between Budapest and Komárom. The retreating Germans blew up the bridge at the end of WW II but reconstruction is now underway with the reopening scheduled for 1995, to coincide with the centenary of the bridge's original construction. Hungary wants to open an international border crossing here but Slovakia is resisting for some

HUNGARY

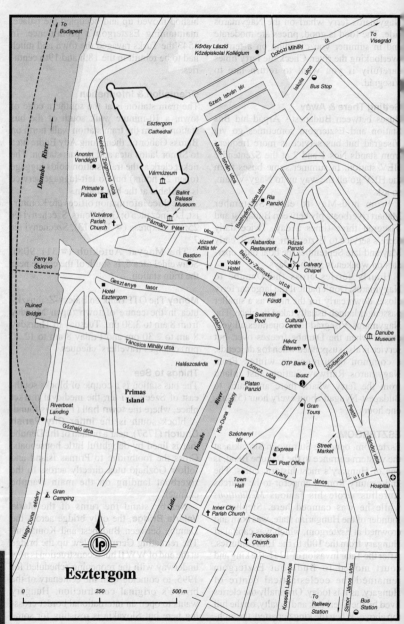

Esztergom

To Budapest

Körösy László
Középiskolai Kollégium

To Visegrád

Doboží Mihály

Szent István tér

Bus Stop

Esztergom
Cathedral

Iskola utca

Danube River

Bétyán Zsigmond utca

Anonim
Vendéglő

Vármúzeum

Mater István utca

Primate's
Palace

Bálint
Balassi
Museum

Ria Pánzió

Vizivaros
Parish
Church

Pázmány Péter
utca

Battyány Lajos utca

Ferry to
Štúrovo

József
Attila tér
Bastion

Alabardos
Restaurant

Rózsa
Pánzió

Volán
Hotel

Bajcsy Zsilinszky utca

Calvary
Chapel

Gesztenye fasor

Hotel Eszergom

Hotel
Fürdő

Ruined
Bridge

Swimming
Pool

Cultural
Centre

Danube
Museum

sétány

Táncsics Mihály utca

Hévíz
Étterem

Vörösmarty

Halászcsárda

Lőrincz utca

OTP Bank

Ibusz

Platan
Pánzió

Riverboat
Landing

Primas
Island

Gran
Tours

Pető utca

Gőzhajó utca

Kis-Duna sétány

Széchenyi
tér

Sándor utca

Express

Street
Market

Post Office

Danube

Liget

Arany

Town
Hall

János

Hospital

Gran
Camping

Nagy-Duna sétány

Inner City
Parish Church

Franciscan
Church

Kossuth Lajos utca

Simor János utca

To Railway
Station

To
Railway
Station

Bus
Station

0   250   500 m

reason. At present only citizens of the neighbouring countries can use the nearby ferry – this may change soon (see the following Getting There & Away section).

Continue north along the river and cross the bridge to **Víziváros Parish Church** (1738). Esztergom's famous **Christian Museum** (closed Monday) is in the adjacent **Primate's Palace** (1882). This is one of the best art collections in Hungary so don't miss it. A plaque on the side of the Primate's Palace bears the name 'József Mindszenty' and is dated 26 December 1948. Cardinal Mindszenty was arrested that day for refusing to allow the Catholic schools of Hungary to be secularised; in 1949 he was sentenced to life imprisonment for treason. Freed during the 1956 uprising, Mindszenty was soon forced to seek refuge in the US embassy in Budapest where he stayed until 1971. In 1974 Mindszenty was sacked as primate of Hungary for his criticism of the Pope's dealings with the communist regime and he died in Vienna in 1975. Nearby at Pázmany Péter utca 13 is the **Bálint Balassi Museum** (closed Monday) with objects of local interest. The lyric poet Bálint Balassi died defending Esztergom from the Turks in 1594.

You can't help noticing **Esztergom Cathedral**, the largest church in Hungary, which is on a high hill above the Danube. The building was rebuilt in the neoclassical style in the 19th century, but the red-marble Bakócz chapel (1510) on the south side was moved here from an earlier church. Underneath the cathedral is a large crypt, but most interesting is the treasury to the right of the altar. Many priceless medieval objects are kept here, including the 13th century Hungarian coronation cross. In summer you can even climb up onto the cathedral's cupola for a sweeping view.

Beside the cathedral, at the southern end of the hill, is the **Vármúzeum** (closed Monday) with remnants of the medieval royal palace (1215). Parts of the complex that were built in an early French Gothic style have been masterfully reconstructed. The views from this hill are great.

If you want to continue on to Visegrád after visiting the cathedral, there's no need to return to the bus station as you can pick up the bus on nearby Iskola utca.

On your way back to the bus or train stations, drop into the **Danube Museum**, Kölcsey Ferenc utca 2, up Vörösmarty utca from near the Bástya Department Store in the middle of town (closed Tuesday). This fine museum provides much information on the river through photos and models, though most of the captions are in Hungarian.

Places to Stay

Camping *Gran Camping* (☎ 311 327) on Nagy-Duna sétány, Primas Island, offers convenient camping with riverside views but little shade (open from May to September). Camping is US$3 per person plus US$3 per tent and there are four double rooms at US$19. In addition, two four-person bungalows without kitchen are US$30, four four-person bungalows with kitchen are US$38, one six-person bungalow with kitchen is US$42 and one eight-person apartment with kitchen is US$46. These units are also complete with shower and TV. In July and August all the rooms may be full, so get ready to unroll the tent.

Private Rooms & Hostel Private rooms are assigned by Ibusz, Lorincz utca 1, and Gran Tours, Széchenyi tér 25, but singles are scarce.

Kőrösy László Középiskolai Kollégium (☎ 312 813), Szent István tér 16, accommodates travellers in its student dormitory at US$5 per person from July to mid-August. You can book through Express, Széchenyi tér 7, or go directly to the hostel.

Hotels *Platán Panzió* (☎ 311 355), Kis-Duna sétány 11, is like a small hotel with excellent prices: US$16 double with bath (no singles). This is only a dollar or two more than a private room and you don't have to contend with a travel agency and landlady. The building is marked only by a blue sign indicating reserved parking but go inside and you'll see the reception on the right.

Esztergom's least expensive hotel is *Rózsa Panzió* (☎ 311 581), Török Ignác utca 11, with rooms with shared bath at US$8/14 single/double. It's not the flashy place right behind Alabardos Restaurant – go further up the street.

At the stately *Hotel Fürdő* (☎ 311 688), Bajcsy-Zsilinszky út 14, you have the choice of a room with bath in the new section (US$36/42 single/double) or a room with shared bath in the old section (US$18/22), all including breakfast. There's a public swimming pool behind the hotel.

Places to Eat

As self-service restaurants go, the *Hévíz Étterem*, upstairs at the back of the shopping centre behind Bástya Department Store on Bajcsy-Zsilinszky út (Monday to Saturday 1 am to 7 pm, Sunday 7 am to 3 pm), is pleasant enough. Check to see if töltött káposzta – a hearty plate of sourkraut with one meat ball – is on the menu.

Pizzerias abound in the centre of Esztergom but for dishes like Hungarian fish soup go to the *Úszófalu Halászcsárda*, Táncsics Mihály utca on Primas Island. The restaurant in *Hotel Fürdő* is very elegant.

Getting There & Away

Trains to Esztergom depart from Budapest's Nyugati Railway Station (53 km, 1¾ hours) about nine times a day. To go to western Transdanubia or Slovakia, take one of four daily local trains from Esztergom to Komárom (53 km, 1½ hours).

Unless you have a railway pass it's faster and more convenient to come by bus and you'll be dropped much closer to the centre of town. Bus services from Budapest's Árpád híd Bus Station are frequent. Buses from Budapest to Esztergom may travel via either Pilisvörösvár, which is the faster, more direct route, or via Visegrád, which is long, slow and scenic. Buses to Budapest run about every half-hour from 5 am to 8 pm, to Visegrád and Szentendre hourly from 6 am to 8.40 pm and to Sopron twice daily.

Mahart riverboats travel to/from Budapest once a day from mid-May to early Septem-

ber with a stop at Visegrád. In April, early May and late September this boat only operates on weekends and holidays. From June to August a nonstop Mahart hydrofoil glides between Budapest and Esztergom on weekends and holidays. All services leave Budapest in the morning and Esztergom in the afternoon, allowing day trippers several hours to visit the cathedral. For Esztergom-based tourists, there's a morning boat to Visegrád from mid-May to early September.

A ferry crosses the Danube to Štúrovo, Slovakia, 10 times a day from mid-February to December (US$0.50). In the past only citizens of Slovakia and Hungary were allowed to use this ferry and the nearest border crossing open to Western tourists was at Komárom. In early 1994 it was announced that the Esztergom-Štúrovo ferry would soon be made available to international travellers, so check.

Western Transdanubia

Beyond the Bakony Mountains, north-west of Balaton Lake, lies the Kisalföld, or Little Plain, which is bounded by the Danube and the Alps. Conquered by the Romans but never occupied by the Turks, this enchanting corner of Transdanubia is surrounded by a string of picturesque small towns with a decidedly European air. The old quarters of Sopron and Győr are brimming with what were once the residences of prosperous burghers and clerics, while Kőszeg offers an intact medieval castle, Szombathely has Roman relics, Fertőd a magnificent Baroque palace and Pannonhalma a functioning Benedictine monastery. This region is also a convenient gateway to/from Austria and Slovakia.

GETTING THERE & AWAY

Many trains link Sopron to Austria and you can walk in/out of Slovakia via Komárom. From Budapest's Déli Railway Station there are trains to Komárom, Győr, Sopron and Szombathely. Rail links to/from the Danube

Bend (Esztergom-Komárom) and Balaton Lake (Székesfehérvár to Komárom and Veszprém to Győr or Szombathely) are also good, though travelling south-east from Sopron and Szombathely is often easier by bus.

KOMÁROM

Komárom is the gateway to Hungary for visitors arriving from Komárno, Slovakia. Until 1920 these two towns were one. In antiquity the Romans had a military post called Brigetio here and the Habsburgs also fortified the area, although their fortresses ended up being used against them by Hungarian rebels during the 1848-49 War of Independence.

Komárom's position behind a large bridge across the Danube is of passing interest and there's a good camping ground next to the public thermal baths, within walking distance of the train station and border crossing. If you arrive in the late afternoon, this is a good place to stop for the night.

Orientation & Information

The train station (with a left-luggage office in a separate building next to the main station) is very near the highway bridge to/from Slovakia. Komturist is at Mártírok útja 19a in the centre of town. Walk straight south from the bridge to the first traffic lights and you'll find it a block to the left and on the right. A map of this vicinity is included in the Komárno section of the Slovakia chapter.

Money The OTP Bank, Mártírok útja 21 next to Komturist, cashes travellers' cheques on Monday from 8 am to 5 pm, Tuesday to Thursday from 8 am to 3 pm and Friday from 8 am to 2 pm. At other times you should be able to change cash at Ibusz Camping or at Hotel Thermál.

Things to See & Do

Right next to Hotel Thermál is a **thermal bathing complex** (open all year, US$1). To get to the thermal baths from the Danube bridge, go south for two blocks and then turn left on Táncsics Mihály utca, a 10-minute walk. A sauna and massage are available in addition to the big thermal pool.

Among the sights of Komárom are two large 19th century fortifications that were built by the Habsburgs. The **Csillag Fortress** is near the river just north of the Thermál Hotel. You can see it from the train as you arrive from Budapest. The **Igmándi Fortress** is on the south side of town.

Places to Stay

Komturist (☎ 341 767), Mártírok útja 19a, should have private rooms at US$6 per person but they're usually fully booked.

The closest hotel to the Danube bridge is the *Beke Hotel* (☎ 340 333), Bajcsy-Zsilinszky út 8, a renovated two-storey building with rooms with shared bath at US$15 single or double.

Right next to the thermal baths is *Ibusz Camping* (☎ 342 551), on Táncsics Mihály utca. Apart from camping, they have bungalows with kitchen and private bath at US$23 for up to four people (often full).

The 39 rooms with bath at *Hotel Thermál* (☎ 342 447), Táncsics Mihály utca 38, cost US$19/22 single/double, breakfast included. Prices include admission to the thermal baths. Next to this attractive resort hotel is a camping ground that is open throughout the year. Motel-style units in the camping ground are US$10/12 single/double without bath or breakfast, but they're only available from mid-April to mid-October.

The newer and more luxurious *Hotel Karát* (☎ 342 222), Czuczor Gergely utca 54, two blocks from the baths, is US$23/25 single/double with bath and breakfast.

Getting There & Away

Train services from Komárom to Budapest (110 km, 1½ hours), Győr (37 km, 30 minutes) and Sopron (122 km, 1½ hours) are fairly frequent. (Most trains on this line depart from Budapest-Keleti but some use Budapest-Déli.) For the Danube Bend, catch a train to Esztergom (four daily, 53 km, 1½ hours), and for Balaton Lake take a train to Székesfehérvár (six daily, 82 km, 1½ hours).

HUNGARY

Komárom is a convenient entry or exit point between Hungary and Slovakia. The highway bridge to Komárno, Slovakia, is just a five-minute walk from Komárom Railway Station and you can easily join the locals crossing between the two countries on foot. Both Hungarian and Slovakian passport controls are together at the Slovakian end of the bridge. Komárno is a much larger town than Komárom and the Slovakian train station is two km from the bridge. While travellers with backpacks will probably enjoy the walk, there's a bus between the two stations every couple of hours. Ask at the information counter in the stations for the departure time of the next bus and pay the driver.

On the Slovakian side you can easily catch a connecting local train to Bratislava (100 km), eliminating the need to buy an international train ticket. International trains usually cross the border here in the middle of the night and require compulsory seat reservations, so forget them. Turn to the Komárno section in the Slovakia chapter for more information.

GYŐR

Győr (Raab) is a historic city midway between Budapest and Vienna, in the heart of the Kisalföld at the point where the Mosoni-Danube, Rábca and Rába rivers meet. Győr-Sopron County is administered from here. In the 11th century, Stephen I established a bishopric here on what was the site of a Roman town named Arrabona. In the mid-16th century a strong fortress was erected at Győr to hold back the Turks.

Győr is Hungary's third-largest industrial centre, home to the Rába Engineering Works, which produces trucks and railway rolling stock. Despite this, the old town centre retains its charm. Less touristy than Esztergom, Sopron or Eger, Győr is well worth a visit.

Orientation

The neo-Baroque city hall (1898) towers above the train station. The left-luggage office at the train station (daily from 5 am to midnight) is next to the exit from one of the two tunnels under the tracks (the one closer to Budapest). This same tunnel leads directly through to the main bus station, which is just south of the train station. The old town is north, at the junction of the Rába and Mosoni-Danube rivers.

Information

Ciklámen Tourist is at Aradi vértanúk útja 22, a block from the train station.

The Magyar Autóklub (☎ 317 400), Bajcsy-Zsilinszky út 47, is a block east of the Express travel office.

Money If Győr is your first stop in Hungary you can change money at the MÁV Tours office upstairs from the main train station hall.

During banking hours you'll get a slightly better rate at the OTP Bank on Árpad út next to the Rába Hotel (Monday to Wednesday 7.45 am to 3 pm, Thursday 7.45 am to 5.30 pm, Friday 7.45 am to 1.30 pm). They change travellers' cheques without commission.

If both of the above are closed, try the Rába Hotel next to the OTP Bank or the reception at Hotel Klastrom which does accept travellers' cheques.

Post & Telecommunications The post office next to the train station is open weekend mornings (as well as during the week). Győr's telephone code is 96.

Things to See

If you follow Aradi vértanúk útja north to Becsi kapu tér, you'll find the enchanting **Carmelite church** (built in 1725) and many fine Baroque palaces. On the far side of the square are fortifications that were built in the 16th century to stop the Turks. In the centre of Becsi kapu tér is a statue of the Romantic playwright Károly Kisfaludy (1788-1830).

Follow the narrow street north up onto Chapter Hill (Káptalan-domb), the oldest part of Győr. The large Baroque **cathedral** (1639) on the hill was originally Romanesque, as you'll see if you look at the exterior of the apse. The Baroque frescoes on the ceiling are fine, but don't miss the Gothic chapel on the south side of the church which contains a glittering 14th century bust of King St Ladislas. Opposite the cathedral is the fortified **bishop's palace** in a mixture of styles. Visit the garden.

The streets behind the cathedral are full of old palaces, and at the bottom of the hill on Jedlik Ányos utca is the outstanding **Arc of the Covenant Monument** (1731). A colourful open-air market unfolds on nearby Dunakapu tér. The view of the rivers from the adjacent bridge is good.

One of the nicest things about Győr is its atmospheric old streets, which seem not to have changed in centuries. Take a leisurely stroll down Apáca utca, Rákóczi Ferenc utca, Liszt Ferenc utca and Király utca where you'll see many fine buildings. The late Renaissance palace at Rákóczi Ferenc utca 6 was once a charity hospital. Go inside to admire the courtyards. Napoleon stayed in the house at Alkotmány utca 4 on 13 August 1809. It has now been turned into an art gallery.

Széchenyi tér is the heart of Győr and features a **Column of the Virgin** (1686) in the middle. **St Ignatius Church** (1641) is the finest church in the city with a superb pulpit and pews. Next door is the Benedictine Convent and next to it, at Széchenyi tér 9, is the **Széchenyi Pharmacy** (closed weekends) – a fully operating Baroque institution! Cross the square to visit the **Xantus János Museum** (closed Monday), Széchenyi tér 5, which is in a palace that was built in 1743. Beside it at Széchenyi tér 4 is Iron Stump House, which still sports the beam into which itinerant journeymen would drive a nail. This building now houses the **Imre Patkó Collection** of paintings and African art, one of the best of Győr's various small museums (closed November to mid-March). You can enter it from the alley.

If you have a half day to spare, it's worth visiting **Pannonhalma Abbey**, on top of a 282-metre hill at the southern edge of the Kisalföld, 21 km south of Győr. Tours of the present Benedictine monastery (closed Monday) take you through the Gothic cloister (1486), into the Romanesque basilica (1225) and down to the 11th century crypt. The 55-metre-high tower was erected in 1830 and the impressive Empire-style library (also included on the tour) dates from the same period. The visit concludes with a look in the one-room 'picture gallery'. Organ recitals are held in the church on Saturday afternoon about once a month. Pannonhalma is best approached from Győr by bus as the train station is a couple of km south-west of the abbey, although local trains between Győr and Veszprém do stop at Pannonhalma every couple of hours.

Activities
West of Rába River are Győr's well-maintained **thermal baths** (open daily May to September). If the first gate you come to is locked, follow the fence along until you reach the main entrance. A variety of large open-air pools are here, some with water as hot as 35°C.

Places to Stay
Camping *Kiskút-liget Camping* (☎ 318 986) is near the stadium, three km north-east of Győr (bus No 8 from beside the city hall). Camping is US$2 per person plus US$2 per tent and there are also 60 three and four-bed cabins at US$11, seven six-bed bungalows at US$28 and 25 three-bedded motel rooms at US$17 single, double or triple. The five four-bedded hotel rooms are US$22. The facilities for campers are in poor shape and there's often no hot water. They do have a restaurant and the site is open from mid-April to mid-October.

Hostels Express, Bajcsy-Zsilinszky út 41 (open weekdays 8 am to 3.45 pm), arranges accommodation in student dormitories year-round at US$9 single or US$5 per person in a four-bed dorm. In July and August ask about the huge student dormitories at Ságvári Endre utca 3 north of the river.

In summer you should be able to get a bed at *Kossuth Kollégium* (☎ 319 244), on the

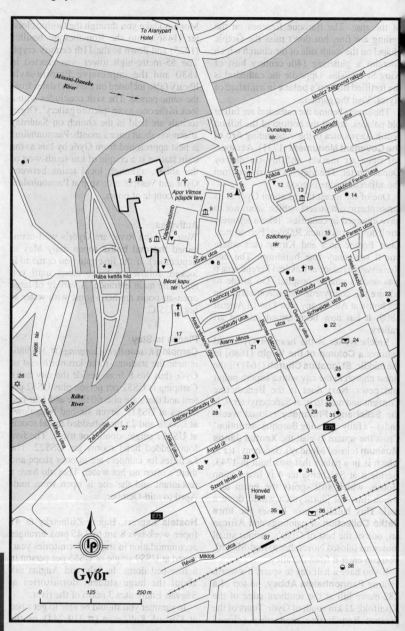

Győr

0   125   250 m

To Aranypart
Hotel

Mosoni-Danube
River

Moricz Zsigmond rakpart

Dunakapu
tér

Vörösmarty
utca

Apáca   utca

Jedlik Ányos utca

Apor Vilmos
püspök tere

Rákóczi Ferenc utca

Széchenyi
tér

Liszt Ferenc utca

Kaptalandomb

Király utca

Kisfaludy   utca

Teleki László utca

Bécsi kapu
tér

Kazinczy utca

Czuczor Gergely utca

Schweidel utca

Kisfaludy utca

Baross Gábor útca

Arany János

Arany vértanúk útja

Bajcsy-Zsilinszky út

Jókai utca

Zechmeister   utca

Rába kettős híd

Petőfi tér

Munkácsy Mihály utca

Rába
River

Árpád út

Szent István út

Honvéd
liget

Réval Miklos   utca

E75

E75

HUNGARY

PLACES TO STAY

17 Hotel Klastrom
20 Kertész Panzió
29 Rába Hotel
35 Hotel Szárnyaskerék

PLACES TO EAT

6 Várkapu Restaurant
7 Vaskakas Taverna
12 Halász Csárda
21 Szürkebarát Borozó
27 Rábaparti Étterem
28 Márka Étterem
32 Magyar Büfé

OTHER

1 Thermal Baths
2 Bishop's Palace
3 Cathedral
4 Jero Disco
5 Casemates Museum
8 Napoleon House
9 Borsos Miklós Collection
10 Arc of the Covenant Monument
11 Margit Kováks Collection
13 Xantus János Museum
14 Former Charity Hospital
15 Széchenyi Cultural Centre
16 Carmelite Church
18 Széchenyi Pharmacy
19 St Ignatius Church
22 Kisfaludy Theatre
23 Express
24 Main Post Office
25 Bartók Cultural Centre
26 Synagogue
30 OTP Bank
31 Ibusz
33 Ciklámen Tourist
34 City Hall
36 Post Office
37 Train Station
38 Bus Station

corner of Erkel Ferenc utca and Kossuth Lajos utca opposite an old synagogue. There are two dormitories here on diagonally opposite sides of the street, the one on Erkel Ferenc for men and the other on Kossuth Lajos for women. Both are only an eight-minute walk from the train station (via Munkácsy Mihály utca) or the centre of town

(via Rába Kettos híd). Express can book you in here.

Private Rooms Private rooms are available at Ciklámen Tourist, Aradi vértanúk útja 22 near the train station (from US$15 double), and Ibusz, Szent István út 31 (from US$11/12 single/double). Singles are scarce and these offices close early.

Hotels The four-storey *Hotel Szárnyaskerék)* (☎ 314 629), Révai Miklós utca 5, directly opposite the train station, is US$17 double with shared bath (no singles).

A British reader wrote in recommending *Kertész Panzió*, Iskola utca 11, in the alley on the north side of Kisfaludy Theatre. A room with private bath and TV will be around US$20 double. A block away at Arany János utca 33, is *Kuckó Pension* (☎ 316 260).

The two-star *Hotel Klastrom* (☎ 315 611), Zehmeister utca 1, has 42 rooms with bath (US$44/46/69 single/double/triple, including breakfast) in the former Carmelite convent (1720). This is great if the price is right for you.

Hotel Aranypart (☎ 326 033), Áldozat utca 12, in Révfalu north of the centre, is a modern one-star sport hotel that charges US$17/18/26 single/double/triple without bath, US$19/20/30 with bath, breakfast included. Show a YHA card here and you'll receive a 10% discount. To get there, cross the bridge from Dunakapu tér, then continue straight ahead for about four blocks till you see the *Revesz Panzió*, Ságvári Endre utca 22, on the right. The Hotel Aranypart is down the next street on the left. Bus No 16 passes near the Hotel Aranypart from beside the city hall.

Places to Eat

For a cheap self-service meal you can't beat *Márka Étterem*, Bajcsy-Zsilinszky út 30 (weekdays 7 am to 5 pm, weekends 7 am to 3 pm).

The *Rábaparti Étterem*, Zehmeister utca 15, serves tasty Hungarian fare in an attrac-

HUNGARY

tive, unpretentious locale at very reasonable prices.

The *Várkapu Restaurant*, Becsi kapu tér 7, has its dishes listed on a blackboard outside.

One of Győr's finest wine cellars is the *Szürkebarát Borozó*, Arany János utca 20 (closed Sunday). A stairway in the courtyard leads down into this vaulted restaurant. Only cold dishes are available at lunch. The ice-cream counter in this same courtyard is one of the best in Győr.

A typical inn near the market is the *Halász Csárda*, Apáca utca 4.

Cafés & Bars For coffee and cakes go to the *Cukrászda*, Baross Gábor út 30.

The *Magyar Büfé*, Árpád út 18, is a very friendly neighbourhood wine cellar where you can taste Balaton wine to your heart's content. Despite the name, no food is served here.

The *Metróz Csárda*, Dunakapu tér 3, is fine for having a glass of wine at the bar.

Entertainment

Győr has one of Hungary's most striking new theatres, the *Kisfaludy Theatre* on Czuczor Gergely utca. You can't miss the Vásárely mosaics covering the exterior walls! The box office is just inside. Győr's ballet company which performs here is internationally recognised.

At Kisfaludy utca 25 is the Országos Filharmonia (closed in summer), where you can enquire about concerts. Also try the *Széchenyi Cultural Centre*, Széchenyi tér 7.

Other events are staged at the *Bartók Cultural Centre*, Czuczor Gergely utca 17.

Jero Disco, in a large pavilion on an island in the river, is open daily except Monday and Wednesday from 10 pm to 4 am, Sunday 10 pm to midnight.

Győr's best disco is *Charlie M* in the Nádorváros district south of the railway line. It opens at 10 pm on weekends, you'll probably have to go by taxi.

Getting There & Away

Győr is well connected by express train to Budapest's Déli and Keleti train stations (131 km, two hours) and to Sopron (85 km, one hour). Other trains run to Szombathely (117 km, 1¾ hours) via Celldömölk. To go to Balaton Lake there's a secondary line with three or four slow local trains a day going south to Veszprém (79 km, 2¾ hours) via Pannonhalma.

To go to/from Vienna's Westbahnhof (126 km) you may have to change trains at Hegyeshalom since some express trains won't pick up passengers at Győr. Check with Ibusz well ahead (you could also hitch from Hegyeshalom). Another route to Austria is through Sopron. To go to/from Slovakia, walk across the bridge at Komárom.

Buses of possible interest include those to Balatonfüred (six daily, 99 km), Budapest (hourly, 123 km), Esztergom (two daily, 87 km), Hévíz (two daily, 214 km), Kecskemét (daily, 208 km), Pannonhalma (hourly or better, 21 km), Pécs (two daily, 241 km), Székesfehérvár (seven daily, 87 km) and Vienna (two daily, 122 km). To go to Fertőd you must take the Sopron bus to Kapuvár and change there for Fertőd.

SOPRON

Sopron (Ödenburg) sits right on the Austrian border, 217 km west of Budapest and only 69 km south of Vienna. In 1921 the town's residents voted to remain part of Hungary, while the rest of Bürgenland (the region to which Sopron used to belong) went to Austria, thus explaining the town's location in a narrow neck of land between Lake Fertő and the green eastern ridges of the Alps.

Sopron (the ancient Scarbantia) has been an important centre since Roman times. The Tatars and Turks never got this far, so numerous medieval structures have come down to the present day intact. In the horseshoe-shaped old quarter, still partially enclosed by medieval walls built on Roman foundations, almost every building is historic. This is Sopron's principal charm and wanderers among the Gothic and Baroque houses are rewarded at every turn. Some of the build-

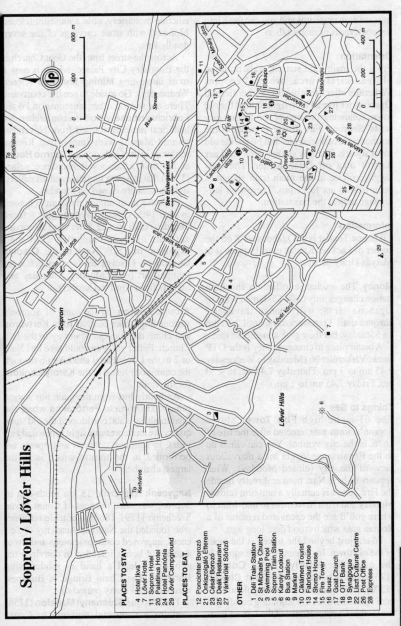

Sopron / Lóvér Hills

PLACES TO STAY

4 Hotel Ikva
7 Lóvér Hotel
11 Sopron Hotel
20 Palatinus Hotel
24 Hotel Pannónia
29 Lóvér Campground

PLACES TO EAT

12 Poncichter Borozó
21 Önkiszolgáló Étterem
23 César Borozó
25 Deák Restaurant
27 Várkerület Söröző

OTHER

1 Déli Train Station
2 St Michael's Church
3 Swimming Pool
5 Sopron Train Station
6 Károly Lookout
8 Bus Station
9 Market
10 Ciklámen Tourist
13 Fabricius House
14 Storno House
15 Fire Tower
16 Ibusz
17 Goat Church
18 OTP Bank
19 Synagogue
22 Liszt Cultural Centre
26 Post Office
28 Express

To Fertőrákos

To Kőváros

See Enlargement

Ikva Stream

Sopron

Lóvér körút

Lóvér Hills

HUNGARY

ings are now museums and you can peek into the courtyards of many others.

Orientation

From the main train station, walk north on Mátyás király utca, which becomes Várkerület after a few blocks. Várkerület and Ógabona tér form a loop right around the old town, following the line of the former city walls. Sopron's Fire Tower is between the northern end of Várkerület and Fő tér, the old town square. The bus station is on Lackner Kristóf utca off Ógabona tér. The left-luggage office in the main train station is open from 3 am to 11 pm. There's no left-luggage area at the bus station.

Information

Ciklámen Tourist is at Ógabona tér 8 on the corner of Lackner Kristóf utca. Express is at Mátyás király utca 7.

Money The exchange office in the train station changes only cash. Ciklámen Tourist, Ógabona tér 8, will change travellers' cheques until 3 pm weekdays, until 2.30 pm on Saturday, but they give a mediocre rate.

A better place to change money is the OTP Bank, Várkerület 96 (Monday to Wednesday 7.45 am to 3 pm, Thursday 7.45 am to 4.30 pm, Friday 7.45 am to 1 pm).

Things to See

The 61-metre-high **Fire Tower** above Sopron's north gate, erected after the fire of 1676, is the city symbol. You can climb up to the Renaissance loggia for a marvellous view of the city (closed Monday). What appears to be a Nazi bunker directly beside the Fire Tower is actually a museum (closed Monday and from November to mid-March) where you'll see the excavated remains of a Roman gate which stood here long ago.

Fő tér, just beyond the tower, is the heart of the old town. In the centre of the square is the magnificent **Holy Trinity Column** (1701) and beyond this the **Goat Church** (1300), built by a goatherd with gold uncovered by his herd! In the adjoining building is the Gothic Chapter House of the former Ben-

edictine monastery, now a museum (closed Monday) with stone carvings of the seven deadly sins.

Across the street from the Goat Church is the Esterházy City Palace, which is now a most interesting **Mining Museum** (closed Wednesday). Go inside to see the courtyard. There are several other museums on Fő tér. **Fabricius House** at No 6 is a comprehensive historical museum (closed from November to mid-March) with impressive Roman sculpture in the Gothic cellar. **Storno House** at No 8 is a famous Renaissance palace (1560) that is now a museum and art gallery. Both houses are closed on Monday.

Sopron's most unique museum is housed in the 14th century **synagogue** (closed Tuesday) at Új utca 22. Jews were an important part of the community until their expulsion in 1526. Next to the **Orsolya Church** on Orsolya tér is a collection of religious art (open Monday, Thursday and Sunday from April to October).

Around Sopron To see some of Sopron's surroundings, take bus No 10 to **Kertváros** and climb the Baroque stairway to the Hill Church. Better yet, you could take bus No 1 or 2 to the Lővér Hotel and hike up through the coniferous forest to the **Károly Lookout** for the view.

An hourly bus from the main bus station runs 10 km north to **Fertőrákos** where the mammoth halls and corridors of the old stone quarry are an impressive sight (open daily all year). In summer, concerts and operas are performed in the theatre which is in the largest chamber.

Nagycenk Nagycenk, 13 km south-east of Sopron, was once the seat of Count István Széchenyi (1791-1860), a notable reformer who founded the National Academy of Sciences, improved communications and wrote a series of books intended to convince the nobility to lend a hand in modernising Hungary. (The Chain Bridge in Budapest was one of his many projects.)

The Baroque **Széchenyi Mansion** (1758) contains a memorial museum to Count

István and a three-star hotel (☎ 99-60 061) with 19 rooms at US$65 double. The café just outside the restaurant (slow service) on the mansion grounds serves great ice cream. Other attractions in Nagycenk include the park with its long avenue of linden trees, the Széchenyi family mausoleum in the local cemetery, a three-km narrow-gauge steam railway to Fertőboz and a 60-horse stud farm. Nagycenk is accessible by bus and train.

Places to Stay

Sopron may be a convenient transit point but it's an expensive place to spend the night, so plan a morning arrival and afternoon departure if at all possible. For example, consider catching the 3 pm bus to Kőszeg where budget accommodation is more plentiful.

Camping No youth hostels or student dormitories exist and from mid-April to mid-October the cheapest accommodation around Sopron is available at the *Lövér Campground* (☎ 311 715), at Pócsi-domb, three km south of the station on Kőszegi út. Camping is US$3/5 single/double and the 129 bungalows here go for US$6/7/10/11 single/double/triple/quad. The atmosphere is friendly and welcoming (for a change). Take bus No 12 in the 'Lövérek fele' direction from either the bus or train stations right to the camping ground.

Private Rooms Ciklámen Tourist, Ógabona tér 8 (weekdays 7.30 am to 4 pm, Saturday 7.30 am to 3.30 pm), has private rooms (from US$15 double). Other private rooms are handled by Volántourist, Lackner Kristóf utca 1, and Ibusz, Várkerület 41 (from US$14 double). Sometimes in summer all rooms are full and singles will have to pay for a double.

You can also find a private room by taking bus No 1 from the train station to the Szieszta Hotel, Lövér körút 37, then walk back down the hill looking for houses with 'zimmer frei' signs. There are quite a few near the hotel and around the public swimming pool. This

procedure is often cheaper than dealing with Ciklámen Tourist.

Hotels Sopron's cheapest regular hotel is two-storey *Ikva* (☎ 332 032), József Attila utca 3-5, on the opposite side of the railway from the old town. It charges US$15 for singles/doubles without bath, US$21 with bath. As you leave the train station, turn left and keep left until you find the level crossing over the tracks. Turn left again and follow the main street up to the hotel.

Sopron's grand old hotel is the *Hotel Pannónia* (☎ 312 180), at Várkerület 75, which opened in 1893. A recent renovation has pushed prices out of sight and effaced much of the Pannónia's old-world flavour.

Places to Eat & Drink

For a tasteless self-service lunch go to *Önkiszolgáló Étterem* at the western end of Széchenyi tér (open from 7 am to 3 pm Monday to Saturday). The food is neither cheap nor good, so only eat here if you're pressed for time.

A local restaurant with Hungarian flavour is the *Várkerület Söröző*, Várkerület 83. César Borozó, Hátsókapu 2, is more touristy; and, though a wine cellar, it serves meals. *Corvinus Pizzeria* on Fő tér, right in front of the Fire Tower, is only reasonably priced if you stick to the pizza.

The *Deák Restaurant*, Deák tér, on the corner of Erzsébet utca, specialises in game dishes like wild boar or venison, though fish is also on the menu. In the evening there's live music and the place is popular with Austrian border-jumpers. There's a large beer garden alongside.

Wine tasters repair to the *Gyógygödör Borozó*, Fő tér 4, opposite the Goat Church (closed Monday), or the *Poncichter Borozó*, Szentlélek utca 13, both great little wine cellars. Try the local Kékfrankos wine.

Entertainment

Posters in the window of the *Liszt Cultural Centre* on Széchenyi tér occasionally announce local events, though the adjacent gambling casino now seems to be the main focus of interest (open after 4 pm). Just around the corner on Petőfi tér is the *Petőfi Theatre*, with drama in Hungarian.

Getting There & Away

Express trains run to Budapest's Déli or Keleti train stations (216 km, three hours) via Győr and Komárom, and local trains run to Szombathely (64 km, 1½ hours) via Nagycenk.

Buses of interest from Sopron include one a day to Balatonfüred (160 km), five to Budapest (210 km), two to Esztergom (174 km), hourly or better to Fertőd and Fertőrákos, hourly to Győr (87 km), three daily to Hévíz and Keszthely (141 km), seven to Kőszeg (53 km), every half-hour to Nagycenk (13 km), daily to Pécs (287 km), two to Szekesfehérvár (174 km) and eight to Szombathely (73 km).

There's also a bus to Vienna from the bus station every morning except public holidays (69 km, 120 Austrian shillings in cash, forint not accepted).

A dozen daily trains run between Sopron and Wiener Neustadt (34 km, 45 minutes, US$4), while eight others use a different line to go to Ebenfurth (33 km, US$4). Trains straight through to Vienna Südbahnhof (84 km, 1½ hours, US$10) are rare so you'll probably have to change trains in one of these two towns to get to Vienna. Tickets to Austria must be purchased with cash hard currency, preferably shillings (forint are not accepted). Other trains go to Deutschkreuz (10 km), Eisenstadt (24 km) and Lackenbach (23 km) in Austria. When boarding for Austria at Sopron, be at the station an hour early to clear customs, which is in a separate hall to one side (customs controls are stricter than usual here).

Ticketing arrangements for both trains and buses leaving Sopron for Austria are poor and you may be forced to buy your ticket directly from an Austrian conductor or driver who may demand Austrian shillings. If you know for sure you'll be catching a train from Sopron to Vienna, you ought to try to buy an open international ticket beforehand at an Ibusz office as the ticket offices

at Sopron Railway Station are unable to carry out this simple transaction for some strange reason.

FERTŐD

Don't miss the 126-room **Esterházy Palace** (1766) at Fertőd, 28 km east of Sopron and readily accessible by bus. This magnificent Versailles-style Baroque palace, easily the finest in Hungary, is open from 8 am to 4 pm all year (closed Monday). You must visit the palace with a guide. On Sunday there's a Haydn or Mozart concert in the music room (variably at noon or 5 pm).

Joseph Haydn was court musician to the princely Esterházy family from 1761 to 1790 and his *Farewell* symphony was first performed in the palace concert hall. A Haydn exhibition is included in the visit. The famous Habsburg queen Maria Theresa stayed in the palace in 1773 and three rooms are dedicated to her. Fertőd was the summer residence of the Esterházys (their winter residence was at Eisenstadt, Austria) and the large French Park behind the palace will help you to visualise the bygone splendour.

Places to Stay & Eat

You can spend the night in the palace. Clean, simple rooms in the *Kastélyszálló* on the 3rd floor are US$13/14 double/triple, US$18 for four, open all year. To find the hostel, look for the arrow near the ticket office that points up to the *szálloda*. For advance reservations have someone who speaks Hungarian call ☎ 370 971 for you. If you arrive to find the Kastélyszálló full don't let yourself be talked into staying at the Esterházy Panzió down the street as it's overpriced and full of drunks. One reader had a camera stolen from a locked room at the Panzió (she did say their restaurant was fine).

In the *Grenadier House* opposite the palace's Rococo wrought-iron gate is a pleasant café (closed Monday) and there are several good restaurants in the village.

KŐSZEG

Kőszeg (Güns) is a lovely medieval town on the Austrian frontier among verdant hills

HUNGARY

between Sopron and Szombathely. Mt Írottkő (882 metres) right on the border south-west of Kőszeg is the highest point in Transdanubia. In 1532 the garrison of Kőszeg's 13th century Jurisich Castle held off a Turkish army of 200,000 and this delay gave the Habsburgs time to mount a successful defence of Vienna, ensuring Kőszeg's place in European history. The houses along the street in front of the castle were erected in a saw-toothed design in order to give defenders a better shot at the enemy.

Jurisich tér, Kőszeg's jewel-box main square, hasn't changed much since the 18th century. It's a pleasant place where fruit and vegetables are left out on the street with little honesty boxes to collect the money. For its good facilities, pleasant atmosphere and wealth of things to see, Kőszeg is probably the nicest little town in all of Hungary.

Orientation & Information

The train station is a 15-minute walk southeast of the centre while buses stop just a block from Várkör. Kőszeg Railway Station doesn't have a regular left-luggage office but

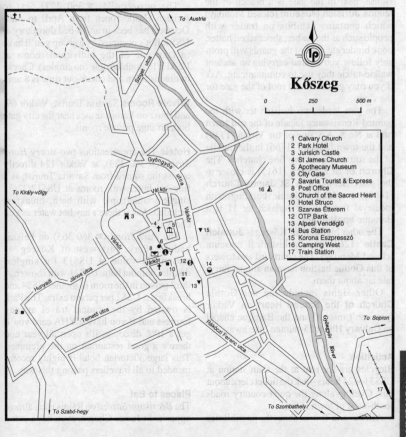

Kőszeg

0   250   500 m

1 Calvary Church
2 Park Hotel
3 Jurisich Castle
4 St James Church
5 Apothecary Museum
6 City Gate
7 Savaria Tourist & Express
8 Post Office
9 Church of the Sacred Heart
10 Hotel Strucc
11 Szarvas Étterem
12 OTP Bank
13 Alpesi Vendéglő
14 Bus Station
15 Korona Eszpresszó
16 Camping West
17 Train Station

To Austria

To Király-völgy

To Sopron

To Szabó-hegy

To Szombathely

the staff will probably agree to hold your bags for the usual fee.

For information try Savaria Tourist, Várkör 69, or Express next door.

Money The OTP Bank, Kossuth Lajos utca 8, behind Hotel Irottkö (Monday 8 am to 5 pm, Tuesday to Thursday 8 am to 3 pm, Friday 8 am to 12.30 pm), changes travellers' cheques.

Things to See

The **City Gate** (1932) bears an exterior relief depicting the 1532 siege. In the 'General's House' next to the gate is a branch of the **Miklós Jurisich Museum** (closed Monday) which contains exhibits on trades with people such as the barber, shoemaker, hatter, book binder etc. One of the guards will probably follow you around carrying an ancient walkie-talkie they use to communicate. Ask if you may go out on the roof of the gate for the view.

The gate leads into Jurisich tér with the painted Renaissance façade of the **old town hall** at No 8. A Statue of the Virgin (1739) and the town fountain (1766) in the middle of the square adjoin two fine churches. The **Church of St Emerich** (1615) is closer to the gate. Behind it is **St James Church** (1403), a splendid Gothic building with medieval frescoes. At Jurisich tér 11 is a Baroque **apothecary**.

The other highlight of Kőszeg is **Jurisich Castle** (1263), now a historical museum (closed Monday). The courtyard and towers of this Gothic bastion have an almost fairy-tale air about them.

Other sights include the neo-Gothic **Church of the Sacred Heart** on Várkör (you can't miss it) and the Baroque chapel on **Calvary Hill**, a 25-minute hike away.

Activities

Bicycles are for rent at the train station at US$3 for 24 hours – ask the ticket clerk about this. Cycling along the quiet country roads south-west of town is fun.

Ask Savaria Tourist about the possibilities

for horse riding at the riding school nea Kőszeg.

Places to Stay

Camping & Hostels *Camping West* (☎ 360 981), Alsó körút 79, next to a public swimming pool *(strand/fürdő)* just across the river from the old town, is one of the nicest places to camp in western Hungary. It's just a five-minute walk east on Kiss János utca from Várkör. Camping is US$2 per person plus US$2 per tent and dormitory accommodation is available in their hostel *(turistaszálló,* at US$4 per person (open from mid-April to October).

The *turistaszálló* (☎ 360 227) next to Jurisich Castle (open from April to mid-October) has beds in an 18-bed dormitory at US$4. If it's occupied by a group you'll have to take one of the individual rooms at US$11/15 double/triple (no singles). Check-in time is 5 pm and check-out time is 8 am.

Private Rooms Savaria Tourist, Várkör 69, and Ibusz on Városház utca near the city gate both arrange private rooms.

Hotels The unpretentious two-storey *Hotel Strucc* (☎ 360 323), at Várkör 124 directly across the square from Savaria Tourist, is a fine old hotel with rooms at US$12/22/31 single/double/triple with bath, breakfast included. Ask if there's any hot water as you check in.

The *Park Hotel* (☎ 360 363) on Felsza-badulás Park, just west of Kőszeg, is reasonable value at US$13 for singles/doubles without bath, US$21 with shower. A third person in the room is another US$4 and breakfast is US$2 per person extra. The Park is owned by the student travel agency Express and if you have a YHA card you'll get a 10% discount. It's open all year and there's a good restaurant on the premises. This large Victorian hotel is highly recommended to all travellers passing this way.

Places to Eat

The *Bécsikapu Söröző* on Rájnis utca, almost opposite St James Church, even has a menu n English! For large portions of tasty Hungarian food with draught beer, you can't beat it.

The *Alpesi Vendéglö*, Munkácsy utca 2, opposite the bus station (closed Sunday and Monday), is more expensive than the Bécsikapu but always crowded with wily Austrians who know a good meal when they taste one.

The *Szarvas Étterem*, Rákóczi Ferenc utca 15, has pizza in addition to the regular menu items.

After dinner, a drink at the bar in the castle is fun (open until midnight daily except Monday year-round).

For coffee and cakes you can't beat *Korona Eszpresszó*, Várkör 18 (daily 8 am to 6 pm).

Getting There & Away

There are frequent trains and buses from Szombathely and less frequent buses from Sopron (53 km). One morning bus goes to Keszthely (129 km).

The train between Szombathely and Kőszeg (18 km, 30 minutes) operates on an honesty system and you must punch your own ticket after boarding (there's a US$3 fine if you fail to do so).

SZOMBATHELY

Szombathely (Steinamanger), pronounced 'som-bat-eye', the seat of Vas County and a major crossroads in western Hungary, was founded as Savaria by the Roman emperor Claudius in 43 AD. It soon became capital of Upper Pannonia and an important stage on the Amber Road from Italy to the Baltic. Destroyed by an earthquake in 455 and pillaged by the Tatars, Turks and Habsburgs, Szombathely only regained its former stature when a bishopric was established here in 1777.

In 1945, just a month before the end of the war, US bombers levelled the town and it's a credit to Hungary that so much has been restored. Although off the beaten tourist track, Szombathely may be a useful stop on your way around the country.

Orientation & Information

The train station is five blocks east of Mártírok tere along Széll Kálmán út. The bus station is on Petőfi Sándor utca, behind the cathedral. Szombathely's busiest square is Fő tér, a long block south of Mártírok tere. For left luggage in the train station ask at the window marked 'poggyász' inside the station hall (open 24 hours).

Savaria Tourist is at Mártírok tere 1. The Magyar Autóklub (☎ 313 945) has an office at Fő tér 19.

Money The OTP Bank at Király utca 10 next to Ibusz is open on Monday from 8 am to 5 pm, Tuesday to Thursday 8 am to 3 pm, and Friday 8 am to 1 pm.

Travel Agencies Railway information and tickets are available from MÁV Tours, Thököly utca 39 near the Isis Hotel.

Things to See

One of the most interesting things to see is the rebuilt neoclassical **cathedral** (1791) on Berzsenyi Dániel tér. Beside the cathedral are the excavated 4th century **remains of Roman Savaria** (Romkert), including mosaics, roads and a medieval castle. On the other side of the cathedral is the Baroque **bishop's palace** (1783), and beyond this on Hollán Ernő utca is the **Smidt Museum** (closed Monday), a fascinating assortment of small treasures collected by a local doctor before his death in 1975.

Head south to Rákóczi Ferenc utca to see the reconstructed 2nd century **temple of the Egyptian goddess Isis**. A festival is held here in August. The **Szombathely Gallery** overlooking the temple is the best modern art gallery in Hungary (closed Monday and Tuesday). A plaque on the front of the **synagogue** (1881) opposite the Szombathely Gallery recalls the 4228 local Jews sent to Auschwitz in 1944.

Also worth visiting is the **Savaria Museum** (closed Monday) on Széll Kálmán út, which is especially strong on archaeology and natural history. There's a large Roman

HUNGARY

Szombathely

Map labels:

Szovo utca

Rohonci út

Bartók Béla körút

Rokonci út

Kondics István utca

Perint Stream

Kópati Kelemen utca

Ady Endre tér

Petőfi Sándor utca

Március 15 tér

Weöseleny Miklos utca

Vörösmarty utca

Szent István park

Szent István utca

Hollán E utca

Templom tér

Mártírok tere

Fő tér

Berzsenyi D tér

Szell Kálmán út

Király utca

Szent Márton út

Hunyadi János út

Kálvária utca

Nárai utca

Thököly Imre utca

Mátyás király út

Rákóczi Ferenc utca

Körmendi út

Jáki út

Rózsa Ferenc

Pálfa utca

Numbered markers: 2, 3, 4, 5, 6, 7, 8, 9, 10, 11, 12, 13, 14, 15, 16, 17, 18, 19, 20, 21, 22

0 250 500 m

---

lapidarium (a collection of architectural fragments) in the basement.

On the western side of Szombathely is a major open-air **ethnographic museum**, or skansen (open from 10 am to 4 pm, closed Monday), with 50 reconstructed folk buildings. It's on a lake near the camping ground (bus No 7 from the train station to the terminus).

Places to Stay

Camping From May to September you can stay at *Tópart Camping* (☎ 314 766) on Kondics István utca 4 by a lake west of town

(bus No 7 from the train station to the end of the line). From the bus stop walk along the causeway across the lake. Bungalows here are US$14 single or double without shower, US$39 with shower. Camping is US$1.50 per person, US$2 per tent. There's a swimming pool nearby.

Private Rooms & Hostels Private rooms are assigned by staff at Savaria Tourist, Mártírok tere 1, and Ibusz, Széll Kálmán út 3. In summer, Express, Király utca 12, may know of youth hostels. These tourist offices are next to one another.

Hotels The 35-room *Liget Hotel* (☎ 314 168), Szent István park 15, west of the city centre, offers motel-style accommodation at US$26/28 single/double with bath and breakfast (no singles). You can get there on bus No 7 from the train station.

Szombathely's nicest hotel by far is the turn-of-the-century *Hotel Savaria* (☎ 311 440), Mártírok tere 4 in the very centre of town. It's open all year but not cheap: rooms cost US$47/51 single/double with shower, US$33 double with shared bath, breakfast included.

Actually, Szombathely, unlike Rome, can be seen in a day and it may be better to go on to less expensive Kőszeg to spend the night.

Places to Eat

Szombathely's most elegant restaurant is in the *Savaria Hotel* on Mártírok tere. They don't sully their menu with prices.

For a less pretentious meal, try the *Gyöngyös Étterem*, Széll Kálmán út 8 nearby. It has a cheap 'menu' at lunch time, but the food

and service are always good. (It's closed on Monday.)

The restaurant in the train station (not the stand-up 'bisztró') is also fine.

Entertainment

The concert hall is opposite the Szombathely Gallery, on Rákóczi Ferenc utca. Also visit the *Cultural & Sports Centre* and a second cultural centre, the *Megyei Müvelődési es Iffusagi Központ* opposite the bus station.

If you have wheels, a popular night spot is *Ciao Amigo* out at the edge of town on the road to Kőszeg. Otherwise check out the *Garden Disco* in the Cultural & Sports Centre.

The symphony orchestra is based in the modern building opposite the Szombathely Gallery on Rakóczi Ferenc utca and concerts are advertised on the board outside.

Getting There & Away

Szombathely is only 13 km from the Austrian border and there are direct trains to/from Graz (146 km, three hours). Some of the Graz services involve a change of trains at the border (Szentgotthárd).

Express trains to Budapest-Déli (236 km, 3½ hours) go via Veszprém and Székesfehérvár. Other express trains run to Győr (117 km, 1¾ hours) via Celldömölk. There are frequent local trains to Kőszeg (18 km, 30 minutes) and Sopron (64 km, 1½ hours). To go to southern Transdanubia or Balaton Lake, take a bus to Keszthely (106 km) via Hévíz (three daily). There's also an early morning express train to/from Pécs (244 km, 4½ hours).

Balaton Lake

In the very heart of Transdanubia, the 77-km-long Balaton Lake (Plattensee) is the largest freshwater lake in central and Western Europe. The south-eastern shore of this 'Hungarian sea' is shallow and in summer the warm, sandy beaches are a favourite family vacation spot. Better scenery and

Balaton Lake

more historic sites are found on the deeper north-western side of the lake.

North of the lake are the Bakony Hills and the extinct volcanoes of the Tapolca Basin. Several ruined castles, such as that at Sümeg, remind visitors that during the Turkish period the border between the Ottoman and Habsburg empires ran down the middle of the lake. The Turks maintained a lake fleet that was based at Siófok. Székesfehérvár and Veszprém, just north of the lake, are old historic towns full of monuments and one of Hungary's finest palaces is at Keszthely. The Benedictine crypt in Tihany Abbey is the oldest existing church in Hungary.

The many towns and villages along both shores have an organic connection to this ancient lake. This is wine-making country. Scenic railway lines encircle the lake and there are no less than 39 camping grounds on its shores. 'Zimmer frei' signs are everywhere. Balaton's very popularity is perhaps its main drawback, though the north-western shore is quieter than the south-eastern one.

To avoid pollution and public nuisances, the use of private motorboats is prohibited, making Balaton a favourite yachting centre. Continuous breezes from the north speed sailors and sailboarders along. Other common activities here are tennis, horse riding and cycling. Any local tourist office will be able to provide information on these activities and the thermal baths of Hévíz are nearby. If you want to spend some time in the area, get hold of the *A Balaton* 1:40,000 topographical map available at Budapest bookshops which illustrates the many hiking possibilities.

GETTING THERE & AWAY

Trains to Balaton Lake leave from Déli Railway Station and buses leave from the Erzsébet tér Bus Station in Budapest. If you're travelling north or south from the lake to/from towns in western or southern Transdanubia, buses are often preferable to trains.

GETTING AROUND

Railway service around the lake is fairly frequent. A better way to see Balaton Lake is by Mahart passenger ferry. These ferries operate on the route between Siófok, Balatonfüred, Tihany, Tihanyi-rév and Balatonföldvár from April to October. During July and August there is a ferry every couple of hours. During the main summer season, which is from mid-June to mid-September, ferries ply the entire length of the lake from Balatonkenese to Keszthely (five hours) with frequent stops on both shores. There are also car ferries across the lake between Tihanyi-rév and Szántódrév (from mid-March to mid-December), and Badacsony and Fonyód (from mid-April to mid-October). Fares are cheap: US$2 will take you anywhere. Of course, in winter there are no boats on the lake.

SZÉKESFEHÉRVÁR

Traditionally, Székesfehérvár (Stuhlweissenburg) is known as the place where the Magyar chieftain Árpád set up camp, therefore it's considered to be the oldest town in Hungary. In 972 the grand duke of Geza established his seat here and his son, Stephen I (later St Stephen), founded a basilica which became the symbol of royal power. Thirty-eight kings of early medieval Hungary were crowned at Székesfehérvár and 18 were buried in the basilica's crypt. It was here in 1222 that Andrew II proclaimed the Golden Bull, Hungary's first constitution.

The Turks captured Székesfehérvár in 1543 and used the basilica to store gunpowder. It exploded during a siege in 1601; by 1688 when the Turks left, the town was just an uninhabited field of ruins. The Habsburgs rebuilt Székesfehérvár in the 18th century, and around 1800 stones from the basilica ruins were used to erect the nearby Episcopal Palace. Only the foundations of the old coronation church are now seen, though the steeples of four huge Baroque churches that were built after liberation from the Turks tower over the old town.

Today Székesfehérvár is the seat of Fejér County, a pleasant little town with a life of its own relatively unaffected by tourism. Although the town's not on Balaton Lake, everyone travelling between Budapest and Balaton passes this way so it's included here for convenience. Székesfehérvár can also be seen as a day trip from Budapest.

Orientation & Information

The bus station is just outside the west wall of the old town, and the train station is a 15-minute walk south-east of the centre. If you arrive by train, march straight up Deák Ferenc utca, then turn left on Rákóczi utca and go through the city gate to Városház tér, the centre of town.

You can leave your bags in the office marked 'csomagmegorző' next to 'Pénztár 5' inside the bus station (weekdays 8 am to 5 pm, Saturday 8 am to 2 pm). The left-luggage office inside the train station is open 24 hours.

Albatours is at Városház tér 6. The Magyar Autóklub (☎ 327 624) is at Deák Ferenc utca 2.

Money The OTP Bank on Várkapu utca off Fő utca (Monday to Thursday 7.45 am to 3 pm, Friday 7.45 am to 12.30 pm) changes travellers' cheques.

Things to See

Székesfehérvár is the sort of place you can visit at leisure – wander up and down the pedestrian promenades, Fő utca and Városház tér. The foundations of the 12th century **royal basilica** where the coronations took place are on Koronázó tér, with St Stephen's sarcophagus to the right, just inside the gate. The 'garden of ruins' is only open from April to October, but you get a good view of it from the street.

Városház tér with the old town hall and **Episcopal Palace** (1801) is the heart of Székesfehérvár. As you stroll north on Fő utca you'll notice the Cistercian church on the left and next door the archaeological collection of the **István Király Museum**, Fő utca 6. The **Black Eagle Pharmacy** is across the street.

The István Király Museum, Országzászló tér 3, off Fő utca (closed Monday), has a small historical collection.

Places to Stay

Private Rooms Private rooms are available from Albatours, Városház tér 6 (US$11 double), and Ibusz, Fő utca on the corner of Ady Endre utca.

Székesfehérvár

0   250   500 m

PLACES TO STAY

2   Magyar Király Hotel
18 Alba Regia Hotel
23 Rév Szálló

PLACES TO EAT

9   Korzo Söröző
15 Ösfehérvár Étterem
24 Viniczai Ice Cream
    Parlour

OTHER

1   Public Swimming Pool
3   Vörösmarty Theatre
4   OTP Bank
5   István Király Museum
6   Ibusz
7   Cistercian Church
8   Black Eagle Pharmacy
10 Törökudvar
    Turistaszálló
11 Franciscan Church
12 Albatours/Town Hall

13 St Stephen Cathedral
14 Bishop's Palace
16 Basilica Ruins
17 Express Travel Agency
19 Fehérvár Department Store
20 Cooptourist
21 Magyar Autóklub
22 Cinema
25 Post Office
26 Carmelite Church
27 St Stephen Monument
28 Bus Station
29 Market

HUNGARY

Hostels Express, Rákóczi utca 4, knows about accommodation in vacant college dormitories, available from July to mid-August only.

The *Törökudvar Turístaszálló* (☎ 324 975), Jókai utca 2 just off Városház tér, is a cheap dormitory open only in the evening.

Hotels The nine-storey *Rév Szálló* (☎ 327 015), Deák Ferenc utca 42, is a Hungarian workers' residence that accepts tourists. Here you pay US$13 for an adequate single, double or triple with a washbasin, but the shower and toilet are down the hall. This conveniently located, inexpensive hotel makes Székesfehérvár attractive as a stopover on the way to/from Budapest.

If you crave luxury, the grand old *Magyar Király Hotel* (☎ 311 262), Fő utca 10, has rooms with private bath at US$37 single or double, breakfast included.

Places to Eat

Korzo Söröző, near the point where Fő utca merges with Városház tér, should satisfy your every need. You can get a huge cooked breakfast with lemon tea, mushroom omelette, bread, butter and jam, and for dinner there's fried cheese or mushrooms (for vegetarians) with cold Czech beer.

Also good is the *Ösfehérvár Étterem* (closed Sunday) on Koronázó tér, opposite the basilica ruins, which has a set lunch 'menu'.

Viniczai, Budai út 17, has some of the best ice-cream cones in town.

There's a pleasant restaurant upstairs in *Fehérvár Department Store* and a large supermarket downstairs. The regular restaurant in the train station is also good.

Entertainment

Check the *Vörösmarty Theatre* on Fő utca beside the Magyar Király Hotel.

Getting There & Away

There are buses from Székesfehérvár to Budapest's Erzsébet tér Bus Station (66 km) about every half-hour, to Balatonfüred (60 km) five times a day, to Veszprém (44 km) every hour, to Komárom (75 km) daily, to Győr (87 km) seven times a day, to Sopron (174 km) twice a day, to Siófok (43 km) seven times a day, to Keszthely (122 km) three times a day, to Hévíz (128 km) four times a day, to Pécs (153 km) three times a day, to Kecskemét (134 km) three times a day and to Szeged (206 km) five times a day.

Local trains between Budapest-Déli and Siófok or Baltonfüred stop at Székesfehérvár frequently. An express line from Budapest-Déli to Szombathely via Veszprém also passes here and there's a local line north to Komárom (82 km, 1½ hours).

BALATONFÜRED

Balatonfüred, an elegant spa town with the easy-going grace that highly commercialised Siófok lacks, is called the 'Mecca of cardiacs' for its curative waters. Located on the northern shore of Balaton Lake between Tihany and Veszprém, it has been the most fashionable bathing resort on the lake since 1772, when a medicinal bathing establishment was set up here. During the early 19th century it became an important meeting place for Hungarian intellectuals and the town still bears an aristocratic air.

Although Balatonfüred is a major spa, the mineral baths are reserved for patients being treated for heart disease, so casual tourists are out of luck. Yet because it's a health resort much is open throughout the year, so it's the best place to visit around the lake in the off season. In the past few years Balatonfüred has become overcrowded with Germans in midsummer.

Orientation & Information

The adjacent bus and train stations are a km north-west of the spa centre. The left-luggage office at the exit from the tunnel at the train station is open from 7.15 am to 9 pm. The small bus information office on the right as you leave the train station is helpful. Buses to/from Tihany also stop near the ferry landing below the Round Church on Jókai Mór utca. Blaha Lujza utca runs from in front

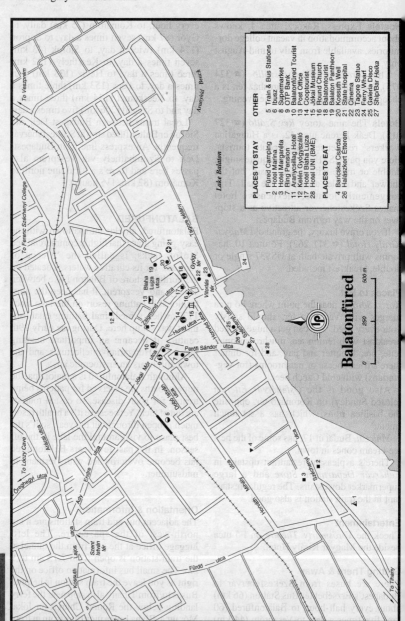

Balatonfüred

0   250   500 m

PLACES TO STAY

1 Füred Camping
2 Hotel Marina
3 Hotel Margaréta
8 Ring Pension
11 Aranycsillag Hotel
12 Kelén Gyógyszálló
17 Hotel Blaha Lujza
28 Hotel UNI (BME)

PLACES TO EAT

4 Baricska Csárda
26 Halászkert Étterem

OTHER

5 Train & Bus Stations
6 Ibusz
7 Supermarket
9 OTP Bank
10 Balatonfüred Tourist
13 Post Office
14 Cooptourist
15 Jókai Museum
16 Round Church
18 Balatontourist
19 Balaton Pantheon
20 Kossuth Well
21 State Hospital
22 Cinema
23 Tagore Statue
24 Ferry Wharf
25 Galéria Disco
27 Ship/Bar Helka

To Veszprém

Aranyhíd Beach

Lake Balaton

To Ferenc Széchényi College

To Lóczy Cave

Öreghegyi utca

Tagore sétány

Gyógy tér

Blaha Lujza utca

Zsigmond utca

Vitorlás tér

Huray utca

Honvéd utca

Jókai Mór utca

Petőfi Sándor utca

Szabó Lőrinc utca

Dózsa István

Arácsi utca

Ady Endre utca

Szent István tér

Lajos utca

Kossuth Lajos utca

Fürdő utca

Horváth Mihály utca

Széchenyi utca

To Tihany

of the church directly into Gyógy tér where the visit begins.

Balatontourist is at Blaha Lujza utca 5.

Money The OTP Bank, Jókai Mór utca 15, next to the supermarket (Monday to Wednesday 7.45 am to 3 pm, Thursday 7.45 am to 5 pm, Friday 7.45 am to 1 pm), changes travellers' cheques.

Things to See

The heart of the spa is Gyógy tér with its **well house** (Kossuth Well), where travellers may freely fill their canteens with radioactive mineral water.

The park along the nearby lakeshore is worth a promenade. Near the wharf you'll encounter the bust of the Bengali poet Rabindranath Tagore before a lime tree that he planted in 1926 to mark his recovery from illness here. The poem 'Tagore' which he wrote for the occasion is reproduced on a plaque in English (the adjacent Hungarian plaque incorrectly identifies Tagore as a Hindi poet).

A little inland, diagonally opposite the **Round Church** (1841), is the **Jókai Museum**, formerly the house of novelist Mór Jókai (closed from November to February and Monday).

Places to Stay

Camping There's only one camping ground at Balatonfüred but it has a capacity for 3700 people. The *Füred Camping* (☎ 343 823), Széchenyi utca 24, is beside *Hotel Marina* on the lake, three km from the train station. Four-person bungalows here cost US$48 from mid-June to August, US$38 from May to mid-June and in early September, and a bargain US$21 in April and from mid-September to mid-October. To get a bungalow you have to arrive before reception closes at 7 pm. The only water-skiing on Balaton Lake is practised here using an electric-powered cable to tow skiers.

Private Rooms As everywhere around Balaton Lake, private room prices are rather inflated. Kádár & Társa Agency (K & T

Tours) at the train station arranges private rooms beginning around US$11/17 single/double (open from April to October only).

Ibusz, Petőfi Sándor utca 4/a, also has private rooms from US$11/17 single/double (open year-round).

Balatonfüred Tourist, Petőfi Sándor utca 8, has the most expensive private rooms (US$24/28 single/double), open year-round. Cooptourist, Jókai Mór utca 23, has only double private rooms (no singles) and they're closed from October to April.

Balatontourist, Blaha Lujza utca 5, has the largest number of rooms, thus they've a better chance of finding something less expensive for you.

Hotels Next to the Ibusz office is *Ring Pension* (☎ 342 884), Petőfi Sándor utca 6/A, so called because the owner is a former champion boxer. Neat, clean singles/doubles with shared bath cost US$35/45, breakfast included (open all year but often full in midsummer). There are several other pensions behind Ibusz, all fairly expensive.

At last report the grand old *Aranycsillag Hotel*, Zsigmond utca 1, was closed. If this is still the case, continue two blocks north to the *Kelén Gyógyszálló* (☎ 342 811), Petőfi Sándor utca 38, a four-storey spa hotel in an attractive park, with reasonably priced rooms at US$20 double without bath, US$27 double with bath, breakfast included. There's only one single room which goes for US$16. The hotel is open year-round and rates are lower in the off season.

There's also the *Hotel Blaha Lujza* (☎ 342 603) behind the Blaha Lujza Restaurant, Blaha Lujza utca 4, opposite Balatontourist. Singles/doubles are US$21/28 with private bath and it's open year-round.

Places to Eat

The *Halászkert Étterem*, on Széchenyi utca next to the ship/bar *Helka*, is expensive and permanently packed with German tourists. The previously mentioned *Blaha Lujza Restaurant* is a much better place to eat.

A number of stand-up food stalls just

below the Round Church towards the wharf sell big pieces of fried fish priced by weight.

Getting There & Away

Balatonfüred is two hours from Budapest-Déli (132 km) by express train and three hours by local train. The line continues to Tapolca via Badacsony. There are Mahart ferries to Siófok from mid-April to mid-October.

Buses depart from the stop in front of the train station for Tihany (10 km) and Veszprém (16 km) about once an hour, to Győr (92 km) six times a day, to Esztergom, Sopron (160 km) and Kecskemét (174 km) daily.

NEAR BALATONFÜRED

The picturesque buildings and scenery at **Veszprém**, 16 km north of Balatonfüred, make it a worthwhile day trip. The old town stands on an abrupt headland overlooking a gorge. From the Baroque Fire Tower (1815) on Ovaros tér follow the old town's one street, Vár utca, through the city gate, reconstructed in 1936, to Veszprém Cathedral. The cathedral was completely rebuilt in a neo-Romanesque style in 1910 but the original Gothic crypt remains. The other massive building on the square is the episcopal palace (1776). A broad stairway behind the cathedral leads down to Benedek Hill, where a sweeping 360° panorama of the Séd Valley awaits you. If you have time, also visit the Bakony Museum, Megyeház tér 5 (open all year, closed Monday), beyond the massive County Hall (1887). Veszprém's train station is on the far north side of town, so take advantage of the frequent bus service (30 minutes) linking Balatonfüred and Veszprém. Balatontourist in the mall between the bus station and the old town may be able to supply a map.

The milky-green Sió River drains Balaton Lake into the Danube at **Siófok**, the largest and busiest town on Balaton's south-eastern shore. It's a useful transit point but there's really no reason to stay. A strip of pricey high-rise hotels, six huge camping grounds, holiday cottages, tacky discos and a seamy nightlife attract big crowds of rowdy German and Austrian tourists. In midsummer bedlam reigns and the confused travel agency staff in charge of issuing private rooms won't even consider stays of one or two nights, and singles are unavailable. In winter Siófok is dead. However the town can be convenient if you're just passing through as the train and bus stations are adjacent in the centre of town and the lake boat terminal is only an easy 10-minute walk away. There's a cheap stand-up buffet in the bus station and the OTP Bank at Fő utca 188 across the street from the stations changes travellers' cheques weekdays from 7.45 am to 3 pm.

TIHANY

The Tihany Peninsula almost bisects the northern end of Balaton Lake. Consensus has it that this is the most beautiful place around and in summer Tihany gets more than its fair share of tourists. After a visit to the famous Benedictine Tihany Abbey, you can easily shake the hordes by hiking out past the hilly peninsula's inner lake, Belsó Lake, with its rare flora, fish and bird life. Külsó Lake has almost dried up.

Orientation

Tihany Abbey sits on a ridge above the Tihany ferry landing on the eastern side of the peninsula's high plateau. The village of Tihany is perched above Belsó Lake, just below the abbey. Lake boats also stop at Tihanyi-rév, the car ferry landing at the southern end of the peninsula.

Things to See & Do

Tihany's magnificent twin-towered **abbey church** (1754) is outstanding for its Baroque altars, pulpit and organ, but pride of place goes to the 11th century crypt at the front of the church. Here is found the tomb (1060) of the abbey's founder, King Andrew I. The earliest written relic of the Hungarian language, dating from 1085, was found here. In summer, organ concerts are given in the church.

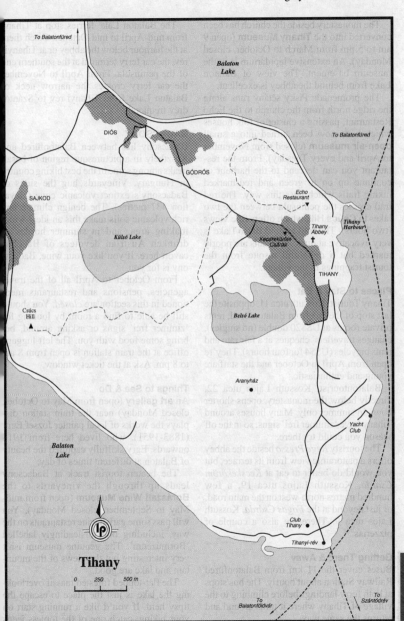

Balaton Lake

To Balatonfüred

DIÓS

GÓDRÓS

To Balatonfüred

Echo Restaurant

Tihany Abbey †

Kecskekörmi Csárdái

Tihany Harbour

TIHANY

SAJKOD

Külsó Lake

Csúcs Hill ▲

Belsó Lake

Aranyház ●

Yacht Club

Balaton Lake

Club Tihany ●

Tihanyi-rév ●

Tihany

0   250   500 m

To Balatonföldvár

To Szántódrév

The monastery beside the church has been converted into the **Tihany Museum** (open 9 am to 5 pm from March to October, closed Monday). An extensive lapidarium is in the museum basement. The view of Balaton Lake from behind the abbey is excellent.

The promenade Pisky sétány runs along the ridge north from the church to the Echo Restaurant, passing a cluster of folk houses which have now been turned into a small **open-air museum** (closed from November to April and every Tuesday). From the restaurant you can descend to the harbour or continue up on to green and red-marked hiking trails which pass this way. The red trail crosses the peninsula between the two lakes to **Csúcs Hill**, which offers fine views (two hours). The trail around Belsó Lake is very evocative at dusk. The trails are poorly marked but a delightful respite from the tourist trappings in the village.

Places to Stay & Eat

Tihany Tourist, Kossuth utca 11, opposite the last stop of the bus from Balatonfüred, rents private rooms at US$20 double (no singles), changes travellers' cheques at a fair rate and rents bicycles (US$4 for four hours). They're open from April to October and the staff are young and enthusiastic.

Balatontourist, Kossuth Lajos utca 22, directly below the monastery, opens shorter hours in summer only. Many houses around Tihany have 'zimmer frei' signs, so in the off season you could try there.

The touristy *Rege Presso* beside the abbey offers a panoramic view from its terrace, but you would do better to eat at *Kecskeköröm Csárda*, Kossuth Lajos utca 19, a few hundred metres north-west on the main road, or just beyond at the *Fogas Csárda*, Kossuth Lajos utca 9. There are also a couple of pizzerias.

Getting There & Away

Buses cover the 11 km from Balatonfüred Railway Station about hourly. The bus stops at both ferry landings before climbing to the village of Tihany where it turns around and returns the same way.

The Balaton Lake ferries stop at Tihany from mid-April to mid-October. Catch them at the harbour below the abbey or at Tihanyi rév, the car ferry terminal at the southern end of the peninsula. From April to November the car ferry crosses the narrow neck of Balaton Lake from Tihanyi-rév to Szántódrév frequently.

BADACSONY

Badacsony lies between Balatonfüred and Keszthely in a picturesque region of basalt peaks among some of the best hiking country in Hungary. Vineyards hug the sides of Badacsony's extinct volcanic cone (elevation 437 metres). The benign climate and rich volcanic soils make this an ideal wine making area, and in summer hordes of drunken Austrian devotees of Bacchus cavort here. If you like your wine, Badacsony is for you.

From October to April all of the travel agencies, pensions and restaurants mentioned in this section are *closed*. You should still be able to find a room by looking for 'zimmer frei' signs or asking around, but bring some food with you. The left-luggage office at the train station is open from 8 am to 8 pm. Ask at the ticket window.

Things to See & Do

An **art gallery** (open from May to October, closed Monday) near the train station displays the works of local painter József Egry (1883-1951), who lived here from 1918 onwards. Egry skilfully captured the beauty of Balaton at different times of day.

The beaten tourist track at Badacsony leads up through the vineyards to the **Borászati Wine Museum** (open from mid-May to September, closed Monday). You will pass some garish wine restaurants on the way, including one misleadingly labelled 'Bormúzeum'. The genuine museum isn't very interesting but the views of the mountain and lake are good.

The flat-topped forested massif overlooking the lake is just the place to escape the tipsy herd. If you'd like a running start on your hiking, catch one of the topless jeeps marked 'Badacsony hegyi járat', which leave Badacsony post office any time from 10 am to 8 pm from May to September whenever at least six paying passengers are aboard (US$2 per person). The jeep driver will drop you off at the Kisfaludy House Restaurant, where a large map outlining the well-marked trails is posted by the parking lot. There are numerous lookouts as well as a tall wooden tower that offers splendid views to the hiker.

Places to Stay

Private rooms are available from a number of agencies, including Balatontourist and Ibusz in the small shopping centre near the ferry wharf, Cooptourist hidden behind some food stalls between the post office and the ABC supermarket, and Miditourist on Park utca behind the train station. Singles are not available and doubles begin around US$15. There are several small pensions among the vineyards on the road above the railway line, a 10-minute walk from the station.

The closest camping ground (☎ 331 091; open from June to mid-September) is by the lake, just under a km west of the station. It's

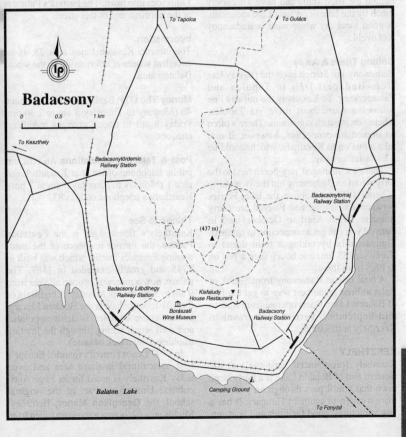

Badacsony

0   0.5   1 km

To Keszthely

To Tapolca

To Gulács

Badacsonytördemic Railway Station

Badacsonytomaj Railway Station

(437 m) ▲

Kisfaludy House Restaurant

Badacsony Lábdihegy Railway Station

Borászati Wine Museum

Badacsony Railway Station

Balaton Lake

Camping Ground

To Fonyód

a casual place but be sure to bring mosquito repellent. Hotplates are available for cooking.

If all this sounds unappealing, you can easily see Badacsony as a stopover on your way around the lake.

Places to Eat

There are no cheap restaurants at Badacsony and the fried fare at the many food stalls near the train station is definitely second rate (although you might try the fried lake fish). Everything is sold by weight and the posted prices are for 100 grams. A better plan is to get picnic food at the ABC supermarket behind the food stalls and have a leisurely lunch by the lake or on top of the mountain. A good local dry white wine is Badacsony Kéknyelű.

Getting There & Away

Badacsony vm Station is on the railway line from Budapest-Déli to Tapolca and Zalaegerszeg. To Keszthely the railway line follows a roundabout route via Tapolca, where you must change trains. There's often an immediate connection, however. If not, take a bus on to Keszthely, which would be a lot faster anyway.

There's a 'managed' pay-beach next to the ferry wharf in Badacsony but the swimming is better at Fonyód across the lake. Ferries between Badacsony and Fonyód are fairly frequent (from April to October) and in Fonyód you can get a connection to southern Transdanubia by taking a train direct to Kaposvár (53 km, one hour), then a bus on to Pécs from there.

A boat ride to Badacsony from Siófok or Balatonfüred is the best way to get the feel of Balaton Lake. Boats operate from June to mid-September. Ferries also travel to Keszthely at this time.

KESZTHELY

Keszthely (pronounced 'cast-eye') at the western end of Balaton Lake is a fairly large town that you'll pass through on your way from western to southern Hungary. It has a few attractions, good facilities and boat services on the lake from June to mid-September. Keszthely is the only town on Balaton Lake which has a life of its own; since it isn't entirely dependent on tourism, it's open all year. The abundance of budget accommodation makes Keszthely a natural stepping stone on your way around this part of Hungary.

Orientation

The bus and train stations are fairly close to the ferry terminal on the lake. The left-luggage office inside the train station is open 24 hours. From the stations follow Mártírok útja up the hill, then turn right on to Kossuth Lajos utca into town. The Festetics Palace is at the northern end of this street.

Information

Tourinform, Kossuth Lajos utca 28, is an excellent source of information on the whole Balaton area.

Money The OTP Bank, Kossuth Lajos utca 40 (Monday to Thursday 8 am to 2.30 pm, Friday 8 am to noon), changes travellers' cheques.

Post & Telecommunications An efficient public telephone office is at Kossuth Lajos utca 1 (Monday to Saturday 9 am to 7 pm). Keszthely's telephone code is 83.

Things to See

Keszthely's finest sight is the **Festetics Palace**, the former residence of the land-owning Festetics family, which was built in 1745 and greatly extended in 1887. The palace, now a museum, is open all year from 9 am to 5 pm except Monday. A highlight of the 101-room palace is the Helikon Library, but the entire complex is richly appointed and well worth seeing (though the hunting trophies show a lack of taste).

In 1797 Count Festetics founded Europe's first agricultural institute here and even today Keszthely is noted for its large Agricultural University. Part of the original school, the **Georgikon Manor**, Bercsényi Miklós utca 67, is now a museum (open from

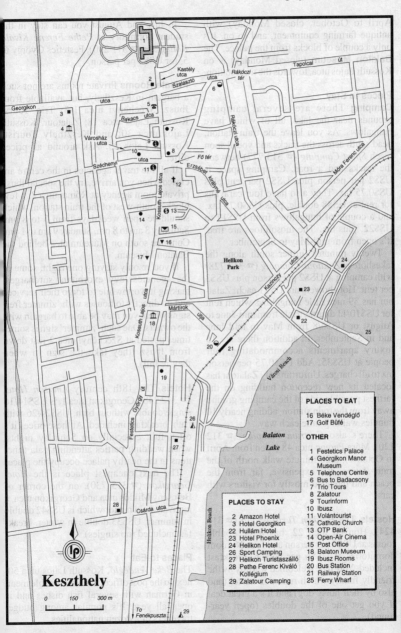

Keszthely

0   150   300 m

To
Fenékpuszta

PLACES TO EAT

16 Béke Vendéglő
17 Golf Büfé

OTHER

1   Festetics Palace
4   Georgikon Manor
    Museum
5   Telephone Centre
6   Bus to Badacsony
7   Trio Tours
8   Zalatour
9   Tourinform
10 Ibusz
11 Volántourist
12 Catholic Church
13 OTP Bank
14 Open-Air Cinema
15 Post Office
18 Balaton Museum
19 Ibusz Rooms
20 Bus Station
21 Railway Station
25 Ferry Wharf

PLACES TO STAY

2   Amazon Hotel
3   Hotel Georgikon
22 Hullám Hotel
23 Hotel Phoenix
24 Helikon Hotel
26 Sport Camping
27 Helikon Turistaszálló
28 Pethe Ferenc Kiváló
    Kollégium
29 Zalatour Camping

Balaton
Lake

Kastély
utca
Rákóczi
tér
Szalasztó   utca
Tapolcai   út

Georgikon   utca

Bakacs   utca

Városház
utca

Széchenyi   utca

Fő tér

Erzsébet királyné utca

Móra Ferenc utca

Kossuth Lajos utca

Rákóczi utca

Helikon
Park

Kazinczy   utca

Mártírok

útja

Városi Beach

Festetics   György   út

Kossuth Lajos utca

Csárda   utca

Helikon Beach

HUNGARY

April to October, closed Monday) with antique farming equipment, and so on. It's only a couple of blocks from the palace. The **Balaton Museum** (closed Monday) is on Kossuth Lajos utca, towards the train station.

Places to Stay

Camping There are several camping grounds near the lake, all of which have bungalows. As you leave the train station, head south across the tracks and you'll soon reach *Sport Camping* (☎ 313 777) between the tracks and a road. Camping space is US$2 per person plus US$2 per tent plus US$0.75 tax. They also have four caravans for rent at US$8 double, plus US$0.75 tax, and a couple of bungalows from US$17 to US$22, plus tax. The mosquitoes are free. It's open from mid-May to September.

Twenty minutes further south along the lakeshore is *Zalatour Camping* (☎ 312 728) with camping at US$2 per person plus US$3 per tent. Hot showers are US$1 each. Zalatour has 39 nice little bungalows which rent for US$10/11 double/triple from mid-June to August or US$6/8 from May to mid-June and in September. In addition there are 15 luxury apartments accommodating four people at US$35. Add US$0.75 per person tax to all charges. Unfortunately Zalatour has located its new reception building on the farthest possible side of the camping ground away from the train station, adding nearly 10 minutes walking time each way.

There's also *Castrum Camping* (☎ 312 120), Móra Ferenc utca 48 (open from April to October), a 20-minute walk north of the train station. It's expensive, far from the beach and intended mostly for visitors with cars.

Hostels The *Helikon Turistaszálló* (☎ 311 424), Honvéd utca 22, has three double rooms at US$7 per person and four 16-room dormitories at US$6 per person, breakfast included. You'll be welcomed warmly by the friendly family which runs this hostel (and also by their noisy dog) and it's a great deal if you get one of the doubles (open year-round).

In July and August you can stay in the student dormitory at *Pethe Ferenc Kiváló Kollégium* (☎ 311 290), Festetics György út 5, for US$5 per person.

Private Rooms Private rooms are not such a bargain in Keszthely, but available from Ibusz, Széchenyi utca 1-3; Trio Tours, Kossuth Lajos utca 18; Zalatour, Kossuth Lajos utca 30; and Keszthely Tourist, Kossuth Lajos utca 25. Ask around as prices differ.

If all the travel agencies in the centre are closed when you arrive, try the special Ibusz private room agency at Római utca 2, a few blocks south-west of the train station, which should be open weekdays from 5 to 8 pm, Saturday 8 am to 8 pm, Sunday 9 am to 1 pm. Continue south on Múzeum utca behind the Balaton Museum.

If you're only staying one night, some of the agencies levy exorbitant surcharges, making it worthwhile to forgo their services and go directly to houses with 'zimmer frei' signs where you may be able to bargain with the owners. One such 'zimmer' sign is sometimes posted at Széchényi utca 2 just down from Ibusz (they take the sign in when they're full).

Hotels The 18th century *Amazon Hotel* (☎ 312 248), Georgikon utca 1, is US$14/16 single/double without bath, US$24/26 with bath, breakfast included. At these prices it's often full, especially on Saturday nights, when wedding parties attending gala functions in the nearby palace occupy the place.

The next cheapest place is the *Hotel Georgikon* (☎ 315 730), on the corner of Bercsény Miklós utca and Georgikon utca, a renovated old manor which is US$42 double in summer, US$33 double in winter, breakfast included (no singles).

Places to Eat

The *Béke Vendéglő*, Kossuth Lajos utca 50, next to the post office, has a reasonable menu in German with several fish dishes and is open all year. It's popular among budget travellers of a dozen nationalities.

The *Golf Büfé*, Kossuth Lajos utca 95, serves grilled meats and pizza. They're only open in the evening after 6 pm and it's something of a youth hang-out. *Easy Rider*, Kossuth Lajos utca 79, also puts out a good beat in the evening.

For real oven-baked pizza and draught beer try *Pizzeria da Francesco*, Szabad nép utca 4 (the backstreet directly behind the main Ibusz office). In recent years da Francesco has become very touristy; colour photos of their offerings are displayed on boards outside without prices.

The *Bár Piccolo*, Szabad nép utca 9 near da Francesco, is just the place to stumble into after dinner, but watch the killer last step!

Entertainment

On Sunday at 8.30 pm from July to mid-August you can see Hungarian folk dancing in the back courtyard at the *Folk Centrum*, Kossuth Lajos utca 28.

Keszthely's top disco is *Club of Colours*, Sömögye dülő 1, three km east of the centre on the road to Badacsony. From mid-June to the end of August it's open nightly from 9 pm to 4 am; the rest of the year, Saturday only (US$2 cover).

Getting There & Away

Keszthely is on a branch line between Tapolca and Balatonszentgyörgy, so railway service is poor. Occasional fast trains arrive from Budapest-Déli (190 km, three hours) via Siófok. For Pécs take a train to Kaposvár, then change to a bus.

The morning train service from Keszthely to Szombathely involves changing trains at Tapolca and Celldömölk but the connections are good. At Tapolca you must go to the ticket window to get a compulsory seat reservation for the Celldömölk-Szombathely leg.

To go to Croatia, take a bus or train to Nagykanizsa where you'll find unreserved local trains to Varaždin (72 km, 1½ hours) twice a day, and buses direct to Zagreb (176 km, US$7), also twice a day.

A bus station with services to most of western Transdanubia adjoins the train station. Some buses for southern Transdanubia leave from in front of the Catholic church in the centre of town, so check carefully. The bus to Badacsony (marked Badacsonytomaj at the stop) leaves seven times a day from Szalasztó utca 20. Always scrutinise the yellow sign boards at the stops and be aware of footnotes. The office marked 'Váró' at Volántourist, Kossuth Lajos utca 43, has information on buses.

From the bus station in front of the Catholic church you can get buses to Budapest (185 km), Szombathely (106 km), Győr, Pécs (158 km) and Sopron (141 km), but most leave only in the very early morning. Buses to Hévíz (six km) from stand No 4 here are frequent. Buses to Sopron and Szombathely leave from the bus station next to the train station around noon.

Mahart ferries travel to Badacsony from June to mid-September. In July and August these boats continue on to Siófok.

HÉVÍZ

In a country with 1500 thermal baths there just had to be a real thermal lake. Lake Gyógy, the second-largest warm-water lake in the world, averages 30°C at the surface and red Indian water lilies blossom in it in summer. Eighty million litres of thermal water gush daily from a depth of one km at a rate of 1000 litres or one cubic metre a second, flushing the lake completely every two days. Radioactive mud from the lake bed is effective in the treatment of locomotor disorders. In winter the steaming waters, which never fall below 24°C, seem almost surreal.

Wooden catwalks have been built over the lake, allowing you to swim in comfort. The **lake baths** (*tófürdő*) are open all year from 8.30 am to 5.30 pm (admission US$2 for three hours, US$3 for all day). A 20-minute massage costs US$7 and a cabin US$2. The indoor **thermal baths** next to the lake function all year from 7 am to 4 pm daily. If you're addicted to the drinking cure, you can get a free fill-up here, but bring a cup.

Post & Telecommunications The post

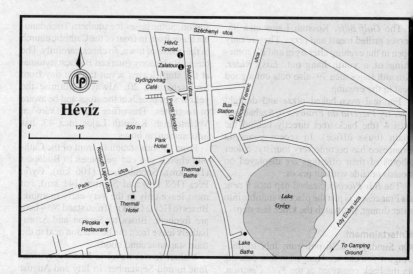

office is on Kossuth Lajos utca near the corner of Széchenyi utca and there are lots of public phones in front of the building.

Places to Stay

The hotels of Hévíz cater mostly to Austrians on short trips who can afford to pay premium prices, or to people on packaged health tours. The camping ground is designed for motorists who pay a flat fee to occupy a large area, a system that works to the disadvantage of backpackers. The restaurants and cafés are also very touristy, so you're far better off staying in Keszthely, six km east, and visiting Hévíz for the day.

If you're determined to stay, your best bet is to visit the agencies renting private rooms, including Hévíztourist and Zalatour, both on Rákóczi utca, or Zala Volántourist in the bus station. Many houses with 'zimmer frei' signs are along Kossuth Lajos utca though you may have to shop around for a good deal.

If you do want to stay at a Hévíz resort for a few days it's cheaper to book ahead through Danubius Travels, Szervita tér 8, Budapest. They have all-inclusive one-week packages at Hotel Thermál which are much cheaper than paying as you go.

Getting There & Away

Hévíz doesn't have a train station, but a bus goes to Keszthely (six km, 30 minutes) almost every half-hour and there are occasional services to Szombathely. Buses run to Badacsony twice daily, to Balatonfüred (73 km) three times daily, to Budapest (191 km) four times daily, to Pécs (164 km) twice daily and to Székesfehérvár (133 km) twice daily. There's no left-luggage office at the bus station.

Southern Transdanubia

Southern Transdanubia close to Croatia is characterised by rolling, forested hills and an almost Mediterranean climate. Near Mohács on the Danube in 1526 the Hungarian armies under King Louis II were routed by a vastly superior Ottoman force. As a result the gracious southern city of Pécs still bears the imprint of 150 years of Turkish rule. The good facilities in Pécs make it a perfect base for day trips to Siklós castles, the spas of Harkány and Sikonda, and hiking trails through the Mecsek Hills. Many people in transit between Croatia and Yugoslavia pass through here.

PÉCS

Pécs (Fünfkirchen), a large historical city in southern Hungary that lies between the Danube and Drava rivers, is the seat of Baranya County. The fine position on the southern slopes of the Mecsek Hills gives Pécs a relatively mild climate and the red-tiled roofs of the houses accentuate its Mediterranean flavour. Zsolnay porcelain and Pannónia champagne are made here. A less appealing activity is the uranium mining on the slopes just north-east of town.

For 400 years Sopianae (Pécs) was the capital of the Roman province of Lower Pannonia. Early Christianity flourished here in the 4th century and by the 9th century the town was known as 'Quinque Ecclesiae' for its five churches. In 1009 Stephen I, Hungary's first king, made Pécs a bishopric. The first Hungarian university (and the sixth in Europe) was founded here in 1367 and the city's humanistic traditions climaxed with the poet Janus Pannonius. City walls were erected after the Tatar invasion of 1241, but 1543 marked the start of 150 years of Turkish rule. The Turks left their greatest monuments in Pécs and these, together with imposing churches and a synagogue, over a dozen museums, possibilities for hiking through the Mecsek Hills, varied excursions and lively student atmosphere, make Pécs the perfect place to spend a couple of days. A direct rail link with Zagreb makes Pécs an excellent gateway city to/from Croatia.

Orientation

The bus and train stations are about three blocks apart on the southern side of the town centre. Find your way north to Széchenyi tér where 12 streets meet. Numerous city buses also run up this way (ask).

The left-luggage office in the main train station is in an obscure building at the far west end of platform No 1. The left-luggage office at the bus station closes at 6 pm, whereas the one at the train station is open around the clock.

Information

Tourinform, Széchenyi tér 9, has information on other parts of Hungary as well as Pécs and the staff are good about answering questions.

The Magyar Autóklub (☎ 324 729) is at Ferencesek utca 22.

Money The OTP Bank, Király utca 11, opposite the National Theatre (Monday to Wednesday 7.45 am to 3 pm, Thursday 9.15 am to 5.30 pm, Friday 7.45 am to 2 pm), changes travellers' cheques.

Post & Telecommunications The main post office is at Jókai Mór utca 10. You can make international telephone calls from there. Pécs's telephone code is 72.

Travel Agencies Advance train tickets and reservations are available at the MÁV ticket office, Rákóczi út 39/c.

Bookshops Corvina on Ferencesek utca between Széchenyi and Jókai squares has one of the best selections of books in English you'll find in Hungary.

Things to See

Széchenyi tér is the bustling heart of Pécs, dominated on the north by the former **Mosque of Gazi Kassim Pasha**, the largest Turkish building in Hungary. Now a Catholic church, Islamic elements such as the mihrab, a prayer niche on the south-eastern side, are easy to distinguish. Behind the ex-mosque is the **Archaeological Museum** with exhibits from prehistory up to the Magyar conquest. Informative summaries in English and German are displayed in each room.

From this museum go west along Janus Pannonius utca for a block to the **Csontváry Museum**, Janus Pannonius utca 11, dedicated to the surrealist painter-philosopher Tivadar Csontváry (1853-1919). His painting of the ruins of Baalbek, Lebanon (1905) is a masterpiece. On the corner opposite this museum is a good little wine cellar that is in front of the men's toilets.

HUNGARY

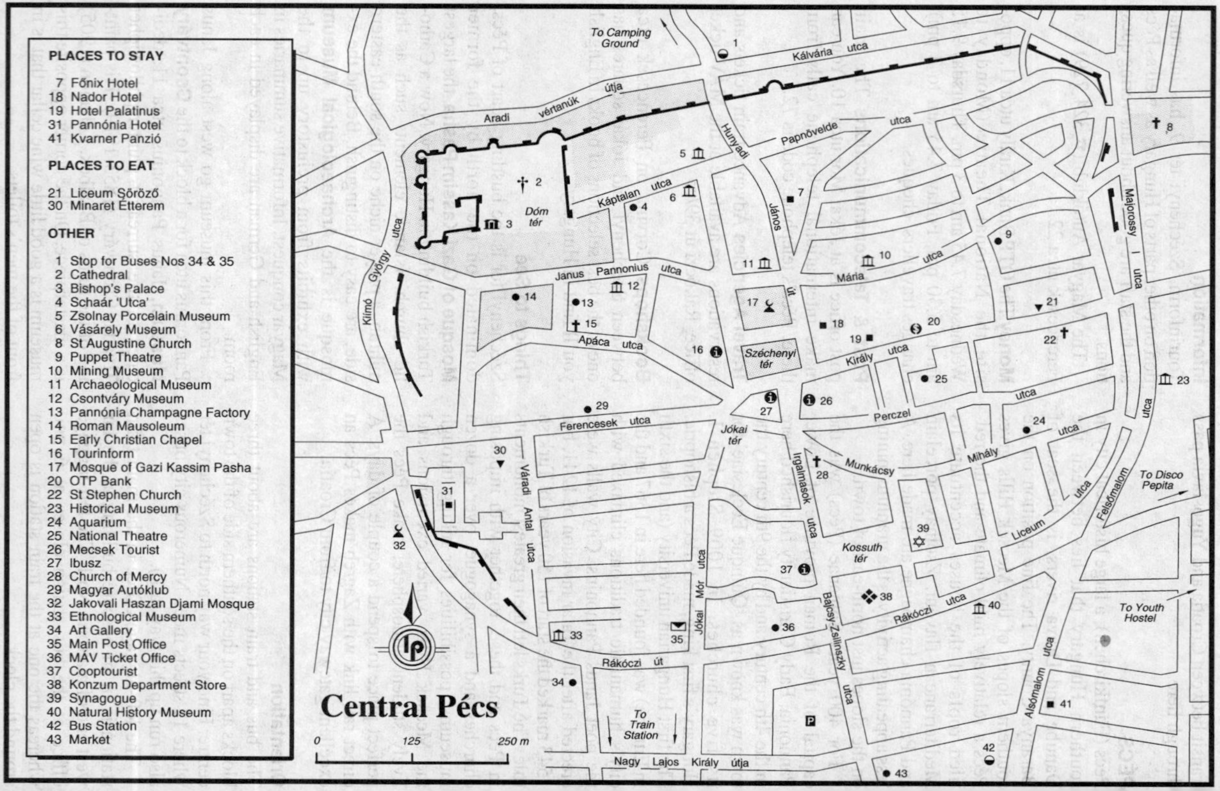

PLACES TO STAY
7 Főnix Hotel
18 Nador Hotel
19 Hotel Palatinus
31 Pannónia Hotel
41 Kvarner Panzió
PLACES TO EAT
21 Liceum Söröző
30 Minaret Étterem
OTHER
1 Stop for Buses Nos 34 & 35
2 Cathedral
3 Bishop's Palace
4 Schaár 'Utca'
5 Zsolnay Porcelain Museum
6 Vásárely Museum
8 St Augustine Church
9 Puppet Theatre
10 Mining Museum
11 Archaeological Museum
12 Csontváry Museum
13 Pannónia Champagne Factory
14 Roman Mausoleum
15 Early Christian Chapel
16 Tourinform
17 Mosque of Gazi Kassim Pasha
20 OTP Bank
22 St Stephen Church
23 Historical Museum
24 Aquarium
25 National Theatre
26 Mecsek Tourist
27 Ibusz
28 Church of Mercy
29 Magyar Autóklub
32 Jakovali Haszan Djami Mosque
33 Ethnological Museum
34 Art Gallery
35 Main Post Office
36 MÁV Ticket Office
37 Cooptourist
38 Konzum Department Store
39 Synagogue
40 Natural History Museum
42 Bus Station
43 Market
Central Pécs
0
125
250 m
To Camping Ground
Kálvária utca
Aradi vértanúk útja
Papnövelde utca
Hunyadi
Káptalan utca
Dóm tér
Klimó György utca
Janus Pannonius utca
János
Mária utca
Apáca utca
Széchenyi tér
Király utca
Perczel utca
Ferencesek utca
Jókai tér
Munkácsy
Mihály utca
Irgalmasok utca
Kossuth tér
Liceum utca
Felsőmalom
To Disco Pepita
Majorossy utca
Váradi Antal utca
Jókai Mór utca
Bajcsy-Zsilinszky utca
Rákóczi utca
Rákóczi út
To Youth Hostel
Alsómalom utca
To Train Station
Nagy Lajos Király útja

Káptalan utca, which climbs east from here, is lined with museums. In a separate pavilion behind the **Endre Nemes Museum**, Káptalan utca 5, is the Erzsébet Schaár *Utca* or 'Street', a complete artistic environment in which the sculptor has set her whole life in stone. The **Vásárely Museum**, Káptalan utca 3, has 150 original examples of op art. Victor Vásárely, a longtime resident of southern France, was born in this house in 1908. Across the street is the **Zsolnay Porcelain Museum**, Káptalan utca 2, which has mostly Art-Nouveau pieces (captions are in German). A room downstairs in the same building contains sculptures by Amerigo Tot.

Return to Szent István tér and the tremendous four-towered **cathedral** (admission costs US$0.50). The oldest part of the building is the 11th century crypt, but the entire complex was rebuilt in a neo-Romanesque style in 1881. In summer there are organ concerts in the cathedral on Friday evenings. Behind the **bishop's palace** (1770), next to the cathedral (and with a metallic statue of Franz Liszt leaning over the balcony), is a 15th century **barbican** that remains from the old city walls.

In the centre of the southern portion of Szent István tér is an excavated 4th century Roman Christian **mausoleum** with striking frescoes of Adam and Eve, and Daniel in the lion's den, certainly a remarkable sight that is unique in central Europe. Nearby at Apáca utca 14 are the ruins of a 4th century Early Christian chapel. It's only open in summer but you can enter the courtyard and peek in through the windows any time.

On the east side of Szent István tér is the **Pannónia champagne factory** with a sales room just inside where you can purchase bottles of all the local wines and champagnes. It's possible to visit the factory and cellars if you come in the morning.

Follow your map south-west a few blocks from Szent István tér to the 16th century **Jakovali Haszan Djami Mosque**, at Rákóczi út 2 (closed Wednesday), the best preserved Turkish monument in Hungary. Also known as the Little Mosque, the build-ing and minaret are perfectly preserved and now form part of a museum of Turkish culture.

After seeing the Little Mosque, follow Péc's most enjoyable pedestrian malls, Ferencesek utca and Király utca, east across the city. You'll pass three beautiful old churches and the ornate **National Theatre** (check for performances). Just beyond the **St Stephen Church** (1741), Király utca 44/a, turn right to Felsőmalom utca 9, where you'll find an excellent **Historical Museum** that will sum up all you've seen.

Visitors to the **synagogue** (1869) on Kossuth tér are offered an informative text on the Jewish faith in a choice of languages (open from May to October, closed Saturday).

All of Pécs' museums except for the Little Mosque and the synagogue are closed on Monday.

Mecsek Hills Every visitor should take a trip up into the Mecsek Hills. Bus No 35 from stand No 2 in front of the train station climbs hourly to the 194-metre **TV tower** on Misina Peak (534 metres). You could also take bus No 35 from Hunyadi út just outside the city wall. There's a restaurant below the viewing balcony high up in the TV tower (open daily) which offers panoramic views. If you order something there, check the prices on the menu beforehand. The observation platform offers an unobstructed view as there is no glass. Bus No 35 also goes past Pécs' **zoo** (open daily all year from 9 am to 6 pm).

There are numerous well-marked hiking trails that fan out from the TV tower. Pick up the 1:40,000 *A Mecsek* topographical map which shows them all. Armed with this map, you could also take a bus from Pécs Bus Station to Orfű (with an attractive lake) or Abaliget (with a large cave) and hike back over the hills. Much of this area has been logged over but doesn't attract nearly as many visitors and you might even see some deer.

Szigetvár Another easy day trip from Pécs by train or bus is to Szigetvár, 33 km west,

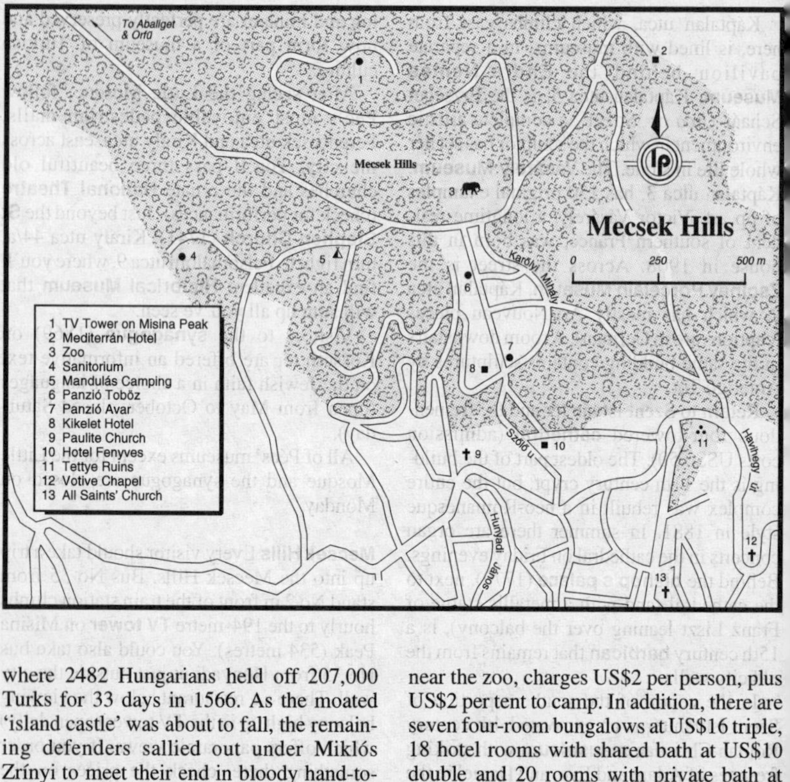

To Abaliget & Orfű
Mecsek Hills
Mecsek Hills
0 250 500 m
Károlyi Mihály
Szőlő u
Havihegy út
Hunyadi János
1 TV Tower on Misina Peak
2 Mediterrán Hotel
3 Zoo
4 Sanitorium
5 Mandulás Camping
6 Panzió Toböz
7 Panzió Avar
8 Kikelet Hotel
9 Paulite Church
10 Hotel Fenyves
11 Tettye Ruins
12 Votive Chapel
13 All Saints' Church

where 2482 Hungarians held off 207,000 Turks for 33 days in 1566. As the moated 'island castle' was about to fall, the remaining defenders sallied out under Miklós Zrínyi to meet their end in bloody hand-to-hand combat. The Turks suffered tremendous losses, including that of Sultan Süleyman I, and their march on Vienna was halted.

Szigetvár's **fortress** (1420) with its four corner bastions contains a museum that focuses on the 1566 battle (open all year from 10 am to 3 pm, closed Monday). Inside the museum is a mosque built soon after the fall of Szigetvár in honour of the sultan. Of the minaret, only the base remains. A second mosque, the **Ali Pasha Mosque** (1569), now a Catholic church, is in the centre of town.

Places to Stay

Camping *Mandulás Camping* (☎ 315 981), Ángyán János utca 2, up in the Mecsek Hills near the zoo, charges US$2 per person, plus US$2 per tent to camp. In addition, there are seven four-room bungalows at US$16 triple, 18 hotel rooms with shared bath at US$10 double and 20 rooms with private bath at US$16/21 single/double. Take bus No 34 right to the door or bus No 35 to the zoo and then walk five minutes to the camping ground (open from mid-April to mid-October).

Hostels In July and August, *Szalay László Kivalo College*, Universitas út 2, accommodates students and YHA members in three-bed dorms at US$5 per person. Go straight to the hostel, a 10-minute walk north-east of the bus station. If they can't accommodate you try *Szent Mór Kollégium*, 48-as tér 4, two blocks back towards the bus station (July and August only).

Express, Bajcsy-Zsilinszky utca 6 near the bus station, knows of other hostels around town.

Private Rooms Mecsek Tourist and Ibusz, two offices that arrange private rooms, face one another at the southern end of Széchenyi tér. Cooptourist, Irgalmasok utcája 22, has more expensive private rooms. These offices close at 4 pm Monday to Thursday and 2 pm Friday, and they don't open on weekends. Unless you stay four nights there's a 30% surcharge on the first night. A tax of US$0.75 per person per night is charged on accommodation in the centre of town (US$0.50 outside the centre), but there's no tax on the first night.

Tourinform, Széchenyi tér 9, can book rooms at hotels and pensions.

Hotels *Kvarner Panzió* (☎ 326 495), Somogyi Béla utca 1, has a very convenient location diagonally opposite the bus station and its prices are also good: US$18 double with shower. There are only a few rooms but if you arrive by bus it only takes a few minutes to try for one. Ask to see the room.

The *Főnix Hotel* (☎ 311 680), Hunyadi János út 2, is a small, modern hotel where singles/doubles/triples with bath cost US$23/34/41, breakfast included. Their restaurant is good.

An excellent place to stay in Pécs is the *Hotel Laterum* (☎ 315 829), Hajnóczy utca 37-39, on the far west side of town. Take bus No 4 from the train station or the market on Bajcsy-Zsilinszky utca near the bus station to the end of the line at Uránváros. From the stop, the green four-storey hotel is visible behind an Afor petrol station. Rooms with shared bath are US$6 per person, with private bath US$8.50 per person, and there's an inexpensive self-service restaurant just off the hotel lobby. Most of the guests are Hungarian workers or student groups but tourists are welcome. Beware of rooms on the west side of the building which face the noisy disco above the restaurant.

Several slightly up-market places to stay are up near the TV tower. The *Hotel Kikelet* (☎ 310 777), Károlyi Mihály utca 1, a former trade union resort still frequented by large numbers of holidaying Hungarians, has rooms without bath at US$13 per person,

with bath at US$21 per person, breakfast included. Because the Kikelet charges per person it's a good bet if you're alone. Buses Nos 34 and 35 run direct to Hotel Kikelet from stand No 2 at the train station. Bus No 34 goes on to the camping ground, while bus No 35 continues to the TV tower.

The 18-room, two-star *Hotel Fenyves* (☎ 315 996), Szőlő utca 64, has a great view of the city (US$21/27 single/double with bath and breakfast). Take bus No 34 or 35 to Hotel Kikelet, then walk down to the hotel.

Tourinform on Széchenyi tér can book you into the *Panzió Toboz* (☎ 325 232), Fenyves sor 5, a clean modern pension just up the street from Hotel Kikelet. Double rooms with bath are US$28, breakfast included.

If you want to stay at the best hotel in Pécs, choose the fine old *Hotel Palatinus* (☎ 433 022), Király utca 5, where a double room with private bath and breakfast will cost US$58 (no singles). It's good for a splurge.

Places to Eat

One of the nicest places in town is *Minaret Étterem*, Ferencesek utca 35, which serves inexpensive meals in the pleasant courtyard of the old Franciscan monastery (1738).

Liceum Söröző, through the back courtyard at Király utca 35, also offers reasonable meals and its draught beer prices are good.

Fiaker Vendéglő, Felsőmalom utca 7 next door to the Historical Museum, is an unpretentious wine cellar with moderate meal prices and a few vegetarian selections such as mushroom stew (gombapörkölt).

A good local restaurant with table service and prices half those charged in the centre is *Csillag Vendéglő*, Hungária utca 27 (a westward continuation of Ferencesek utca). The menu is translated into German.

The local beer is called 'Szalon sör'.

Entertainment

Pécs has famous opera and ballet companies. If you're told that tickets to the *National Theatre* on Király utca are sold out, try for a cancellation at the box office an hour before the performance. This theatre is closed all summer so ask Tourinform about concerts and other events.

The Cultural Centre or *Művészetek Háza*, Széchenyi tér 7-8 behind Ibusz, advertises its programmes outside. This is the place to ask about Philharmonia concerts (which only occur once or twice a month).

One of Pécs' most popular discos is *Club Pepita* next to the Tennis Club off Zsolnay Vilmos út on the east side of town (Tuesday, Thursday, Friday and Saturday from 9 pm). You can walk here from the centre in about 15 minutes.

Getting There & Away

Express trains run regularly to Budapest-Déli (229 km, three hours) and one early morning express goes to Szombathely (via Gyékényes). Some trains to Budapest carry compulsory seat reservations.

Daily buses departing from Pécs include two to Hévíz (164 km), seven to Kaposvár (67 km), two to Kecskemét (176 km), hourly to Siklós (32 km), three to Siófok (122 km), one to Sopron (287 km) and six to Szeged (189 km, four hours). The bus is more direct than the train on all these routes.

Croatia-bound, a daily train runs between Pécs and Zagreb (267 km, five hours, US$16), leaving Pécs in the very early morning and Zagreb in the late afternoon. Buses run five times a day from Barcs to Zagreb (202 km, US$14) and there are also two afternoon buses a day from Pécs to Osijek (US$6 or DM10 in cash – pay the driver).

HARKÁNY

The hot springs at Harkány, 26 km south of Pécs, feature medicinal waters with the richest sulphuric content in Hungary. There's a large open-air thermal pool and you can also receive a mud bath which is said to alleviate various obscure afflictions. The baths are open to the public daily year-round.

Harkány is a major transit point for people travelling between Croatia and Yugoslavia. The Drávaszabolcs/Donji Miholjac border crossing to/from Croatia is just eight km south of the town.

Information

Both Mecsek Tourist and Ibusz have offices at the entrance to the baths on Bajcsy-Zsilinszky utca, just up from the bus station.

The left-luggage office at the bus station is open Monday to Thursday from 8 am to 4 pm, Friday from 8 am to 2 pm.

Money The OTP Bank has a kiosk between the bus station and the baths changing travellers' cheques weekdays from 7.45 am to 3.30 pm (open May to September only).

Numerous individuals on the street near the bus station offer to change money, an indication of the proximity of Yugoslavia.

Places to Stay & Eat

Both Mecsek Tourist and Ibusz rent private rooms but for a one-night stay you may be better going to a hotel.

The *Baranya Hotel* (☎ 380 160), Bajcsy-Zsilinszky utca 5 opposite the baths, has doubles with shared bath at US$16, breakfast included (no singles). It's popular among transients from ex-Yugoslavia.

Before checking in at the Baranya check out the adjacent three-storey *Hotel Napsugár* (☎ 380 300), Bajcsy-Zsilinszky utca 7, which looks expensive but has 42 rooms at US$13/18 single/double with bath and breakfast.

Another block down the road is *Thermál Camping* (☎ 380 117), Bajscy-Zsilinszky utca 4. Camping here is US$3 per person plus US$3 per tent, and they also have 20 hotel-style rooms with shared bath at US$13 double, 26 rooms with private bath at US$19 double and 21 four-person bungalows with bath and kitchen at US$38 (open from mid-April to mid-October).

Getting There & Away

All buses between Pécs and Siklós stop here. Four buses a day link Harkány to Croatia, two to Osijek (87 km) and one each to Našice (71 km) and Slavonski Brod (125 km). Three buses a day run from Harkány to Belgrade (US$19). Since the border between Croatia and Yugoslavia closed in 1991, numerous travellers from former Yugoslavia have used Harkány as a transit point.

SIKLÓS

Siklós, south of the red wine-producing Villány Hills and six km east of Harkány, is the southernmost town in Hungary. On a hill top overlooking the surrounding farmland stands a well-preserved 15th century **castle**, the only one in Hungary continuously in use since the Middle Ages, now a museum (open daily except Monday year-round). A section of the museum is dedicated to the 1848 Revolution and especially to the progressive lord of Siklós Castle, Casimir Batthyány, who freed his serfs in 1847. The tomb of this gentleman may be seen in the castle's Gothic chapel. There's also a small but excellent collection of 19th century costumes.

Place to Stay & Eat

The *Hotel Központi* (☎ 352 513), Kossuth tér 4, just below the castle, is an old hotel with adequate rooms with shared bath at US$6 per person. The hotel restaurant is also reasonable.

The hotel and hostel in the castle itself have closed.

Getting There & Away

Siklós is connected to Pécs (32 km) by hourly bus (via Harkány), which makes it an easy day trip from Pécs.

The bus and train stations are on opposite sides of Siklós, each about a 10-minute walk from the castle which is visible from afar.

The Great Plain

South-eastern Hungary, the Great Plain (Nagyalföld), is a wide expanse of level puszta (prairie) drained by the Tisza River. This rich farming area bears barley, corn, oats, potatoes, rye, sugar beet and wheat. Perhaps no other region of Hungary has a place in Hungarian folklore like the Great Plain. The poet Sándor Petőfi wrote of the puszta: *Börtönéböl szabadult sas lelkem, Ha*

a rónak végtelenjét látom (that his soul soars like an eagle released from a cage, every time he sees this endless plain). In the blazing heat of summer many have witnessed mirages shimmering over the blonde plains.

Visitors to the region are introduced to the lore of the Hungarian cowboys and their long-horned grey cattle or the nomadic shepherds and their tiny sheepdogs. Two national parks, Kiskunság in the Bugac puszta and Hortobágy in the Hortobágy puszta, preserve this unique environment. Kecskemét, Szeged and Debrecen are centres of the western, southern and eastern puszta.

KECSKEMÉT

Exactly halfway between Budapest and Szeged, near the geographical centre of Hungary, Kecskemét is a clean, healthy city famous for its potent *barack pálinka* (apricot brandy) and level puszta. It's known as the garden city of Hungary for the million fruit trees in the surrounding area; wine is also produced. Bács-Kiskun County is administered from here. Among Kecskemét's most renowned native sons are József Katona (1791-1830), author of the historical play *Bánk bán*, and the composer Zoltán Kodály (1882-1967).

Orientation & Information

The adjacent bus and train stations are on the north-eastern side of town. The left-luggage office at the train station is open from 7 am to 7 pm. From the train station follow the yellow brick pavement of Nagykőrösi utca to Szabadság tér and Kossuth tér, the centre of town.

Pusztatourist is between Szabadság tér and Kossuth tér. Express is upstairs at Dobó István körút 11.

The Magyar Autóklub (☎ 482 188) is at Jász utca 26.

Money The OTP Bank, Szabadság tér 5 next to the former synagogue (Monday to Wednesday from 7.45 am to 3.30 pm, Thursday 7.45 am to 4.30 pm, Friday 7.45 am to 1 pm), changes travellers' cheques without commission.

HUNGARY

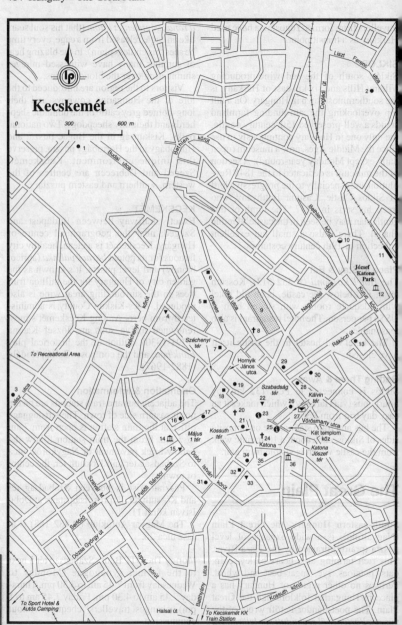

Kecskemét

0   300   600 m

Post & Telecommunications The main post office on Katona József tér is open weekdays from 8 am to 7 pm, Saturday from 8 am to 2 pm and holidays from 8 am to noon. This is the best place from which to make international telephone calls. Kecskemét's telephone code is 76.

Things to See
Kossuth tér is surrounded by historic build-ings. Dominating the square is a massive Art-Nouveau **town hall** (1897) with a caril-lon that 'gives concerts' every hour on the hour. Half hidden among the bushes right in front of the town hall is a split stone cube bearing the inscription 'here broke the heart of Kecskemét's most famous son', for on this spot in April 1830 playwright József Katona died of a heart attack. Also in front of the town hall is a statue of the 19th century politician Lajos Kossuth, who led the strug-gle for independence from Austria, and a monument bearing the distances to towns everywhere in Hungary.

Flanking the town hall are two fine churches: the neoclassical **Old Church** (1806) and the earlier **St Miklós Church** with a Baroque calvary (1790) before the door. Close by on Katona József tér is the magnificent **Katona József Theatre** (1896) with a Baroque statue of the Trinity (1742) standing in front of it.

Of the many other museums and art gal-leries around Kecskemét, the most interesting is the **Museum of Naive Artists** (closed Monday) in the 'Stork House' (1730), surrounded by a high white wall just off Petőfi Sándor utca. In the art gallery directly below the museum one can purchase original paintings almost as good as those on display upstairs at very reasonable prices. Next to this museum is a toy museum with all the pieces jumbled together in imagina-tive displays.

Places to Stay
Camping *Autós Camping* (☎ 329 358) is on Sport utca, on the south-western side of Kecskemét, nearly five km from the train station. City Busz No 101 and Volán buses Nos 1 and 11 run there from the train station. Camping costs US$2 per person plus US$2.50 per tent and there are 25 neat little bungalows with cooking facilities and cold showers at US$23 for up to four people. The restaurant here is good. Adjacent to the camping ground is an attractive public swim-ming pool (often empty) surrounded by manicured lawns. The camping ground is open from mid-April to mid-October.

Hostels About three blocks from the camping ground is Kecskemét's youth hostel, the *Gémpari és Automatizálási Műszaki Főiskola* or 'GAMP' (☎ 321 916), Izsáki út 10. A bed in a four-bedded room here is US$3. Officially it's only open in July and August but you can sometimes get in during other months. Buses Nos 1 and 11 from the train station run directly to this pleasant university complex south of the centre.

In summer you may be able to get a room in the *Tanítóképző Főiskola Lőveiklára Kollégiuma* (☎ 321 977), Jókai tér 4. In fact, it's worth trying this eight-storey student dormitory right in the centre of town any time – you could be lucky.

Private Rooms Pusztatourist (☎ 483 493), opposite the town hall on Kossuth tér (closed weekends) charges US$12 single or double for a private room for one night. Cooptourist, Ket templom köz 9, is slightly cheaper with singles for US$10. Also try Ibusz on Széchenyi tér opposite the Aranyhomok Hotel.

Hotels *Color Panzió* (☎ 324 901), Jókai utca 26, is a small pension with rooms above a chemist's at US$21 double (no singles).

Caissa Panzió (☎ 481 685), Gyenes tér 18, 5th floor, has 11 rooms varying in price from US$12/16 single/double without bath to US$20/26 with bath. Two larger rooms for up to five people are also available. The location is excellent so it's always worth a try.

The 45-room *Hotel Három Gúnár* (☎ 483 611), Batthyány utca 3, is expensive at US$32/38 single/double with bath and breakfast, but it has a certain charm and is minutes from the centre of town. A bowling alley and bar are in the hotel basement.

Two blocks south of the 'GAMP' youth hostel is the *Sport Szálló* (☎ 323 090), Izsáki út 15/a, a neat two-storey hotel with rooms with bath at US$20 single or double.

Places to Eat
If all you want is a fast feed the *Szalag*

Ételbár, Petőfi Sándor utca 1, can provide it. Otherwise, eat elsewhere.

The *Jalta Restaurant*, Batthyány utca 2, right opposite the Hotel Három Gúnár, is a rather homy wine cellar with a menu in English and German. Their speciality is grilled meat and they have Kaiser beer on tap.

The *Kisbugaci csárda*, Munkácsy utca 10, serves regional dishes.

To taste the local wines go through the door marked *Borozó* at Rákóczi út 3 and take your choice from the row of pitchers on the counter. The price shown is for a litre and if you point to the smallest wine glass you'll pay a tenth of that. Drinking from these small glasses, you should be able to try all the wines for less than a dollar.

Entertainment
The ticket office of the *Katona József Theatre* on Katona József tér is on the side of the building (open Tuesday to Friday from 10 am to 1 pm and 5 to 7 pm). Operettas are often staged here.

Flash Dance Club on Liszt Ferenc utca north of the train station is a large modern disco open Wednesday to Sunday from 9.30 pm to 5 am. *Club Robinson*, Akadémia körút 2 (closed Monday and Tuesday) is similar.

Galaxis Disco Club, Szilády Károly utca 6, on a back street behind the concert hall (Wednesday to Sunday from 9 pm), isn't nearly as high-tech as the other places but it is a bit cheaper and right in the centre of town.

Getting There & Away
Kecskemét is on the main railway line from Budapest-Nyugati to Szeged.

There are almost hourly buses to Budapest (85 km), every couple of hours to Szeged (86 km) and two a day to Pécs (176 km).

Buses run to Arad, Romania, about four times a week (191 km, US$11), but check with information. The bus to Subotica, Yugoslavia, is twice daily (130 km, US$6), but take the earlier one as the second one scheduled usually arrives from Budapest full. Tickets are available from the drivers.

Getting Around

There are two competing municipal bus systems. City Busz runs pink microbuses and tickets are available from the drivers. The larger Volán buses are about two forint more expensive and you must buy a ticket at a kiosk.

BUGAC

Bugac, an accessible corner of the 306-sq-km Kiskunság National Park south-west of Kecskemét, is a good place to get close to the Great Plain. Great herds of fork-horned Hungarian grey cattle and flocks of twisted-horned sheep (racka), some black, some white, roam across the sandy puszta, while the adjacent juniper forest invites hikers.

Things to See & Do

The Bugaci Csárda, an eight-minute walk from Bugac-Felső Railway Station, is a very touristy folkloric restaurant where there's also a camping ground.

It's three km from the Csárda to Kiskunság National Park and the **Shepherd Museum** (closed from November to March and every Monday). The real reason to come is the **horse shows** which are performed daily at 1 pm in summer and more often when tour groups are present. You'll see real whip-snapping Hungarian cowboys working their horses and exciting 'five-in-hand' riding during which one man makes five horses gallop around a field at full speed while standing on the backs of the rear two horses.

You can see many fine animals in the nearby stables, so Bugac is a must for horse lovers. To get in some horse riding yourself you should make prior arrangements through Bugac Tours, Szabadság tér 1, Kecskemét.

Admission to the park and horse shows is US$1.50. Avoid the 30-minute horse-cart rides which are certainly not worth US$7 per person. The eight-minute helicopter rides are also a rip-off.

Getting There & Away

The fun way to get to Bugac is on the narrow-gauge railway from Kecskemét which rumbles 40 km south between vineyards, sunflower fields and apple orchards. The little carriages have hard wooden seats and a stove for heating in winter. This train departs from Kecskemét KK Railway Station, not the main station. To get there, walk south on Batthyány utca from the Három Gúnár Hotel and continue straight across a large bridge until you see the small station on the right. Get the 7.55 am train which reaches Bugac at around 9 am, but don't get off at Bugacpuszta or Bugac – you want Bugac-Felső. It's best to get the times of trains returning to Kecskemét before setting out as no information is available at Bugac-Felső.

If the return train times are inconvenient, catch a bus from the highway near the Bugaci Csárda to Kiskunfélegyháza (18 km), where there are frequent buses back to Kecskemét.

SZEGED

Szeged (Segedin), the paprika and 'Pick' salami capital of Hungary, straddles the Tisza River just before it enters Yugoslavia. The Maros River from Arad, Romania, enters the Tisza just east of the centre. In March 1879 a great flood burst upon Szeged, damaging almost every building in the city. Afterwards, the city was redesigned with concentric boulevards and radial avenues. Sections of the outer boulevard are named for cities which provided aid after the flood: Vienna, Moscow, London, Paris, Berlin, Brussels and Rome. Szeged is large and lively with lots of students, and in midsummer the city really comes to life for the famous Szeged Festival. It's the seat of Csongrád County and an important gateway to/from Yugoslavia and Romania.

Orientation

The train station is a 15-minute walk south of the centre, and the bus station is 10 minutes west of Széchenyi tér. Tram No 1 connects the train station to town. The left-luggage office at the train station is open from 4 am to 11 pm.

HUNGARY

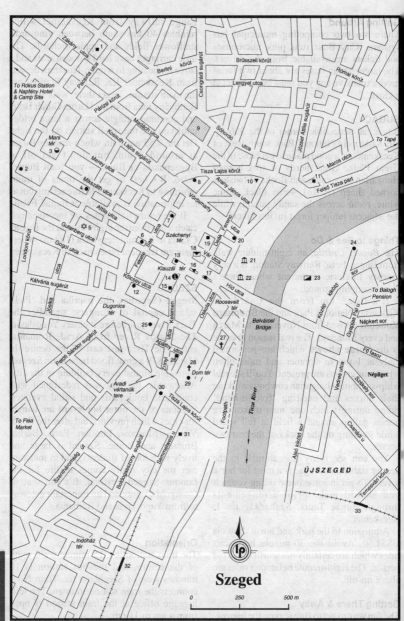

Szeged

0   250   500 m

HUNGARY

PLACES TO STAY

1	Sára Panzió
11	Hotel Hungária
15	Royal Hotel
19	Tisza Hotel
26	Apáthy István College
31	Semmelweis Ignac College

PLACES TO EAT

10	Ciao Pizzeria
16	Étel Bár

OTHER

2	Sing Sing Discoteque
3	Bus Station
4	Magyar Autóklub
5	New Synagogue
6	Express
7	Old Town Hall
8	Public Baths
9	Market
12	Reök Palace
13	Ibusz
14	Szeged Tourist
17	Festival Ticket Office
18	Main Post Office
20	National Theatre
21	City Museum
22	Móra Ferenc Museum
23	Public Swimming Pools
24	Partfürdő
25	University/Jaté Klub
27	Serbian Church
28	Votive Church
29	Site of Summer Festival
30	Heroes Gate
32	Szeged Train Station
33	Újszeged Train Station

Information

Szeged Tourist is at Klauzál tér 7. The Magyar Autóklub is at Bartók tér 6. The Autóklub has a service centre opposite Rókus Railway Station.

Money The OTP Bank, Klauzál tér 5 (Monday from 7.45 am to 4.30 pm, Tuesday to Thursday 7.45 am to 3 pm, Friday 7.45 to 11.30 am), changes travellers' cheques.

Post & Telecommunications A couple of public telephones are in the cramped main post office, Széchenyi tér 1 (weekdays 8 am to 7 pm, Saturday 8 am to 2 pm, Sunday 8 am to noon). Szeged's telephone code is 62.

Things to See

The one sight of Szeged not to be missed is the neo-Byzantine **Votive Church**, built between 1913 and 1930 in remembrance of the 1879 flood. The dome of this huge red-brick structure is 53 metres high, and the twin neo-Romanesque towers soar 92 metres. The church's cavernous interior is covered with frescoes and the organ (1930) has 11,500 pipes.

Beside the church is the 13th century **Demetrius Tower** remaining from the previous church, which was demolished to make room for the present one. The old **Serbian Church** (1745) behind the Votive Church provides a good contrast.

By the Belvárosi Bridge over the Tisza River is the **Móra Ferenc Museum** (closed Monday) in a huge neoclassical building (1896). Downstairs is a good collection of Hungarian painting (including several representations of the 1879 flood) and a new exhibit on the Avar people who occupied the Carpathian Basin from the 5th to 8th centuries (captions in English). The upper floor is dedicated to the folk art of the region. Behind this museum, in an **old gate** remaining from Szeged's 18th century fortress, is a very informative city historical museum.

There are many fine buildings around Széchenyi tér in the centre of town, including the neo-Baroque **old town hall** (1883). In summer this park is Szeged's prettiest place.

Surprisingly, Szeged's most compelling sight is the **New Synagogue** (1903), a few blocks west of Széchenyi tér. The names of the many Jewish deportees from this area are inscribed in stone on the synagogue walls. This building with its great blue dome has a captivating Oriental atmosphere.

Places to Stay

Camping *Partfürdő Camping Ground* (☎ 430 843) is on Közép kikötő sor, right beside the river, opposite the city centre. You can see the tents from the Belvárosi Bridge.

Camping is US$2 per person plus US$1.50 per tent and there are 26 hotel rooms at US$7/10/11 single/double/triple with shared bath. Guests have free use of the many swimming pools and one thermal pool in this area. This is your best bet for camping (open May to September).

A second camping ground, *Napfény Camping* (☎ 325 800), Dorozsmai út 2, is across a large bridge from Rókus Railway Station and the western terminus of tram No 1. In addition to camping, double rooms are available in a series of 20-room wooden barracks at US$9 with shared bath (available year-round). From May to August bungalows with kitchen and private bath are US$30 for three persons, US$37 for four. The modern hotel here has rooms at US$23/28 single/double with bath and breakfast.

Hostels In July and August the student dormitories of *Apáthy István College*, Apáthy István utca 4 right next to the Votive Church, and *Semmelweis Ignác College*, Semmelweis utca 4 between the train station and town, are opened as youth hostels. If Semmelweis is full, try *Ëotvös Loránd College*, Tisza Lajos körút 103 just around the corner. Go directly to the hostels or ask for information at Express, Kígyó utca 3. Some hostels in Szeged charge unusually high prices (US$18 double).

Private Rooms If you want a private room, your best bet is Szeged Tourist, Klauzál tér 7. During the Summer Festival it's open from 9 am to 7 pm daily and rooms are available. Ibusz, Klauzál tér 2, also has private rooms, but not as many.

Hotels The fine old two-star *Tisza Hotel* (☎ 478 278), Wesselényi utca 1 at Széchenyi tér, costs US$12/23 for singles/doubles without bath and US$31 double with bath. Beware of rooms directly above the disco.

If you arrive by bus you'll be within walking distance of *Sára Panzió* (☎ 314 920), Zákány utca 13, where rooms are US$17/23 single/double. If it's full there's a similar place around the corner at Pacsirta utca 17a.

Places to Eat

The *Boszorkanykonyha étélbár*, Híd utca 8, just off Széchenyi tér, is a cheap self-service. It's a little complicated because you have to pay first and get a ticket. Hang around until you see someone getting a plate of something you fancy and then point to it.

Festival Étélbár, in the modern building on Oskola utca directly across the street from the entrance to the Votive Church (daily 10 am to 9 pm), is a more expensive self-service with a pleasant terrace on which you can eat. It's easy since you pay at the end of the line.

Ciao Pizzeria, downstairs at Tisza Lajos körút 12 (daily from 11 am to midnight, Friday and Saturday until 2 am), has the best pizza in Szeged. It's real freshly baked pizza (not some microwave concoction) but order the 'maxi' size if you're at all hungry.

The *Virág Cukrászda*, Klauzál tér 1, opposite Szeged Tourist, serves great cakes and pastries. *Kis Virág* across the square is cheaper if you're willing to eat standing up. The ice cream is the best in town.

For a tasty treat upon arrival in Szeged look for the *lángos* shop (yellow sign) across the street from the train station and order a big Hungarian doughnut with cheese (*sajtos*).

Entertainment

The *National Theatre* (built in 1883) is on Tanácsköztársaság útja on the corner of Vörösmarty utca.

The Szeged Summer Festival (held from mid-July to mid-August) unfolds on Dóm tér with the two great towers of the Votive Church as a backdrop. The open-air theatre here seats 6000 people. Main events include an opera, an operetta, a play, folk dancing, classical music, ballet and a rock opera. Festival tickets and information are available from Szabadtéri Játékok Jegyiroda (☎ 471 466), Deák Ferenc utca 30 (weekdays 10 am to 5 pm).

Daily organ concerts are given in the

Votive Church during the festival period at 12.30 pm (US$1).

Jate Klub, Toldi utca 2 in the centre, is a student disco with live music Thursday to Saturday from 8 pm to 2 am.

Sing Sing Discotheque occupies a huge pavilion on Mars tér near the bus station. It's open Friday and Saturday from 10 pm to 4 am. Unlike some other clubs in this area, this one is safe.

Getting There & Away

Direct express trains travel from Budapest-Nyugati (191 km, 2½ hours) via Kecskemét.

Seven buses travel daily to Pécs (189 km), two daily to Eger (245 km), two daily to Győr (294 km), two daily to Siófok (224 km) and two daily to Debrecen (224 km). On most buses you pay the driver (but ask at the ticket window).

From mid-June to August, on Saturday and holidays only, a Mahart riverboat plies the Tisza River between Szeged and Csongrád (70 km, five hours), leaving Szeged in the early morning, Csongrád in the afternoon.

To/From Yugoslavia There are about two buses a day to Subotica (44 km, US$2.50 – pay the driver) but they're not listed on the departures board at the station and trying to get information about them is a struggle, so you're better off taking the train. (The people working at Szeged Bus Station seem to hate their jobs, so don't expect much help from them.)

Three local trains a day run to Subotica in Yugoslavia (45 km, 1½ hours, US$2). Buy your ticket at the train station.

To/From Romania There are daily buses to Arad (106 km, US$5) and Timişoara/Temesvár (157 km), departing from platform No 4 at the bus station (check with information). These buses are listed on the departures board.

Getting to Romania by train is complicated, as you must change at Békéscsaba (seven local trains a day go from Szeged to Békéscsaba, 97 km). This connection is not good. If you are adventurous and don't mind walking or hitching, you could take one of nine daily local trains from Ujszeged Station (across the Tisza River from central Szeged) to Nagylak (47 km, 1¼ hours), which is right on the Romanian border, halfway to Arad. The highway border crossing is near Nagylak Station and it's only a six-km walk from there to the first Romanian town, Nădlac, which has local trains to Arad four times a day (52 km, 1½ hours). Hitching from the border is easy.

Northern Hungary

Northern Hungary is the most mountainous part of the country. The southern ranges of the Carpathian Mountains stretch east along the Slovakian border in a 1000-metre-high chain of woody hills from the Danube Bend almost to the Ukrainian border. Miskolc is heavily industrialised but historic Eger offers an ideal base for sightseers and wine tasters. Day trips to the nearby Mátra and Bükk mountains are possible. Farther north, right beside Slovakia, are the caves near Aggtelek, Hungary's most extensive caves. To the east is the famous Tokaj wine-growing area.

EGER

Eger (Erlau), the seat of Heves County, is a lovely Baroque city full of historic buildings. It was at Eger Castle in 1552 that 2000 Hungarian defenders temporarily stopped the Turkish advance into Europe and helped to preserve the Hungarian identity. The Turks returned in 1596 and captured the castle but were themselves thrown out by the Austrians in 1687. Later Eger was a centre for Ferenc Rákóczi's unsuccessful 1703-11 War of Independence against the Habsburgs.

It was the bishops and later the archbishops of Eger who built the town you see today. The many handsome 18th century palaces and churches along Kossuth Lajos and Széchenyi streets deserve special attention. Eger possesses some of Hungary's finest

HUNGARY

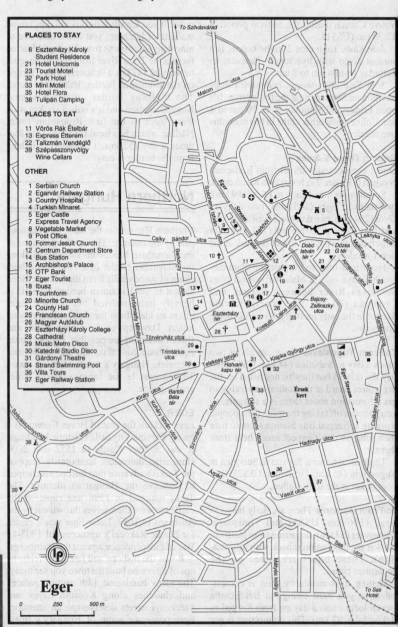

PLACES TO STAY

6   Eszterházy Károly
     Student Residence
21 Hotel Unicornis
23 Tourist Motel
32 Park Hotel
33 Mini Motel
35 Hotel Flora
38 Tulipán Camping

PLACES TO EAT

11 Vörös Rák Ételbár
13 Express Étterem
22 Talizmán Vendéglő
39 Szépasszonyvölgy
     Wine Cellars

OTHER

1   Serbian Church
2   Egarvár Railway Station
3   Country Hospital
4   Turkish Minaret
5   Eger Castle
7   Express Travel Agency
8   Vegetable Market
9   Post Office
10 Former Jesuit Church
12 Centrum Department Store
14 Bus Station
15 Archbishop's Palace
16 OTP Bank
17 Eger Tourist
18 Ibusz
19 Tourinform
20 Minorite Church
24 County Hall
25 Franciscan Church
26 Magyar Autóklub
27 Eszterházy Károly College
28 Cathedral
29 Music Metro Disco
30 Katedrál Studio Disco
31 Gárdonyi Theatre
34 Strand Swimming Pool
36 Villa Tours
37 Eger Railway Station

Eger

0   250   500 m

examples of Zopf architecture, a late Baroque-Rococo style found only in Central Europe. Nineteenth-century railway builders left Eger to one side, so it retained its historic form and character.

Today Eger is more famous for its potent Egri Bikavér (Bull's Blood) red wine. Literally hundreds of wine cellars are to be seen in Szépasszonyvölgy (the Valley of Beautiful Women), just a 20-minute walk west of the cathedral.

Orientation & Information

The train station is a 15-minute walk south of town on Deák Ferenc utca, while the bus station is just above Széchenyi István utca, Eger's main drag. The left-luggage office at the train station is open from 6.30 am to 6.30 pm only (ask at the ticket window). At the bus station, the left-luggage office is only open as long as the ticket window functions (until 6 pm weekdays, 5 pm Saturday, 4 pm Sunday and holidays).

Tourinform, Dobó tér 2, can supply all the brochures you care to carry and the staff answer questions in fluent German.

The Magyar Autóklub (☎ 317 590) is nearby at Jókai utca 5.

Money To change a travellers' cheque go to the OTP Bank, Széchenyi utca 2 (weekdays 7.45 am to 3 pm).

Post & Telecommunications Both card and coin phones are available at the main post office, Széchenyi utca 22. Eger's telephone code is 36.

Emergency If you have an urgent medical or dental problem try the county hospital (megyei kórház) near the Turkish minaret.

Things to See

The first thing you see as you come into Eger from the bus or train station is the huge neoclassical **cathedral** (1836) on Eszterházy tér. Opposite this is the Rococo **Eszterházy Károly College** (1785). Buy a ticket just inside the college door to see the frescoed library in room No 48 on the 1st

floor and the **Museum of Astronomy** (open Tuesday to Sunday from 9.30 am to noon) on the 6th floor of the tower at the back of the building. On the 9th floor of the tower is the periscope, a unique apparatus which allows you to spy on all of Eger unobserved (use the same ticket for this). Along Kossuth Lajos utca is the Baroque **county hall** at No 9, which has elegant wrought-iron gates (1761) and an old prison in the courtyard (now a museum).

At the eastern end of Kossuth Lajos utca, across Dózsa György tér, is **Eger Castle**, erected after the Tatar invasion of 1242. Inside this great fortress are the foundations of St John's Cathedral, which was destroyed by the Turks. Models and drawings in the castle's **Dobó István Museum** give a clear idea of how the cathedral once looked. This museum, housed in the Gothic bishop's palace (1470), is named after the Hungarian national hero who led the resistance to the Turks in 1552. Below the castle are underground chambers (kazamata) hewn from solid rock, which you may tour with a guide. As soon as you arrive at the castle, ask the person at the ticket window when the next tour of the casemates will begin.

The Baroque **Minorite church** (1771) on Dobó tér was designed by the famous Prague architect Dientzenhofer. In front of the church is a statue of Dobó István and sculptures that depict a battle against the Turks. In the shadow of the castle in the old town is a climbable 35-metre **Turkish minaret** – the northernmost Turkish monument in Europe.

After so much history, unwind in **Népkert Park**, once the private reserve of the bishops. Opposite Népkert Park is the **Strand**, with relaxing hot thermal swimming pools open year-round. Masseurs (male and female) are on duty. Unfortunately the 17th century **Turkish baths** (török fürdö) nearby are reserved for patients under medical supervision.

Places to Stay

Camping A new private camping ground has opened on Szépasszonyvölgy utca just at the entrance to the Valley of the Beautiful

HUNGARY

Women. *Tulipán Camping* (☎ 410 580) offers two-bed caravans (US$11) and four-bed bungalows (US$18) with shared bath, as well as luxurious five-bed bungalows with private bath (US$33). Camping is US$6 for two people. This site can get crowded but it's an obvious first choice for those on foot as both the train station and the centre of town are less than a km away (the town's wine cellars are within easy stumbling distance). It's open from April to September, or whenever there's demand, and there's a snack bar on the premises.

Eger's other camping ground at Rákóczi utca 79, four km north of Eger, is only of interest to people with cars.

Hostels In July and August for US$5 you can stay in the vacant student dormitories of *Eszterházy Károly Tanárkepzo Fóiskola* (☎ 321 415), Leányka utca 2, just up the hill from Eger Castle. There are actually two hostels here. The sign over the door of the first hostel says 'üdvözöljük vendégeiket'. If it's full continue up the hill, past the phone booth on Leányka utca, to a stairway on the left which leads straight back. The last building on the right is also a hostel.

Express, Széchenyi utca 28, may have information about other summer student hostels.

Private Rooms For private rooms visit Eger Tourist, Bajcsy-Zsilinszky utca 9 in the centre of town (from US$11/12 single/double). Ibusz, in the alley behind Eger Tourist, also has private rooms (from US$11 single or double).

Villa Tours, Deák Ferenc utca 53, a four-minute walk from the train station, is a private travel agency that arranges private rooms (US$18 double).

Hotels The *Sas Hotel* (no phone), Sas út 96, a km south-east of the train station, is a four-storey workers' hostel which offers beds in four-bedded rooms without bath at US$5 per person, or doubles with bath at US$12. From the train station, walk back along the tracks to the level crossing, turn left and you're on Sas út. It's open year-round.

The central *Mini Motel* (☎ 311 388), Deák Ferenc utca 11, costs US$7/10/14 single/double/triple. Lock your window in this single-storey building. The modern *Hotel Unicornis* (☎ 312 455) on Kossuth Lajos utca is US$13/14 single/double without bath, US$19/20 with bath. And finally, the *Tourist Motel* (☎ 310 014), Mekcsey István utca 2, is US$11 double (no singles). On summer weekends, accommodation in Eger is tight, so arrive early.

Places to Eat
Bottom End *Express Étterem*, Pyrker tér 4 just below the north-east side of the bus station parking lot, is a large self-service cafeteria open until 8 pm. You can take your own beer from the cooler here and if you dig deep enough you should find a cold one.

Some of Eger's cheapest food, including fried chicken or fish, barbecued ribs and sausages, are consumed standing up (weekdays from 10 am to 3 pm) at the various buffets upstairs in the indoor vegetable market on Katona István tér behind the main post office. No alcohol is served here.

At the attractive *Kondi Saláta Bár*, Széchenyi utca 2, you can get a deli-style lunch, or just coffee with delicious desserts, which you can carry out onto their terrace or a plastic tray.

Top End A good selection of places to eat is around Dobó tér. *Vörös Rák Etelbár*, Szent János utca 11 near Dobó tér, has a few inexpensive chicken and carp dishes, as well as the usual pork. Despite the name, don't expect to get any red lobster here.

Bajor Sörház, Bajsy-Zsilinszky utca 19, just off Dobó tér, offers up-market meals with big mugs of beer.

In summer you can dine at any of five rather touristy restaurants over the bridge at the north end of Dobó tér. They set their tables out on the square and there's even a keyboarder providing live music. Some of the restaurants here serve good traditional food while others are a rip-off. Vegetarians should check out the self-service *Salátabár* here.

The *Talizmán Vendéglő*, Kossuth Lajos utca 19, is a trendy wine cellar that's always packed with European tourists. The restaurant at the nearby *Hotel Unicornis* is cheaper. The *Kopcsik Cukrászda* across the street from Talizmán has a great selection of cakes which you can have with coffee on their terrace.

Many wine restaurants haunt the cellars of Szépasszony völgy utca. The most famous is the *Ködmön Csárda*, where live Hungarian folk music accompanies dinner. The menu is in Hungarian, but ask to see it anyway to get an idea of the prices. There are many other similar places and the noisiest is probably the best – great atmosphere. To get there, walk west on Telekesy István and Király streets. When you come to a fork in the road, go left down the incline and straight ahead.

Entertainment

The Gárdonyi Géza Theatre ticket office, Széchenyi utca 5, should know about local events.

Music Metro Disco is on the corner of Trinitárius utca and Törvényház utca. A block south on Trinitárius utca is the *Katedrál Studio Disco* where laser lights flash as you dance inside a huge Baroque former church dating from 1782 (Thursday, Friday and Saturday from 10 pm).

Getting There & Away

Eger is connected to Budapest's Keleti Railway Station by express train (142 km, two hours). It's sometimes quicker to take a local train to Füzesabony (17 km), where you can catch a connecting express train to Budapest.

Buses leave Eger's bus station to Budapest (128 km) about once an hour, to Szilvásvárad (24 km) about twice an hour, to Jósvafö/Aggtelek (2½ hours) once in the morning, to Szeged (245 km) twice a day and to Kecskemét (158 km) three times a day. The times are irregular so look at the posted schedule (*indul*), then check with information.

SZILVÁSVÁRAD

Just to the north of Eger are the Bükk Mountains, much of which fall within the 388-sq-km **Bükk National Park**. A good place to begin a visit to the forests of Bükk is the village of Szilvásvárad, 28 km north of Eger on the road to Aggtelek.

Szilvásvárad has the dual attraction of being an ideal base for hiking and the centre of horse breeding in Hungary, with some 250 prize Lipica horses in local stables. Horse riding can be arranged at about US$10 per hour, and in summer there are horse-cart rides, in winter horse-drawn sleigh rides.

Szilvásvárad also makes a good base for visiting the Aggtelek Caves as you can pick up the bus from Eger to the caves here and shave almost an hour off your travelling time in each direction.

Things to See

The best time to come to Szilvásvárad would be during the Lipicai Horse Festival in early September when the racecourse in the centre of town becomes the scene of major events. **Horse shows** (*lovasbemutató*) are also put on throughout the year, a couple of times a week in winter and almost daily in summer, in the smaller horse pavilion (*lovarda*) near the racecourse. Check on this as soon as you arrive.

From this pavilion, a chestnut-lined road leads up the Szalajka Valley to hiking trails into the hills. You can also ride on a **narrow-gauge railway** which takes 15 minutes to cover the five km about hourly from 9 am to 5 pm on weekends and holidays from April to October. On weekdays there are a couple of afternoon trains.

Among the varied attractions up the **Szalajka Valley** are waterfalls, a lake and an open-air museum of forest industries. From this museum you can climb to the **Istállóskő Cave** where evidence of habitation by early man was uncovered. Nearby **Istállós-kö** (958 metres) is the highest peak in the Bükk Mountains. Serious hikers can follow trails along the ridge all the way to Lillafüred near Miskolc. Some paved roads through the national park are now closed to motorised vehicles which makes this an excellent area for cycling. Eger Tourist and Tourinform in Eger sells a detailed map of this area.

Back in Szilvásvárad, you can see some of the famous Lipica horses in the stable adjoining the **Horse Museum** *(Lovaskiállítás)* at Park utca 8, next to Hotel Szilvás.

The **Orbán-Ház Museum** (closed on Monday), Miskolci út 58, at the north end of town, has exhibits on the flora and fauna of the Bükk Mountains in a typical farmhouse of this region dating from 1880. Opposite the museum is an impressive circular neoclassical **Lutheran church**.

Places to Stay & Eat

Camping *Hegyi Camping* (☎ 355 207), Egri út 36a, a five-minute walk from Szilvásvárad-Szalajkavölgy Railway Station, has neat bungalows at US$12/15/18 double /triple/quad. In addition, a US$0.65 per person per day resort tax is collected. This camping ground run by Eger Tourist is open from May to mid-October and there's a snack bar on the premises. (Freelance camping is not allowed in the national park.)

Hotels *Hotel Lipicai* (☎ 355 100), Egri út 14, a modern two-storey hotel, has rooms with bath and breakfast at US$10 per person.

The *Szalajka Vendéglő* (☎ 355 257), Egri út 2, has hotel rooms with shared bath at US$8/9 single/double, but it's usually full in summer. It serves substantial meals, often accompanied by live music, on the front porch.

At US$14/18 single/double the *Hotel Szilvás* (☎ 355 211), Park utca 6, a 40-room Baroque palace overlooking a park in the centre of town, is a real bargain, but in summer it's usually full. This palace once belonged to Count Pallavicini whose family owned the entire region but after 1945 it became a trade-union holiday house.

Getting There & Away

Szilvásvárad is easily accessible from Eger by train (six daily, 31 km, one hour) or bus. Get on/off the train at Szilvásvárad-Szalajka völgy Station. In Eger the Szilvásvárad train stops at Egarvár Station, which you may find more convenient if you're making it a day trip. The Aggtelek bus to/from Budapest passes here.

AGGTELEK

Hungary's largest and most famous scenic caves are the **Baradla Caves** in Aggtelek National Park on the Slovakian border, north of Eger and Miskolc. The caves stretch 25 km underground, 18 km of which is in Hungary and seven km in Slovakia. The easiest way to get there is to take the morning Volán bus from Eger to Aggtelek (2½ hours US$4). The same bus returns to Eger in the afternoon, allowing you plenty of time to see the Aggtelek caves. It doesn't, however, give you time to see the Jósvafő Caves. Alternatively, spend the night at Aggtelek and visit the three different sections of the caves. One reader commented that he didn't like the way the walking paths within the caves had been hacked out and cemented up.

Things to See & Do

The short tour at Aggtelek (one hour US$1.75, students half-price, open year-round) includes recorded music in the 'concert hall'. There you will see beautiful karst formations and an underground lake. There's another entrance to the Baradla Caves near **Jósvafő**, six km east of Aggtelek, where you can go on different short tours (US$2, students half price). Two-hour trips (US$2.75) begin at **Vöröstó** between Aggtelek and Jósvafő, and in summer there's even an epic five-hour cave tour (US$9) during which visitors must carry lamps. All tours are led by Hungarian-speaking guides who only set out when 10 tickets have been sold, so you may have to buy the extra tickets when things are slow (the one-hour Aggtelek tour begins at 10 am, 1 and 3 pm even when fewer people are waiting).

Next to the Aggtelek entrance to the Baradla Caves is a **terrárium** with a small collection of local reptiles and insects (open mid-May to mid-September). **Hiking trails** begin behind this museum and even on a brief visit it's well worth climbing the hill for a view of the countryside. A trail marked with a green pine tree on a white base leads from here to the Jósvafö entrance (7½ km). The trail begins at the viewpoint above the cave entrance but soon swings right past a wooden electricity pole (don't charge straight up the hill on the main trail marked by blue triangles). You can swim in a small lake a five-minute walk from the Jósvafö entrance.

Places to Stay & Eat

The bus from Eger stops in front of the modern four-storey *Cseppkő Hotel* (☎ 343 075) at Aggtelek, where the 73 rooms with bath cost US$17/24 single/double including breakfast. The hotel has a restaurant with an English menu. The hotel reception changes cash only (no travellers' cheques).

Also at the Aggtelek entrance is pleasant *Baradla Camping* (☎ 343 073; open from mid-April to mid-October) with 3rd-class cabins at US$9 (two beds) and 1st-class bungalows at US$17. Camping is US$1.50 per person plus US$3 per tent.

The camping ground reception also controls the tourist hostel *(turistaház)* (US$3 per person) above the terrárium at the entrance to the caves (said to be open year-round). It has beds in eight-bed dorms at US$3 per person (plus 25% tax if you stay longer than one night). If you have a car there will be a parking fee. Cooking facilities are provided but you may have to walk to the end of the camping ground for a hot shower. The check-out time at the hostel is 10 am.

The *Tengerszem Szálló* (☎ 312 700) is a rustic 22-room lodge at the Jósvafö Caves, a km or so west of Jósvafö village. All the buses stop here.

Getting There & Away

Only one bus a day travels between Budapest, Eger and Aggtelek, leaving Budapest and Eger in the morning and Aggtelek in the afternoon. Buses travel from Aggtelek to Jósvafö every couple of hours and a morning bus goes from Miskolc to Aggtelek, returning to Miskolc in the afternoon. (Throughout Hungary, Aggtelek is listed on posted bus schedules as 'Jósvafö'.)

You can also come by train from Miskolc to Jósvafö-Aggtelek Railway Station where a bus is usually waiting to carry you the 22 km on to the caves at Aggtelek. At Miskolc look for one of the seven daily trains bearing the sign 'Tornanádaska'.

Though the caves in Aggtelek are only a five-minute walk from the Slovakian border, only Hungarians and Slovaks may cross here. There's a morning bus from Aggtelek to Rožňava in Slovakia, but Westerners are not allowed to take it (the Hungarian government wants this changed, but for some reason the Slovakian government doesn't). The nearest highway border crossing open to everyone is at Banréve, 30 km south-west, and if you don't have a car or bicycle you'll probably have to go all the way around via Miskolc to get to Košice.

MISKOLC

This large industrial city between Budapest and Košice often serves as a transit point between Hungary and Slovakia. Two unreserved local trains a day shuttle between Miskolc and Košice (84 km), and there are another six connections through Sátoraljaújhely/Slovenské Nové Mesto. At Tiszai pu Railway Station in Miskolc you should be able to change dollars or Deutschmarks in cash at the international ticket window No 7. If it's closed, use a coin to tap on the glass until someone comes.

A hundred metres from this train station is the *MTM Szálló* (☎ 340 043), to the right of the city buses and across a parking lot, with beds in four-bedded rooms at US$4 per person. In winter the rooms are tremendously overheated, so ask for one upstairs so you can open the window.

Macedonia (Македонија)

Macedonia is a Slovenia-sized country at the south end of what was once the Yugoslav Federation. Its position in the centre of the Balkan Peninsula between Albania, Bulgaria, Serbia and Greece has often made it a political powder keg. Alternating Islamic and Orthodox overtones tell of a long struggle which ended in 1913 when the Treaty of Bucharest divided geographical Macedonia among its four neighbours. Serbia got the northern part while the southern half went to Greece. Bulgaria and Albania each received much smaller slices. Only in 1992 did ex-Yugoslav Macedonia become fully independent.

For travellers Macedonia is a land of contrasts, ranging from space-age Skopje with its ultramodern shopping centre and time-worn Turkish bazar, to the many medieval monasteries of Ohrid. Macedonia's fascinating blend of Orthodox mystery and the exotic Orient combine with the world-class beauty of Ohrid Lake to make the country much more than just a transit route on the way to somewhere else.

Facts about the Country

HISTORY

Historical Macedonia (from whence Alexander the Great set out to conquer the ancient world in the 4th century BC) is today contained mostly in present Greece, a point Greeks are always quick to make when discussing contemporary Macedonia's use of that name. The Romans subjugated the Hellenic Greeks of ancient Macedonia and the territory to the north in the mid-2nd century BC, and when the empire was divided in the 4th century AD this region became part of the Eastern Roman Empire ruled from Constantinople. Slav tribes settled here in the 7th century, changing the ethnic character of the area.

In the 9th century the region was conquered by the Bulgarian tsar Simeon (893-927) and, under Tsar Samuel (980-1014), Macedonia was the centre of a powerful Bulgarian state. Samuel's defeat by Byzantium in 1014 ushered in a long period when Macedonia passed back and forth between Byzantium, Bulgaria and Serbia. After the final defeat of Serbia by the Turks in 1389, the Balkans became part of the Ottoman Empire and the cultural character of the region again changed.

In 1878 Russia defeated Turkey, and Macedonia was ceded to Bulgaria by the Treaty of San Stefano. The Western powers, fearing the creation of a powerful Russian satellite in the heart of the Balkans, forced Bulgaria to give Macedonia back to Turkey. In 1893 Macedonian nationalists formed the Internal Macedonian Revolutionary Organisation (IMRO) to fight for independence from

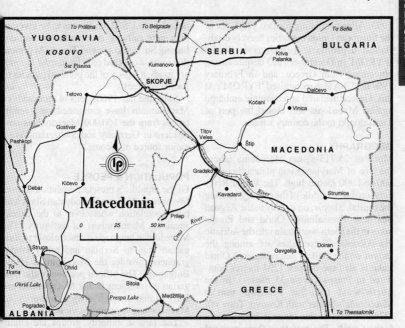

Turkey, culminating in a revolt led by Goce Delčev in 1903 which was brutally suppressed.

The First Balkan War in 1912 brought Greece, Serbia and Bulgaria together against Turkey. In the Second Balkan War in 1913 Greece and Serbia ousted the Bulgarians and split Macedonia between themselves. Frustrated by this result IMRO continued the struggle against royalist Serbia, to which the interwar government responded by banning the Macedonian language and even the name Macedonia. Though some IMRO elements supported the Bulgarian occupation of Macedonia during WW II, many more joined Tito's partisans, and in 1943 it was agreed that postwar Macedonia would have full republic status in future Yugoslavia. The first Macedonian grammar was published in 1952 and an independent Macedonian Orthodox church was allowed to form. By recognising Macedonians as an ethnic group distinct from both Serbs and Bulgarians the Belgrade

authorities hoped to weaken Bulgarian claims to Macedonia.

On 8 September 1991 a referendum on independence was held in Macedonia and 74% voted in favour of independence, so in January 1992 the country declared its full independence from former Yugoslavia. For once Belgrade cooperated by ordering all federal troops present to withdraw and, because the split was peaceful, road and rail links were never broken. In mid-1993, however, about a thousand United Nations troops were sent to Macedonia as a precaution to monitor the border with Yugoslavia.

Greece delayed diplomatic recognition of Macedonia by demanding that the country find another name, alleging that the term Macedonia implied territorial claims on northern Greece. At the insistence of Greek officials, Macedonia was forced to use the absurd 'temporary' title FYROM (Former Yugoslav Republic of Macedonia) for the purpose of being admitted to the UN in April

1993. After vacillating for two years, six of the European Union countries bravely established diplomatic relations with the 'FYROM' in December 1993 despite strong objections from Greece, and in February 1994 the USA also recognised 'FYROM'. At this, Greece declared an economic embargo against Macedonia and closed the port of Thessaloniki to the country's trade.

GEOGRAPHY

Much of 25,713-sq-km Macedonia (about the size of Maryland) is a plateau between 600 and 900 metres high. The Vardar River cuts across the middle of the country, passing the capital, Skopje, on its way to the Aegean Sea near Thessaloniki. Ohrid and Prespa lakes in the south-west drain into the Adriatic via Albania. These lakes are among the largest on the Balkan peninsula, and Ohrid Lake is also the deepest (294 metres compared to Prespa Lake's 35 metres). In the north-west the Šar Planina marks Macedonia's border with Kosovo; Titov vrh (2748 metres) in this range is Macedonia's highest peak. The country's three national parks are Pelister west of Bitola, Galičica between Ohrid and Prespa lakes and Mavrovo between Ohrid and Tetovo.

ECONOMY

Macedonia is a rich agricultural area which feeds itself and exports tomatoes and cucumbers to Western Europe. Cereals, rice, cotton and tobacco are also grown and Macedonian mines yield chromium, manganese, tungsten, lead and zinc. The main north-south trade route from Western Europe to Greece via the valleys of the Danube, Morava and Vardar rivers passes through the country. Tourism is concentrated around Ohrid Lake. At present Macedonia is suffering serious economic difficulties due to UN sanctions against Yugoslavia and bad relations with Greece are hindering trade with the EU.

With the changes in Eastern Europe and especially with the separation of Macedonia from Yugoslavia, a new east-west trading route is developing from Turkey to Italy via Bulgaria, Macedonia and Albania. Over the next decade US$2.5 billion is to be invested in a new railway and motorway corridor linking Sofia, Skopje and Tirana. At present this route is covered only by narrow secondary roads, a legacy of the political policies of former regimes.

Since the late 1960s, tens of thousands of Macedonians have emigrated, and remittances from the 100,000 Macedonians now resident in Germany and Switzerland are a major source of income.

POPULATION & PEOPLE

Of the republic's present population of over two million, 68% are Macedonian Slavs who bear no relation whatsoever to the Greek-speaking Macedonians of antiquity. The Macedonian language is much closer to Bulgarian than to Serbian and many ethnographers consider the Macedonians ethnic Bulgarians. The official position of the Bulgarian government is that Macedonians are Bulgarians, though only a minority of Macedonians support this view.

The largest minority groups are ethnic Albanians (22%), Serbs (5%), Gypsies (3.6%) and Turks (3.4%). The birth rate of the mostly rural Albanians is three times the national average. Albanians are in a majority in the region between Tetovo and Debar in the north-western part of the republic and there have been demonstrations in defence of the right to education in Albanian. Most of the Albanians and Turks are Muslim; the Slavs, Orthodox.

The 50,000 Slavic Macedonians living in northern Greece are subject to assimilatory pressures by the Greek government which calls them 'Slavophone Greeks'. Education in Macedonian is denied and human rights groups such as Helsinki Watch have documented many cases of police harassment of Greek Macedonians who publicly protested these policies.

ARTS

Music In Macedonian folk music the drone of the *gajda* (bagpipe) and chords of the *tambura* (two-stringed lute) provide a background for the *kaval* (flute) and *tapan* (cylindrical drum).

LANGUAGE

Macedonian is a South Slavic language divided into two large groups, the western and eastern Macedonian dialects. The Macedonian literary language was based on the central dialects of Titov Veles, Prilep and Bitola. Macedonian shares all the characteristics which separate Bulgarian from the other Slavic languages, evidence that it's a dialect of Bulgarian. Since WW II there has been a conscious effort to eliminate Serbian and Bulgarian usage from the language taught in the schools.

The Cyrillic alphabet is based on the alphabet developed by two Greek brothers, St Cyril and St Methodius, in the 9th century. It was taught by their disciples at a monastery in Ohrid, Macedonia, whence it spread across the eastern Slavic world.

Although both the Cyrillic and Roman alphabets are official in Macedonia, Cyrillic is predominantly used. Main signs and street names are printed either in Cyrillic script only, or in both alphabets.

Lonely Planet's *Mediterranean Europe Phrasebook* contains a complete chapter on Macedonian with Cyrillic spellings provided.

Pronunciation

The spelling of Macedonian is phonetically based: almost every word is written exactly as it is pronounced and every letter is pronounced. With regard to the position of the stress accent, only one rule can be given: the last syllable of a word is never stressed. There are 31 letters in the Cyrillic alphabet. The pronunciation of the Roman or Cyrillic letter is given to the nearest English equivalent.

Cyrillic Alphabet – Macedonia

Cyrillic	Roman	Pronunciation
Аа	a	'a' as in 'rather'
Бб	b	'b' as in 'brother'
Вв	v	'v' as in 'vodka'
Гг	g	'g' as in 'got'
Дд	d	'd' as in 'do'
Ѓѓ	gj	the 'dj' sound in 'verdure'
Ее	e	the 'e' sound in 'bear'
Жж	ž	'zh' as in 'treasure'
Зз	z	'z' as in 'zero'
Ѕѕ	zj	'z' plus 'y'
Ии	i	'i' as in 'machine'
Јј	j	'y' as in 'young'
Кк	k	'k' as in 'keg'
Лл	l	'l' as in 'lad'
Љљ	lj	the 'ly' sound in 'colliery'
Мм	m	'm' as in 'map'
Нн	n	'n' as in 'no'
Њњ	nj	'ny' as in 'canyon'
Оо	o	'o' as in 'shawl'
Пп	p	'p' as in 'pop'
Рр	r	'r' as in 'rock'
Сс	s	's' as in 'loss'
Тт	t	't' as in 'too'
Ќќ	ḱ	the 'tch' sound in 'future'
Уу	u	'oo' as in 'book'
Фф	f	'f' as in 'fat'
Хх	h	the 'gh' sound in 'hot'
Цц	ts	'ts' as in 'cats'
Чч	č	'ch' as in 'chop'
Џџ	dz	'j' as in 'just'
Шш	š	'sh' as in 'hush'

Greetings & Civilities

hello	zdravo
good morning	dobro utro
good evening	dobra večer
goodbye	prijatno
please	ve molam
thank you	fala
excuse me/forgive me	izvini
I am sorry.	žal mi e
yes	da
no	ne

Small Talk

I don't understand.	Ne razbiram.
Could you write it down?	Napiši go?
What is it called?	Kako se vika?

Where do you live?	Kade živeeš?
What work do you do?	Što rabotiš?
I am a student.	Jas sum student.
I am very happy.	Jas sum mnogu sreḱen.

Accommodation

youth hostel	mladinski dom
camping ground	kamp
private room	privatna soba
How much is it?	Kolku košta?
Is that the price per person?	Dali e za edna osoba?
Is that the total price?	Dali e ova totalna cena?
Are there any extra charges?	Dali ima dodatni plaḱanja?
Do I pay extra for showers?	Dali plaḱam ekstra za banja?
Where is there a cheaper hotel?	Kade ima eftin hotel?
Should I make a reservation?	Može li da rezerviram soba?
single room	soba za eden
double room	soba za dvajca
It is very noisy.	Premnogu ima bučava.
Where is the toilet?	Kade e klozet?

Getting Around

What time does it leave?	Koga zaminuva?
When is the first bus?	Koga e prviot avtobus?
When is the last bus?	Koga e posledniot avtobus?
When is the next bus?	Koga e sledniot avtobus?
That's too soon.	Toa e premnogu skoro.
When is the next one after that?	Koga e sledniot posle ovoj?
How long does the trip take?	Kolku vreme trae patuvanjeto?
arrival	stignuva
departure	poagja
timetable	vozen red

Where is the bus stop?	Kade e avtobuskata stanica?
Where is the train station?	Kade e železničkata stanica?
Where is the left-luggage room?	Kade e garderobata?

Around Town

Just a minute.	Počekaj malce.
Where is ... ?	Kade e ...
the bank	banka
the post office	pošta
the tourist information office	informacionen centar
the museum	muzej
Where are you going?	Kade odiš?
I am going to ...	Jas odam kaj ...
Where is it?	Kade e?
I can't find it.	Nemožam da go najdam.
Is it far?	Dale e daleku?
Please show me on the map.	Pokaži mi na kartava.
left	levo
right	desno
straight ahead	pravo napred
I want ...	Jas sakam ...
Do I need permission?	Mi treba li odobruvanje?

Entertainment

Where can I buy a ticket?	Kade možam da kupam bilet?
Where can I refund this ticket?	Kade možam da go unovčam biletov?
Is this a good seat?	Dali ova e dobro mesto?
at the front	napred
ticket	bilet

Food

I do not eat meat.	Ne jadam meso.
self-service cafeteria	samoposlužuvanje
grocery store	samoposluga
fish	riba
pork	svinsko

MACEDONIA

soup	*supa*
salad	*salata*
fresh vegetables	*taze zelenčuk*
milk	*mleko*
bread	*leb*
sugar	*šeker*
ice cream	*sladolet*
coffee	*kafe*
tea	*čaj*
mineral water	*mineralna voda*
beer	*pivo*
wine	*vino*
hot/cold	*toplo/ladno*

January	*Januari*
February	*Fevruari*
March	*Mart*
April	*April*
May	*Maj*
June	*Juni*
July	*Juli*
August	*Avgust*
September	*Septemvri*
October	*Oktomvri*
November	*Noemvri*
December	*Dekemvri*

Shopping

Where can I buy one?	*Kade možam da kudam?*
How much does it cost?	*Kolku čini?*
That's (much) too expensive.	*Toa e preskapo.*
Is there a cheaper one?	*Dali ima poeftino?*

Time & Dates

today	*denes*
tonight	*večer*
tomorrow	*utre*
the day after tomorrow	*zad utre*
What time does it open?	*Koga se otvara?*
What time does it close?	*Koga se zatvara?*
open	*otvoreno*
closed	*zatvoreno*
in the morning	*nautro*
in the evening	*navečer*
every day	*sekoj den*
At what time?	*Vo kolku saat?*
when?	*koga?*

Monday	*Ponedelnik*
Tuesday	*Vtornik*
Wednesday	*Sreda*
Thursday	*Četvrtok*
Friday	*Petok*
Saturday	*Sabota*
Sunday	*Nedela*

Numbers

1	*eden*
2	*dva*
3	*tri*
4	*četiri*
5	*pet*
6	*šest*
7	*sedum*
8	*osum*
9	*devet*
10	*deset*
11	*edinaeset*
12	*dvanaeset*
13	*trinaeset*
14	*četirinaeset*
15	*petnaeset*
16	*šesnaeset*
17	*sedumneaset*
18	*osumneaset*
19	*devetneaset*
20	*dvaeset*
21	*dvaeset i eden*
22	*dvaeset i dva*
23	*dvaeset i tri*
30	*trieset*
40	*četirieset*
50	*pedeset*
60	*šeeset*
70	*sedumdeset*
80	*osumdeset*
90	*devedeset*
100	*sto*
1000	*iljada*
1,000,000	*milion*

Facts for the Visitor

VISAS

British passport holders require no visa. Canadians, Americans, Australians and New Zealanders need a visa but it's issued free of charge at the border.

The Greek border guards will stamp 'cancelled' across any Macedonian visas, used or unused, they find in your passport – a nice souvenir of friendly Greece.

MONEY

Macedonian denar banknotes come in denominations of 10, 20, 50, 100 and 500 and there are coins of one, two and five denars. In mid-1993 US$1 was worth 25 Macedonian denars in Macedonia. Outside Macedonia the denar is worthless.

Travellers' cheques can be changed into Macedonian denars at most banks with no commission deducted. There's a small black market which buys cash US dollars or Deutschmarks for just slightly more than the bank rate. Shopkeepers will often perform this service, otherwise watch for men at markets or on the street with thick wads of banknotes in their hands. The only real advantage of changing this way is that you avoid the lines at the banks. These people probably won't try to cheat you.

CLIMATE

Macedonia's summers are hot and dry and in winter warm Aegean winds blowing up the Vardar Valley moderate the continental conditions prevailing farther north.

SUGGESTED ITINERARIES

Depending on the length of your stay, you might want to see and do the following things in Macedonia:

Two days
    Visit Skopje.
One week
    Visit Skopje, Ohrid and Bitola.

Two weeks
    As above, plus some hiking in Pelister National Park between Ohrid and Bitola.

HOLIDAYS

Public holidays in Macedonia are New Year (1 and 2 January), Orthodox Christmas (7 January), Old New Year (13 January), Easter Monday and Tuesday (March/April), Labour Day (1 May), Ilinden or Day of the 1903 Rebellion (2 August), Republic Day (8 September) and 1941 Partizan Day (11 October).

POST & TELECOMMUNICATIONS

Receiving Mail

Mail addressed c/o Poste Restante, 91000 Skopje 2, Macedonia, can be claimed at the post office next to Skopje Railway Station, weekdays from 8 am to 1 pm.

Mail addressed c/o Poste Restante, 96000 Ohrid, Macedonia, can be picked up at Ohrid's main post office near the bus station.

Telephones

Long-distance phone calls cost less at main post offices, much more at hotels. To call Macedonia from abroad dial the international access code, 389 (the country code for Macedonia), the area code (without the initial zero) and the number. Area codes include 091 (Skopje), 096 (Ohrid) and 097 (Bitola). For outgoing calls the international access code in Macedonia is 99.

TIME

Macedonia goes on daylight-saving time at the end of March when clocks are turned one hour ahead. On the last Sunday of September they're turned back an hour. Bulgaria and Greece are always one hour ahead of Macedonia while Yugoslavia and Albania keep the same time as Skopje.

ACTIVITIES

Macedonia's top ski resort is Popova šapka (1845 metres) on the southern slopes of the Šar Planina west of Tetovo.

ACCOMMODATION

Macedonia's hotels are very expensive but

there are camping grounds and private-room agencies in Ohrid and Skopje. Skopje's convenient youth hostel is open throughout the year, and the Ohrid hostel opens in summer. Beds are available at student dormitories in Skopje in summer.

FOOD

Turkish-style grilled mincemeat is available almost everywhere and there are self-service cafeterias in most towns for the less adventurous. Balkan *burek* (cheese or meat pie) and yoghurt makes for a cheap breakfast. Watch for Macedonian *gravče na tavče* (beans in a skillet) and Ohrid trout, which is priced according to weight.

Getting There & Away

AIR

With the demise of JAT Yugoslav Airlines a number of local carriers have popped up offering direct flights from Skopje to cities in Germany and Switzerland. Companies like Avioimpex, Makedonija AS, Vardar Air and Palair cater mostly to Macedonians resident in those countries and fares average US$250 one way, US$400 return. Makedonija AS also has a flight to Zagreb (US$175). Prices vary on flights to Ljubljana, so it's worth comparing Palair (US$140), Avioimpex (US$190) and Adria Airways (US$240). Palair also serves Amsterdam (US$250). Any travel agent in Skopje or Ohrid can book these flights. Ask about travel insurance: in March 1993 a Palair flight crashed at Skopje killing 81 people and in November the same year 115 died when an Avioimpex flight from Geneva crashed at Ohrid.

The airport tax at Skopje is US$13.

LAND

Bus

To/from Croatia you must transit Belgrade and Hungary. To/from Bulgaria the bus service between Sofia and Skopje (216 km, six hours, US$10) runs daily except Sunday.

Ask about overnight buses from Skopje to Belgrade and Podgorica. Buses between Skopje and Prizren in Kosovo, Yugoslavia (117 km), are fairly frequent. To/from Albania you can travel between Skopje and Tirana by bus or walk across the border at Sveti Naum (see the Ohrid section).

Train

Express trains run five times a day between Skopje and Belgrade, via Niš (472 km, seven hours, US$17). Sleepers are available on the overnight Skopje-Belgrade train. Trains run twice a day to/from Greece.

Sample 2nd-class international train fares from Skopje are US$16 to Thessaloniki (285 km, five hours), US$47 to Athens (795 km, 14 hours), US$22 to Sofia (401 km via Niš), US$64 to Vienna (20 hours) and US$91 to Salzburg (22 hours).

Greece-bound it's cheaper only to buy a ticket to Thessaloniki and get another on to Athens from there. There's no direct rail link between Macedonia and Bulgaria and the train is not recommended for travel between Sofia and Skopje as you must change trains in Yugoslavia and a visa may be required.

Car & Motorbike

There are several main highway border crossings into Macedonia from neighbouring countries.

To/From Yugoslavia You can cross at Blace (between Skopje and Uroševac) and Tabanovci (10 km north of Kumanovo).

To/From Bulgaria The main crossings are Kriva Palanka (between Sofia and Skopje), Delčevo (26 km west of Blagoevgrad) and Novo Selo (between Kulata and Strumica).

To/From Greece There are crossings at Gevgelija (between Skopje and Thessaloniki), Doiran (just east of Gevgelija) and Medžitlija (16 km south of Bitola).

To/From Albania The crossings are Sveti Naum (29 km south of Ohrid), Čafa San (12

MACEDONIA

km south-west of Struga) and Blato (five km north-west of Debar).

Getting Around

BUS
Bus service is well developed in Macedonia with fairly frequent service from Skopje to Ohrid and Bitola. Always book buses to/from Ohrid well in advance.

TRAIN
You won't find Macedonia's trains of much use, except perhaps for the overnight train from Skopje to Belgrade and trains to Greece. The local train from Skopje to Bitola takes four hours to cover the 229 km.

CAR & MOTORBIKE
Petrol coupons can be purchased at the border crossings with Yugoslavia and Greece 24 hours a day (payment in cash Deutschmarks only). During business hours (weekdays from 7 am to 3 pm) coupons can also be purchased at Automoto Sojuz offices in Bitola, Gevgelija, Gostivar, Kavadarci, Kičevo, Kočani, Kumanovo, Prilep, Ohrid, Skopje, Štip, Strumica, Tetovo and Titov Veles. The regulations surrounding petrol coupons change frequently, so check at the border.

Motorway tolls can be paid either in cash or for coupons purchased at the border.

Speed limits for cars and motorcycles are 120 km/h on motorways, 80 km/h on the open road and from 50 to 60 km/h in towns. Speeding fines are high (from US$90 to US$200) and inflexibly enforced by radar-equipped highway police, so never speed! Not wearing a seat belt costs US$40 and parking tickets average US$90.

The Macedonia-wide number for emergency highway assistance is ☎ 987.

Around the Country

SKOPJE (СКОПЈЕ)
Macedonia's capital, Skopje (population 600,000), is strategically set on the Vardar River at a crossroads of Balkan routes almost exactly midway between Tirana and Sofia, capitals of neighbouring Albania and Bulgaria. Thessaloniki, Greece, is 260 km south-east, near the point where the Vardar flows into the Aegean. The Romans recognised the location's importance long ago when they made Scupi the centre of Dardania Province. Later conquerors included the Slavs, Byzantines, Bulgarians, Normans and Serbs, until the Turks arrived in 1392 and managed to hold onto Uskup (Skopje) until 1912.

After a devastating earthquake in 1963 which killed 1066 people, aid poured in from the rest of Yugoslavia to create the modern urban landscape we see today. It's evident that the planners got carried away by the money being thrown their way, and erected oversized, irrelevant structures which are now crumbling due to lack of maintenance and function. Fortunately, much of the old town survived, so Skopje offers the chance to see the whole history of the Balkans in one shot, almost as if it had been cut in half with a knife. Do try to get beyond the tourist sights and feel the pulse of this vibrant Balkan metropolis.

Orientation
Most of central Skopje is a pedestrian zone with the 15th century Turkish stone bridge over the Vardar River linking the old and new towns. South of the bridge is Ploštad Maršal Tito, which gives into ulica Maršal Tito leading south. The relatively new elevated train station is a 15-minute walk south-east of the stone bridge. The bus station is a few minutes' walk north of the bridge. Farther north is Čaršija, the old Turkish bazar.

The left-luggage office at the bus station is open from 5 am to 10 pm. Left luggage at the train station is open 24 hours.

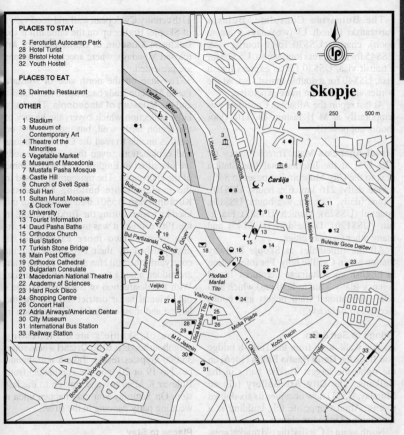

PLACES TO STAY
2 Feroturist Autocamp Park
28 Hotel Turist
29 Bristol Hotel
32 Youth Hostel

PLACES TO EAT
25 Dalmettu Restaurant

OTHER
1 Stadium
3 Museum of
   Contemporary Art
4 Theatre of the
   Minorities
5 Vegetable Market
6 Museum of Macedonia
7 Mustafa Pasha Mosque
8 Castle Hill
9 Church of Sveti Spas
10 Suli Han
11 Sultan Murat Mosque
    & Clock Tower
12 University
13 Tourist Information
14 Daud Pasha Baths
15 Orthodox Church
16 Bus Station
17 Turkish Stone Bridge
18 Main Post Office
19 Orthodox Cathedral
20 Bulgarian Consulate
21 Macedonian National Theatre
22 Academy of Sciences
23 Hard Rock Disco
24 Shopping Centre
26 Concert Hall
27 Adria Airways/American Centar
30 City Museum
31 International Bus Station
33 Railway Station

Skopje

0   250   500 m

Čaršija

Information

The tourist information office is opposite the Daud Pasha Baths on the viaduct between the Turkish bridge and Čaršija.

The office of the Automoto Sojuz or Automobile Club of Macedonia (☎ 116 011) is at Ivo Ribar Lola 51 just west of the downtown area. Petrol coupons are available here.

Money The Stopanska Banka facing the Turkish bridge opposite the bus station changes travellers' cheques weekdays from 7 am to 7 pm, Saturday 7 am to 1 pm.

Most black-market moneychanging occurs along the main drag in Čaršija.

Post & Telecommunications Poste restante mail is held at the train station post office, not the main post office. The telephone centre in the main post office near the centre is open 24 hours. Skopje's telephone code is 091.

Foreign Embassies The American Centar (☎ 116 623), ulica Dame Gruev 7, is open weekdays from 10 am to 4 pm.

MACEDONIA

The Bulgarian Consulate, Bulevar Partizanski Odredi 13 (weekdays 9 am to noon), charges US$30 for a tourist visa, US$45 for an express tourist visa, US$20 for a transit visa, US$30 for an express transit visa, US$40 for a double transit visa. At the border visas are even more expensive.

At last report the Albanian Consulate was temporarily at M H Jasmin 14, 11th floor (hours not posted).

Travel Agencies Mata Travel Agency (☎ 239 175) at the International Bus Station next to the City Museum has buses to Sofia (twice daily, 216 km, 6½ hours, US$10), Tirana (daily, 129 km, 9½ hours, US$10), Istanbul (US$23), Munich (US$87), Frankfurt (US$120), Düsseldorf (US$145) and many other German cities.

All the timetables at Skopje Railway Station are in Cyrillic only. For information in English go upstairs to Feroturist Travel Agency (daily 7 am to 8.30 pm) which also sells international train tickets and books sleepers to Belgrade.

Things to See & Do

As you walk north from the Turkish bridge you'll see the **Daud Pasha Baths** (1466) on the right, the largest Turkish baths in the Balkans. The **City Art Gallery** (closed Monday, US$1) now occupies its six domed rooms. Almost opposite this building is a functioning Orthodox church.

North again is Čaršija, the old market area, which is well worth exploring. Steps up on the left lead to the tiny **Church of Sveti Spas** with a finely carved iconostasis done in 1824 (US$1). It's half buried because when it was constructed in the 17th century no church was allowed to be higher than a mosque. In the courtyard at Sveti Spas is the tomb of Goce Delčev, a mustachioed IMRO freedom fighter killed by the Turks in 1903.

Beyond the church is the **Mustafa Pasha Mosque** (1492), with an earthquake-cracked dome. The US$1 ticket includes the right to ascend the 124 steps of the minaret. In the park across the street from this mosque are the ruins of the castle, **Fort Kale**, with an

11th century Cyclopean wall and good views of Skopje. Higher up on the same hill is the lacklustre **Museum of Contemporary Art** (closed Monday), where special exhibitions are presented.

The lane on the north side of Mustafa Pasha Mosque leads back down into Čaršija and the **Museum of Macedonia**. This has a large collection which covers the history of the region fairly well, but much is lost on visitors unable to read the Cyrillic captions and explanations, even though the periods are identified in English at the top of some of the showcases. The museum is housed in the modern white building behind the **Kuršumli Han** (1550), a caravanserai or inn used by traders during the Turkish period. In the 19th century it was turned into a notorious prison. Two more caravanserais distinguished by their two-storey interior courtyards, the Suli Han and the Kapan Han, are hidden among the streets of old Čaršija. With the destruction of Sarajevo, Skopje's old Oriental bazaar district has become the largest and most colourful of its kind left in Europe.

One of Skopje's most interesting neighbourhoods is **Suto Orizari** where some 35,000 Gypsies reside. Take a northbound bus No 19 or 20 (pay the conductor) from Bulevar K Misirkov and stay on to the last stop. On Saturday you may happen upon a wedding party dancing in the street.

Places to Stay

Camping From April to mid-October you can pitch a tent at *Feroturist Autocamp Park* (☎ 228 246) for US$4 per person and US$4 per tent. Basic camping caravans are for hire year-round at US$11 per person (mosquitoes free). Late-night music from the restaurant can be a problem. This camping ground is between the river and the stadium, a 15-minute walk upstream from the Turkish stone bridge along the right (south) bank. It's always a good bet.

Hostels The HI *Dom 'Blagoj Šošolčev' Youth Hostel* (☎ 115 519), Prolet 25, is near the train station. The two, three and four-bed dorms are US$10 for members, US$11 for non-members. New, fully renovated double rooms with private bath are US$15 per person for members, US$17 for non-members (including breakfast). Open all year, 24 hours a day, it's often full with groups.

In July and August you can stay at the *Studentski dom Goce Delčev* (☎ 258 004 or 363 306), ulica Ivo Lola Ribar off Bulevar Partizanski Odredi on the west side of Skopje (too far to walk). Double rooms with bath are US$6 per bed, but you can only check in after 3 pm. Take bus No 5 westbound from Veljko Vlahovič or 11 Oktomvri and ask.

Private Rooms The tourist information office (☎ 116 854), on the viaduct two blocks north of the Turkish stone bridge, has singles/doubles in private homes beginning at US$20/35 but they're in short supply and there's no reduction for stays longer than one night. At this price insist on something in the centre.

Hotels There are no cheap or even moderately priced hotels in Skopje. The cheapest of the expensive ones is the old 33-room *Bristol Hotel* (☎ 114 883) opposite the City Museum which charges US$52/84 single/double with breakfast. The newer 91-room *Hotel Turist* (☎ 114 434) just up ulica Maršal Tito is US$57/84 single/double. At these prices you needn't worry about getting a room (hard currency only, please). At a pinch, ask taxi drivers if they know of any cheaper places to stay.

Places to Eat

Colourful small restaurants in Čaršija serving kebab and *aevapčiai* reflect a Turkish culinary heritage still dear to the stomachs of many Macedonians.

There are two good restaurants in the modern city centre beyond Ploštad Maršal Tito at the south side of the Turkish stone bridge. The *Dalmettu Restaurant* is fairly obvious across the square at the beginning of ulica Maršal Tito, on the left as you come

from the bridge. Vegetarians will like the salad bar and the pizza is also good. *Ishrana Self-Service* is half a block away down the next street over to the right. Look for the vertical sign reading 'restaurant' in large blue letters.

Women will feel comfortable at the *Baghdad Café* in the old Bezisten in Čaršija and there's sometimes music in the evening here. Most of the other cafés in this area are male domains.

Entertainment

Check the concert hall, ulica Maršal Tito 12. *Hard Rock*, facing the river behind the Academy of Sciences, is a large modern discotheque which opens nightly except Monday at 10 pm during the school year (closed July and August).

Club MHT, downstairs below the Macedonian National Theatre, also cranks up around 10 pm and is open in summer,

Getting There & Away

Bus There are buses to Ohrid, Bitola, Priština, Prizren, Pea, Podgorica and Belgrade. Book a seat on the bus of your choice the day before, especially if you're headed for Ohrid Lake. There are two bus routes from Skopje to Ohrid Lake: the one through Tetovo (167 km) is much faster and more direct than the bus that goes via Titov Veles and Bitola (261 km). If you just want to get to the Adriatic from Skopje, catch the overnight bus to Podgorica (382 km).

If for some reason you can't take the direct bus to Sofia (see Travel Agencies above) there are 12 buses daily to Kriva Palanka (96 km), 13 km short of the Bulgarian border. Onward hitching should be possible.

Train All trains between central Europe and Greece pass through Skopje. There are two daily trains to/from Thessaloniki (285 km, five hours, US$16) and Athens (795 km, 14 hours, US$47 one-way).

Fast trains run to Belgrade (472 km, seven hours, US$17), and local trains run to Bitola (229 km, four hours). Couchettes are available to Belgrade. Feroturist Travel Agency upstairs in Skopje Railway Station sells international tickets and books couchettes and sleepers (US$13).

Getting Around
City buses in Skopje use tokens (getone) which you must buy at kiosks at major stops.

To/From the Airport The Adria Airways airport bus (US$2) leaves from the International Bus Station next to the City Museum 1½ hours before Adria flights

OHRID (ОРИД)
Ohrid Lake, a natural tectonic lake in the south-west corner of Macedonia, is the deepest lake in Europe (294 metres) and one of the oldest in the world. A third of its 450-sq-km surface area belongs to Albania. Nestled amid mountains at an altitude of 695 metres, the Macedonian section of the lake is the more beautiful, with striking vistas of the open waters from the beach and hills.

The town of Ohrid is *the* Macedonian tourist mecca and signs in the windows of market cafés offer *hollandse koffie*. Some 30 'cultural monuments' in the area keep visitors busy. Predictably, the oldest ruins readily seen today are Roman. Lihnidos (Ohrid) was on the Via Egnatia, which connected the Adriatic to the Aegean, and part of a Roman amphitheatre has been uncovered in the old town.

Under Byzantium Ohrid became the episcopal centre of Macedonia. The first Slavic university was founded here in 893 by Bishop Clement of Ohrid, a disciple of St Cyril and St Methodius, and from the 10th century until 1767 the patriarchate of Ohrid held sway. The revival of the archbishopric of Ohrid in 1958 and its independence from the Serbian Orthodox Church in 1967 were important steps on the road to modern nationhood. Many of the small Orthodox churches with intact medieval frescoes have now been adapted to the needs of ticketed tourists. Nice little signs in Latin script direct you to the sights, but even the cellophane wrapping doesn't spoil the flavour of enchanting Ohrid.

Orientation
Ohrid Bus Station is next to the post office in the centre of town. To the west is the old town and to the south is the lake.

The left-luggage office at the bus station is open from 5 am to 8.20 pm daily. Ask at the ticket windows.

Information
'Biljana' Tourist Office is at Partizanska 3 beside the bus station.

Automoto Sojuz (☎ 22 338) is on Galičica at Lazo Trpkoski, backstreets behind the large 'Mini Market' on the corner of Jane Sandanski and Bulevar Turistička, a major intersection on the east side of town.

Money The Stopanska Banka agency (green sign), Sveti Kliment Ohridski 110 (Monday to Saturday from 8 am to 8 pm, Sunday 7 am to 1 pm), changes travellers' cheques without commission.

Post & Telecommunications The telephone centre at the post office near the bus station is open Monday to Saturday 7 am to 9 pm, Sunday 9 am to noon and 6 to 8 pm. Ohrid's telephone code is 096.

Travel Agencies Putnik, Partizanska 2 opposite the bus station, sells train tickets.

Things to See & Do
The picturesque old town of Ohrid rises from Sveti Kliment Ohridski, the main pedestrian mall, up towards Sveti Kliment Church and the citadel. A medieval town wall still isolates this hill from the surrounding valley. Penetrate the old town on Car Samuil as far as the **Archaeological Museum** in the four-storey dwelling of the Robevu family (1827) at No 62. Further along Car Samuil is 11th century **Sveti Sofija**, also worth the US$1.25 admission price. Aside from the frescoes there's an unusual Turkish *mimbar* (pulpit) remaining from the days when this was a mosque, and an upstairs portico of real architectural interest.

From near here ulica Lindenska climbs to the North Gate, to the right of which is the

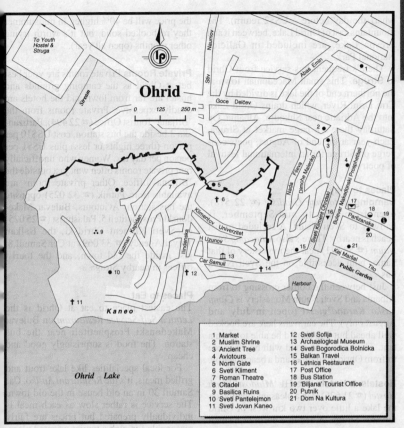

To Youth
Hostel &
Struga

Ohrid

Stream

Stiv

Naumov

Goce Delčev

Abas Emin

0   125   250 m

Nada Fileva

Dimche Malenko

Bulevar Makedonski Prosphetiteli

Kuzman Kapidan

Klimentov Univerzitet

Ilindenska

H Uzunov

Car Samuil

Sveti Kliment Chridski

Kej Maršal Tito

Partizanska

Public Garden

Harbour

Ohrid Lake

Kaneo

1 Market
2 Muslim Shrine
3 Ancient Tree
4 Aviotours
5 North Gate
6 Sveti Kliment
7 Roman Theatre
8 Citadel
9 Basilica Ruins
10 Sveti Pantelejmon
11 Sveti Jovan Kaneo
12 Sveti Sofija
13 Archaelogical Museum
14 Sveti Bogorodica Bolnicka
15 Balkan Travel
16 Letnica Restaurant
17 Post Office
18 Bus Station
19 'Biljana' Tourist Office
20 Putnik
21 Dom Na Kultura

13th century **Church of Sveti Kliment**, almost covered inside with vivid frescoes of biblical scenes. An icon gallery is opposite this church and there's a fine view from the terrace. The walls of the 10th century **citadel** to the west offer more splendid views.

In the park below the citadel are the ruins of an Early Christian **basilica** with 5th century mosaics covered by protective sand and nearby is the shell of **Sveti Pantelejmon**, now a small museum. Tiny 13th century **Church of Sveti Jovan Kaneo**, on a point overlooking the lake, occupies a very pleasant site even if you don't pay to go

inside. There's a beach at the foot of the cliffs. (All churches and museums at Ohrid are closed on Monday.)

The better part of a second day at Ohrid could be spent on a pilgrimage to the Albanian border to see the 17th century **Church of Sveti Naum** on a hill above the lake, 29 km south of Ohrid by bus. From here you get a view of the Albanian town of Pogradec across the lake and inside the church is a finely carved iconostasis. In summer you can also come by boat (it only goes when a group is present, so ask about times at the Putnik office opposite the bus station and at the wharf the day before – US$2 return). The mountains east of Ohrid Lake, between it and Prespa Lake, are included in Galičica National Park.

There's frequent bus service from Ohrid to **Struga**. This small Macedonian town at the northern end of the lake is divided by the Crni Drim River, which drains Ohrid Lake into the Adriatic near Shkodra, Albania. On Saturday there's a large market at Struga. Each year at the end of August, poets converge on Struga for an international festival of poetry.

Places to Stay

Camping *Autocamp Gradište* (☎ 22 578), open from June to mid-September, is halfway to Sveti Naum. A secluded nudist beach is nearby. There's also *Autocamp Sveti Naum* (☎ 58 811) near the monastery of that name, both accessible on the Sveti Naum bus.

Just between the border crossing to/from Albania and Sveti Naum Monastery is *Camp Vasko Karandžgleski* (open in July and August only). The caravans here are booked well ahead but you should be able to pitch a tent. The location is good with boat service to/from Ohrid in summer and a beach nearby.

Hostels & Hotels The HI *'Mladost' Youth Hostel* (☎ 21 626) is in a pleasant location on the lake a little over two km west of Ohrid towards Struga. A bed in a dorm or a small four-berth caravan will cost around US$6 per person. Even if all the caravans are full they'll let you pitch a tent for US$2 per person, US$3 per tent, US$1 per person tax. The hostel is open from April to mid-October and YHA membership cards are not essential. In midsummer it will be full of preteens. Get there on the Struga bus or if you're walking, turn left at the fifth minaret counting from the one opposite the old tree at the top of Sveti Kliment Ohridski.

The *Mladinski Centar* (☎ 21 671), a modern hotel next to the youth hostel, is US$16 per person in three-bedded rooms, including three meals daily, provided you have a youth hostel card. Without the card

the price will be 40% higher. In midsummer they're booked solid, but it's worth trying other months (open all year).

Private Rooms Private rooms are your best bet at Ohrid as the camping grounds and hostel are far from town and the hotels are deadly expensive. Private rooms from the 'Biljana' Tourist Office (☎ 22 494), Partizanska 3 beside the bus station, cost US$10 per person (three nights or less) plus US$1 per person per day tax. Women who unofficially rent private rooms often wait just outside the 'Biljana' office. Other private rooms are available from Putnik (☎ 32 025) opposite the bus station; Aviotours, Bulevar Makedonski Prosphetiteli 5; Palasturist (☎ 25 025) on Sveti Kliment Ohridski; the Balkan Travel Agency (☎ 33 069) at Car Samuil 8, just inside the old town; and the tourist offices in nearby Struga.

Places to Eat

The easiest place to eat at Ohrid is the *Letnica Self-Service Restaurant* on Bulevar Makedonski Prosphetiteli near the bus station. The food is surprisingly good and cheap.

For local specialities like lake trout and grilled meats, it's the *Restaurant Antiko*, Car Samuil 30 in an old house in the old town. The service is rather slow as each meal is individually prepared but prices are fairly reasonable for such a tourist-oriented place. Watch the cost of the lake trout if you want it prepared Ohrid-style as it's charged by weight and the bill can work out 50% higher than expected. Check this with the waiter when ordering.

Entertainment

The Balkan Festival of Folk Dances & Songs held at Ohrid in early July draws folkloric groups from around the Balkans. The Ohrid Summer Festival from mid-July to mid-August features classical concerts in the church of Sveti Sofija as well as many other events.

Ohrid's movie theatre is Dom Na Kultura

Grigor Prlicev facing the lakeside park. Various cultural events are also held here.

Getting There & Away

Air Palair has flights from Ohrid to Ljubljana (US$140) and Düsseldorf (US$250).

Bus Some buses between Ohrid and Skopje run via Tetovo (167 km, three hours, US$4), others via Bitola (261 km). The former route is much shorter, faster and more scenic, so try to take it. It pays to book a seat the day before.

Overnight buses from Ohrid to Belgrade (694 km) leave Ohrid around 3.30 and 5.45 pm, reaching Belgrade about 14 hours later. Adriatic-bound, take a bus to Skopje, then another to Podgorica.

Buses to Struga (seven km) leave about every 20 minutes from stand No 1 at the bus station (enter through the back doors and pay the conductor).

To/From Albania To go to Albania catch a bus or boat to Sveti Naum Monastery which is very near the border crossing (cut up the hill through the tennis courts at the camping ground next to the monastery). In summer there are six buses a day from Ohrid to Sveti Naum (29 km), in winter three daily. From Albanian customs it's six km to Pogradec but hitching is easy (and it's an interesting walk, if necessary).

To/From Greece To get to Greece you can take a bus from Ohrid to Bitola (80 km), then hitch 16 km to the Medžitlija highway border crossing to Florina. It's much easier,

however, to go to Skopje and pick up a train to Thessaloniki (US$16) from there.

BITOLA (БИТОЛА)

Bitola, the southernmost city of former Yugoslavia and second-largest in Macedonia, sits on a 660-metre-high plateau between the mountains 16 km north of the Greek border. The old bazar area (Stara Čaršija) is colourful but the facilities at Bitola are poor. Private rooms are unavailable and the hotels overpriced. No left-luggage office is provided at either the bus or train stations and the city is useless as a transit point to/from Greece as there's no bus or train to the border (Medžitlija). You must hitch the 16 km. Bus service to Ohrid (80 km) and Skopje (181 km), on the other hand, is good.

It's probably not worth totting your luggage two km into town just to see Bitola's Turkish mosques and bazar but the **Heraclea ruins** beyond the old cemetery, one km south of the bus station, are recommended (admission US$1.20, photos US$6 extra). Founded in the 4th century BC by Philip II of Macedonia, Heraclea was conquered by the Romans two centuries later and became an important stage on the Via Egnatia. From the 4th to 6th centuries AD it was an episcopal seat. Excavations continue but the Roman baths, portico and theatre can now be seen. More interesting are the two Early Christian basilicas and the episcopal palace, complete with splendid mosaics. There's also a small museum through the refreshment stand, and a nice terrace on which to have a Coke or beer.

Poland

In both area and population, 312,683-sq-km Poland is by far the largest country in Eastern Europe. The next largest, Romania, is only two-thirds the size of Poland and none of the 10 other countries covered in this book are more than a third as big. Poland is just a bit smaller than reunified Germany and about the same size as the US state of New Mexico.

Always open to invaders from east and west, Poland has had a tumultuous past. The weight of history is on Kraków, the illustrious royal city; Gdańsk (Danzig), the former Hanseatic trading town where WW II began; Auschwitz, a reminder of the depths to which humanity can descend; and rebuilt Warsaw, symbol of the resilient Polish spirit. In 1939 Poland displayed great courage in being first to say 'no' to Hitler and half a century later it again changed the course of history by becoming the first Eastern European state to break free of communism.

Apart from the historical and cultural sides to this subtle land of Chopin and Copernicus, there's the gentle beauty of Baltic beaches, quiet north-eastern lakes and forests, and the majestic mountains in the south, all requiring time to be appreciated. Each of the separate regions of Poland has its own character: Mazovia (around Warsaw), Małopolska ('Little Poland', in the south-east), Silesia (in the south-west), Wielkopolska ('Big Poland', in the west), Pomerania (in the north-west) and Mazuria (in the north-east). Palpable differences remain between the areas once controlled by Austria, Germany and Russia; yet bound together by Catholicism, language, nationality and a common experience, Poland has a unity few other nations in the region can match.

In 1944 Stalin commented that fitting communism to Poland was like putting a saddle on a cow and now that the saddle has been removed, the pace of economic change goes faster in Poland than anywhere else in Eastern Europe. Though the full benefits of

the changes are still in the future, Poland has already taken on new life as goods reappear in the shops and Polish small businesspeople spread their wares in the streets. The psychological change is tremendous.

For visitors, Poland is now a much nicer place than it was under communism. The shortages of food and drink are gone, it's much easier to find a cheap place to stay and most of the annoying paperwork previously involved in a visit (compulsory exchange, police registration, currency declarations, and, in many cases, visas) have been abolished. The old suspicion has also disappeared and foreigners are now accepted everywhere on the same footing as Poles. Of course prices have gone up, but tourists have been freed from the nuisance of having to deal on the black market to get fair value for their money and, compared to any Western European country, Poland is still excellent value. This is one of the only countries in Eastern Europe where you won't be charged

POLAND

Poland

0   50   100 km

two or three times more than the locals for hotel rooms. Once you have a visa (where required) there are few additional hassles.

Facts about the Country

HISTORY

In the 6th and 7th centuries AD the West Slavs pushed north and west and occupied most of what is now Poland. By the 10th century the leaders of the Polanian tribe in western Poland were uniting other Slavic tribes under their rule. Mieszko I adopted Christianity in 966, a date considered to mark the formation of the first Polish state, and in the year 1000 the Gniezno Archbishopric was founded. Boleslav the Brave took the title of king in 1025 and his descendant, Boleslav the Bold, consolidated the power of the Piast dynasty over a territory very similar to the Poland of today.

There was constant pressure from the west as the Germans pushed into Pomerania and Silesia, so, to be less vulnerable, from the 11th century onwards Polish kings were no longer crowned in Poznań but in Kraków. In the mid-12th century the country was divided into four principalities and a weakened Poland soon fell prey to invaders. In 1226 the Teutonic Knights, a Germanic military and religious order, were invited to come to Poland by the prince of Mazovia to subdue the restive Prussians of the northeast. Once the knights had subjugated the Baltic tribes they turned their attention to the Poles. The order set up a state in the lower Vistula area east of Gdańsk/Toruń, ruled from their castle at Malbork. Tatar invasions devastated southern Poland in 1241 and 1259. Though Poland was reunified in 1320, the knights held onto Pomerania and Prussia.

From the 14th to 17th centuries Poland was a great power. It's said that the 14th century king, Casimir III the Great, last of the Piast dynasty, 'found a Poland made of wood and left one made of masonry'. His administrative reforms increased the significance of towns like Kraków, Lublin and Poznań. When Casimir died without an heir, the throne passed to the daughter of the king of Hungary, Princess Jadwiga, who in 1386 married the duke of Lithuania, uniting the two countries under the Jagiello dynasty.

In 1410 the combined Polish, Lithuanian and Ruthenian (Ukrainian) forces under Ladislaus Jagiello defeated the Teutonic Knights at Grunwald, south of Olsztyn. After the Thirteen Years' War (1454-66) the Teutonic order was broken up and in 1525 the secular Duchy of Prussia became a fiefdom of the Polish crown. In 1490 King Casimir IV of Poland also assumed the Hungarian throne.

The early 16th century monarch Sigismund I the Old brought the Renaissance to Poland and in 1543 Nicolaus Copernicus published his immortal treatise *De Revolutionibus Orbium Coelestium*. At a time when much of Europe was being torn apart by religious wars and persecutions, there was relative peace and tolerance in Poland. Lithuania and Poland were formally united as one country in 1569, to oppose Russian expansion, and the Polish-Lithuanian Commonwealth became the largest

country in Europe, stretching from the Black Sea to the Baltic Sea.

After the death of Sigismund Augustus in 1572, the Jagiello dynasty became extinct and the Sejm (parliament) decided future kings would be elected by the entire gentry (about 10% of the total population), a system which greatly increased the power of the feudal nobility. In the early 17th century Sigismund III, an elected king from the Swedish Vasa line, moved the capital from Kraków to Warsaw. Sigismund III also embroiled Poland in Swedish dynastic wars and, though the country successfully held off Sweden and Moscow for a time, in 1655 a Swedish invasion ('the Deluge') devastated Poland's towns. King Jan III Sobieski, builder of Warsaw's Wilanów Palace, led a crusade against the Turks which resulted in their removal from Hungary after 1683.

Weak leadership, constant wars and the domination of the gentry over the middle class led to the decline of Poland in the 18th century. In the first partition of Poland in 1772, Russia, Prussia and Austria took 29% of the national territory. Poland's last king, Stanislaus Poniatowski, tried to reverse the situation with reforms, but the powerful magnates resisted strongly, leading to civil war and a pretext for foreign intervention. In 1791 the king granted Poland a democratic constitution (the second in the world) but the magnates again revolted, leading to a second partition in 1793. A year later Tadeusz Kościuszko, a veteran of the American Revolution, led a war of independence against the invaders but was defeated in 1795. A subsequent third partition that year wiped Poland right off the map of Europe until 1918.

The oppressed Poles supported Napoleon, who set up a duchy of Warsaw in 1807 from where he led his Grand Army to Moscow in 1812 (the beginning of a special Franco-Polish relationship which has continued until today). After 1815 Poland again came under tsarist Russia. There were unsuccessful uprisings against this in 1831, 1848 and 1864 with Poland's position worsening after each one. A Russification and Germanisation policy was enforced in the areas controlled by those powers; Poles were permitted to maintain their identity only in the Austrian-occupied part around Kraków.

The 20th Century

Poland was completely overrun by the Germans during WW I, but in 1919 a Polish state was again established by the Treaty of Versailles. Then the Polish military struck east and took big chunks of Lithuania, Belorussia and Ukraine, inhabited by non-Polish majorities, from a weakened Soviet Union. In 1926 Marshal Józef Piłsudski, ex-commander of the Polish Legions which had fought alongside Austria in WW I, staged a military coup and set himself up as dictator. Poland gained a measure of prosperity under Piłsudski, but by the time of his death in 1935 Poland had been ruined by the depression and soon fell victim to Hitler.

WW II began in Gdańsk (at that time the Free City of Danzig) where 182 Poles at Westerplatte held out for a week against the battleship *Schleswig Holstein*, Stuka dive bombers and thousands of German troops. To the west the Polish Pomorska Brigade of mounted cavalry met General Guderian's tanks – medieval lances against modern armour – in a final suicidal charge. Polish resistance continued for almost a month and German losses during the campaign were as great as subsequent losses during the 1940-41 invasions of Western Europe, the Balkans and North Africa combined. As these events took place in the west, the Soviet Union invaded from the east and took back the territories lost in the 1919-21 Polish-Soviet War. Poland had been partitioned for the fourth time.

During WW II Poland was the only country in Europe which never produced any quislings (collaborators) willing to serve in a German-dominated puppet government. The Nazi governor general, Hans Frank, ruled those areas not directly incorporated into the Reich, and Poles resident in the areas which had been annexed by Germany were deported east. Yet two resistance groups, the London-directed Armia Krajowa (Home

Army) and the communist Gwardia Ludowa (People's Guard), later the People's Army, fought on inside Poland. In July 1944 the Red Army liberated Lublin and set up a communist-led provisional government.

Six million Poles – a fifth of the population – died during the Nazi terror, half of them Jews. During the Warsaw Ghetto uprising of 1943, some 70,000 poorly armed, starving Jews led by Mordechai Anielewicz held out against the full weight of the Nazi army for 27 days. The Warsaw uprising was begun on 1 August 1944 by the Home Army as Soviet forces approached the right bank of the Vistula River. The intention was to evict the retreating Germans from Warsaw and have a non-communist force in place to greet the Soviet army, but the uprising was premature. The Nazis brought up reserves to halt the Red Army in Praga across the river, then engaged the 50,000 Polish irregulars in house-to-house combat.

By 2 October, when the remaining partisans surrendered with honour, some 250,000 Poles had died, many of them civilians slaughtered en masse by SS troops. All the remaining inhabitants were then expelled from the city and German demolition teams levelled Warsaw street by street. The Soviet armies which entered the city three months later encountered only desolation. Ironically the Germans set the stage for a post-war communist Poland by physically eliminating the bulk of the non-communist resistance within the country.

At the Teheran Conference in November 1943, Churchill, Roosevelt and Stalin decided that everything east of the Odra (Oder) and Nysa (Neisse) rivers – which meant Silesia, Pomerania and Mazuria – was to be returned to Poland after centuries of German control. At the same time the Soviet Union was to get the eastern territories, reducing Poland's land area to four-fifths of the prewar size. Millions of people were dislocated by these changes which brought Poland's borders back to where they had been eight centuries earlier. Poland's postwar borders were guaranteed by the creation of the Warsaw Pact in 1955, and in

1970 Chancellor Willy Brandt signed a treaty accepting the Oder-Neisse border.

Recent History

After the war a Soviet-style communist system was installed in Poland and the country was run according to five and six-year plans. The emphasis on heavy industry led to chronic shortages of consumer goods while the *nomenklatura* of party bureaucrats enjoyed many privileges. Intellectual freedom was curtailed by the security apparatus and individual initiative stifled. In 1956, when Nikita Khrushchev denounced Stalin at the Soviet 20th Party Congress, Bolesław Bierut, the Stalinist party chief in Poland, died of a heart attack!

In June 1956 workers in Poznań rioted over low wages, and in October, Władysław Gomułka, an ex-political prisoner of the Stalin era, took over as party first secretary. Gomułka introduced a series of superficial reforms reducing Soviet domination of Poland and freeing political prisoners, but the basic system continued unchanged. After the Arab-Israeli War of 1967, party hardliners used an 'anti-Zionist' purge to enforce discipline, but by December 1970 living conditions had declined to the point where workers in northern Poland went on strike over food price increases. When 300 of them were shot down during demonstrations, Edward Gierek replaced Gomułka as party leader and persuaded the strikers to return to work by promising sweeping changes.

Gierek launched Poland on a reckless programme of industrial expansion to produce exports which could be sold on world markets. Money to finance this was supplied by 17 capitalist governments and 501 banks, and by 1981 the country had run up a hard-currency debt of US$27 billion. Many of the ill-founded heavy industry schemes ended in failure as a recession in the West shrank the markets for Polish exports at the end of the 1970s.

This decade of mismanagement left Poland bankrupt. Living standards fell sharply as Poland was forced to divert goods to export from domestic consumption, to earn hard currency with which to service the debt. The election of a Pole to the papacy in October 1978, and the visit to Poland by John Paul II in June 1979, also changed the atmosphere in a country where the party was supposed to play the 'leading role'.

In 1980 a wave of strikes over sharp food price increases forced Gierek out and marked the emergence of Lech Wałęsa's Solidarity trade union which soon had 10 million members (a million of them also Communist Party members). Solidarity said all it wanted was self-management of the factories by workers' councils instead of central planning. At first the Polish government was conciliatory, recognising Solidarity in November 1980, and conceding to a five-day work week. In September 1981, many of Solidarity's demands for reduced central planning and greater worker control over enterprises were met.

Things soon got out of hand as union militants challenged government authority. Strikes and obstruction threatened Poland with economic collapse and a Soviet military intervention which could have led to a bloody civil war. On 13 December 1981 martial law was declared by General Wojciech Jaruzelski, who had become prime minister in February 1981, and thousands were interned as the government broke up the union. In October 1982 Solidarity was dissolved by the courts and by July 1983 martial law could be lifted.

A year after the imposition of martial law, General Jaruzelski introduced economic reforms of his own based on greater autonomy for state corporations. In April 1986, the government set in motion 'second stage' reforms providing for decentralisation, worker control of companies, greater competition, incentives, a market economy and some political pluralism. These ·initiatives lacked public support, and in a November 1987 referendum Poles cast a vote of no confidence in the communist government.

Meanwhile Solidarity had been biding its time, and in 1988 fresh strikes followed government attempts to remove food subsidies.

The big pay increases won by the striking workers clearly revealed government weakness, and officials agreed to meet with Solidarity to discuss reform, realising that without a compromise Poland would explode.

In April 1989, nine weeks of round-table talks between Solidarity and the communists ended in an accord which legalised Solidarity and the other opposition groups. A 100-seat senate was to be created, giving Poland a two-house parliament for the first time since 1946. Both the senate and the new president would have veto power over a 460-seat Sejm, though these vetoes could be overridden by a two-thirds majority vote in the lower house. The Polish United Workers Party (PZPR) and allied parties were guaranteed 65% of the seats in the lower house, while the other 35% of the Sejm and the entire senate were to be chosen in Eastern Europe's first Western-style elections.

The sweeping Solidarity victory in the June 1989 elections soon caused the communist coalition to fall apart, and in August 1989 Tadeusz Mazowiecki was picked to head a Solidarity-led coalition, thus becoming the first non-communist prime minister of an Eastern European country in over four decades. Though General Jaruzelski had been elected to serve as a transitional president by parliament in July 1989, the communist era in Poland had come to an end, and the two-million-member Polish United Workers Party dissolved itself at its congress in February 1990.

The Mazowiecki government adopted a 'shock therapy' economic programme to switch Poland from a planned to a free-market economy. On 1 January 1990 price and currency exchange controls were removed, allowing both to find their real levels. During the first month, prices jumped 79% but the markets suddenly filled with products. Inflation was eventually brought under control as the złoty stabilised against Western currencies, though at the cost of wages losing 30% of their purchasing power in 1990 and industrial production falling by 25%. The Mazowiecki team also prepared

for privatisation by cutting subsidies to over-staffed state industries, thereby sending unemployment up from zero to 7.5% in 1990.

In September 1990 General Jaruzelski stepped down and Lech Wałęsa was elected president three months later. Parliamentary elections with no allotted seats were held in October 1991, but Poland's system of proportional representation resulted in 29 political parties winning seats although only two got over 10% of the vote. In January 1992 Jan Olszewski formed a centre-right coalition government which was defeated after only five months in office and in July 1992 Hanna Suchocka of the centrist Democratic Union (UD) cobbled together a coalition of seven parties to become Poland's first woman prime minister.

Abortion had been legal in Poland since 1956 but parliament came under intensive lobbying from the Catholic Church and in January 1993 an anti-abortion law was pushed through by the Christian National Union, one of Suchocka's coalition partners. Abortion became illegal except in cases of incest, rape, deformed foetus or serious danger to the mother. Public opinion surveys showed a large majority of Poles against this move and the conservative politicians strongly resisted having the matter put to a referendum. Moderates did manage to have amendments attached to the law requiring that contraceptives be made available and that Polish schools begin providing sex education for the first time.

Political instability combined with lowered living standards and soaring unemployment had made the successive centrist governments highly unpopular among those hardest hit by economic austerity, especially pensioners, industrial workers and low-ranking civil servants. When Suchocka's government was defeated in a vote of no confidence over a labour dispute in May 1993, President Wałęsa ordered fresh elections to be held under a new rule restricting parliamentary representation to parties winning over 5% of the vote (8% for coalitions).

The parliamentary elections of September 1993 saw a strong swing to the left as voters abandoned the Catholic parties which had pushed through the anti-abortion and religious education legislation. Of the six parties represented in the new parliament, the largest was the Democratic Left Alliance (SLD), a party of ex-communist social democrats. Second place went to the Polish Peasant Party (PSL) whose leader, Waldemar Pawlak, became prime minister (and at age 34, the youngest to hold the post in Polish history), but the real power in the new parliament seems to be SLD leader Aleksander Kwaśniewski. The Solidarity-descended parties together obtained less than a quarter of the seats. The new government has promised to continue economic reform, but more slowly and with more attention for those most affected by the changes.

On 18 September 1993, the last 24 Russian soldiers left Poland by train, almost 54 years to the day after Stalin ordered his armies into the country on 17 September 1939.

GEOGRAPHY

Poland is divided into 49 provinces (voivodships) and 2383 local administrative units (gmina). It's a low, square-shaped country with sides about 550 km long with call of the mountains in the south. The Sudeten Mountains south of Jelenia Góra in Silesia are 280 km long and 50 km wide, with a medium height of 1200 metres culminating in Śnieżka (1605 metres). The Beskidy and Pieniny mountains in the Western Carpathians run along the Slovakian border north of the Tatras. The Bieszczady Mountains in the Eastern Carpathians are open grassy peaks which reach 1346 metres at Tarnica.

Poland's highest mountains are the rocky Tatras, a section of the Carpathian range that Poland shares with Slovakia. The Polish Tatras (150 sq km) are 50 km long and rise to Rysy (2499 metres), and the Slovakian Tatras (600 sq km) culminate in Gerlachovský Štít (2654 metres). Poland's lowest point is actually 1.8 metres below sea level in the Vistula delta.

Lowland predominates in central Poland, a land of great north-flowing rivers such as the Vistula, Odra, Warta and Bug. The entire drainage area of the 1047-km Vistula, the mother river of Poland, lies within Poland's boundaries and most of the rest of the country is drained by the Odra. Poland has more post-glacial lakes than any country in Europe except Finland. West of the Vistula is the Pomeranian lake district, and east are the picturesque Mazurian Lakes. The coastal plain along the broad, sandy, 524-km Baltic coast is spotted with sand dunes, bays and lakes, separated from the sea by narrow sand bars.

ECONOMY

After WW II, Poland was a patchwork of small farms with 38% of the economy in ruins and in the rebuilding process the emphasis was placed on heavy industry, leading to perennial shortages of consumer goods. Heavy industries include steel mills (at Warsaw, Kraków and Katowice), shipbuilding (at Gdańsk), mining machinery and chemicals. Textile production is centred at Łódź.

Zinc, lead, silver and copper are extracted in southern Poland. Poland is the fourth-largest producer of hard bituminous coal in the world, most of it from Silesia. This quality low-sulphur coal is mostly exported while dirty brown lignite is burned locally for electricity and to fuel industry. In 1990 Poland halted construction of its first nuclear power plant which was being built near Gdańsk using outmoded Soviet technology.

The communists sought increased production with scant regard to quality or cost, creating tremendous environmental problems. Some 20 million tonnes of toxic wastes are dumped in unregulated sites annually. The Odra and Vistula rivers discharge thousands and millions of tonnes of heavy metals, nitrogen, phosphorous, oil and highly toxic chloride compounds (PCBs) into the Baltic Sea every year, causing fish catches and tourism to plummet. Half the 813 towns and villages along the Vistula have no sewage-treatment facilities at all and 6000 factories also use the river as an open sewer.

In the south the steel mills and other coal-burning industries have caused severe air pollution, including the acid rain which is stunting Poland's forests and dissolving Kraków's medieval monuments. Heavy metals such as cadmium, copper, lead and mercury have contaminated the soil in the southern industrial zones, making fruits and vegetables inedible. The life span of the average Silesian is three years shorter than the national average and the infant mortality rate there is 30 per 1000 live births compared to 17 nationwide.

Poland is the world's second-largest producer of rye. Barley, oats, oilseed, potatoes, sugar beet and wheat are also important. Though an exporter of livestock and sugar, Poland still imports grain. Throughout the communist period Poland was unique in Eastern Europe in that most agricultural land was privately farmed by small holders. Today 76% of farm land is privately owned but 83% of these farms consist of less than 10 hectares, limiting productivity.

Until recently Poland exported machinery, coal, transportation equipment and chemicals to the former communist countries, particularly the USSR which supplied Poland with raw materials such as metals and phosphates for industry, plus 80% of its crude oil. Trading patterns changed rapidly after 1 January 1991 when Poland began accepting only hard currencies (not 'accounting roubles') for its exports and today Poland's largest trading partner by far is Germany, accounting for over a quarter of imports and exports, followed by the ex-Soviet states, the UK, Austria, Switzerland and Italy.

In December 1991 Poland became an interim associate member of the European Community (now the European Union) and the following March an interim trade agreement came into effect. These moves are seen as the beginning of a 10-year transitional period which should see Poland fully integrated into the European Union by the year 2002. By 1993, 58% of Poland's foreign trade was already with the European Union, compared with just 32% in 1989. Though the EU maintains tariff barriers against Polish agricultural products, textiles, chemicals and steel, Poland has a trade surplus with the West.

Current Trends

In 1990 the Polish economy contacted 12%, followed by a further production drop of 7.5% in 1991. In 1992 this decline bottomed out and in 1993 Poland was the only Eastern European country to register net growth (of 5%). Production is still well below 1989 levels and real income has declined 25%, but things are getting better. Since 1989 two million new jobs have been created in the private sector and together new and privatised firms now account for 45% of the gross domestic product and over 60% of the total workforce.

Privatisation has moved fastest in the retail trade where 80% of the turnover is now in private hands. Most large industries are still state owned but construction, commerce and publishing are now largely in private hands. About 20 National Investment funds have been set up to facilitate the privatisation of larger firms. Shares have been distributed free to pensioners and civil servants, and for token amounts to others. With privatisation, employment in services has increased sharply as the importance of industry declines.

Initially Germany was the largest foreign investor in Poland, but the USA has now far surpassed the Europeans. In March 1991 Western governments forgave a big chunk of Poland's foreign debt, though at US$49 billion it remained the largest in the region by far. In March 1994 a group of Western commercial banks gave Poland additional relief by writing down another US$13 billion in defaulted loans by 43% on the condition that the remainder would be repaid.

In 1989 only half of the prices were based on supply and demand, in 1990 it was 90%, and in 1991, 100%. Deregulation at first led to soaring prices but inflation has been brought under control by strictly limiting government spending. Despite the economic rebound, by 1993 unemployment had reached 16% or three million and a third of the population was living in poverty. Much of the unemployment was linked to the loss of trade with the former Soviet bloc which has put heavy pressure on companies unable to adapt to Western markets. Unemployment may continue to rise as inefficient state monopolies are restructured or closed down, putting heavy pressure on both the government and people.

In mid-1993 a 22% value added tax (VAT) was imposed (7% on energy, transportation, food and construction materials). For visitors, the economic changes still haven't affected the accommodation situation much, but a whole new generation of restaurants, bars and discos has appeared.

POPULATION & PEOPLE

Over half the 38 million inhabitants of Poland live in towns and cities, the six largest of which are Warsaw (1,700,000), Łódź (850,000), Kraków (750,000), Wrocław (650,000), Poznań (600,000), Gdańsk (500,000) and Szczecin (425,000). The south-west is the most densely populated part, especially the area around Łódź and Katowice, while the north-east is the least populated. There's a serious housing shortage forcing many young families to live with in-laws. Literacy is 98%.

At the end of WW II 2,300,000 Germans were evicted from East Prussia, Pomerania and Silesia, their places taken by further 2,000,000 Poles from the L'vov region of the Ukraine. Half a million Ukrainians, Belorussians and Lithuanians were resettled in the USSR. In the 18th century a third of the world's Jews lived in Poland but tragically few of Poland's 3.5 million prewar Jews survived the Nazis, and only five or six thousand Jews remain in Poland today.

These forced migrations and exterminations created a homogeneous population. Before the war, minorities accounted for 30% of the population of Poland. Today only 1.5% are minorities, mostly Ukrainians and

Belorussians. Ten million Poles live abroad in North America, the former Soviet Union, France and Brazil, and Chicago is the second-largest Polish city in the world. Poles refer to the overseas Polish community as 'Polonia' and overseas Poles as 'Polonians'.

ARTS

Poland is a land of remarkable individuals, so many in fact that visitors often lose their way among the unfamiliar names. Apart from Copernicus and Chopin one soon becomes acquainted with Jan Matejko (1838-93), whose monumental historical paintings hang in galleries all around Poland. By creating dramatic visual images of decisive moments in Polish history, Matejko inspired his compatriots at a time when Poland was under foreign yokes.

A kindred spirit was the Romantic poet Adam Mickiewicz (1798-1855) who sought the lost motherland in his writings. Mickiewicz explored the ethical and moral problems of a Poland subject to Russia and held out the hope of eventual redemption, in the same way that Christ was resurrected.

Henryk Sienkiewicz (1846-1916) wrote historical novels which gave Poles a new sense of national identity and won the author a Nobel Prize. His book *The Knights of the Teutonic Order* published in 1900 makes fascinating reading in light of the Nazi attack on Poland four decades later.

One contemporary Polish writer who abandoned Socialist Realism in the 1950s is Kazimierz Brandys (1916-). His best known novel is *Rondo* which deals with theatrical life in Warsaw during WW II. Although written in 1976, it was only published in 1982 after Brandys went into exile in Paris.

Tadeusz Konwicki (1926-) also started out as a Stalinist but after Stalin's crimes were revealed in 1956 turned to depicting Polish life under a hollow system. Recent Konwicki works such as *The Polish Complex* (1982) and *Moonrise, Moonrise* (1987), both translated into English, again explore the theme summed up in the 1797 Polish national anthem: *Jeszcze Polska nie zginęła póki my yjemy* (Poland has not yet perished as long as we live).

Music & Dance

Polish folk music goes back far beyond the first written records of mid-16th century mazurka rhythms. Throughout Europe, most folk dances developed from medieval court dances. The *krakowiak* is an old folk dance from the Kraków region, while the mazurka, a spirited Mazovian folk dance similar to a polka, originated in central Poland. Danced by a circle of couples in three-four time with much improvisation, mazurkas were originally accompanied by goatskin bagpipes (*kozial*).

The *polonaise* is a dignified ceremonial dance that originated as a formal march in the 16th century. During the 17th and 18th centuries the polonaise was used to open functions at the royal court. Arrayed according to their social station, the couples would promenade around the ballroom in three-four time, knees bending slightly on every third gliding step.

The Bohemian composer Jan Stefani (1746-1829), who spent most of his working life in Warsaw, created a unique sentimental style by writing over 100 polonaises for orchestra. Together with playwright Wojciech Boguslawski (1757-1829), Stefani wrote *Krakowiacy i Górale* (1794), a classical opera based on Polish folklore.

The romantic composer Frédéric Chopin in Polish, Fryderyk Szopen) (1810-49) raised this dance music (mazurkas, polonaises and waltzes) to the level of concert pieces. Written at a time when central Poland was under Russian domination, Chopin's music displays the melancholy and nostalgia which became hallmarks of the Polish national style.

Composer Stanisław Moniuszko (1819-72) 'nationalised' 19th century Italian opera music by introducing folk songs and dances onto the stage. His *Halka* (1858) about a peasant girl abandoned by a young noble was the first Polish national opera, and many of Moniuszko's operatic characters now belong to Polish national 'mythology'. Chopin and Moniuszko are the forefathers of Polish art music.

The 20th century composer Karol Szymanowski (1882-1937) strove to merge the traditions of Polish music with those of Europe. His ballet *Harnasie*, based on the folklore of the *Górale*, the highlanders of the Tatra Mountains, employed modern technical devices also used by the Russian Igor Stravinsky.

CULTURE

Poles greet each other by shaking hands much more than is done in the English-speaking world. Men also shake hands with women, though it's customary for the woman to extend her hand first. Poles bump into each other a lot and never apologise. They're not being rude, it's just what they're accustomed to.

If a Polish family befriends you, you'll be smothered with hospitality, in which case just submit and feel right at home going along with their suggestions. When the time comes, propose a toast to the health of the hostess, and be sure to take flowers and perhaps chocolates for the lady of the house whenever you're invited for dinner at a Polish home. Never arrive early for a dinner engagement, preferably arrive a little late, and be prepared to stay later than you'd planned. At the end of a meal always say *dziękuję* (thank you) as you get up, even in restaurants when sharing a table with strangers.

In this strongly Catholic country Easter is just as important as Christmas, and the most remarkable Easter event is the seven-day Passion Play at Kalwaria Zebrzydowska, 23 km south-west of Kraków. A re-enactment of Christ's entry into Jerusalem on Palm Sunday is followed by a crucifixion on Good Friday and a resurrection on Easter Sunday witnessed by hundreds of thousands of people. At times the crowd has become so excited that it has attempted to rescue Christ from the 'Roman soldiers'! Forty-two Calvary chapels representing the Stations of the Cross have been set up on this hilly site near the 17th century Bernardine monastery.

Of the few mystery cycles still performed in Europe, this is the oldest and most renowned – don't miss it if you're in Kraków around Easter.

On All Souls' Day (November 1) people visit the cemeteries and adorn the graves with candles and flowers. In the mid-19th century, Poles adopted the custom of the Christmas tree from Western Europe. Before Christmas Eve dinner, hay is put under the tablecloth. When everyone is seated, each pulls out a blade of hay at random. To get a long blade signifies a long life, while a shorter one indicates a more complicated future. Traditionally an extra place is set at the table for an unexpected guest. There will be 12 courses, one for each of the 12 apostles. At midnight on Christmas Eve, a special mass is celebrated in all churches, while New Year's Eve is marked by formal balls.

RELIGION

In 966 AD Poland became the easternmost Roman Catholic country in Europe, while Russia and most of the Balkan countries converted to Eastern Orthodox Christianity. Archbishops are seated at Kraków, Poznań, Warsaw and Wrocław. The Polish Church often had a distant relationship with Rome until 1978, when a Pole was elected Pope. Today the overwhelming majority of Poles are fervent Catholics and on Sunday every church is full to overflowing. The Catholic university in Lublin (founded in 1918) and the Academy of Catholic Theology in Warsaw are leading church-controlled institutions. Częstochowa with its Black Madonna is one of the most important pilgrimage centres in Europe.

The narrow line between church and state has always been difficult to define in Poland. The church openly supported Solidarity throughout the years when it was banned, and the overthrow of communism was as much a victory for the Catholic Church as it was for democracy. It's no coincidence that Catholic religious instruction was reintroduced in the public schools just as the teaching of Marxist ideology was dropped. Legislation passed in 1993 requires both public and private radio and TV to espouse 'Christian values' in their broadcasts. The church has demanded the return of property confiscated not only by the communists but also by the Russian tsars!

LANGUAGE

English speakers are less common in Poland than in some other Eastern European countries – German and Russian are often more useful. While trying to make yourself understood you'll greatly increase comprehension by writing the word or message down on a piece of paper. A pocket English-Polish dictionary will come in handy; consider bringing one with you as they're often hard to find in Poland. Best of all, check out a set of 'learn Polish' language tapes or records from your local library and listen to them a couple of times before leaving home.

The first words a visitor to Poland should learn are *proszę* (please) and *dziękuję* (thank you). Also be aware of *tak* (yes), *nie* (no) *dzień dobry* (good morning), *do widzenie* (goodbye), *wejście* (entrance), *wyjście* (exit and *nieczynne* (closed). You'll quickly learn *remont* which means something like 'under repair'. You'll see this word posted frequently on museums, hotels and restaurant which close for extended renovations. Other common words are *nie ma* which mean something like 'nothing' or 'not available'.

Public toilets (or 'WC') are marked with a circle for women *(panie)* and a triangle for men *(panowie)*. When holding up fingers to indicate numbers in Poland, remember to begin with the thumb, otherwise you'll get one more item than you want.

Lonely Planet's *Eastern Europe Phrase book* provides far more extensive coverage of the Polish language than is possible here and it's well worth taking along.

Pronunciation

Some of the 32 letters in the Polish alphabet are pronounced quite differently than they are in English.

c	'ts'
ć	'ch'

ci	'ch' (before a vowel)
cz	'ch'
ch	'kh'
dź	'j' as in 'jelly'
dż	'j' as in 'jelly'
dzi	'j' as in 'jelly' (before a vowel)
j	'y'
ł	'w'
ń	'ny' as in 'canyon'
rz	's' as in 'pleasure'
ś	'sh'
si	'sh' (before a vowel)
sz	'sh'
w	'v'
y	'i' as in 'sit'
ż	's' as in 'pleasure'
ź	's' as in 'pleasure'
zi	's' as in 'pleasure' (before a vowel)

The ogonek below ą and ę makes those vowels nasal. The vowels a, e, i, o and u are pronounced as in Italian or Spanish and r is always trilled. There are many refinements to the above which would take several pages to outline. In almost all Polish words, the stress falls on the next-to-last syllable.

When consulting indexes in Polish books or maps be aware that letters with acute, ogonek and overdot accents are considered distinct from the same letter without an accent, so if you don't find the word immediately, check further down the column. The nine accented letters are ą, ć, ę, ł, ń, ó, ś, ź and ż.

Greetings & Civilities

hello	*cześć (very informal)*
hello/good morning	*dzień dobry*
good evening	*dobry wieczór*
goodbye	*do widzenia*
please	*proszę*
thank you	*dziękuję*
excuse me/forgive me	*przepraszam*
yes	*tak*
no	*nie*

Small Talk

I don't understand.	*Nie rozumiem.*

Could you write it down?	*Czy mógł byś to zapisać?*
What is it called?	*Yak to się nazywa?*
Where do you live?	*Gdzie mieszkasz?*
What work do you do?	*Jaką wykonujesz pracę?*
I am a student.	*Jestem studentem.*
I am very happy.	*Jest mi bardzo przyjemnie.*

Accommodation

youth hostel	*schronisko młodzieży*
camping ground	*kemping*
private room	*kwatera prywatna*
How much is it?	*Ile to kosztuje?*
Is that the price per person?	*Czy to jest cena od osoby?*
Is that the total price?	*Czy to jest ostateczna cena?*
Are there any extra charges?	*Czy są jakieś dodatkowe opłaty?*
Do I pay extra for showers?	*Czy płacę dodatkowo za prysznic?*
Where is there a cheaper hotel?	*Gdzie jest tańszy hotel?*
Should I make a reservation?	*Czy mam zrobić rezerwację?*
single room	*pokój jednoosobowy*
double room	*pokój dwuosobowy*
It is very noisy.	*Jest bardzo głośny.*
Where is the toilet?	*Gdzie jest toaleta?*

Getting Around

What time does it leave?	*O której odjeżdża?*
When is the first bus?	*O której jest pierwszy autobus?*
When is the last bus?	*O której jest ostatni autobus?*
When is the next bus?	*O której jest następny autobus?*
That's too soon.	*To za wcześnie.*
When is the next one after that?	*O której jest następny po nim?*
How long does the trip take?	*Jak długo trwa podróż?*
arrival	*przyjazdy*
departure	*odjazdy*
timetable	*rozkład jazdy*

POLAND

Where is the bus stop?	*Gdzie jest przystanek autobusowy?*
Where is the train station?	*Gdzie jest stacja kolejowa?*
Where is the left-luggage room?	*Gdzie jest przechowalnia bagażu?*

Around Town

Just a minute.	*Chwileczkę.*
Where is ...?	*Gdzie jest ...?*
the bank	*bank*
the post office	*poczta*
the tourist information office	*informacja turystyczna*
the museum	*muzeum*
Where are you going?	*Dokąd idziesz?*
I am going to ...	*Idę do ...*
Where is it?	*Gdzie to jest?*
I can't find it.	*Nie mogę (tego) znaleźć.*
Is it far?	*Czy to daleko?*
Please show me on the map.	*Proszę pokazać mi to na mapie.*
left	*lewo*
right	*prawo*
straight ahead	*prosto*
I want ...	*chcę ...*
Do I need permission?	*Czy potrzebuję pozowolenie?*

Entertainment

Where can I buy a ticket?	*Gdzie mogę kupić bilet?*
Where can I refund this ticket?	*Gdzie mogę zwrócić ten bilet?*
Is this a good seat?	*Czy to jest dobre miejsce?*
at the front	*z przodu*
ticket	*bilet*

Food

I do not eat meat.	*Nie jadam mięsa.*
self-service cafeteria	*bar samoobsługowy*
grocery store	*sklep warzywniczy*
fish	*ryba*
pork	*wieprzowina*

soup	*zupa*
salad	*sałatka*
fresh vegetables	*świeża jarzyna*
milk	*mleko*
bread	*chleb*
sugar	*cukier*
ice cream	*lody*
coffee	*kawa*
tea	*herbata*
mineral water	*woda mineralna*
beer	*piwo*
wine	*wino*
hot/cold	*gorący/zimny*

Shopping

Where can I buy one?	*Gdzie mogę to kupić?*
How much does it cost?	*Ile to kosztuje?*
That's (much) too expensive.	*To jest zbyt drogie.*
Is there a cheaper one?	*Czy jest coś tańszego?*

Time & Dates

today	*dzisiaj*
tonight	*dzisiaj wieczorem*
tomorrow	*jutro*
the day after tomorrow	*pojutrze*
What time does it open?	*O której się otwiera?*
What time does it close?	*O której się zamyka?*
open	*otwarte*
closed	*zamknięte*
in the morning	*rano*
in the evening	*wieczorem*
every day	*codziennie*
At what time?	*O której godzinie?*
when?	*kiedy?*

Monday	*poniedziałek*
Tuesday	*wtorek*
Wednesday	*środa*
Thursday	*czwartek*
Friday	*piątek*
Saturday	*sobota*
Sunday	*niedziela*

January	*styczeń*
February	*luty*
March	*marzec*
April	*kwiecień*
May	*maj*
June	*czerwiec*
July	*lipiec*
August	*sierpień*
September	*wrzesień*
October	*październik*
November	*listopad*
December	*grudzień*

Numbers

1	*jeden*
2	*dwa*
3	*trzy*
4	*cztery*
5	*pięć*
6	*sześć*
7	*siedem*
8	*osiem*
9	*dziewięć*
10	*dziesięć*
11	*jedenaście*
12	*dwanaście*
13	*trzynaście*
14	*czternaście*
15	*piętnaście*
16	*szesnaście*
17	*siedemnaście*
18	*osiemnaście*
19	*dziewiętnaście*
20	*dwadzieścia*
21	*dwadzieścia jeden*
22	*dwadzieścia dwa*
23	*dwadzieścia trzy*
30	*trzydzieści*
40	*czterdzieści*
50	*pięćdziesiąt*
60	*sześćdziesiąt*
70	*siedemdziesiąt*
80	*osiemdziesiąt*
90	*dziewięćdziesiąt*
100	*sto*
1000	*tysiąc*
10,000	*sto tysięcy*
1,000,000	*milion*

Facts for the Visitor

VISAS & EMBASSIES

You must have a passport and in some cases a visa to enter Poland. Your passport must be valid six months after the expiry of the visa. You're supposed to obtain the visa at a consulate, although many travellers report success in buying one at the border. Still, it's cheaper to get the visa beforehand and you eliminate the possibility of problems with the border guards.

Citizens of Austria, Belgium, Denmark, Finland, France, Germany, Italy, Luxembourg, the Netherlands, Norway, Sweden, Switzerland, the UK and the USA do not require visas for a stay of up to 90 days. Other nationals should check with one of the Polish consulates listed in this section or at any LOT Polish Airlines office. By phone it's much easier to get through to LOT than to a consulate and they'll have the latest information in their computer.

Polish tourist visas cost about US$25 and two photos are required (US$35 at the border). Canadians are charged visa fees 50% higher than other nationalities due to a refusal by the Canadian government to lift visa requirements for Polish tourists wishing to enter Canada. In Eastern Europe visas are generally issued in 24 hours, with a one-hour express visa service available if you pay 50% more. Polish embassies in Western Europe tend to charge more for visas than those in Eastern Europe. For example, the Polish Embassy in Paris asks US$45 per entry. A multiple-entry visa valid for up to four entries costs four times the usual fee. Students who are 23 years of age and under are charged a reduced visa fee. A cheaper, 48-hour transit visa is also available (onward visa required).

If you apply to the consulate in your home country by registered mail it could be several weeks before you get your passport back. Ask about express service when you write in for the application forms. Some consulates only give seven-day visas if you apply by

POLAND

POLAND

mail. Otherwise call one of the consulates listed below which are generally open weekday mornings. Some consulates are tremendously overcrowded or charge unusually high fees, so get your visa well in advance, allowing yourself the opportunity to try elsewhere if need be.

If you're asked how long you wish to stay in Poland when you apply for the visa, say one month even if you plan to stay less. That way you won't have to worry about visa extensions should you decide to stay a little longer. Since you must personally register with the police if you stay over a month, it's best to limit your stay to 30 days maximum though you can get a regular visa for a stay of up to 90 days. If you overstay your visa for any reason you'll be fined US$22 when you depart for every additional day.

Polish visas may be used any time within three or six months from the date of issue. If you have to extend your tourist visa within Poland, go to the local passport office (biuro paszportowe) on a weekday morning. Any tourist office will have the address. Extensions cost about US$35.

Polish Embassies & Consulates

Polish embassies and consulates are found in Belgrade, Bratislava, Bucharest, Budapest, Prague, Sofia and Zagreb, as well as these:

Australia
  7 Turrana St, Yarralumla, Canberra, ACT 2600
  (☎ 062-273 1208)
  10 Trelawney St, Woollahra, Sydney, NSW 2025
  (☎ 02-363 9816)
Canada
  443 Daly St, Ottawa 2, ON K1N 6H3 (☎ 613-236 0468)
  1500 Avenue des Pins Ouest, Montreal, PQ H3G1B4 (☎ 514-937 9481)
  2603 Lakeshore Blvd West, Toronto, ON M8V 1G5 (☎ 416-252 4171)
  1177 West Hastings St, Suite 1600, Vancouver, BC V6E 2K3 (☎ 604-688 3530)
Netherlands
  Alexanderstraat 25, 2514 JM ,The Hague
  (☎ 070-360 5812)
New Zealand
  17 Upland Rd, Kelburn, Wellington
  (☎ 712 456)

UK
  73 New Cavendish St, London W1N 7RB
  (☎ 0171-580 0476)
  2 Kinnear Rd, Edinburgh EH3 5PE
  (☎ 131-552 0301)
USA
  2640 16th St NW, Washington, DC 20009
  (☎ 202-234 3800)
  233 Madison Ave, New York, NY 10016
  (☎ 212-889 8360)
  1530 North Lake Shore Dr, Chicago, IL 60610
  (☎ 312-337 8166)
  3460 Wilshire Blvd, Suite 1200, Los Angeles
  CA 90010 (☎ 213-365 7900)

MONEY

One of the successes of the Mazowieck government was the establishment of the złoty (zł) as a convertible currency. By legalising private currency trading (the former 'black market') in 1990 and allowing the country's currency to find its own value on the open market, Poland took a giant step along the road to economic reform.

You can pay for everything (except visas, duty-free goods and international transportation tickets) directly in Polish złoty with no exchange receipts and changing money is the easiest thing in the world, provided you have cash. You'll find private exchange offices known as 'kantory' all around Poland offering excellent commission-free exchange rates, but they rarely accept travellers' cheques. These offices stay open long hours, occasionally around the clock, and they're so numerous we don't usually bother listing them herein: when you need one you'll probably find one.

Travellers' cheques are not welcome in Poland. Only a few main banks will accept them and commissions (prowizya) of 1% to 2% with a minimum charge of US$2 to US$3 are standard. Main branches of the Narodowy Bank Polski (NBP) and the Polska Kasa Opienki or PKO Bank (also known as the Bank Pekao SA) change travellers' cheques, but you have to search for a branch willing to do it, line up and wait while they complete the paperwork. After that you'll get a rate lower than that you'd have got in seconds without commission for cash at a private kantor. The PKO Bank is usually more efficient than the NBP and keeps longer hours. Most other banks simply refuse to change travellers' cheques at all, so bring cash if you possibly can.

Some Polish banks insist on seeing the original purchase receipt you got when you bought your travellers' cheques, even though such receipts are supposed to be carried separately for security. Rather than argue it's best to adopt a condescending attitude and humour these quaint officials by carrying your receipts together with your travellers' cheques (keep a record of the numbers elsewhere).

If you neglected to bring sufficient hard currency in cash, it's useful to know that the PKO bank will change dollar travellers' cheques into dollars cash for a half percent commission (minimum US\$2). You can then take the cash dollars to any private kantor and buy złoty with no commission. The first chance you get, change enough travellers' cheques into dollars cash to cover your entire remaining stay in Poland (then guard the money with your life).

Credit cards are only accepted in Orbis hotels and expensive restaurants and shops which cater mostly to tourists. The best known cards are American Express, Visa, Diners Club, Eurocard and Access/MasterCard. In late 1990 an American Express office offering all the usual services opened in Warsaw.

Before you leave Poland it's usually no problem changing złoty back into hard currency at private exchange offices. Don't leave it to the last minute to do this, however, as some exchange offices right on the border may be unwilling to change back and the złoty is not recognised outside Poland. You might want to take the opportunity to pick up some Czech or Slovakian currency, to ease your entry into those countries. Poland's private exchange offices are also perfect places to unload all those leftover Turkish, Bulgarian and Romanian banknotes you've been carrying around!

You used to have to fill out a currency declaration upon arrival to inhibit you from changing the declared money on the black market. Now if they ask to see your money it's because they suspect that you may not have enough to support yourself while in Poland. Only cash in excess of US\$10,000 must be declared in writing upon arrival. Keep any Polish or other Eastern European banknotes out of sight at the border, however, as they may still be forbidden to import/export.

Thanks to the deregulation of foreign exchange, trading on the black market in Poland is dead and if you change money with someone on the street, you're likely to get *less* than you would at a private exchange office and run the risk of being ripped off.

Currency

Poland may have a greater variety of banknotes in circulation than any other country. Depicted on the banknotes are the commander in chief of the International Brigades during the Spanish Civil War, Karol Świerczewski (50 złoty); 19th century socialist activist Ludwik Waryński (100 złoty); Paris Commune commander in chief Jarosław Dąbrowski (200 złoty); 18th century patriot Tadeusz Kościuszko (500 złoty); 16th century astronomer Mikołaj Kopernik (1000 złoty); 10th century king Mieszko I (2000 złoty); 19th century composer Frédéric Chopin (5000 złoty); early 20th century artist Stanisław Wyspiański (10,000 złoty); radium co-discoverer Maria Skłodowska-Curie (20,000 złoty); 18th century geologist Stanisław Staszic (50,000 złoty); 19th century opera composer Stanisław Moniuszko (100,000 złoty); author Henryk Sienkiewicz (500,000 złoty); author Wladyslaw Reymont (1,000,000 złoty), and composer/pianist Ignacy Jan Paderewski (2,000,000 złoty). The 200,000 note has been withdrawn.

When you first arrive, study Poland's banknotes carefully as the high denominations and great variety of bills can be confusing. The similar colour and appearance of the 200 and 20,000 and the 1000 and 100,000 notes doesn't help either! Watch out for counterfeit banknotes. Genuine notes have a watermark you can see if you hold the

POLAND

bill up to the light and the lettering on the notes has a slightly elevated texture you can feel. Carefully check all bills of a half million złoty or more. Złoty banknotes printed before 1975 are worthless.

Exchange Rates

In 1981 one US dollar was worth 34 złoty; in 1986, 160 złoty; in November 1987, 310 złoty; in May 1989, 3750 złoty; and in July 1989, 6000 złoty. By late 1990 it was relatively stable at 9000 to the dollar, but by early 1994 it had devalued further to 22,000 to the dollar. Inflation was 251% in 1989, 586% in 1990, 70% in 1991, 45% in 1992 and 35% in 1993.

There's only one market exchange rate now, which is somewhere between what the old official and black market rates would have been. This makes accommodation cheaper while all other prices are still very manageable in hard currency terms. There's no systematic cheating in Poland and everyone pays the same price for food, accommodation, transport and admissions – quite a contrast to most other Eastern European countries where foreigners are often charged prices several times higher than those paid by locals.

Costs

You should be able to see Poland in relative comfort following the recommendations in this book for under US$25 per person per day. That includes a room at a budget-priced hotel, at least one meal a day at a regular restaurant, and admissions and 2nd-class transportation by train. Couples, families and small groups will spend less, and if you camp or sleep in youth hostels, and eat only at self-services you could easily end up spending under US$15 per person per day. Museum admission fees are usually under US$1 (US$0.50 for students). Before congratulating yourself on how cheap it is, remember that Polish workers only make the equivalent of about US$200 a month.

Aside from being a bonanza for budgeteers, the low prices open other possibilities. If you're tired of travelling and want to hang out somewhere for a while, you can live very well in Poland on US$20 a day, provided you stay in one place. Ask any tourist office to find you a Polish language tutor, then just pass your time reading, writing, studying, painting or whatever. The friends you make during that time could end up being friends for life.

Tipping

Poles generally tip waiters, taxi drivers and hairdressers by rounding up the bill to the next even figure as they're paying. Rounding up by much over 10% is unusual but failing to round up at all suggests dissatisfaction with the service. Tips are never left on restaurant tables. If a 10% service charge is added to a restaurant bill there's no need to tip, although you could still round up slightly if it's only a small amount. Cloakroom and toilet attendants collect a small fee which is usually posted, otherwise put the equivalent of about US$0.10 in the bowl.

CLIMATE & WHEN TO GO

Poland has a moderate continental climate with considerable maritime influence along the Baltic coast, which makes conditions variable from year to year. Spring is a time of warm days and chilly nights, while summer (from June to August) can be hot. Autumn (September to November) brings some rain and there can be snow from December to March. In the mountains the snow lingers until mid-April. From late October to February it gets dark around 5 pm.

The sea coast is the sunniest part of the country in summer; the Carpathian Mountains are sunnier in winter. July is the hottest month, February the coolest. Warsaw has average daily temperatures above 14°C from May to September, above 8°C in April and October and below freezing from December to February. Expect Poland to be cooler and rainier than Western Europe.

In the mountains the ski season runs from December to mid-March, though between Christmas and New Year all the facilities will be packed. Spring (April and May) is a good time for sightseeing. Another major advantage of visiting Poland in spring is that the theatre and concert season will be in full swing, allowing you to see outstanding performances almost every night. Mountain hiking and camping are good and uncrowded in June and September; late August and early September are a relatively dry, sunny time to tour the Great Mazurian Lakes. To swim in the Baltic you'll have to come in July and August. The cities are visitable all year, and winter is sometimes even preferable as most theatres and concert halls are closed throughout summer.

SUGGESTED ITINERARIES
Depending on the length of your stay, you might want to see and do the following things in Poland:

Two days
    Visit Kraków.
One week
    Visit Kraków, Warsaw and Gdańsk.
Two weeks
    Visit Kraków, Zakopane, Warsaw, the Great Mazurian Lakes, Gdańsk and Wrocław.
One month
    Visit most of the places included in this chapter.

TOURIST OFFICES
Most cities have municipal tourist offices, such as Syrena in Warsaw and Wawel Tourist in Kraków, often identified by the letters IT (*Informacja Turystyczna*) on the door. These places are usually good sources of information and some also try to cover costs by selling various tickets and arranging private-room accommodation. Gromada, Juventur, Sports-Tourist and Turysta are tourism cooperatives catering exclusively to the domestic market. They don't usually arrange accommodation, sell train tickets or speak English.

Orbis is the largest travel agency in Poland with offices in cities and towns all around the country. Like commercial travel agencies in the West, its main functions are to make reservations, sell transportation tickets and book rooms at luxury hotels. Its staff will also give information if they're not too busy, and in most offices there's somebody who

speaks English. They're not paid to provide free information, however, so don't hold it against them if they won't (try asking general questions about budget travel at an American Express office and see how far you get).

The Polish Tourists & Country-Lovers' Association (PTTK) has offices in towns and resort areas which often know about accommodation in city dormitories, camping grounds and mountain huts, and even have information on hitchhiking *(autostop)*. But English is seldom spoken, and what the staff tell you about facilities outside their immediate area may be unreliable. They often sell excellent indexed city or hiking maps of both their own and other areas, so always have a look inside whenever you see the letters PTTK.

Student Travel
Almatur is the Travel & Tourism Bureau of the Union of Polish Students. Its offices issue ISIC student cards (US$5) and know about student accommodation in July and August.

The ISIC (International Student Identity Card) card is valid in Poland for student reductions *(ulgowa)* on museum admissions and train or ferry tickets.

Almatur organises excellent weekly horse riding and sailing holidays which foreign students may join. In July and August there are Almatur International Camps of Labour in which participants work 46 hours a week as construction, agricultural, or forest labourers. After work there are excursions, sporting and cultural events etc. Get details from Orbis offices abroad or the Almatur office in Warsaw.

Orbis Offices Abroad
Orbis offices outside Poland include:

Netherlands
    Orbis, Leidsestraat 64 (upstairs)
    1017 PD Amsterdam (☎ 020-625 3570)
UK
    Polorbis, 82 Mortimer St, London W1N 7DE
    (☎ 0171-637 4971)
USA
    Orbis, 342 Madison Ave, Suite 1512, New York, NY 10173 (☎ 212-867 5011)

POLAND

USEFUL ORGANISATIONS

Every November the Polish globetrotters club, Travel-Bit (Box 258, 30-965 Kraków 69, Poland), organises a weekend meeting called OSOTT (Ogólnopolskie Spotkania Organizatorów Turystyki Trampingowej) to which all travellers are cordially invited. Every participant gets 15 minutes to show his/her slides and sessions have been known to continue until 5 am! Write at least two months in advance for the exact place and date of this years OSOTT.

The Exploration Society, another Polish travel club, meets in Warsaw every Friday afternoon at 6.30 pm. Call ☎ 022-227 436 or 022-224 870 for more information.

BUSINESS HOURS & HOLIDAYS

Banking hours are weekdays from 8 am to 1 pm with main branches open until 5 pm. Stores are generally open weekdays from 11 am to 7 pm, although this can vary an hour or two either way. Grocery stores open earlier and open Saturday until 1 pm. In smaller towns almost everything is closed on Sunday. Many businesses post their hours on the door.

Milk bars tend to open between 6 and 9 am and close between 5 and 8 pm. Restaurants stay open later. With privatisation and increased competition, businesses keep longer hours than they did.

Museums usually open at 9 or 10 am and close anywhere from 3 to 6 pm, with slightly shorter hours in winter. Most museums close on Monday, although a few maverick institutions close on Tuesday and occasionally both days. Most are also closed on days following public holidays. Most live theatres are closed on Monday and from the end of June to the end of September.

Public holidays in Poland include New Year (1 January), Easter Monday (March/April), Labour Day (1 May), Constitution Day (3 May), Corpus Christi (a Thursday in May or June), Assumption Day (15 August), All Saints' Day (1 November), Independence Day (11 November) and Christmas (25 and 26 December).

Independence Day commemorates 11 November 1918 when Poland reappeared on the map of Europe. Poland is a poor place to spend New Year's Eve as virtually every restaurant and bar except those in the luxury hotels will be rented out for private parties or closed.

As many as a dozen trade fairs and exhibitions a year are held in Poznań, the largest of which are the International Technical Fair in June and the Consumer Goods Fair in October. For information about the fairs contact: Poznań International Fair (☎ 061-692 592, fax 061-665 827), Głogowska 14, 60-734 Poznań. An international book fair is held in Warsaw in May.

CULTURAL EVENTS

Poland's many annual festivals provide the opportunity to experience the best in music, film and folklore amid an exciting cultural milieu. All the annual events referred to in the following paragraph are listed in the city sections under 'entertainment'; also ask at local tourist information offices.

Classical music festivals are held in Łańcut (May), Toruń (September) and Wrocław (December), while contemporary music festivals are held at Wrocław (February), Poznań (March), Zakopane (July), Warsaw (September) and Kraków (November). For organ music it's Kraków (April) and Gdańsk (July and August). Singing can be heard at Kraków (April), Opole (June), Gdańsk (from June to August), Sopot (August) and Wrocław (September).

Jazz festivals are held at Wrocław (May), Warsaw (October) and Kraków (September and October). Poland's leading folk festivals are those of Toruń (May), Żywiec (August) and Zakopane (August). Film festivals are held at Kraków (May) and Gdańsk (September). Annual street fairs take place in Poznań (June or July) and Gdańsk (June and August).

POST & TELECOMMUNICATIONS

Main post offices (poczta) are open from 8 am to 8 pm weekdays and in large cities one post office stays open around the clock. Always use airmail, even for parcels. Most mail boxes are red.

Receiving Mail

A good place to have mail sent is c/o Poste Restante, Poczta Główna, ulica Święto-krzyska 31/33, 00-001 Warszawa 1, Poland. Mail can be picked up there daily from 8 am to 8 pm at window No 12.

American Express card holders can have mail sent c/o American Express Travel, Dom Bez Kantow, Krakowskie Przedmieście 11, 00-068 Warszawa, Poland. You must show your American Express card when collecting mail.

For the addresses of other potential mail drops, turn to Post & Telecommunications in the Kraków, Wrocław and Gdańsk sections of this book.

Telephone

Improvements to Poland's antiquated telephone system have been announced several times, but as yet not much has materialised. It's said the Polish joke originated among people trying to communicate by phone.

The easiest way to make calls is with a telephone card purchased at a post office. These cards cost US$2 for 50 units or US$4 for 100 units, and are valid for domestic or international calls. Tokens (US$0.05) are used for local calls and some old phones still accept a C token for international calls.

Blue card telephones (often found outside post offices) can be used for all types of calls, though only half of them will be in actual working order at any given time and even those that do work only successfully make international connections one try in five. You'll often get a number you didn't dial or a busy signal which probably means that all the lines are engaged – try again.

In Warsaw and Zakopane the blue card phones work well, while in Poznań and Gdańsk they're hopeless. In Kraków card phones are so rare that the few that do exist always have a queue of people waiting. Card phones in hotel lobbies are the ones most likely to work and you've a better chance of getting though outside business hours.

If you place a call through an operator at a main post office it should go through right away, but will be more expensive than it would have been using a telephone card (US$4 for three minutes to Western Europe). The price of calls placed from hotels is much higher again than what you'd pay to call from a main post office.

To call Poland from abroad, dial the international access code (different from each country), then 48 (the country code for Poland), the area code (without the initial zero) and the number. Important area codes include 2 (with seven-digit phone numbers in Warsaw), 22 (with six-digit numbers in Warsaw), 12 (Kraków), 34 (Częstochowa), 56 (Toruń), 58 (Gdańsk and Gdynia), 59 (Łeba), 61 (Poznań), 71 (Wrocław), 81 (Lublin), 84 (Zamość), 89 (Olsztyn) and 165 (Zakopane).

Inside Poland, add 0 before the Polish area code for domestic intercity calls or 00 (the Polish international access code) before the country code for international calls.

TIME

Time in Poland is GMT/UTC plus one hour. Poland goes on summer time at the end of March when clocks are turned forward an hour. At the end of September they're turned back an hour.

ELECTRICITY

The electric current is 220 V AC, 50 Hz. A circular plug with two round pins is used.

BOOKS & MAPS

Bookshops and tourist offices in Poland sell excellent city and regional maps, often complete with indexes, for under US$2. Tram and bus routes are shown on the maps, which is handy. The *Samochodowa Mapa Polski* is the best map of the country. Also watch for the comprehensive, 316-page *Polska Atlas Samochodowy*.

Lonely Planet's *Poland – a travel survival kit* by Krzysztof Dydyński is easily the best travel guide to Poland. The information was compiled independently of *Eastern Europe on a shoestring* and it's well worth picking up if you'll be spending much time in Poland. *Poland: The Rough Guide* is also excellent. A traditional guidebook strong on art and history is *Nagel's Encyclopedia-Guide Poland* (Nagel Publishers, Geneva, 1986), though the practical information is scanty.

The Polish Way by Adam Zamoyski (John Murray, London, 1987) is a superb cultural history of Poland full of maps and illustrations which bring the past 1000 years to life. This book reads as smoothly as a novel though it's 100% factual.

The Struggles for Poland by Neal Ascherson (Michael Joseph, London, 1987) developed from a television series on Polish history in the 20th century. Ascherson provides much information on the formative 1930s and 1940s when the physical shape of modern Poland was decided.

Isaac Bashevis Singer's masterful novel *Shosha* gives some insight into the lives and attitudes of Polish Jews prior to WW II.

Mad Dreams, Saving Graces by Michael T Kaufman (Random House, New York, 1989) is a fascinating insider's look at Poland from the imposition of martial law in 1981 to the eve of the fall of Polish communism in 1988. Kaufman, the *New York Times* correspondent in Warsaw those years, really brings to life Father Jerzy Popiełuszko, Marek Edelman (the only surviving leader of the Warsaw Ghetto Uprising), government movers and Solidarity shakers.

The Captive Mind is a collection of essays by Nobel Prize-winning Polish poet and novelist Czesław Miłosz, who left Poland in 1951 and now lives in California. Published in 1953, the book shows how intellectuals were co-opted by communism.

Poland, A Novel by James A Michener (Ballantine Books, New York, 1983) is a readable dramatisation of the history of Poland.

MEDIA

Poland's English-language weekly is *The Warsaw Voice*, published by the Polish Inter-

press Agency. To subscribe for 26 weeks send US$78 to: The Warsaw Voice, PO Box 28, 00-950 Warszawa 1, Poland. This well-written paper is hard to find outside Warsaw so grab it when you see it.

Poland Today Monthly (Aleje Stanów Zjednoczonych 53, 04-028 Warsaw, Poland), published every two months by the Polish Information Agency, presents a sanitised official picture of Poland. Annual subscriptions are US$29 to Europe, US$34 to North America and US$43 to Australia.

Of the British papers, the *Guardian* is cheaper and more readily available than the *Times* because it's printed in Frankfurt and on sale the same day.

HEALTH

Most foreigners have to pay for medical treatment, although in emergencies it's often free. Citizens of the UK receive free treatment if they can prove coverage back home. Speaking English often helps to jump hospital queues as Polish doctors are all keen to practise their English. In Warsaw call your consulate for the name of a private doctor experienced in treating foreigners. Orbis offices abroad can arrange stays at Polish health spas.

As of mid-1993 there were 130 AIDS victims and another 2500 HIV-positive persons in Poland, most of them infected as a result of sharing needles or syringes during drug abuse.

DANGERS & ANNOYANCES

Many Poles are chain smokers, so choose your seating in restaurants, bars and trains with this in mind.

Don't establish eye contact with the colourfully dressed women you see sitting on the pavement begging, often with small children, as they can quickly become aggressive.

While Poland is a lot safer than most large US or Western European cities, be aware of your surroundings on lonely streets in big cities and watch out for pickpockets in crowded train stations, especially in Warsaw. Most of the violent crime is perpetrated by persons from the former Soviet Union, not

Poles. Watch out for small groups of robust, poorly dressed men hanging around train stations or at street markets, and avoid men standing in front of private exchange offices, as you never know what they're up to. If you stay clear of types like this and keep your eyes open, you'll be okay.

It's unwise to leave money and valuables unattended in hotel rooms. Lock your luggage if you can. By removing the temptation you'll usually eliminate the danger.

Drunks can sometimes be a nuisance, especially for women, and about all you can do is try to steer clear of them. They're not usually dangerous.

If you go to the police to report a crime, expect to encounter indolence and indifference. In small towns English-speaking police are rare, so it's best to take along an interpreter. Be both persistent and patient, and once the police see you're not about to simply go away they'll go through the motions of making an investigation. Don't expect a lot: the police earn next to nothing and they can be rather cynical about a 'rich' foreigner complaining about losing a few dollars.

Clerks in self-services and fast-food outlets will sometimes cheat you out of small amounts (US$0.10 etc). Defend yourself by asking the clerk to write down the amount due on a piece of paper before you produce any money (offer him/her a pen and paper). Often you'll be able to see the amount rung up on the cash register.

ACTIVITIES

Zakopane, Poland's premier southern mountain resort, features hiking in summer and skiing in winter. With a little effort you could also get in some rafting on the Dunajec River near Zakopane. Hikers less interested in meeting their fellows along the trails should consider instead the Bieszczady Mountains south of Przemyśl.

Mikołajki in the Great Mazurian Lakes district of north-east Poland is a major yachting centre with boats available for rent. Canoeists and kayakers will be quite at home here, and this part of Poland is flat enough

also to appeal to cyclists, as is most of northern Poland.

See Tours under Getting Around (later in this chapter) for information on tour packages built around the above activities and horse riding.

Courses

Since 1969, Jagiellonian University (fax 48-12-227 701), Rynek Główny 34, 31-010 Kraków, Poland, has organised a summer school of Polish language and culture in July and August. The three, four, and six-week courses are taught in English by university faculty members. Write for information well ahead.

HIGHLIGHTS OF POLAND
Nature

Poland excels in mountains, lakes and coast. Those wishing to commune with the Baltic will find the beaches of Łeba unending and the sand dunes inspiring. Mikołajki is a fine place to begin exploring the 3000 Mazurian lakes, while Zakopane is the launching pad for hikes into the Tatras, Poland's most magnificent mountain range. The Białowieska Forest in Poland's far east is home to the largest remaining herd of European bison and other wildlife. Each of these environments is distinct and equally worth experiencing.

Museums & Galleries

Warsaw's National Museum holds Poland's largest and finest art collection, though Kraków's Czartoryski Art Museum has individual works which are unsurpassed. The Musical Instruments Museum in Poznań will delight music lovers, as will Chopin's birthplace at Żelazowa Wola, 50 km west of Warsaw. Finally, the Auschwitz Museum at Oświęcim is perhaps the most meaningful of them all.

Castles

Malbork Castle, one-time seat of the Teutonic Knights, is perhaps the largest surviving medieval castle in Europe, while another 14th century castle at Lidzbark Warmiński is less known but equally impressive. For hundreds of years Kraków's Wawel Castle sheltered Polish royalty, most of whom are still buried in the adjacent cathedral. Lublin Castle intrigues us with its remoteness and memories of Nazi atrocities committed within its walls. True castle lovers will seek out Pieskowa Skała Castle and nearly a dozen others along the Eagles' Nests Route from Kraków to Częstochowa.

Palaces

It's not surprising that Poland's capital, Warsaw, contains Poland's two most magnificent royal palaces: the 17th century Wilanów Palace and the 18th century Łazienki Palace. In the countryside feudal magnates built splendid Renaissance, Baroque and Rococo palaces such as the Branicki Palace at Białystok, the Rogalin Palace near Poznań, and Łańcut Palace.

Historic Towns

Of all Poland's cities, only Kraków, the de facto capital till 1596, survived WW II relatively untouched. The historic cores of Poznań, Toruń and Gdańsk have been masterfully restored. All three grew rich from trade in the Middle Ages, as the homes of rich burghers around their central squares and the magnificent churches attest. Zamość in south-east Poland is unique as a perfectly preserved 16th century Renaissance settlement.

ACCOMMODATION
Camping

There are hundreds of camping grounds in Poland, many offering small timber cabins which are excellent value. IFCC card holders get a 10% discount on camping fees. Theoretically most camping grounds are open from May to September, but they tend to close early if things are slow. The opening and closing dates listed in official brochures (and this book) are only approximate. The yellow *Polska Mapa Campingów* map lists most camping grounds.

Hostels

Poland is the only country in Eastern Europe with youth hostels similar to those of Western Europe. Although there's no maximum age limit, persons under 26 years have priority. Children under 10 years cannot use the hostels. Groups larger than five persons must book a month in advance and Polish school groups crowd the hostels from mid-May to mid-June. Persons without YHA membership cards are readily accepted though they pay a little more. Many hostels are open only in summer although the main ones operate all year. The hostels are closed from 10 am to 5 pm and you must arrive before 9 pm.

All 1100 HI hostels in Poland are run by the Polskie Towarzystwo Schronisk Młodzieżowych (PTSM) and have a green triangle over the entrance. A large percentage are located in school buildings. They're categorised as 1st, 2nd or 3rd class, with overnight charges at 1st-class hostels costing about US$4 for members 26 and under, US$5 for members aged over 26, and US$6 for non-members. Second and 3rd-class hostels are about US$1 cheaper. Some hostels have kitchens where you can cook your own food. In cities where there's more than one youth hostel, if the first hostel you visit is full they may be willing to call around to the others to find you a bed.

International Student Hotels

In July and August the Polish student travel agency, Almatur, arranges accommodation in vacant student dormitories in 17 university towns. The Almatur hotels tend to be far from the centre of town and the addresses change annually, so you'll have to ask about them at local Almatur offices. You share a room of one to four beds and there are usually cooking facilities, cheap cafeterias and even disco clubs on the premises. Accommodation costs about US$11 single, US$9 for a bed in a double or US$7 per person in a triple. If you take the triple rate you'll often have the room to yourself anyway.

Private Rooms

It's possible to stay in private rooms (*prywatny pokój*) in Poland, though they're less common than in Hungary or Croatia. A few municipal tourist offices (*Biuro Zakwaterowań*) arrange private rooms but their prices are sometimes high, almost what you'd pay for a budget hotel. The agencies classify the rooms according to 1st, 2nd or 3rd category. Singles are scarce and during busy periods all their rooms could be full.

Sometimes you're offered a private room by an individual on the street outside a tourist office or private room agency. Their prices may be lower and open to bargaining. In some cities like crowded Kraków and Gdańsk these 'black' rooms are good places to stay. Beware of rooms far from the centre of town.

Hotels

Hotels are graded from one to five stars, and unlike the Czech Republic and Slovakia where foreigners are charged double or triple, in Poland everyone pays the same price for rooms. Orbis hotels are all in the expensive, three and four-star category and a few hotels belonging to international chains such as Inter-Continental and Marriott are five-star. Municipal hotels are usually cheaper, and the PTTK has a chain of 'Dom Turysty' and 'Dom Wycieczkowy' which have hotel rooms and dorm beds. A country inn is called a *zajazd* or *gościniec*.

Hotel prices vary according to the season and these are different in the various regions of Poland. At Zakopane the high ski season is from mid-December to March, while in Poznań hotel rates increase dramatically at trade fair time. The low season runs from October to April in northern Poland and Wrocław, or from November to March in Kraków. In Warsaw hotel prices are the same throughout the year. Rooms booked from abroad through a travel agency or Orbis are much more expensive than what you'd pay locally.

Rates are usually posted on a board at hotel reception desks. Compare the price of a room with private bath to one with shared bath. Sometimes it's only a slight difference, other times it's a lot. If in doubt about the quality ask to *see* a room before checking in, in which case it's unlikely they'll give you their worst room. On arrival day, hotel rooms cannot be occupied until after noon, 2 or 4 pm, so leave your things at the station.

FOOD

Milk Bars

In Poland the word 'bar' is almost always used in the sense of snack bar or refreshment bar, and 'cocktail' means fruit cocktail or something similar. The cheapest places to eat in Poland are milk bars (*bar mleczny*) which are also good places to try local dishes not available at expensive restaurants. If you want an inexpensive fruit juice with your meal ask for *kompot*. Avoid the meat dishes at milk bars, however, as they're priced three or four times higher than anything else so most Poles don't take them and you could end up with something that's been on display for quite a while.

Milk bars are self-service (*samoobsługa*). You either pay at the end of the line cafeteria-style or, more often, you pay first and get a receipt which you hand to the person dispensing the food. This can be confusing if you don't know the Polish name of whatever it is you want, but most cashiers are patient and will try to understand if you point to something someone else is eating. Try asking the person in line behind you what a particular dish is called. Sometimes you'll order the wrong thing, which adds to the excitement.

The cashiers at milk bars are often apprehensive about dealing with unpredictable foreigners and you yourself may be slightly intimidated by the unfamiliar food and surroundings. A smile and a sense of humour will go a long way here. You'll make yourself popular with milk bar staff by carrying your dirty dishes back to the counter, as you see others doing. Milk-bar lines usually move quickly, so don't be put off.

Some milk bars close on Saturday afternoon and all day Sunday. Breakfast is a bit of a problem as most milk bars only open at

9 am. Keep in mind that the difference in price between a fast-food stand and a 1st-class restaurant is much less in Poland than it is in the west. Eat at self-service cafeterias to save time, not money, and whenever you have the time to enjoy a proper meal, go to one of the better restaurants listed herein or any top-end hotel, not a milk bar. Now that milk bars have to make a profit they're having a hard time competing and it's sad to see them being replaced by US-style fast-food outlets serving bland unappetising fare on plastic plates.

Restaurants

Restaurants and coffee shops at the luxury Orbis hotels have the widest selection of dishes and the best service, although the atmosphere can be pretentious and even dull. These are the *only* places in Poland where you can get a reasonable English breakfast of ham and eggs with juice, but it's expensive at about US$5. Ask your hotel if they have some arrangement for breakfast vouchers. Elsewhere you may have to settle for soup.

Always ask to see the menu and have a look at the prices. Waiters who speak English or German and simply tell you what's available will charge extra for the service. If a waiter wants to be helpful, ask him or her to translate the menu or tell you what's available, as very few Polish restaurants offer everything listed. Soup is *zupy* and a main course is *dania*. Watch for the *obiad firmowy* (recommended meal) on restaurant menus.

When ordering seafood keep in mind that you will be charged by weight, and the price on the menu may only be for 100 grams. Expect to be charged extra for the bread, butter, sauces and vegetables with the meals. If beer prices aren't listed on the menu expect them to be much higher than usual. Beware of accepting things you didn't order, such as a sliced tomato salad, as this could be a ploy to double your bill. Also beware of waiters who come back five minutes after they've taken your order to tell you something isn't available. If you accept their suggestion of a substitute without asking to see the menu again and re-checking prices, your bill will be substantially increased. Many Polish waiters have worked out what 'Wow, that's cheap!' means and do their best to hear it less often.

In Polish restaurants it's customary to occupy any vacant seat, which can be a problem if you don't smoke. If you're wearing a coat you must deposit it at the coat check whenever there is one. It's also customary to round restaurant bills up to the next higher unit (but only in places with table service, not in milk bars). Write what you want to pay on the bill. If you feel you've been overcharged pay the exact amount asked and don't bother rounding up.

It may be cheap to eat in Poland (for tourists) but too often the quality reflects the price. Menus are usually only in Polish, occasionally in German and very seldom in English. Many things on the menu will not be available anyway, and whole categories such as soups and desserts may be unavailable. Salads are almost never fresh but pickled, and fresh fruit and vegetables are rare. Almost every dish includes some meat, so vegetarians will have a problem. Salt and pepper are usually not on the table, so you must either catch the waiter's attention or get up and search the other tables yourself.

The main meal in Poland is eaten at lunch time. As a result, restaurants often close unexpectedly early (at 8 pm), forcing you to dine on cake and ice cream if you left it too late. Many restaurants have live music and 'dancing' after 7 pm, bringing food service to an end. It can also be hard to find an inexpensive restaurant open on Sunday, and many restaurants are closed for wedding receptions on weekends. The political changes in Poland have at least made it much easier to get a beer with your meal. Restaurant difficulties due to a poor supply situation may be understandable but the low level of service is not.

Cafés & Bars

Few restaurants serve dessert, so for cake and ice cream go to a *kawiarnia* (café). Alcohol is also served at these. Polish cafés are social meeting places where people sit around and talk. A *winiaria* is a wine bar. Polish ice cream *(lody)* is excellent.

Polish Specialities

Poland is a land of hearty soups such as *botwinka* (beet greens soup), *kapuśniak* (cabbage soup), *krupnik* (potato soup), *rosół* (bouillon with little dumplings stuffed with meat), *zacierka* (noodle soup) and *żurek* (sour cream soup). Many traditional Polish dishes originated farther east, including Russian borsch or *barszcz* (red beet soup), Lithuanian *chłodnik* (cold pink cream soup), *kołduny* (turnovers with meat) and *kulebiak* (cabbage and mushroom loaf).

Two world-famous Polish dishes are *bigos* (sauerkraut and meat) and *pierogi* (ravioli-like dumplings served with potatoes and cheese or sauerkraut and mushrooms). If you've got a strong stomach *fasolka po bretónska* (Brittany beans) is a heavy-duty dish, but don't consume a plate of it just before embarking on a long train trip as it may backfire and make you very unpopular.

A few special Polish dishes to watch for on restaurant menus are *kaczka* (roast duck) or *gęś* (goose) with apples, *zraz* (pound steak in cream sauce), *kotlet schabowy* (breaded pork cutlet), *golonka* (pea purée with pig's leg and sauerkraut), *flaki* (tripe Polish style) and sauerkraut with sausage and potatoes. *Zawijasy słowiańskie* is a meat roll of spicy stuffing wrapped in ham and deep fried. Beefsteak tartar is raw minced meat with a raw egg, sardine, chopped onions and seasoning. Only sample this at a 1st-class establishment where you can be sure of the quality. A favourite Polish fast food is *zapiekanka,* a long bread roll baked with onions, cheese and mushrooms on top.

Mushrooms *(grzyby)* have always been great favourites in Poland, either boiled, pan-fried, stewed, sautéed, pickled or marinated. Cucumbers are served freshly sliced and seasoned with honey, pepper or cream as a salad *(mizeria)*. *Ćwikła* is a salad of red beetroot with horseradish. Potatoes are made into dumplings, patties or pancakes *(placki ziemniaczane)*. *Kopytka* is chunks of dough served with a semi-sweet sauce – good for

breakfast at milk bars. *Pyzy* is similar to *kopytka* except that the chunks are stuffed with meat. A traditional Polish dessert is *mazurek* (shortcake). In early summer you can get fresh strawberries, raspberries or blueberries with cream. Hot chocolate is called *kakao.*

DRINKS

Some restaurants have certain rooms in which alcoholic drinks are not served (beware of signs reading *sala bezalko-holowa*). Alcoholism has long been a big problem in Poland and is getting bigger still. The minimum drinking age is 18 years.

Under the communists the only alcoholic beverage you could usually get was vodka. Now excellent beer in healthy half-litre bottles is available everywhere, though it's still hard to find it cold. If you don't say *zimne piwo* (pronounced 'jimne pivo') when ordering you'll automatically get it at room temperature, even in 1st-class restaurants. When ordering beer at restaurants always ask for Polish beer, unless the price of imported beer is clearly indicated on the menu. Otherwise you could end up paying 50% more for German or Czech beer than you would for an acceptable Polish equivalent such as Żywiec, Leżajsk, Okocim or Piast. Pool halls usually have bars where you can get a beer and other drinks at normal prices. Watch for the name *bilard.*

Red and black currant juices are popular non-alcoholic drinks. All wine is imported so pay attention to the price which may be for a glass, not a bottle. Vodka (served chilled) is the national drink, which the Poles claim was invented here. Other notable drinks include *myśliwska* (vodka flavoured with juniper berries), *śliwowica* (plum brandy) and *winiak* (grape brandy). The favourite Polish toast is *na zdrowie* (to your health), sometimes followed by a rendition of *Sto lat*, a popular hymn which means 'may you live 100 years'.

ENTERTAINMENT

A section near the back of the daily papers carries announcements of concerts, plays etc, plus cinema times and even museum hours. It doesn't take any knowledge of Polish to understand these listings, as Handel is Handel and Schubert Schubert in any language. The name and address of the theatre are usually given, and a quick stop there to check the information and pick up tickets clinches the matter. When checking theatre listings it's important to check *both* local papers, as the list in one may be incomplete.

Discos are common in Poland, usually opening around 9 pm from Thursday to Saturday. Also ask about jazz clubs, operetta, opera, concerts, special events and so on at your hotel reception or at local tourist offices. Operetta performances will be in Polish, opera in the original language.

Cinemas

Movies are usually shown in the original language with Polish subtitles, and the admission is cheap. Unfortunately, most are Hollywood productions and films by outstanding Polish directors such as Andrzej Wajda, Krzysztof Zanussi and Waldemar Krzytek are a rarity. (One Hollywood film *about* Poland which you won't want to miss is Steven Spielberg's *Schindler's List*.)

Every year from mid-April to May there's a nationwide film festival called 'Konfrontacje' with 15 award-winning movies shown in the original language at selected cinemas around the country. A different film is shown each night during two 15-day cycles. This is one Polish institution other countries would do well to imitate!

THINGS TO BUY

Cepelia shops belonging to the Folk Art & Crafts Cooperatives Union sell authentic local handicrafts such as tapestries, rugs, embroidery, lace, hand-painted silks, sculptures in wood, pottery, paper cut-outs, folk toys, icons, glassware, wrought-iron objects, silver jewellery and amber necklaces. Works by living professional artists are sold at Desa shops. Amber necklaces are an excellent portable souvenir typical of Poland, and a good necklace shouldn't cost over US$25. If

buying amber see the Malbork Castle exhibits first.

Desa shops have information on complicated Polish export regulations, so check before making large purchases. Basically, it's forbidden to take out any item manufactured before 9 May 1945, works of art and books included. Otherwise you're allowed to export goods from Poland up to a value of US$100 duty-free. Large quantities of crystal or amber will be scrutinised. Official sales receipts should be kept for valuable items.

Since 1989 the retail trade in Poland has come out of the shops into the streets with thousands of small pavement vendors displaying wares they often purchased on 'tourist' trips to other countries. Almost two-thirds of all music recordings sold in Poland are unauthorised 'pirate' copies.

Getting There & Away

AIR

The national carrier, LOT Polish Airlines, flies to Warsaw from Bangkok, Beijing, Cairo, Chicago, Damascus, Dubai, Istanbul, Larnaca, Montreal, Newark, New York, Singapore, Tel Aviv, Toronto and numerous European cities. In recent years LOT has retired its fleet of gas-guzzling, maintenance-intensive Tupolevs and Ilyshins and now flies mostly Western aircraft.

Regular one-way fares to Warsaw are not cheap: US$450 from Frankfurt/Main, US$535 from Amsterdam, US$550 from Paris and US$475 from London. Ask travel agents about special excursion and advance purchase excursion fares on LOT and note the restrictions. People aged 22 years and under get a 25% discount on flights from Western Europe.

LOT has 'Super Saver' fares from New York to Warsaw ranging from US$588 return in the low season to US$848 return in the high season. The minimum stay is seven days, the maximum one month. One-way fares are US$499 to US$1064. These prices are for midweek departures; weekend departures are about US$60 more per return ticket. In the USA call LOT for information at ☎ 800-223 0593 toll free (in Canada ☎ 800-361 1017).

A US travel agency specialising in Poland is Fregata (☎ 212-541 5707, fax 212-262 3220), 250 West 57th St, New York, NY 10107.

Bucket shops in Europe and Asia sell LOT tickets at deep discounts, usually on fares from Asia to Western Europe or vice versa with a free stopover in Warsaw. Ask around the budget travel agencies in Singapore, Penang, Bangkok, London and Amsterdam for deals.

Travel Agencies

Although Poland isn't a mecca for people in search of cheap long-distance flights, a few Polish travel agencies such as Sawa Tour, ulica Wspólna 65a, Warsaw, and World Computer Travel (☎ 061-481 342), ulica Dąbrowskiego 5, 60-848 Poznań, try to offer competitive fares. Of course, you could probably do better in Berlin, Amsterdam or London, but you'll have to add the cost of getting there and your expenses while shopping around and waiting for a reservation.

Departure Tax

The airport tax on international flights is US$10 at Warsaw, US$8 at Gdańsk and Kraków and US$7 at all other airports. There's no airport tax on domestic flights.

LAND

Bus

The cheapest way to travel to Poland from the UK, Holland and many other Western European countries is by bus, costing much less than a train or plane ticket. In Britain, the companies to call are Eurolines National Express (☎ 0171-730 8235), 52 Grosvenor Gardens, Victoria, London SW1W 0AC; Fregata (☎ 0171-734 5101), 100 Dean St, London W1V 6AQ; Fregata (☎ 0161-226 7227), 117 Withington Rd, Manchester MI6 7EU; and the Buchananan Bus Station, Killermont St, Glasgow. The Fregata bus

leaves the Victoria Coach Station weekly year-round (three times a week from June to September). Fares from London to Warsaw are £70 one way, £110 return (30 hours) with reductions for those aged under 26 and over 59 years.

Budget Bus/Eurolines (☎ 020-627 5151), Rokin 10, Amsterdam, runs buses twice a week year-round from Amsterdam to Kraków, Warsaw and Gdańsk. All services depart from each end in the late afternoon and arrive at their destination by midmorning (17 hours). The fare on all these services is US$88 one way, US$140 return (10% reduction for students and persons aged under 26 or over 59 years). For information on similar buses from Brussels to Warsaw (27 hours) contact Eurolines (☎ 217 0025), Place de Brouckere 50, Brussels.

Polish buses leave regularly for Western European cities and they're also cheaper than the train. Many of the companies selling international bus tickets are listed under the heading Travel Agencies in the main city sections of this chapter.

A Hungarian Volanbus runs daily between Budapest and Zakopane (nine hours, US$14).

Some Polish buses to Ukraine, Belorussia, Lithuania and Russia use border crossings still closed to Western tourists, so be sure to confirm that the border crossing you intend to use is in fact open to you when you pick up your visa (a list of places reliably open is provided under Car & Motorbike in this section).

To/From Lithuania Beware of travelling from Poland to Lithuania by train as the 425-km railway line from Warsaw to Vilnius via Grodno passes through Belorussia for 27 km and the Belorussian border guards come aboard and slap unsuspecting tourists with a US$30 Belorussian transit visa fee which is reportedly valid for a return trip. Avoid this rip-off by taking a bus from Poland direct to Lithuania. Orbis, Bracka 16, Warsaw, sells tickets for buses from Warsaw to Vilnius, otherwise catch one of the two morning buses (marked 'Wilno') to Vilnius from

POLAND

Suwałki in north-eastern Poland (209 km, US$7). They often sell out so make getting a ticket a priority. An unreserved local train leaves Suwałki every morning for Šeštokai, Lithuania, along a secondary line which also avoids Belorussia. Arrive at Suwałki in good time to get a ticket.

Train

It's important to keep in mind that there are three price levels for tickets on Polish trains. The most expensive are tickets to Poland bought in Western Europe. Avoid these by breaking your journey in the Czech Republic, from where you pay the much cheaper rate for travel between Eastern European countries. Cheaper still are domestic fares within Poland itself. You can easily take advantage of these by breaking your journey at the first city inside Poland (Poznań, Wrocław, Katowice, Kraków, Nowy Sącz etc). Many of the 'name trains' mentioned below have compulsory seat reservations available at Orbis offices and train stations. International tickets should be purchased in advance at Orbis.

Almatur sells discounted Eurotrain tickets for train trips to Western Europe to persons under 26 years. Holders of students cards are supposed to get a 25% discount on train tickets for travel within the Eastern European countries but you may be told that the reduction only applies if your student card was issued in Eastern Europe. Turn to the Warsaw and Kraków sections of this book for the addresses of the special Almatur offices handling these tickets. The Inter-Rail pass (sold to European residents only) is valid in Poland.

To/From Western Europe The *Ost-West* express train leaves Paris-Nord daily for Warsaw (22 hours) via Poznań. Portions of other trains from Ostend and the Hook of Holland are attached to the *Ost-West* somewhere in Germany, providing direct connections to/from London's Liverpool Street Station (29 hours from Warsaw). Amsterdam passengers join the train at Amersfoort and a one-way 2nd-class ticket

from Amsterdam to Poznań is US$105. Only 2nd-class seats are available though the train also carries sleeping cars. At Rzepin you can change for Wrocław.

If you're coming from London, catch the morning train that goes straight through to Poland and not the evening train which involves a train change in Germany.

A through train from Basel, Switzerland, to Warsaw (25 hours) via Wrocław runs five times a week but only sleepers are available (no seats).

To/From Germany Many trains run between Berlin-Lichtenberg and Warsaw (569 km, eight hours) via Frankfurt/Oder and Poznań. The Eurocity *Berolina* covers the distance in only 6½ hours, leaving Warsaw in the morning and Berlin-Hauptbahnhof in the afternoon. If you really want to save money only get a ticket from Berlin to Rzepin, the first major junction inside Poland. There you could buy a cheap onward ticket with złoty and connect for Poznań, Wrocław or Kraków.

The nightly *Gedania* express with seats and sleeping cars runs from Berlin-Lichtenberg to Gdynia (10 hours) via Szczecin. An overnight train runs from Cologne to Warsaw (16 hours) via Poznań. Trains from Cologne to Kraków (24 hours) travel via Leipzig, Dresden and Wrocław. Another line goes from Frankfurt/Main to Warsaw (22 hours) via Leipzig, Dresden and Wrocław.

To/From the Czech Republic & Austria The overnight *Bohemia* express train between Prague and Warsaw (740 km, 12 hours) travels via Wrocław. Between Wrocław and Prague (339 km) the journey takes about six hours. The *Silesia* express travels via Katowice between Prague and Warsaw (10 hours). The *Baltic* express train runs overnight from Prague to Gdańsk (16 hours) via Wrocław and Poznań.

The *Sobieski* and *Chopin* express trains both travel from Vienna-Süd to Warsaw via Břeclav and Katowice, the *Sobieski* taking nine hours by day, the *Chopin* 11 hours by night in both directions (753 km).

To/From Slovakia, Hungary & Beyond

From Budapest the overnight *Báthory* express train runs daily to Warsaw (837 km, 13 hours) via Komarno, Púchov and Katowice. The *Polonia* express from Belgrade goes via Budapest, Komarno, Žilina and Katowice to Warsaw (21 hours from Belgrade). Change at Katowice for Kraków. Both these trains are routed through a short stretch of the Czech Republic, so beware of taking them if you require a Czech visa as you'll be put off the train at the border.

A different route through Košice in eastern Slovakia is followed by the overnight *Cracovia* express train from Budapest to Kraków (598 km, 12 hours). The *Karpaty* express train from Bucharest to Warsaw (31 hours) also travels via Košice, Nowy Sącz and Kraków (missing Budapest).

To western Poland there's the *Bem* express train from Budapest to Szczecin (1027 km, 18 hours) via Žilina, Wrocław and Poznań.

In addition, there are three unreserved local trains a day which take 20 minutes to hop across the border between Plaveč, Slovakia, and Muszyna, Poland. On the Slovakian side, these trains connect with other local trains to/from Prešov and Poprad-Tatry. Ask about the unreserved *Poprad* fast train from Kraków to Muszyna which doesn't run every day.

To/From China

Orbis, ulica Bracka 16, Warsaw, sells train tickets to Beijing, China, via the Trans-Siberian Railway. The one-way fare with a 2nd-class sleeper is US$125 – the best deal you're likely to get on this route anywhere. First class is about 50% more. Orbis will need a day or two to make all the necessary reservations, then you can start visa hunting. These fares could change, so if you're thinking of coming to Poland primarily to take advantage of these prices, try calling Orbis in Warsaw at ☎ 022-270 105 to check the current situation.

Car & Motorbike

The names of the Polish border posts at the main highway crossings into Poland are given below. Other highway border crossings may be restricted to local residents and closed to Western tourists.

To/From Germany You can cross at Kołbaskowo (20 km west of Szczecin), Świecko (at Frankfurt/Oder), Olszyna (24 km east of Cottbus) and Zgorzelec (at Görlitz).

To/From the Czech Republic You may cross at Jakuszyce (between Liberec and Jelenia Góra), Kudowa-Zdrój (43 km east of Kłodzko), Chałupki (12 km north of Ostrava) and Cieszyn (31 km east of Ostrava).

To/From Slovakia It's Chyżne (west of Zakopane), Łysa Polana (east of Zakopane), Piwniczna (31 km south of Nowy Sącz) and Barwinek (between Rzeszów and Prešov).

To/From the Former Soviet Union You can use Medyka (14 km east of Przemyśl) to enter Ukraine, Terespol (opposite Briest) and Kuźnica Białostocka (between Białystok and Grodno) to enter Belorussia, and Ogrodniki (13 km north-east of Sejhy) to enter Lithuania. The line of cars waiting to cross at Ogrodniki can be several km long, in which case a detour via Belorussia may be worth the transit-visa fee.

On Foot

If you want to avoid the hassle or increasing expense of getting an international train ticket, consider walking across the border. From Germany you can easily walk across the bridge over the Neisse/Nysa River from Görlitz to Zgorzelec, where there are frequent onward train services to Wrocław (163 km). Turn to the Silesia section of this chapter for a complete description.

The best place to walk across the Czech/Polish border is between Cieszyn (Poland) and Český Těšín (Czech Republic), virtually one city cut in half by the Olza

River. On the Czech side the onward train connections to/from Prague and Žilina are good. More information on this crossing is provided at the end of the Małopolska section of this book.

If you'd like to walk across to/from Slovakia, the easiest place to do it is at Łysa Polana with frequent bus service from Zakopane and one bus a day from Kraków. For more information turn to the Zakopane section in this chapter and the Vysoké Tatry section in the Slovakia chapter.

SEA
Ferries

Polferries offers regular year-round service to Świnoujście and Gdańsk from Denmark, Sweden and Finland. Any travel agent in Scandinavia will have tickets; in Poland ask at an Orbis office.

There are services to Świnoujście from Copenhagen, Denmark, five times a week (nine hours, US$43 one way), and from Ystad, Sweden, twice a day (seven hours, US$33 one way). The service to Świnoujście from Rønne on Bornholm Island, Denmark, runs weekly from June to August only (five hours, US$23 one way).

Ferries sail to Gdańsk from Oxelösund, Sweden, weekly from October to May, three or four times a week from June to September (19 hours, US$38 one way), and from Helsinki, Finland, twice a week (35 hours, US$44 from mid-August to June and US$66 one way from July to mid-August).

Reservations are recommended for car or cabin accommodation although deck space is almost always available. Return tickets (valid for six months) are 20% cheaper than two one ways. Holders of ISIC student identity cards and pensioners receive a 20% discount on ferry tickets. Other reductions are available to families of three or more persons. Bicycles are carried free.

The Corona Line runs car ferries from Karlskrona, Sweden, to Gdynia year-round. In July the service is daily and the rest of the year it's about three times a week (15 hours, US$37).

Getting Around

AIR

LOT Polish Airlines operates domestic flights daily from Warsaw to Rzeszów, Kraków, Wrocław, Poznań, Szczecin and Gdańsk. The fare from Warsaw on all these flights is US$35 one way during the week, US$30 on weekends, and there's a 50% discount for those aged 24 years and under. Standby fares are not available. You must check in at least 30 minutes before domestic flights and passports must be shown.

BUS

Long distances are better covered in Poland by train (PKP) than by bus (PKS). Buses are used mostly in mountainous areas, such as around Zakopane, or along routes where there are no direct train connections. Seats on long-distance buses can and should be booked ahead. Baggage is allowed aboard free of charge.

Always check the footnotes on posted bus schedules as some buses don't operate daily. First look at the *odjazdy* column on the departures board to pick a bus that might suit you. Then write down the destination and time, and show it to the person at information to confirm that this bus really will run. Try to buy a ticket (sometimes you can do this the day before, sometimes only on the same day), then check the board again to find out which platform your bus will leave from, locate the platform, and check that your bus is listed on the board there (if any). If you follow this procedure you'll have few problems with Polish buses. Often you can also buy the ticket from the driver.

When asking for the bus station, write PKS on a piece of paper; for the train station write PKP.

TRAIN

The Polskie Koleje Panstwowe (PKP) operates over 27,092 km of railway line allowing you to reach almost every town by rail. Express trains (*expresowy*) with seat reserva-

POLAND

BALTIC SEA

LITHUANIA

To Vilnius &
St Petersburg

RUSSIA

Leba
Ustka
Reda Hel
Gdynia
Słupsk
Kołobrzeg
Gdańsk

Koszalin
Elbląg
Kętrzyn
Suwałki
Giżycko
Augustów

Świnoujście
Szczecin
Tczew
Malbork
Olsztyn
Elk

Mikołajki
Ruciane-Nida

Stargard
Szczeciński
Iława
BELO-
RUSSIA

Piła
Sokółka

Bydgoszcz
Działdowo

To
Berlin
Toruń
Białystok

Kostrzyn
Gniezno
Białowieża

Rzepin
Poznań
Nasielsk

GER-
MANY
Kutno
WARSAW
Siedlce
To Moscow

Zielona
Góra
Łowicz
Łuków
Brest

Cottbus
Leszno
Łódź
Koluszki

To
Dresden
Ostrów
Wielkopolski
Dęblin
To
Kiev

Zgorzelec
Radom
Lublin

Legnica
Wrocław

Kluczbork
Częstochowa
Kielce

Zamość

Opole
Tarnobrzeg
Stalowa
Wola

PRAGUE
Kłodzko
Katowice

Międzylesie
Tarnów
Rzeszów
Przemyśl
Lvov

CZECH
REPUBLIC
Kraków
Jasło

To Kiev
& Odessa

Rabka
Nowy Sącz

Polish Railways
Zakopane
Muszyna

SLOVAKIA
UKRAINE

0   50   100 km

To Vienna
To Budapest

tions are the best way to travel. Direct trains (*pośpieszne*) are also fast and don't usually require reservations, but are much more crowded. Local trains (*osobowe* or *normalne*) are OK for short trips and never require reservations. Polish trains and buses usually run on time.

The best trains are the 'name trains' which usually run to and from Warsaw. To use one of these express trains you must reserve a seat, but reservations are easily made up to two months in advance in main train stations or at Orbis offices (US$1.50). On departure day, reservations can only be made at the

train station. The name trains have Wars dining cars and comfortable compartments – even 2nd class is quite luxurious. We list these trains throughout this chapter – be sure to take them whenever possible. Intercity trains are being introduced in Poland, for example, the IC *Lech* which travels from Warsaw to Poznań in three hours (308 km) and the IC *Sawa*, *Krakus* and *Kościuszko* from Warsaw to Kraków in 2½ hours (325 km). On some of these trains a light meal is included in the price.

As in other European countries, train departures (*odjazdy*) are usually listed on a yellow board while arrivals *(przyjazdy)* are on a white board. Express trains are in red, local trains in black. Watch for the symbol R enclosed in a box, which indicates a fully reserved train. Departure boards also indicate whether a train offers both 1st and 2nd-class accommodation, plus the train number and departure track *(peron)*. The Polish railway system goes on its summer timetable (with extra services) around 1 June.

Tickets for express trains are 50% more expensive than tickets for local stopping trains, so make sure you've got the correct ticket for your train (by writing your destination and the departure time on a piece of paper to show the cashier, for example). Otherwise the conductor will charge you a supplement. In large stations, tickets for different trains are sometimes sold at different windows. Check the train number over the window to make sure you're in the right line and ask information. If you're forced to get on a train without a ticket, find the conductor right away and he/she will sell you one with only a small supplement instead of the heavy fine you'd pay if he/she found you first. Tickets *are* checked on Polish trains.

Both 1st-class and 2nd-class train travel is inexpensive with 1st class costing 50% more than 2nd class. Sample fares for a 100-km trip are US$2 in 2nd class by local train, US$3 in 1st class by local train, US$3 in 2nd class by direct train, US$4.50 in 1st class by direct train, US$4 in 2nd class by express train or US$6 in 1st class by express train.

A Polrailpass providing unlimited travel on trains throughout Poland is available from North American travel agencies through Rail Europe (not for sale in Poland). The passes come in durations of eight days (US$40/59 2nd/1st class), 15 days (US$45/69), 21 days (US$50/70) and one month (US$55/85). Persons aged under 26 years on the first day of travel can buy a 'Junior' pass for about 20% less. Seat reservation fees are not included.

Couchettes & Sleepers

Overnight trains are a good way of saving money in Poland while getting to your destination. A 2nd-class ticket and couchette are often less than the price of a hotel, and you arrive in the next city early in the morning. The attendant in the sleeping car sells soft drinks and coffee and express trains often carry good stand-up dining cars. You can't beat a breakfast of *flaki* (tripe) and coffee (US$1.75).

Second-class couchettes (US$9) contain six beds to the compartment, three to a side. First-class sleepers (US$19) have only two beds. There's a third type called 'special' 2nd-class sleeper which has three beds to the compartment (US$14). It used to be very hard to book these, involving over an hour in line at an Orbis office. Sharply increased prices have cut demand and most train stations are now computerised, allowing you to book your couchette or sleeper at the reservation window at any train station in minutes. Main stations have special 'Polres' offices to do this. Orbis, the Polish travel agency, also books couchettes and sleepers for the same price and its staff are more likely to speak English.

One reader commented that he found it cheaper to take a 1st-class seat on overnight trains rather than a 2nd-class couchette, and that he usually had the 1st-class seating compartment all to himself while the 2nd-class couchettes were full. This is probably only true during the middle of the week.

Train Stations

Train stations in Poland have good facilities: left-luggage rooms open round the clock, cafeterias, waiting rooms, newsstands, posted timetables etc. There are public toilets in all train stations (and in many other places) and you're expected to pay around US$0.10 to use them.

When you check your baggage at railway cloakrooms *(przechowalnia bagażu)* you must declare the value of the object in złoty and sign the form (have the amount written down on a piece of paper ready to show the clerk). You're charged 1% of the declared value which includes insurance. This makes it fairly expensive if you declare anything near the real value, though in small stations you can easily forgo the insurance and just pay the standard US$0.35 fee. If you say 'million' when the baggage handler asks you how much your bag is worth, you'll still pay under US$1. We've never heard of anyone actually losing luggage properly checked at a Polish train station. You pay the left-luggage charge when you pick the item up, not when you deposit it (useful to know if you arrive in the country with no Polish currency).

CAR & MOTORBIKE

Poland's 258,588 km of roads are generally narrow but in good condition and there isn't too much traffic. Over the next 15 years Poland is to build a 2000-km network of toll roads stretching from Gdańsk to the Czech border and Germany to Ukraine. The World Bank and Western banks have promised loans covering 65% of the US$5 billion cost.

To drive a car into Poland you'll need your driver's licence, the car registration card and liability insurance (the 'green card'). If your insurance isn't valid for Poland you must buy an additional policy at the border. The car registration number will be entered in your passport.

Always use 94-octane 'yellow' petrol or 98-octane 'red' (super), as the 86-octane 'blue' fuel can damage your engine. Unleaded 95-octane petrol (benzyna bezołowiowa) is becoming easier to find. If one station doesn't have unleaded fuel, ask them for the address of another which does.

In recent years petrol has become readily available at service stations around Poland, rendering obsolete such quaint communist inventions as petrol coupons purchased for hard currency and quick capitalist solutions like slipping the pump attendant a hard-currency tip.

Petrol stations are sometimes few, so plan ahead and expect queues, especially in the south. Elsewhere the lines at the fuel pumps are much shorter. Most petrol stations are open from 6 am to 10 pm (Sunday 7 am to 3 pm), though some work around the clock.

You're allowed to import or export fuel up to a maximum of 10 litres in a spare tank.

When asking directions of people along the road, always write the place name on a piece of paper to avoid any misunderstanding. Car theft is a problem in Poland and most cars are fitted with alarm systems which go off at the slightest provocation. Drive carefully as Poland has the fourth highest incidence of motor-vehicle fatalities per capita in the world.

The Polski Związek Motorowy (Polish Motoring Association) with offices in all large cities can provide breakdown service (pomoc drogowa) and other assistance to motorists. If you're a member of an automobile club at home, bring along your membership card with an international letter of introduction, as this could entitle you to free breakdown service and legal advice from the PZM. The nationwide PZM emergency breakdown number is ☎ 981.

Road Rules

The speed limit is 110 km/h on expressways, 90 km/h on other open roads and 60 km/h in built-up areas. Motorcycles cannot exceed 90 km/h in any case. At the entrance to small towns, if the background of the sign bearing the town name is white you must reduce speed to 60 km/h. If the background is green there's no need to reduce speed.

Radar-equipped police are very active, especially in villages where you must slow down to 60 km/h, and speeding fines ranging from US$7 to US$32 are levied frequently. Approaching cars often flash their lights in warning. Seat belts are compulsory in the front seat. Parking tickets (US$7) are also common and having one person sitting in the car while the other pops into a shop doesn't exempt you.

Cyclists are not allowed to ride two abreast on highways.

Car Rental

Avis, Budget and Hertz/Orbis are now well represented in Poland. Their economy models begin around US$37 a day plus US$0.38 a km or US$100/550 daily/weekly with unlimited mileage. Add 5% tax and US$13 per day for compulsory Loss Damage Waiver (LDW) insurance. If the car is stolen you may be charged US$100 or more despite having theft covered by the insurance. It's usually cheaper to prebook your car from abroad rather than just front up at an agency inside Poland.

The minimum age to rent a car is 21 years at Budget and Hertz, 23 years at Avis. Budget and Hertz allow you to drop the car off at any of their offices around Poland at no additional charge but their unlimited mileage cars cannot be taken out of Poland. Avis allows one-way rentals from Warsaw to Prague.

Some of the cars are in pretty poor shape so check the vehicle carefully before you drive off. If the lights aren't in order, for example, you could be fined. Insist on exchanging the car at the next rental office if you discover that they've unloaded a lemon on you.

If you had thought of renting a car in Berlin and driving it into Poland, think again as most German car rental agencies will not allow their vehicles to be taken to Poland. This is because of a report circulated by the Federal Office of Criminal Investigations in Wiesbaden about 'criminal organisations which have specialised in stealing new vehicles'. Call the car rental chains directly for the latest information.

HITCHING

Hitchhiking is a practical way of getting around and even Polish women regularly travel 'autostop'. There's even an official 'autostop' card complete with coupons for drivers available from PTTK offices! Large commercial vehicles that pick up hitchhikers expect to be paid the equivalent of a bus fare but car drivers will also stop, leaving the question of payment at your discretion.

BOAT
Local Boats

A pleasant way to sightsee is from a ship, and local cruises on the Vistula River are offered at Kraków, Warsaw and Toruń. Other local river cruises are available at Gdańsk and

Wrocław. The day excursion from Gdańsk or Sopot to Hel across the Gulf of Gdańsk is recommended. Most of these trips operate only in summer.

Enthusiasts for canal cruising by narrow boat won't want to miss a trip on the Elbląg Canal from Elbląg to Ostróda where the boats are carried up and down ramps on rail-mounted platforms. Also in northeastern Poland, excursion boats of the Mazurian Shipping Company's White Fleet run daily from May to September between Giżycko, Mikołajki and Ruciane-Nida, while other tourist boats operate out of Augustów and Ostróda.

LOCAL TRANSPORT

Local buses, trolley buses and trams cost about US$0.25 a ride, but tickets must be purchased in advance at kiosks or Ruch newsstands. Buy a bunch of them as drivers don't sell tickets. You punch the ticket as you board. Public transport operates from 5.30 am to 11 pm. Express buses *(pośpieszny)* are double fare, night buses after 11 pm triple fare. Luggage is an extra fare. Though tickets aren't checked often, you will receive a stiff fine if you're caught without one at a spot check.

Taxi

Since the Polish złoty became a 'hard' currency, taxis are a lot easier to find. There are always regular taxi stands in front of train stations and near markets, plus other strategic points around town. It's also possible to flag down taxis on the street. Beware of taxis waiting in front of the tourist hotels, and unmarked, unmetered 'pirate' taxis as these will try to overcharge. Always insist that the meter be turned on and carry small bills (otherwise you won't get proper change). If there's no meter agree on the price beforehand. Metered taxis operate on tariff No 1 from 6 am to 10 pm, tariff No 2 from 10 pm to 6 am. Make sure the meter is set to the correct level during the day.

Taxi meters have difficulty keeping up with inflation. At last report taxis charged from 400 to 600 times the meter fare. This could change as the meters are adjusted, so check by asking your hotel receptionist or any Polish acquaintance. Outside city limits and after 11 pm taxis charge double. Luggage and the number of passengers don't affect the fare. A short trip around town may cost US$2, while an hour-long search for a youth hostel including a 10-km drive out of town may cost up to US$10, tip included. It never hurts to round the fare up and if a driver is especially helpful in finding a cheap place to stay, tip generously.

TOURS

Of the package tours to Poland offered by travel offices abroad, the most interesting cater to special interests such as horse riding, skiing, yachting, health resorts etc, which are hard to organise on your own.

Almatur (☎ 022-262 639), ulica Kopernicka 23, Warsaw, offers one-week sailing trips on the Mazurian Lakes at US$135 per person. Horse riding in Silesia is US$132 for one week, US$197 for two weeks. These trips are intended mainly for young people and are only available in July and August.

Pegrotour (☎ 022-243 676), ulica Emilii Plater 47 (upstairs), opposite the Palace of Culture in Warsaw, arranges horse riding at Szczawno Zdroj in Silesia, 90 km from Wrocław. Their stable is three km from a train station with taxis to the door and it's open all year. Pegrotour packages cost about US$40 per person a day (double occupancy), half board and one hour in the saddle included. Additional riding is about US$5 an hour. Pegrotour can make all the arrangements for individuals who just walk into their Warsaw office.

The OZGT (☎ 089-275 156; fax 089-273 442), above tourist information at the High Gate in Olsztyn, runs regular 10-day canoe tours along the Krutynia canoe route from June to August and occasionally in spring and fall. The US$125 price includes canoe, food, lodging and a Polish-speaking guide. You can just show up at their Olsztyn office and hope they can fit you into one of their scheduled tours, or fax them before you leave for Poland and fit one of their departures into your schedule. Either way, it's worth the effort.

Orbis offices and private travel agencies around Poland offer organised city sightseeing tours in Warsaw, Kraków and other cities. The best of the Warsaw trips are to Wilanów Palace and Chopin's birthplace at Żelazowa Wola, while at Kraków you have the salt mines and Auschwitz-Birkenau to choose from. Most operate from mid-May to September only.

New Millennium Holidays (☎ 0121-711 2232), 20 High St, Solihull, West Midlands B91 3TB, England, offers low-cost bus tours from the UK to Gdynia and Zakopane year-round.

Warsaw

Warsaw (Warszawa), a city of nearly two million inhabitants in the north-east corner of Eastern Europe, is almost equidistant from Berlin (590 km), Prague (620 km), Vienna (678 km) and Budapest (700 km). Viewed another way, Warsaw is almost the same distance from London (1590 km), Paris (1610 km) and Sofia (1660 km). The Vistula (Wisła) River cuts a curving course across Poland, from the Carpathian Mountains in the south to the Baltic in the north, and halfway down sits Warsaw, off-centre now that the country's borders have moved west.

The strategic location in the centre of the Mazovian lowland led to the site being fortified in the 14th century, and in 1596 King Sigismund III Vasa had the capital transferred here from Kraków. Warsaw has long resisted foreign domination: by the Swedes in the 17th century, tsarist Russia in the 19th century and Nazi Germany and the USSR in the 20th century.

Many of Warsaw's finest avenues, parks and palaces were built in the 18th century, whereas the 19th century was a period of decay with the city as a mere provincial centre of the Russian Empire. Yet this was nothing compared to WW II when hundreds of thousands of residents were killed and all

POLAND

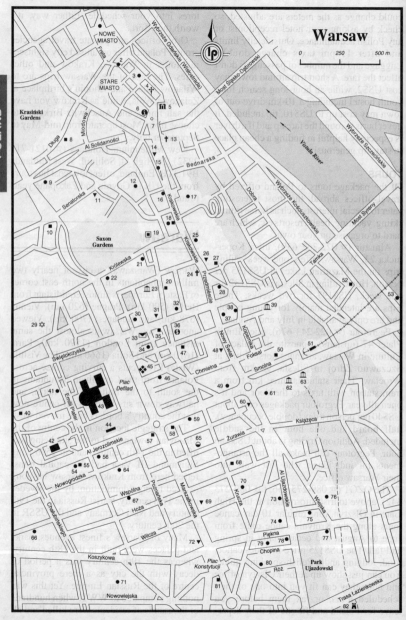

Warsaw

NOWE
MIASTO

STARE
MIASTO

Krasiński
Gardens

Saxon
Gardens

Plac
Defilad

Al Jerozolimskie

Plac
Konstytucji

Park
Ujazdowski

Wisła/Vistula River

POLAND

PLACES TO STAY

8	Pokoje Gościnne
10	Saski Hotel
18	Europejski Hotel
20	Hotel Garnizonowy
27	Hotel Harenda
35	Hotel Warszawa
40	Holiday Inn Hotel
47	Hotel Dom Chłopa
50	Smolna Youth Hostel
52	Hotel Belfer
55	Marriott Hotel
57	Metropol & Polonia Hotels
58	Forum Hotel
68	Grand Hotel
81	MDM Hotel

PLACES TO EAT

11	El Popo Restauracja Meksykańska
14	Pizzeria Giovanni
26	Uniwersytecki Milk Bar
31	U Matysiaków Restaurant
48	Familijny Milk Bar
60	Szwajcarski Milk Bar
69	Steak & Salad Bar Dolce Vita
72	Złota Kurka Milk Bar

OTHER

1	New Town Square
2	Barbican
3	Old Town Square
4	St John's Cathedral
5	Royal Palace
6	'IT' Tourist Information
7	Plac Zamkowy
9	Jewish Historical Institute
12	Wielki Opera House
13	St Anne's Church
15	Café Studio M
16	Kino Kultura
17	Radziwiłł Palace
18	American Express
19	Tomb of the Unknown Soldier
21	Zachęta Art Gallery
22	Orbis (Train Tickets)
23	Ethnological Museum
24	Church of the Holy Cross
25	University of Warsaw
28	Academy of Sciences
29	Synagogue
30	Klub Europa Voltaire
32	Antykwariat Warszawski
33	Post Office/Telephone Centre
34	Filharmonia Concert Hall
36	NBP Bank
37	Wagon-lits Travel
38	Almatur
39	Chopin Museum
41	Akwarium Club/Pegrotour
42	Central Railway Station
43	Palace of Culture & Science
44	Śródmieście Railway Station
45	Department Stores
46	Bar Hybrydy
49	Orbis (International Tickets)
51	Powiśle Railway Station
53	Excursion Boats
54	LOT Polish Airlines
56	Polski Związek Motorowy
59	Kasy Teatralne
61	Former Party House
62	National Museum
63	Armed Forces Museum
64	Operetta
65	Pekaes Bus Office
66	Klub Medyków
67	Sawa Tour
70	Syrena Tourist Office
71	Politechnical University
73	Bulgarian Consulate
74	American Embassy
75	Canadian Embassy
76	Parliament
77	French Embassy
78	Hungarian & Yugoslavian Consulates
79	Romanian Consulate
80	Czech Republic Consulate
82	Ujazdów Castle

the survivors finally expelled before the city was levelled block by block. Before WW II a third of the population of Warsaw was Jewish but only a handful of Jews remain today.

In a way, Warsaw reborn from wartime destruction epitomises the Polish nation. The masterful rebuilding of old Warsaw and its harmonious union with the new symbolise the determination of the Polish people to develop and build without sacrificing an identity which has always been their greatest strength. You'll witness that identity in the museums and churches, but more directly in the surprisingly candid people. Warsaw is a fascinating layer cake you'll need several days to digest.

Orientation

If you're coming by train you'll probably arrive at Central Station beside the Palace of Culture & Science near the corner of Aleje

Jerozolimskie and Marszałkowska. Dump your things in the baggage room and start hostel or hotel hunting using the listings in this section. More information on Central Station is given under Getting There & Away following. If you arrived by plane, the airport transportation possibilities are described under Getting Around.

Warsaw has many focal points but you'll soon become acquainted with Plac Zamkowy, the gateway to old Warsaw, and the Royal Way, which runs 10 km south-east from this square to Wilanów Palace with changing names: Krakowskie Przedmieście, Nowy Świat, Aleje Ujazdowskie, Belwederska, Jana Sobieskiego and Aleja Wilanowska. Plan your sightseeing around this corridor.

Information

Tourist Offices Tourist information is available from the information-cum-souvenir shop marked 'IT' (☎ 635 1881) at Plac Zamkowy 1/13 in the old town. Stock up on maps of cities all around Poland here.

Just opposite Central Station is the Polski Związek Motorowy (Polish Motoring Association, ☎ 210 788), Aleje Jerozolimskie 63, where you should be able to buy a good indexed map of Warsaw.

If you'll be staying longer than a day or two it's a good investment to buy the indexed 48-page *Warszawa Plan Miasta* map book (US$3), available at bookstores all around Poland. It will make using public transport easy and will save you a lot of time and money.

Pick up a copy of the free monthly magazine *Warszawa, What, Where, When* at tourist information or at a luxury hotel. It includes an excellent centrefold map and current information about tourist facilities.

The Incoming Bureau at Orbis, ulica Marszałkowska 142, can answer questions about standard tourist facilities such as up-market hotels, sightseeing excursions, river cruises, festivals and activities etc.

A map listing all youth hostels in Poland is available from PTSM (Polskie Towarzystwo Schronisk Młodzieżowych), at ulica Chocimska 28 near Łazienkowski Park, 4th floor, suite 426 (weekdays 8 am to 3 pm).

Money A convenient place to change travellers' cheques is the Bank Pekao SA, on the 3rd floor of the Marriott Hotel opposite Central Station (weekdays 9 am to 2 pm). Their commission is 2% with a US$2 minimum, and they'll change dollar travellers' cheques into dollars cash for half a per cent commission (minimum US$2).

The NBP Bank on Plac Powstańców Warszawy (upstairs), a couple of blocks from Central Station (weekdays 8 am to 6 pm, Saturday 8 am to 1 pm), changes travellers' cheques for 1.5% commission.

Of course, the numerous private exchange offices around town are much faster but they only accept cash. For exchange facilities at the airport and train station see Getting There & Away following.

American Express, opposite Hotel Europejski (weekdays 9 am to 5 pm, Saturday 10 am to 2 pm), is not a good place to change money. They change all types of travellers' cheques without commission, but give a lower rate than the banks. Ironically, they *do* charge commission to change cash. American Express will change dollar travellers' cheques into dollars cash but you lose about 3% on the transaction. There's an American Express automatic cash dispenser outside the office and clients' mail is held inside.

Post & Telecommunications Poste restante mail is held at window No 12 in the main post office, ulica Świętokrzyska 31/33 (daily 8 am to 8 pm). A 24-hour post and telephone centre functions in the same building.

There's a branch post office/telephone centre at Rynek Starego Miasta 15, but it's only open during business hours. They have some of the cheapest postcards in town and you can buy stamps right there.

Warsaw's telephone code is 02 with seven-digit numbers, 022 with six-digit numbers.

Western Embassies Embassy row stretches along Aleje Ujazdowskie between Aleje Jerozolimskie and Łazienki Park. The American Embassy (☎ 283 041), Aleje Ujazdowskie 29/31, and the Canadian Embassy (☎ 298 051), ulica Matejki 1/5, are only a block apart, and the French Embassy (☎ 628 8401), Piękna 1, is just behind the Canadian Embassy.

The British Embassy is two blocks south of these, on the corner of Aleje Ujazdowskie and Aleje Róż, but only diplomatic business is dealt with there. British and New Zealand travellers must trek out to the British Consulate, ulica Wawelska 14 (weekdays 9 am to noon and 2 to 4 pm), in an inconvenient south-western suburb of Warsaw.

The Australian Embassy (☎ 176 081) is at ulica Estońska 3/5 on the east side of the Vistula (take any eastbound tram on Aleje Jerozolimskie and get off at the first stop across the river). They're open weekdays from 9 am to 1 pm.

Eastern Embassies Most of the Eastern European embassies are in the same area. The Bulgarian Consulate, Aleje Ujazdowskie 35 (open Monday, Wednesday and Friday 10 am to noon), issues tourist visas valid three months from the date of issue for US$32 and one photo, but you have to wait five working days. If you want a tourist visa on the spot it's a whopping US$70. Thirty-hour transit visas are always issued on the spot: US$22 for one entry, US$44 for two entries (no photos required).

Visas for the other Eastern European countries are more easily obtained. The Yugoslav and Hungarian consulates are side by side on Aleje Ujazdowskie, a block south of the American Embassy, and both are open Monday, Wednesday and Friday from 9 am to noon. Yugoslav visas are issued on the spot free of charge. Hungarian visas cost US$20 and two photos for one entry, US$33 and four photos for two entries, and are issued at once. Be sure to get a tourist and not a transit visa.

The Romanian Consulate, around the corner at ulica Chopina 10, keeps the same hours. Romanian visas are issued immediately at US$35 for Canadians, Americans, New Zealanders and Australians, and US$45 for British. No photos are required.

Nearby at ulica Koszykowa 18, on the corner of Aleje Róż, is the Czech Republic Consulate (Monday to Friday 9 am to noon). You'll receive a tourist or transit visa right away upon payment of US$23 and one photo for one entry, US$54 and one photo for multiple entries, though some nationalities are charged more (such as Canadians – US$48 for one entry). Transit visas are the same price.

The Slovak Embassy, ulica Litewska 6 off Aleja Jana Szucha (Monday, Wednesday, and Friday 9 am to noon), is three blocks south of the Czech Consulate. At last report they were charging exactly the same prices for exactly the same visas (but Slovakian visas are not accepted in the Czech Republic and vice versa).

Of the four former components of the USSR which have land borders with Poland, Lithuania is by far the easiest to visit. The Lithuanian Consulate, Aleje Szucha 5 (weekdays 10 am to noon and 2 to 4 pm), issues visas for US$20 plus US$7 for 24-hour express service (otherwise you must wait 10 days). Visas are free for US citizens and British nationals don't require visas. A Lithuanian visa is valid for two days transit through Latvia and Estonia, and stays in those countries can be extended upon arrival. See Getting There & Away in the introduction to this chapter for information of transportation to Lithuania.

At last report the Ukrainian Consulate was in temporary quarters at Aleja Szucha 7, next door to the Lithuanian Consulate. Ukrainian visas are US$50, but be prepared for all sorts of nasty communist-era requirements such as prepayment of rooms at expensive hotels.

The Consulate of the Russian Federation, ulica Belwederska 25, building C (Monday, Wednesday, Friday 8 am to noon), continues to enforce all the old USSR visa requirements, which makes independent travel to

POLAND

Russia a real drag. Check anyway, as things can only get better.

The Albanian Consulate, Słoneczna 15 across the park behind the Russian Embassy, is theoretically open weekdays from 8 to 10 am, but visiting them is usually a waste of time.

The Belorussian Embassy, Ateńska 67, is in an isolated suburb east of the Vistula.

Travel Agencies Student travel is handled by Almatur, ulica Kopernika 23 (weekdays 9 am to 5 pm, Saturday 10 am to 2 pm), and they're generally helpful. They'll be able to tell you about the International Student Hotels which are open in July and August only. Also ask about one-week Almatur sailing and horse-riding trips in July and August.

As many as 20 travel agencies in Warsaw sell international bus tickets from Poland to Western Europe and many such buses leave from the parking lot behind Central Railway Station. Service is more frequent from May to October.

Almatur, ulica Kopernika 23, has bus tickets to Amsterdam (US$91), Cologne (US$59), London (US$113), Paris (US$94) and Zürich (US$94).

Orbis, Bracka 16, sells bus tickets from Warsaw to Belgium, Britain, France, Germany, Holland, Italy, Norway, Spain and Sweden. This is the place to ask about buses to Vilnius, Lithuania.

Other companies with bus tickets to Western Europe include Anna Travel (☎ 255 389), on the top floor at Central Station (weekdays 8 am to 6 pm, Saturday 9 am to 3 pm), the Syrena Tourist Office, ulica Krucza 16/22, and Pekaes, ulica Żurawia 26.

International train tickets are available from Orbis, ulica Bracka 16. This is a good place to pick up discounted student train tickets to other Eastern European countries. Seat reservations for domestic express trains, sleepers and couchettes can also be booked at this Orbis office or at Central Station.

The Orbis office at Marszałkowska 142 also sells both domestic and international train tickets and it's sometimes less crowded.

This is the only Orbis office that accepts Visa cards.

A special Almatur office at the University of Warsaw, Krakowskie Przedmieście 26/28, sells discounted Eurotrain international tickets to persons under 26 years (student card not required). This office (open weekdays from 9 am to 3.30 pm) is in room No 19, upstairs in the building to the right as you go through the gate. Eurotrain tickets are valid for two months.

Wagon-lits Travel, Nowy Świat 64, sells train and air tickets to points outside Eastern Europe.

Sawa Tour, ulica Wspólna 65a, can book cheap flights to anywhere departing from Berlin (they need a week to get the tickets).

Newspapers Klub MPK, ulica Marszałkowska 122 at ulica Sienkiewicza (next to Junior Department Store), has foreign newspapers and magazines.

Laundry Alba Self-Service Laundry, on the corner of Aniele wicza and Karmelicka (weekdays 9 am to 7 pm, Saturday 9 am to 1 pm), charges US$5 to wash and dry up to six kilos. You're asked to call ☎ 317 317 two days ahead to make a reservation. Bring your own detergent.

Things to See
The Old Town From Plac Zamkowy you enter the old city (Stare Miastro) along ulica Świętojańska. You'll soon come to 14th century Gothic **St John's Cathedral**, and then the **Rynek Starego Miasta**, the old town square. Try to catch the 15-minute film at the **City Historical Museum**, Rynek Starego Miasta 42 (free Sunday, closed Monday), which unforgettably depicts the wartime destruction of the city. It's hard to believe that all the 17th and 18th century buildings around this square have been completely rebuilt from their foundations. Stroll around, visiting the shops, galleries and restaurants.

Continue north a block on ulica Nowomiejska to the **Barbican** (1548), part of the medieval walled circuit around Warsaw.

Walk towards the river inside the walls a bit to find the city's symbol, the **Warsaw Mermaid** (1855). (Once upon a time a mermaid, Syrena, rose from the river and told a fisherman, Wars, and his wife, Sawa, to found a city here.) Everything north of this wall is New Town (Nowe Miasto). Straight ahead on Freta, beyond several historic churches, is **Rynek Nowego Miasta** with more churches. At ulica Freta 5 is the Asian Gallery of the **Asia & Pacific Museum** (closed Monday) with interesting exhibitions. The delightful streets and buildings in both Old and New towns are best explored casually on your own without a guidebook.

The Royal Way On a tall pillar (1644) in the centre of Plac Zamkowy is a statue of King Sigismund III. The **Royal Castle** (1619) on the east side of the square developed over the centuries as successive Polish kings added wings and redecorated the interior. In 1945 all that remained was a heap of rubble but from 1971 to 1974 the castle was carefully rebuilt. The entrance is on the north side of the building, but castle tickets must be purchased at the Zamek Kasy Biletowe, around the corner on ulica Świętojańska (closed Monday, free Thursday, reduced admission Sunday). For US$1.50 you can see the 'Konmaty Pokoje Dworskie' (courtiers' lodgings) with the parliament chamber and historic paintings by Jan Matejko. To see the 'Apartamenty Królewskie' (king's apartments) with the Canaletto paintings a further US$3 must be paid (except on Sunday when you can see everything for US$2). Students get half price. A guided tour in English or French is US$7 extra. In summer demand outstrips supply, so arrive early and be prepared to wait.

On the south side of Plac Zamkowy is **St Anne's Church** (1454), one of the most beautiful churches in the city. Continue south on Krakowskie Przedmieście where there are many aristocratic residences, especially the **Radziwiłł Palace** (1643), on the left beside a church. The Warsaw Pact was signed in this building on 14 May 1955. Next to this palace is the elegant secessionist

Bristol Hotel (1901) with the neoclassical **Hotel Europejski** (1877) across the street. Behind the Europejski are Saski Gardens with the **Tomb of the Unknown Soldier**, occupying a fragment of an 18th century royal palace destroyed in WW II. The ceremonial changing of the guard here takes place Sunday at noon.

On the north side of the square is the massive **Wielki Opera House** (1833, rebuilt in 1965), while to the south is the modern Hotel Victoria Inter-Continental. On the west side of this hotel is the **Zachęta Art Gallery** (closed Monday) which often stages great art shows in summer. South a block beyond the circular **Evangelical Church** (1781) is the **Ethnological Museum** (closed Monday), ulica Kredytowa 1. This large museum has collections of tribal art from Africa, Oceania and Latin America, as well as Polish folklore.

From this museum follow ulica Traugutta east a block back to the Royal Way. Just around the corner on the right is the 17th century **Church of the Holy Cross**. The heart of Frédéric Chopin is preserved in the second pillar on the left-hand side of the main nave of this church (though Chopin left Warsaw when he was 20 years old and died of tuberculosis in Paris aged only 39, he was a Polish nationalist to the end). In front of the 19th century **Academy of Sciences** (Staszic Palace) nearby stands the famous statue (1830) of Polish astronomer Nicolaus Copernicus by the Danish sculptor Bertel Thorvaldsen. Below the Academy towards the river is the **Chopin Museum**, ulica Tamka 41 (closed Tuesday), with memorabilia such as Chopin's last piano and one of the best collections of Chopin manuscripts in the world. They'll play recordings of his music if you ask.

More Museums Return to the Royal Way and then head south along Nowy Świat (New World St), crossing Aleje Jerozolimskie (Jerusalem Ave) to the former **Party House** (1951). This is where the Central Committee of the Polish United Workers Party (PZPR) used to meet. In 1991 the top floor of this

POLAND

POLAND

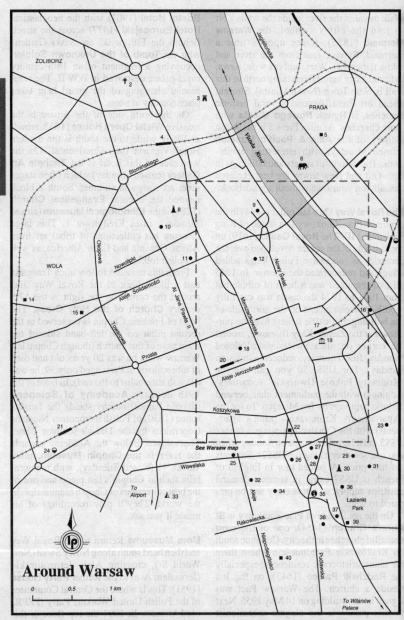

ŻOLIBORZ

PRAGA

Vistula River

Jagiellońska

Słomińskiego

Okopowa

Nowolipki

WOLA

Al. Jana Pawła II

Aleje Solidarności

Towarowa

Prosta

Plac Starynkiewicza

Marszałkowska

Marchlewska

Nowy Świat

Koszykowa

Aleje Jerozolimskie

See Warsaw map

Wawelska

Wawelska

Aleje

Rakowiecka

Niepodległości

Puławska

Łazienki Park

To Airport

To Wilanów Palace

Around Warsaw

0   0.5   1 km

POLAND

PLACES TO STAY

5	Nowa Praga Hotel
14	Hotel Syrena
15	Karolkowa Youth Hostel
22	MDM Hotel
33	Camping OST 'Gromada'
39	Hotel Uniwersytet Warszawski
40	Hotel Agra

OTHER

1	Praga Railway Station
2	Church of Św Stanisława Kostki
3	Citadel
4	Gdańska Railway Station
6	Zoo
7	Wileńska Railway Station
8	Warsaw Ghetto Monument
9	Old Town Square (Rynek)
10	Alba Self-Service Laundry
11	Warsaw Chamber Opera
12	Wielki Opera House
13	Stadion Bus & Railway Stations
16	Excursion Boat Landing
17	Powiśle Railway Station
18	Palace of Culture & Science
19	National Museum
20	Central Railway Station
21	Zachodnia Railway Station
23	Stadion 'Legia'
24	Central Bus Station
25	British Consulate
26	Disco Remont
27	Slovak Consulate
28	Lithuanian Consulate
29	Orangerie
30	Chopin Monument
31	Łazienki Water Palace
32	Disco Park
34	Disco Stodoła
35	Youth Hostel Association Office
36	Belvedere Palace
37	Russian Consulate
38	Albanian Consulate

building became the Warsaw Stock Exchange. (After rising 820% in dollar terms in 1993, the Warsaw index crashed 50% in early 1994.)

The large building beside this on Aleje Jerozolimskie is the **National Museum** (closed Monday, free Thursday) which has a magnificent collection of paintings including *The Battle of Grunwald* by Jan Matejko.

During WW II this huge painting was evacuated to Lublin and secretly buried. The Nazis offered a reward of 10 million Reichsmarks for information leading to its discovery but no one accepted. After the war Matejko's work was uncovered and restored.

Towards the riverside next to the National Museum is the **Armed Forces Museum** (closed Monday and Tuesday) with a large assortment of old guns, tanks and planes on the terrace outside. A gate beyond the planes on the south side of this terrace opens into Park Kultury where a footpath leads south through the greenbelt all the way to Łazienki Park, a pleasant 25-minute walk (if the gate is locked you'll have to circle back around Party House).

The Royal Palaces Łazienki Park is best known for its 18th century neoclassical **Water Palace** (closed Monday and during bad weather), summer residence of Stanislaus Augustus Poniatowski, the last king of Poland. This reform-minded monarch, who gave Poland the world's second written constitution in 1791, was deposed by a Russian army and a confederation of reactionary Polish magnates in 1792.

The **Orangerie** (1788) in the park is also well worth seeing for its theatre and gallery of sculpture (closed Monday). The striking **Chopin Monument** (1926) is just off Aleje Ujazdowskie but still within the park. On summer Sundays at noon and 5 pm excellent piano recitals are held here. Poland's Head of State resides in the neoclassical **Belvedere Palace** (1818), just south of the monument.

Six km farther south on bus No 180 or B (from the next intersection south of the massive Russian Embassy) is **Wilanów Palace** (1696), the Baroque summer residence of King John III Sobieski who defeated the Turks at Vienna in 1683, ending their threat to Central Europe forever. In summer it's hard to gain admission to the palace (closed Tuesday, US$2) due to large groups and limited capacity, but even the exterior and 18th century French-style park are worth the trip. One-hour guided tours in Polish begin every 15 minutes from 9.30 am to 2.30 pm but only 35 people are admitted each time, and on weekdays tour groups often pre-book all the tickets. Summaries in English and French are posted in most rooms. On Saturday, Sunday and holidays the palace is reserved for individuals so these are good days to come, but arrive early and be prepared to stand in line. Don't come on Tuesday or the day following a public holiday as not only the palace but also the park behind the palace will be locked. While you're at Wilanów the **Poster Museum** (Muzeum Plakatu) in the former royal stables beside the palace is worth a visit (closed Monday). There are two fancy restaurants between the bus stop and the palace where you could have lunch.

Other Sights Warsaw's **Palace of Culture** (1955) near the Central Station is an impressive Stalin-era building with an elevator which will carry you up to the observation terrace on the 30th floor for a panoramic view (US$2). Poles often joke that this is the best view in the city because it's the only one which doesn't include the Palace of Culture itself! There's also a **Technical Museum** (closed Monday), several theatres and a congress hall in the palace. The large street market selling everything from imported beer to car tyres in the park around the palace and the large department stores, Junior, Wars and Sawa, on the east side of the Palace of Culture, are good places to get a feel for the current state of Polish consumerism.

Most of the **Citadel** (1834) on the north side of the city is still occupied by the military; however, part of it may be visited through the Brama Straceń, the large gate near the middle of the Citadel wall on the river side. This large fortress was built by the Russians after a Polish uprising in 1830. There's a museum (closed Monday and Tuesday) and plaques recalling the Poles executed here by the tsarist forces a century or more ago. Buses Nos 118 and 185 stop near the Citadel entrance.

Within walking distance north-west of the citadel near Plac Wilsona is the **Church of Św Stanisława Kostki** with the red-granite tomb of Father Jerzy Popiełuszko in the yard. Prior to his murder by the secret police in October 1984 the 37-year-old priest had earned the enmity of communist hardliners by giving sermons in support of Solidarity. The government cooled the passions aroused by Father Popiełuszko's death by publicly trying and sentencing the four officers responsible to long prison terms. Don't miss the photo display on Father Popiełuszko's political activities inside behind the altar. Solidarity pins are sold at the church souvenir counter. Also in the churchyard is a moving memorial to those who died in Nazi death camps during WW II.

Activities
Organised Tours The 'Incoming Bureau' at Orbis, ulica Marszałkowska 142, books Orbis sightseeing tours, but this is more easily done at the reception desks of the Bristol, Europejski, Forum, Grand, Holiday Inn, Marriott, Sobieski and Victoria hotels. Five-hour city tours depart daily except Sunday, while the Wednesday tour to Wilanów Palace would ensure that you actually get inside and are shown around by an English-speaking guide. The tours cost anywhere from US$15 to US$19 per person and operate from mid-May to September.

Orbis and the hotels take bookings for the Sunday 'Polish landscape countryside tour'. For US$44 you visit palaces, farms, forests and villages, hear a live piano recital at Chopin's birthplace at Żelazowa Wola, 50 km west of Warsaw, and get a typical Polish lunch with vodka. (You can also get to Chopin's family home, now a museum, on your own by train from Warszawa Śródmieście Station to Sochaczew, then by bus No 6 hourly to Żelazowa Wola.)

Mazurkas Travel in the lobby of the Forum Hotel runs a very good four-hour city sightseeing tour daily year-round departing at 9 am (US$21). Included is the old town, the Royal Way and Wilanów Palace.

From May to September the Biała Flota runs six one-hour cruises a day (US$2) on the Warsaw reach of the Vistula River from a landing below the bridge at the east end of Aleje Jerozolimskie.

Festivals
Annual events worth asking about include the 'Złota Tarka' (Golden Washboard) Jazz Festival in June, the Mozart Festival from mid-June to mid-July, the Festival of Contemporary Music 'Warsaw Autumn' in September and the 'Jazz Jamboree' in late October.

Places to Stay
Camping From May to September one of the best places to stay in Warsaw is *Camping OST 'Gromada'* (☎ 254 391), ulica Żwirki i Wigury 32, south-east of town on the road in from the airport (bus No 175 between the airport and town stops at the gate). Tent space is US$2.50 per person and bungalows are US$8 a double or US$15 for four persons. Rooms in a large pavilion on the grounds are available for the same price when all the bungalows are full. The atmosphere is informal and welcoming.

Hostels The *youth hostel* (☎ 278 952) at ulica Smolna 30 is on the top floor of a large concrete building a few minutes' walk from Warsaw Powiśle Railway Station in the centre of the city. Go in the entrance with the green sign and up to the top of the stairs. It's dusty, crowded and 110 steps up, but the charge will be only US$4 and there are even two hot showers. Stow your gear in a locker during the day. The curfew is 11 pm.

The ulica Karolkowa 53a *youth hostel* (☎ 328 829), just off Aleje Solidarności, is less convenient. To get there catch a north or westbound tram No 1, 13, 20, 24, 26 or 27. Get off at the 'Centrum-Wola' department store, then walk back on the right and look for a three-storey building among the trees beyond Gepard Disco (which puts out a heavy beat all night). The baggage room is open from 6 am to 9 pm but the hostel itself is closed from 10 am to 5 pm.

Directly across the street from Camping Gromada are two 11-storey student dormito-

ries at Żwirki i Wigury 95/97 and 97/99 which rent spare rooms in July and August at US$10/12 double/triple. Each building has its own individual reception so if the first one doesn't work out, try the next. For reservations call ☎ 222 407 weekdays from 9 am to 2 pm.

Private Rooms The Syrena Travel Office (☎ 628 7540), ulica Krucza 16/22, arranges accommodation in private homes for US$10/16 single/double. Although the office stays open till 7 pm daily you should try to get there before 4 pm. You cannot occupy the room until 6 pm, so leave your luggage at the station.

Cheaper Hotels The best of the regular hotels is the *Hotel Saski* (☎ 204 611), Plac Bankowy 1, on the square opposite Warsaw Town Hall. Rooms without bath are US$18/30 single/double; ask for one facing the interior courtyard, away from tram noise. You can usually get a US$2 per person reduction on the quoted rate by asking for a room without breakfast. This 141-bed hotel has real character and a fine location.

A few blocks away from the Saski is the *Pokoje Gościnne* of the Federacja Metalowcy (☎ 314 021), ulica Długa 29 near Stare Miasto. No English is spoken but the rooms are among the cheapest in Warsaw at US$10 single without bath, US$13/19 single/double with bath, and US$25 for a four-bedded room with bath.

The recently renovated *Hotel Harenda*, formerly the PTTK Dom Turysty Hotel (☎ 260 071), Krakowskie Przedmieście 4/6 opposite the Academy of Sciences, has rooms at US$16/25 single/double without bath, US$25/47 with bath. A bed in a three-bed room is US$9, a bed in a four-bed dorm US$6. The reception is up on the 2nd floor and the hotel is often full.

A few blocks west at ulica Mazowiecka 10 is the *Hotel Garnizonowy* (☎ 683 3569), an older hotel formerly reserved for military officers but now open to everyone. Rooms without bath or breakfast here are US$16/23/26 single/double/triple.

POLAND

The *Hotel Belfer* (☎ 625 2600), ulica Wybrzeże Kościuszkowskie 31/33 on the Vistula Embankment, has singles/doubles at US$14/25 without bath, US$22/30 with bath. Some of the rooms on the upper floors have excellent views of the river. Breakfast is US$3 extra. Occasionally there are water problems with the showers only running for a couple of hours in the evening. This modern hotel was formerly Dom Nauczyciela ZNP, a hostel for visiting school teachers. It's complicated to reach by public transport, so take a taxi the first time.

The seven-storey *Hotel Syrena* (☎ 321 256), ulica Syreny 23 off Górczewska, is on the far west side of Warsaw but there's a frequent bus service. Singles/doubles are US$13/24 without bath, US$31 a double with bath, breakfast included.

A similar but somewhat better place is the *Nowa Praga Hotel* (☎ 191 577), ulica Brechta 7, in a working-class neighbourhood east of the zoo on the far east side of the river. The Nowa Praga charges US$13/20/21 for singles/doubles/triples without bath, US$16/29/35 with bath.

The four-storey *Hotel Uniwersytet Warszawski* (☎ 411 308), Belvederska 26/30, just south of Łazienki Park, has singles/doubles with shared bath at US$18/29, with private bath US$24/36, breakfast included. The cheaper rooms are usually full and the others are overpriced.

A few blocks west of here is the *Hotel Agra* (☎ 493 881), ulica Falęcka 9/11, at US$15/19/22 single/double/triple. Every two rooms share a toilet and shower in this clean four-storey hotel owned by Warsaw Agricultural University. Nearby at ulica Madalińskiego 38 is a large vegetarian restaurant.

Expensive Hotels Most of Warsaw's other hotels are in the luxury tourist bracket. Right opposite the Palace of Culture, a block from Central Station, is the old *Hotel Polonia* (☎ 628 7241), Aleje Jerozolimskie 45, at US$21/34 single/double without bath, US$31/52 with bath, breakfast included. The newer *Metropol Hotel* (☎ 294 001), ulica Marszałkowska 99, is similarly priced.

Hotel Dom Chłopa (☎ 279 251), Plac Powstańców Warszawy 2, is a modern hotel owned by the Polish travel agency Gromada. Rooms are US$23/41 single/double without bath, US$47 double with bath, breakfast included. The entrance is a little hard to find, around on the north side of this white four-storey place, but the hotel itself is very convenient to everything.

Nearby is *Hotel Warszawa* (☎ 269 421), a three-star, 17-storey Stalinist erection at Plac Powstańców Warszawy 9, near the centre of town. It's US$35/42 single/double without bath, US$42/57 with bath, breakfast included.

Jumping up-market, there's the four-star *Europejski Hotel* (☎ 265 051), Krakowskie Przedmieście 13. Erected in 1877, this was Warsaw's first modern hotel and Marlene Dietrich was once a guest. Be prepared for rates beginning at US$69/100 single/double for a small room, US$75/113 for a large room, all with bath and breakfast included. (The Europejski is soon to be renovated, which may mean you'll find it closed or the prices sharply increased.)

The five-star *Bristol Hotel* (☎ 625 2525), across the street at ulica Krakowskie Przedmieście 42/44, is also excellent, though the 209 rooms begin at US$180/220 single/double with breakfast. It's owned by the British Forte hotel chain which completed a US$36 million renovation in 1993. The US$27 Sunday brunch here (from noon to 5 pm) is superb with unlimited champagne and a buffet that includes smoked salmon, caviar, salads, cheeses, meats, six main dishes, sweets and coffee. Reservations are required.

Places to Eat

In the Old Town Many of Warsaw's tourist restaurants are on Rynek Starego Miasta, the old town square. Most famous is the *Bazyliszek Restaurant*, Rynek Starego Miasta 5 (upstairs), where game dishes like wild boar and venison are served. Sloppy dressers are not welcome. *Winiarnia Fukier*,

Rynek Starego Miasta 27, is an up-market wine restaurant with old world atmosphere. The *Kamienne Schodki Restaurant*, Rynek Starego Miasta 26, specialises in roast duck with apples (menu in English and German).

Another slightly pretentious place is the *Swietoszek Klub*, ulica Jezuicka 6/8 just off Rynek Starego Miasta, with gourmet creations such as bline with black caviar and sour cream.

The *Zapiecek Restaurant*, Zapiecek at Piwna, posts its reasonable menu outside.

Several excellent, cheap places to eat are just north of Rynek Starego Miasto. *Bar Murzynek*, ulica Nowomiejska 3, is perfect for a plate of self-service spaghetti and a big bottle of Żywiec beer, or just coffee and cakes. The menu on the wall is in English, yet prices are low! The main clientele here is Polish students.

Pod Barbakanen, Mostowa 27/29 just north of the old town gate (Barbikan), is a cheap milk bar. *Pod Samsonem,* ulica Freta 3, serves more substantial meals. *Nowy Miasto*, Rynek Nowego Miasta 13, specialises in vegetarian food though the portions are a bit small.

One of Poland's most bizarre culinary concoctions is without doubt *El Popo Restauracja Meksykańska*, ulica Senatorska 27, not far from Plac Zamkowy. It offers a cuisine which could best be termed microwave Mexican, and the chef seems to have got his training out of a Mexican cook book which forgot to mention that south of the border French fries don't come with every meal. Even the name is wrong: Mexicans call parrots *papagayos*, not 'popos'. Still, for us *gringos*, it's good fun. The menu is in English and Spanish, the décor is bright and the staff friendly and there's cold beer. Prices are high for Poland or Guadalajara but *no problema para Americanos ricos*. Vegetarians will get by here.

Along the Royal Way There are many places to eat at along this busy corridor. *Pizzeria Giovanni*, Krakowskie Przedmieście 37, serves real pizza at good prices. *Uniwersytecki Milk Bar*, Krakowskie

Przedmieście 20, is easy since you pay at the end of the line.

The elegant *Staropolska Restaurant*, Krakowskie Przedmieście 8 beside Hotel Harenda, gives a taste of old Warsaw as you dine by candlelight (moderately expensive).

U Matysiaków, ulica Świętokrzyska 18, offers unpretentious meals with full table service (beer!) though there's little selection. *Familijny Milk Bar*, Nowy Świat 39, is cheap and open Sunday, and farther south near the National Museum is *Szwajcarski Milk Bar*, Nowy Świat 5.

In the City Centre A cheap place to eat near Central Station is *Milk Bar Srednicowy*, Aleje Jerozolimskie 49.

For a big splurge indulge in the all-you-can-eat buffet at the *Lila Weneda Restaurant*, just beyond the casino on the 2nd floor of the 42-storey Marriott Hotel, Aleje Jerozolimskie 65, opposite Central Station (enter through the main entrance and take the lift). Lunch is US$11 (Monday to Saturday noon to 4 pm) and dinner US$15 (daily 4.30 pm to midnight). Sunday brunch (US$15) runs from noon to 5 pm while an orchestra plays. Each night there's a different theme: Monday Indian, Tuesday Polish, Wednesday and Saturday Tex-Mex, Thursday Middle Eastern, Friday Oriental and Sunday international. You probably won't enjoy this place unless you're presentably dressed.

Steak & Salad Bar Dolce Vita, ulica Marszałkowska 68/70, is an attractive private self-service where you can get big mugs of draught beer and Polish specialties. In summer there are tables out on the pavement – recommended.

Złota Kurka Milk Bar, Marszałkowska 55/57, down near the MDM Hotel on Plac Konstytucji, and *Bambino Milk Bar*, Krucza 21, beside Air France diagonally opposite the Grand Hotel, both offer typical Polish food at low prices.

Bars & Cafés In summer the tables come out onto Rynek Starego Miasta, especially in front of *Gessler* at No 19 where you'll hear more English than Polish spoken. At last

POLAND

POLAND

report there were still a few public benches scattered around the square from which you could take in the scene for free.

The cafés on Rynek Nowego Miasta are less pretentious than those on Rynek Starego Miasta, and the *Kawiarna Nove Miasto* at Rynek Nowego Miasta 15 often has a few musicians playing in the evening. *Bar Boruta*, ulica Freta 38 on the corner of Rynek Nowego Miasta, is also a good place to sit and chat over drinks in the evening.

Café Literacka, Krakowskie Przedmieście 87/89, just off Plac Zamkowy, becomes a pavement café in summer.

Café Studio M, Krakowskie Przedmieście 27, is an elegant café-cum-art gallery with additional seating upstairs.

Café Ambasador, Aleje Ujazdowskie 8, opposite the US Embassy, is just the place to sit and ponder the complexities of diplomatic life.

An all-night liquor store called *Delikatesy* functions at ulica Nowy Świat 53. Join the queue of hard-core alcoholics inside.

Entertainment

You'll find theatre, concert and cinema offerings in the daily newspapers. If you're after theatre tickets, go to Kasy Teatralne, Aleje Jerozolimskie 25, which has tickets for many events. The *Filharmonia* booking office is at ulica Sienkiewicza 12. If you're attending a concert in the smaller 'sala kameralna', enter by the ulica Moniuszki entrance on the other side of the building. Warsaw's National Philharmonic Orchestra is Poland's finest.

Tickets for the *Wielki Opera House*, Plac Teatralny, and the *Warsaw Operetta*, ulica Nowogrodzka 49 near Central Station, are sold at the theatres. The Wielki Opera is often sold out a few days in advance. You may have better luck at the smaller *Warsaw Chamber Opera*, at Al Solidariności 76b (in the back courtyard). The Kasy Teatralne handles its tickets.

Nightly at 8 pm from June to September there's a folklore show accompanied by traditional Polish cuisine in the restaurant at the *Europejski Hotel* (about US$16 per person).

Reservations should be made in advance at the Europejski reception.

The *Akwarium Club*, Emilii Plater 49, across the street from the Palace of Culture, is the place for live jazz (nightly at 8 pm). There's no cover charge to sit downstairs.

The *Opus One Pub & Restaurant*, Plac Emila Młynarskiego, on the west side of Filharmonia Concert Hall, has live folk music every Thursday, live jazz every Friday, both from 10 pm to 1 am (admission US$4).

The cinema where you're the most likely to see quality films is *Kino Kultura*, ulica Krakowskie Przedmieście 21/23.

Discos On Friday, Saturday and Sunday there's a disco at *Bar Hybrydy*, ulica Złota 7/9 (downstairs), behind the department stores a block east of the Palace of Culture. At street level nearby is a good pub with food and drink all day.

Also central is *Klub Europa Voltaire*, ulica Szkolna 2/4, a block from the main post office. This glossy up-market disco opens at 10 pm on Thursday, Friday and Saturday; admission costs US$8.

A much larger locale with high-tech features such as strobe and laser lighting, artificial smoke etc, is *Gepard Disco* (☎ 321 857), Aleje Solidarności 128, west of the centre. The Fosters emblems are reassuring and people of all ages will feel comfortable here but the drinks are quite expensive, so have something before you arrive. It's open Thursday to Sunday from 7 pm till late; admission costs US$5.

Warsaw's three most popular student discos are a couple of km south of the Palace of Culture. *Remont*, on the corner of Aleje Armii Ludowej and Waryńskiego, functions from 9 pm to 4 am Thursday to Sunday. The cover charge is US$2 for students with ISIC, US$6 for others (includes one drink). *Stodoła*, ulica Batorego 10, about a km south-west of Remont, is open Friday and Saturday from 8 pm to 5 am; admission costs US$4. The liveliest of the student clubs is probably *Disco Park* at Aleje Niepodległosci 196, in the centre of a park about midway between Studoła and Remont. It's open Friday, Saturday and Sunday from 10 pm on, cover charge US$4 for men, US$2 for women. The crowd at all three places is mostly aged under 30 and drinks are normal-priced.

Also check the posters in the pedestrian underpass in front of Warsaw University on Krakowskie Przedmieście for rock concerts, discos and happenings.

Spectator Sports Wednesday and Saturday at 5 pm you can often see soccer matches at the Stadion Wojska Polskiego 'Legia', ulica Łazienkowska 3 near Łazienki Park. Check the daily papers to make sure there's a game and cheer the local team, CWKS Legia.

Things to Buy

Good places to shop for souvenirs, amber jewellery, clothing etc, are Cepelia and Jubiler in the ulica Krucza 23/31 block, directly across from the Orbis Grand Hotel. Other shopping possibilities exist along Nowy Świat.

The Poles are noted graphic designers, and poster shops such as Galeria Plakatu, Rynek Starego Miata 23, offer real bargains. The store at ulica Nowomiejska 17 beside the Barbican in the old town sells a greater variety of kitsch than you ever thought existed in Poland.

A better selection of genuine Polish hand-crafts is available at Cepelia, ulica Chmielna 8 off Nowy Świat. For antiques try Desa, ulica Nowy Świat 51 (but ask about export restrictions).

Antykwariat Logos and Kosmos, Aleje Ujazdowskie 16 near the US Embassy, has a fascinating assortment of old books, maps, prints and paintings for sale (though export-ing books printed before 1945 is officially prohibited).

Getting There & Away

Air The LOT Polish Airlines office is in the Marriott Hotel building on Aleje Jerozolimskie opposite the Central Railway Station.

Train International trains depart from Warsaw Central Station for Basel, Belgrade, Berlin, Bucharest, Budapest, Cologne, Frankfurt/Main, the Hook of Holland, Leipzig, Ostend, Paris, Prague and Vienna. These are described in the chapter introduc-tion. Domestic expresses run to every part of Poland. For information on 'name train' expresses leaving Warsaw for cities around Poland turn to the section of this book dealing with the city you wish to reach. All these trains carry mandatory seat reserva-tions.

Train Station Central Railway Station, Aleje Jerozolimskie 54, has four levels. Your train will arrive on the lowest level and you'll go up an escalator to a network of passageways where you'll also find a 24-hour, cash-only currency exchange and left-luggage office. Note carefully the two hours a day when the baggage room is closed (*przerwy*). Beware of pickpockets on this crowded intermediate level. (Uniformed police patrol the station regularly, so if you're directly threatened, start screaming 'police' and you'll put your assailants on the defensive.) Above this is the main station hall where you can buy domes-tic tickets and reserve couchettes to any city in Poland (long queues). The posted time-tables are easy to follow. Here you'll also find 24-hour stand-up coffee bars and a cur-rency exchange (open 8 am to 10 pm daily) offering a slightly better rate than the offices downstairs in the passageways. This office will also change travellers' cheques but they take 10% commission (no commission on cash). On a balcony about this spacious hall are the international ticket windows and, on the opposite balcony, a travel agency which sells international bus tickets.

Reader Norm Mathews of Western Aus-tralia sent us this:

I was robbed by pickpockets whilst boarding the train to Gdańsk. Two men hopped on before me, two after. I was jostled and lost the wallet in my hip pocket with day-to-day money. They tried to get at my waist belt but luckily it was under my jacket. The train moved off just after. I reported it to the conductor and later to the railway police in Gdańsk but they spoke no

POLAND

English and weren't interested. Later we heard of three other robbery episodes at Warsaw Central Station.

Reader Brian Moore of West Midlands, England, sent this:

One travelling companion had his pocket picked on the Warsaw-Kraków train by a well-organised pair. They had obviously selected their target at the Central Station. They followed him onto the train, one in front and one behind. As the target entered his carriage the first one bent down to pick up something whilst the one behind used the distraction to take his wallet and then bundled past as if in a hurry.

Bus The Central Bus Station serving western and southern Poland is on the west side of the city near Warsaw Zachodnia Railway Station.

For north-eastern Poland, including the Lake District, you must go to the Stadion Bus Station on the east side of the Vistula. An easy way to get there is to take a commuter train from Warsaw Śródmieście Railway Station in front of the Palace of Culture east to Warsaw Stadion Railway Station which adjoins the bus terminal.

Tickets for these buses are only sold at the stations and it's all a little complicated, so you're probably better off leaving Warsaw by train.

Getting Around

To/From the Airport The AirportCity 'linia specjalna' express bus runs to Terminal No 1 at the international airport from Aleje Jerozolimskie in front of Central Railway Station, every 20 minutes from 5.30 am to 10.30 pm (US$2, pay the driver). This bus also picks up near the hotels Bristol, Victoria and Forum (ask).

It's also possible to get there on bus No 175, which goes to Terminal No 1 from outside Central Station opposite the LOT office (punch a regular ticket). For the domestic airport take bus No 114 from Plac Trzech Krzyży at the south end of Nowy Świat. To get between the terminals (about three km) take either bus up ulica Żwirki i Wigury a few stops, cross the street and take the other bus back.

Airport Okęcie International Airport, 10 km south-west of central Warsaw, has arrivals downstairs, departures upstairs. Only change a small amount of money here as the exchange offices give a very poor rate. As little as US$1 should be enough to get into town if you're using public transport. Departing, there are no exchange facilities beyond passport control. The left-luggage office on the arrivals level is open 24 hours (US$3 per piece per day). To use bus No 114 or 175 to town you must purchase a ticket at a newsstand downstairs on the arrivals level inside the terminal building. Remember to get an extra ticket for your luggage. Both the AirportCity express bus and bus No 175 leave from the arrivals level (after dropping passengers at the upper departures level). A taxi from the airport to town will be US$20 (after bargaining).

Bus & Tram In Warsaw, city buses of the 100, 200, 300, 400 and 500 series and express buses with a letter instead of a number plus all trams and trolley buses require only a single US$0.25 ticket (punch both ends). Suburban buses of the 700 and 800 series require two US$0.25 tickets, both punched at each end. Night buses of the 600 series operating between 11 pm and 5 am call for four US$0.25 tickets, all punched at both ends – a total of eight punches! Heavy baggage is an additional US$0.25 on all services.

You must purchase tickets at a newsstand (Ruch) before boarding the service, then validate them once aboard by punching them in a device near the door. Drivers don't sell tickets. You're liable for a stiff fine if caught without a valid ticket during a spot check.

Transit passes are available from the MZK Dział Sprzedaży Biletów office, ulica Senatorska 37 opposite the Saski Hotel, and at other locations. A one-day ticket (bilet yednodniowy) is US$1, a one-week ticket (bilet tygodniowy) US$5 and a one-month ticket (*bilet sieciowy*) US$13 (one photo required).

Watch out for pickpockets on crowded city buses and trams. Some are highly skilled and can easily zip open a bag you thought was in front of you. Don't become separated from your companion by people reaching between you to grab hold of the handrail. The pleasant looking young man who says hello may only be trying to distract you.

Metro Plans for a Warsaw underground railway were drawn up in 1925 but construction was interrupted by WW II. Work resumed in the 1960s but due to budgetary limitations progress has been slow and the metro still hadn't opened at press time. The initial north-south route linking Żurawia ulica in central Warsaw to Kabaty, a southern suburb, is scheduled to be completed by 1995 but it may take another 15 years for a second line to be built.

Taxi Some taxi drivers are friendly and just trying to make a living, while others will rip you off. Ask the driver to explain the meter system to you and judge his intentions by his response. At last report the meter reading was multiplied by 600, but this could change (any Warsaw resident should know the current multiplier). Beware of taxis parked at the Central Railway Station, the airport, the Palace of Culture, Plac Zamkowy and all the luxury hotels as they charge up to 1500 times the meter reading. Some taxis have new meters which show the exact fare. Avoid problems by making sure the meter is switched on.

Taxis with 'radio taxi 919' or 'super taxi 9622' on the side of the vehicle are far less likely to cause problems than unmarked 'pirate' taxis. If you take a taxi parked at a taxi stand you may be asked to pay double to allow the driver to return to the same stand (ask).

Car Rental The main Hertz office (☎ 211 360) is in the nine-storey car park at ulica Nowogrodzka 27, across the street from the Forum Hotel. Hertz also has desks at the Holiday Inn and Victoria Inter-Continental hotels. Avis (☎ 630 7316) and Budget (☎ 630 7280) both have reservations counters at the Marriott Hotel. All three companies are represented in the arrivals hall at Terminal No 1 at Okęcie International Airport. Turn to Getting Around in the introduction to this chapter for more information on car rentals.

There's a guarded parking lot between the Central Railway Station and the Holiday Inn Hotel.

Małopolska

Much of south-eastern Poland still bears a gentle bucolic air. Here in Małopolska ('Little Poland') you'll see people working the fields as they have for centuries, and long wooden horse carts along the roads. Until 1918 the region was divided into two parts. Everything north of the Vistula and a line drawn east from Sandomierz (including Lublin and Zamość) came under Russian control in 1815. South of this was 'Galicia' under the Habsburgs of Austria. Kraków remained semi-independent until 1846 when it was annexed by Austria. After an abortive uprising in 1863-64 tsarist Russia suppressed Polish culture in the territory it occupied, while the southern areas enjoyed considerable autonomy under the Austro-Hungarian empire. In 1915 Germany evicted the Russians and in 1918 the whole area once again became Polish. The impact of this chequered history can still be seen.

While nearby industrial cities like Katowice and Łódź have little to offer the average tourist, nearly every foreign visitor makes it to Kraków, one of the great art centres of Europe. Some also join the hordes of Polish excursionists on their way to the mountains around Zakopane. There's much more to south-eastern Poland, however, such as the holy sanctuary of Jasna Góra at Częstochowa, perfectly preserved Renaissance Zamość, the superb Baroque palace at Łańcut, and the horrors of Auschwitz,

POLAND

Birkenau and Majdanek. It's easy to lose the crowds in the unspoiled mountains along the southern border. Here is Poland to be savoured.

LUBLIN

Long a crossroads of trade, Lublin was an important point of contact between Poland and Lithuania. In 1569 a political union of these kingdoms was signed here, creating the largest European state of the time. Beginning in the 17th century, Lublin saw repeated foreign invasions by Swedes, Austrians, Russians and Germans, culminating in the Nazi death camp at Majdanek. For a time in 1944 Lublin was capital of liberated Poland.

Somehow the compact old town (Stare Miasto) retains the flavour of this turbulent past with its narrow crumbling streets, defensive towers and ominously isolated castle, long a prison. During the 19th century the city expanded west to Plac Litewski and under the communists spectacular growth mushroomed in all directions. Many foreign students study at the Lublin Catholic University, Poland's oldest private university. Lublin is slightly off the beaten track so people are interested to meet you, which is half the reason for coming.

Orientation

The train station with its architecture echoing Lublin Castle is several km south of the city centre, so catch a trolley bus No 150 or bus No 13 to the 'centrum'. If you want one of the hostels on the west side of town, get out at the next stop after the Orbis Unia Hotel. The left-luggage office at the train station is open 24 hours. Left-luggage at the main bus station on Aleje Tysiąclecia is opposite stand No 11 (open daily from 6.30 am to 7 pm).

Plac Łokietka in front of Kraków Gate marks the boundary between the old and new towns. Go through the gate and you'll soon reach Rynek, the old market square. Krakowskie Przedmieście extends west from Kraków Gate, and most of Lublin's hotels, restaurants and large stores line this slightly decadent old avenue. The Orbis Unia

Hotel, universities, parks and modern buildings are on Aleje Racławickie, its westward continuation.

Information

The tourist office (☎ 24 412) at ulica Krakowskie Przedmieście 78 (open weekdays 9 am to 5 pm, Saturday 10 am to 2 pm) sells good maps and is generally helpful.

In the old town, the PTTK, ulica Grodzka 3, may also provide information.

The Polski Związek Motorowy is at ulica Prusa 8 next to the PZM Motel. If you're having car trouble, this is the place to come.

Money To cash travellers' cheques you have a choice of the NBP Bank, Krakowskie Przedmieście 37, opposite Hotel Lublinianska (weekdays 8 am to 3 pm, Saturday 8 to 11.30 am), and the hectic PKO Bank, ulica Królewska 1 opposite Kraków Gate (weekdays 7.30 am to 6 pm, Saturday 7.30 am to 2 pm).

Post & Telecommunications The telephone centre on one side of the main post office, Krakowskie Przedmieście 48/50, is open around the clock. Lublin's telephone code is 081.

Travel Agencies Orbis, ulica Narutowicza 31, sells international bus tickets to Western Europe, makes seat reservations on express trains and books couchettes.

Things to See

Old Town The 14th century **Kraków Gate**, built to protect Lublin from Tatar invasions, is now the **City History Museum** (closed Monday and Tuesday). You'll get a good view of Lublin from the top floor. Rather than enter the old town straight away, go south-east a block on ulica Królewska to reach the Baroque **cathedral** (1596). Beside the cathedral is the 19th century neo-Gothic **Trinitarian Tower** with a religious art museum and another 360° panorama of Lublin, and below, a passage into the old city.

Walk straight ahead to Market Square (Rynek) with the 16th century **Tribunal**, for-

POLAND

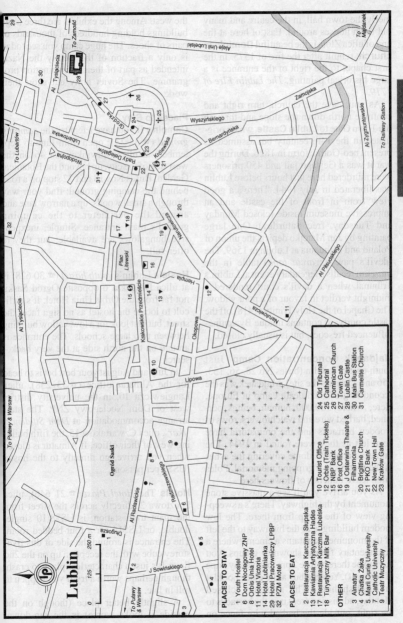

Lublin

0   125   250 m

To Puławy
& Warsaw

To Puławy & Warsaw

To Lubartów

To Zamość

Aleje Unii Lubelski

To Majdanek

To Zygmuntowskie

To Railway Station

To Lublin

Al Tysiąclecia
Al Tysiąclecia
Lubartowska
Lubelska
Rady Delegatów
Wodopojna
Królewska
Grodzka
Plac
Litewski
Krakowskie Przedmieście
Hempla
Narutowicza
Okopowa
Lipowa
Radziszewskiego
Al Racławickie
Ogród Saski
J Sowińskiego
Dlugosza
Al Piłsudskiego
Narutowicza
Okopowa
Bernardyńska
Wyszyńskiego
Zamojska

PLACES TO STAY

1   Youth Hostel
6   Dom Noclegowy ZNP
8   Orbis Unia Hotel
11 Hotel Victoria
14 Hotel Lublinianka
29 Hotel Pracowniczy LPBP
32 PZM Motel

PLACES TO EAT

2   Restauracja Karczma Słupska
17 Kawiarnia Artystyczna Hades
18 Restauracja Karczma Lubelska
18 Turystyczny Milk Bar

OTHER

3   Almatur
4   Chatka Żaka
5   Marii Curie University
7   Catholic University
9   Teatr Muzyczny
10 Tourist Office
12 Orbis (Train Tickets)
15 NBP Bank
16 Post Office
19 J Osterwina Theatre &
    Filharmonia
20 Brigittine Church
21 PKO Bank
22 New Town Hall
23 Kraków Gate
24 Old Tribunal
25 Cathedral
26 Dominican Church
27 Town Gate
28 Lublin Castle
30 Main Bus Station
31 Carmelite Church

merly the town hall, in the centre and many old town houses around. East of here at the end of ulica Złota is the beautiful **Dominican church**, rebuilt after the fire of 1575. In the first chapel to the right of the entrance is a large historical painting, *The Lublin Fire of 1719*.

As you leave the church, turn right and continue north down the slope and through the Town Gate to **Lublin Castle**, which originated in the 14th century but assumed its present neo-Gothic form in 1826. During the war it was a Gestapo jail and 450 prisoners were murdered here just hours before Lublin was liberated in July 1944. There's a good view from in front of the castle and an impressive museum inside (closed Monday and Tuesday, free Saturday). One large painting by Jan Matejko depicts the union of Poland and Lithuania at Lublin in 1569. The 'devil's paw' *(czarcia łapa)* table in the museum recalls a legendary event at Lublin's Tribunal when a devil's court rendered a midnight verdict in favour of a poor widow. The Chapel of the Holy Trinity (1418) off the castle courtyard contains unique Byzantine-influenced frescoes, but is usually closed.

Majdanek Concentration Camp Just south-east of Lublin (buses No 28, 56, 153, 156 and 158 pass the site), Majdanek was the second-largest Nazi death camp in Europe. Here, where 360,000 human beings perished, barbed wire and watchtowers, rows of wooden barracks and the crematoria have been left as they were found in 1944. The immense concrete dome covering the ashes of the victims is a gripping memorial. Poles often leave bunches of flowers here.

As you arrive you'll see a massive stone monument by the highway. There's a sweeping view of the camp from there. The low modern building near the highway to the left of the monument contains a cinema where a documentary film is shown to groups (you have to be there before 2 pm to have any hope of seeing it). You can buy a site guide booklet in English here. The museum (closed Monday, admission free) is in the barracks to the right, outside the barbed wire fence on

the west. Among the exhibits are three large buildings holding hundreds of thousands of pairs of shoes. The huge camp you see today is only a fraction of the facility the Nazis intended as part of their extermination programme. The Soviet army cut short their work.

Places to Stay

Camping If you have a tent try the *camping ground* (☎ 32 231; open from June to September) at ulica Słowinkowska 46 on the west side of the city, up beyond the Botanical Garden. Buses Nos 18 and 32 stop on a road behind the camping ground: find your way through a small woods, up a narrow lane and around the perimeter to the camping ground's main entrance. Simple, inexpensive bungalows are available, but they're often full.

Hostels Lublin's *youth hostel* (☎ 30 628) is at ulica Długosza 6 opposite Ogród Saski, not far from the Orbis Unia Hotel. It's difficult to locate the hostel as no sign faces the street, but just look for a low, yellow building between two large schools. The entrance is around on the north side at the very back – search.

In July and August your best bet is to head for the Almatur office (☎ 33 238), ulica Langiewicza 10, in the university district west of Dom Noclegowy ZNP. The staff arrange accommodation at *Dom Studencki 'Ikar'*, ulica Czwartaków 15, the fifth building west of their office. If Almatur is closed when you arrive, go directly to the hostel (US$3 per person).

Hotels The *Hotel Piast* (☎ 21 646), ulica Pocztowa 2, directly across the street from the main train station, is US$8/10 single/double, or US$14 for a four-bedded room. The entrance is around the side of this five-storey cube with the reception up on the 2nd floor. It's just a characterless place to crash, though perhaps worth a try if you happen to roll in late.

A slightly better place (though on the outside it looks worse) is the run-down,

POLAND

three-storey *Hotel BYT* (☎ 26 215), ulica 1-go Maja 16, with rooms at US$9 single or double. It's about two blocks from the train station.

Lublin's cheapest hotel is the *Hotel Pracowniczy LPBP* (☎ 774 407), ulica Podzamcze 7, a five-minute walk north-east of the main bus station. A double room in this nine-storey former workers dorm will set you back US$4. The main clientele is Ukrainian and Russian street-market vendors.

Dom Noclegowy ZNP (☎ 38 285), ulica Akademicka 4, also known as Dom Nauczyciela, is in a much nicer area close to the Orbis Unia Hotel beside the university (US$7/9 single/double with shared bath). If coming by bus from the train station, ask to be dropped near the Orbis Unia Hotel. This neat, eight-storey teachers' hotel is cheap but busloads of excited Polish tourists often fill the place. A good cinema and bar are behind the hotel and the biggest danger here – depending on who your neighbours are – is the radios found in every room.

Lublin's oldest hotel is the *Hotel Lublinianka* (☎ 24 261), ulica Krakowskie Przedmieście 56, which opened in 1900. Rooms here are US$13/19 single/double without bath, US$36 double with bath. The location is excellent. There used to be a cheap hotel nearby at Krakowskie Przedmieście 29 – check to see if they're reopened.

If you're driving you might consider the *PZM Motel* (☎ 34 232), ulica Prusa 8, on the north side of town. Rooms are US$9/15 single/double without bath, US$12/19 with bath, and breakfast costs US$2 per person extra. This place is owned by the Polish Automobile Association and there's a large auto service centre next door, but be prepared, this six-storey hotel is not all the name implies. Truck drivers often stay here.

Places to Eat

Turystyczny Milk Bar, ulica Krakowskie Przedmieście 29, is cheap. Another place in this vein is the *Staromiejski Milk Bar*, ulica Jezuicka 1 just inside the Kraków Gate in the old town.

The *Powszechna Restaurant* in the Lublinianka Hotel serves filling meals accompanied by good white wine and, in the evening, live music. The *Karczma Lubelska*, Plac Litewski 2, is another folksy restaurant.

The *Kawiarnia Artystyczna Hades*, ulica Peowiaków 12, downstairs in the Centrum Kultury w Lublinie, a block back from Hotel Lublinianka, is a private club where foreigners are always welcome. The bar opens at 10 am, the restaurant at 1 pm (menu in English and French), and on weekends there's usually live music (including jazz) and dancing. Sharp and modern yet reasonably priced, it's a little hard to find but worth the effort.

The restaurant in the *Orbis Unia Hotel*, Aleje Racławickie 18, is the best in Lublin and the only place in town where you can order eggs and toast for breakfast or be sure of a cold beer. Its menu is in English and French. The *Restauracja Karczma Słupska*, Aleje Racławickie 22, just west of the Orbis Unia Hotel, is a folkloric restaurant with live music in the evening (cover charge). It's open for dinner only (closed Wednesday).

The local Perła beer is not Poland's best, but it is cheap.

Cafés *Pod Czarcia Łapa*, ulica Bramowa between the Kraków Gate and the Tribunal, is an elegant café which plays on the devils' paw theme. Half a block away, *U Rajcy*, Rynek 2, is similar. *Café Trzosik*, ulica Grodzka 5a, also in the old town, is another nice place to sit.

Entertainment

For Filharmonia tickets check the ticket office at ulica Kapucyńska 7. Concerts are most likely on Saturday nights. Opposite the Brigittine Church just around the corner is the ticket office of the *J Osterina Theatre* (1886). Although it presents mostly drama in Polish, you might attend until the first intermission to see the theatre and sample the acting.

Teatr Muzyczny operettas are performed at the new theatre at ulica Skłodowskiej 5. Check the daily papers which list performances at all these theatres.

On the weekend there's usually a student disco at the *Chatka Żaka*, ulica Radziszewskiego 16 at Marii Curie University. Almost everything that's happening around Lublin is advertised on posters at the Chatka Żaka.

Getting There & Away

Bus Be aware that there are three bus stations in Lublin: the main bus station on Aleje Tysiąclecia, one near the main train station and another two km east of town. You don't need to bother with either of the latter to get out of town, but you need to be aware of them in case you happen to arrive at one. Frequent city buses link all stations to the 'centrum'.

Buses from the main bus station run west to Kazimierz Dolny (40 km) and Łódź (260 km), south-west to Kraków (269 km), Częstochowa (288 km) and Zakopane (376 km), south-east to Zamość (89 km) and north-west to Warsaw (161 km). Buses to Zamość leave from stands Nos 13, 14 and 15. It's always a good idea to buy an advance ticket with a reserved seat the day before, especially on weekends and holidays.

Train The *Bystrzyca* express runs daily between Lublin and Warsaw (175 km, three hours), leaving Lublin in the morning and Warsaw in the afternoon. Reservations are required. From Lublin there are overnight trains with sleepers to Gdynia and Wrocław (but not to Kraków). There is an overnight train with couchettes from Kraków. Two fast trains a day, the *Jadwiga* and *Jagiełło*, depart from Lublin for Kraków, one in the early morning and another in the afternoon (five hours via Radom).

Railway connections from Lublin to Zamość and southern Poland are poor because the lines were originally laid down before WW I when this area was under Russia while the area around Kraków was Austrian. Local trains to Zamość are painfully slow – take a bus.

ZAMOŚĆ

Zamość hasn't changed much since the 16th century when its chessboard street pattern was laid down by the Italian architect Bernardo Morando. The intact town square has an almost Latin American flavour with its long arcades and pastel shades.

Jan Zamoyski, chancellor and commander in chief of Renaissance Poland, founded Zamość in 1580 as an ideal urban settlement and impregnable barrier against Cossack and Tatar raids from the east. Its position on a busy trade route midway between Lublin and L'vov prompted merchants of many nationalities to settle here. Zamość's fortifications withstood Cossack and Swedish attacks in 1648 and 1656 but by the 18th century its military value had dwindled. Later it was used as a military prison.

The Nazis renamed Zamość 'Himmlerstadt' and expelled the Polish inhabitants from 292 nearby villages. Their places were taken by German colonists to create an eastern bulwark for the Third Reich. Surrounded by parks and totally unspoiled today, Zamość is unique in Eastern Europe. Unlike overpromoted cities like Prague Zamość doesn't get a lot of Western visitors which is refreshing.

Orientation

The bus and train stations are on opposite sides of Zamość, each about two km from the centre. From in front of the bus station take bus No 0, 22 or 59 to the centre of town. The left-luggage office at the bus station is next to the information counter. There's also left-luggage at the train station. The marketplace is on the north edge of the old town along ulica Przyrynek.

Information

The tourist information office (☎ 22 92) is in a corner of the old town hall directly off Rynek Wielki.

The Polski Związek Motorowy (☎ 34 71) is at ulica Peowiaków 9, a few blocks north-east of the old town. There's an auto service centre here.

Money Change travellers' cheques at the Bank Pekao SA, ulica Grodzka 2 (weekdays 7.30 am to 5 pm, Saturday 7.30 to noon).

Post & Telecommunications The post office and telephone centre is at ulica Kościuszki 9 (Monday to Saturday 7 am to 9 pm). Zamość's telephone code is 084.

Travel Agencies Orbis, ulica Grodzka 18, has information on trains and sells tickets.

The PTTK, ulica Staszica 31, can provide an English-speaking guide for a four-hour city walking tour, including a visit to the passageways at the L'vov Gate, for US$30 per group.

Things to See

Zamość is a pleasant small town with all the sights an easy stroll apart. You'll want to begin on **Rynek Wielki**, an impressive square surrounded by Italian-style arcaded dwelling houses once owned by wealthy Greek and Armenian traders. The curving exterior stairway was added to the 16th century **town hall** in 1768. The House 'Under the Angel' (1634), Ormiańska 24 on Rynek Wielki, is a **museum** (closed Monday) which presents the opportunity to see a good collection of historical paintings plus the interior of an Armenian merchant's house. Just off the south-west corner of this square, at ulica Staszica 37, the famous German revolutionary, Rosa Luxemburg, was born in 1870.

Continue west a bit to **St Thomas' Cathedral** (1598), a three-aisled Mannerist basilica. South-west of this church is the old **Arsenal** (1583), now a museum of old weapons (closed Monday). The nearby **Zamoyski Palace** (1585) lost much of its character when it was converted into a military hospital in 1831. North again on ulica Akademicka is the **former Academy** (1648). The fortifications opposite this building have been beautifully landscaped and made into a park extending east along the north side of Zamość to the **open-air theatre**.

Re-enter the town south from the theatre to see the old **synagogue** (1620), now a public library, on the corner of Zamenhofa and Bazyliańska. Do go inside. East on Zamenhofa you come again to the bastions of Zamość. Turn right and walk south towards **L'vov Gate** (1820) where you'll find a 16th century bastion with endless passageways which groups may enter. Russians and Ukrainians often set up a street market near the gate.

Return to Rynek Wielki and follow ulica Moranda south from the square. Cross the park and go over the train tracks and a bridge till you get to the **Rotunda** (1831), a circular gun emplacement where the Nazis executed 8000 local residents. Today it's something of a Polish national shrine.

Places to Stay

Bottom End The *PTTK Camping* (☎ 24 99) on ulica Królowej Jadwigi, one km west of town, is US$2 per person to camp. There's plenty of shade, an appealing bar on the premises, and bungalows are available.

In summer the *Schronisko Turystyczne 'Relax'* (☎ 71 553), ulica Szczebrzeska 10 next to the zoo directly across the street from the train station, also operates as a basic dormitory-style hostel.

In July and August there's also a 50-bed *youth hostel* (☎ 79 125) in the school at ulica J Zamoyskiego 4, behind Hotel Jubilat a few blocks north of the bus station.

The *PTTK Dom Wycieczkowy* (☎ 26 39), beside the old synagogue at ulica Zamenhofa 13, isn't cheap at US$13 per person in three to eight-bed dormitories.

No private rooms are available in Zamość.

Middle The nicest place to stay is the modern 73-room *Hotel Renesans* (☎ 20 01), ulica Grecka 6 in the old city. A pleasant room with private bath is US$12/19/23 single/double/triple. Rooms at the Renesans have a shower but the toilets are down the hall. Try to get a room on the 2nd floor to be farther away from the disco beat downstairs. Their breakfast is good value at US$3 per person extra.

The *Sportowy Hotel* (☎ 60 11), on ulica Królowej Jadwigi behind the stadium between the camping ground and town, has

POLAND

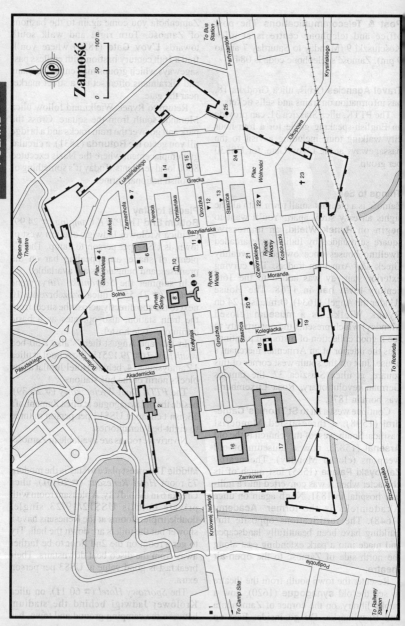

Zamość

To Bus Station

To Rotunda

To Railway Station

To Camp Site

Open-air Theatre

Market

Plac Stefanidesa

Rynek Solny

Rynek Wielki

Plac Wolności

Rynek Wodny

Grecka

Bazyliańska

Kolegiacka

Zamkowa

Akademicka

Solna

Piłsudskiego

Bohaterów

Pereca

Kolłątaja

Grodzka

Staszica

Staszica

Zamenhofa

Ormiańska

Pereca

Grodzka

Żeromskiego

Kościuszki

Moranda

Łukasińskiego

Królowej Jadwigi

Podgroble

Szczebrzeska

Partyzantów

Kryształkiego

Okrzowa

POLAND

PLACES TO STAY

1 Sportowy Hotel
5 PTTK Dom Wycieczkowy
14 Hotel Renesans

PLACES TO EAT

12 Bar Lech
13 Milk Bar Popularno
22 Restaurajca Centralka

OTHER

2 Old Lublin Gate
3 Former Academy
4 Market
6 Public Library
7 Jazz Club Kosz
8 Town Hall
9 Tourist Office
10 Museum
11 Orbis
15 Bank Pekao
16 Zamoyski Palace
17 Arsenal Museum
18 St Thomas' Cathedral
19 Post Office
20 PTTK Office
21 Royal Night Club
23 St Nicholas' Church
24 Cinema
25 Old L'vov Gate

rooms at US$10/12 single/double with bath, US$4 per person in an eight-bed dorm, or US$29 double for an apartment. Most of the rooms at the Sportowy are dormitories with three to eight beds and it's usually booked by sports groups.

The unfriendly *Hotel Pracowniczy No 4* (☎ 51 64), ulica Młodzieżowa 6 just off ulica Partyzantów between the bus station and town, is a former workers' dormitory which rents rooms at US$10 double (no singles) or US$13 for a four-bedded room.

The three-storey, three-star *Hotel Jubilat* (☎ 64 01), Aleje Wyszyńskiego 52 right beside the bus station, is more expensive (US$24/33 single/double with bath and breakfast) and less convenient to the sights. These drawbacks mean it almost always has free rooms.

Places to Eat

Bar Lech, ulica Grodzka 7, has a self-service milk bar on one side, a stand-up beer bar on the other. You could try it for breakfast as it theoretically opens at 7 am.

Milk Bar Popularno, ulica Staszica 10, is open for lunch weekdays and it's easy since you pay at the end of the line.

The *Centralka*, ulica Żeromskiego 3, is a full-service restaurant with a menu in English (weird translations!). Try the żurek (cream soup with egg and sausage) and kotlet po zamojsku (pork roll). Prices are good and they're open late (for Zamość). An older crowd comes here to dance on Thursday, Friday and Saturday nights.

Around the corner from the Centralka is *Pizza Italiana*, ulica Bazyliańska 30, with barely passable pizza and ice cream.

If all else fails, try the restaurant in the *Renesans Hotel* which is open until 10 pm.

The local beer is Warka Hetman.

Entertainment

Royal Night Club, ulica Żeromskiego 22, offers disco dancing nightly except Monday from 8 pm to 3 am.

Jazz Club Kosz, in the rear courtyard at Zamenhofa 5, is a cozy little bar open from 1 pm daily, with a disco on Friday, Saturday and Sunday from 7 pm to midnight.

Piwnica Pod Arkadami, Staszica 25 on Rynek Wielki, is a subterranean students' hang-out.

Annual events include a jazz festival during the last week of May and an 'International Meeting of Jazz Vocalists' during the last weekend in September. In late June and early July theatrical performances (in Polish) are staged on the curving main stairway of the old town hall. If you decide to come to Zamość for any of these, call tourist information at ☎ 22 92 well in advance to verify the dates, then call one of the hotels for reservations.

Getting There & Away

There are trains and buses between Lublin and Zamość. The train takes over three hours to reach Zamość from Lublin on a roundabout route, so you're better off coming by bus as these run every half-hour and are faster.

Buses leave Zamość Bus Station for Lublin about every half-hour until 7.30 pm (89 km). There's one morning bus to Kraków (318 km, eight hours, US$9) and four buses to Warsaw (250 km). Some buses aren't listed on the departures board, and those that are listed aren't necessarily daily, so it pays to ask at information. If you want to continue south from Zamość plan your escape immediately upon arrival by booking an onward ticket as train service in this direction is terrible.

The three daily trains between Zamość and Kraków are all slow and inconvenient. One leaves around 5 am and the other two arrive in the middle of the night. About the only useful train leaving Zamość is the daily fast train to Warsaw, departing around 7 am and reaching Warszawa-Zachodnia Station five hours later. Check the times at Orbis.

It's possible to visit Zamość as a day trip from Lublin by bus if you get an early start and book your return bus ticket as soon as you arrive.

SOUTH-EAST POLAND

The south-eastern corner of Poland near Slovakia and Ukraine is off the beaten track but not without attractions. The border town of **Przemyśl** on the San River, just 14 km short of Ukraine, is sometimes used as an entry/exit point (buses to L'vov, 92 km). Six huge churches and their towers loom above the main town and there's the usual assortment of small hotels.

South-west of Przemyśl are the **Bieszczady Mountains**, beckoning youthful hikers in summer and cross-country skiers in winter. Youth hostels (summer only), tourist hostels and camping grounds (with cabins) make bases for exploring this sparsely populated region of enormous mountain pastures. A bus from Przemyśl to Ustrzyki Dolne, then another to Ustrzyki Górne, will bring you into the heart of the mountains. Costs in this area are very low.

The south-east's polished jewel is the

magnificent Renaissance palace (1629) at **Łańcut**, 67 km north-west of Przemyśl on the road to Kraków. Now it's a Museum of Interior Decoration (closed Monday and Tuesday), worth getting off your bus to see. Lots of buses cover the 17 km from Łańcut to **Rzeszów**, the regional capital, with a few old streets and many ugly apartment blocks.

If you're arriving by train from Slovakia over the Muszyna border crossing you'll pass **Stary Sącz**, a sleepy little town of single-storey dwellings with high, sloping roofs lining the quiet, cobbled streets. For a place to stay you'll probably have to continue eight km north-east to **Nowy Sącz**, pronounced 'nove-sonch', which has an old town square, several hotels and a good restaurant in the *Panorama Hotel*.

KRAKÓW

Kraków (population 800,000) is the third largest city in Poland. Over a millennium ago Prince Krak founded a settlement on Wawel Hill, above a bend of the legendary Vistula River. Boleslav the Brave built a cathedral here in 1020 and transferred the capital here from Poznań shortly after. The kings of Poland ruled from Wawel Castle until 1596, but even afterwards Polish royalty continued to be crowned and buried in Wawel Cathedral.

At this crossing of trade routes from Western Europe to Byzantium and from Southern Europe to the Baltic, a large medieval city developed. Kraków was devastated during the 13th century Tatar invasions, but rebuilt. In January 1945 a sudden encircling manoeuvre by the Soviet army forced the Germans to quickly evacuate the city, and Kraków was saved from destruction. Today Stare Miasto, the old town, harbours world-class museums and towering churches while Kazimierz, the now silent Jewish quarter, tells of a sadder recent history, and Auschwitz is close by (see the separate entry later in this chapter).

Kraków was a medieval students' town. Jagiellonian University, established at Kraków in 1364, is Poland's oldest; Copernicus the astronomer studied here. It is still the second-largest university in Poland (after Warsaw) and 10% of the present population are higher education students. This is the one Polish city you simply cannot miss.

Reader Anne Small of Tauranga, New Zealand, who was in Kraków in 1992, sent us this:

I'm not a 'spiritual' person but sitting enjoying rests in the city square in Kraków was one of the really special experiences in my life. There were no jarring Western influences and no architecture obtruded. The cathedral meets the populace with its ground level entrances. Plenty of people but no crush of humanity and no groups of gawking tourists. I am so glad I took heed of the advice in your book and saw Kraków in that way because it could well be the last summer of innocence. I regret very much that I did not spend more than eight days in Poland.

Orientation

The main train and bus stations are next to one another just outside the north-east corner of the old town. There's no left luggage in the bus station but the left-luggage office at the adjacent train station is open 24 hours.

Ulica Pawia, with the tourist office and several hotels, flanks the stations to the west. To walk into town follow the crowds into the underpass on the corner of Pawia and Lubicz, then bear slightly right and lose yourself in the old streets until you come out on Rynek Główny, Kraków's glorious Market Square.

Trains on the Przemyśl-Wrocław line usually call at Kraków Płaszów Railway Station south of the city centre, not Kraków Główny. If there isn't a connecting train leaving immediately for the main station, take tram No 3 or 13 from ulica Wielicka, a few minutes' walk straight ahead from Kraków Płaszów, to 'Poczta Główna', the main post office on Westerplatte.

Information

There's an excellent tourist information office (☎ 220 471) at ulica Pawia 8, a few minutes' walk from the stations. They'll sell you maps and brochures, and direct you to the accommodation service next door. If you're staying longer than two days it's wise to invest in an indexed city map.

A poorly marked tourist information office is in the Cloth Hall on Rynek Główny, near the entrance to the National Museum (weekdays 9 am to 5 pm). They're seldom busy and good at answering questions.

The office of the Polski Związek Motorowy (☎ 220 215 or 223 490) is at ulica Dietla 67.

Kodak Express, Rynek Główny 41, does one-hour colour film developing.

Money Kraków's private exchange offices are open shorter hours than those in other major cities, but the one at Wawel Tourist, ulica Pawia 8, is open daily from 8 am to 8 pm.

To change travellers' cheques go to the Bank Pekao SA, Rynek Główny 31 (weekdays 7.30 am to 6.15 pm, Saturday 7.30 am to 1.45 pm), or the NBP Bank, ulica Basztowa 20 (weekdays 7.45 am to 1 pm).

Post & Telecommunications Any mail addressed care of Poste Restante, Poczta Główna, 30-960 Kraków 1, Poland, is collected at window No 1 in the main post office, Westerplatte at Starowislna.

American Express card holders can receive mail addressed c/o American Express, Orbis, Hotel Cracovia, ulica Focha 1, 30-111 Kraków, Poland.

There's a crowded telephone centre in the main post office on Westerplatte, open weekdays 7.30 am to 9 pm, Saturday 8 am to 2 pm, Sunday 9 to 11 am. Kraków's telephone code is 012.

Consulates There are five: the Austrian Consulate, ulica Św Jana 12, the German Consulate, ulica Stolarska 7, the US Consulate (☎ 229 764), ulica Stolarska 9, and the French Consulate, ulica Stolarska 15.

The Russian Consulate, Westerplatte 11 (Monday, Wednesday and Friday 8.30 am to noon), issues visas for US$20 and four photos, but one must first obtain an accommodation voucher from Orbis at the Hotel

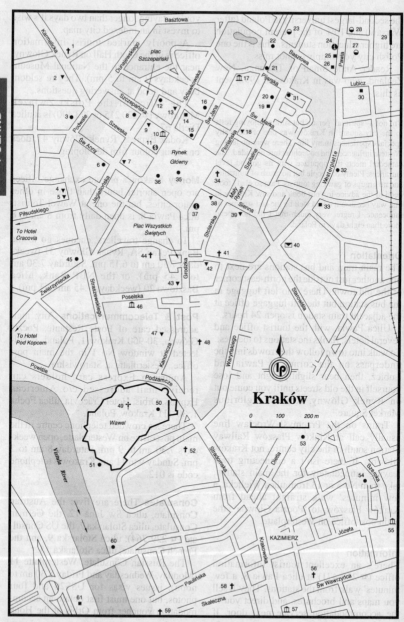

Basztowa

Karmelicka

plac
Szczepański

Dunajewskiego

Szczepańska

Podwale

Szewska

Św Anny

Jagiellońska

Piłsudskiego

To Hotel
Cracovia

Zwierzyniecka

Straszewskiego

Poselska

To Hotel
Pod Kopcem

Powiśle

Podzamcze

Wawel

Viscula River

Sławkowska

Św Jana

Rynek
Główny

Grodzka

Kanonicza

Szczepańska

Basztowa

Pijarska

Floriańska

Szpitalna

Św Marka

Sienna

Mały
Rynek

Sławkowska

Lubicz

Westerplatte

Pawia

Starowiślna

Wielopole

Dietla

Stradomska

Starowiślna

Skawińska

KAZIMIERZ

Krakowska

Paulińska

Skałeczna

Szeroka

Józefa

Św Wawrzyńca

Kraków

0   100   200 m

LP

1 2 3 6 4 5 7 8 9 10 11 12 13 14 15 16 17 18 19 20 21 22 23 24 25 26 27 28 29 30 31 32 33 34 35 36 37 38 39 40 41 42 43 44 45 46 47 48 49 50 51 52 53 54 55 56 57 58 59 60 61

PLACES TO STAY	OTHER	
14 Hotel Saski	1 Carmelite Church	34 Church of Our Lady
19 Hotel Pollera	3 Księgarnia Elefant Bookshop	35 Cloth Hall (Sukiennice)
25 Hotel Warszawski	6 Collegium Maius	36 Town Hall Tower
26 Hotel Polonia	8 Stary Teatr	37 Almatur
30 Hotel Europejski	10 City Historical Museum	40 Post Office
33 PTTK Dom Turysty	11 Bank Pekao SA	41 Dominican Church
61 Forum Hotel	12 Strawberry Club	44 Franciscan Church
	15 Orbis (Train Tickets)	45 Filharmonia
PLACES TO EAT	16 Cartoon Gallery	46 Archaeological Museum
2 Bar Rybny	17 Czartoryski Art Museum	48 St Peter & Paul Church
4 Różowy Słoń Salad Bar	20 Blue Box Disco	49 Wawel Cathedral
5 Bar Uniwersytecki	21 St Florian's Gate	50 Wawel Castle
7 Pizzeria Grace	22 Barbican	51 Dragon Statue
9 Bistro Piccolo	23 Bus No 100/Jadłoderia Snack Bar	52 Bernardine Church
13 Lody u Jacka i Moniki	24 Tourist Office	53 Polski Związek Motorowy
18 Żywiec Restaurant	27 Bus Station	54 Jewish Cemetery
38 Złoty Smok Self-Service	28 Bus No 208 to Airport	55 Jewish Museum
39 Jadłodajnia	29 Kraków Główny Station	56 Corpus Christi Church
42 Restauracja Orientalna Andalous	31 Teatr Im J Słowackiego	57 Ethnographic Museum
43 Balaton Restaurant	32 Russian Consulate	58 St Catherine's Church
47 Café U Literató		59 Pauline Church
		60 Excursion Boats

Cracovia (US$57/74 single/double a day and up). Interestingly, Orbis will also issue an 'open voucher' at US$30 for two weeks, US$60 for four weeks, which gets you nothing at all except the visa. The consulate may insist on seeing a Belorussian or Ukrainian visa if you plan to transit those countries on your way to Russia and such visas are only obtainable in Warsaw, so plan ahead.

Travel Agencies For bus tickets to Western Europe try Wawel Tourist, ulica Pawia 8, or Intercrac, Rynek Główny 14.

Dana Air Travel, ulica Szpitalna 40, and Fregata, ulica Szpitalna 32, sells cheap bus tickets to Western Europe and discounted air tickets to cities around the world.

Almatur, Rynek Główny 7 (upstairs on the 2nd floor from the courtyard), sells discounted Eurotrain tickets to Western Europe to persons aged under 26 years.

Both international and domestic train tickets, reservations and couchettes are available at regular prices from Orbis, Rynek Główny 41 on the north side of Market Square, and the staff speak English. From May to September, this same Orbis office offers rather rushed city sightseeing tours (three hours, US$15), plus day trips to the salt mines (five hours, US$15) and Auschwitz-Birkenau (daily, five hours, US$19).

Intercrac, Rynek Główny 14, runs daily sightseeing tours of Kraków (four hours, US$15), the Wieliczka salt mines (US$20) and Auschwitz (US$18). On Wednesday, Friday and Saturday nights they offer a typical Polish dinner with folk dancing at a local inn for US$25 per person including transfers. Ask about the 20% student discounts.

Bookshops Księgarnia Elefant, ulica Podwale 5/6, has books in English and the latest English-language newspapers.

For Carpathian Mountains hiking maps check the PTTK, ulica Jagiellońska 6, and Wierchy Sklep Górski, ulica Szewska 23, around the corner.

Things to See

Around Market Square You'll probably want to begin your visit on Rynek Główny, Kraków's wonderful Market Square, the largest medieval town square in Europe. It was here on 24 March 1794 that Tadeusz Kościuszko proclaimed a nationwide armed uprising to save Poland from partition. The 16th century Renaissance **Cloth Hall** (Sukiennice) dominates the square and there's a large craft market under the arches. Upstairs is the National Museum (closed Monday and Tuesday, free Thursday) with 19th century paintings, including several well-known historical works by Jan Matejko.

The 14th century **Church of Our Lady** fills the north-east corner of Rynek Główny. The huge main altarpiece (1489) by Wit Stwosz (Veit Stoss) of Nuremberg is the finest sculptural work in Poland. The altar's wings are opened daily at noon. A trumpet call sounded hourly from one of the church towers recalls a 13th century trumpeter cut short by a Tatar arrow.

On the opposite side of the Cloth Hall is the 14th century **Town Hall Tower**, complete with a café serving hot honey wine or mead (*miód*) and apple cider in the cellar. The town hall itself was demolished in 1820. Take ulica Św Anny (the street running west from the corner of the square closest to the tower) a block to the 15th century Collegium Maius, the oldest surviving part of **Jagiellonian University**. Enter the Gothic courtyard. Also visit the **City Historical Museum** at Rynek Główny 35 (closed Monday and Tuesday). Go north from the Cloth Hall to the **Galeria**

Autorska Andrzeja Mleczki at ulica Św Jana 14 which seems to specialise in pornographic comic books. Farther up at Św Jana 17 is the **Czartoryski Art Museum** (closed Wednesday and Thursday, free Friday), the collection of a wealthy Polish family donated to Kraków over a century ago. The most famous works here are Leonardo da Vinci's *Lady with an Ermine* and Rembrandt's *Landscape with the Good Samaritan*. Raphael's *Portrait of a Young Man*, stolen from this museum during WW II, has never been recovered. Captions are provided in French.

The Royal Way Around the corner from the Czartoryski Art Museum on ulica Pijarska is a remaining stretch of the medieval city walls which once surrounded Kraków, where the greenbelt is today. Go through **St Florian's Gate** (1307) to the **Barbican**, a defensive bastion built in 1498. Kraków's **Royal Way** runs south from St Florian's Gate to Wawel Castle.

Re-enter the city and follow ulica Floriańska south to Rynek Główny, then south again on ulica Grodzka. The **Jan Matejki Museum** (closed Wednesday and Thursday) is at Floriańska 41. At Plac Wszystkich Świętych, where the tram tracks cut across Grodzka, are two large 13th century **monastic churches**, Dominican on the east and Franciscan on the west. Cardinal Karol Wojtyła resided in the Episcopal Palace across the street from the Franciscan church for over a dozen years until he was elected Pope John Paul II in 1978. South on ulica Grodzka is the 17th century Baroque Jesuit **Sts Peter & Paul Church**. The Romanesque **Church of St Andrew** (1086) alongside was the only building in Kraków which resisted the Tatar attack of 1241, and where those who had taken refuge inside survived.

Continue south another block, then take the lane on the right (ulica Podzamcze) which leads to the ramp up to **Wawel Castle**, Poland's Kremlin. The huge equestrian statue of Tadeusz Kościuszko above this

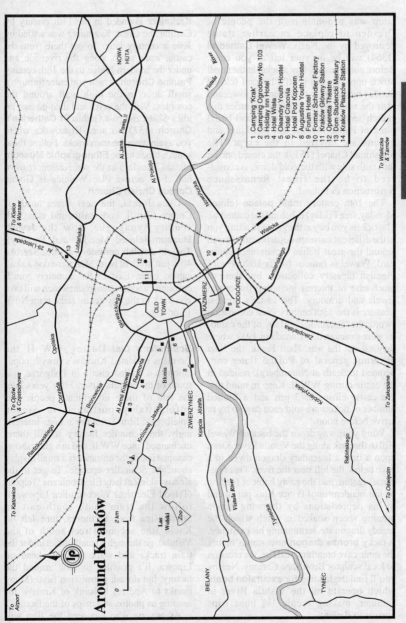

Around Kraków

1 Camping 'Krak'
2 Camping Ogrodowy No 103
3 Holiday Inn Hotel
4 Hotel Wisła
5 Oleandry Youth Hostel
6 Hotel Cracovia
7 Hotel Pod Kopcem
8 Augustine Youth Hostel
9 Forum Hotel
10 Former Schindler Factory
11 Kraków Główny Station
12 Operetta Theatre
13 Dom Dziecki Merkury
14 Kraków Płaszów Station

ramp was a donation of the people of Dresden to replace an earlier statue destroyed by the Nazis. **Wawel Cathedral** (1364) will be on your left as you enter. Before going inside, buy a ticket at the small office opposite and a little beyond (closed Sunday morning) to climb the bell tower and visit the main crypt. For four centuries this church served as the coronation and burial place of Polish royalty, and 100 kings and queens are interred in the crypt. The Sigismund Chapel (1539), the closed one on the south side with the gold dome, is considered to be the finest Renaissance construction in Poland.

The 16th century **main palace** (closed Monday, free Friday) is behind the cathedral. The tickets you buy at the gate will admit you to the different museum departments arrayed around the great Italian Renaissance courtyard. Wawel is famous for its 16th century Flemish tapestry collection, but there is much else of interest including the crown jewels and armoury. The castle's greatest treasure is the 13th century Piast coronation sword, the 'Szczerbiec'. Many of the exhibits were evacuated to Canada in 1939 where they sat out the war. Hans Frank, the Nazi governor general of Poland (later condemned to death at Nuremberg), resided in the castle during WW II. Keep in mind that the castle closes at 3 pm and a limited number of tickets are sold each day, so try to arrive before noon.

Wind your way down the back of Wawel Hill to the park along the Vistula River. Once upon a time a legendary dragon dwelt in a cave below the hill near the river. This fearsome creature had the nasty habit of feeding on fair maidens until Prince Krak put an end to his depredations by throwing him a burning sheep soaked in pitch which the greedy dragon ate, terminating his existence. A tacky **bronze dragon** now stands before the same cave breathing real fire, the creation of local sculptor Bronisław Chromy. Nearby you'll find the landing for **excursion boats** which operate on the Vistula River in summer, making scenic 1½ hour trips upriver to Bielany.

Kazimierz Founded in the 14th century by Casimir the Great, Kazimierz was settled by Jews a century later. To get there from the castle, walk south along the riverside and under the modern bridge to the 18th century **Pauline Church**, which you enter through a small door in the high wall around the complex. Visit the crypt and then go east on ulica Skałeczna past Gothic **St Catherine's Church** (1373) to ulica Krakowska where you again meet the tram tracks. Follow these south a block to the **Ethnographic Museum** (closed Tuesday) in the old Kazimierz town hall. East across Plac Wolnica is Gothic **Corpus Christi Church**.

Ulica Józefa, the next street north of Corpus Christi, ends eastbound at a 15th century synagogue, now the **Jewish Museum** (closed Monday and Tuesday). The old **Jewish cemetery** at ulica Szeroka 40 is just north of here. Men must don a skull cap to enter. East of the cemetery you'll encounter another tram route which will take you back to the city centre (take tram No 3, 13 or 43).

Schindler's List During WW II the Germans relocated Kraków's Jewish population to a walled ghetto in Podgórze, just south of the Vistula River. Fifty years later the fate of these unfortunate people was unforgettably portrayed in Steven Spielberg's film *Schindler's List*. Interestingly, the Schindler factory is still there, unchanged since WW II, and in a glass showcase just inside the entrance is a small display about the Schindler episode. To get to the Krakowskie Zakłady Elektroniczne 'Telpod' (Telpod Electrical Works), ulica Lipowa 4, follow the tram route south-east on Starowiślna from Kazimerz, turn left on Kącik (the second street south of the Vistula), go through a small tunnel under the train tracks and walk straight ahead on Lipowa. It's possible to look around the factory, but do ask permission first. (Many thanks to Andrzej Urbanik of Kraków for sending us photos and maps of the factory.)

As anyone who has seen the film will

POLAND

know, towards the end of the war Schindler moved his Jewish workforce to Moravia.

According to reader Larry Bailey of Huntington Beach, California, the new factory was at Březová nad Svitavou (formerly Brinnlitz), a village on the railway line from Brno to Česká Třebová.

Nowa Huta Just east of Kraków is the industrial community of Nowa Huta with its ex-Lenin Steel Works, built by the communists in the early 1950s to balance the clerical/aristocratic traditions of the old capital. All of the raw materials have to be carted in. Far from acting as a bulwark of the regime, a May 1988 strike by 20,000 steelworkers here contributed greatly to that government's eventual fall. The tens of thousands of tonnes of carbon monoxide, sulphur dioxide and particulates emitted annually by the steel mill have seriously damaged Kraków's monuments but now a restructuring program is underway to cut both the workforce and pollution while improving the quality of the product by investing in new equipment.

Wieliczka The **salt mines** at Wieliczka, 13 km south-east, are a popular day trip from Kraków. Try to arrive before 2 pm to be sure of getting on a tour (open daily, 2½ hours, admission US$5, students and children US$3). Taking videos is an additional US$3.50. The basic charge includes a guided tour in Polish and you shouldn't have to wait over an hour for one to start. For a tour in English an additional US$22 per group must be paid. The tour in Polish can be rather tedious, so you might want to invest in the mine guide booklet in English sold at the souvenir shop.

You enter the mines down an elevator shaft, then follow a guide five km through the many chambers carved from solid salt. The mine's 11 levels of galleries stretch 300 km – some 20 million tonnes of rock salt were extracted over 700 years. According to a local legend the deposits were discovered in the 13th century by a Hungarian princess named Kinga whose lost ring was found in a block of salt extracted here. Thus it's not surprising that the largest underground chamber should be the **St Kinga Chapel**; it took 30 years to carve, measures 54 by 17 metres and is 12 metres high.

Another feature of Wieliczka is a health resort 200 metres below the surface where patients under medical supervision are treated for bronchial asthma and diseases of the respiratory tract. It's certainly a change of pace from museums and churches!

There are two train stations at Wieliczka. Due to an earthquake in 1992 which damaged the line (and the mine) most trains from Kraków terminate at Wieliczka Station. Wieliczka Rynek Station is about a km farther along, beyond the bus station. From Wieliczka Station follow the crowd south along the railway tracks until you see the bus station on your right. Walk through the bus station and continue a few minutes west up the hill to the mine.

If the line has been repaired and your train continues to Wieliczka Rynek, stay on as it's closer. As you come out of Wieliczka Rynek Station turn right and go north through the park. Just beyond the red brick Miejski Dom Kultury, turn left up the street to the mine. Either way, follow any signs reading 'Kopalnia Soli Wieliczka'. The times of trains back to Kraków are posted at the mine ticket window. If these are inconvenient you can also return by bus No FB (ticket from the conductor) which departs from a stop on ulica Piłsudskiego, up the hill on the opposite side of Wieliczka Rynek Station from the mine. Bus No FB only goes as far as Kraków Płaszów Station from which you must take a tram on into Kraków.

Festivals

Kraków has one of the richest cycles of annual events in all of Poland. Ask about the Organ Music Days and Student Song Festival in April, the Polish Festival of Short Feature Films in May, the 'Kraków Days' and wreath-letting on the Vistula River in June, 'Music in Old Kraków' in August, the Folk Art Fair and the 'Solo-Duo-Trio' Festival of Small Jazz Groups in September, the

'Polonez' dancing contest in October, the Halloween Jazz Festival and the International Review of Modern Ballet in November, and the exhibition of nativity scenes around Christmas.

During Easter week there's the famous week-long Passion Play at nearby Kalwaria Zebrzydowska; on Assumption Day(15 August) a solemn procession in folk costumes is held in the same village. The 'Kraków Days' are opened on Corpus Christi (a Thursday in May or June) by the 'Lajkonik', a legendary figure disguised as a Tatar riding a hobbyhorse!

Places to Stay

Kraków is Poland's premier tourist attraction and the city's hotels are expensive and heavily booked, so if you can skip a night by arriving in the morning or leaving in the afternoon, so much the better.

Camping From June to September *Camping 'Krak'* (☎ 372 122), in the far north-west corner of Kraków at the junction of the highways arriving from Katowice and Częstochowa, offers good camping facilities. The traffic noise here is considerable. The bar of the adjacent four-star motel is handy (bus No 238 from Kraków Railway Station).

A quieter camping ground is *Camping Ogrodowy No 103* (☎ 222 011), ulica Królowej Jadwigi 223, west of Kraków on the way to the zoo. Open from mid-May to September, it's US$4 per person to camp here and there's almost always space for tents (but no bungalows). Buses Nos 102, 134, 152, 452 and B all pass nearby.

Youth Hostels Both year-round HI youth hostels are west of the old town. The closest to the city centre is in a functional concrete building at ulica Oleandry 4 (☎ 338 822). Take tram No 15 from the train station to Hotel Cracovia. The hostel is on the street to the right of the tram line, west of the hotel. There are hot showers! Although this is the largest hostel in Poland it's often full in summer. Prices vary according to the size of the room and the staff may shift you around

from one room to another charging a different price each time. We've heard of people being kicked out halfway through their stay because someone else had booked their bed! (The comments we receive from readers about this hostel are highly contradictory: some say it was the best hostel they stayed at, while others say it was the worst.) The hostel does serve a good breakfast. Upstairs in the building directly across the street from this hostel is the excellent and inexpensive *Oleandry Restaurant* – not the student dining hall downstairs.

There's a second, less expensive hostel (☎ 221 951) behind the large Augustine Church at Tadeusza Kościuszki 88, just west of the city (tram No 1, 2, 6 or 21, direction 'Salwator' to the terminus). Members stay in a functioning convent (mixed dorms!) overlooking the Vistula River. In summer it's also overcrowded. Ask about the direct bus to Auschwitz which leaves from across the street from this hostel around 8.30 am.

Both charge US$6 per person in a double room or US$4 for a bed in a six to 12-person dormitory, US$5 in a five-bed dorm. Everyone is welcome (no hostel card required).

Other Hostels The big, crowded *PTTK Dom Turysty* (☎ 229 566), ulica Westerplatte 15/16, an eight-minute walk from the stations, is a sort of glorified youth hostel. Singles/doubles are overpriced at US$19/24 without bath, US$28/34 with bath – you pay for the location. The only real reason to come here is if you're interested in a bed in one of the dormitories, which go for US$7 per person in a four-bedded room, US$6 in an eight-bedded room. Breakfast is US$2 extra. There's a noisy disco downstairs (open from 10 pm to 4 am).

Almatur (☎ 226 352), Rynek Główny 7 (upstairs on the 2nd floor from the courtyard), arranges accommodation in student dormitories at US$5 per person in two to seven-bedded rooms. Though many more beds are available in July and August they'll try to find something for you year-round.

The *Zaczek Student's Hotel* (☎ 335 477), Aleje 3 Maja 5 diagonally across the park from the Orbis Hotel Cracovia, is US$11 single, US$8 for a hard bed in a double, US$7 for a hard bed in a triple. This six-storey student residence belonging to Jagiellonian University is run as a regular hotel from July to September only. During other months the huge 'hotel' signs on the front of the building are only someone's idea of a joke. The Zaczek is a great place to stay if you want to meet Polish students, and there always seems to be a lot happening here. The 'Rotunda' disco is in the same building, and one of Kraków's HI youth hostels is just around the corner.

In July and August only the 11-storey *Dom Studencki Merkury*, Aleje 29-Listopada 48a, a couple of km north of the train station, operates as an international student hotel.

Private Rooms At ulica Pawia 8, near the bus and train stations, is an office arranging stays in private homes for around US$8/13 single/double 1st class, US$6/10 in 2nd class. The rooms are often far from the city centre, so ask first. This office or the one next door can also help you find a hotel.

You may also be offered a private room by someone on the street outside. Ask them to point out the location on a good map of Kraków before agreeing to go.

Hotels The *Hotel Warszawski* (☎ 220 622), ulica Pawia 6, right next to the private room office, is about US$13/18/21 single/double/triple without bath, US$15/22/27 with bath. The more appealing *Hotel Polonia* (☎ 221 281), ulica Basztowa 23, just around the corner from the Warszawski, is US$14/21/25 single/double/triple without bath, US$17/26/30 with bath. Ask for a room facing the quieter back garden. There's even an elevator that works! It's often full. The *Hotel Europejski* (☎ 220 911), ulica Lubicz 5 opposite the train station, is US$17/26/30 single/double/triple with bath.

To be sure of a room at one of these three hotels in summer you'll have to call ahead and make a reservation. The receptionists usually speak English, but you may have to call a couple before finding one with an available room. From September to May it should be enough to arrive before 2 pm to get a room on the spot. Beware of tram noise at these hotels.

The *Hotel Pollera* (☎ 221 044), ulica Szpitalna 30 in the old city, is US$17/25/30 single/double/triple without bath, US$20/27/36 with bath, a satisfying breakfast included – quiet and good value.

A step up from these is the convenient *Hotel Saski* (☎ 214 222), ulica Sławkowska 3 just off Rynek Główny: US$22/34 single/double without bath, US$26/40 single/double with bath.

The elegant old *Hotel Polski* (☎ 221 144), ulica Pijarska 17, charges US$22/32/35 single/double/triple without bath, US$29/41/50 with bath. For couples this is a good choice.

Right next to the Holiday Inn is the six-storey *Hotel Nauczycielska* (☎ 377 304), ulica Armii Krajowej 9, with 140 rooms with bath at US$18 single/double. If you don't mind commuting, this teachers' hotel is a good place to stay with a restaurant and disco on the premises.

The *Hotel Wisła* (☎ 334 922), ulica Reymonta 22, part of a large sports complex a km back towards town from the Nauczycielska, is also US$18 single or double, but it's not as convenient a place to stay.

By far the most unusual place to stay in Kraków is the *Hotel Pod Kopcem* (☎ 222 055), Aleje Waszyngtona, in a massive 19th century Austrian fortress on a hill top overlooking the city. There's a cool forest surrounding the hotel, plus a coffee shop and restaurant. Room rates begin at US$31/35 single/double without bath, US$40/44 single/double with bath, breakfast included. There are only 36 rooms, so it might be worth calling ahead to make sure they'll have one for you. If you wanted to splurge once in Poland, this is it! Bus No 100 from Plac Matejki 2, opposite the Barbican, ends in front of the hotel (hourly). Even if you're not staying, the Hotel Pod Kopcem merits a visit. There's a splendid view from the Kościuszki mound above the hotel.

POLAND

Places to Eat
Around Market Square Privatisation has eliminated all of old Kraków's cheap proletarian milk bars but many excellent little places to eat have popped up in their place offering superior fare at prices any foreigner will find very affordable. Pushcart vendors sell obwarzanki, a doughnut-shaped pretzel or bagel which makes a tasty snack.

Złoty Smok (Golden Dragon), ulica Sienna 1, in a red brick building just off Rynek Główny, is a self-service for tourists with all prices clearly marked. Farther down the street, *Jadłodajnia*, ulica Sienna 11, provides basic fare to a local clientele.

For Polish haute cuisine try *Restauracja Staropolska*, ulica Sienna 4 (opens at 1 pm). Kraków's most exclusive restaurant is *Wierzynek*, Rynek Główny 15, allegedly founded in 1364. Since then the likes of Charles de Gaulle, Indira Gandhi and Mikhail Gorbachev have dined here. Drop by beforehand for reservations if you want to be sure of getting a table. The Wierzynek's immaculate service and excellent food are inexpensive by Western standards but you're expected to be neatly dressed.

The *Żywiec Restaurant*, ulica Floriańska 19, has a sharp, elegant appearance but the meals are substantial and inexpensive if you order correctly. There's a menu in English and the service is good.

West of Market Square *Bistro Piccolo*, ulica Szczepańska 2, is a great place to have a half chicken and chips.

The *Restauracja 'Cechowa'*, ulica Jagiellońska 11, is an old-style Polish restaurant with beer on tap. *Pizzeria Grace*, ulica Św Anny 7, serves good pizza at good prices. Vegetarians will like *Salad Bar Chimera*, ulica Św Anny 3 (downstairs), although it's weak on leafy green vegetables. The staff speak English.

Bar Rybny, ulica Karmelicka 16, dishes out huge pieces of fried fish at the counter.

The only genuine milk bar left in the centre of Kraków is *Bar Uniwersytecki*, on the corner of Piłsudskiego and Podwale (open daily).

Vegetarians will like *Różowy Stoń Salad Bar*, ulica Straszewskiego 24, where the salads are charged by weight.

The *Karczma Pod Blacha*, ulica Piastowska 22, just across the street from the western terminus of trams Nos 15 and 18, is a traditional inn serving typical Polish food (daily 10 am to 10 pm). There's sometimes folk dancing here.

A 24-hour convenience store (with beer) operates at ulica Szewska 10.

South of Market Square The *Restauracja Orientalna Andalous*, Plac Dominikański 6, offers North African dishes such as couscous.

For better Hungarian food than you'll get in Hungary try the *Balaton Restaurant*, ulica Grodzka 37 (menu in Polish only). The tipsy waiters tend to cause hilarity in the first hour, irritation and frustration the second hour.

North of the Old Town One of the best places for your money is *Jadłoderia Snack Bar*, Plac Matejki 3, next to the Grunwald monument just north of the Barbican (Monday to Saturday 8 am to 8 pm, Sunday 10 am to 5 pm). The menu is in Polish and you must order at the counter, but just hang around and watch what others are getting. Huge plates of well-prepared food and cold beer are offered, and the dining area is tastefully decorated with modern art. It's just off the tourist track, so most of the patrons are locals.

Bar Smok next to the bus and train stations is neither cheap nor good but it does open at 6 am.

Dessert *Rio Bar Kawowy*, ulica Św Jana 2, has the best coffee in Kraków. Locate this place early in your visit.

For Kraków's top ice cream get in line at *Lody u Jacka i Moniki*, ulica Sławkowska 8.

Cafés *Jama Michalika*, ulica Floriańska 45, is the elegant turn-of-the-century café you'd expect to find in Kraków. Many famous artists and dramatists have sat on the forest green velvet couches surrounded by Art-

Déco chandeliers, stained glass and dark wood. Certain nights there's a cabaret show at Jama Michalika. And as if that weren't enough, there's no smoking in the main section at the back. On a summers' day, a nice place to sit outside and have a drink is the café straight through the arch at Rynek Główny 17. From the pavement café on Mały Rynek behind the Church of Our Lady you can watch the trumpeter in the church tower on the hour.

For coffee and ice cream you can't beat *Kawiarnia 'Alvorada'*, Rynek Główny 30. A less touristed place for coffee and cakes is *Kawiarnia U Zalipianek*, ulica Szewska 24. In summer you can relax on its open terrace facing a park.

There's a good little bar down in the basement of *Galeria Krzysztofory*, ulica Szczepańska. No sign faces the street but go down anyway. Jazz concerts sometimes happen here.

The *Café U Literatów*, ulica Kanonicza 7, has a nice garden where you can sit in summer.

The *Piwiarnia pod Beczkami*, ulica Dietla 46, between Wawel and Kazimierz, is just the place for a mug of cold Żywiec (the only woman in there is the barmaid).

Entertainment

Check the listings in the daily papers. One of the first things to do in Kraków is visit the *Filharmonia* booking office, ulica Zwierzyniecka 1 (weekdays 9 am to noon and 5 to 7 pm), for tickets to any concerts which happen to coincide with your stay. Don't be fooled by the price of the ticket; this orchestra ranks with the best in the world.

The renovated *Teatr Im J Słowackiego*, ulica Szpitalna, offers classical theatre, opera and ballet. It's worth attending a performance just to see the gilded interior of this splendid neo-Baroque theatre erected in 1893. The *Teatr Miniatura* is just behind and shares the same box office.

Kraków's *Operetta Theatre,* ulica Lubicz 48, is a 10-minute walk east of the train station. Lots of trams pass this theatre for the return trip.

Lighter Fare On Tuesday and Sunday nights there's jazz at the *Pod Jaszczurami Student Club*, Rynek Główny 8 (admission US$3, students US$1.50). *Jazz Club U Muniaka*, ulica Floriańska 3, has live jazz concerts on Friday and Saturday from 9.30 pm to 2 am.

Films and other events happen at the *Cultural Centre* (Pałac Pod Baranami), Rynek Główny 27. The *Institute Français de Cracovie*, ulica Św Jana 15, screens quality films (in French).

Discos Kraków's top disco is *Blue Box*, ulica Szpitalna 38 (open nightly, admission US$5). *Maxime*, ulica Floriańska 32, is another disco (dancing from 9 pm to 4 am, admission US$3). The cabaret show at *Feniks*, Św Jana 2, is also fun. The *Strawberry Club*, ulica Św Tomasza 1, is a sharp modern bar with a disco downstairs.

The *'Rotunda' Students' Cultural Centre*, ulica Oleandry 1 opposite the youth hostel near Hotel Cracovia, has a good disco from 8 pm on weekends. Posters outside Rotunda advertise special events.

Getting There & Away

Air The LOT Polish Airlines office is at ulica Basztowa 15 on the north side of the old town.

Bus Buses departing from Kraków Bus Station include one every half hour to Zakopane (100 km), nine a day to Oświęcim (60 km), one daily to Lublin (269 km), two daily to Zamość (318 km), seven daily to Cieszyn (Czech border, 121 km) and one daily to Łysa Polana (Slovakian border, 109 km). In June, July and August there's a nonstop morning bus to Częstochowa (114 km). Always check the footnotes on the posted schedule and try to buy an advance ticket.

Train Kraków is on the main railway line between Przemyśl and Szczecin via Katowice, Opole, Wrocław and Poznań. Another important line through the city is Warsaw to Zakopane. The overnight *Cracovia* express train arrives direct from

Budapest via Košice (Slovakia) and Nowy Sącz. Coming from Prague or Vienna you usually change at Katowice, although in summer there's a daily train direct from Vienna. From Germany there are direct trains from Berlin-Lichtenberg, Cologne, Frankfurt/Main and Leipzig.

The *Sawa* and *Tatry* express trains depart from Warsaw in the morning, reaching Kraków Główny (325 km) about three hours later. The return trips are in the evening. The *Krakus* and *Pieniny* express trains do the opposite, leaving Warsaw in the late afternoon and Kraków in the early morning. The *Kościuszko* departs from both ends in the afternoon while the *Małopolska* runs during the middle of the day. Reservations are required on these excellent trains which ensure fast, easy transport between the two cities.

The *Lajkonik* express train runs direct between Kraków Główny and Gdańsk (621 km, seven hours), leaving Kraków in the early morning and Gdańsk in the afternoon. This train also services Warsaw, Malbork, Sopot and Gdynia, and reservations are required.

Other fast trains departing from Kraków include the *Kasprowy* to Zakopane (147 km, 2½ hours), the *Giewont* to Częstochowa (two hours) and Zakopane and the *Jadwiga* and *Jagiełło* to Lublin (five hours). Reservations are not required on these.

There are seven trains daily between Kraków Główny and Oświęcim, four of them in the early morning and none during the middle of the day. To Wieliczka trains run about once an hour (every two hours in late morning). Carefully check the times beforehand.

Getting Around

Trams and city buses use the same US$0.25 tickets (punch both ends), so buy a bunch as soon as you arrive. Most places in the centre are easily accessible on foot.

To/From the Airport Balice Airport is 18 km west of Kraków on the road to Katowice. Bus No 208 from the train station runs directly

there at least once an hour from 4.30 am to 10.30 pm (45 minutes).

Car Rental Hertz (☎ 371 120) is at Hotel Cracovia, ulica Focha 1. Budget (☎ 370 089) is at Motel Krak, ulica Radzikowskiego 99 on the north-west side of the city.

THE TATRA MOUNTAINS & ZAKOPANE

Poland is a flat, open land of lakes and rivers, but in the south the Sudeten and Carpathian mountain ranges break through the plains. The Tatra Mountains 100 km south of Kraków are the highest knot of these ranges with elevations averaging 2000 metres. Here, folded granite and limestone were shaped by glaciation to create a true Alpine environment. The Slovakian border runs along the ridges of these jagged Carpathian peaks.

The entire Polish portion of the range is included in Tatra National Park (217 sq km, entry US$0.50). Zakopane, the regional centre, is known as the winter capital of Poland due to its popularity as a ski resort. The noted Polish composer Karol Szymanowski lived at Willa Atma in Zakopane from 1930 to 1936. Because so many Polish tourists come here, everything is very well organised and there are lots of facilities. For summer visitors it's a chance to do some hiking and meet the Poles in an unstructured environment. Many students come here on holidays, and your conversations with them may be as memorable as the rugged landscape itself.

Orientation

Zakopane, nestling below Mt Giewont at an altitude of 800 to 1000 metres, will be your base. The bus and train stations are adjacent on the north-east edge of town. The left-luggage office in the train station is open around the clock but the bus station left luggage functions only from 7.30 am to 7 pm. If you want to leave your luggage somewhere in town, the cloakroom beside the restaurant in the PTTK Dom Turysty is open from 8 am to 9 pm.

From the train station, cross the street and

POLAND

To Gubałówka

To Kraków

To Hotel Kasprowy

To Mt Giewont & Dolina Strążyska

To Dolina Białego

To Jaszczurówka & Morskie Oko

To Kuźnice

Zakopane

0   200   400 m

PLACES TO STAY

7   Dom Turysty PTTK
9   Hotel Gromada-Gazda
13 Hotel Orbis-Giewont
14 Juventur-Słoneczny Hotel
15 Youth Hostel
17 Hotel Gladiola
24 Hotel Warszawianka
27 Ermitage Hotel
29 Pod Krokwią Campground
33 Imperial Hotel

PLACES TO EAT

3   Restauracja U Wnuka
5   Karcma Redykołka
25 Restauracja Wierchy
28 Karczma Obrochtówka
32 Bistro Pod Smrekami

OTHER

1   Funicular Station
2   Willa Koliba
4   Old Wooden Church
6   Tatra Museum
8   Willa Atma
10 Post Office

11 Orbis
12 Sokół Cinema
16 Wilkiewicza Theatre
18 Bank Pekao SA
19 Centralne Biuro FWP
20 Tourist Office
21 PKS Bus Station
22 Railway Station
23 Hasior Art Gallery
24 Tatratourist
26 Trip Travel Agency
30 National Park Museum
31 Park Information Office

take ulica Kościuszki past the bus station straight up into town. You'll pass Hotel Giewont on the right before reaching the post office, your reference point in Zakopane.

Ulica Krupówki, Zakopane's pedestrian mall, is always jammed with throngs of Polish tourists parading in trendy ski or hiking gear. The cable car to Mt Kasprowy Wierch is at Kuźnice, four km south of the stations. 'Rondo', a roundabout midway between the train station, or town, and Kuźnice, is another good reference point.

Information

The Centrum Informacji Turystyczny (☎ 12 211) is at ulica Kościuszki 23 in the five-storey Kolejarz Hotel next to the bus station. It claims to be open 24 hours a day!

The Tatra National Park Information Office, ulica Chałubińskiego 44 at 'Rondo', sells good maps and can answer hiking questions, often in English. The National Park Museum, among the trees just behind this office, sells the same maps.

The PTTK office at Krupówki 12 arranges mountain guides from US$25 to US$50 a day per group depending on the difficulty of the hike. One guide, Mr Tadeusz Gąsienica (☎ 12 421), speaks perfect English and it would be worth calling him up beforehand to make sure he'll be available if you're sure you want a guide.

Money The only bank that will change travellers' cheques is the Bank Pekao SA, ulica Gimnazjalna 1, behind the bus station (open weekdays 10.15 am to 2.30 pm).

The currency exchange counter in the Hotel Giewont changes travellers' cheques on weekends, but deducts 5% commission.

Post & Telecommunications The telephone centre around the side of the main post office, on the corner of Kościuszki and Krupówki streets, is open weekdays from 7 am to 9 pm, Saturday 8 am to 9 pm and Sunday 8 am to noon. There are lots of blue card phones around town, and they work! Zakopane's telephone code is 0165.

Travel Agencies Orbis (☎ 15 051), ulica Krupówki 22 beside the post office, books couchettes and sleepers on overnight trains (as does the ticket office at the train station). Orbis is also the American Express representative.

For bus tickets to Western Europe go to Trip Travel Agency, ulica Zamoyskiego 1.

Things to See & Do

Zakopane Founded in 1888, the **Tatra Museum** (closed Monday), ulica Krupówki 10, is hidden among the trees just down from the post office. Downstairs are displays on the folklore of the region including paintings on glass, peasant costumes, farm implements and dwelling interiors. Upstairs is natural history, including an excellent relief map of the Tatras.

From here walk down ulica Krupówki and turn left on ulica Kościeliśka to reach an old **wooden church** (1851) with a pioneer cemetery behind. If you continue west on ulica Kościeliśka you'll pass a number of traditional Zakopane-style houses, especially **Willa Koliba** (1892) across a wooden bridge to the right.

Return to the corner of ulica Krupówki and proceed west under the overpass to the **funicular railway** (built in 1938) up Mt Gubałówka (1123 metres). There's a fine view from the top (US$1.50 return trip) and a trail south-west along the ridge with spectacular mountain views on one side and quaint wooden farm houses on the other.

Kuźnice The work of Polish avant-garde artist Władysław Hasior can be seen at the **Hasior Art Gallery**, ulica Jagiellońska 7, up the hill from the train station (closed Monday and Tuesday).

For an introduction to the natural history of this area visit the **Przyrodnicze Museum of Tatra National Park** (open Tuesday to Sunday 9 am to 2 pm) in the forest just below 'Rondo' on the road up to the Kuźnice cable car.

Since it opened in 1935, almost every Polish tourist has made the **cable-car trip** from Kuźnice to the summit of **Mt**

KasprowyWierch (1985 metres) where you can stand with one foot in Poland and the other in Slovakia. There's a great view from here, clouds permitting, and also a restaurant. Many people return to Zakopane on foot down the Gąsienicowa Valley, and the most intrepid walk the ridges all the way across to Morskie Oko Lake via Pięć Stawów, a very strenuous hike taking a full day in good weather.

In July and August the cable car operates from 7.30 am to 8 pm; in other months it's more like 8 am to 5 pm. Tickets cost US$4 for the return trip. When you buy a return-trip ticket you automatically get a reservation for a return two hours later. Advance cable-car tickets are sold at Orbis, ulica Krupówki 22 beside the post office. You can also usually get one at the terminal itself, though at busy times you risk running into a long line and having to wait an hour or more to go up, so it's best to book through Orbis the day before. In midsummer it may be faster to walk up (2½ hours).

Mountain Climbing One of the best things to do in Zakopane is to climb **Mt Giewont** (1909 metres), a jagged peak overlooking the town. From the cable-car terminus at Kuźnice follow the blue trail up the Kondratowa Valley past the *Hala Kondratowa Hostel* where refreshments are sold. From the cross on top of Mt Giewont (2½ hours from Kuźnice) you get a sweeping view of Zakopane and the Tatras, a truly magnificent spectacle on a clear day.

Return to Zakopane down the steeper red trail through the forested Strążyska Valley, along a foaming river beneath striking rock formations and past a flower-filled meadow, finishing at ulica Strążyska a couple of km south of the centre. The whole circle trip can be done in about six hours without too much difficulty.

Morskie Oko One of the highlights of a visit to Zakopane is the bus trip to Morskie Oko Lake, the largest lake in the Tatras (34.54 hectares in area and 53 metres deep). The name means 'eye of the sea' from a legend-

ary tunnel said to connect the lake to the Adriatic. It's wise to book return bus tickets a few days in advance at the bus station, although tickets are often available on the bus itself (you want the 'Polana Palenica' bus). A couple of hours at the lake is enough.

From Polana Palenica it's still nine km (not steep) to the lake, though 20-passenger horse carts are available at US$4 per person to go up (two hours), US$3 to come down (one hour). It's best to pay each way separately so you can return whenever you like. Arrive early if want to be sure of finding a cart. At the lakeside is a large tea shop serving *bigos* (boiled cabbage).

A stone path runs around this mountain-girdled glacial lake – a lovely 40-minute stroll. You can climb to an upper lake, Czarny Staw, in another 20 minutes or so. **Mt Rysy**, the highest point in the Polish Tatras (2499 metres), rises directly above this upper lake. In late summer, when the snow has finally gone, you can climb it in about four hours from the tea shop. Lenin climbed Mt Rysy in 1913.

Side Trip West Take a bus (they depart frequently) west from Zakopane to **Chochołów**, an interesting village with large log farmhouses along the roadside for quite a distance. It's like an open-air museum of traditional architecture, except that all the houses are inhabited and the farming people have retained their age-old ways. There's a small museum (closed Monday and Tuesday) by the store opposite the church, and you can walk around the village.

On the way back to Zakopane get off at Kiry and walk up the **Kościeliska Valley** to the Hala Ornak Hostel. A broad stone road runs right up the valley. From the hostel you can climb the black trail to idyllic Smreczyński Lake in about 15 minutes. Buses from Kiry back to Zakopane are frequent.

Places to Stay
Camping The camping ground *Pod Krokwią* (☎ 12 256, open year-round), on ulica Żeromskiego between town and Kuźnice,

POLAND

has eight large bungalows, each containing several double and triple rooms (US$4 per person without bath, US$5 per person with bath), as well as camping space among the pines. The camping staff rents mountain bikes at US$9 a day and in winter you can rent skis to use on the ski slopes near Pod Krokwią from the outdoor shop on Rondo for about US$8.

Hostels Zakopane has a convenient year-round *youth hostel* (☎ 66 203) at ulica Nowotarska 45. From the train station walk straight up ulica Kościuszki to a bridge across a small stream. Here, turn right and follow ulica Sienkiewicza down to the corner of ulica Nowotarska, an easy 10-minute walk. You risk meeting large groups of preteens here.

The *Hotel Warszawianka* (☎ 63 261), ulica Jagiellońska 7/18, functions as a sort of youth hostel (sheets not provided and there's a 10 pm curfew), but they do have double rooms with shared bath at US$4 per person. They cater mostly to school groups and the signs outside are ambiguous, but look for a three-storey building between the road and the Hasior Art Gallery. The reception is inside: ring the bell at the counter and hope that someone's around. There are only hot showers when groups are present. In the basement is *Night Club Pstrąg* which opens at 8 pm.

Private Rooms People peddling private rooms often approach passengers getting off the buses from Kraków and lots of houses around Zakopane have *pokoje, noclegi* or *zimmer frei* signs outside, indicating the availability of private rooms. You'll also see signs for new private *pensjonaty* all around Zakopane.

The tourist office (☎ 12 211), ulica Kościuszki 23 (open 24 hours a day), has private rooms at US$5 per person with shared bath, US$7 per person with private bath, but they only rent for stays of two nights or more. Some of the rooms are rather far from town.

Kozica Travel Bureau (☎ 12 212), ulica

Jagiellońska 1, just across the park from the stations, rents private rooms at US$5 per person (one-night stays OK).

The Orbis office (☎ 15 051), ulica Krupówki 22, arranges room and board at small *pensjonaty* in Zakopane.

Holiday Hotels The Centralne Biuro Funduszu Wyzasów Pracowniczych (☎ 12 763), ulica Kościuszki 19, in Dom Wcyzasowy 'Podhale' just up from the bus station (Monday to Saturday 7 am to 4 pm), rents rooms in FWP holiday hotels around Zakopane. Rooms with bath and full board (three meals) cost US$14/26 single/double in 1st-class properties such as the *Hyry, Sienkiewiczówka* and *Roztoka*, while rooms with shared bath and full board are US$12/23 in 2nd-class places like the *Bristol, Postęp* and *Manru*. Without meals the rooms are about US$5 per person cheaper. A total of 11 hotels are available and the FWP office has a booklet with colour photos of each to help you choose. This is excellent value, so drop into their office as soon as you arrive.

Hotels The *Dom Turysty PTTK* (☎ 63 207), ulica Gen Zaruskiego 5, is a few minutes' walk from the post office along the road running towards the mountains. Rooms are US$10/18/27 single/double/triple with a bath tub, US$15 double with a shower, US$13 double without bath, or you can get a bed in dormitories with four beds (US$4), eight beds (US$3) or 28 beds (US$2.50). There's a restaurant in the building open from 8 am to 9 pm. Unfortunately, Dom Turysty is so swamped by excited groups of preteens that you should consider it as a last resort only. There's an 11 pm curfew.

At the modern three-star *Hotel 'Gromada-Gazda'* (☎ 15 011), ulica Zaruskiego 6 next to the post office, bright, clean rooms are expensive at US$22 single with toilet but no shower or US$35 double with bath, and breakfast included.

The *'Orbis-Giewont' Hotel* (☎ 12 011) across the street from the Gazda has rooms at US$13/18 single/double without bath,

US$18/24 with bath, breakfast US$4 per person extra.

The *'Juventur-Słoneczny' Hotel* (☎ 66 253), ulica Słoneczna 2a off ulica Nowotarska, is a large modern hotel that caters mostly to students and young people (US$8/15 single/double without bath, US$12/23 with bath, breakfast included). It's only a block from Zakopane's youth hostel, so keep it in mind as the next place to try if you arrive to find the hostel full.

Comparatively few Westerners come here so prices are geared towards the Polish market which makes staying cheap if you shop around. Most hotels assume Westerners want a room with private bath and you have to specifically request one without bath. All accommodation rates are considerably lower in the off season, from October to mid-December and April to May. During the ski season (from mid-December to March) prices double. Zakopane is one of Poland's most popular tourist centres (for Poles) and, despite the variety of accommodation available, on weekends and holidays everything could be full.

Mountain Huts There are a number of 'mountain huts' (large hostels) in Tatra National Park offering inexpensive accommodation for the hiker (US$4 per person in a dormitory or US$10 per person in a double room). All the huts serve basic meals. The hostels are in high demand at certain times and to protect the environment camping isn't allowed in the park (there are also bears!), so before setting out it's a good idea to check with the Biuro Obsługi Ruchu Turystycznego PTTK (☎ 12 429), ulica Krupówki 12 next to the Tatra Museum. It controls all the hostels and will know for sure which ones are open.

Alternatively, you could just take pot luck that there'll be a bed for you (don't arrive too late in this case). No one is ever turned away though you may have to crash on the floor if it's very crowded. The huts often close for repairs in November so be sure to check that month. Otherwise they're open all year. The best weather for hiking is in August; until the end of May expect to encounter ice on the trails (boots required).

The easiest 'hut' to get to from Zakopane is the giant *Hala Kalatówki Hostel* (84 beds, US$10 per person, breakfast included), a 30-minute walk from the Kuźnice cable-car station (more like a hotel). Half an hour beyond Kalatówki on the trail to Giewont is the *Hala Kondratowa Hostel* (20 beds). For location and atmosphere it's great, but note the small size.

Hikers wishing to traverse the park could begin at the *Roztoka Hostel* (96 beds, accessible via the Morskie Oko bus. An early start from Zakopane, however, would allow you to visit Morskie Oko in the morning and continue through to the *Pięć Stawów Hostel* (70 beds), a couple of hours' walk on the blue trail over a high pass from Morskie Oko. Pięć Stawów (Five Lakes) is the highest (1700 metres) and by far the most scenically located hostel in the Polish Tatras.

A good day's walk west of Pięć Stawów is the *Hala Gąsienicowa Hostel* (100 beds), from which one can return to Zakopane. In midsummer the most crowded hostels are Pięć Stawów and Hala Gąsienicowa. In the western part of the park are the *Ornak* (75 beds) and *Chochołowska* (161 beds) hostels, connected by trail.

Places to Eat
Bottom End *Bar Fis* across the street from the bus station is a cheap self-service open from 8 am to 8 pm.

At a pinch the *Bar Semafor* in the train station (open daily 6.30 am to 10 pm) is not bad and serves a good bowl of flaki (tripe soup).

Several pizzerias, a Chinese restaurant and a host of snack bars have sprung up along ulica Krupówki during the past few years – take your pick.

Bistro Pod Smrekami at Rondo is the closest self-service to the camping ground.

Top End Zakopane's finest restaurant is in the *Hotel 'Orbis-Giewont'*, ulica Kościuszki 1 diagonally across from the post office. The menu is in English and German, the service

POLAND

POLAND

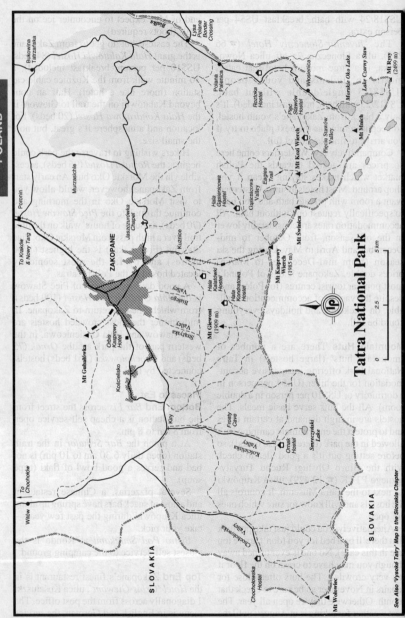

Tatra National Park

0   2.5   5 km

See Also 'Vysoké Tatry' Map in the Slovakia Chapter

good and there's even cold beer. Try a dish with bryndza (sheep cheese). The café serves a good breakfast. Though theoretically this place is open until 10 pm, the head waiter may deny you entry unless you have a reservation. *Restauracja Świarna* (also known as Grill Bar 'Dom Podhala'), ulica Kościuszki 4, across the street from the Giewont, is less pretentious and offers a set regional meal of cream soup and pork cutlet. The *Karcma Redykołka*, on the corner of Kościeliśka and Krupówki streets, is a rather touristy folkloric restaurant where the folk dances of the *górale* highlanders are performed some evenings at 8 pm (US$4 cover charge). A similar yet less touristically inundated place is *Restauracja U Wnuka*, ulica Kościeliśka 8, a block west of the old wooden church. This picturesque log edifice dating from 1850 and decorated with old glass folk paintings also contains a good café.

For regional dishes try the socialist-modern *Restauracja Wierchy*, ulica Tetmajera 2 at Krupówki. The menu is in English and German. From 8 pm to 2 am the Wierchy is a disco (US$3 admission, live music weekends).

A folklore-style restaurant worth seeking out is the *Karczma Obrochtówka*, ulica Kraszewskiego 10, a small street running between Zamoyskiego and Chałubińskiego streets halfway between 'Rondo' and town (coming from town, turn left at ulica Zamoyskiego 13a). Traditional Polish dishes are served in the basement of a large log house (Tuesday to Sunday noon to 10 pm). The menu is in English, French and German. This is perhaps the best of the various folkloric restaurants around Zakopane, though the beer is a little pricey. One reader reported that he had his four best meals in Poland here.

Cafés *Cocktail Bar Zakopaniański*, Krupówki 40, is a good place to have ice cream out on the terrace and watch the passing parade.

Entertainment

Concerts occasionally take place at the *Ośrodek Kultury*, ulica Kościuszki 4, as advertised on posters outside.

Your most reliable entertainment option is probably a movie at *Kino Sokól*, ulica Orkana 2, next to the fire hall just off ulica Krupówki.

The Karol Szymanowski Musical Days in July and the Festival of Highland Culture in August are local events to ask about.

Things to Buy

Street vendors in Zakopane sell woollen sweaters, caps, gloves and socks at reasonable prices. Bargaining should get you 25% off the first price but check the quality carefully.

Cepelia below the Hotel Gromada-Gajda sells a variety of folk handicrafts, amber jewellery, icons etc.

Getting There & Away

The *Tatry* express train (for which reservations are required) takes just over six hours to cover the 472 km from Warsaw to Zakopane via Kraków, departing from Warsaw in the early morning, Zakopane in the afternoon. It's seasonal, so check to see if it's operating at the time you wish to travel.

Two unreserved fast trains operate daily to/from Kraków (147 km, 2½ hours), the *Kasprowy* departing from Kraków in the morning, Zakopane in the afternoon, the *Giewont* doing the opposite. The *Giewont* also serves Częstochowa departing from Zakopane in the early morning, Częstochowa in the afternoon. Several other trains also operate between Zakopane and Częstochowa (five hours).

Overnight trains with couchettes and sleepers run between Zakopane and Gdańsk, Wrocław, Poznań and Warsaw. In July and August there's an overnight train between Zakopane and Olsztyn.

From Kraków to Zakopane it's often shorter, faster and cheaper to take a bus (100 km, 2½ hours, US$3) instead of the train, but book advance tickets at the bus station. The bus driver may charge you a small amount for baggage. Two buses a day run between

Zakopane and Lublin (a route poorly covered by train).

There's a direct Hungarian Volánbus daily from Zakopane to Budapest (364 km, nine hours, US$14), an excellent way to get from Poland to Hungary (Slovakian transit visa required by some). Get your ticket from the driver (reservations not possible).

Ask about buses direct to Poprad-Tatry, Poland.

To/From Slovakia Pedestrians may use the Łysa Polana highway border crossing off the road to Morskie Oko. All the Polana Palenica buses (eight daily in June and September, 13 daily in July and August, five daily the rest of the year) from Zakopane pass here. From Łysa Polana there's a road around to Tatranská Lomnica via Ždiar (30 km) with 15 buses a day. Pick up a few dollars worth of Slovakian crowns at an exchange office in Zakopane to pay your onward bus fare as there's no bank on the Slovakian side of the border. The exchange office on the Polish side of the border gives a poor rate but they will take travellers' cheques. Southbound this route is easy but northbound you could find the Polana Palenica bus to Zakopane crowded with daytrippers from Morskie Oko (in which case hitch, as the taxi drivers want 20 times the bus fare).

Getting Around
There are buses to Kuźnice several times an hour from stand No 7 in front of the bus station. Buy your ticket (US$0.25) inside the terminal.

The minibuses you see parked opposite the stations operate like large taxis (you must charter the entire vehicle) and unfortunately they do not compete with buses.

THE DUNAJEC GORGE
Every year tens of thousands of people go rafting on the Dunajec River, along a stretch where the river cuts through the Pieniny Mountains just before turning north to flow up towards the Vistula. The river runs right along the Polish-Slovakian border here, winding through a lovely wooded gorge with high cliffs on both sides. The mix of deciduous trees and conifers makes for lovely colour patterns. This is not a white-water experience: the rapids are gentle and you won't get wet (accidents are unheard of).

The Dunajec Gorge is an easy day trip from Zakopane. First take a bus from Zakopane to Nowy Targ (frequent service, 21 km, 30 minutes, US$1), then one of the six daily Sromowce Niżne buses from Nowy Tary to Kąty (31 km, one hour, US$1), a couple of km east of Sromowce Wyżne. The landing at Kąty is fairly obvious with a large parking lot and entrance pavilion on the left.

The 2½ hour raft trips operate from mid-May to mid-September with boats leaving as soon as 10 people sign up (US$7 per person). If you arrive in the morning you're almost certain to be able to go (weather and water level permitting). Each 10-seat raft consists of five wooden coffin-like sections lashed together, guided by two boatmen dressed in embroidered velvet folk costumes. At the other end the sections are taken apart, loaded onto a truck and carried back to Kąty.

The trip ends at Szczawnica, a health resort, from whence you'll easily be able to catch one of the 25 daily buses back to Nowy Targ (35 km, US$1). They stop up on the main highway, a five-minute walk from the raft landing (not in the tourist bus parking lot near the landing). If you leave Zakopane just before 8 am and catch an onward bus to Kąty by 9 am, you'll easily be back in Zakopane in time for dinner.

Dunajec raft trips are also offered from Červený Kláštor in Slovakia, but the Slovakian trips are shorter and not as easily arranged.

OŚWIĘCIM
Auschwitz (Oświęcim) and Birkenau (Brzezinka), two deadly Nazi concentration camps 60 km west of Kraków, have been preserved as memorials to the 1.5 million people of 28 nationalities who perished here, the overwhelming majority of them Jews. From all Europe the fascists brought their victims for slave labour purposes in the nearby armaments factories. Apart from the

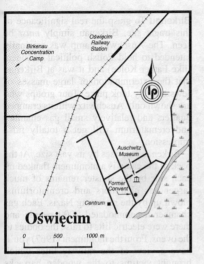

Birkenau
Concentration
Camp

Oświęcim
Railway
Station

lp

Auschwitz
Museum

Former
Convent

Centrum

Oświęcim

0   500   1000 m

main camps there were 40 subcamps scattered throughout the area. As one group of starving prisoners became too weak to continue, they were led into the gas chambers, their places taken by new arrivals off the trains. It's difficult to conceive of the minds that could invent such a system. Children (especially twins) were held in the camps for medical experimentation.

Today the main Auschwitz camp contains a museum, information centre, cinema and restaurant, while the Birkenau camp has been left more or less as it was found. Due to their enormous historical significance, these camps are an essential part of any trip to Europe and something not to be missed. Yet you should be aware that many of the present inhabitants of Oświęcim are not overjoyed about the connotations associated with their town and it's role as a focus of 'death camp tourism', so it's best to be as considerate in your dealings with them as possible.

Orientation

Oświęcim Railway Station is about two km north of the main Auschwitz camp. Birkenau is three km north-west of Auschwitz or two km south-west of the train station. The left-luggage office at the train station is open 24 hours a day.

As you come out of the train station turn right and follow ulica Wyzwolenia south-west along the railway line, then head south on ulica Stanisławy Leszcsyńskiej to the 'muzeum', a 20-minute walk.

Things to See

Auschwitz Established in May 1940 in what used to be Polish army barracks, Auschwitz was the original extermination camp, though the number of people held here was much smaller than in some other camps such as nearby Birkenau. The museum occupies the various prison blocks, with different blocks dedicated to victims from different countries.

Over the years different groups have tried to exploit Auschwitz for their own purposes. The museum itself was conceived during the communist era as an anti-fascist exhibition and the fact that most of the victims were Jewish was played down (as all ethnic, racial or religious divisions were minimised under communism). The various national pavilions dedicated to the countries which lost citizens to Auschwitz were seen as a means of fostering international solidarity against fascism.

The Catholic Church has also been accused of attempting to 'use' Auschwitz and something of a cult has formed around Father Maximilian Kolbe, an inmate who voluntarily took the place of another Catholic prisoner sentenced to death in 1941. In 1982 Pope John Paul II dispensed with the usual requirement of verifiable miracles and abruptly declared Father Kolbe a saint even though prior to WW II he had been an ultra-nationalist who edited an anti-Semitic Catholic newspaper.

In 1984 a Carmelite convent was established right against the camp walls, sparking protests from Jewish organisations which considered its presence a sacrilege. In 1987 the Catholic Church agreed to move the convent within two years and when this deadline was not met, seven US Jewish activists climbed over the convent fence and staged a sit-in in July 1989. The beating and forcible eviction inflicted on the seven Americans and further delays led to much bitterness, and only in 1993 did the nuns finally agree to move to a new building about a km away after receiving a direct order to do so from the pope. The old building is still there, complete with its security fence and warning signs in English, just around the corner from the museum entrance in the opposite direction to the train station.

In the past the exhibitions at Auschwitz have been criticised by Jewish writers for giving undue prominence to the 75,000 Polish Catholics killed here at the expense of the Jewish dead. One Canadian reader of this book wrote that he was shocked when he suddenly realised that the thousands of individual ID photos of the dead on display at the museum were all Catholic Poles! This approach seems to be changing and pavilion No 27 dedicated to the 'suffering and struggle of the Jews' already presents Auschwitz with chilling accuracy as the place of martyrdom of European Jewry.

The Auschwitz Museum (admission free) opens daily at 8 am and closes at 7 pm in June, July and August; at 6 pm in May and September; at 5 pm in March and November; at 4 pm in April and October; and at 3 pm in December, January and February. English-speaking guides can be hired at the museum information window, US$12 per group for one to 10 persons to visit Auschwitz, US$21 to visit both Auschwitz and Birkenau. The national pavilions are closed from October to April and can only be visited at that time with a guide (although pavilion No 27 is supposed to be open year-round). Pick up the guidebook which contains maps of the sites, plus information and photos. Near the museum entrance is a flower shop if you'd like to leave a token.

The museum cinema (US$0.35) shows a 15-minute Soviet film taken just after the 1945 liberation. Ask when they'll be showing the English version. If you pay US$5 they'll schedule an English showing just for you, although the film's message is clear in any language.

Birkenau To grasp the real significance of this tragic site, Birkenau simply *must* be seen. The Auschwitz camp was originally intended to hold Polish political prisoners (like Father Kolbe) and it was at Birkenau that the extermination of large masses of Jews actually took place. Tour groups who are shown only Auschwitz with its cramped quarters and relatively small gas chamber and crematorium will get a totally false impression.

Birkenau surprises by its vast size. At the back of the camp is a monument flanked on each side by the sinister remains of much larger gas chambers and crematoriums, blown up by the retreating Nazis. Each gas chamber accommodated 2000 people and there were electric lifts to raise the bodies to the ovens. From the monument (1967) you'll have a view of the railway lines which brought victims to the wooden barracks stretching out on each side, almost as far as the eye can see. The camp could hold 200,000 inmates at a time.

In summer a bus runs direct from Auschwitz to Birkenau five times a day. There are also taxis (parked to the left as you leave the museum) which will drive you around Birkenau and back to the train station for about US$5. It's preferable to see it on foot but you'll need two or three hours at least.

Places to Stay & Eat
A Catholic institution, the *Centrum* (☎ 0381-31 000), ulica Św M Kolbergo 1, offers clean accommodation in a four-storey building next to the new Carmelite convent, about a km south-west of Auschwitz. There are seven two-to-five-bedded rooms at US$10 per person for bed and breakfast (students US$5). In the evening group discussions are sometimes held here.

A large self-service cafeteria, *Bar Smak*, is next to the museum entrance. The buffet in the train station is also inexpensive.

Getting There & Away
Oświęcim is fairly easy to reach. There are six local trains a day from Kraków Główny Station (1½ hours), 12 trains a day from

Kraków Płaszów Station and 15 trains a day from Katowice (one hour). Check the times the day before as the services are irregular. Direct buses from Kraków (60 km, 1½ hours, US$2) pass the Auschwitz camp gate, although some terminate at a bus station on the opposite side of town (buses from there to the train station should pass the camp). The last bus back to Kraków leaves around mid-afternoon. There's fairly frequent bus service from the Auschwitz Museum to the train station. If there are a few of you, consider hiring a taxi at Kraków Bus Station for the excursion to Auschwitz and Birkenau (US$40 should be enough).

CZĘSTOCHOWA

Częstochowa (Tschenstochau) is the spiritual heart of Poland and pilgrims from every corner of the country come to Jasna Góra (Luminous Mountain) Monastery to worship the image of the Black Madonna, Poland's holiest icon. The best time to arrive is at dawn when the churches are overflowing with nuns in silent prayer. This could be the most sacred place you'll ever visit.

History

Częstochowa was first mentioned in 1220. In 1382 Duke Władysław of Opole invited the Paulites of Hungary to establish Jasna Góra Monastery, and the famous icon of the Black Madonna was brought from the east in 1384. The story goes that it had been painted at Jerusalem by St Luke. In 1430 the image was cut by invading Protestant Hussites and during restoration a scar from the sword blow was left on the Madonna's face as a reminder.

Early in the 17th century the monastery was fortified and subsequent Swedish (1655) and Russian (1770) sieges were resisted. Rebuilding took place after a fire in 1690, and centuries of patronage have increased the richness of Jasna Góra. Industry developed in the town at the end of the 19th century with the building of the railway from Warsaw to Vienna, and the communists built Częstochowa into a major industrial centre

to balance the clerical influence at Jasna Góra. Today Częstochowa has a steel works with 30,000 employees, plus clothing, chemical and paper industries.

Orientation

The main train station (shown on our map) is undergoing renovation and the baggage room (open 24 hours except for three 30-minute breaks) has been moved several times recently – just keeping looking. Alternatively use the left-luggage office at information in the bus station (open from 7 am to 6 pm).

From the main train station, walk north a block to Aleje Najświętszej Marii Panny, locally known as Aleje NMP. Jasna Góra is on a low hill at the end of this important avenue, one km due west. If you're arriving in the early morning darkness you'll see a bright light high above the monastery.

A few local trains to Wrocław and Poznań use Częstochowa Stradom Railway Station on the south side of town (check).

Information

A very helpful tourist information office (☎ 41 360) is at Aleje NMP 65. It sells maps of many other cities in Poland.

The Polski Związek Motorowy (☎ 43 413 or 42 169), Aleje NMP 4, assists motorists.

Money The NBP Bank, Piłsudskiego 5 near the train station (weekdays 8 am to 1 pm, Saturday 8 to 11 am), changes travellers' cheques for 1.5% commission. The PKO Bank, Aleje NMP 19 (Monday to Saturday 8 am to 6 pm), also changes travellers' cheques.

The reception of the Orbis Patria Hotel will change travellers' cheques for 3% commission daily from 7 am to 7 pm.

Post & Telecommunications There's a telephone centre in the main post office next to the bus station (weekdays 7 am to 9 pm, weekends 8 am to 9 pm). Częstochowa's telephone code is 034.

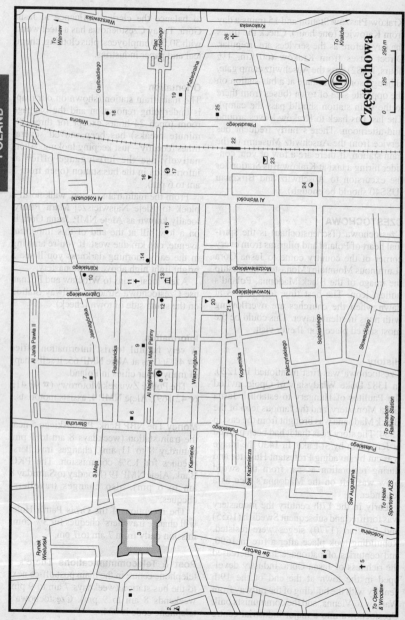

Częstochowa

To Warsaw

Warszawska

Krakowska

To Kraków

Plac Daszyńskiego

Garibaldiego

Katedralna

26

19

18

25

Piłsudskiego

Wilsona

22

23

24

16

17

Al Kościuszki

Al Wolności

15

14

Modzelewskiego

10

11

13

Nowowiejskiego

Kilińskiego

Dąbrowskiego

12

20

21

Sobieskiego

Kopernika

Słowackiego

Al Jana Pawła II

Jasnogórska

Radławicka

9

Waszyngtona

Paczyńskiego

Pułaskiego

To Stradom Railway Station

Starucha

8

6

Al Najświętszej Marii Panny

Pułaskiego

Św Kazimierza

To Hotel Sportowy AZS

3 Maja

Rynek Wieluński

3

7 Kamienic

Św Augustyna

Kościelna

To Opole & Wrocław

Św Barbary

Św Barbary

1

2

4

5

250 m

125

0

PLACES TO STAY

1	Dom Pielgrzyma
2	Camping Oleńka No 76
4	Dom Rekolekcyjny
6	Orbis Patria Hotel
7	Summer Youth Hostel
9	Logos Foundation
19	Hotel Miły
25	Hotel Centralny-Polonia

PLACES TO EAT

16	Pizzeria La Bussola
20	Restauracja Wiking
21	Bar Jedyny

OTHER

3	Jasna Góra Monastery
5	Church of St Barbara
8	Tourist Office
10	Theatre
11	Church of St Andrew
12	Art Gallery
13	City Museum
14	Orbis
15	Almatur
17	PKO Bank
18	Filharmonia Concert Hall
22	Railway Station
23	Post Office
24	Bus Station
26	Cathedral

POLAND

Travel Agencies For express train tickets, couchettes and information try Orbis, Aleje NMP 40.

Things to See

Today **Jasna Góra Monastery** retains the appearance of a fortress, a vibrant symbol of Catholicism tossed in a secular sea. Inside the compound are two churches. The large Baroque church you enter first is beautifully decorated, but the image of the Black Madonna is on the high altar of the smaller, less ornate church. It's hidden behind a silver curtain (1673) and only exposed during the frequent religious services. This makes it difficult to have a close look. Upstairs in the convent adjacent to the churches is the Sala Rycerska where you can examine a copy of the icon up close.

There are also three museums to visit within the monastery's defensive walls (open daily). You can't miss the **Arsenal** (open 9 am to noon and 2 to 6 pm). The **600 Year Museum** (open 11 am to 4.30 pm), containing Lech Wałęsa's 1983 Nobel Prize, is just beyond. The **Treasury** or *Skarbiec* (open 9 am to noon and 3 to 5 pm) is rather hidden. It's above and behind the two churches and you enter from an outside terrace. You can also climb the monastery tower.

On weekends and holidays there are long lines to enter all three museums, and the crowds in the smaller church may be so thick you're almost unable to enter, much less get near the icon. A great 10-day pilgrimage on foot from Warsaw reaches here on Assumption Day (15 August).

The **City Museum** (closed Monday and Tuesday) in the old town hall (rebuilt 1908) on Plac Biegańskiego has an excellent historical collection and much information on the chain of ruined castles perched on top of sandstone crags along the 'Eagles' Nests Route' between Częstochowa and Kraków, once the border between Poland and Bohemia. The local **art gallery** (closed Monday and Tuesday) nearby at Aleje NMP 47 is also well worth visiting.

Places to Stay

Camping On the far side of the tour-bus parking lot behind the monastery is pleasant *Camping Oleńka No 76* (☎ 47 495; open from May to September). It's US$1.25 per person to pitch a tent, and rooms are US$4/7 single/double without bath, US$14/18/22 for three/four/five people with bath. There's a snack bar.

Summertime Hostels In July and August a seasonal *youth hostel* (☎ 43 121) functions in the three-storey school building at ulica Jasnagórska 84/90 (entry around the back).

POLAND

Also in July and August, it's possible to get a dorm bed for US$2 at the *Logos Foundation* (☎ 42 925), Aleje NMP 56, provided all the rooms are not occupied by groups. No bedding is provided.

Check with Almatur, Aleje NMP 37, for information on accommodation in student dormitories in summer. There's no office renting private rooms in Częstochowa (hopefully a landlady will find you).

Catholic Hostels *Dom Pielgrzyma* (☎ 43 302), the large building on the north side of the parking lot behind the monastery, has beds in double and triple rooms at US$10 per person (check-in from 3 to 8 pm, doors close at 10 pm). This church-operated facility is probably what you want if you came for strictly religious reasons.

Dom Rekolekcyjny, ulica Św Barbary 43 a couple of blocks south of Jasna Góra, also shelters pilgrims (doors closed from 10 pm to 5 am).

Hotels The three-storey *Hotel Centralny-Polonia* (☎ 44 067), at ulica Piłsudskiego 9 opposite the eastern exit from the train station, is US$12/20/25 single/double/triple without bath, US$22/28/35 with bath, breakfast included.

The *Hotel Miły* (☎ 43 391), nearby at ulica Katedralna 18, is US$10/12 double/triple without bath, US$14/15 with bath (no singles). It's often full.

A km south of Dom Rekolekcyjny is *Hotel Sportowy AZS* (☎ 55 247), ulica Św Andrzeja 8/10, in a neat white two-storey building. If you happen to arrive at Częstochowa Stradon Railway Station you'll find this hotel about halfway to the monastery. It's US$10/14 double/triple (no singles) and if there's no one at the reception, check the back room downstairs. Since this place isn't often used by pilgrims, it's more likely to have rooms.

Places to Eat

Pizzeria La Bussola, Aleje NMP 16, services genuine pizza and beer, while *Restauracja Sir*, Aleje NMP 24, features Polish dishes.

Restaurajca Wiking, ulica Nowowiejskiego 10, has two sections: an up-market dining room facing the main street and a cheaper bar with a few tables on the terrace around the side. Both serve Wiking Brok beer.

Farther up the same street is Częstochowa's last old fashioned milk bar, *Bar Jedyny*, ulica Nowowiejskiego 14.

Other than the *Orbis Patria Hotel* there's nowhere decent to eat up around the monastery. The tired staff of the cafeteria/bar adjacent to *Dom Pielgrzyma* dispense cheap, tasteless food to a pushy, queue-jumping crowd from 7 am to 9 pm.

A 24-hour convenience store is at Aleje NMP 67.

Getting There & Away

There are direct trains to Częstochowa from Warsaw (235 km, 3½ hours), Opole (95 km), Katowice (86 km, two hours), Kraków (two hours) and Zakopane (five hours). Local trains run almost hourly to Katowice where there are connections to Kraków and Wrocław. An overnight train with couchettes departs for Gdańsk-Sopot-Gdynia around 10 pm nightly year-round. Warsaw-bound trains from Budapest, Vienna and Prague also stop here.

The *Opolanin* express train runs daily all year between Częstochowa and Warsaw (three hours), departing from Warsaw in the late afternoon and Częstochowa in the morning. Reservations are required.

To go to Cieszyn (Czech border) you'll probably have to change trains at Katowice and Bielsko-Biała (allow six hours by local train, including the two changes). There's one morning train direct to Bielsko Biała (141 km, three hours).

Buses departing from Częstochowa include three daily to Kraków (114 km), three daily to Wrocław (176 km) and one a day to Zakopane (222 km).

BIELSKO-BIAŁA

On your way to/from the Czech Republic border at Cieszyn you may pass through Bielsko-Biała which has three daily trains to

Kraków, 11 to Cieszyn, 30 to Katowice (55 km) and two express trains direct to Warsaw (376 km). From the train station a pedestrian bridge leads across to Bielsko-Biała Bus Station where you have a choice of 12 buses a day to Cieszyn (35 km) and 17 to Kraków (86 km).

Several large city maps are posted outside the bus and train stations. If connections force you to spend the night here the *PTTK Dom Wycieczkowy* (☎ 23 018), ulica Krasińskiego 38, about three blocks west of the bus station, has double rooms at US$8 and beds in six and seven-bed dorms at US$4 per person. It's closed from 10 pm to 6 am. There's also a year-round *youth hostel* (☎ 27 466) at ulica Komorowicka 25, about six blocks east of the train station. Otherwise all the hotels of Bielsko-Biała are expensive.

CIESZYN

The Polish border town, Cieszyn, sits in a verdant valley, separated from Český Těšín, Czech Republic, by the Olza River. The town has a quaint central square and some old churches but the only real reason to come here is to walk across one of the two one-way bridges linking the countries.

In Cieszyn the bus and train stations are adjacent about one km from the border, but the bus station has two sections a block apart. The left-luggage area at the train station is open 24 hours excepting two one-hour breaks. Ten trains a day link Cieszyn to Bielska-Biała and one goes on to Katowice, but there are none to points beyond. Buses move faster than the trains and you can choose from among 10 buses a day to Bielsko-Biała (35 km), 14 to Katowice (76 km) and six to Kraków (121 km).

Camping Olza is at Aleje Łyska 13, by the river a few blocks south of Rynek. At last report the old *Hotel 'Pod Brunatnym Jeleniem'*, Rynek 20, was closed for renovations and the other hotels of Cieszyn are expensive. You'll probably find a cheaper room in Český Těšín across the river (for more information turn to the Český Těšín section at the end of the Czech Republic chapter of this book).

The Bank Śląski, ulica Mennicza 1 just off Rynek (weekdays 8 am to 5 pm, Saturday 8 am to 1 pm), changes travellers' cheques, and there are several cash-only exchange offices around town. Change excess złoty into crowns at one of these before crossing over.

If you need a Czech visa, the nearest Czech consulate (☎ 518 576) is at ulica Pawła Stelmacha 21, Katowice.

Silesia

Silesia (Śląsk) in south-western Poland is the industrial heart of the country. Although Silesia accounts for only 6% of Poland's area, it provides a fifth of its wealth, including half its steel and 90% of its coal (8% of the world supply). The Upper Silesian Basin around Katowice, source of both the Vistula and Odra rivers, is densely developed, populated and polluted. Lower Silesia stretches north-west along the Odra past Wrocław. The fertile farming area between Opole and Wrocław is known as 'Green Silesia' while the coal-mining region of Upper Silesia is called 'Black Silesia'.

Silesia was originally inhabited by Slavic tribes, the largest of which, known as the Ślęzanie, gave their name to the region. Medieval Silesia was autonomous under Piast princes. In 1335 Silesia was annexed to Bohemia and from 1526 to 1742 it was under Austria's Habsburgs. Frederick the Great took Silesia for Prussia in 1742. Throughout the German period the large Polish minority was subjected to 'Germanisation'. After WW I Polish nationalist uprisings resulted in most of Upper Silesia going to Poland while Lower Silesia remained part of Germany until 1945. That year the German population was expelled and Silesia returned to Poland after a lapse of six centuries.

While tourists may not be attracted to the industrial wonders of Katowice and its vicinity, Wrocław is an old historic city with an intense cultural life. The Sudeten Mountains west of Kłodzko (the 'Góry Stołowe') and

POLAND

POLAND

south of Jelenia Góra (Karkonoski Park Narodowy) lure hikers.

WROCŁAW

Wrocław (pronounced 'vrotslau'), historic capital of Lower Silesia, was German Breslau from 1742 until 1945. In the 13th century Wrocław had been capital of a local Piast dynasty, then the town passed from Bohemia to the Habsburgs and finally Prussia. During the final phase of WW II, the Nazis fortified the area and though surrounded, the 40,000 German soldiers at 'Festung Breslau' held out from 15 February to 6 May, only surrendering after Berlin fell on 2 May 1945. In the course of this 81-day siege 70% of the city was destroyed.

Immediately after the war, any German residents who hadn't already fled were deported and the ruins were resettled by Poles from L'vov in Ukraine. People in Wrocław still have a sentimental attachment to L'vov and you'll sometimes see historical displays on that city in the museums, or advertising for tourist trips to L'vov. Even the local beer brewed in Wrocław is called 'piwo Lwów' (though Wrocław's 'Piast' beer is better).

Today this enjoyable big city by the Odra offers good museums, historic buildings, concert halls, theatres, parks and over 120 canals, plus a picturesque central square and a memorable cluster of churches by the river. Wrocław is a lively cultural centre, a students' city, and the clubs are packed if anything's happening. It's all conveniently located so you can do most of your sightseeing on foot.

Orientation

Wrocław Główny Railway Station buzzes with activity 24 hours a day and most of the hotels are conveniently nearby. The left-luggage area inside the train station is open 24 hours. To walk to Rynek, the old market square, turn left on ulica Piłsudskiego and walk three blocks to ulica Świdnicka. Turn right and continue straight into town.

The addresses of buildings around the edge of the square are given as 'Rynek' while the block in the middle of the square is called 'Rynek-Ratusz'.

Information

The 'Odra' tourist information office, ulica Piłsudskiego 98, is below Hotel Piast I diagonally opposite the train station.

The PTTK tourist information centre, Rynek 38, is closed weekends and holidays.

The Polski Związek Motorowy, ulica Hauke-Bosaka 20, is the place to go for information if you're having car problems.

Money There are several exchange offices in the train station changing cash 24 hours a day. One is marked by a circular yellow sign next to the left-luggage office. Another with a red sign 'Kantor Korona' just a little farther down gives a slightly better rate. Compare.

To change a travellers' cheque you must go to the PKO bank, Plac Solny 16 (weekdays 8 am to 5.30 pm, Saturday 8 am to 3 pm).

Post & Telecommunications Mail addressed to Poste Restante, ulica Krasińskiego 1, 50-415 Wrocław, Poland, is kept at window No 2 in the main post office at that address. A branch post office is at Rynek 28.

There's a telephone centre at ulica Malachowskiego 1, to the right as you leave the train station, which is open 24 hours a day. Wrocław's telephone code is 071.

Travel Agencies Orbis, at ulica Piłsudskiego 62, is where you go to buy international train tickets, reserve seats, couchettes etc.

The Orbis offices at Rynek 29 and ulica Piłsudskiego 62 sell international bus tickets to Munich (twice weekly, US$50), Frankfurt/Main (twice weekly, US$50), Cologne (twice weekly, US$45), Amsterdam (twice weekly, US$75), Paris (three times a week, US$82), Brussels (twice weekly, US$75) and London (weekly, 27 hours, US$100). These services operate year-round and on return tickets the return portion is 50% cheaper than a one way.

Haisig & Knabe, Rynek 45, also sells

international bus tickets to many European cities, such as London, Vienna, Brussels, Lyon, Paris, Athens, Amsterdam, Geneva, Zürich, Rome and others. They also know about buses to Scandinavian cities departing from Poznań.

Bookshops Foreign books are available from the bookstore at Rynek 59. The map store at ulica Oławska 2, behind the Orbis office Rynek 29, has maps of many Polish cities. For hiking maps try the PTTK, ulica Wita Stwosza 15.

You can get the *Warsaw Voice* from the newsagent at Plac Kościuszki 21/23.

Things to See
The Old Town As you walk along ulica Świdnicka into town you'll pass **Corpus Christi Church** on the right and the neoclassical **Opera House** (1872) on the left. Next to the Monopol Hotel is **St Dorothy's Church**. When you reach the pedestrian underpass turn left a block to the Ethnographic and Archaeological **museums** (both are closed Monday and Tuesday). They have separate entrances but are in the same complex at ulica Kazimierza Wielkiego 34/35. Unfortunately, only Polish captions are posted in the Archaeological Museum, making the exhibits rather meaningless to foreigners.

Continue west again in the same direction and turn right across the street the first chance you get, then straight around into Plac Solny, the old salt market which is now a flower market and spills into Rynek, the medieval marketplace with its Renaissance and Baroque burgher houses. Wrocław's Gothic **Ratusz** (town hall), built between 1327 and 1504, is one of the most intricate in Poland and now contains a museum (closed Monday and Tuesday, free Wednesday) in the arched interior. On the north-west corner of Rynek is 14th century **St Elizabeth's Church** with its 83-metre tower. The two small houses on the corner, connected by a gate, are known as Hansel and Gretel.

Walk east from this church along the north side of Rynek and continue due east on ulica Wita Stwosza, with a digression to visit the Gothic **Church of St Mary Magdalene** on the right. Note the 12th century Romanesque portal on the far side of the church.

Museums & Churches Keep straight on ulica Wita Stwosza till you reach the Orbis Panorama Hotel. The **Museum of Architecture** (closed Monday, free Wednesday) in the 15th century convent across the street from the hotel has a scale model of Wrocław as it appeared in 1740.

In the park around behind this museum is the **Panorama Racławicka**, a huge 360° painting of the Battle of Racławice (1794) near Kraków during which the national hero, Tadeusz Kościuszko, led the Poles against Russian forces intent on partitioning Poland. Created by Jan Styka and Wojciech Kossak for the centenary of the battle in 1894, the painting is 120 metres long and 15 metres high. It was displayed at L'vov until 1939, then held in storage for over four decades due to political considerations (might have offended Poland's erstwhile Soviet allies) and only reopened at Wrocław in 1985. You're given headphones with an English or German commentary, but they screech and the story is difficult to follow.

You may have difficulty getting panorama tickets (admission US$4, students US$2, closed Monday) as visitors are only admitted 17 times a day in groups of 40 persons, and tour groups often book all the showings a couple of days in advance. Check for tickets early during your stay. Someone standing at the door may offer to sell you a ticket purchased earlier which they cannot use.

Just east beside the park is the **National Museum** (closed Monday, free Thursday) with a large collection of masterpieces of medieval Silesian art. The Panorama Racławicka admission ticket is also valid for a same-day visit to this museum. Cross the bridge over the Odra beside the museum, taking a glance upstream at the **Most**

POLAND

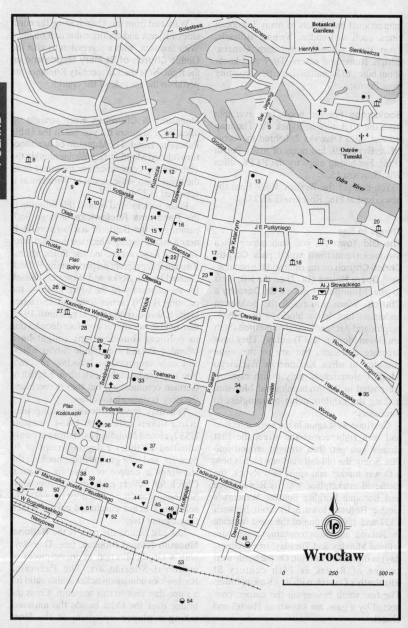

Wrocław

0   250   500 m

POLAND

PLACES TO STAY	52	Cocktail Bar	21	Ratusz (Town Hall)
			22	Church of St Mary
14	Teachers' Hostel	**OTHER**		Magdalene
23	Hotel Saigon		25	Post Office
24	Orbis Panorama	1	Botanical Gardens	27	Archaeological
	Hotel	2	Archdiocesan		Museum
26	PTTK Stacja		Museum	29	St Dorothy's Church
	Turystyczna	3	Church of the Holy	31	Opera House
28	DaiMen Hotel		Cross	32	Corpus Christi
30	Monopol Hotel	4	Cathedral		Church
40	Hotel Polonia	5	Church of the	33	Puppet Theatre
41	Savoy Hotel		Virgin Mary on	34	Bastion
43	Hotel Piast II		the Sands	35	Polski Związek
45	Hotel Europejski	6	Jesuit Church		Motorowy
46	Hotel Piast I	7	Collegium Maximum	36	Centrum Depart-
47	Grand Hotel	8	Arsenal (Military		ment Store
			Museum)	37	Pałacyk Student
PLACES TO EAT	9	Rura Jazz Club		Club & Almatur
		10	St Elizabeth's	38	Orbis
11	Miś Milk Bar		Church	39	Casino
12	Café Pod	13	Market	46	Tourist Office
	Kalamburen	17	Art Gallery	48	Old Bus Station
15	Rancho Pizzeria	18	Museum of	49	Teatr Polski
16	Café Studnią		Architecture	50	Happy 7 Night Club
42	Cyganeria	19	Panorama	51	Operetka Theatre
	Restauracja		Racławicka	53	Railway Station
44	Wzorcowy Milk Bar	20	National Museum	54	New Bus Station

Grunwaldzki (1910), the most graceful of Wrocław's 90 bridges.

On the north side of the river, turn left when the tram tracks bend right and walk west into Ostrów Tumski, an old quarter inhabited since the 9th century. In the 10th century the ducal palace was here. The chapels at the rear of the Gothic **Cathedral of St John the Baptist** deserve special attention, though they're usually kept securely locked. The **Archdiocesan Museum** (closed Monday) is at ulica Kanonia 12 between the cathedral and the **Botanical Gardens** (admission US$1.50). The gardens (established in 1811) are a lovely, restful corner of the city well worth seeking out.

West again from the cathedral is the two-storey Gothic **Church of the Holy Cross**. Keep straight and cross the small bridge to the 14th century **Church of the Virgin Mary on the Sands** which has a stunning Gothic interior.

Southbound now, follow the tram tracks across another small bridge to the huge, red-brick **city market** (1908). Then follow the riverbank downstream a block or two till you reach a large **Jesuit Church** (1755) with the **Collegium Maximum** (1741) just beyond. Inside this ornate Baroque building is the magnificent Aula Leopoldina, now used for formal university functions.

Parks & Zoo Take a taxi or tram No 1, 2, 4, 10, or 12 east to Wrocław's enjoyable **zoo** (US$1.50), Poland's oldest. In summer, **excursion boats** operate on a branch of the Odra several times a day from the landing beside the zoo.

Across the street from the zoo is a famous early work of modern architecture, **Centenary Hall** or 'Hala Ludova', erected in 1913 by the noted German architect Max Berg to commemorate the defeat of Napoleon in 1813. Enter to appreciate this great enclosed space. The steel needle beside the hall was

POLAND

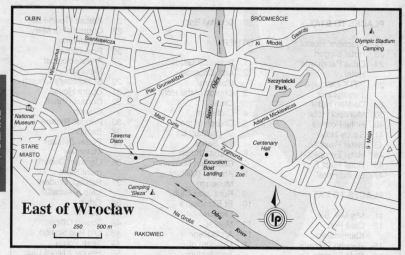

OLBIN

ŚRÓDMIEŚCIE

H. Sienkiewicza

J. Wróżki

Al. Młodej Gwardii

Olympic Stadium
Camping

Plac Grunwaldzki

Odra

Szczytnicki
Park

National
Museum

Marii Curie

Stara Odra

Adama Mickiewicza

9 Maja

STARE
MIASTO

Tawerna
Disco

Centenary
Hall

Zygmunta

Excursion
Boat
Landing

Zoo

Camping
'Sleza'

East of Wrocław

0   250   500 m

Na Grobli

Odra   River

RAKOWIEC

the symbol of the 1948 Exhibition of the
Regained Territories. The **Szczytnicki Park**
beyond includes an attractive Japanese
garden.

Circle Trip Provided there are no obstruc-
tions due to road works, tram No 0 makes a
complete loop around Wrocław in about 45
minutes, the best city tour you'll ever get for
US$0.25. You can pick it up in front of the
train station.

Places to Stay

Camping Wrocław's *camping ground*
(☎ 484 651) is near the Olympic Stadium
across Szczytnicki Park from the zoo on the
east side of the city (trams Nos 9, 16, and 17
pass the entrance). There's a row of simple,
clean bungalows (US$4 per person), and
from May to September foreigners wishing
to pitch a tent (US$2 per person plus US$1
per tent) are *never* turned away. English and
German are spoken.

Hostels The *youth hostel* (☎ 38 856) at ulica
Kołłotaja 20, just behind the Grand Hotel, a
few minutes' walk from the train station, is
US$3 for the first night, US$2 for subsequent

nights. Only dorm beds are available and it's
usually full in midsummer but a good bet the
rest of the year (open all year). The receptionist will hold your luggage until they open
at 5 pm.

The PTTK runs a *Stacja turystyczna*
(☎ 443 073) at ulica Szajnochy 11 (upstairs)
just off Plac Solny in the old town. The hostel
reception is only open from 5 to 9 pm and a
bed in a six, 10, or 18-bed dormitory will be
around US$4. It's open all year.

The *Ośrodek Zakwaterowań Nauczycieli*
(☎ 443 781), ulica Kotlarska 42 right in the
middle of town, is a teachers' hostel with
rooms at US$10 single or double, or US$6
for a bed in a three-bed dorm, US$5 for a bed
in a four-bed dorm. This place is really
intended for teachers only but it will take
others if space is available.

Almatur, ulica Kościuszki 34, will know
about accommodation in student dormitories
in summer.

Private Rooms Odra Tourist, ulica Piłsudskiego 98 opposite the train station, can
arrange private rooms at US$7 per person.
Before paying ask them to point out the
location on their map.

Hotels Near the Station A whole row of relatively inexpensive hotels line ulica Piłsudskiego, to the left as you come out of the train station. The *Grand Hotel* (☎ 33 983), ulica Piłsudskiego 102 right across from the station, is US$14/20 single/double without bath, US$17/25 with bath, breakfast included. *Hotel Piast I* (☎ 30 033), just west on the next corner, is US$10/19 single/double without bath, US$23 double with bath.

The *Hotel Europejski* (☎ 31 071), at ulica Piłsudskiego 94/96, charges US$20/32 single/double for a 2nd-class room, US$27/40 for a 1st-class room, private bath and breakfast included in all. Quieter is the *Hotel Piast II* (☎ 445 447) around the corner at ulica Stawowa 13 (US$10/19 single/double without bath, US$23 double with bath, breakfast not included).

Hotel Polonia (☎ 31 021), ulica Piłsudskiego 66, is more expensive than any of the hotels just mentioned (US$24/36 single/double with bath and breakfast). Wrocław's casino is beside the Polonia.

Rooms facing the street in the Grand, Piast I, Europejski and Polonia hotels get a lot of tram noise; the Piast II is on a quiet side street.

Hotels in Town The five-storey *Hotel Savoy*, Plac Kościuszki 19, is a bargain at US$10/13/15 single/double/triple with bath. It's free of streetcar noise.

The old three-storey *Hotel DaiMen*, ulica Kazimierza Wielkiego 45, has rooms with shared bath at US$16/22 single/double, including breakfast.

Of the four Orbis hotels the stylish *Monopol Hotel* (☎ 37 041), ulica Modrzejewskiej 2 beside the Opera House, is the most colourful (from US$22/35 single/double without bath, US$32/50 with bath, breakfast included). The Monopol was erected in 1890 and Hitler would stay here whenever he visited Breslau and would address the crowds from the balcony.

The *Hotel Saigon* (☎ 442 881), ulica Wita Stwosza 22/23, has rooms beginning at US$19/35 single/double with bath plus US$3 per person for breakfast (extra charge for a TV or king-size bed). This renovated five-storey hotel near the centre of town is a good medium-priced choice. Their Vietnamese restaurant is good.

Places to Eat
Near the Station Wrocław doesn't shine in the food department, and there's no good middle-level place to eat near the train station (*Mamma Mia Pizza* inside the train station itself is open 24 hours a day). The *Europejski* and *Polonia* hotels both have restaurants; ask what's available before struggling with the Polish/German menu.

Fast-food places have mushroomed in Wrocław in recent years and the numerous establishments of this kind along ulica Piłsudskiego near Hotel Polonia need no introduction. *Wzorcowy Milk Bar*, ulica Piłsudskiego 86, a block from the station (closed Sunday), would be great if they didn't tend to overcharge foreigners.

The *Cyganeria Restaurant*, ulica Kościuszki 37, looks bad at first – full of men drinking warm beer and vodka straight – but actually the food is quite good and the staff are friendly.

In the Old Town Most of the city's best eating and drinking places are conveniently located around Rynek. *Vega Bar Wegetariański*, Rynek Ratusz 27a, on the corner of Sukiennice behind the old town hall, has cheap cafeterias upstairs and down. Students feast on Polish peasant specialities here. You're supposed to return your tray to the counter. Look for a green building, part of the block in the middle of the square – it's worth taking a few minutes to locate.

Other cheap places around here include *Miś Milk Bar*, ulica Kuźnicza 48, a typical self-service, and *Rancho Pizzeria*, ulica Szewska 59/60. *Café Mona Liza*, Rynek 16/17, offers borsch, steak, and ice cream.

Zorba Bar, Przejście Garncarskie 8, hidden right in the middle of the block in the centre of Rynek, grills great souvlaki and other Greek dishes. It's visible through the passage at Rynek-Ratusz 15.

The *Piwnica Świdnicka Restaurant*, in a basement of the old town hall, serves reasonable meals in a medieval setting which dates back to the 14th century. Unfortunately, the cacophony of rock music directed at you from several directions obliterates most of the atmosphere (though some readers say they like it).

Spiż, Rynek-Ratusz 2, diagonally opposite the old town hall, is a subterranean German-style restaurant where they brew their own beer. The restaurant is up-market but a mug of their rich 13% brew or 12% pils in the wood-panelled bar should fit into almost anyone's budget and belly. You can even get huge one-litre mugs of rich black beer. The bar opens at 8 am and there's a beer garden on the square outside.

If you assumed from the American Express stickers in the window that the *Królewska Restaurant* at Dwór Wazów, Rynek 5, might be expensive, you'd be right. If price means anything to you at all, skip the meal and go upstairs to the very elegant café where you can get ice cream and a glass of wine for a more manageable sum. The elegant dining room in the *Monopol Hotel* is good for a splurge and there are even a few vegetarian dishes on the menu.

Cafés & Bars *Herbowa*, Rynek 19, is a teahouse serving excellent desserts. On weekend evenings it becomes a disco. *U Prospera*, Rynek 27, is a billiard bar open around the clock.

Pod Papagami, ulica Sukiennice 9a, is a students pub which opens at 5 pm daily. It's a great place to go for a beer and unless there's live entertainment no cover charge is payable. The entrance is under the archway directly behind Spiż in the centre of Rynek.

Bar U Prasoła, Plac Solny 11 (through the archway), is open from noon to 11 pm. Avoid the *John Bull Pub*, Plac Solny 6, which is expensive and only for tourists. A 24-hour bottle shop is at Plac Solny 8/9.

Pod Kalamburen, ulica Kuźnicza 29a, is an elegant Art Nouveau-style café.

Cafe Studnią, ulica Szewska 19, is a students' bar with a good atmosphere. In the cellar below Cafe Studnią is the *Club 'Pod Studnią'* where there's sometimes live music. There's even a no-smoking section! The two bars are under separate management so you might have to enter the club through the yellow door around the corner on ulica Kotłarska.

There are three unpretentious places at the *Pałacyk Student Club*. The *Klub Samo Zycie* in the basement is a pub where a rock band is often playing. The billiard bar on the main floor is good for a game or just a drink and upstairs there's a lively disco.

The *Cocktail Bar*, ulica Komandorska 4a off Piłsudskiego, serves about the best coffee and ice cream in town.

Entertainment

Wrocław is a major cultural centre and during the winter season you'll have a lot to choose from. Check the listings in the morning papers, *Słowo Polskie* and *Gazeta Robotnicza*, or the evening paper, *Wieczór Wrocławia*.

At the *Operetka Theatre*, ulica Piłsudskiego 67, actors, actresses, costumes, music, scenery – everything is superb. The *Teatr Polski*, nearby at ulica Zapolskiej 3 off Piłsudskiego, also offers excellent performances in Polish. If Wrocław's *mime theatre* performs here during your stay, don't miss it. Also check *Filharmonia Hall*, ulica Piłsudskiego 17, and the *Opera House*, ulica Świdnicka 35. The architectural splendour of the opera complements the excellence of the performances.

The *Wrocławski Teatr Lalek*, Plac Teatralny 4, offers puppet theatre for kids several times a week at 10 and 11 am.

Annual musical events include the Festival of Polish Contemporary Music held in February, the 'Jazz of the Odra' jazz festival in May, the Flower Fair in July, the International Oratorio and Cantata Festival, 'Vratislavia Cantans', in September and the Days of Old Masters' Music in early December.

Discos What Wrocław loses in the food department it more than makes up with its varied and lively nightlife. A good place to start is the *Klub Związków Twórczyca*, Rynek Ratusz 24, Wrocław's most popular disco among the city youth (opens at 9 pm, US$5 admission). From noon to 9 pm the locale is an expensive-looking but reasonably priced restaurant with a menu in English.

A slightly older crowd frequents *Bachus Disco Club*, Rynek 16 (open from 4 pm to 5 am daily). It's downstairs through the café.

Be sure to attend any jam sessions at the *Rura Jazz Club*, ulica Łazienna 4. Great! This club is to move to a new location in the near future, so check the address at the tourist office.

On Friday and Saturday nights there's a disco at the *Pałacyk Student Club*, ulica Kościuszki 34 (8 pm to 3 am).

Wrocław's up-market disco is *Happy 7 Night Club* (☎ 442 332), ulica Świdnicka 53 (open daily from 10 pm, cover US$4). Dress sharp to feel comfortable here.

If you don't mind paying extra for taxi fares, *Bravo* in Centenary Hall (Hala Ludowa) is another popular disco. Halfway back to town from Bravo is the *Tawerna Disco*, ulica Wybrzeże Wyspiańskiego 40 (closed Sunday), across the street from the Politechnika Wrocławska.

Things to Buy

Wrocław's shopping is concentrated around Plac Kościuszki and along ulica Świdnicka to Rynek. The largest of the department stores is Centrum, ulica Świdnicka 40 at Plac Kościuszki. Have a look around.

Cepelia, Plac Kościuszki 12, has an excellent selection of Polish handicrafts and some amber jewellery. Right next door is the Philatelic Bureau at No 11 with some unusual bargains. Hitler stamps issued by the Nazi 'General Government' in Kraków are sold here. For antiques it's Desa, Plac Kościuszki 16.

Pro Musica, Rynek 49, has Polish CDs and cassettes.

Getting There & Away

Train Main lines from Szczecin to Przemyśl (via Poznań and Kraków), and Warsaw to Jelenia Góra (via Łódź), cross at Wrocław. Other direct trains come from Gdynia or Gdańsk (via Poznań). There's service from Katowice (180 km), Poznań (165 km, three hours, US$5) and Rzepin (224 km) every couple of hours.

Several trains a day arrive from Berlin (329 km via Rzepin), Cologne, Frankfurt/Main and Hannover in Germany (via Dresden and Leipzig). The daily *Bohemia* express to/from Prague (339 km) arrives and departs in the middle of the night. Dresden and Prague are each about seven hours away.

The *Odra* express runs daily all year between Warsaw and Wrocław (390 km, five hours), departing from Warsaw in the afternoon and Wrocław in the early morning. Reservations are required.

Car Rental Orbis (☎ 34 780), Rynek 29, is the Hertz agent. Budget is represented by Haisig & Knabe (☎ 38 969), Rynek 45.

Vitesse (☎ 447 385), Plac Kościuszki 19 below the Savoy Hotel, also has rental cars.

GÖRLITZ TO ZGORZELEC

If you've got a taste for adventure and want to save a little money by walking in or out of Poland, the easiest border crossing for pedestrians to/from Germany is at Zgorzelec, 163 km west of Wrocław by train. Trains run between Wrocław and Zgorzelec every couple of hours with some services requiring a change of trains at Wegliniec. Only buy a ticket as far as Zgorzelec, the Polish border town, then walk across the bridge over the Nysa River to the neighbouring town of Görlitz where there are frequent trains to Dresden-Neustadt (102 km, US$10) and Berlin-Lichtenberg (212 km, US$20). If you have a Eurail pass Görlitz is the perfect place to begin using it.

Arriving from Western Europe, go out the main entrance from Görlitz Railway Station and head north up Berliner Strasse to Postplatz. Proceed east on Schützen Strasse (the street behind the main post office), turn right at the park and go down Am Stadpark to the bridge to Poland – an easy 15-minute

POLAND

walk. City maps posted at Görlitz Railway Station and there's also a left-luggage office if you'd like to look around the old town. Don't miss medieval **Peter-Pauls Cathedral**.

You'll find several small exchange offices at the Polish end of the bridge where you can easily swap currencies (cash only). The train station in Zgorzelec is a 10-minute walk from the bridge. Go straight up the main street, turn right onto another main street and ask. You want Zgorzelec Station, not Zgorzelec Miasto Station which is farther away.

The only hotel in Zgorzelec is the five-storey *Hotel 'Pod Orłem'* (☎ 24 53), ulica Warszowska 17 between the bridge and Zgorzelec Railway Station. At US$22/40 single/double with bath and breakfast, it's expensive for Poland but good value compared to the places across the river. The pleasant *Görlitz Youth Hostel* (☎ 03581-406 510) is at Goethe Strasse 17. Go out the south exit from Görlitz Railway Station, turn left on Sattig Strasse, and walk east five minutes to Goethe Strasse where you turn right. As for hotels in Görlitz, the *Hotel Stadt Dresden* (☎ 03581-407 131), Berliner Strasse 37 opposite the station, is expensive at US$60/75/85 single/double/triple. A better bet is the old 28-room *Hotel Prinz Friedrich Karl/Monopol* (☎ 03581-403 361) on Postplatz in the centre of town. It's US$32/50 single/double with breakfast (shared bath).

Wielkopolska

Western Poland, or Wielkopolska ('Great Poland'), was the cradle of the Polish nation. Here on a plateau along the Warta River lived the Polanians, a Slavic tribe which gave its name to the whole country. In 966 Mieszko I, duke of the Polanians, was baptised at Gniezno. Mieszko's son, Boleslav the Brave, was crowned king in 1025, establishing the Piast dynasty which ruled Poland until 1370.

In 1253 Prince Przemyśl I granted Poznań municipal rights and the city became a regional centre. Wars in the 18th century seriously weakened Poland, and in 1793 Western Poland was annexed to Prussia. After Bismarck set up the German Empire in 1871, Germanisation and German colonisation became intense. Returned to Poland in 1919, the area was seized by the Nazis in 1939 and devastated during the liberation battles of 1945.

Today the rebuilt regional capital Poznań is a great industrial, commercial and historical city, well worth a stop on the way to or from Berlin. Gniezno can easily be visited on the way to Toruń, an enchanting old riverside town by the Vistula. Though the German influence is still evident, western Poland is as Polish as you can get.

POZNAŃ

Poznań (Posen), on the main east-west trade route between Berlin and Warsaw, has long been a focal point of Polish history. A wooden fort stood on Ostrów Tumski (Cathedral Island) in the 9th century, and from 968 to 1039 Poznań was capital of Poland. In 1253 Stare Miasto (Old Town) was founded on the left bank of the Warta River and it continued to play a major role in the life of the country. By the 15th century Poznań was already famous for its fairs, and despite Swedish assaults in the 17th century the city remained an important trading centre. In 1815 the Congress of Vienna created the Grand Duchy of Poznań under Prussian suzerainty, but after 1849 the Germans took direct control. From 1918 to 1939 Poznań was part of Poland and the 1945 battle to liberate the city lasted over a month.

The 1956 strike for higher wages by workers at the huge Cegielski Engineering Works was one of the first of its kind in Poland. The works, founded by Hipolit Cegielski in 1846 and still the city's largest employer, manufactures railway rolling stock, diesel engines and machinery. Since 1925 Poznań has been the site of Poland's largest international trade fairs, although the good restaurants, historic places and varied museums draw visitors all year. Poznań's Żytnia rye vodka is Poland's best.

Orientation

Poznań Główny Railway Station is a 20-minute walk from the centre of the city. The left-luggage area is upstairs in the main hall between tracks Nos 1 and 4 (open 24 hours). Exit the station from this hall and walk north to the second street, ulica Św Marcin, which you follow east. Turn left with the tram tracks at Aleje Marcinkowskiego, then right and straight ahead to Stary Rynek, the old town square.

If you want to catch a tram from the station to town, go out the exit beyond track No 6, buy a ticket at the Ruch kiosk beside the stop and board tram No 5 which will take you to the Rzymski Hotel.

Information

The tourist office (☎ 526 156) at Stary Rynek 59 is extremely helpful and sells maps. It has *IKS*, the monthly entertainment magazine which details everything that's happening.

The Polski Związek Motorowy, Cześnikowska 30 off Grunwaldzka, in a distant western suburb, assists motorists.

Money Glob-Tour in the main hall between tracks Nos 1 and 4 at the train station changes cash 24 hours a day. It also sells maps and the staff will answer general questions if they're not too busy. Two other exchange offices (cash only) are in the smaller station hall beyond track No 6.

The PKO Bank, Stary Rynek 44 (weekdays 8 am to 6 pm, Saturday 10 am to 2 pm), changes travellers' cheques for 1.5% commission (US$3 minimum). Cash is changed at a better rate without commission.

The PKO Bank, ulica Masztalarska 8a, a block off the north-west corner of Stary Rynek (weekdays 7.30 am to 5 pm, Saturday 7.30 am to 1.30 pm), also changes travellers' cheques and their commission is slightly lower than that taken by the Stary Rynek office. You must go to 'Sala B', a small back office at the rear of a courtyard next to the main bank.

Post & Telecommunications The main post office is at ulica 23 Lutego 28. Avoid using the chaotic poste restante service here.

The telephone centre just outside the west exit from the train station is open daily from 7 am to 9 pm. Poznań's telephone code is 061.

Consulates The US Consulate (☎ 529 586) is at ulica Chopina 4.

Travel Agencies Book domestic and international train tickets and couchettes at the Orbis office below the Orbis Poznań Hotel (weekdays 8 am to 6 pm, Saturday 8am to 2 pm). It also has international bus tickets from Poznań to Amsterdam, Barcelona, Brussels, London, Lyon, Madrid, Oslo, Paris, Vienna, and many German cities. This is a good place to get train information in English.

Agencja Eurostop (☎ 520 344), ulica Fredry 7, also has bus tickets to cities all across Europe and sells ISIC student cards.

World Computer Travel (☎ 481 342), at ulica J Dąbrowskiego 5A, has one-way flights to North America (US$500) and Melbourne, Australia (US$850), departing from Warsaw. They have a second office next to the US consulate.

Things to See

Museums There are half a dozen museums in the historic buildings on or near Stary Rynek. Begin with the one in the Renaissance **old town hall** (closed Thursday and Saturday) which will envelop you in Poznań's medieval past. The coffered ceiling in the vestibule dates from 1555. Every day at noon a bugle sounds and butting heraldic goats appear above the clock on the town hall façade opposite Proserpina's fountain (1766). The **Musical Instruments Museum** (closed Monday and Thursday, free Friday), Stary Rynek 45, is one of the best of its kind in Europe.

Nearby at the south-eastern corner of the square is the **Archaeological Museum**

POLAND

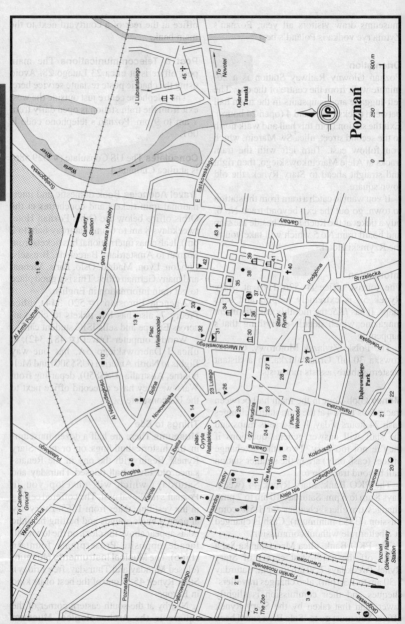

Poznań

Garbary Station

Garbary

Strzelecka

Stary Rynek

Plac Wielkopolski

Plac Wolności

Podgórna

gen T Tadeusza Kutrzeby

Al Armii Poznań

Strzegomska

Warta

Citadel

Ostrów Tumski

To Novotel

J Lubratskiego

E Estkowskiego

Al Niepodległości

Solna

Nowowolejska

23 Lutego

Grudnia

Gwarna

Św Marcin

Aleje Nie podległości

Kościuszki

Ratajczaka

Dąbrowskiego Park

Powiejska

plac Cyryla Ratajskiego

Libelta

Karola

Aleksandra

Fredry

Franklin Roosevelta

Dworcowa

Towarowa

Bogdanka

Poznań Główny Railway Station

Poznań Główny Railway Station

To Camping Ground

Weikopolska

Pułaskiego

Poznańska

J Dąbrowskiego

Chopina

To The Zoo

500 m

250

0

PLACES TO STAY

2	Orbis Mercury Hotel
9	Hotel Garnizonowy
10	Orbis Hotel
17	Lech Hotel
19	Wielkopolska & Savoy Hotels
22	Orbis Poznań Hotel
27	Rzymski Hotel
35	Dom Turysty PTTK

PLACES TO EAT

23	Smakosz Restaurant
24	Restauracja Indyjska
26	Pod Arkadami Milk Bar
28	U Marcina
32	Pekin Restaurant
42	Pizzeria Tivoli

OTHER

1	World Computer Travel
3	International Fairgrounds
4	Biuro Zakwaterowania
5	Stajenka Pegaza Pub
6	Solidarity Monument
7	Opera House
8	US Consulate
11	Commonwealth War Cemetery
12	Polish War Memorial
13	Carmelite Church
14	Studio Jack Disco
15	Agencja Eurostop
16	Palace of Culture
18	Filharmonia
20	PKS Bus Station
21	Musical Theatre
25	Polski Theatre 'Naród Sobie'
29	St Martin's Church
30	National Museum
31	Post Office
33	Vegetable Market
34	Decorative Arts Museum
36	Franciscan Church
37	Tourist Office
38	Old Town Hall
39	Musical Instruments Museum
40	Parish Church
41	Archaeological Museum
43	Dominican Church
44	Archdiocesan Museum
45	Cathedral

(closed Monday) in a 16th century Renaissance palace. Make a side trip to the end of ulica Świętosławska from beside this museum to visit the Baroque **parish church**, originally a Jesuit church. There's a peculiar **Military Museum** (closed Monday) full of little lead soldiers in one of the incongruous modern buildings in the very centre of Stary Rynek itself. Notice the art gallery opposite. There are two more museums, one literary (Stary Rynek 84) and the other political (Stary Rynek 3), on the west side of the square.

Go up ulica Franciszkańska from the latter to the beautiful 17th century **Franciscan church**. In the Castle of Przemyśl on the hill opposite is the **Decorative Arts Museum** (closed Monday and Tuesday). Go around the church and west on ulica Paderewskiego to the **National Museum** (closed Monday), with Poland's best collection of Dutch and Spanish paintings.

Other Sights The historic centre of Poznań has a lot more to offer than just museums, most of which you'll be able to discover for yourself without a guidebook. However, a few sights just outside the centre deserve your attention.

Walk north from the National Museum to the end of Aleje Marcinkowskiego, then turn right, then left on ulica Działowa, the first street. You'll pass two old churches before reaching the striking **Polish War Memorial**, commemorating the Polish army's heroic resistance to the Nazi onslaught in 1939. Pass it and continue north on Aleje Niepodległości to the 19th century Prussian **citadel**. Though Poznań fell to the Soviet army in January 1945, 20,000 German troops held out inside this fortress for another two months and the city was badly damaged by artillery fire. There's much to see around the citadel, including a couple of war museums (closed Monday), monuments to the Soviet liberators, and the **Commonwealth War Cemetery** (to the right). Many of the Soviet and Polish soldiers who died in the battle are buried along the hillside. The last name on the bronze plaque below the central obelisk is Marshall J Stalin.

Poznań's towering red-brick Gothic **cathedral** is at Ostrów Tumski on the east

POLAND

side of the Warta River. Any eastbound tram from Plac Wielkopolski will take you there. The Byzantine-style Golden Chapel (1841), mausoleum of Mieszko I and Boleslav the Brave, is behind the main altar. The **Archdiocesan Museum** (closed Sunday) at the north end of ulica Lubrańskiego near the cathedral is surprisingly rich.

Poznań's most compelling sight is the large bronze **monument** in the park beside the Palace of Culture, which you may have noticed on your way in from the train station. Erected in 1981 by supporters of the trade union Solidarity, the monument commemorates 'Black Thursday', 28 June 1956, when rioting by workers demanding higher wages was put down by force with as many as 70 killed and hundreds injured. The two huge crosses, bound together, symbolise the struggle of Polish workers for 'bread, peace and freedom', and the dates recall various popular upheavals: 1956 (Poznań), 1968 (Warsaw), 1970 (Gdańsk), 1976 (Radom), and 1980 (Gdańsk). Next to the monument is a statue of the Romantic poet Adam Mickiewcz.

Kórnik & Rogalin Each of these small towns 20 km south of Poznań boasts a large palace of the landed nobility in expansive parks. The two are similar, so unless you've got plenty of time or your own transport, one might be representative of the other. Kórnik is the easiest to reach with frequent bus service from Poznań. Buses between Kórnik and Rogalin run only a couple of times a day, but maybe you'll be lucky! There's a bus from Rogalin directly back to Poznań every couple of hours.

The 19th century English-style country manor at Kórnik (closed Monday) was rebuilt on the site of an earlier palace by the famous Berlin architect Karl Friedrich Schinkel. A highlight at Rogalin is the small art gallery (closed Monday and Tuesday) hidden behind the 18th century Rococo palace. Its collection of 19th century German and Polish paintings is quite good. Some of the oak trees in the surrounding park are almost nine metres around and 1000 years old. The three largest trees are named for the legendary brothers Lech, Czech and Rus who founded Poland, Bohemia and Russia.

Places to Stay

Poznań's hotels use the 12 annual trade fairs as a pretext for doubling prices, but when you ask what that week's trade fair is about they haven't a clue (typical themes include printing equipment, burglar alarms, medical equipment, computers, furniture, mining, agriculture, construction, packaging, advertising media and garbage collection). During the main trade fair in June all accommodation will be fully booked, so check the dates carefully before heading this way. The price increases are also in effect a few days before and after the fairs. One way to check the dates beforehand would be to call the Fair Agency (☎ 692 592) or Poznań tourist information (☎ 526 156).

Camping You'll find *Poznań-Strzeszynek Camping* (☎ 47 224), at ulica Koszalińska 15, inconveniently located on the far northwest edge of Poznań (bus No 95). It's open from June to September.

Hostels The 56-bed *youth hostel* (☎ 663 680) is at ulica Berwińskiego 2/3, the tall yellow brick building opposite Kasprzaka Park. To get there leave the train station by the west exit and go left along ulica Głogowska till you come to the park (five minutes). The doors are locked at 9 pm.

Agencja Europstop (☎ 520 344), ulica Aleksandra Fredry 7 behind the Palace of Culture, may have information on International Student Hotels (open July and August).

Private Rooms The Przemysław Biuro Zakwaterowania (☎ 663 560 or 663 983), ulica Głogowska 16, can arrange accommodation in private homes at US$10/14 single/double.

At trade fair times the prices double and the offices stay open extra long hours (normal hours are weekdays from 9 am to 6 pm, Saturday 10 am to 3 pm). Look for this office at the end of the long white building across from the west exit from the train station. If the first door you try is locked go to the next one along the row.

The Orbis Biuro Obsługi Cudzoziemców (BOC) office downstairs in the Orbis Poznań Hotel also has expensive private rooms at US$25/32 single/double, but only during the trade fairs.

Hotels The *Hotel Royal* (☎ 537 884), ulica Św Marcin 17 between the train station and the centre, through the archway and at the back of the courtyard, is US$13/19/22 single/double/triple with shared bath. There can be long waits to use the one communal shower.

The *Wielkopolska Hotel* (☎ 527 631), ulica Św Marcin 67, charges US$15/29 single/double without bath, US$29/33 with bath. The seven-storey *Lech Hotel* (☎ 530 151), ulica Św Marcin 74, is way overpriced at US$44/60 single/double with bath and breakfast.

Also good is the *Rzymski Hotel* (☎ 528 121), Aleje Marcinkowskiego 22, charging US$14/24 single/double without bath, US$23/32 with bath, breakfast included. In all of the above hotels except the Royal the rooms facing the street are noisy.

Dom Turysty PTTK (☎ 523 893) at Stary Rynek 91 (entry from Wroniecka 91), a 19th century building right on Poznań's main square, is US$19/32 single/double without bath, US$22/38 with bath, US$7 per person in a five-bed dorm, US$5 per person in a seven-bed dorm (no breakfast). The location can't be beaten and the restaurant downstairs is good.

The *Hotel Garnizonowy* (☎ 492 671), a modern, 10-storey hotel on Solna just north of downtown, has rooms with bath at US$22/32 single/double. The Garnizonowy was originally intended to house military officers but it's now open to anyone.

The *Hotel Miejski Ósrodek Sportowy* (☎ 332 444), ulica Churałkowskiego 34, is a white four-storey sports hotel with rooms with shared bath at US$13 per person. The triple rooms have private bath. It's just

beyond the stadium, south-east of the Orbis Poznań Hotel. From the train station follow our map east along Towarowa, which becomes Królowej Jadwigi, pass the Orbis Poznań, and look for the stadium on the right beyond the park after the next main street. Otherwise catch tram No 12 from the west side of the train station. There's a good snack bar upstairs in the adjoining gym.

Places to Eat
Old Town The *Stara Ratuszowa Wine Cellar*, Stary Rynek 55, is for real: you go down into the cellar to get wine. The downstairs restaurant is good for an atmospheric splurge.

Club Elite, in the basement of the old Weight House in the centre of Stary Rynek directly behind the old town hall, posts their menu outside in English and German. It's good for solid meat dishes.

Avanti Buffet, Stary Rynek 76, serves tasty platefuls of spaghetti but there's always a long line. The *Spaghetti Bar* on ulica Rynkova off the north-west corner of Stary Rynek is slightly cheaper.

Pizzeria Tivoli, ulica Wroniecka 13, serves pizza and beer until 11 pm. It's three blocks off the north end of Stary Rynek.

West of the Old Town There are several good places to eat in the streets and squares west of the old town. *Bistro Apetit*, Plac Wolności 1 below Hotel Rzymski, is a cheap milk bar.

Just two blocks west of here is the full-service *Smakosz Restaurant*, ulica 27 Grudnia 9, an old-style European restaurant with impeccable service, excellent food, good prices and an English menu. It's open till 11 pm.

Smak Coop, Św Marcin 73, and *Pod Kuchcikiem*, Św Marcin 75, both offer basic self-service meals with beer. *U Marcina*, Św Marcin 34, is a rather chic self-service popular with the city youth.

The *Restauracja Indyjska*, Kantaka 8/9, serves fairly expensive Indian curries and has cold beer to cool you down (open daily until midnight).

POLAND

For an up-market Chinese meal there's the *Pekin Restaurant*, ulica 23 Lutego 29 opposite the main post office.

The *Pod Arkadami Milk Bar*, Plac Cyryla Ratajskiego 10, is great for a snack or a full meal. Whole groups of workers crowd in here – recommended.

Cafés & Bars When it's time for coffee, cakes and ice cream, stop at *Sukiennicza*, Stary Rynek 100. *Loger*, Stary Rynek 93, specialises in a sweet honey wine known as miód (mead). *Herbaciarnia*, Stary Rynek 68, is a place for having a pot of tea. *Pod Piwoszem*, ulica Wrocławska 12, off the south end of Stary Rynek, is a working man's pub with cold beer on tap.

Lech is a good local beer to try here, but beware of the sweet, low-alcohol Czarna Perła beer. The *Stajenka Pegaza*, a small pub on ulica Aleksandra Fredry midway between the opera house and the train tracks, is a nice place to drop in after the opera or before going to a disco.

A 24-hour liquor store is at 27 Grudnia 13.

Entertainment

The *Opera House*, ulica Aleksandra Fredry 9, is in the park behind the Solidarity monument (ticket office open Tuesday to Saturday 1 to 7 pm, Sunday 4 to 7 pm).

Poznań's symphony orchestra plays at the *Filharmonia*, ulica Św Marcin 81 opposite the Palace of Culture. Check there for performances by the famous Poznań Boys' & Men's Philharmonic Choir which specialises in old music.

Also check the *Polski Theatre 'Naród Sobie'*, ulica 27 Grudnia, which presents plays in Polish.

The *Musical Theatre* next to the Orbis Poznań Hotel features Broadway shows like *Hello Dolly* and *Me and My Girl*.

St John's Fair in June or July and the Poznań Musical Spring in March are annual events to enquire about.

Discos Though you'll have a better selection of places to eat than in Wrocław, the nightlife in Poznań isn't as good.

Poznań's top disco is *Studio Jack* (☎ 520 522), ulica Działyńskich. It opens nightly with a billiard bar downstairs from 4 pm to 5 am and disco upstairs from 10 pm to 5 am.

Akumulatory, ulica Zwierzyniecka 7, in the 12-storey building directly across the street from the Orbis Mercury Hotel, is a students disco which opens at 9 pm.

Things to Buy

There's an Antykwariat (second-hand) bookstore at Stary Rynek 54, and Desa, Stary Rynek 48, has antiques plus old jewellery and paintings. Keep in mind that books and works of art produced before 1945 cannot be exported. Jubiler, Stary Rynek 40, has contemporary Polish amber jewellery. You can see more amber at Stary Rynek 81.

Księgarnia, ulica Gwarna at 27 Grudna near the Lech Hotel, has a large selection of cassettes and CDs. Also visit the large flower and vegetable market in Plac Wielkopolski in the old town.

Getting There & Away

Direct trains arrive at Poznań from Berlin (261 km), Copenhagen, the Hook of Holland, Kiev, Moscow, Ostend and Paris abroad, and Ełk, Gdynia-Gdańsk, Kraków, Olsztyn, Rzepin, Szczecin, Toruń, Warsaw and Wrocław in Poland. As you see, it's quite a crossroads! If you're arriving in Poland from Western Europe via Berlin, stop here instead of going straight through to Warsaw.

The *Warta* and *Lech* express trains run daily all year between Warsaw and Poznań (311 km, 3½ hours). The *Warta* departs from Warsaw in the morning and Poznań in the late afternoon, whereas the *Lech* does the opposite. The Eurocity *Berolina* links Poznań to Berlin-Hauptbahnhof in just three hours, departing from Poznań in the morning, Berlin in the afternoon. Reservations are required on all these trains.

Buses to Kórnik and Rogalin leave frequently from the PKS bus station on Towarowa. First get a departure time from the Informacja window inside the station (offer the staff a piece of paper on which to write it down), then ask them which gate *(stanowiska)* your bus leaves from as it's different every time. Gate numbers are also indicated by the blue footnotes on the white departures board posted in the station. Buy your ticket at any window, then go to the gate to check that your bus really is listed on the board there.

Getting Around

Tram tickets come in two varieties, one type valid for a single trip lasting up to 10 minutes, and another (costing double) for a 30-minute trip.

Car Rental The Hertz office (☎ 332 081) is at the Orbis Poznań Hotel, Plac Dąbrowskiego 1.

Taxi Taxis wait on ulica Rynkova, the street off the north-west corner of Stary Rynek. The fare will be 400 times the meter reading if it hasn't been increased).

GNIEZNO

Gniezno, a small town 50 km east of Poznań, was the birthplace of the Polish nation. Here the legendary hero Lech found the white eagle now represented on the Polish flag. Already in the 8th century the Polanian tribe had their main fortified settlement at Gniezno, and in the 10th century, when Mieszko I converted to Christianity, a kingdom was established here.

In the year 1000 Boleslav the Brave and the German emperor Otto III had a historic meeting at Gniezno. These events are retold in the **Museum of the Origin of the Polish State** (closed Monday) on Jelonek Lake, a little over a km west of the train station.

In the centre of town a bit back towards the station is the 14th century Gothic **cathedral** with the silver sarcophagus (1662) of St Adalbertus on the main altar. The life story of this saint appears on the cathedral's famous Romanesque bronze doors (1170), inside below the tower. The Bohemian monk Adalbertus arrived at Gniezno in 996 on his way to the lands east of the mouth of the Vistula River where he intended to convert

the heathen Prussians. Instead the tribesmen killed the monk, whose remains were bought back by Boleslav the Brave for their weight in gold. Pope Sylvester canonised Adalbertus in 999, elevating Gniezno to an archbishopric at the same time.

Getting There & Away

Gniezno is a day trip from Poznań or a stop on the way to Toruń. The town is on the main railway line from Wrocław to Gdynia via Poznań, Inowrocław and Bydgoszcz. Through trains from Poznań to Olsztyn via Toruń and Iława also pass here. Otherwise, to go from Gniezno to Toruń you must change at Inowrocław. Local trains to/from Poznań (52 km) are frequent and these stop at Poznań-Garbary Station as well as Poznań Główny.

TORUŃ

Halfway between Poznań and Gdańsk (or Warsaw and Gdańsk), Toruń (Thorn) was founded by the Teutonic Knights in 1233 and its position on the Vistula River at a crossing of trade routes made it an important member of the medieval Hanseatic League.

The wealth this brought is reflected in Toruń's three towering Gothic churches. Two are near Rynek Staromiejski, the old town square in the merchants' quarter, while the third adjoins Rynek Nowomiejski, the new town square in the craftsmen's quarter. The ruins of the knights' castle can still be seen by the river between these two districts.

Fortunately medieval Toruń, still enclosed in surviving sections of the city walls, was not seriously damaged in WW II. It offers a chance to step briefly back in history without a lot of other tourists on your heels. Look for gingerbread *(pierniki)*, a local speciality made with honey using 18th century moulds.

Orientation

There are several train stations in Toruń. Although Toruń Miasto is closer to the centre of town, most trains stop at Toruń Główny, the main station on the south side of the river. Here you'll find the left-luggage office and

POLAND

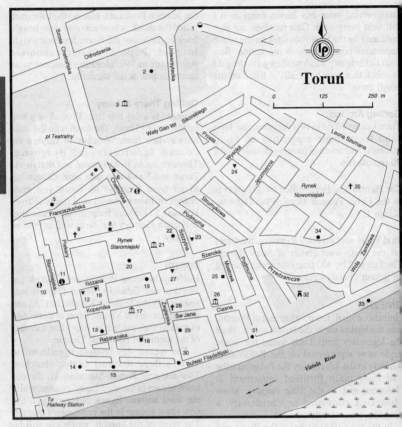

Toruń

0   125   250 m

(map labels)
Odrodzenia
Szosa Chełmińska
Uniwersyhecka
Sikorskiego
Wały Gen Wł Sikorskiego
pl Teatralny
Chełmińska
Prosta
Wysoka
Leona Szumana
Jęczmienna
Franciszkańska
Piekary
Rynek
Staromiejski
Strumykowa
Podmurna
Szczytna
Szeroka
Mostowa
Podmurna
Przedzamcze
Wola Zamkowa
Rynek
Nowomiejski
Różana
Staromiejska
Kopernika
Żeglarska
Św Jana
Rabiańska
Ciasna
Bulwar Filadelfijski
Vistula River
To Railway Station

a restaurant between tracks Nos 2 and 3. Taxis park just outside this hall. To catch bus No 22 or 27 to town, go through the subterranean passage towards track No 4 and buy a ticket at the Ruch kiosk near the stop. Get off the bus at the first stop across the bridge and walk east from the stop, and within minutes you'll be on Rynek Staromiejski, the old town square. The main bus station is near the northern edge of town, an easy walk.

Information
Tourist Office Tourist information (☎ 10 931) is on the west side of the town hall

building in the centre of Rynek Staromiejski. The enthusiastic staff here go out of their way to be helpful.

The PTTK Tourist Office (☎ 28 228), Plac Rapackiego 2, is at the west end of ulica Różana just by the passage into the old town. This PTTK office sells a good selection of maps from all over Poland but they aren't very good about answering questions, for this go to the town hall office.

The Youth Hostel Association has an information office selling hostel guidebooks at ulica Kopernicka 27 (weekdays 10 am to 1 pm).

PLACES TO STAY

6	Hotel Polonia
8	Hotel Trzy Korony
25	Hotel Orzeł
29	Hotel Zajazd Staropolski

PLACES TO EAT

12	Pizzeria
18	Bar Mleczny
23	Staromiejska Restaurant
24	Restauracja Hungaria
27	Pod Gołębiem Restaurant

OTHER

1	Bus Station
2	Ethnographic Park
3	Ethnographical Museum
4	Municipal Theatre
5	Copernicus University
7	PKO Bank
9	St Mary's Church
10	NBP Bank
11	PTTK Tourist Office
13	Kawiarna Pod 'Atlantem'/ Auto Club
14	Crooked Tower
15	Monastery Gate
16	Czarna Oberża Pub
17	Copernicus Museum
19	Orbis (Train Tickets)
20	Old Town Hall
21	Oriental Art Museum
22	Elana Klub
26	Archaeological Museum
28	St John's Church
30	Sailor's Gate
31	Bridge Gate
32	Castle Ruins
33	Excursion Boat Landing
34	Club 'Stary Brower'
35	St James' Church

The Toruń Automobile Club (☎ 28 691) is at Ducha Św 5 in the old town.

Money The Narodowy Bank Polski (NBP Bank), on Plac Rapackiego next to the PTTK office on the west side of the old town (weekdays 8 am to 5 pm, Saturday 8 to 11 am), changes travellers' cheques for 1.5% commission.

The PKO Bank, ulica Podmurna 81-83,

also changes travellers' cheques for the same commission (US$3 minimum) and it's far less crowded than the NBP Bank.

Post & Telecommunications The main post office and telephone centre is conveniently located at Rynek Staromiejski 15 (open weekdays 8 am to 8 pm, Saturday 8 am to 1 pm). At last report they still didn't have any card phones. Toruń's telephone code is 056.

Travel Agencies Seat reservations for express trains can be made at Orbis at ulica Żeglarska 31 on Rynek Staromiejski or at Toruń Główny Station.

Things to See

The Old Town Begin your sightseeing on Rynek Staromiejski with the **historical museum** (closed Monday) in the 14th century old town hall, one of the largest of its kind in the Baltic states. From May to September you can climb the tower. The statue of Copernicus beside the town hall was erected in 1853. Don't miss the nearby **Oriental Art Museum** (free Sunday, closed Monday) in 15th century Pod Gwiazdą house at Rynek Staromiejski 35, featuring a hanging wooden staircase dated 1697.

Just off the north-west corner of the square is 14th century **St Mary's Church**, a typical Gothic hall church with all naves of equal height – but what a height! The presbytery, stained glass windows, organ (1609) and decoration of this church are fine.

Gothic **St John's Church**, on ulica Żeglarska south of Rynek Staromiejski, is remarkable for its soaring white interior and the richness of its altars. West at ulica Kopernika 15 from this church is the **birthplace of astronomer Nicolaus Copernicus** (born in 1473), now a museum dedicated to the man who moved the earth and stopped the sun (closed Monday). You must buy two tickets here, one to see the scale model of Toruń and another for the rest of the museum, though the two add up to under a dollar. Copernicus stayed in Toruń until his

17th birthday when he left to study in Kraków.

Go around the corner beyond the museum and walk straight down to the riverside. Here you'll see the **medieval walls and gates** which once defended Toruń. Walk east along the river past the castle ruins. To reach the ruins turn left, then left again on ulica Przedzamcze. The **Castle of the Teutonic Knights** was destroyed in 1454 but its massive foundations are visible. Early 14th century **St James' Church** is off Rynek Nowomiejski in the north-east section of the old town. The flying buttresses on this church are rare in Poland.

If you're enchanted by Toruń's old Teutonic charm and have a good cheap place to stay, consider extending your stay by a day and visiting nearby Chełmo and Golub-Dobrzyń, both easily accessible by bus. **Chełmo**, near the Vistula 45 km north-west of Toruń, is completely surrounded by a 14th century city wall protecting the same sort of picturesque **central square** and **Gothic churches** seen in Toruń. **Golub-Dobrzyń**, 43 km north-east of Toruń, has a red-brick castle erected by the Teutonic Knights.

Places to Stay

Camping Toruń's convenient camping ground makes this a good place to unroll the tent. *Camping 'Tramp'* (☎ 24 187; open year-round), near the south end of the highway bridge over the Vistula River, is a five-minute walk from Toruń Główny Railway Station. Bungalows are US$5 single or US$10 for up to four people, while hotel-style rooms in the building adjoining the restaurant are US$4/8 single/double. The public toilets and showers could do with a cleaning but camping is just US$2 per person. Bring mosquito repellent. The camping-ground restaurant is open till midnight.

Hostels Toruń's *youth hostel* (☎ 27 242) is at ulica Rudacka 15, across the river east of Toruń Główny Railway Station (bus No 13). The doors don't open until 5 pm.

The *PTTK Dom Wycieczkowy* (☎ 23 855),

ulica Legionów 24, a continuation of ulica Uniwersytecka several blocks north of the bus station, is a three-storey building in a pleasant suburb a 15-minute walk from the old town. Double rooms are US$12, a bed in a four-bed dormitory US$5, but it's sometimes fully booked by groups.

Hotels The old *Hotel Trzy Korony* (☎ 26 031), Rynek Staromiejski 21, is rather basic for US$10/14 single/double without bath or breakfast, though the location is great, right on the old town square. Don't stay here if you're a light sleeper as loud music from the downstairs bar continues late into the night.

The four-storey *Orzeł Hotel* (☎ 25 024), ulica Mostowa 15 (US$10/16 single/double without bath, US$22 double with bath), is still cheap but nicer.

The *Hotel Polonia* (☎ 23 028), Plac Teatralny 5, a fine old four-storey hotel opposite the municipal theatre, is US$13 single or double, US$17 triple without bath or US$16 single with bath (no doubles with bath). The rooms up on the top floor are about a dollar cheaper. The hotel restaurant is good.

For a mild splurge consider the *Zajaz Staropolski* (☎ 26 061), ulica Żeglarska 14, a tasteful small hotel owned by the Polish travel agency Gromada. There are several different types of rooms with varying prices; back rooms are US$17/28 single/double while doubles with a street view go for US$32. Rooms with TV are about US$5 more and in midsummer all prices are increased about US$10. All rooms include bath and breakfast. The hotel restaurant has a nice open atmosphere and the menu is clearly written in German.

Places to Eat

There are three cheap places in a row on ulic Różana just off Rynek Staromiejski. *Bar Mleczny*, ulica Różana 1 (behind the ice cream place on the corner), has genuine Polish dishes at low prices though it's difficult to order as you must point or just take chance and pick anything on the menu. *Mini Bar Makary*, ulica Różana 3, has cheap spa ghetti and lasagne, while the self-service pizza place at ulica Różana 5 serves assembly-line pizza covered with ketchup.

Restauracja Hungaria, Prosta 19, offers Hungarian cuisine at very reasonable prices. Their menu is in German and there's full bar service. Nearby at Prosta 20 is a place dispensing soggy self-service pizza to hordes of young Poles.

For more sedate dining with proper table service try *Pod Gołębiem*, ulica Szeroka 37. The *Staromiejska Restaurant*, at ulica Szczytna 4, is an up-market Italian restaurant.

Cafés & Gingerbread *Kawiarnia Pod 'Atlantem'*, Ducha Św 3 near the Copernicus Museum, is a nice informal place for coffee and cakes in plush surroundings. Authentic Toruń gingerbread can be purchased at *Kopernik*, ulica Żeglarska 25 near St John's Church. Join the queue of eager Polish tourists waiting to buy this treat.

Entertainment

The *Municipal Theatre* is on Plac Teatralny at the north entrance to the old town. Every second Friday at 7 pm there's a concert in the old town hall. Festivals include the Meeting of Folk Bands in May and the International Old Music Festival in September.

Bars & Discos *Pub Kuranty*, Rynek Staromiejski 29, is a popular drinking place for the town youth. Go through the café and down the stairs in back.

Czarna Oberża, ulica Rabiańska 9, is a German-style pub with billiard tables.

A mixed crowd frequents *Orion Night Club* (☎ 27 962), Plac Teatralny 7, which is open for drinks from 6 pm and functions as a disco from 10 pm to 5 am. The disco downstairs at the *Elana Klub*, ulica Szczytna 15, opens at 10 pm.

The *Club 'Stary Brower'*, ulica Browarna 1, is a students' bar with live music and disco dancing on Friday and Saturday nights. The downstairs bar opens around 5 pm nightly. There's no name outside – just look for the

beer advertisements on what appears to be an 'old brewery'.

Getting There & Away

There are direct services from Gdańsk, Malbork, Olsztyn (via Iława), Poznań and Warsaw. Most trains to Warsaw carry mandatory seat reservations, so ask. Services between Gdańsk and Poznań require Toruń passengers to change trains, southbound at Bydgoszcz, northbound at Inowrocław.

The *Kujawiak* express train runs daily all year between Warsaw and Toruń (242 km, three hours), departing from Warsaw in the afternoon and Toruń in the morning. Reservations are required.

Buses to Chełmno and Golub-Dobrzyń depart from Toruń's bus station every hour or two. For more distant destinations you're probably better off taking a train, although one early morning bus does depart from Toruń for Gdańsk (181 km). The information and ticket windows inside the bus station are open from 6 am to 8.30 pm.

Pomerania

The Polish Baltic coast stretches 694 km from Germany to the Russian border, a region of rugged natural beauty where endless beaches and shifting dunes alternate with vast bays, lagoons and coastal lakes. Most of Pomerania (north-western Poland between the Vistula and Odra rivers) was part of Germany until 1945, though the area from Bydgoszcz to Gdynia belonged to Poland from 1918 on.

Here Baltic beach resorts such as Świnoujście, Łeba, Hel and Sopot join historic Gdańsk to put Pomerania on most Polish itineraries. Ferries from Denmark, Sweden and Finland call at Świnoujście and Gdańsk. Szczecin (Stettin), near the mouth of the Odra River, was once the main port of Berlin but the old town was largely destroyed in WW II and it's now just another seedy industrial city. Świnoujście is much nicer

POLAND

and nearby Międzyzdroje is the gateway to Wolin National Park. Słowiński National Park west of Łeba is another area of special interest to naturalists.

HISTORY

Northern Poland has long been a battleground between Poles and Germans. Poland never really controlled the Slavic tribes of western Pomerania, and beginning in the 12th century the area was absorbed by the margraves of Brandenburg. In eastern Pomerania the Germanic Teutonic Knights, invited here in 1226 to help subdue the restive Prussian tribes, played a similar role. From their castles at Malbork and Toruń, the knights defied the king of Poland until their defeat in the 15th century by combined Polish and Lithuanian forces. Although the Duchy of Prussia was a vassal of Poland in the 16th century, wars with Sweden and internal dissent weakened Poland's position in the 17th century.

In 1720 the Kingdom of Prussia reoccupied all of western Pomerania, and the first partition of Poland (1772) brought everything south as far as Toruń under Prussian control (Toruń itself wasn't annexed by Prussia until 1793). After the Congress of Vienna in 1815, Poland south-east of Toruń came under tsarist Russia, a situation that persisted until WW I. In 1919 the Treaty of Versailles granted Poland a narrow corridor to the sea, separating East Prussia from Pomerania. Since the Free City of Danzig (Gdańsk) was populated mostly by Germans, the Polish government built Gdynia from scratch after 1922.

In 1939 Hitler's demand for a German-controlled road and rail route across Polish territory to East Prussia and the incorporation of Danzig into the Third Reich sparked WW II. In 1945 the German inhabitants were expelled from Pomerania and East Prussia. Poland got Pomerania and the southern half of East Prussia (Mazuria) while the USSR took the northern half of East Prussia including the capital Königsberg (Kaliningrad), now part of Russia.

INFORMATION

The 1:400,000 *Pobrzeże Bałtyku* map of north-western Poland available at bookshops and tourist offices is well worth having.

GDAŃSK

The Tri-City conurbation, Gdańsk-Sopot-Gdynia, stretches 30 km along the west side of the Gulf of Gdańsk on the Baltic Sea. Gdańsk (Danzig) on the Motława River, a stagnant arm of the Vistula, about four km from the sea, is Poland's largest port, a major shipbuilding centre, and the birthplace of Solidarity. Though in existence as early as the 9th century, the beautiful historic centre dates from the Hanseatic period when medieval Gdańsk was one of the richest ports in Europe providing access to the Baltic for much of Central Europe.

From 1454 to 1793 Gdańsk belonged to the Polish crown, and the largely German population was pacified by the autonomy and many privileges granted by Poland's kings. A famous 17th century resident was astronomer Jan Hevelius, after whom the local brewery is named. Physicist Daniel Fahrenheit and philosopher Arthur Schopenhauer also hailed from here.

After WW I, the Treaty of Versailles created the Free City of Danzig, with Poland administering essential services such as the port, post and railways, and the German residents dominating municipal government. What could have developed into a profitable commercial relationship for both sides was soured by petty nationalism.

At 4.45 am on 1 September 1939 the first shots of WW II were fired as the battleship *Schleswig-Holstein* opened up on a Polish military depot at Westerplatte near Gdańsk. Gdańsk was 55% destroyed during the war and the entire historic core had to be rebuilt, but you'd hardly know it today, so well was the job done. Now, with industrialisation and billowing smokestacks, central Gdańsk has a serious pollution problem.

Orientation

Gdańsk Główny Railway Station is a 10-

POLAND

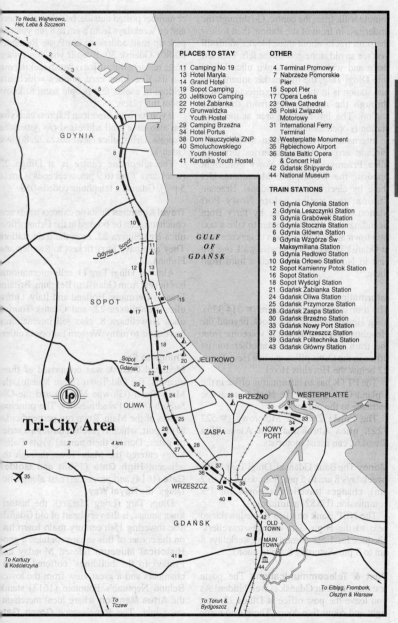

PLACES TO STAY

11 Camping No 19
13 Hotel Maryla
14 Grand Hotel
19 Sopot Camping
20 Jelitkowo Camping
22 Hotel Żabianka
27 Grunwaldzka
   Youth Hostel
34 Hotel Portus
38 Dom Nauczyciela ZNP
40 Smoluchowskiego
   Youth Hostel
41 Kartuska Youth Hostel

OTHER

4 Terminal Promowy
7 Nabrzeże Pomorskie
   Pier
15 Sopot Pier
17 Opera Leśna
23 Oliwa Cathedral
26 Polski Związek
   Motorowy
31 International Ferry
   Terminal
32 Westerplatte Monument
35 Rębiechowo Airport
36 State Baltic Opera
   & Concert Hall
42 Gdańsk Shipyards
44 National Museum

TRAIN STATIONS

1 Gdynia Chylonia Station
2 Gdynia Leszczynki Station
3 Gdynia Grabówek Station
5 Gdynia Stocznia Station
6 Gdynia Główna Station
8 Gdynia Wzgórze Św
   Maksymiliana Station
9 Gdynia Redłowo Station
10 Gdynia Orłowo Station
12 Gdynia Kamienny Potok Station
16 Sopot Station
18 Sopot Wyścigi Station
21 Gdańsk Żabianka Station
24 Gdańsk Oliwa Station
25 Gdańsk Przymorze Station
28 Gdańsk Zaspa Station
30 Gdańsk Brzeźno Station
33 Gdańsk Nowy Port Station
37 Gdańsk Wrzeszcz Station
39 Gdańsk Politechnika Station
43 Gdańsk Główny Station

minute walk from the centre. Go through the underpass in front of the station, then follow the tram tracks about three blocks south till you see an old stone gate on the left. Turn left there and walk straight down ulica Długa into Długi Targ, the old market square. The bus station is in the opposite direction, west through the main tunnel from the train station. The left-luggage area at the train station is open 24 hours.

International ferries from Sweden and Finland arrive at the Polferries terminal, ulica Przemysłowa 1 at Nowy Port right opposite the Westerplatte Monument. Get there by electric train to Gdańsk Brzeźno Station, the station before Nowy Port Station. If you're arriving by ferry from Scandinavia it might be better to take a taxi into town as no tram or train tickets are sold at Gdańsk Brzeźno. Otherwise walk one km east to Nowy Port and catch a tram from there.

Information

The tourist information centre (☎ 314 355), ulica Heweliusza 27, is a block beyond the Hevelius Hotel, on the left as you come from the train station. There's another tourist office in the Orbis office at ulica Heweliusza 22 below the Hevelius Hotel.

The PTTK has an information office in the Upland Gate next to the High Gate at the entrance to the old town.

The Polski Związek Motorowy (☎ 522 722), ulica Abrahama 7 at Aleja Wita Stwosza, can assist motorists.

Money The Bank Gdański, Długi Targ 14/16 (weekdays 8 am to 5 pm, Saturday 8 am to 2 pm), changes travellers' cheques for 1% commission (US$2 minimum).

The NBP Bank on ulica Bogusławskiego next to the High Gate changes travellers' cheques for 1.5% commission (weekdays 8 am to 3 pm, Saturday 8 am to noon).

Post & Telecommunications The poste restante office in Gdańsk is well hidden! As you leave the post office at Długa 22, turn right and count five doors. There's no name

or number posted outside, but it's really there and on weekdays from 8 am to 8 pm you can pick up mail addressed c/o Poste Restante, 80-801 Gdańsk 50. Even if you don't want poste restante this office is worth seeking out for its five blue card phones which are seldom in use as few people seem to know about this place.

If you have an American Express card you can also have mail addressed c/o American Express, Orbis, ulica Heweliusza 22, 80-890 Gdańsk.

The telephone centre is at Długa 22 (weekdays 7 am to 9 pm, weekends 9 am to 5 pm). Gdańsk's telephone code is 058.

Travel Agencies Seats on express trains and couchettes can be booked at the Orbis office ulica Heweliusza 22, or at the train station. They also have ferry tickets to Sweden and Finland.

Almatur, Długi Targ 11, sells international bus tickets from Gdańsk to Belgium, Britain, France, Germany, Holland and Italy. Orbis, ulica Heweliusza 22, and Gdańsk-Tourist, ulica Heweliusza 8, also sell international bus tickets to many Western European cities.

Things to See

Medieval Gdańsk was comprised of three quarters: the Old Town (Stare Miasto), the Main Town (Główne Miasto) and the Old Suburb (Stare Przedmieście). The principal streets of the Main Town run perpendicular to the port, which is reached through a series of gates. During their annual visits Polish kings entered the Main Town through the adjacent **High Gate** (1588) and **Golden Gate** (1614) and proceeded east along ulica Długa, the **Royal Way**.

Długi Targ (Long Market), the historic town square, is the very heart of old Gdańsk. The towering 15th century **main town hall** on the corner of this square contains a good **Historical Museum** (closed Monday and Friday) in the buildings' coffered Gothic chambers and a great view from the tower. Behind Neptune's Fountain (1613) stands the **Artus Mansion** where local merchants once met. The Renaissance **Green Gate**

(1568) at the east end of the square gives access to the old harbour on the Motława River. The excursion boats departing from the landing near the gate are highly recommended (see the Excursion Boats section that follows).

Two blocks north along the harbour is the Mariacka Gate with the **Archaeological Museum** (closed Monday) and through this gate is ulica Mariacka, the most picturesque street in Gdańsk, lined with 17th century burgher houses. Follow it west to the Gothic **Church of Our Lady**, the largest brick church in Poland. You may climb the 78-metre tower for US$0.25.

Continue west on ulica Piwna (Beer Street!) to the Dutch Renaissance **Armoury** (1609), and take the street running north straight to Gothic **St Catherine's Church** in the Old Town. Opposite this church is the 14th century **Great Mill**. Just behind St Catherine's is **St Bridget's Church** (1514), Lech Wałęsa's place of worship. At the back of the church are some Solidarity mementos including a memorial to Father Jerzy Popiełuszko. Solidarity and Wałęsa pins are sold at the souvenir counter inside the church.

Near Gdańsk On the north side of Gdańsk at the entrance to the **Gdańsk Shipyards**, just north-east of Gdańsk Główny Railway Station, is a tall **monument** with three steel crosses and anchors dedicated to 45 workers killed during a December 1970 strike. The monument, erected in 1980, stood here throughout the period of martial law. Nearby at the shipyard entrance is a souvenir stand selling Solidarność stickers, pins, T-shirts and even umbrellas.

Individuals are not allowed inside the shipyard but Almatur (☎ 312 403), Długi Targ 11, can organise guided tours at US$20 per group of up to 25 people. Almatur must obtain special permission from the shipyard authorities, so you'll need to book at least five days in advance.

From the post office on ulica Długa walk south four blocks to the former Franciscan monastery (1514) in the Old Suburb, south of the Main Town. The monastery now houses the **National Museum** (closed Monday), ulica Toruńska 1 at Rzeźnicka, with porcelain and paintings. The highlight of this large collection is Hans Memling's *Last Judgement*.

At Oliwa between Gdańsk and Sopot is a soaring 13th century **Cistercian cathedral** in a large park, with a museum (closed Monday) in the adjacent monastery. The cathedral's Rococo organ (1788) is one of the best in Europe – ask about organ concerts (often weekdays at noon and Sunday at 3 pm). Get there on tram No 6, 12 or 15, or by electric train to Gdańsk Oliwa Station.

Excursion Boats From April to October excursion boats to Westerplatte (US$3 single, US$4 return, a third off for students) depart several times daily from the landing near Gdańsk's Green Gate. At the beginning and end of the season the 10 am and 2 pm departures to Westerplatte are the most likely to be operating. This is one of the best trips of its kind in Poland, allowing a fine cross-section view of Gdańsk's harbour. At **Westerplatte** a towering monument (1968) with sweeping views commemorates the heroic resistance of the Polish naval garrison here which held out for a week against ferocious attacks in September 1939. Bus No 106 also connects Gdańsk to Westerplatte.

From mid-May to September there are boats across the Baltic from Gdańsk to the fishing village of **Hel** on the Hel Peninsula (US$5 single, US$7 return). From June to August, boats go to Gdynia. Alternatively, take a boat from Gdańsk to Hel, then a second from Hel to Gdynia or Sopot. Be sure to get out on the water if you're in the area in season.

Places to Stay
Camping If you arrive on the international ferry from Scandinavia, the closest camping ground to the wharf is *Camping Brzeźna* (☎ 566 531), Aleje Józefa Hallera 234 (tram No 7 or 15 from the wharf).

Hostels There are four youth hostels in the

POLAND

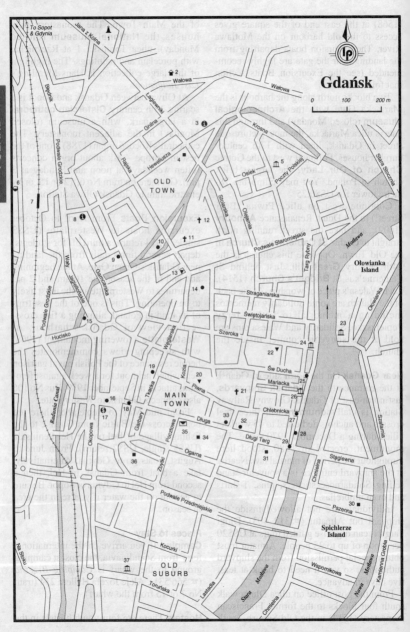

Gdańsk

0   100   200 m

To Sopot & Gdynia

Wałowa

Wałowa

OLD TOWN

MAIN TOWN

OLD SUBURB

Ołowianka Island

Spichlerze Island

Motława

POLAND

PLACES TO STAY

2 Wałowa Youth Hostel
4 Orbis Hevelius Hotel
30 Novotel Hotel
31 Jantar Hotel
34 Hotel Zaułek
36 Dom Harcerza

PLACES TO EAT

13 Restauracja Tan-Viet
20 Pod Wieza
22 Pod Łososiem Restaurant

OTHER

1 Solidarity Monument
3 Tourist Office
5 Postal Museum
6 Bus Station
7 Gdańsk Główny Railway Station
8 Gdańsk-Tourist
9 Old Town Hall
10 Great Mill
11 St Catherine's Church
12 St Bridget's Church
14 Hala Targowa Market
15 Club Żak
16 High Gate
17 NBP Bank
18 Golden Gate
19 Armoury
21 Church of Our Lady
23 Museum Ship Soldek
24 Big Crane & Maritime Museum
25 Holy Ghost Gate
26 Mariacka Gate & Archaeological Museum
27 Chlebnicka Gate
28 Excursion Boats
29 Green Gate
32 Artus Mansion
33 Main Town Hall
35 Post Office
37 National Museum

Gdańsk area. Most convenient is the hostel (☎ 312 313) at ulica Wałowa 21, a large red-brick building set back from the road, only a five-minute walk from Gdańsk Główny Railway Station. You have to ask for the key to use the showers (at the bottom of the back stairs next to the dining room). The reception is closed from 10 am to 5 pm.

The other three hostels are between Gdańsk and Sopot, too far to walk. First is the hostel (☎ 323 820) at ulica Smoluchowskiego 11 (take tram No 12 or 13 north from the train station).

The friendly Aleje Grunwaldzka 238/240 hostel (☎ 411 660) is in a small sports complex near Oliwa (open in July and August only). Take a northbound tram No 6, 12 or 15 to 'Abrahama' – ask someone where to get off.

The hostel (☎ 324 187) at ulica Kartuska 245 is about three km west of Gdańsk Railway Station (open July and August only). Catch a southbound tram No 10 or 12 outside the station, stay on to the end of the line, then walk west along the road about 10 minutes till you see a grey three-storey building with a gabled roof on the right.

Dom Harcerza (☎ 313 621), ulica Za Murami 2-10, is a large Boy Scout hostel with dormitory beds at US$5, double rooms with shared bath at US$12, doubles with private bath at US$25. The problem is, it's almost always full up with groups, but the excellent location right next to the old town makes it well worth trying anyway.

From June to September the student travel agency Almatur (☎ 314 403), Długi Targ 11 (open year-round weekdays 9 am to 5 pm, Saturday 9 am to 3 pm), rents rooms in student dormitories at US$10/15 single/double. The same office will book beds at local youth hostels.

Private Rooms Private rooms (US$10/16 single/double) are arranged by Gdańsk-Tourist (☎ 312 634), ulica Heweliusza 8 near the Gdańsk Główny Railway Station. A US$1 per person tax is charged the first night only and some of their rooms are in the old town. Freelancers on the street outside this office may have an unofficial private room to offer you, perhaps in the centre – bargain hard if their prices are higher than those asked inside.

The tourist office at Orbis in the Hevelius Hotel (weekdays 9 am to 5 pm, Saturday 10 am to 4 pm) has more expensive private rooms (US$16/22/29 single/double/triple),

POLAND

all in the centre of town. They have an album with colour photos of their rooms which you can thumb through.

Hotels The old *Jantar Hotel* (☎ 312 716), Długi Targ 19, has singles/doubles at US$18/26 without bath, US$37 double with bath, breakfast included. You couldn't ask for a more central location but it can be noisy due to the band playing downstairs.

The *Hotel Zaułek* (☎ 314 169), ulica Ogarna 107/108 (go into the courtyard), is cheap at US$6/9/12 single/double/triple and the location in the heart of old Gdańsk is fine, but it's usually fully booked weeks ahead.

One of Gdańsk's best bargains is the no-frills four-storey *Hotel Portus* (☎ 439 624), ulica Wyzwolenia 48/49, in Nowy Port. Plain rooms with shared bath are US$7 single or double. Take tram No 10 north from the train station and get out when you see the large Morski Dom Kultury on the right. The Portus will be just across the street. Otherwise it's a five-minute walk from Gdańsk Nowy Railway Station, or a 15-minute walk from the international ferry terminal. Many of the rooms are permanently occupied by Polish seamen but the staff is friendly to the very few travellers who happen to arrive. It's an interesting, totally untouristed area in which to stay.

Dom Nauczyciela ZNP (☎ 419 116), ulica Uphagena 28, is a school teachers' hotel which accommodates visitors at US$9/17/21 single/double/triple with shared bath, US$16/25/25 with private bath. This is good value but breakfast in the hotel restaurant is extra. It's a pleasant red-brick building a five-minute walk from Gdańsk Politechnika Railway Station.

The *Hotel Żabianka* (☎ 522 772), ulica Dickmana 14/15, is a functional five-storey hotel a five-minute walk from Gdańsk-Żabianka Railway Station in Oliwa. The reception is up on the 3rd floor. At US$16/18 single/double with bath and breakfast, it's fair value and they'll probably still have rooms when all the other places are full. Although convenient for those commuting by train, in about every other way the

Żabianka is uninspiring and you get a lot of train noise here (ask for a room on the side facing west).

Places to Eat
Bottom End *Neptun Milk Bar*, ulica Długa 32-34, serves hearty, cheap cafeteria-style meals with no language problems since you pick up the food first and pay at the end of the line. It's a good place for breakfast since it opens at 7 am weekdays (closed Sunday). Unfortunately the choice for vegetarians is limited.

Meals at *Złoty Kur*, ulica Długa 4 near the Golden Gate, are also cheap. Cheap self-service pizza is dispensed at *Starówka*, ulica Długa 74.

Krewctka, ulica Elzbietańska 10/11 near the train station, is a cheap seafood self-service where you pay at the end of the line. It's worth going in just to see the long wooden mural of old Gdańsk along one wall.

Top End All of the up-market restaurants of Gdańsk are highly touristy and when ordering fish you must keep in mind that the menu price is probably only for 100 grams. The portion you'll be served could weigh anywhere from 200 to 300 grams, so to avoid getting a shock when you see your bill, ask first.

A picture of a salmon is in the window of *Pod Łososiem*, ulica Szeroka 52, Gdańsk's most famous seafood restaurant. The *Restaurant Retman*, ulica Stagiewna 1, across the bridge beyond the Green Gate, is another trendy seafood restaurant with prices somewhat lower than Pol Łososiem. Their menu is posted outside (in Polish).

The restaurant downstairs in the *Jantar Hotel*, Długi Targ 19, serves unpretentious, filling meals. After 7 pm a dance band plays for an older crowd and it's rather amusing to watch the action as you have dinner, just don't sit in that section or you'll be charged US$2 cover.

Pod Wieza, Piwna 51, is inexpensive as long as you stick to the traditional Polish meat dishes. Beware of the price of the beer. The *Restauracja Tan-Viet*, at ulica

Podmłyńska 1/5, which is diagonally opposite the Targowa market, is a rather expensive Vietnamese restaurant.

Artus beer, brewed by Hevelius Breweries, is Gdańsk's star suds.

Cafés The *Palowa Coffee House* in the basement of the main town hall on Długi Targ is a good place to sit and read, or eat cakes and ice cream. Sometimes it's reserved for tour groups. The *Cocktail Bar*, Długa 59/61, also has excellent coffee and ice cream. The *Café Nad Motława* next to the Chlebnicka Gate has a nice riverside terrace where you can sit in summer. There are several romantic little bars and cafés along ulica Mariacka, such as *Podkolendrem* at No 38 and *Mariacka* at No 23.

Entertainment
Check the local papers and ask tourist information about events. The *Wybrzeże Theatre*, ulica Św Ducha 2, behind the armoury in the Main Town, presents mostly drama in Polish.

The *State Baltic Opera & Concert Hall*, Aleje Zwycięstwa 15, is near Gdańsk Politechnika Railway Station (take tram No 12 or 13 north from the train station). The opera ticket office is open weekdays from 10 am to 7 pm, Saturday 2 to 7 pm, and two hours before the performance. It's usually no problem getting in.

Gdańsk-Tourist, ulica Heweliusza 8, can reserve seats at the Musical Theatre in Gdynia.

Annual events to ask about include the Gdańsk Days in June, the International Choral Meetings from June to August, the International Festival of Organ and Chamber Music in July and August, the Dominican Fair in early August and the Festival of Polish Feature Films in September.

Lighter Fare *Club Zak* (☎ 314 115), the large red brick building on the corner of Wały Jagiellońskie and Hucisko, is a student club which includes an art cinema, a jazz club, pool tables, an art gallery, a café (open from 5 pm to 2 am), two discos (both opening at

9 pm) and a pub with live music. The downstairs disco has a lower cover charge but it's better to go upstairs where a live band will be playing on Thursday, Friday and Saturday nights. Other nights there could be live jazz, plays and perhaps even a rock concert. Decent meals are served at the bar in the upstairs disco. Unaccompanied women should have no problems upstairs at Club Zak and everyone is welcome.

Kino Neptune, Długa 57, usually shows reasonable films and upstairs through the adjacent entrance are the smaller *Kameralne* and *Helikon* cinemas with different programmes.

Things to Buy
Cepelia, Długa 48/49, sells authentic folk items including costumed dolls, embroidered table cloths, inlaid jewellery boxes, amber necklaces, costume jewellery, wall hangings, icons, leather goods, bedspreads, ceramics, walking sticks, spinning wheels and more. Jubilar, Długa 15, also has amber necklaces and jewellery.

Getting There & Away
Bus Buses leaving Gdańsk Bus Station include hourly services to Krynica Morska (58 km) and Elbląg (59 km), five daily to Malbork (56 km), four daily to Lębork (81 km) and daily to Giżycko. To go to Łeba from Gdańsk you must first take a train to Gdynia and change to a bus there (or go by bus via Lębork).

Train All long-distance trains arriving in the Tri-City area call at Gdańsk, Sopot and Gdynia. Southbound trains usually originate in Gdynia while trains to Szczecin begin in Gdańsk.

Direct trains arrive at Gdynia/Gdańsk from Berlin-Lichtenberg (via Szczecin), Poznań, Szczecin, Wrocław, Warsaw (via Malbork) and Olsztyn (also via Malbork). Couchettes are available to Prague, Warsaw, Szczecin and Berlin.

The *Neptun, Słupia* and *Kaszub* express trains run from Warsaw to Gdańsk (333 km, 3½ hours) daily all year, with the *Neptun*

POLAND

POLAND

departing from Warsaw in the morning and Gdańsk in the evening. The *Kaszub* and *Słupia* do the opposite, leaving Gdańsk in the morning and Warsaw in the late afternoon. The *Lajkonik* express train runs direct between Kraków Główny and Gdańsk (621 km, seven hours), leaving Kraków in the early morning and Gdańsk in the afternoon. All these trains also service Sopot and Gdynia, and reservations are required.

Ferry Large car ferries arrive at Gdańsk once or twice a week throughout the year from Oxelösund, Sweden, and Helsinki, Finland. The ferry from Karlskrona, Sweden, docks at Gdynia. Turn to Getting There & Away in the chapter introduction for a description of routes and fares.

Getting Around
To/From the Airport Bus No B to Rębiechowo Airport leaves from the stop on ulica Wały Jagiellońskie between Gdańsk-Tourist and the train station. Service is from 5 am to 6 pm with long gaps, so check the schedule posted at the stop well ahead.

Tram & Train Transport around the Tri-City area is easy. Tram lines carry you north from Gdańsk to Oliwa and Jelitkowo. To go to Westerplatte you can take a bus or boat. Cheap SKM electric commuter trains run constantly between Gdańsk, Sopot, Gdynia and Wejherowo (Inter-Rail valid). Frequencies vary from every six minutes during weekday rush hours to every half-hour on weekends. At Reda change for Hel. Commuter train tickets are sold at counters and you must punch your own ticket before going onto the platform. Tram tickets (sold at kiosks) are hard to find on Sunday or in outlying areas, so buy an adequate supply.

Car Rental The Avis Rent-a-Car agent in Gdańsk is Almatur, Długi Targ 11. Budget (☎ 315 611) is at the Novotel Hotel, ulica Pszenna 1 two blocks east of Długi Targ, and at Rębiechowo Airport. Orbis (☎ 314 045) at Hotel Hevelius, ulica Heweliusza 22, is the Hertz agent.

SOPOT
Sopot (Zoppot), north of Gdańsk by electric train, has been Poland's most fashionable seaside resort since Napoleon's former doctor, Jean Haffner, erected baths here in 1823. During the interwar period, Sopot belonged to the Free City of Danzig, only fully joining Poland in 1945. Sopot has a greater abundance of budget accommodation than either Gdańsk or Gdynia, and the resort atmosphere makes for a pleasant stay. The resort hotels lining the wide, white sandy shores stretching north from Jelitkowo are expensive, but budget accommodation is also available. Unfortunately, the Vistula River flushes thousands of tonnes of pollutants into the Gulf of Gdańsk every year, so swimming here is definitely not recommended.

Orientation
Turn left as you leave the train station and in a few minutes you'll reach Bohaterów Monte Cassino, Sopot's attractive pedestrian mall which leads straight down to the 'molo', Poland's longest pier, jutting 512 metres out into the Gulf of Gdańsk. North of the pier and the Orbis Grand Hotel is a seaside promenade, while behind the town, west of the railway line, is a large forest.

Information
The tourist office is at ulica Dworcowa 4 near the train station.

Travel Agencies For train tickets with seat reservations, sleepers and couchettes try Orbis, Bohaterów Monte Cassino 49. They also have international bus tickets and ferry tickets to Scandinavia.

Places to Stay
Camping *Jelitkowo Campground* (☎ 532 731) is near the beach between Gdańsk and Sopot, a seven-minute walk from the northern terminus of trams Nos 2, 4 and 6. Twenty-five three-bed bungalows are available. It's open from May to September.

There's a cheaper camping ground, *Sopot Camping*, open June to August, at ulica

Bitwy pod Płowcami 79, about one km north of Jelitkowo on the main highway. It doesn't have any bungalows but is closer to the beach.

The *Camping No 19* (☎ 518 011, extension 252) is a convenient five-minute walk from Sopot-Kamienny Potok Railway Station. The seven bungalows here are US$13 each (up to three people) but it can get crowded in the summer (open from May to September). A good bar with four pool tables is on the premises.

Hotels & Private Rooms The *Dworcowy Hotel* (☎ 511 525) near the Sopot Railway Station is US$7/12/15/18 single/double/triple/quad without bath or breakfast.

The Biuro Zakwaterowań beside the Dworcowy arranges stays in private rooms. In the off season they're closed weekends. If they can't help, hang around outside the office looking lost, baggage in hand, and wait until someone approaches you.

One of the few European-style pensions in Poland, *Pensjonat Irena* (☎ 512 073), ulica Chopina 36, in a large mansion just down the hill from Sopot Railway Station, is US$10/15/19 single/double/triple without bath or breakfast.

The 112-room, four-star *Orbis Grand Hotel* (☎ 510 041), by the pier right on Sopot Beach, is US$35/47 single/double and up with breakfast. During July and August these prices double. This neo-Baroque resort hotel built in 1926 hosts Sopot's gambling casino and it's becoming rather pretentious.

Hotels at Sopot-Kamienny Potok In front of Camping No 19 near Sopot-Kamienny Potok Railway Station is the *Hotel Miramar* (☎ 518 011), ulica Zamkowa Góra 25, formerly the PTTK Dom Turysty. Rooms with bath in the newer 'pavilion A' are US$19/30 single/double, while in the older 'pavilion B' they're US$17/28. Double rooms without bath are US$19 in both buildings and there is one single room without bath in pavilion A which costs US$8. Breakfast is included. There are also three, four, five and six-bed dormitories costing US$4 per person without

breakfast. Though it does receive many groups and is very busy in the summer, the Miramar has 327 beds – hopefully including one for you. A disco called *Bungalow* is just down the street.

The *Maryla Hotel* (☎ 516 053), a couple of blocks away at ulica Sepia 22, is rather plush with a bar and restaurant on the premises. The Maryla sort of looks like a country club but not only yuppies will like it here. Rooms with bath in the main building are US$19/25/32 single/double/triple and from June to August the adjacent 'camping bungalows' rent for US$16 double or US$22 for four persons without bath, US$29 for four with bath.

Next door to the Maryla is *Hotel Magnolia* (☎ 513 419), ulica Haffnera 100, with rooms at US$12/16/19 single/double/triple (shared bath).

Across the street from the Maryla and Magnolia is the 104-room *Sopot Lucky Hotel* (☎ 513 296), ulica Haffnera 81/85, with rooms with bath at US$25/32/35 double/triple/quad (no singles). This modern three-storey building is a former holiday complex owned by the Gdynia shipyard.

All four hotels are on a hill a five-minute walk from Sopot-Kamienny Potok Railway Station and 10 minutes from the beach. Hotel prices at Sopot are greatly increased in July and August, so expect to pay considerably more than the rates quoted here at that time.

Places to Eat
The *Albatros Restaurant* in the Dworcowy Hotel not far from the Sopot Railway Station is one of the least expensive in town. The service is good and the portions large, but there may not be any printed menu so ask the waiter to write down the prices while ordering. The restaurant at *Pensjonat Irena* is also good and inexpensive.

Cafés The artists' club, *Spatif*, ulica Bohaterów Monte Cassino 54 (upstairs), has a great bar and meals are served, but this is a private club and the door is kept securely locked. If you knock you'll be scrutinised through a

POLAND

tiny window and only if the members present like what they see will you be admitted.

At the terrace at Złoty Ul, Bohaterów Monte Cassino 33, you'll be among visitors who like to sip as they sit and watch the passing parade. Sopot's most popular café among students is Café Bazar, Bohaterów Monte Cassino 5.

Entertainment

Summer activities centre around the open-air Opera Leśna in the forest, 15 minutes' walk straight west from Bohaterów Monte Cassino. The Opera and Musical Theatre Festival is held here in July and the International Song Festival during the last 10 days of August. Rock groups appear on the programme of the latter.

Plays in Polish are staged at the Scena Kameralna, Bohaterów Monte Cassino 55/57. Kino Bałtyk, Bohaterów Monte Cassino 28, is Sopot's best cinema.

For tickets to the Opera Leśna check with the Bałtycka Agencja Artystyczna-BART (☎ 510 115), ulica Kościuszki 61 a couple of blocks south of Sopot Railway Station. Orbis, Bohaterów Monte Cassino 49, may also have summer opera tickets.

Getting There & Away

All long-distance trains stop here.

GDYNIA

Gdynia (Gdingen), the northernmost of the Tri-City three, is the base for much of Poland's merchant and fishing fleet. Unlike Gdańsk which is on a river, Gdynia is a real Baltic port looking out onto the open sea, with sailors on the streets and seagulls flying above.

In 1922 the Polish parliament decided to build a port on the site of a small village here to give Poland an outlet to the sea at a time when Gdańsk was still the Free City of Danzig. With the help of French capital, Gdynia had become one of the largest ports on the Baltic by the outbreak of WW II. Unlike most other towns along the north coast which are German in origin, Gdynia is Polish through and through.

Orientation & Information

Gdynia Railway Station shelters a left-luggage office and cash-only exchange facilities, both open 24 hours a day. The tourist information office (daily 9 am to 6 pm) in the train station is well hidden down near the PKS bus ticket window, beyond the video games to one side from the main station hall.

The ferry from Karlskrona, Sweden, arrives/departs from the Terminal Promowy, ulica Kwiatkowskiego 60, five km north-west of Gdynia Railway Station. Ask about the free shuttle bus between the terminal and Gdańsk when you book your ticket.

Post & Telecommunications There's a telephone centre in the main post office on ulica 10 Lutego (weekdays 7 am to 8 pm, Saturday 9 am to 5 pm, Sunday and holidays 11 am to 6 pm). If the main entrance is closed go in through the door around the corner on ulica Władysława IV. Gdynia's telephone code is 058.

Travel Agencies Orbis, ulica Świętojanska 36, has the usual international bus, train and ferry tickets, and can book couchettes.

Things to See

Sightseeing centres around Gdynia's broad main pier, Nabrzeże Pomorskie, pointing out into the Gulf of Gdańsk. Along it runs an attractive walkway past museum ships, local ferry terminals, an aquarium and finally a monument to the writer Joseph Conrad.

Two historic **museum ships** (closed Monday) are stationed on this pier. The Błyskawica, a WW II warship, is permanently moored at the pier. The Dar Pomorza, a three-masted sailing vessel built at Hamburg in 1909, was christened the Prinzess Eitel. In 1919 France got the ship for reparations and it was purchased by Poland as a naval training ship in 1929. The Dar Pomorza spent the war years in Stockholm. It's still an active training ship and often travels abroad to show the flag, so there's no assurance it will be there when you are.

POLAND

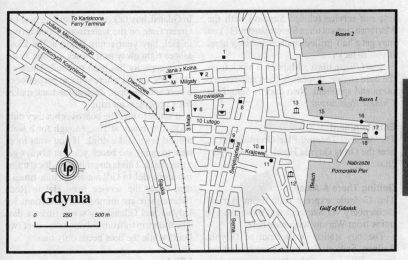

Gdynia

0   250   500 m

1	Hotel Garnizonowy	10	Orbis Gdynia Hotel
2	Dom Rybaka	11	Musical Theatre
3	Market	12	Naval Museum
4	Gdynia-Główna Railway Station	13	City Museum
5	Nord Turus	14	Fishing Boats
6	Sapri Pizza	15	Museum Ship Bryskawica
7	Post Office	16	Museum Ship Dar Pomorza
8	Hotel Lark	17	Joseph Conrad Monument
9	Orbis	18	Oceanographic Museum & Aquarium

Most attractions around Gdynia are closed on Monday.

Places to Stay

Private Rooms A good place to try first is Nord Turus (☎ 209 287), ulica Starowiejska 47 (entrance from ulica Dworcowa) near Gdynia Główna Railway Station, which arranges accommodation in private homes for US$5/9 single/double (higher in mid-summer). It's open from 8 am to 6 pm Monday to Saturday.

Hotels Rooms at the *Lark Hotel* (☎ 218 046), an old-style hotel conveniently located at ulica Starowiejska 1, is US$9/12/16 single/double/triple with shared bath. It's the kind of place a seaman might appreciate and the earthy atmosphere will also appeal to any rough-and-ready traveller looking to get off the beaten track.

If the Lark is fully booked try *Dom Rybaka* (☎ 208 723), ulica Jana z Kolna 27, a five-storey red-brick hotel with rooms at US$10/13 single/double.

The *Hotel Garnizonowy* (☎ 266 472), ulica Jana z Kolna 6, is a six-storey hotel formerly reserved for military personnel. Double rooms are US$19 (no singles).

Places to Eat

For cheap basic meals check out the nameless self-service (closed Sunday) with the Marlboro signs at ulica Świętojanska 11. You may get a half-grilled chicken and beer here, if you're lucky.

Sapri Pizza, ulica 3 Maja 21, a block from the train station, dispenses good self-service pizza and spaghetti. Next door is *Song Lam Chinese Restaurant*.

Entertainment
The *Musical Theatre*, Plac Grunwaldzki 1, near the Orbis Gdynia Hotel, presents operettas.

Getting There & Away
The *Gedania* express train from Berlin-Lichtenberg via Szczecin and most express trains from Warsaw terminate here.

The bus station is in front of Gdynia Railway Station. Bus tickets are sold at the 'kasy PKS' near the train reservation windows inside the train station. Buses of possible use to visitors include those to Hel, Łeba and Świnoujście.

HEL
Hel, a real Baltic fishing village near the tip of the narrow peninsula separating the Gulf of Gdańsk from the sea, is the favourite day-trip destination for Tri-City area visitors.

Things to See & Do
The local **fishing museum** is in the old red church opposite the harbour. There's a beach on the bay just west of the harbour, or walk a little over one km across the peninsula to the sea beach.

Places to Stay & Eat
There are no hotels at Hel, though the PTTK Tourist Office, Generała Waltera 80 near the harbour, might be able to suggest a place to stay. Next to the PTTK is the *Kaszubska Bar* with big mugs of draught beer.

Getting There & Away
On summer mornings excursion boats to Hel leave from the end of the long wooden pier at Sopot, and less frequently from Gdańsk.

In Gdańsk buy tickets at the landing near the Green Gate on the waterfront. Upon arrival in Hel, buy your return ticket at the kiosk ashore right away as it closes as soon as the ship's capacity has been reached. There's a small bar aboard where you can get coffee or a beer and the open deck at the back makes for a very pleasant trip.

It's nice to take the boat over but they only allow 2½ hours at Hel, enough for a walk around town and a drink. If you want more time to enjoy the beach you can always get a train back. This is no problem as local trains run from Hel to Gdynia about four times a day, while the service from Hel to Reda (where there are immediate connections for Gdynia and Gdańsk) is seven times a day. The train trip to/from Gdynia takes over two hours while the boat needs only one.

ŁEBA
If you're looking for a Baltic beach resort you won't have to share with thousands of holidaying Polish workers and their families, where the small town ambience still prevails and the surrounding nature is relatively undisturbed, you won't go wrong by choosing Łeba (pronounced 'weba'). The beach here stretches in both directions as far as the eye can see, and only one old mansion breaks through the forest crowning the beachside sand dunes. Unlike the polluted waters around Gdańsk, you can swim in the open Baltic here. Łeba is too far to do as a day trip from Gdańsk – don't bother coming if you can't stay the night.

Orientation
Trains and buses from Lębork terminate at Łeba Railway Station two blocks west of ulica Kościuszki, Łeba's main drag. This shopping street runs north a few hundred metres, crosses the Chełst Canal, and ends in a park which you walk through to reach the sea. A town plan is posted outside the train station.

Things to See
Łeba is on a brief stretch of the Łeba River which joins Łebsko Lake to the sea. Just

before dusk, people head down to the river mouth to join the fisher folk in watching the sunset. The river divides Łeba's beach in two. The town is nestled back out of the way behind the eastern beach, while the beach on the west side of the river is far less crowded. The broad white sands of this western beach stretch back 75 metres to the dunes – one of the best beaches on the entire Baltic.

Farther west of town and the river, a sand bar of white pine-covered dunes separates shallow Lake Łebsko from the Baltic. Here one finds **Słowiński National Park**, where the largest shifting sand dunes in Eastern Europe create a striking desert landscape. During WW II, Rommel's Afrika Korps trained in this desert, and a small Polish military base is still hidden among the dunes. V-1 rockets were fired at England from here, and you can still find what appear to be the old concrete launching pads.

The road into the park runs along the north shore of Lake Łebsko for 2.5 km to the Rabka park entry gate (pedestrians free, cars US$3), then another 4.5 km to Wydmy Ruchome where vehicular traffic ends. In July and August there are buses from Łeba to Wydmy Ruchome (seven km) every two hours. From the end of the road it's a two-km walk to a magnificent, 42-metre-high sand dune which simply must be climbed for a sweeping view of desert, lake, beach, sea and forest. You can return to Łeba on foot along the beach with perhaps a stop for a swim – something you can't do in the Sahara!

Places to Stay

Camping The *Intercamp* (☎ 61 206), a five-minute walk west from the train station (signposted), has camping space or rooms in a central building. In 1984 the International Camping and Caravanning Jamboree was held here. The facilities are good but there's little shade.

There are two more camping grounds a few hundred metres west of the Intercamp, to the right on ulica Turystyczna, and these have more shade and are closer to the beach. The first is *Camping 'Przymorze' No 21 'Leśny'*. The second is run by the PTTK and has lots of pretty little three-bed wooden cabins among the pine trees.

Camping No 21 and the Intercamp both have a bar and store, and all three are open from mid-May to mid-September. On a hot summer weekend every bed at Łeba will be occupied by people from the Tri-City area, so have your tent ready.

Private Rooms & Hotels The Przymorze Biuro Wczasów on Plac Dworcowy opposite the train station can arrange private rooms and provide general information.

Dom Wycieczkowy PTTK (☎ 661 324), ulica 1-go Maja 6 on the corner of ulica Kościuszki, just two blocks from the train station, has 28 rooms with private bath (but no hot water) at US$4 per person.

Pensjonat Angela (☎ 662 647), Plac Dworcowy 2 near the train station, is a new three-storey building, open only during the summer season. It's about US$8 per person. Ring the bell if it looks closed.

The three-storey *Hotel Morska* (☎ 661 468), beside the cinema between town and the beach, is US$10 single or double.

The *Dom Wypoczynkowy 'Kowelin'* (☎ 661 440), ulica Nad Ujścien 6, is an attractive four-storey building with 24 rooms with bath at US$8 per person. As you walk down ulica Kościuszki towards the beach, turn right after the small bridge over the canal. There's a restaurant downstairs in this former holiday home for workers from the copper mining industrial complex.

There are a number of other seasonal hotels and pensions around Łeba which the tourist office should know about.

Places to Eat

Try the *Restaurant Morska* in the hotel of the same name. You can't miss the *Karczma Słowińska Restaurant & Café*, ulica Kościuszki 28, overlooking the canal. Neither of these places is very good and there's nowhere to get breakfast before 9 am in Łeba, so it's best to buy groceries the night before.

Getting There & Away

Coming and going you'll probably transit Lębork, a town on the main railway line from Gdańsk to Szczecin, where you'll have to change for Łeba. Trains only run from Lębork to Łeba every three or four hours (28 km). If you're unlucky, check the bus station across the street from Lębork Railway Station where there are buses to Łeba every hour or so from platform No 3 (ticket from the office inside, US$0.75).

The *Słupia* express train runs daily all year between Warsaw and Lębork (409 km, five hours). It leaves Lębork in the very early morning and Warsaw in the late afternoon, travelling via Gdynia, Gdańsk and Malbork; reservations are required. Unfortunately neither schedule connects with a bus to/from Łeba, so unless you're willing to spend a night at the *Miejski Hotel* (☎ 21 903), ulica 10 Marca 9, Lębork, you can't use this train.

Trains between Lębork and Wejherowo (and the electric train line to Gdańsk) run every couple of hours. Several buses a day also go from Lębork to Wejherowo. A couple of buses a day go from Łeba direct to Gdynia (59 km).

MALBORK

From 1309 to 1457 Malbork (Marienburg) was the headquarters of the Teutonic Knights and one of the largest medieval fortified castles in Europe. The Teutonic Knights with their white robes and black crosses originated during the Third Crusade (1198), and with the Templars and Hospitallers became one of the three great military/religious orders of the time. In 1271 Monfort Castle in Palestine was lost and the order began searching for a new headquarters.

Construction of Malbork Castle began in 1276 and in 1309 the order's capital was shifted here from Venice. Constant territorial disputes with Poland and Lithuania finally culminated in the Battle of Grunwald in 1410. The order was defeated but continued to hold the castle until 1457. From 1772 to 1945 Malbork was incorporated into Prussia and extensive restorations were carried out in the years prior to WW I when Malbork

was viewed as a romantic symbol of the glory of medieval Germany. After WW II the Polish authorities in turn continued the work to preserve this great monument of Gothic culture. The museum here was opened in 1960.

Orientation

As you leave the train station turn right and cut across the busy highway, then straight down ulica Kościuszki to the castle. Lots of taxis park in front of the train station, otherwise it's a 15-minute walk though the modern town. A left-luggage service is available at the train station.

Things to See

One highlight is **Malbork Castle**, overlooking the Nogat River, an eastern arm of the Vistula, was badly damaged during WW II but has now been largely restored. It consists of the service facilities of the 15th century Lower Castle (between the railway line and the main gate), the 14th century Middle Castle where the Grand Master lived and the 13th century High Castle.

The first courtyard features an outstanding museum of Polish amber. Three floors of exhibits are to be seen in the rooms around the second courtyard (High Castle). One hall contains a superb collection of inlaid antique weapons. In the far corner a passageway leads to the Gdanisko Tower. Yes, the gaping hole in the floor was the toilet.

At least four hours are required to explore this imposing monument (open from 8.30 am to 5 pm May to September, 9 am to 2.30 pm October to April, closed Monday). The compulsory, two-hour guided museum tour with a Polish-speaking guide in a group of up to 40 persons is US$3 per person. For a tour in English (or French or German) an additional US$30 per group must be paid. On Monday all the exhibition halls are closed but you're allowed to wander around the courtyards and corridors in relative peace for a US$0.50 fee. You must arrive at least three hours before closing time if you want to get on a tour.

The best view of Malbork Castle is from

the train. Coming from Gdańsk it's on the right immediately after you cross the river; northbound towards Gdańsk it's on the left just beyond Malbork Station. Have your camera ready.

Places to Stay & Eat

The cheapest place to stay is the *Hotel Noclegownia PKP*, ulica Dworcowa 1a, just up the street from the train station as you head for the castle. It's the yellow brick building on the left just before the busy highway. A basic room with shared facilities will be US$4 per person and adjacent to this hotel is the self-service *PKP Bar Express* with cheap food.

Across the highway at ulica Kościuszki 43 is the functional, four-storey *Hotel Zbyszko* (☎ 25 11), a five-minute walk from the train station. At last report it was US$8 per person with shared bath but the hotel is gradually being renovated which could boost prices. The hotel restaurant may be worth patronising by daytrippers and there's also an inexpensive pizza place on the corner across the street at ulica Kościuszki 25.

The *Hotel Zamek* (☎ 27 38) offers rooms in a restored medieval building of the Lower Castle. At US$30/60 it's a splurge. The hotel restaurant (closed Monday) is a good place for lunch, however, but check their opening hours if you were thinking of having dinner there.

In July and August there's a *youth hostel* (☎ 25 11) in the big red school house at ulica Żeromskiego 45, a 10-minute walk from the station.

There's also a camping ground (open from June to August) on ulica Portowa about two km beyond the train station, away from the train station. The Hotel Sportovy (☎ 24 13) behind the camping ground has rooms and is open year-round.

Getting There & Away

It's quite easy to visit Malbork as a stopover between Warsaw and Gdańsk or vice versa using the half-dozen express trains which pass through every day. If you're travelling north from Warsaw you can arrive on the *Neptun, Posejdon* or *Lajkonik* express trains in the morning and continue to Gdańsk on the *San, Stoczniowiec* or *Słupia* express trains (or a local train) in the afternoon. Southbound, leave Gdańsk on the *Słupia* or *San* express trains (or any local train) in the morning and carry on to Warsaw on the *Stoczniowiec, Lajkonik, Neptun* or *Posejdon* in the afternoon.

Ask an Orbis office to help you work out an itinerary using these trains with a stopover of three or four hours in Malbork. Malbork is 282 km and three hours by express train from Warsaw. Some trains are seasonal and reservations are required on all except the *San* and the *Stoczniowiec*. Ask Orbis to make the reservations for you and check the onward time as soon as you arrive in Malbork.

Otherwise visit Malbork as a day trip from Gdańsk (58 km) or on the way to/from Olsztyn. Sometimes to go between Malbork and Olsztyn (126 km) you must change trains at Elbląg or Bogaczewo or both; other times you change at Iława.

Mazuria

Mazuria stretches from the Vistula to the Russian, Lithuanian and Belorussian borders north of the Mazovian plain. Here the Scandinavian glacier left behind a typical postglacial landscape, and many of the 3000 lakes are linked by rivers and canals to create a system of waterways well favoured by yachtspeople. The winding shorelines with many peninsulas, inlets and small islands are surrounded by low hills and forests, making the picturesque lake districts of north-eastern Poland one of the most attractive and varied touring areas in the country. Add to this the many fascinating historical remains and the opportunity to venture into places which seldom see English speakers, and you'll have all the reasons you need to visit.

HISTORY

The historic regions of Warmia and Mazuria

were the southern half of German East Prussia until 1945 (the northern half is now part of Russia). Originally inhabited by heathen Prussian and Jatzvingian tribes, the area was conquered in the 13th century by the Germanic Teutonic Knights who had been invited in by the Polish Prince Conrad of Mazovia in 1225. The intention was that the knights would convert the Baltic tribes and depart, but instead they created a powerful religious state on the north-east border of Poland.

The Battle of Grunwald, fought in 1410 just south-west of Olsztyn, turned out to be a pivotal showdown between the knights and the Polish Crown. The knights' defeat at the battle was followed by other long wars which led to the Treaty of Toruń (1466) which gave Warmia (Ermeland), the area between Olsztyn and Frombork, to Poland for over three centuries. It was during this period that the famous Polish administrator and astronomer lived in Warmia, and today we can follow the Copernicus Trail from Olsztyn to Lidzbark Warmiński and Frombork.

Mazuria came under the Hohenzollerns of Brandenburg in the 16th century and in 1772 Warmia was also annexed to the Kingdom of Prussia. In a 1918 plebiscite, Warmia and Mazuria voted to remain German while the area around Suwałki went to Poland. During WW II the Nazis militarised Mazuria, which became a base for Hitler's dreams of conquest. This policy brought seven centuries of German involvement in the area to an ignominious end. However, even today, Lutheran Protestantism is alive in central Mazuria whereas Warmia remains more stolidly Catholic.

OLSZTYN

Olsztyn, 177 km south-east of Gdańsk, is the capital of Mazuria and a regional transportation hub. For travellers, Olsztyn is important as a jumping-off point for Lidzbark Warmiński, Grunwald, the Elbląg Canal and the Great Mazurian Lake District rather than as a destination in itself. Though the food and

accommodation are good, you can see the city's historic sites in a couple of hours.

From 1466 to 1772 the town belonged to the Kingdom of Poland, and none other than Nicolaus Copernicus, administrator of Warmia, commanded Olsztyn Castle from 1516 to 1521. Here he made astronomical observations and began writing *On the Revolutions of Celestial Bodies*. With the first partition of Poland, Olsztyn became Prussian Allenstein and remained so until 1945.

Orientation

Olsztyn Główny Railway Station and the bus station are adjacent on the north-east side of town, a 15-minute walk from the centre.

Walk south-west on ulica Partyzantów past Plac Gen Bema to Aleje Dąbrowszczaków on the left. When this street terminates in the city centre, cross the street and look for ulica 22 Lipca which takes you to High Gate and the old town. Olsztyn Zachodni Railway Station is just a short walk west of the castle.

Information

The tourist office (☎ 272 738) in the PTTK complex beside the High Gate is helpful in providing maps of the Mazurian lakes and advice. It's open weekdays from 9 am to 4 pm, Saturday from 10 am to 2 pm. The adjacent sporting goods store has an excellent selection of maps.

The automobile club is at 'Polmozbyt' on ulica Sielska near the Novotel west of town.

Money Travellers' cheques can be changed at the PKO Bank, ulica Dąbrowszczaków 30 (weekdays 8 am to 6 pm, Saturday 8 am to 1 pm).

Post & Telecommunications A telephone centre is in the post office at ulica Partyzantów 39 next to the train station (weekdays 7 am to 9 pm, Saturday 9 am to noon). Olsztyn's telephone code is 089.

Travel Agencies Orbis, Aleje Dąbrowszczaków 1, has international bus, train and ferry tickets.

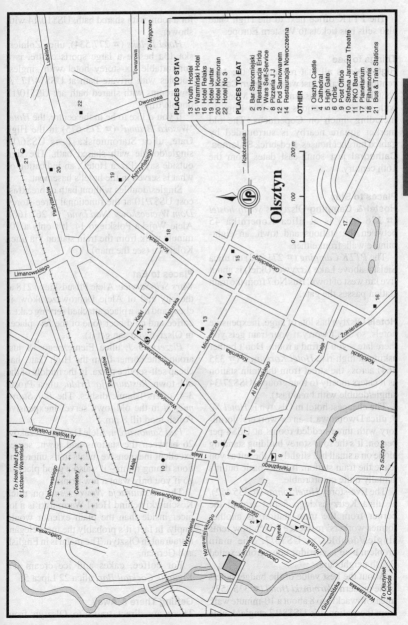

Olsztyn

PLACES TO STAY

13 Youth Hostel
15 Warmiński Hotel
16 Hotel Relaks
19 Hotel Jantar
20 Hotel Kormoran
22 Hotel No 3

PLACES TO EAT

2 Bar Staromiejski
3 Restauracja Eridu
7 Wars Self-Service
8 Pizzeria J
12 Pod Samowarem
14 Restauracja Nowoczesna

OTHER

1 Olsztyn Castle
4 Cathedral
5 High Gate
6 Orbis
9 Post Office
10 Stefana Jaracza Theatre
11 PKO Bank
17 Planetarium
18 Filharmonia
21 Bus & Train Stations

POLAND

The PTTK office next to the High Gate also sells bus tickets to Western Europe.

Things to See

High Gate is all that remains of the 14th century city walls. Just west, **Olsztyn Castle** contains a good museum (closed Monday) with some explanations posted in English, including much on Copernicus. The old market square nearby is surrounded by gabled burgher houses. Red-brick **St James' Cathedral** just south-east dates from the 16th century.

Places to Stay

Hostel & Camping Olsztyn's *youth hostel* (☎ 276 650) is at ulica Kopernika 45 between the stations and town, an eight-minute walk from either.

The *PTTK Camping* (☎ 271 253) on ulica Sielska above Lake Krzywe (Ukiel) is about five km west of town. Bus No 7 from the train station passes the gate.

Hotels Olsztyn has lots of large, inexpensive hotels, so don't worry if your train gets you there late – you'll find a room. Don't bother asking at high-rise *Hotel Kormoran* (☎ 335 864) across the street from the train station as it caters mostly to tour groups (US$27/34 single/double with breakfast).

The cheapest hotel in Olsztyn is *Hotel No 3*, ulica Dworcowa 1, an ex-workers' dormitory with three-bedded rooms at US$4 per person. It's the four-storey building standing alone on a small hill slightly to the left as you leave the train station. It looks basic but it's actually quite comfortable.

The five-storey *Hotel Jantar* (☎ 335 452), at ulica Kętrzyńskiego 5 just around the corner from the train station, is another former workers' residence which now rents singles/doubles at US$5/7. The main problem here is corridor noise from excited Polish neighbours.

About the best value of the budget hotels is the modern *Warmiński Hotel* (☎ 335 353), ulica Głowackiego 8 about a 10-minute walk from the station. It's US$8/12 single/double

for a room with shared bath, US$10/14 with shower.

Hotel Relaks (☎ 277 534), ulica Żołnierska 13a beside a large sports centre, is a comfortable six-storey hotel with singles/doubles with private bath at US$14/17. A few rooms with shared bath are US$10/12 double/triple.

If you'd like to be in the centre, the *Hotel 'Wysoka Brama'* (☎ 273 675) in the High Gate, ulica Staromiejska 1, is US$6/10 single/double with shared bath. The sign outside says 'Pizza Hotel', an indication of what is served in the hotel's basement.

Singles/doubles without bath or breakfast cost US$7/10 at the functional three-storey *Dom Wycieczkowy 'Nad Łyną'* (☎ 267 166), Aleje Wojska Polskiego 14. It's only a 10-minute walk from the train station via ulica Kolejowa (see the map).

Places to Eat

Wars Self-Service, Aleje Piłsudskiego 218 at the city end of Aleje Dąbrowszczaków, is cheap and has a place attached serving cakes, coffee and cold beer (one of the few places in Olsztyn you can get it).

Pizzeria J J, ulica Pieniężnego 18 just around the corner from the High Gate, has cheap self-service pizza. In the middle of the old town *Restauracja Eridu*, ulica Prosta 3-4, offers Islamic dishes. The *Bar Staromiejski* in the old town serves inexpensive Polish food till 8 pm.

Pod Samowarem, Aleje Dąbrowszczaków 26 between the stations and town, serves excellent inexpensive meals in its unpretentious dining room – it's also a good place to go if you only want a few drinks.

The *Restauracja Nowoczesna* on ulica Kościuszki behind Hotel Warmiński is a lot nicer inside than the plain exterior would imply. In fact, it's probably the most elegant restaurant in Olsztyn. The menu is in English and German.

For coffee, cakes and ice cream it's *Yogurcik Cocktail Bar*, ulica 22 Lipca 5.

Getting There & Away

There are direct trains to Olsztyn from

Gdynia/Gdańsk (179 km via Malbork), Poznań (via Iława, Ostróda and Toruń) and Warsaw (237 km via Działdowo). If the timing doesn't allow you to use the Gdańsk train, you may have to change trains at Elbląg, Bogaczewo or Iława to travel between Malbork and Olsztyn (no direct buses). For Frombork or Kaliningrad you must change at Braniewo. For Lidzbark Warmiński change at Czerwonka (though the bus is much faster and more frequent on this route). For the Mazurian lakes look for a train to Ełk and get off at Giżycko, Mikołajki or Ruciane-Nida.

The *Kormoran* express train runs daily all year between Warsaw and Olsztyn (three hours), departing from Olsztyn in the morning, Warsaw in the afternoon. Reservations are required.

Numerous buses depart from Olsztyn, including nine daily to Elbląg (97 km), eight to Gdańsk (156 km), nine to Giżycko (120 km), eight to Kętrzyn (89 km), 43 to Lidzbark Warmiński (46 km) and four to Warsaw (213 km). Check the footnotes and ask at information, then try and purchase an advance ticket to be sure you selected a bus that really is going that day.

THE ELBLĄG CANAL

A fascinating excursion is a trip on the 81-km Elbląg Canal built in 1848-60 from Elbląg to Ostróda. The difference in water level between these towns is 100 metres, and to bridge this gap the boats pass through two locks and are carried up and down five slipways on rail-mounted platforms or 'ramps', a technical solution unique in Europe!

Theoretically, the excursion boats leave Elbląg for Ostróda at 8 am daily from mid-May to mid-September (11 hours, US$16) but captains often cancel the trip if not enough passengers are around. You should be OK from mid-June to August and on weekends. Bring your own food as what's sold on board is very expensive. (If the trip is cancelled consider going to Frombork instead.)

You can do the canal trip en route between

Gdańsk and Olsztyn, though you'll have to catch the 6 am bus from Gdańsk (59 km) in order to be there in time. Get out at the first stop after the canal in Elbląg, otherwise you'll have to walk back from the bus station. The boat dock is to the left as the bus crosses the bridge.

To do the canal as a day trip from Olsztyn involves a very early start. Check the 4.40 am train from Olsztyn to Elbląg (97 km) and the 9.06 pm train from Ostróda to Olsztyn (39 km), but remember, these times could change! In midsummer Orbis, ulica Dąbrowszczaków 1, Olsztyn, organises day excursions on the Elbląg Canal with bus transfers from Olsztyn (US$40).

It's probably better to spend the previous night in Elbląg and the *PTTK Dom Wycieczkovy* (☎ 24 307), ulica Krótka 5, is a good bet at US$5/8 single/double without bath. Otherwise there's the *Hotel Dworcowy* (☎ 27 011) opposite the bus/train station. The *PTTK camping ground* (☎ 24 307), ulica Panieńska 14, is right near the bridge over the canal. Elbląg was destroyed in WW II and the only reason to come is the canal trip.

THE COPERNICUS TRAIL

Though he was born in Toruń and studied at Kraków, astronomer Nicolaus Copernicus spent the last 40 years of his life in Warmia. From 1503 to 1510, Copernicus served as an adviser to his uncle, Bishop Łukasz Watzenrode, at **Lidzbark Warmiński**, episcopal seat of the Polish bishops who ruled the Duchy of Warmia under the Polish crown from 1466 to 1772. In the 14th century a strong castle was built here which the bishops later adopted as their residence, adding a neoclassical palace to the complex in the 17th century. The vaulted chambers of the castle interior now house a world-class museum (closed Monday) with Gothic sculpture and painting in the grand refectory downstairs, a large art gallery and exhibition on the restoration of historic monuments upstairs. Also to be seen are a gilded chapel, old weapons in the cellars and a splendid arcaded interior courtyard. Just 46 km north

POLAND

of Olsztyn, Lidzbark Warmiński is an easy day trip by bus.

Frombork (Frawenburg), on the south-east shore of the Vistula Lagoon (Zalew Wiślany) between Lidzbark Warmiński and Gdańsk, was founded by colonists from Lübeck, Germany, in the 13th century. From 1512 to 1516, and again from 1522 until his death in 1543, Copernicus lived and worked in Frombork and his unmarked grave is in Frombork's red-brick Gothic cathedral (erected in 1388), beneath the aisle by the second pillar on the right as you stand below the organ. On the opposite side of this pillar is a statue of the astronomer and in the former bishop's palace next to the cathedral is a Copernicus Museum (closed Monday). Just below Cathedral Hill is a tall statue of Copernicus which makes him look rather like Chairman Mao.

The easiest way to get to Frombork is by bus from Gdańsk (93 km – train connections from Gdańsk are bad). To/from Olsztyn (105 km) you must change trains at Braniewo. There isn't a lot of accommodation at Frombork, though you could try the *PTTK Dom Wycieczkowy* (☎ 72 51) in the park just west of Cathedral Hill which also serves meals. The year-round *youth hostel* (☎ 74 53), ulica Elbląska 11, is a couple of blocks west of the centre of town.

THE GREAT MAZURIAN LAKES

The Great Mazurian Lake District north-east of Olsztyn is a verdant land of rolling hills interspersed with glacial lakes, healthy little farms, scattered tracts of forest and many small towns. There are literally thousands of postglacial lakes to the north and south of Mikołajki. A fifth of the surface of this area is covered by water and another 30% by forest. Lake Śniardwy (110 sq km) is the largest lake in Poland, and Lake Mamry and adjacent waters total an additional 102 sq km. The large, clean lakes and abundant forests are an irresistible beacon for boaters, anglers and nature lovers. Polish tourists also arrive in great numbers though it's much less crowded after 15 August.

Orientation & Information

Pick up the 1:60,000 *Jezioro Śniardwy* map or the 1:120,000 *Wielkie jeziora mazurskie* map at a bookstore before you visit. These maps can be frustratingly difficult to find in the area itself.

Activities

The Great Mazurian Lakes are well connected by canals, rivers and streams, making this a paradise for canoeists and kayakers. Established kayak routes follow the Krutynia River near Ruciane-Nida, and the Czarna Hańcza River in the Augustów area. People arriving by train with folding kayaks could get on the Krutynia River Kayak Trail near Spychowo Railway Station between Olsztyn and Ruciane-Nida. There's a water-side hostel *(stanica wodna)* at ulica Juranda 30, Spychowo, open from May to September. Check with the PTTK in Olsztyn to make sure it's open and ask about other such riverside hostels at Krutyń, Ukta and Nowy Most. Otherwise begin at Ruciane-Nida itself or at Sorkwity on the railway line between Olsztyn and Mrągowo. Canoes can be rented at Sorkwity (☎ 81 24).

Yachtspeople will want to sail on the larger lakes, and boats with or without captains can usually be hired at the yacht harbours in Giżycko, Mikołajki, Ruciane-Nida and Węgorzewo. If you have difficulty making the arrangements, ask your hotel or pension manager for help or go to a tourist office.

Getting There & Away

Communications are good, with three different west-east railway lines running across the region from Olsztyn (the gateway city) to Ełk via Giżycko, Mikołajki or Ruciane-Nida. Frequent buses link the settlements on north-south routes, so getting around is easy. To/from Warsaw there are direct buses which are faster than the train.

Getting Around the Lakes

Theoretically, excursion boats of the Mazurian Shipping Company's White Fleet run between Giżycko, Mikołajki and Ruciane-

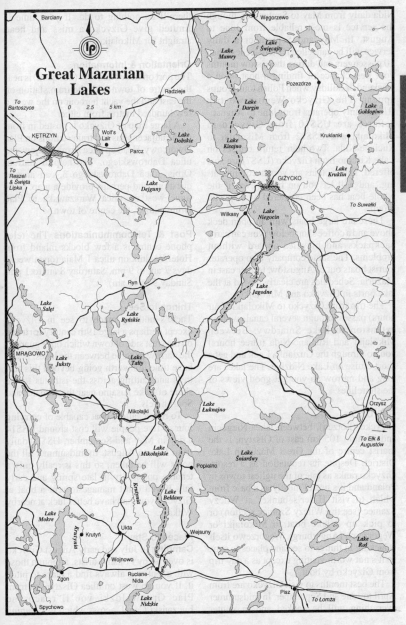

Great Mazurian Lakes

0   2.5   5 km

To Bartoszyce

To Reszel & Święta Lipka

KĘTRZYN

Wolf's Lair

Parcz

Barciany

Radzieje

Lake Mamry

Lake Święcajty

Węgorzewo

Pozezdrze

Lake Dargin

Lake Gołdopiwo

Lake Dobskie

Lake Kisajno

Kruklanki

Lake Kruklin

Lake Dejguny

GIŻYCKO

Wilkasy

Lake Niegocin

To Suwałki

Lake Salęt

Ryn

Lake Ryńskie

Lake Jagodne

Lake Juksty

MRĄGOWO

Lake Tałty

Mikołajki

Lake Łuknajno

Orzysz

To Ełk & Augustów

Lake Mikołajskie

Popielno

Lake Śniardwy

Lake Mokre

Krutynia

Ukta

Lake Bełdany

Wejsuny

Lake Roś

Krutyń

Wojnowo

Zgon

Spychowo

Ruciane-Nida

Lake Nidzkie

Pisz

To Łomża

Nida daily from May to September, though the service is most reliable from June to August. In May and September a daily service will be cancelled if there are less than 10 passengers and during these slow months your best chance of finding a boat is on a weekend or holiday when Polish tour groups appear. The Giżycko-Węgorzewo trip (US$7) only operates from June to August.

Fares are US$10 from Giżycko to Mikołajki and US$12 from Mikołajki to Ruciane-Nida. Two-hour return cruises on Lake Kisajno from Giżycko (US$7) are also offered. The captains are very accommodating, and will let you on board even if the whole boat has been chartered by a special group.

These are large boats with an open deck above and a coffee shop below; you can carry backpacks and bicycles aboard without problems. The same company also operates tourist boats out of Augustów, farther east in Mazuria. Schedules are clearly posted at the lake ports in Giżycko and Mikołajki.

The trip from Giżycko to Mikołajki (four hours) passes through several canals with an extension to Lake Śniardwy. Between Mikołajki and Ruciane-Nida (three hours) you go through the Guzianka Lock and get a short cruise on Lake Nidzkie. The lakes are long and narrow so you get good views of the shorelines.

GIŻYCKO

Giżycko (Lötzen), between lakes Niegocin and Kisajno 105 km east of Olsztyn, is the tourist centre of the Great Mazurian Lake District. Despite its reputation as a resort, Giżycko ranks as one of the ugliest towns in Poland and it's useful mostly as a base from which to visit Hitler's bunker at Wilczy Szaniec (see the Wilczy Szaniec section) or to pick up a lake boat to Mikołajki or Węgorzewo (Angerburg). Węgorzewo itself is lacking in things to see and places to stay, so it's not worth visiting except as a day trip from Giżycko by boat.

The best months to visit Giżycko are from April to June and September. In midsummer everything will be packed and in winter there'll be nothing to do. If your time is limited give Giżycko a miss and head straight for Mikołajki.

Orientation & Information

The port on Lake Niegocin (26 sq km) is near the centre of town with the train station on the east and the yacht harbour on the west, a few hundred metres from either.

A large map of Giżycko is posted in front of the adjacent bus and train stations on Plac Dworcowy. Head up ulica Armii Krajowej to ulica Dąbrowskiego. The helpful staff at Orbis, ulica Dąbrowskiego 3, can answer questions and perhaps provide a map. Continue west on ulica Warszawska to Plac Grunwaldzki, the centre of town.

Post & Telecommunications The telephone centre is a few blocks inland from Hotel Wodnik on ulica 1 Maja (open weekdays 7 am to 9 pm, Saturday 8 am to 1 pm, Sunday 9 to 11 am).

Things to See

There's nothing much to see in Giżycko except perhaps a large 19th century **fortress** on the west side of town which once guarded the narrow passage between the lakes. If you have time it's worth going beyond this fortress and cutting across the isthmus to the shore of Lake Kisajno near the Almatur and Sport hotels.

To rent a sailing boat capable of carrying four or five people will cost around US$14 a day in May and September, US$20 daily from June to August. In midsummer all the boats will be taken, so this is really only a tenable possibility in late spring and early fall. If you can't manage to rent a boat at Giżycko you may have better luck at nearby Wilkasy.

Places to Stay

Camping In July and early August Giżycko is overrun by Polish tourists, although those with a tent will always find a place to pitch it. If you go west on ulica Olsztyńska from Plac Grunwaldzki you'll reach the Łuczański Canal, across which is *Camping*

C1, just before the railway tracks. At the Mazurski Yacht Club beyond the tracks is a small harbour where you can rent a sailing boat. In summer there's also camping here.

Private Rooms Centrum-Mazur (☎ 33 83) at Hotel Wodnik may be willing to find you a private room. Also ask them about boat rentals, though they only speak Polish and German and are only there weekdays from 8 am to noon. Otherwise the hotel desk clerk may be able to help you find a private room.

Gromada, ulica Warszawska 21 (weekdays 8 am to 3.30 pm), rents private rooms at US$4 per person.

Hostels In July and August ask about youth hostel accommodation in the school at ulica Mickiewicza 27, a block back from Hotel Wodnik. If this is closed the staff may be able to refer you to another hostel that's open.

You can usually rent a cheap room in the two-storey drivers' examination centre or *Ośrodek Egzaminowania Kierowćw* (☎ 25 30), Lotnicza 4, by the lake to the west of the Mazurski Yacht Club. The person in the small office at the level crossing over the train tracks here should know about this, otherwise just wait around the hostel itself until someone shows up. Rooms are US$5 per person.

Hotels The modern, four-storey *Hotel Wodnik* (☎ 38 71), ulica 3 Maja 2 just off Plac Grunwaldzki in the centre of town, offers clean, comfortable rooms with private bath at US$29/50 single/double from mid-May to mid-September, US$19/35 the rest of the year (breakfast US$4 per person extra). Foreign bus tour groups always stay at the Wodnik – it's their kind of place.

The *Hotel Garnizonowy*, ulica Olsztyńska 10a (behind the apartment buildings), is primarily intended for visiting military personnel and in the past they have not accepted tourists, though this could change. Ask, as a room here should be half what you'd pay at the Wodnik.

The *PTTK Dom Wycieczkowy* is between the train tracks and the lake right beside the Łuczański Canal, but on the town side across the canal from the camping grounds. It's closed in the off season.

Just beyond the bridge over the Łuczański Canal is *Motel Zamek* (☎ 24 19), ulica Moniuszki 1, with 12 rooms with bath at US$35 double. When it's cold outside, a log fire will be burning in the small bar at the reception.

Farther west a km or two is the stadium where a road leads off to the right towards Lake Kisajno and two hotels. The *COS Sport Hotel*, ulica Moniuszki 22, has inexpensive rooms. You can also camp here (bungalows available) and it's a quieter site than the one previously mentioned. The *Almatur Hotel* is nearby. When no groups are present the receptions of both hotels close early in the day, so don't expect to get a room if you arrive late. Boat rentals are possible.

Places to Eat
A couple of good self-service snack bars are right opposite the train station. The *Omega Bar*, ulica Olsztyńska 4, is a cheap self-service (open daily).

In the centre of town is the cavernous, socialist-modern *Mazurska Restaurant*, ulica Warszawska 2. In the evening there's sometimes live music here. For more familiar food and surroundings try *Pizza Nicola*, ulica Warszawska 14. The *Hotel Wodnik* has a reasonable restaurant with a German menu.

WILCZY SZANIEC
History buffs will certainly want to visit **Hitler's wartime headquarters**, the Wolfschanze or Wolf's Lair (Wilczy Szaniec in Polish), at Gierłóż, 30 km west of Giżycko or 10 km east of Kętrzyn. Hitler spent most of his time here from 24 June 1941 to 20 November 1944 and the base had its own train station and airfield surrounded by minefields, anti-aircraft guns and camouflaging.

The Germans blew up the Wolfschanze on 24 January 1945 and only cracked concrete bunkers remain, but it's significant as the site of the 20 July 1944 assassination attempt by Colonel Claus von Stauffenberg (a plaque now marks the spot). A heavy wooden table saved Hitler and as many people died and as much property was destroyed in the last year of war as during the first five combined.

Things to See & Do

Over 70 reinforced bunkers are scattered through the forest. A large map of the site is posted at the entrance and all the bunkers are clearly numbered: Bormann No 11, Hitler No 13, Goering No 16 etc. The roofs of the eight most important ones are eight metres thick! Bring along a torch (flashlight) if you want to explore inside the bunkers (although large signs warn you that it is dangerous to do so).

Admission to Wolfschanze is US$3 per person, plus another US$3 if you have to park a vehicle. English and German-speaking guides wait at the entrance and charge US$13 per group for a one-hour tour of the site. The guides also sell booklets about Wilczy Szaniec, priced according to language: Polish US$1, German US$2 and English US$3.

Some buses between Olsztyn and Kętrzyn pass the photogenic Baroque church of **Święta Lipka** from which onward buses to Kętrzyn run hourly. It's well worth stopping to see the remarkable organ if you have the time.

Places to Stay & Eat

The recently renovated *Dom Wycieczkowy* (☎ 44 29) at the site is US$27 double with bath and breakfast (no singles). Rooms without bath are US$17 triple or US$23 for four persons, also including breakfast. The *Restaurant 'Michel'* behind the Dom serves reasonably good food. The hotel is open year-round but the restaurant is only open in summer. A basic *camping ground* is nearby – check in at the hotel reception.

Getting There & Away

Kętrzyn (Rastenburg), a large town on the railway line from Olsztyn to Ełk via Giżycko, is the starting point for most visits to Wilczy Szaniec. Trains from Kętrzyn to Węgorzewo pass right through the site but

only stop at Parcz, two km east – walk back along the paved highway towards Kętrzyn. You can see Goering's bunker (No 16) from both the train and the road.

Eight buses a day on the route from Kętrzyn to Węgorzewo via Radzieje stop right at the gate. At Kętrzyn buy bus tickets in an office near the stop. From June to August city bus No 5 also runs hourly between Kętrzyn and the site.

MIKOŁAJKI

During summer the best gateway to the lakes for hikers and campers is Mikołajki (Nikolaiken), 86 km east of Olsztyn on a railway line to Ełk. Perched on a picturesque narrows crossed by three bridges, there are scenic views on all sides of this pearl of Mazuria. The red-roofed houses of Mikołajki stretch along the shore of narrow Lake Mikołajskie just north of the Mazurian Landscape Park and Lake Śniardwy. Wild horses are in the forests to the south. Lakes Ryńskie, Tałty, Mikołajskie and Bełdany together fill a postglacial gully 35 km long.

German tourism promoters have discovered Mikołajki and new developments are blossoming on all sides. Especially horrendous is the five-star Hotel Gołębiewski erected by a German company in 1992, a couple of km west of Mikołajki on the road to Olsztyn. The 280-room Gołębiewski comes complete with helicopter shuttles, disco, three restaurants, indoor swimming pool and an elderly clientele bused in from Germany. Thankfully, you can't see it from town.

Orientation & Information

The bus station is beside a large Evangelical church near the bridge in the centre of town. The train station, several blocks east down ulica Kolejowa, provides left-luggage service.

In late July ask about the International Festival of Country Music, or the 'Country Picnic', in nearby Mrągowo.

Post & Telecommunications The post office and telephone centre at ulica 3-go

Maja 8 is open weekdays from 8 am to 6 pm and Saturday from 9 to 11 am.

Things to See

Europe's largest surviving community of **wild swans** is at nearby Lake Łuknajno. The 1200 to 2000 swans nest in April and May but stay at the lake all summer. The young birds are brown, the adults white. The 'Rezerwat Łuknajno' is about four km east of Mikołajki, beyond the Osiedle 'Łabędzia' suburb. Several observation towers beside the lake make viewing possible.

Activities

Mikołajki is an important yachting centre with a large Schronisko Żeglarskie (waterside hostel) overlooking the yacht harbour. Boats capable of carrying up to four people rent from around US$14 daily.

Agencja Sagit (☎/fax 16 470), Plac Wolności 3, can organise horse riding (US$13 an hour), buggy rides in the Pisz Forest (US$7 an hour for up to four people), yacht charter (US$13 to US$32 a day), canoe rental (US$7 a day), row boats (US$2 an hour) and waterskiing (US$7 an hour). In winter there's cross-country skiing. For those unfamiliar with sailing Sagit can organise lessons at US$4 an hour per group. In midsummer they should be able to get you a canoe, row boat or motorboat, but yacht hire at that time is difficult if you didn't reserve ahead. The Sagit office is open year-round (9 am to 4 pm in the off season, 8 am to 8 pm in summer) and the staff speak good English, so it's a good starting point.

Places to Stay

Camping Camping 'Wagabunda' (☎ 16 018), ulica Leśna 2, is across the bridge and two km west of town. In addition to camping space there are 60 neat little bungalows varying in price from US$16 for a four-bed unit without water to US$49 for a six-bed unit with private bath, They're open from April to October.

Hostels Ask about dormitory accommodation at the Schronisko Żeglarskie or waterside hostel (☎ 16 040), overlooking the yacht harbour (summer only).

In July and August a youth hostel functions in the Szkoła Podstanowa, a large school next to the tennis courts on ulica Łabędzia.

Pensions & Hotels Pension owners in Mikołajki are forced to charge high prices in summer because from October to April the town is virtually empty. Unless you have a tent, it's risky to arrive late in the day in midsummer as you could be forced to pay a lot for your room.

Pensjonat Ada, ulica Kolejowa 8, and Pensjonat Natalis (☎ 16 311), ulica Kościuszki 2a (US$25 double), are side by side on the way from the train station into town.

About the cheapest hotel in Mikołajki is the Hotel 'Żeglarsz' (☎ 16 144), ulica Dąbrowskiego 2. It's next to the large red-brick building with circular windows you see on the right as you walk into town along ulica Kowalska from the train station. Rooms are US$7 per person, it's open all year and looks better inside than out.

The Hotel Król Sielaw (☎ 16 323), ulica Kajki 5, has rooms with shared bath at US$15 double, with private bath US$19 double (no singles). Breakfast is US$4 extra. This friendly little hotel is open year-round (except in November and December) and their restaurant is the most reliable eating place in town although the drinks at the bar are expensive.

Pensjonat 'Mikołajki' (☎ 16 437), ulica Kajki 18 near the centre of town, is Mikołajki's finest pension (US$16/32 single/double). The double rooms have private baths. A big breakfast is US$3 per person extra and other meals (US$7) are available, perhaps the best home cooking you'll get in Poland. The rooms are often fully booked but the owner speaks perfect English so call him up for reservations (open from April to October only).

Pensjonat 'Na Skarpie' (☎ 16 418), ulica Kajki 96, is one km beyond Pensjonat

'Mikołajki'. Some rooms have excellent lake views.

Agencja Sagit (☎ /fax 16 470), Plac Wolności 3, books rooms at pensions around Mikołajki for US$22/44 single/double with breakfast from mid-June to mid-September, US$19/38 in spring and fall. Sagit handles bookings for *Pensjonat 'Tałty'* (☎ 16 398), four km north of town, which has four-person bungalows with cooking facilities at US$32 out of season, US$44 in season. Bungalows for up to six persons cost US$44 out of season, US$57 in season.

Places to Eat

All the tour groups eat at the *Restaurant Portowa* (open from May to September only) just above the lake-boat landing. The food is nothing special but prices are reasonable. Also keep in mind the *Król Sielaw* mentioned under Hotels above.

In summer tourists sit on the terrace of *Café Mocca* on ulica Kowalska just off the square and sip one of the 14 varieties of coffee. You can also get pizza here (but no alcohol).

Cold draught beer is on tap at *Mini-Bar Kufelek*, ulica Kajki 9. You probably won't see many tourists in there.

Entertainment

On summer weekends *Disco ABC* cranks up from 9 pm to 3 am in the basement of the big yellow schoolhouse building at ulica Kolejowa 6.

Things to Buy

Several small boutiques have sprung up in Mikołajki selling knockout amber jewellery with prices to match. Have a look at Bernstein, ulica 3-go Maja 17, and the two adjacent shops at ulica 3-go Maja 2/3. If you can resist buying amber here, you're safe from seduction in Poland.

Getting There & Away

There's only one bus a day to Ruciane-Nida (23 km) but there's bus service to Mrągowo every couple of hours (25 km) and several buses a day to Giżycko (31 km) and Suwałki (134 km). Buses to other points are rare. Trains run to Olsztyn (89 km) and Ełk (62 km) three times a day in either direction.

RUCIANE-NIDA

Hiking trails lead 23 km south from Mikołajki through the forest past many lake-side camping grounds to Ruciane-Nida (Rudschanny), in the heart of the Pisz Forest between picturesque Bełdany and Nidzkie lakes. Lake Nidzkie (18.3 sq km) is considered the most beautiful of the Mazurian lakes for its small forested islands. Ruciane-Nida is the right place to end a trip through the lake district by excursion boat, yacht, bicycle or foot as train service back to Olsztyn is good.

Orientation & Information

The adjacent bus and train stations are a five-minute walk from the lake-boat landing.

Places to Stay

Places to stay include the *PTTK Dom Wycieczkowy*, ulica Mazurska 16 (four-person cabin US$11), and *Pensjonat 'Bełdan'*, both north of the train station, and the more expensive *Orbis Pensjonat 'Kowaljik'* across the bridge. The 'Kowaljik' looks south down Lake Nidzkie. The *PTTK camping ground* is on Lake Nidzkie, a 20-minute walk south-west of the train station.

Getting There & Away

Train service to Olsztyn (90 km) and Ełk (70 km) is every couple of hours. There's a daily bus to Mikołajki via Ukta.

Romania

Romania, a little-known Latin country straddling the Carpathian Mountains, offers surprising variety, ranging from alpine peaks and Black Sea beaches to the mighty Danube River. The towns of Transylvania are straight out of medieval Hungary or Germany, whereas the exotic Orthodox monasteries of Moldavia and Bukovina suggest Byzantium. Western Romania bears the imprint of the Austro-Hungarian empire whereas Constanţa is heavily Roman and Turkish, and Bucharest has a Franco-Romanian character all of its own. Fine museums and churches are scattered throughout the country – few Eastern European countries feature such a kaleidoscope of cultures as Romania.

Romania is the 'Wild West' of Eastern Europe; if you come expecting fast efficiency and the conveniences of home, you will be disappointed. You'll often be thoroughly exasperated by the level of service you receive but you'll have encounters that would be inconceivable in the West. By accepting some of the hardships, you stand a better chance of capturing part of the essence of this colourful, perplexing land. In the opinion of the author (and the overwhelming majority of readers' letters we receive), Romania is the most exciting, best-value destination for the adventurous budget traveller in the whole of Eastern Europe.

Reader Andrew Warmington of Middlesex, England, UK, sent us this:

Any Hungarian or Bulgarian – and quite a lot of travellers – will tell you not to go [to Romania], that it's dirty, unsafe, hell on earth, etc, etc. Don't believe it. Easy it isn't and inexperienced travellers may find it too much (hope that doesn't sound snobbish!) but Romania is a real experience. More happened there in five days than during three times as long in twee little Hungary. Romania hides nothing from you and the people are mostly friendly and curious – remember it's not that long that they've been allowed to talk to foreigners, and many travellers find themselves given a bed and treated like kings.

Reader Philip Offer of Witney, England, UK, had this to add:

Generally, after the first few days, I found travelling in Romania much easier than I'd expected and the rewards far greater than in previous Eastern European countries I've visited. Every day I had a story for my diary and it made me hope I can return sometime in future.

Facts about the Country

HISTORY

Ancient Romania was inhabited by Thracian tribes. The Greeks called them the Getae, the Romans called them Dacians, but they were actually a single Geto-Dacian people. From the 7th century BC the Greeks established trading colonies along the Black Sea at Callatis (Mangalia), Tomis (Constanţa) and Histria. In the 1st century BC, a Dacian state was established to meet the Roman threat.

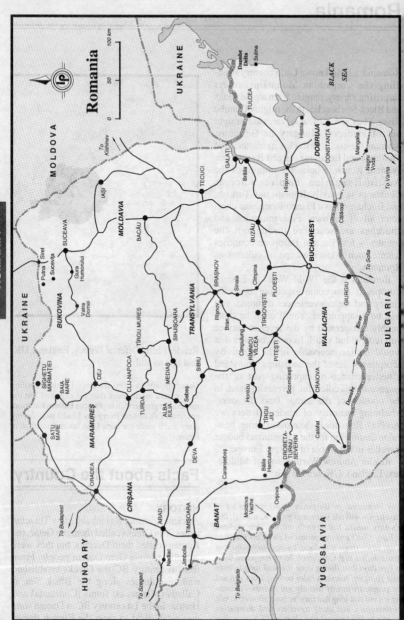

The last king, Decebalus, consolidated this state but was unable to prevent the Roman conquest in 105-6 AD.

The Romans recorded their expansion north of the Danube on two famous monuments: Trajan's Column in Rome and the 'Tropaeum Trajani' on the site of their victory at Adamclisi in Dobruja. Most of present Romania, including the Transylvanian plateau, came under their rule. The slave-owning Romans brought with them a superior civilisation and mixed with the conquered tribes to form a Daco-Roman people speaking a Latin tongue. A noted visitor during the Roman period was the Latin poet Ovid, who was exiled to the Black Sea by the Emperor Augustus. (The precise reason for his exile is unknown.)

Faced with Goth attacks in 271, Emperor Aurelian decided to withdraw the Roman legions and administration south of the Danube, but the Romanised Vlach peasants remained in Dacia. Waves of migrating peoples, including the Goths, Huns, Avars, Slavs, Bulgars and Hungarians, swept across this territory from the 4th to the 10th centuries. The Romanians survived in village communities and gradually assimilated the Slavs and other peoples who settled there. By the 10th century a fragmented feudal system ruled by a military class had appeared.

From the 10th century the Hungarians expanded into Transylvania, north and west of the Carpathian Mountains, and by the 13th century all of Transylvania was an autonomous principality under the Hungarian crown, although Romanians remained a majority of the population. After devastating Tatar raids in 1241 and 1242, King Bela IV of Hungary invited Saxon Germans to settle in Transylvania as a buffer against further attacks.

When the Turks conquered Hungary in the 16th century, Transylvania became a vassal of the Ottoman Empire, retaining its autonomy by paying tribute to the sultan. This semi-independence meant that Catholicism was not reimposed as it was in the areas under Habsburg control and many of the Hungarians and Germans in Transylvania converted from Catholicism to Protestantism in the 16th century. The Austrian Habsburgs conquered Transylvania at the end of the 17th century and suppressed an independence struggle led by the Transylvanian prince Ferenc Rákóczi II from 1703 to 1711.

The Romanian-speaking feudal principalities of Wallachia and Moldavia formed south and east of the Carpathian Mountains in the 14th century and throughout the 15th century they offered strong resistance to Turkish expansion north. Mircea the Old, Vlad Ţepeş and Stefan the Great became legendary figures in this struggle. Vlad Ţepeş 'the Impaler', ruling prince of Wallachia from 1456 to 1462 and 1476 to 1477, inspired the tale of Count Dracula by his habit of impaling his enemies on stakes. (Vlad Ţepeş was called Dracula or 'son of the dragon' after his father, Vlad Dracul, a knight of the Order of the Dragon, although today 'drac' means 'devil' in Romanian. The vampires originated in the imagination of 19th century Irish novelist Bram Stoker.)

After the Hungarian defeat, Wallachia and Moldavia also paid tribute to the Turks but maintained their autonomy. This indirect control explains why the only Turkish buildings seen in Romania today are in Dobruja, the area between the Danube and the Black Sea. In 1600 the three Romanian states were briefly united under Michael the Brave (Mihai Viteazul) at Alba Iulia. There were major peasant uprisings in 1437, 1514 and 1784. In 1812 Russia took Bessarabia, the eastern half of Moldavia, from the Turks.

Turkish suzerainty persisted in Wallachia and the rest of Moldavia well into the 19th century despite unsuccessful revolutions in 1821 and 1848. After the Russian defeat in the Crimean War (1853-56), Romanian nationalism grew, and in 1859, with French support, Alexandru Ioan Cuza was elected to the thrones of Moldavia and Wallachia, creating a national state which took the name Romania in 1862. The reform-minded Cuza was forced to abdicate in 1866 and his place was taken by the Prussian prince Carol I. With Russian assistance, Romania declared independence from the Ottoman Empire in

1877 and, after the 1877-78 War of Independence, Dobruja became part of Romania.

In 1916 Romania entered WW I on the side of the Triple Entente (Britain, France and Russia) with the objective of taking Transylvania, where two-thirds of the population was Romanian, from Austria-Hungary. During the fighting, the Central Powers (Germany and Austria-Hungary) occupied Wallachia but Moldavia was staunchly defended by Romanian and Russian troops. With the defeat of Austria-Hungary in 1918, the unification of Banat, Transylvania and Bukovina with Romania was finally achieved.

In the years leading up to WW II, Romania, under the able guidance of foreign minister Nicolae Titulescu, sought security in an alliance with France and Britain, and joined Yugoslavia and Czechoslovakia in the Little Entente. It signed a Balkan Pact with Yugoslavia, Turkey and Greece, and established diplomatic relations with the USSR. These efforts were weakened by the Western powers' appeasement of Hitler and by King Carol II, who declared a personal dictatorship in February 1938. After the fall of France in May 1940, Romania was isolated, and in June 1940 the USSR occupied Bessarabia, which had been taken from Russia after WW I. On 30 August 1940, Romania was forced to cede northern Transylvania (which covers 43,500 sq km) and its 2.6 million inhabitants to Hungary by order of Nazi Germany and Fascist Italy. In September 1940, southern Dobruja was given to Bulgaria.

These setbacks sparked widespread popular demonstrations. To defend the interests of the ruling classes, General Ion Antonescu forced Carol II to abdicate in favour of his (Carol's) son Michael and imposed a fascist dictatorship with himself as *conducătór*. German troops were allowed to enter Romania in October 1940 and in June 1941 Antonescu joined Hitler's anti-Soviet war. Some 400,000 Romanian Jews and 36,000 Gypsies were sent to Auschwitz and other such camps. (After the war, Antonescu was executed as a war criminal.)

Deep-seated anti-Nazi resentment smouldered among the Romanian soldiers and people. As the war went badly and the Soviet army approached Romania's borders, a rare national consensus was achieved. On 23 August 1944, Romania suddenly changed sides, captured 53,159 German soldiers who were in Romania at the time, and declared war on Nazi Germany. By this dramatic act, Romania salvaged its independence and shortened the war. By 25 October the Romanian and Soviet armies had driven the Hungarian and German forces from Transylvania. The Romanian army went on to fight in Hungary and Czechoslovakia. Appalling losses were sustained: half a million Romanian soldiers died while their country was on the German side and another 170,000 died after it joined the Allies.

Post WW II

Prior to WW II the Romanian communists had little influence; their postwar ascendancy was a consequence of backing from Moscow. The Soviet-engineered return of Transylvania greatly enhanced the prestige of the left-wing parties which won the parliamentary elections of November 1946. A year later the monarchy was abolished and a Romanian People's Republic proclaimed. The Communist and Social Democratic parties united as the Romanian Workers' Party in 1948, the name being changed back to Romanian Communist Party in 1965. (The name 'Rumania' was replaced by 'Romania' about the same time, to emphasise Romania's Roman heritage.) Industry was nationalised in June 1948 and a planned economy instituted.

The last Soviet troops were withdrawn from Romania in 1958 and after 1960 Romania adopted an independent foreign policy under two 'national' communist leaders, Gheorghe Gheorghiu-Dej (ruled 1952-65) and his protégé Nicolae Ceauşescu (ruled 1965-89), both of whom had been imprisoned during WW II. Although this policy was officially based on disarmament, détente and peaceful coexistence with all countries, in practice it meant deviating from the Soviet line. While it remained a member of the Warsaw Pact, Romania did not participate in the pact's military manoeuvres after 1962. Although Romania never broke with the USSR, as did Tito's Yugoslavia and Mao's China, it refused to assist in the intervention in Czechoslovakia in 1968 and President Ceauşescu publicly condemned the invasion. Years later, Soviet intervention in Afghanistan was similarly denounced and Romania participated in the 1984 Los Angeles Olympic Games despite a Soviet-bloc boycott. This nationalistic approach won the government domestic popular support and opportunistic approval in the West. (Ceauşescu was decorated by Queen Elizabeth II.)

In contrast to its skilful foreign policy, Romania suffered from increasingly inept government at home during the 25-year reign of Nicolae Ceauşescu. In 1974 the post of president was created for Ceauşescu, who placed members of his immediate family in high office during the 1980s. Thus his wife, Elena, became first deputy prime minister; his son, Nicu, became head of the communist youth organisation and later political boss of Transylvania; and three brothers were assigned to key posts in Bucharest. This amounted to 'socialism in one family', as opposed to 'socialism in one country', the pre-WW II situation in the USSR.

Ceauşescu's megalomania is illustrated by the various grandiose projects that he initiated: the functionless Danube Canal from Agigea to Cernavodă which opened in 1984; the Transfăgăraşan Highway; the disruptive redevelopment of south Bucharest into a new political centre (1983-89); the building of the Bucharest Metro (opened in 1985); the destruction of the Danube Delta through agricultural development; and the unrealised plans to 'systematise' Romanian agriculture by transferring the inhabitants of 7000 of the country's 13,000 villages into hastily constructed concrete apartment blocks, despite the cultural and social upheaval this would have caused. In March 1989 Ceauşescu arranged lavish public celebrations to mark the paying-off of Romania's US$10 billion

foreign debt. His greatest blunder, however, was the decision to export Romania's food to help pay the debt, as this created serious food shortages within Romania.

By the late 1980s, with the Soviet bloc quickly disintegrating, the USA no longer required an independent Romania and withdrew the 'most favoured nation' trading status that it had previously granted the country. Ethnic tensions simmered and the population endured prolonged scarcities of almost everything. In November 1987, 10,000 workers rioted in Braşov in support of better conditions. In late 1989, as the world watched one communist regime after another tumble, it seemed only a matter of time before Romania's turn would come. However, on 20 November 1989, during a six-hour address to the 14th Congress of the Romanian Communist Party, Ceauşescu denounced the political changes in the other Eastern European countries and vowed to resist them. His speech was interrupted by 60 standing ovations and the Congress re-elected him as general secretary.

Revolution The revolution in Romania was carried out with Latin passion and intensity. The spark that ignited Romania came on 15 December 1989 when Father Lászlo Tökés spoke out publicly against the dictator from his small Hungarian church in Timişoara. The following evening people gathered outside Father Tökés' home to protest against the decision of the Reformed Church of Romania to remove him from his post, and by 9 pm this had turned into a noisy demonstration. When the police began to make arrests, the unrest spread to other parts of the city and armoured cars began patrolling the streets.

At noon on 17 December a huge crowd on Timişoara's Bulevardul 30 decembrie between the Opera House and the Orthodox cathedral, was confronted by Securitate (secret police) units and regular army troops. When demonstrators broke into the Communist Party's district headquarters and threw portraits of Ceauşescu out of the windows, the army used tanks and armoured cars to clear the vast square. Despite this, further clashes took place in nearby Piaţa Libertăţii.

Back in Bucharest later that afternoon, the Executive Political Committee condemned the 'mild' action taken by the army and ordered that real bullets be used; this was the start of civilian casualties. The Securitate continued mopping-up operations all night and the dead were collected and buried in mass graves or sent to Bucharest to be cremated. The resistance continued, however, and on 19 December the army in Timişoara went over to the side of the demonstrators.

On 20 December negotiators from Bucharest arrived in Timişoara to buy time until fresh troops could be sent to the city, and newly arrived Securitate units began firing on the demonstrators once again. At 6 pm Ceauşescu arrived back in Romania from a state visit to Iran and proclaimed martial law in Timiş County. Train-loads of elite troops were dispatched to the city with orders to crush the rebellion.

On 21 December a remarkable thing happened. Ceauşescu decided that he would address a mass rally in front of the Central Committee building in Bucharest to show the world that the workers of Romania supported him and approved his action against the 'hooligan' demonstrators in Timişoara. What went on behind the scenes may never be known but it's possible that Ceauşescu was set up by conspirators within the Communist Party who wanted to engineer his downfall. Factories around Bucharest dutifully sent their most trusted cadres to applaud Ceauşescu as they had done so many times before, but upon their arrival early in the morning at Piaţa Gheorghe Gheorghiu-Dej (now Piaţa Revoluţiei), these people were told that Ceauşescu had changed his mind about the speech and that they could go home. A few hours later the word went out again that the speech would in fact be held at noon and that the workers should reassemble. However, the reliable party supporters had already left and the factory bosses were forced to be less selective as they scrambled to send the required number of people to the square.

At 12.30 pm as Ceauşescu began to speak to the assembly from the balcony of the Central Committee building, youths who were being held back by three cordons of police a block away started booing. Tension mounted in the silent crowd and suddenly Ceauşescu was cut off in mid-sentence by shouts of disapproval. For a second the dictator faltered, amazement at being directly challenged written across his face as recorded on live TV. Pandemonium erupted as the youths attempted to break through the police lines and the assembled workers tried to escape. Urged on by his wife, Ceauşescu attempted to continue his speech even as police cleared the square, finally ending as the tape with prerecorded applause and cheers was switched off.

Meanwhile, the anti-Ceauşescu demonstrators retreated to the wide boulevard between Piaţa Universităţii and Piaţa Romană. At about 2.30 pm reinforcements of special riot police with clubs and shields arrived down Calea Victoriei and plainclothes police began making arrests. As more police and armoured cars arrived, the growing number of demonstrators became concentrated in these two piaţas (squares). Around 5 pm, when the crowds still refused to disperse, the police at Piaţa Romană first fired warning shots and then used gunfire and armoured cars to brutally crush the demonstration.

In front of the Inter-Continental Hotel on Piaţa Universităţii armoured cars also drove into the crowd. Drenched by ice-cold water from fire hoses, the demonstrators there refused to submit and began erecting barricades under the eyes of Western journalists in the adjacent hotel. At 11 pm the police began their assault on Piaţa Universităţii, using a tank to smash the barricades. By dawn the square had been cleared and the bodies of those killed removed.

At 7 am on 22 December, demonstrators began assembling in Piaţa Romană and Piaţa Universităţii once more. By 11 am huge crowds faced the phalanx of army troops in their tanks with Securitate behind them blocking the way to the Central Committee building where Ceauşescu was still believed to be. Rumours then began circulating about General Milea, the minister of defence, who allegedly had been forced to commit suicide by Ceauşescu because he had refused to order his troops to fire on the people. Gradually the crowd began to chant 'The army is with us!' and to mix with the troops arrayed against them, offering the soldiers flowers and cigarettes.

As the demonstrators swarmed up onto the unresting tanks and fraternised with the crews, the Securitate forces withdrew towards the site of the previous day's speech. At 11.30 am Bucharest Radio announced the 'suicide' of the 'traitor' Milea and the proclamation of a state of emergency. As thousands of people moved towards the Central Committee building, the Securitate continued to draw back. At around noon Ceauşescu again appeared on the balcony and attempted to speak, but people began booing and throwing objects at him, forcing him to duck back quickly inside the building. At this point the crowd surged in through the main doors past unresting police, but, with the crowd just a few dozen metres away, Ceauşescu, his wife and several others managed to escape by helicopter from the roof. Soon after, the radio and TV stations were taken by the rebels, who did not meet any resistance.

The helicopter took the Ceauşescus to their villa at Snagov, just north of Bucharest. The plan was that they would proceed to an air base near Piteşti, where a waiting jet would take them into exile outside Romania. Halfway to Piteşti, however, the helicopter pilot feigned engine trouble and set the chopper down beside a highway where the two Securitate officers present commandeered a passing private car. The party then drove on to Tîrgovişte, where the Ceauşescus were arrested and taken to a military base.

On 23 December Nicolae and Elena Ceauşescu were tried together by an anonymous court, condemned and summarily executed by a firing squad. (The army general who presided over the court committed suicide two months later.) The next day their bodies were exhibited on TV, allegedly to stifle resistance by die-hard Securitate units attempting to rescue them. News reports at the time told of fierce resistance by the Securitate, but anyone who visited Bucharest during the months immediately following the revolution would have seen that virtually all the buildings pockmarked with bullet holes were Securitate strongholds around the Central Committee building and TV station. This indicates that they were mostly on the receiving end of fire from young army conscripts who opened up at the slightest provocation. (This damage has now been repaired.) With their modern weapons, the Securitate officers could have caused tens of thousands of casualties had they so desired.

It is now believed that the Ceauşescus' speedy trial had much more to do with controlling the revolution and saving former Communist Party members than in stopping the Securitate. Clearly, Nicolae and Elena knew too much and many people still in high office today might have been dragged down with them had they been given an open trial. Among the charges brought against the Ceauşescus by the kangaroo court was that they had deposited US$470 million in Swiss banks, yet none of this mysterious money has ever been found.

Evidently, reformers in the Communist Party had been preparing a coup d'état against Ceauşescu and his family for at least six months when the December 1989 demonstrations forced them to move their schedule forward. When Ceauşescu fell, therefore, the National Salvation Front was ready to take over. Most of its leaders, including President Ion Iliescu, were former party members.

Reports of casualties in the revolution were wildly exaggerated. At the Ceauşescus' trial it was claimed that 64,000 people died in the revolution (alleged 'genocide'); a few days later it was changed to 64,000 deaths in the entire 25-year Ceauşescu era. After a week the number of victims had been reduced to 7000 and the final count was

ROMANIA

1033. In Timişoara, 115 people died, not the 4000 reported.

The Sequel When the National Salvation Front (FSN) took over, it claimed to be only a caretaker government until elections could be held and that it would not field candidates. However, on 25 January 1990, the FSN announced that it would in fact run. This prompted mass demonstrations both for and against the front amid accusations of neo-communism.

The 20 May 1990 elections were contested by 88 political parties. In the presidential race Ion Iliescu of the FSN won 85% of the vote, Radu Câmpeanu of the National Liberal Party won 10.6% and Ion Ratiu of the National Peasant Party won 4.3%. The FSN also won control of the National Assembly and Senate.

In the meantime, students had occupied Piaţa Universităţii to protest against the FSN's ex-Communist Party leadership. On 13 June 1990, after police cleared demonstrators from the square, extremist youths burned police headquarters and attacked the Ministry of the Interior in what the government called a 'fascist coup attempt'. This prompted 20,000 coal miners from the Jiu River area near Tîrgu Jiu to travel to Bucharest for a counter-riot in which many injuries were sustained among student and opposition supporters. It was later revealed that secret police had infiltrated the miners and provoked the worst violence.

In September 1991 the miners returned to Bucharest to force the resignation of Prime Minister Petre Roman, whose free-market economic reform programme had led to worsening living conditions. Roman's departure was a serious setback for the whole reform process and again, ex-Securitate elements were involved in the rioting that ensued.

The September 1992 elections were won by the left-wing Democratic National Salvation Front (DFSN, successor to the FSN) which formed a coalition government with several smaller communist or ultra-nationalist parties and promised to slow economic reforms. In October 1992, Iliescu was re-elected president. Despite the organised thuggery by the miners, public criticism of the government is allowed.

Romania Today Since the revolution, Romanians have been allowed to have more contact with foreigners, to accommodate them in their homes, to hold foreign currency and to speak fairly freely. For travellers, the general atmosphere of increased personal freedom certainly makes Romania more pleasant, though hotels still charge foreigners higher prices and visa regulations are unchanged. Queues are still long at petrol stations and some shops.

Previously, there were only government stores with empty shelves, but now flourishing street markets have sprung up where farmers sell their produce and small traders peddle contraband consumer goods smuggled in from abroad. In May 1993 subsidies on food, transportation and energy were scrapped and prices jumped four or five times. Romanians only earn around US$75 a month and inflation has made travelling around Romania much more expensive for them, so trains, buses, hotels, cable cars etc are now far less crowded than they were in 1990. For foreigners it's very inexpensive whenever the local Romanian price is charged and, unlike most other Eastern Europe countries, Romania hasn't increased museum admission prices at all in recent years.

Many Romanians are disillusioned by the lack of progress since 1989 and by declining living standards, rampant inflation and 9% unemployment. They'll joke that when a Romanian goes on hunger strike nobody notices. Many students have little hope of finding work after graduation and young couples must often live with their parents now that government investment in new apartments has almost ceased. Prior to 1989 contraception and abortion were prohibited but now three out of every four pregnancies is aborted. Most Romanians would gladly emigrate if they could find a Western country willing to take them, and very few have much hope that things will improve in the near future. Romanians value and appreciate their new personal freedoms and, despite the present economic problems, few would wish to be back in the suffocating grip of the old communist system. Yet it's fascinating to ask people what they think of Ceauşescu and to hear them compare the present to the recent past. Be prepared for a few comments you didn't expect.

GEOGRAPHY

Covering 237,500 sq km, oval-shaped Romania is larger than Hungary and Bulgaria combined (and just a bit bigger than the Australian state of Victoria). The Danube River drains the whole of Romania except the Black Sea coast and completes its 2850-km course through nine countries in Romania's Danube Delta. South of the delta is the Black Sea coast and south-west of it, along the Bulgarian border, stretch the Danube lowlands.

Most of central and northern Romania is taken up by the U-shaped Carpathian Mountains. The highest point in the Romanian Carpathians is Mt Moldoveanu at 2544 metres in the Făgăraş Mountains south-east of Sibiu. The Transylvanian Plain (Cîmpia Transilvaniei), an eroded plateau with hills and valleys, occupies the centre of the U, and the Moldavian plateau lies to the east. Earthquakes are common in the south and south-west.

The Carpathian Mountains account for about a third of the country's area, with alpine pastures above and thick forests below. Another third of Romania is covered by hills and tablelands full of orchards and vineyards. The final third is a fertile plain where cereals, vegetables, herbs and other crops are grown. Eleven per cent of the land is irrigated.

German companies have been heavily involved in toxic waste exports to Eastern Europe, and after Poland banned this trade in 1990 the focus shifted to Albania and Romania. In 1992 the environmental organisation Greenpeace mounted a campaign to force the German government to return 500 tonnes of obsolete pesticides and industrial wastes from the Sibiu area. Italian firms have dumped wastes in the Danube Delta. Legislation has been enacted to prevent these practices from continuing.

ECONOMY

Under the communists the economy was centrally planned, and the change to a market economy has been slow in coming. Romania exports minerals, chemicals, machinery and manufactured goods. Under Ceauşescu, self-sufficiency became a major goal, and from 1980 every effort was made to eliminate Romania's foreign debt of US$10 billion. This was partly done by exporting food at the expense of domestic consumption, creating hunger in what had once been the granary of Europe. Although this policy has now ceased, Romania and Albania still have the lowest living standards in Europe. Since 1989 the government has accumulated a new debt of US$4 billion.

The communists promoted heavy industry and infrastructure projects such as the huge Iron Gate Hydropower Project at Drobeta-Turnu Severin on the Danube River, which was opened in 1972. The Ploieşti oilfields north of Bucharest have been pumping oil since 1860, but the giant iron and steel works at Galaţi has only been operating since WW II. Other energy resources include natural gas from Transylvania, lignite coal from Tîrgu Jiu and the nuclear power station at Cernavodă, at the mouth of the Danube Canal. Fortunately this station was built with Canadian rather than Soviet technology and is relatively safe. Three-quarters of Romania's electricity comes from thermal power stations, over half of which are powered by natural gas. Dwindling oil reserves and increased world fuel prices since 1973 have handicapped Romania's chemical and petrochemical industries.

Two types of car are manufactured in Romania. The popular Oltcit is a home-grown Citroën put together at Craiova, and the more up-market Dacia is in fact a Renault 12 built at Piteşti. The 4WD Aro jeep is made in Cîmpulung.

ROMANIA

Romania is still a developing country. The emphasis on heavy industry was in line with Romania's long-range goal of self-reliance but it led to shortages of food and consumer goods and has left Romania with uneconomic industries that are technologically unable to compete on world markets. Between 1989 and 1992 industrial production dropped 50%. In the absence of adequate bankruptcy laws, inefficient firms continue to accumulate massive debts and hold on to redundant personnel. Privatisation is hampered by official corruption and resistance from entrenched bureaucrats. In 1991 the government announced that 85% of collective farm land would be returned to private ownership but two years later only 10% had actually changed hands.

Many Romanians fear chaos if the social safety net is removed, and economic change has been slowed to shield the people from high inflation and unemployment. Many wages are indexed to inflation (which ran at 200% in 1992 and 300% in 1993), thus fuelling more inflation. In mid 1993 there were major mine and railway workers strikes. The ruling Party of Social Democracy in Romania (formerly called the Democratic National Salvation Front) floats along without an effective programme.

POPULATION & PEOPLE

Romania has a population of 23 million, 43% of whom live in towns and cities. Bucharest (2.3 million) is by far the largest city, followed by Braşov, Timişoara, Iaşi, Cluj-Napoca, Constanţa, Galaţi and Craiova, all of them with just over 300,000 inhabitants. The main educational centres are in Bucharest, Iaşi, Cluj-Napoca and Timişoara.

Romania is the only country with a Romance language that does not have a Roman Catholic background. Seventy per cent of the population is Romanian Orthodox, 6% Protestant, 6% Catholic and 3% Greek Orthodox (Uniate).

The country's largest ethnic minorities are Gypsies (9%) and Hungarians (7.1%). The number of Germans in Romania has steadily dwindled. During WW II, 175,000 Romanian Germans were killed or left the country and since then many Transylvanian Germans have emigrated to Germany. Some 227,000 left between 1976 and 1991, reducing the number of Germans in Romania from 745,000 in 1930 to 130,000 in 1991. An estimated two million Gypsies live in Romania – the largest Gypsy community in the world – although official statistics give a much lower number because many Gypsies declare themselves Romanians at censuses. Unfortunately there is much anti-Gypsy sentiment, largely because Gypsies provide a convenient scapegoat for Romania's economic problems. Gypsy villages have been burned by Romanian nationalists with official complicity.

In the past, the situation of the 1.7 million Hungarians in Romania has soured relations with neighbouring Hungary. Under Ceauşescu, all Hungarian-language newspapers and magazines in Romania were closed down, and official plans to relocate 7000 Romanian villages, many of them in Transylvania, threatened Romania's Hungarians with cultural assimilation. Since 1989 things have improved. The 1991 constitution includes articles guaranteeing minority rights and the Hungarian Democratic Union is represented in both the Romanian Senate and House of Representatives.

Most accounts of ethnic conflicts in Romania published in the West show quite justified concern for the Hungarian minority, yet tend to ignore the fact that the Romanian majority in Transylvania was subjected to forced 'Magyarisation' under Hungarian rule prior to WW I. While Hungarians and Bulgarians tend to look down on Romanians, the Romanians consider themselves the direct heirs of ancient Rome and thus on a higher plain than the descendants of barbaric Slav and Hungarian tribes. Interestingly, Romania has always had friendly relations with Yugoslavia and there are parallels between the personality cults of Ceauşescu and Marshal Tito, and the dominance today of neo-communists like Ion Iliescu and Slobodan Milošević.

ARTS

The Romantic poet Mihai Eminescu (1850-89) captured the spirituality of the Romanian people in his work. The painter Nicolae Grigourescu (1838-1907) absorbed French impressionism and created canvases alive with the colour of the Romanian peasantry. You can see Grigourescu's work in art galleries in Bucharest, Iaşi and Constanţa. In his plays, satirist Ion Luca Caragiale (1852-1912) decried the impact of precipitous modernisation on city life and showed the comic irony of social and political change.

Although primarily a resident of France after 1904, abstract sculptor Constantin Brâncuşi (1876-1957) endowed his native Tîrgu Jiu with some of his finest works in 1937. Brâncuşi revolutionised sculpture by emphasising essential forms and the beauty of the material itself. Perhaps the best-known Romanian writer internationally is playwright Eugene Ionesco (1912-1994), a leading exponent of the 'theatre of the absurd', who lived in France after 1938.

Music

Traditional Romanian folk instruments include the *bucium* (alphorn), the *cimpoi* (bagpipe), the *cobză* (a pear-shaped lute) and the *nai* (a panpipe of about 20 cane tubes). Many kinds of flute are used, including the *ocarina* (a ceramic flute) and the *tilinca* (a flute without finger holes). The violin, which is of more recent origin, is today the most common folk instrument. Romania's best known composer, George Enescu (1881-1955), was himself a virtuoso violinist and used Romanian folk themes in his work.

The *doină* is an individual, improvised love song, a sort of Romanian blues with a social or romantic theme. The *baladă*, on the other hand, is a collective narrative song which reflects the conditions or feelings of the people, often with some historic content. Many group songs are vestiges of archaic rites, such as weddings, funerals or harvest festivals. Flute and bagpipe music originated with shepherds.

Couples may dance in a circle, a semicircle or a line. In the *sîrbă* males and females

dance quickly in a closed circle with their hands on each other's shoulders. The *horă* is another fast circle dance, while in the *brîu* or 'belt dance' the dancers form a chain by grasping their neighbour's belt. In the waist dance the line of dancers have their arms around each others' waists.

Modern Gypsy or 'Tzigane' music has absorbed many influences and professional Gypsy musicians play whatever their village clients desire. The *lăutari* (musicians) circulate through the village inviting neighbours to join in weddings, births, baptisms, funerals and harvest festivals. Improvised songs *(cîntec)* are often directed at a specific individual and are designed to elicit an emotional response (and a tip). No two renditions of the same piece by the same player are ever identical. To appeal to older people, the lăutari sing traditional ballads (baladă) or epic songs *(cîntece epice)* in verse, often recounting the exploits of Robin Hood-style *haiducs* (outlaws) who apply justice through their actions. The legendary haiducs combat Turkish invaders, force wicked priests to return money obtained under false pretences and rob evil landlords and redistribute the wealth to the poor.

Professional Gypsy ensembles or *tarafs*, such as the famous Taraf de Haiducs from Clejani village south-west of Bucharest, use the violin, accordion, guitar, double bass, *ţambal* (hammered dulcimer), *nai*, *fluier* (flute), and other instruments. At village weddings the dance music was originally provided by goatskin bagpipes, though today the accordion, percussion, and electric guitar are almost universally used.

The folk music of Transylvania is briefly discussed in the introduction to the Hungary chapter. In general, the music of the Hungarians of Transylvania is heavier and more serious than the light-hearted Romanian melodies. Romanian folk dancers wear shoes while their Hungarian counterparts in Transylvania wear black riding boots.

During the communist era an urbanised folk music was promoted by state folkloric ensembles such as the Romanian Radio Folk Music Orchestra to bolster the Romanian national identity. In this genre virtuoso nai and *ţambal mare* (concert cymbalum or dulcimer) players are backed up by large orchestras seldom seen in Romanian villages. The Romanian folk songs played by panpipe virtuoso Gheorghe Zamfir are carefully orchestrated for New Age ears.

LANGUAGE

English and French are the first foreign languages taught in Romanian schools and German is useful in Transylvania. You'll often be surprised to meet fluent English speakers in remote areas. This is one Eastern European country where Russian won't get you very far.

Romanian is much closer to classical Latin than the other Romance languages and the grammatical structure and basic word stock of the mother tongue are well preserved. Some Slavic words were incorporated in the 7th to 10th centuries as the Romanian language took definite shape. Speakers of French, Italian and Spanish won't be able to understand much spoken Romanian but will find written Romanian more or less comprehensible.

A few terms of use in getting around are *aleea* (avenue), *bulevardul* (boulevard), *calea* (road), *piaţa* (square), *şoseaua* (highway) and *strada* (street). In Romania, as in Bulgaria, you can use the French *merci* to say 'thank you' – many locals do.

Lonely Planet's *Eastern Europe Phrasebook* is very handy with plenty of useful words and phrases translated into Romanian. In a sometimes difficult country like Romania, the value of such a resource should not be underestimated.

Pronunciation

Until the mid-19th century, Romanian was written in the Cyrillic script. Today Romanian employs 28 Latin letters, some of which bear accents. It is spelt phonetically, so once you learn a few simple rules you'll be able to read aloud the expressions that follow. Vowels without accents are pronounced as they are in Spanish or Italian. In Romanian there are no long and short vowels, but e, i,

o and u form a diphthong or triphthong with adjacent vowels. At the beginning of a word, 'e' and 'i' are pronounced 'ye' and 'yi', while at the end of a word an 'i' is almost silent. At the end of a word 'ii' is pronounced 'ee'. The stress is usually on the penultimate syllable.

ă	'ea' as in 'pearl'
â	'i' as in 'river'
c	'k'
c	'ch' before 'e' and 'i'
ch	'k' before 'e' and 'i'
g	'g' as in 'good'
g	'g' as in 'gentle' before 'e' and 'i'
gh	'g' as in 'good'
î	'i' as in 'river'
ş	'sh'
ţ	'tz'

Greetings & Civilities

hello	*bună*
goodbye	*la revedere*
good morning	*bună dimineaţa*
good day	*bună ziua*
good evening	*bună seara*
please	*vă rog*
thank you	*mulţumesc*
I am sorry./Forgive me.	*Iertaţi-mă.*
Excuse me.	*Scuzaţi-mă.*
yes	*da*
no	*nu*

Small Talk

I don't understand.	*Nu înţeleg.*
Could you write it down?	*Puteţi să notaţi?*
What is it called?	*Cum se cheamă?*
Where do you live?	*De unde sînteţi?*
What work do you do?	*Cu ce vă ocupaţi?*
I am a student.	*Sînt student.*
I am very happy.	*Sînt foarte fericit.*

Accommodation

youth hostel	*camin studentesc*
camping ground	*camping*
private room	*cameră particulară*
How much is it?	*Cît costă?*

ROMANIA

Is that the price per person?	*Preţul acesta este per persoană?*
Is that the total price?	*Acesta este preţul total?*
Are there any extra charges?	*Mai este ceva de plătit?*
Do I pay extra for showers?	*Trebuie să plătesc în plus pentru duş?*
Where is there a cheaper hotel?	*Unde este un hotel mai ieftin?*
Should I make a reservation?	*Pot face o rezervare?*
single room	*o cameră pentru o persoană*
double room	*o cameră pentru două persoane*
It is very noisy.	*Este foarte zgomotos.*
Where is the toilet?	*Unde este toaleta?*

Getting Around

What time does it leave?	*La ce oră este plecarea?*
When is the first bus?	*Cînd este primul autobuz?*
When is the last bus?	*Cînd este ultimul autobuz?*
When is the next bus?	*Cînd este următorul autobuz?*
That's too soon.	*Foarte curînd.*
When is the next one after that?	*Cînd este următorul după acesta?*
How long does the trip take?	*Cît timp durează excursia?*
arrival	*sosire*
departure	*plecare*
timetable	*mersul/orar*
Where is the bus stop?	*Unde este staţia de autobuz?*
Where is the train station?	*Unde este gară?*
Where is the left-luggage room?	*Unde este biroul pentru bagaje de mînă?*

Around Town

Just a minute.	*Un moment.*
Where is ...?	*Unde este ...?*
the bank	*banca*
the post office	*poşta*
the tourist information office	*birou de informatii turistice*
the museum	*muzeu*
Where are you going?	*Unde mergeti?*
I am going to ...	*Merg la ...*
Where is it?	*Unde este?*
I can't find it.	*Nu pot să găsesc.*
Is it far?	*Este departe?*
Please show me on the map.	*Vă rog arătaţi-mi pe hartă.*
left	*stînga*
right	*dreapta*
straight ahead	*drept înainte*
I want ...	*Vreau ...*
Do I need permission?	*Am nevoie de aprobare?*

Entertainment

Where can I hear live music?	*Unde pot asculta muzică în concert?*
Where can I buy a ticket?	*Unde pot cumpăra un bilet?*
I'm looking for a ticket.	*Nu aveţi un bilet în plus?*
I want to get a refund on this ticket.	*Aş vrea să renunţ la acest bilet.*
Is this a good seat?	*Este un loc bun?*
at the front	*în primele rînduri*
ticket	*bilet*

Food

I do not eat meat.	*Nu consum carne.*
self-service cafeteria	*autoservire*
grocery store	*băcănie*
fish	*peşte*
pork	*porc*
soup	*ciorbă*
salad	*salată*
fresh vegetables	*legume proaspete*
milk	*lapte*
bread	*pîine*
sugar	*zahăr*
ice cream	*îngheţată*
coffee	*cafe*
tea	*ceai*
mineral water	*apă minerală*

ROMANIA

beer	bere
wine	vin
hot/cold	cald/rece

Shopping

Where can I buy one?	Unde aş putea cumpăra?
How much does it cost?	Cît costă?
That's (much) too expensive.	Este (mult) prea scump.
Is there a cheaper one?	Pot găsi ceva mai ieftin?
there is	există
there isn't	nu există

Time & Dates

today	azi
tonight	deseară
tomorrow	mîine
the day after tomorrow	poimîine
What time does it open?	La ce oră se deschide?
What time does it close?	La ce oră se închide?
open	deschis
closed	închis
in the morning	dimineaţa
in the evening	seară
every day	în fiecare zi
At what time?	La ce oră?
when?	cînd?

Monday	luni
Tuesday	marţi
Wednesday	miercuri
Thursday	joi
Friday	vineri
Saturday	sîmbătă
Sunday	duminică

January	ianuarie
February	februarie
March	martie
April	aprilie
May	mai
June	iunie
July	iulie
August	august

September	septembrie
October	octombrie
November	noiembrie
December	decembrie

Numbers

1	unu
2	doi
3	trei
4	patru
5	cinci
6	şase
7	şapte
8	opt
9	nouă
10	zece
11	unsprezece
12	doisprezece
13	treisprezece
14	patrusprezece
15	cincisprezece
16	şaisprezece
17	şaptesprezece
18	optsprezece
19	nouăsprezece
20	douăzeci
21	douăzeci şi unu
22	douăzeci şi doi
23	douăzeci şi trei
30	treizeci
40	patruzeci
50	cincizeci
60	şaizeci
70	şaptezeci
80	optzeci
90	nouăzeci
100	o sută
1000	o mie
10,000	zece mii
1,000,000	milion

Facts for the Visitor

VISAS & EMBASSIES

All Western visitors require a tourist or transit visa to enter Romania. Visas are easily obtained at the border or you can pick one up beforehand at a Romanian embassy. Either way, the price will be from US$35 to US$40 (US$45 for British nationals), regardless of how long you intend to stay, and no photos are required. The best way to compensate for this high admission fee is to stay longer in the country. Five-day transit visas are US$23 (not available at the border).

When you receive your visa, you'll have to specify exactly how many days you wish to remain in Romania. Always ask for a 30-day visa, even if you intend to stay for a shorter duration. (Some embassies will give up to 60 days.) That way you won't need to worry about an extension should you decide to stay longer. Check to make sure the correct number of days has been entered on your visa. You may use the visa any time within three months of the date of issue.

Don't lose the 'exit card' the official will put in your passport upon arrival or you'll have problems upon departure. It's best to keep the card in your money belt together with your travellers' cheques and not leave it in the passport as it could fall out.

Once inside Romania, it's possible to extend your stay by reporting to a passport office – any local tourist office will have the address. The Bucharest office is at Strada Nicolae Iorga 7 near Piaţa Romană. You must apply before your current visa expires. However, you would be much better off asking for enough time in the first place.

Romanian Embassies

In addition to the Romanian embassies in Belgrade, Budapest, Bratislava, Prague, Sofia, Warsaw and Zagreb listed elsewhere in this book, Romanian embassies around the world include the following:

Australia
    333 Old South Head Road, Bondi, NSW
    (☎ 02-365 015)
Canada
    655 Rideau St, Ottawa, ON K1N 6A3
    (☎ 613-789 5345)
    111 Peter St, Suite 530, Toronto, ON M5V 2H1
    (☎ 416-585 5802)
Netherlands
    Catsheuvel 55, 2517 KA, The Hague
    (☎ 070-354 3796)

UK
    4 Palace Green, London W8 4QD
    (☎ 0171-937 9666)
USA
    1607 23rd St NW, Washington, DC 20008
    (☎ 202-232 4829)
    573-577 Third Ave, New York, NY 10016
    (☎ 212-682-3273)

MONEY

At last report, the Romanian leu was officially worth 1500 lei to the US dollar. There are coins of one, three, five, 10, 20, 50 and 100 lei and notes of 100, 200, 500, 1000 and 5000 lei. Beware of receiving obsolete 5000 lei notes issued just after WW II. (All US dollar prices in this chapter were obtained by converting to lei at the bank rate.)

The only banks that consistently change travellers' cheques are main offices of the Banca Comercială Română (a division of the National Bank of Romania) and the less numerous branches of the Banca Romană de Comerţ Exterior. Both banks are only open weekdays from 9 am to noon and deduct commissions of from 3% to 5% on travellers' cheques with a US$2 to US$5 minimum (passport required). No commission is charged to change cash.

In Bucharest some private exchange offices offer a premium of up to 25% above the bank rate for cash US dollars or Deutschmarks. (Other Western currencies are less enthusiastically accepted.) They often post the official rate outside and you have to ask the clerk for the true rate. If an office seems especially busy they probably have a good rate. In provincial cities such rates are generally much lower than those in Bucharest while the bank rate is uniform across the country.

Apart from up-market hotel receptions, most exchange offices around Romania (including those in major hotels) will change only cash. The exception is the Bucharest Exchange Office chain with branches all around Romania which changes travellers' cheques at the standard official rate. Before signing your cheque ask what rate they're giving for cash, as it may be much more. Considering how difficult it is just to change

ROMANIA

a travellers' cheque, trying to get a cash advance on a credit card is almost impossible.

When you change money at a bank or tourist office, you're given a receipt which you should keep for reference, although almost everything can be paid for in lei without this receipt. Occasionally a hotel clerk from the old school will ask to see a bank receipt when you pay for your hotel room in lei and at other times you'll need one if you book a sightseeing tour or rent a car. Receipts are always required to change excess lei back into hard currency but doing this is usually impossible. (Some readers have reported success in reconverting lei at Bucharest Airport.) Bulgarian leva cannot be changed in Romania, and Hungarian forint are only accepted by black marketeers in Transylvania.

Officially, you're allowed to import hard currency up to a maximum of US$50,000 but amounts over US$1000 in cash are supposed to be declared upon arrival. If you're carrying more than US$1000 in cash upon departure (which you did not declare on arrival) keep it out of sight to be on the safe side. You are only allowed to export 5000 lei in Romanian banknotes and then only in notes of 1000 lei or smaller.

By law, Romanians are only allowed to purchase US$125 in foreign currency a year, which is why there's a black market offering 25% above the official bank rate for cash dollars or Deutschmarks (though often they'll only want to give you 10% more). Be aware that using the black market is extremely dangerous, as many of the individuals who offer to change money on the street are professional thieves who only want to trick you out of your cash. The amount of money you will be given the first time will always be 'short' and in the process of correcting the 'error' the real money disappears. The moneychangers flash a thick wad of notes, count out the agreed price for your dollars or Deutschmarks, roll the money up into a tight little roll, then switch rolls at the last instant. Later, when you take the money out to count it again, you discover a roll of newsprint or worthless Yugoslav banknotes with a lei note on top. These operators will insist that you change at least US$50 or DM 100 (even in lei, US$10 doesn't make much of a roll), so that's one way to recognise them.

Another favourite trick is to take your dollars and give you the correct amount, then just as you're walking off, they will rush back shouting, 'Not good, not good'. The operators will then insist on giving you 'your' money back in exchange for theirs. As soon as they have the lei in hand again, they'll quickly disappear and you'll find that your US$20 and US$50 bills have been swapped for US$1 bills or counterfeit notes. Beware of anyone who's too pushy, wears flashy clothing or works with a partner. Given any chance at all, they'll rob you.

This book has included warnings on this subject since the first edition but we still get letters from readers who thought they knew what they were doing and ended up being cheated.

Reader William Redgrave of Maidenhead, England, sent us this:

Romania was the one place where the 'change money' men were 100% untrustworthy. The locals continually warned us not to talk to them and when we occasionally dabbled we could see their sleight-of-hand tricks and walked away. Worryingly, these rogues seem to have the run of the place: the police and exchange office workers seem unable to do anything and even the public seemed scared of them, warning us with covert shakes of the head. Perhaps they're ex-Securitate men! Coming out of an official exchange office (in which we'd been continually hassled by dubious characters, provoking no response from the bona fide staff behind the counter) we were physically grabbed and an attempt was made, though rather half-heartedly it seemed, by a group of black marketeers to mug us – in broad daylight on a busy road in Constanţa! Passersby shouted at them and eventually beat them off but the police showed no interest. It evoked memories of India, but not my favourite ones!

Reader Michael van Verk of Dordrecht, The Netherlands, sent this:

I heard of an unusual trick being used at Constanţa and Neptun. A man will walk up to you and ask if you want to change money. If you say 'no' and walk on another man will appear and 'arrest' the first man. He'll flash some fake ID-card at you telling you that he is from the 'tourist police' and that he wants to see your passport and check your money. If you give them to him he'll say he needs them as 'evidence' and they'll both be off. I think the best bet is not even to take out your wallet and just ignore them, and if they become really persistent to ask a uniformed police officer for advice or to offer to go with them to the police station.

If you're set on cutting your costs by 25%, deal with people you meet in camping grounds or hotels rather than on the street. Take the money from them, re-examine it carefully, put it away and only then show your money. Don't be in a hurry. Wait till you meet someone who can't run away. At best, you only have to be cheated one time in four to have all your profits cancelled and more, so approach this whole business with extreme caution.

Costs
With the collapse of the leu, which was officially valued at nine to the US dollar when the first edition of this book was published in 1989, Romania has become an inexpensive country for foreigners. Room prices at tourist hotels are based on hard currency and are thus still high, but almost everything else now costs much less than it did just a few years ago. Restaurant meals, drinks, public transport, museum admissions, theatre tickets and private rooms (outside Bucharest) are less expensive in Romania than they are in any other Eastern European country. This is one of the few chapters in this book where the quoted hotel prices are lower than those in the 1991 edition. However, it must always be kept in mind that Romanians only earn the equivalent of US$75 a month and when discussing these matters with Romanians it's far better to express your sympathy with their situation instead of raving about how cheap you find everything. To do otherwise is to breed resentment and encourage overcharging of foreigners.

Tipping
At restaurants, if the service charge is included, there's no need to tip extra though you should always round the bill up a little. If you give a tip for preferential treatment somewhere, don't let the Romanians who are also waiting see you do it, otherwise you could provoke an irate response. While working wonders with service industry personnel, tips should not be offered to officials, including train conductors, as this could create a serious nuisance for future travellers.

CLIMATE & WHEN TO GO
Romania has a variable continental climate. It can be cold in the mountains, even in midsummer. The average annual temperature is 11°C in the south and on the coast, but only 2°C in the mountains. Romanian winters can be extremely cold and foggy with lots of snow from mid-December to mid-March. In summer there's usually hot, sunny weather on the Black Sea coast. Annual rainfall is 600 to 700 mm, much of it in spring. The mountains get the most rain and the Danube Delta the least.

SUGGESTED ITINERARIES
Depending on the length of your stay, you might want to see and do the following things in Romania:

Two days
    Visit Bucharest.
One week
    Visit Bucharest, Sinaia, Braşov, Bran and perhaps Sighişoara.
Two weeks
    Visit Bucharest, Sinaia, Braşov, Bran, Sighişoara, Sibiu, Alba Iulia, Cluj-Napoca and Oradea with at least one mountain hike.
One month
    Visit many (but not all) of the places included in this chapter.

WHAT TO BRING
Romanian customs regulations are complicated but not often enforced. Gifts worth up to a total of US$100 may be imported duty-free. Duty-free allowances are four litres of wine, one litre of spirits, 200 cigarettes and 200 grams each of coffee and cocoa, but only

for personal use, not for resale. If you're coming from Bulgaria, bring BT cigarettes, which are greatly appreciated by Romanians. Bring some matches, too, as the Romanian variety is hopeless. A water bottle, water-purification pills, insect repellent and a roll of toilet paper will come in handy.

Motorists intending to camp would be wise to stock up on canned foods, powdered soups, tea bags, cooking oil, sugar and salt in Hungary, as these are hard to find in Romania. You're not allowed to bring in uncanned meats and dairy products, however. What you can usually find in Romania are tomatoes, peppers, onions, potatoes, carrots, apples, dusty bottles of pickled beets and bread.

Most important of all, bring Western currency in cash. Travellers' cheques are accepted at banks, tourist offices and large hotels, but at low rates. Cash US dollars and Deutschmarks are like gold in Romania.

TOURIST OFFICES

The Carpaţi National Tourist Office (Oficiul Naţional de Turism – ONT) is the government agency that controls tourism in Romania. Visit the ONT offices for free travel brochures, but don't expect the staff to help you to save money, as their function is exactly the opposite. It's usually better to go directly to hotels, rather than have ONT make accommodation bookings for you.

County tourist offices called Oficiul Judeţean de Turism (OJT) are sometimes more helpful than ONT, although they cater mostly for Romanian tourists. They'll often just refer you to the tour desk at the nearest 1st-class hotel. It's always worth trying them, however, as some will provide information if they're not too busy. Romania's student travel organisation, the Biroul de Turism Pentru Tîneret (BTT), has nothing to offer individual foreign students (a policy of the old regime which has persisted). You'll often have to fend for yourself in Romania.

Touring ACR, the travel agency of the Romanian Automobile Club (Automobil Clubul Român), has desks in several hotels around Romania and these are very helpful in reserving accommodation at up-market hotels and providing general information for visiting motorists (and others). ACR offices will usually give you a free copy of their highway map of Romania. You'll often recognise these offices by the large Hertz signs. (They rent Hertz cars as a sideline.) These are all listed in this chapter.

Since 1989 private travel agencies have opened up all across Romania but their main business is organising packaged holidays for Romanians. Some will also arrange private rooms, plus sightseeing tours in a private car with an English-speaking guide, either in the city or surrounding countryside, for less than ONT would charge in a bus.

ONT Offices Abroad
Romanian National Tourist Office addresses abroad include:

Netherlands
  Weteringschans 165, 1017 XD, Amsterdam (☎ 020-623 9044)
UK
  83a Marylebone High St, London, W1M 3DE (☎ 0171-224 3692)
USA
  342 Madison Ave, Suite 210, New York, NY 10173 (☎ 212-697 6971)

BUSINESS HOURS & HOLIDAYS
Banking hours are weekdays from 9 am to noon. Some shops close for a mid afternoon siesta – after all, this is a Latin country! Theatrical performances and concerts usually begin at 7 pm, except on Monday and in summer, when most theatres are closed. Sporting events are usually on Wednesday, Saturday and Sunday. Almost all museums in Romania are closed on Monday.

The public holidays in Romania are New Year (1 and 2 January), Easter Monday (March/April), National Unity Day (1 December) and Christmas (25, 26 and 27 December).

CULTURAL EVENTS
Many folklore festivals take place along the coast in summer, including one in Tulcea in August. Autumn is the time for musical fes-

tivals in Transylvania, such as Sibiu's Cibinium in September, Braşov's Cerbu de Aur Festival also in September, and Cluj-Napoca's Musical Autumn in October. In December the Days of Bihor Culture takes place in Oradea. The Bucharest International Fair in October is Romania's main trade fair.

POST & TELECOMMUNICATIONS

The main post offices are open from Monday to Saturday until 8 pm, Sunday until noon. Mailboxes are yellow and labelled *poşta*. When mailing purchases home from Romania, you may be asked to pay an export duty of 20% of their value. The Romanian postal service is slow and unreliable – mail your things from another country.

Romanian postal clerks are often confused about the postal rates to places outside Romania, so buy your stamps at a main post office in a large city.

Receiving Mail

Mail addressed c/o Poste Restante No 1, 70700 Bucureşti, Romania, can be collected at the post office on Strada Matei Millo, in the room with the post office boxes (weekdays 7.30 am to 8 pm, Saturday 8 am to 1 pm).

The American Express representative next door to the ONT office holds mail addressed c/o ONT Carpaţi SA, American Express Representative, 7 Bulevardul Magheru, Bucureşti, Romania. They kindly allow you to sort through the box of letters yourself and take any that you like.

Telephone & Telegraph

The telephone service in Romania is by far the worst in Eastern Europe. Even Poland and Albania shine in comparison. It's best not to count on being able to make any international calls at all; if you succeed, good for you!

To place an international call at a telephone centre you must put up a deposit equivalent to the cost of your call and if no connection is made for any reason (nobody home, line busy, no connection etc), a US$1 service charge is deducted from your refund.

Since you've only got a fifty-fifty chance of getting through in the first place, this can be very frustrating. To make a collect call is *cu taxâ inversâ*. The high level of static on the lines usually forces you to shout, so everyone in the telephone centre will hear your call.

Alternatively, try sending your contact a telegram with a number where you can be reached, as incoming calls go through much more easily. It's very easy to send a telegram from any main post office.

To call Romania from Western Europe dial the international access code, 40 (the country code for Romania), the area code and the number. Important area codes in Romania include 90 (Bucharest), 91 (Constanţa), 92 (Sibiu, Bran and Rîşnov), 95 (Cluj-Napoca), 96 (Timişoara), 915 (Tulcea and Sulina), 917 (Eforie Nord, Neptun and Mangalia), 918 (Mamaia), 921 (Braşov), 943 (Calafat), 950 (Sighişoara), 957 (Hunedoara), 966 (Arad), 968 (Alba Iulia), 973 (Sinaia), 978 (Drobeta-Turnu Severin), 981 (Iaşi), 987 (Suceava and Gura Humorului), 989 (Rădăuţi) and 991 (Oradea). Within Romania, you must add an initial 0 before the area code.

TIME

Romanian time is GMT/UTC plus two hours, which means there's a one-hour difference between Romania and Hungary or Yugoslavia, but no difference between Romania and Bulgaria. Romania goes on summer time at the end of March, so clocks are turned forward an hour. At the end of September, they're turned back an hour.

WEIGHTS & MEASURES

The electric current is 220 V, 50 Hz AC.

BOOKS

Nagel's Encyclopedia-Guide (Nagel Publishers, Geneva) is strong on historical and artistic information but of limited practical use. Tim Burford has written two guides which are meant to be used: *A Hiking Guide to Romania* (Bradt Publications) and *A Rough Guide to Romania* (Rough Guides). *Kiss the Hand You Cannot Bite: the Rise and Fall of the Ceauşescus* by Edward Behr provides fascinating background information on the 1989 revolution. Another pivotal figure of 1989 is the subject of *With God, for the People: the Autobiography of László Tökés* as told to David Porter (Hodder & Stoughton, London, England, UK).

Marie, Queen of Romania by Hannah Paluka focuses on this half-English, half-Russian granddaughter of Queen Victoria whose persuasive charm at the 1919 Trianon Peace Conference helped Romania obtain Transylvania. For a colourful portrait of Romania at the outbreak of WW II read Olivia Manning's 1960 novel *The Balkan Trilogy*.

Former dissident Paul Goma, born in 1935, is Romania's best known contemporary novelist. His *My Childhood at the Gate of Unrest* recently appeared in Britain in an English translation but all of his books are worth reading. Also watch for books by Ana Blandiana, born in 1942, and Mircea Dinescu.

MEDIA

More than 1000 newspapers appeared after the revolution, precipitating a newsprint crisis. Important daily papers are *Adevărul* and *Tineretul Libera*, both of which favour the DFSN, *România Libera*, an opposition voice, and *Evenimentul Zilei*, a popular mainstream paper.

Nine O'Clock (1 Piaţa Presei Libere, Central Building, 1st floor, Bucharest) is Romania's English-language newspaper, although it's hard to find a copy anywhere.

HEALTH

Foreigners must pay dearly for medical treatment in Romania. This is the Eastern European country where diarrhoea is most likely to be a problem, so take extra care of what you eat and drink, and bring a remedy, just in case.

One-third of all European sources of mineral or thermal waters are concentrated in Romania. There are 160 spas. The mud baths on Lake Techirghiol at Eforie Nord go well with the salty lake water and the nearby

Black Sea. Other important spas are Băile Felix (near Oradea) and Băile Herculane (known since Roman times). Ask for the brochure *Health Sources & Original Treatments in Romania* at ONT offices abroad.

Some of the spas offer special treatments using the unique Romanian products Gerovital H3, Aslavital, Boicil Forte, Pellamar, Covalitin and Ulcosilvanil. Gerovital H3 and Aslavital are drugs used against ageing effects; Pell-amar, extracted from sapropel mud, treats rheumatism; Covalitin dissolves kidney stones; Boicil Forte, which is extracted from medicinal herbs, relieves ankylosis and rheumatic pains; and Ulcosilvanil is used for the treatment of gastroduodenal ulcers. Gerovital H3 beauty cream rejuvenates the body.

DANGERS & ANNOYANCES

The Romanians' egocentric Latin temperament is apparent when they do things like turning on loud music without consulting those nearby, butting in front of others in line, monopolising the pavement and generally insisting on being served first. Some bad-mannered Romanians rudely interrupt conversations at ticket and information windows. On the other hand, many Romanians go out of their way to assist foreign visitors and that goes a long towards compensating for these disadvantages. Surprisingly, Romanians are considerate about smoking on trains and will usually get up and have their cigarette in the corridor.

Romanians are disorderly queuers and they will try to cut in front of you in line every time. Don't make it easy for them to do this by giving a lot of space, but at the same time don't let it upset you too much – a minute or two is not worth a nasty scene.

Be aware of theft in Romania. This is a poor country, so it's unwise to display your wealth. Be on guard wandering around late at night as muggings are not unknown. Keep to well-lit streets and look purposeful. If you are attacked, don't expect much help from bystanders or the police. Apart from the danger of having things stolen while camping or being ripped off while changing money on the street, you also have to take care in hotels by locking your things in your pack or suitcase when you go out.

If you have a car, it's safer to carry your valuables into your hotel room rather than to leave them in the car overnight. (The Black Sea coast and Braşov are said to be the worst areas in this regard.) It's safer to park in a well-lit town centre than in an isolated area. Always check that your car doors and windows are properly closed. Don't get paranoid, though. With a little care, nothing at all will be lost. During half a dozen extensive trips around Romania over the years, this author has never had anything stolen.

Women travellers may be unnerved by the way some Romanian men eye them constantly and deliberately bump into them on trains or on the street. We would appreciate having female readers write in and compare their experiences in Romania with what happened in other Eastern European countries.

Occasionally beggars can be a nuisance and, unless you're sure it's someone temporarily in dire need, it's best to avoid them, especially professional beggars like the colourfully dressed women with babies in their arms. Watch out for beggar children who may try to kick you or grab something if you don't give. Avoid eye contact with such types. Be prepared for some distressing sights of disabled people begging, especially in Braşov.

ACTIVITIES
Skiing
Romania's most famous ski resorts are Sinaia, Buşteni, Predeal and Poiana Braşov in the Carpathian Mountains, between Bucharest and Braşov. All are fully developed with cable cars, chair lifts and modern resort hotels. The ski slopes at Sinaia vary in altitude from 400 to 2800 metres, with level differences up to 585 metres. On top of the Bucegi Plateau above the Sinaia resort is an eight-km cross-country route, and there is also a 13-bend bobsled track.

Poiana Braşov boasts 20 km of ski slopes and sledding runs at varying degrees of difficulty. As this resort is off the main railway

line, it's less crowded and preferable for serious skiers. Other lesser known Romanian ski resorts include Păltiniş south-west of Sibiu; Borşa, between Suceava and Baia Mare; and Semenic near Reşita, south-east of Timişoara.

The ski season runs from December to March and you can hire gear at the main hotels. Courses at the ski school at Poiana Braşov last from four to six days and run for four hours a day, with about 12 students in each class. Special courses for children are available.

Hiking
Romania's Carpathian Mountains offer endless opportunities for hikers, with the Bucegi and Făgăraş ranges south and west of Braşov being the most popular areas. Other choice Carpathian hiking zones include the Retezat National Park, northwest of Tîrgu Jiu; the Şureanu Mountains, between Alba Iulia and Tîrgu Jiu; the Apuseni Mountains, south-west of Cluj-Napoca; and the Ceahlău Massif, between Braşov and Suceava. Good hiking maps are hard to come by, so buy them when you see them.

Courses
Several Romanian universities offer two-or three-week summer courses (cursuri de vară) in Romanian language and civilisation for foreigners. Tuition includes about 20 hours of instruction a week, accommodation in double rooms at student dormitories, meals at student cafeterias, cultural events and other activities. Registration (by mail or fax) generally closes around 1 June and anyone with a serious interest in Romanian culture is welcome. Programmes for beginners are offered and there are no age restrictions. These courses are a great way to add depth to your visit and meet some interesting people in the process.

The three-week course in July at the Universitatea 'Al I Cuza' Iaşi (fax 40-98-146 330), Secretariat Relaţii Internaţionale, Bulevardul Copou No 11, 6600 Iaşi, costs US$350, which includes a three-day excursion to Bukovina. Babes-Bolyai University (fax 40-95-111 905), Secretariatul Cursurilor de Vară, Strada M Kogălniceanu 1, 3400 Cluj-Napoca, also has a three-week course in July (US$500).

The three-week international summer course (mid-July to early August) of Ovidius University (fax 40-91-618 372), Bulevardul Mamaia 124, 8700 Constanţa, is US$600. In late August and early September the University of Timişoara (fax 40-96-116 722), Bulevardul V Parvan, 1900 Timişoara, offers specialised two-week courses in a variety of fields (US$425).

The most distinguished summer school is that of the Universitatea Bucureşti (☎ 40-90-615 1942), Bulevardul M Kogălniceanu 64, 70609 Bucharest, in operation since 1959. Their three-week course for students of Romance languages at Sinaia in late July and early August costs US$1050, but you are accommodated at a 1st-class hotel and lectures by prominent academics are scheduled.

HIGHLIGHTS
Museums & Galleries
Constanţa's Archaeological Museum has one of the best collections of Greek and Roman artefacts in Eastern Europe. The Ethnographical Museum in Cluj-Napoca, Museum of Popular Techniques at Sibiu and Bucharest's Village Museum will be appreciated by anyone interested in Romanian folklore. Romania's oldest and finest art gallery is the Brukenthal Museum in Sibiu. Finally, the Danube Museum in Drobeta-Turnu Severin is outstanding for history and natural history, with the added bonus of an aquarium of fish from the Danube. Always ask for the museum lights to be turned on, otherwise they may not be.

Castles
Bran Castle near Braşov is everyone's idea of a fairy-tale castle (even if Count Dracula never slept there). Hunedoara Castle is easily the finest Gothic castle in Romania, but it's spoiled by the ugly steel mill next door. Alba Iulia Citadel has deep significance to Romanians as the place where the country was finally reunited. Peleş Castle at Sinaia is actually a royal palace, but what a brilliant palace!

Historic Towns
It may come as no surprise that Romania's best preserved medieval towns, Sighişoara, Sibiu, Braşov and Cluj-Napoca, are all in Transylvania. Oradea is an elegant 19th century Habsburg town.

ACCOMMODATION
You may pay all accommodation charges in lei. There's no bureaucratic requirement to register with the police, get hotel stamps on a visa form or account for every night spent in the country.

Camping
As there are no youth hostels in Romania, camping is one of the few ways to see the country on a low budget. Of course you'll need a tent and will have to come in summer. Dozens of official camping grounds have been set up along the Black Sea coast, the perfect place to relax for a few days and meet young Romanians. Camping grounds with bungalows are called *popas turisticas*. Many Romanian camping grounds are in bad condition. Some are without toilets and showers and most only open from June to mid-September. When choosing your place at a camping ground keep in mind that your Romanian neighbours will probably have their radios on fairly loud at night.

Freelance camping is prohibited in cities, but not necessarily elsewhere. Such camping on the Black Sea coast, unthinkable during the Ceauşescu era, is now fairly common. If you see Romanian tourists camping in an open field or on a beach, there's nothing to prevent you from joining them. If you're camping alone, try to keep out of sight of the road. If you wish to sleep in your car or van, it's safer to go to a camping ground or park near a hotel, as vehicles parked along roads can attract unwelcome attention. If anyone hints that there could be a problem about camping somewhere, believe them and go elsewhere. Wherever you camp, take care of your gear.

Mountain Hostels

Although you can pitch a tent anywhere you like in the mountains, you may find it too cold to do so. In most mountain areas there's a network of cabins or chalets *(cabane)* with restaurants and dormitories where hikers can stay for the night. Prices are much lower than hotels and no reservations are required, but arrive early if the *cabana* is in a popular location, for example next to a cable car terminus. Expect to find good companionship rather than cleanliness or comfort at these hostels.

Private Rooms

Only since 1990 have Romanians been allowed to rent rooms in their homes to foreigners. This type of accommodation is so new that it's not fully organised yet, but always ask about private rooms at tourist offices. Private rooms are very easy to find in Braşov and Sinaia, but hard to find along the Black Sea coast and very expensive in Bucharest. A few agencies offering private rooms are mentioned in this chapter. You have the best chance of getting the much lower local price by renting from landladies you meet at train stations or on the street. As you get off the beaten track, you'll sometimes be invited to stay with local people you meet on trains or elsewhere.

Waiting Rooms

At a pinch, railway station waiting rooms are viable places to spend the night, especially if you arrive somewhere very early or late. It helps to have a train ticket, used or unused, in case security personnel ask you to show it, and it wouldn't hurt to check in your bag at the left-luggage office if you plan to get some sleep. You'll gain colourful insights into rural life in terms of noise and smell.

Hotels

Rooms in a good modern hotel will often only cost about US$10 more than a flea pit, so this is one country where the cheapest

isn't always the best value. Some hotels charge you extra to use the communal shower. Ask first as it may be better value in the long run to take a room with a private bathroom (though even 1st-class hotels sometimes have total water failures).

All accommodation prices in this chapter were calculated at the official rate. If you're paying with lei obtained at an exchange house which paid a premium above the bank rate, you'll pay that much less. You can always pay for hotels in lei, but receptionists will occasionally ask to see an exchange receipt to verify that you changed your money legally.

Many Romanian hotels have been reclassified as 1st-class hotels simply to increase the prices, so a 1st-class hotel in no way ensures a 1st-class room. In addition, the lowest category of hotel is second class, so all third-and fourth-class hotels are listed as second class automatically.

On the positive side, Romanian hotel keepers will go out of their way to find you a room, even in hotels with large 'no vacancy' *(nu avem locuri)* notices on the door. This is mostly because Western tourists must pay four times more than Romanians for the same rooms. Still, it's comforting to know that you'll almost always be able to find something. Breakfast *(mic dejun)* is sometimes included in the price (ask).

Hotel Coupons If you want to visit Romania in reasonable comfort, the hotel coupons issued by the Romanian Automobile Club (Automobil Clubul Român) are recommended. You can only purchase these at ONT offices abroad, some foreign travel agencies, Touring ACR desks in certain Romanian hotels, highway border crossings and the Automobil Clubul Român/Hertz (☎ 090-611 0408), Strada Cihoschi 2, just off Piaţa Romană, Bucharest (travellers' cheques are accepted). In Romania, the coupons can be purchased with lei calculated at that day's official rate.

Each coupon guarantees you a room at a 1st-class hotel with bath, breakfast included. Reservations are not required as the participating hotels are required to hold a certain number of rooms free until 7 pm every day for coupon-holders who may show up. The price is US$29/44 single/double per coupon, which is usually less than what you would pay for the same rooms without coupons. Once purchased, the coupons are valid until March the next year.

Hotel coupons will often get you rooms in hotels, especially along the Black Sea coast, which are otherwise 'full', but be aware that many 1st-class hotels don't accept coupons and luxury category hotels are not included. Before turning over your coupon, ask how much it would be if you paid cash, as in some cases it's slightly cheaper. There will be occasions when a hotel coupon is a lifesaver.

Even if you decide to use the coupons as a means of acquiring accommodation around the country, don't buy too many as there are lots of other places where you can stay. If you are left with any unused coupons, however, they will be refunded in lei less a 40% penalty. As a rule of thumb, buy one coupon for every three nights you plan to spend in Romania. Camping coupons are also available, but they are expensive and of no use.

FOOD

Unlike most hotel accommodation you'll find the restaurants of Romania very affordable. This is because foreigners pay four or five times more than locals for rooms, but food is the same price for everyone (though roguish waiters sometimes try to change this). Whenever you have trouble finding a decent place to eat, try the dining room of a major hotel. As foreigners tend to offer better tips, waiters in good restaurants will compete to seat you. Dining at places with table service involves some waiting, so patronise the self-service cafeterias if you don't have time for a leisurely meal. Many of the cheaper restaurants close early.

Even at up-market restaurants you'll rarely pay over US$10 for dinner for two, a bottle of wine included, and one person alone drinking only mineral water can have a good meal for US$2. All restaurant meals, including those at hotel restaurants, can be paid for

in lei. If the waiter asks you to pay in hard currency, he or she is trying to cheat you. You should always show your appreciation for good, honest service by rounding the bill up to the next even figure as you're paying.

Away from the hotels, the state-owned restaurants are often pretty grim and quality private restaurants have been slow to appear because most Romanians simply can't afford to eat out. In many places the hotel restaurants are still the only ones serving proper meals from regular menus. In the morning it's best to patronise the restaurant of a large hotel where a good breakfast of cheese omelette, toast, butter, jam and tea will be under US$1.50.

Always have a look at the menu, even a menu in Romanian. If it's a first-class place and you're told there's no menu with prices clearly listed (usually untrue), consider walking out rather than being forced to ask the price of every dish. If the waiter wants to be helpful ask him or her to point out recommendations on the menu. Many cheaper places don't have menus but are still quite OK, however. If the drinks are not listed on the menu, expect them to be expensive and order a bottle of mineral water which is always cheap (or ask to see the wine menu). You could also just point at something on someone else's plate and ask for the same, though you'd have to trust the waiter to charge you the correct price in that case.

Many of the things on the menu won't be available but most restaurants do have soup and it's usually good. Vegetarians are going to have a problem, as almost every restaurant dish is based on meat and there aren't many alternatives. Look for dishes based on cheese (*brînză*), tomatoes (*roşii*), peppers (*ardei*) and eggs (*ou*). At a pinch, most restaurants will prepare *ciorbă de legumă* (vegetable soup) upon request. When you order a salad at a restaurant you've got a good chance of getting a plate of sliced pickles unless you tell the waiter *nu vreau castraveţi* (I don't want pickles). Pastries and cakes are available everywhere.

Always check your bill for 'mistakes', but remember that the vegetables and bread are often extra. If the menu lists the separate weights of two or three of the components of the meal, chances are the menu price will be the full charge for that dish. In other words, if you order a dish that specifies 100 grams of this and 150 of that, your bill will be a lot closer to what you expected to pay because everything will be included.

Take care what you eat in Romania or you could end up with Ceauşescu's Revenge!

Romanian Specialities

Romanian favourites include *ciorbă de perişoare* (a spicy soup made with meatballs and vegetables), *ciorbă de burtă* (tripe soup), *ghiveciu* (vegetable stew), *tocană* (onion and meat stew), *ardei umpluti* (stuffed peppers), *mititei* or *mici* (pronounced 'meech' – highly seasoned grilled meatballs), *sarmală* (cabbage or vine leaves stuffed with spiced meat and rice) and *pastramă* (smoked goat meat). *Mămăligă* is a cornmeal porridge that goes well with everything. Typical desserts include *plăcintă* (turnovers) and *cozonac* (a brioche). Turkish sweets such as *baclavă*, *cataif* and *halva* are common. Unfortunately, it's hard to find any of these dishes at Romanian restaurants. Usually they will only have a pork cutlet served with chips (French fries) and if you're lucky, a Balkan salad (cucumbers and tomatoes dusted with white cheese).

DRINKS

Romania is noted for its excellent wine, while the local beer is notable only for its low price and you get what you pay for. Imported Hungarian beer is often available. Among the best Romanian wines are Cotnari, Murfatlar, Odobesti, Tîrnave and Valea Calugareasca. Red wines are called *negru* in Romanian. A bottle of chilled white wine at the restaurant of a two-star hotel shouldn't be over US$2. *Must* is a fresh unfermented wine available during the wine harvest. *Tuica* (plum brandy) is taken at the beginning of a meal. *Palinca* is a stronger variety of *tuica*. *Crama* refers to a wine cellar, while a *berarie* is a pub or beer hall. A couple of toasts are *poftă bună* (bon appétit) and *noroc!* (cheers!).

Romanians drink Russian-style tea and Turkish coffee. Beware of 'ness', an awful type of imitation instant coffee made from vegetable extracts. It's always served super sweet and is usually cold. In proper cafés always ask for Turkish coffee which is much better and if that's not available, you're better off ordering tea. Mineral water is cheap and easily available in Romania.

ENTERTAINMENT

Ask at tourist offices about local festivals or cultural events. Ask too about local events at the main theatre and concert hall of the town you're in, and visit any theatre ticket offices you can find. Opera companies exist in Bucharest, Cluj-Napoca, Iaşi and Timişoara. In large towns buy the local paper and try to decipher the entertainment listings. The hotel bars are often pretentious and dull, and non-hotel discos often feature erotic shows that make for a sleazy atmosphere. If nothing at all seems to be happening, just go to bed and get an earlier start the next day!

THINGS TO BUY

Traditional purchases in Romania include plum brandy, Gerovital H3 and Pellamar cosmetics, embroidered blouses and handicrafts. Romarta stores sell glassware, textiles, women's clothing and ceramics, and Muzică stores sell Romanian records. Pirate rock music cassettes are cheap. You're not supposed to export books printed before 1973.

Consumer scarcities have developed a predator instinct among Romanian consumers. Sometimes you'll notice a shop with no-one in it which looks marginally interesting and stop to go in for a look. Immediately a dozen passers-by, sensing that you've spotted something, will crowd in behind you and stand peering at what's behind the counter. Often people will suddenly change direction and try to beat you to the counter, queue or seat. When a scarce item does become available, the hoarding instinct takes over and huge crowds gather to buy as much of the item as they can possibly carry. Romanians often carry a small cloth shopping bag around with them everywhere for just such emergencies.

If in doubt about a price at stores, offer the vendors a pen and paper and ask them to write it down. Always count your change.

Getting There & Away

AIR

TAROM (Transporturile Aeriene Române), Romanian Air Transport, has flights to Bucharest from Abu Dhabi, Amman, Bahrain, Bangkok, Beijing, Beirut, Cairo, Calcutta, Chicago, Damascus, Delhi, Dubai, Istanbul, Karachi, Kuwait, Larnaca, New York, Tel Aviv and many European cities. The flights between Bucharest and New York have been operating since 1974. From Western Europe and the USA, a package tour to Romania with flights, hotels and all meals included may be cheaper than a regular return plane ticket. Also ask the price of the 'camping flight'. Bucket shops (unbonded travel agencies) in Asia sell TAROM tickets at a discount.

For information on Romavia flights from Timişoara to Switzerland and Cyprus turn to the Timişoara section in this chapter. There's no airport departure tax in Romania.

LAND

Bus

To/from Hungary the cheapest option by far is a Hungarian Volanbus and these leave daily from Budapest's Népstadion Bus Station. For example, Budapest-Oradea is US$10 (246 km). Turn to Getting There & Away in the introduction to the Hungary chapter and the Cluj-Napoca, Oradea, Arad and Timişoara sections of this chapter for details.

Numerous buses shuttle between Bucharest and Istanbul (turn to Travel Agencies in the Bucharest section for details). There are no buses to/from Bulgaria but the Istanbul buses can be used for this purpose and the low US$13 fare makes this a practical alter-

native. The thick cigarette smoke is a definite minus of these buses.

Buses from Bucharest to Kishinev, Moldova, are also covered in the Bucharest section.

Train

Railway fares to/from Hungary are more expensive than those to/from Bulgaria. A one-way ticket from Arad or Oradea to Budapest costs US$18, while Bucharest-Ruse costs only US$3 and Bucharest-Sofia is US$11. When bound for Hungary, you can save a little money by going across Romania on a domestic ticket, although Bucharest-Budapest is only US$31 one way, which is still cheap. (This fare may soon change as it's only a third what is being charged in Hungary for Budapest-Bucharest.)

International train tickets must be purchased in advance at CFR (Romanian State Railways) travel agencies *(agentii de voiaj)* as they're not usually available at train stations. Since the Bucharest ticket offices are crowded, try picking up an open international train ticket to get you out of the country at a provincial CFR Travel Agency. (Many are listed in this chapter.) Students are supposed to get a 25% reduction on international train travel within Eastern Europe.

Most of the daily, year-round international trains listed here have compulsory seat reservations. If you already have your ticket, you may be able to make reservations at the station an hour before departure, though it's preferable to do so at a CFR Travel Agency at least one day in advance. Expect any train in transit across Romania which originated in Hungary or Bulgaria to run several hours late due to delays at the border. Consequently, when leaving it's best to book only on trains originating in Romania.

To/From Hungary & Beyond The *Balt-Orient* express from Berlin-Lichtenberg, the *Carpaţi* express from Warsaw, the *Dacia* express from Vienna and the *Pannonia* express from Prague, all go via Hungary and Arad on their way to Bucharest, taking about

17 hours to travel from Budapest to Bucharest (873 km).

The easiest way to enter or leave Romania by train to/from Hungary is on one of the two daily local Hungarian trains which shuttle between Oradea and Budapest-Nyugati (249 km, five hours). At last report these trains left Oradea at 12.10 and 6.10 pm, and Budapest-Nyugati at 6.10 am and 1.30 pm. No reservations are required, but in Romania try to buy an open Oradea-Budapest ticket at a CFR Travel Agency well ahead. If this is impossible, board the train at Episcopia Bihor, following the instructions given in the Oradea section of this chapter.

Local unreserved trains depart from Békéscsaba, Hungary, for Oradea (90 km) and Arad (68 km) once or twice a day.

To/From Yugoslavia The *Bucureşti* express shuttles daily between Beograd-Dunav Railway Station and Bucharest (693 km, 13 hours) via Timişoara, leaving both cities in the evening and travelling overnight.

If you can't get a ticket or reservation for this train, you can get an unreserved early morning train from Timişoara-Nord to Jimbolia (39 km), where you change to another local train to go to Kikinda, Yugoslavia. Two unreserved local trains a day run from Timişoara to Vršac (76 km) on the line to Belgrade.

To/From Bulgaria The train service between Romania and Bulgaria is terrible. Between Sofia and Bucharest (513 km) there's only one overnight train, passing Ruse northbound in the very early morning. It's incredibly overcrowded but reservations are not possible and unless you board early, you'll stand up all the way. Several other trains such as the *Vitoşa* express originating in Ukraine or Russia pass through Romania on their way to/from Bulgaria, but you're not allowed to use them. (In an emergency a US$10 banknote to the conductor might do the trick.)

There's a railway line from Negru Vodă, Romania, to Kardam, Bulgaria, but no passenger trains operate along it.

Car & Motorbike

When crossing the Romanian border by car, expect long queues of cars at the Romanian checkpoint. There are fewer cars on Monday, Tuesday and Wednesday than on weekends, however. With varying success, some foreigners drive right past the long lines of Romanian vehicles waiting to cross and jump to the head of the queue. Avoid the temptation to bribe the Romanian officials and beware of unauthorised persons charging dubious 'ecology', 'road' or 'bridge' taxes at the border. (Ask for a receipt.)

Trying to leave Romania for Bulgaria by car is a disaster, with long, slow-moving lines of vehicles at all borders. (Have some food and drink with you as eight-hour waits are routine.) The unusually heavy traffic is a result of the UN economic embargo against Yugoslavia – much traffic between Europe and Turkey is now routed through Romania. If you have a private car, a Yugoslavian visa and a taste for adventure it may even be preferable to take your chances with the Serbian police and swing down through Yugoslavia to Bulgaria. Re-entering Romania from Bulgaria is much easier as the problem lies with the inefficient Romanian customs officials. They're forced to process vehicles arriving from Bulgaria faster to avoid bottlenecks at the border gate.

The Romanian highway border crossings open to all nationalities are listed here in an anticlockwise direction around Romania. All are open 24 hours a day, except those to/from Ukraine and Moldova, which are open from 8 am to 8 pm.

To/From Hungary There are border crossings at Petea (11 km north-west of Satu Mare), Borş (14 km north-west of Oradea), Vărşand (66 km north of Arad) and Nădlac (between Szeged and Arad).

To/From Yugoslavia You may cross at Jimbolia (45 km west of Timişoara), Stamora Moraviţa (between Timişoara and Belgrade), Naidăş (120 km east of Belgrade) and Porţile de Fier (Iron Gate) (10 km west of Drobeta-Turnu Severin).

ROMANIA

To/From Bulgaria You can cross at Calafat (opposite Vidin, Bulgaria), Giurgiu (opposite Ruse), Călăraşi (opposite Silistra), Negru Vodă (37 km north-east of Tolbuhin) and Vama Veche (10 km south of Mangalia).

To/From the former USSR If you're going to/from Moldova there's Albiţa (65 km south-east of Iaşi), and to/from Ukraine it's Siret (between Suceava and Cernăuţi).

On Foot

If you don't want to bother picking up an international train ticket and have a taste for adventure, consider walking out of Romania. Take one of the four daily local trains from Arad to Nădlac (52 km, 1½ hours), then walk or take a taxi the last six km to the Hungarian border. In Hungary there are nine local trains a day from Nagylak to Szeged (47 km).

To travel to/from Bulgaria, you could take bus No 14 south 10 km from Mangalia to Vama Veche. There you can walk across into Bulgaria and look for onward transport to Balchik, 62 km south-west. Pedestrians are not allowed to use the so-called 'Friendship Bridge' to/from Ruse, Bulgaria, but you could take a train from Bucharest-Progresu to Giurgiu-Nord (nine daily, 58 km, 1½ hours). Follow the line of cars three km to the bridge and hitch across.

RIVER

Ferry

A regular passenger ferry between Calafat, Romania, and Vidin, Bulgaria, crosses the Danube River hourly throughout the year (US$2 in hard currency, 30 minutes). Both these towns are well connected to the rest of their countries by rail, so this route is practicable for travellers without vehicles. It's best to have your onward Bulgarian or Romanian visa already, and not expect to get one at the border.

From Craiova to Calafat by local train takes 2½ hours (five daily, 107 km). It's only a few blocks from Calafat Railway Station to the Romanian ferry terminal, where you can easily obtain ferry tickets. Turn to the

Calafat and Vidin sections of this book for more information on this interesting and quite feasible route.

Getting Around

AIR

TAROM has an extensive network of domestic flights out of Bucharest and Constanţa. Many of the Constanţa flights operate only in July and August, but you can fly out of Bucharest's Băneasa Airport to every part of the country all year. Very few TAROM flights operate on Sunday.

Foreigners pay much higher fares than Romanians on TAROM's domestic flights, which makes it very expensive. Sample one-way fares from Bucharest are: Arad US$52, Cluj-Napoca US$44, Constanţa US$30, Iaşi US$44, Oradea US$52, Satu Mare US$54, Sibiu US$32, Suceava US$44, Timişoara US$48 and Tulcea US$30. From Constanţa it costs US$74 to Arad, US$54 to Cluj-Napoca, US$68 to Oradea and US$66 to Timişoara. Only 10 kg of luggage is carried free but overweight charges are minimal.

BUS

Romanian buses are less reliable and more crowded than the trains and on rural routes only one or two buses may run a day. The schedules posted in bus stations are often incomplete or out of date, so always ask at information or the ticket window. You usually have to purchase your ticket before boarding and if you haven't done so at a bus station (*autogară*), you could have problems with the driver. If the bus is the only way to get there, try to reserve a seat by buying a ticket the day before and arrive early at the stop. With the advent of private buses (such as those from Braşov to Bran Castle), things are slowly improving.

TRAIN

The CFR (Căilor Ferate Române), Romanian State Railways, runs trains over 11,106 km of track. There are two types of trains:

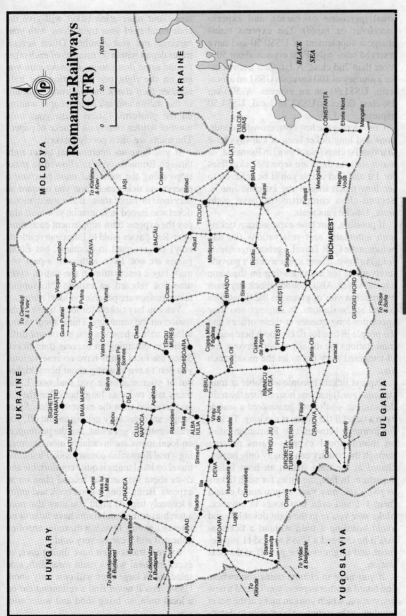

local (persoane or cursă), and express (accelerat or rapid). The express trains charge a supplement of US$0.50 and have reserved seats only. First class is about 50% more than 2nd class. A 1st-class train ticket for a journey of 100 km costs US$1 on a local train, US$1.60 on an express. A 500-km 1st-class ticket is US$3.75 local, US$4.50 express.

Considering the low cost, crowded conditions and long ticket lines, it's always wise to travel 1st class (clasă întîi) in Romania. At major stations there are separate ticket lines for 1st and 2nd class; you'll be relieved to see how much shorter the 1st-class line is. Second-class compartments have eight seats, 1st-class six seats.

If possible, purchase express train tickets with automatic seat reservations the day before at the CFR Travel Agency (agenţie de voiaj) in town. These agencies can't provide reservations for trains leaving on the same day, however. Also, double-check any train information you're given on the timetables posted at the stations. In summer you may encounter long queues at these offices and the people in line for tickets both here and at train stations are usually rather nervous and ill-tempered – try not to let the mood catch you.

Express tickets become available at train stations (gară) just one hour before the train departs, but you're not guaranteed a seat or even a ticket if the queue is too long. Tickets for journeys between two Romanian cities on international express trains passing through the country can usually only be purchased at the train station an hour before departure. In fact, the times for such tickets to go on sale may vary, so you could obtain them 1½ and even two hours in advance. Make sure you're in the right ticket line and avoid boarding a train without a ticket as you'll be charged a US$8 to US$11 supplement, and might even be put off at the next station.

If you have to change trains somewhere and board another express you'll need a new reservation, which you can make at the ticket window in the station an hour prior to departure. Your reservation ticket will give the code number of your train along with your carriage and seat number. Often several trains depart within 30 minutes of each other for the same destination, so make sure you get on the right one by noting the train number, then check the electronic indicator in the station and ask other people waiting on the platform. (Show them your train number written clearly on a piece of paper.) The trains are often poorly marked.

If you have an international ticket right through Romania, you're allowed to make stops along the route but must purchase a reservation ticket each time you reboard an accelerat or rapid train. If the international ticket was issued in Romania, you must also pay the express train supplement each time. Inter-Rail passes (sold to European residents only) are accepted in Romania, but Eurail passes are not. Even with such a pass you must buy a reservation in the station every time you reboard an express. No supplements or fees are payable on local trains.

You can buy tickets for local trains at the station on the same day. Think about taking a local train whenever you encounter difficulties in obtaining an express train ticket. Since the local trains have no reservations, you don't have to worry about being kicked out of your seat once you find one. Local trains take twice as long, but often they're less crowded than the express trains. Since people are constantly getting on and off, you will eventually get a seat, and the passengers on local trains are invariably more interesting – real Romanian country folk. First-class travel on local trains is quite comfortable and costs about the same as second class on an express. Bring along a good book and enjoy a leisurely trip. At night you may also need a torch as some local trains have little or no interior lighting. In winter the trains are often unheated and it can be very cold.

Express trains often have dining cars; an excellent meal with a main meat dish, side salad and a large beer will cost only about US$4. You'll never find a restaurant car on a local train, so bring food and water with you.

Sleepers (*vagon de dormit*) are available between Bucharest and Arad, Cluj-Napoca, Oradea, Timişoara, Tulcea and other points, and are a good way to cut accommodation expenses. First-class sleeping compartments have two berths, second-class sleepers three berths and second-class couchettes six berths. Book these well in advance at a CFR Travel Agency in town. Overnight trips on unreserved local trains are also good if you buy a 1st-class ticket and board the train early at the originating station. You can travel from Braşov to Iaşi this way.

If you'll be travelling much in Romania, look out for the railway timetable booklet, the *Mersul Trenurilor*, which is sometimes sold at CFR travel agencies. It only costs about a dollar and is invaluable. On posted timetables, *sosire* means arrivals and *plecare* means departures.

Important Railway Routes

Most visitors use one of the two main railway routes across Transylvania from Bucharest to Hungary or vice versa. The two routes are in fact one as far as Braşov (166 km and three hours from Bucharest by express). Here one line branches off west towards Arad (621 km and 10 hours from Bucharest by express) via Sibiu, though many of the Arad trains go via Sighişoara and Alba Iulia. A more important line continues north-west past Sighişoara and Cluj-Napoca to Oradea (651 km and 13 hours from Bucharest by express).

Other main lines are from Bucharest to Mangalia (269 km, five hours by express), Bucharest to Galaţi (230 km, four hours by express), Bucharest to Iaşi (462 km, seven hours by express), Bucharest to Suceava (450 km, seven hours by express) and Bucharest to Timişoara (533 km, eight hours by express). A useful route across the top of the country is Iaşi to Timişoara via Suceava and Cluj-Napoca. Beyond Cluj-Napoca some trains on this route go via Oradea and Arad, others via Simeria.

Some important domestic express trains which leave from Bucharest's Gara de Nord are the *Timişoara* running to Timişoara-Nord, the *Braşovia* to Braşov (originating in Constanţa), the *Transilvania* to Cluj-Napoca, the *Ştefan cel Mare* to Suceava-Nord and the *Moldova* to Iaşi. These trains are all classed as rapid and are the best that Romania has to offer. (All carry dining cars.) Reservations are required.

CAR & MOTORBIKE

Generally speaking the roads are in poor condition with unexpected potholes and irregular signposting. Secondary roads can become dirt tracks and after rain the mountain roads often become impassable. Concrete roads (such as the Bucharest ring road) were often constructed without gaps for expansion and are now quickly deteriorating. Level crossings over railway lines should be approached with caution as the roads can become very rough at these points. Open manhole covers are a hazard in cities like Bucharest and Constanţa. Check the pressure of your tyres before entering Romania because it's often impossible to do so at Romanian petrol stations. Punctures can be repaired at shops labelled *vulcanizare*.

Drive carefully as roadwork warnings are not posted and vehicles tend to stop suddenly in the middle of the road. You'll come across slow-moving tractors pulling wagons loaded with personnel, produce, factory output, cement and manure. Trucks and bicycles sometimes don't have any lights, and many drivers lack discipline. On the other hand, you'll find the Romanians very friendly and helpful and always eager to meet foreign motorists. Traffic is comparatively light.

The Automobil Clubul Român (ACR) emergency road service number throughout Romania is ☎ 12 345.

Fuel

Petrol is no longer rationed in Romania but there are still long lines at the fuel pumps. The types of petrol available are normal or regular (88-90 octane), unleaded (95 octane), premium or super (96-98 octane) and diesel. Don't use normal petrol as this can damage your car. Occasionally you'll find that water has been mixed with the petrol.

Fill up with unleaded petrol (*benzină fără plumb*) whenever possible as it's available only at a total of about 15 PECO petrol stations around the country. The stations often receive their supplies on Monday or Tuesday and are sold out by Thursday or Friday, so top up whenever you can. The morning is the busiest time. Station attendants are sometimes reluctant to sell unleaded fuel to foreigners when the locals have to wait hours and even days for leaded fuel. Discreetly offer a pack of cigarettes and be patient. Romanians always travel with an extra supply of petrol in the boot, so bring an empty fuel container with you. (You're not allowed to bring in a full container and there's a 200% tax on fuel exported in containers.)

Here's a list of a few PECO stations that are supposed to have unleaded petrol:

Piaţa Vasile Roaltă, near Arad Railway Station
Dîrste, south-east of Braşov
Bulevardul Schitu Măgureanu 15 near Cişmigiu Park, Bucharest
Strada Aurel Vlaicu 140, east side of Cluj-Napoca
Bulevardul Alexandru Lăpuşneanu 32, Constanţa
Bulevardul 1 Mai 25, west side of Suceava
Calea Dorobanţilor near Pădurea Verde, Timişoara

Needless to say, the root cause of the problems mentioned above is that fuel is too cheap; if prices were allowed to float to their real market level without government interference, supply would soon equal demand. Official price increases usually take effect on Monday, in which case all stations will close for the preceding weekend. At last report foreigners paid for fuel in lei at the same rate as Romanian motorists. Petrol coupons have been abolished and foreign vehicles are no longer allowed to cut to the front of the queue at petrol stations (though in practice many still do). Ask about coupons at the border so you'll know for sure if station attendants are just trying to rip you off if they demand payment in hard currency. However, if paying in US dollars or Deutschmarks

allows you to avoid a long wait, you may feel it's worth it.

Road Rules

The speed limit for cars is 60 km/h in built-up areas or 80 km/h on the open road. Motorbikes are limited to 40 km/h in built-up areas and 50 km/h on the open road.

If you are fined for a traffic violation insist on a receipt before producing any money. Don't accept only a written statement that doesn't specify the exact amount, otherwise the money will go straight into the police officer's pocket.

Car Rental

ONT rents Dacia 1300 cars for US$17 a day, plus US$0.22 a km. With unlimited km the charge is US$204 for the cheapest Dacia for three days, US$363 for a week. You can pay with lei but must show an official exchange receipt to cover the amount. The daily insurance charge on Dacia cars is US$9, or US$17 daily on better models. Credit card insurance is not accepted – everyone must pay the daily fee.

The Carpaţi National Tourist Office (ONT) represents Europcar. In Bucharest you can get a car from the main ONT office, Bulevardul Magheru 7, or the ONT counter at Otopeni Airport. Cars are also available at ONT desks in large tourist hotels, such as the Inter-Continental in Bucharest, the Aro Palace in Braşov, the Continental in Constanţa, the Transilvania in Cluj-Napoca, the Continental in Sibiu, the Bucovina in Suceava and the Continental in Timişoara. It's possible to pick up a car at one ONT office and drop it off at another with no additional charge. You must leave a cash deposit if you want to pay cash.

Hertz Rent-a-Car is represented by the Automobil Clubul Român desks at Hotel Park in Bucharest, Hotel Capitol in Braşov, Hotel Alcor in Mamaia, Hotel Europa in Eforie Nord and Hotel Belvedere in Neptun, with a main office at Strada Cihoschi 2, just off Piaţa Romană, Bucharest.

HITCHING

The hitchhiking in Romania is variable as the small cars are usually full and there isn't much traffic on secondary roads where you may really need a ride. Your chances will improve if it's obvious that you're a Westerner. Hitching from near bus stops is the best option as you can always jump on any bus that comes along. Some drivers will expect you to pay the equivalent of the bus fare and occasionally they even solicit business at bus and train stations as a way of covering their fuel costs.

You may be able to guess where a car is going by the letters on its licence plate: AB (Alba Iulia), AR (Arad), BV (Braşov), B (Bucharest), CJ (Cluj-Napoca), CT (Constanţa or Mangalia), DJ (Craiova), GL (Galaţi), GR (Giurgiu), IS (Iaşi), BH (Oradea), PH (Ploieşti), SB (Sibiu), SV (Suceava), TM (Timişoara) and TL (Tulcea).

BOAT

Navrom offers regular passenger boat service on the Danube River from Sulina on the Black Sea inland to Tulcea and Galaţi, daily throughout the year. Turn to the Tulcea section for details.

LOCAL TRANSPORT

Public transport within towns and cities is fairly good, though often overcrowded. Service is usually from 5 am to 11 pm daily. Most routes have numbers and if you ask the best-dressed person at the stop for advice on which number to take, you'll find that getting around is no problem. You must purchase tickets at kiosks and tobacconists, and then validate them once aboard. The Bucharest Metro takes coins which you insert in a turnstile.

Taxi

Government taxis are distinguished by a chequered design on the side and have meters (you pay what the meter displays). Unmetered private taxis with the letters 'P' or 'PO' on the roof are more expensive but often easier to find. If there's no meter, always bargain for a price beforehand.

TOURS

ONT sightseeing tours are sometimes useful if you want to visit out-of-the-way attractions, but they generally operate only in summer. Your best chance of getting on a day tour is on a Sunday. Book ONT tours at ONT offices or at the reception desk of luxury hotels. You can pay for sightseeing tours in lei but must show an exchange receipt. Be aware that with tourism to Romania down, most advertised sightseeing tours will be cancelled and foreigners are not permitted to join tours intended for Romanians.

If you want to travel around the country as part of an organised group you should come on a package tour, as group travel is difficult to arrange and extremely expensive after arrival. ONT offices abroad can arrange three-week stays at Romanian health resorts and offer package tours to ski resorts such as Sinaia, Buşteni, Predeal and Poiana Braşov. All package tours are based on dual-occupancy hotel rooms. (If you can't or don't wish to share a room, you must pay a single supplement.)

From May to September, New Millennium Holidays (☎ 0121-711 2232), 20 High St, Solihull, West Midlands B91 3TB, England, UK, runs inexpensive bus tours from Britain to Băile Felix and Predeal, sometimes in combination with Hungary. If you don't mind group travel, this is one of the cheapest ways to visit Romania from Britain.

Bucharest

Founded by a legendary shepherd named Bucur, Bucharest (Bucureşti), on the plains between the Carpathian foothills and the Danube, became the capital of Wallachia in 1459, during the reign of Vlad Ţepeş (Dracula). Now a city of over two million people, roughly the size of Budapest, Bucharest is the metropolis of Romania and has been its capital since 1862.

The broad, tree-lined boulevards, park-girdled lakes, pompous public buildings and

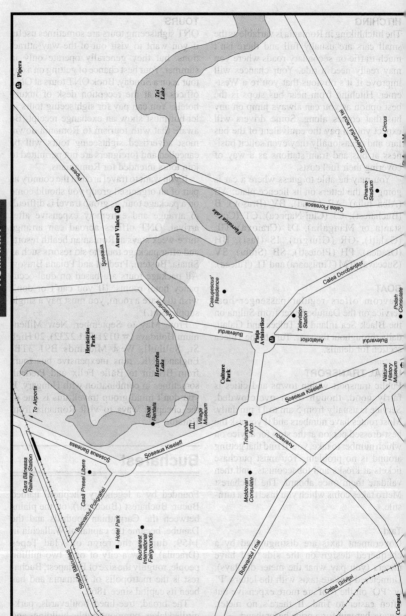

Pipera

Tei Lake

Floreasca Lake

Dinamo Stadium

Bulevardul Lacul Tei

Circus

Calea Floreasca

Calea Dorobanților

Ceaușescus' Residence

Polish Consulate

Aviaitor

Herăstrău Park

Herăstrău Lake

Television Station

Piața Aviatorilor

Bulevardul

Bulevardul

Aviatorilor

Șoseaua

Aurel Vlaicu

Boat Rentals

Village Museum

Culture Park

Șoseaua Kiseleff

Natural History Museum

To Airports

Triumphal Arch

Aviatorilor

Aviaitor

Șoseaua Băneasa

Șoseaua Kiseleff

Gara Băneasa Railway Station

Moldovan Consulate

Casa Presei Libere

Bulevardul Poligrafiei

Strada Baiculești

Bucharest International Fairgrounds

Hotel Park

Bulevardul 1 mai

Calea Griviței

Crângași

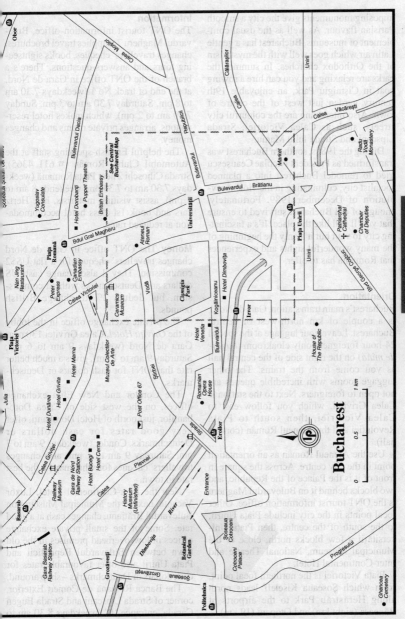

ROMANIA

Bucharest

LP

imposing monuments give the city a smooth Parisian flavour. As well as the usual complement of museums, Bucharest has a gentle Latin air which goes well with the mysticism of the Orthodox churches. In summer the parks are relaxing and you can hire a rowing boat in Cişmigiu Park, an enjoyable 19th century garden just west of the centre of town. Also interesting are the colourful city streets, such as Calea Victoriei, Strada Lipscani and Strada Iuliu Maniu.

During the 1980s, southern Bucharest was transformed as President Nicolae Ceauşescu tried to remodel Bucharest into a planned socialist city, culminating in the violent revolution of December 1989. Fortunately, enough of old Bucharest survived to ensure that you'll still like the place. It's a fascinating city to visit but it's only the beginning of the many wonderful sights and experiences that Romania has to offer.

Orientation

Bucharest's main train station, Gara de Nord, is a couple of km north-west of central Bucharest. Leave your luggage at the special 24-hour foreigners-only cloakroom (*bagaje de mîňa*) on the right side of the central hall as you come from the trains. The other luggage rooms with incredible queues are not open to foreigners. Next to the station is Calea Griviţei, which you follow east to Calea Victoriei, then south to Piaţa Revoluţiei and the Ateneul Român (concert hall).

Use the Ateneul Român as an orientation point in the city centre. Across the square in front of it is the Palace of the Republic, and two blocks behind it on Bulevardul Magheru is the ONT tourist information office. Other focal points in the city include Piaţa Unirii, to the south of the centre, then Piaţa Universităţii a few blocks north, close to the Municipal Museum, National Theatre and Inter-Continental Hotel.

Piaţa Victoriei is the northern focal point, from which Şoseaua Kiseleff leads north along Herăstrău Park to the airports at Băneasa (eight km) and Otopeni (19 km).

Information

The ONT tourist information office, Bulevardul Magheru 7, supplies travel brochures, changes travellers' cheques, books sightseeing tours and answers questions. There's a branch of the ONT office in Gara de Nord, at the end of track No 1 (weekdays 7.30 am to 8 pm, Saturday 7.30 am to 3 pm, Sunday 7.30 am to 2 pm), which makes hotel reservations, arranges private rooms and changes money.

The helpful English-speaking staff at the Automobil Clubul Român (☎ 611 4365), Strada Cihoschi 2 near Piaţa Romană (weekdays 7.30 am to 7.30 pm, weekends 8 am to 2 pm), assist visiting motorists, hire Hertz cars and book 1st-class hotel accommodation at reduced rates.

Money   The ONT office in Gara de Nord changes travellers' cheques for a flat US$2 commission. They'll also change cash US dollars and Deutschmarks without commission, but deduct 2% to change British pounds.

The private exchange office in the lobby of the *Griviţa Hotel*, Calea Griviţei 130 near Gara de Nord (weekdays 9 am to 6 pm, Saturday 9 am to 1 pm), gives a much better rate than ONT for cash dollars or Deutschmarks.

The Condor and New Elita exchange offices, on the west side of Calea Dorobanţilor, just north of Hotel Dorobanţi, offer very good rates for cash dollars or Deutschmarks. Condor (weekdays 9 am to 7 pm, Saturday 9 am to 1 pm) also changes travellers' cheques for what may be the best rate in town.

Near the Inter-Continental Hotel, Luxor Vacanta, next to the Municipal Museum on Bulevardul Brătianu, changes cash at a good rate. Some of the small private exchange offices in low-overhead premises in the old town between Bulevardul Republicii and Piaţa Unirii also offer favourable rates for cash dollars or Deutschmarks – shop around.

The Banca Romană de Comerţ Exterior, corner of Strada Lipscani and Strada Eugen Carada, entrance 'B' (weekdays 8.30 am to

12.30 pm), changes travellers' cheques for 1.5% commission.

Don't risk changing money on the street in Bucharest as rip-offs are common. As you approach the Inter-Continental Hotel you'll be accosted by some of the most seasoned confidence men in Eastern Europe, expert in tricking tourists with 'packets' – stacks or rolls of paper with a few real notes on top. Travellers with backpacks, who can't give chase, are the preferred victims of people like this.

Post & Telecommunications To mail a parcel you must take it unsealed to Post Office No 67, Strada Virgiliu 45, between Gara de Nord and Eroilor (weekdays 8 am to 2.30 pm). All packages are carefully inspected. Express Mail Service (EMS) is available here weekdays from 8 am to 6 pm.

The Oficiul Telefonic de Cabina telephone centre, on Strada Matei Millo in the city centre, is open 24 hours a day, but there's not much else that's good about it. Push your way through the crowd hanging around the counter and write your number on a form, pay a deposit and cross your fingers. You've a much better chance of getting a call through with less hassle if you go at odd hours.

If you don't connect (as often happens), walk down Strada Matei Millo a block to the small post office on the right where telegrams are easily sent. If you have a phone in your hotel room give your contacts the hotel's telephone number and your room number, and ask them to call you. Poste restante mail is held in the next office. Bucharest's telephone code is 090.

Foreign Embassies The US Consulate (☎ 312 4042, extension 269) is on Strada Snagov, directly behind the Inter-Continental Hotel (Monday to Thursday 8 am to noon and 1 to 3 pm, Friday 8 am to noon). The British Embassy is at Strada J Michelet 24, off Bulevardul Magheru (weekdays 9 am to noon). The Canadian Embassy (☎ 312 8345) is at Strada Nicolae Iorga 36, off Piaţa Romană (weekdays 9 am to 5 pm). New Zealanders must use the British Embassy, Australians the Canadian Embassy.

The Hungarian Consulate, on the corner of Strada I C Frimu and Bulevardul Dacia near the Canadian Embassy just off Piaţa Romană (Monday, Tuesday, Thursday and Friday 8.30 to 11.30 am), issues tourist visas (US$24) on the spot. You may encounter tremendous crowds here and may even have to queue up for the forms, but just be patient.

The Yugoslav Consulate is at Calea Dorobanţilor 34 (open weekdays 10 am to 1 pm).

The Consulate of Slovakia, is at Strada Oţelari 3, a few blocks east of the Inter-Continental Hotel (weekdays 9 am to noon).

A block east of the Slovakian Consulate is the Bulgarian Consulate, Strada Vasile Lascar 32 (weekdays 10 am to noon). Obtaining a Bulgarian tourist visa entails a seven-day wait unless you pay double the normal fee for same-day service. Transit visas (US$11) are issued on the spot.

The Consulate of Croatia, Hristo Botev 3, 6th floor, is in the same general area, south of Bulevardul Republicii.

Right in the city centre in Strada Ion Ghica next to the Russian Church is the Consulate of the Czech Republic (weekdays 8 to 11 am). Czech tourist visas are US$25 (Canadians US$50).

North-east of Piaţa Victoriei Metro Station is the Polish Consulate, Aleea Alexandru 23 (open weekdays 9 am to 2 pm). This is a good place to pick up a Polish visa.

The Albanian Embassy, Strada Modrogan 4 off Bulevardul Aviatorilor (weekdays 10 am to 2 pm), is also north of the centre.

The Consulate of Moldova, Strada Cîmpina 47 near the Arcul de Triumf (Monday 10.30 am to 1 pm, Tuesday to Friday 9 am to 1 pm and 2 to 5 pm), issues tourist visas within three days for US$25 and one photo. As a special favour they may agree to issue an urgent visa the same day from US$50. The procedure is straightforward and everyone other than Romanians needs a visa. Keep in mind that a new Romanian visa will be required if you want to return the way you came.

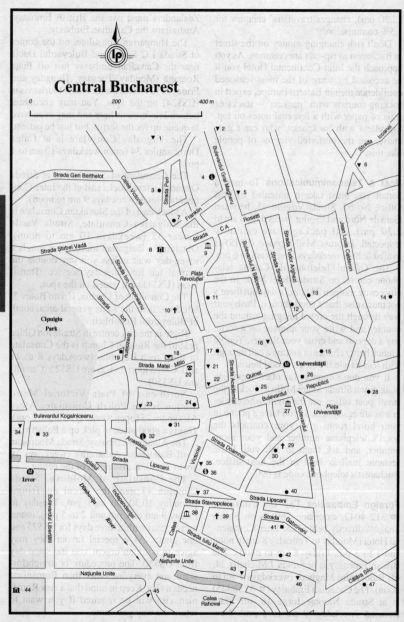

Central Bucharest

0   200   400 m

PLACES TO STAY		37	Caru cu Bere Beer Hall	15	National & Operetta Theatres
17	Hotel Muntenia	43	Lacto Rahova	18	Telephone Centre
19	Hotel Opera	45	Bucur Restaurant	20	Post Office
26	Inter-Continental Hotel	46	Hanul Manuc Inn	24	Vox Maris Disco
33	Hotel Dîmbovița			25	University
41	Hotel Universal	**OTHER**		27	Municipal Museum
43	Hotel Rahova			28	Croatian Consulate
		3	Hard Currency Shop	29	Russian Church
PLACES TO EAT		4	ONT Tourist Information Office	30	Czech Republic Consulate
1	Alicom Amezi Bar	7	Ateneul Roman	31	Paralela 45 Travel Agency
2	Efes Pub	8	Palace of the Republic	32	CFR & TAROM Ticket Agency
5	Cofetăria Ambasador	9	Theodor Aman Museum	36	Banca Romana de Comerț Exterior
6	Restaurant Moldova	10	Crețulescu Church	38	Museum of History
16	Restaurantul Pescarul	11	Former Central Committee Building	39	Stavropoleos Church
21	Gustari Minuturi Lacto-Bar	12	US Consulate	40	Rapsodia Romana
22	Casă Capșa	13	Policlinic Batistei	42	Old Princely Court
23	Berarie Gambrinus	14	Consulates of Slovakia & Bulgaria	44	House of the Republic
34	Restaurantul Cireșica			47	Market
35	Cofetăria Victoria				

Travel Agencies There are two TAROM airline offices in Bucharest. The domestic booking office is beside Galeria Edmond on Piața Victoriei, while the international TAROM office is above the CFR Travel Agency on Strada Domnița Anastasia in the city centre.

Half a dozen companies working out of small offices on the square between Gara de Nord and Hotel Cerna have daily buses to Istanbul (711 km, 14-22 hours, US$13 one way), many travelling overnight. Compare prices at a couple (or haggle!) and remember that you may need a Bulgarian transit visa which is more expensive if obtained at the border. The price is low enough that you could even use the Istanbul buses just to get to Bulgaria, disembarking once you've cleared Bulgarian customs and taking a local bus into Ruse. If you're going right through to Istanbul, be prepared for a gruelling trip as the Romanians and Turks smoke like fiends, music tapes will be blasting and winter heating may be seen as optional. Half the journey is spent waiting at borders or at

meal stops. (If you don't have Bulgarian currency, bring food.) One reader sent us this:

After a boring four-hour wait at Romanian customs we underwent a meticulous search for consumer goods and they confiscated a lot. Then, after 'negotiations' with our Turkish bus crew, they returned it all. The Romanians were overjoyed and cheered 'revolution!' but I couldn't imagine a bigger waste of time. At the crossing into Turkey I was drafted into carrying my full quota of Marlboro and Johnny Walker. The Romanians couldn't believe that I wasn't interested in hawking duty-free goods in Istanbul.

As well as buses to Istanbul, Royal Turism below Hotel Cerna has a daily bus to Kishinev (Chișinău), Moldovan Republic (435 km, US$9 plus US$2 for baggage), a weekly bus to Budapest (US$13) and another weekly bus to Dortmund, Germany (US$82 one way). Some of these agencies near the station also have buses to Poland (US$10).

Double 'T' Travel Agency, Piața Națiunile

Unite, has a bus from Bucharest to Istanbul twice daily (US$12 one way). Double 'T' also has a bus to Rome twice a week (US$125) and one to Athens three times a week (US$75).

The CFR Travel Agency on the north side of Piaţa Unirii, near the corner of Bulevardul Brătianu, handles international train tickets. Railway fares are US$3 to Ruse, US$11 to Sofia and US$31 to Budapest. A seat reservation costs an extra US$0.25. You must pay for international tickets in hard currency.

The CFR Travel Agency (downstairs) and the TAROM international department (upstairs) share a building on Strada Domniţa Anastasia, behind the Central Hotel, off Bulevardul Kogălniceanu (Monday to Friday 7.30 am to 7 pm). Come here to purchase tickets for domestic trains or sleepers. You can also make reservations on domestic express trains here, but you must do this at least one day ahead.

Domestic train tickets are also sold by the CFR Travel Agency beside the Hotel Nord at Calea Griviţei 139, two blocks south of Gara de Nord.

Bookshops Bucharest's best bookstore is Libraria Academiei, Calea Victoriei 12. Downstairs is an interesting antiquarian bookstore and upstairs you'll find English books in the self-service section at the back. You may even find the occasional translation of Romanian literary classics into English!

Vendors in front of the university building on Bulevardul Republicii sell excellent maps of Bucharest, mountain areas, Romania and other places.

Emergency Foreigners with medical problems are referred to the Policlinic Batiştei, Strada Tudor Arghezi 28, opposite the American Embassy near the Inter-Continental (weekdays 7 am to 7 pm). Consultations begin at US$30.

Things to See
Ceauşescu's Bucharest In the last Ceauşescu years the southern section of Bucharest around Piaţa Unirii was 'systematised' to create a new Civic Centre. From Piaţa Unirii Metro Station walk over to the large ornamental **fountain** in the middle of the square to get your bearings. On the north-east side of the square is the **Unirea Department Store** (good photos of the fountain can be taken from the top floor); the main **city market** is behind it.

South-west of the fountain, an older street, Aleea Dealul Mitropoliei, climbs to the **Patriarchal Cathedral** (1658) and **Patriarch's Palace** (1875). Surrounding the church are the **Chamber of Deputies** (1907), a belfry (1698) and three 16th to 17th century stone crosses, a most impressive complex.

West from the fountain runs Bulevardul Unirii, Bucharest's Champs Élysées, directly towards the massive **House of the Republic**, an incredible Stalinist structure which was almost finished when Ceauşescu was overthrown in 1989. Some 20,000 workers and 400 architects toiled for six years on this massive palace at a cost of 16 billion lei. Virtually all of the materials used were Romanian. Inside are two monumental neo-Baroque galleries that are 150 metres long and 18 metres high. At a height of 101 metres, it's one of the largest buildings in the world and many historic structures had to be demolished to make way for it.

Nicolae Ceauşescu intended to house the Central Committee of the Communist Party, the State Council and the government of Romania in his grandiose House of the Republic and on the converging streets surrounding it are great rows of apartment buildings to house the *nomenklatura* of privileged bureaucrats employed in nearby ministries. On the south side of the House of the Republic is the huge **National Institute for Science & Technology** of which Elena Ceauşescu was president. West is the new **Ministry of Defence**.

In the massive square facing the House of the Republic, huge mass rallies were to have been held with Ceauşescu himself addressing the throng from the first balcony. Ceauşescu planned to have the remodelling of Bucharest complete by the end of 1990 and literally hundreds of gigantic, almost finished buildings are seen around the city, especially in this southern part. Before work on this vast complex began, Ceauşescu had smaller political-administrative centres similar to this built in each of Romania's district capitals!

Central Bucharest On the north-east side of Piaţa Unirii on the corner of Bulevardul Brătianu, is the CFR international railway ticket office. Penetrate the old city on the lane beside this office and veer left on Strada Iuliu Maniu. Enter the **Hanul Manuc** (1808), an old inn on the left, and peruse the nearby ruins of the **Old Princely Court** (Palatul Voievodal) and the oldest church (1546) in Bucharest, on the right. In the 16th century, Prince Mircea Ciobanul ordered a palace to be built here. Continue west on Strada Iuliu Maniu a few blocks, and when you see a large white church turn right on to Strada Poştei and continue to **Stavropoleos Church** (1724), one of the city's most typical churches.

Stavropoleos Church is almost behind Bucharest's most important museum, the **Museum of History** (closed Monday) in the former Post Office Palace (1900) on Calea Victoriei. The 41 rooms on the 1st and 2nd floors tell the story of the country from prehistoric times to WW I. The highlight of the museum is the fabulous treasury in the basement, which is full of objects of gold and precious stones created over the ages. There's also a complete plaster cast of Trajan's Column that depicts the conquest of Dacia by Rome. Summaries in English and French are posted in most rooms.

Proceed north on Calea Victoriei, Bucharest's main shopping street. After four or five blocks you'll see **Creţulescu Church** (1722) on the left, then the massive **Palace of the Republic** (1937), formerly the king's palace and the seat of the State Council until 1989. The palace was the scene of heavy fighting during the revolution, and the extensive collection of European and Romanian art in the palace's four-storey **Fine Arts Museum** was badly damaged. The palace

has since been repaired but only a small part of the museum is open again (closed Monday and Tuesday).

Piaţa Revoluţiei was the very heart of the 1989 revolution. Ceauşescu made his last fateful speech from the balcony of the **building of the Central Committee of the Communist Party** (1950), the long white stone building across the square from Creţulescu Church. Underground passages connected the Central Committee building to the Palace of the Republic. The Securitate had occupied most of the buildings next to the Central Committee and these were pockmarked with bullet holes by fire from army troops. The **University Library** (1895), between the Central Committee and the Ateneul Român, was gutted but has since been rebuilt.

Across the square from the palace is the neo-classical **Ateneul Român** (1888), the city's main concert hall, with a statue of Romantic poet Mihai Eminescu in front. North again at Calea Victoriei 107 is the **Ceramics Museum**. The nearby **Muzeul Colecţilor de Arte**, Calea Victoriei 111 (closed Monday and Tuesday), was formed from several private art collections. Note the many fine works by the 19th century painter Nicolae Grigourescu.

Northern Bucharest A brisk walk north on Calea Victoriei will bring you to Piaţa Victoriei and the **government of Romania** building (1938), which is on the north-east side of the square. On the north-west side of Piaţa Victoriei is the **Natural History Museum** with a large collection of stuffed animals.

If you don't mind walking another km or so, Şoseaua Kiseleff will lead you north to the **triumphal arch** (1936), erected to commemorate the reunification of Romania in 1918. Alternatively, take the Metro one station north to Piaţa Aviatorilor, beyond which is one of Bucharest's most appealing attractions. The **Village Museum**, first opened in 1936, includes three churches and 42 houses and farms, 297 rural Romanian buildings in all, assembled here in a rich

ROMANIA

mixture of styles. The north entrance to the Village Museum opens into **Herăstrău Park** with a lake plied by all manner of boats in summer.

While you're in the area, you may wish to see the former personal residence of Nicolae and Elena Ceauşescu, the **Primavera Palace**, not far from Piaţa Aviatorilor. To get there, walk north-east up Bulevardul Primăverii to the corner of Bulevardul Mircea Eliade. The Ceauşescu mansion is the one on the south-west, right-hand corner. There may be a guard at the gate. Just across Bulevardul Mircea Eliade from the entrance to the Ceauşescus' mansion is the former residence of Gheorghe Gheorghiu-Dej, Romania's communist ruler until Ceauşescu took over in 1965. Until late 1989 this neighbourhood was reserved for the party elite and all nonresidents were kept out by police, but today only the flowers along Bulevardul Primăverii are still red.

On Calea Dorobanţilor, also near Piaţa Aviatorilor, is the headquarters of **Romanian Television**, with a small memorial in front to those killed here during the 1989 fighting.

As you're returning to the city by Metro, you may wish to get out at **Piaţa Romană** to see the plinth of an unfinished monument intended to glorify the Ceauşescu regime. In December 1989 student demonstrators clashed with police here and there's now a small memorial to the revolution on the site.

Western Bucharest Nicolae Ceauşescu was determined to leave an indelible mark on Bucharest and during his last decade in power he really succeeded. In order to make Bucharest a great capital like Paris or Moscow, Ceauşescu decided that his new city needed a river, so he ordered that the Dîmboviţa River be rechannelled through southern Bucharest in a tremendous engineering project. To ensure a regular supply of water for the Dîmboviţa, he had a massive dam built across the river on the west side of Bucharest, thereby creating **Dîmboviţa Lake**. Crîngaşi Metro Station is only about 500 metres from the dam, which is visible

from the station. Notice how Ceauşescu's name has been moved from the dedicatory inscription on the dam.

From the Dîmboviţa Dam or Crîngaşi Metro board a southbound tram No 41 to the end of the line. From there it's two stops east on tram No 8 or 48 to **Ghencea Cemetery**. (You could also walk.) The burial place of the Ceauşescus was supposed to have remained secret but it's now common knowledge that they're buried in Ghencea Cemetery, Bulevardul Ghencea 18, to the south-west of the city centre. Their clearly marked graves are on opposite sides of the main avenue leading to the church in the centre of the cemetery, Nicolae to the left and Elena to the right. The family wants to have these remains moved to Nicolae's ancestral village, Scorniceşti, but for some reason the present authorities will not allow this, so for now the two graves serve as pilgrimage points for the Ceauşescus' remaining admirers. You'll see candles burning and many flowers on the tombs.

From the cemetery take an eastbound tram No 48 as far as the stop called 'Razoare', just where the tram turns for the second time. Walk straight ahead two long blocks on Bulevardul Geniului (the road made from stone bricks), then turn right at the T-junction onto Şoseaua Cotroceni. For the last half of this walk you'll be following the high grey wall of the 17th century **Cotroceni Palace**, restored by Ceauşescu as a personal residence but never occupied by him. You may visit the palace (closed Monday) through a small but clearly marked door on the south side of Şoseaua Cotroceni.

The entrance to Bucharest's **Botanical Garden** is on the north side of Şoseaua Cotroceni, a little further to the east. The garden is divided into sections, with the flora of the different regions of the country each in its own area. The garden opens from 7 am to 8 pm in summer and from 8 am to 5 pm in winter, but you may only visit the Botanical Museum and greenhouse on Tuesday, Thursday and Sunday from 9 am to 1 pm.

From the Botanical Garden follow Şoseaua Cotroceni east again until you reach the Dîmbovița River which you should not cross just yet, but follow south-east a block to the unfinished structure of the **Museum of Romanian History** on the opposite bank. This massive stone building resembling the ancient Egyptian palaces of Luxor was intended to house Ceaușescu's tomb amid the entire history of Romania! Every 23 August, Ceaușescu would take the salute from the long reviewing stand in the front of the building during the annual Liberation Day Parade. In the park opposite this structure is the Stalinist **Romanian Opera House** (1954). Eroilor Metro Station is nearby.

Southern Bucharest After all these grandiose monuments to megalomania, you'll want to visit the **Heroes Cemetery**, where many of the victims of the December 1989 revolution are buried. As you come out of Eroii Revoluției Metro Station, south of the city, you'll see the neat rows of white marble graves across Calea Șerban Vodă. Photos of the dead are attached to their graves – a most moving sight. In 1993 a memorial church was erected here.

A few blocks north of this cemetery on Calea Șerban Vodă are the high red marble arches of the **Memorial to the Heroes of the Struggle for the People's and the Homeland's Liberty, for Socialism** (1963) in Parcul Carol. Gheorghe Gheorghiu-Dej and other early Romanian communists are buried here. Go down the stairway and walk north through Parcul Carol to a square where you can pick up tree-lined Strada 11 Iunie, which will bring you into Bulevardul George Coșbuc and Piața Unirii once again.

Places to Stay
Camping *Camping Băneasa*, in the forest beyond Băneasa Airport, north of the city, is being used to house displaced persons and is closed to tourists. The nearest camping ground is now the one at Snagov Lake.

Private Rooms The person at the ONT tourist office at Gara de Nord can arrange private rooms at US$15 per person, breakfast included. The main ONT office, Bulevardul

Magheru 7, also has private rooms. The quality of these rooms varies considerably. If you're not satisfied with what you get, go back and ask for something else. Occasionally people at the station or on the street outside offer private rooms, but evaluate these people carefully and ask them to point out the location of their rooms on a map. Make sure that you understand the price before you agree to take a room.

Peter Express (☎ 650 2567), Bulevardul Ana Ipătescu 17 near Piața Romană, arranges private rooms in the vicinity of its office at US$16/20 single/double.

Hotels There are lots of old 2nd-class hotels in Bucharest and it's usually no problem finding a room, even in midsummer. Prices average US$15/25 single/double (shared bath) with a slightly lower rate from November to mid-December. Avoid accepting a room that faces onto a busy thorough- fare where the traffic could wake you at 5 am and ask if breakfast is included. If you're not fully satisfied, compare the price and appearance with the next hotel before deciding. They all want to have you, because the official price you pay is many times higher than what locals pay for the same room. There are two clusters of inexpensive hotels: one around the train station and another in the city centre.

Near Gara de Nord The hotels closest to the train station are on your right as you come out of the station's main entrance. The *Hotel Bucegi* (☎ 637 5225), Strada Witing 2, is US$12/19/23 single/double/triple without bath, US$23 double with bath, while the *Hotel Cerna* (☎ 637 7540), across the street, is US$12/19 single/double without bath, US$19/30 with bath.

To your left from the station is the noisy *Hotel Dunărea* (☎ 617 3220), Bulevardul G Duca 2 (US$14/23 single/double with shared bath). Go down the avenue to the *Grivița Hotel* (☎ 650 2327), Calea Griviței 130 (US$12/19/23 single/double/triple without bath).

Two blocks down and around the corner

ROMANIA

to the left is the *Hotel Marna* (☎ 650 2675), Strada Buzeşti 3. It's US$15/23/30 single/double/triple with shared bath, US$32 double with bath, and showers are free but get a room at the back to escape the noise of trams.

In the Centre There are a few hotels near Cişmigiu Park. The *Hotel Veneţia* (☎ 615 9148), Piaţa Mihail Kogălniceanu 2 (US$21/34 single/double with shared bath), and *Hotel Dîmboviţa* (☎ 615 6244), Bulevardul Schitu Măgureanu 6 (US$21/34 single/double without bath, US$23 single with bath), are south-west of the park.

East of the park are the *Hotel Opera* (☎ 614 1075), Strada Brezoianu 37 (US$13/23 single/double without bath, US$15/27 with bath), and *Hotel Muntenia* (☎ 614 6010), Strada Academiei 21 (US$22/35 single/double without bath, US$40 double with bath). The Hotel Muntenia is in a great location.

South in the oldest part of the city are the *Hotel Rahova* (☎ 515 2617), Calea Rahovei 2 (US$20 single or double), and *Hotel Universal* (☎ 614 8533), Strada Gabroveni 12. At US$5 per person with shared bath, the Universal is obviously the best deal in town, but bargains like this have a way of disappearing overnight in Romania. It's on a quiet street.

Expensive Hotels The only hotel in Bucharest accepting hotel coupons is the 14-storey, two-star *Hotel Parc* (☎ 618 0950), Bulevardul Poligrafiei 3, near Piaţa Presei Libere on the way to the airport. Though the rooms are dimly lit, it's a good choice if you want something better than the places mentioned above. Get a room on one of the upper floors to escape the disco beat from the restaurant. You can use the pool at the adjacent Hotel Flora. Just make sure you have coupons, otherwise it's US$62/96 single/double. The Automobil Clubul Român desk (weekdays 9 am to 2 pm) next to reception usually sells coupons, but it's safer to buy them at the Automobil Clubul Român/Hertz (☎ 611

4365), Strada Cihoschi 2 (Metro: Piaţa Romană).

Places to Eat
Bottom End A cheap milk bar in the vicinity of the train station is *Lacto Marna* below Hotel Marna, Strada Buzeşti 3. If it's closed another place to try near the train station is the restaurant in the *Griviţa Hotel*, Calea Griviţei 130, though the service is slow.

Lacto Rahova, on the corner of Strada Iuliu Maniu and Calea Rahovie in the old town, serves simple Romanian meals at low prices. Just point at dishes you see on other tables. The *Columbia Restaurant* across the street has a regular menu and higher prices, but it's also good.

If you don't mind eating standing up *Gustari Minuturi Lacto-Bar*, Calea Victoriei 40, serves a good local meal for under a dollar. Avoid the soup which could give you the runs.

The *Café de l'Université*, in the pedestrian underpass just above Universităţii Metro Station, has a small salad bar and other rare treats for vegetarians, though you have to eat standing up. It's a good choice for a fast breakfast.

One of Bucharest's last remaining proletarian self-service cafeterias is on Bulevardul Dacia beside the Hotel Dorobanţi (Metro: Piaţa Romană). It's closed Sunday.

Some readers have reported being overcharged at the restaurant in the train station.

Restaurants in the Centre *Casă Capşa*, Calea Victoriei 36 (closed on Sunday), is perhaps Bucharest's finest restaurant. A local institution since 1852, it will allow you to dine in style.

Since 1875 the *Caru cu Bere*, a large Munich-style beer hall on Strada Stavropoleos close to the Museum of History, has served mititei (grilled meatballs) and other tasty treats along with big mugs of draught beer. Beware of overcharging here.

Though rather touristy, the restaurant at the *Hanul Manuc*, a historic old inn at Strada Iuliu Maniu 62, near Piaţa Unirii, has some atmosphere. Service in the beer garden is errible and the indoor restaurant closes at 8 pm. Fried cheese is available for vegetarians.

A good medium-priced restaurant near Cişmigiu Park is the *Restaurantul Cireşica*, Bulevardul Kogălniceanu 45.

Restaurants North of the Centre There's a good choice of places to eat along the boulevard leading north from the Inter-Continental Hotel on Piaţa Universităţii. The *Restaurantul Pescarul*, Bulevardul Nicolae Bălcescu 9a, across the street from the Inter-Continental, offers a range of fish dishes in an attractive setting (closed Sunday).

The *Restaurant Moldova*, Strada Icoanei 2, off Strada Jean Louis Calderon east of Bulevardul Nicolae Bălcescu, serves the cuisine of Moldavia in a garden setting.

Efes Pub, Bulevardul Magheru at Strada George Enescu (Metro: Piaţa Romană), has a clean, modern beer garden where you can drink mug after mug of Efes Pilsner and consume fresh grilled chicken. It's more expensive than many other places around here but you're paying for the quality.

A block west of Efes Pub along Strada Tache Ionescu is the *Alicom Amzei Bar*. Their pizza tastes like a thick cheese omelette but you'll enjoy the music they play if you like loud rock and roll. The market area just beyond this place is worth a stroll.

Berarie Turist, on the south side of Piaţa Romană, only serves a few dishes but you can get spicy little hamburg patties (mici) and big mugs of draught beer.

The up-market *Nan Jing Restaurant* in the Hotel Minerva on Bulevardul Ana Ipătescu, between Piaţa Romană and Piaţa Victoriei, serves exquisite Chinese food, and there's no smoking in the dining room!

Pizza Julia, Şoseaua N Titulescu 16, between Piaţa Victoriei and Gara de Nord, doesn't serve hand-tossed pizza but at least each thick-crust pie is made to order and comes out hot. Until a real pizzeria opens in Bucharest, this is the best you'll find. Half the pleasure here is dining on their outdoor terrace (in summer).

Cafés & Bars *Cofetăria Victoria*, Calea

Victoriei 18, has some incredibly rich cakes that will please the sweetest tooth. The *Pasaguil Victoria Restaurant*, in the passageway next to Hotel Muntenia, serves good chocolate-pudding ice cream.

Cofetăria Ambasador, next to Hotel Ambasador, Bulevardul Magheru 10 almost opposite the ONT tourist office, serves some of the best coffee and cakes Bucharest has to offer.

A favourite local drinking place is *Berarie Gambrinus*, Bulevardul Kogălniceanu 18. It's a bit of a dive, but still OK.

The *Restaurantul Bucur*, just south of Piaţa Naţiunile Unite, has a nice beer garden in summer.

Entertainment

Theatres The shiny new *National Theatre*, at Bulevardul N Bălcescu 2 (Metro: Universităţii), is opposite the Inter-Continental Hotel. The ticket office of the National Theatre is on the south side of the building, facing Bulevardul Republicii (Monday to Saturday 11 am to 6 pm). Next to the National Theatre is the *'Ion Dacian' Operetta Theatre* (tickets daily 11 am to 6.30 pm).

Rapsodia Romană (Teatrul Pan), Strada Lipscani 53 in the old town, is a folkloric theatre offering a programme that combines music, poetry and dancing – well worth visiting.

If at all possible, attend a performance at the *Ateneul Român*, the main concert hall in Bucharest. Tickets are sold in the office on the north side of the building.

The *Teatrul Satiric Muzical 'C Tanase'*, Calea Victoriei 33, offers variety shows.

The *Teatrul de Marionete si Papusi 'Tandarica'*, (Puppet Theatre), just off Piaţa Lahovari near the Dorobanţi Hotel (Metro: Piaţa Romană), presents innovative, amusing puppet shows, sometimes in the afternoon.

The *Romanian Opera House*, Bulevardul Kogălniceanu 70-72, is west of Cişmigiu Park, a little out of the way (Metro: Eroilor).

Bucharest's *circus* (closed in July and August) is on Aleea Circului, off Şoseaua

Ştefan cel Mare (Metro: Ştefan cel Mare). The ticket office opens from 1 to 8 pm.

All theatres are closed in July and August.

Discos Bucharest's classiest disco is *Vox Maris*, below the stairway leading up to the Cercul Militar National on the corner of Calea Victoriei and Bulevardul Kogăl-niceanu (daily 10 pm to 4 am). There's a US$2 cover charge and neat dress is required. People of all ages will fit in here.

A disco club popular among Bucharest teens and punks is downstairs from the Pasagiul Victoriei, a passageway that runs from Strada Academiei to Calea Victoriei next to Hotel Muntenia. Break out your black apparel and leathers.

From Thursday to Sunday beginning around 8 pm, there's a student disco in the *Casă de Cultură a Studenţilor*, Calea Plevnei 61, directly behind the Romanian Opera House (Metro: Eroilor).

Things to Buy

Unirea Department Store on Piaţa Unirii is the largest of its kind in Bucharest. There's a Kodak Express one-hour colour-film developing facility inside Unirea.

Muzica, Calea Victoriei 41-43, has the city's best selection of CDs and cassettes, including some by Zamfir.

Calea Victoriei is Bucharest's most fashionable shopping street, but more interesting is Strada Lipscani in the old town with many small shops and itinerant Gypsy hawkers.

Stock up on imported cigarettes, coffee and liquor in the hard-currency shop at Strada Gabriel Peri 3, near the Ateneul Român.

Getting There & Away

Air TAROM has flights several times a week throughout the year from Bucharest to Arad, Cluj-Napoca, Iaşi, Oradea, Satu Mare, Sibiu, Suceava and Timişoara. In summer there are also flights to Constanţa and Tulcea. Fares are quoted in the introduction to this chapter but don't expect any bargains. (The addresses of the two Bucharest TAROM

offices are given under the previous Travel Agencies section.)

The Otopeni Airport information number (to check if a flight is on time) is ☎ 633 6602

Bus For information on international buses to Istanbul, Budapest and beyond see Bucharest, Travel Agencies.

Train Almost all express trains and many local trains use Bucharest's Gara de Nord, the most important train station by far. Many other unreserved local trains to/from Braşov, Craiova, Piteşti, Sibiu, Suceava, Timişoara, and so on, arrive at and depart from Gara Basarab, which is a long block north-west of Gara de Nord.

Some local trains to/from Feteşti and Constanţa use Bucureşti-Obor Railway Station, which is east of the city centre. Local trains to/from Snagov and a couple of seasonal accelerat trains to/from Mangalia sometimes use Gara Băneasa, on the north side of town. All local trains to/from Giurgiu arrive at Gara Progresul, on the far south side of Bucharest (take tram No 12 to Gara Basarab).

At Gara de Nord different windows sell tickets for different trains, as noted on small signs. There are separate ticket halls for 1st and 2nd class, but express train tickets are only sold at the station an hour before departure and then only if there are unsold seats. Don't count on being able to buy an international ticket at the station! One of the only posted railway timetables at Gara de Nord is in the ONT tourist office there.

The Railway Museum (closed Monday and Saturday) on Calea Griviţei, directly behind Gara de Nord, may provide some useful information for your trip.

For the offices selling international or advance express train tickets see Travel Agencies above. For specific train routes to/from Bucharest see Romania, Getting There & Away at the start of this chapter.

Getting Around

To/From the Airport Every 30 minutes from 6.30 am to 9 pm you can catch the red bus

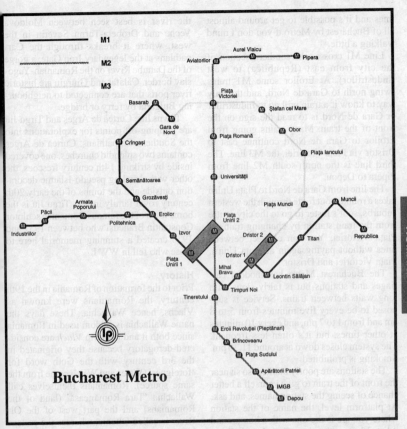

Bucharest Metro

No 783 for Băneasa Domestic Airport and Otopeni International Airport from Piaţa Unirii (US$0.20, pay the driver). You can also pick this bus up in front of the old church on the east side of Bulevardul Brătianu just south of Piaţa Universităţii (though it may not stop if it's already full). Allow adequate time if you go this way.

Trolleybus No 131 also terminates at Băneasa Domestic Airport.

Public Transport To use the Metro you drop coins in a turnstile. If you don't have the coins you must line up at a booth for change.

Get into the habit of changing a bill for coins whenever you see a booth without a queue.

You must purchase tickets for other forms of public transport at a kiosk and validate them once aboard. It costs US$0.05 for trams, trolleybuses and regular buses (same tickets). Tickets are checked regularly by inspectors and there's a US$6 fine if you're caught without one. All services can be extremely crowded, so hang on to your wallet.

Underground The Bucharest Metro, built during the last Ceauşescu years, has three lines and it's possible to get around almost all of Bucharest by Metro if you don't mind walking a little.

Line M1 crosses the southern section of the city from east (Republica) to west (Industriilor). At Eroilor some M1 trains swing north to Gara de Nord, and the only way to know if a train will go to Industriilor or Gara de Nord is to read the sign on the front of the train. Many trains going from Eroilor to Gara de Nord continue east to Dristor via Piaţa Victoriei, the M3 line. The third line is the north-south M2 line from Pipera to Depou.

The line from Gara de Nord to Piaţa Unirii takes a roundabout route through the western suburbs, so it's faster to go to the city centre from the train station by changing trains at Piaţa Victoriei. You can connect between lines without paying again at Piaţa Unirii, Piaţa Victoriei and Dristor.

The Bucharest Metro has modern carriages and stations but is fairly slow, with long waits between trains. Service is supposed to be every five minutes from 5 to 8 am and from 1 to 7 pm, and every 10 minutes at other times, but it's often less frequent. The system closes down at around 11.30 pm. Smoking is prohibited.

The stations are poorly marked, so sit near the front of the train to give yourself a better chance of seeing the station names, and ask. At platform level, the name of the station where you are is the one with a box around it listed last on the sign. The others indicate in which direction the train is going.

Taxi Government radio taxis have the phone number 953 on the rear door. If the taxi doesn't have a meter agree on a price before getting in.

Wallachia

Wallachia occupies the Danube plain north to the crest of the Carpathian Mountains. Although the mighty Danube River flows right along the southern edge of Wallachia,

the river is best seen between Moldova Veche and Drobeta-Turnu Severin in the west, where it breaks through the Carpathians at the legendary Iron Gate, a gorge of the Danube River on the Romanian-Yugoslav border. Calafat and Giurgiu are historic river ports that are connected to neighbouring Bulgaria by ferry or bridge.

Towns like Curtea de Argeş and Tîrgu Jiu are jumping-off points for explorations into the Southern Carpathians. Curtea de Argeş contains two splendid churches, one covered inside by striking 14th century frescoes, the other with dazzling pseudo-Islamic decoration outside and the tombs of the early 20th century royal family inside. Tîrgu Jiu is the home town of the famous Romanian sculptor Constantin Brâncuşi who between 1937 and 1938 created a stunning memorial here to those who fell in WW I.

History

Prior to the formation of Romania in the 19th century, the Romanians were known as Vlachs, hence Wallachia. These days the name Wallachia is seldom used in Romania since both it and the term *Vlach* are considered derogatory because they originated in the 3rd century with the Goth word for 'foreigner' (Wales and Welsh come from the same source). Romanians themselves call Wallachia 'Tara Românească' (land of the Romanians) and the part west of the Olt River is called Oltenia, whereas the eastern half is known as Muntenia.

Founded by Radu Negru in 1290, this principality was subject to Hungarian rule until 1330, when Basarab I defeated the Hungarian king Charles I Robert and declared Wallachia independent. The Wallachian princes *(voivode)* built their first capitals – Cîmpulung, Curtea de Argeş and Tîrgovişte – close to the protective mountains, but in the 15th century Bucharest gained the ascendancy, a role it has maintained to the present day. Medieval Wallachia prospered from agriculture and trade between Western Europe and the Black Sea.

After the fall of Bulgaria to the Turks in

1396, Wallachia faced a new threat, and in 1417 Mircea the Old was forced to acknowledge Turkish suzerainty. By paying tribute to the Turks, Wallachia remained largely autonomous, although trade and foreign policy were controlled by the Turks. Other Wallachian princes such as Vlad Ţepeş the Impaler and Michael the Brave became national heroes by defying the Turks and refusing to pay tribute. In the 18th and early 19th century, Wallachia suffered instability, first as the Turks placed Phanariote Greeks on the throne, and then as the Russians dictated policy. The serfs were only freed in 1864, five years after Wallachia was united with Moldavia.

SNAGOV

Snagov, 34 km north of Bucharest, is a favourite picnic spot for city dwellers, with a famous 16th century church on an island in Snagov Lake. The first monastery was built on the island in the 11th century, and in 1456 Vlad Ţepeş the Impaler, the notorious 'Count Dracula', built fortifications and a prison near the church. The present church dates from 1521, with paintings done in 1563. The body of Vlad Ţepeş himself was reputedly buried below the dome, just in front of the church's wooden iconostasis, but when the grave was opened in 1931 it was found to be empty. (Dracula's head was sent to the Turkish sultan who exhibited it on a stick.) A printing press was operating in the monastery as early as 1695.

The early 20th century Snagov Palace, just across the lake from the island, was built by Prince Nicolae, brother of King Carol II, in the Italian Renaissance style. During the Ceauşescu era it was used for meetings of high-level government officials and today it is a restaurant. Ceauşescu had a summer home on Snagov Lake, Villa No 10, which is now rented out to wealthy tourists at US$1000 a day. Villa No 1, the former abode of King Michael I, is now the summer residence of the prime minister. Ceauşescu's two large yachts, both named *Snagov*, are used to take tourists around the lake for US$5 a head. If you rent a rowing boat to get over to the island, allow an hour each way. There are two camping grounds in the lakeside oak forest. The *Restaurant Vinatorul* is said to be good.

Getting There & Away

From June to September three unreserved local trains a day run from Gara de Nord to Snagov Plajă (43 km, one hour). In winter these trains may depart from Bucharest's Gara Băneasa, so check.

CALAFAT

The small town of Calafat, on the Danube opposite Vidin, Bulgaria, makes a convenient entry/exit point to/from Bulgaria. Car ferries cross the river hourly, and there are trains to/from Craiova where one joins the main railway line between Bucharest and Timişoara. Apart from the **Museul de Arta** on Strada 22 decembrie and a monument to the 1877-78 war of independence against the Turks, there isn't much to see or do in Calafat.

Orientation & Information

The ferry landing is right in the centre of Calafat, about four blocks from the train station. To use the left-luggage office at the train station, first buy a baggage ticket at the ticket window, then look for the baggage room in a small building just down the track.

Money It's impossible to change a travellers' cheque in Calafat. As you get off the ferry you'll see several exchange kiosks near customs. Don't change at the first ones as they give a poor rate and deduct 5% commission. The last exchange office marked 'bank' right at the gate changes cash at the official rate without commission and is open 24 hours. The Banca Agricola opposite the post office on the way from the ferry to the train station gives exactly the same rate for cash with no commission.

Post & Telecommunications There's a telephone centre (daily 6 am to 10 pm) on Strada Traian at the top of the hill. Just follow the line of cars waiting to board the Vidin

ROMANIA

ferry back until you see it on the right. Calafat's telephone code is 0943.

Places to Stay & Eat

The *Hotel Calafat* (☎ 231 303), on a slight hill near the ferry terminal, is US$24/37 single/double with bath (but no hot water). At last report the old two-storey *Hotel Carpaţi*, 100 metres from the Calafat, was closed. The accommodation situation is better in Vidin, so continue on if it's not too late.

Getting There & Away

There are six local trains a day to/from Craiova (107 km, 2½ hours). If you're continuing through to Bucharest or elsewhere, buy a ticket to your final destination and as soon as you reach Craiova, go into the station and purchase a compulsory seat reservation for your onward express train. There are separate lines for 1st and 2nd class.

To/From Bulgaria The car ferry crosses the Danube hourly all year round (30 minutes, US$2 or DM3 in cash hard currency only). Bicycles are sometimes US$2, sometimes free. For information on conditions on the other side, turn to the Vidin section in the Bulgaria chapter.

The queue of southbound cars waiting at Calafat to board the ferry to Bulgaria is often pretty horrendous. Northbound it's not so bad and pedestrians can just walk past all the lines in both directions. Cars can spend anywhere from 12 to 24 hours in the queue on the Romanian side. Look at the brighter side: this is a chance to get to know the other motorists in line around you and, if you have some folding chairs or mats to put out on the pavement, it can almost be pleasant. There are small cafés along the line where you can buy drinks, though one person will have to remain sober to shift the car down the line.

DROBETA-TURNU SEVERIN

Drobeta-Turnu Severin, on the Danube between Bucharest and Timişoara, is the administrative centre of Mehedinţi County. Yugoslavia lies on the opposite river bank.

Though of ancient origin, the present town was laid out in the 19th century and has a pleasant series of parks in the centre. A four-hour stop is enough to see the best of Drobeta-Turnu Severin.

Things to See

Follow Bulevardul Republicii above the station east about two km to the **Muzeul Porţile de Fier** (Iron Gate Museum) (closed Monday), a large museum with a fine exhibit on the natural history of the Danube River, including an aquarium with fish from the Danube. Other sections of the museum cover history and ethnography. There's a good deal on the Roman period, including a scale model of the **Roman bridge** constructed across the Danube in 103 AD by Apolodorus of Damascus on the orders of the emperor Trajan. The bridge stood just below the site of the present museum, and alongside the museum are the ruins of **Castrul Drobeta**, a 2nd to 3rd century Roman fort which protected the bridge. You can also see the foundations of a 14th century basilica in the same area.

West of Drobeta-Turnu Severin, the train runs along the north bank of the Danube through the famous **Iron Gate**, passing a huge concrete hydroelectric power station (1972), on top of which is a road that links Romania to Yugoslavia. You get a good view of everything from the train window. The dam has tamed the whirling Danube 'cauldrons' west of Orşova, once a major navigational hazard as the river raced through a narrow defile.

Places to Stay

The *Hotel Parc* (☎ 978-12 853), a large modern hotel at Bulevardul Republicii 2, has rooms at US$31/46 single/double including a miserable breakfast (hotel coupons are accepted). There's no camping ground at Drobeta-Turnu Severin.

Getting There & Away

All express trains between Bucharest and Timişoara stop here. Local trains make shorter, more frequent trips in both directions. The canal, opened by President Ceauşescu in 1984, shortens the sea route to Constanța by 400 km.

Dobruja

Dobruja (Dobrogea), the squat neck of land between the Danube and the Black Sea, was joined to Romania in 1878 when a combined Russo-Romanian army drove the Turks from Bulgaria. This relatively recent accession accounts for the many Islamic buildings in the area. In antiquity the region was colonised first by the Greeks and then by the Romans, who left behind a great deal for visitors to admire. Histria, 70 km north of Constanța, is the oldest ancient settlement in Romania, founded by Greek merchants in 657 BC. From 46 AD, Dobruja was the Roman province of Moesia Inferior. At Adamclisi (Tropaeum Traiani) the Romans scored a decisive victory over the Geto-Dacian tribes which made possible their expansion north of the Danube. Later, Dobruja fell under Byzantium, and in 1418 it was conquered by the Turks.

Today, the soft, sandy beaches along the southern half of Romania's 245 km of tideless Black Sea coast are the country's main focus of tourism. Each summer the trains are jammed with hordes of Romanians in search of fine white sand, warm water, from 10 to 12 hours of sunshine and freedom from dangerous fish, sharks or undersea rocks. Far from being a nuisance, the crowds of vacationers have motivated the Romanian government to provide proper facilities, and in midsummer things become lively.

There are nine modern resorts: Mamaia, Eforie Nord, Eforie Sud, Costinești, Neptun-Olimp, Jupiter, Venus-Aurora, Saturn and Mangalia. Mamaia and Neptun-Olimp are popular with young people because of their varied entertainment possibilities, whereas Saturn, Venus, Aurora and Jupiter attract families. Eforie Nord is frequented by an older clientele attracted to the nearby spa, although lots of families and young people come here too. Costinești is one gigantic

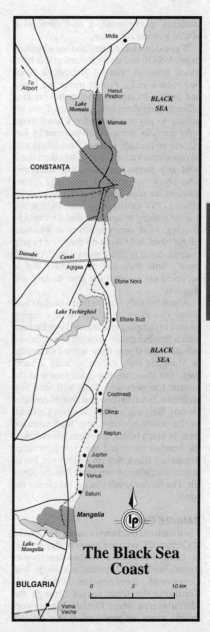

The Black Sea Coast

ROMANIA

students' playground, a real carnival if you're looking for action.

If you don't have a tent and are unwilling to pay US$30 and up for a comfortable hotel room, however, visiting Romania's Black Sea coast is risky. Private rooms are scarce and hard to locate, with no central booking office renting them out. And even if you are willing to pay top dollar for a hotel room, most are fully occupied all summer by foreigners on package tours or Romanians with advance reservations, and most hotels don't hold any rooms for individual foreigners who show up without bookings. Hotel coupons are your best bet in this case, as the official ONT tourist offices are useless and will do nothing to help you find a room. The Touring ACR representatives at Mamaia, Eforie Nord and Olimp do their best to help coupon-holders find something, though there's little they can do if every bed is occupied (as is often the case in July and August).

About the only way to find a cheap room along this coast is to go from camping ground to camping ground until you find one with a free bungalow. You may be offered a private room if you hang around Constanţa or Mangalia train station wearing a backpack, but there are few such rooms at the resorts. Campers with tents will have few problems, but everyone else should consider visiting Bulgaria's Black Sea coast instead, as the accommodation and food situation there is much better, the room prices lower, the beaches nicer and the crowds smaller. Romania's Black Sea isn't black yet, but in places it's rather brown from Danube River silt. The further south you go, the clearer the water.

DANUBE CANAL

The train from Bucharest crosses the Danube at Cernavodă, on a great iron bridge erected in 1895. Romania's first nuclear power station, built with Canadian technology, is at Cernavodă. Between the Danube and Constanţa the train passes through the Murfatlar area, where Romania's best sweet dessert wines are produced. It then follows the new Danube Canal for almost its entire 64.2 km length. The canal, opened by President Ceauşescu in 1984, shortens the sea trip from Constanţa to Cernavodă by 400 km. There are two locks of 310 metres in length and water from the canal is used for irrigation.

The Danube Canal took 30,000 people nine years to construct, but the one activity you probably won't see on it is shipping. This canal was only part of a centuries-old European dream to build an inland waterway linking the North and Black seas, which was finally realised in 1992 when a 171-km canal between the Main and Danube rivers in Germany was inaugurated. Yet although navigation is now possible between Constanţa and Rotterdam (3500 km), few barges or riverboats are to be seen on Ceauşescu's canal, for reasons that are not clear.

TOURS

The ONT tourist office offers various bus excursions from the beach resorts, for example, wine tasting at Murfatlar. Information should be available at any hotel or camping ground reception. Foreigners still aren't allowed to travel in the same tour groups as Romanians, so when there aren't enough foreign tourists around, the sightseeing tours for foreigners are cancelled.

Tour desks booking sightseeing tours are located in Hotel Continental at Constanţa (all year round), Hotel Perla at Mamaia (mid-May to September), Hotel Europa at Eforie Nord (all year round), Hotel Anfiteatru at Olimp (mid-May to September) and Hotel Mangalia at Mangalia (mid-May to September).

CONSTANŢA

Constanţa, midway between Istanbul and Odessa, is Romania's largest port. In ancient times the Greek town of Tomis, which the Romans renamed Constantiana, was the main port in these parts. After Küstendje (the name of the town under Turkish rule) was taken by Romania in 1877, Constanţa grew in importance, with a railway line being built to it from Bucharest.

Much remains today from every period of Constanţa's colourful history. Despite ugly industrial development to the north and west, the picturesque old town has a charming Mediterranean air and the excellent museums are within easy reach of crowded city beaches.

Orientation

Constanţa Railway Station is about two km west of the old town. The left-luggage office at the train station is just down inside the passageway from the main hall to the tracks (open 24 hours). Constanţa's main city beach is at the east end of Bulevardul Republicii. From the Hotel Continental, Bulevardul Tomis runs south-east to Piaţa Ovidiu, in the heart of old Constanţa.

Information

The ONT tourist information desk is inside the Hotel Continental, Bulevardul Republicii 20, on the corner of Bulevardul Tomis.

The Automobil Clubul Român (☎ 11 849), at Bulevardul Tomis 141 between Constanţa and Mamaia, can assist motorists.

Money The Banca Comercială Romană, diagonally opposite the Archaeological Museum on Piaţa Ovidiu (weekdays 9 am to noon), changes travellers' cheques for 4.5% commission.

The ONT tourist information desk in Hotel Continental changes travellers' cheques for a whopping 8% commission. The exchange office at TAROM, nearby at Ştefan cel Mare 15, is slightly better at 6% commission.

Post & Telecommunications The telephone centre is in the main post office, Bulevardul Tomis 79 (daily 7 am to 10 pm). Constanţa's telephone code is 091.

Travel Agencies You can purchase train tickets at the CFR Travel Agency at Aleea Vasile Canarache 4, near the Archaeological Museum. They also sell international tickets.

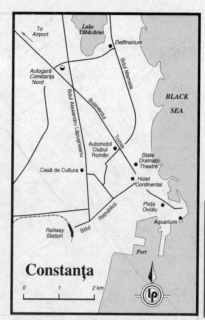

Constanţa

Things to See

Constanţa's most renowned attraction is the **Archaeological Museum** on Piaţa Ovidiu, with exhibits on three floors. Most of the cases have captions in English and German. The most unusual objects are kept in the treasury downstairs. Don't miss the 2nd century AD sculpture of a Glykon, which is a serpent with the muzzle of an antelope and the eyes, ears and hair of a human. Also outstanding is the Goddess Fortuna, a horn of plenty in her arms, with Pontos, God of the Black Sea, leaning on a ship at her feet. The exhibits on the top floor covering the period from 1940 onwards have been removed and the museum guide booklet has 34 pages rudely torn out of it, just when it starts to get interesting!

The archaeological fragments of Roman Tomis spill over onto the surrounding square. Facing these is another museum, which shelters a gigantic 3rd century **Roman mosaic** discovered in 1959 and left *in situ*.

ROMANIA

ROMANIA

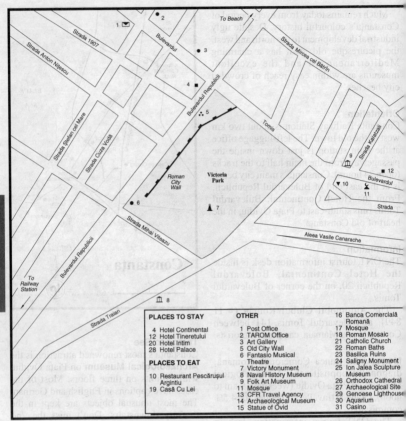

PLACES TO STAY

4 Hotel Continental
12 Hotel Tineretului
20 Hotel Intim
28 Hotel Palace

PLACES TO EAT

10 Restaurant Pescăruşul Argintiu
19 Casă Cu Lei

OTHER

1 Post Office
2 TAROM Office
3 Art Gallery
4 Old City Wall
6 Fantasio Musical Theatre
7 Victory Monument
8 Naval History Museum
11 Mosque
13 CFR Travel Agency
14 Archaeological Museum
15 Statue of Ovid
16 Banca Comercială Romană
17 Mosque
18 Roman Mosaic
21 Catholic Church
22 Roman Baths
23 Basilica Ruins
24 Saligny Monument
25 Ion Jalea Sculpture Museum
26 Orthodox Cathedral
27 Archaeological Site
29 Genoese Lighthouse
30 Aquarium
31 Casino

The statue of Ovid, erected on Piaţa Ovidiu in 1887, commemorates the Latin poet, who was exiled to Constanţa in 8 AD and is thought to have been buried there.

A block south of this square on Strada Muzeelor is a large **mosque** (1910) with a 140-step minaret you may climb. Two blocks farther down the same street you'll find the **Orthodox cathedral** (1885) and one block to the right is the **Saligny monument** from which you'll get an excellent view of the modern harbour. Go east on the lovely waterfront promenade till you reach the **casino** (1904) and **aquarium**, which are face to

face. Farther along the promenade is the **Genoese lighthouse** (1860) and the pier, with a fine view of old Constanţa.

The other worthwhile sights can be covered by returning to Piaţa Ovidiu and Bulevardul Tomis, which you follow northwest to the Hotel Continental. Halfway up Bulevardul Tomis you will pass another mosque and the **Folk Art Museum**, in an ornate building on the right.

Some good examples of the Romanian art of painting on glass are displayed here. When you reach the hotel, turn left and explore Victoria Park, which has remains of

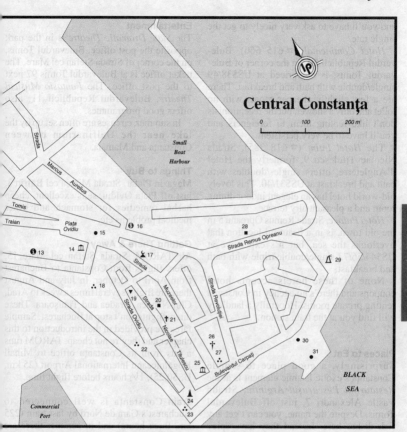

Central Constanța

0   100   200 m

Small Boat Harbour

Strada

Marcus Aurelius

Tomis

Traian

Piața Ovidiu

Strada Remus Opreanu

Strada Muzeelor

Strada Revoluției

Strada Ovidiu

Strada

Nicolae Titulescu

Bulevardul Carpați

BLACK SEA

Commercial Port

the 3rd century **Roman city wall**, pieces of Roman sculpture and a modern **Victory monument**. From the terrace across the street from the monument, you'll have another good view of the modern commercial port.

The **Naval History Museum** (closed Monday), Strada Traian 53, offers exceptionally informative exhibits on early Romanian history. Although the captions are all in Romanian, much can be gained from the illustrations alone.

Constanța's **Art Gallery**, at Bulevardul Tomis 22, opposite the Hotel Continental, has a large collection of paintings by Nicolae Grigourescu and other well-known Romanian painters.

Places to Stay

There are no cheap hotels in Constanța (or anywhere else on the Romanian Black Sea coast, for that matter) and in summer accommodation is tight. The best you'll find is the *Hotel Tineretului* (☎ 613 590), Bulevardul Tomis 24, a new five-storey hotel with neat, clean rooms at US$27/35 single/double with bath and breakfast. All the rooms are doubles and you'll have to ask very nicely to get the single rate.

Hotel Continental (☎ 615 660), Bulevardul Republicii 20, on the corner of Bulevardul Tomis, is overpriced at US$38/49 single/double with bath and breakfast. There are a few slightly cheaper rooms with no toilet and only a shower, but the receptionists don't like renting them to foreigners and you'll have to be very persistent.

The *Hotel Intim* (☎ 618 285), Strada Nicolae Titulescu 9, formerly the Hotel d'Angleterre, offers singles/doubles with bath and breakfast at US$31/40. This lovely old-world hotel has an elegant indoor dining room and a pleasant airy terrace.

Hotel Palace, Strada Remus Opreanu 5 in the old town, is in a beautiful location that overlooks the sea, but it's expensive at US$44/56/72 single/double/triple with bath and breakfast.

None of these hotels accepts hotel coupons and there's no agency in Constanţa renting private rooms. Hopefully a landlady will find you at the train station.

Places to Eat

Surprisingly, a good place to sample Constanţa's exotic Islamic element is at the *Restaurant Pescăruşul Argintiu*, Strada Vasile Alexandri 7, just off Bulevardul Tomis. Despite the name, you can't get any fish dishes here. Instead they have spicy Middle Eastern meat dishes and after 10 pm a band belts out the type of music you'd expect to hear in Istanbul or Damascus. The service, prices and portions are good, so if you've got the time it's better to sit down to a regular meal here instead of patronising their adjacent fast food outlet which dispenses similar fare that you must eat standing up.

If the occasion calls for something better, try the *Casă Cu Lei* or House of the Lions, Strada Nicolae Titulescu 27, an 1898 building not far from the mosque in the old town. (You might notice the sign while visiting the mosaic museum.) Even if you're not eating, the bar there is an agreeable oasis.

Entertainment

The *State Dramatic Theatre* is in the park opposite the post office, Bulevardul Tomis, on the corner of Strada Ştefan cel Mare. The ticket office is at Bulevardul Tomis 97 next to the post office. The *Fantasio Musical Theatre*, Bulevardul Republicii 11, also offers good programmes.

In summer, circuses are often set up by the lake near the Delfinarium between Constanţa and Mamaia.

Things to Buy

Magazin Plafar, Strada Mircea cel Bătrîn 3, just off Piaţa Ovidiu, sells excellent, cheap herbal remedies for stomach and other medical problems etc.

Getting There & Away

Air TAROM, Strada Ştefan cel Mare 15, offers flights from Constanţa to Bucharest from April to October. In July and August there are flights several times a week to Arad, Cluj-Napoca, Oradea and Timişoara. These direct flights don't stop at Bucharest. Sample fares are provided in the introduction to this chapter and they're not cheap. TAROM runs a bus from its Constanţa office to Mihail Kogălniceanu International Airport (25 km, US$0.25), 1½ hours before flight time.

Train Constanţa is well connected to Bucharest's Gara de Nord by fast train (225 km, three hours) and in summer there are direct trains to Oradea, Timişoara, Arad, Iaşi, Suceava, Braşov and Satu Mare, and points between. The *Ovidius* express train runs overnight between Constanţa and Budapest-Keleti (1069 km, 17 hours) via Arad. Book tickets on these trains a day ahead at the CFR Travel Agency listed under the previous Travel Agencies section. (Same-day tickets are sold at the station an hour before departure.)

Unreserved local trains run north to Tulcea (179 km via Medgidia), south to Mangalia (43 km) and west to Bucureşti-Obor and Braşov. For northern Romania take a Bucharest-bound train west to Feteşti (79 km) and change for Făurei (for Iaşi) or

Buzău (for Suceava). Try to board at the originating station (Constanţa or Mangalia) with a 1st-class ticket. As there are no reserved seats, you'll have to be quick. Trains to Tulcea cannot be booked ahead.

There are no buses or trains from Constanţa to nearby Bulgaria, an indication of the poor relations between these neighbouring countries. The only connection is described in the Mangalia section.

Getting Around

From in front of the train station, trolleybus Nos 40, 41 and 43 run to the centre of town (tickets from a kiosk at the stop). On trams and buses around Constanţa beware of small groups of young men who create artificially crowded conditions as a means of picking your pocket.

MAMAIA

Mamaia, a congested eight-km strip of sand between Lake Mamaia (or Siutghiol) and the Black Sea, just north of Constanţa, is Romania's Miami, with 57 hotels and countless tourists. The abundant greenery and park-like environment makes Mamaia restful despite the crowds. The main thing to do here is swim and enjoy the sun, though historic Constanţa is just a bus ride away. Romania's original casino is here.

Post & Telecommunications

A small post office/telephone centre is between Hotel Alcor and the main highway (in summer, weekdays 8 am to 8 pm, weekends 11 am to 7 pm). The telephone code is 0918.

Things to See & Do

An excursion boat ferries tourists across freshwater Lake Mamaia to **Ovidiu Island** every hour or two in the afternoon during the summer season. The boat leaves from the wharf near Mamaia Casino, on the lake side of the strip behind the Casino Bazar. Try the local seafood in the thatch-roofed restaurant on the island if you have time.

All kinds of activities such as sailboarding, water-skiing, yachting, rowing, pedal boats and tennis are laid on along the main beach at Mamaia.

Organised Tours The Litoral Agentia de Turism International (☎ 831 344) at Hotel Perla, near the south entrance to Mamaia, organises one-day excursions to the Danube Delta (US$47 including lunch and dinner), wine tasting at Murfatlar (US$18 including lunch) and a tour of the coastal resorts as far south as Neptun (US$25 including lunch). The tours only operate from May to September and at least 20 people must sign up, but there's usually something going in midsummer.

Places to Stay

Camping The *camping ground* at Mamaia is at the northern end of the Black Sea coast six-km strip. However, it's small and always chock-a-block in summer.

The *Hanul Piraţilor Campground* is between the main road and the beach, three km north of Mamaia (bus service). There's always tent space here but there are no bungalows. Across the road is the *Hanul Piraţilor Restaurant* where a band plays on a stage designed like a pirate ship. You can enjoy a good mixed grill and plenty of wine. Book a table ahead if you can, though English speakers are usually admitted promptly without reservations. Ask what time the main show begins. There's another camping ground with less shade between Mamaia and this one, but just ask for the Hanul Piraţilor, which everyone knows.

Hotels The hotels of Mamaia are being privatised and there's no longer a central booking office, but you can find some good bargains if you shop around. A good place to begin is the *Casino Bazar*, right in the centre of the resort. In summer the two wings of the casino operate as private mini-hotels with basic rooms with shared bath overlooking the beach at US$12 double (closed in winter). The location is great, but check both wings as prices and conditions differ (the rooms are actually converted dressing rooms, so don't expect much more than four bare walls and a mattress on the floor). Romanians pay less than US$2 to stay here but even at that price most of them won't accept the austere conditions at the casino, so this is one place where you've got a chance of finding something even in mid-summer. While making enquiries here you may be offered a private room.

If you want a proper hotel room with private bath you'll have to ask around. Avoid hotels with information boards set up in the lobby by Western tour operators as these will be more expensive or fully booked by groups. Instead, ask at hotels which usually cater to Romanians as they'll be delighted to rent you a room at five times the local price, if they have one, and you'll still find it relatively cheap.

For example try *Hotel Perla* (☎ 31 670), a high-rise at the southern end of the Mamaia strip, where foreigners pay US$20/30/32 single/double/triple. If they're full the receptionist may help you find something else.

The modern, four-storey *Hotel Dobrogea* (☎ 67 014) on Lake Tabacarie at Sat Vacanta Beach, just south of Mamaia (tram No 100 from the train station to the terminus), has rooms with bath at US$26/32 double/triple (no singles). It's usually full but you can reserve a room by calling a few days in advance.

Hotel coupons are supposed to be accepted at the *Hotel Alcor* (☎ 831 202), near the trolleybus terminus at the northern end of Mamaia (open June to September only). Ask if the Hertz/Touring ACR representative (☎ 831 171) is on duty, as he or she may be willing to help you. The Alcor is often full and even if you have coupons you may not get in. There's no way you'll get a room here without a coupon.

Places to Eat

Restaurant service is poor compared with that in the rest of the country and the staff tend to be irritable. One British reader reported that a waiter at the *Miorita*, supposedly a 1st-class restaurant, threw his starter onto his main course because he was eating too slowly! The *Cherhana Fish Restaurant*, on Lake Mamaia a bit south of the Ovidiu Island ferry, was the only exception he found.

Entertainment

In summer there are lots of discos at Mamaia, such as *Holiday Disco* (popular among the younger set) near Hotel Patria or *Disco Club 33* at Hotel Bucureşti, both a little north of the Casino Bazar. Further north is *Hotel Rex*, Mamaia's top hotel, which has an up-market disco.

Getting There & Away

Travelling between Constanţa and Mamaia by trolleybus is easy. Trolleybus No 40 runs from the train station to Constanţa and on to the Pescarie bus stop near Hotel Parc, Mamaia. Here you change to trolleybus No 47 which runs right up the Mamaia strip. Otherwise take tram No 100 from the train station to Sat Vacanta and walk north along the beach.

EFORIE NORD

Eforie Nord, 17 km from Constanţa, is the first large resort south of the city. The beach is below 20-metre cliffs along the eastern side of the town, and walls built out into the sea trap additional sand. Tiny Lake Belona, just behind the southern end of the sea beach, is a favourite bathing place, as its water is much warmer than the Black Sea. Because Eforie Nord is close to Constanţa it tends to be overcrowded, and the beaches are better and cleaner further south.

Just south-west of this is Techirghiol Lake, a former river mouth famous for its black sapropel mud baths, which are effective against rheumatism. The cold mud baths are the only place in Romania where mud-covered nudism is allowed (separate areas are designated for women and men). The lake's waters are four times as salty as the sea; the lake is in fact two metres below sea level.

Orientation

The train station is only a few minutes walk from the post office but the route isn't obvious, so study one of the large city maps posted around town or ask. To use the left-luggage room at the train station ask the stationmaster.

Post & Telecommunications In summer the telephone centre at the main post office on Bulevardul Republicii is open daily from 7 am to 10 pm and it's very crowded. Eforie Nord's telephone code is 0917.

Travel Agencies The CFR Travel Agency next to the post office in Eforie Nord sells tickets for express trains.

Places to Stay
Camping The low-budget traveller's first stop should be *Camping Sincai* (no phone), a few hundred metres west of Eforie Nord Railway Station. The shortest way to get there is to walk west to the far end of the railway platform, cross the tracks and follow a path to a breach in the wall. As well as camping space, there are five two-room huts at US$4 per person and a lovely but dilapidated old villa right by the lake with five two-bed rooms, eight four-bed rooms and four six-bed rooms, all US$5 per person. Expect to live at close quarters with Romanians on budgets far lower than yours – they're curious and friendly, and you'll like it if you don't mind a bit of noise. This privately owned camping ground is only reliably open in July and August, but if you're at the station anyway it's always worth a try. It's right on Techirghiol Lake, but rather far from the Black Sea beaches.

Better camping facilities are available at *Camping Meduza* behind Hotel Minerva on the north side of Eforie Nord. It's closer to the beach but much farther from the train station.

Hotels The Touring ACR desk (☎ 742 599), in the lobby of the Europa Hotel, Bulevardul Republicii 19 in the centre of town (open June to mid-September only), sells hotel coupons and will help you find a hotel room. The Europa itself doesn't accept coupons.

The *Hotel Bega* (☎ 41 468), a pleasant four-storey hotel down from the post office towards the beach, is US$34/43 single/double with bath (hotel coupons accepted). The Bega is open all year round.

Places to Eat
The *Cofetăria Pescărus* opposite the post office has great cakes, but avoid the adjacent restaurant of the same name which has no printed menu. In front of the post office back across the street is a shop which dispenses wretched mass-produced pizza to those in the queue. You're probably better off eating at a hotel restaurant.

Restaurant Neon next to Hotel Bega offers 1950s-style dancing to a B-grade band. Try to reserve a table as Romanian holiday-makers pack the place.

Getting There & Away
All trains between Bucharest and Mangalia stop at Eforie Nord.

Bus Nos 10, 11 and 12 leave for Eforie Nord from the street beyond the tram stop, just south of Constanţa Railway Station.

NEPTUN-OLIMP
Before the 1989 revolution, Neptun and Olimp formed an exclusive tourist complex under the direct control of the Central Committee of the Communist Party of Romania. The resorts of Jupiter, Aurora, Venus and Saturn were administered separately from Mangalia and this administrative division still exists. Opened in 1960, Neptun-Olimp was formerly reserved for foreign tourists and important Romanians, but the hotels are now open to everyone. Because of its unique history, Neptun-Olimp is perhaps the nicest and most chic of Romania's Black Sea resorts.

Money The Banca Romană de Comerţ Exterior, next to Hotel Decebal at Neptun (weekdays 10 am to 1 pm), will change travellers' cheques for a flat US$2 commission.

Post & Telecommunications The post office/telephone centre is a block north of

Hotel Decebal, Neptun. Neptun's telephone code is 0917.

Travel Agencies The CFR Travel Agency in Hotel Apollo at Neptun books express trains (in summer only).

Things to See

Ceauşescu had a summer residence at Neptun, the **Villa Nufar**, and all of the luxury villas in its immediate area were once reserved for members of the Ceauşescu family or for high-level party officials. Right after the 1989 revolution you could visit the Ceauşescu villa and rent an apartment in one of the nearby buildings, but most are now occupied by government leaders once again and armed guards have reappeared.

Places to Stay

There are three camping grounds. *Camping Olimp* is at the northern end of the Olimp tourist strip, and *Neptun Camping* and nearby *Zodiak Camping* are by the lagoon, at the southern end of Neptun.

In Neptun, there's an office upstairs in the shopping arcade, across the street from Hotel Decebal, which is supposed to find hotel rooms for visitors, but in midsummer they adopt a couldn't-care-less attitude and just tell you everything is full.

If you have hotel coupons, go directly to the Touring ACR desk (☎ 731 873) at Hotel Belvedere in Olimp (open from June to mid-September only). The friendly English-speaking staff there will do their best to find you a room at a 1st-class hotel in Olimp, or you can pay an extra US$12 to upgrade your coupon and stay at the luxury category *Hotel Amfiteatru*. If you don't already have hotel coupons, they can sell them to you (see Accommodation in the introduction to this chapter for details).

At Olimp, two km north of Neptun, hotel coupons are accepted at the 15-storey *Hotel Transilvania* (☎ 731 123). Without coupons it's US$38/47 single/double with bath. You can also stay at the three-star *Hotel Belvedere* (☎ 731 256) nearby, but a supplement of US$12 per person must be paid in addition

to your coupon. Rooms at the Belvedere are good, with balcony, refrigerator and private bath. Both hotels are open from June to September only.

Getting There & Away

Halta Neptun Railway Station is within walking distance of the Neptun-Olimp hotels, midway between the two resorts. All of the trains that travel between Bucharest and Mangalia, local and express, stop here.

Bus Nos 15 and 20 go nine km south to Mangalia; bus No 20 also runs 38 km north to Constanţa. Private taxi buses also cover these routes for about the same fares.

MANGALIA

Mangalia, at the southern end of the Romanian Black Sea strip, was founded by Dorians from Heraclea Pontica at the end of the 6th century BC and Callatis (now Mangalia) offers several minor archaeological sites. More of a draw are the resorts along the Romanian Riviera to the north: Saturn, Venus, Aurora and Jupiter. Saturn is right next to Mangalia and thus is crowded with locals, with long queues at the food stalls. Beach hopping's the thing to do, and on a hot summer's day the area really becomes a zoo.

Information

Left Luggage The left-luggage office at Mangalia Railway Station is in a separate building at the south end of the main platform, to the left (open 24 hours).

Post & Telecommunications The telephone centre is in the main post office at Ştefan cel Mare 16, within sight of the Sultan Esmahan Mosque (daily 7 am to 10 pm). Mangalia's telephone code is 0917.

Travel Agencies The CFR Travel Agency in Mangalia is inside the post office at Strada Ştefan cel Mare 16. At Venus, the CFR Travel Agency is in the post office beside the Hotel Adriana.

Things to See & Do

As you leave the train station turn right and

walk south on Şoseaua Constanţei about 600 metres till you reach a roundabout, with the new Casă Tineretului on the right. A street on the left runs from the roundabout straight down to Hotel Mangalia and the beach, with the ruins of a 6th century **Palaeo-Christian basilica** and a fountain dispensing sulphurous mineral water behind the hotel. The numerous apartment blocks around Hotel Mangalia were built by the Ceauşescu regime in the 1980s.

Return to the roundabout and continue south on Şoseaua Constanţei. You'll soon reach the **Callatis Archaeological Museum** on the left with a good collection of Roman sculpture. This small museum is often inexplicably closed. Just past the high-rise building next to the museum are some remnants of a 4th century necropolis, which once stood on the site of the high-rise.

Continue straight south on Şoseaua Constanţei another 500 metres to the centre of town. On most summer evenings cultural events take place in the **Casă de Cultură** with the large mural on the façade which you'll see on the right. Further ahead on the same street is the Turkish **Sultan Esmahan Mosque** (1460). All these sights can easily be seen in a couple of hours.

Mineral Springs Across the street from Hotel Adriana at Venus, just north of Mangalia, is a thermal bath using hot sulphurous water and medicinal mud, recommended for rheumatism, nervous disorders, skin problems, constipation and many other conditions listed on a board at the entrance. It's open daily from May to September, with separate entrances for women and men, admission US$0.50.

Places to Stay

Camping *Popas Saturn* (☎ 751 380), less than a km from Mangalia Railway Station, offers camping space. They also have 56 small cabins which rent for US$4 per person, though in midsummer you've only got a fifty-fifty chance of getting one. You can see the tents from the train window as you're arriving at Mangalia and it's walking dis-

tance from the station, otherwise take bus No 14, 15 or 20 two stops north, right to the camping ground entrance. Though it does get crowded, there's almost always space for people staying in tents. This camping ground offers shady trees, snack and beer bars, occasional warm showers and easy access to coastal buses and the beach. It's open from mid-June to mid-September.

Alternatively, there are similar camping grounds in the string of tourist resorts to the north – Venus, Jupiter, Neptun, Saturn and Olimp – all of which are accessible by frequent bus and operate beyond capacity.

Hotels There are countless luxury tourist hotels along the Black Sea coast strip, for example, the *Hotel Adriana* (☎ 731 506) on the beach at the entrance to Venus, near Venus Camping. The Adriana has rooms at US$18/36 single/double with bath, but it's usually full in midsummer (open May to September only).

The circular *Hotel Raluca* (☎ 731 502), a few blocks from the Adriana and the beach, is US$23/33 single/double and also likely to be full (open in summer only).

Getting There & Away

At the end of the line on the Black Sea route, Mangalia is easily accessible by fast train from Bucharest's Gara de Nord (269 km, 4½ hours). Local trains arrive from Constanţa several times a day (43 km, 1¼ hours). Through express trains depart from Mangalia for Arad, Bucharest, Craiova, Galaţi, Iaşi, Oradea, Sibiu, Suceava and Timişoara, some only in summer. (Check with the CFR Travel Agency mentioned previously.) Every afternoon one unreserved local train leaves for Braşov – board early with a 1st-class ticket.

Bus Nos 12 and 20 operate between Mangalia and Constanţa. Bus No 12 goes along the main highway, while bus No 20 stops at all the beach resorts as far north as Olimp, terminating at Constanţa Railway Station.

Private buses also run between Constanţa and Mangalia. On the private lines you pay the driver, whereas for the numbered buses you must buy a ticket at a kiosk, then cancel it once aboard.

To/From Bulgaria Bus No 14 runs from Mangalia Railway Station to the Bulgarian border at Vama Veche, 10 km south of Mangalia, 10 times a day. After crossing on foot, be prepared for a six-km hike to Durankulak, the first settlement inside Bulgaria, if you can't manage to hitch a ride.

Getting Around
In summer, open-sided jeeps haul wagon-loads of tourists back and forth infrequently between Mangalia and Olimp for US$0.20 a short ride or US$0.60 for a complete trip, a fun way to familiarise yourself with what the area has to offer. The jeeps stop at all the beaches.

The receptionist at the Mangalia Hotel, Strada Costache Negri 2, books sightseeing tours with activities such as wine tasting at Murfatlar (US$21), a Romanian evening (US$18) and trips to the Danube Delta (US$51 for one day, US$92 for two days, meals included).

The Danube Delta

The triangular 4340-sq-km Danube Delta on the Black Sea, just south of the Ukrainian border, is the youngest land in Europe. Here the mighty Danube splits into three arms, the Chilia, Sulina and Sfintu Gheorghe channels. It's an ever-changing environment of marshes, reeds and sand bars, as the river carries over two tonnes of silt a second, making Romania 40 metres longer each year.

The flora and fauna are unique. The only large pelican colony in Europe is found here, along with another 250 species of birdlife. The converging migratory bird routes make this the richest area of its kind in Europe. Among the dazzling variety of insects are mosquitoes, which you'll encounter everywhere from May to July. Locals come to the delta to fish for carp and sturgeon. Small

boats are required to see the wildlife, as hydrofoils drive the birds away from the main channels.

About 10% of the delta is included in nature reserves, but these are poorly managed. In 1983 President Ceauşescu approved plans to reclaim 38.4% of the Danube Delta for agriculture, fish farming and forestry. Six years later, with less than half the project complete, President Iliescu cancelled the plan, which was seriously affecting the ecological balance at the Danube mouth.

GETTING AROUND
Passenger boats regularly ply the Danube Delta, making access relatively easy. 'Rapid' hydrofoils *(nave rapide)* run daily from Tulcea to Sulina and Galaţi, leaving Tulcea mid-morning and Sulina mid-afternoon, but departures are often cancelled without notice. Hydrofoil fares are about 50% higher than the 'classical' ferries and the service only operates from May to September.

A better choice would be the classical ferries from Galaţi to Tulcea and Sulina, operating all year round. Heading east, these depart from Galaţi for Tulcea at 8.45 am on Monday, Wednesday and Friday (three hours), connecting with the boat from Tulcea to Sulina leaving at 1.30 pm daily (three hours). Heading west, they depart from Sulina for Tulcea at 7 am daily, connecting for Galaţi on Tuesday, Thursday and Saturday. In winter the Sulina ferry only operates four times a week. Ferry service upriver from Galaţi to Brăila has been suspended.

Six times a week the ferry from Tulcea to Sulina connects at Crişan, with a smaller ferry to Mila 23 or Caraorman going to one or the other on alternate days.

There are also Navrom ferries from Tulcea to Periprava (103 km) four times a week, and to Sfintu Gheorghe (113 km) three times a week. Foreign tourists are now allowed on these services on the north and south arms of the Danube.

Ferry tickets go on sale at the terminals about two hours before departure. In summer the queues are long, so get in the correct line

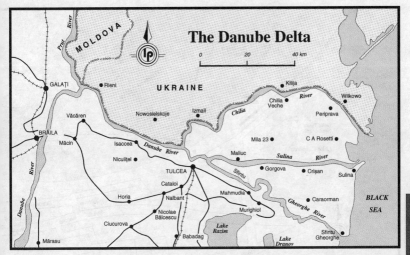

The Danube Delta

early. The classical ferries have 1st and 2nd class, though it's unlikely you'll want to stay in the stuffy 1st-class lounge for long. If it's a nice day take 2nd class and sit outside.

TULCEA

Tulcea, the seat of Tulcea County, which includes the Danube Delta, is a modern industrial city with little to detain you more than a couple of hours. Accommodation is a problem in Tulcea, so try to schedule your visit so that you don't have to stay there. Tulcea's position on the Danube at a crossing of transport routes makes this possible, provided you arrive before 1 pm, allowing you to catch an onward ferry the same day. The riverfront was cleaned up and remodelled in one of Ceauşescu's much-maligned 1980s systematisations and its setting is rather attractive, despite the polluting aluminium smelter.

Orientation

Tulcea's bus and train stations, and the Navrom riverboat terminal, are next to each other by the Danube. Lake Ciuperca near the train station is completely surrounded by a park. Central Tulcea focuses on the river-front promenade, where you will see boats and people constantly coming and going. The promenade stretches eastward along the river to the Delta Hotel. Inland a block is Piaţa Civică, the modern centre of rebuilt Tulcea.

The left-luggage office at the train station opens daily from 6.45 am to 11 pm. Left luggage at the bus station is open weekdays from 6.30 am to 6.30 pm.

Information

Try the tour desk of the Delta Hotel, Strada Isaccea 2. Ask for the excellent tourist map *The Danube Delta*.

Travel Agencies Advance train tickets are sold at the CFR Travel Agency on Strada Babadag, opposite Piaţa Civică.

From May to September, Eurodelta Tours (☎ 0915-16 604) in the Delta Hotel has daily boat tours through the delta from Tulcea (US$30, including lunch at Crişan). Their main office is just across the street from the hotel.

The Automobil Clubul Român (☎ 0915-15 151), Strada Gării 7, assists motorists and organises Danube boat trips. For about

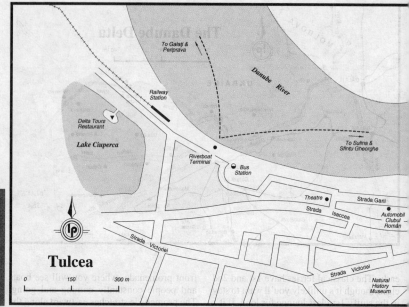

Tulcea

US$35 they'll provide a small cargo boat with captain and crew for a five-hour tour, including exploration of small channels in a rowboat.

Things to See

As you stroll along the river, you'll see the **Independence Monument** (1904) on Citadel Hill at the far eastern end of town. You can reach this by following Strada Gloriei from behind the Egreta Hotel to its end. You'll find an **historical museum** just below the monument and the view is worth the trip. Some ruins of ancient Aegisos are seen here. On your way back, look out for the minaret of the Turkish **Azizie Mosque** (1863) down Strada Independenţei.

The **Natural History Museum & Aquarium**, Strada Progresului 32, west of Piaţa Civică, behind Patria Cinema, should certainly be visited if you have time for its good collection of Danube fish. In front of the Greek Orthodox church opposite the

museum is a memorial to local victims of the 1989 revolution.

Places to Stay

Camping A no-camping regulation within Tulcea's city limits is strictly enforced by police. At a pinch, take the hourly passenger ferry across the Danube and follow the path downstream a km or two past the beach. There are places to pitch a tent along the river there, though you'll have to contend with stray dogs and people walking around in the morning.

The closest official camping ground is the *Pelicanul* near Murighiol (Independenta), 40 km south-east of Tulcea by bus, and then three km on foot. The facilities here are abysmal and the only return bus to Tulcea departs from Murighiol at 5 am! Give it a miss.

Hotels Of Tulcea's two high-rise hotels, the *Egreta Hotel* (☎ 0915-517 103), at Strada

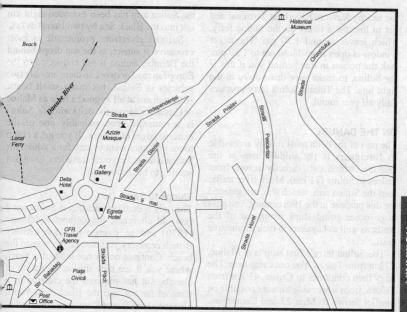

Pǎcii 1, is the cheaper, but at US$34/43 for a single/double it's no bargain. All the rooms at the *Delta Hotel* (☎ 0915-514 720), Strada Isaccea 2, cost US$46/59 single/double including breakfast. The Delta accepts hotel coupons.

The receptionist at Hotel Egreta can arrange pricey private rooms (US$23/32 single/double).

Places to Eat

The *Calypso Restaurant* on Strada Babadag, a long block south-west of the post office and just a bit past the synagogue, is an attractive private restaurant with good food and service at reasonable prices. The menu is in English.

Dinner at the *Delta Hotel* is good and it's wise to prebook a table.

The *Delta Tours Restaurant*, on a small island in Lake Ciuperca near the train station, has a nice terrace where you can eat or drink outdoors in summer.

Entertainment

The *Disco Fun Club Elevilor*, in the large theatre on the river between the stations and Hotel Delta, is open daily in summer from 6.30 to 11 pm.

Getting There & Away

There are four local trains from Constanţa via Medgidia (179 km, four hours). The daily express train from Bucharest's Gara de Nord takes five hours (335 km). The overnight local train to/from Bucharest is bearable if you go 1st class and arrive early to get a seat.

There's a direct daily bus from Tulcea to Buzǎu (198 km) in Moldavia. Other buses leaving Tulcea include five to Constanţa (123 km), one to Brǎila (93 km), one to Iaşi (374 km) and one to Bucharest (263 km). Times are clearly posted on the platforms and tickets for long-distance buses can be purchased up to five days in advance.

If you arrive in Tulcea around noon on a train from Bucharest or Constanţa, hurry to the nearby Navrom Riverboat Terminal and get in line for a ticket on the Sulina ferry, which leaves around 1.30 pm. The ticket window is open from 11.30 am to 1.30 pm. Ask the person in line behind you if this is for Sulina, to make sure that you're in the right line. The Tulcea-Sulina ferry operates daily all year round.

ON THE DANUBE

The part of the delta most readily accessible to foreigners is the middle arm of the Danube, which cuts directly across from Tulcea to Sulina (71 km). Much river traffic uses the Sulina arm, which was straightened for this purpose in the 19th century. You pass huge ocean-going ships rising out of the water as well as kayakers in their diminutive craft.

The Sulina ferry's first stop is at Maliuc, 27 km from Tulcea. You can camp here. The ferry then continues to Crişan, 43 km from Tulcea, from where side trips are possible on smaller ferries to Mila 23 and Caraorman. The 1st-class *Lebăda Hotel*, on the opposite side of the Danube from the Crişan ferry landing and a km upstream, is US$4 double for Romanians and US$46 double for foreigners (hotel coupons are accepted). You may camp in the vicinity of the hotel. Rowing boats to explore the side channels are sometimes available at Crişan and Maliuc. Take some food and water with you on your expedition into the delta.

SULINA

Sulina is the highlight of the ferry trip from Tulcea and you get a great view of it as the ship sails through the middle of town on its way to the landing. You'll pass derelict old dredges and freighters – many noble ships have ended their careers at Sulina's scrapyard. A canal dug from 1880 to 1902 shortened the length of the Sulina arm from 83.3 to 62.6 km. After WW I Sulina was declared a free port and trade boomed, a period that Jean Bart describes in his novel *Europolis*. Greek merchants dominated business here until their expulsion in 1951. Now

the Sulina arm has been extended eight km out into the Black Sea by two lateral dykes.

Sulina's riverfront promenade is most evocative at sunset, as the sun drops behind the Danube. Sulina is not connected to the European road network so there are only two vehicles in Sulina, but many small boats. Although not at all as good a base as Maliuc or Crişan for seeing the delta wildlife, Sulina is a romantic spot, palpably one of the extreme edges of Europe. If you get a cheap room you may want to stay for a while, for Sulina is an archetypical travellers' town just waiting to be discovered.

Things to See & Do

The only specific attractions at Sulina are a few old churches, the defunct lighthouse (1870) and an overgrown 19th century British cemetery you pass on the way to the beach. Continue on for one km to this beach where you'll see how the accumulation of Danube silt has required the creation of a channel far out into the Black Sea. You'll also see a long line of Romanian radar installations among the dunes, pointed at the former Soviet Union. This broad beach continues 30 km south, all the way to Sfîntu Gheorghe.

Places to Stay & Eat

Camping & Private Rooms You can camp in the cow pasture opposite the Sulina Hotel, and lots of people also camp free along the beach, though it can be rather windy. It's best to befriend the Romanian campers here and pitch your tent near theirs for security. They're sure to give you a warm welcome and in the evening there'll be a bonfire.

As you're getting off the ferry watch for people offering private rooms, your best bet for a long stay. You should be able to get a room somewhere even in midsummer.

Hotels The three-storey *Hotel Europolis*, next to the Sulina Cinema, a few minutes' walk to the right from the ferry wharf, is US$5 per person for a spacious but plain room with shared bath. You'll spot it as your ship is arriving. The Europolis even has a few rooms with balconies overlooking the river.

A couple of hundred metres west along the riverfront from the Europolis, past the bookshop, is a small sign pointing to the *Hotel Ochiş* (☎ 0915-43 379) which you enter from the rear. It's opposite an old church on the backstreet. Rooms here are US$4 per person and the management staff are very friendly. The Ochiş has a nice little restaurant, but if you want fish put in your order the day before. They promise always to have water for bathing, something the Europolis sometimes lacks.

The government-owned *Sulina Hotel* (☎ 0915-43 017), Strada Deltei 207, charges foreigners US$30/46/69 single/double/triple with bath. Unless you want cold, oily food with a side salad of sliced pickles, avoid the hotel restaurant, where the waiters will try to cheat you.

Entertainment

Club Pif and *Bar Atlantis II* are local hangouts along the riverfront. Sulina may seem light years from the muggings in big cities like New York or Los Angeles, but as you're strolling around late at night take care – undesirables hanging around here may look upon you as a target of opportunity.

Getting There & Away

It's possible to go straight through from Sulina to Galaţi or vice versa on Navrom classical ferries which connect at Tulcea, a seven-hour trip. Through tickets Between Sulina and Galaţi are sold, saving you the major inconvenience of having to line up again in Tulcea. You sometimes change boats at Tulcea and may have a few hours to look around.

UPRIVER FROM TULCEA

The ferry trip between Tulcea and Galaţi is especially interesting since the Danube here marks the boundary between Romania and Ukraine. You get a fine continuous view of Rieni, perhaps the best free peek possible into Ukraine. Rieni is the second most important Ukrainian Danube port (the most

important being Izmail, on the northern arm of the Danube),

Galaţi is a large industrial city with a steel mill and docks and shipyards scattered for km along the riverside. Massive housing complexes fill the city and cover entire hillsides. Inexpensive accommodation is hard to find here, so walk straight through the town to the railway station which has four daily local trains to Bîrlad (109 km, 2½ hours) where you change for Iaşi. If your timing doesn't coincide with these trains, take one of the 13 daily trains to Tecuci (85 km, two hours) where there are more connections for Iaşi and Suceava. Many of the Tecuci trains continue on to Mărăşeşti, Adjud or Bacău, which is better if you're headed for Suceava. Four express trains a day run from Galaţi to Bucharest (230 km, 3½ hours) and there's an overnight local train.

Moldavia

Moldavia, one of the three original principalities of Romania, is a land rich in folklore. It is known for its excellent horses. Many famous Romanian poets, artists, writers and musicians hail from Moldavia. Some of Romania's best vineyards are at Cotnari, between Iaşi and Suceava. In 1859, Moldavia, where the empires of the tsars, Habsburgs and Ottomans met, became the birthplace of modern Romania when Prince Alexandru Ioan Cuza united Moldavia and Wallachia for defensive purposes against these three encroaching powers.

Prince Bogdan won Moldavian independence from Hungary in 1349, and the centre of the medieval principality became Bukovina (which means beech wood) in the easily defended Carpathian foothills. From Suceava, Ştefan cel Mare (Stefan the Great), called the 'Athlete of Christ' by Pope Pius VI, led the resistance against the Turks from 1457 to 1504. This prince and his son, Petru Rareş, erected fortified monasteries throughout Bukovina. On the exteriors were stunning frescoes intended to educate the illiterate masses. Only with the defeat of Petru Rareş by the Turks in 1538 did Moldavia's golden age wane, as the principality began paying tribute to the Ottoman Empire.

After Bukovina was ceded to Austria by the Turks in 1775, the emphasis shifted to the Moldavian Plateau, an inclined plain stretching north from Galaţi. Romanian Moldavia is only the western half of the medieval principality. Bessarabia, the portion east of the Prut River, was taken by Russia in 1812, at a time when Moldavia was a vassal state of the Ottoman Empire under Phanariote Greek rule (1711-1821).

Although recovered by Romania from 1918 to 1940 and again from 1941 to 1944, Bessarabia was subjected to brutal divide-and-conquer surgery by Stalin after WW II. Northern Bukovina (around Cernăuţi) and Hertza Land (north of the Danube) were detached and handed to Ukraine despite their large Romanian majority, while Trans-Dniestria (east of the Dniester River) was taken from Ukraine and added to Bessarabia despite its Ukrainian population. Large numbers of Russians were brought in to work in newly established industries and today Moldova's three million ethnic Romanians comprise just 65% of the total population (Moldova is the Slavic version of Moldavia).

In June 1990 the newly elected parliament of Soviet Moldova switched its official language from Russian to Romanian and adopted the Romanian tricolour as the republic's official flag. Moves towards reunification with Romania led to ethnic fighting and the secession of Trans-Dniestria which set up its own government backed by Russian troops. On 27 August 1991 former Soviet Moldova, proclaimed its independence, but reincorporation into Romania seems as far off as ever (although Romanians and Moldovans may now cross the border without formalities). Ethnic Russians control Moldova's bureaucracy and the new state is economically bound to Russia and Ukraine.

Although Bukovina attracts lots of tour groups, the rest of Moldavia, Iaşi included, is well off the beaten track.

IAŞI

Iaşi (pronounced 'yash') became capital of Moldavia in 1565. When the principalities of Moldavia and Wallachia were united in 1859, Iaşi served as the national capital until it was replaced by Bucharest in 1862. This illustrious history accounts for the city's great monasteries, churches, public buildings and museums which surprise visitors who have never heard of the place. Always a leading intellectual centre, Romania's first university was founded here in 1860. It's a happening city with a better than average selection of restaurants, bars and night spots. Since tourists are rare, people are interested in meeting you and will go out of their way to be helpful. You'll need a full day at least to visit Iaşi.

Orientation

To reach Piaţa Unirii, the city's heart, from the train station, walk north-east two blocks on Strada Gării, then turn right into Strada Arcu. From Piaţa Unirii, Bulevardul Ştefan cel Mare runs south-east past the Moldavian Metropolitan Cathedral to the massive Palace of Culture, one of Romania's finest buildings. Calea Copou runs north-west to the university and Botanical Garden.

To reach the left-luggage office at the train station (open 24 hours), turn right as you leave the station and walk over to the adjacent 11-storey apartment building. Left luggage is below it, facing the parking lot. At the bus station you can leave luggage at the information window on the outer side of the station (open 6 am to 7 pm).

Information

The tourist office is on Strada Anastasie Panu next to Hotel Moldova. (Don't expect much from them.)

The Automobil Clubul Român (☎ 112 345), Strada Gării 13-15, two blocks from the train station, assists motorists.

Money Bucharest Exchange Office, inside Restaurant Select opposite Hotel Continental (weekdays 8 am to 8 pm, Saturday 8 am to noon), changes travellers' cheques.

Post & Telecommunications Iaşi has a nice, new telephone centre opposite Cinema Tineretului on Strada Lăpuşneanu (daily 7 am to noon). Iaşi's telephone code is 0981.

Travel Agencies The CFR Travel Agency is on Piaţa Unirii, across from the Hotel Traian.

The Agentia de Turism Moldova (☎ 15 309), in the TAROM office at Strada Arcu 3/4, offers a variety of bus tours around north-eastern Romania, varying from three to 10 days. Although these are designed for Romanians, foreigners are welcome to participate when space is available. Some of the tours include hiking, and all offer a great chance to see a bit of the country while getting to know some of its people. Prices are reasonable. Ask for their director, Professor Al Murgu, who speaks some English.

Things to See

On Piaţa Unirii, in the centre of Iaşi, is a statue (1912) of Prince Alexandru Ioan Cuza (1820-73), the founder of modern Romania, who achieved the union of Wallachia and Moldavia in 1859. Walk up the pedestrian street beside Hotel Traian to the residence of this man, a large neoclassical building (1806) that is now the **Museum of the Union**, Strada Lăpuşneanu 14.

The broad, tree-lined Bulevardul Ştefan cel Mare leads directly south-east from Piaţa Unirii towards the monumental Palace of Culture. Along the way you'll pass two magnificent churches on the right: first the **Moldavian Metropolitan Cathedral** (1886) with four towers and a cavernous interior, and then the fabulous **Church of the Three Hierarchs** (1639), the exterior of which is completely covered with intricate decorative patterns in stone. Inside are the tombs of the church's founder, Prince Vasile Lupu, and the aforementioned Prince Alexandru Ioan Cuza. The unmarked white stone building

beside this church is a gallery of 17th century frescoes.

The giant neo-Gothic **Palace of Culture** (1906-25), formerly the administrative palace, stands on the site of the 15th century princely court. There are four museums in the building – historical, fine arts, ethnological and technical – and special exhibitions are held here. Separate tickets are sold for each museum and exhibition, so you could end up with five or six tickets if you visit everything. As with most of Iaşi's museums, they're all closed on Monday. You'd probably have to be a specialist to appreciate the neolithic Cucuteni pottery in the Historical Museum, but it's worth noting for its importance to European prehistory.

On the square in front of the Palace of Culture is an equestrian statue of Stefan the Great (1883). Also on the square is **St Nicolae Domnesc Church** (1492), Iaşi's oldest building, and an old stone building called **Dosoftei House** in which the Orthodox church leader Dosoftei printed the first major work in verse to appear in the Romanian language (1673).

Find your way a few blocks north past the Central Market to **Golia Monastery** (1660) on Strada Cuza Vodă which overlooks Tîrgu Cucu. The monastery's walls and 30-metre tower shelter a 17th century church that has twin domes, frescoes, intricate carved doorways and iconostasis.

From Tîrgu Cucu take a westbound tram No 1, 4 or 8 and get out when you see a building marked 'Stadionul Emil Alexandrescu' on the left. Iaşi's 80-hectare **Botanical Garden** (Gradina Botanica), on the far side of Parcul Expositiei from this stop, is Romania's largest by far and there are greenhouses and many shady lanes to explore.

Follow the tramline back a few blocks to **Copou Park**, a nice place to sit and write postcards or update your diary. The poet Mihai Eminescu (1850-1889) was especially fond of this park and the linden tree under which he wrote some of his best works still stands beside the monument with the lions. (Mihai Eminescu was born in Ipoteşti, near

ROMANIA

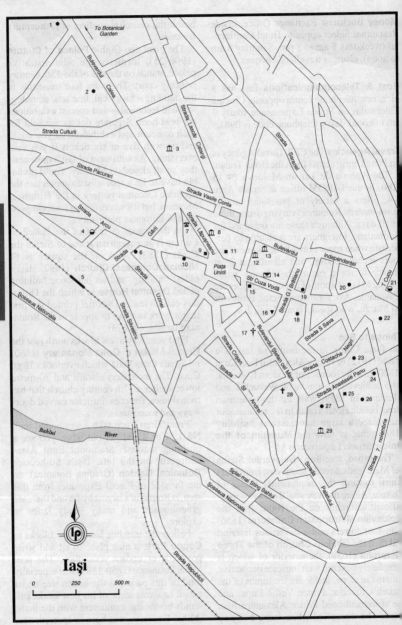

Iaşi

0   250   500 m

Botoşani, in northern Moldavia, but his great love, Veronica Micle, was from Iaşi, and he consequently spent a lot of time there.)

Walk back down Bulevardul Copou, past the huge neoclassical **university** (1897), and just before the statue in the middle of the street, turn left to the 1858 mansion which houses the **Casă Pogor Literary Museum**, Strada Vasile Pogor 4. Many well-known Romanian writers who have lived in Iaşi, including the poet Vasile Alecsandri (1821-90), are honoured here.

Places to Stay

All of Iaşi's low-budget accommodation is

at Lake Ciric, near Iaşi Airport, about six km north-east of town. The camping ground here has closed but the *Baza Sportiva si de Agrement Ciric* (☎ 179 304), across the dam and right, offers simple cabins *(casuţa)* at US$2 single or double (open May to September). The other holiday camps around the lake are private, but you might get a room if you talk to the right person and they have space. It should also be possible to pitch a tent freelance in the forest, but keep well out of sight unless you see others camping. On the lake is a restaurant that's usually closed. To get to the lake, take a tram to Tîrgu Cucu and then wait for bus No 25 to Lake Ciric, which leaves from the stop opposite the building marked 'Complexul Tîrgul Cucului' at Tîrgu Cucu. This bus leaves about once an hour, but the times are irregular.

The only regular hotel in Iaşi which approaches cheapness is the *Hotel Continental* (☎ 114 320), Strada Cuza Vodă 4. Rooms in this older four-storey hotel are US$16/24/29 single/double/triple with shared bath, US$19/29 single/double with private bath. The rooms vary in quality, so you might ask to see a couple before checking in. Hot water is available and the management staff are friendly.

A block away is the elegant old *Hotel Traian* (☎ 143 330), Piaţa Unirii 1, with singles/doubles at US$33/49 with bath and breakfast (hotel coupons accepted). The video games in the lobby are rather jarring. Both the Traian and Continental suffer from tram noise in the very early morning.

The modern 13-storey high-rise *Hotel Unirea* (☎ 142 110), Piaţa Unirii 5, is more expensive at US$47/75 single/double with bath and breakfast. It's only worth considering if you have hotel coupons.

The 14-storey *Hotel Moldova* (☎ 142 225), Piaţa Palatului 1, near the Palace of Culture, charges exactly the same as the Unirea (coupons accepted). Behind it is the smaller *Hotel Orizont* (☎ 112 700) with overpriced rooms at US$28/46 single/double. This is a 'youth tourism' hotel of the student travel organisation BTT, so everything is just a little more spartan except the

ROMANIA

price (no discounts for individual foreigners).

Places to Eat

The *Restaurant Iaşul* behind the Hotel Traian is one of the city's best dining rooms. The restaurant in *Hotel Unirea* is a reliable place to eat (good breakfast) and on the 13th floor is a café with an open terrace that overlooks the city (fine for a beer).

The *Restaurant Select*, opposite the Hotel Continental, serves pizza and cake downstairs, and there's a casino upstairs. Select is open 24 hours a day and their terrace is very much *the* place to see and be seen. Next door to the Restaurant Select is the unpretentious *Restaurant Miorita* with draught beer and little else.

Pera Metro Pizza, Strada G I Brătianu 32 near the National Theatre, serves fairly reasonable pizza by the slice, and at *Cofetăria Opera* next door you can get good ice cream for dessert. (There are several places around Iaşi called Metro Pizza – don't mix them up.)

Entertainment

On the east side of Bulevardul Ştefan cel Mare, nearly opposite the Moldavian Metropolitan Cathedral, is the neo-Baroque *Vasile Alecsandri National Theatre* (1896), which was designed by the famous Viennese architects Fellner and Hellmer. Also check the nearby *Filharmonica*.

There are three cinemas right in the centre of town, the *Tineretului* and *Republica* on Strada Lăpuşneanu, and *Cinema Victoria* on Piaţa Unirii. Don't buy any popcorn at the Victoria as it attracts rats, which begin scampering beneath the seats as soon as the lights go out.

Discos The disco scene focuses on *Hotel Moldova*, although the hotel disco itself is smoky and colourless and is only crowded because admission is free. A better disco is the one in the basement at the *Scala Restaurant*, opposite the Central Market (Hala Centrală) on Strada Anastasie Panu (daily 6 pm to 4 am). It's preferable, however, to skip both these places and head for *Cocktail Night*

Club (closed Monday) below the apartment blocks behind Luceafarul Theatre. The flashing lights and chic crowd are fun, and you can pick up your own drinks at the bar (no need to order through a stuffy waiter).

Iaşi's hottest student disco is *Metro Pizza* at the Complexul Studentesc 'Tudor Vladimescu' east of town (five stops from Piaţa Unirii on tram No 8). It's closed on Monday and Tuesday and from August to mid-September.

Getting There & Away

There are TAROM flights to Iaşi from Bucharest.

Iaşi is on the main line between Bucharest and Kiev which goes via Kishinev (Chişinău), the capital of Moldova. The Ungheni border crossing is only 21 km away. Reservations are required on the four daily trains from Iaşi to Kishinev (131 km).

Express trains to Bucharest (462 km, seven hours) and Suceava (138 km, 1½ hours) leave several times a day. Several *accelerat* trains a day travel from Iaşi to Timişoara (793 km, 16 hours) via Suceava and Cluj-Napoca – a useful transverse route. For Galaţi you may have to change trains at Bîrlad or Tecuci.

There's a daily overnight persoane (local) train in each direction between Iaşi and Braşov, which is quite acceptable if you go 1st class. It is a cheap, easy connection between these points. Just be on the platform an hour early to grab a seat, as no reservations are accepted.

One daily bus runs from Iaşi to Tulcea (374 km), another to Braşov (326 km) and another to Rădăuţi.

Bukovina

The painted churches of Bukovina are among the greatest artistic monuments of Europe. Erected at a time when northern Moldavia was threatened by Turkish invaders, the monasteries were surrounded by strong defensive walls. Great popular armies

ROMANIA

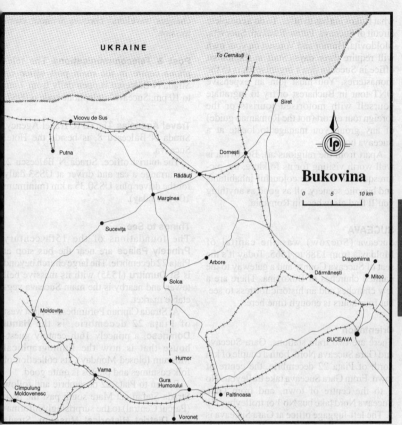

would gather inside these walls, waiting to do battle. To educate, entertain and arouse the interest of the illiterate soldiers and peasants who were unable to enter the church or understand the Slavic liturgy, well-known biblical stories were portrayed on the church walls in cartoon-style frescoes – a unique mass media. The exterior of the church at Sucevița Monastery is almost completely covered with these magnificent 16th century frescoes.

What catches the attention is the realistic manner of painting human figures in vast compositions against a backdrop not unlike the local landscape of the forested Carpathian foothills. Over the centuries the freshness of the colours has been preserved, from the greens of Sucevița, to the blues of Voroneț and the reds of Humor. The church domes are a peculiar combination of Byzantine pendentives and Moorish crossed arches with larger-than-life paintings of Christ or the Virgin peering down from inside.

If your time is limited, the Voroneț and Moldovița monasteries, both quite accessible by bus and train (see the Moldovița and Gura Humorului Getting There & Away sections), provide a representative sample of what Bukovina has to offer. To do a complete circuit of Suceava, Putna, Rădăuţi, Suceviţa, Moldoviţa, Humor and Voroneţ on your own will require three days. Staff at the tourist office in Suceava don't organise tours to the monasteries. You must join an expensive ONT tour in Bucharest or try to ingratiate yourself with motorised tourists or the foreign tour escort (not the Romanian guide) of any group you manage to locate at a Suceava hotel.

Apart from the religious art, Bukovina is well worth visiting for its folklore, the picturesque villages, the colourful inhabitants and bucolic scenery, all as good as anything you'll find elsewhere in Romania.

SUCEAVA
Suceava (Soczow) was the capital of Moldavia from 1388 to 1565. Today it's the seat of Suceava County and a gateway to the painted churches of Bukovina. There are a few churches and an historic fortress to see, but four hours is enough time here.

Orientation
There are two train stations, Gara Suceava and Gara Suceava Nord, both a couple of km north of Piaţa 22 decembrie, the centre of town. From Gara Suceava take trolleybus No 2 to the centre of town, and from Gara Suceava Nord take bus No 1 or trolleybus No 5. The left-luggage office at Gara Suceava is at the information window on the main platform (open 24 hours). There's no left-luggage office at the bus station in the centre of town.

Information
The tourist office, Strada N Bălcescu 2, is beside Hotel Suceava on Piaţa 22 decembrie.

Motorists are assisted by the Automobil Clubul Român (☎ 10 997), Strada N Bălcescu, on the west side of the main post office.

Money Bucharest Exchange, in a kiosk directly behind the Casă de Cultură (weekdays 8 am to 8 pm, Saturday 9 am to 5 pm),

changes travellers' cheques without commission.

Post & Telecommunications The telephone centre in the main post office on Strada N Bălcescu is open daily from 7 am to 10 pm. Suceava's telephone code is 0987.

Travel Agencies The CFR Travel Agency, Strada N Bălcescu 8, is beside the Hotel Suceava.

The tourist office, Strada N Bălcescu 2, can arrange a car and driver at US$3 daily for the driver plus US$0.35 a km (minimum 100 km a day).

Things to See
The foundations of the 15th century **Princely Palace** are near the bus stop at Piaţa 22 decembrie. The large church beyond is **St Dumitru** (1535) with its massive bell tower, and nearby is the main Suceava vegetable market.

At Strada Ciprian Porumbescu 5, just west of Piaţa 22 decembrie, is the **Hanul Domnesc**, a princely 16th century guesthouse that is now the Ethnographical Museum (closed Monday). Its collection of folk costumes and photos is quite good.

Return to Piaţa 22 decembrie and follow Strada Ştefan cel Mare south past the park (Parcul Central) to the surprisingly informative **District Historical Museum**, Strada Ştefan cel Mare 33 (closed Monday). The presentation comes to an abrupt end at 1945 and old paintings now hang in the rooms which formerly glorified the communist era. The captions are only in Romanian.

Backtrack a little to the park and take Strada Mitropoliei south-east to the **Monastery of Sfintu Ioan cel Nou** (1522). The paintings on the outside of the church are badly faded, but they do give you an idea of the painted churches Bukovina is famous for.

Continue on Strada Mitropoliei, keeping left on the main road out of town, till you see a large wooden gate marked 'Parcul Cetatii' on the left. Go through it and, when the ways divide, follow the footpath with the park

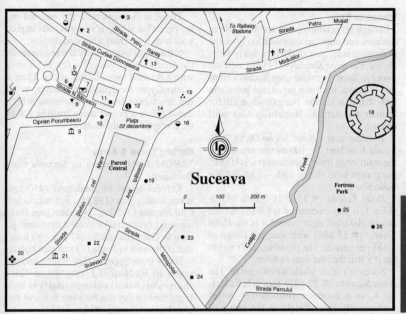

Suceava

0   100   200 m

PLACES TO STAY

4 Hotel Arcasul
11 Hotel Suceava
22 Hotel Bucovina
24 Hotels Balada & Tineret

PLACES TO EAT

2 Roti-Bar
8 Restaurant National
14 Restaurant Bucuresti

OTHER

1 Bus Station
3 Market
5 Synagogue
6 Automobil Clubul Român
7 Post Office
9 Hanul Domnesc
10 Casă de Cultura
12 Tourist Office
13 St Dumitru Church
15 Princely Palace Ruins

16 Buses to the Train Stations
17 Mirăuţi Church
18 Cetatea de Scaun
19 Municipal Theatre
20 Universal Department Store
21 District Historical Museum
23 Sfintu Ioan cel Nou Monastery
25 Statue of Ştefan cel Mare
26 Cemetery

benches around to the left to the huge **equestrian statue** (1966) of the Moldavian leader, Ştefan cel Mare. Twenty metres back on the access road to the monument is another footpath on the left which descends towards the **Cetatea de Scaun** (1388), a fortress which in 1476 held off Mehmed II, conqueror of Constantinople.

On the hillside opposite the fortress is **Mirăuţi Church** (1390), the original Moldavian coronation church, which was rebuilt in the 17th century. Get there by taking the path down through the park on the west (left) side of the fortress. Mirăuţi Church is only a short walk from your starting point.

Places to Stay

Although no private rooms are available in Suceava and other accommodation is on the expensive side, you do have a fairly large choice. *Camping Ștrand* (☎ 14 958), near the Suceava River, between Gara Suceava Nord and Suceava, has been privatised but it's in bad shape, with the bungalows unfit for human habitation. Hopefully this will change.

The five-storey *Hotel Socim* (☎ 58 297), Strada Jean Bart 24, 100 metres straight up the main street from Gara Suceava, is US$15 per person with shared bath – a lot for this basic place.

Hotel Balada (☎ 23 198), Strada Mitropoliei 1, is way overpriced at US$37 double (no singles), but right behind it is the *Hotel Tineret* (☎ 15 886) with spacious rooms at US$7 per person. The plumbing isn't so hot but it's still the best deal in town.

Suceava's other hotels are expensive. The *Hotel Suceava* (☎ 22 497), Strada N Bălcescu 4, is a modern four-storey hotel conveniently located right in the centre of everything. The 101 rooms with bath are US$23/33/42 single/double/triple, breakfast not included.

Hotel Arcașul (☎ 10 944), Strada Mihai Viteazul 4-6, is US$29/44 single/double with bath, and the 10-storey *Hotel Bucovina* (☎ 717 048), Strada Ana Ipătescu 5, charges US$27/42/59 single/double/triple with bath but without breakfast (hotel coupons accepted).

Places to Eat

Restaurant National, opposite the main post office (PTTR), is probably Suceava's most attractive restaurant and its terrace is fine for a beer if you have some time on your hands. There's no menu but the waiter may be willing to write out your bill in advance as you order. Only a few dishes are offered, but they're good value.

The *Restaurant București*, on the northeast corner of Piața 22 decembrie, serves basic meals to your table. Unfortunately there's no written menu here either, so try pointing at dishes you see on other tables.

The *Roti-Bar*, opposite the bus station, isn't great but at least it's easy as you can pick your own food from what's on display.

If these fail to please try the restaurant in the *Arcașul Hotel*, one of the few in Suceava with a detailed menu listing prices. There's often a Gypsy band playing for diners. Avoid the restaurant in *Hotel Bucovina* which doesn't have a proper menu, putting you at the mercy of greedy waiters.

Getting There & Away

TAROM flights operate to Suceava from Bucharest.

Express trains to Bucharest (450 km, seven hours), Iași (138 km, 1½ hours) and Cluj-Napoca (325 km, 7½ hours) are fairly regular. Local trains of interest to visitors go west to Gura Humorului (47 km, one hour) and north-west to Putna (73 km, two hours).

Buses from Suceava Bus Station include seven to Rădăuți (62 km), 10 to Gura Humorului (30 km) and one to Iași (141 km). Eight buses a day run between Suceava and Cernăuți in Ukraine (90 km, US$5).

PUTNA

Putna Monastery, founded in 1466, is still home to a very active religious community with groups of monks chanting mass just before sunset. A text posted just inside Putna's church reads:

The monastery of Putna, the first foundation of Stefan the Great, princely necropole and a real centre of Romanian culture through the centuries, represents a living testimony of the cultural and artistic traditions of the Romanian people and by that is a remarkable school of patriotism.

Stefan the Great himself is buried in the church. The large building behind the church contains a rich museum of medieval manuscripts and rare 15th century textiles. Place of honour goes to the *Tetraevanghel* of 1473, which has a portrait of the prince offering the book to the Virgin.

Places to Stay & Eat

Just outside the monastery gate is a large

ROMANIA

tourist complex with a medium-priced hotel that is open all year round. Adequate meals are served in the hotel restaurant. Beside the hotel are many small bungalows and a camping ground. These are open from May to mid-September.

Some people camp freelance in the field opposite the rock-hewn hermit's cave at Chilia near the train station. To get there, follow the river upstream to a wooden bridge which you cross, and then continue straight ahead. The spiritually inclined could ask special permission to stay in the monastery.

Getting There & Away
Local trains travel to Putna from Suceava eight times a day (73 km, two hours), making Putna Monastery one of the most accessible in Bukovina. The large monastic enclosure is at the end of the road, just under two km from the station.

You can hike the 20 km due south from Putna to Suceviţa Monastery in about four hours of steady going. Follow the trail marked with blue crosses in white squares which starts near the hermit's cave. About four km down the road you turn off to the left.

RĂDĂUŢI
This not very touristy town has several buses a day to Suceviţa Monastery. If you don't arrive in time for a convenient departure, take a bus to Marginea and walk or hitchhike the last nine km to the monastery.

Orientation
The bus station on Bulevardul Ştefan cel Mare is a block from Rădăuţi Railway Station on Strada Gării. The centre of town is an eight-minute walk from either of these stations.

The left-luggage office in the bus station is open until 8 pm. The left-luggage area at the train station is open 24 hours.

Information
There's a tourist office next to Hotel Nordic but it doesn't rent private rooms and is of little help.

Travel Agencies The CFR Travel Agency is behind Hotel Nordic, around the block.

Things to See
There's a **Muzeul Etnografik** opposite the hotel (open daily) which features local folk pottery and embroidered coats. In the central courtyard of the museum is a workshop where traditional pottery is made and items can be purchased.

The long park in the centre of town has a functioning Orthodox church at the south end and a functioning synagogue at the north end. A large market is held in Rădăuţi on Friday.

Places to Stay & Eat
Rădăuţi would be a good base from which to visit Arbor, Putna and Suceviţa if the accommodation situation were not so poor. The only hotel, the three-storey *Hotel Nordic* (☎ 0989-61 643), erected in 1910, Strada Piaţa Unirii in the centre of town, is US$19 double with shared bath (no singles).

The *Restaurant Nordic* around the corner from the hotel is the best Rădăuţi has to offer.

Getting There & Away
Buses from Rădăuţi include four a day to Suceava (62 km) and another four to Suceviţa (17 km), but none to Putna. Don't trust the departure times posted in the bus station – instead ask the friendly dispatcher in his office at the back of the building. Bus tickets are sold only an hour prior to departure.

SUCEVIŢA
Suceviţa is the largest and finest of the Bukovina monasteries. The church inside the fortified monastic enclosure (1586) is almost completely covered in frescoes inside and out. As you enter you first see the *Virtuous Ladder* fresco covering most of the north exterior wall, which depicts the 30 steps from hell to paradise (one step for each year of Christ's life). On the south exterior wall is a tree symbolising the continuity of the Old and New Testaments. The tree grows from the reclining figure of Jesse, who is flanked

by a row of ancient philosophers. To the left is the Virgin as a Byzantine princess, with angels holding a red veil over her head. Apart from the church, there's a small museum to visit at Sucevita Monastery.

It's worth spending a night here and doing a little hiking in the surrounding hills. The hill opposite the monastery offers a splendid view. Freelance camping is possible in the field at the foot of this hill, across the stream from the monastery. There's also the *Hanul Sucevita* (☎ 141), a restaurant about a km back towards Rădăuți, which offers rooms in the main two-storey building at US$14 per person and neat little cabins behind the hotel at US$6 per person. The Hanul's restaurant will sell you bread, cheese, tomatoes etc if you're planning a hike and it's open all year round. You could also ask around for a private room.

Getting There & Away

Sucevita is the most difficult monastery to reach on public transport. There are four buses from Rădăuți (17 km), one in the morning and three in the afternoon. Two daily buses connect Sucevita to Moldovita (36 km), one in the early morning and another around mid-afternoon. The west-bound highway winds up and over a high mountain pass, through forests which enclose both the Sucevita and Moldovita monasteries. It's possible to hike the 20 km north to Putna in about four hours.

MOLDOVITA

Moldovita Monastery (1532) is right in the middle of a quaint Romanian farming village with a life of its own. As at Sucevita, Moldovita consists of a strong fortified enclosure with towers and gates, and a magnificent painted church at its centre. Both monasteries are in the care of pious nuns and have undergone careful restoration in recent years.

Several of the paintings at Moldovita are unique. For example, on the south exterior wall of the church is a depiction of the defence of Constantinople in 626 against Persians dressed as Turks, and on the porch is a representation of the Last Judgment. Inside the sanctuary, on a wall facing the original carved iconostasis, is a portrait of Prince Petru Rareș (the founder) and his family offering the church to Christ. All of these works date from 1537. In the small museum at Moldovita Monastery is Petru Rareș' original throne.

Places to Stay & Eat

Popas Turistic (open mid-June to mid-September), between the train station and the monastery, has attractive little cabins with electric lighting at US$3 per person. You can also camp here. There's no running water at all, but you can draw water from the caretaker's well on his farm next door.

A simple restaurant in the Complex Commercial near the camping ground, on the road to Vama, serves *mititei* (grilled meat patties) and draught beer.

Getting There & Away

Moldovita Monastery is much easier to reach than Sucevita Monastery since it's right above Vatra Moldoviței Railway Station, on a 14-km branch line from Vama off the Suceava-Cluj main line. There are three trains a day in each direction.

GURA HUMORULUI

This small logging town, 36 km west of Suceava on the main railway line to Cluj-Napoca, is an ideal centre for visiting the monasteries. Most trains stop here and the adjacent train and bus stations are a seven-minute walk from the centre of town. The **Ethnographical Museum**, Bulevardul Bucovina 21 (closed Monday), is on the main street, east of the post office.

There are eight buses a day to the painted churches of Humor and Voroneț, each about six km from Gura Humorului. On Sunday, however, bus service is greatly reduced. The walk back to town from Voroneț is enjoyable, as you will pass many large farm houses. In summer both churches stay open until 8 pm.

There's no left-luggage office at the bus station.

Travel Agencies The CFR Travel Agency, Piaţa Republicii 10, is across the street from Cinema Lumina.

Things to See

Voroneţ The Last Judgment, which fills the entire west wall at Voroneţ, is perhaps the most marvellous, unified composition of all the frescoes on the Bukovina churches. At the top angels roll up the signs of the zodiac to indicate the end of time. The middle fresco shows humanity being brought to judgment. On the left St Paul escorts the believers, while on the right Moses brings forward the non-believers. From left to right the latter are Jews, Turks, Tatars, Armenians and Negroes – a graphic representation of the prejudices of the time. Below is the resurrection. Even the wild animals give back pieces of bodies to complete those rising from the graves. The sea also gives forth its victims.

At the top of the north wall is Genesis, from Adam and Eve on the left to Cain and Abel on the right. The south wall features another tree of Jesse with the genealogy of biblical personalities. In the vertical fresco to the left of this is the story of the martyrdom of St John of Suceava. This saint is buried in the Monastery of Sfintu Ioan cel Nou in Suceava. Inside, facing the iconostasis, is the famous portrait of Stefan the Great offering Voroneţ Church to Christ. This prince ordered that Voroneţ be erected in 1470, although the paintings date from 1547.

Humor At Humor (1530) the best paintings are on the church's south exterior wall. There's a badly faded depiction of the siege of Constantinople, with the parable of the return of the prodigal son beside it to the right. Notice the feast scene and five dancers. Above this is the devil as a woman (the figure with wings but no halo). On the porch is a painting of the Last Judgment and, in the first chamber inside the church, scenes of martyrdom. In the middle chamber is the tomb of Toader Bubuiog, who ordered the church be built, with his portrait (offering the church to Christ) just above and to the left of the tomb.

Places to Stay

The four-storey *Hotel Carpaţi* (☎ 0987-31 103), Strada 9 mai 3, the street beside the post office, has rooms for US$11 per person.

Otherwise try the *Cabana Ariniş* (☎ 0987-30 414) at the foot of the wooded hills, a km south of town (US$5 per person). Coming from the stations on foot, don't cross the river and enter town but follow the right embankment downstream till you reach a bridge at the entrance to Parc Dendrologic. Go through the park to a suspension bridge which leads directly to the cabana. By car the cabana is accessible from the Voroneţ road (turn left just south of the bridge) and you could easily walk from here to Voroneţ in under an hour. Many people camp freelance upstream from the cabana. Meals are served at the cabana and in the large terrace restaurant by the suspension bridge. This is a very nice area in which to stay.

Places to Eat

The two main restaurants in town are the *Moldova*, on the left just after the bridge as you come from the stations, and the *Bucovina*, on the right behind the cinema. Both are pretty dismal. You should at least be able to get a piece of cake at the *cofetăria* below Restaurant Moldova.

Getting There & Away

Gura Humorului is on the main railway line between Suceava and Cluj-Napoca. Buses from Gura Humorului include seven to Humor, eight to Voroneţ, one to Arbor and two to Rădăuţi. On weekends the service is greatly reduced. If you have limited time, you can bargain with taxi drivers here for tours to the monasteries.

Transylvania

To most people, the name Transylvania conjures up images of haunted castles, werewolves and vampires. Certainly the 14th century castles of Bran and Hunedoara appear ready-made for a Count Dracula movie, but Vlad Țepeș – Dracula – was a real prince who led Romanian resistance to Ottoman expansion in the 15th century. His habit of impaling slain Turkish foes on stakes may seem extreme, but Transylvania has had a tumultuous past.

For 1000 years, right up to WW I, Transylvania was associated with Hungary. In the 10th century a Magyar tribe, the Szeklers, settled here 'beyond the forest', followed in the 12th century by Saxon merchant-knights, invited in to help defend the eastern frontiers of Hungary. The seven towns the Saxons founded, Bistrița (Bistritz), Brașov (Kronstadt), Cluj-Napoca (Klausenburg), Mediaș (Mediasch), Sebeș (Muhlbach), Sibiu (Hermannstadt) and Sighișoara (Schässburg), gave Transylvania its German name, Siebenbürgen. Hungarians still number 1.7 million in Transylvania, and until recently 200,000 ethnic Germans were also present (most have now left for Germany). Scattered through the countryside around Sibiu and Sighișoara are many small villages which seem to have been lifted directly out of 19th century Germany.

Medieval Transylvania was an autonomous unit ruled by a prince responsible to the Hungarian crown. The indigenous Romanians were mere serfs whose presence is only noted in the chronicles in relation to peasant revolts. After the defeat of Hungary by the Turks in 1526, the region became independent in practice, while recognising Turkish suzerainty after 1566 (and paying tribute). This independence was maintained in the 17th century by playing the Ottoman sultan off against the Habsburg emperor.

In 1683 Turkish power was broken at the gates of Vienna and in 1687 Transylvania came under Habsburg rule. The Catholic Habsburg governors sought to control the territory by favouring first the Protestant Hungarians and Saxons, and then the Orthodox Romanians. In 1848, when the Hungarians revolted against the Habsburgs, the local Romanian population sided with the Austrians. After 1867, Transylvania was fully absorbed into Hungary to the dismay of the increasingly nationalist Romanians, who massed at Alba Iulia in 1918 to demand Transylvania's union with Romania.

Transylvania's absorption into Romania has never been fully accepted in Hungary and from 1940 to 1944 much of the region was annexed by fascist Hungary. After the war the communists put a tight lid on nationalist sentiments, but since 1989 rightist politicians in Hungary have attempted to score points by beating the Greater Hungary drum. Consequently the position of the large Hungarian minority in Transylvania remains a topic of controversy.

Although easily accessible from Hungary, the Transylvanian Plateau is still one of the travel frontiers of Europe. Facilities such as camping grounds, hotels, restaurants, trains and buses do exist, however, and aside from the enchanting old towns there are rugged mountains to climb all round. For lovers of medieval art and history, it's an unparalleled chance to escape the tourist hordes in Budapest and Prague and have an untamed corner of the old Austro-Hungarian empire all to themselves.

SINAIA

This well-known winter ski resort snuggles at an altitude of 800 to 930 metres in the narrow Prahova Valley sliced between the fir-clad Bucegi Mountains. Sinaia and nearby Bușteni are perfect starting points for summer hikes into the Bucegi Carpathians and in winter the Bucegi Plateau is a favourite cross-country ski area. Cable cars carry you effortlessly up to the crest from points on the main railway line between Bucharest and Brașov.

Although a monastery had existed here since the 17th century, Sinaia only developed into a major resort after King Carol I selected it as his summer residence in 1870 and had a railway built from Bucharest in 1879. The local elite soon followed suit, constructing imposing residences and villas along the wooded slopes. Until 1920 the Hungarian-Romanian border ran along Predeal Pass just north of Sinaia. For convenience this area has been included with Transylvania in this book even though it belongs with Wallachia.

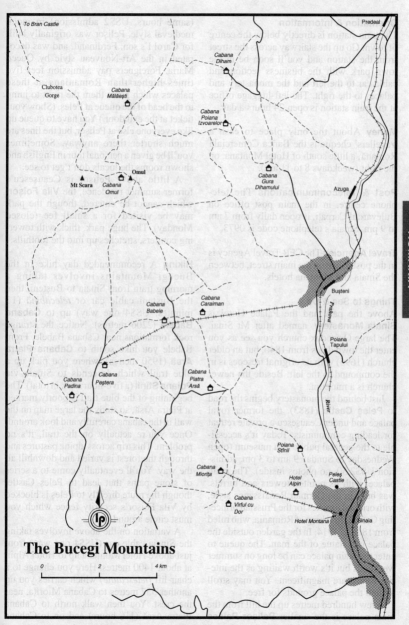

The Bucegi Mountains

0   2   4 km

To Bran Castle

Predeal

Clubotea Gorge

Cabana Diham

Cabana Mălăești

Cabana Poiana Izvoarelor

Omul

Mt Scara

Cabana Omul

Cabana Gura Dihamului

Azuga

Bușteni

Cabana Caraiman

Cabana Babele

Poiana Tapului

Cabana Padina

Cabana Peștera

Cabana Piatra Arsă

Prahova River

Poiana Stînii

Poiana Stînii

Cabana Miorița

Peleș Castle

Hotel Alpin

Cabana Virful cu Dor

Hotel Montana

Sinaia

Orientation & Information

The train station is directly below the centre of town. Go up the stairway across the street from the station and you'll soon be in the town park with the business section and cable car to the left and the monastery and palaces to the right. The left-luggage office at the train station is open 24 hours a day.

Money About the only place to cash a travellers' cheque is the Banca Comercială Romană, a little south of Hotel Montana, on the right (weekdays 8 to 11 am).

Post & Telecommunications The telephone centre, in the main post office on Bulevardul Carpați, is open daily from 7 am to 9 pm. Sinaia's telephone code is 0973.

Travel Agencies The CFR Travel Agency is in the post office on the main street, between the Sinaia and Montana hotels.

Things to See & Do

Above the park and the Palace Hotel is **Sinaia Monastery**, named after Mt Sinai. The large Orthodox church you see as you enter the town dates from 1846, but an older church (1695) with its original frescoes is in the compound to the left. Beside the newer church is a museum.

Just behind the monastery begins the road to **Peleş Castle** (1883), the former royal palace and under Ceauşescu a private retreat for leading communists. Today it's accessible to the general public as a museum (open Wednesday to Sunday 9 am to 3 pm, admission US$2.50, no photos inside). The main palace, with its pointed towers and turrets, was built in the German Renaissance style, with oriental touches for the Prussian princeling Carol I, first king of Romania, who ruled from 1866 to 1914. In the garden outside the palace is a statue of the man. The queue to enter the main palace can be long on summer weekends but it's worth waiting as the interior rooms are magnificent. You may stroll around the palace grounds for free.

A few hundred metres up the hill from the main palace is the smaller **Pelişor Palace**

(same hours, US$2 admission) in mock medieval style. Pelişor was originally built for Carol I's son, Ferdinand, and was decorated in the Art-Nouveau style by Queen Maria. Foreigners pay admission fees five times higher than Romanians at these palaces which gives them the right to jump to the head of the queue at Peleş. (Show your ticket at the exit door.) You have to queue up like everyone else at Pelişor, but the lines are much shorter there anyway. Sometimes you'll be given a personal tour in English and shown rooms the locals don't get to see.

A little above Pelişor is Ceauşescu's former summer residence, the **Vila Foişor**, which cannot be entered, though the park may be visited for a small fee (closed Monday). The huge park, thick with towering conifers, stretches up into the foothills.

Hiking A recommended day hike in the Bucegi Mountains involves taking a morning train from Sinaia to Buşteni, then the Buşteni cable car or *telecabină* (13 minutes, US$4 one way) up to **Cabana Babele** (2206 metres). Notice the strange rock formations near Cabana Babele. From Babele you hike south to **Cabana Piatra Arsă** (1950 metres), where you pick up a blue trail which descends to Sinaia via **Poiana Stînii** (a five-hour walk in total). The beginning of the blue trail is poorly marked at Piatra Arsă, so study the large map on the wall in the cabana carefully and look around. Once you're actually on the trail, it's no problem. This trip across alpine pastures and through the forest is varied and downhill all the way. You'll eventually come to a series of stone paths that lead to Peleş Castle, though the route directly to Peleş is blocked by Vila Foişor's security fence which you must circle around.

A variation on the above involves taking the Sinaia cable car (US$4 one way) from just above Hotel Montana up to Hotel Alpin at about 1400 metres. Here you change to a chair lift *(telescaune)* which carries you up another 557 metres to Cabana Mioriţa, near the crest. You then walk north to Cabana Piatra Arsă (1½ hours) and on to Cabana

Babele (another hour), where there's a second cable car (US$4 one way) back down to the railway at Buşteni. The main disadvantage of this route is that you have to use two cable cars and they don't operate every day (see the section Getting Around which follows). At last report the Mioriţa chair lift was closed.

To Bran Castle A more ambitious expedition into the Carpathian Mountains involves taking one of the two cable cars mentioned above up to the mountain crest and hiking north-west across the mountains all the way to Bran Castle, where there are buses to Braşov. You can do this in one strenuous day if you get an early start from Babele, but it's preferable to take two days and spend a night at Cabana Omul.

As you look north from Babele, you'll see a red-and-white TV transmitter on a hill top, which looks like a rocket about to take off. To the right of this is a trail marked with a cross which leads to a large monument that offers a great view of Buşteni (45 minutes each way from Babele). To the left is a yellow-marked trail which leads to **Cabana Omul** (two hours) right on the summit (2505 metres). North of Babele the scenery gets better, with great drops into valleys on either side. Accommodation is usually available at Omul on dormitory platforms with mattresses, and meals (soup, bread and omelette) are served, but it's best to bring some food and water. Although blankets are provided, a sleeping bag would be useful here as the gas heater is turned off as soon as you're asleep. There are good views on all sides from Omul, and the sunsets and sunrises are great.

To go from Omul to Bran Castle takes five hours or more and involves a tough 2000-metre drop. (To climb up from Bran Castle to Omul would be murder!) The trail is easy to follow, as it has yellow triangle markers, and chances are that you and the mountain goats will have this surprisingly beautiful landscape all to yourselves. From Omul you begin by crossing Mt Scara (2422 metres) and you then begin the descent down the

Ciubotea Gorge. Your legs will remember this trip for many days! After a couple of hours you come out on a logging road beside a river (wash up!), which you follow for two hours right down to Bran Castle. If it's getting late, you can camp in the forest here. This invigorating hike is a great way to experience the mountains with few of the logistical problems you'll encounter elsewhere.

Places to Stay

Camping There's a *camping ground* at Izvorul Rece, four km south of central Sinaia, but only three buses a day go there from a stop on Bulevardul Carpaţi just south of Hotel Montana.

If you don't have your own transport, a better bet is to ask permission to camp in the front yard of house No 26 right next to the lower cable car station at Sinaia. Many people camp freelance in the fields around the lower cable car station near Hotel Silva at Buşteni.

Camping Fulg de Nea at Predeal is a five-minute walk from Predeal Railway Station, and you can see the tents from the train on the right-hand side, just before Predeal as you arrive from Sinaia. The road to the chair lift up Mt Clăbucet begins here. Don't expect much in the way of facilities.

Mountain Huts You can also stay at *Cabana Babele* (☎ 973-311 751, interior extension 329) and *Cabana Piatra Arsă* (☎ 973-311 751, interior extension 334), mentioned under Hiking above. You'll pay anywhere from US$2 to US$10 per person, depending on whether you get a bed in a double room or stay in the dormitory at the tourist or local price. Cabana Piatra Arsă is a large, modern chalet offering better accommodation than Cabana Babele – it may look closed when it's actually not. Both of the above (and Cabana Mioriţa further south) serve inexpensive meals and drinks.

On weekends the cabanas become crowded with young people from Bucharest and some places even have discos, so it's a good opportunity to meet people and have

ROMANIA

fun. Arrive by Thursday as the double rooms fill quickly, though you'll usually be able to squeeze in to the dormitory.

Private Rooms Women renting private rooms frequent the train station. Hang around looking confused for a few minutes and you'll probably be approached. At about US$4 a double, the price is right.

Hotels There are two modern, high-rise hotels on Bulevardul Carpaţi, both with indoor swimming pools and saunas. *Hotel Sinaia* (☎ 311 551), opposite Cinema Perla, is US$27/42/50 single/double/triple with bath, while *Hotel Montana* (☎ 12 751), near the cable car, is US$19/33/41 single/double/triple with bath.

Both of the above places accept hotel coupons, but you're better off spending your coupon at the luxury-category *Hotel Palace* (☎ 312 051), Strada Octavian Goga, founded in 1911. Without a coupon, the Palace's old-world elegance costs US$48/61 single/double in a three-star room with one large bed, breakfast included. The Touring ACR representative at Hotel Palace sells hotel coupons.

The old *Hotel Caraiman* (☎ 313 551), across the park from the Hotel Palace, is US$30/38 single/double in a room with a shower and one bed, US$50 twin (coupons accepted).

Places to Eat
There's a basic self-service restaurant in *Hotel Montana*. You enter the restaurant from the road which leads up to the cable car station.

Pizza Carpaţi, attached to Magazin Central across the street from Hotel Montana, has a more pleasant atmosphere than the Hotel Montana self-service and it even has a type of cheese pastry for vegetarians.

Visit the colourful open-air market on Piaţa Unirii, the street descending towards the railway line from Hotel Montana. Several places to eat, drink and change money (cash only) are here.

The restaurant in *Hotel Sinaia* is good to fall back on if none of the other places meets your fancy. The service here is usually fine. The *Palace Hotel* restaurant is about 50% more expensive than the one in Hotel Sinaia, if you want to splurge.

Entertainment
Check out the *Disco Club* in Hotel Montana or *Blue Angel Disco* directly across the street.

Getting There & Away
Sinaia is on the main railway line from Bucharest to Braşov – 126 km from the former and 45 km from the latter. All express trains between Bucharest and Transylvania stop here, and local trains to Buşteni (eight km), Predeal (19 km) and Braşov are quite frequent.

Getting Around
The cable cars at both Sinaia and Buşteni operate all year, but the one at Sinaia is closed on Monday. At Buşteni they close on Tuesday. Neither cable car will run if fewer than 20 passengers are present. Both charge foreigners US$4 one way and stop operating at 4 pm. With prices having sharply increased the lines are a lot shorter than they used to be.

BRAŞOV
Braşov (Brassó) is a pleasant medieval town flanked by verdant hills on both sides. The original German mercantile colony was protected by the walls of old Kronstadt (now Braşov). The Romanians lived at Scheii, just outside the walls to the south-west of the town. Strategically situated at the meeting point of three principalities, Braşov was a major medieval trading centre.

Contemporary Braşov is Romania's second-largest city, although it's still only one-sixth the size of Bucharest. Today the city's tractor, truck and textile factories have more importance than commerce, and endless rows of concrete apartment blocks have risen to house the proletariat. Fortunately, these buildings are far enough away not to spoil the charm of Braşov's quaint old town.

Orientation

The train station is to the north-east, far from the centre of town, so take bus No 4 (buy your ticket at the kiosk) to Parcul Central if you're looking for a hotel or to the Black Church if you're sightseeing. Strada Republicii, Braşov's pedestrian promenade, is crowded with shops and cafés from Parcul Central to Piaţa Sfatului. At the train station, the left-luggage office (open 24 hours) is in the underpass that leads out from the tracks.

Information

The tourist information office is in the lobby of the Aro Palace Hotel, Bulevardul Eroilor 25, on Parcul Central.

The Touring ACR desk (☎ 118 920) in Hotel Capitol can provide assistance for motorists.

For concerts and theatre, ask for details at the theatre ticket agency, Strada Republicii 4, just off Piaţa Sfatului.

Money Bucharest Exchange Office 181, next to the self-service restaurant below Hotel Capitol (weekdays 8 am to 8 pm, Saturday 9 am to 6 pm, Sunday 9 am to 2 pm), changes travellers' cheques without commission but for the low official rate.

The Banca Romană de Comerţ Exterior, Strada Republicii 20 (weekdays 9 am to noon), changes travellers' cheques at a slightly better rate than Bucharest Exchange but deducts 1.5% commission.

Post & Telecommunications Braşov's telephone centre is on Bulevardul Eroilor between the Capitol and Aro Palace hotels (daily 7 am to 9 pm). Braşov's telephone code is 0921.

Travel Agencies The CFR Travel Agency is at Strada Republicii 53, opposite the Hotel Postăvarul. This is a good place to pick up an open international train ticket (valid two months).

Things to See

In the middle of Piaţa Sfatului is the town hall (1420), now the **Historical Museum** (closed Monday). The 58-metre Trumpeter's Tower above the building dates from 1582. The Gothic **Black Church** (1384-1477), still used by German Lutherans, looms just south of the square. The church's name comes from its appearance after a fire in 1689. As you walk around the building to the entrance, you'll see statues on the exterior of the apse. The originals are now inside at the back of the church, and Turkish rugs hang from every balcony. In summer, recitals are given on the 1839 organ at 6 pm on Tuesday, Thursday and Saturday (US$0.25). The church is closed to sightseers on Sunday.

Go south-west a little to the neoclassical **Schei Gate** (1828), then walk 500 metres up Strada Prundului to Piaţa Unirii. As soon as you pass through Schei Gate the urban landscape changes from the sober rows of Teutonic houses lining the streets of the old town to the lighter, separate houses of the Romanian settlement. On Piaţa Unirii you'll find the black-spired Orthodox Church of **St Nicolae din Scheii** (1595). Beside the church is the **First Romanian School Museum** which houses a collection of icons, paintings on glass, old manuscripts, and so on. The clock tower (1751) was financed by Elizabeth, empress of Russia. There's a picturesque cemetery opposite.

Go back as you came and turn right before Schei Gate to reach the 16th century **Weaver's Bastion**, which is a little hidden above the sports field. This corner fort on the old city walls has a museum with a fascinating scale model of Braşov as it was in the 17th century. The model itself was created in 1896. Above the bastion is a pleasant promenade through the forest overlooking the town. Halfway along you'll come to the **Timpa Cablecar** (open daily until 8 pm in summer, closed Monday in winter, US$1.50), which rises from 640 metres to

ROMANIA

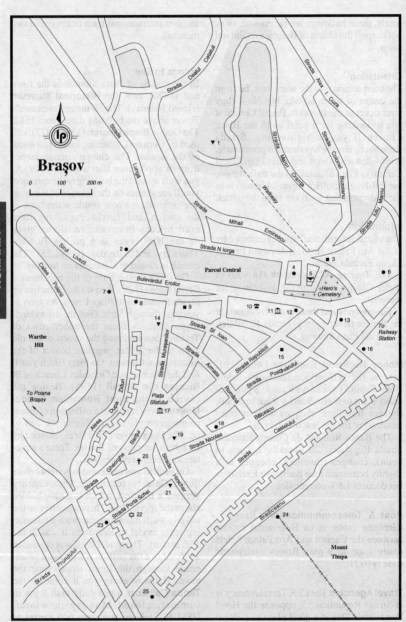

Braşov

0   100   200 m

ROMANIA

960 metres, offering a stunning view of the entire area.

The **Art Gallery**, Bulevardul Eroilor 21, next to the Hotel Capitol, has a good Romanian collection upstairs.

Prejmer Prejmer (Taertlauer) is an unspoilt Saxon town with a picturesque 15th century citadel surrounding the 13th century Gothic church in its centre. The 275 small cells on four levels lining the inner citadel wall were intended to house the local population during sieges. It makes an interesting side trip from Braşov but there are only about four local trains during the day, so careful planning is required to avoid being stuck there for hours.

To reach Prejmer Citadel (Cetatea Prejmer), 16 km north-east of Braşov, take a train to Ilieni on the line to Ciceu. As you arrive at Ilieni Railway Station from Braşov look for the high pointed tower of the citadel church to the right (south) of the railway line. Walk south on Strada Nouă about 500 metres, then left on Strada Alexandru Ioan Cuza which you follow to the end. Turn left to reach Strada Scolii on the right which will bring you directly to the citadel.

Places to Stay

Private Rooms & Camping If you want a private room, go to the Biroul de Cazari EXO, Strada Postăvarului 6 (Monday to Saturday 11 am to 8 pm, Sunday 11 am to 2 pm). Their rooms average US$7 to US$13 per person. Women on the street outside the Aro Palace, Capitol and Postăvarul hotels also offer private rooms. You'll usually have no problem finding a private room in Braşov and it's definitely the cheapest way to go.

The most convenient camping ground around Braşov is at Rîşnov (see the Rîşnov & Bran section which follows).

Hotels The only medium-priced hotel is the *Aro Sport Hotel* (☎ 142 840), Strada Sf Ioan 3, behind the Aro Palace Hotel (from US$21/34 single/double with shared bath). *Hotel Parc* (☎ 119 460), Strada N Iorga 2, is greatly overpriced at US$29/54 single/double with bath.

Of the 1st-class hotels, the one with the most character is the *Hotel Postăvarul* (☎ 144 330), Strada Republicii 62 (from US$55/70 single/double with bath), founded in 1906. Beware of being given a lower-category room with shared bath in the annexe. (We've received complaints about this.)

The Postăvarul is often full in summer, in which case you'll be sent to the nearby high-rise *Hotel Capitol* (☎ 118 920), at Bulevardul Eroilor 19, with singles/doubles for US$62/71. Ask for a room on one of the top floors at the Capitol as it's rather noisy and smelly on the lower floors. Both hotels accept hotel coupons. (If you don't have any coupons you can pick them up at the Touring ACR desk in Hotel Capitol.)

Places to Eat

The easiest place to eat is *Autoservire* below Hotel Capital, Bulevardul Eroilor 19, though the food tends to be cold and it's not especially cheap.

Crama Postăvarul on Strada Republicii, opposite the Hotel Postăvarul, is a wine cellar that serves typical Romanian dishes. Go back to the kitchen at the rear and pick what you want from the pots. It's a bit of a dive but the food and drink are cheap, there's often local music and all sorts of local characters and drunks. Great atmosphere.

Istanbul Impex, Strada Republicii 22, has the best fresh bagels in Braşov.

Braşov's most famous restaurant is the *Cerbul Carpaţin* in Hirscher House (1545), Piaţa Sfatului 12. There's a wine cellar that opens from 7 pm to 2 am, and a large restaurant upstairs that serves meals from 11 am to 11 pm. The folklore programme downstairs at the Cerbul Carpaţin is daily except Monday at 10 pm (US$1.50 cover charge).

Sirena Gustari, Piaţa Sfatului 14, next to the Cerbul Carpaţin, offers good food and service for a reasonable price and you can eat outside on the square.

The expensive *Restaurant Chinezesc*, also on Piaţa Sfatului, is good for a change from the bland international cuisine often served up in Romania. Appealing features include the authentic Oriental décor, excellent service, menus in English and German and the choice of wines. There's even a selection of fish and vegetable dishes. Be prepared to find several unexpected extras added to your bill, however, including a 12% service charge and a fee for the condiments on the table.

Restaurantul Nemaco is a cheap restaurant on the corner of Strada Porta Schei and Strada Hirscher.

Dessert *Casata*, Piaţa Sfatului 12, is the place to go for coffee and ice cream. Ice-cream freaks can also pig out at *Mamma Mia*, Strada Mureşenilor 25.

Entertainment

Two of Braşov's best discos are near the County Library: *Number One Disco*, next to Cinema Astra (Tuesday to Sunday 8 pm to 4 am), and the *Student Club*, beside Transylvania University, Bulevardul Eroilor 29 (Tuesday to Sunday 7 pm to 2 am).

Getting There & Away

Braşov is well connected to Bucharest (166 km, three hours), Sighişoara (128 km, two hours), Cluj-Napoca (331 km, six hours) and Oradea (484 km, eight hours) by fast trains. Local trains to/from Sinaia (45 km, one hour) are fairly frequent. Local trains along the line from Braşov to Sibiu (149 km, four hours) drop off hikers headed for the Făgăraş Mountains. The *Corona* express runs overnight between Braşov and Budapest-Nyugati (783 km, 14 hours) via Oradea.

Private buses marked 'Moeciu' direct to Rîşnov and Bran leave from in front of the County Library every hour on the hour (US$0.25, pay the driver).

POIANA BRAŞOV

Take bus No 20 from the Biblioteca Judeteana (County Library) at the western end of Parcul Central in Braşov to the winter ski resort of Poiana Braşov (1020 metres), which is 13 km away. From Poiana Braşov you can reach the **Postăvarul Massif** (1799 metres) on the Telecabina Teleferic Cable Car which operates daily all year round (US$4 one way, US$7 return for foreigners). There's a splendid view of the Carpathian Mountains from the summit.

From Postăvarul it's possible to hike down to Timişu de Jos Railway Station on the line from Sinaia to Braşov in four hours. Otherwise hike back down to Poiana Braşov via Cabana Cristianul Mare and Cabana Postăvarul in under two hours. A direct nine-km road links Poiana Braşov to Rîşnov, a pleasant downhill walk.

Places to Stay & Eat

Hotel coupons are accepted at the huge *Ciucaş* (☎ 262 111) and *Piatra Mare* (☎ 262 226) hotels and the smaller *Hotel Bradul*. Without coupons the Piatra Mare is US$42/53 single/double.

The *Cabana Cristianul Mare* (☎ 186 545), below the upper cable-car terminus at 1704 metres altitude, offers beds in rooms with two to 10 beds at US$5 per person. This large wooden chalet is open all year round, though it closes in November for annual maintenance. People sometimes camp free in the cow pasture just below Cristianul Mare.

Fifteen minutes back down the hill from Cristianul Mare is the cheaper *Cabana Postăvarul* (☎ 186 356), at 1602 metres altitude, which has a better atmosphere than Cristianul Mare with fewer cable-car tourists. Meals are served at both cabanas but all the beds are sometimes taken.

The *Restaurantul Şura Dacilor*, just beyond the west end of the small lake in the centre of Poiana Braşov, between the hotels Caraiman and Teleferic, is a picturesque folkloric restaurant with a pleasant outdoor terrace.

RÎŞNOV & BRAN

Both Rîşnov and Bran, in the foothills southwest of Braşov, on the main road to Piteşti, are well known for their castles. It's hard to visit Romania without seeing Bran Castle in travel brochures or on postcards. The tour buses rarely visit Rîşnov Castle, which is less accessible than Bran Castle.

Rîşnov

Rîşnov offers the dual attraction of a ruined castle (closed Monday) and a convenient camping ground. From the train station, you'll see the large 14th century castle on a distant hill top. To reach it, climb up the stairs behind the Casă de Cultură on Piaţa Unirii, about a km up Strada Republicii from the station.

The camping ground, *Camping Valea Cetatii* (☎ 092-186 346), is directly below Rîşnov Castle on the road to Pioana Braşov, less than a km from Piaţa Unirii or about two km from the bus stop to/from Braşov. There are 30 neat little cabins at US$5 per person and camping is US$2.50 per tent. This central camping ground is a good base from which to visit Bran Castle, Braşov and even

Pioana Braşov, but it's reliably open from June to August only.

Nearby is the *Cabana Cetate Rîşnov* (☎ 092-230 266), a modern restaurant/hotel next to a large public swimming pool. The six rooms with bath are US$19 per person (open all year round).

Bran

Bran Castle (1378) originated as a toll station erected by the German merchants of Braşov to regulate trade between Transylvania and Wallachia. Though this fairy-tale castle is impressive in itself, don't be taken in by tales that Bran is Count Dracula's castle as it's unlikely the real Vlad Ţepeş ever stayed here. In his 1897 novel, Bram Stoker placed Dracula's castle far away on the Tihuta Pass in northern Romania, exactly halfway between Cluj-Napoca and Suceava (there's nothing to see there other than a garish hotel, custom-built on a ridge for Dracula freaks).

Still, it's fun to run through Bran Castle's 57 newly restored rooms (if the crowds aren't too thick). The best thing about it is that you're not forced to join a group and endure a monologue in Romanian, but may wander around at will. Beside the entrance to the castle is an ethnographic village museum with a collection of Transylvanian farm buildings. Your ticket (US$0.75) admits you to the farmhouses, the castle and the Vama Bran Museum below the castle (all open 9 am to 4 pm, closed Monday).

Places to Stay & Eat

You can camp free in the field across the stream from the Vama Bran Museum, just below the castle.

Cabana Bran Castel (☎ 092-236 404), a rustic chalet on the hillside about 600 metres from the castle, provides accommodation at US$8/12 single/double, or US$5 per person in a three-or four-bed room, US$3.50 per person in a five-bed room. Meals are served and it's open all year round, but in summer it's often full.

The old *Hotel Bran* (☎ 092-236 556), two blocks from the castle, has rooms at US$11

ROMANIA

per person. The front terrace is a good place for a meal.

Getting There & Away

Getting to Bran Castle on public transport used to be a major hassle involving a local train from Braşov to Rîşnov (seven daily, 16 km), then an infrequent bus on to Bran (another 12 km). Now Bran and Rîşnov are easily accessible from Braşov, with private buses departing from central Braşov every hour on the hour (departing from Bran for Braşov on the half-hour).

SIGHIŞOARA

Sighişoara (Schässburg), birthplace of Vlad Ţepeş, is a perfectly preserved medieval town in beautiful hilly countryside. No less than 11 towers remain on Sighişoara's intact city walls, inside which are sloping cobbled streets lined with 16th century burgher houses and untouched churches. All trains between Bucharest and Budapest (via Oradea) pass here, so watch for it from the window if you're foolish enough not to get off. Many readers have written in saying this was their favourite town in Romania.

Orientation

Follow Strada Gării south from the train station to the Soviet war cemetery, where you turn left to the large Orthodox church. Cross the Tîrnava Mare River on the footbridge here and take Strada Morii to the left, then keep going right, all the way up to Piaţa Hermann Oberth and the old town. Many of the facilities you'll want to use are found along a short stretch of Strada 1 decembrie to the left off Strada Morii.

The left-luggage office and information share premises on the main platform at the train station (open 24 hours).

Information

The OJT tourist office is at Strada 1 decembrie 10, beside the Steaua Hotel.

Money The Banca Comercială Romană, Strada Justiţiei 7 (weekdays 8 to 11 am),

changes travellers' cheques for 3% commission.

Bucharest Exchange Office 121, Piaţa Hermann Oberth 1 (weekdays 8 am to 8 pm, Saturday 9 am to 1 pm), changes travellers' cheques for the usual official rate, but gives a much better rate for cash.

Post & Telecommunications

The telephone centre, in the main post office on Piaţa Hermann Oberth, is open daily from 7 am to 9.30 pm. Sighişoara's telephone code is 0950.

Travel Agencies

You can buy tickets for express trains at the CFR Travel Agency, Strada 1 decembrie 2.

Things to See

The first tower you reach above Piaţa Hermann Oberth is the massive **clock tower** on Piaţa Muzeului. The 1648 clock still keeps time and the 14th century tower is now a **museum** (closed Monday) with a very good collection of local artefacts, a scale model of the town and a superb view from the walkway on top. Note the photos of the 1989 revolution at the top of the first stairs. Next to the tower is the **monastery church** (1515), which has a collection of Oriental rugs hanging on each side of the nave (usually closed). Nearby on Piaţa Muzeului is the house in which Vlad Ţepeş, second son of Vlad Dracul, was born in 1431, now a restaurant. (See Places to Eat following.) A house between the restaurant and the clock tower contains a small collection of firearms and a small Dracula exhibition (closed Monday).

Piaţa Cetăţii, complete with benches and fine old houses, is the heart of old Sighişoara. Go left up Strada Şcolii from the square to the 172 steps of the **Covered Stairway** (1642). This leads to the Gothic **Bergkirche** (1345) with its frescoes of knights in armour rescuing damsels in distress. The old German tombstones in the church and adjacent **cemetery** are fascinating.

Sighişoara

0   125   250 m

1	Railway Station
2	Bus Station
3	Soviet War Cemetery
4	Orthodox Church
5	Piaţa Cetăţii
6	Vlad Dracul's House
7	Clock Tower & Museum
8	Steaua Hotel
9	CFR Travel Agency
10	Bergkirche
11	Post Office
12	Banca Comercială Romană

Strada Libertăţii

Strada Gării

Strada Nicolae Titulescu

Târnava Mare River

Strada

3

Strada G Lazar

Strada

Andrei Şaguna

✝ 4

Şoseaua Mihai Viteazul

Strada

Strada Zaharie Boiu

Morii

Horia Teculescu

Bastionul

Strada Anton Pann

Strada Scolii

5
6

7

Strada 1 decembrie

■ 8

ℹ 9

✝ 10

Piaţa
Hermann
Oberth

✉ 11

ℹ 12

ROMANIA

Places to Stay

Camping You can camp on a hill top above the town, but it's a stiff half-hour hike up from the train station. Walk east along the train tracks to a bridge, then cross the tracks and turn left to a road leading up. At the end of this road is the *Dealul Gării Restaurant* (☎ 71 046), where you can camp or rent a bungalow. The bungalows (US$10 double) are OK, but facilities for those staying in tents are poor to nonexistent.

There's a better camping ground at Hula Daneş (☎ 71 052), but it's four km out of town on the road to Mediaş, with 11 buses a day marked 'Cris' from the *autogară* (bus terminal) beside the train station. Bungalows cost US$9 double and the site is not crowded.

Private Rooms & Hotel The OJT tourist office, Strada 1 decembrie 10 (open weekdays 8 am to 3.30 pm), can supply the address of a private home where you can rent a room for about US$12 double.

The *Steaua Hotel* (☎ 71 594), Strada 1 decembrie 12 (from US$13/23/33 single/double/triple without bath, US$16/28/40 with bath), is Sighişoara's only hotel. This comfortable 1st-class hotel takes hotel coupons, but it's much cheaper to pay in cash. The Steaua does fill up, so it might be wise to call ahead for a reservation. The TV sets in every room make for some noise.

Places to Eat

Dracula freaks can indulge their ghoulish hunger by dining in Vlad Dracul's house in the upper town, now a good restaurant upstairs and *berarie* (pub) downstairs. The Vlad Dracul does have a typewritten Romanian menu, but everything on it is only available in the evening. Insist on seeing it anyway. Most readers report eating very well in there! There's also a restaurant at the Steaua Hotel.

A self-service restaurant open weekdays from 8 am to 4 pm only is at Piaţa Hermann Oberth 34. A cheap beer bar is next door and there's an adjacent pastry shop.

Entertainment

Try *Super Sound Disco* across the street from the post office on Piaţa Hermann Oberth.

Getting There & Away

All trains between Braşov and Cluj-Napoca stop at Sighişoara. For Sibiu (95 km) you'll probably have to change trains at Mediaş or Copşa Mică.

From the adjacent bus station there's one very early morning bus to Sibiu (92 km) and another to the town of Făgăras (86 km), but most other services are of no interest.

SIBIU

Sibiu is just far enough off the beaten track to be spared the tourist tide that occasionally engulfs Braşov. Founded in the 12th century on the site of the former Roman village of Cibinium, Sibiu (Hermannstadt) has always been one of the leading cities of Transylvania. Destroyed by the Tatars in 1241, the town was later surrounded by strong walls which enabled the citizens to resist the Turks. Under the Habsburgs from 1703 to 1791 and again from 1849 to 1867, Sibiu served as the seat of the Austrian governors of Transylvania. Much remains from this colourful history and Sibiu is also a gateway to the

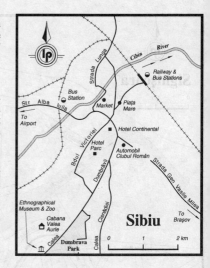

Făgăraş Mountains, Romania's best hiking area.

Orientation

The adjacent bus and train stations are near the centre of town. The left-luggage office at Sibiu Railway Station is clearly marked at the west end of the main platform (open 24 hours). Stroll up Strada General Magheru four blocks to Piaţa Mare, the historic centre. From the opposite corner of the square, Strada Nicolae Bălcescu continues south-west to Piaţa Unirii, another focal point.

Information

The ONT tourist office is in the lobby of Hotel Bulevard on Piaţa Unirii.

The Automobil Clubul Român (☎ 47 259), Strada General Vasile Milea 13, is two blocks east of Hotel Continental.

Money The Banca Comercială Romană, Strada Mitropoliei 16, next to the post office (weekdays 8.30 to 11.30 am), changes travellers' cheques for US$3 commission.

Post & Telecommunications Sibiu's telephone centre is at Strada Nicolae Bălcescu

13 (daily 7 am to 10 pm). Sibiu's telephone code is 092.

Travel Agencies The CFR Travel Agency is at Strada Nicolae Bălcescu 6, next to the Împăratul Romanilor Hotel.

Bookshops The Librărie Dacia Traian, Piaţa Mare 7, often stocks useful Romanian maps and guidebooks.

A map of the Făgăraş Mountains is sold at Librărie Mihai Eminescu, Strada N Bălcescu 11.

Things to See

Central Sibiu is a perfectly preserved medieval monument, and there's no better place to begin your visit than at the top of the council tower (1588) on Piaţa Mare, now the **City Historical Museum** (closed October to April and every Monday). The old maps and photos complement the view of red roofs, with the Făgăraş Mountains beckoning to the south.

After this visual treat, walk along the square past the Baroque **Catholic cathedral** (1728) to the **Brukenthal Museum** (closed Monday), the oldest and finest art gallery in Romania. Founded in 1817, the museum is in the aristocratic Baroque palace (1785) of Baron Samuel Brukenthal, former governor of Transylvania. Apart from the paintings, there are excellent archaeological and folk-art collections housed in the same building. Note especially the folk paintings on glass. Pick up the handy guide booklet to all of Sibiu's museums here. Just west along Strada Samuel Brukenthal is the **Primaria Municipiului** (1470), now a historical museum (closed Monday).

Nearby on Piaţa Griviţa is another of Sibiu's many highlights, the Gothic **Evangelical church** (1300-1520), its great five-pointed tower visible from afar. As you enter, you will see four magnificent Baroque funerary monuments on the upper nave, and the organ with 6002 pipes (1772). The tomb of Mihnea Vodă cel Rău, son of Vlad Ţepeş (Dracula) is in the closed-off section behind the organ. This prince, who ruled Wallachia

from 1507 to 1510, was murdered on the square in front of the church after attending a service in March 1510. His name translates 'Prince Mihnea the Bad' in English. Don't miss the fresco of the Crucifixion (1445) up in the sanctuary – a splendid work. The church opens weekdays from 9 am to 1 pm, and from July to September organ concerts are held on Wednesday at 6 pm.

From here you have the choice of going down the 13th century **Staircase Passage**, on the opposite side of the church from where you entered, into the lower town, which is thick with local characters and popular scenes. Also extremely picturesque is nearby Piaţa Mică with its **Iron Bridge** (1859), popularly known as the 'Liar's Bridge' because it is thought it will collapse if anyone tells a lie while standing on it.

Continue south-west along Strada Mitropoliei to the **Orthodox cathedral** (1906), a monumental building styled after the Hagia Sofia in Istanbul. Strada Tribunei, around the corner to the left, will lead to Piaţa Unirii, where you'll find the beginning of a pleasant walk north-east along a section of the 16th century **city walls**.

If you've got an extra afternoon, it's worth taking in the **Museum of Popular Techniques** (open May to October, Tuesday to Sunday 10 am to 6 pm) in Dumbrava Park (take trolleybus No T1 from the station to get there). A great number of authentic old rural buildings and houses have been reassembled around several lakes in the park to create an open-air ethnographical museum. Ask about guided tours of the site in English. At the Dumbrava **zoo** here you can hire a boat and row yourself around the lake.

If you've got an extra day, take a bus 32 km south-west to the winter ski resort of **Păltiniş** (1450 metres altitude) from where there are many hiking trails into the Cindrel Mountains.

Places to Stay

Camping There are two camping grounds near Sibiu. The closest is *Popas Turistic* (☎ 422 831), beside the Hanul Dumbrava Restaurant, four km south-west of town (take

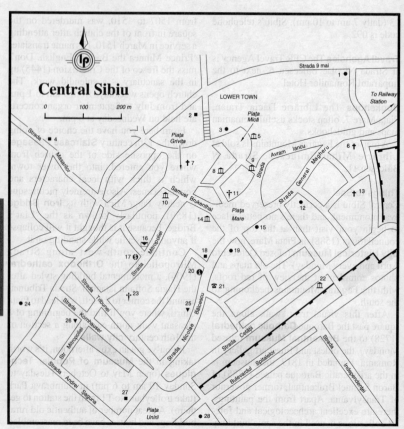

Central Sibiu

0   100   200 m

LOWER TOWN

To Railway Station

Strada 9 mai

Piaţa Mică

Piaţa Griviţa

Piaţa Mare

Piaţa Unirii

Avram Iancu

Samuel Brukenthal

Strada Mitropoliei

Str. Mitropoliei

Strada Tribunei

Strada Kornhauser

Strada Andrei Şaguna

Strada Nicolae Bălcescu

Strada General Magheru

Strada Cetăţii

Bulevardul Spitalelor

Strada Independenţei

---

trolleybus No T1 from the train station direct to the site). They have 204 rooms in worn-out little cabins with damp cardboard-thin walls spread around the grounds at US$13 single or double. Camping on their shady lawn (own tent) is US$10 for one to three persons. There's plenty of space and it's open from June to September. Bring insect repellent.

Fourteen km north of Sibiu on the railway line to Copşa Mică is Băile Ocna Sibiului, with a large camping ground in the forest. The camping ground is right next to the station and all trains stop here. The many natural pools and geological curiosities around Ocna Sibiului make it a popular bathing resort. The Lacul Fără Fund (Bottomless Lake) here is the flooded shaft of a former salt mine.

Private Rooms To find a private room, try the small office marked *'birou de cazare'* (☎ 417 971) in the passageway at Strada Nicolae Bălcescu 1, just off Piaţa Mare (open 2 to 10 pm). The sign on the street says *'rooms – camere de inchiriat'*. If they're closed knock on the apartment door directly opposite the office (the manager's personal residence). You'll pay about US$8/13 single/double for a room with shared bath in the centre of town.

Hotels in the Centre The privately run *Hotel La Podul Minciunilor* (☎ 417 259), a small pension at Strada Azilului 1, the first side street below the Iron Bridge on Piaţa Mică, has three rooms with a total of 10 beds at US$13/18 single/double.

A similar place is the three-room *Hotel Halemadero* (☎ 412 509), Strada Măsarilor 10, charging US$20/23 single/double.

Sibiu's most colourful hotel is the central three-star *Împăratul Romanilor* (☎ 416 490), Strada Nicolae Bălcescu 4. Founded in 1555 as 'La sultanul turcilor', the name was changed to Împăratul Romanilor in 1773 after a visit by Habsburg emperor Josef II. In 1790, Johannes Brahms and Franz Liszt both stayed here. The present hotel dates from the early 19th century and each of the 102 rooms has a private bath and colour TV, and costs US$41/71 single/double and up.

Another appealing old place is the imposing *Hotel Bulevard* (☎ 412 140), Piaţa Unirii 10, with rooms of differing prices, beginning around US$22/36 single/double. Though expensive, the Bulevard is an excellent hotel, with unlimited quantities of hot water and a cosy breakfast room.

The nearby 15-storey *Hotel Continental* (☎ 416 910), Calea Dumbrăvii 2-4, is a poor choice at US$28/43 single/double with bath and breakfast, though it does accept hotel coupons (none of the other hotels will).

Hotels South of the Centre There is a cluster of hotels next to the municipal stadium, a couple of blocks south of Hotel Continental (a taxi from the train station will cost about a dollar). The largest is the eight-storey *Hotel Parc* (☎ 424 455), Strada Scoala de Înot 3, Sibiu's 'youth tourism' hotel, with rooms at US$24/37 single/double with bath. Their disco is lively during the school year and the hotel restaurant is good.

Just west of the Hotel Parc is the modern three-storey *Hotel Silva* (☎ 442 141), Strada Aleea M Eminescu 1, at US$27/34 single/-double.

Much better value than either of these is the old two-storey *Hotel Sport* (☎ 422 472), Strada Octavian Goga 2, on the east side of Hotel Parc. Rooms here are US$3 per person, though it's often fully booked by sporting groups. Even then, if you are polite and explain that you're a student they may let you in.

Dumbrava Park The *Hanul Dumbrava* (☎ 422 920), a rustic inn four km south-west of town, is overpriced at US$24/35/39 single/double/triple without bath, US$40/56 double/triple with bath – far too much for this basic place. You can expect a lot of noise until the large restaurant downstairs closes at around 9 pm, and on disco nights the beat goes on till dawn. It's open all year round.

There's also a *motel* nearby at US$19 single or double, and the facilities are much better than at the inn. The reception of the camping ground mentioned earlier handles accommodation at the motel (open May to September only). All three places to stay at Dumbrava sometimes experience water problems.

Less expensive accommodation is available at the *Cabana Valea Aurie* (☎ 482 090), a two-storey wooden chalet between Dumbrava Park and a new apartment complex. There are only six rooms, each with two to four beds, at US$7 per person. Their restaurant has a nice terrace overlooking the lake in Dumbrava Park. Get there on trolley bus No T1 from the train station and get off one stop before the end of the line (ask). It's open all year round.

Places to Eat

Sibiu has a shortage of places to eat and most of the places around town that call themselves restaurants are little more than rather depressing drinking places. The three large hotels all have restaurants, though the one in the *Împăratul Romanilor* is rather stuffy, with a sign at the entrance requesting patrons to come properly dressed. (Several readers have commented that they found this restaurant superb.) Less pretentious is the restaurant in the *Bulevard*, but insist on seeing the Romanian menu to know how much things cost. As well as its regular restaurant, *Hotel Continental* has a self-service around the side of the building, but it closes very early.

Lacto Bar Liliacul, Strada Nicolae Bălcescu 18, is a good place for breakfast on weekdays, if you don't mind consuming your mămăligă and yoghurt standing up.

Dori's Bistro, Piața Mică 3, is a pleasant place for a coffee and you can get sandwiches, hamburgers and ice cream as well.

If you intend to visit Dumbrava Park plan on having lunch on the terrace of the *Hanul*

Dumbrava. (Expect to be overcharged slightly.)

Sibiu's 'Trei Stejari' beer is one of Romania's better brews.

Entertainment

Check the Agentie Teatrala, Strada Bălcescu 17, for events.

Disco Bar Mega Vox, downstairs in the Casă de Cultură in front of Hotel Continental on Piața Unirii (entry from the rear of the building), opens early – 5 pm daily!

During the school year there's a student's disco in the same building as the *Cocktail Bar* at the west end of the park beside Hotel Bulevard.

Getting There & Away

Sibiu is on a secondary railway line from Arad to Brașov and local trains bound for Brașov stop at the Făgăraș trailheads. Some trains to Bucharest travel via Brașov, while others go via Piatra Olt. For Sighișoara (95 km), you may have to change at Copșa Mică or Mediaș, although some trains go direct, so ask. For Alba Iulia (92 km) you must change at Vințu de Jos. Ask the other passengers where you have to change trains.

Trains departing from Sibiu include seven trains to Brașov (149 km), three trains to Arad (254 km, five hours), one morning express train to Cluj-Napoca (198 km), one afternoon express train to Timișoara, seven local trains to Copșa Mică (45 km, one hour), five express trains to Bucharest (335 km, six hours), two local trains to Bucharest and one overnight train to Iași. From mid-June to mid-September there's a direct train to Mangalia.

One afternoon bus to Sighișoara (92 km) leaves from the bus station next to the train station.

THE FĂGĂRAȘ MOUNTAINS

In summer, hordes of backpackers descend on the Făgăraș Mountains, a section of the Carpathian Mountains in central Romania. Here they soon get lost in alpine glory, for Făgăraș is the most spectacular hiking area in the country. First, get a proper map at a

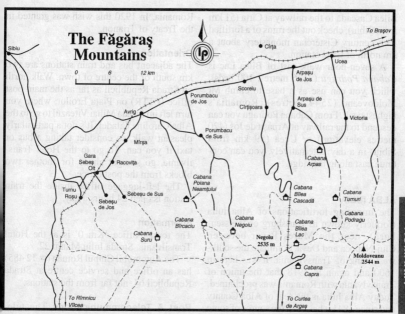

The Făgăraş Mountains

Sibiu

0   12 km

To Braşov

Cîrţa

Ucea

Arpaşu de Jos

Scoreiu

Porumbacu de Jos

Arpaşu de Sus

Cîrţişoara

Avrig

Victoria

Porumbacu de Sus

Mîrşa

Gara Sebeş Olt

Racoviţa

Cabana Arpaş

Turnu Roşu

Sebeşu de Sus

Cabana Poiana Neamţului

Cabana Bîlea Cascadă

Cabana Tumuri

Sebeşu de Jos

Cabana Podragu

Cabana Bîrcaciu

Cabana Negoiu

Cabana Bîlea Lac

Cabana Suru

Negoiu 2535 m

Moldoveanu 2544 m

Cabana Capra

To Rîmnicu Vîlcea

To Curtea de Argeş

ROMANIA

bookshop, tourist office or luxury hotel reception. Just keep looking until you find one

To hike Făgăraş you must be in good physical shape and have warm clothing and sturdy boots. The trails are well marked, but keep the altitude in mind and be prepared for cold and rain at any time. From November to April these mountains are snow-covered; August and September are the best months. Basic food is available at the cabanas but carry a supply of biscuits and keep your water bottle full. You'll meet lots of other hikers eager to tell you of their adventures, and with the help of a good map you'll soon know exactly where to go.

Unless you have a car, getting to the Făgăraş trailheads is much more difficult than it is in the Bucegi Mountains around Sinaia. Unfortunately there are no buses from Sibiu in this direction and it's quite a hike from the railway line just to the bottom of the hills.

Routes & Places to Stay

The easiest access is from Sibiu, and local trains on the Făgăraş line to Braşov pass many starting points. One of the best places to get off at is Gară Sebeş Olt (24 km from Sibiu), from where you can hike to *Cabana Suru* (1450 metres elevation, 60 beds) in about five hours via Sebeşul de Sus (450 metres). *Cabana Negoiu* (1546 metres, 170 beds) is seven hours east of Suru across peaks up to 2306 metres high. From Porumbacu de Jos Railway Station (41 km from Sibiu) you can hike up to Cabana Negoiu in about seven hours.

Eight strenuous hours east of Cabana Negoiu is *Cabana Bîlea Lac* (2034 metres, 170 beds), where there's a cable car down to *Cabana Bîlea Cascadă* (1234 metres, 63 beds) and to the road leading out of the mountains. On this section you will pass Mt Negoiu (2535 metres), the second-highest peak in Romania. If you decide to end your trip here by hitching or hiking north from

Bîlea Cascadă to the railway at Cîrţa (51 km from Sibiu), check out the ruins of a fortified 13th century Cistercian monastery about a km north of Cîrţa station.

A seven-hour walk east of Bîlea Lac is *Cabana Podragu* (2136 metres, 100 beds), which you can use as a base to climb Mt Moldoveanu (2544 metres), Romania's highest peak. From Cabana Podragu you can descend to the railway at Arpaşu de Jos (420 metres elevation) or Ucea (59 km from Sibiu) in a day; alternatively, you can continue east along the ridge.

ALBA IULIA

The imposing fortifications of Alba Iulia (formerly known as Karlsburg or Weissenburg), near the Mureş River between Cluj-Napoca and Deva, dominate the southwest flank of Transylvania. It was here in 1600 and again in 1918 that the union of Transylvania with Romania was proclaimed. Today Alba Iulia is the seat of Alba County and since 1841 it has been the source of some of Romania's best champagne. Three million bottles a year are produced.

In Roman times, Apulum (now Alba Iulia) was an important town and headquarters of the 13th legion. From 1542 to 1690, Alba Iulia served as the capital of the principality of Transylvania. Michael the Brave, ruler of Romania from 1593 to 1601, entered Alba Iulia on 1 November 1599, unifying the three Romanian principalities of Wallachia, Moldavia and Transylvania under his rule, a union that endured until he was assassinated a year later. The present Vauban-style citadel with its seven bastions and six gates, designed by the Italian architect Giovanni Visconti, was erected between 1714 and 1741. Previous fortifications on this site had been destroyed by the Tatars in 1241 and the Turks in 1661.

Alba Iulia is best remembered by Romanians for the 'Great Assembly' which occurred here on 1 December 1918, when some 100,000 Romanians from Transylvania, Banat, Crişana and Maramureş gathered to express their wish to be united with

Romania. In 1920 this wish was granted in the Treaty of Trianon.

Orientation

The adjacent bus and train stations are two km south of the centre of town. Walk north on Strada Republicii as far as the main post office (PTTR) on Piaţa Eroilor, where you turn left up Strada Mihai Viteazul to go to the Alba Carolina Citadel. It's not a particularly pleasant walk, so consider taking a bus or taxi if you can. To go to the Hotel Transilvania, go straight ahead for another two blocks from the post office.

The left-luggage office inside the train station is open 24 hours a day.

Information

The tourist office 'Km 0' is at the Hotel Transilvania, Strada Iuliu Maniu 22.

The Automobil Clubul Român (☎ 12 485) has an office and service centre at Strada Republicii 64, not far from the stations.

Post & Telecommunications The telephone centre, in the main post office on Piaţa Eroilor, is open daily from 7 am to 9 pm. Alba Iulia's telephone code is 0968.

Travel Agencies The CFR Travel Agency is on Strada Moţilor, opposite Magazin Universal, a block from Hotel Transilvania.

Things to See & Do

Strada Mihai Viteazul leads up from the lower town to a ramp which brings you to the Baroque east gate of the **Alba Carolina Citadel** (1735). An obelisk opposite this gate commemorates the peasant uprising of 1784 led by Cloşca, Crişan and Horea, who were imprisoned here. (Crişan committed suicide and the other two were tortured to death.) Above the gate is Horea's cell.

Enter the citadel and continue straight ahead to the large equestrian statue of Mihai Viteazul (Michael the Brave). The statue faces **Unification Hall**, where the act of unification between Romania and Transylvania was signed on 1 December 1918. Across the street is the **Museum of the Unification**

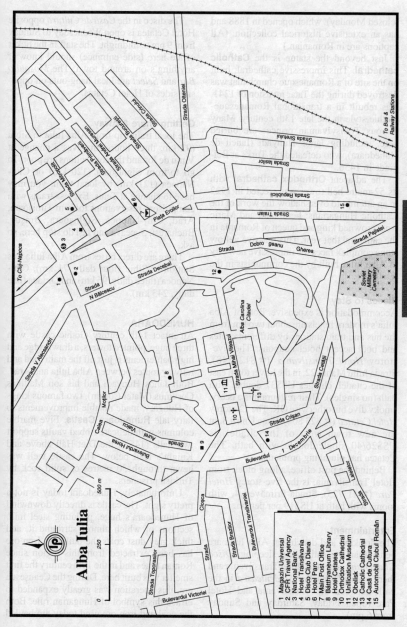

Alba Iulia

1 Magazin Universal
2 CFR Travel Agency
3 National Bank
4 Hotel Transilvania
5 Disco Club Diana
6 Hotel Parc
7 Main Post Office
8 Bátthyaneum Library
9 Hotel Cetatea
10 Orthodox Cathedral
11 Unification Museum
12 Obelisk
13 Catholic Cathedral
14 Casa de Cultura
15 Automobil Clubul Român

(closed Monday), which opened in 1888 and has an extensive historical collection. (All captions are in Romanian.)

Just beyond the statue is the **Catholic cathedral**. This impressive cathedral, built on the site of a Romanesque church that was destroyed during the Tatar invasion of 1241, was rebuilt in a transitional Romanesque-Gothic style in the late 13th century. Many famous Transylvanian princes are buried here, including János Hunyadi (Iancu de Hunedoara), who defeated the Turks at Belgrade in 1456.

The adjacent **Orthodox cathedral** with its 52-metre bell tower was erected in 1922 in an attempt to overshadow the work of the Catholic Hungarians; Ferdinand and Marie were crowned king and queen of Romania in the cathedral that year. This massive yellow stone complex faces the impressive new city of Alba Iulia, built by the communists in the 1980s.

Places to Stay

Accommodation is expensive. Both of Alba Iulia's modern hotels are about two km from the bus and train stations by different routes and both accept hotel coupons. The five-storey *Hotel Transilvania* (☎ 812 548), Strada Iuliu Maniu 22, in the lower town east of the citadel, charges US$37 double with bath (no singles). Their restaurant is a beery, smoky dive but otherwise OK. The 12-storey *Hotel Cetatea* (☎ 823 804), Piaţa Unirii 3, in the new town west of the citadel, is US$26/40 single/double with bath. The Cetatea has plumbing problems.

Behind the post office, a long block from Hotel Transilvania, is the five-storey *Hotel Parc* (☎ 11 723), Strada Primăveri 4, with rooms with bath at US$19 per person.

Entertainment

The drinking and dancing at Alba Iulia are better than the eating and sleeping. *Disco Club Diana* is next to Hotel Transilvania and there's also *Disco Bar Studenteasca* in the park between the Transilvania and Hotel Parc (open Friday, Saturday and Sunday from 6 pm).

The disco in the *Casă de Cultură* opposite Hotel Cetatea is open Wednesday to Sunday from 9 pm to midnight. The staff in the ticket office here (side entrance) should know if anything's on around town. The *Mosquito Bar* and *Select* are local hang-outs on opposite sides of Hotel Cetatea.

Getting There & Away

The local train trip from Alba Iulia to Sibiu (92 km, three hours) involves a change at Vinţu de Jos and the connections are poor. To go to/from Sighişoara (120 km) or Cluj-Napoca (121 km) by local train, you may have to change at Teiuş. Express trains with compulsory reservations to/from Timişoara, Arad, Cluj-Napoca, Sighişoara, Braşov, Bucharest, Suceava and Iaşi do stop here, so ask.

There are direct buses from Alba Iulia Bus Station to Sibiu (four daily, 71 km), Cluj-Napoca (three daily, 96 km) and Oradea (one daily, 243 km).

HUNEDOARA

An intact 14th century Gothic castle with three huge, pointed towers, a drawbridge and high battlements is just off the main road and railway routes between Alba Iulia and Arad. Both János Hunyadi and his son Matthias Corvinus (Matei Corvin), two famous kings of Hungary, made notable improvements to fairy-tale **Hunedoara Castle**. Five marble columns with delicate ribbed vaults support two halls (1453), the Diet Hall above and Knight's Hall below. The castle well was hewn through 30 metres of solid rock by Turkish prisoners.

Unfortunately, Hunedoara today is not a pretty sight. The castle is directly downwind of Hunedoara's huge, polluting steel mill, sections of which almost surround it, and thick grey dust coats the building. Iron ore has been extracted from this region since Roman times and in the 19th century the first smelter was built here. During the Ceauşescu era, this operation was greatly expanded to efface this symbol of Hungarian rule. Both the coal and iron ore used today are hauled in and the mill could easily have been located elsewhere.

Although Hunedoara is now mostly of interest to Greenpeace activists seeking to document cases of historical and environmental devastation, if you still want to visit, there are 10 local trains a day from Simeria to Hunedoara (15 km) and an overnight express with sleepers to/from Bucharest. Buses run hourly to Deva (13 km) from the bus station next to Hunedoara Railway Station. The castle (closed Monday) is two km south of the stations.

CLUJ-NAPOCA

Cut in two by the Someşul Mic River, Cluj-Napoca is as Hungarian as it is Romanian. Its position near the middle of Transylvania made it a crossroads, which explains its present role as an educational and industrial centre. Known as Klausenburg to the Germans and Kolozsvár to the Hungarians, the old Roman name of Napoca has been added to the city's official title to emphasise its Daco-Roman origin.

The history of Cluj-Napoca goes back to Dacian times. In 124 AD, during the reign of Emperor Hadrian, Napoca attained municipal status and Emperor Marcus Aurelius elevated it to a colony. Documented references to the medieval town date back to 1183. German merchants arrived in the 12th century and after the Tatar invasion of 1241 the medieval earthen walls of *castrenses de Clus* were rebuilt in stone. From 1791 to 1848 and again after the union with Hungary in 1867, Cluj-Napoca served as capital of Transylvania.

Alhough Cluj-Napoca has far fewer historical relics than Sibiu and is in a less picturesque location than Braşov, it has several good museums and a large botanical garden. To the south-west are the Munti Apuseni, or Western Carpathians, a favourite hiking area for the locals that is almost unknown to foreigners.

Orientation

The train station is some distance north of the centre of town, so catch a trolleybus or take any southbound bus on Strada Horea and get off at the first stop after crossing the river. From the bridge here, Strada Gheorghe Doja climbs slightly to Piaţa Unirii, the heart of the city. The left-luggage office inside the train station is near the restaurant (open 24 hours).

Cluj-Napoca has two bus stations. Autogară No 2 (with buses to Hungary) is over the bridge from the train station north of town. Autogară No 1 is on Strada Aurel Vlaicu on the far east side of town (no left luggage). Trolleybus No 4 connects Autogară No 1 to the centre of town and the train station.

Information

The English-speaking staff at Agentia de Turism 'Km 0', Piaţa Unirii 10 (weekdays 9 am to 6 pm, Saturday 10 am to noon), are very helpful with information and can also book things for you.

The tourist office on the corner of Strada Memorandumului and Strada Şincai, three blocks west of Piaţa Unirii, sells old maps listing all the camping grounds and mountain huts in Romania.

The Automobil Clubul Român (☎ 116 503), Strada Memorandumului 27, is almost next to this tourist office.

Ziare Newsstand, Strada Gheorghe Doja 1, sometimes has the English newspaper *Nine O'Clock*.

Money To change a travellers' cheque try the Banca Romană de Comerţ Exterior, Strada Gheorghe Doja 8 (weekdays 8 am to noon; US$5 commission to change up to US$300 or 1.5% commission on larger amounts), or the Banca Comercială Romană, Piaţa Unirii 7 (weekdays 9 am to noon; 4.5% commission with a US$3 minimum).

Black-market moneychangers hang out on the street in front of Agentia de Turism 'Km 0', Piaţa Unirii 10.

Post & Telecommunications Cluj's telephone centre (daily 7 am to 10 pm) is in a

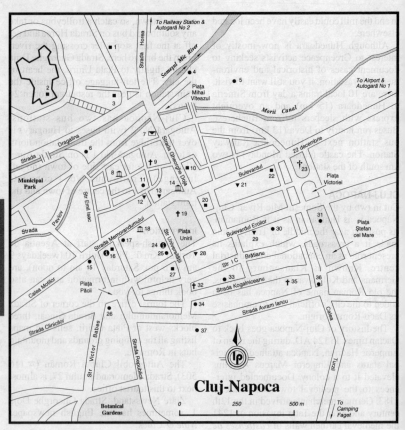

ROMANIA

Cluj-Napoca

new building directly behind the main post office, Strada Gheorghe Doja 33. Cluj-Napoca's telephone code is 095.

Travel Agencies You can buy international train tickets at the CFR Travel Agency at Piaţa Unirii 9, opposite the Continental Hotel.

The CFR Travel Agency selling domestic train tickets is at Piaţa Mihai Viteazul 20 near the market.

Albatros Travel Agency, in the courtyard at the Vlădeasa Hotel, has a bus to Budapest

twice a week (currently Thursday and Sunday).

Things to See

St Michael's Church, a 15th century Gothic hall church with a neo-Gothic tower (1859), sits in the centre of Piaţa Unirii. Flanking it on the south is a huge equestrian statue (1902) of the famous Hungarian king Matthias Corvinus (ruled 1458-90), son of János Hunyadi (Iancu de Hunedoara). On the east side of the square is the **Fine Arts Museum** (closed Monday and Tuesday) in the Baroque Banffy Palace (1785). A **phar-**

PLACES TO STAY

1 Hotel Casa Alba
2 Hotel Transilvania
3 Hotel Astoria
10 Hotel Vlădeasa
16 Hotel Siesta
20 Hotel Central-Melody
22 Hotel Victoria
27 Continental Hotel

PLACES TO EAT

12 Restaurantul Intim
13 Berarie
21 Hubertus Restaurant
28 Cafeteria Carpaţi
29 Pizza Restaurant

OTHER

4 CFR Travel Agency (Domestic)
5 Market
6 Hungarian State Theatre & Opera
7 Post Office
8 History Museum of Transylvania
9 Franciscan Church
11 Birthplace of Matthias Corvinus
14 Pharmaceutical Museum
15 Town Hall
16 Tourist Office
17 Automobil Clubul Român
18 Ethnological Museum
19 St Michael's Church
20 Banffy Palace
23 Orthodox Cathedral
24 Agentia de Turism 'KM 0'
25 CFR Travel Agency (International)
26 Student Club
30 Agenţie Teatrala (Theatre Ticket Office)
31 National Theatre
32 Piarist Church
33 State Philharmonic Orchestra
34 Disco Bianco e Nero
35 Reformed Church
36 Tailor's Bastion
37 Házsongárd Cemetery

maceutical museum is diagonally across the street at Strada Gheorghe Doja 1 (open Monday to Friday 9 am to 4 pm), on the site of Cluj-Napoca's first apothecary (1573).

Strada Matei Corvin leads from the northwest corner of the square to **Corvinus'**

birthplace (in 1440) at number 6. A block ahead is the beautifully decorated **Franciscan Church**. Left on Piaţa Muzeului is the **History Museum of Transylvania** (closed Monday) which has been open since 1859 and has an extensive collection on display. Unfortunately no explanations in English are provided but it's still worth walking through. The **Ethnographical Museum**, with its Transylvanian folk costumes and farm implements, is at Strada Memorandumului 21.

South at Strada Republicii 42 is the large and varied **Botanical Gardens**, which includes greenhouses, a museum and a Japanese garden. In summer allow several hours to explore it. For an overall view of Cluj-Napoca, climb up the steps behind Hotel Astoria to the Hotel Transilvania in the **citadel** (1715).

Places to Stay

Camping *Camping Făget* (☎ 116 234) is up in the hills, seven km south of Cluj-Napoca. The 143 bungalows on the site go for US$6/7 double/triple, or it's US$3/4/5 single/double/triple to camp with a tent. The restaurant here closes at 9 pm.

To get there take bus No 35 from Piaţa Mihai Viteazul 29 up Calea Turzii to the end of the line. You must still walk the last two km uphill to the camp site (which is open from May to mid-October).

Private Rooms Agenţia de Turism 'Km 0' (☎ 116 557), Piaţa Unirii 10, has private rooms at US$4 per person.

Hotels Cluj-Napoca has one of the best selections of hotels in Romania. The five-storey *Hotel Delta* (☎ 132 507) at Autogară No 2, across the bridge from the train station, is convenient if you're catching a bus to Budapest, but it's only a place to crash. Few foreigners have ever stayed here so the 'tourist price' is in flux.

The basic *Hotel Pax* (☎ 136 101), Piaţa Gării 2, opposite the train station, is US$10/23 single/double without bath, US$27/39 double/triple with bath.

ROMANIA

The old *Hotel Vlădeasa* (☎ 118 491), Strada Gheorghe Doja 20, is good value at US$11/22/32 single/double/triple without bath, US$13/26/34 with bath, but beware of rooms within earshot of the video games downstairs unless you want to relive the movie *Star Wars* in your dreams. The desk clerk here is fluent in six languages.

The *Hotel Astoria* (☎ 130 166), Strada Horea 3, is US$17/26/38 single/double/triple with shared bath, US$20/30/41 with private bath, plus an additional charge for showers. In the same category is the *Hotel Central-Melody* (☎ 117 465), Piaţa Unirii 29, overpriced at US$18/27/39 single/double/triple with shared bath, US$32/42 double/triple with private bath.

A step up in price is the elegant old *Continental Hotel* (☎ 111 441), on the southwest corner of Piaţa Unirii, with singles/doubles from US$22/34 with shared bath, US$32/50 with private bath.

The newer *Hotel Siesta* (☎ 195 582), Strada Şincai 4, behind the tourist office, is US$30/47 single/double with bath and breakfast.

Cluj-Napoca's finest hotel is the three-star *Hotel Transilvania* (☎ 134 466), on Citadel Hill overlooking the city. This modern hotel is expensive at US$78 double with bath and breakfast, but hotel coupons are accepted. Rooms at the *Hotel Casă Alba*, Strada Racoviţă 22, just below the Transilvania, are also highly expensive but their terrace is a good place for an up-market meal.

Places to Eat
Many good eating places are found on or near Piaţa Unirii. *Expres*, Piaţa Unirii 23 (closed Sunday), is a cheap self-service with fare slightly better than is usual at such places.

Berarie, Piaţa Unirii 19, is a beer garden with a good self-service restaurant at the back. *Mititie* (grilled meatballs) are available in the cool vault downstairs.

Despite the name, most of the dishes served at the *Lacto-Vegetarian Restaurant*, Piaţa Unirii 12 (closed Sunday), are meat-based.

The dining room at the *Continental Hotel* has great atmosphere and is frequented by some interesting underworld characters. If you like seafood, try the *Restaurantul Pescarul* on Strada Universităţii, next to Cinema Arta, behind the Continental Hotel.

The *Pizza Restaurant*, Bulevardul Eroilor 26 (closed Sunday), serves mass-produced pizza but it's cheap, fast and easy. If you want game meat go to *Hubertus*, Bulevardul 22 decembrie 22 (closed Sunday).

Theoretically the *Dacia Restaurant*, Strada Memorandumului 13, is the place to try local specialities, though there's no guarantee they'll have anything other than pork chops. The serving staff here dress in traditional attire.

Restaurantul Intim on Strada Matei Corvin is a rare beast: it's a women's restaurant and bar where (almost) no men are allowed.

By 9 pm all of these places will be closed, in which case try the *Restaurant Specializat*, Strada Gheorghe Doja 16, which stays open a bit later.

Cafés For coffee and cakes try *Cofetăria Carpaţi*, Piaţa Unirii 3.

Café Urania on Strada Horea, diagonally across the street from Hotel Astoria, serves a good cup of filter coffee (avoid the 'ness' here).

Entertainment
The neo-Baroque *National Theatre* (1906) on Piaţa Victoriei was designed by the famous Viennese architects Fellner and Hellmer. The *Hungarian State Theatre & Opera* is at the northern end of Strada Emil Isac, near the river. Also check the *Puppet Theatre* in the courtyard at Bulevardul Eroilor 8.

The Agenţia Teatrala, Bulevardul Eroilor 36, has tickets for most events.

Discos *Disco Bianco e Nero* in the Clubul Cultural Studenţesc, corner of Universităţii and Kogălniceanu, is open after 9 pm from Thursday to Sunday all year round. *Disco*

Ciao is nearly next to Cinema Arta on Strada Universităţii (open nightly).

The *Student Club*, in the Casă de Cultură Studenţească on Piaţa Pacii, has a disco Thursday to Sunday from 6 to 11 pm (closed May to September). A student card may be required to get in.

Getting There & Away

There are express trains from Cluj-Napoca to Oradea (153 km, 2½ hours), Sighişoara (203 km, three hours), Braşov (331 km, five hours), Timişoara (331 km, six hours) and Bucharest (497 km, eight hours). Through trains run to Iaşi via Gura Humorului and Suceava. For Sibiu you may have to change at Copşa Mică. For Alba Iulia you sometimes have to change at Teiuş. Sleepers are available to Bucharest.

A Hungarian Volanbus to Budapest leaves from Autogară No 2, across the bridge from the train station, three times a week (399 km, US$7). At last report it left Cluj-Napoca at 7 am on Monday, Thursday and Friday (check). Tickets are sold at the bus station.

Buses departing from Autogară No 1, on Strada Aurel Vlaicu, east of the centre of town, include one bus a day to Alba Iulia (96 km) and another to Sibiu (173 km).

Crişana & Banat

The plains of Crişana and Banat merge imperceptibly into Yugoslavia's Vojvodina and the Hungarian Great Plain. In Romania the Mureş River roughly divides Crişana (to the north) from Banat (to the south). Until 1918 the whole region was one, and although Subotica (Yugoslavia), Szeged (Hungary) and Timişoara now belong to three different nations, all three cities bear the unmistakable imprint of the old Habsburg Empire, which is strongly felt in Arad and Oradea as well.

Oradea, Arad and Timişoara all had large military fortresses intended to defend Austria-Hungary's south-eastern flank. For political reasons, the Habsburgs built up these cities around the turn of the century;

also for strictly political reasons, they were handed to Romania after WW I, despite their predominantly Hungarian populations. The Hungarian element is still strong throughout the region and in Banat you'll see the influence of the Serbs.

It's logical that Romania's 1989 revolution should have begun in the west, where the ethnically mixed population had always been at the margin of communist economic development. Drained of food and resources to finance Ceauşescu's great projects around Bucharest, facing increasing marginalisation of national minorities and bombarded with Hungarian and Yugoslav TV coverage of the political changes in East Germany, Czechoslovakia etc, the west exploded in December 1989. Pilgrims following the 'freedom trail' will want to visit the little Hungarian church in Timişoara where it all began.

Western Romania is Romania's front door and all the trains from Hungary and Yugoslavia pass through the three gateway cities of Timişoara, Arad and Oradea. Each city offers a touch of fading imperial glory, easy accommodation and a place to stop and get your bearings. If you're leaving Romania and have spare lei and an extra hotel coupon or two, this is your last chance to use them.

ORADEA

Oradea (Nagyvárad in Hungarian, Grosswardein in German), only a few km east of the Hungarian border and 153 km west of Cluj-Napoca, is the seat of Bihor County. It's the centre of the Crişana region, a fertile plain drained by the Crişul Alb, Crişul Negru and Crişul Repede rivers at the edge of the Carpathian Mountains and the Great Hungarian Plain. Oradea's stately city centre area straddles both banks of the Crişul Repede River.

Of all the cities of the old Austro-Hungarian Empire, Oradea is probably the one that retains best its fin de siecle elegance unmarred by modern developments. Ceded to Romania in 1920, this splendid example of Habsburg majesty became the backwater it remains today, a time capsule preserved for romantics in search of a simpler world. Băile

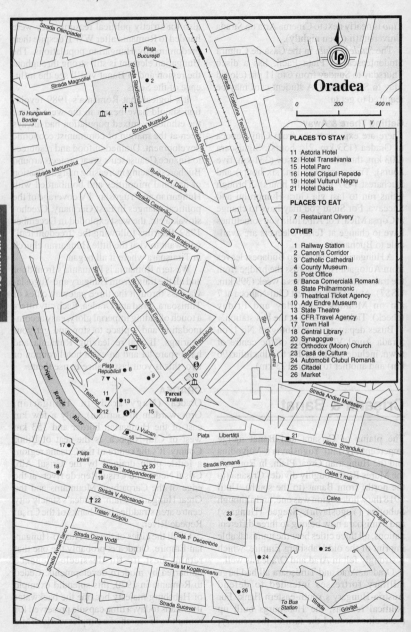

Oradea

0   200   400 m

PLACES TO STAY

11 Astoria Hotel
12 Hotel Transilvania
15 Hotel Parc
16 Hotel Crişul Repede
19 Hotel Vulturul Negru
21 Hotel Dacia

PLACES TO EAT

7 Restaurant Olivery

OTHER

1 Railway Station
2 Canon's Corridor
3 Catholic Cathedral
4 County Museum
5 Post Office
6 Banca Comercială Romană
8 State Philharmonic
9 Theatrical Ticket Agency
10 Ady Endre Museum
13 State Theatre
14 CFR Travel Agency
17 Town Hall
18 Central Library
20 Synagogue
22 Orthodox (Moon) Church
23 Casă de Cultura
24 Automobil Clubul Romană
25 Citadel
26 Market

Felix with its hot springs is almost a suburb of Oradea and those who get bored quickly can mellow out in a sulphurous pool. All in all, it's a great place to stop and spend your remaining Romanian currency and to prepare yourself for a return to the ruthless West.

Orientation
The train station is a couple of km north of town, so take tram No 1 to Piaţa Unirii. Piaţa Republicii with the tourist office, hotels and State Theatre is just across the bridge over the Crişul Repede River. Strada Republicii, the main pedestrian mall, runs north-east from beside the State Theatre.

The left-luggage office at the train station is beside the restaurant on the main platform (open 24 hours).

Information
Crişul Travel Agency, Piaţa Republicii 4, is Oradea's makeshift tourist office.

The Automobil Clubul Român (☎ 30 725) is in one of the high-rise buildings at the east end of Piaţa 1 decembrie.

Money The Banca Comercială Romană, Parcul Traian 8 (weekdays 8 to 11.30 am), changes travellers' cheques.

Post & Telecommunications Oradea's telephone centre is well hidden in the back courtyard behind Complexul Comercial Merkur on Strada Republicii, just off Piaţa Republicii (daily 7 am to 9 pm). Expect to spend a long time in there waiting. Oradea's telephone code is 0991.

Travel Agencies The CFR Travel Agency is at Strada Republicii 2.

Crişul Travel Agency, Piaţa Republicii 4, has buses to Budapest (US$8) and Kraków (US$20) about four times a week, but long delays at the border are routine.

Things to See
Oradea's most imposing sights are on the two city-centre squares, Piaţa Unirii and Piaţa Republicii. The **Orthodox church** (1792) on Piaţa Unirii is also known as the 'Moon Church' for a three-metre sphere on the tower which shows the phases of the moon. The other fine churches and palaces on this square are an interesting mix of Rococo, Baroque, Renaissance, Art Nouveau and various other eclectic styles.

Across the bridge over the Crişul Repede River is the magnificent **State Theatre** (1900), dominating Piaţa Republicii. The famous Viennese architects Fellner and Hellmer designed this building in the neoclassical style. Nearby on Parcul Traian is a small museum dedicated to the Hungarian poet Endre Ady.

Oradea's other worthy buildings are found along Strada Stadionului, just a block from the train station. The **Catholic cathedral** (1780) here is the largest Baroque church in Romania. The adjacent former **episcopal palace** (1770) with its 100 rooms and 365 windows was modelled after the Belvedere Palace in Vienna. Now it's the County Museum. The side that faces away from the cathedral is the most impressive. The **Canon's Corridor** with its series of archways along Strada Stadionului also dates back to the 18th century.

Places to Stay
Camping From May to mid-September you can camp at Băile 1 mai, nine km south-east of Oradea. Take a southbound tram No 4 (black number) from the train station or an eastbound tram No 4 (red number) from Piaţa Unirii south to the end of the line, then bus No 15 to the end of the line right at *Campare Venus* (☎ 261 507) where the 32 cabins rent for US$3 per person. In midsummer they'll probably all be full, in which case walk 500 metres along the road beyond the bus terminus to *Camping 1 mai* which is more likely to have cabins for the same price and always has tent space. There's a large thermal swimming pool very near these camping grounds and Băile Felix is only 30 minutes walk away.

Hotels There are several reasonably priced hotels in Oradea. The yellow Art-Nouveau

Hotel Vulturul Negru (☎ 135 417), Strada Independenţei 1, erected in 1908, is an architectural curiosity in itself. Rooms are US$15/22/25 single/double/triple without bath, US$30/33 double/triple with bath.

The friendly *Hotel Parc* (☎ 111 699), Strada Republicii 5, an older two-storey hotel right on Oradea's main pedestrian promenade, has singles/doubles/triples with shared bath for US$15/23/26, with private bath for US$27/30 double/triple.

Two other fine old hotels are the *Astoria* (☎ 31 663), Strada Teatrului 1 (US$14/22 single/double without bath, US$33/42 double/triple with bath), and the *Transilvania* (☎ 130 508), Strada Teatrului 2 (US$16/24/28 single/double/triple). Both the Astoria and Transilvania are popular drinking places and the Transilvania especially throbs to a rock beat when a band is playing in the restaurant downstairs.

Some rooms at the *Hotel Crişul Repede* (☎ 132 509), Strada Libertăţii 6, also overlook the action. Rooms with bath and breakfast at the Crişul Repede are US$19/27/33 single/double/triple, while doubles without bath are US$22. All these hotels have great atmosphere and will delight Habsburg-era romantics.

Spend your hotel coupon at the nine-storey *Hotel Dacia* (☎ 18 656), Aleea Ştrandului 1, where singles/doubles with private bath begin at US$48/75.

Places to Eat

The restaurant at *Hotel Transilvania* is good, or you can try the *Restaurant Oradea*, Strada Iosif Vulcan 1, just across the square – a most elegant dining room with a specific menu printed in four languages. Their prices are good.

The *Starel Com Rotiserie*, on a corner of Piaţa Unirii facing the Central Library, has tasty grilled chicken which you eat standing up.

Restaurant Olivery, Strada Moscovei 12 (daily until 10 pm), is an unpretentious local restaurant with good food at reasonable prices.

The *Café Orient Express* at the train station has good coffee and cakes, and is open 24 hours. If you're catching a train to Hungary you can spend your remaining lei here.

Entertainment

The theatre ticket agency is at Strada Republicii 6.

The disco at *Hotel Dacia* is a bit of a boring joke, but get a room on an upper floor to avoid losing any sleep over it.

Getting There & Away

Many trains run north to Satu Mare (133 km, 2½ hours), south to Arad (121 km, 2½ hours) and east to Cluj-Napoca (153 km, three hours).

Oradea's bus station is inconveniently located at Strada Războieni 81 on the south-eastern side of town, far from the train station (bus No 12 from Piaţa Unirii). A bus to Debrecen, Hungary (68 km, US$3), departs daily at the crack of dawn. Ask about the daily bus to Budapest (246 km, six hours, US$10). The international ticket window here is open from 5 am to noon.

To/From Hungary Among the fully reserved express trains crossing into Hungary from Oradea are the *Claudiopolis* and the *Corona*, both to Budapest.

Local Hungarian trains shuttle twice daily between Budapest-Nyugati and Oradea (249 km, four hours). Fares from Oradea are US$7 to Püspökladány or US$18 to Budapest. These unreserved trains sometimes use the names *Partium* and *Varadinium*. Also ask about the three daily local trains from Oradea to Békéscsaba (90 km). International train tickets cannot be purchased at Oradea's chaotic train station, so pick them up at a CFR travel agency beforehand.

If you don't already have an open international train ticket, take bus No 11 from in front of Oradea Station directly to the Episcopia Bihor border train station where you can easily buy a ticket to Hungary with lei and board the first westbound train. The information window at Oradea Railway Station should be able to give you the times of trains leaving Episcopia Bihor for Hungary.

BĂILE FELIX

Băile Felix, a famous year-round health spa only eight km south-east of Oradea, has facilities for treating rheumatism and diseases of the nervous system. There's a large open-air swimming pool of thermal water here and several smaller thermal pools covered by the rare *Nymphea lotus thermalis*, a white water lily which dates back to the Tertiary period of three million years ago.

Places to Stay & Eat

The *Hotel Thermal* (☎ 261 215) near the train station accepts hotel coupons and has a hot thermal swimming pool right in the hotel (it's outdoors in summer and indoors in winter).

The *Poienita* (☎ 261 172) and *International* (☎ 261 445) hotels at Băile Felix also accept hotel coupons.

The nearest official camping grounds are three km away at Băile 1 mai.

Getting There & Away

Three local trains a day run from Oradea to Băile Felix (11 km, 20 minutes), but an easier way to get there is to take tram No 4 (red number) east from Piaţa Unirii or tram No 4 (black number) south from Oradea Railway Station to the end of the line at Cartierul Nufărul, from where bus No 14 runs directly to the spa.

ARAD

Arad sits in wine-making country on the Mureş River, which drains much of central Transylvania. The city's streets are lined with huge turn-of-the-century buildings that were constructed while this was still part of the Austro-Hungarian empire. The river loops around Arad's 18th century citadel before flowing west to Szeged in Hungary. Arad Citadel itself is still occupied by the military and can't be visited, but the surrounding parks are crowded all summer with bathers in the river and pools. After crushing

the liberal revolution of 1848, the Habsburgs had 13 Hungarian generals executed outside the citadel. (An obelisk commemorating them is in front of the camping ground.)

Only 20 km south of the Hungarian border by rail, Arad is an entry point to Romania. Hunedoara Castle, Sibiu and Sighişoara are on the main line east of Arad and Timişoara is just south.

Orientation

The train station is a couple of km north of the centre of town. Take a bus (buy a ticket at the kiosk in front of the station) down Bulevardul Revoluţiei into town.

The bus station is two blocks west of the railway station along the main boulevard. The left-luggage office at the train station is in the main building (open 24 hours).

Information

Zarandul Travel Agency, Bulevardul Revoluţiei 76, opposite the town hall, is the closest thing you'll find to a tourist information office in Arad.

The Automobil Clubul Român office (☎ 12 445) is at Strada 1 decembrie 2 next to Hotel Astoria.

Money The Banca Comercială Romană, Bulevardul Revoluţiei 72 (weekdays 8.30 am to noon), changes travellers' cheques.

Bucharest Exchange Office, Bulevardul Revoluţiei 55 (weekdays 8 am to 8 pm, Saturday 8 am to 2 pm), also changes travellers' cheques.

Post & Telecommunications The telephone centre, in the main post office, Bulevardul Revoluţiei 44, is open daily from 7 am to 9 pm. Arad's telephone code is 0966.

Travel Agencies International train tickets can be purchased at the CFR Travel Agency at Bulevardul Revoluţiei 99, beside the State Theatre. Such tickets aren't sold at the station.

Marco Polo Travel Agency in the Mureşul Hotel sells tickets for buses to Budapest

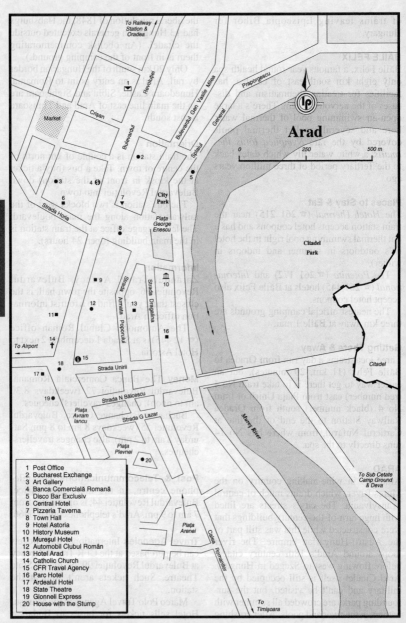

Arad

0   250   500 m

1 Post Office
2 Bucharest Exchange
3 Art Gallery
4 Banca Comercială Romană
5 Disco Bar Exclusiv
6 Central Hotel
7 Pizzeria Taverna
8 Town Hall
9 Hotel Astoria
10 History Museum
11 Mureşul Hotel
12 Automobil Clubul Român
13 Hotel Arad
14 Catholic Church
15 CFR Travel Agency
16 Parc Hotel
17 Ardealul Hotel
18 State Theatre
19 Gionneli Express
20 House with the Stump

To Railway
Station &
Oradea

Market

Crişan

Bulevardul

Revoluţiei

Bulevardul Gen Vasile Milea

Spitalul

General

Praporgescu

Strada Horia

City
Park

Piaţa
George
Enescu

Citadel
Park

Strada Amata

Strada Drapalina

Strada Poporului

To Airport

Strada Unirii

Strada N Bălcescu

Strada G Lazar

Piaţa
Avram
Iancu

Piaţa
Plevnei

Piaţa
Arenei

Mureş River

Citadel

Calea Romanilor

To Sub Cetate
Camp Ground
& Deva

To
Timişoara

(US$11), Munich (US$50) and many German cities.

Things to See

The neoclassical **town hall** (1876) on Bulevardul Revoluţiei is Arad's most impressive building. On Piaţa George Enescu, behind the town hall, is the **History Museum** (closed Monday) in the Palace of Culture (1913). The museum's large display covers the entire history of the area (captions in Romanian only).

Walk south on the attractive Bulevardul Revoluţiei to the neoclassical **State Theatre** (1874). On a corner at Piaţa Plevnei, two blocks beyond the theatre, is a stump (against the outside wall of the house) in which apprentice blacksmiths used to hammer a nail to symbolise their acceptance into the guild. Your attention will be drawn to it by the large padlock alongside.

Places to Stay

Camping If you're headed for the safe, well-run *Sub Cetate Campground* (☎ 11 314), Strada 13 Generali 13, cross the bridge near the Parc Hotel, turn right and follow the river downstream 1.5 km until you reach 'Popas Turistic'. No public transport passes this way but it's a fairly pleasant walk. Sixty cabins are available at US$7 per person and camping with your own tent costs exactly the same, so obviously it's worth taking a cabin. There's a restaurant/bar on the premises, which is open from March to mid-October.

Hotels Hotels in Arad are often crowded with Romanians coming from or going to Hungary. Since they get a very cheap rate at hotels inside Romania, most stop here for the night. Despite this, you should still be able to find a room.

Arad's best value is the *Central Hotel* (☎ 31 226) on Strada Horia, a modern five-storey building formerly used as a guesthouse for visiting communist leaders. Rooms with bath and breakfast are US$22/35/42 single/double/triple.

Since the 2nd-class *Hotel Mureşul* (☎ 11 540), Bulevardul Revoluţiei 88, was completely renovated in 1993, there are no longer any really cheap hotels in Arad. Spacious rooms at the Mureşul are now US$23/36/37 single/double/triple, breakfast included. Some rooms have private bath, others don't, but all cost the same.

The *Ardealul Hotel* (☎ 11 840), Bulevardul Revoluţiei 98, beside the State Theatre (US$29 double with bath, no singles), is a fine old neoclassical building (1841) with a music room where Brahms, Liszt and Strauss once gave concerts.

The *Hotel Arad* (☎ 13 663), Strada Armata Poporului 9, behind Hotel Astoria, is US$24/35 single/double without bath, US$25/39 with bath and breakfast. This large three-storey mansion was erected in 1898.

If you have hotel coupons, go to the nine-storey, 210-room *Parc Hotel* (☎ 12 628), Strada Dragalina 25 (US$40/62/66 single/double/triple with bath if you don't have coupons). Every room has a TV and many also have a fridge, but the lower floors suffer from disco noise on weekends.

Places to Eat

Gionneli Expres, Bulevardul Revoluţiei 104, offers hot self-service meals around the clock.

The *Palace Restaurant*, Strada Mihai Eminescu 1, next to the Mureşul Cinema behind the Ardealul Hotel, is an attractive private restaurant which posts its extensive, inexpensive menu outside. The service is excellent – this is easily one of Romania's best restaurants.

Some of Romania's best pizza is served at *Pizzeria Taverna*, Bulevardul Revoluţiei 73 (downstairs on the side of the building facing the town hall). The well-lit restaurant is ventilated by three fans so cigarette smoke shouldn't be a problem. The pizzas are individually produced and not churned out en masse, as is usually the case in Romania.

For up-market coffee and cakes, try *Casă Vernieri*, Bulevardul Revoluţiei 84.

ROMANIA

Entertainment

Arad's theatrical agency, with tickets to local performances, is at the back of the State Theatre (Tuesday to Sunday 11 am to noon and 5 to 6.30 pm).

In summer *Disco Bar Exclusiv*, beside the river beyond City Park, blasts rock music across their terrace while in a back room inside there's a strip show (US$2 cover plus pricey drinks). Before paying anything check the upper rear terrace around the building where there's a drinking terrace for ordinary Romanians. Sometimes there's a live band playing there – no cover charge.

There are discos in both the Parc and Astoria hotels.

Getting There & Away

Arad is an important stop for the *Balt-Orient, Carpaţi, Dacia, Ovidius* and *Pannonia* express trains between Budapest and Bucharest via Curtici. Reservations are required. You can also get to Hungary on one of the two daily local trains from Arad to Békéscsaba (68 km), but check the times carefully and pick up your open ticket at a CFR Travel Agency beforehand.

Other local trains run north to Oradea (121 km, 2½ hours), east to Deva (149 km, four hours) and, more frequently, south to Timişoara (57 km, 1½ hours). There's an overnight train with sleepers between Bucharest and Arad (589 km, 11 hours).

A number of buses to Hungary depart from Arad Bus Station. There's a daily afternoon bus to Szeged (106 km, US$5), an afternoon bus three times a week to Békéscsaba (87 km, US$3) and an early morning bus four times a week to Budapest (276 km, seven hours, US$8). Tickets for Budapest and Békéscsaba are available at the ticket window but for Szeged you pay the driver. Don't go by the times posted at the station – ask.

Alternatively, take one of four daily local trains from Arad to Nădlac (52 km, 1½ hours), walk, hitch or take a taxi the six km to the border crossing, walk across, and catch one of the nine daily trains from Nagylak, Hungary, to Szeged (47 km, 1¼ hours).

TIMIŞOARA

The Banat plain around Timişoara (Temesvár in Hungarian, Temeschburg in German) is an eastward extension of Yugoslavia's Vojvodina, and the Bega Canal, which curves through the city, leads into the Tisa River in Yugoslavia. The Serbian influence is evident in a few of the churches, and the inhabitants are a mix of Romanians, Germans, Hungarians and Serbs. Although it's Romania's fourth-largest city, central Timişoara has a garden-like, Mediterranean air. Timiş County, of which Timişoara is the administrative centre, is the richest agricultural area in Romania. If you're coming from Yugoslavia, you'll probably enter Romania through Timişoara.

Orientation

Timişoara-Nord Railway Station is just west of the city centre. If you're on foot, walk east on Bulevardul Republicii to the Opera House, then north a block to the verdant Piaţa Libertăţii. Piaţa Unirii, the old town square, is two blocks farther north.

If you'd rather ride, catch the tram with the black No 1 just outside the station, which does a great scenic loop through the centre of town. It doesn't matter if you're too enthralled to get off because they all come back the same way.

The left-luggage office at the train station is at the beginning of the underground passageway to the tracks (open 24 hours).

Timişoara's bus station is beside the Idsefin Market, three blocks from the train station. Take Strada General Dragalina south to the canal, which you cross and follow west to the next bridge.

Information

Cardinal Travel Agency, Bulvardul Republicii 6, functions as Timişoara's unofficial tourist information office (no private rooms).

The office of the Automobil Clubul Român (☎ 15 819), Strada Hector 1, is opposite Beraria Bastion in the old city wall, a block from Hotel Continental.

ROMANIA

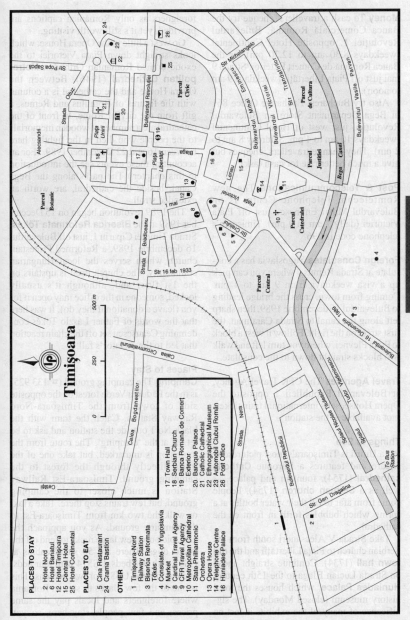

Timişoara

PLACES TO STAY
2 Hotel Nord
6 Hotel Banatul
12 Hotel Timişoara
15 Hotel Central Hotel
25 Hotel Continental

PLACES TO EAT
5 Cina Restaurant
24 Crama Bastion

OTHER
1 Timişoara-Nord
    Railway Station
3 Biserica Reformată
    Tőkés
4 Consulate of Yugoslavia
7 Market
8 Cardinal Travel Agency
9 CFR Travel Agency
10 Metropolitan Cathedral
11 State Philharmonic
    Orchestra
13 Opera House
14 Telephone Centre
16 Huniades Palace
17 Town Hall
18 Serbian Church
19 Banca Romana de Comert
    Exterior
20 Baroque Palace
21 Catholic Cathedral
22 Ethnographical Museum
23 Automobil Clubul Român
26 Post Office

0   250   500 m

Money To cash a travellers' cheque try the Banca Comercială Romană, Bulevardul Revoluţiei 1, opposite Hotel Continental (weekdays 8.30 am to 12.30 pm), or the Banca Romană de Comerţ Exterior, Strada 9 mai just off Piaţa Libertăţii (weekdays 9 am to noon).

Also try Bucharest Exchange Office 861 in Bega Department Store on Bulevardul Revoluţiei, just west of Hotel Continental (weekdays 10 am to 4 pm, Saturday 8 am to 2 pm). They change travellers' cheques but give a much better rate for cash (ask).

Post & Telecommunications The new Romtelecom Telephone Centre is on Bulevardul Mihai Eminescu just off Piaţa Victoriei (daily 7 am to 9 pm). Timişoara's telephone code is 096.

Foreign Consulates Yugoslavia has a consulate at Strada Remus 4 where you can pick up a visa weekdays from 9 am to 1 pm. Coming from town, cross the bridge leading to Bulevardul 16 decembrie 1989, then sharp left along the canal to Strada Caraiman, the first street on the right. Follow it west a block to Piaţa Plevnei, where you turn left and walk two blocks straight down to the consulate.

Travel Agencies The CFR Travel Agency, at Bulevardul Republicii 1 opposite the Opera House, sells international train tickets (not available at the station).

Things to See

Piaţa Unirii is Timişoara's most picturesque square and features a Baroque **Catholic cathedral** (1754), fountain and palace, as well as a **Serbian church** (1754). People come from afar to fill their water bottles at a spring which bubbles forth in front of the cathedral.

Take Strada V Alecsandri south from the Serbian church to Piaţa Libertăţii and the **old town hall** (1734). Continue straight ahead on Strada Lucian Blaga to the 15th century **Huniades Palace**, which houses the local history museum (closed Monday). The significance of many of the exhibits is lost on

foreigners as only Romanian captions are provided, yet it's still worth visiting.

Go west a little to the Opera House, which looks straight down Piaţa Victoriei to the exotic domed Romanian Orthodox **Metropolitan Cathedral** (1946). Between the Opera House and the cathedral is a column with the figures of Romulus and Remus, a gift from the city of Rome. In front of the cathedral are a number of wooden memorials to the people who died in the fighting here between 16 and 22 December 1989. (For an account of these events see the introduction to this chapter.) The parks along the Bega Canal, beside the cathedral, are worth an extended stroll.

The 1989 revolution began on 15 December 1989 at the **Biserica Reformata Tökés**, Strada Timotei Cipariu 1, just off Bulevardul 16 decembrie 1989, a Reformed Protestant church which serves the local Hungarian community. The church itself is upstairs on the 1st floor and, although it's usually locked, someone in the office may open it for you (leave a donation if they do). It was here that the words of Father László Tökés condemning Ceauşescu set off the chain reaction that led to the dictator's fall.

Places to Stay

Camping The camping ground (☎ 133 925) is in the Pădurea Verde forest on the opposite side of town from the Timişoara-Nord Railway Station. Catch the tram with the black No 1 outside the station and ask to be let off at the 'camping'. The route from the tram stop is unmarked, but take one of the trails directly through the forest to the camping ground. Timişoara-Est Railway Station is much closer to the camping ground, but few trains stop there. Take a taxi or walk the two km from Timişoara-Est to the camping ground. As you approach the gate, pick up a few large rocks to fend off the guard dogs. There are 50 small cabins at US$7 with two beds, US$14 with four beds, and camping is US$2 for two persons. This is one of the few places to stay in Romania where foreigners and locals pay the same prices, and few people stay here, so you should have no problem getting a cabin. There's a good restaurant on the premises. It's open from mid-May to mid-September.

Hotels Accommodation in Timişoara can sometimes be tight as Romanians in transit to/from Yugoslavia or Hungary often spend the night here to take advantage of the low hotel rates available to them (about 20% of the prices paid by foreigners).

The cheapest regular hotel rooms are available at the *Casă Tineretului* (☎ 162 419) or 'House of Youth', a large, modern building on Strada Arieş, about two km south of the centre. Rooms with shared bath are US$6 per person. Get there on trolleybus No 15 or 16 from Strada Grozavescu near Hotel Continental or tram No 8 from the train station (on either ask to be let out at Strada Arieş).

Of Timişoara's five downtown hotels only the Nord and Banatul are reasonably priced, while the Timişoara, Central and Continental are expensive. The *Hotel Nord* (☎ 112 308), Strada General Dragalina 47, around the corner from Timişoara-Nord Railway Station, is US$14/26 single/double without bath, US$18/32 with bath. They're the most likely to have singles available late in the day. It's rather run-down but the management tries to be helpful and breakfast is conveniently served from 6.30 to 9 am, allowing you to get an early start.

Hotel Banatul (☎ 136 030), Bulevardul Republicii 5, is much better than the Hotel Nord yet charges lower prices (US$12/19 single/double without bath, US$13/25 with bath), though the singles are often full.

The six-storey *Central Hotel* (☎ 190 091), Strada Lenau 6, is US$33/40 single/double with bath and breakfast (coupons not accepted). It doesn't have much going for it.

If you have hotel coupons, your choice should be the modern 11-storey *Hotel Timişoara* (☎ 137 815), Strada 1 mai 2, next to the Opera House (US$34/45 single/double without coupons), you enter from the rear. It's often full with groups.

Places to Eat

There's a self-service restaurant in the *Hotel*

Central, Strada Lenau 6. US-style hot dogs and hamburgers are dispensed at *Extraplus*, Strada V Alexandri 8, just off Piaţa Unirii.

The *Restaurantul Bulevard* in Piaţa Victoriei opposite the opera is very elegant, but you're more likely to see people actually eating in the restaurant at *Hotel Banatul*, nearby on Bulevardul Republicii, which has a menu in Romanian posted on the door.

The *Cina Restaurant*, Strada Piatra Craiului 4, is one of the best in the city.

The *Crama Bastion*, in a section of the city's 18th century fortifications, is a wine restaurant but there's also a large beer garden here.

Entertainment

The Agenţia Teatrala (the theatre ticket office) is at Strada Mărăşeşti 2, beside the Hotel Timişoara.

From October to May there's a disco in the *Casă de Cultură a Studenţilor*, Bulevardul Tinereii 9, near the corner of Strada General Dragalina, a couple of blocks from the train station (opening Tuesday to Sunday at 8 pm). Tram No 1 passes this way.

Getting There & Away

Romavia at Hotel Continental has flights from Timişoara to Zürich, Switzerland, twice a week, and to Larnaca, Cyprus, weekly, US$186 one way on either.

Timişoara is 1½ hours south of Arad by local train (57 km). Service to Bucharest is fairly frequent via Băile Herculane, Orşova, Drobeta-Turnu Severin and Craiova. Sleepers are available to/from Bucharest (534 km, eight hours). Direct express trains link Timişoara to Iaşi via Cluj-Napoca and Suceava.

Daily buses connect Timişoara to Békéscsaba (138 km), Baja (257 km), Szeged (157 km) and Nuremberg. To Budapest (327 km, eight hours, US$14) the service is weekly. The international ticket window is open weekdays from 9 am to 5 pm, otherwise you can usually pay the driver.

To/From Yugoslavia The daily *Bucureşti* express train from Belgrade (159 km, six hours) arrives at Timişoara around midnight and returns to Yugoslavia early the next morning. Reservations are required. It's also possible to get to Yugoslavia by taking a local train to Jimbolia (39 km, one hour) and then a connecting train to Kikinda (twice daily, 19 km). International tickets must be purchased in advance at a CFR Travel Agency.

Hitchhiking in Yugoslavia is much worse than in Romania but if you want to try it, take one of the six daily local trains 56 km south to the border station, Stamora Moraviţa, walk across and stick out your thumb – Belgrade is 98 km south-west. Take any ride offered as far as Vršac, 14 km south of the border, as there are six cheap local trains a day from there to Pančevo Glavna Station near Belgrade. Two of the six unreserved Stamora Moraviţa trains continue on to Vršac (76 km from Timişoara).

Getting Around

Tram and trolleybus tickets are very difficult to find, so pick some up at the kiosk across the street from the train station as soon as you arrive.

Taxis in Timişoara are metered and quite cheap.

Slovakia

Europe's youngest country Slovakia only emerged from 74 years of junior partnership in Czechoslovakia in 1993. Though just half the size of the Czech Republic in area and population, Slovakia's strategic position as a bridge between Austria, Ukraine, Hungary and Poland ensures it a pivotal role in the new Europe.

The country has much to offer those who enjoy outdoor activities. The rugged High Tatra Mountains are an attraction of European stature and there's also the gentler natural beauty of the Malá Fatra near Žilina and the Slovenský raj east of Poprad. The possibilities for hikers are so numerous this book can only scratch the surface. In winter this is easily the best ski country in Europe when viewed in terms of value for money.

Slovakia is also rich in specific things to see. In East Slovakia a string of unspoiled medieval towns shelter Gothic artworks of the first order while Bratislava is a cosmopolitan city with a rich cultural life. There are 180 quaint castles and castle ruins in Slovakia, the largest of which are Spišský hrad, east of Levoča; Orava Castle, above the village of Oravský Podzámok, 28 km north of Ružomberok; and Trenčín Castle in West Slovakia.

Best of all, much of Slovakia is well off the beaten tourist track. The facilities are good, yet few visitors stray beyond the Prague-Bratislava-Budapest corridor. This certainly works to the advantage of the clever few willing to make the long detour east to see the magnificent mountain ranges along the Polish border and the 13th century towns founded by Saxon Germans on what was then Hungary's eastern frontier.

The rural Slovaks are a people apart from the urbane Czechs and the peasant traditions of Slovakia are a clear transition from the more Germanised culture of Bohemia and Moravia to Ukraine. This background is evident in the folk costumes you'll see in remote Slovak villages on Sunday, the tradi-

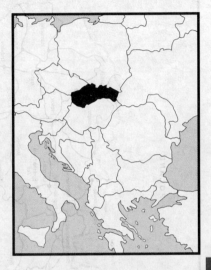

tional meal of roast goose with potato pancakes and the country's colourful handicrafts. For 1000 years Slovakia was Hungarian and many ethnic Magyars still reside here. You'll find the Slovaks an extremely warm, friendly people prepared to go out of their way to make sure you'll never regret including their country in your European tour.

Facts about the Country

HISTORY
Slavic tribes occupied what is now Slovakia in the 5th century AD. In 833 the prince of Moravia captured Nitra and formed the Great Moravian Empire which included all of present Central and West Slovakia and Moravia in the Czech Republic. To counter Frankish influence from the west, the Great Moravian prince invited the Byzantine king

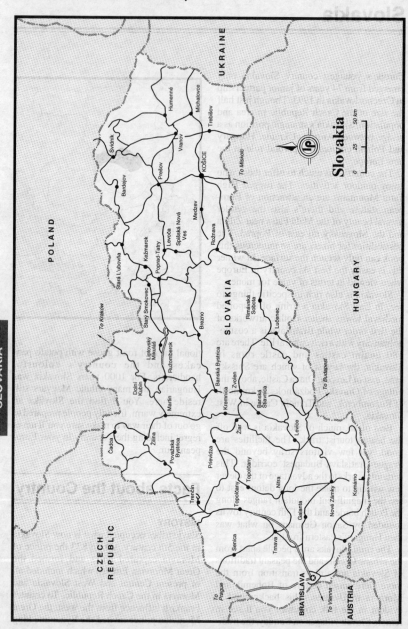

SLOVAKIA

to send missionaries to the area and in 863 the famous Greek brothers, Cyril and Methodius, arrived to implant Christianity. To facilitate the translation of liturgical texts and the Holy Scriptures, Cyril created the first Slavic alphabet here, the forerunner of contemporary Cyrillic.

In 907 the empire collapsed due to the political intrigues of its rulers and external pressure from the Germans and the Hungarians. The invading Hungarian tribes settled southern Slovakia and, after the creation of a unified Hungarian kingdom in the year 1000, the whole of Slovakia was annexed to Hungary in 1018. To gain influence in the Latinised west, the Hungarian monarch reoriented his realm away from Byzantium and towards Catholic Rome.

The Hungarians developed mining (of silver, copper and gold) and trade (in gold, amber and furs). After a Tatar invasion in the 13th century, the Hungarian king invited Saxon Germans to settle the eastern borderlands (present East Slovakia) to provide a buffer against further such attacks. The Slovak language emerged as a separate Slavic language between the 12th and 15th centuries.

Slovakia remained part of Hungary until 1918, although the Spiš region of East Slovakia belonged to Poland from 1412 to 1772. When the Turks overran Hungary in the early 16th century, the Hungarian capital moved from Buda to Bratislava. The Austrian Habsburg dynasty assumed the Hungarian throne and the entire territory of former Czechoslovakia was brought together under one rule for the first time since the 9th century. Only in 1686 was the Ottoman Empire finally driven from Hungary south of the Danube.

In the mid-19th century, the poet L'udovít Štúr (1815-56) instigated the creation of a literary Slovak language and the democratic revolution of 1848 further stimulated Slovak national consciousness. Yet the formation of the dual Austro-Hungarian monarchy in 1867 made Hungary autonomous from Austria in matters of culture and a policy of enforced Magyarisation was instituted in

Slovakia between 1868 and 1918. In 1907 Hungarian became the sole language of elementary education.

As a reaction to this, Slovakian intellectuals cultivated closer cultural relations with the Czechs who themselves were being subjected to Austrian domination. The old concept of a single Czecho-Slovakian tribe was revived for political purposes and, after Austria-Hungary's defeat in WW I, Slovakia, Bohemia and Moravia united as Czechoslovakia.

The centralising tendencies of the sophisticated Czechs alienated many Slovaks and, after the 1938 Munich agreement which forced Czechoslovakia to cede territory to Germany, Slovakia declared its autonomy within a federal state. Hungary took advantage of the instability of the time to annexe a strip of southern Slovakia including Košice and Komárno. When Hitler's troops invaded Czechoslovakia in March 1939, a clerofascist puppet state headed by Monsignor Jozef Tiso (executed in 1947 as a war criminal) was set up in Slovakia under German 'protection'.

Tiso led Slovakia into WW II alongside Germany but in August 1944 Slovak partisans (both communist and non-communist) overthrew his regime in the Slovakian National Uprising (SNP), an event which is today a source of national pride. Although the Germans sent in forces to crush the uprising, fighting continued until late October. In the wake of Soviet advances in early 1945, a government of free Czechoslovakia was established at Košice two months before the liberation of Prague.

The second Czechoslovakia established after the war was intended to operate on the basis of equality between the two peoples, but after the communist takeover in February 1948 the administration once again became centralised in Prague. Slovakian communists who resisted were brought to trial accused of advocating 'bourgeois nationalism'. Although the 1960 constitution granted Czechs and Slovaks equal rights, only the 1968 'Prague Spring' reforms introduced by Alexander Dubček (a rehabilitated

SLOVAKIA

Slovakian communist) actually implemented this concept. In August 1968 Soviet troops quashed the democratic reforms and although the Czech and Slovakian republics theoretically became equal partners in a federal Czechoslovakia in 1969, the real power remained in Prague.

The fall of communism in Czechoslovakia in 1989 led to a resurgence of Slovakian nationalism and agitation for Slovakian autonomy. In February 1992 the Slovakian parliament rejected a treaty which would have perpetuated a federal Czechoslovakia.

The rift deepened with the results of the June 1992 elections which brought to power the left-leaning Movement for a Democratic Slovakia (HZDS) headed by ex-boxer Vladimír Mečiar. The 150-seat Slovakian parliament was divided between the HZDS with 74 seats, the (ex-Communist) Party of the Democratic Left (SDL') with 29 seats, the Christian Democrats (KDH) with 18 seats, the ultra-nationalist Slovak National Party (SNS) with 14 seats and the Hungarian Minority Party (MKDH-E) with 14 seats. In July this parliament voted to declare sovereignty.

Mečiar held negotiations with his Czech counterpart Václav Klaus, with Mečiar calling for a loose confederation with a common currency, army and president, while Klaus insisted on a federation with a central government. By May 1992 unemployment was 11.8% in Slovakia compared to just 3.2% in Bohemia and Moravia and only 10% of foreign investment had gone to Slovakia. To alleviate hardship, the Slovaks wanted to slow economic reform and, with both sides refusing to compromise, in August 1992 it was agreed that the federation would peacefully dissolve at the end of the year. Thus on 1 January 1993 the Czech and Slovak Federative Republic separated into two fully independent states.

With the Slovakian economy in trouble, Mečiar was ousted from the prime ministership by a parliamentary vote of no-confidence in March 1994 after it became apparent that his only clear policy was separation from Czechoslovakia. At the present

Slovakia faces an uphill struggle to keep economic pace with its neighbours in an increasingly competitive Europe.

GEOGRAPHY

Slovakia sits in the very heart of Europe straddling the north-western end of the Carpathian mountain range. This hilly 49,035-sq-km country (just a bit smaller than Nova Scotia, Canada) forms a clear physical barrier between the plains of Poland and Hungary. Almost 80% of Slovakia has an altitude of over 750 metres above sea level.

Slovakia south of Nitra is a fertile lowland stretching down to the Danube River which forms the border with Hungary from Bratislava to Štúrovo/Esztergom. The Váh River joins the Danube at Komárno and together they flow south-east to the Black Sea.

Žilina is caught between the Beskydy of Moravia and the Malá Fatra (Little Fatra) of Central Slovakia, and to the east are the Vysoké Tatry (High Tatra). At 2655 metres Gerlachovský štít (Gerlach in German) is the highest of the mighty peaks in this spectacular alpine range which Slovakia shares with Poland. The Nízke Tatry (Low Tatra) are between Poprad-Tatry and Banská Bystrica.

There are five national parks: Malá Fatra (east of Žilina), Nízke Tatry (between Banská Bystrica and Poprad-Tatry), Vysoké Tatry (north of Poprad-Tatry), Pieniny (along the Dunajec River) and Slovenský raj (near Spišská Nová Ves). In this book we provide practical information on visiting all of these parks except Nízke Tatry.

ECONOMY

For centuries this was a backward agricultural area from which people sought to escape through emigration (nearly two million people of Slovak origin live in the USA today). In 1918 Slovakia united with the far more advanced Czech lands, stimulating limited industrial development. During WW II, however, most existing Slovakian factories were adapted to the needs of the German war effort and later the communists developed arms production into a key industry. Actually, 65% of former Czechoslovakia's military production came from Slovakia. Attempts since 1989 to convert these plants to other uses have led to widespread unemployment in Central Slovakia and created severe problems for Slovakia's heavy engineering and metallurgy industries. In early 1994 unemployment in Slovakia stood at 14.4% and inflation was 25% a year.

Under the communists, agriculture was neglected and the natural connection of the farmers to their land was disturbed by Soviet-style collectivisation. State subsidies kept production and consumption high but since 1990 agricultural output has plummeted as subsidies were removed and the purchasing power of the general public reduced. Slovakia's cooperative farms are now owned by those who work on them and the state farms are soon to be privatised but as yet private farms account for only 4% of the land.

Heavy industry was developed throughout former Czechoslovakia, with Slovakia being industrialised almost from scratch. By 1989 Slovakia accounted for a fifth of former Czechoslovakia's industrial output with oil refineries at Bratislava, textile mills at Bratislava, Trenčín, Žilina and Prešov, cement works at Banská Bystrica and an iron works at Košice. In 1991 the chemical industry alone accounted for 67.5% of industrial production, textiles 16% and leather and shoe-making a further 8%.

The heavy industry concentrated here is experiencing the biggest difficulties in Eastern Europe today due to a combination of lost markets in the former Soviet bloc and intense protectionism in Western Europe which is keeping out Slovakian chemicals, iron, textiles and agricultural products. Not only is Slovakia unable to sell its armaments in Europe but Western countries also object to sales to the Third World. Inefficient, debt-ridden companies without saleable products are not prime candidates for privatisation and the choice between endless state subsidies and mass bankruptcy is daunting. And to make matters worse, trade between

Slovakia and the Czech Republic has plummeted. This is a much bigger problem for Slovakia which relies on the Czech Republic for 40% of its trade than it is for the Czechs who only conduct 20% of their foreign business with Slovaks.

The big investors in Slovakia to date have been Austria, Germany, the USA and the Czech Republic, in that order. Slovakia offers investors competitive advantages in the form of a highly trained workforce (over 10% of Slovakian workers have a university education and 36.4% are high school graduates) and low wages (averaging just US$200 a month), but some Western investors claim there are many bureaucratic obstacles to doing business here. The Slovakian government defines its goal as a 'socially oriented' market economy.

Slovakia's first nuclear generating station was built at Jaslovské Bohunice near Trnava in the 1970s and a second plant is nearing completion at Mochovce east of Nitra. These Soviet-designed VVER-440 facilities supply nearly half of Slovakia's electricity but the safety of the Jaslovské Bohunice facility has been questioned.

The Gabčíkovo hydroelectric project on the Danube west of Komárno became highly controversial after Hungary backed out of the joint project in 1989 due to environmental considerations. By October 1992 the Danube River had been partially diverted near Bratislava and in November the power plant and navigational route at Gabčíkovo were put into operation (turn to the Visegrád section in the Hungary chapter for more information). Gabčíkovo produces enough electricity to cover the needs of every home in Slovakia and the canal allows even the largest river vessels to reach Bratislava year-round.

POPULATION & PEOPLE

Slovakia has a population of 5,300,000 of which 85.6% are Slovaks, 10.7% Hungarians, 1.5% Gypsies and 1% Czechs. The 600,000 ethnic Hungarians live mostly in southern and eastern Slovakia. The September 1992 Slovakian constitution

SLOVAKIA

guarantees the rights of minorities and three-quarters of Hungarian children receive schooling in their mother tongue. For historical reasons, some antagonism exists between Slovaks and Hungarians but leaders on both sides have tried to minimise confrontations.

Eighty thousand Slovakian Gypsies managed to escape Nazi extermination because the Germans didn't actually occupy Slovakia until after the uprising in late 1944 and there wasn't time to send them to Auschwitz. The communists gave the Gypsies homes and jobs, and most of them now lead normal lives, though their nomadic culture has been destroyed in the process. Lately, as heavy industrial jobs disappear, many Slovakian Gypsies have migrated to the Czech Republic. As elsewhere in Eastern Europe, there is much prejudice against Gypsies.

Slovakia's Jews weren't as lucky as the Gypsies and beginning in March 1942 60,000 of them were deported to Nazi death camps in Poland by the Slovakian fascists while another 30,000 were rounded up in the Hungarian-occupied part of southern Slovakia. Many of those who survived emigrated to Palestine after the war and the number of Jews in Slovakia today is small.

Catholics are in a majority but Evangelicals are also numerous and in East Slovakia there are many Greek Catholics and Orthodox believers. Religion is taken rather more seriously by the folksy Slovaks than it is by the secular Czechs.

The largest cities are Bratislava (440,000), Košice (236,000), Žilina (97,000), Nitra (91,000), Prešov (89,000), Banská Bystrica (87,000) and Trnava (73,000).

ARTS
Music

Traditional Slovakian folk instruments include the *fujara* (a two-metre-long flute), the *gajdy* (bagpipe), and the *konkovka* (a strident shepherd's flute). Folk songs helped preserve the Slovak language during the millennium of Hungarian control and in East Slovakia the ancient folk traditions are still a living part of village life. The songs tell of love, lament, anticipation and celebration as vigorous dancing dispels the uncertainty of life.

The locally available compact disc *Spievajme si, dievky* (OPUS 9157 2186) by the female folk choir Vajana makes a good souvenir, although the songs are highly orchestrated and not pure folk music.

LANGUAGE

Although many people working in tourism have a good knowledge of English, in rural Slovakia very few people speak anything other than Slovakian. German is probably the most useful non-Slavic language to know.

An aspect of Slovakian nationalism is pride in the language and Slovaks can get a little hot under the collar when Slovak is given short shrift in comparison with other Slavic languages. As a visitor, you won't be taken to task if you mix your 10 words of Czech with your five words of Slovak, but any effort to communicate in the language of the land will be most appreciated.

Pronunciation

The 43 letters of the Slovak language are pronounced similarly to those of Czech. In words of three syllables or less the stress falls on the first syllable. Longer words generally also have a secondary accent on the 3rd or 5th syllable. The number of syllables is the same as the number of vowels (a, á, ä, e, é, i, í, o, ó, u, ú, y, ý), semi-vowels (l, l', r) or diphthongs (ia, ie, iu, ou, ô). Letters and diphthongs pronounced somewhat differently from their English equivalents include the following:

c	'ts' as in 'cats'
č	'ch' as in 'chain'
dz	'ds' as in 'pads'
dž	'j' as in 'jaw'
ia	'yo' as in 'yonder'
ie	'ye' as in 'yes'
iu	as in 'you'
j	'y' as in 'yet'
ň	'ni' as in 'onion'
o	'wo' as in 'won't'

SLOVAKIA

ou	'ow' as in 'know'
š	'sh' as in 'show'
y	'i' as in 'machine'
ž	'z' as in 'azure'

Greetings & Civilities

hello	*ahoj*
good morning	*dobré ráno*
good day	*dobrý deň*
good evening	*dobrý večer*
goodbye	*dovidenia*
please	*prosím*
thank you	*d'akujem*
excuse me/forgive me	*prepáčte mi/odpuste mi*
I am sorry.	*Ospravedlňujem sa.*
yes	*áno*
no	*nie*

Small Talk

I don't understand.	*Nerozumiem.*
Could you write it down?	*Môžeš mi to napísat'?*
What is it called?	*Ako sa do volá?*
Where do you live?	*Kde bývaš?*
What work do you do?	*Čo robíš?*
I am a student.	*Som študent.*
I am very happy.	*Som vel'mi šťastný.*

Accommodation

youth hostel	*mládežnícka ubytovňa*
camping ground	*kemping*
private room	*súkromné izby*
How much is it?	*Kol'ko to stojí?*
Is that the price per person?	*Je to cena za jednu osobu?*
Is that the total price?	*Je to celková cena?*
Are there any extra charges?	*Sú tam ešte iné položky?*
Do I pay extra for showers?	*Platím zvlášť za sprchu?*
Where is there a cheaper hotel?	*Kde tu je lacnejší hotel?*
Should I make a reservation?	*Môžem si to rezervovat'?*
single room	*jednolôžková izba*
double room	*dvojlôžková izba*

| It is very noisy. | *Je to vel'mi hlučné.* |
| Where is the toilet? | *Kde je toaleta?* |

Getting Around

What time does it leave?	*O ktorej to odchádza?*
When is the first bus?	*Kedy ide prvý autobus?*
When is the last bus?	*Kedy odchádza posledný autobus?*
When is the next bus?	*Kedy ide ďalší autobus?*
That's too soon.	*To je vel'mi skoro.*
When is the next one after that?	*Kedy ide najbližší spoj po tomto?*
How long does the trip take?	*Ako dlho trvá výlet?*
arrival	*príchod*
departure	*odchod*
timetable	*cestovný poriadok*
Where is the bus stop?	*Kde je autobusová zastávka?*
Where is the train station?	*Kde je vlaková stanica?*
Where is the left-luggage room?	*Kde je úschovňa batožín?*

Around Town

Just a minute.	*Počkajte chvíl'u.*
Where is ... ?	*Kde je ...?*
the bank	*banka*
the post office	*pošta*
the tourist information office	*turistické informácie*
the museum	*múzeum*
Where are you going?	*Kam ideš?*
I am going to ...	*Ja idem do ...*
Where is it?	*Kde to je?*
I can't find it.	*Nemôžem to nájst'.*
Is it far?	*Je to d'aleko?*
Please show me on the map.	*Prosím, ukážte mi to na mape.*
left	*vl'avo*
right	*vpravo*
straight ahead	*rovno*
I want ...	*Ja chcem ...*
Do I need permission?	*Potrebujem povolenie?*

SLOVAKIA

Entertainment

Where can I buy a ticket?	*Kde si môžem kúpiť lístok?*
Where can I refund this ticket?	*Kde môžem vrátiť lístok?*
Is this a good seat?	*Je to dobré miesto?*
at the front	*vpredu*
ticket	*lístok*

Food

I do not eat meat.	*Ja nejem mäso.*
self-service cafeteria	*samoobslužný bufet*
grocery store	*potraviny*
fish	*ryba*
pork	*bravčovina*
soup	*polievka*
salad	*šalát*
fresh vegetables	*čerstvá zelenina*
milk	*mlieko*
bread	*chlieb*
sugar	*cqkor*
ice cream	*zmrzlina*
coffee	*káva*
tea	*čaj*
mineral water	*minerálka*
beer	*pivo*
wine	*víno*
hot/cold	*horúci/studený*

Shopping

Where can I buy one?	*Kde to môžem kúpiť'?*
How much does it cost?	*Koľko to stojí?*
That's (much) too expensive.	*To je veľmi drahé.*
Is there a cheaper one?	*Kde to kúpim lacnejšie?*

Time & Dates

today	*dnes*
tonight	*dnes večer*
tomorrow	*zajtra*
the day after tomorrow	*pozajtra*
What time does it open?	*Kedy otvárajú?*
What time does it close?	*Kedy zatvárajú?*

open	*otvorené*
closed	*zatvorené*
in the morning	*ráno*
in the evening	*večer*
every day	*každý deň*
At what time?	*O ktorej?*
when?	*kedy?*

Monday	*pondelok*
Tuesday	*utorok*
Wednesday	*streda*
Thursday	*štvrtok*
Friday	*piatok*
Saturday	*sobota*
Sunday	*nedeľa*

January	*január*
February	*február*
March	*marec*
April	*apríl*
May	*máj*
June	*jún*
July	*júl*
August	*august*
September	*september*
October	*október*
November	*november*
December	*december*

Numbers

1	*jeden*
2	*dva*
3	*tri*
4	*štyri*
5	*päť*
6	*šesť*
7	*sedem*
8	*osem*
9	*deväť*
10	*desať*
11	*jedenásť*
12	*dvanásť*
13	*trinásť*
14	*štrnásť*
15	*pätnásť*
16	*šestnásť*
17	*sedemnásť*
18	*osemnásť*
19	*devätnásť*
20	*dvadsať*

SLOVAKIA

21	*dvadsat'jeden*
22	*dvadsat'dva*
23	*dvadsaľt'tri*
30	*tridsat'*
40	*štyridsat'*
50	*pät'desiat*
60	*šest'desiat*
70	*sedemdesiat*
80	*osemdesiat*
90	*devät'desiat*
100	*sto*
1000	*tisíc*
10,000	*desat'tisíc*
1,000,000	*milión*

Facts for the Visitor

The official separation of Slovakia and the Czech Republic only occurred in January, 1993, and much of the practical information contained in the Facts for the Visitor section of the Czech Republic chapter also applies to Slovakia. Rather than repeat information, in this section we've tried to focus on differences between the countries. For this reason, you should read the previously mentioned part of the introduction to the Czech Republic chapter even if you have no intention of going there.

VISAS & EMBASSIES

At last report entry requirements were the same as for the Czech Republic (visas not required by most Europeans and US citizens). Visas cost US$25 for Australians and New Zealanders, or US$50 for Canadians, and two photos are required. The visa consists of a full-page stamp in your passport and two separate sheets (make sure the clerk doesn't forget to give you these), one of which should include your photo. Slovakian visas cannot be used to visit the Czech Republic, nor vice versa, and if you have only a Czech visa you'll be refused entry at the Slovakian border. Don't count on getting your Slovakian visa at the border.

Slovakian Embassies

Apart from the Slovakian embassies in Belgrade, Bucharest, Budapest, Prague, Sofia, Warsaw and Zagreb listed elsewhere in this book, diplomatic missions for Slovakia include:

Australia
47 Culgoa Circuit, O'Malley, Canberra, ACT 2606 (☎ 062-90 1516)

Canada
50 Rideau Terrace, Ottawa, ON K1M 2A1 (☎ 613-749 4442)

Netherlands
Parkweg 1, 2585 JG, The Hague (☎ 070-355 7566 or 355 8097)

UK
25 Kensington Palace Gardens, London W8 4QY (☎ 0171-243 0803)

USA
2201 Wisconsin Ave NW, Washington, DC 2000 (☎ 202-965 5161)

MONEY

The Slovakian crown or *Slovenská koruna* (Sk) is worth about 10% less than the Czech crown; US$1 = 32 Sk. In late 1993 Slovakia issued its own distinctive currency with coins of 10, 20 and 50 hellers (halierov) and 1, 2, 5 and 10 crowns (Sk). Banknotes come in denominations of 20, 50, 100, 500, 1000 and 5000 crowns. The old Czechoslovakian notes and coins are now worthless.

The easiest place to change a travellers' cheque is at a branch of the Všeobecná Úverová Banka (General Credit Bank) or the Investičná Banka (Investment Bank) where you'll be charged a standard 1% commission. Satur offices (see Tourist Offices) deduct 2% and may only accept cash. Post office exchange windows never change travellers' cheques and take 2% weekdays and 3% weekends to change cash. Banks often give a slightly better rate for travellers' cheques than for cash.

If you'll be arriving from Poland you might think about purchasing a small amount of Slovakian currency at a Polish exchange office to make your entry easier (keep them out of sight at the border). Poland-bound, you can easily get rid of excess crowns at any Polish exchange office, at a loss of about

10%. Otherwise, it's best to spend all your Slovakian currency before you leave.

Because Slovakia has been slower to privatise than the Czech Republic it's likely to remain a bargain for travellers far longer than its neighbour, whatever the economic logic of the situation. You'll find food, admissions and transport cheap and accommodation manageable except in Bratislava. The value added tax (VAT) in Slovakia is 25%.

CLIMATE & WHEN TO GO
Slovakia experiences hot summers and cold winters. The warmest, driest and sunniest area is the Danube lowland east of Bratislava. Due to the altitude there are really only two seasons in the High Tatra Mountains with spring and fall each lasting less than two weeks. The High Tatras also experience the highest rainfall.

SUGGESTED ITINERARIES
Depending on the length of your stay, you might want to see and do the following things in Slovakia:

Two days
    Visit Bratislava.
One week
    Visit Košice, Levoča and the Tatra Mountains.
Two weeks
    Visit most of the places included in this chapter.

TOURIST OFFICES
The old Czechoslovakian tourism monopoly Satur (called Čedok until early 1994) is well represented in Slovakia. Turn to them whenever you require the assistance of a commercial travel agency. Other commercial travel agencies with offices around Slovakia include Tatratour and Slovakoturist. CKM Student Travel also has offices in most towns. In Bratislava the Bratislava Information Service (BIS) is an excellent source of general information on both city and country.

BUSINESS HOURS & HOLIDAYS
Public holidays in Slovakia are New Year's Day (1 January), Three Kings Day (6 January), Easter Friday and Easter Monday (March/April), Labour Day (1 May), Liberation Day (8 May), Cyril and Methodius Day (5 July), Feast of the Assumption (15 August), SNP Day (29 August), Constitution Day (1 September), All Saints Day (1 November) and Christmas (from 24 to 26 December).

Things are really quiet in Slovakian towns from Saturday afternoon to Monday morning as the locals evacuate to their cottages in the country. Don't plan on doing any business at this time although most museums will be open. All grocery stores (*potraviny*) are shut tight from noon Saturday until Monday morning and even the kiosks are closed.

CULTURAL EVENTS
The Bratislava Lyre in May or June features rock concerts. During June or July folk dancers.from all over Slovakia meet at the Východná Folklore Festival, 32 km west of Poprad-Tatry. The Bratislava Jazz Days are held in September.

POST & TELECOMMUNICATIONS
Receiving Mail
Mail addressed c/o Poste Restante, 81000 Bratislava 1, Slovakia, can be picked up at window No 6 in the main post office, námestie SNP 34, weekdays from 7 am to 8 pm, Saturday 7 am to 1.30 pm.

American Express cardholders can have their mail sent c/o Tatratour, Frantiákánske námestie 3, 81509 Bratislava, Slovakia.

Telephones
The telephone system isn't quite as good as the one in the Czech Republic and it's sometimes hard to get even local calls through. Calls are most easily placed from main post offices or telephone centres although you can also make them from blue coin phones on the street. A three-minute telephone call from Slovakia will cost about US$3.50 to the UK, US$6.50 to the USA or Australia.

To call Slovakia from abroad, dial the international access code, 42 (the country code for Slovakia), the area code and the number. Important area codes include 7 (Bratislava), 89 (Žilina or Vrátna), 91 (Prešov), 92 (Poprad-Tatry), 95 (Košice), 819 (Komárno), 831 (Trenčín or Trenčianské Teplice), 935 (Bardejov), 965 (Spišská Nová Ves), 966 (Levoča or Spišské Podhradie) and 969 (Starý Smokovec, Štrbské Pleso or Tatranská Lomnica). When dialling from within Slovakia you must add a 0 before the area code.

TIME

In Slovakia time is GMT/UTC plus one hour. At the end of March Slovakia goes on summer time and clocks are set forward an hour. At the end of September they're turned back an hour.

WEIGHTS & MEASURES

The electric current is 220 V, 50 Hz AC. The metric system is used in Slovakia.

HEALTH
Thermal Baths

Public thermal swimming pools exist at Trenčianské Teplice and Komárno. Most of Slovakia's other spas are reserved for patients under medical supervision, but Slovakoterma, Radlinského 13, 800 00 Bratislava, can organise stays at health resorts such as Bardejovské Kúpele and Trenčianské Teplice. New Millennium Holidays (☎ 0121-711 2232), 20 High St, Solihull, West Midlands B91 3TB, England, UK runs inexpensive bus tours from the UK to Trenčianské Teplice from May to October.

ACTIVITIES
Hiking

Slovakia is one of Eastern Europe's prime hiking areas and full information is provided in the sections of this chapter devoted to Malá Fatra, Vysoké Tatry and Slovenský raj.

Rafting

For information on rafting on the Dunajec River in Pieniny National Park turn to the section on the Dunajec Gorge. The hiking is also good here.

Skiing

Slovakia contains some of Europe's top ski resorts and this really is the place to come skiing on a budget. The ski season runs from December to April in the Vysoké Tatry, Nízke Tatry and Malá Fatra. Quality ski gear is hard to find in Slovakia though you can usually rent the local variety at very competitive rates. Sometimes the waits at the ski lifts can be excruciatingly long. The runs are colour coded: black (difficult), red (moderate) and blue (easy).

Cycling

Slovakia offers some of the best cycling terrain in Eastern Europe with uncrowded roads and beautiful scenery. East Slovakia especially is prime cycling territory. Several places at the Vysoké Tatry resorts rent mountain bikes and the possibilities there are endless.

HIGHLIGHTS
Museums & Galleries

Epicureans will enjoy Bratislava's wine museum. The Šarišské Museum at Bardejovské Kúpele has one of the best collections of reassembled traditional dwellings in Eastern Europe. The Slovak National Uprising Museum in Banská Bystrica, a 'political' museum built by the communists, survives because of the crucial period it documents in Slovakia's history. Finally, at the museum of the Tatra National Park at Tatranská Lomnica, you have the rare opportunity of stepping out the door and exploring the very things you saw in the exhibits.

Castles

Spišský hrad, in remote Spišské Podhradie, is the largest castle in the country, and Trenčín Castle is well known as having been perhaps the most strategic. Bratislava Castle had to be rebuilt from the ground up after wartime destruction.

Historic Towns

Three of Slovakia's most picturesque historic towns are Bardejov, Košice and Levoča. Old Bratislava is also lovely.

ACCOMMODATION

Since 1990, hotel prices for Slovaks have remained fairly steady while those for foreigners have doubled and tripled. Much of the accommodation information in the introduction to the Czech Republic chapter also applies here.

Hostels

CKM Student Travel often has information on youth hostels and can often make advance bookings at CKM 'Juniorhotels' in Bratislava, Banská Bystrica, Horný Smokovec (Vysoké Tatry) and Jasná pod Chopkom (Nízke Tatry). A youth hostel card is not required but it should get you a discount at these. In July and August vacant student dormitories are often converted into temporary youth hostels and CKM is the most likely to know.

FOOD

Once again, check the introduction to the Czech Republic chapter for general information on eating out here. As in the Czech Republic, always insist on seeing a menu with prices listed before ordering a meal at a regular restaurant.

The Slovaks serve their meals with paprika and *halušky* (small dumplings topped with grated cheese and bits of bacon). A real treat to watch for is *palačinky so zavareninou* (peach pancakes). *Langoše* is a large round fried doughnut with garlic and oil brushed on which makes a great snack. It's usually possible to get fairly good salads in Slovakia.

DRINKS

Two-thirds of former Czechoslovakia's vineyards are on the southern and eastern slopes of the Little Carpathian Mountains north of Bratislava. Slovakian wine is good and cheap and there are also some excellent sparkling wines.

Getting There & Away

AIR

Czechoslovak Airlines (ČSA) flies from Bratislava to Prague several times a day with immediate connections twice a week to Chicago, Montreal, New York and Toronto. ČSA links Bratislava directly to Moscow once a week.

From Prague, ČSA flies daily to Bratislava (US$66), Poprad-Tatry (US$77) and Košice (US$87). Weekdays there are also flights from Bratislava to Košice (US$54). These overpriced services are mostly intended for international passengers connecting with long-haul ČSA flights in Prague.

In addition, a local carrier called Tatra Air has daily flights from Bratislava to Košice and Zürich.

A US$2.50 airport tax is charged on all flights except Bratislava-Košice.

LAND
Bus

There's a bus several times a day from Vienna (Mitte Busbahnhof) to Bratislava (64 km, two hours, US$9). For more information on international buses turn to Getting There & Away in the Bratislava section.

Eurolines has a weekly bus year-round between Amsterdam and Bratislava (22 hours, US$86 one way, US$139 return) via Brussels and Vienna (Czech transit visa not required). A 10% reduction is available to those aged under 26 or over 59 years. Tickets are available from Budget Bus (☎ 020-627 5151), Rokin 10, Amsterdam, and Europabus (☎ 2-217 0025), Place de Brouckere 50, Brussels.

Train

To/From Western Europe Vienna (Südbahnhof) to Bratislava is a 64-km hop done four times a day (two hours, US$8). All trains to/from Germany pass through Prague and a Czech transit visa is required by some nationals.

To/From Eastern Europe Bratislava is linked to Budapest (215 km, three hours, US$23) by the *Hungária, Balt-Orient* and *Pannónia* express trains from Budapest-Keleti and the *Metropol* express train from Budapest-Nyugati, all via Štúrovo. From Budapest, the morning Eurocity *Hungária* and the afternoon *Metropol* are your best bet because the *Balt-Orient* and *Pannónia* often arrive late from Romania. Ask about reservations when you book your ticket.

Surprisingly, there are no direct trains from Bratislava to Poland and all connections are via the Czech Republic. Several express trains pass through West Slovakia between Hungary and Poland, for example the *Bem* to Wrocław, Poznań and Szczecin, and the *Polonia* to Katowice and Warsaw, both passing Žilina in the middle of the night. The *Báthory* express train, which travels between Warsaw and Budapest via Katowice, calls at Trenčín in the middle of night in both directions. Reservations are mandatory on all these trains and you should avoid them if you require a Czech visa as they transit the Czech Republic for a short distance and you could be put off at the Czech border.

Train services from East Slovakia to Poland and Hungary avoid the Czech Republic. The *Rákóczi* express train shuttles daily between Budapest and Košice (270 km, 4½ hours, US$22), continuing to Poprad-Tatry on certain days (ask). The *Rákóczi* leaves Budapest-Keleti in the early morning, Košice in the late afternoon. Reservations are optional. The *Cracovia* express train from Budapest-Keleti to Kraków transits Košice around midnight northbound, around 4 am southbound. The *Karpaty* express train to Kraków and Warsaw passes Košice during the day, but northbound it often arrives late from Romania and southbound it only goes to Hatvan (not Budapest). Reservations are required on both the *Cracovia* and *Karpaty*.

Unreserved local trains run three times a day between Muszyna, Poland, and Plaveč, Slovakia (16 km, 20 minutes). In Plaveč there are train connections to/from Prešov (54 km, 1½ hours) and Poprad-Tatry (61 km,

two hours); from Muszyna trains run to Nowy Sącz (50 km) and (less frequently) to Kraków (217 km). Approximate times of this cross-border train are given in the Prešov section.

Unreserved local trains connect Košice and Miskolc, Hungary, twice a day (88 km, 2½ hours, US$9). Six times a day there are unreserved local trains between Slovenské Nové Mesto, Slovakia, and Sátoraljaújhely, Hungary, with connections to/from Košice and Miskolc.

Both daily trains to/from Moscow, the *Dukla* to/from Prague and the *Slovakia* to/from Bratislava (2325 km, 44 hours), pass through Košice. From Košice 2nd-class fares are from US$46 to Kiev and US$66 to Moscow.

Car & Motorbike

Some highway border crossings are only open to citizens of Slovakia, Hungary and Poland, though this could change. The following crossings (listed clockwise around the country) are open to everyone. In each case, the name of the Slovakian border post is provided.

To/From Poland You can cross at Trstená (west of Zakopane); Javorina (east of Zakopane); Mníšek nad Popradom (31 km south of Nowy Sącz); and Vyšný Komárnik (between Rzeszów and Prešov).

To/From Ukraine You can cross at Vyšné Nemecké (94 km east of Košice).

To/From Hungary The border crossings are at Slovenské Nové Mesto (opposite Sátoraljaújhely); Hraničná pri Hornáde (21 km south of Košice); Kráľ' (45 km northwest of Miskolc); Šiatorská Bukovinka (just north of Salgotarjan); Slovenské Ďarmoty, Šahy (80 km north of Budapest); Komárno (opposite Komárom); Medveďov (13 km north of Győr); and Rusovce (16 km southeast of Bratislava).

To/From Austria The only crossing is at Petržalka (at Bratislava).

SLOVAKIA

On Foot

Walking in and out of Slovakia is cheap, easy and fun. By crossing on foot you avoid the hassle of buying an expensive international ticket and end up with a memorable experience.

To/from Poland, the most convenient place to cross is at Łysa Polana/Javorina between Starý Smokovec and Zakopane. Turn to the Vysoké Tatry section of this chapter and Zakopane in the Poland chapter for a description of how it's done.

To/from Hungary, you can easily walk across the bridge over the Danube River between Kormárno and Komárom. This route is described in the Kormárno section of this chapter and the Komárom section in the Hungary chapter.

To/from Austria, you could hitch towards Vienna from Bratislava and a few details of the route are provided in the Bratislava section.

Getting Around

BUS

Buses are more expensive than trains and on weekends bus services are more sharply reduced than rail services. Plan on doing most of your travel by train with side trips by bus. Bus tickets in Slovakia cost US$0.50 for 25 km, US$1 for 50 km, US$2 for 100 km and US$4 for 200 km.

When trying to decipher posted bus schedules beware of departure times bearing footnotes you don't completely understand as these buses often don't show up. Check the time at the information window whenever possible. It is helpful to know that *premáva* means 'it operates' and *nepremáva* means 'it doesn't operate'.

TRAIN

The Slovak Republic Railways or Železnice Slovenskej republiky (ŽSR) provides efficient service at low rates. Most of the places covered in this chapter have been selected precisely because they're on or near the main

railway line between Bratislava and Košice. By express train from Bratislava it's 123 km and 1¾ hours to Trenčín, 203 km and three hours to Žilina, 344 km and five hours to Poprad-Tatry, 370 km and 5½ hours to Spišská Nová Ves and 445 km and 6½ hours to Košice.

Most train stations in Slovakia have a left-luggage office where you can check your bag for US$0.20.

CAR RENTAL

Europcar has offices in Bratislava and Košice, as well as at Bratislava airport (US$10 service charge at this outlet). Their cheapest Škodas begin at US$40 a day plus US$0.40 a km, or US$98/480 daily/weekly with unlimited mileage, 25% tax included. A weekend rate of US$128 runs from 3 pm Friday to 9 am Monday with unlimited mileage. Add about US$10 daily for collision insurance and another US$10 for theft coverage. Europcar allows one-way rentals between Bratislava and Prague or Košice at no additional charge.

Also check Budget, Hertz, Pragocar and other car rental agencies in Bratislava as their rates could well be lower (ask the Bratislava Information Service for a list of companies).

Bratislava

Bratislava (Pozsony in Hungarian, Pressburg in German) is Slovakia's largest city. Here the Carpathian Mountains, which begin at the Iron Gate of Romania, finally come to an end. As you arrive at the main train station, you'll see vineyards on the slopes of the Little Carpathian Mountains which meet the Danube River here. The Austrian border is almost within sight of the city and Hungary is just 16 km away.

Founded in 907 AD, Bratislava was already a large city in the 12th century. Commerce developed in the 14th and 15th centuries and in 1467 the Hungarian Renaissance monarch Matthias Corvinus founded a

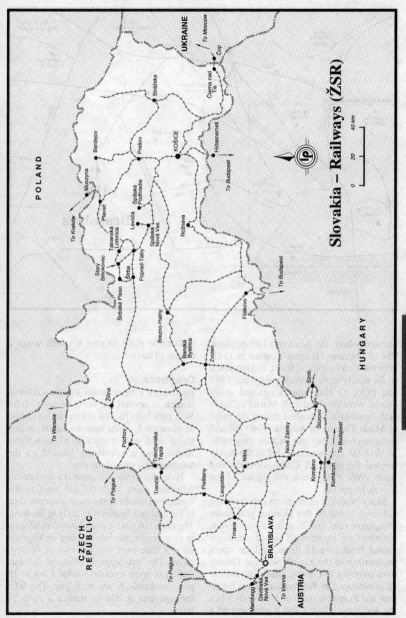

Slovakia – Railways (ŽSR)

SLOVAKIA

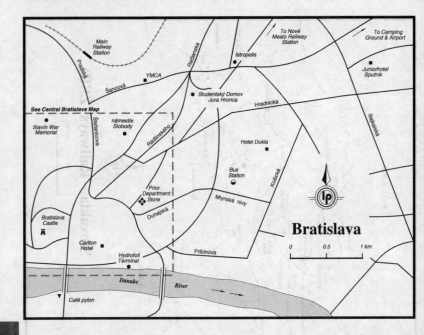

Bratislava

0   0.5   1 km

university here, the Academia Istropolitana. The city became Hungary's capital in 1541, after the Turks captured Buda, and remained so for nearly three centuries. Between 1563 and 1830, 11 Hungarian kings and seven queens were crowned in St Martin's Cathedral. Bratislava flourished during the reign of Maria Theresa of Austria (1740-80) and some imposing Baroque palaces were built. In 1918 the city was included in the newly formed Republic of Czechoslovakia and since 1969 it has been the capital of the Slovak Republic.

Many beautiful monuments survive in the old town to tell of this glorious past under Hungarian rule, and Bratislava's numerous museums are surprisingly rich. Franz Liszt visited Bratislava 15 times, and the opera productions of the Slovak National Theatre rival anything in Europe. Bratislava isn't at all as swamped by Western tourism as Budapest and Prague (except on weekends when the Austrians invade), and if you can find a

reasonable place to stay it's well worth a couple of days.

Orientation

Bratislava's main train station, Hlavná stanica, is several km north of town. Tram No 1 runs from the lower level at this station to námestie L Štúra near the centre. A few trains also use stanica Bratislava-Nové Mesto, less conveniently located on the north-eastern side of the city.

Hviezdoslavovo námestie is a convenient reference point, with the old town to the north, the Danube to the south, Štúrova ulica to the east and Bratislava Castle to the west. The main bus station (autobusová stanica) is in a convenient modern building on Mlynské nivy, a little over one km east of Štúrova ulica. The left-luggage office at the bus station is open weekdays from 5 am to 10 pm, weekends 6 am to 6 pm. The left-luggage area at Hlavná stanica is open 24 hours.

Information

General information about the city is supplied by the Bratislava Information Service or BIS (☎ 333 715), Panská 18 (open weekdays from 8 am to 6 pm, Saturday from 8 am to 1 pm). They sell an indexed city map and are very helpful. *Kam v Bratislave* (Where in Bratislava) available at BIS provides detailed information about what's on around Bratislava.

Map freaks can go to the source and buy maps of almost anywhere in Slovakia at Slovenská Kartografia, Pekná cesta 17 off Račianska (eastbound tram No 3, 5 or 11). Geodézia Bratislava, Pekná cesta 15, has topographical maps of western Slovakia.

Money The Všeobecná Úverová Banka has a poorly marked exchange office at Hlavná stanica open daily from 7.30 am to 6 pm. It's hidden to one side of the corridor, around behind the 'Internationale Kasse' on the opposite side of the main hall from the left-luggage office. Their rate is as good as anything in town and they take the usual 1% commission on cash and travellers' cheques.

The Všeobecná Úverová Banka upstairs in the bus station is open Monday to Thursday from 8 am to noon and 1 to 5 pm, Friday 8 am to noon.

The Všeobecná Úverová Banka, námestie SNP 14 (weekdays 8 am to 5 pm, Saturday 8 am to noon), also charges 1% commission to change travellers' cheques.

An automatic currency-exchange machine able to convert the banknotes of 14 countries is outside the Slovenská Štátna Sporiteľňa, Štúrova ulica 11 near the ČSA office (accessible 24 hours).

Post & Telecommunications Mail addressed c/o Poste Restante, 81000 Bratislava 1, can be collected at window No 6 at the main post office námestie SNP 34 (weekdays from 7 am to 8 pm, Saturday 7 am to 1.30 pm). Letters from abroad are held one month. To mail a parcel you must go to the office marked 'podaj a výdaj balíkov' through the next entrance at námestie SNP 35.

You can make international telephone calls at Kolárska ulica 12 (open 24 hours a day).

Bratislava's telephone code is 07.

Embassies The American Embassy (☎ 335 932) is at Hviezdoslavovo námestie 4 (weekdays 8.30 am to noon and 2 to 4 pm).

The British Embassy (☎ 364 420; open weekdays from 8.30 am to 12.30 pm and 1.30 to 5 pm) and the French Embassy (☎ 361 727) are in the same building at Grösslingová 35. The Croatian Embassy is nearby at Grösslingová 47.

The Czech Embassy is at Panenská 33, off Hodžovo námestie (Monday and Wednesday 9 am to noon and 2 to 4 pm, Tuesday and Thursday 9 am to noon).

Nearby are the Hungarian Embassy, Palisády ulica 54 (open Monday, Wednesday and Friday from 9 am to noon), and the Embassy of Bulgaria, Kuzmányho 1 off Palisády ulica (open Monday, Wednesday and Friday from 9 am to noon).

Also in this area is the Russian Embassy, Maróthyho ulica 3 off Palisády ulica (Monday, Wednesday and Friday 9 am to 1 pm), and the Romanian Embassy, Fraňa Kráľa 11 (Monday, Wednesday and Friday 9 am to noon).

The Polish Embassy, Hummelova 4, is in the residential area north-west of Bratislava Castle. To get to the Polish Embassy (open Monday to Friday from 9 am to 12.30 pm), take trolley bus No 213, 216 or 217 from Hodžovo námestie to 'Hummelova'.

In the same neighbourhood as the Polish Embassy is the Ukrainian Embassy, Radvanská ulica 35 (Monday, Wednesday and Friday from 9 am to 1 pm), which issues one-month tourist visas for US$50.

Travel Agencies CKM Student Travel, Hviezdoslavovo námestie 16, sells HI youth hostel cards (US$6) and ISIC student cards (US$7). If you're under 26 years old, ask CKM about Eurotrain tickets for reduced international train travel to Western Europe.

The American Express representative in Bratislava is Tatratour (☎ 335 852), Frantiákánske námestie 3.

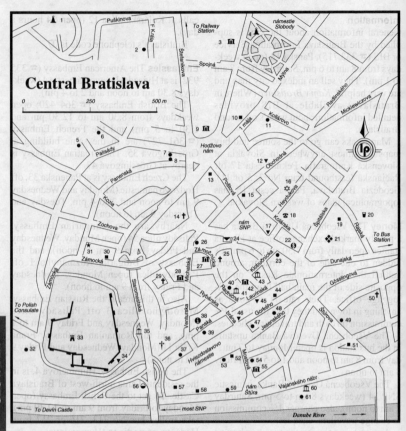

Central Bratislava

0   250   500 m

Staff at Slovakoterma, Radlinského 13, can arrange stays at health spas throughout Slovakia (from US$50/80 single/double all-inclusive).

For information on travel to the former USSR visit Intourist, Ventúrska 2 (weekdays 8 am to 4 pm).

Bookshops Knihy Slovenský, on the corner of Rybárska brána and Laurinská, sells useful hiking maps.

Visa Extensions Any visa or passport enquiries should be directed to the foreigners' police, conveniently located at Svoradova ulica 11 (Monday, Tuesday, Thursday and Friday 7 am to noon, Wednesday 8.30 am to noon and 1 to 5 pm).

Things to See

Begin your visit with the **Slovak National Museum** (1928) opposite the hydrofoil terminal on the river. The museum features anthropology, archaeology, natural history and geology exhibits – notice the large relief map of Slovakia. A little farther up the riverfront is the ultramodern **Slovak National Gallery** (admission US$1.50),

PLACES TO STAY

10	Hotel Tatra/Kino Tatra
13	Hotel Forum
15	Palace Hotel
19	Hotel Kyjev
30	Chez David Pension
44	Gremium Pension/Café
51	Krym Hotel
52	Carlton Hotel
57	Hotel Danube
58	Hotel Devín

PLACES TO EAT

12	Picco Pizza
17	Cukráreň Jezbera
34	Modrá Hviezda Restaurant
45	Diétna Jedáleň
46	Food Market

OTHER

1	Slavín War Memorial
2	Romanian Embassy
3	Archbishop's Summer Palace
4	Site of the Klement Gottwald Monument
5	Russian Embassy
6	Bulgarian Consulate
7	Hungarian Consulate
8	Czech Embassy
9	Grassalkovich Palace
11	nová scéna
14	Church of the Holy Trinity
16	Synagogue
18	International Telephone Office
20	Charlie's Pub
21	Prior Department Store
22	Všeobecna Úverová Banka
23	Old City Market
24	Main Post Office
25	Franciscan Church
26	Michael Tower
27	Mirbach Palace
28	Palace of the Royal Chamber
29	Church of the Clarissine Order
31	Foreigners' Police
32	Slovak National Parliament
33	Bratislava Castle
35	Decorative Arts Museum
36	St Martin's Cathedral
37	CKM Student Travel
38	Bratislava Information Service
39	City Art Gallery
40	Old Town Hall
41	Museum of Wine Production
42	Primate's Palace
43	Hummel Music Museum
47	Slovak National Theatre
48	Pokladňa Kassa (Theatre Ticket Office)
49	ČSA Airline Office
50	Hungarian Church
53	American Embassy
54	Slovenská filharmonia
55	Reduta Palace
56	Bus to Devín Castle
59	Slovak National Gallery
60	Slovak National Museum
61	Hydrofoil Terminal

Bratislava's major art collection with a good Gothic section. The gallery building itself is interesting because of the daring incorporation of an 18th century palace into the design.

Backtrack slightly to námestie L Štúra where, on the corner of Mostová, you'll find the Art-Nouveau **Reduta Palace** (1914), now Bratislava's concert hall. Go north up Mostová to the neo-Baroque **Slovak National Theatre** (1886) on the right with Ganymede's Fountain (1888) in front.

Crowded, narrow Rybárska brána penetrates the old town to Hlavní námestie, at the centre of which is Roland's Fountain (1572). To one side is the old town hall (1421), now the **Municipal Museum** with torture chambers in the casemates and an extensive collection housed in finely decorated rooms. You enter the museum from the picturesque

inner courtyard where concerts are held in summer.

Leave the courtyard through the east gate and you'll be on a square before the **Primate's Palace** (1781). Enter to see the Hall of Mirrors where Napoleon and the Austrian emperor Franz I signed a peace treaty in 1805. In the municipal gallery on the 2nd floor are rare English tapestries (1632). St George's Fountain stands in the courtyard. On Saturday the palace is crowded with couples being married, but it's still open to visitors. Just beyond this palace is the **Hummel Music Museum**, Klobučnícka 2, in the former home of the German composer and pianist Johann Hummel (1778-1837).

Return through the old town hall courtyard and turn left into Radničná 1 to get to

SLOVAKIA

the **Museum of Wine Production** (closed Tuesday) in the Apponyi Palace (1762). Buy the museum guide book in English if you're at all interested in the subject. Next head north on Frantiákänske námestie to the **Franciscan Church** (1297). The original Gothic chapel (1297) with the skeleton of a saint enclosed in glass is accessible through a door on the left near the front. Opposite this church is the **Mirbach Palace** (1770), at Frantiákánske námestie 11, a beautiful Rococo building housing a good art collection.

From the palace continue around on narrow Zámočnícka ulica to the **Michael Tower** (closed Tuesday), which has a collection of antique arms. There's a great view from the tower. Go north through the tower arch into the old barbican, out the north gate and across the street, to the **Church of the Holy Trinity** (1725), an oval edifice with fine frescoes.

Return to the Michael Tower and stroll down Michalská to the **Palace of the Royal Chamber** (1756) at Michalská 1. Now the university library, this building was once the seat of the Hungarian parliament. In 1848 serfdom was abolished here, marking the end of feudalism in Hungary.

Take the passage west through the palace to the Gothic **Church of the Clarissine Order** with a unique pentagonal tower (1360) supported on buttresses. Continue west on Farská, then turn left into Kapitulská and go straight ahead to the 15th century coronation church, **St Martin's Cathedral**. Inside you'll find the bronze statue (1734) of St Martin cutting off half his robe for a beggar.

Castles on the Danube The busy motorway in front of St Martin's follows the moat of the former city walls. Construction of this route and the adjacent bridge was rather controversial as several historic structures had to be pulled down and vibrations from the traffic have structurally weakened the cathedral. Find the passage under the motorway and head up towards Bratislava Castle, built above the Danube on the southernmost spur of the Little Carpathian Mountains. At the foot of the hill is the **Decorative Arts Museum** (closed Tuesday).

Since the 9th century, **Bratislava Castle** has been rebuilt several times; it served as the seat of Hungarian royalty until it finally burnt down in 1811. Reconstructed between 1953 and 1962, the castle now houses a large historical museum. Climb up to the castle for a great view. The Slovakian National Parliament meets in the modern complex that overlooks the river, just beyond the castle.

As you return from the castle, take a stroll on one of the pedestrian walkways across the sweeping **most SNP** (SNP Bridge) (1972) over the Danube. On the far side you can take a lift (US$0.50) up one of the pylons to an expensive café that sits 80 metres above the river. Even the toilets have a view.

Below the Bratislava end of most SNP is a city bus terminal where you can catch city bus No 29 west along the Danube to the Gothic ruins of **Devín Castle** (open from May to October, closed Monday), which is on a hill where the Morava and Danube rivers meet. The castle withstood the Turks but was blown up in 1809 by the French. Stay on the bus to the end of the line and walk back to the castle. Austria is just across the rivers from Devín.

From the 1st to 5th centuries AD, Devín and Bratislava castles were frontier posts of the Roman Empire, manned by the 14th Legion. In the 9th century Devín Castle was a major stronghold of the Great Moravian Empire, and today both castles are regarded as symbols of the Slavic peoples who maintained their identity despite centuries of foreign rule.

Post-Communist Bratislava To see a bit of the Bratislava built by the communists, head north from the Michael Tower across Hodžovo námestie to the Baroque **Grassalkovich Palace** (1760), previously the House of Pioneers. Continue north-east towards námestie Slobody, previously known as Gottwaldovo námestie. An impressive monument to Klement Gottwald (1980), the man instrumental in implanting communism in Czechoslovakia, once stood on the platform in the north-west corner of the square but the massive marble figures of Gottwald and others were destroyed during the political upheaval of late 1989. Some of the new buildings on the square belong to the **Technical University**. On the western side of námestie Slobody is what used to be the **archbishop's summer palace** (1765), now the seat of the Government of the Slovak Republic.

If you go west down Spojná and north up Štefánikova ulica 25, you'll come to the former **Lenin Museum**, now an art gallery. Continue north a little, then head west up the steps of Puškinova towards the **Slavín War Memorial** (1965). This is where 6847 Soviet soldiers who died in the battle for Bratislava in 1945 are buried. There's a good view of modern Bratislava from here.

Unless otherwise noted, all of Bratislava's galleries and museums are closed on Monday.

Hiking

To get out of the city and up into the forested Little Carpathian Mountains, take trolley bus No 213 north-east from Hodžovo námestie to the end of the line at Koliba, then walk up the road to the **TV tower** on Kamzík Hill (440 metres) in about 20 minutes. Here an elevator (US$0.50) lifts you to a viewing platform overlooking three countries. The revolving café just below the platform has no food but the drinks are quite affordable. The tower is closed on Monday from October to February.

Maps posted at the tower outline the many hiking possibilities of this area. For example, head north from the Koliba EXPO Restaurant near the tower down a road closed to vehicular traffic to 'Lanovka'. When you get to a main road at the foot of the hill, turn right to reach a favourite weekend picnic area for Bratislava locals. Bus No 33 runs back to town from here (ask the driver where you have to change to trolley bus No 212 to return to Hodžovo námestie).

Places to Stay

Hostels Staff at CKM Student Travel, Hviezdoslavovo námestie 16, may be able to tell you about summer youth hostels and perhaps reserve a bed for you at the *Juniorhotel Sputnik* (☎ 294 167) at Drieňová 14 in the eastern suburbs (tram No 8, 9 or 12 or bus No 34, 38 or 54). The Juniorhotel Sputnik, a modern hotel beside a large pond, is open all year and comfortable double rooms are US$14 per person for YHA or student-card holders (or several times that for others). Ask if breakfast is included. This place is often full up with groups.

The *YMCA* (☎ 498 005), on the corner of Šancová and Karpatská, has 13 doubles at US$13, six triples at US$20 and one five-bedded room at US$33 but they're often full. It's conveniently located just an eight-minute downhill walk from the main train station, so you could always give it a try upon arrival.

In July and August the 12-storey *Študentský Domov Jura Hronca* (☎ 497 721), Bernolákova ulica 1, about five blocks east of the main train station, rents beds in doubles at US$7 per person. There's a swimming pool and disco (audible throughout the building). Ask CKM about this gigantic student dormitory or just go there direct.

Študentský domos 'Mladá Garda' (☎ 253 136), Račianska 103, north-east of town (tram No 3, 5, 7 or 11), provides accommodation in this large student dormitory complex from July to mid-September only. The communal showers are hidden way down in the basement.

Private Rooms Satur, Jesenského 1-3, arranges private room accommodation for about US$10/15 single/double. The rooms are 20 minutes by tram from the centre.

Your best all-round accommodation stop is the Bratislava Information Service, Panská 18, which rents private rooms near the centre at US$15/18 single/double and knows about cheaper hotels out in the suburbs where rooms begin around US$6 per person. In July and August they can tell you about student hostels where beds cost from US$3 to US$6 per person.

Reditour (☎ 335 174), Ursulínská 11, next

SLOVAKIA

to the Primate's Palace, has pricey private rooms at US$13 per person.

Hotels With the closure of the Carlton Hotel for reconstruction and the upgrading of the Palace Hotel, the already critical budget hotel situation in downtown Bratislava has become almost hopeless. The only moderately priced hotel in the centre is now the *Krym Hotel* (☎ 325 471), Šafárikovo námestie 7 (US$23/35 single/double without bath, US$28/45 with bath), but it's noisy and usually full.

Better is the *Gremium Pension* (☎ 321 818), Gorkého 11, at US$20/31 single/double including breakfast. Considering the alternatives and the excellent location it's a good bet if you can get one of the five rooms.

In the splurge category is *Chez David Pension* (☎ 313 824), Zámocká 13, a clean, modern hotel on the site of the old Jewish ghetto directly below the castle. The eight double rooms are US$52/65 single/double with bath and breakfast – the right choice if price isn't a big consideration.

The white, two-storey *Športhotel Trnávka* (☎ 223 497), Nerudova 8, next to a small stadium north-east of town, is seedy and the rooms are small but at US$12/16/23 single/double/triple with shared bath it's good value. Get there on trolleybus No 215 from Cintorínska ulica near Hotel Kyjev or trolley bus No 219 eastbound from Palárikova ulica just down the hill from the train station. On Friday and Saturday nights ask for a room away from the disco. In winter there's the constant sound of water trickling through the ancient radiators. It's often crowded with people from the former USSR waiting for onward visas.

Ask the Bratislava Information Service about the *Hotel Ineks* (☎ 277 2195), Nobelova 16 north-east of the centre, which sometimes rents rooms at US$6 per person. Going directly there is risky as they're often closed and it's a long way to go for nothing (BIS can sell you a map to help you find the place). Also ask BIS about the *Clubhotel*, Odbojárov 3 off Vajnorská, which also has a tendency to close at the most unexpected times.

The hostel of the *Institute for Adult Education in the Building Industry* or 'Ústav Vzdelávania v Stavebníctve' (☎ 372 060), Bardošová 33, on a hill 1.5 km north-west of the main train station, is not breathtaking value at US$17 per person but the accommodation is good. This place is often full, so ask someone to help you call ahead before going there (trolley bus No 212 from Hodžovo námestie).

Zlaté piesky There are bungalows, a motel, a hotel and two camping grounds at Zlaté piesky (Golden Sands), which is near a clear blue lake seven km north-east of Bratislava. Trams No 2 (from the main train station) and No 4 (from the city centre) terminate right at Zlaté piesky. You can hire rowing boats and sailboards here in summer and there are also tennis courts.

As you cross the bridge from the tram stop you'll see *Hotel Flora* (☎ 257 988) on your left. Double rooms here are US$27 with shower (no singles) and the hotel restaurant is open until 10 pm daily. Next to the Flora is a lakeside camping ground (☎ 257 373) with 50 four-bed cottages without bath at US$18 for the unit and 20 three-bed bungalows with private bath at US$31. Tent camping is possible and the facility is open from mid-April to mid-October. A second, poorer camping ground with run-down three-bed bungalows at US$20 triple is nearby (but not on the lake). Camping here is handled at the reception but the bungalows are controlled by *Motel Evona Zlaté Piesky* (☎ 257 365) a couple of minutes away. The 35 double rooms with bath at the motel are US$22 (no singles). Motel Evona is open year-round but the bungalows are only available from mid-May to September.

Places to Eat

Budget One of the few places to get an early breakfast is *Cukráreň Jezbera*, námestie SNP 11, which opens at 6.30 am Monday to Saturday, 8 am Sunday. The stand-up buffet in the basement, which you enter from around the corner, opens an hour later and not at all on weekends. On weekends the upstairs section of the Jezbera is a good choice for lunch or dinner and the menu is in English.

The *Food Market* found on the corner of Hviezdoslavovo námestie and Rybárska brána (open daily from 9 am to 10 pm), caters for a dozen cuisines at individual counters in the stand-up section or you can sit down and order spaghetti or pizza in the adjacent full-service restaurant.

The *Diétna Jedáleň Restaurant*, Laurinská 8, is a great place for lunch (open weekdays only from 11 am to 4 pm). Ask the person in line behind you to translate the menu. It's self-service but you can get beer and there's a pleasant dining room where you sit down to eat. Note the floral arrangements hanging from the walls. Next door is the similar *Vegetariánská Jedáleň* which keeps identical hours.

Another self-service vegetarian restaurant is in the passageway at Obchodná 68 (Monday to Thursday 11.30 am to 3.30 pm, Friday 10 am to 3 pm only). It's one of the least expensive places to eat in Bratislava and really is vegetarian!

The pizzas served at *Picco Pizza*, Obchodná 45 (closed Sunday), are small and dry (most people douse them in ketchup), and the drinks expensive. An excellent beer garden is directly behind Picco but unfortunately you can't get takeaway pizza to carry back there. A stand adjacent to Picco sells *piróžky*, a sweet Slovakian doughnut.

At the bus station, the *Bistro Express* on the outer back side of the station facing the buses is much better than the self-service inside the station itself.

In summer check out the *Občerstvenie Beer Garden* at námestie SNP 28/30.

Top End A slightly up-market but still affordable place for a better meal is the *Korzo Restaurant*, Hviezdoslavovo námestie 11. Gypsy musicians occasionally play here.

A wine restaurant worth trying is *Vináreň Veľký františkáni*, Frantiákánske námestie 10, in the old monastery beside the Mirbach Palace. Other typical smoky wine-cellars, known as *pod viechou*, where Gypsy music is often played, are found in Baštová and Zámočnícka alleys near the Michael Tower.

The *Modrá Hviezda Restaurant*, Beblavého ulica 14 on the way up to the castle, features local dishes such as cheese pie. The menu is in English.

Chez David Kosher Restaurant, Zámocká 13 directly below the castle, is up-market but not intolerably so. Carp served in the Jewish manner is a speciality.

Stará Sladovňa, Cintorínska 32 (daily until 11 pm), between the Prior Department Store and the bus station, is a large, modern restaurant complex-cum-beer hall dating back to 1872 but reconstructed in 1980 as an eating and drinking place for the masses. The service is variable, the menu only in Slovak and the waiters will tell you the cheaper dishes are unavailable, then bring you things you didn't order merely to inflate your bill. Treat Stará Sladovňa strictly as a drinking place and eat elsewhere.

Cafés *Espresso Cukráreň*, Hviezdoslavovo námestie 25 (closed Monday), is just the place for coffee and cakes.

Another good coffee, cakes and ice cream place is *Atlantis*, Stúrovo 13 (daily until 9 pm). They have Bratislava's best ice cream and on Sunday afternoon the queue runs out the door and down the pavement.

The *Gremium Art Galerie Café*, Gorkého 11, is the place to sip a pseudo-intellectual cup of Viennese coffee *(Viedenská káva)* without having to be pretentious. The atmosphere is good.

Entertainment

Opera and ballet are presented at the *Slovak National Theatre* (1886), on Hviezdoslavovo námestie (often closed Sunday). The local opera and ballet companies are outstanding. Tickets are sold at the 'Pokladňa Kassa' office (open weekdays from noon to 6 pm) on the corner of Jesenského ulica and Komenského námestie, behind the National Theatre. An hour before the performance begins ticket sales are at the theatre itself, but they're usually sold out by then, especially on weekends.

The *nová scéna*, Kollárovo námestie 20, presents operettas, musicals – and drama in Slovak – so you have to check. The ticket office is open weekdays from 12.30 to 6 pm and an hour before the performance but they're usually sold out *(vypredané)*.

The *Slovenská filharmonia* is based in the neo-Rococo Reduta Palace (built in 1914) on Palackého on the corner of Mostová, across the park from the National Theatre. The ticket office (open weekdays from 1 to 5 pm) is inside the building.

The PKO Predpredaj Vstupeniek, Hviezdoslovo námestie 24, has tickets for special events such as rock concerts.

The *Štátne Bábkové Divadlo*, Dunajská 36, puts on puppet shows for kids, usually at 9 or 10 am and sometimes again at 1 or 2 pm. It's good fun.

There's often something happening at Dom Kultury, námestie SNP 12.

Charlie's Pub, Špitálska 4 near Hotel Kyjev (daily from 4 pm to 4 am), is like a disco without the dancing (and without the cover charge). It's probably the most popular meeting and drinking place in town for the city youth.

Discos *Danglár Klub VŠVU-Friedl*, Hviezdoslavovo námestie 18 (downstairs through the smaller entrance to one side), is a student club open weekdays from 11 am to 3 am, weekends 6 pm to 3 am. Friday nights from 8 pm to midnight there's live jazz here (US$1 cover charge on Friday, other nights US$0.50). Apart from the bar and friendly staff, Danglár is a good place to eat and the kitchen stays open until midnight. Prices are reasonable. On Saturday night the locale is often booked by wedding parties.

Klub Rock-Pop-Jazz, Jakubovo námestie 12, a few blocks east of Hotel Krym, is one of the best places near the centre (opens at 8.30 pm).

MM Night Club 'Dimitrovec', on Nobelova (tram No 3, 5, 7 or 11 north-east to Vinohrady Railway Station), is a laser disco open daily from 8 pm to 5 am (US$2 cover). It's spacious and has four bars, but only expensive small cans of beer are available so you ought to have a couple of drinks at the adjacent *Queen's Pub* before going in.

Cinemas In the same complex as Charlie's Pub, Špitálska 4, are cinemas Marilyn and Charlie, Bratislava's best art cinemas. Other cinemas in the centre include Kino Mladosť, Hviezdoslavovo námestie 17, Kino Mier, Grösslingová ulica 23, Kino Slovan, námestie SNP 14, Kino Tatra, námestie 1 mája 5, and Kino Hviezda, námestie 1 mája 9. Near the train station, there's a cinema at the YMCA, Karpatská 2. Films are shown in the original language with Slovak subtitles and admission prices are low.

Getting There & Away

Bus At Bratislava's main bus station you can usually buy your ticket from the driver, but check first at the information counter. Advance tickets may be purchased for the buses marked 'R' on the posted timetable. The footnotes on this timetable are in English.

Ten express buses a day run to Prague (one hour faster than the train for about the same price) and there are 13 buses a day to Komárno (104 km). Other buses leaving Bratislava include six to Košice (402 km), four to Bardejov (457 km), three to Prešov (429 km) and two each to Banská Štiavnica and Tatranská Lomnica.

Six buses a day connect Vienna (Mitte Busbahnhof) to Bratislava (63 km, US$9). In Bratislava buy your ticket for this bus at the ticket window inside the bus station.

Other international buses posted at the bus station are those to Brussels (weekly, US$72), Budapest (three a week, US$9), Cologne (weekly, US$96), Frankfurt (weekly, US$88), Kraków (two a week, US$12), London (weekly, US$108), Munich (weekly, US$52), Paris (weekly, US$75), Salzburg (weekly, US$38), Sofia (two a week, US$47), Stockholm (weekly, US$119) and Thessaloniki (weekly, US$85). Tickets may be purchased for crowns at any of the ticket windows in the bus station or at the adjacent office with the yellow sign 'Obchodná agentúra'. If you require a Czech visa beware of buses which transit that country as you could be 'bumped off' at the border.

Trains All express trains between Budapest and Prague call at Bratislava. Train services from Košice to Bratislava (via Poprad-Tatry, Žilina and Trenčín) are fairly frequent and couchettes are available on the night train.

If you can't find a reasonable place to stay in Bratislava, go to the train station and book a couchette or sleeper to Košice (445 km) or Prague (398 km) for that night. Don't forget that you'll need a regular train ticket along with the couchette ticket. In total a 1st-class sleeper and ticket shouldn't cost you more than you would have had to pay for a hotel room anyway.

There are four local trains a day between Vienna (Südbahnhof) and Bratislava Hlavná stanica (64 km, 1½ hours, US$8). One nightly train departs for Moscow but there's no direct service to Poland. International train tickets are available at Hlavná stanica.

Two local trains a day run from Bratislava Nové Mesto Station to Györ, Hungary (90 km, two hours, US$9) via Rajka. The ticket office in Nové Mesto Railway Station will only sell you a ticket as far as the border (US$0.50) and you must pay the Hungarian conductor the balance. Otherwise buy a through ticket at Hlavná stanica or from Satur the day before.

Walking into Hungary or Austria If you don't want to bother getting an international train ticket, take a local train or bus to Komárno and walk across the bridge to Komárom in Hungary. See the Komárno section for details.

The Austrian border is about four km beyond most SNP along Viedenská cesta. Take bus No 47 from Hodžovo námestie southbound across the bridge and get off at the next stop after high-rise Hotel Incheba. Walk two km to the border, clear customs

and stick out your thumb: Vienna is 64 km west.

Boat From mid-April to September, Raketa hydrofoils ply the Danube between Bratislava and Vienna twice a day for US$19 one way, US$30 return (1¼ hours). In October the service is only daily. Children aged 15 years and under and students pay half-price. Tickets and information are available at the hydrofoil terminal in Bratislava. In late summer the service can be interrupted because of low water levels.

It makes an interesting day trip if your visa allows you to return to Slovakia; a day in Vienna is probably enough, especially considering how outrageously expensive it is. The scenery between Bratislava and Vienna is surprisingly dull and there are no boats downriver to Budapest, a much more scenic trip.

Getting Around

Public transport around Bratislava is based on an extensive tram network that is complemented by buses and trolley buses. Orange automats at tram and trolley bus stops sell tickets, but make sure that the green light is on before inserting any coins.

Toqrist tickets *(turistické cestovné lístky)* valid for 24 hours (US$1), 48 hours (US$2) or seven days (US$3) are sold at the DPHMB office in the underground passageway below Hodžovo námestie (weekdays from 7 am to 6 pm). At Bratislava Hlavná stanica these tickets are sold at the window marked 'Cestovné Lístky' next to the taxi stand in front of the station. The validity of the ticket begins immediately upon purchase, so only buy one when you need it.

Bratislava's taxis all have meters and they're far less likely to try to overcharge you than those in Prague. Downtown Bratislava is small enough for you to be able to walk almost anywhere.

To/From the Airport Airport buses leave from the ČSA office, Štúrova ulica 13 (three or four a day, US$0.20). You can also get to

Ivanka International Airport on city bus No 24 from the train station (eight km).

Car Rental Budget Rent-a-Car is represented by Tatratour, Frantiákánske námestie 3. Pragocar (☎ 333 233) is at Hviezdoslovo námestie 14 (in the courtyard) and Europcar (☎ 340 841) is in the lobby of nearby Hotel Danube. Hertz has a desk in the lobby of Hotel Forum. Hertz and Europcar also have desks at Ivanka airport.

West Slovakia

KOMÁRNO
This Danube border town opposite Komárom, Hungary, is a convenient entry/exit point for travellers in transit between Slovakia and Hungary. Frequent trains with low domestic fares run between these twin cities and their respective capitals, Bratislava and Budapest, and it costs nothing to walk across the massive river bridge erected in 1892. By coming this way you not only avoid the hassle and expense of an international train ticket but you have a chance to compare conditions on both sides of the border up close.

Three-quarters of the inhabitants of Komárno are Hungarian and it's mostly Hungarian you hear spoken in the shops. Komárno serves as the cultural and political centre of the large Hungarian community in south Slovakia, and all street signs in Komárno are written in Slovak and Hungarian. Across the river in Komárom they're in Hungarian and German. Of the two cities, Komárno is by far the more interesting and less touristy, although you don't have the thermal baths found in Komárom.

As at Komárom, the Habsburgs erected impressive fortifications here between 1541 and 1592 to hold back the Turks, who never managed to capture the town. The defensive system was rebuilt and greatly expanded during the Napoleonic wars. The large shipyards at Komárno founded in 1898 build both river and ocean-going vessels.

Orientation
The bus and train stations in Komárno are close to one another. To get to the border from the stations, walk due south on Petöfiho ulica to the end of the street, then left a block and right at Azia Centrum Department Store. Continue south past Hotel Európa to the bridge, a 20-minute walk from the stations. The left-luggage office in the train station is open irregularly (try your luck with one of the coin lockers).

Slovakian and Hungarian customs are together on a peninsula in the middle of the river. For conditions on the Hungarian side, turn to the Komárom section in the Hungary chapter.

Information
Money The Všeobecná Úverová Banka has an exchange office on Tržničné námestie midway between hotels Európa and Danubius, just as you come into town from the bridge. They change travellers' cheques for 1% commission weekdays from 7.30 am to noon and 1 to 5 pm.

The VUB also runs an exchange office right next to customs on the bridge itself (open 7 am to 6 pm and 7 pm to 6 am daily). Their rate for cash is as good as any in town.

The exchange office in the post office behind Hotel Európa will change excess crowns into forints weekdays from 8 am to noon and 2 to 6 pm and Saturday 8 am to noon. They deduct 2% commission weekdays, 3% on Saturday.

Post & Telecommunications The main post office directly behind Hotel Európa contains a telephone centre open weekdays from 8 am to 6 pm and Saturday 8 am to 1 pm. Komárno's telephone code is 0819.

Things to See
The two tall towers of **St Andrew's Church** (1734) on Palatínova ulica are visible from afar. Directly opposite the church is the **Danube Museum** (closed Sunday and Monday) with a small historical collection and one room of paintings. East on

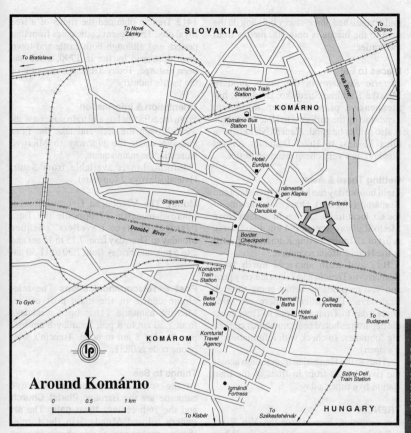

Around Komárno

0   0.5   1 km

Palatínova is námestie gen Klapku with several attractive monuments and the **town hall** (1875). East again in the same direction is the massive 18th century **fortress** near the junction of the Váh and Danube rivers. It's still occupied by the military and is inaccessible.

Komárno's most interesting museum (closed Monday) is the one dedicated to composer Ferenc Lehár and novelist Jókai Mór which is right next to the approach to the bridge to Hungary. Admission includes the adjacent 18th century Serbian Orthodox church with its interesting woodcarvings.

Places to Stay

Your best bet is the *Hotel Danubius* (☎ 44 91), Dunajské nábrežie 12, on the corner of Lehárova ulica (US$10 single or double without bath). As you're walking north across the bridge from Hungary you'll see a yellow three-storey building down on the right with the words 'Spoločenský dom' on the roof. This is the hotel.

The 57 rooms at *Hotel Európa* (☎ 42 51), námestie Štefánika 1, are overpriced at US$22/36/45 single/double/triple with bath and breakfast. Rooms with only a shower and no toilet are a few dollars cheaper. This undistinguished, three-storey building on the road to the bridge is only 500 metres from the border.

Places to Eat

Pizzeria Rigoletto in the sharp, modern Mestské Kultúrne Stredisko, Hradná 1, has inexpensive pizza and beer. *Restaurant Lehár* facing the park next to Hotel Danubius is also said to be good. *Zlata Ryba*, Lehárova ulica 12 next to Hotel Danubius (closed Sunday), is a very cheap stand-up buffet.

Getting There & Away

Eight buses a day run between Bratislava and Komárno (104 km). Otherwise take one of the six local trains to/from Bratislava Nové Mesto Railway Station (94 km, two hours). A list of all trains leaving Komárno is posted at the Hotel Európa reception.

Bus and train services north from Komárno to Trenčín and Žilina are very poor and you're probably better going through Bratislava. Theoretically there are three buses a day to Trnava and one to Trenčín but the departures board bears numerous confusing footnotes, so check with information (if it's open).

A bus to the Hungarian train station across the river leaves from in front of the train station five times a day.

TRENČÍN

For centuries, here where the Váh River valley begins to narrow between the White Carpathians and the Strážov Hills, Trenčín Castle guarded the south-west gateway to Slovakia and one of the routes from the Danube to the Baltic. Laugaricio, a Roman military post – the northernmost Roman camp in central Europe – was established here in the 2nd century AD. A rock inscription at Trenčín dated 179 AD mentions the stay of the Roman 2nd Legion and its victory over the Germanic Kvad tribes.

The mighty castle which now towers above the town was first mentioned in 1069 in a Viennese illustrated chronicle. In the 13th century the castle's master, Matúš Čák, held sway over much of Slovakia and in

1412 Trenčín obtained the rights of a free royal city. The present castle dates from that period, and although both castle and town were destroyed by fire in 1790, much has been restored. Today Trenčín is a centre of the textile industry.

Orientation & Information

From the adjacent bus and train stations walk west through the park and take the Tatra Passage under the highway to Mierové námestie, the main square.

Information is available from Satur, Hviezdoslavova 2 (upstairs).

Money The Všeobecná Úverová Banka, Mierové námestie 37 opposite the Tatra Passage, changes travellers' cheques Monday to Thursday from 7.15 to 11 am and 2 to 5 pm, and Friday from 7.30 to 11.30 am only.

Post & Telecommunications The telephone centre in the main post office, Mierové námestie 21, is open weekdays from 7.30 am to 8 pm, Saturday 8 am to 2 pm, Sunday 8 am to noon. Trenčín's telephone code is 0831.

Things to See

At the south-western end of Mierové námestie are the Baroque **Piarist Church** and the 16th century **town gate**. The **art gallery** (closed Monday) in the former Piarist convent next to this church features works by local artists, especially the realist painter M A Bazovský.

A covered stairway from the corner of the square opposite the Piarist church leads up to the Gothic **parish church** and the entrance to **Trenčín Castle** (open daily all year). The so-called 'Well of Love' on the first terrace is a fantastic construction that is 70 metres deep. Above is the castle's great central tower which provides a sweeping view of the whole area. At night the castle is illuminated with fairy tale green and purple lights.

The famous Roman inscription of 179 AD is behind the Tatra Hotel at the north-eastern

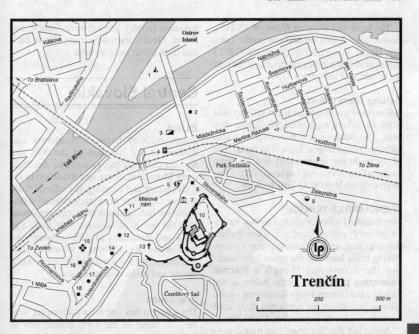

Trenčín

1	Camping Ground	7	Trenčín Museum	14	Satur
2	Sports Stadium	8	Railway Station	15	Prior Department
3	Swimming Pool	9	Bus Station		Store
4	Car Parking Lot	10	Trenčín Castle	16	Hotel Laugaricio
5	Všeobecná	11	Piarist Church	17	Cultural Centre
	Úverová Banka	12	Town Gate	18	Trenčan Hotel
6	Tatra Hotel	13	Parish Church		

end of Mierové námestie and not directly accessible from the castle. The **Trenčín Museum** (closed Monday), Mierové námestie 46, is next to the Tatra Hotel.

Places to Stay

Camping The *Vodácky Klub Ostrove Camping Ground* (☎ 34 013) is on Ostrov, an island in the Váh River, opposite the large sports stadium near the city centre. Camping is US$1 per person, US$1.50 per tent, and nice little two and four-bed cabins are US$3 per person. Singles are accommodated for

the same price aboard the ex-hydrofoil *Raketa*, now permanently moored at the camping ground. Though the rooms are often full, this place is well worth trying if you arrive between June and August.

Hotels Rooms at the nine-storey *Hotel Laugaricio* (☎ 37 841), on Vajanského námestie, next to the Prior Department Store on the edge of the old town, a 10-minute walk from the train station, cost US$17 single without bath, US$34 double with bath.

SLOVAKIA

The basic old *Trenčan Hotel* (☎ 33 117), Braneckého 7, just around the corner from the Hotel Laugaricio, costs US$18/23 triple/quad (no singles or doubles). Use of the communal showers is US$1.50.

Getting There & Away

All express trains on the main railway line from Bratislava to Košice via Žilina stop here. The *Báthory* and *Bem* express trains to/from Poland stop at Trenčín in the middle of the night but reservations and (in some cases) a Czech visa are required. Take a bus to go to/from Brno (134 km).Trenčín

TRENČIANSKE TEPLICE

Trenčianske Teplice, a spa in a narrow valley 14 km north-east of Trenčín, is a worthwhile day trip and an alternative place to stay. Hiking trails lead into the green hills flanking the resort and there's a **thermal swimming pool** open to the public at the Zelená žaba (Green Frog) Restaurant on the hillside just above the spa (open daily until 6 pm from May to September, US$0.50).

Also visit the 'hamman', an exotic neo-Moorish bathhouse (1888) in the middle of town. The five hot sulphur springs at the spa are used to treat rheumatic and nervous system diseases. There are many attractive parks and from June to September a varied cycle of musical programmes is presented at Trenčianske Teplice. You can buy the circular spa wafers (and see them being made) at Kúpel'né Oblátky, ulica Masaryka 14.

Places to Stay

The *Hotel Jalta* (☎ 29 91), a modern five-storey hotel near the train station, is US$21/33 single/double with bath.

The Satur office (☎ 23 61) inside the Liečebny dom Pol'nohospodárov Spa House, ulica 17 novembra 14, has private rooms, but there's a minimum stay of one week (US$42/56 single/double for the week).

Getting There & Away

Trenčianske Teplice is accessible via a six-km branch line from Trenčianska Teplá on the main railway line between Trenčín and Žilina. Electric tram-type trains shuttle back and forth about once an hour.

Central Slovakia

ŽILINA

Žilina, midway between Bratislava and Košice, at the junction of the Váh and Kysuca rivers, is the gateway to the Malá Fatra Mountains. Since its foundation in the 13th century at a crossing of medieval trade routes, Žilina has been an important transportation hub, a status that was confirmed with the arrival of railways from Košice in 1871 and Bratislava in 1883. Though the third largest city in Slovakia, it's still a pleasant, untouristy town with an attractive main square and many interesting shops.

Orientation

The adjacent bus and train stations are near the Váh River on the north-eastern side of town, a five-minute walk from Mariánske námestie, Žilina's old town square. Another five minutes south from Mariánske námestie is Štúrovo námestie, with the Cultural Centre and the luxurious Hotel Slovakia.

Information

Satur (☎ 48 512) is at Štúrovo námestie 3, but don't expect much from them.

CKM Student Travel, Hodžova ulica 8, is just off Mariánske námestie.

Tatratour, Mariánske námestie 21, is the American Express representative.

Money The Všeobecná Úverová Banka, Na bráne 1, changes travellers' cheques (weekdays from 7.30 to 11 am and 1 to 5 pm, Wednesday 7.30 am to noon only).

Post & Telecommunications The telephone centre in the post office next to the train station is open weekdays from 7 am to 8.30 pm, Saturday 7 am to 3 pm, Sunday 8 am to 2 pm. Žilina's telephone code is 089.

Things to See

Žilina's central square with its picturesque church and covered walkway all around could have been lifted straight out of Mexico. Other than this, the only sight worth seeking out is the **Regional Museum** (closed Monday) in the Renaissance castle (zámok) across the river in Budatín, a 15-minute walk north-west from the train station. As you come out of the train station, turn right and go straight ahead for a few minutes, then go right under the train tracks and straight again till you reach the bridge over the river. The white castle tower is visible from there.

Places to Stay

The *Metropol Hotel* (☎ 29 300), right opposite the train station, is the least expensive at US$8 per person without bath – a triple is the same price as three singles. The rooms have a sink and double doors which keep out corridor noise but use of the communal showers is US$0.50 extra. They almost always have rooms.

Also opposite the train station is the more up-market *Hotel Polom* (☎ 21 152) which charges US$18/26 for singles/doubles with private bath and breakfast. Žilina's casino is here.

The *Športklub Hotel* (☎ 22 164), Na strelnici 1, beyond the stadium on the back side of the train station, has rooms at US$8 per person. You check in at the restaurant.

If these places are full, you can always resort to the recently renovated *Hotel Slovan* (☎ 20 556), Kmetova 2, behind the Prior Department Store, back towards the train station (US$25/30 double/triple with bath, TV and breakfast, no singles).

Places to Eat

If you want to eat standing up, try the *Potravinárske Centrum L'udová Jedáleň* in a white four-storey building on a corner near the bus station. It serves hearty breakfasts of goulash soup and beer from 5 am weekdays, from 6 am Saturday (closed Sunday).

The trendy *Vegetariánska Reštaurácia*, Mariánska námestie 11, is fine for what it is, though some of the dishes are pretty unimaginative (for example, lentils and rice with a fried egg).

Non-vegetarians may prefer the *Reštaurácia na bráne*, Bottova 10. The beer hall downstairs and the wine restaurant upstairs are mostly drinking places, but the menu is extensive.

In summer the tables come outside at the *Záhradná Reštaurácia*, ulica Hurbana 24 (through the alley), and it becomes a great place to sit at picnic tables and guzzle draught beer.

Piccollo Pizzeria, Zaymusova 4 near Satur, is a new private place with a nice back terrace where you can down pseudo-pizza and cheap red wine to the beat of rock music.

Getting There & Away

Žilina is on the main railway line from Bratislava to Košice via Trenčín and Poprad-Tatry, and is served by fairly frequent express trains. Most trains between Prague and Košice also stop at Žilina. Express trains from Žilina take six hours to reach Prague (466 km), 1½ hours to Trenčín (80 km), three hours to Bratislava (203 km), two hours to Poprad-Tatry (141 km) and three hours to Košice (242 km).

There are several buses a day to Brno (134 km), but none to Prague.

To/from Poland, if you don't require a Czech visa you can take a local train from Žilina to Český Těšín (69 km) and walk across the border (see the Český Těšín section in the Czech Republic chapter). If you do need a separate Czech visa you will have to avoid that route and go via Poprad and the Javorina/Łysa Polana border crossing to Zakopane.

Both of the express trains between Hungary and Poland which call at Žilina in the middle of the night, the *Bem* and the *Polonia*, also transit the Czech Republic and require mandatory seat reservations.

THE MALÁ FATRA

The Malá Fatra (Little Fatra) Mountains stretch 50 km across north-western Slovakia; Vel'ký Kriváň (1709 metres) is the highest

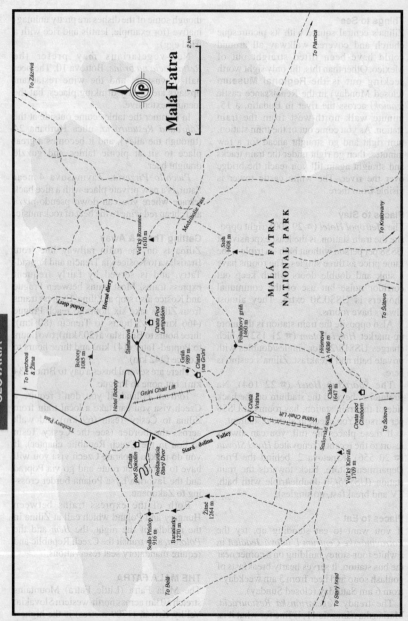

Malá Fatra

To Párnica

To Zázrivá

0 1 2 km

MALÁ FATRA NATIONAL PARK

To Kraľovany

Meitznohle Pass

Veľký Rozsutec 1610 m

Stoh 1608 m

Poludňový grúň 1460 m

To Šútovo

Horné dlery

Dolné dlery

Chata Pod Lampášom

Štefanová

Grúň 989 m

Chata na Grúni

Hromové 1636 m

Boboty 1085 m

Hrnčiarky 1270 m

Grúni Chair Lift

Hotel Boboty

Chľab 1647 m

Vrátna Chair Lift

Chata Vrátna

Chata pod Chlebom

To Šútovo

Tiesňavy Pass

Stará dolina Valley

Sninovské sedlo

Veľký Kriváň 1709 m

Chata pod Sokolím

Reštaurácia Starý Dvor

Žinné 1264 m

To Terchová & Žilina

Sedlo Príslop 916 m

Baraniarky 1270 m

To Belá

To Starý hrad

peak. Two hundred sq km of this scenic range, north of the Váh River and east of Žilina, are included in the Malá Fatra National Park. At the heart of the park is Vrátna, a beautiful mountain valley enclosed by forested slopes on all sides.

Noted for its rich flora, the Vrátna Valley has something for everyone. The hiking possibilities vary from easy tourist tracks through the forest to scenic ridge walks. There are plenty of places to stay and eat, though in midsummer accommodation is tight. The valley is an easy day trip from Žilina. In winter Vrátna becomes a popular ski resort and has many lifts operating.

Information

The Mountain Rescue Service (Horská Služba), on the access road to Hotel Boboty, can provide detailed information on the park.

Things to See & Do

The bus from Žilina enters the Vrátna Valley just south of Terchová where it runs through the **Tiesňavy Pass** which has rocky crags on both sides. One rock resembles a person praying (look back after you've gone through the pass).

Stay on the bus until **Chata Vrátna** (750 metres) where detailed maps of the area are posted. From just above Chata Vrátna, a two-seater chair lift climbs 770 metres to the Snilovské sedlo (1520 metres), a saddle midway between Chleb (1647 metres) and Vel'ký Kriváň (1709 metres). Take along a sweater or jacket as it will be a lot cooler on top. The chair lift (US$2 return) only runs if at least 20 people are present – no problem in summer when there may be a queue. In rain the chair lift doesn't operate at all as there's no protection.

From Snilovské sedlo you can follow the red trail south-east along the mountain ridges past Hromové (1636 metres), then north-east to Poludňový grúň (1460 metres) and Stoh (1608 metres) to the **Medziholie Pass** (1185 metres) right below the rocky summit of **Vel'ký Rozsutec** (1610 metres). An orange trail skirting the side of Stoh allows you to avoid a 200-metre climb. From Medziholie

it's easy to descend another green trail to **Štefanová**, a picturesque village of log houses with private rooms available (ask around). You can do the hike from Snilovské sedlo to Štefanová via Medziholie in about four hours. Other possible hikes from Snilovské sedlo are the blue trail to Starý Dvor via the ridges (three hours) and the red trail west to Strečno Railway Station via the Starý hrad castle ruins (6½ hours).

A good alternative if the chair lift isn't operating, or you don't have much time, is to take the yellow trail from Chata Vrátna to **Chata na Grúni** at 970 metres (45 minutes). This mountain chalet has 30 beds and a restaurant but it's often closed or full. From Chata na Grúni the blue trail descends to Štefanová (45 minutes), where you can get buses back to Žilina.

Places to Stay & Eat

No camping is allowed in the Vrátna Valley. The nearest camping grounds are at Nižné Kamence, three km west of Terchová, and at Varín, both on the way to/from Žilina.

Chata Vrátna (☎ 95 223), a large wooden chalet at 750 metres elevation with 88 beds, is usually full up with hikers in summer and skiers in winter. In spring and late autumn, groups of school children pack the dormitories. Regular hotel rooms at Chata Vrátna are US$15/19/22 double/triple/quad, while the *turistická ubytovňa* dormitory is US$4 to US$7 per person. A good self-service restaurant faces the bus stop below the hotel.

Chata pod Sokolím on the hillside above Reštaurácia Starý Dvor has 60 beds and a large restaurant. The view from here is great. It it's closed try *Pension Vahostav* about a km further up the valley.

The *Chata Pod Skalným Mestom* (☎ 95 363), a few minutes up the green trail in Štefanová village, charges US$14 per person for bed, breakfast and dinner. A few hundred metres beyond is the similar *Chata Pod Lampá Šom*. Both are open year-round.

Reštaurácia Štefanová (☎ 95 325) at Štefanová rents cabins in the forest at US$5 per person year-round except in November.

The *Hotel Boboty* (☎ 95 227), a fairly

luxurious mountain hotel, a five-minute walk up from a bus stop near Štefanová, costs US$19/29 single/double with shower and breakfast (higher in midsummer). The hotel also has a sauna, swimming pool and restaurant.

Getting There & Away

A bus from Žilina to Chata Vrátna, 32 km east (US$1), leaves from platform No 10 at the Žilina Bus Station about once an hour. The bus travels via Krasňany, which has a natural history museum, and Terchová, where a folk festival is held in July.

If you come on a day trip, check the times of afternoon buses returning to Žilina from Štefanová at the information counter in Žilina Bus Station before setting out.

East Slovakia

East Slovakia is one of the most attractive touring areas in Eastern Europe. In one compact region you can enjoy superb hiking in the High Tatra Mountains, rafting on the Dunajec River, historic towns such as Levoča and Bardejov, the great medieval castle at Spišské Podhradie, the lovely spa of Bardejovské Kúpele and city life in the capital Košice. The proximity of Ukraine gives the region an exotic air. Getting around is easy with frequent trains and buses to all these sights plus easy access to Poland and Hungary. In spite of all these advantages, exciting East Slovakia is still well off the beaten track.

THE VYSOKÉ TATRY

The Vysoké Tatry (High Tatras) are the only truly alpine mountains in Central Europe and one of the smallest high mountain ranges in the world. This 27-km-long granite massif covers 260 sq km, forming the northernmost portion of the Carpathian Mountains. The narrow, rocky crests soar above wide glacial valleys with precipitous walls. At 2655 metres, Gerlachovský štít (Mt Gerlach) is the highest mountain in the entire 1200-km Carpathian Mountains, and several dozen other peaks exceed 2500 metres.

Enhancing the natural beauty packed into this relatively small area are 30 valleys, almost 100 glacial lakes and bubbling streams. The lower slopes are covered by dense coniferous forests. From 1500 to 1800 metres altitude, there's a belt of brushwood and knee pines, and above this are alpine flora and bare peaks. (In short, the Slovakian High Tatras is the most appealing mountain resort area in Eastern Europe.)

Since 1949 most of the Slovakian portion of this jagged range has been included in the Tatra National Park (TANAP), the first national park to be created in former Czechoslovakia, which complements a similar park in Poland. A network of 600 km of hiking trails reaches all the alpine valleys and many peaks. The red-marked Tatranská Magistrála Trail follows the southern crest of the Vysoké Tatry for 65 km through a striking variety of landscapes. The routes are colour-coded and easy to follow. Park regulations require you to keep to the marked trails and refrain from picking flowers. A park entry fee of US$0.50 is collected in July and August.

Orientation

The best centre for visitors is Starý Smokovec, a turn-of-the-century resort that is well connected to the rest of the country by road and rail. Tram-style electric trains run frequently between the three main tourist centres in the park: Štrbské Pleso (1320 metres), Starý Smokovec (990 metres) and Tatranská Lomnica (850 metres). At Poprad-Tatry these trains link up with the national railway system. Buses also run frequently between the resorts. Cable cars, chair lifts and a funicular railway carry you up the slopes to hiking trails which soon lead you away from the throng. During winter, skiers flock to this area which offers excellent facilities.

All three main train stations have left-luggage offices, with those at Starý Smokovec and Tatranská Lomnica open 24 hours a day and the one at Štrbské Pleso Station open from 5 am to 10.30 pm.

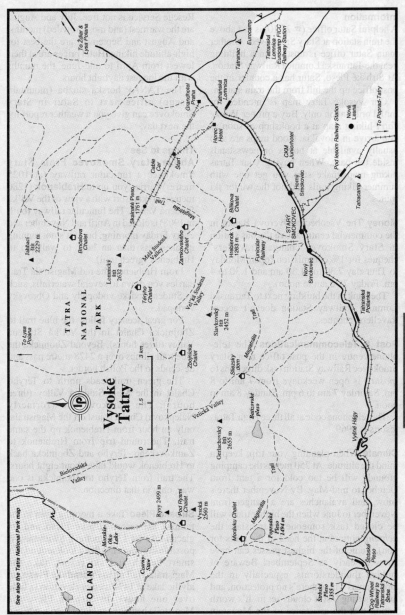

Information

A helpful Satur office (☎ 27 10) is just above the train station at Starý Smokovec. Another main Satur office is upstairs in a building near the Tatranská Lomnica Railway Station. At Štrbské Pleso, Satur has a counter in the post office up the hill from the train station.

Our Vysoké Tatry map is intended for initial orientation only. Buy a proper *Vysoké Tatry* hiking map at a bookshop as soon as you arrive in Slovakia. Good maps are also usually available at hotels or newsstands inside the park. When buying your Tatras hiking map, make sure you get one with summer hiking trails and not the winter ski routes.

Money The Všeobecná Úverová Banka in the commercial centre above the bus station in Starý Smokovec changes travellers' cheques for 1% commission (open Monday to Thursday 7.30 to 11.30 am and 1.30 to 4 pm, Friday 7.30 am to noon).

The bank in the building next to Tatranská Lomnica Railway Station doesn't accept travellers' cheques.

Post & Telecommunications The telephone centre in the post office near Starý Smokovec Railway Station (ask directions to *'pošta'*) is open weekdays from 7 am to 8 pm, Saturday 7 am to 6 pm, Sunday 8 am to noon.

The telephone code at all three High Tatras resorts is 0969.

Climate When planning your trip, keep in mind the altitude. At 750 metres the camping grounds will be too cold for a tent from October to mid-May. By November there's snow, and avalanches are a danger from November to June when the higher trails will be closed (ask someone to translate the *achtung* notices at the head of the trails for you). Some of the highest passes can have snow as early as September! Beware of sudden thunderstorms, especially in the alpine areas where there's no protection, and avoid getting lost if clouds set in. It's worth noting that the assistance of the Mountain

Rescue Service is not free. July and August are the warmest (and most crowded) months, and August and September are the best for high-altitude hiking. Hotel prices are at their lowest from April to mid-June, the months with the longest daylight hours.

The TANAP horská služba (mountain rescue) office next to Satur in Starý Smokovec can give you a weather report for the next day.

Things to See

Above Starý Smokovec From Starý Smokovec a funicular railway (at 1025 metres) carries you up to **Hrebienok** (1280 metres), a ski resort with a view of the Veľká Studená Valley. The funicular railway (built in 1908) is closed in April and November and every Friday morning, but if it's not running it takes less than an hour to walk up to Hrebienok (green trail).

From Hrebienok the red Magistrála Trail carries you down to several waterfalls, such as Studenovodské vodopády and Obrovský vodopád.

For great scenery follow the blue trail to Zbojnícka Chalet in the Veľká Studená Valley (three hours). Beyond Zbojnícka the blue trail climbs over a 2428-metre pass and descends to the Polish border.

The green trail leads north to Téryho Chalet in the Malá Studená Valley (three hours). The Zamkovského (formerly Nálepkova) Chalet is just off the Magistrála, only an hour from Hrebienok up the same trail. The round trip from Hrebienok to Zamkovského, Téryho and Zbojnícka back to Hrebienok would take about eight hours. The trail from Téryho to Zbojnícka is one way, only in that direction.

Štrbské Pleso Take a morning train to the famous ski resort Štrbské Pleso and its glacial lake (at 1355 metres). Swimming is possible in summer. After a look around this smart health and ski resort, take the Magistrála Trail up to **Popradské Pleso**, an idyllic lake at 1494 metres elevation (a little over one hour). In Štrbské Pleso the Magistrála begins near Hotel Patria, where a pedestrian bridge crosses the main road at the entrance to Helios Sanatorium. Have lunch at the Morávku Chalet right next to Popradské Pleso. From here the Magistrála zigzags up the mountainside towards Sliezsky dom and Hrebienok. A better bet is to hike up the blue trail from Popradské Pleso to the Hincovo lakes in another hour and a half.

Via Tatranská Lomnica A recommended round trip begins with a morning train from Starý Smokovec to Tatranská Lomnica. In 1937 a **cable car** able to carry 30 people at a time began operating, going from the resort up to **Skalnaté Pleso** (1751 metres); an extension to Lomnický štít (2632 metres) was completed in 1941. As soon as you arrive, visit the cable-car station near the Grandhotel Praha in Tatranská Lomnica to pick up tickets (US$2 one way) for the ride to Skalnaté Pleso. The cable car (closed Tuesday) is very popular with tourists, so you have to get to the office early to book the trip.

In 1973 a second, smaller cable-car line (closed Monday) with four-seat cabins was built to Skalnaté Pleso via Štart from above the Horec Hotel in Tatranská Lomnica. It doesn't operate when there's too much wind (at last report this cable car was closed for reconstruction).

While you're waiting for your departure time to roll around, visit the **Museum of Tatra National Park**, a few hundred metres from the bus station at Tatranská Lomnica (open weekdays from 8.30 am to 5 pm, weekends from 8 am to noon). The exhibition on the natural and human histories of this area is excellent.

There's a large observatory at Skalnaté Pleso and a smaller cable car (US$4 return) to the summit of **Lomnický štít** where you get a sweeping view of the entire High Tatra Range. If you're lucky the service will be running, the sky will be clear and you won't have to wait too long to go. You're only allowed 30 minutes at Lomnický štít and if you miss your car down you'll have to wait around until another car has room for you

(maximum capacity 15 persons). From Skalnaté Pleso it's only two hours down the Magistrála Trail to Hrebienok and the funicular railway back to Starý Smokovec.

If you visit the High Tatra Mountains during a peak period when the place is overflowing with tourists, you can do the Skalnaté Pleso-Hrebienok trip in reverse. It's a lot easier to get in the cable car at Skalnaté Pleso for a ride down than at Tatranská Lomnica for a ride up. Hundreds of people may be waiting to get on at Tatranská Lomnica.

Activities
In summer Satur offers several interesting bus excursions from the Vysoké Tatry resorts. The weekly trip to the Demänovská jaskyňa Caves near Liptovský Mikuláš also includes a chair-lift ride to Chopok Peak (2024 metres) in the Nízke Tatry (US$13). Rafting on the Dunajec River is offered four times a week from June to September (US$13). You can make bookings at Satur offices in any of the three High Tatras resorts but the trips don't happen unless at least 30 people sign up.

Mountain Climbing You can reach the summit of Slavkovský štít (2452 metres) in nine hours on a round trip via the blue trail from Starý Smokovec. Rysy Peak (2499 metres), right on the Polish border, is about nine hours away on a round trip from Štrbské Pleso (via Popradské Pleso and Pod Rysmi Chalet). These you can do on your own, but to scale the peaks without marked hiking trails (Gerlachovský štít included) you must hire a mountain guide. Members of recognised climbing clubs are exempt from this requirement.

The TANAP horská služba (mountain rescue) office in Starý Smokovec charges US$65 per day for a mountain guide for up to five people.

Places to Stay
Camping There's no camping within the Tatra National Park. The nearest commercial camping ground to Starý Smokovec is the

SLOVAKIA

Tatracamp (☎ 24 06) near the Pod lesom Railway Station, three km down the road to Poprad-Tatry. Six-person bungalows cost US$30 (open from June to September).

There's also a camping ground at Tatranská Štrba (open from May to September) below Štrbské Pleso.

Three camping grounds are a couple of km from Tatranská Lomnica (near the Tatranská Lomnica-Eurocamp Railway Station on the line to Studený Potok). The largest of these is the *Eurocamp FICC* (☎ 967 741), a five-minute walk from the train station, with 120 four-person luxury bungalows with private bath at US$49, plus regular hotel rooms with shared bath at US$17 double (no singles). Camping is US$3 per person, US$3 per tent. The Eurocamp features restaurants, bars, shops, a supermarket, a swimming pool, tennis, sauna, disco, hot water and row upon row of parked caravans. One reader wrote in with lavish praise for the folkloric Kolibar Restaurant here. The 1975 rally of the International Camping & Caravaneering Federation was held here. This place is open all year.

An eight-minute walk south of the Eurocamp is the less expensive *Športcamp* (☎ 967 288) where camping is US$2 per person plus US$2 per tent. Bungalows here are US$19 for up to four persons or US$24 for five persons, but in summer they're usually taken (open year-round).

Halfway between the Eurocamp and Tatranská Lomnica is the *Tatranec Campground* where bungalows are also available, but there's no train station nearby so it's more for people with cars.

Chalets Up on the hiking trails are eight mountain chalets *(chata)* but given the popularity and limited capacity of this area, the chalets could all be full in midsummer. Staff at the TANAP horská služba (mountain rescue) office next to Satur in Starý Smokovec will be able to tell you if a certain chalet is open and may even telephone ahead to see if there's a place for you. Many of the chalets close for maintenance in November and May. Although food is available at the chalets, you should take along some of your own supplies.

Basically, the chalets come in three varieties, as explained in the following examples. The *Morávku Chalet* (1500 metres, 82 dorm beds) on Popradské Pleso and *Sliezsky dom* (1670 metres, 79 dorm beds) are large mountain hotels. To stay at Morávku is US$9 per person in three, four and six-bed dorms. Sliezsky dom (☎ 23 545) is US$34/45 double/triple (no singles) in individual rooms with toilet and shower, or US$11 per person in a six to 12-bed dorm. Breakfast and dinner at both Morávku and Sliezsky dom cost US$8 per person for the two.

Bílikova (1255 metres, 68 beds), *Zamkovského* (1475 metres, 20 beds) and *Brnčalova* (1551 metres, 52 beds) are rustic wooden buildings on the Magistrála Trail. Bílikova is only five minutes from Hrebienok and room prices have been jacked up to US$32 double, so you'd be well advised to hike one hour down into the forest and stay in four-bedded rooms at the much friendlier Zamkovského Chalet which is US$10 per person with breakfast and dinner. Brnčalova is US$9 per person including breakfast and dinner in four, six and 12-bed dorms.

Pod Rysmi (2250 metres, 19 beds), *Zbojnícka* (1960 metres, 16 beds) and *Téryho* (2015 metres, 21 beds) are high mountain chalets built of stone. Pod Rysmi is US$8 per person including breakfast and dinner in the one 19-bed dorm, while both Zbojnícka and Téryho are US$9 per person in their dorms including breakfast and dinner. These three places make perfect bases for alpine exploration, but make sure they're open and available before you set out.

Satur in Starý Smokovec handles chalet bookings at Sliezsky dom and Morávku. Slovakoturist (☎ 20 31), just above the Pekná vyhliadka Railway Station in Horný Smokovec, a 10-minute walk east from Satur in Starý Smokovec, can reserve beds at all eight of the chalets.

Actually, staying at a chalet is a far better mountain experience than a hotel room at one of the resorts and it's cheaper. You're also more likely to meet interesting local people at the chalets and you'll have ample time in the evening to chat. Leave your backpack at a left-luggage office at a train station and carry basic essentials in a day pack.

Reader Tony English of Sunderland, England, sent us this:

One of the best things I did in Slovakia was to climb Mt Rysy on the Polish border. The day I climbed up there the Pod Rysmi hut was being resupplied with food and booze and there was considerable rivalry as to who had carried the heaviest pack up to the hut. Two porters astonishingly managed to carry in packages weighing 75 kg. The strength and courage needed to carry in such a load, tied to a special backpack frame, up steep snow-covered slopes and over rocky scrambles, is quite mind boggling. There was a good atmosphere in the hut that night!

Private Rooms Satur doesn't have any private rooms at Starý Smokovec but can arrange rooms with families in the village of Nová Lesná for US$11/17 double/triple. Unless you have a car this is not convenient. Slovakoturist (☎ 20 31) in Horný Smokovec has private rooms at US$13/18 double/triple (no singles).

Private rooms are advertised by 'zimmer frei' signs outside numerous houses in Ždiar village on the north side of the High Tatras and easily accessible from Poprad-Tatry or Starý Smokovec on the Łysa Polana bus. Several small restaurants and pensions are also here. Ždiar is a pretty little village with sheep grazing in the fields and it makes a good base for exploring the High Tatras from this less-frequented side.

Hotels Many of the hotels you see in this area are owned by the trade unions and are only open to their members. Other hotels are reserved for groups. Hotel prices are almost double in the high seasons (mid-December to February and mid-June to September) as compared to the low seasons (March to mid-June and October to mid-December). Be aware that most prices quoted in this section are those charged in the low season.

Staff at the Satur office (closed on Satur-day afternoon and Sunday) near the train station at Starý Smokovec will help you to find a room. Satur controls many hotel rooms around Smokovec, so it's sometimes easier to go there for a booking than to tramp around looking on your own. The staff can arrange rooms in all categories from low budget to deluxe.

Smokovec If the price doesn't deter you, you'll like the three-star *Grandhotel* (☎ 21 54) at Starý Smokovec. This majestic turn-of-the-century building has a certain elegance the high-rise hotels lack. Since many of the 83 rooms (both single and double) have shared bath, it's not as expensive as you might think. In the low season it's US$18/28 single/double without bath, US$28/44 with bath; in the high season you'll pay US$29/45 without bath, US$48/74 with bath. Breakfast and use of the indoor swimming pool are included.

The nearby *Hotel Crocus* (☎ 27 41) just above the train station at Starý Smokovec is overpriced at US$16/31/46 single/double/triple without bath but with breakfast. This hotel may be cheaper if booked through Satur.

The *Park Hotel* (☎ 23 42), a circular five-storey hotel that opened just above the Nový Smokovec Railway Station in 1970, charges US$22/35 single/double including breakfast in the low season, or US$37/58 without breakfast in the high season. All 96 rooms have private bath. Avoid the hotel restaurant.

The log cabin-style *Hotel MS 70* (☎ 20 61), just west of the Park Hotel, is one of the least expensive around at US$6/12 single/double with shared bath.

One of the best deals at Starý Smokovec is *Pension Vesna* (☎ 27 74), a white two-storey building behind the large sanatorium opposite Nový Smokovec Railway Station. Spacious rooms with shared bath and private balcony are US$8 per person and there's a kitchen where you can cook. There's a short-cut through the sanatorium grounds to get there (ask).

Another inexpensive hotel at Starý Smokovec is the four-storey, B-category

Hotel Šport (☎ 23 61; US$8/18 single/double with shared bath), a five-minute walk east from Starý Smokovec train station. It's popular with noisy youth groups and the hotel restaurant is not recommended.

Pension Pol'ana (☎ 25 18), across the street from the Sports Centrum at Pekná Vyhliadna Railway Station, is US$8/13 single/double with shared bath. The rooms are small but comfortable, each with a sink, and many also have a balcony. The cosy little bar downstairs serves a spicy bowl of tripe soup. The Pol'ana is often full.

The cheapest place to stay at if you have a YHA or ISIC card is the *CKM Juniorhotel Vysoké Tatry* (☎ 26 61), just below the Horný Smokovec Railway Station. The regular charge will be around US$10 per person including breakfast. Students and youth-hostel card holders should get a 50% discount if they book direct (not through an agency). Guests are accommodated in half a dozen single-storey pavilions spread around the hotel grounds. The hotel is open all year, but it's often full with noisy school groups.

Tatranská Lomnica *Hotel Lomnica* (☎ 967 251), an older two-star hotel with quaint folk architecture between the train and bus stations in Tatranská Lomnica, is expensive at US$21/27 double/triple without bath, US$28/36 with bath, breakfast included (no singles). Only one or two rooms with bath are available.

The newer *Hotel Horec* (☎ 967 261), a five-minute walk up the hill from the train station, is US$22 double without bath, US$24 with bath, breakfast included (no singles).

One of Slovakia's most romantic hotels is the 91-room *Grandhotel Praha* (☎ 967 941), built in 1905, up the hill beside the cable-car terminal. In the high season singles/doubles with bath cost US$47/72, or US$28/43 in the low season, bath and breakfast included. By all means stay there if price isn't a big consideration and you want to go in style.

Štrbské Pleso The 11-storey *Hotel Panorama* (☎ 92 111) next to the Prior Department Store, above the Štrbské Pleso Railway Station, costs US$17/26 single/double without bath, US$20/31 with bath, breakfast included. This hotel has 42 single and 50 double rooms.

The 150-room *Hotel Patria* (☎ 92 591), a huge A-frame hotel overlooking the lake, a 10-minute walk uphill from the train station, costs US$43 double (no singles).

Hotel FIS (☎ 92 221) opposite the huge ski jumps, five minutes beyond the Patria Hotel, is US$20/29 single/double with bath. The FIS is a modern sports hotel and both it and ski jumps were built for the 1970 International Ski Federation world championships.

Places to Eat
Almost all the hotels and chalets of this region have their own restaurants.

Just above the bus station at Starý Smokovec are two adjacent restaurants. The *Tatranská Kúria* is a folk-style restaurant but it's nothing special. The neighbouring *Reštaurácia Tatra* is cheaper, better and more likely to be open. They even have a vegetarian section in their menu. If you'd like to splash out, there's the elegant restaurant in the *Grand Hotel* (you're expected to dress up).

Pizza Piccola, right beside the Tatranská Lomnica Railway Station, has a great variety of pizzas. Right next door is the *Slovenská Reštaurácia* with national dishes. The *Vínna Pivnička* in Hotel Lomnica serves light local meals and cold beer.

There's an excellent self-service restaurant in *Prior Department Store* next to Štrbské Pleso Railway Station (open daily from 8 am to 5.45 pm).

Entertainment
The *Stella Bar* between Satur and Starý Smokovec Bus Station operates as a disco Friday, Saturday and Sunday from 8 pm to 2 am. There's also a disco at the *Park Hotel*.

Getting There & Away
Bus There are regular express buses from

Bratislava to Tatranská Lomnica via Nitra, Banská Bystrica and Starý Smokovec.

From Starý Smokovec there are 15 buses a day to Łysa Polana (38 km, one hour), 26 to Ždiar, seven to Levoča (38 km), three to Bardejov, four to Prešov, six to Žilina, five to Trenčín, three to Bratislava and two to Brno.

The Hungarian Volánbusz bus from Budapest to Tatranská Lomnica runs twice a week (311 km, seven hours, US$13).

Train To come by train, take one of the express trains running between Prague or Bratislava and Košice and change at Poprad-Tatry (couchettes are available). There are frequent narrow-gauge electric trains between Poprad-Tatry and Starý Smokovec (13 km).

Alternatively, get off the express train at Tatranská Štrba, a station on the main line from Prague to Košice, and take the cog-wheel railway up to Štrbské Pleso (there are over 20 services daily), which climbs 430 metres over a distance of five km. Also known as the 'rack railway', this service opened in 1896.

The booking offices in Starý Smokovec and Tatranská Lomnica train stations can reserve sleepers and couchettes from Poprad-Tatry to Prague, Karlovy Vary, Brno and Bratislava.

To/From Poland For anyone interested in walking between Slovakia and Poland there's a highway border crossing near Javorina, 30 km from Tatranská Lomnica via Ždiar by bus. The Slovakian bus to/from Starý Smokovec is never crowded and the bus stop is just a hundred metres from the border (bus times posted). On the Polish side buses can be full up with people on excursions between Morskie Oko Lake and Zakopane, so this route is easier southbound than northbound.

You'll find a bank at Łysa Polana on the Polish side where you can change money, but there's no Slovakian bank at Javorina. The rate offered at the border is about 10% worse than you'll get in Zakopane. Southbound

travellers should buy a few dollars worth of Slovakian crowns at an exchange office in Poland to pay the onward bus fare to Starý Smokovec or Poprad, as this may not be possible at the border. Northbound, excess crowns are easily unloaded at exchange offices in Poland (at a loss). (See the Tatra Mountains section in the Poland chapter of this book for information on conditions on the Polish side.)

A bus direct to Zakopane leaves Starý Smokovec Bus Station weekdays at 7 am (60 km, US$3 one way, pay the driver). This bus isn't listed on the posted schedule but Satur knows about it. Also ask Satur about its excursion buses to Zakopane and Kraków.

Getting Around

You can experience virtually every type of mountain transportation here: funicular railway, cog-wheel or rack railway, narrow-gauge electric trains, cable cars and chair lifts. The most used are the electric trains which run from Poprad-Tatry to Starý Smokovec (13 km) and Štrbské Pleso (29 km) about every half-hour. Trains also travel from Starý Smokovec to Tatranská Lomnica (six km) every 30 minutes. These trains make frequent stops along their routes; when there isn't a ticket window at the station, go immediately to the conductors upon boarding and buy your ticket from them.

POPRAD-TATRY

Poprad-Tatry is a modern industrial city with little to interest visitors. However, it's an important transportation hub that you'll pass through at least once. The electric railway from here to Starý Smokovec was built in 1908 and was extended to Štrbské Pleso in 1912.

Information

Money Change travellers' cheques at the Všeobecná Úverová Banka, ulica Mnohel'ova 9, next to Hotel Satel two blocks from the train station (weekdays 7 am to noon and 1 to 5 pm, Wednesday 7 am to noon only, Saturday 8 am to noon).

Places to Stay & Eat

If you arrive late, you could stay at the old *Hotel Európa* (☎ 092-32 744; US$6/8 single/double with shared bath) just outside the Poprad-Tatry Railway Station. The hotel restaurant is quite good (the menu is in German).

Getting There & Away

Bus There are buses to almost everywhere else in Slovakia from the large bus station next to the train station. Banská Bystrica (124 km), Łysa Polana (via Starý Smokovec), Červený Kláštor, Levoča (26 km), Spišské Podhradie (41 km), Bardejov (125 km) and Prešov (84 km) are most easily reached by bus. Ask about buses to Zakopane, Poland.

Train Poprad-Tatry is a major junction on the main railway line from Bratislava or Prague to Košice. Express trains run to Žilina (141 km, two hours) and Košice (101 km, 1½ hours) every couple of hours. Electric trains climb 13 km to Starý Smokovec, the main Vysoké Tatry resort, every half-hour or so. A feeder railway line runs north-east to Plavec (61 km, two hours by local train) where you can get a connection to Muszyna, Poland, three times a day (see the Prešov section for approximate times).

DUNAJEC GORGE

Pieniny National Park (21 sq km), created in 1967, combines with a similar park in Poland to protect the nine-km Dunajec River gorge between the Slovakian village of Červený Kláštor and Szczawnica, Poland. The river here forms the international boundary between the two countries and the 500-metre limestone cliffs are impressive.

At the mouth of the gorge is a 14th century fortified **Carthusian monastery**, now a park administrative centre and museum with a good collection of statuary and old prints of the area (open daily from May to September, closed Sunday and Monday from October to April).

From June to mid-September, Dunajec raft trips (US$6) depart from two locations

at Červený Kláštor: a landing opposite the monastery and a second landing a km upriver west of the village. A raft only sets out when 12 passengers gather and when business is slow you may have to wait around for the quorum to be reached. From the downriver terminus you can hike back to the monastery in a little over an hour, or rent a bicycle (US$4) and peddle back. Actually, the rafting operation on the Polish side is larger and better organised, so you might wait to do your rafting there (see under Dunajec Gorge in the Poland chapter for details). The raft trip in Slovakia is much shorter than the one in Poland.

Even if you don't go rafting, it's still worth coming to Červený Kláštor to hike along the riverside trail through the gorge on the Slovakian side (no such trail exists on the Polish side). In midsummer a US$0.30 'trail fee' is charged to enter the national park but this fee includes a brochure in English.

Places to Stay

Just across a small stream from the monastery is a camp site that is open from mid-June to mid-September. No bungalows are available.

A couple of km up the road to Vel'ký Lipník from the monastery is the *Hotel Dunajec* with some bungalows across the road. A few km further along in the same direction is the more up-market *Dunajec Motorest* camping ground with more bungalows (often full in summer).

Near Lesnica, a bit inland from the downriver end of the gorge where the raft trips end, is the inexpensive *Pieniny Chata* (☎ 0963-97 530) which is often full in summer. In this case the hostel manager has two rooms for rent in his private residence at US$12 double including a terrific breakfast.

Getting There & Away

Direct buses go to Červený Kláštor from Poprad-Tatry. Although Poland is just across the river, there's no official border crossing here, so you must take a bus from Červený Kláštor to Stará L'ubovňa (25 km), and then a train to Plavec (16 km), where a local train goes to Muszyna, Poland (16 km) three times a day (see Getting There & Away in the Prešov section). From Muszyna there are Polish trains to Nowy Sącz (50 km) and Kraków. Check connecting train times beforehand. There are also buses from Stará L'ubovňa to Bardejov, Prešov, and Košice. Alternatively use the Łysa Polana crossing directly to Zakopane.

SPIŠSKÁ NOVÁ VES
Spišská Nová Ves, the administrative centre of the Spiš region, is a modern city with a history dating back to 1268. The long central square is nice to walk around and the many large apartment complexes built here by the communists are impressive. Spišská Nová Ves makes a good base from which to visit Levoča, Spišské Podhradie and nearby Slovenský raj National Park.

Orientation & Information
The bus station is about 200 metres west of Spišská Nová Ves Railway Station. A 24-hour left-luggage office is available at the train station.

Money You can change travellers' cheques at the Všeobecná Úverová Banka, Letná ulica 33 (Monday 9 am to 4 pm, Tuesday to Friday 9 am to 5 pm).

Post & Telecommunications There's a telephone centre in the main post office, Štefánikovo námestie 7 opposite Dom Kultury (Monday to Saturday 7 am to 8 pm, Sunday 8 am to 4 pm). Spišská Nová Ves's telephone code is 0965.

Things to See & Do
Just south-west of Spišská Nová Ves is **Slovenský raj** (the Slovak Paradise), a national park created in 1988, with cliffs, caves, canyons, waterfalls and 1896 species of butterflies. This mountainous karst area is accessible via **Čingov**, eight km west of Spišská Nová Ves by bus. The closest train station to Slovenský raj is **Spišske Tomášovce**, less than an hour from

Tomášovský výhl'ad on the green trail. Only local trains stop at this station.

From Čingov (elevation 494 metres) the blue trail leads up the Hornád River gorge, passing below Tomášovský výhl'ad, to Letanovský mlyn. The trail up the river is narrow and there are several ladders and ramps where hikers can only pass one by one. This can cause delays if you happen to meet a large group at such a place and during peak periods hikers are only allowed to travel in an upstream direction from Čingov (returning over the mountain).

A km beyond Letanovský mlyn, a green trail leaves the river and climbs sharply to **Kláštorisko** (elevation 755 metres) where there's a restaurant (☎ 0965-90 307), open daily year-round, with cabins at US$5 per person. If you'd like to stay there, call ahead to check availability in midsummer. From Kláštorisko you can follow another blue trail back down the ridge towards Čingov.

From Čingov to Kláštorisko via Letanovský mlyn and the gorge takes a good three hours and to return to Čingov down the ridge takes another two hours, so a minimum of at least six hours are required to do this entire circuit, lunch at Kláštorisko included.

Places to Stay
The modern, 10-storey *Metropol Hotel* (☎ 22 241), Štefánikovo námestie 2 next to Dom Kultury, three blocks south of the train station, charges US$16/25 single/double with shower and breakfast.

The *Šport Hotel* (☎ 26 753), on ulica T Vansovej, next to the Zimný Štadión, is US$6 per person with shared bath. From Hotel Metropol continue south a few blocks and you'll see this neat, clean five-storey building off to the left. The hotel restaurant is reasonable.

Satur opposite Dom Kultury near the Metropol knows of private rooms, but at US$9 per person with breakfast they're no bargain.

Čingov The *Hotel Flora* (☎ 91 129), a large three-storey establishment at Čingov, has rooms at US$13/25 single/double with bath.

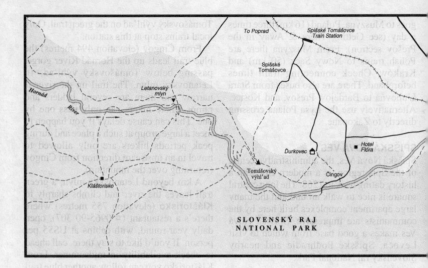

SLOVENSKÝ RAJ
NATIONAL PARK

SLOVAKIA

Cheaper accommodation is available at the *Chatová osada Ďurkovec* on a hill about a 20-minute walk from the bus stop at Čingov. There's also camping at Ďurkovec, which is good as camping is not allowed in the park itself. There are many other places to stay at Čingov, so ask around.

In Spišské Tomášovce, about a km south of the train station, is a large 65-bed *Ubytovnacie zariadenie* 'Touristic hut' (☎ 91 184).

Getting There & Away

Spišská Nová Ves is on the main railway line from Žilina to Košice with trains from Poprad-Tatry (26 km) every hour or so. All trains stop here. A feeder line runs 13 km north to Levoča with services every two or three hours.

Buses leave Spišská Nová Ves for Čingov every couple of hours. There are morning buses to Spišské Podhradie, Tatranská Lomnica, Starý Smokovec and Štrbské Pleso.

LEVOČA

In the 13th century the king of Hungary invited Saxon Germans to colonise the Spiš region on the eastern borderlands of his kingdom as a protection against Tatar incursions and to develop mining. One of the towns founded at this time was Levoča (Leutschau), 26 km east of Poprad-Tatry. Granted urban privileges in 1271, the merchants of Levoča grew rich in the 14th century.

To this day the medieval walls, street plan and central square of Levoča have survived, unspoiled by modern developments. The town is an easy stop on the way from Poprad-Tatry to either Prešov or Košice. A large community of Gypsies resides here.

Orientation & Information

The train station is a km south of town, down the road beside the Faix Hotel. A left-luggage service is available if you ask the stationmaster. Satur is at námestie Majstra Pavla 46.

Money The Všeobecná Úverová Banka, námestie Majstra Pavla 28 (Monday, Tuesday, Wednesday and Friday 9 am to noon and 1.30 to 4 pm, Thursday 8.30 am to noon), changes travellers' cheques for 1% commission (US$2 minimum).

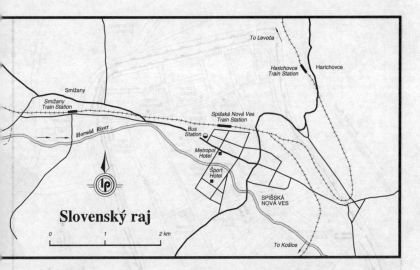

Slovenský raj

0   1   2 km

Post & Telecommunications The telephone centre in the post office at námestie Majstra Pavla 42 is open weekdays from 7 am to 8 pm, Saturday 8 am to 1 pm. Levoča's telephone code is 0966.

Things to See
Bastions and 15th century walls greet the traveller arriving by bus at námestie Slobody. The old town begins just through **Košice Gate** with the **new Minorite church** (1750) on the left.

Námestie Majstra Pavla, Levoča's central square, is full of things to see. In the 15th century **St James' Church** (closed Monday, admission US$1) is a gigantic Gothic high altar (1517) by Master Pavol, one of the largest and finest of its kind in Europe. The Madonna on this altar appears on the new 100 Sk banknote. Next to St James is the Gothic **town hall**, enlivened by Renaissance arcades, today the **Museum of the Spiš Region** (closed Monday). Beside the old town hall is a 16th century cage where prisoners were once exhibited.

There's an **art museum** (closed Monday) in the 15th century house at námestie Majstra Pavla 40. While you're there have a peek in

the courtyard of námestie Majstra Pavla 43. The **Evangelical church** (1837), which once served the German community, is in the Empire style, as is the former **district council** (1826), námestie Majstra Pavla 59. Thurzov dom (1532), námestie Majstra Pavla 7, now the **State Archives**, is another fine building. At námestie Majstra Pavla 20 is the **Master Pavol Museum** (closed Monday).

On a hill a couple of km north of town is the large neo-Gothic **Church of Mariánska hora** where the largest Catholic pilgrimage in Slovakia is held on 2 July.

From October to April, St James Church and all the museums of Levoča are open on Saturday and Sunday only.

Places to Stay
Camping *Levočská Dolina Autocamp* (☎ 27 01) is five km north of námestie Slobody on the road to Závada. Bungalows are available (open from mid-June to August only).

Autocamping Starý mlyn (☎ 36 51), with deluxe bungalows and a restaurant on the premises, is more convenient, about five km west of Levoča on the road to Poprad.

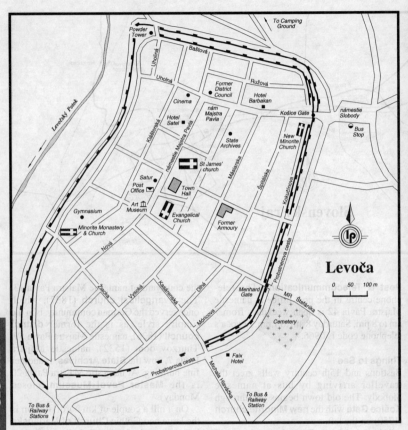

Levoča

0   50   100 m

Hotels Your best bet is the 25-room *Hotel Faix* (☎ 23 35), Probstnerova cesta 22, between the train station and the old town. Rooms in this recently renovated hotel are US$11/14 single/double with shared bath, US$14/21 with private bath. The hotel restaurant is good.

The *Hotel Barbakan* (☎ 43 10), Košická 15, offers comfortable rooms with private bath (US$35/38 single/double) in a newly renovated building in the centre of town. Guests are required to purchase US$6 per person in compulsory meal coupons to ensure that they won't stray from the restaurant.

An even more expensive place is the Austrian-owned *Hotel Satel*, námestie Majstra Pavla 55. Tourism development plans call for Levoča to be converted into the 'Slovak Prague' so there'll probably be a few more up-market establishments around town by the time you get there.

Places to Eat

Levoča's best restaurant is the *Restaurant u 3 Apostolov*, námestie Majstra Pavla 11. For coffee and cakes go to *Mliečne Lahodky*, námestie Majstra Pavla 9.

A reader wrote in recommending a vegetarian restaurant which recently opened at Vholňa 3, just off the north-west corner of the main square behind the cinema.

Getting There & Away

Levoča is connected by 11 daily local trains to Spišská Nová Ves, a station 13 km south on the main line from Bratislava to Prague and Košice (the main line bypassed the town decades ago because local landowners refused to sell their property for railway construction). Bus travel is more practical as there are frequent services to Poprad-Tatry (26 km), Spišské Podhradie (15 km) and Prešov (58 km). All buses stop at námestie Slobody and some local buses also stop at the train station at the southern end of town.

SPIŠSKÉ PODHRADIE

Spišské Podhradie, 15 km east of Levoča, is midway between Poprad-Tatry and Prešov in the centre of East Slovakia. In the 12th century a settlement appeared below the neighbouring castle, developing into an artisans' town in the 13th century. The town itself is not outstanding but adjacent Spišský hrad and Spišská Kapitula are sights of prime importance. Spišská Kapitula was built by the clergy and from the 13th century an abbot resided there. After 1776 Spišská Kapitula became the seat of a bishop. Spišské Podhradie is a typical Slovakian country town, still remarkably unaffected by tourism despite its attractions and central location.

Things to See & Do

If you're arriving by bus from Levoča, ask the driver to drop you at **Spišská Kapitula**, on a ridge a km west of Spišské Podhradie. This 13th century ecclesiastical settlement is completely encircled by a 16th century wall and the single street running between two medieval gates is lined with picturesque Gothic houses. At the upper end of this street is magnificent **St Martin's Cathedral** (1273) with twin Romanesque towers and a Gothic sanctuary. Inside are three folding Gothic altars (1499) and, near the door, a Romanesque white lion. Unfortunately, the church is often closed. On opposite sides of the cathedral are the seminary and the Renaissance bishop's palace (1652).

On the opposite side of Spišské Podhradie is **Spišský hrad** (Zipser Burg), the largest castle in Slovakia. Spišský hrad is directly above and east of the train station, a km south of Spišské Podhradie's bus stop. Cross the level crossing over the tracks near the station and follow the yellow markers up to the castle (closed Monday and from October to April). The first gate is always locked, so carry on to the second one higher up. Even if both are closed, the exterior still justifies a visit. (If you're driving or cycling, the access road is off the Prešov highway east of town.)

In winter Spišský hrad is often shrouded in mist and invisible from the train station which it rises above.

Spišský hrad occupies a long ridge 180 metres above Spišské Podhradie. The castle was founded in 1209 and reconstructed in the 15th century (the defenders of Spišský hrad repulsed the Tatars in 1241). Until 1710 the Spiš region was administered from here. Although the castle burnt down in 1780, the ruins and the site are spectacular. The highest castle enclosure contains a round Gothic tower, a cistern, a chapel and a rectangular Romanesque palace perched over the abyss. Instruments of torture are exhibited in the dungeon (explanations in Slovak only). On the south side of Spišský hrad is the Dreveník karst area featuring caves, cliffs and ravines.

Places to Stay & Eat

At last report the *Spiš Hotel*, Palešovo námestie 50, opposite the cinema and post office near the bus stop in the middle of Spišské Podhradie, was closed.

A better bet than Hotel Spiš is the *Hotel Pod Hradom* (☎ 86 19), formerly known as the Turistická Ubytovňa Družstevný Klub or Hotel Raj, with beds at US$6 per person. Some rooms have excellent views of the castle. It's a red three-storey building behind some apartment blocks on a backstreet, a five-minute walk from the bus stop.

The only restaurant in Spišské Podhradie is the one in Hotel Pod Hradom and its menu consists of pork chops with potatoes and not

SLOVAKIA

much else. The supermarket you pass on the way from the post office to the train station has large quantities of a few items.

Getting There & Away

A secondary railway line connects Spišské Podhradie to Spišské Vlachy (nine km), a station on the main line from Poprad-Tatry to Košice. Departures are scheduled to connect with the Košice trains. You can leave your bags at the left-luggage office in the Spišské Podhradie Railway Station (ask the stationmaster).

Buses from Prešov (43 km), Levoča (15 km), Spišská Nová Ves (25 km) and Poprad-Tatry (41 km) are quite frequent.

PREŠOV

This busy market centre, 36 km north of Košice, is the centre of the Slovakian Ukraine, the breadbasket of Slovakia. Prešov (Preschau) received a royal charter in 1374 and, like Bardejov to the north and Košice to the south, was once an eastern bulwark of the Kingdom of Hungary. In June 1919 a Slovak Soviet Republic was proclaimed at Prešov, part of a larger socialist revolution in Hungary. This movement was quickly suppressed by the big landowners, whose holdings were threatened, and in 1920 the region was incorporated into Czechoslovakia. The accommodation situation is poor but you may wish to stop off when travelling between Košice and Bardejov.

Orientation & Information

Hlavná ulica, Prešov's central square, is a 20-minute walk north up Masarykova from the adjacent bus and train stations (or take trolley bus No 4 to/from 'železničná stanica').

The left-luggage office at Prešov Railway Station is open 24 hours except for two half-hour breaks. Satur is at Hlavná ulica 1.

Money The Všeobecná Úverová Banka, Masarykova 13 just south of Prior, changes travellers' cheques for 1% commission (open weekdays from 7.30 am to 12.30 pm

and 1.30 to 5 pm, Wednesday from 7.30 am to 12.30 pm only).

The Investičná Banka, Hlavná ulica 82, changes travellers' cheques Monday and Friday from 8 am to 1.30 pm, and Tuesday, Wednesday and Thursday from 8 am to noon and 1.30 to 3 pm.

Post & Telecommunications There's a telephone centre in the post office at Masarykova 2 opposite Prior (daily 6 am to 10 pm). Prešov's telephone code is 091.

Things to See

The most imposing structure in the city is 14th century **St Nicholas Church** with its Gothic structure and Baroque organ and altars. Behind it is the **Evangelical church** (1642). To one side is the **Prešov Museum** (closed on weekend afternoons and every Monday), inside Rákóczi House, Hlavná ulica 86. In addition to the archaeology, history and natural history displays, there's a large fire-fighting exhibit. The Slovak Soviet Republic was declared on 16 June 1919 from the iron balcony of the **old town hall** (1533), Hlavná ulica 73.

Places to Stay

The nine-storey *Penzión ZPA* (☎ 23 206), Budovatelská 14, is about the only inexpensive option. The 40 rooms with bath in this pleasant workers hostel are US$9 single or double. It's about a 10-minute walk from the train station: walk north on Masarykova and turn left on Škultétyho ulica which crosses the railway line. The second street on the left is Budovatelská. Expect some noise from the adjacent Victoria Night Club on Friday and Saturday nights. Actually the music probably won't bother you as much as the drunken dancers leaving.

Prešov has two high-rise tourist hotels, the cheaper of which is the eight-storey Interhotel Šariš (☎ 46 351) at US$22/42/53/triple with bath and breakfast. The 39-room *Dukla Hotel* (☎ 22 741), Hlavná ulica 2, charges US$22/33 single/double without bath, US$26/46 with bath. This five-storey hotel erected in 1952 just isn't worth it.

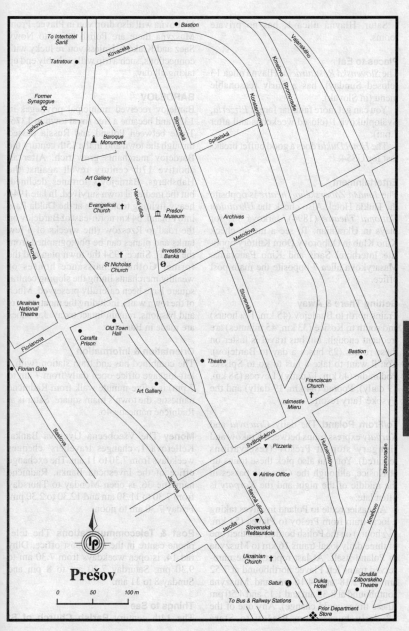

Prešov

0   50   100 m

To Interhotel
Šariš

To Interhotel
Šariš

● Bastion

Kovacska

● Tatratour

Valanského

Kmetovo

Stromradie

Kováčská

Former
Synagogue
✿

Jarková

Konstantinova

Baroque
Monument
♦

Spitalská

Slovenská

Art Gallery ●

Hlavná ulica

Evangelical
Church †

Archives ●

🏛 Prešov
Museum

Metodova

Jarková

Investičná
Banka
$

St Nicholas
Church †

Slovenská

Ukrainian
National
Theatre ●

● Old Town
Hall

Florianova

● Caraffa
Prison

● Theatre

● Bastion

● Florian Gate

Bastova

Art Gallery ●

Franciscan
Church †

námestie
Mieru

Stromoradie

Jarková

Svätoplukova

▼ Pizzeria

Hunaislavov

● Airline Office

Hlavná ulica

Kmetovo

Jaroša

▼ Slovenská
Reštaurácia

Ukrainian
Church †

Jonáša
Záborského
Theatre

● Satur 🛈

Dukla
Hotel ■

To Bus & Railway Stations

Prior Department
✶ Store

SLOVAKIA

Satur, Hlavná ulica 1, has no private rooms.

Places to Eat

The *Slovenská Reštaurácia*, Hlavná ulica 13 (closed Sunday), has a fairly reasonable menu (in Slovak).

You can get more familiar fare at *Pizzeria*, Svätoplukova 1 (closed weekends and after 7 pm).

The *Hotel Dukla* does a good buffet breakfast for US$4.

Entertainment

The *Jonáša Záborského Theatre* is opposite the Dukla Hotel. Also check the *Ukrainian National Theatre* (1894), Jarková 77, for plays in Ukrainian. To see a movie check Kino Klub in Odborový Dom Kultúry opposite Interhotel Šariš and Kino Panoráma, Masarykova ulica 7 opposite the main post office.

Getting There & Away

Trains north to Bardejov (45 km, 1¼ hours) and south to Košice (33 km, 45 minutes) are frequent enough, but bus travel is faster on these routes (25 buses a day to Bardejov). You'll want to take a bus to go to Spišské Podhradie (43 km, 17 daily), Levoča (58 km, 19 daily), Poprad (84 km, 19 daily) and the Vysoké Tatry resorts.

To/From Poland The daily *Cracovia* and *Karpaty* express trains between Kraków and Hungary stop at Prešov (reservations required). You can also pick these trains up at Košice, although the *Cracovia* passes in the middle of the night and the *Karpaty* is often late.

An easier route to Poland involves taking a local train from Prešov to Plaveč (54 km, 1½ hours) on the Polish border, and then one of three daily local trains 16 km to Muszyna in Poland itself. At last report, these unreserved trains left Plaveč northbound at 7.52 am and 2.18 and 4.16 pm and Muszyna southbound at 8.35 am and 1.15 and 4.50 pm (these times could change). Any one of the 18 daily buses from Prešov to Stará

Ľubovňa will also drop you in Plaveč. From Muszyna there are Polish trains to Nowy Sącz and Kraków. Unless you're lucky with connections, such a trip will probably end up taking all day.

BARDEJOV

Bardejov received municipal privileges in 1320 and became a free royal town in 1376. Trade between Poland and Russia passed through the town and in the 15th century the Bardejov merchants grew rich. After an abortive 17th century revolt against the Habsburgs, Bardejov's fortunes declined, but the medieval town survived. In late 1944 heavy fighting took place at the Dukla Pass into Poland, 54 km north-east of Bardejov on the road to Rzeszów (the wrecks of a few tanks and planes can be photographed from the road). Since 1954 the town plan and the former Gothic-Renaissance houses of wealthy merchants lining the sloping central square have been carefully preserved. Much of the town walls, including the moat, towers and bastions, remain intact today. Jas shoes are made in Bardejov.

Orientation & Information

The combined bus and train station (with a left-luggage office open daily from 7 am to 7 pm) is a five-minute walk from Radničné námestie, the town's main square. Satur is at Radničné námestie 46.

Money The Všeobecná Úverová Banka, Kellerova 1, changes travellers' cheques weekdays from 7.30 to 11 am. The exchange office of the Investičná Banka, Radničné námestie 36, is open Monday to Thursday from 7.30 to 11.30 am and 12.30 to 2.30 pm, Friday 7.30 am to noon.

Post & Telecommunications The telephone centre in the main post office, Dlhý rad 14, is open weekdays from 7.30 am to 9.30 pm, Saturday 7.30 am to 8 pm and Sunday 8 to 11 am.

Things to See

The 14th century **Parish Church of St**

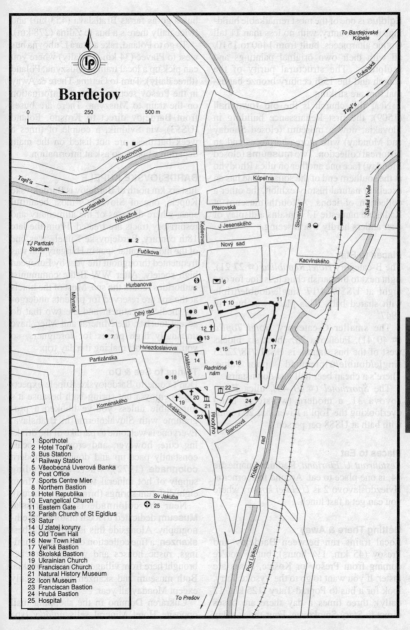

Bardejov

0   250   500 m

To Bardejovské Kúpele

Topľa

Dukejská

Kutuzovova

Topľa

Toplianska

Nábrežná

Kellerova

Kúpelna

Přerovská

J Jesenského

Nový sad

Slovenská

Slabská Voda

Kacvinského

TJ Partizán Stadium

Fučíkova

Hurbanova

Dlhý rad

Mlynská

Partizánska

Hviezdoslavova

Kláštorská

Radničné nám

Rhodno

Siancová

Komenského

Jiráskova

Krátky rad

Pod Lipkou

Sv Jakuba

To Prešov

1   Športhotel
2   Hotel Topľa
3   Bus Station
4   Railway Station
5   Všeobecná Úverová Banka
6   Post Office
7   Sports Centre Mier
8   Northern Bastion
9   Hotel Republika
10 Evangelical Church
11 Eastern Gate
12 Parish Church of St Egidius
13 Satur
14 U zlatej koruny
15 Old Town Hall
16 New Town Hall
17 Veľká Bastion
18 Školská Bastion
19 Ukrainian Church
20 Franciscan Church
21 Natural History Museum
22 Icon Museum
23 Franciscan Bastion
24 Hrubá Bastion
25 Hospital

Egidius is one of the most remarkable buildings in the country, with no less than 11 tall Gothic altarpieces, built from 1460 to 1510, all with their own original paintings and sculptures. The structural purity of the church and the 15th century bronze baptismal font are striking.

Near this church is the **old town hall** (1509), the first Renaissance building in Slovakia, now a museum (closed Sunday and Monday) with more altarpieces and an historical collection. Two **museums** (closed Monday) face one another on ulica Rhodyho at the southern end of the square. One has an excellent natural history exhibit, the other a collection of icons. A fourth museum at Radničné námestie 13 contains a display of deer antlers hardly worth seeing.

Places to Stay

The B-category *Hotel Republika* (☎ 27 21), right next to the parish church, is fine for one night at US$9/14/17 single/double/triple with shared bath. This place was built in 1947.

The smaller C-category *Hotel Topl'a* (☎ 40 41), Fučíkova 25, about six blocks west of the bus station, is US$11/18/22/25 single/double/triple/quad – poor value. There's a cheap beer hall just downstairs.

The *Športhotel* (☎ 49 49), ulica Kutuzovova 31, a modern two-storey hotel overlooking the Topl'a River, has 20 rooms with bath at US$8 per person.

Places to Eat

Restaurant U Floriána, Radničné námestie 44, is one place to eat. Around the corner at Hviezdoslavovo 2 is *U zlatej koruny* where you can get a fast lunch.

Getting There & Away

Local trains run between Bardejov and Prešov (45 km, 1¼ hours), but if you're coming from Prešov or Košice, buses are faster. If you want to go to the Vysoké Tatry, look for a bus to Poprad-Tatry (125 km, 12 daily); three times a day there are buses direct to Starý Smokovec. Four times a day

buses go as far as Bratislava (453 km) and twice daily there's a bus to Žilina (278 km).

To go to Poland, take a Stará L'ubovňa bus west to Plaveč (34 km, 13 daily) where you can pick up a local train to Muszyna, Poland (three daily). Turn to Getting There & Away in the Prešov section for more information on the train to Muszyna. There are buses from Bardejov direct to Krosno, Poland (US$3), via Svidník, a couple of times a week but these are not listed on the main departures board, so ask at information.

BARDEJOVSKÉ KÚPELE

Just six km north of Bardejov is Bardejovské Kúpele, one of Slovakia's most beautiful spas, where diseases of the alimentary and respiratory tracts are treated. From the late 18th century, Bardejovské Kúpele was one of the most popular spas in Hungary and was frequented throughout the year by European high society. After WW II the communist authorities rebuilt the spa. Most of the hotels at the spa are reserved for patients undergoing medical treatment and the two that do accept tourists, the Mineral and Mier, have unusually high prices for foreigners, so you're better off making it a day trip.

Things to See & Do

Don't come to Bardejovské Kúpele expecting to enjoy a hot-spring bath because it's impossible unless you've booked a programme with Slovakoterma in Bratislava. Everyone is welcome to partake of the drinking cure, however, and crowds of locals constantly pace up and down the modern **colonnade** (1972), where an unending supply of hot mineral water streams from eight different springs (bring your own cup).

Near the colonnade is the **Šarišské Museum** dedicated to local history and ethnography. Alongside this is Slovakia's best **skanzen**, a fine collection of old farm buildings, rustic houses and wooden churches brought here from villages all over Slovakia. Both museum and skanzen are open daily except Monday all year.

Cukráreň Domino in the shopping mall opposite Hotel Mineral sells *oplátky* (spa wafers), a local treat not to miss. Domino also dispenses *grog* (rum with hot water).

Getting There & Away

There's no train station, but Bardejovské Kúpele is connected to Bardejov by the city buses Nos 1, 2, 6, 7, 10 and 11. Some long-distance buses for places as far away as Bratislava begin here.

KOŠICE

Košice (Kassa in Hungarian) is the second-largest city in Slovakia and is the capital of the eastern portion of the republic. Before WW I, Košice was a Hungarian city where Slovak was seldom heard and the historic and ethnic influence of nearby Hungary remains strong. The Transylvanian prince Ferenc Rákóczi II had his headquarter s at Košice during the Hungarian War of Independence against the Habsburgs from 1703 to 1711. The town became part of Czecho-slovakia in 1918 but was recovered by Hungary from 1938 to 1945. From 21 February to 21 April 1945, Košice served as the capital of liberated Czechoslovakia. On 5 April 1945 the Košice Government Programme was announced here, outlining the future socialist development of the country.

Although now a major steel-making city with vast new residential districts built by the communists, there is much in the old town to interest visitors. Churches and museums abound, and there's an active State Theatre. The city is a good base for excursions to other East Slovakian towns. Daily trains between Kraków and Budapest stop here, making Košice the perfect beginning or end to a visit to Slovakia.

Orientation

The adjacent bus and train stations are just east of the old town, a five-minute walk down Mlynská ulica. This street will bring you into námestie Slobody, which becomes Hlavná ulica both north and south of the square. Much of your time in Košice will be spent on this colourful street. Large indexed city maps are posted at various locations around town.

The left-luggage office *(úschovňa)* in the train station is open 24 hours, except for three 45-minute breaks (note the times of these).

Information

Satur (☎ 622 3123) is in the Slovan Hotel, Rooseweltova 1.

There are no Hungarian, Polish or Ukrainian consulates in Košice, so be sure to get your onward visas beforehand in Bratislava.

Money The Investičná Banka exchange office upstairs in the train station is open weekdays from 7.30 am to 5 pm (no commission).

The Všeobecná Úverová Banka, Hlavná ulica 112 (Monday to Thursday 7.30 to noon and 1 to 5 pm, Friday 7.30 am to noon), changes travellers' cheques for 1% commission.

The reception at Hotel Slovan, Rooseweltova 1, will change travellers' cheques at a reasonable rate from 8 am to 10 pm daily. A large sign says this service is for hotel guests only but they'll usually make an exception of the few English-speakers who stray in.

Post & Telecommunications There's a 24-hour telephone centre in Poštova 2, about 500 metres north of the train station at the end of the park. Košice's telephone code is 095.

Travel Agencies Satur, Rooseweltova 1, reserves sleepers and couchettes and sells international train tickets. The 'Pokladnica Ares' office upstairs in the train station also arranges these tickets.

Satur, Rooseweltova 1, has international bus tickets to Athens, Cologne, Düsseldorf, Istanbul, London, Milan, Munich, Rome, Salzburg, Stockholm, Stuttgart and Zürich. Many of these buses actually leave from Bratislava and some transit the Czech Republic (check visa requirements). Prominent Travel Agency, Mlynská ulica 18, Tatratour, Alžbetina ulica 6, and Autoturist,

SLOVAKIA

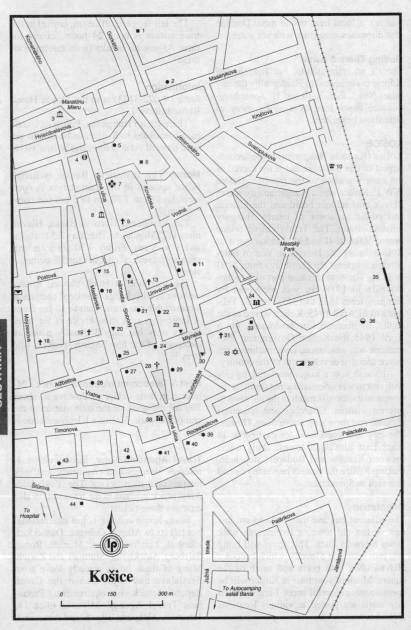

Košice

0   150   300 m

PLACES TO STAY	4	Všeobecná	26	Art Gallery
		Úverová Banka	27	Tatratour
1	Hutník Hotel	5	Autoturist	28	Cathedral of
6	Hotel Coral	7	Prior Department		St Elizabeth
33	Hotel Európa		Store	29	Košice Programme
40	Slovan Hotel	8	Slovak Technical		House
44	TJ Metropol		Museum	31	Evangelical
	Turistická	9	Franciscan Church		Church
	Ubytovná	10	Pošta 2 Telephone	32	Former
			Centre		Synagogue
PLACES TO EAT	11	Executioner's	34	Jakub's Palace
			Bastion	35	Railway Station
15	Aida Espresso	12	Miklušova Väznica	36	Bus Station
20	Piváreň U	13	Jesuit Church	37	Swimming Pool &
	Dominikánov	14	Plague Column		Sauna
23	Grill Dětva	16	Ursuline Convent	38	Forgach Palace
30	Reštaurácia Ajvega	17	Main Post Office	39	Bábkové Divadlo
		18	Ukrainian Church	40	Satur
OTHER	19	Dominican Church	41	ČSA Airline Office
		21	State Theatre	42	Thália Hungarian
2	Dom kultúry	22	Former Town Hall		Theatre
3	East Slovak	24	Urban Tower	43	Dom Umenia
	Museum	25	CKM Student Travel		Concert Hall

Továrenská 1, also sell international bus tickets.

For reduced student and under-26 train tickets to places outside Slovakia try the 'Medzinárodná Pokladnica' window upstairs in the train station.

CKM Student Travel, Alžbetina ulica 11, also has international train tickets with student and youth discounts and they sell ISIC student and youth hostel cards.

The American Express representative in Košice is Tatratour (☎ 24 872), Alžbetina ulica 6.

Bookshops Petit, Hlavná ulica 41, and Kníhkupectivo, Hlavná ulica 38, have a good selection of hiking maps and town plans.

Visa Extensions The Úradovňa Cudzineckej Polície a Pasovej Služby, across the street from the huge Okresný Úrad Košice/Mestský Magistrát building on trieda Slovenského Národného Povstania (Monday and Wednesday 10 am to noon and 12.30 to 6 pm, Tuesday, Thursday and Friday 7 am to noon), is the place to apply for visa extensions, complete police registration or

report a lost passport or visa. Several trams pass here (ask).

Things to See

Košice's top sight is the **Cathedral of St Elizabeth** (1345-1508), a magnificent late-Gothic edifice a five-minute walk west of the train station. In a crypt on the left side of the nave is the tomb of Ferenc Rákóczi (tickets are sold at the adjacent Urban Tower). Duke Rákóczi was exiled to Turkey after the failed 18th century Hungarian insurgency against Austria and only in 1905 was he officially pardoned and his remains reburied here.

Beside the cathedral is the 14th century **Urban Tower**, with a museum of metalwork. On the opposite side of the cathedral is the 14th century **St Michael's Chapel** and the **Košice Programme House**, Hlavná ulica 27, where the 1945 National Front programme was proclaimed. The building dates from 1779 and is now an art gallery (closed Monday) with a large collection by local painter Július Jakoby (1903-1985).

Most of Košice's other historic sites are north along Hlavná ulica. In the centre of the square is the ornate **State Theatre** (1899)

SLOVAKIA

with a musical fountain in front. Beside it at Hlavná ulica 59 is the Rococo former **town hall** (1780), now a cinema, and north of the theatre is a large **plague column** (1723). The Jesuit and Franciscan churches are also on the square. Farther north at Hlavná ulica 88 is the **Slovak Technical Museum** (closed Monday and Saturday).

The **East Slovak Museum** (1912) is on námestie Maratónu mieru at the northern end of Hlavná ulica. The 1st and 2nd floors are dedicated to archaeology and prehistory. Don't miss the Košice Gold Treasure in the basement, a hoard of over 3000 gold coins dating from the 15th to the 18th centuries and discovered by chance in 1935. In the park behind the museum building is an old wooden church.

Walk back along Hlavná ulica to the State Theatre and take the narrow Univerzitná ulica beside the Jesuit church east to the **Miklušova Väznica**, ulica Pri Miklušovej Väznici 10. This connected pair of 16th century houses once served as a prison equipped with medieval torture chambers and cells. If the houses are closed, ask for the keys at the **Zoology Museum** beside the nearby church. The Zoology Museum is housed in the Executioner's Bastion, part of Košice's 15th century fortifications.

Most museums and galleries in Košice are closed on Sunday afternoon and Monday.

Places to Stay

Camping South of the city is the *Autocamping salaš Barca* (☎ 58 309). Take tram No 3 south along Južná trieda from the train station until the tram turns left at an underpass, then walk west on Alejová (the Rožňava Highway) for about 800 metres till you see the camping ground on the left. It is open from 15 April to 30 September and there are cabins (US$10/14 double/triple or US$24 for five beds) and tent space (US$1 per person, US$1 per tent). The cabins are available year-round and there's a restaurant on the premises.

Hostels CKM Student Travel, Alžbetina ulica 11, arranges hostel accommodation

year-round. For example, they can book you in to the *Domov Mládeže* (☎ 429 334), Medická 2, on the west side of town, at US$6 per person in two and three-bedded rooms (student card not required). If CKM is closed when you arrive you could try going directly there. CKM can also make advance bookings for you at other hostels and budget hotels around Slovakia.

Hotels Because Košice is not a major tourist centre, hotel prices are lower than those in Bratislava but Satur in the *Slovan Hotel* has no private rooms.

The recently renovated *Hotel Európa* (☎ 622 3897), a grand old three-storey building just across the park from the train station, costs US$15/26/35 single/double/triple with shared bath.

The *Hotel Coral* (☎ 622 6819), Kasárenské námestie 5 behind Prior Department Store, is good value at US$12/24 single/double. Every two rooms in this new five-storey building share a shower.

The *TJ Metropol Turistická Ubytovňa* (☎ 55 948), Štúrova 32, is an attractive sports complex with cheerful rooms with shared bath at US$9/11/15 single/double/triple. It's an easy walk from town but is often full with groups. You get a lot of tram noise here in the very early morning.

The proletarian *Hotel Strojár* (☎ 54 406), Južná trieda 93, has double and triple rooms with a bathroom shared between every two rooms at US$6 per person. Apartments are US$19 double. This workers' dormitory is a little run-down but usually has rooms. Get there on tram No 3 from the stations.

The 12-storey *Hutník Hotel* (☎ 37 780), Tyršovo nábr 6 (US$18/28 single/double with bath), is there as a last resort.

Places to Eat

One of the cheapest and best places to eat at is *Grill Detva*, Mlynská ulica 8. You'll be served tasty wholesome meals promptly (ask for the English menu). You can get a good breakfast here.

Reštaurácia Ajvega, Orlia 10, is an inexpensive, friendly vegetarian restaurant with an English menu. The portions are large but the meals are only so-so and carnivores would do well to eat elsewhere.

The *Zdroj Grill*, Hlavná ulica 83, offers succulent barbecued chicken which you eat standing up. The *Veverická Grill*, Hlavná ulica 95, is good for grilled meats and fish.

A local beer hall worth checking out is *Piváreň U Dominikánov*, Mäsiarska ulica 15 near the market.

A better restaurant for more leisurely dining is the *Zlatý ducat*, Hlavná ulica 16 (upstairs). You'll find less expensive wine (vináreň) and beer (piváreň) restaurants are downstairs. The *Madárská Hungarian Restaurant*, Hlavná ulica 65 (closed on Sunday), features a bright, attractive décor, an extensive menu, good food and a relaxed atmosphere – recommended. It's in Levoča House, a 16th century warehouse reconditioned into a restaurant, café and nightclub.

Aida Espresso on Poštová ulica through the passage at Hlavná ulica 74 (daily 9 am to 10 pm) has the best ice cream in town (and perhaps the best in Eastern Europe).

Entertainment

The *State Theatre* on námestie Slobody is currently closed for renovations. In the meantime performances are being held at *Dom kultúry* near the Hutník Hotel.

The *Thália Hungarian Theatre* and the *State Philharmonic Dom Umenia* are both in the south-west corner of the old town, but performances are only held once or twice a week. Recitals are sometimes given at the Konzervatórium, Hlavná ulica 89.

The *Bábkové Divadlo*, Rooseweltova ulica 1, puts on puppet shows for children weekday mornings and Sunday afternoon.

You can buy theatre tickets from the box office at Štúdio SMER, Hlavná ulica 76.

Cinemas include Kino Tatra, Hlavná ulica 8, and Kino Slovan, Hlavná ulica 59.

The first Sunday in October runners from many countries participate in an International Marathon Race for Peace here.

Discos Try the *Hacienda Disco Club*, Hlavná ulica 65.

The *Valtická Vináreň*, Hlavná ulica 97, functions as a disco Friday and Saturday from 9 pm to 2 am, but it's better known as a pub open nightly until 11 pm. If there are any English-speaking beer drinkers in town you'll probably find them here.

Things to Buy

Úl'uv, Hlavná ulica 76, has a good selection of local handicrafts.

A large street market operates along ulica Cyrilometodejská from the Ukrainian to the Dominican churches.

Getting There & Away

Train Two morning trains depart from Košice for Kiev (1013 km, US$46) and Moscow (1880 km, US$66). Tickets for these trains must be purchased from Satur before 10 am the day before.

Overnight trains with sleepers and couchettes are available between Košice and Prague (708 km), Brno (493 km), Bratislava (445 km), Děčín (807 km), Karlovy Vary (897 km), Plzeň (896 km) and Frantiákovy Lázně (1081 km). Daytime express trains connect Košice to Prague (via Poprad-Tatry and Žilina) and Bratislava (via Banská Bystrica or Žilina).

Bus For shorter trips to Prešov (several an hour, 36 km), Bardejov (14 daily, 77 km, 1¾ hours), Bardejovské Kúpele (six daily, 83 km) and Spišské Podhradie (eight daily, 64 km), you're better off taking a bus. A bus to Užgorod, Ukraine (200 km, three hours, US$3), leaves Košice on Tuesday, Thursday and Saturday at 7 am.

To/From Poland The daily *Cracovia* and *Karpaty* express trains between Hungary and Kraków pass through Košice (reservations required). Northbound the *Cracovia* travels overnight, the *Karpaty* in the late afternoon. A ticket Košice-Kraków costs US$17. For information about unreserved local trains to Poland, see the sections on Prešov and Bardejov.

There's a bus from Košice to Nowy Targ early every Thursday and Saturday morning, to Rzeszów every afternoon. Both are US$5 and you pay the driver. Check the exact times with information as they're not listed on the departures board.

To/From Hungary Local trains run the 88 km from Košice to Miskolc, Hungary (2½ hours, US$9), via Hidasnémeti every morning and afternoon. This is an easy way to cross the border as no reservations are required. If you take the morning train, get a ticket right through to Budapest (if you're going there!) as you will only have five minutes to change trains at Miskolc and no time to change money and buy another ticket.

Alternatively, there are six unreserved local trains a day between Slovenské Nové Mesto, Slovakia, and Sátoraljaújhely, Hungary, with connections to/from Košice and Miskolc.

The *Rákóczi* express train links Košice to Budapest (270 km, 4½ hours, US$21) daily, departing from Budapest-Keleti in the morning, Košice in the late afternoon (reservations optional).

There's a bus from Košice to Miskolc on Wednesday, Friday and Saturday at 6.30 am (84 km, US$3). Book your ticket the day before at window No 1 in the bus station.

Car Rental Autoturist (☎ 622 4066), Továrenská 1, represents Europcar.

Slovenia

Slovenia (Slovenija) sits on the edge of Eastern and Western Europe. The cities bear the imprint of the Italian Counter-Reformation, while up in the Julian Alps you sense the proximity of Austria. The two million Slovenes were the best off among the peoples of former Yugoslavia and the relative wellbeing on this 'sunny side of the Alps' is apparent. The wooded slopes, fertile valleys, scenic rivers and neat little villages are reminiscent of Bavaria. If you're arriving from Italy or Austria, Slovenia may be your gateway to the Balkans, but you'll feel you're still in central Europe.

For travellers Slovenia is one of Eastern Europe's nicest surprises. Fairy-tale Bled Castle, breathtaking Bohinj Lake, the scenic Postojna and Škocjan caves, Venetian Piran and vibrant Ljubljana are outstanding attractions, all accessible at a fraction of the cost of their counterparts in northern and Western Europe. The amazing variety of environments packed into a small area makes this country a Europe in miniature.

The political problems of ex-Yugoslavia only touched Slovenia briefly in July 1991, and since then this independent republic has been a peaceful, safe place to visit. Luckily, Slovenia escaped war damage, but the bad publicity scared off the masses of Western Europeans who formerly holidayed there and only now are they beginning to realise that things are back to normal. Meanwhile, you can enjoy Slovenia without the huge crowds of tourists found in Western Europe and minus most of the hassles encountered further east. You'll probably agree by the time you leave that Slovenia is one of the most delightful little countries in Europe.

Facts about the Country

HISTORY

The Slovenes settled here in the 6th century AD and accepted Christianity in the 7th century (the first Slavic people to do so). In 745, Slovenia was brought under Germanic rule, first with Bavaria in the Frankish empire of Charlemagne, then as part of the Holy Roman Empire in the 9th century. The Austrian Habsburgs took over in the 13th century and continued to rule this region right up until 1918 with only brief interruptions. During this long period, the upper classes became totally Germanised, though the peasantry retained their Slavic identity. The Slovenian language diverged from Croatian in the 8th century, and although the Bible was translated into Slovene in 1584 during the Reformation, only in the 19th century did Slovene come into common use as a written language.

In 1809, Napoleon set up the 'Illyrian Provinces' (Slovenia, Dalmatia and part of Croatia) with Ljubljana as the capital to isolate Austria from the Adriatic. Though the Habsburgs returned in 1814, French reforms

Slovenia
(Slovenija)

in education and public administration endured. The democratic revolution of 1848 also increased political consciousness and in 1918 Slovenia was included in the Kingdom of Serbs, Croats and Slovenes. During WW II most of Slovenia was annexed by Germany, though Italy and Hungary got smaller slices off the sides. Slovenian partisans fought courageously against this from mountain bases and when Italian Istria was formally presented to Yugoslavia in 1947, Slovenia obtained a 47-km stretch of Adriatic coastline between Trieste and Portorož. Koper was then developed to give previously landlocked Slovenia a major port.

Moves by Serbia in the late 1980s to reassert its leading role within Yugoslavia worried Slovenes, who were shocked by the cancellation of Kosovo's autonomy in 1989, something they feared could also happen to them. For some years, Slovenia's interests had been shifting to the west and north. As a member of Alpen-Adria, a regional grouping

bringing together Austria, Hungary, Croatia, Bavaria and adjacent regions of Italy for multilateral cooperation in many fields, Slovenia had established excellent relations with all its neighbours. The Yugoslav connection, on the other hand, was deteriorating into a burden and a threat.

In early 1990, Slovenia became the first Yugoslav republic to hold free elections and slough off 45 years of communist rule and, on 23 December 1990, the inhabitants voted overwhelmingly in favour of independence. The Slovenian government began stockpiling weapons and on 25 June 1991 it pulled the republic out of the Yugoslav Federation. To dramatise their bid for independence and to generate foreign sympathy, the Slovenian leaders deliberately provoked fighting with the 'thuggish' federal army by attempting to take control of the border crossings. Belgrade's conscript army soon began to melt before determined resistance from the Slovenian militia. As no territorial claims or minority issues were involved, the Yugoslav government agreed to a truce brokered by the European Community (EC). This took effect on 8 July, and 10 days later it was announced that all federal troops would be withdrawn within three months. Slovenia implemented its Fundamental Sovereignty Act on 8 October, got a new constitution in December, and on 15 January 1992 the EC formally recognised the country – Slovenia became an independent state for the first time in its history! Slovenia was admitted to the United Nations on 22 May 1992 and full membership in the European Union is anticipated by the year 2000.

GEOGRAPHY

Slovenia is pinched between Austria and Croatia, with much shorter borders with Italy and Hungary. Measuring just 20,256 sq km, Slovenia is the smallest country in Eastern Europe, about the size of the US state of Massachusetts or Wales. Much of it is mountainous, culminating in the north-west at Mt Triglav (2864 metres) in the Julian Alps. From this jagged knot the main Alpine chain continues east along the Austrian border, while the Dinaric range runs south-east along the coast into Croatia. Below the limestone plateau between Ljubljana and Koper is Europe's most extensive network of karst caves. (The Slovenian karst is the original 'karst' after which all other karst regions around the world are named.)

The coastal range forms a barrier isolating the Istrian Peninsula from Slovenia's corner of the Danube Basin. Much of the interior east of the Alps is drained by the rivers Sava (which originates in Bohinj Lake) and Drava (which passes Maribor), both tributaries of the Danube. The Soča drains western Slovenia and flows into the Adriatic.

ECONOMY

Slovenia's furniture, textile and paper industries produce high-quality products exported to Germany, Italy and France. There are major coal mines east of Ljubljana and mercury mines to the west, a steel mill at

Jesenice and textile mills at Kranj. Slovenia has a nuclear power plant at Krško on the Sava River between Ljubljana and Zagreb. Agriculture is important with the emphasis on apples, pears, potatoes, grapes and wheat. Over a quarter of ex-Yugoslavia's milk came from Slovenia and the number of poultry and cattle here is disproportionately high. The fishing industry is based at Izola, with much of the catch taken in Croatian waters.

Though Slovenia had only 8% of former Yugoslavia's population, it accounted for 16.5% of the country's gross domestic product and 30% of exports to the West. Since 1991, Slovenia has suffered serious economic difficulties resulting from the loss of its markets in the other ex-Yugoslav republics, which absorbed 48% of Slovenia's exports in 1990 but only 16.7% in 1992. In 1991, production was down by 12.4%, unemployment increased by 60% and inflation was 124.1%. In 1993, unemployment stood at 14%.

The negative side effects of independence now seem to have bottomed out and by mid-1992 inflation had been reduced to a mere 2% through sharp cutbacks in government spending. This success has a price, of course, and the population faces continuing austerity. Yet at US$438 a month, the average wage in Slovenia is the highest in Eastern Europe. Many Slovenes, like Hungarians, hold two jobs and a third of the national income is derived from the 'black' economy associated with this moonlighting.

In mid-1992, 84.9% of employees still worked for 'socially owned' companies inherited from the communist past but in November 1992 parliament passed a new privatisation law which took effect in April 1993. The complex plan envisions the free distribution of 60% of shares and the sale of the rest but actual privatisation was put off until mid-1994 to allow companies time to prepare. Light industry is reviving but the unwieldy heavy industry built up by the communists remains a liability. The shake-out of unprofitable, heavily indebted enterprises will be painful but with its advantageous location, good infrastructure and

SLOVENIA

industrious workforce, Slovenia has a bright future.

POPULATION & PEOPLE

This tiny country was the most homogeneous portion of former Yugoslavia. About 86% of the two million inhabitants are Slovenes, 3% Croats and 2% Serbs, with smaller groups of Muslims, Hungarians, Italians and others. Roman Catholics account for over 80% of the total. The largest cities are Ljubljana (330,000), Maribor (108,000), Celje (42,000) and Kranj (37,000).

ARTS

Slovenia's best known writer is the Romantic poet France Prešeren (1800-49) whose lyric poems combined folk rhythms with the literary forms of his day to inspire a national consciousness. Disappointed in love, Prešeren wrote sensitive love poems, and he's also known for his satirical verses and epic poetry. There's a drawing of him on the 1000 tolarji banknote.

Many notable buildings and public squares in Ljubljana were designed by the architect Jože Plečnik (1872-1957), a member of the school of Otto Wagner of Vienna. Plečnik's portrait appears on the 500 tolarji note.

The avant-garde Slovenian art movement 'Neue Slowenische Kunst' (NSK) typifies the iconoclastic mood in post-communist Eastern Europe. For example, the Ljubljana rock group Laibach organises its concerts as if they were Nazi mass rallies. During one skit by the theatre troupe Red Pilot (now renamed Noordung), the audience is herded into boxcars by actors in military uniform. In the rock ballet *Thieves of Wet Hankies*, the members of the Betontanc Dance Company murder one another and then are resurrected. Back in the Yugoslavia days, the designer group 'New Collectivism' became notorious when they won a Belgrade poster competition with a plagiarised Nazi poster in which the swastika was replaced by a red star. The five-member artists' collective IRWIN (founded in 1983) spurns the sacred myth of the individual artist by exhibiting only as an anonymous group with jarring ideological or historical symbols juxtaposed in such a way as to bring out new meanings. The sometimes strident aesthetic provocations of NSK have caused reactions for speaking the unspeakable but the cleansing power of their work has left its mark on the contemporary European art scene.

Music

Since WW II, many Slovenian folk traditions have been lost, but Mira and Matija Terlep of the trio Trutamora Slovenica have dug into the literature and made field surveys in an attempt to rediscover the roots of Slovenian popular culture, as young Hungarians did a decade ago. Their compact disc *Sound Image of Slovene Regions No 4* features reconstructions of old Slovenian folk songs played on original folk instruments such as the dulcimer or cimbalom (the ancestor of the piano), zither, *zvvegla* (wooden cross flute), *ocarina* (a clay flute), *šurle* (Istrian double flute), panpipes, Jew's harp, *gudalo* (earthenware bass) and even a dried-up pumpkin rattle. Accompanied by a detailed English text, this outstanding recording can be purchased at DZS music shops in Ljubljana.

LANGUAGE

Slovene is a Slavic language distinct from Croatian but also written with Roman characters. Apart from singular and plural word forms, it also has a dual number – a very rare phenomenon in linguistics.

Most Slovenes speak a second language. English and German are widely spoken by people involved in tourism and you can speak Italian anywhere on the Slovene Riviera.

Pronunciation

Slovene sounds are not difficult to learn. The alphabet consists of 25 letters, most of which are very similar to English. It does not have the letters q, w, x and y, but the following letters are added: č, š and ž. Each letter has only one sound, with very few exceptions,

SLOVENIA

and the sounds are pure and not diphthongal. The letters 'l' and 'v' at the end of syllables and before vowels are both pronounced like the English 'w'. Though words like *trn* (thorn) look unpronounceable, most Slovenes add a short vowel like an 'a' or the German 'ö' (depending on dialect) in front of the 'r' to give a Scot's pronunciation of 'tern' or 'tarn'. Here is a list of letters specific to Slovene.

c	'ts' as in 'pizza'
č	'ch' as in 'chocolate'
ê	'a' as in 'apple'
e	'er' as in 'opera' (when unstressed)
é	'ay' as in 'day'
j	'y' as in 'yellow'
ó	'o' as in 'more'
r	'rrrim' (rolled)
š	'sh' as in 'ship'
u	'oo' as in 'good'
ž	'zh' as the 's' in 'vision'

Greetings & Civilities

hello	*zdravo*
good morning	*dobro jutro*
good day	*dober dan*
good evening	*dober večer*
goodbye	*na svidenje*
please	*prosim*
thank you	*hvala*
I am sorry.	*oprostite*
yes	*da*
no	*ne*

Small Talk

I don't understand.	*Ne razumem.*
Could you write it down?	*Lahko to napišete?*
What is it called?	*Kako se to imenuje?*
Where do you live?	*Kje živite?*
What work do you do?	*Kaj delate?*
I am a student.	*Sem študent/študentka.*
I am very happy.	*Sem zelo srečen/srečna.*

Accommodation

youth hostel	*mladinski dom*
camping ground	*autokamp*
private room	*zasebna soba*
How much is it?	*Koliko to stane?*
Is that the price per person?	*Ali je ta cena po osebi?*
Is that the total price?	*Ali je to končna cena?*
Are there any extra charges?	*Ali je potrebno še doplačati?*
Do I pay extra for showers?	*Moram doplačati za prho?*
Where is there a cheaper hotel?	*Kje je cenejši hotel?*
Should I make a reservation?	*Ali je potrebna rezervacija?*
single room	*enoposteljna soba*
double room	*dvoposteljna soba*
It is very noisy.	*Je zelo glasno.*
Where is the toilet?	*Kje je stranišče?*

Getting Around

What time does it leave?	*Kdaj je odhod?*
When is the first bus?	*daj pelje prvi avtobus?*
When is the last bus?	*Kdaj pelje zadnji avtobus?*
When is the next bus?	*Kdaj pelje naslednji avtobus?*
That's too soon.	*To je prezgodaj.*
When is the next one after that?	*Kdaj gre naslednji po tem?*
How long does the trip take?	*Kako dolgo traja potovanje?*
arrival	*prihod*
departure	*odhod*
timetable	*vozni red*
Where is the bus stop?	*Kje je avtobusna postaja?*
Where is the train station?	*Kje je železniška postaja?*
Where is the left-luggage room?	*Kje je garderoba?*

Around Town

Just a minute.	*Samo trenutek.*

SLOVENIA

Where is ... ?	Kje je ... ?
the bank	banka
the post office	pošta
the tourist information office	turistični biro
the museum	muzej
Where are you going?	Kam greš?
I am going to ...	Grem v ...
Where is it?	Kje je to?
I can't find it.	Ne morem ga/je najti.
Is it far?	Je daleč?
Please show me on the map.	Prosim, pokažite mi na zemljevidu.
left	levo
right	desno
straight ahead	naravnost
I want ...	Želim ...
Do I need permission?	Potrebujem dovoljenje?

Entertainment

Where can I buy a ticket?	Kje lahko kupim vstopnico?
I want to refund this ticket.	Kje lahko refundiram vstopnico?
Is this a good seat?	Je to dober sedež?
at the front	spredaj
ticket	vstopnica

Food

I do not eat meat.	Ne jem mesa.
self-service cafetaria	samopostrežna restavracija
grocery store	trgovina
fish	riba
pork	svinjina
soup	juha
salad	solata
fresh vegetables	sveža zelenjava
milk	mleko
bread	kruh
sugar	sladkor
ice cream	sladoled
coffee	kava
tea	čaj
mineral water	mineralna voda
beer	pivo

wine	vino
hot/cold	vroče/mrzlo

Shopping

Where can I buy one?	Kje lahko to kupim?
How much does it cost?	Koliko to stane?
That's (much) too expensive.	To je predrago.
Is there a cheaper one?	Se je kje kaj cenejše?

Time & Dates

today	danes
tonight	nocoj
tomorrow	jutri
the day after tomorrow	pojutrišnjem
What time does it open?	Kdaj se odpre?
What time does it close?	Kdaj se zapre?
open	odprto
closed	zaprto
in the morning	zjutraj
in the evening	zvečer
every day	vsak dan
At what time?	Ob kateri uri?
When?	Kdaj?

Monday	ponedeljek
Tuesday	torek
Wednesday	sreda
Thursday	četrtek
Friday	petek
Saturday	sobota
Sunday	nedelja

January	januar
February	februar
March	marec
April	april
May	maj
June	junij
July	julij
August	avgust
September	september
October	oktober
November	november
December	december

SLOVENIA

Numbers

1	*ena*
2	*dva*
3	*tri*
4	*štiri*
5	*pet*
6	*šest*
7	*sedem*
8	*osem*
9	*devet*
10	*deset*
11	*enajst*
12	*dvanajst*
13	*trinajst*
14	*štirinajst*
15	*petnajst*
16	*šestnajst*
17	*sedemnajst*
18	*osemnajst*
19	*devetnajst*
20	*dvajset*
21	*enaindvajset*
22	*dvaindvajset*
23	*triindvajset*
30	*trideset*
40	*štirideset*
50	*petdeset*
60	*šestdeset*
70	*sedemdeset*
80	*osemdeset*
90	*devetdeset*
100	*sto*
1000	*tisoč*
10,000	*desettisoč*
1,000,000	*en milijon*

Facts for the Visitor

VISAS & EMBASSIES

No visa is required by citizens of the European Union, Scandinavian countries, Australia, Canada or the USA for a stay of 90 days. New Zealanders still require a tourist visa (US$12) but it's available at the border. Passport controls on entry into Slovenia are relaxed (EU citizens don't even need a passport) and the Italian or Austrian authorities will probably scrutinise your passport more closely when you return to those countries.

Slovenian Embassies

In addition to the embassies listed following, Slovenia has honorary consuls in Sydney, Australia (☎ 02-314 5116 or 604 5133), and Cleveland, Ohio, USA (☎ 0216-589 9220), and embassies in Budapest, Prague, Skopje and Zagreb.

Australia
    60 Marcus Clarke St, Canberra, ACT 2601
    (☎ 062-43 4830)
Canada
    150 Metcalfe St, Suite 2101, Ottawa, ON K2P
    1P1 (☎ 0613-565 5781)
UK
    Suite One, Cavendish Court, 11-15 Wigmore St,
    London W1H 9LA (☎ 0171-495 7775)
USA
    1525 New Hampshire Ave NW, Washington, DC
    20036 (☎ 0202-667 5363)
    600 Third Ave, 24th Floor, New York, NY 10016
    (☎ 0212-370 3006)

MONEY

In October 1991, Slovenia issued its own currency, the tolar (SIT), which is pronounced something like 'dollar'. Counting goes one tolar, two tolarja, three tolarji (and up). The original tolar coupons bearing a photo of Mt Triglav were replaced in late 1992 by new tolar notes depicting famous Slovenes. Slovene currency is easy to understand as the denominations are manageable. There are coins of 50 stotinov and one, two and five tolarji and banknotes of 10, 20, 50, 100, 200, 500, 1000 and 5000 tolarji. In mid-1994 the rate was US$1 = 133 tolarji.

There's no black market but different exchange offices offer slightly different rates, so it pays to keep your eyes open. Commissions *(provizija)* also vary, with up to 5% deducted at hotels, so ask. Some travel agencies take 2% commission, others none. Banks pay a higher rate for travellers' cheques than cash but some private exchange offices (not travel agencies) do the reverse, paying better rates than the bank for cash. Post offices are not good places to change money as they may only accept cash,

SLOVENIA

and if they do take travellers' cheques it will be at a very poor rate (the posted rate may be only for cash). If in doubt, enquire about the rate before signing your cheque.

You can usually change excess Slovenian tolarji back into hard currency but exchange receipts may be required. Some offices will refuse to change them back and tolarji are nearly impossible to change outside Slovenia, so only change what you need and spend what's left over on long-distance telephone calls or something similar. You're allowed to import/export tolar banknotes up to a value of about US$50. Slovenia is a good place to trade your travellers' cheques for cash dollars or Deutschmarks. Most Slovenian banks will carry out the transaction for a flat 3% commission. Prices in Slovenia are fixed and well posted and it's unlikely that people will try to cheat you very often.

CLIMATE & WHEN TO GO

As elsewhere around the Mediterranean, from April to September are the best months to be in Slovenia as the days are long and the weather is warm. Snow can linger in the mountains as late as June, but spring (April and May) is a good time to be in the lowlands as everything is fresh and in blossom. In July and August, hotel rates are increased and there will be lots of other tourists. September is an excellent month as the summer crowds will have vanished, despite this being the best mountain-hiking month.

SUGGESTED ITINERARIES

Depending on the length of your stay, you might want to see and do the following in Slovenia:

Two days
    Visit Ljubljana.
One week
    Visit Ljubljana, Bled, Bohinj and Piran.
Two weeks
    Visit all the places covered in this chapter.

TOURIST OFFICES

Ljubljana has an excellent municipal Tourist Information Centre (TIC), and travel agencies in most other towns are much more willing to offer assistance to individual visitors than commercial travel agencies in Western Europe. The companies to watch for are Atlas, Generaltourist, Globtour, Kompas, Slovenijaturist and any office marked 'Turist Biro'.

Tourist Offices Abroad

The Slovenian Tourist Office (☎ 0171-495 4688 or 499 7488), Moghul House, 57 Grosvenor St, London W1X 9DA, England, UK, mails out free brochures on the country. In the USA try Double A International Inc, Slovenia Group (☎ 212-421 0551), P O Box 192, New York, NY 10044.

Additionally, representatives abroad of the Slovenian travel agency Kompas should be able to provide information on tourism in Slovenia. Here are a few Kompas offices to contact:

Australia
    Suite 401, 115 Pitt St, Sydney, NSW 2000
    (☎ 02-233 4197)
Canada
    Suite 535, 4060 Ste-Catherine W, Montreal, PQ
    H3Z 2Z3 (☎ 0514-938 4041)
France
    23-25 Rue Singer, 75016 Paris (☎ 01-4525 5715)
USA
    2826 E Commercial Blvd, Fort Lauderdale, FL
    33308 (☎ 0305-771 9200)
    10662 El Adelante Ave, Fountain Valley, CA
    92708 (☎ 0714-378 0510)

BUSINESS HOURS & HOLIDAYS

Normal banking hours are on weekdays from 8 am to 6 pm and Saturday from 8 am to noon. Main post offices are open weekdays similar hours. Some government offices close at 3 pm and large stores at 7 pm on weekdays and 1 pm on Saturday.

Public holidays in Slovenia include New Year (1 and 2 January), Prešeren Day (8 February), Easter Monday (March/April), Insurrection Day (27 April), Labour Days (1 and 2 May), Statehood Day (25 June), Assumption Day (15 August), Reformation Day (31 October), All Saints' Day (1 November), Christmas (25 December) and Independence Day (26 December). If any of these falls on a Sunday, then the following Monday becomes a holiday.

Though not a public holiday, St Martin's Day (11 November) is important for on this day *must* officially becomes wine and can be sold as such. That evening families dine on goose and some restaurants offer a *martinovanje* dinner of goose with fresh wine accompanied by folk music. On Palm Sunday (the Sunday before Good Friday), people carry complex arrangements of leaves and ribbons called *butare* to church and Slovenia really looks like Bali. On the eve of St Gregory's Day (3 September), village children set afloat hundreds of tiny boats bearing candles.

CULTURAL EVENTS

The cultural highlights of Slovenia's summer season are the International Summer Festival at Ljubljana and the Piran Musical Evenings at Piran and Portorož, both in July and August. Many events in old Ljubljana accompany the International Wine Fair in late August or early September. In early October there's a festival of Baroque music in Maribor.

POST & TELECOMMUNICATIONS
Receiving Mail

American Express card members can have their mail addressed c/o Atlas Ambassador, Mestni trg 8, 61000 Ljubljana, Slovenia. Other mortals should have mail sent c/o Poste Restante, 61101 Ljubljana, Slovenia (held for 30 days).

Telephones

To call Slovenia from Western Europe, dial the international access code, 386 (the country code for Slovenia), the area code (without the initial zero) and the number. Slovenian area codes include 061 (Ljubljana), 064 (Bled and Bohinj), 065 (Nova Gorica), 066 (Koper, Portorož and Piran) and 067 (Postojna).

Magnetic phonecards come in denominations of 100 impulses (US$2) and 200 impulses (US$3.25), and can be purchased at post offices. Both phonecards and tokens may only be useable in the local area, so ask.

Public telephone booths are found at all post offices and the cards are easy to use and fairly inexpensive. A local call absorbs about five impulses, and a three-minute call from Slovenia will cost about US$3 to the UK or US$6.75 to the USA or Australia. If you want to call abroad, the international access code in Slovenia is 00.

Many of the people working at accommodation facilities around Slovenia speak English, so don't hesitate to use your phonecard to call some of the places listed in this chapter for current information. After the first call you'll get the hang of it.

TIME

Slovenia is one hour ahead of GMT/UTC. Slovenia goes on summer time at the end of March when clocks are turned forward an hour. At the end of September they're turned back an hour.

ELECTRICITY

The electric voltage is 220 V AC, 50 Hz. Plugs are the standard European two-pronged type.

WEIGHTS & MEASURES

Slovenia uses the metric system.

ACTIVITIES
Skiing

Slovenia has many well-equipped ski resorts in the Julian Alps, especially Vogel (1922 metres) above Bohinj, Kranjska gora (810 metres), Krvavec (1853 metres) east of Kranj, and Pohorje (1543 metres) near Maribor. World Cup trials are held at Kranjska gora (where the Winter Olympic Games will be held in 2002) and the current world ski-jumping record (194 metres) was set at nearby Planica. Every fourth Slovene is an active skier!

All of these resorts have multiple chair lifts, cable cars and large resort hotels. Ski schools are found at Pokljuka west of Bled, Kranjska gora and Pohorje. For information about special all-inclusive ski tours to

SLOVENIA

Slovenia, consult a travel agency. Turn to the Bohinj section in this chapter for specific information about skiing at Vogel. December to March is the main ski season.

Hiking

Next to skiing, hiking is the national sport of Slovenia and one of the nicest things about it is that it gives you a chance to meet the locals in an informal environment. No less than 120,000 Slovenes are members of mountaineering clubs and there are 9000 km of marked hiking trails and 140 mountain huts in this small country. You'll experience the full grandeur of the Julian Alps in Triglav National Park at Bohinj, and for the veteran mountaineer there's the Slovenian Mountain Transversal, which crosses all the highest peaks – one of the oldest tracks in Europe.

Cycling

Mountain bikes are for rent at Bled and Bohinj and the uncrowded roads around these resorts are a joy to cycle.

White-Water Rafting

Exciting white-water rafting is practised on the Soča River in north-western Slovenia, one of only five rivers in the European Alps whose upper waters are still unspoiled. The agency organising the trips is based at the Hotel Alp (☎ 065-86 040) in Bovec and trips leave at 10 am and 2 pm daily in July and August (weekends only in April, May, June, September and October). Expect to pay about US$35 for a 1½-hour trip along 10 km of the river (call ahead for information and reservations).

ACCOMMODATION
Camping

In summer camping is the cheapest way to go and there are conveniently located camping grounds in all areas of Slovenia covered in this chapter. Of course, you'll need a tent. The two best camping grounds for those who want to experience Slovenia's combination of mountains and sea are Zlatorog at Bohinj and Jezero at Piran.

Hostels

Slovenia's only authentic year-round youth hostel is the one in Bled although student dormitories in Ljubljana and Koper admit YHA members all year.

Private Rooms & Pensions

Private rooms arranged by tourist offices and travel agencies are only slightly more expensive than camping, but a 30% surcharge is sometimes levied if you stay only one or two nights (the surcharge is always levied along the coast). You can often bargain for rooms without the surcharge by going directly to houses in resort areas bearing *sobe* (room) signs. Small pensions are also good value, though in July and August you may be required to take dinner and the rates are higher. Pensions are good value for solo travellers as rooms are often priced per person.

Farm Houses

The agricultural cooperatives of Slovenia have organised a unique programme to accommodate visitors on working farms. It's like staying in private rooms except that the 120 participating farms are in picturesque rural areas and may offer activities such as horse riding (US$9 an hour), kayaking, skiing and cycling. The farm of Anton Kovač (☎ 061-801 508) at Osilnica between Ljubljana and Rijeka, for example, offers a special weekend programme including horse riding and canoeing to groups of six people or more (US$50 per person all-inclusive). Anton speaks German and Italian and takes guests all year but book ahead from Ljubljana.

Prices at the other farm houses range from US$12 per person for a 2nd-category room with shared bath and breakfast in the low season (from September to mid-December and mid-January to June) to US$25 per person for a 1st-category room with private bath and all meals in the high season (July and August). Apartments for groups of up to eight people are also available. There's a 30% surcharge on stays of less than three nights. Bookings should be made through the Cooperative Tourist Agency VAS

(☎ 061-125 3282), Miklošičeva 4, 61000 Ljubljana. The UK agent is Slovenia Pursuits (☎ 01763-852 387), Brummels, Guilden Morden, Royston, Herts SG8 0JP, England, UK.

Hotels

Hotels are more expensive than any of the other accommodation options and the rates vary according to season, with July and August being the peak season and June and September the shoulder season. In Ljubljana, prices are constant all year. Many resort hotels are closed in winter. As hotels seldom levy a surcharge for stays of one or two nights they're worth considering if you're only passing through.

FOOD

In Slovenia you can enjoy some of the best food in Eastern Europe at very reasonable prices. You'll taste the Germanic flavour in the sausages with sauerkraut *(kranjske klobase s kislim zeljem)*, game dishes and meats with mushrooms. Other neighbours have contributed Austrian strudel *(zavitki)*, layer cake *(torte)* and omelette *(palačinke)*, and that old Balkan standby, *burek* (a greasy layered cheese or meat pie), is served at take-aways everywhere.

There are many types of dumplings, of which walnut and cheese dumplings are a delicacy. Try also the baked delicacies: best known is *potica*, walnut roll, and *gibanica*, pastry filled with apples, cheese and poppy seeds, baked in cream and eaten warm. No Slovene lunch is complete without a soup such as *goveja juha* (beef broth), *kisla juha* (sour soup), *ribji brodet* (Istrian fish soup), *jota* (sauerkraut soup) and *ričet* (pork and barley broth). Goulash is considered a main dish and not a soup. Traditional dishes are most easily found at inns *(gostilna)*. Watch for the daily menu *(dnevna kosila)*, a set meal often advertised on a blackboard on the street outside.

DRINKS

The wine-growing regions of Slovenia are Podravje in the east (noted for its champagne and white wines such as Riesling), Posavje in the south-east (excellent dry rosé wines) and Primorska near Koper (where the 'terra rossa' yields hearty red wines). Wines are classed *vrhunsko* (top quality), *kakovostno* (quality wine) and *namizno* (table wine) whether they be *suho* (dry), *polsuho* (semi-dry) or *sladko* (sweet). Beware of wines marked *uvoz* (import) as any wine imported without an original label will be of inferior quality. If the bottle has a metal or plastic stopper instead of a cork it only means the wine will not age and it's not necessarily bad.

According to a local reader of this book, Tomaž Lovrenčič, Slovenia's finest white wines are Laški Rizling, Šipon, Beli Pinot, Traminec and Cviček, and the top red wines are Merlot, Refošk and Kraški Teran. Tomaž claims the best beers are Zlatorog (from Laško), Union (from Ljubljana) and Gambrinus (from Maribor), in that order. Prove him wrong!

Two herbal liqueurs are hermelika and 1000 rož. Pelinkovec is made from wormwood. The most unusual local liqueur is Pleterska hruška made by ingenious Carthusian monks who let a pear grow in a bottle, then pick bottle and pear together and pour brandy inside. This concoction is sure to give you a vision of hell.

Getting There & Away

AIR

The national airline, Adria Airways (☎ 061-131 8155), has nonstop flights from Ljubljana to Frankfurt, London, Manchester, Moscow, Munich, Paris, Rome, Skopje, Split, Tirana, Vienna and Zürich. They also fly from Maribor to Skopje and Tirana.

An airport tax of US$14 is collected on all flights departing from Slovenia (usually included in the ticket price).

LAND
Bus

Koper is the easiest entry/exit point to/from Italy as there are 15 buses a day going from the bus station next to Trieste Railway Station to Koper Railway Station (21 km, US$2). From Koper there's a frequent bus and train service to/from Ljubljana.

To/from Hungary you can catch a bus between Ljubljana and Lenti twice a week (235 km, five hours, US$12). Otherwise take one of the six daily buses from Ljubljana to Lendava (204 km, four hours), then walk the five km through Lendava to the Hungarian border. The first Hungarian railway station, Rédics, is only two km beyond the border (eight trains a day to Zalaegerszeg, from where there are connections to Budapest).

For information on buses to Germany see the Ljubljana section (these are much cheaper than the train).

Train

The main train routes into Slovenia from Austria are Vienna to Maribor and Salzburg to Jesenice. Tickets cost US$30 from Ljubljana to Salzburg (300 km, 4½ hours), US$41 from Ljubljana to Vienna (460 km, six hours) and US$196 Ljubljana-Amsterdam (1429 km, 18 hours). To Austria, it's cheaper to take a local train to Maribor and buy your ticket on to Vienna from there. Similarly, from Austria only buy a ticket as far as Jesenice or Maribor as domestic fares are much lower than the international ones.

There are two trains a day between Munich and Ljubljana (453 km, seven hours, US$54) via Salzburg. The *Eurocity Mimara* travels by day, while *Intercity 296/297* express goes overnight in each direction (sleeping carriage available). A US$5.50 supplement is payable on the *Mimara* and this includes a seat reservation if made the day before or earlier. Reservations (US$3.50) are required on *Intercity 296/297* southbound, but not northbound. Northbound the *Mimara* carries on to Nuremberg and Leipzig.

Five trains a day run from Trieste, Italy, to Ljubljana (165 km, three hours, US$10) via Pivka. From Croatia it's Zagreb to Ljubljana (160 km, 2½ hours, US$8) via Zidani Most, or Rijeka to Ljubljana (155 km, 2½ hours, US$7) via Pivka. Services between Slovenia

and Croatia require a change of trains halfway but the connections are immediate. The *Drava* express train links Ljubljana directly to Budapest (500 km, 7½ hours, US$33) via Croatia.

Car & Motorbike

Slovenia maintains 65 border crossings to Italy, 48 to Austria, 34 to Croatia but only two to Hungary. Thanks to the policies of former regimes only rough secondary roads link Slovenia to Hungary and there are long lines of trucks waiting to cross on each side at the two border crossings.

Following is a list of selected international highway entry/exit points clockwise around Slovenia, with the Slovenian border post named.

To/From Italy The crossings are at Lazaret (between Trieste and Ankaran), Škofije (between Trieste and Koper), Kozina (between Trieste and Rijeka), Lipica (near Trieste), Fernetiči/Sežana (between Trieste and Ljubljana), Vrtojba (near Nova Gorica), Rožna dolina (between Gorizia and Nova Gorica), Robič (32 km north-east of Udine), Učeja (16 km west of Bovec), Predel (13 km south of Tarvisio) and Rateče (12 km east of Tarvisio).

To/From Austria There's Korensko sedlo (20 km south-west of Villach), Karavanke (at the seven-km tunnel between Jesenice and Villach), Ljubelj (between Klagenfurt and Kranj), Jezersko (35 km north-east of Kranj), Holmec (49 km east of Klagenfurt), Vič (between Klagenfurt and Maribor), Radelj (43 km west of Maribor), Jurij (13 km north-west of Maribor), Šentilj (17 km north of Maribor), Trate (16 km east of Šentilj), Gornja Radgona (41 km north-east of Maribor), Gederovci (10 km west of Murska Sobota) and Kuzma (28 km north of Murska Sobota).

To/From Hungary & Croatia You can cross at Hodoš (west of Zalaegerszeg) and Dolga vas (between Lendava and Rédics). Most of the 26 highway border crossings to/from Croatia may be used by everyone.

Getting Around

BUS
Bus is about the easiest way to get around Slovenia, with fares averaging US$2 for every hour of travel. Departures are frequent. Bus is the only way to get to Bled, Bohinj and Istria, whereas other routes such as Ljubljana to Koper, Rijeka and Zagreb are served by both bus and train. If your bag has to be checked in to the luggage compartment below the bus it will be US$0.50 extra though most drivers don't mind you carrying it on the bus if it can fit between your legs. In Ljubljana you can buy your ticket (with seat reservation) the day before, but many people simply pay the conductor on the bus itself. The one time you really will need a reservation is Friday afternoon, when many students travel from Ljubljana to their homes.

Footnotes you may see on Slovenian bus schedules include *vozi vsak dan* (runs daily), *vozi ob delavnikih* (runs on weekdays), *vozi ob sobotah* (runs on Saturday) and *vozi ob nedeljah in praznikih* (runs on Sunday and holidays).

TRAIN
The Slovenske železnice (SŽ) operates over 1198 km of track. Slovenia's most scenic rail route runs from Jesenice to Nova Gorica. This 108-km route through the Julian Alps and down the Soča River opened for service in 1906. A 6327-metre tunnel south of Bohinjska Bistrica cuts between the drainage basin of the Danube River and that of the Adriatic. Five local trains a day cover this route in each direction.

The 160-km train ride from Ljubljana to Zagreb is also worth taking as the line follows the Sava River along most of its route through a picturesque gorge. Sit on the right side eastbound, the left side westbound.

Local trains leave Ljubljana regularly for Jesenice (74 km, 1½ hours), Maribor (178 km, three hours), Zagreb (160 km, 2½ hours), Karlovac (175 km, four hours), Rijeka (155 km, 2½ hours), Pula (258 km, five hours) and Koper (175 km, three hours). Express trains also operate on these routes.

On posted timetables in Slovenia, *prihodi* means arrivals and *odhodi* means departures. If you don't have time to buy a ticket, seek out the conductor who will sell you one with a supplement of US$1. Otherwise you'll be subject to a US$10 fine. If you couldn't buy a ticket because your connecting train was late no supplement is payable.

CAR & MOTORBIKE
A toll is payable on the motorways from Ljubljana to Kranj (25 km), Ljubljana to Postojna (41 km) and Maribor to Celje (51 km) but it's under US$2 for cars and motorbikes. Speed limits for cars are 60 km/h in built-up areas, 80 km/h on secondary roads, 100 km/h on main highways and 120 km/h on motorways. In large towns illegally parked vehicles are routinely towed away.

Slovenia's automobile club is the Avto-Moto Zveza Slovenije (AMZS). For emergency road assistance, motorists should call them on ☎ 987.

Car Rental
Car rentals from Avis, Budget/Globtour and Hertz/Kompas begin around US$21 a day plus US$0.21 a km, or US$350 a week with unlimited km for the cheapest car, usually a Renault 4. Optional collision insurance is about US$8 a day extra, theft insurance another US$8 a day and there's 15% tax. Hertz will rent to drivers aged from 18 to 23 years, but insurance is mandatory. Budget rents to those aged 19 years and over, Avis only to those 23 and over. Ask about one-way rentals with free drop-offs at other offices in Slovenia (Bled, Ljubljana, Maribor or Portorož).

HITCHING
Hitchhiking from bus stops is fairly common in Slovenia and even practised by young women.

SLOVENIA

Ljubljana

Foggy Ljubljana (Laibach), capital of Slovenia, is a pleasant, small city. The most beautiful part is along the Ljubljanica River below the castle. Ljubljana began as the Roman town of Emona, and the Italian influence continued under the Catholic Habsburgs during the Counter-Reformation when many churches were built. From 1809 to 1814, Ljubljana was the capital of the 'Illyrian Provinces', a Napoleonic puppet state.

Despite the Austrian imperial overtones, contemporary Ljubljana has a vibrant Slavic air all its own. It's like a little Prague without the hordes of tourists but with all the facilities you'll need. Over 25,000 students attend Ljubljana University's 13 faculties and three art academies. Though you can easily see the best of the city in a day, it's is a nice place to linger – and don't worry, the fog usually clears by mid-morning.

Orientation

The bus and train stations are adjacent on the north side of town. The left-luggage office (*garderoba*) is on the platform inside the train station (open 24 hours a day). A smaller garderoba is inside the bus station (open from 5.30 am to 8.30 pm).

Information

Tourist Office The Tourist Information Centre (TIC) is at Slovenska cesta 35. It's open weekdays from 8 am to 7 pm, weekends from 8 am to noon and from 4 to 7 pm. They're well worth visiting to pick up free maps and brochures.

The Cultural Information Center, Trg francoske revolucije 7, gives out a free booklet describing all local museums and galleries.

For information on hiking in the Julian Alps and excellent trail maps and guides, visit the Slovene Alpine Association, Dvoržakova 9 (in the wooden house at the back of the yard).

Motorists in need of assistance or advice can turn to the Avto Moto Zveza (☎ 341 341) at Dunajska cesta 128, about three km north of the centre.

Money The currency exchange office inside the train station is open 24 hours a day (no commission charged). They accept travellers' cheques and give as good a rate as any. Make sure you sign your cheque while the clerk is watching, otherwise it will be refused. Upon departure they'll change excess tolarji back into Deutschmarks or dollars.

There's an automatic currency exchange machine outside the SKB Banka, Trg Ajdovščina 4, in the very centre of the modern shopping mall, which changes the banknotes of 18 countries (accessible 24 hours a day).

Post & Telecommunications Poste restante mail is held 30 days at the post office at Slovenska cesta 32 diagonally opposite the tourist office (open from 7 am to 8 pm weekdays and from 8 am to 1 pm Saturday). There's a small charge to pick up letters.

To mail a parcel you must go to the special customs post office at Trg osvobodilne fronte 5 opposite the bus station (weekdays 8 am to 2 pm). Bring your parcel open for inspection (maximum weight about 15 kg depending on destination).

International telephone calls can be made at the Pošta Center, Pražakova ulica 3 (open 24 hours a day). The telephone code for Ljubljana is 061.

Foreign Embassies The most convenient are the American Embassy (☎ 301 427), Pražakova ulica 4 (open Monday, Wednesday and Friday from 9 am to noon), and the British Embassy (☎ 125 7191), Trg republike 3 (on the 4th floor of the tall tower with the Union Jack flying outside).

North of town near the entrance to the Ljubljana fairgrounds is the Hungarian Embassy, Dunajska cesta 22, 4th floor (open Monday, Wednesday and Friday from 9 am to noon), and the Macedonian Embassy,

Dunajska cesta 104 (Monday and Friday 9 am to noon, Wednesday noon to 6 pm).

The Czech Republic Embassy, Kolarjeva 30 (weekdays 10 am to noon), is also in a northern suburb of Ljubljana. Ask the tourist office to mark it on one of their free maps.

The Croatian Embassy, Gruberjevo nabrežje 6 off Karlovška cesta (weekdays 10 am to 3 pm), is south of the castle.

For the addresses of the Bulgarian, Polish, Romanian and Slovakian embassies ask at the Tourist Information Centre as all are presently in remote locations and the addresses may change.

Travel Agencies Tourist Office Eros on the main platform at the train station sells bus tickets to Belgrade (US$35) and Skopje (US$53), departing daily at 3.30 pm.

Slovenijaturist, Slovenska cesta 58, sells BIJ international train tickets to persons aged under 26 years (40% cheaper than regular fares).

Mladi Turist, Celovška cesta 49 (weekdays 9 am to 3 pm), is the office of the Slovenian Youth Hostel Association. They sell youth hostel cards (US$10), ISIC student cards (US$3) and can make bookings at youth hostels in Ljubljana (a good idea).

The American Express representative is Atlas Ambassador (✆ 222 711), Mestni trg 8, Ljubljana 61000. They will hold clients' mail but don't cash travellers' cheques.

Bookshops Ljubljana's best bookshop is Mladinska Knjiga on Slovenska cesta near Šubičeva ulica (upstairs). They also have a branch on Miklošičeva cesta 40, opposite the bus station, and another at Nazorjeva 1.

Hiking maps are available from the Inštitut za Geografijo Univerze, Trg francoske revolucije 7 opposite the Town Museum, and at Mladinska Knjiga, Nazorjeva 1.

For the latest newspapers and magazines in English try the gift shop just inside the Grand Hotel Union, Miklošičeva cesta 1.

Emergency You can see a doctor at the Klinični Centar, Niegoševa cesta 4, near Zaloška, just east of Hotel Park. Once you reach this huge complex ask directions to 'urgenca' (emergencies), which is open 24 hours a day.

Things to See
The most picturesque sights of old Ljubljana are along the Ljubljanica River, a tributary of the Sava, which curves around the foot of imposing Castle Hill. From the TIC on Slovenska cesta, follow Čopova ulica down to Prešernov trg with its inviting **Franciscan church** (1660), a statue (1905) of poet France Prešeren and the famous 'three bridges' over the river. In 1931, architect Jože Plečnik added the side bridges to the original bridge dating from 1842.

Cross one of these bridges and continue straight ahead to the Baroque fountain (1751) in front of the **Town Hall** (1718) on Mestni trg. Italian sculptor Francesco Robba designed this fountain and numerous monumental altars in the city's churches. Enter the town hall to see the two courtyards, then visit the **Municipal Gallery**, Mestni trg 5, which has changing exhibits. To the south of this is Stari trg, atmospheric by day or night. North-east are the twin towers of **Ljubljana Cathedral** (1708), which contains impressive frescoes. Behind the cathedral is Ljubljana's colourful open-air **vegetable market** (closed Sunday) and a colonnade (1942) along the riverside designed by Plečnik.

Študentovska ulica, opposite the Vodnik statue in the market square, leads directly up to **Ljubljana Castle** (closed Monday). The castle has been undergoing reconstruction for many years, but the wing above the castle café is now open, having been rebuilt in an ultramodern glass-and-marble style for use as a wedding hall. Climb the castle tower for the view. Reber ulica beside Stari trg 17 also leads up to the castle, and you should be able to find your way back down this way.

There's a second interesting area worth exploring on the west side of the Ljubljanica River. The **Town Museum**, Gosposka ulica 15 (open Tuesday to Friday from 10 am to 1 pm and 4 to 6 pm, and Saturday and Sunday

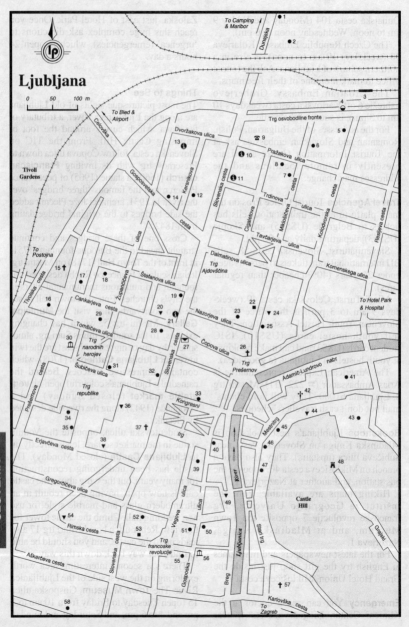

Ljubljana

0   50   100 m

To Camping
& Maribor

To Bled &
Airport

Tivoli
Gardens

To
Postojna

To Hotel Park
& Hospital

Castle
Hill

To
Zagreb

Dunajska

Trg osvobodilne fronte

Dvoržakova ulica

Gosposvetska

Kersnikova

Slovenska cesta

Pražakova ulica

Trdinova

Mikloš ičeva cesta

Kolodvorska cesta

Resljeva cesta

Cigaletova ulica

Tavčarjeva ulica

Komenskega ulica

Dalmatinova ulica

Trg
Ajdovščina

Čopova ulica

Nazorjeva ulica

Štefanova ulica

Župančičeva

Cankarjeva
cesta

Tomšičeva ulica

Trg
narodnih
herojev

Šubičeva ulica

Slovenska cesta

Trg
republike

Kongresni
trg

Erjavčeva cesta

Gregorčičeva ulica

Rimska cesta

Aškerčeva cesta

Slovenska cesta

Prešernova cesta

Tivolska cesta

Celovška

Trg
Prešernov

Adamič-Lundrovo nabr

Mestni trg

River

Stari trg

Ljubljanica

Breg

Gosposka

Trg
francoske
revolucije

Vegova ulica

Karlovška cesta

Grajski

SLOVENIA

PLACES TO STAY	7	Hertz Rent-a-Car	32	Mladinska Knjiga
	8	American Embassy	33	Babilon Disco
22 Grand Hotel Union	9	Telephone Centre	34	British
53 Pension Pri Mraku	10	Slovenijatourist		Embassy
	11	Golfturist	35	Cultural &
PLACES TO EAT	12	Klub K-4		Congress Centre
	13	Slovene Alpine	37	Ursuline Church
20 Daj-Dam		Association	39	University
24 Samopostrež	14	Adria Airways	40	Filharmonija
Restaurcija	15	Serbian Orthodox	41	Vegetable Market
36 Maximarket		Church	42	Cathedral
38 Pizzeria Parma	16	Modern Art Gallery	43	Puppet Theatre
44 Gostilna pri	17	National Gallery	45	Town Hall
Kolovratu	18	Budget Rent-a-Car	46	Municipal Gallery
49 Bistro Pri Zlati	19	'Skyscraper'	47	Atlas Ambassdor/
Ladjici	21	Tourist Information		American Express
54 Pizzeria pod Lipo		Centre	48	Castle
	23	Kino Union	50	Academy of
OTHER	25	Tourist Agency VAS		Sciences
	26	Franciscan Church	51	National Library
1 Hungarian Embassy	27	Post Office (Poste	52	Glej Theatre/
2 Ljubljana Fair		Restante)		Galerija Equrna
Grounds	28	Kino Komuna	55	Ljubljana Festival
3 Railway Station	29	Opera House		Theatre
4 Bus Station	30	National Museum	56	Town Museum
5 Kino Dvor	31	Parliament	57	St James Church
6 Kino Kompas		(Skupščina)	58	Roman City Wall

from 10 am to 1 pm), is a good place to start. The museum has a well-presented collection of Roman artefacts, plus a scale model of Emona (Ljubljana) to help it all make sense Upstairs are period rooms. At Gosposka ulica 14 near the Town Museum is the **National & University Library** (1941) designed by Plečnik, and north on Gosposka ulica at Kongresni trg is the **university** building (1902), formerly the regional parliament. The **Ursuline Church** (1726) with an altar by Robba is nearby.

If you still have time, go west on Šubičeva ulica to the recently renovated **National Museum**, Trg herojev 1 (closed Monday, entry US$1.25), which includes prehistory, natural history and ethnography collections. The highlight is an ancient Celtic situla (pot) from the 6th century BC sporting an evocative relief. Unfortunately, the captions aren't in English but the museum building, erected in 1885, is impressive. The museum shop sells cassettes of Slovenian folk music.

The **National Gallery**, Cankarjeva 20 (closed Monday, free Saturday after 2 pm), offers 19th century portraits and landscapes, as well as copies of medieval frescoes. You enter the upstairs rooms through a closed, unmarked door. Diagonally opposite is the **Modern Art Gallery**, at Cankarjeva 15 (closed Monday), where the International Biennale of Graphic Art is held every other summer (1995, 1997 etc). The Serbian Orthodox **Church of Sts Cyril & Methodius** between the two art galleries is well worth entering to see the beautiful modern frescoes (open Tuesday to Saturday from 3 to 6 pm). Through the underpass from the Modern Art Gallery are the relaxing **Tivoli Gardens**.

Places to Stay

Luckily, reasonably priced accommodation is easy to find in Ljubljana. You should plan on spending at least two nights in this enjoyable city.

SLOVENIA

Camping *Camping Ježica* (☎ 371 382) is by the Sava River at the north end of Dunajska cesta (bus No 8 to the terminus), six km from the city centre. There's a large, shady camping area (US$5 per person, US$5 per tent) and 38 deluxe three-bed bungalows at US$40/60 double/triple. It's clean and quiet with hot water, a restaurant, currency exchange and some tourist information. This recommended site is open from May to September.

Private Rooms The TIC (☎ 224 222 or 215 412), Slovenska cesta 35 (hours listed in the Information section), has private rooms for about US$10/18 single/double, but they aren't usually in the city centre and if you're staying too far outside town you won't be able to attend any of the wonderful theatrical presentations and concerts. There's no surcharge for one-night stays but only there are only 10 rooms available and they're often full.

Hostels The *Diješki Dom Bežigrad* (☎ 342 864 or 342 867), Kardeljeva ploščad 28, a three-storey student dormitory just off Dunajska cesta, north of the city (bus No 6 or 8 to Centralni Stadion), has rooms at US$13/18/21 single/double/triple. In July and August, 150 beds are available, but for the rest of the year there are only 15 available. To get in you must arrive on a weekday between 7 am and noon and talk to the 'director'. The hostel itself is open on weekends but you won't be admitted then. Otherwise have Mladi Turist book a bed for you.

In July and August the *Dijaški Dom Tabor* (☎ 321 067), Vidovdanska cesta 7, opposite Hotel Park, functions as a 59-bed youth hostel with beds at US$8 per person. Other months it's a student dormitory. The location is excellent if you can get in.

Hotels The *Super Li Bellevue Hotel* (☎ 133 4057), Pod gozdom 12, is in an old yellow building with character and a terrace overlooking the city north of Tivoli Gardens. The 15 rooms with shared bath are US$20/38/51

single/double/triple including breakfast. If you stay at the Super Li Bellevue on a Friday or Saturday night, get a room on the top floor to be further away from the disco in the basement.

The 13-storey, C-category *Hotel Park* (☎ 133 1306), Tabor 9 in a quiet residential area just east of the centre, offers 122 simple, functional rooms at US$21/33 single/double without bath, US$27/41 with bath, breakfast included.

The 30-room *Pension Pri Mraku* (☎ 223 412), Rimska cesta 4 to the south of the centre, has singles/doubles/triples with bath from US$35/48/55, or US$24/34/40 for the seven rooms without bath; breakfast included. It has more atmosphere than the Park for only a few dollars more.

The three-star *Grand Hotel Union* (☎ 125 4133), Miklošičeva cesta 1, manages to preserve some of the elegance of its inaugural year, 1905. At US$51/72 single/double and up with bath and breakfast, rooms at the Grand Union are half the price of those in the adjacent Holiday Inn.

Places to Eat

The *Samopostrežna Restauracija*, Miklošičeva cesta 10 at the back of the passage opposite the Holiday Inn, is a pleasant, modern, self-service restaurant open daily until 9 pm all year.

There's another self-service restaurant labelled 'Maximarket' downstairs in the shopping arcade on Trg republike (open weekdays from 9 am to 6 pm, Saturday 9 am to 3 pm). At the south end of the corridor from it is *Pizzeria Parma*, downstairs in the mall off Erjavčeva cesta. The pizza here is fairly cheap so you may have to stand around waiting for a seat (come at odd hours). It's open from 8 am to 9 pm weekdays, to 5 pm Saturday, closed Sunday.

Bistro Pri Zlati Ladjici, at Jurčičev trg 1, near the river (closed Sunday), is a much better place for low-price pizza and beer.

Daj-Dam, at Cankarjeva cesta 4, around the corner from the tourist office, (closed Sunday) is pleasant and inexpensive. You can either pay the cashier near the door for the set menu *(kosilo)* then pick up your meal at the counter and eat standing up or, if you have more time, walk into the rear dining room where there's regular table service.

In the old town, the *Gostilna pri Kolovratu*, Ciril Metodov trg 14, next to the cathedral, serves Slovene national dishes.

Union pivo has been brewed in Ljubljana since 1864.

Cafés For coffee and cakes it's *Slaščičarna Slon*, Slovenska cesta 34 (closed Monday), directly across the street from the tourist office.

Entertainment

Ljubljana enjoys a rich cultural life, so ask the TIC for its monthly programme of events. 'Summer in Old Ljubljana' from mid-July to August features three or four free events a week in the old town.

The ticket office of the neo-Rococo *Opera House* (1892), Župančičeva ulica 1, is open weekdays from 11 am to 1 pm and from 5 to 7 pm, Saturday from 11 am to 1 pm, and an hour before the performance. The best seats cost US$16.

Ljubljana's ultramodern *Cultural & Congress Centre 'Cankarjev dom'* includes four theatres. The symphony orchestra often appears in the Big Hall. For tickets and information look for the office downstairs in the adjacent shopping mall (weekdays from 1 to 8 pm, Saturday 9 am to 1 pm, and an hour before performances). Also check for concerts at the *Filharmonija* (1891) at Kongresni trg 10.

From July to September things happen in the *Ljubljana Festival Open-Air Theatre* on Trg francoske revolucije opposite the Town Museum. The poorly marked festival ticket office is right next to the memorial pillar in the centre of the square (open weekdays from 11 am to 1 pm, 6 to 7 pm and one hour before performances).

The *Puppet Theatre* is at Krekov trg 2 near the vegetable market.

Avant-Garde Ljubljana's experimental theatre is *Theatre Glej*, Gregorčičeva ulica 3,

with three resident companies: Grapefruit, Betontanc and Tomaž Štrucl. They're often on tour and the theatre is closed in July and August; other months your best chance to see a performance is on Thursday or Friday at 9 pm. The adjacent *Galeria Equrna* often exhibits works by IRWIN (see the introductory Arts sections of this chapter) and other NSK artists, so this really is the place to come if you want to get in touch with Ljubljana's vibrant underground art scene. The *Škuc Gallery*, Stari trg 21, also exhibits NSK art.

Discos The most popular disco is *Babilon*, Kongresni trg 2 (open Tuesday to Saturday from 10 pm to 4 am).

Ljubljana's student disco is *Klub K-4*, Kersnikova 4. There's a different programme every night and the cover charge varies according to what's on, but it's always half-price for students. The doors open at 10 pm nightly (Sunday night is usually a gay/lesbian scene).

Cinemas Among the most central cinemas are Kino Komuna, Cankarjeva cesta 1, and Kino Union, Nazorjeva 2. Near the train station are Kino Dvor, Kolodvarska 29, and Kino Kompas, Miklošićeva 38. The Kinoteka, Miklošićeva 28, screens classic films at 6 and 8 pm. Film admissions are about US$3.50 and most films are shown in the original language with Slovene subtitles.

Spectator Sports On Sunday at 3 pm there's often a soccer game in the Centralni Stadion, a 20-minute walk north from the centre up Dunajska cesta. (The stadium itself was erected by Jože Plečnik in 1937.)

Things to Buy

Nazorjeva ulica, the street which begins opposite the tourist office, is a good shopping street. DZS at Šubičeva ulica 2 and Trg francoske revolucije 6 has a good selection of Slovenian compact discs. The largest department store in town (with a supermarket in the basement) is Maximarket on Trg republike.

Getting There & Away

Bus There's a bus to Trieste, Italy, each morning (103 km, US$7). For Lenti, Hungary, a bus leaves Ljubljana on Tuesday and Thursday at 5.30 am (235 km, five hours, US$12). For Germany you can take an evening bus to Munich on Monday, Tuesday, Thursday, Friday and Sunday (US$32); to Stuttgart on Wednesday, Thursday and Sunday (US$62); to Frankfurt on Wednesday and Sunday (US$74) and to Berlin on Wednesday and Saturday (US$91). Obtain details at the bus station. Be ready for a quick change of buses at the Austrian or German border.

Direct buses to Belgrade via Hungary (26 hours, US$29) leave from stand No 30 at the bus station every afternoon around 5.45 pm.

If you're headed from Ljubljana to Bled or Bohinj in the Julian Alps, be sure to take a bus, as Lesce-Bled Railway Station is far from the action. Choose the bus to Postojna for the same reason. Buses to Bled leave every hour on the hour from 6 am to 7 pm daily. Other buses from Ljubljana include 26 to Postojna (41 km), 14 to Koper (104 km), 13 to Nova Gorica (116 km), nine to Piran (125 km), eight to Zagreb (138 km), six to Lendava (204 km, four hours), three to Varaždin (179 km), two to Rijeka (128 km) and Pula (211 km) and one each to Poreč (175 km) and Rovinj (189 km). One overnight bus runs daily to Split (532 km).

Train The *Eurocity Mimara* and *Intercity 296/297* express trains run between Munich and Ljubljana daily. There are five through trains to Trieste, Italy (165 km, US$10). A train ticket from Ljubljana to Zagreb costs US$8 (some services with a change of trains at Zidani Most).

From Ljubljana to Koper (175 km, US$5) you have a choice of train and bus. To Rijeka (155 km), Zagreb (160 km) and Maribor (178 km) you're better off by train. For more information on trains leaving Ljubljana turn

to the introductory Getting There & Away section of this chapter.

Getting Around

To/From the Airport The bus to Brnik Airport (Letališče), 26 km north of Ljubljana, leaves from platform No 28 at the bus station (US$1.50) every hour from 5 am to 8 pm weekdays and every two hours from 6 am to 7 pm on weekends. Buy your ticket from the driver.

Bus From 1898 to 1958, public transport around Ljubljana was provided by trams. Then the trams were swapped for electric trolley buses, and in 1971 these were replaced by the diesel buses that carry commuters around the city today. You can drop the exact change in the fare box next to the driver or buy bus tokens *(žeton)* in advance at a newsstand. The two red kiosks marked LPP on the pavement at Slovenska cesta 55 sell a transit day pass *(enodnevna vozovica)* for US$1.25.

Car Rental The international car-rental chains are Budget (☎ 126 3118), Štefanova ulica 13; Hertz (☎ 311 241), Miklošičeva ulica 11; and Avis (☎ 168 7204), Dunajska 160. All three also have counters at Brnik Airport. Ask the Tourist Information Centre about cheaper local operators, such as Golfturist Rent a Car (☎ 315 353), Trdinova ulica 3.

Around Ljubljana

POSTOJNA

The much-touted **Postojna Caves** between Ljubljana and Rijeka are a bit of a rip-off. For US$15 a head, hordes of tourists are taken on a miniature train ride between the colourfully lit karst formations. Of the 27 km of caves, only five km are visited – one km on foot, the rest on the miniature electric train. Near the exit, tourists gawk at blind salamanders in a pool.

Orientation & Information

The caves are within walking distance of Postojna bus or train stations (both of which have left-luggage offices). The train station is on the east side of town, one km from the centre. The bus station is right in the centre and the caves are another km west of it. Visits are daily at 9.30 am and 1.30 pm all year, with more frequent tours from April to October and on Sunday. Dress warmly as the cave is a constant 8°C all year.

The tour takes 1¼ hours and you'll hear a commentary in your own language. Don't worry if you see countless masses waiting impatiently to enter. Most people will go around with their German or Slovene-speaking guides – the English groups are much smaller. There's no use joining in the pushing to be the first one in, as everyone is divided up inside anyway.

Getting There & Away

Postojna can be a day trip from Ljubljana or a stopover on the way to/from Istria. There are direct trains to Postojna from Ljubljana (76 km), Rijeka, Croatia, (79 km) and Koper (99 km). The bus station in Postojna is much more conveniently located and all buses between Ljubljana and the coast call there.

ŠKOCJAN CAVES

The Škocjan Caves, 10 km from Divača between Postojna and Koper, have been heavily promoted since 1986 when they were entered on UNESCO's World Heritage list. There's a visit at 10 am daily all year and more frequent visits in summer (US$15 per person). These caves are in more natural surroundings than those at Postojna but it's really only feasible to visit them if you have your own transport. It's over an hour's walk along a busy highway from Divača Railway Station just to the access road to the caves.

Julian Alps

Slovenia shares with Italy the Julian Alps in the north-west corner of the country. Three-headed Mt Triglav (2864 metres), the country's highest peak, is scaled regularly by hundreds of summer weekend mountaineers, but there are countless less ambitious hikes. Lakes Bled and Bohinj make ideal starting points – Bled with its chic resort facilities, Bohinj right beneath the rocky crags themselves. The tall wooden racks called *kozolci* on which local farmers dry their hay are found nowhere else in Europe. Most of this spectacular area falls under **Triglav National Park** (founded in 1924). The park administration has valiantly resisted pressure to allow tour buses into the valleys and to upgrade the roads. A few of the many existing routes are mentioned in the following sections.

BLED

Bled, a fashionable resort at 501 metres altitude, is set on an idyllic, two-km-long emerald lake which you can walk around in under two hours. Trout and carp proliferate in the crystal-clear lake water, which is surprisingly warm and a pleasure to swim in. The climate is also good: there's no fog at Bled during the summer. To the north-east, the Karavanke Range forms a natural boundary with Austria. Bled has been a favourite destination for decades, but somehow you couldn't call it spoiled.

Orientation

The village is at the east end of the lake below Castle Hill. The bus station is also here, but Lesce-Bled Railway Station is about five km east. In addition there's Bled-Jezero, a branch-line train station west of the lake, where the camping ground is also found. There's no left-luggage office at Bled Bus Station but the ticket seller may agree to hold your bag in an emergency.

Information

The tourist office is the very helpful Turistično Društvo souvenir shop below the Park Hotel Bled, Cesta svobode 15. Ask for the useful booklet *Bled Tourist News*. Kompas at the Trgovski Shopping Mall, Ljubljanska cesta 4, sells good hiking maps.

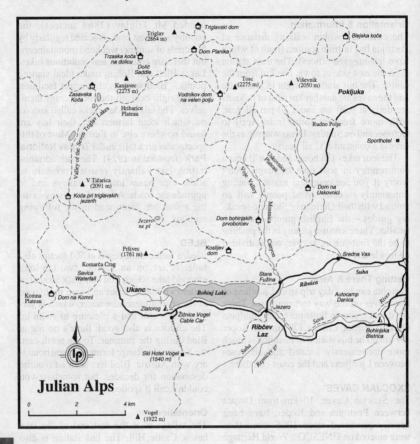

Julian Alps

0   2   4 km

SLOVENIA

Motorists can turn to the Avto-Moto Društvo Bled, Grajska cesta 24, in case of problems. The Triglav National Park office is midway along the lake's north shore.

Money The Ljubljanska Banka, Cesta svobode 15 below Hotel Park, changes travellers' cheques weekdays from 8 am to 6 pm, Saturday 8 am to noon.

Post & Telecommunications The telephone centre in the post office at Ljubljanska cesta 10 is open weekdays from 7 am to 7 pm, Saturday from 7 am to noon. Bled's telephone code is 064.

Things to See & Do
The neo-Gothic **parish church** (1904) with frescoes painted in 1937 is just above the bus station. Follow the road north-west to the youth hostel where there's a trail up to the castle *(grad)*. **Bled Castle** (open daily, US$3 admission) was the seat of the bishops of Brixen (South Tyrol) for over 800 years. Set on top of a steep cliff 100 metres above the lake, it offers magnificent views in clear weather. The castle museum presents the

history of the area and allows a peep into the 16th century chapel. By the altar is a fresco of the Holy Roman emperor Henry II presenting the church to Christ in 1004. You get free admission to the castle if you eat at the restaurant (a US$5 deposit against your meal must be paid at the gate).

The other feature of Bled which immediately strikes the eye is a tiny **island** at the west end of the lake. From the massive red-and-white belfry rising above the dense vegetation, the tolling 'bell of wishes' echoes across the lake. It's said that all who ring this bell will be successful in love. Underneath the present Baroque church are the foundations of a pre-Romanesque chapel, unique in Slovenia. Most people reach the island on one of the large hand-propelled gondolas called *pletna* (or *pletne* if it's plural), which let you off for a half-hour visit (US$7 return per person, admission to church and belfry included). If there are two or three of you it would be cheaper to hire a rowing boat from the bathing establishment below the castle (US$10 an hour for three people, US$14 for five people). Rowing boats are also available on the shore in front of Grand Hotel Toplice (US$8 an hour for three people) – compare prices, as they fluctuate a lot.

Kompas in the Trgovski Shopping Mall rents mountain bikes at US$7 a day, US$4 a half day or US$1.50 an hour. Scooters are US$23 a day or US$16 a half day (petrol extra). No special licence is required to rent or drive a scooter.

Hiking An excellent half-day hike from Bled features a visit to the **Vintgar Gorge** (Soteska Vintgar). Begin by taking the Krnica bus from Bled to Zgornja-Gorje. From beside the 'Gostilna' stop opposite the church follow the signposted road through lovely alpine countryside to Vintgar (two km), where you pay US$1.50 to enter the gorge. The clear, trout-filled Radovna River roars below the wooden walkways and high cliffs. At the far end of the gorge a trail climbs over the hill to St Catherine's Chapel, from which you can walk down the road through Zasip straight back to Bled. From June to September a tourist bus runs direct from Bled Bus Station to Vintgar every morning (US$1.50 one way).

Places to Stay

Camping *Camping Zaka* (☎ 77 325; open from May to September) is in a quiet valley at the west end of Bled Lake about two km from Bled Bus Station. The location is good and there's even a beach, supermarket and restaurant, but at US$8 per person it's not cheap.

Hostels The family-operated *'Bledec' Youth Hostel* (☎ 78 230), Grajska cesta 17 (closed from mid-October until the end of November), is conveniently situated in pleasant surroundings just up the hill from the bus station. The overnight charge at this pleasant 28-bed hostel with two, three, four and six-bed rooms is US$11 per person. Couples are given double rooms (when available) at no extra charge and in the off season you'll probably have the room to yourself unless you happen to coincide with a school group. Although everyone pays the same (youth hostel card not required) YHA members don't have to pay the US$1.25 per person per day tourist tax. There's no supplement for a one-night stay. The rooms are heated in winter and there are plentiful free showers. Breakfast (optional) is US$3 extra and it's US$5 to use the washing machine (three kilos). The hostel is open all day and there's no curfew. At a pinch it's possible to arrive late in the evening as the friendly managers live on the premises.

Private Rooms Finding a private room at Bled is fairly easy. Not only are all the travel agencies eager to help you but lots of houses around the village have sobe or zimmer signs.

Kompas Tourist Agency (☎ 77 245) in the Trgovski Shopping Mall rents private singles/doubles for US$17/25 (2nd category) or US$20/31 (1st category), less 30% if you stay three or more nights. Private rooms from Globtour (☎ 77 909) at Hotel Krim, Ljubljanska cesta 7, are about a dollar

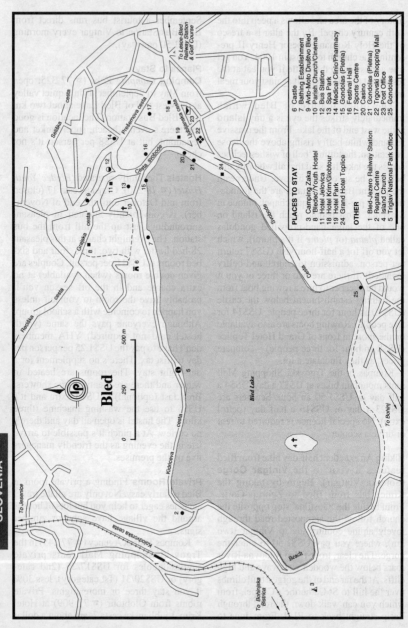

Bled

PLACES TO STAY

3 Camping Zaka
8 'Bledec'/Youth Hostel
11 Hotel Jelovica
18 Hotel Krim/Globtour
19 Hotel Park
24 Grand Hotel Toplice

OTHER

1 Bled-Jezero Railway Station
2 Regata Centre
4 Island Church
5 Triglav National Park Office
6 Castle
7 Bathing Establishment
9 Avto-Moto Društvo Bled
10 Parish Church/Cinema
12 Bus Station
13 Spa Park
14 Medical Clinic/Pharmacy
15 Gondolas (Pletna)
16 Festival Hall
17 Sports Centre
20 Casino
21 Gondolas (Pletna)
22 Trgovski Shopping Mall
23 Post Office
25 Gondolas

To Lesce-Bled
Railway Station
& Golf Course

Prešernova cesta

Seliška cesta

Ljubljanska cesta

Cesta svobode

Grajska cesta

Cesta svobode

Rečiška cesta

Kidričeva cesta

Kolodvorska cesta

Bled Lake

To Jesenice

To Bohinj

To Bohinjska
Bistrica

Beach

500 m

250

0

more expensive. Complete apartments accommodating up to six people are also available. Private room rates are slightly lower at Bled during the off seasons from mid-March to June and during September. Forget Bled's hotels which start at US$56 a single.

Places to Eat

The *Gostilna Pri Planincu*, Grajska cesta just up from the bus station, offers grilled meats and pizza. It's also a nice place just for a glass of beer. The *Slaščičarna Šmon Franci*, a little farther up the same way, has burek.

The *Hambi Fast Food Hut* (open from 7 am to 8 pm daily all year) behind the buses parked in front of the bus station serves cheap hamburgers and burek, and there are four picnic tables.

There's a vegetable market near the bus station and a supermarket in the Trgovski Shopping Mall. *Taverna Bella Bled* in the Trgovski Shopping Mall is a slightly up-market spaghetti house.

Entertainment

All summer there are concerts and fireworks by the lake on Saturday evenings. During mid-August folklore performances accompany the 'peasant wedding'.

Maxim Cezare Night Club (Monday to Saturday 10 pm to 4 am) is directly behind the Festival Hall. *Dancing Kazina* in the Casino opposite Hotel Park puts on a sexy floorshow nightly (open 9 pm to 2 am).

The Bled Cinema beside the parish church is your best budget choice.

There's a beautiful 23°C **thermal pool** downstairs at the Grand Hotel Toplice, Cesta svobode 20, which you can use all day for US$4. Information is available from the hotel desk (☎ 77 222).

The Bled Golf & Country Club (☎ 78 282) is just east of the Sava River, a 20-minute walk from Bled. Built in 1938, renovated in 1972 and expanded in 1993, this is Slovenia's original 18-hole, par-73 golf course. Green fees are US$35 daily, club rentals US$10, hand cart US$4, driving

range with 36 balls US$9 (open mid-April to mid-October).

Getting There & Away

The easiest way to get to Bled is by bus (hourly service from Ljubljana, 54 km, 1½ hours, US$4). Bus service between Bled and Bohinj (28 km, US$2) is also good and two morning buses leave for Zagreb (203 km). There are six buses a day to Jesenice.

Express trains between Munich and Zagreb stop at Lesce-Bled station. Local trains from Ljubljana to Jesenice also pass this way. There are frequent buses from this train station to Bled.

Bled-Jezero Station is on a secondary line between Jesenice and Nova Gorica, border stations for Austria and Italy. Five local trains a day in each direction follow this scenic route.

Car Rental Globtour (☎ 77 909) at Hotel Krim represents Budget Rent a Car. The Avis agent is Generalturist (☎ 77 795) opposite Hotel Park. Kompas (☎ 77 245) in the Trgovski Shopping Mall represents Hertz.

BOHINJ

Bohinj, 28 km south-west of Bled, is a more nature-oriented place to stay than Bled. Bohinj Lake (475 metres elevation) is exceedingly beautiful, with high mountains rising directly from the basin-shaped valley. There are secluded beaches for nude swimming off the trail along the north shore. There are many hiking possibilities at Bohinj, including an ascent of Mt Triglav. Bohinj often has a morning fog which clears before noon.

Orientation & Information

The area's main tourist centre is Jezero at the east end of the lake. All in a row just up from the bus stop at Jezero are the post office/telephone centre, Turist biro, Mercator Supermarket, Tourist Agency Alpinium, a good pizzeria and Club Amor Discoteka, most of them open all year. One km north across the Sava River sits the old town, Stara Fužina, at the mouth of the Mostnica

Canyon. Hotel Zlatorog is at Ukanc at the west end of the lake near the camping ground and the Vogel cable car.

Post & Telecommunications The telephone centre in the post office at Jezero is open weekdays from 8 am to 6 pm, Saturday from 8 am to noon. The telephone code for Bohinj is 064.

Things to See & Do

A footpath leads over the 'Devil's Bridge' and up the **Mostnica Canyon** into the Voje Valley just north of Stara Fužina. The *Dom bohinjskih prvoborcev* (also known as Planinski dom Uskovnica), an hour's hike up this deep gorge from Stara Fužina, is a beginning point for climbing Mt Triglav. It costs US$10 per person to stay at the Dom (open from late May until October).

The 'Žičnice Vogel' cable car, above the camping ground at the west end of Bohinj Lake, can carry you 1000 metres up into the mountains. It operates daily every 30 minutes (US$6 return, closed in November). From the Ski Hotel Vogel (1540 metres) on top you can scale **Mt Vogel** (1922 metres) in a couple of hours for a sweeping view of everything. Be careful in fog.

In winter, skiers can use the lifts for US$20 daily and rent skis and boots at the Ski.Hotel Vogel for US$10 daily, but there are no heavy coats for hire.

The Hotel Zlatorog reception rents mountain bikes at US$2.50 an hour or US$12 a day.

Places to Stay

Camping The *Zlatorog Camping Ground* (☎ 723 482; open from mid-May to mid-September) is at the west end of the lake – one of the best situated camping grounds in Europe. At US$9 per person it's expensive, but the location right on a lake beach is lovely and it's a good base for hiking.

Private Rooms & Pensions The Turist Biro (☎ 723 370) at Jezero has private rooms for US$11 per person for one or two nights, US$9 per person for three or more nights.

Ask if there's anything cheaper if the first room they offer seems too expensive. Many houses here and in Stara Fužina village bear *sobe* signs.

Pension Park (☎ 723 300) is a seven-room pension right beside the Sava River just across the bridge from Hotel Zlatorog. Formerly owned by the Croatian Communist Party, the Park now accommodates regular tourists at US$20 per person including a good breakfast. They're open all year.

About 150 metres beyond Pension Park is *Pension Stare* (☎ 723 403). The nine rooms with bath in this attractive mountain hotel are US$26/40 single/double with breakfast (plus 20% if you only stay one or two nights). Several houses advertising private rooms are also in this lovely area.

From mid-December to April skiers can stay at the *Ski Hotel Vogel* (☎ 721 471) for US$32 per person including breakfast and dinner.

Places to Eat

The pizzeria behind the Turist biro at Jezero is not overpriced and has cold beer on tap.

If staying in the vicinity of the Zlatorog Hotel, try the nearby *Restaurant Erlah Anica 'Ukanc'*.

Getting There & Away

Buses are fairly frequent between Bohinj and Ljubljana (83 km, two hours, US$6). These buses stop at Jezero then run right along the south shore of Bohinj Lake, terminating at the Hotel Zlatorog at the west end of the lake. The closest train station is Bohinjska Bistrica on the Jesenice-Nova Gorica line, six km east of Jezero.

TREKKING MT TRIGLAV

The Julian Alps are one of the finest hiking areas in Eastern Europe. A mountain trip here is also an excellent way to meet young Slovenes, so take advantage of this opportunity if you're in the country during the hiking season. Mountain huts *(planinska koča)* are scattered throughout the range, normally less than five hours' walk apart. The huts in the higher regions are open from July to September, and in the lower regions from June to October. No reservations are possible at the huts but the ones around Mt Triglav become crowded on Friday and Saturday nights. A bed for the night shouldn't be over US$10 per person (members of alpine clubs get a 10% discount). Meals are also sold, so you don't need to carry a lot of gear. Leave most of your things below. Warm clothes, sturdy boots and good physical condition are indispensable.

The best months for hiking are August and September, though above 1500 metres you can encounter true winter weather conditions any time. Keep to the trails that are well marked with red-and-white circles. Before you come, pick up the 1:25,000 *Triglav* map, the 1:50,000 *Triglavski Narodni Park* map or something similar at a bookshop. These maps are available in Jezero at the Turist Biro and at Alpinum Tourist Agency (compare prices before buying).

The circular three-day route described here is not the shortest or the easiest way to climb Slovenia's highest mountain, but it is one of the most rewarding. Try to get hold of the brochure *An Alpine Guide*, which provides more detail than can be included here.

The Route

An hour's hike west of the Zlatorog Hotel at Bohinj is the **Savica Waterfall**, source of the Sava River, which gushes from a limestone cave and falls 60 metres into a narrow gorge. From here, a path zigzags up the Komarča Crag. From the top of this cliff (1340 metres) there's an excellent view of the lake. Farther north, three hours from the falls, is the *Koča pri triglavskih jezerih* hut (1683 metres, 120 beds) at the south end of the fantastic **Valley of the Seven Triglav Lakes**. Spend the night here. If you're still keen and it's not too late, you can climb nearby **Mt Tičarica** (2091 metres, one hour from the hut) for a sweeping valley view. An alternative route from Bohinj to the Seven Lakes is via the Komna Plateau to the south, a major WW I battlefield (Hemingway described it in *A Farewell to Arms*). *Dom na Komni* there stays open all year.

The next morning you hike up the valley past the largest glacial lakes, then north-east to the desert-like Hribarice Plateau (2358 metres). You descend to the Dolič Saddle (2164 metres) where the *Tržaška koča na doliču* hut (2120 metres, 60 beds, four hours from Koča pri triglavskih jezerih) offers a night's rest. You could well carry on to *Dom Planika* (2408 metres, 80 beds), 1½ hours beyond, though on weekends Dom Planika is packed. From this hut it's just over another hour to the summit of Triglav (2864 metres), a well-beaten path. If you decide to do the trip in reverse, Dom Planika is a seven-hour climb from Stara Fužina or about six hours from the Sporthotel, Pokljuka. Getting back down from Triglav's summit can be slightly hairy if you meet a large group going up as not everyone can hold onto the pegs and cables at the same time.

The way down passes the *Vodnikov dom na Velem polju* hut (1805 metres, 50 beds), less than two hours from Dom Planika. There are two routes between Vodnikov dom and Stara Fužina: down the Voje Valley or over the Uskovnica Plateau. Uskovnica is a little longer but allows better views. The way to Rudno Polje and the Sporthotel, Pokljuka, branches off the Uskovnica route. Stara Fužina (546 metres, four hours down from Vodnikov) is back near Bohinj Lake.

BOHINJSKA BISTRICA

This village is a good place to stay if you're catching an early train towards Austria or Istria. It can also be used as a base for visiting Bled and Bohinj as the bus service is good. Since it's between the main tourist centres, Bohinjska Bistrica is less affected by tourism, thus is cheaper and friendlier. It's a good choice for escaping the tourists yet still being close to everything.

Information

Money The Ljubljanska Banka in the village centre is open weekdays from 8 am to 6 pm, Saturday from 8 am to noon.

Post & Telecommunications The post

office at the bus stop is open weekdays from 8 am to 6 pm, Saturday from 8 am to noon.

Places to Stay & Eat

Autocamp Danica, a few minutes' walk from the bus stop in Bohinjska Bistrica, is US$7 per person to camp.

Slovenijaturist (☎ 721 032), Triglavska 37, opposite the bus stop in Bohinjska Bistrica, has private rooms at US$11/20 single/double. It also sells hiking maps.

The *Almira Buffet* (closed Sunday) beside Špecerija Supermarket is cheap, but there are only two or three things listed on a board by the bar to choose from.

Getting There & Away

All the buses between Bled and Bohinj stop here, as do the Bohinj buses to/from Ljubljana (two hours, US$5).

Five trains daily run between Jesenice and Nova Gorica with a stop in Bohinjska Bistrica. This mountain railway, one of the most picturesque in Slovenia, was built by the Habsburgs between 1900 and 1906 to provide a direct rail route from Austria to Trieste. To/from Austria you connect at Jesenice (32 km) for Villach. To/from Italy you connect at Nova Gorica (76 km) for Gorizia. Going from Bohinjska Bistrica to Nova Gorica, sit on the right-hand side of the train to see the valley of the emerald-green Soča River at its best.

NOVA GORICA

This medium-sized border town has grown up since 1918 when the region was partitioned, with Italy getting the old town of Gorizia and Yugoslavia its hinterland to the east. Modern Nova Gorica contains little of interest to visitors but it is a convenient stop between the Julian Alps and Istria or entry/exit point to/from Italy.

Orientation & Information

Nova Gorica Railway Station is right on the Italian border and there's a secondary border crossing just near the station, but foreigners on foot must use the Rožna dolina/Casa Rossa crossing about 1.5 km away. As you leave the train station you look across the fence into Italy and the footpath to Casa Rossa follows the border south. The travel agency in the train station changes money and provides information.

The bus station is a 15-minute walk from the train station (turn left as you leave the train station and left again at the secondary border crossing.

Getting There & Away

There are frequent bus connections from Nova Gorica to Postojna (62 km) and Ljubljana (116 km) but far fewer to Koper (95 km). For Istria change buses at Postojna. From Nova Gorica Bus Station you can catch a city bus to Gorizia, Italy.

Five local trains a day run from Nova Gorica to Bohinjska Bistrica (76 km), Bled-Jezero (96 km) and Jesenice (108 km). Two trains a day link Nova Gorica to Gorizia Centrale, Italy. To go from Nova Gorica to Ljubljana (170 km) you must change trains at Sežana or Divača, so take a bus instead.

The Coast

KOPER

Koper, only 21 km south of Trieste, is the first of three quaint old Italian towns along the north side of the Istrian Peninsula. The town's Italian name, Capodistria, recalls its former status as capital of Istria. After 1945, Koper's port was developed to provide Slovenia with an alternative to Italian Trieste and Croatian Rijeka, the existing major ports in this area.

Once an island but now firmly connected to the mainland, the old town's medieval flavour lingers despite the surrounding industry, container ports, high-rise buildings, superhighways and developments. This administrative centre and largest town on the Slovene Riviera makes a good base for exploring the coast and the frequent bus service to/from nearby Trieste makes it an easy entry/exit point to and from Italy.

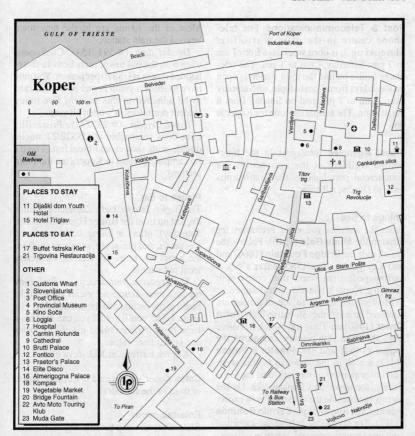

Koper

GULF OF TRIESTE

Beach

Belveder

Old Harbour

PLACES TO STAY
11 Dijaški dom Youth Hotel
15 Hotel Triglav

PLACES TO EAT
17 Buffet 'Istrska Klet'
21 Trgovina Restauracija

OTHER
1 Customs Wharf
2 Slovenijaturist
3 Post Office
4 Provincial Museum
5 Kino Soča
6 Loggia
7 Hospital
8 Carmin Rotunda
9 Cathedral
10 Brutti Palace
12 Fontico
13 Praetor's Palace
14 Elite Disco
16 Almerigogna Palace
18 Kompas
19 Vegetable Market
20 Bridge Fountain
22 Avto Moto Touring Klub
23 Muda Gate

Port of Koper
Industrial Area

Titov trg

Trg Revolucije

Argame Reforme

Gimnaz trg

Dimnikarska   Sabinjeva

To Railway & Bus Station

To Piran

Vojkovo   Nabrežje

Orientation

The bus and train stations are adjacent about two km south of the old town. There's a left-luggage office in the train station (open daily from 5.30 am to 10 pm, US$0.65).

Information

Slovenijaturist is at Ukmarjev trg 7 opposite the small boat harbour.

The Avto Moto Touring Klub (☎ 22 084) is on Prešernov trg just inside the Muda Gate.

Money The Slovenijaturist counter inside the train station (daily 6 am to 7.30 pm)

changes traveller's cheques for a 2% commission.

The Splošna Banka Koper, Kidričeva ulica 21 right next to the Provincial Museum, changes travellers' cheques without commission weekdays from 8 am to noon and from 4 to 6 pm, and Saturday from 8 am to noon. Compare the rate at the private exchange office at Kidričeva 41 as it's higher than the bank for cash.

Maki Turizem, Pristaniška ulica 13 (open weekdays from 7.30 am to 7.30 pm, and Saturday from 7.30 am to 1 pm), also offers a good rate for cash.

Post & Telecommunications The telephone centre in the main post office, Muzejski trg 3, is open weekdays from 7 am to 7 pm, Saturday 7 am to 1 pm. The telephone centre behind the train station is open on weekdays from 7 am to 8 pm, on Saturday from 7 am to 7 pm, and on Sunday from 8 am to noon. The telephone code for Koper is 066.

Travel Agencies Interagent in the Intereuropa Building at the entrance to the commercial port handles the Transeuropa ferry to Durrës, Albania.

Things to See

From the stations you enter Prešernov trg through the **Muda Gate** (1516). Follow the crowd past the **Bridge Fountain** (1666) and into Čevljarska ulica (Shoemaker's St), a narrow pedestrian street that opens onto Titov trg, Koper's historic central square.

Most of the things to see in Koper are clustered around the 36-metre-high **Town Tower** (1480) on Titov trg, which is visible from afar. The 15th century **cathedral**, the **loggia** (1464) and the **Praetor's Palace** (1452) are all in the Venetian Gothic style. The lower portion of the cathedral façade is Gothic, the upper part Renaissance. On the narrow lane beside the cathedral is an earlier building, the Romanesque **Carmin Rotunda** (1317). Trg revolucije behind the cathedral contains several more old Venetian palaces.

The **Provincial Museum** (open Tuesday to Sunday from 9 am to noon) is in the Belgramoni-Tacco Palace on Kidričeva ulica between Titov trg and the old boat harbour. The museum features old maps and photos of the area, Italianate sculpture and copies of medieval frescoes.

Places to Stay

Slovenijaturist (☎ 21 358), Ukmarjev trg 7 opposite the small boat harbour, has private rooms. More private rooms are available from Kompas (☎ 21 581), Pristaniška ulica 17 opposite the vegetable market. Both levy a 30% surcharge if you stay only one night.

Most of the rooms are in the new town beyond the train station.

Dijaški dom (☎ 391 154), Cankarjeva ulica 5 in the old town, rents beds in three-bedded rooms at US$10 per person. You may have to show a youth hostel or student card to be admitted to this modern five-storey student dormitory. It's open all year.

Hotel Triglav (☎ 23 771), Pristaniška ulica 3, is reasonable at US$20/27 single/double with shower and breakfast. There's no camping ground in Koper (see the Piran section).

Places to Eat

The *Buffet 'Istrska klet'*, Župančičeva ulica 39, just up from the Bridge Fountain, (closed Saturday), offers a filling US$4 set lunch weekdays, and glasses of wine straight from the barrel any time. Try Refošk, the hearty local red wine.

The *Trgovina Restauracija* on Prešernov trg lists three-course set meals on a blackboard at the entrance to the dining room. For about US$5 you'll get all you can eat plus a large beer. It's patronised mostly by locals and is excellent value.

A burek buffet is at Kidričeva ulica 8.

Cafés

Koper's finest café is *Kavana Loggia* in front of the cathedral.

Entertainment

Elite Disco, Carpacciov trg 6 (closed Sunday), is just off the old harbour.

There's also the *Camel Club* (opens at 10 pm) next to the Snack Bar at Hotel Žusterna, about two km west of Koper on the road to Izola.

Kino Soča is on Trubarjeva ulica, near the cathedral.

Getting There & Away

There are 15 buses daily from Trieste to Koper (21 km, US$2). In Trieste look for this bus in the bus station next to Trieste Train Station (buy a ticket at the office inside).

Buses connect Koper to Postojna (57 km) 13 times a day, to Poreč (70 km) six times a day and to Pula (104 km) three times a day.

To Ljubljana there's both a bus (104 km) and a train (175 km, four daily, 2½ hours, US$5). The train is much more comfortable than the bus. To go from Koper to Zagreb by train involves two changes, so in that case it's better to take one of the two daily buses (253 km).

Getting Around

There's a bus about every half-hour between Koper and Piran (16 km, US$1), calling at Izola and Portorož. This bus begins at Koper Railway Station; you can also catch it beside the vegetable market in Koper. Enter through the rear doors to pay the conductor.

IZOLA

Izola, between Koper and Piran, is the centre of Slovenia's fishing industry and has its own cannery. The area of the old town was once an island, hence the name. All the coastal buses stop there. Izola doesn't live only from tourism, so it's more natural than Portorož or Piran, as long as you don't mind a slightly fishy smell.

Orientation & Information

The bus from Koper/Piran stops on the edge of the old town, just around the corner from the Turist Biro, Kidričevo nabrežje 4.

Money The Splošna Banka Koper, Drevored 1 Maja 5 next to Pizzeria Palma, changes travellers' cheques weekdays from 7.30 am to 6 pm, and Saturday from 7.30 am to noon. A better rate for cash only is offered by Fiba, Pittonijeva ulica 1, just up the small street from the bus stop marked 'Slavnik Koper' (weekdays from 8 am to noon and 4 to 6 pm, Saturday from 8 am to noon).

Post & Telecommunications The telephone centre in the post office facing the bus stop is open weekdays from 7.30 am to 7 pm, Saturday from 7.30 am to 1 pm.

Places to Stay

Autocamp Jadranka (☎ 61 202; open from June to September) is conveniently located on the waterfront one km west of Izola (if

you're coming from Koper get off at the next stop after you see the caravans). It costs US$6 per person. Unfortunately, it's unbelievably noisy because of the adjacent highway, so you're much better off going on to the camping grounds in Portorož or Piran.

The Turist Biro (☎ 62 901), Kidričevo nabrežje 4, facing the waterfront, has private rooms. There's a 50% surcharge if you stay only one or two nights.

In July and August the *Hotel Riviera* (☎ 62 921), near the Turist Biro, offers singles/doubles at US$30/54. During other months this hotel is a tourism school and the rooms are occupied by students. The *Hotel Marina* (☎ 65 325) facing the small boat harbour is open all year, charging US$48/74 single/double in July and August and US$35/54 other months.

Places to Eat

There's a rather poor self-service cafeteria, the *Restauracija Izola*, at Cankarjev Drevored 17, just east of the post office on the road to Koper. In the evening it's a pizzeria (closed Sunday). *Pizzeria Palma*, about 100 metres along the road to Piran, is better, and there's also a large restaurant in *Hotel Riviera*.

Entertainment

Izola's top disco is the *CC Club* behind Hotel Simonov Zaliv, about two km west on the road to Piran.

The Odeon Cinema is hidden behind Caffé Bar Odeon across the street from the police station near Hotel Riviera.

PORTOROŽ

Portorož (Port of Roses) is a chic resort on a sandy bay five km south-east of Piran. Whereas Koper, Izola and Piran have history going back hundreds of years, Portorož only grew up around the Grand Palace Hotel established in 1891. Obala (Beach Road), the main drag, is a solid strip of high-rise hotels, restaurants, bars, travel agencies, shops, discos, 'managed' beaches, parked cars and tourists. There's even a casino for those with spare cash. If you're after a fast social scene and don't mind spending a little money to be part of it, Portorož is for you.

Information
The Turist Biro is at Obala 16 near the bus station. There's no left-luggage facility at the bus station.

Money The Splošna Banka Koper, Obala 33 near the Grand Palace Hotel (open weekdays 8.30 to 11.30 am and 4 to 6 pm, Saturday 8 am to noon), has an automatic machine outside the office which changes the banknotes of 18 countries.

Post & Telecommunications The telephone centre beside Grand Palace Hotel is open weekdays from 8 am to 7 pm, Saturday from 8 am to 1 pm. There's a row of public telephones outside. The telephone code for Portorož is 066.

Activities
The beaches of Portorož are 'managed' so you'll pay about US$2 (US$1.50 after 1 pm) to use them. On a hot summer's day it really becomes a zoo.

The **Terme Palace** behind the Grand Palace Hotel at Portorož offers warm sea-water baths (US$6 per half-hour), brine baths (US$19) and mud baths (US$16) Monday to Saturday from 7 am to 2 pm. The public swimming pool here is open daily except Monday from 7 am to 7 pm all year (US$3 admission, sauna US$6 for two hours). This spa uses mud and brine from the nearby salt pans as well as sea water; Austro-Hungarian officers began coming to Portorož for treatment as long ago as 1830.

Places to Stay & Eat
From May to September there's *Autocamp Lucija* (☎ 71 027), beyond the marina at the south end of Portorož. It's on the Seča Peninsula, near the Forma Viva Sculpture Park, (ask for the 'marina' bus stop). Not only is it cramped but you can expect to pay US$9 per person to pitch a tent and it's always full of caravans.

Many travel agencies along Obala offer private rooms, including Slovenijaturist (☎ 75 670), Obala 18a, near the bus station, the Turist Biro (☎ 73 155), Obala 16, Kompas (☎ 73 167) near the Grand Palace Hotel, Globtour (☎ 73 356) near Hotel Slovenija, and Top Line Service (☎ 73 281), Obala 22, at Metropol Beach. Some of the rooms are up on the hillside, quite a walk from the beach. Getting a room for less than three nights or a single any time is difficult and in winter the landladies don't wish to rent at all due to the low off-season rates in force at that time. In winter, most of the travel agencies close at 1 pm.

There's a self-service restaurant at Plaza Beach. Another *Self-Service Grill* faces the beach behind the Beltours office. Both only open in summer.

Entertainment
The foremost disco on the Slovene Riviera is said to be *Arcadia*, near the old church tower in the centre of the Bernardin Tourist Complex between Portorož and Piran (opens daily at 10 pm). There's also *Club Venus* below Hotel Riviera, Obala 31, (closed Monday) and the *Tivoli Club*, opposite the Grand Palace Hotel.

The *Avditorij*, Senčna pot 10, only a block back behind the bus station, is a modern theatre which serves as Portorož's cinema. During summer, there are special events in the large open-air theatre.

Getting There & Away
Portorož airport is a few km south of town very near the Croatian border, and the Portorož bus station is in the middle of things just off the strip. Buses to Piran, Izola and Koper run every half-hour; to Ljubljana (122 km) via Postojna 12 times a day; to Poreč (54 km) and Zagreb (268 km) three times a day; to Rovinj (68 km) and Pula (90 km) twice a day and to Nova Gorica (114 km) daily. On weekdays there are eight direct buses from Portorož to Trieste (35 km).

Car Rental The international chains represented here are Budget/Globtour (☎ 74 075), Obala 33, and Hertz/Kompas (☎ 76 170),

Obala 41. Many smaller local companies have offices on Obala, so stroll along comparing prices.

PIRAN

Set on a point at one end of the Istrian Peninsula, three km beyond Portorož, picturesque Piran (Pireos) is the pearl of Istria, a gem of Venetian architecture. The name derives from the Greek word 'pyr' (fire), referring to fires on the ancient lighthouse here. Piran has a long history dating from the time of the ancient Greeks, and town walls still protect it to the east.

Because it's at the end of the peninsula, tourists tend to pile up in Piran, but fortunately traffic is restricted. All cars entering the town for over an hour must pay a stiff parking fee (the parking lot 100 metres back towards Portorož from the bus station is much cheaper). If you can put up with a little bustle, the tiny lanes and squares of the old town are well worth exploring.

Orientation

The bus station (no left luggage) is just south of Piran harbour, an easy walk from town. Tartinijev trg, Piran's heart, is just north of this harbour.

Information

The Turist Biro is at Tartinijev trg 44 (closed in winter).

Money The Splošna Banka Koper, Tartinijev trg 12, changes travellers' cheques weekdays from 7.30 am to 6 pm and Saturday from 7.30 am to noon. Outside their office is an automatic machine that changes the banknotes of 13 countries 24 hours a day.

Post & Telecommunications The telephone centre in the post office on Tartinijev trg is open weekdays from 7.30 am to 7 pm, Saturday from 7.30 am to 1 pm. Piran's telephone code is 066.

Things to See

The **Maritime Museum** (closed Monday, US$1), in a 17th century palace on the harbour, is an excellent museum with detailed descriptions of the salt-collecting basins near Piran, antique model ships, paintings and photos. The captions are in Italian and Slovene. Piran's **aquarium** (US$1.50 per person) on the other side of the small boat harbour may be small but there's a tremendous variety of life packed into the 25 tanks.

The **town hall** and **court house** stand on Tartinijev trg, in the centre of which is a statue of the violinist and composer Giuseppe Tartini, who was born here in 1692. Deeper in the medieval town is Trg 1 maja with a Baroque fountain.

The compact old town is dominated by the tall tower of the **parish church of St George** on a hill overlooking the sea. This church was founded in 1344 and rebuilt in the Baroque style in 1637. It's wonderfully decorated with frescoes, marble altars and a large statue of St George slaying the dragon. The freestanding bell tower (1609) is modelled on the tower of San Marco in Venice, and the 17th century octagonal **baptistery** next door contains a wooden medieval crucifix (1300).

The **town walls** to the east can be climbed for a superb view of Piran and the sea.

Places to Stay

Camping The best camping ground on the Slovene Riviera is *Camping Jezero* (☎ 73 473) at Fiesa, one km east of the old town. It's in a quiet valley by a small lake just a few minutes' walk from a pebble beach. A lovely path below the bluffs on the north side of the peninsula brings you into town. Camping is US$8 per person. It's open from May to September.

Private Rooms The Turist Biro (☎ 73 680), Tartinijev trg 44, the pink building in the far corner of the square, has private rooms for US$11/17 single/double, with a 50% surcharge if you only stay one or two nights. The price is always 50% higher in July and August and in winter they're closed.

The Maona Tourist Agency (☎ 75 592), Cankarjevo nabrežje 7 facing the small boat

SLOVENIA

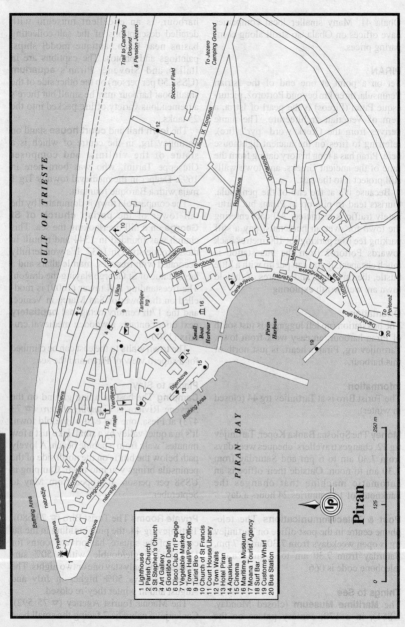

GULF OF TRIESTE

To Camping Ground & Pension Jezero

Trail to Camping Ground & Pension Jezero

To Jezero Camping Ground

Soccer Field

Ulica IX. Korpusa

Rozmanova

Gortanova

Mancova

Bonini

Rozmanova

Ulica Svobode

Tartinjev trg

Cankarjevo nabrežje

Zdravljiška

Tomšiča

Ulica IX. Korpusa

Cankarjevo

Piran Harbour

Small Boat Harbour

To Portorož

Danilejeva ulica

Presernova

nabrežje

Adamičeva

Bonistanova

Gregorčičeva

Presernova

nabrežje

Verdijeva

Trg 1 maja

1 maja

Stjenkova

Bathing Area

Bathing Area

Bathing Area

PIRAN BAY

Piran

1 Lighthouse
2 Parish Church
3 St Stephen's Church
4 Art Gallery
5 Gostišče Delfin
6 Visco Club Trr Papige
7 Vegetable Market
8 Town Hall/Post Office
9 Tourist Biro
10 Church of St Francis
11 Court House/Library
12 Town Walls
13 Hotel Piran
14 Aquarium
15 Cinema
16 Maritime Museum
17 Moana Tourist Agency
18 Surf Bar
19 Customs Wharf
20 Bus Station

250 m

125

0

SLOVENIA

harbour, and Student Tours (☎ 73 773) next to Hotel Piran also have private rooms from June to September.

Hotels Your best bet is *Pension Jezero* (☎ 73 473) at Fiesa, in the building above the restaurant right next to Camping Jezero. This pleasant four-storey hotel overlooking the sea has 40 rooms at US$20/37 single/double with bath and breakfast from October to May, 50% more in summer (no supplement if you stay only one night). Theoretically they're open all year but in winter call ahead

to make sure they're open and in summer to make sure they have a room available.

Remember that there's a US$1.25 per person per night tourist tax which will be added to all accommodation charges in Piran or Portorož.

Places to Eat
Affluent tourists consume conspicuously at the waterfront seafood restaurants along Prešernovo nabrežje. *Gostišče Delfin*, Kosovelova 4, off Trg 1 maja, at least posts an illustrated menu outside with prices.

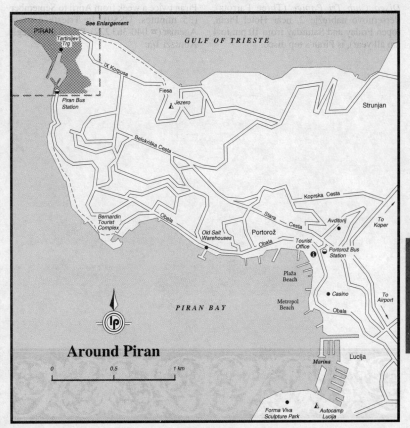

PIRAN

GULF OF TRIESTE

Tartinijev Trg

See Enlargement

IX Korpusa

Fiesa

Piran Bus Station

Jezero

Strunjan

Belokriška Cesta

Koprska Cesta

Bernardin Tourist Complex

Obala

Stara Cesta

Avditorij

To Koper

Old Salt Warehouses

Portorož

Obala

Tourist Office

Portorož Bus Station

Plaža Beach

Casino

To Airport

Metropol Beach

Obala

PIRAN BAY

Around Piran

0   0.5   1 km

Marina

Lucija

Forma Viva Sculpture Park

Autocamp Lucija

SLOVENIA

A good bet is the *Surf Bar*, Grudnova 1, on a backstreet not far from the bus station (watch for the signs). Its unique album menu contains colour photos of all their dishes. The pizza is excellent and draught beer is served in big glass mugs. In the morning you can get ham and eggs. You'll enjoy the pub-like atmosphere, and the polyglot staff will speak to you in any language you like, so it's worth stopping by for a drink at the bar even if you're not hungry. It's open Monday to Saturday from 8.30 am to 10 pm, Sunday from 11 am to 10 pm.

Entertainment

Disco Club Tri Papige (Three Parrots), Peršernovo nabrežje 2, near Hotel Piran, (open Friday and Saturday from 10 pm to 4 am all year), is Piran's top disco.

Events of the Piran Musical Evenings in summer take place in the cloister of St Francis Church.

Getting There & Away

Local buses between Piran, Portorož, Izola and Koper are frequent. Tickets are sold on the bus (enter via the back door). Buses from Piran include nine to Postojna and Ljubljana, six to Trieste (weekdays only) and one each to Nova Gorica, Zagreb, Poreč and Rovinj. More long-distance buses pass through nearby Portorož Bus Station.

The Adriatica Navigazione fast motor vessel *Marconi* glides between Trieste and Piran twice a week from April to September (35 minutes, US$9). In Trieste contact Agemar (☎ 040-363 222), Piazza Duca degli Abruzzi 1/a.

Yugoslavia (Југославија)

The new Federal Republic of Yugoslavia (SRJ), made up of Serbia and Montenegro, occupies the heart of the Balkan Peninsula astride the main road, rail and river routes from Western Europe to Asia Minor. Since the withdrawal of Croatia, Slovenia, Bosnia-Hercegovina and Macedonia in 1991, Yugoslavia (Jugoslavija) seems to have become a mere 'Greater Serbia', with oppressed Hungarian, Muslim and Albanian minorities in the north and south.

This tragic outcome and the continuing ethnic strife have cast a pall over a country still rich in mountains, rivers, seascapes, climates, cultures, customs, cuisines and peoples. Now shorn of most of its coastal tourist resorts, rump Yugoslavia seems destined to be forgotten by the world of mass tourism.

Awaiting those select few who stray beyond the transit corridors to Turkey and Greece are the glorious gorges and beaches of Montenegro, the mystical Orthodox monasteries of southern Serbia and Kosovo, the imposing fortresses along the Danube and hundreds of other tangible traces of a tumultuous history stretching back thousands of years.

In this book we use the term Yugoslavia ('The Land of the South Slavs') to refer to either pre-1991 Yugoslavia or present Yugoslavia (Serbia and Montenegro), depending on the context. By ex-Yugoslavia we mean the whole territory of pre-1991 Yugoslavia as it is today. We make no judgment on whether present Yugoslavia is entitled to continue using the name Yugoslavia. If that's what they want to call their country, so be it. The same applies to Macedonia.

At the time of going to press United Nations (UN) sanctions were in effect against Yugoslavia, yet most of the country is peaceful and safe. We leave it up to the individual to decide whether he or she wishes to visit and limit ourselves to providing factual information.

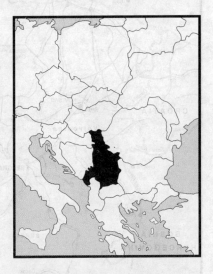

Facts about the Country

HISTORY

The original inhabitants of this region were the Illyrians, followed by the Celts who arrived in the 4th century BC. The Roman conquest of Moesia Superior (Serbia) began in the 3rd century BC and under Augustus the empire extended to Singidunum (Belgrade) on the Danube. In 395 AD Theodosius I divided the empire and what is now Serbia passed to the Byzantine Empire, while Croatia remained part of the Western Roman Empire.

In the middle of the 6th century, Slavic tribes (Serbs, Croats and Slovenes) crossed the Danube in the wake of the Great Migration of Nations and occupied much of the Balkan Peninsula. In 879 the Serbs were converted to the Orthodox Church by Sts Cyril and Methodius. In 969 Serbia broke

Yugoslavia (Jugoslavija)

HUNGARY

Baja
Horgoš SZEGED
SUBOTICA
PÉCS

Sprska
Crnja TIMIŞOARA

CROATIA

NOVI SAD
Danube
Tisa River
River

Vojvodina

Vatin

Vršac

ROMANIA

Sava River

Bijeljina

Drina River

BELGRADE

Smederevo

Golubac

Kladovo

Zvornik

BOSNIA-HERCEGOVINA

SERBIA

Manasija

Negotin

River

Danube

Čačak

Požega

Čuprija

Zaječar

Vidin

Kraljevo

Morava River

Ušće
Studenica

Brus
Kruševac

Ibar River

NIŠ

Raška
Kapaonik
(2017 m)

Pljevlja

Sandžak

Žabljak

Bijelo Polje

Novi
Pazar

Dimitrovgrad

MONTENEGRO

Mojkovac
Rožaj

Kosovo

Klisura

Nikšić

Ivangrad

Kolašin

Herceg-Novi
Kotor
Cetinje

Peć

Priština

BULGARIA

Tivat
Skadar Lake
Podgorica
Budva

Kosovo
Polje

Bay of Kotor

Dečani

Sveti
Stefan
Bar

Shkodra Lake
SHKODRA

Prizren

Šar Planina

Kumanovo

Ulcinj

ALBANIA

Kukës

SKOPJE

ADRIATIC SEA

MACEDONIA

0   50   100 km

free from Byzantium and established an independent state; however, Byzantium re-established its authority in the 11th century.

An independent Serbian kingdom reappeared in 1217 and during the reign of Stefan Dušan (1346-55) Serbia was a great power including much of present Albania and northern Greece within its boundaries. Numerous frescoed Orthodox monasteries were erected during this Serbian 'Golden Age'. After Stefan's death Serbia declined, and at the Battle of Kosovo on 28 June 1389 the Serbian army was defeated by the Ottoman Turks, ushering in 500 years of Islamic rule. The Serbs were pushed north as the Turks advanced into Bosnia in the 15th century and the city-state of Venice occupied the coast. By 1459 Serbia was a Turkish *pashalik* (province) and the inhabitants had become mere serfs. In 1526 the Turks defeated Hungary at the Battle of Mohács, adding territory north and west of the Danube to their realm.

The first centuries of Turkish rule brought stability to the Balkans but, as the power of the sultan declined, local Turkish officials and soldiers began to oppress the Slavs. After their defeat at Vienna in 1683, the Turks began a steady retreat. By 1699 they had been driven out of Hungary and many Serbs moved north into Vojvodina, where they enjoyed Habsburg protection. Through diplomacy the sultan regained northern Serbia for another century, but a revolt in 1815 led to de facto Serbian independence in 1816. Serbia's autonomy was recognised in 1829, the last Turkish troops departed in 1867, and in 1878, after the defeat of Turkey by Russia in a war over Bulgaria, complete independence was achieved. Montenegro also declared itself independent of Turkey in 1878. Macedonia remained under Turkish rule into the 20th century.

Tensions mounted after Austria's annexation of Bosnia-Hercegovina in 1908, with Russia backing Serbia. In the First Balkan War (1912), Serbia, Greece and Bulgaria combined against Turkey for the liberation of Macedonia. The Second Balkan War (1913) saw Serbia and Greece join forces against Bulgaria, which had claimed all of Macedonia for itself. At about this time Serbia wrested control of Kosovo from Albania with the help of the Western powers.

WW I was an extension of these conflicts as Austria-Hungary used the assassination of Archduke Ferdinand on 28 June 1914 as an excuse to invade Serbia. Russia and France came to Serbia's aid. In the winter of 1915-16 a defeated Serbian army of 155,000 retreated across the mountains of Montenegro to the Adriatic from where it was evacuated to Corfu. In 1918 these troops fought their way back up into Serbia from Thessaloniki, Greece.

After WW I, Croatia, Slovenia and Vojvodina were united with Serbia, Montenegro and Macedonia to form the Kingdom of Serbs, Croats and Slovenes under the king of Serbia. In 1929 the name was changed to Yugoslavia. The Vidovdan constitution of 1921 created a centralised government dominated by Serbia. This was strongly opposed by the Croats and other minorities, forcing King Alexander to end the political turmoil by declaring a personal dictatorship in 1929. The assassination of the king by a Macedonian nationalist in 1934 led to a regency which continued the Serbian dictatorship. Corruption was rampant and the regent tilted towards friendship with Nazi Germany.

On 25 March 1941, Yugoslavia joined the Tripartite Alliance, a fascist military pact, after being promised Greek Macedonia and Thessaloniki by the Germans. This sparked mass protest demonstrations and a military coup that overthrew the profascist regency. Peter II was installed as king and Yugoslavia abruptly withdrew from the alliance. Livid, Hitler ordered an immediate invasion and the country was carved up between Germany, Italy, Hungary and Bulgaria. In Croatia a fascist puppet state was set up which massacred hundreds of thousands of ethnic Serbs and Jews.

Almost immediately the Communist Party under Josip Broz Tito declared an armed uprising. There was also a monarchist resistance group, the Četniks, but they proved far less effective than Tito's partisans, and after 1943 the British gave full backing to the communists. A 1943 meeting of the Antifascist Council of National Liberation of Yugoslavia (AVNOJ) at Jajce laid the basis for a future communist-led Yugoslavia.

The partisans played a major role in WW II by tying down huge Italian and German armies, but Yugoslavia suffered terrible losses, especially in Croatia and Bosnia-Hercegovina where most of the fighting took place. According to the Serbian author Bogoljub Kočović some 487,000 Serbs, 207,000 Croats, 86,000 Muslims, 60,000 Jews, 50,000 Montenegrins, 32,000 Slovenes, 7000 Macedonians and 6000 Albanians died in the war. The resistance did, however, guarantee Yugoslavia's postwar independence.

Recent History

In 1945 the Communist Party (which had been officially banned since 1920) won control of the national assembly, which in November abolished the monarchy and declared Yugoslavia a federal republic. Serbia's size was greatly reduced when Bosnia-Hercegovina, Montenegro and Macedonia were granted republic status within this 'second' Yugoslavia. The Albanians of Kosovo and Hungarians of Vojvodina were denied republics of their own, however, on the pretext that they were not nations because their national homelands were outside the boundaries of Yugoslavia. Under Tito's slogan *bratstva i jedinstva* (brotherhood and unity) nationalist tendencies were suppressed.

Tito broke with Stalin in 1948 and, as a reward, received US$2 billion in economic and military aid from the USA and UK between 1950 and 1960. For the West this was a cheap way of protecting NATO's southern flank, but for Yugoslavia the Western subsidies alleviated the need for reform, contributing to the economic problems of today.

After the break with the USSR, Yugoslavia followed its own 'road to socialism' based on a federal system, self-management,

personal freedom and nonalignment. The decentralisation begun in 1951 was to lead to the eventual 'withering away of the state' of classical Marxism. Yugoslavia never became a member of either the Warsaw Pact or NATO, and in 1956 the country played a key role in the formation of the nonaligned movement.

The 1960s witnessed an economic boom in the north-west accompanied by liberalisation throughout the country, and in July 1966 Tito fired his hardline secret police chief Alexander Ranković. The growing regional inequalities led, however, to increased tension as Slovenia, Croatia and Kosovo demanded greater autonomy within the federation. In 1971 Tito responded with a 'return to Leninism', which included a purge of party reformers and a threat to use military force against Croatia.

With the most talented members of the leadership gone, Yugoslavia stagnated through the 1970s while borrowing billions of recycled petrodollars in the West. A 1970 constitutional amendment declared that the federal government would have control of foreign policy, defence, trade, the national economy and human rights, and all residual powers were vested in the six republics (Croatia, Bosnia-Hercegovina, Macedonia, Montenegro, Serbia and Slovenia) and two autonomous provinces of Serbia (Kosovo and Vojvodina). The 1974 constitution strengthened the powers of the autonomous provinces.

Tito died in 1980 and the state presidency became a collective post rotated annually among nine members elected every four years by the national assembly, the six republics and the two autonomous provinces. This cumbersome system proved unable to solve Yugoslavia's deepening economic problems or to control regional antagonisms.

In 1985 a working group of the Serbian Academy of Sciences prepared a memorandum calling on Serbia to reassert its hegemony in Yugoslavia and a year later Slobodan Milošević took over as party leader in Serbia by portraying himself as the champion of an allegedly persecuted Serbian minority in Kosovo. Milošević hoped to restore the flagging popularity of the League of Communists by inciting the Serbs' latent anti-Albanian sentiments. When moves by Serbia to limit Kosovo's autonomy led to massive protest demonstrations in the province in late 1988 and early 1989, the Serbian government unilaterally scrapped Kosovo's autonomy. Thousands of troops were sent to intimidate Kosovo's 90% Albanian majority, and in direct confrontations with the security forces dozens of civilians were shot dead.

Milošević's vision of a 'Greater Serbia' horrified residents of Slovenia and Croatia, who elected non-communist republican governments in the spring of 1990. These called for the creation of a loose Yugoslav 'confederation' which would allow Slovenia and Croatia to retain most of their wealth for themselves, and threatened to secede from Yugoslavia if such reforms were not forthcoming. In the Serbian elections of December 1990, however, Milošević's policies paid off when the communists won 194 of 260 seats (the Albanians boycotted the election). In the other republics the communists held Montenegro but lost Bosnia-Hercegovina and Macedonia.

Meanwhile, the federal prime minister, Ante Marković (a Croat), tried to steer clear of the ethnic turmoil. In late 1989 Marković introduced major economic reforms to control inflation. Though Western governments verbally supported the Marković reforms, few came forward with material support in the form of new loans or investments. With the Soviet empire disintegrating Yugoslavia was no longer of prime strategic importance.

In early 1991 Serbian nationalists staged provocations in several Croatian towns in the hope of triggering a military coup or martial law which might halt separatist moves by Slovenia and Croatia and reimpose the authority of Belgrade. In March 1991 Serbia's state-controlled media broadcast false reports of a massacre of ethnic Serbs in Croatia in an attempt to precipitate a crisis leading to a military takeover. This outraged prodemocratic Serbian students who, led by

Serbian Renewal Movement leader Vuk Drašković , massed outside the TV studios in Belgrade demanding that those responsible be sacked.

On 25 June 1991 Slovenia and Croatia declared themselves independent of Yugoslavia. This soon led to heavy fighting as the federal army moved into Slovenia. Fearing the unleashing of a tidal wave of refugees, the European Community (EC) rushed a delegation of foreign ministers to Yugoslavia to negotiate a truce which, however, soon broke down. In Belgrade, Milošević went on TV to reaffirm his support for Yugoslavia and the right of people to continue to live in it. He said the Yugoslav People's Army would intervene to defend Serbs wherever they lived.

On 7 July federal and republican leaders met on Brijuni Island off Istria in the hope of preventing a full-scale civil war as the EC imposed a weapons embargo on Yugoslavia and froze US$1 billion in aid and credits. It soon became clear that the matter would be decided in Croatia and on 18 July the Yugoslav government announced that all federal troops would be withdrawn from Slovenia within three months.

Intervention by the federal army on the side of Serb separatists in Croatia led to months of fighting, with widespread property damage and thousands of casualties. The EC sent unarmed cease-fire monitors to the trouble areas in September and organised a peace conference in the Netherlands but this failed, and in November the EC applied economic sanctions against Serbia and Montenegro. On 20 December 1991 the federal prime minister, Ante Marković, resigned after the army demanded 81% of the 1992 budget.

In December it was agreed that a UN peacekeeping force would be sent to Croatia and from 3 January 1992 a cease-fire generally held. On 15 January the EC recognised Croatia's and Slovenia's independence, whereupon Macedonia and Bosnia-Hercegovina demanded recognition of their own independence. Montenegro alone voted to remain in Yugoslavia. The secession of

Bosnia-Hercegovina sparked bitter fighting as Serb militants with army backing again used force to seize territory, as they had done in Croatia.

On 27 April 1992 a 'third' Yugoslav federation was declared by Serbia and Montenegro in a rushed attempt to escape blame for the bloodshed in Bosnia-Hercegovina. The rump state disclaimed responsibility for the federal army in Bosnia-Hercegovina and announced that all soldiers hailing from Serbia and Montenegro would be withdrawn. In practice this manoeuvre didn't amount to much as 80% of the federal troops in the breakaway state were Bosnian Serbs. Meanwhile, the federal army purged its ranks of officers who still supported the old concept of Yugoslavia and replaced them with Serb hardliners.

In May 1992, with Sarajevo under siege and the world losing patience with what was seen as Serbian aggression, the UN Security Council passed a sweeping package of economic and diplomatic sanctions against Yugoslavia, and in mid-July US and Western European warships began patrolling the Adriatic off Montenegro to monitor the embargo. Yugoslavia was denied the old Yugoslavia seat at the UN in September 1992 and in November a UN naval blockade was imposed. Sanctions against Yugoslavia were greatly strengthened in April 1993 after the Serb side rejected a peace plan for Bosnia-Hercegovina. Yet despite the severe economic hardship, the socialists won the December 1993 elections.

At the time of going to press the dream of a 'Greater Serbia' seems about to become reality, stained with the blood of tens of thousands of unfortunate people and soiled by the ashes of their burned homes. The new constitution of rump Yugoslavia invites 'other republics' to join the new state, which is undoubtedly what the Serb mini-states in Bosnia-Hercegovina and Croatia intend to do at the first opportunity (see the Bosnia-Hercegovina chapter for more information). The constitution makes no mention of 'autonomous provinces', and the Albanian majority in Kosovo is being brutally repressed by Serb officials with a real danger of a bloody uprising and Bosnia-style genocide (see the Kosovo section).

GEOGRAPHY

Mountains and plateaus account for the lower half of this 102,173-sq-km country (the size of the US state of Virginia), the remainder being the Pannonian Plain drained by the Sava, Danube and Tisa rivers in the north-east. Yugoslavia's interior and southern mountains belong to the Balkan range, and the coastal range is an arm of the Alps. Most of the rivers flow north into the Danube, which runs through Yugoslavia for 588 km. In the south many smaller rivers have cut deep canyons in the plateau which make for memorable train rides.

When the country split up in 1991, most of the Adriatic coast went to Slovenia and Croatia, though the scenically superb 150-km Montenegrin coast remains in Yugoslavia. The Bay of Kotor here is the only real fjord in southern Europe, and Montenegro's Durmitor National Park has ex-Yugoslavia's largest canyon. Between Ulcinj and Albania is one of the longest beaches in the eastern Adriatic.

ECONOMY

The importance of agriculture to Serbia and Montenegro is indicative of a backwardness that is in sharp contrast to Slovenia and Croatia. After WW II, Yugoslavia was a war-torn land of peasants, but from 1948 to 1951 a concentrated attempt was made to form agricultural cooperatives. This failed, however, and most of the land continued to be worked privately by small farmers. In 1953 individual private holdings were reduced to a maximum of 10 hectares.

During the 1950s, state property was handed over to the workers in a reaction against Stalinist state socialism. The economy was thus reorganised on the basis of 'self-management', and elected workers' councils began running the factories and businesses with coordination from producers' councils on a regional level. State control was limited to the broadest economic planning.

This system soon led to inefficiencies and an expensive duplication of services without the full benefits of open competition. Since socially owned property had no clear owner, it was impossible to enforce economic efficiency or to guarantee profits. Initiative was stifled and employees often used self-management to improve their own financial standing without feeling any responsibility towards their property. Income was spent on higher wages and, with little or no capital left for development, companies turned to the banks. The cycle of inefficiency and dependency deepened as companies borrowed with little hope of ever paying off the loans.

The crisis of 2000% inflation in 1989 shattered the self-management ideal and led reformers to consider a return to private property inevitable. At the beginning of 1990 the government attempted to halt inflation by stopping the printing presses of the Belgrade mint and declaring a wage freeze. Prices still jumped by 75% but by mid-1990 inflation had levelled off to 13% a year. However, by 1992 hyperinflation had returned as the government again turned to printing money to finance government operations and the war in Bosnia-Hercegovina. UN economic sanctions did the rest.

Trade between the five ex-Yugoslav states has almost ceased, and 250% a month inflation, economic inefficiencies, bankruptcies by major firms and astronomical military expenditures spell economic disaster. In 1993 incomes were a tenth what they had been three years previously, industrial output had dropped 40% from that of a year before and 60% of factory workers were unemployed. Over 80% of Yugoslav property is still socially owned and if normal bankruptcy procedures were applied most of these firms would go broke. Instead, freshly printed banknotes from the public purse keep them going and everyone pays the price in the form of inflation. People get by on remittances from relatives overseas or by subsisting on their gardens and livestock.

The end of the Cold War has greatly reduced the strategic importance of the entire Balkan region and Western countries are unlikely to rush in with 1950s-style aid or 1970s-style loans, even assuming that peace and stability do somehow return. Yugoslavia owes foreign governments and banks about US$16 billion, most of it dating back to the 1970s.

POPULATION & PEOPLE

The 11 million people of the 'third' Yugoslavia include Serbs (62.3%), Albanians (16.6%), Montenegrins (5%), Hungarians (3.3%) and Slavic Muslims (3.1%), plus a smattering of Croats, Gypsies, Slovaks, Macedonians, Romanians, Bulgarians, Turks and Ukrainians. The Montenegrins are officially considered ethnic Serbs. In 1991 an estimated 170,000 Gypsies lived in Yugoslavia, 100,000 of them in Kosovo. About half a million war refugees from Croatia and Bosnia-Hercegovina are present in Serbia and another 64,000 are in Montenegro.

Nearly a quarter of the population of Vojvodina is Hungarian, and 90% of Kosovars are Albanian. Around 200,000 Serbs also live in Kosovo and there are large Muslim and Albanian minorities in Montenegro. In total there are 1,800,000 ethnic Albanians in present Yugoslavia, a large number considering that the population of Albania itself is only 3,200,000. Some 250,000 Muslims live in the Sandžak region of Serbia and Montenegro between Novi Pazar and Ivangrad (part of Bosnia until 1918). The human rights of all minorities are challenged by an increasingly nationalistic Serbia. The Serbs and Montenegrins are Orthodox, whereas the Hungarians are Roman Catholic and the Albanians predominantly Muslim.

Yugoslavia's largest cities are Belgrade (1,500,000), Novi Sad (250,000), Niš (230,000), Priština (210,000) and Subotica (160,000).

ARTS

The artistic group FIA (☎ 011-347 355), Hilandarska 4, 11000 Belgrade, founded in 1989 by Stavislav Sharp and Nada Rajičić, explores the connection between Serbia's tumultuous present and art through 'Phobjects', suggestive images juxtaposed against folk art, political symbols and provocative quotations.

At exhibitions, group members dress in black paramilitary uniforms and show videos of skits in which FIA 'conspiracies' are acted out. Their 1992 Belgrade exhibition was visited by over 50,000 people in two weeks before being suddenly closed by force. Phobjects have been exhibited in the ruins of the train station in Sarajevo and at the bombed-out zoo in Osijek (Croatia). Surrealist 'posters of conscience' bring the FIA message to the streets. Their works are often prophetic.

Music

Serbia's vibrant dances merge with those of neighbouring Bulgaria. Serbian folk musicians use the *caraba* (small bagpipe), *gadje* (larger bagpipe), *frula* (small flute), *duduk* (large flute) and fiddle. The gadje employed in much Balkan music probably dates back to the 4th century Celtic invasions; unlike the Scottish sheepskin bagpipe, the gadje is made from goatskin. The music of the Albanians of Kosovo bears the deep imprint of five centuries of Turkish rule, with the high whine of an Arab *zorna* (flute) carrying the tune above the beat of a goatskin drum. The *kolo* (round dance) is often accompanied by Gypsy musicians.

'Blehmuzika' or brass music has become the national music of Serbia. Though documented as far back as 1335, blehmuzika evolved under the influence of Turkish and later Austrian military music. During the early 20th century the trumpet became a symbol of Serbian resistance to foreign domination. The instrumentation is said to have come out of Austrian army bands. Old or damaged copper instruments were taken home by local farmers working for the army and there they 'brewed' their own combination of Austrian 'umpapa' and local song styles. In the 1920s, orchestras of eight to 10 musicians were formed, and right up to the present Serbian brass music is played mostly

by village farmers in their spare time. The heartland of blehmuzika is the area around Guča, a village south of the railway line between Kraljevo and Pozega. Each year around the end of August more than 100,000 people attend the three-day Guča trumpet festival to hear 20 competing bands. A second centre for Serbian brass music is the Niš region, where Gypsy bands play wild Eastern-inspired dance music.

A *bleh orkestar* or *banda* will include *fligorni* (trumpets), *truba* (bass), *dobo* (drum), *bubanj* (bass drum), clarinet, saxophone and perhaps a frula. An unfortunate side effect of the popularity of the bleh or *duvacki* orchestras is that groups using traditional folk instruments have been overpowered, and even the old combination of accordion and frula has lost ground.

LANGUAGE

Ordinary Yugoslavs are most likely to know German as a second language, though educated people in Kosovo and Serbia often speak French. Serbian is the common language, and Albanian is spoken in Kosovo.

Serbian and Croatian are almost the same language, although Serbian is written in Cyrillic and Croatian is written in Latin characters (see the Croatian Language section in the Croatia chapter). Before the break-up of the Yugoslav Federation, the language was referred to as Serbo-Croatian, but this term is now obsolete.

The Latin alphabet is used by the Albanians in Kosovo and the Hungarians in Vojvodina. In Montenegro you'll encounter a mixture of Latin and Cyrillic, but in Serbia most things are written only in Cyrillic. It's well worth spending an hour or two studying the Cyrillic alphabet (see the Language section of the Macedonia chapter).

Facts for the Visitor

VISAS & EMBASSIES

Most visitors require visas and these are issued promptly at Yugoslavian consulates, usually free of charge (New Zealanders are charged US$10). Before the current troubles began you could get a Yugoslav visa at the border but this is no longer possible and you must obtain your Yugoslav visa in advance at a consulate. We've heard of travellers who arrived at the Yugoslav border without a visa and were hauled off the train and interrogated by guards who demanded as much as US$60 for the right to proceed. Get your free visa in advance. (Don't confuse Yugoslavia with Macedonia and Croatia, where visas *are* readily available at the border.)

Don't count on obtaining a Yugoslavian visa in Slovenia, Croatia or Macedonia. A one-entry Yugoslavian visa is just that and if you go to Macedonia you will need a new visa to return to Belgrade.

Yugoslavian Embassies

Besides those listed below, Yugoslav consulates or embassies are found in Bucharest, Budapest, Prague, Sofia, Timişoara, Tirana and Warsaw. Try to avoid the chaotic Tirana consulate.

Australia
    11 Nuyts St, Canberra, ACT 2603
    (☎ 062-95 1458)
Canada
    17 Blackburn Ave, Ottawa, Ontario, K1N 8A2
    (☎ 233 6289)
Netherlands
    Groot Hertoginnelaan 30, 2517 EG, The Hague
    (☎ 070-363 6800)
UK
    5-7 Lexham Gardens, London, W8 5JJ
    (☎ 0171-370 6105)
USA
    2410 California St NW, Washington, DC 20008
    (☎ 202-462 6566)

MONEY

All banks and travel agencies will change cash hard currency into Yugoslav dinars at the standard official rate of exchange; unlike Western Europe, you won't be given a worse rate at the fancy hotels or on Sunday. Be aware, however, that as long as UN economic sanctions remain in force, travellers' cheques cannot be changed anywhere in Yugoslavia and credit cards are also not

accepted. In emergencies your embassy in Belgrade may agree to change US$100 in travellers' cheques for you as a special favour, but don't count on it.

Instead bring cash, preferably Deutschmarks, as black-market moneychangers buy US dollars at about 10% less than their corresponding value. Almost everyone in Yugoslavia changes money on the street and unlike in Budapest, Bucharest and Prague, it's fairly straightforward to do so and you probably won't be ripped off (but still take care). You'll often hear men on the street whisper *devize, devize* (hard currency, hard currency). Expect to get 20% above the official rate for cash on the street (this could change). Ask around for the current rate, though you usually don't have to bargain.

A few private exchange offices offer the equivalent of the black-market rate for cash only and, of course, there's no risk at all dealing with them. Only change enough money for one or two days at a time, as you'll get more and more dinars every time you change. It's usually a waste of time trying to change money at a bank.

Only change what you're sure you'll need, as it's *impossible* to change dinars back into hard currency.

Currency

With the Belgrade mint working overtime to print money to finance an oversized military and subsidise de facto Serb governments in Bosnia-Hercegovina and Croatia, the Yugoslav dinar has suffered repeated devaluations, and in December 1993 Yugoslavia experienced the highest inflation in the history of Europe (higher even than the 32,000% a month record set in Weimar Germany in 1923). To most of us, such a situation is inconceivable but the Yugoslavs are experienced at dealing with inflation.

In 1990 four zeros were knocked off the Yugoslav dinar, so 10,000 old dinars became one new dinar, and in mid-1993 another six zeros were dropped. When this currency in turn inflated into obsolescence, a 'super dinar' was issued in January 1994 with a value of one to 12 million old dinars. At the time of going to press the 'novi dinar' was still holding at the rate of one to one German mark, effectively terminating the black market. How long this will last is anyone's guess but for now there are coins of five, 10, 25 and 50 para and one novi dinars. The current 'economic miracle' is the result of a stabilisation plan introduced by central bank governor Dragoslav Avramović to avoid economic collapse by cutting inflation and restoring confidence to the market. Pressure to turn on the printing presses again to fuel Serbia's dirty little wars may eventually restart the whole inflationary cycle. You'll find out when you arrive.

CLIMATE & WHEN TO GO

The interior areas have a more extreme continental climate than the Adriatic coast of Montenegro. Belgrade has average daily temperatures above 17°C from May to September, above 13°C in April and October and above 7°C in March and November. In winter a cold south-east wind *(koshava)* often blows across Belgrade.

SUGGESTED ITINERARIES

Depending on the length of your stay, you might want to see and do the following things in Yugoslavia:

Two days
    Visit Subotica and Belgrade.
One week
    Visit Subotica, Belgrade, Bar, Budva and Cetinje.
Two weeks
    Visit all areas covered in this chapter except Kosovo.
One month
    Visit all areas covered herein plus Kopaonik.

TOURIST OFFICES

All of the overseas offices of the Yugoslav National Tourist Office closed in 1991, but municipal tourist offices still exist in Belgrade, Novi Sad and Podgorica. Commercial travel agencies such as Montenegroturist or Putnik will often provide general information on their area.

BUSINESS HOURS & HOLIDAYS

Banks in Yugoslavia keep long hours, often from 7 am to 7 pm weekdays, 7 am to noon Saturday. Most government offices are closed on Saturday, though shops stay open on Saturday until 2 pm. On weekdays many shops close for lunch from noon to 4 pm but stay open until 8 pm. Department stores, supermarkets and self-service restaurants generally stay open throughout the day. On Saturday many businesses close at 3 pm.

Public holidays include New Year (1 and 2 January), Orthodox Christmas (6 and 7 January), Labour Days (1 and 2 May), Partisan Day (4 July), and Republic Days (29 and 30 November). In addition, 7 July (Uprising Day) is a holiday in Serbia and 13 July is a holiday in Montenegro. If any of these should fall on a Sunday, then the following Monday or Tuesday is a holiday.

CULTURAL EVENTS

Belgrade hosts a film festival in February, an international theatre festival in mid-September, a festival of classical music in October and a jazz festival in November. The Novi Sad Agricultural Fair is in mid-May. Budva has a summer festival in July and August.

POST & TELECOMMUNICATIONS

To mail a parcel from Yugoslavia take it unwrapped to a main post office where the staff will wrap and seal it. You then fill out six or seven forms, stand in line for a while and with luck, it will be sent off. Not all post offices will do this, however. Allow several hours to complete the transaction.

Inflation is so high in Yugoslavia that the post office has trouble printing stamps of higher and higher denominations fast enough to keep up. You'll probably have to go to a post office to have your postcards meter-mailed rather than use stamps.

Receiving Mail

You can receive mail addressed to poste restante in all towns for a small charge per letter.

Mail addressed c/o Poste Restante, 11101 Belgrade 1, Yugoslavia, will be held for one month at window No 2 at the main post office, Takovska 2.

Telephones

To place a long-distance phone call in Yugoslavia you usually go to the main post office. Avoid doing this on weekends as the office may be jammed with military personnel waiting to call home. International calls placed from hotels are much more expensive. Calls placed at post offices go straight through and cost about US$1.50 a minute to the USA and Australia, with no minimum.

Magnetic telephone cards purchased at post offices or news kiosks are an inexpensive, easy way of placing international calls, but only in Belgrade as card phones are hard to find elsewhere. The international access code for outgoing calls is 99. To call another town within Yugoslavia dial the area code with the initial zero and the number.

To call Yugoslavia from Western Europe dial the international access code (which varies from country to country), 381 (the country code for Yugoslavia), the area code (without the initial zero) and the number. Yugoslavia's area codes include 011 (Belgrade), 021 (Novi Sad), 024 (Subotica), 029 (Prizren), 039 (Peć), 083 (Žabljak), 085 (Bar and Ulcinj), 086 (Budva and Cetinje) and 0871 (Rožaj).

TIME

Yugoslavia is one hour ahead of GMT/UTC. The country goes on summer time at the end of March when clocks are turned forward an hour. At the end of September they're turned back an hour.

ELECTRICITY

The electric voltage is 220 V AC, 50 Hz. Plugs are of the standard European two-pronged type.

WEIGHTS & MEASURES

Yugoslavia uses the metric system.

BOOKS & MAPS

Rebecca West's *Black Lamb & Grey Falcon* is a classic portrait of prewar Yugoslavia.

Former partisan leader (and regime ideologist until purged in 1954) Milovan Djilas has written many fascinating books about history and politics in Yugoslavia, most of them published in English translations. Any good library will have a couple of them. One of the best contemporary Serbian writers is Danilo Kiš.

A highly recommended recent (updated to July 1991) book on the region's current political upheaval is *Remaking the Balkans* by Christopher Cviic (Pinter Publishers, 25 Floral St, London WC2E 9DS). The precise background information contained in this slim volume offers a clear explanation of present events. *The Destruction of Yugoslavia* by Branka Magaš (Verso Publishers, London and New York) offers many insights on the period from the death of Tito in 1980 to the end of 1992.

MEDIA

Until publication was suspended in 1993 as a consequence of UN sanctions, the English-language *International Weekly* carried the best stories of the week from the Serbian daily *Politica*. Now the Monday issue of the Serbian edition of *Politica* carries a four-page supplement in English every other week. It's worth reading to get a glimpse of things from the Serbian perspective.

The *Review of International Affairs*, a magazine published 12 times a year, carries scholarly articles on the problems in ex-Yugoslavia. An annual subscription by surface mail costs US$25 from Nemanjina 34, Belgrade. The *Review*'s Belgrade office sells issue-oriented books in English (though most are out of date).

FILM & PHOTOGRAPHY

Bring all your own film, as that sold locally is expensive and unreliable. You're only allowed to bring five rolls per person, and because this isn't enforced, it's possible to distribute larger quantities through your luggage. Keep your camera stowed away while crossing the border and be careful about taking pictures of anything other than obvious tourist attractions, as you could arouse unwelcome curiosity. Taking photos from a train or bus is not advisable and photographing soldiers or military facilities will cause serious problems if you're caught. The funny little signs with a camera crossed out should be taken seriously.

HEALTH

The cost of medical treatment in Yugoslavia is very low and if you're covered at home by a regular health insurance plan which includes treatment abroad, special travel medical insurance is unnecessary and a waste of money. This could change if medical care is privatised but for now you can enjoy the benefits of socialised medicine.

DANGERS & ANNOYANCES

Belgrade is a remarkably safe city, even late at night. The seediest area is around the train station but even there there's no particular danger. Throughout Yugoslavia theft is rare.

Many Yugoslavs are chain smokers who can't imagine that anyone might be inconvenienced by their habit, so choose your seat in trains, restaurants, bars and other public places carefully. It's harder to avoid smokers on the bus than it is on the train.

If the subject turns to politics, it's best to listen to what the Yugoslavs say rather than tell them what you think, as nationalist passions can be unpredictable. It's striking the way Serbs who seem to be reasonable, nice people suddenly become tense and defensive as soon as the subject of Kosovo comes up.

If the police think you're a journalist or human rights activist you'll be taken to the station for questioning. In this case all your belongings will be searched and every piece of paper in your possession meticulously examined. As soon as it's established that you're only a tourist you'll be sent on your way with apologies, so just be patient and don't get worried or upset. This is unlikely to happen in Belgrade or along the Adriatic coast.

ACTIVITIES

Skiing

Serbia's largest ski centre is Kopaonik (2017 metres), south of Kraljevo, with 26 different runs covering a total of 54 km. Get there from Belgrade by taking a bus to Brus (246 km, five hours), then a local bus to the resort at Brzecé (18 km). Otherwise take a bus from Belgrade to Kruševac (194 km) and another from there to Brus (52 km). Kopaonik has a 150-bed youth hostel (☎ 037-833 176) with three, four and five-bedded rooms at US$15 per person, open year-round.

On the north side of the Šar Planina which separates Kosovo from Macedonia is Brezovica (1750 metres), Kosovo's major ski resort. Montenegro's main ski resort is at Žabljak. The season is roughly from December to March.

White-Water Rafting & Hiking

White-water rafting is sometimes offered on the Tara River in Montenegro's Durmitor National Park. Turn to Travel Agencies in the Belgrade section for a contact address. For high-altitude lakes and one of the world's deepest canyons, Durmitor can't be beaten. This is also a popular hiking area.

HIGHLIGHTS

Yugoslavia has a wealth of castles, such as Smederevo Castle on the Danube, Serbia's last medieval fortress. Petrovaradin Citadel at Novi Sad is one of Europe's great Baroque fortresses and Belgrade's Kalemegdan Citadel must be mentioned for its historic importance. At Kotor the Venetian city walls creep right up the mountainside behind the town. The old Montenegrin capital Cetinje will please romantics. Of the beach resorts, Budva is chic but Ulcinj has more atmosphere and is much cheaper.

ACCOMMODATION

Hotel prices are set in US dollars or Deutschmarks and you won't find many inexpensive hotels. Foreigners pay four to eight times as much as locals at the state-owned hotels. Food prices are the same for everyone, so at resort hotels compare the price of room with all meals against the price of a room only as it may only be a few dollars more.

In summer you can camp along the

Montenegrin coast; organised camping grounds are few and many of those that do exist are closed due to the absence of tourists. There's a youth hostel in Belgrade but it's far from the centre, overcrowded and over-priced. Other HI hostels exist at Kopaonik and Ulcinj (summer only). At last report the Novi Sad hostel was being used to house refugees. Youth hostel charges for foreigners are fixed in Deutschmarks and thus staying in hostels could be more expensive and often less convenient than taking a private room.

Private rooms are usually available along the coast but seldom inland. There are steep surcharges on private rooms if you stay less than three nights. If you plan to stay that long, Budva and Bar make good central bases from which to make side trips to Cetinje and Ulcinj.

An overnight bus or train can sometimes get you out of an accommodation jam. Book a sleeper or couchette on the train between Belgrade and Bar or buy a bus ticket with a seat reservation between Belgrade and Skopje/Ohrid as far ahead as possible. It will cost less than the cheapest hotel room and you'll reach your destination as well.

FOOD

The cheapest breakfast is Balkan *burek*, a greasy layered pie made with cheese *(sir)* or meat *(meso)* available everywhere. *Krompirusa* is potato burek. Food is cheaper in the interior than along the coast and national meat dishes can be very cheap in the Turkish-influenced areas.

Regional Dishes

Yugoslavia's regional cuisines range from spicy Hungarian goulash in Vojvodina to Turkish kebab in Serbia and Kosovo. A speciality of Vojvodina is *alaska čorba* (fiery river fish stew). In Montenegro try the pastoral fare such as boiled lamb or *kajmak* (cream from boiled milk which is salted and turned into cheese).

Serbia is famous for grilled meats such as *ćevapčići* (small patties of spiced, minced meat, grilled), *pljeskavica* (a large spicy hamburger steak) and *ražnjići* (a shish kebab

of chunks of pork or veal with onions and peppers grilled on a skewer). If you want to try them all at once, order a *mešano meso* (a mixed grill of pork cutlet, liver, sausage and minced meat patties with onions). Serbian *duveč* is grilled pork cutlets with spiced stewed peppers, zucchini and tomatoes in rice cooked in an oven – delicious.

Other popular dishes are *musaka* (aubergine and potato baked in layers with minced meat), *sarma* (cabbage stuffed with minced meat and rice), *kapama* (stewed lamb, onions and spinach served with yoghurt), *punjena tikvica* (zucchini stuffed with minced meat and rice) and peppers stuffed with minced meat, rice and spices, cooked in tomato sauce.

Most traditional Yugoslav dishes are based on meat so vegetarians will have problems, though every restaurant menu will include a Serbian salad *(Srpska salata)* of raw peppers, onions and tomatoes, seasoned with oil, vinegar and chilli. Also ask for *gibanica* (a layered cheese pie) and *zeljanica* (cheese pie with spinach).

DRINKS

Beer is always available. Nikšićko pivo brewed at Nikšić in Montenegro is terribly good when imbibed ice-cold at the beach on a hot summer day. Its taste is far richer than that of the Bip beer served around Belgrade.

Yugoslav cognac (grape brandy) is called Vinjak. Coffee is usually served Turkish-style, boiled in a small individual pot, 'black as hell, strong as death and sweet as love'.

Getting There & Away

AIR

JAT Yugoslav Airlines used to operate flights from Belgrade to cities around the world, but since the UN sanctions took effect in June 1992 all international flights have been cancelled.

Departure Tax

In principle, the airport departure tax on

YUGOSLAVIA

international flights is US$7 (though no flights are operating) and US$2 on domestic flights.

LAND

Train

Only buy a ticket as far as your first stop in Yugoslavia, as domestic fares are much cheaper than international fares. Consider breaking your journey in Subotica, Niš or Skopje for this purpose alone. A student card will get you a reduction on train fares from Yugoslavia to other Eastern European countries.

All the international 'name trains' mentioned here run daily all year unless otherwise stated.

To/From Hungary & Beyond All trains between Western Europe and Belgrade run via Budapest, Subotica and Novi Sad. About six trains a day cover the 354 km between Budapest and Belgrade (six hours, US$28). The *Avala* and *Beograd* express trains originate in Vienna, the *Skopje Istanbul* in Munich, the *Balkán* in Warsaw and Istanbul and the *Meridian* in Berlin and Sofia. Belgrade is 11 hours from Vienna (627 km) and 17 hours from Munich (US$95). Reservations are usually required on these trains.

An unreserved local train runs between Szeged and Subotica three times a day (45 km, 1½ hours, US$2).

To/From Croatia In mid-1991 all rail and road links between Croatia and Serbia were cut, making it necessary to do a loop through Hungary to travel from Zagreb to Belgrade. You can take a direct train from Zagreb to Budapest (US$26), then change to another train to Belgrade (US$28). Otherwise take the daily train from Zagreb to Pécs, a bus from Pécs to Szeged and a train from Szeged to Subotica in Vojvodina. You would have to spend at least one night somewhere along the way. See also the Harkány section in the Hungary chapter.

To/From Romania From Romania the overnight *Bucureşti* express train runs between Bucharest and Belgrade-Dunav (693 km, 13 hours, US$44) via Timişoara. Reservations are required. Two daily unreserved local trains on this route connect Timişoara to Vršac (76 km).

Apart from this, there's an unreserved local train from Jimbolia, Romania, to Kikinda, Yugoslavia, twice a day (19 km). From Kikinda there are four local trains a day to Pančevo Glavna Station (161 km, 3½ hours), with hourly trains from there to Belgrade (23 km, 30 minutes). Four daily trains run between Jimbolia and Timişoara (39 km, one hour).

To/From Bulgaria & Turkey The most reliable service to/from Bulgaria is the *Meridian* express train from Sofia to Berlin via Niš, Belgrade, Novi Sad and Budapest. If bound for Bulgaria you can board this overnight train in Novi Sad. Reservations are not required.

There's also the *Istanbul* express train between Istanbul and Munich via Sofia, Belgrade, Vienna and Salzburg, and the *Balkan* express from Budapest to Istanbul via Belgrade and Sofia. From Belgrade it's nine hours to Sofia (417 km, US$16) and 26 hours to Istanbul (1051 km). This train runs four times a week and reservations are required.

To/From Greece The southern main line between Belgrade and Athens (1267 km, 22 hours) is through Skopje and Thessaloniki, with two trains a day. Reservations are not required.

Car & Motorbike

Following are the main highway entry/exit points clockwise around Yugoslavia with the Yugoslav border post named.

To/From Hungary There are crossings at Bački Breg (32 km south of Baja), Kelebija (11 km north-west of Subotica) and Horgoš (between Szeged and Subotica).

To/From Romania You may cross at Sprska Crnja (45 km west of Timişoara), Vatin (between Timişoara and Belgrade),

Kaluđerovo (120 km east of Belgrade) and Kladovo (10 km west of Drobeta-Turnu Severin).

To/From Bulgaria You have a choice of Negotin (29 km north-west of Vidin), Zaječar (45 km south-west of Vidin), Gradina (at Dimitrovgrad between Sofia and Niš) and Klisura (66 km west of Pernik).

To/From Macedonia You can cross at Preševo (10 km north of Kumanovo) and Đeneral Janković (between Uroševac and Skopje).

To/From Albania There are crossings at Vrbnica (18 km south-west of Prizren) and Božaj (24 km south-east of Podgorica).

SEA

In normal times a ferry service operates between Bari (Italy), and Bar in Montenegro. Until UN sanctions are lifted, this service is cancelled.

Getting Around

AIR

JAT domestic flights operate from Belgrade to Tivat four to six times daily and to Podgorica twice daily, both US$25 one way, plus US$2 airport tax. These flights are heavily booked.

Only 15 kg of checked baggage is allowed on domestic flights. JAT runs inexpensive buses to the airports from city centres.

BUS

Though present Yugoslavia depends on railways far more than the other four countries of ex-Yugoslavia, there are also many buses. You'll depend on buses to travel along the Montenegrin coast from Bar to Budva and Ulcinj, to go from Montenegro to Kosovo and to get to Durmitor National Park and the monasteries of southern Serbia. On the long hauls, overnight buses can be exhausting but they do save you time and money.

As a result of petrol shortages resulting from UN sanctions, bus services have been sharply reduced and those buses that do exist often run late. This is especially a problem in Montenegro where buses are essential for getting around.

TRAIN

The Jugoslovenske Železnice (JŽ) provides adequate railway service along the interior main line from Subotica to Novi Sad, Belgrade, Niš, Priština and Skopje and there's a highly scenic line from Belgrade down to the coast at Bar, especially between Kolašin and Bar. There are four classes of train: *ekspresni* (express), *poslovni* (rapid), *brzi* (fast) and *putnicki* (slow). Make sure you have the right sort of ticket for your train.

Overnight trains from Belgrade to Bar, Peć and Skopje all have couchettes which cost US$4.50 in 2nd class in a three-bed compartment, US$3.50 in a four-bed compartment, US$2.50 in a six-bed compartment; 1st-class sleepers are US$7. Train tickets are also inexpensive, with the Belgrade-Bar journey costing US$4.50 2nd class, US$5.50 1st class (524 km, 7½ hours).

The train is cheaper than the bus, you don't have to pay for luggage and it's also more comfortable. It's usually only possible to make seat reservations in the train's originating station unless reservations are mandatory, in which case try to book the day before. Most trains have 'no smoking' compartments. Inter-Rail passes are valid in Yugoslavia, but Eurail passes are not.

All train stations (except in Kosovo) have left-luggage offices where you can dump your bag (passport required).

CAR & MOTORBIKE

Yugoslavia's motorways *(autoput)* run south-east through Belgrade, Niš and Skopje towards Greece. Yugoslavs pay low tolls in dinars but foreign-registered vehicles must pay much higher prices in Deutschmarks: US$10 from the Hungarian border to Belgrade and US$40 from Belgrade to the Bulgarian border. Toll charges are posted at the motorway exit, not at the entrance. All other roads are free and, with a little time and planning, you can avoid the motorways.

Speed limits for private cars and motorcycles are 120 km/h on motorways, 100 km/h on 1st-class roads, 80 km/h on 2nd-class roads and 60 km/h in built-up areas.

Members of foreign automobile clubs get a reduced rate on towing services provided by the Automoto Savez Jugoslavije (AMSJ). It has branches in almost every town with repair facilities available. Call ☎ 987 for AMSJ emergency assistance.

Petrol is available in regular (86 octane), super (98 octane) and unleaded or *bezolovni* (95 octane). There are no petrol coupons but tremendous queues form at government-owned Jugopetrol and Beopetrol stations which sell fuel at artificially low rates. Avoid this by asking another motorist for the location of a private petrol station *(privatna benzinska pumpa)* where prices are higher but the lines shorter. UN sanctions have led to serious petrol shortages.

This is not the best time to drive around Yugoslavia. Although all borders are open except the one with Croatia and the large towns and the coast are quiet, there's a lot of paranoia and if you ventured into a sensitive area and didn't have a good reason for being there when stopped by the police, there could be trouble. Travelling by bus or train you'll be less conspicuous.

LOCAL TRANSPORT

Public-transport strip tickets or tokens are available from newsstands in Belgrade. Punch your ticket as you board the vehicle. If you pay a city bus or tram driver directly it will be about double the fare.

Vojvodina

Vojvodina (21,506 sq km) was an 'autonomous province' until 1990 when Serbia scrapped this arrangement and annexed Vojvodina to the Republic of Serbia. Slavs settled here in the 6th century, followed by Hungarians in the 10th century. Vojvodina

became depopulated after the 16th century Turkish conquest, but when the Habsburgs drove back the Turks in the late 17th century the region reverted to Hungary, where it was to remain until 1918.

In the 18th century many Serbs fled to this Hungarian-controlled area to escape Ottoman rule in the lands farther south, and today ethnic Serbs make up most of the population. Minorities include Hungarians (24%), Croats (8%), Slovaks (4%) and Romanians (3%). Some 170,000 ethnic Germans were expelled from Vojvodina after WW II and large numbers of Serbs immigrated here to occupy the areas they formerly inhabited. As a result, the percentage of Serbs in the total population of Vojvodina increased from 37% in 1921 to 57.2% in 1991.

Until Serbian nationalists took control of the Vojvodina government in October 1988, the province's 345,000 Hungarians had fared better than Hungarian minorities in Romania and Slovakia, but since then they have come under increasing pressure. In July 1991 the Serbian parliament required all public signs to be written in Cyrillic, and teaching in Hungarian is being phased out in the schools. Some 25,000 Hungarians have fled to Hungary to escape war propaganda and forced mobilisation, and as they left the Serbian government resettled some of the 140,000 Serbian refugees in Vojvodina in their homes. The 100,000 Croats of Bačka in northern Vojvodina are also suffering extreme repression as the Serbian government attempts to force them to leave.

This low-lying land of many rivers merges imperceptibly into the Great Hungarian Plain and Romania's Banat. The Tisa River cuts south across the middle of the region, joining the Danube midway between Novi Sad and Belgrade. The Sava and Danube rivers mark Vojvodina's southern boundary with Serbia, while to the west the Danube also separates Vojvodina from Croatia. Numerous canals crisscross this fertile plain which provides much of Yugoslavia's wheat and corn. Most of Yugoslavia's crude oil comes from wells here. Vojvodina's two hilly regions are the Fruška gora just south of Novi Sad, which reaches 539 metres at Crveni čot, now a national park, and a 641-metre hill between Vršac and the Romanian border.

SUBOTICA (СУБОТИЦА)

Subotica, Vojvodina's second city, is a large Hungarian-speaking city 10 km from the Hungarian border. Over half the 180,000 inhabitants are of Hungarian origin and another quarter are Croats. Subotica serves as a useful transit point to/from Szeged, Hungary, and the train station is just a short walk from the centre of town.

The left-luggage office at the train station is open 24 hours (passport required). You pay when you collect your luggage later (useful to know if you've just arrived from Hungary and haven't had a chance to change money).

Information

Putnik (☎ 25 400), Borisa Kidriča 4, is helpful with information and sells train tickets. Subotica's telephone code is 024.

Money The Vojvođanska Banka has an exchange office in the old town hall (weekdays 7 am to 7.30 pm, Saturday 7 am to 1.30 pm). It's much faster to change your money with one of the men on the street outside or below the town hall tower nearby.

Things to See

The Art-Nouveau **town hall** (1910) contains an excellent **historical museum** (closed Sunday and Monday) on the 1st floor (captions in Serbian and Hungarian). Entry to the museum is through the rear entrance to the town hall. Check to see if the exquisitely decorated council chambers on the same floor as the museum are open.

Places to Stay & Eat

The only hotel is the seven-storey, B-category *Hotel Patria* (☎ 26 312), on Đure Đakovića, three blocks from the train station. Singles/doubles are US$22/36 with bath and breakfast.

Stara Pizzeria, Engelsova 7 off Borisa Kidriča, is a good choice for eating out.

Palić Palić, eight km east of Subotica on the railway line to Szeged, is the city's recreation centre with a zoo, lake, sporting facilities, restaurants and pleasant walks. The attractive park was laid out in 1912 and the pointed water tower is visible from the train.

There are three hotels at Palić. The best is the *Park* near the train station. The *Jezero* is also near the station, but the less expensive *Sport* is close to the camping ground, a 10-minute walk away. In winter only the Park will be open. The train to/from Szeged stops near these hotels and you can also get there on bus No 6 from the main bus station near Hotel Patria in Subotica.

Getting There & Away

There are three local trains a day to/from Szeged, Hungary (45 km, 1½ hours, US$2). Several daily buses also shuttle between Szeged and Subotica (US$2.50), but the train is more convenient. A daily bus links Subotica to Budapest (216 km, US$9).

Three express trains a day run north to Budapest (274 km, six hours) and there are 12 trains a day to Novi Sad (99 km, two hours).

NOVI SAD (НОВИ САД)

Novi Sad (Neusatz), capital of Vojvodina, is a friendly, modern city at a strategic bend of the Danube. The city developed in the 18th century when a powerful fortress was built on a hill top overlooking the river to hold the area for the Habsburgs. Novi Sad remained part of the Austro-Hungarian empire until 1918 and it still has a Hungarian air about it today. The main sights can be covered in a couple of hours or you can make a leisurely day of it.

Orientation & Information

The adjacent train and bus stations are at the end of Bulevar Oslobođenja, several km north-west of the city centre. The people at the Turistička Agencija Žeta, to the right as

Novi Sad

0   200   400 m

To Railway Station

To Youth Hostel

To Autocamp

1 Market/City Bus Station
2 Tourist Office
3 Vojvodanski Museum
4 Museum of the Revolution
5 Trg slobode
6 Serbian National Theatre
7 Putnik Travel Agency
8 Hotel Vojvodina
9 Main Post Office
10 Art Galleries
11 Ferijalni Savez Novog Sada
12 Administration Building
13 Petrovaradin Citadel

you come out of the train station, are helpful with information.

Catch bus No 4 (enter through the rear doors and pay the conductor) from the train station to Bulevar Mihajla Pupina, then ask directions to the tourist office at Dunavska 27, in a quaint old part of town. This office has brochures on many parts of Yugoslavia besides Novi Sad.

The Automoto Klub Vojvodine is at Arse Teodorovića 15 off Pap Pavla.

Post & Telecommunications The telephone centre next to the main post office in the centre is open 24 hours.

The telephone code for Novi Sad is 021.

Travel Agencies Putnik (☎ 29 210), Kraja Aleksandra 8 just off Trg slobode, sells train tickets.

Things to See

There are three **museums** on Dunavska near the tourist office: paintings at No 29 (closed Monday and Tuesday), archaeology at No 35 (closed Monday) and the history of the 1941-45 revolution at No 37. The latter museum is very close to the Danube. Officially, the

Museum of the Revolution is closed for rearrangement but the old exhibits are still in place and the staff will let you see them if you say you're especially interested in Yugoslavia's WW II history.

Walk across the old bridge to majestic **Petrovaradin Citadel** (built 1699-1780), the 'Gibraltar of the Danube', designed by the French architect Vauban. The stairs beside the large church in the lower town lead up to the fortress. Today the citadel contains an expensive hotel, restaurant and two small museums (closed Monday), but the chief pleasure is simply to walk along the walls enjoying the splendid free view of the city, river and surrounding countryside. There are up to 16 km of underground galleries and halls below the citadel, but these can only be visited by groups.

Other sights of Novi Sad include three substantial **art galleries** (closed Monday and Tuesday) side by side on Vase Stajića, not far from trg Sobode, and the ultramodern **Serbian National Theatre** (1981), also close by.

Places to Stay
Camping There's a large *Autocamp* (☎ 368

400) near the Danube at Ribarsko Ostrvo, with bungalows (US$29/30/42 single/double/triple) available all year. Bus No 4 runs frequently from the train station to Liman via the city centre. From the end of the line walk two km towards the river. If you walk all the way from the centre of town, it will take one hour.

Hostels If you arrive during business hours, visit Ferijalni Savez Novog Sada (☎ 25 339), Mihajla Pupina 19. The staff here will know if the HI hostel at Donji put 79, on the south side of the river, has reopened (at last report the building was occupied by refugees). Even if the hostel is still closed the staff will do their best to find some other inexpensive place for you to stay.

Hotel Subotica's oldest hotel, the *Vojvodina* (☎ 622 122), trg Slobode 2, looks run-down on the outside but the interior was renovated in 1980. The 62 rooms with private bath are US$12/18 single/double, breakfast included. Noise from the restaurant downstairs can be heard in the rooms.

Places to Eat

The *Atina Restaurant* next to the large church on trg Slobode has a self-service section for a quick lunch and a full-service restaurant at the back. It's nothing special but at least there's a menu with prices clearly listed (avoid the pizza).

The *Sloboda Express Grill* on Modene in the centre is cheap but it's hard to order as you must pay first and no menu is posted.

Getting There & Away

Novi Sad is on the main railway line between Belgrade, Budapest and Sofia. In the evening you can easily pick up the overnight *Meridian* express train to Sofia (485 km, 12 hours). Trains to Subotica (99 km, two hours) and Belgrade (80 km, 1½ hours) run every two hours.

Serbia (Србија)

The dominant role of Serbia (Srbija) in the former Yugoslav Federation was suggested by the inclusion within its boundaries of two formerly 'autonomous provinces', Vojvodina and Kosovo, and the national capital, Belgrade. At 88,361 sq km it's by far the largest of Yugoslavia's six former republics, though if you subtract the area of the two former provinces it's only 55,968 sq km, slightly smaller than 56,538-sq-km Croatia. Northern Serbia along the Danube is an extension of the lowland plains of Hungary, while the mountainous centre and south merge into Montenegro, Kosovo, Macedonia and Bulgaria.

BELGRADE (БЕОГРАД)

Belgrade (Beograd) is strategically situated on the southern edge of the Carpathian basin where the Sava River joins the Danube. Just east of the city is the Morava Valley, route of the famous 'Stamboul Road' from Turkey to Central Europe. At this major crossroads a city developed which has long been the flash point of the Balkans. It might be an interesting place to look around for a few days if most accommodation weren't so absurdly expensive.

Until WW I Belgrade was right on the border of Serbia and Austria-Hungary and its citadel has seen many battles. Destroyed and rebuilt 40 times in its 2300-year history, Belgrade has never managed to pick up all the pieces. As well swarms of polluting vehicles and transiting travellers will test your nerves. Do your business, have a look around, and move on.

History

The Celtic settlement of Singidunum was founded in the 3rd century BC on a bluff overlooking the confluence of the Sava and Danube rivers. The Romans arrived in the 1st century AD and stayed till the 5th century. The present Slavic name Beograd ('White City') first appeared in a papal letter dated

Belgrade (Beograd)

Map legend:

1. Grand Hotel Zemun
2. Contemporary Art Museum
3. Kalemegdan Citadel
4. Terazije
5. Beograd-Dunav Railway Station
6. Automoto Savez Jugoslavije
7. Hungarian Consulate
8. Main Railway Station
9. Novi Beograd Railway Station
10. Hippodrome
11. Grave of Marshal Tito
12. Autocamp Košutnjak
13. Topčider Railway Station
14. 'Mladost' Hotel

16 April 878. Belgrade became the capital of Serbia in 1403, as the Serbs were pushed north by the Turks. In 1456 the Hungarians under János Hunyadi succeeded in defeating a Turkish advance in this direction but in 1521 the Turks finally took Belgrade. In 1842 the city again became the capital of Serbia and in 1918, the capital of all Yugoslavia. In April 1941, 17,000 lives were lost in a Nazi bombing raid on Belgrade. Soon after, on 4 July 1941, Tito and the Communist Party's Central Committee meeting at Belgrade decided to launch an armed uprising. Since Belgrade was liberated on 20

October 1944, the population has grown sixfold to over a million and a half.

Orientation

You'll probably arrive at the train station on the south side of the city centre or at the adjacent bus station. The left-luggage office at the train station (open 24 hours) is just past the kiosks at the end of track No 9. The left-luggage room at the bus station is open from 6 am to 10 pm. Putnik Garderoba across the street from the train station opens from 6 am to 9 pm. A passport is required at all of these. Allow plenty of time to pick up your

YUGOSLAVIA

bag. For information on other facilities at the train station see Getting There & Away at the end of this section.

To walk into town from the station, go along Milovanovića east a block, then straight up Balkanska to Terazije, the heart of modern Belgrade. Kneza Mihaila, Belgrade's lively pedestrian boulevard, runs north-west through Stari Grad (the old town) from Terazije to Kalemegdan Park, where you'll find the citadel. The crowds are surprisingly chic, but notice the vendors selling fascist-style emblems, books and even cassette recordings of patriotic music designed to arouse base instincts.

Information

The friendly, helpful tourist office (☎ 635 622), open weekdays from 9 am to 8 pm, Saturday 9 am to 4 pm, is in the underpass below Jugoslovenska Knjiga bookshop at the beginning of Terazije, on the corner of Kneza Mihaila. (Note the public toilets down there for future reference.) There's also a tourist office at the airport open daily from 7 am to 11 pm.

Information on HI youth hostels around Yugoslavia is available from Ferijalni Savez Jugoslavije, Moše Pijade 12, 3rd floor.

Motorists are assisted by the English-speaking staff at the special Informativni Centar around the corner from the Automoto Savez Jugoslavije (☎ 419 822), Ruzveltova 18, a little south-east of Tašmajdan Park.

Money The JIK Banka is across the park in front of the station (open from 8 am to 8 pm weekdays, and from 8 am to 3 pm Saturday). The exchange window in the train station gives a poor rate.

There are four private exchange offices in the street-level shopping arcade at Kolarčeva 7 very near the tourist office on Terazije (open weekdays from 9 am to 9 pm, Saturday 9 am to 5 pm). They offer something approaching the black-market rate for cash only. The Red Star Exchange kiosk on Balkanska directly behind Hotel Moskva gives a slightly lower rate.

Black marketeers patrol the pavement between the bus and train stations and Terazije near Hotel Moskva.

Post & Telecommunications The main post office, Takovska 2, holds poste restante mail at window No 2 for one month. International telephone calls can be placed from here from 7 am to 10 pm daily. This is the only place you can send a fax (one page to the USA or Australia costs US$4). A more convenient telephone centre (open 24 hours a day) is in the post office at Zmaj Jovina 17 in the centre of town.

The telephone centre in the large post office on the right (south) side of the train station opens weekdays from 7 am to midnight, weekends from 7 am to 10 pm.

The telephone code for Belgrade is 011.

Foreign Embassies Most of the consulates and embassies are on or near Kneza Miloša, a 10-minute walk south-east from the train station (visas payable in cash, hard currency only). The Polish Consulate is at Kneza Miloša 38 (weekdays from 8 am to noon, visas US$40 for same-day service, US$25 with a three-day wait). The American Embassy (☎ 645 655) is at Kneza Miloša 50. The Albanian Embassy (☎ 646 864) is at Kneza Miloša 56 (weekdays 9 am to 1 pm). The Romanian Consulate is at Kneza Miloša 70 (weekdays from 9 am to 1 pm, visas US$31, issued on the spot). The Canadian Embassy (☎ 644 666) is at Kneza Miloša 75. (Note the tremendous queues of Yugoslavs applying for visas at the US and Canadian embassies – an indication of this country's disastrous economic situation.)

The UK Embassy (☎ 645 034 or 645 055) is at Generala Ždanova 46. The Bulgarian Consulate is at Birčaninova 26 (weekdays from 9 am to noon, visas cost US$30 with a one-week wait or US$45 for same-day service). The Hungarian Consulate, Ivana Milutinovića 74 (weekdays from 9 am to noon, visas US$20), is a few blocks east, while the Czech Republic Consulate, Bulevar Revolucije 22 (weekdays from 9 am to noon), is near the main post office. The Australian Embassy (☎ 624 655) is conve-

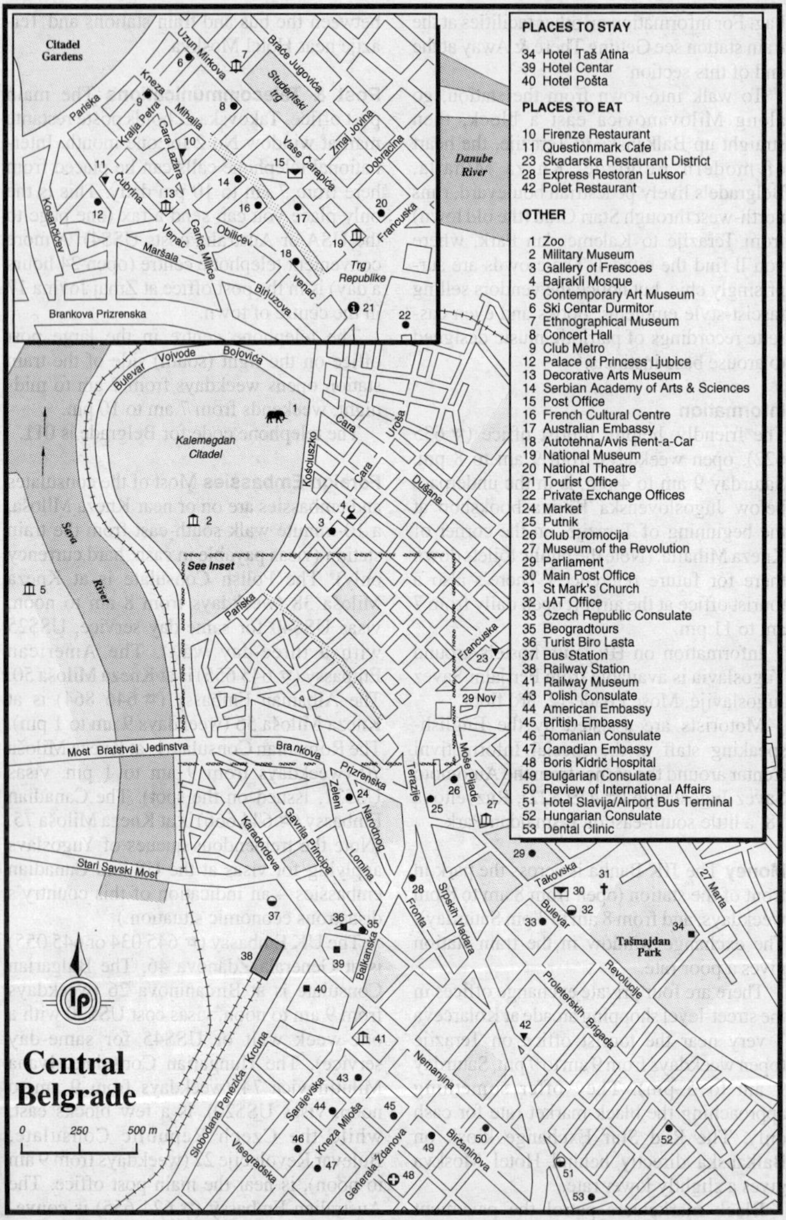

PLACES TO STAY
34 Hotel Taš Atina
39 Hotel Centar
40 Hotel Pošta
PLACES TO EAT
10 Firenze Restaurant
11 Questionmark Cafe
23 Skadarska Restaurant District
28 Express Restoran Luksor
42 Polet Restaurant
OTHER
1 Zoo
2 Military Museum
3 Gallery of Frescoes
4 Bajrakli Mosque
5 Contemporary Art Museum
6 Ski Centar Durmitor
7 Ethnographical Museum
8 Concert Hall
9 Club Metro
12 Palace of Princess Ljubice
13 Decorative Arts Museum
14 Serbian Academy of Arts & Sciences
15 Post Office
16 French Cultural Centre
17 Australian Embassy
18 Autotehna/Avis Rent-a-Car
19 National Museum
20 National Theatre
21 Tourist Office
22 Private Exchange Offices
24 Market
25 Putnik
26 Club Promocija
27 Museum of the Revolution
29 Parliament
30 Main Post Office
31 St Mark's Church
32 JAT Office
33 Czech Republic Consulate
35 Beogradtours
36 Turist Biro Lasta
37 Bus Station
38 Railway Station
41 Railway Museum
43 Polish Consulate
44 American Embassy
45 British Embassy
46 Romanian Consulate
47 Canadian Embassy
48 Boris Kidrič Hospital
49 Bulgarian Consulate
50 Review of International Affairs
51 Hotel Slavija/Airport Bus Terminal
52 Hungarian Consulate
53 Dental Clinic
Citadel Gardens
Uzun Mirkova
Braće Jugovića
Studentski trg
Kneza Mihaila
Pariska
Kralja Petra
Cara Lazara
Zmaj Jovina
Vase Čarapića
Dobračina
Cubrina
Kosančićev
Venac
Maršala
Carice Milice
Obilićev
Francuska
Trg Republike
Venac
Birjuzova
Brankova Prizrenska
Danube River
Bulevar Vojvode Bojovića
Kalemegdan Citadel
Cara Uroša
Kosciuszko
Cara Dušana
Sava River
See Inset
Pariska
Francuska
29 Nov
Most Bratstvai Jedinstva
Brankova
Prizrenska
Terazije
Moše Pijade
Zeleni
Narodnog
Karađorđeva
Gavrila Principa
Lomina
Stari Savski Most
Takovska
27 Marta
Fronta
Srpskih Vladara
Bulevar
Revolucije
Tašmajdan Park
Balkanska
Proleterskih Brigada
Nemanjina
Birčaninova
Sarajevska
Kneza Miloša
Slobodana Penezića - Krcuna
Generala Ždanova
Višegradska
Central Belgrade
0 250 500 m

niently located at Čika Ljubina 13 in Stari Grad. The Slovak Consulate (☎ 222 2432) is at Bulevar Umetnosti 18, far away in Novi Beograd.

Travel Agencies Until 1992 American Express was represented by Atlas Tours, Kosovska 8, 6th floor, but although the office is still there they can no longer provide any American Express services nor cash travellers' cheques.

Ski Centar Durmitor, Uzin Mirkova 7, has information on white-water rafting, skiing and hiking in Montenegro's Durmitor National Park.

Basturist, the office with the JAT sign in the window between the bus and train stations, sells tickets for international buses, daily to Vienna (US$40) and Munich (US$82), and weekly to Lyon (US$84), Paris (US$114), Stockholm (US$174) and Zürich (US$98).

Turist Biro Lasta on Milovanovića and the adjacent Putnik office sell international bus tickets to Ljubljana, Munich, Stuttgart, Frankfurt, Paris, Copenhagen and other cities.

Beogradtours, Milovanovića 5, a block up the hill from the train station, will book couchettes and sleepers and offers ISIC student-card holders discounted international train tickets to other Eastern European countries (but not Greece). The English-speaking staff provide reliable train information and sell tickets at the same prices charged in the station, but without the crowds.

Putnik Travel Agency, Terazije 27, also sells train tickets and makes advance reservations. International tickets can be purchased here with Yugoslav dinars.

Laundry The dry cleaners at Generala Ždanova 6 just off Bulevar Revolucije (weekdays 7 am to 8 pm, Saturday 8 am to 3 pm) can do your laundry in 24 hours but they charge per piece.

Emergency The Boris Kidrič Hospital, Pasterova 1, has a special clinic for foreigners open Tuesday to Saturday from 7 am to 1 pm (consultations US$3). It's also possible to consult the doctors in the regular clinic here until 7 pm daily. At other times go to the Klinički Centar, Pasterova 2, which is open 24 hours.

A dental clinic for foreigners is at Ivana Milutinovića 15 behind the Slavija Hotel (daily 7 am to 7 pm).

Things to See & Do
From the train station take tram No 1, 2 or 13 north-west to **Kalemegdan Citadel**, a strategic hill-top fortress at the junction of the Sava and Danube rivers. This area has been fortified since Celtic times and the Roman settlement of Singidunum was on the flood plain at the foot of the citadel. Much of what is seen today dates from the 17th century, including medieval gates, Orthodox churches, Muslim tombs and Turkish baths. Ivan Meštrović's *Monument of Gratitude to France* (1930) is at the citadel's entrance and on the ramparts overlooking the rivers stands his 1928 statue *The Winner*. The large **Military Museum** on the battlements of the citadel presents a complete history of Yugoslavia in 53 rooms. The benches in the park around the citadel are relaxing and on summer evenings lots of people come strolling here.

Next to Kalemegdan Citadel is Stari Grad, the oldest part of Belgrade. The best museums are here, especially the **National Museum**, Trg Republike, which has archaeological exhibits downstairs, paintings upstairs. The collection of European art is quite good. A few blocks away at Studentski trg 13 is the **Ethnographical Museum**, with an excellent collection of Serbian costumes and folk art. Detailed explanations are provided in English. Not far away is the **Gallery of Frescoes**, Cara Uroša 20, with full-size replicas of paintings in remote churches of Serbia and Macedonia. Belgrade's most memorable museum is the **Palace of Princess Ljubice**, on the corner of Svetozara Markovića and 7 jula, an authentic Balkan-style palace (1831) complete with period furnishings.

Among the things to see in the modern city

east of Terazije is the **Museum of the Revolution**, Trg Nikole Pašića 11, one of the last surviving communist-era political museums in Eastern Europe. This alone makes it a curiosity of the first order. The imposing edifice just east of this museum is **Skupština**, the Yugoslav parliament (built 1907-32). East again behind the main post office is **St Mark's Serbian Orthodox Church** (built in 1932-39), with four tremendous pillars supporting a towering dome. There's a small Russian Orthodox church behind it.

If you'd like to visit the white marble **grave of Marshal Tito** (open from 9 am to 4 pm), it's within the grounds of his former residence on Bulevar Mira a few km south of the city centre (take trolleybus No 40 or 41 south from Kneza Miloša 64). This tomb and all of the museums are closed on Monday.

Escape the bustle of Belgrade on **Ada Ciganlija**, an island park in the Sava River just upstream from the city. In summer you can swim in the river (naturists walk a km upstream from the others), rent a bicycle or just stroll among the trees. Many small cafés overlooking the beach dispense cold beer at reasonable rates.

Places to Stay

Accommodation in Belgrade is very expensive, with most places in the budget category both inconvenient and overpriced. Try to arrange an early morning arrival and a late evening departure.

Camping *Autocamp Košutnjak* (☎ 555 127), Kneza Višeslava 17, is about eight km south-west of the city centre. Camping is possible from May to September only, but there are expensive new bungalows open all year (US$30 per person with private bath). The older, cheaper bungalows are permanently occupied by locals. It's a fairly pleasant wooded site with lots of shade, but pitch your tent far from the noisy restaurant. To get there take tram No 12 or 13 south from beside the train station to Kneza Višeslava, the next stop after you see the horse-racing

track (hippodrome) on the left. From the tram stop it's a km up the hill.

Hostels Belgrade's HI youth hostel is the *'Mladost' Hotel* (☎ 237 2560), a modern three-storey building opposite Bulevar JNA 253 on the south side of the city. At US$15 for a bed in a six-bed dorm it's expensive but breakfast is included. A YHA card is not required. Individual rooms are US$46/64 single/double. It's open all day (check in from noon) and there's no curfew or rules. From Beograd-Dunav Railway Station take bus No 47 directly to the hostel. From the main train station take tram No 9 from outside the station to Vojvode Stepe 274, then walk back to Vojvode Stepe 266, turn left and go straight ahead.

Private Rooms Turist Biro Lasta (☎ 641 251), closed Sunday, on Milovanovića below the Astorija Hotel in front of the station, sometimes has private rooms at US$7 per person but this cannot be relied upon. There are only two single rooms, for example, and neither is in the city centre. If the person delegated to rent private rooms doesn't happen to be in the office no private rooms will be rented. Also, they won't reserve private rooms for future return visits. You must take your chances, which aren't good. If you're lucky, someone on the street outside Lasta will offer you an unofficial private room.

Hotels Belgrade is full of state-owned B-category hotels charging US$45/65 single/double and up (locals only pay a fraction of that). The only privately owned B-category hotel to appear so far is the *Hotel Taš Atina* (☎ 343 507), Beogradska 71, and here everyone pays the same: US$7/11 single/double. The Taš Atina has only one single room and 18 doubles, and it's often full (and occasionally noisy). Take tram No 12 from the train station to the end of the line, then walk across the park.

The next cheapest place is the *Hotel Centar* (☎ 644 055), Savski trg 7 opposite the train station. It's US$13 per person in a four-bed dorm, US$16 per person in a double room with bath. The only advantage of having to pay more than twice as much as a local is that they won't put a local in the room with you, which means you'll probably have it to yourself. This place is usually full.

The shabby *Hotel Pošta* (☎ 642 046), Slobodana Penezića-Krcuna 3 right beside the train station, charges foreigners US$25 per person – eight times more that Yugoslavs. The 24-hour traffic roar outside is a big problem.

A Valuable Tip Save a day's travelling time, a night's hotel bill and a lot of aggravation by booking a sleeper or couchette out of Belgrade at the train station. This is easily done and costs only around US$7. Just try getting a room for that! There are overnight trains to Bar, Skopje and Peć. If you arrive in Belgrade in the morning, you'll have all day to look around before boarding the train late that evening and the main sights can be seen in a busy day. Don't forget that a train ticket is required in addition to the couchette ticket.

If for some reason you can't get a couchette, consider an overnight bus with a seat reservation to your next destination. It's cheaper than the train and advance tickets are easily purchased at the bus station, but it's much more tiring.

Places to Eat
A great breakfast place near the train station is the burek counter at Nemanjina 5 just below Hotel Beograd (open weekdays from 5 am to 1 pm, Saturday from 5 to 11 am). Avoid the food kiosks right opposite the train station as they overcharge.

Expres Restoran Luksor, Balkanska 7 on the street leading up from the train station to Hotel Moskva, is the cheapest self-service in town.

Just up from Luksor is the *Lesnja Bašta Moskva*, Balkanska 5, where grilled meats are served on a pleasant terrace in summer. There's always a line at the adjacent *Leskovac* takeaway window where authentic Balkan-style hamburgers are sold.

The *Boulangerie et Café Français*, Terazije 4 near the tourist office, is perfect for a cappuccino with croissants.

For inexpensive seafood try the *Polet Restaurant*, Njegoševa 1. The attractive maritime décor is designed to resemble the interior of a large ship. The menu is only in Serbian but all prices are clearly listed. On weekdays from 1 to 6 pm there's a special set menu of spicy fish soup (čorba), salad, bread, main dish of fish and vegetables. The portions are large and the service good – recommended.

Vegetarians and all those who appreciate great pizza and pasta will love *Firenze*, Cara Lazara 11. The prices are reasonable for such a smart place and it's so popular you may not get a table. The beer is expensive so order a bottle of wine instead. All prices are clearly listed on the Italian menu – recommended.

The *Questionmark Cafe*, Kralja Petra 6 opposite the Orthodox church, is in an old Balkan inn with an English/German menu, traditional meat dishes, side salads and flat draught beer.

For local colour, try the more expensive folkloric restaurants near the fountain on ulica Skadarska, a street full of summer strollers. In the evening, open-air folkloric, musical and theatrical performances are often staged here.

Entertainment
During the winter season opera performances take place at the elegant *National Theatre* (1869) on Trg Republike. Their box office opens from 10 am to 1 pm Tuesday to Sunday and from 3 pm onwards on days of performances. The Yugoslavs aren't pretentious about theatre dress and jeans are OK even at the opera.

Concerts are held at the *Concert Hall* of Kolarčev University, Studentski trg 5 (box office open 10 am to noon and 6 to 8 pm). In October a festival of classical music is held here. The *Belgrade Philharmonia* is hidden at the end of the passageway at Studentski trg 11, directly across the street from the Ethnographical Museum.

Concerts also take place in the hall of the

Serbian Academy of Arts & Sciences, Kneza Mihaila 35. The *French Cultural Centre*, Kneza Mihaila 31 (closed weekends), often shows free films and videos. In the evening throngs of street musicians play along Kneza Mihaila.

The Bilet Servis, Trg Republike 5, has tickets to many events and the friendly English-speaking staff will search happily through their listings for something musical for you. Ask them about the *Teatar T*, Bulevard Revolucije 77a, which stages musicals several times a week (theatre closed Wednesday and Thursday).

Belgrade doesn't have a lot of discos and most people do their socialising in the many fashionable cafés around Trg Republike. One disco called *Club Promocija* is reached through a dark lane at Nušićeva 8 just off Terazije (open from 9 pm daily except Sunday).

From May to October there's horse racing at the hippodrome (*Trkalište*) every Sunday afternoon (take tram No 12 and 13 from the train station).

Getting There & Away

Bus Bus ticketing is computerised at the bus station and there are overnight buses to many places around Yugoslavia. Buy your ticket as far ahead as you can to be assured of a good seat.

Train Belgrade is on the main railway lines from Istanbul and Athens to Western Europe. International trains on these routes are discussed under Getting There & Away in the chapter introduction. Overnight domestic trains with couchettes or sleepers run from Belgrade to Bar (524 km, 8½ hours), Peć (490 km, 9½ hours) and Skopje (472 km, nine hours). Most of the above depart from the main station on Savski trg. Trains to Romania depart from Beograd-Dunav Station, Đure Đakovića 39.

Train Station At the main railway station, windows Nos 31 to 38 are in the smaller building facing the end of the tracks, whereas windows Nos 1 to 26 are inside the main station building next to track No 1. The person at window No 31 or 32 provides train information in English, tourist information and information about cheaper places to stay. In the main building buy international tickets at windows Nos 3 and 4, regular tickets at windows Nos 7 to 20, and get train information in Serbian at window No 25. The posted timetables are in Cyrillic. Sleepers and couchettes are purchased in the office marked 'prodaja kuset i spavacim kolima' next to the waiting room directly accessible from track No 1.

Getting Around

To/From the Airport The JAT bus (US$1.50) departs from Hotel Slavija, trg D Tucovića, 1½ hours before flight time. Surčin Airport is 18 km west of the city. If you're stuck at the airport waiting for a flight, visit the nearby Yugoslav Aviation Museum (closed Monday).

Public Transport Because Belgrade lacks a metro the streetcars are tremendously overcrowded. Six-strip public transport tickets are sold at tobacco kiosks and you validate your own ticket by punching a strip once aboard. Tickets purchased from the driver are more expensive. Night buses between midnight and 4 am charge double fare. A *dnevna karta* allows you to ride all services for one day (US$0.25).

Car Rental Autotehna/Avis (☎ 620 362), Obilićev venac 25, has cars beginning at US$28 a day plus 7% tax, 100 km included. Their cars are only for use within Yugoslavia.

Montenegro

The Republic of Montenegro (Crna Gora) occupies a corner of south-western Yugoslavia directly north of Albania, close to where the Dinaric Alps merge with the Balkan range. The republic's Adriatic coastline attracts masses of Serbian sunseekers, but there are also the spectacular Morača and

Tara canyons in the interior. Between Podgorica and Kolašin a scenic railway runs right up the Morača Canyon with fantastic views between the countless tunnels. West of Mojkovac, the next station after Kolašin, is the 100-km-long Tara Canyon, thought to be the second-largest in the world. Other striking features of this compact, 13,812-sq-km republic are the winding Bay of Kotor, the longest and deepest fjord in southern Europe, and Skadar Lake, the largest lake in the Balkans, which Montenegro shares with Albania. There are no major islands off the Montenegrin coast but the sandy beaches here are far longer than those farther north in Croatia. Now cut off from northern Europe by troubled areas of Croatia and Bosnia-Hercegovina, Montenegro is a bit of a backwater.

History

Only tiny Montenegro kept above the Turkish tide which engulfed the Balkans for over four centuries. Medieval Montenegro was part of Serbia, and after the Serbian defeat in 1389 the inhabitants of this mountainous region continued to resist the Turks. In 1482 Ivan Crnojević established an independent principality at Cetinje ruled by *vladike* (bishops) who were popularly elected after 1516. Beginning in 1697 the succession was limited to the Petrović Njegoš family (each bishop being succeeded by his nephew) which forged an alliance with Russia in 1711.

The intermittent wars with the Turks and Albanians continued until 1878, when the European portion of the Ottoman Empire largely collapsed and Montenegrin independence was recognised by the Congress of Berlin. Nicola I Petrović, Montenegro's ruler from 1860, declared himself king in 1910. In 1916 the Austrians evicted the bishop-king and in 1918 Montenegro was incorporated into Serbia. During WW II Montenegrins fought valiantly in Tito's partisan army and after the war the region was rewarded with the status of a republic within Yugoslavia. In 1946 the administration shifted from Cetinje

to Podgorica (formerly Titograd), a modern city with little to interest the visitor.

The history of Montenegro is hard to follow unless you remember that, like the Albanians, the Montenegrins were divided into tribes or clans, such as the Njegoš clan west of Cetinje and the Paštrović clan around Budva. While blind obedience to the clan leader helped Montenegrins resist foreign invasions, it has not made the transition to democracy easy. During recent elections, the Bar region was fiercely anti-Milošević while the inland population, traditionally in the opposite camp, sided with Milošević mainly for reasons of inter-clan rivalry.

Getting There & Away

In the past the overwhelming majority of visitors arrived in Montenegro from Dubrovnik by car or bus. The 1991 fighting closed this route and until the situation normalises the easiest way to get there will be by train from Belgrade to Bar. You can also fly directly to Tivat or Podgorica airports from Belgrade.

BAR (БАР)

Bar (Antivari) is a modern city backed by the barren coastal range, the terminus of the railway from Belgrade and (in better times) a ferry line to/from Bari, Italy. The development of Bar to provide landlocked Serbia with an Adriatic outlet was first proposed in 1879, yet it was not until 1976 that the dream became a reality with the opening of the Belgrade-Bar line, the only railway routed exclusively through ethnic Serbian areas to the sea.

As long as the border between Croatia and Yugoslavia remains closed, Bar will probably be your gateway to Montenegro. An overnight train arrives each morning from Belgrade. All transport along the coast radiates from here and if you find a cheap private room it makes a good base for day trips to Ulcinj, Podgorica, Cetinje, Kotor and Budva.

Orientation

The ferry terminal in Bar is only a few

hundred metres from the centre of town, but the adjacent bus and train stations are about two km south-east of the centre. The beach is north of the port.

The left-luggage office at the train station is open from 7 am to 9 pm.

Information

The tourist office next to Putnik near the port has a few brochures and the adjacent Montenegro Express office is good about answering questions in English. Bar's telephone code is 085.

Money Moneychangers hang around in front of the market building, two blocks back towards the mountains from the large circular supermarket in the centre of town.

Places to Stay

At last report *Autocamp Susanj*, two km north of the ferry landing along the beach, was closed. Putnik Turist Biro opposite the ferry landing arranges private room accommodation at US$5 per person. Putnik is only open weekdays during business hours; if you arrive at other times you must go on to Ulcinj to find a private room.

Hotel Topolica (☎ 21 122), a modern five-storey hotel on the beach a few hundred metres north of the port, is US$29/48 single/double with bath and breakfast or US$35/60 single/double with full board.

Getting There & Away

There are four trains a day to/from Belgrade (two with couchettes, 524 km, eight hours, US$6) and buses to Ulcinj. Until strict UN sanctions were imposed in April 1993, a ferry linked Bar to Bari, Italy, from March to December. In midsummer all transport to/from Bar is very crowded as all Serbia heads for the beach.

ULCINJ (УЛЦИНЬ)

A broad military highway tunnels through the hills between olive groves for 26 km from Bar to Ulcinj (Ulqin in Albanian, Dulcigno in Italian) near the Albanian border. The Turks held Bar and Ulcinj for over 300 years,

and most of the ethnic Albanian inhabitants are Muslims. You'll notice the difference in people right away from the curious direct looks you get and the lively bazar atmosphere in the many small shops lining the streets. Many older women at Ulcinj still wear traditional Islamic dress, especially on market day (Friday). It's a popular holiday resort for Serbs, who seem to arrive en masse on the Belgrade-Bar train, and in July and August it can get very crowded although accommodation is always available.

Orientation

You'll arrive at Ulcinj Bus Station about two km from Mala Plaža, the small beach below the old town. It's an interesting walk up ulica 26 novembar to Mala Plaža and you'll pass several buildings with *sobe* and *zimmer* (room) signs where you can rent a room.

Velika Plaža (Great Beach), Ulcinj's famous 12-km stretch of unbroken sand, begins about five km south-east of town (sporadic bus service to 'Ada').

Information

Adriatours, ulica 26 novembar 18, is about 500 metres from the bus station on the way into town. The telephone code for Ulcinj is 085.

Money Money changes hands on ulica 26 novembar in front of Robna Kuća Ulcinj.

Post & Telecommunications The telephone centre in the main post office, at the foot of ulica 26 novembar not far from the bus station, is open Monday to Saturday from 7 am to 9 pm, Sunday 9 am to noon.

Things to See & Do

Founded by the Greeks, Ulcinj gained notoriety as a base for North African pirates from 1571 to 1878. There was even a slave market from which the few resident Black families are descended. The ancient ramparts of old Ulcinj overlook the sea, but most of the buildings inside were shattered by earthquakes in 1979 and later reconstructed. The **museum** (closed Monday) is by the upper

Dubrovnik to Ulcinj

gate and you can walk among the houses and along the wall for the view.

Places to Stay

Camping There are two camping grounds on Velika Plaža, *Milena* and *Neptun*. On Ada Island, just across the Bojana River from Albania, is *Camping Ada Bojana FKK*, a nudist camping ground accessible by bus (guests only).

Private Rooms Adriatours (☎ 52 057), ulica 26 novembar 18, halfway between the bus station and Robna Kuća Ulcinj, is a private travel agency where the helpful English-speaking staff will find you a private room at about US$3 per person a night. They're open all year. If you arrive outside business hours knock on the door of the adjacent house with the *zimmer frei* signs (owned by the same family) and if they can't accommodate you they'll suggest somewhere else that can.

If you continue into town towards Mala Plaža, you'll pass Olcinium Travel Agency (more private rooms) nearly opposite Kino Basta (Basta Cinema). Facing Mala Plaža itself is Turist Biro 'Neptun' Montenegroturist with another selection of private rooms (US$4 per person).

Hotels The least expensive hotel is the 240-room *Mediteran* (☎ 81 411), a pleasant modern hotel which is a five-minute walk uphill from Mala Plaža. Rooms with private bath and breakfast are US$17/25 single/double and most have a balcony overlooking the sea. It's open all year.

Places to Eat

There are numerous inexpensive restaurants around town offering cheap grilled meat or more expensive seafood. Try the *Dubrovnik Restaurant* next to the unfinished Cultural Centre on ulica 26 novembar.

Getting There & Away
Buses to/from Bar (26 km, US$1) run every couple of hours.

BUDVA (БУДВА)
Budva is Yugoslavia's top beach resort. A long, sandy beach curves around from the old town with its adjacent harbour all the way to Sveti Stefan, with the high coastal mountains forming a magnificent backdrop. Budva caters mostly to people on cheap package tours and it's not cheap for individuals. Though Bar is better positioned transport-wise as a base for making coastal day trips, Budva is far more beautiful and worth the extra effort and expense if you're not in a hurry.

Orientation & Information
The route from the bus station to town is confusing and poorly marked, so ask directions to the main post office (pošta), a 10-minute walk away. The old town is five minutes beyond there. There's no left-luggage office at Budva Bus Station.

The people at Montenegro Express on Trg Republike near the old town are good about answering questions. The telephone code for Budva is 086.

Money Moneychangers are found in the parking lot between the post office and the market. Maestral Tours, Mediteranska 18, changes cash for the equivalent of the black-market rate.

Things to See
Budva's big attraction is its glorious beach which curves around the bay. The old walled town of Budva was levelled by two 1979 earthquakes after which the residents were permanently evacuated. Since then it has been completely rebuilt as a tourist attraction and the main square with its three churches, museum and fortress (great view from the ramparts) is so picturesque it seems almost contrived. It's possible to walk three-quarters of the way around the top of the town wall. The Stara Budva Café in the old town

has large photos of the earthquake damage on the walls.

Only a few km south-east of Budva is the former village of **Sveti Stefan**, an island now linked to the mainland. During the 1960s the entire village was converted into a luxury hotel but unlike Budva, which you may enter free, to set foot on the hallowed soil of Sveti Stefan costs US$6. Settle for the long-range picture-postcard view and keep your money.

Places to Stay
Camping If you have a tent, try *Autocamp Avala* (☎ 51 205), behind Hotel Montenegro, two km east along the shore (through a small tunnel). It's crowded with caravans but at least it's near the beach. No bungalows are available but the manager may help you find a private room nearby. Avala is open from June to September. Right next to Avala is *Autokamp Boreti* which is less secure.

Private Rooms Maestral Tours (☎ 52 250), Mediteranska 18, just down from the post office, rents private rooms at US$13 double (no singles) in July and August only. Emona Globetour nearby may also have private rooms and a third place to try is Montenegro Express (☎ 51 443) on Trg Republike closer to the old town. Their rooms are US$7/10 single/double in June and September, US$10/14 in July and August. Single rooms are scarce and they don't rent rooms for one or two nights. From October to May finding a private room may take some searching.

Hotels The modern 440-bed *Aleksandar Hotel* (☎ 44 969) on the beach at Budva is US$22/38 single/double in the low season, US$32/50 in the high season, all meals included (hotel open from May to October only). The Aleksandar is owned by the Yugoslav Automobile Association and claims to be one of the only hotels where Yugoslavs and foreigners pay the same.

Places to Eat
Restoran Centar is upstairs beside the supermarket above the vegetable market, just

inland from the post office. Unfortunately the bars and restaurants of Budva don't display their prices, so always ask to see a menu before ordering.

Getting There & Away
There's a bus service to Podgorica (74 km, 20 daily), Cetinje (31 km) and Bar (38 km, 16 daily).

If coming from Belgrade, get off the train at Podgorica and catch a bus from there to Budva. In the other direction it's probably best to take a bus from Budva to Bar and pick up the train to Belgrade there.

Getting Around
From May to September a small tourist train shuttles up and down the beach from Budva to Bečići at US$1 a ride.

Ask around the harbour for tourist boats to Sveti Stefan.

CETINJE (ЦЕТИЊЕ)
Cetinje, perched on top of a high plateau between the Bay of Kotor and Skadar Lake, is the old capital of Montenegro, subject of songs and epic poems. The open, easily defended slopes help to explain Montenegro's independence, and much remains of old Cetinje, from museums to palaces, mansions and monasteries. At the turn of the century all the large states of Europe had embassies here. Short hikes can be made in the hills behind Cetinje Monastery. It's well worth spending the night here if you can find an inexpensive place to stay.

Things to See & Do
The most imposing building in Cetinje is the **State Museum**, the former palace (1871) of Nicola I Petrović, the last king. Looted during WW II, only a portion of its original furnishings remain, but the many portraits and period weapons give a representative picture of the times. Nearly opposite this is the older 1832 residence of the prince-bishop Petar II Petrović Njegoš, who ruled from 1830 to 1851. This building, now a museum, is also known as **Biljarda Hall** because of a billiard table installed in 1840.

Around the side of Biljarda Hall is a large glass-enclosed pavilion containing a fascinating relief map of Montenegro created by the Austrians in 1917 for tactical planning purposes. Ask one of the Njegoš Museum attendants to let you in. Beyond the map is **Cetinje Monastery**, founded in 1484 but rebuilt in 1785. The monastery treasury contains a copy of the *Oktoih* or 'Octoechos' (Book of the Eight Voices) printed near here in 1494 – one of the oldest collections of liturgical songs in a Slavic language. Vladin Dom, the former Government House (1910) and now the **National Gallery**, is not far away.

Twenty km away at the summit of **Mt Lovčen** (1749 metres), the 'Black Mountain' which gave Montenegro its Italian name, is the mausoleum of Petar II Petrović Njegoš, a revered poet as well as ruler. The masterful statue of Njegoš inside is by Croatian sculptor Ivan Meštrović. There are no buses up Lovčen and taxis want US$30 return; the building is visible in the distance from Cetinje. From the parking lot you must climb 461 steps to the mausoleum and its sweeping view of the Bay of Kotor, mountains and coast. The whole of Mt Lovčen has been declared a national park.

Places to Stay & Eat
For a private room ask at Intours (☎ 21 157), the place marked 'Vincom Duty Free Shop' next to the post office. Chances are they'll send you to Martinović Petar who lives a block away at Bajova Pivljanina 50 next to Belveder Mini Market.

If this fails you have a problem as the only hotel is the *Grand Hotel* (☎ 21 104), a modern so-called five-star hotel that would barely rate two anywhere else. It's US$36/60 single/double with bath and breakfast. It's just a five-minute walk from the centre.

Getting There & Away
Some 25 buses a day shuttle between Podgorica and Cetinje (45 km), and there's also frequent service to/from Budva (31 km).

You can easily make Cetinje a day trip from Bar by catching an early train to

Podgorica where you'll connect with a bus to Cetinje. An early afternoon bus down to Budva will give you some time at the beach and a chance to look around the reconstructed old town before taking a late afternoon bus back to Bar.

DURMITOR NATIONAL PARK

Montenegro's Durmitor National Park is a popular hiking and mountaineering area just west of Žabljak, a ski resort which is also the highest town in Yugoslavia (1450 metres). There's a chair lift from near Hotel Durmitor which operates in winter towards Mt Štuoc (1953 metres). Žabljak was a major partisan stronghold during WW II, changing hands four times.

Some 18 mountain lakes dot the slopes of the Durmitor Range south-west of Žabljak. You can walk right around the largest lake, **Crno jezero** or 'Black Lake', three km from Žabljak, in an hour or two, and swim in its waters in summer. The rounded mass of Međed (2287 metres) rises directly behind the lake, surrounded by a backdrop of other peaks, including Savin kuk (2313 metres) to the left. You can climb Savin kuk in eight hours there and back. The national park office next to Hotel Durmitor sells good maps of the park.

Durmitor's main claim to fame is the 1067-metre-deep **Tara Canyon** which cuts dramatically into the mountain slopes and plateau for about 100 km. The edge of the Tara Canyon is about 12 km north of Žabljak, a three-hour walk along a road beginning near Hotel Planinka. Yugoslav tourist brochures maintain that this is the second-largest canyon in the world after the Grand Canyon in the USA, a claim other countries such as Mexico and Namibia also make for their canyons, but any way you look at it, it's a top sight.

White-Water Tours

Travel agencies sometimes offer rubber raft trips on the clean, green water, over countless foaming rapids, down the high, forested Tara Gorge. These put in at Splavište near the

Đurđevića Tara bridge. Three-day raft expeditions go right down the Tara from Đurđevića Tara to the junction with the Piva River at Šćepan Polje (88 km).

For advance information on white-water rafting on the Tara River contact Ski Centar Durmitor, Uzin Mirkova 7, Belgrade. At last report two-day, one-night raft trips departed from Žabljak every Monday from June to August, US$100 per person including transfers, meals and gear. There's a 10-person minimum to run a trip, so enquire well ahead. In winter the same Belgrade office will know all about ski facilities here.

Places to Stay

The Turist Biro in the centre of town is not much help – t arranges expensive private rooms at US$14 a single and hands out brochures written in Serbian.

Žabljak has four hotels owned by Montenegroturist. The *Planinka* (☎ 083-88 344) and *Jezera* (☎ 083-88 226) are modern ski hotels charging US$30/54 single/double with bath and breakfast in summer. The *Hotel Žabljak* (☎ 083-88 300) right in the centre of town also offers rooms with bath and breakfast at US$24/40 single/double.

The cheapest of the bunch is the old four-storey wooden *Hotel Durmitor* (☎ 083-88 278), past Hotel Jezera at the entrance to the national park, a 15-minute walk into town. Singles/doubles with shared bath here are US$20/34, breakfast included. Although the Durmitor seems to have the reputation of being run-down and unfit for foreigners, some of the rooms are quite pleasant with balconies facing the mountains. Just be aware that there's no hot water or shower in the building.

On a hill top a five-minute walk beyond the national park office is *Autocamp Ivan-do* which is little more than a fenced-off field. People around here rent private rooms at rates far lower than those charged in town and you'll get an additional discount if you have a sleeping bag and don't require sheets. Set right in the middle of the forest, Ivan-do is a perfect base for hikers.

Places to Eat

The *Restoran Sezam* next to the small market just below the Turist Biro bakes its own bread and is one of the only places besides the hotels that serves meals.

Getting There & Away

The easiest way to get to Žabljak is to take a bus from Belgrade to Pljevlja (334 km), then one of the two daily buses from Pljevlja to Žabljak (57 km). On the return, these buses leave Žabljak for Pljevlja at 5 am and 5 pm, connecting for Mojkovac and Podgorica at Đurđevića Tara where there's a spectacular bridge over the canyon. If you have to change buses at Pljevlja, be fast as they don't wait long.

As soon as you arrive at Žabljak enquire about onward buses to Belgrade, Pljevlja, Mojkovac and Podgorica at the red kiosk marked 'Turist Biro' beside the bus stop. Seats should be booked the day before.

Another jumping-off point is Mojkovac on the Belgrade-Podgorica line. About four trains daily run from Bar to Mojkovac (157 km, two hours); catch the earliest one for the best connections. At Mojkovac you must walk two km from the train station to the bus station where you can pick up buses running from Podgorica to Pljevlja. They'll usually drop you at Đurđevića Tara and from there you may have to hitch the remaining 22 km to Žabljak.

Kosovo

A visit to Kosovo can be a traumatic experience. Probably nowhere in Europe are human rights as flagrantly and systematically violated as they are here. The inhabitants have an uninhibited friendliness and curiosity which sets them apart from other Yugoslavs and the direct looks you get are at first disconcerting. The region's poverty and backwardness are also apparent, as is the watchful eye of the Serbian government. Police posts have taken the place of left-luggage facilities in the region's bus and train stations. Your presence won't go unnoticed.

Until recently an 'autonomous province', Kosovo is now an integral part of the Republic of Serbia. Isolated medieval Serbian monasteries tell of an early period which ended in 1389 with the Battle of Kosovo just outside Priština (Prishtinë in Albanian). After this disaster the Serbs moved north en masse, abandoning the region to the Albanians, descendants of the ancient Illyrians who had inhabited this land for thousands of years.

In the late 19th century the ethnic Albanians, who make up 90% of the population today, struggled to free themselves of Ottoman rule. Yet in 1913 when the Turkish government finally pulled out, Kosovo was handed over to Serbia. Over half a million ethnic Albanians emigrated to Turkey and elsewhere to escape Serbian rule and, by 1940, 18,000 Serbian families had been settled on the vacated lands. During WW II, Kosovo was incorporated into Italian-controlled Albania, then in October 1944 it was liberated by communist partisans from Albania who turned the area over to Tito's forces in early 1945.

After the war Tito wanted Albania itself included in the Yugoslav Federation as a seventh republic with Kosovo united to it. This never came to pass and thus began two decades of pernicious neglect. Between 1954 and 1957 another 195,000 Albanians were coerced into emigrating to Turkey. After serious rioting in 1968 (and with the Soviet invasion of Czechoslovakia pushing Yugoslavia and Albania closer together), an 'autonomous province' was created (in 1974) and economic aid increased. Due to these concessions Kosovo is one of the only parts of ex-Yugoslavia where Marshall Tito is still warmly remembered. You see his portrait in restaurants and cafés everywhere and the main street in Peć is still named for him.

Yet the changes brought only cosmetic improvements and the standard of living in Kosovo (which has some of the most fertile land in the Balkans) remained a quarter the Yugoslav average. Kosovo was treated as a colony, its mines providing raw materials for industry in Serbia. In 1981 demonstrations calling for full republic status were put down by military force at a cost of over 300 lives. The 7000 young Albanians subsequently arrested were given jail terms of six years and up. This brutal denial of equality within the Yugoslav Federation sowed the seeds which led to the violent break-up of the country a decade later.

Trouble began anew in November 1988 as Albanian demonstrators protested against the sacking by Belgrade of local officials, including the provincial president Azem Vllasi, who was later arrested. A Kosovo coal miners' strike in February 1989 was followed by new limits imposed by Serbia on Kosovo's autonomy, a curfew and a state of emergency. This resulted in serious rioting, and 24 unarmed Albanian civilians were shot dead by the Yugoslav security forces.

On 5 July 1990 the Serbian parliament cancelled Kosovo's political autonomy and dissolved its assembly and government. The only Albanian-language daily newspaper, *Rilindja*, was banned and TV and radio broadcasts in Albanian ceased. In a process termed 'differentiation' some 115,000 Albanians suspected of having nationalist sympathies were fired from their jobs and Serbs installed in their places. At Priština University, founded in 1969, 800 Albanian lecturers were sacked, effectively ending teaching in Albanian and forcing all but 500 of the 23,000 Albanian students to terminate their studies. Albanian secondary school teachers are forced to work without salaries, otherwise the schools will close. All Albanians on state hospital staffs were sacked, creating a growth industry in private clinics where most Albanian women now give birth. (This happened after rumours that the survival rate for male Albanian babies born in hospitals had suddenly dropped.)

Large numbers of Albanians went abroad after losing their jobs and a third of adult male Kosovars now work in Western Europe. Ironically, with Yugoslavia now in an economic tailspin, the families of the émigrés are fairly well off thanks to the hard currency their men send home, while the Serbs who took their government jobs are paid in super-soft Yugoslav dinars. The 20% of Kosovars who do have jobs in Kosovo itself work almost exclusively in private businesses.

In September 1991 Serbian police and militia mobilised to block a referendum on independence for Kosovo, turning voters away and arresting election officials. The vote went ahead anyway and, with a 90% turnout, 98% voted in favour of independence from Serbia. In further elections on 24 May 1992, also declared illegal by Serbia, the writer Ibrahim Rugova was elected president of Kosovo. The unrecognised parliament of the 'Republic of Kosovo' elected with Mr Rugova is attempting to create a parallel administration that can offer passive resistance to Serbia and has requested UN peacekeeping troops for Kosovo.

An Albanian national uprising would certainly unleash the bloodiest of former Yugoslavia's current series of civil wars and the Kosovars are intensely aware of how Western countries stood by and tolerated ethnic genocide in Bosnia, so to date they've resisted Serb aggression with non-violence. Yugoslavia has an estimated 40,000 troops and police in Kosovo and no one doubts its readiness to use them. Serb nationalists are firmly convinced they have an historic right to Kosovo as part of a 'Greater Serbia' and a plan already exists to colonise Kosovo with Serbs. In December 1992 Kosovo Serbs elected to parliament a thuggish militia leader named Arkan whose troops have been accused of murdering 3000 Muslims in northern Bosnia.

Given Albania's increasing ties with Islamic countries, a major disturbance in Kosovo would have serious repercussions and both presidents Bush and Clinton have warned Serbia that any repetition of the Bosnian scenario there could lead to US intervention. At the very least, a conflict would see tens of thousands of Kosovars fleeing towards Western Europe before the notorious Serbian ethnic cleansing machine, probably via Macedonia where ethnic Albanians historically make up 20% of the population. This would quickly destabilise that small country and Greece has warned that it will take decisive action if its northern border is breached, possibly leading to military involvement by Bulgaria and Turkey. Considerations such as these have made even the rabble-rousers in Belgrade proceed with caution, at least until they've got what they want in Bosnia-Hercegovina.

Just under two million people occupy Kosovo's 10,887 sq km, making it the most densely populated portion of Yugoslavia with the highest birth rate. The Albanians adopted Islam after the Turkish conquest and today the region has a definite Muslim air, from the inhabitants' food and dress to the ubiquitous mosques. The capital, Priština, is a depressing, redeveloped city with showplace banks and hotels juxtaposed against squalor, but in the west the Metohija Valley between Peć and Prizren offers a useful transit route from the Adriatic to Macedonia or Belgrade to Albania, plus a chance to see another side of this troubled land.

Warning Your luggage will probably be searched by the Serbian police as you enter Kosovo. They're looking mostly for arms and printed matter published abroad about the conflict in ex-Yugoslavia. Anything printed in Albania or Albanian will raise a lot of questions and be confiscated. If the police suspect you're a journalist or human rights activist you'll be taken to the station for questioning and your belongings especially notebooks and other papers (put the names and addresses of any local contacts in code) will be carefully scrutinised again. If you are briefly detained look upon it as a unique experience. Once you convince them you're a harmless tourist you'll be released and have no further problems.

You may ask, why visit such a place? Although you should certainly not become involved in local politics, by coming here and observing conditions first-hand you'll gain a better understanding of the tragedy of ex-Yugoslavia. Although the Albanians of

Kosovo are cheerful, they mention their 'situation' to foreigners whenever they get the chance and it's impossible not to feel the resentment. Listen, but beware of getting yourself and others into trouble by making statements. Individuals seen with you may later be questioned by the police. Be careful about taking photos.

Getting There & Away

Getting to Kosovo from Serbia and Macedonia is easy as there are direct trains from Belgrade to Peć (490 km, 9½ hours), and lots of buses from Skopje to Prizren (117 km).

Getting through from the Adriatic coast to Kosovo, on the other hand, takes a full night or day. From Budva or Cetinje catch a bus to Podgorica and look for a direct bus to Peć from there. However only three buses a day run between Podgorica and Peć (244 km), crossing the 1849-metre Čakor Pass. Alternatively, take one of the 16 daily buses between Podgorica and Ivangrad (152 km). If you're leaving from Ulcinj, take an early bus to Bar, then a train 186 km to Bijelo Polje (this scenic ride takes you across Skadar Lake and up the Morača Canyon). Minibuses to Ivangrad await the trains at Bijelo Polje.

From Ivangrad to Peć is the most difficult part of the trip, possibly involving a wait of a few hours for an onward bus. *Autocamp Berane* (☎ 084-61 822) is less than one km from Ivangrad Bus Station if you get stuck. Otherwise go on to Rožaj (32 km) and spend the night at the comfortable *Rožaje Hotel* (☎ 0871-54 335; US$18/34 single/double) near the Rožaj Bus Station. An early bus will carry you the 37 km from Rožaj to Peć the next morning. There's nothing much to see in Rožaj other than the view of the mountains from the white war memorial.

For the route to/from Albania, turn to the Prizren section.

PEĆ

Peć (Pejë in Albanian), below high mountains between Podgorica and Priština, is a friendly, untouristed town of picturesque dwellings with some modern development. Ethnic Albanian men with their white felt skullcaps and women in traditional dress crowd the streets, especially on Saturday market day. The horse wagons carrying goods around Peć share the streets with lots of beggars.

Orientation

The bus and train stations are about 500 metres apart, both in the east part of Peć about a km from the centre. Neither station has a left-luggage room. Follow Rruga Marshall Tito west from the bus station into the centre of town.

Information

Try Kosmet Tours at Marshall Tito 102, Putnik, Marshall Tito 64, and Metohija Turist, Marshall Tito 20.

Post & Telecommunications The main post office and telephone centre is opposite the Hotel Metohija. The telephone code for Peć is 039.

Things to See

There are eight well-preserved, functioning mosques in Peć, the most imposing of which is the 15th century **Bajrakli Mosque**. Its high dome rises out of the colourful **bazar** (*čaršija*), giving Peć an authentic Oriental air.

By the river two km west of Peć is the **Patrijaršija Monastery**, seat of the Serbian Orthodox patriarchate in the 14th century, from 1557 to 1766 and again after 1920. The rebirth of the patriarchate in 1557 allowed the Serbs to maintain their identity during the darkest moments of Ottoman domination, so this monastery is of deep significance to contemporary Serbs. Inside the high-walled compound are three mid-13th century churches, each of which has a high dome and glorious medieval frescoes. There is a detailed explanation in English in the common narthex (admission US$4). Two km west of the monastery along the main highway is the **Rugovo Gorge**, an excellent hiking area.

Peć's most impressive sight, however, is 15 km south, accessible by frequent local bus. The **Visoki Dečani Monastery** (1335) with its marvellous 14th century frescoes is a two-km walk from the bus stop in Dečani (Deçan in Albanian) through beautifully wooded countryside. This royal monastery built under kings Dečanski and Dušan survived the long Turkish period intact. From Dečani you can catch an onward bus to Prizren.

Places to Stay

Camping *Kamp Karagač* (☎ 22 358), over the bridge and a km up the hill from the Metohija Hotel, is quiet and rather pleasant with lots of shade. This camping ground has been privatised and their main business is now the restaurant. It doesn't really cater to campers any more, though this could change so ask.

Hotels None of the travel agencies in town offers private rooms. The A-category *Metohija Hotel* (☎ 22 611), Marshall Tito 60, is a budget-breaker at US$45/70 single/double with private bath and breakfast. The 50-room *Hotel Korzo*, Marshall Tito 55, erected in 1929, has been closed for renovations for several years.

The B-category *Hotel Park* (☎ 21 864), just beyond the Kamp Karagač, is your best bet. Prices here vary but it's not expensive. Also try *Motel Dardanija* which you can see from the train just before you arrive at Peć station.

Getting There & Away

Bus Bus service from Prizren (73 km) and Skopje (190 km) is good and there's a night bus to/from Belgrade (388 km). In July and August buses run direct to Peć from Ulcinj (279 km).

Train Express trains stop at Kosovo Polje, a junction eight km west of Priština, from where there are branch lines to Peć (91 km, two hours) and Prizren (125 km, three hours). There's an overnight train with couchettes to/from Belgrade.

PRIZREN

Prizren, the most Albanian-looking city in Yugoslavia, is midway between Peć and Skopje. The road to Shkodra reaches the Albanian border at Vrbnica, 18 km west of Prizren. A big military base with lots of armoured vehicles is just outside Prizren on the way to Skopje.

Prizren was the medieval capital of 'Old Serbia' but much of what we see today is Turkish. Colourful houses climb up the hillside to the ruined citadel *(kaljaja)*, from which the 15th century Turkish bridge and 19 minarets are visible.

The Bistrica River emerges from a gorge behind the citadel and cuts Prizren in two on its way into Albania. East up this gorge is the Bistrica Pass (2640 metres), once the main route to Macedonia. Wednesday is market day when the city really comes alive.

Orientation

The bus and train stations are adjacent on the west side of town, but there's no left-luggage facility in either. From the bus station follow Rruga Metohjska towards the mountains, then take Rruga Vidovdanska up the riverside into town.

Information

Try the Tourist Association of Prizren, Rruga Vidovdanska 51, or Putnik on Trg Cara Dušana in the centre of town.

Post & Telecommunications The main post office and telephone centre is next to the Theranda Hotel. Prizren's telephone code is 029.

Things to See

On your way into town from the bus station you'll see the huge white-marble Bankkos Prizren building facing the river. On a backstreet behind the bank is the **Church of Bogorodica Ljeviška** (1307), which has an open bell tower above and frescoes inside. Nearby, a tall square tower rises above some Turkish baths, now the **Archaeological Museum** (usually closed).

The **Sinan Pasha Mosque** (1561) beside the river in the centre is closed, as are the **Gazi Mehmed Pasha Baths** (1563) beyond the Theranda Hotel. A little back from these is the large dome of the beautifully appointed 16th century **Bajrakli (Gazi Mehmed) Mosque**, which is still in use. Behind this mosque, on the side facing the river, is the **Museum of the Prizren League**, a popular movement which struggled for Albanian autonomy within the Ottoman Empire from 1878 to 1881. In 1881 Dervish Pasha suppressed the League, killing thousands of Albanians and exiling thousands more to Asia Minor.

The largest Orthodox church in Prizren is **Sveti Georgi** (1856) in the old town near the Sinan Pasha Mosque. Higher up on the way to the **citadel** is **Sveti Spas**, with the ruins of an Orthodox monastery.

Places to Stay & Eat

Unfortunately, no private rooms are available in Prizren. The B-category *Theranda Hotel* (☎ 22 292), by the river in the centre of town, is US$19/25 single/double with private bath and breakfast.

Motel Putnik (☎ 43 107), near the river three blocks from the bus station (ask directions), charges similar prices for foreigners and locals, which makes it relatively cheap (prices vary). The camping ground which should exist behind the motel has been officially closed for years but they'll probably let you pitch a tent there at no cost.

Several good ćevapčići places lie between Sveti Georgi and Sinan Pasha.

Getting There & Away

Bus service is good from Priština (75 km), Peć (73 km) and Skopje (117 km). Only slow local trains to Metohija junction (64 km, 1½ hours) and Kosovo Polje (125 km, three hours) leave from Prizren, so you're much better coming and going by bus.

Buses to the Albanian border leave from the street beginning at Rruga Vidovdanska 77. Some buses run directly to the border post *(dogana)* at Vrbnica (18 km) but none cross into Albania. If you can't find a bus to

Vrbnica take a local bus to Zhur, from which it's a six-km walk downhill to the border. It's only 200 metres between the Yugoslav and Albanian checkpoints, then you should be able to hitch a ride the 16 km to Kukës without difficulty.

Appendix I – Alternative Place Names

The following abbreviations are used:

(A) Albanian
(B) Bulgarian
(C) Czech
(Ce) Celtic
(Cr) Croatian
(D) Dutch
(E) English
(G) German
(Gk) Greek
(H) Hungarian
(I) Italian
(L) Latin
(M) Macedonian
(MGk) Medieval Greek (Byzantine)
(P) Polish
(R) Romanian
(Rus) Russian
(Se) Serbian
(Slav) Slav
(Slk) Slovak
(Sle) Slovene
(T) Turkish

ALBANIA
Shqipëri (A)

Apolonia (L) – Pojan (A)
Berat (A) – Antipatria (L)
Butrint (A) – Buthroton (Gk)
Durrës (A) – Durazzo (I), Epidamnos (Gk), Dyrrhachium (L)
Elbasan (A) – Skampa (L), El Basan (T)
Gjirokastër (A) – Gjirokastra (A), Argyrokastron (Gk)
Ioannina (Gk) – Janinë (A)
Korçë (A) – Korça (A), Koritsa (Gk)
Kruj (A) – Kruja (E)
Lezhë (A) – Alessio (I)
Sarandë (A) – Saranda (E), Onchesmos (Gk)
Tiranë (A) – Tirana (E)
Vlorë (A) – Vlora (E), Avlon (L)

BULGARIA
Bâlgariya

Bachkovo Monastery (E) – Bachkovski Manastir (B)
Balchik (B) – Krunoi (Gk), Dionysopolis (L)
Golden Sands (E) – Zlatni Pyasâtsi (B), Goldstrand (G)
Hisarya (B) – Augusta (L), Hisar (T), Toplitsa (MGk)
Nesebâr (B) – Mesembria (Gk)
Plovdiv (B) – Philipopolis (Gk), Philibe (T)
Rila Monastery (E) – Rilski Manastir (B)
Ruse (B) – Rouschouk (T)
Shumen (B) – Chumla (T)
Sofia (E) – Sofiya (B), Serdica (L), Sredets (Slav), Triaditsa (MGk)
Sozopol (B) – Apollonia (Gk)
Stara Planina (B) – Balkan Mountains (E)
Sunny Beach (E) – Slânchev Bryag (B), Sonnenstrand (G)
Varna (B) – Odessos (Gk)
Vidin (B) – Dunonia (Ce), Bononia (L)

CROATIA
Hrvatska (Cr)

Dalmatia (E) – Dalmacija (Cr)
Danube (River) (E) – Dunav (Cr)
Dubrovnik (Cr) – Ragusa (I)
Hvar (Island) (Cr) – Lesina (I)
Korčula (Cr) – Curzola (I)
Krk (Island) (Cr) – Veglia (I)
Kvarner (Gulf of) (E) – Quarnero (I)
Lošinj (Island) (Cr) – Lussino (I)
Mljet (Island) (Cr) – Melita (I)
Plitvice Lakes (E) – Plitvicer Seen (G)
Poreč (Cr) – Parenzo (I), Parentium (L)
Pula (Cr) – Polensium (L)
Rab (Island) (Cr) – Arbe (G)
Rijeka (Cr) – Fiume (I)
Rovinj (Cr) – Rovigno (I)
Split (Cr) – Spalato (I)
Trogir (Cr) – Trau (G)
Zadar (Cr) – Zara (I), Iader (L)
Zagreb (Cr) – Agram (G)

CZECH REPUBLIC
Česká republika

Brno (C) – Brünn (G)

897

Česke Budějovice (C) – Budweis (G)
Český Krumlov (C) – Krumau (G)
Cheb (C) – Eger (G)
Danube (River) (E) – Dunáj (C)
Hluboká nad Vltavou (C) – Frauenberg (G)
Karlovy Vary (C) – Karlsbad (G)
Krkonoše (C) – Giant Mountains (E)
Krusne Hory (C) – Ore Mountains
Labe (River) (C) – Elbe (G)
Mariánské Lázně (C) – Marienbad (G)
Plzeň (C) – Pilsen (G)
Prague (E) – Praha (C), Prag (G)
Telč (C) – Teltsch (G)
Vltava (River) (C) – Moldau (G)
Zlaté piesky (C) – Golden Sands (E)
Znojmo (C) – Znaim (G)

HUNGARY
Magyarország

Balaton Lake (H) – Plattensee (G)
Debrecen (H) – Debrezin (G)
Eger (H) – Erlau (G)
Great Plain (E) – Nagyalföld (H)
Győr (H) – Raab (G), Arrabona (L)
Kisalföld (H) – Little Plain (E)
Komárom (H) – Brigetio (L)
Kőszeg (H) – Guns (G)
Pécs (H) – Fünfkirchen (G), Sopianae (L)
Sopron (H) – Ödenburg (G), Scarbantia (L)
Szeged (H) – Segedin (G)
Székesfehérvár (H) – Stuhlweissenburg (G)
Szombathely (H) – Steinamanger (G),
    Savaria (L)
Tata (H) – Totis (G)
Transdanubia (E) – Dunántúl (H)
Vác (H) – Wartzen (G)

MACEDONIA

Ohrid (M) – Lihnidos (L)
Skopje (M) – Uskup (T), Scupi (L)

POLAND
Polska

Brzezinka (P) – Birkenau (G)
Bydgoszcz (P) – Bromberg (G)
Częstochowa (P) – Tschenstochau (G)
Frombork (P) – Frawenburg (G)

Gdańsk (P) – Danzig (G)
Gdynia (P) – Gdingen (G)
Gniezno (P) – Gnesen (G)
Kołobrzeg (P) – Kolberg (G)
Giżycko (P) – Lötzen (G)
Gniezno (P) – Gnesen (G)
Ktrzyn (P) – Rastenburg (G)
Kraków (P) – Krakau (G), Cracow (E)
Lidzmark Warmiński (P) – Heilsberg (G)
Lvov (E) – Lwów (P), Lemberg (G)
Malbork (P) – Marienburg (G)
Małopolska (E) – 'Little Poland' (E)
Mikołajki (P) – Nikolaiken (G)
Nowy Sącz– Neusandez (G)
Nysa (River) (P) – Neisse (G)
Odra (River) (P) – Oder (G)
Olsztyn (P) – Allenstein (G)
Opole (P) – Oppeln (G)
Oświęcim (P) – Auschwitz (G)
Poznań (P) – Posen (G)
Ruciane-Nida (P) – Rudschanny (G)
Silesia (E) – Śńęsk (P), Silesien (G)
Świnoujście (P) – Swinemünde (G)
Szczecin (P) – Stettin (G)
Sopot (P) – Zoppot (G)
Tannenberg (G) – Stębark (P)
Toruń (P) – Thorn (G)
Vistula (River) (E) – Wisła (P), Weichsel (G)
Warsaw (E) – Warszawa (P), Warschau (G)
Węgorzewo (P) – Angerburg (G)
Wielkopolska (P) – 'Great Poland' (E)
Wilczy Szaniec (P) – Wolfschanze (G),
    Wolf's Lair (E)
Wrocław (P) – Breslau (G)

ROMANIA
Romania

Alba Iulia (R) – Karlsburg (G), Weissenburg
    (G), Apulum (L)
Brașov (R) – Kronstadt (G)
Bucharest (E) – București (R)
Chernovtsy (Rus) – Cernăuţř(R), Czerno-
    witz (G)
Cluj-Napoca (R) – Klausenburg (G),
    Koloszvár (H), Napoca (L)
Constanţa (R) – Constantiana (L), Tomis
    (Gk), Küstendje (T)
Dobruja (E) – Dobrogea (R), Moesia Inferior
    (L)

Hunedoara (R) – Eisenmarkt (G)
Iaşi (R) – Jassy (G)
Mangalia (R) – Callatis (L)
Mediaş (R) – Mediasch (G)
Oradea (R) – Grosswardein (G), Nagyvárad (H)
Sebeş (R) – Muhlbach (G)
Sibiu (R) – Hermannstadt (G), Cibinium (L)
Sighişoara (R) – Schässburg (G)
Suceava (R) – Soczow (G)
Timişoara (R) – Temeschburg (G), Temesvár (H)
Transylvania (R) – Siebenbürgen (G)

SLOVAKIA
Slovenská

Banská Bystrica (Slk) – Neusohl (G)
Bratislava (C) – Pressburg (G), Pozsony (H)
Gerlachovskńy Štít (Slk) – Mt Gerlach (E)
Košice (Slk) – Kaschau (G)
Levoča (Slk) – Leutschau (G)
Mala Fatra (Slk) – Little Fatra (E)
Nízke Tatry (Slk) – Low Tatra (E)
Prešov (Slk) – Preschau (G)
Slovenské rudohorie (Slk) – Slovak Ore Mountains (E)
Slovenskńy raj (Slk) – Slovak Paradise (E)

Spišský hrad (Castle) (Slk) – Zipser Burg (G)
Vysoké Tatry (Slk) – High Tatra (E)
Zvolen (Slk) – Altsohl (G)

SLOVENIA
Slovenija

Koper (Sle) – Capodistria (I)
Ljubljana (Sle) – Laibach (G), Emona (L)
Piran (Sle) – Pireos (Gk)
Postojna Caves (E) – Adelsberger Grotten (G)
Vintgar Gorge (E) – Soteska Vintgar (Sle)

YUGOSLAVIA
Jugoslavija

Bar (Se) – Antivari (I)
Belgrade (E) – Beograd (Se)
Kotor (Se) – Cattaro (I)
Montenegro (E) – Crna Gora (Se)
Novi Sad (Se) – Neusatz (G)
Pejë (A) – Peć (Se)
Prishtinë (A) – Priština (Se)
Serbia (E) – Srbija (Se)
Titograd (Se) – Podgorica (Se)
Ulcinj (Se) – Ulqin (A), Dulcigno (I)

Appendix II – International Automobile Signs

The following is a list of official country abbreviations that you may encounter on vehicles in Eastern Europe. Other abbreviations are likely to be unofficial, and often refer to a particular region, province or city. A motorised vehicle entering a foreign country must carry a sticker identifying its country of registration, though this rule is not always enforced.

A – Austria
AL – Albania
AND – Andorra
AUS – Australia
B – Belgium
BG – Bulgaria
CC – Consular Corps
CD – Diplomatic Corps
CDN – Canada
CH – Switzerland
CZ – Czech Republic
CY – Cyprus
D – Germany
DK – Denmark
DZ – Algeria
E – Spain
EST – Estonia
ET – Egypt
F – France
FL – Liechtenstein
GB – Great Britain
GR – Greece
H – Hungary
HKJ – Jordan
HR – Croatia

I – Italy
IL – Israel
IR – Iran
IRL – Ireland
IRQ – Iraq
IS – Iceland
J – Japan
L – Luxembourg
LAR – Libya
LT – Lithuania
LV – Latvia
M – Malta
MA – Morocco
MC – Monaco
N – Norway
NL – Netherlands
NZ – New Zealand
P – Portugal
PL – Poland
RL – Lebanon
RO – Romania
RSM – San Marino
RUS – Russia
S – Sweden
SF – Finland
SK – Slovakia
SLO – Slovenia
SYR – Syria
TN – Tunisia
TR – Turkey
USA – United States of America
V – Vatican
VN – Vietnam
YU – Yugoslavia
ZA – South Africa

Appendix III – Climate Charts

Belgrade

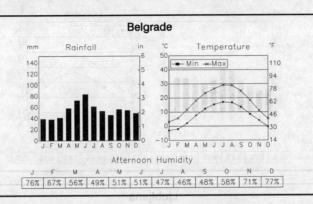

	J	F	M	A	M	J	J	A	S	O	N	D
Afternoon Humidity	76%	67%	56%	49%	51%	51%	47%	46%	48%	58%	71%	77%

Bratislava

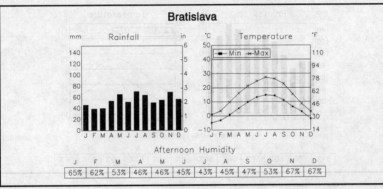

	J	F	M	A	M	J	J	A	S	O	N	D
Afternoon Humidity	65%	62%	53%	46%	46%	45%	43%	45%	47%	53%	67%	67%

Bucharest

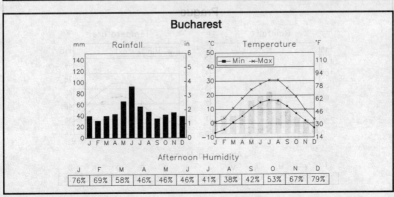

	J	F	M	A	M	J	J	A	S	O	N	D
Afternoon Humidity	76%	69%	58%	46%	46%	46%	41%	38%	42%	53%	67%	79%

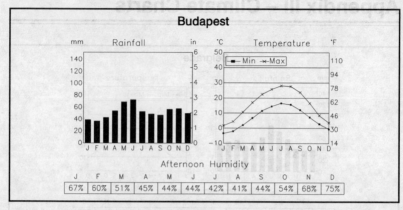

Budapest

	J	F	M	A	M	J	J	A	S	O	N	D
	67%	60%	51%	45%	44%	44%	42%	41%	44%	54%	68%	75%

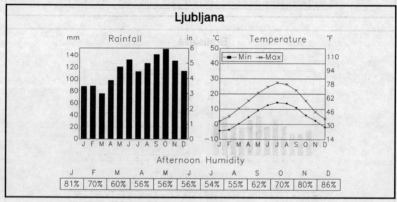

Ljubljana

	J	F	M	A	M	J	J	A	S	O	N	D
	81%	70%	60%	56%	56%	56%	54%	55%	62%	70%	80%	86%

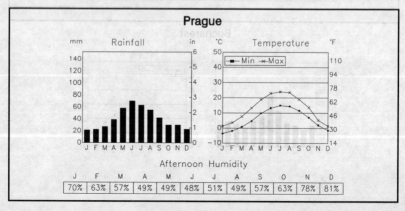

Prague

	J	F	M	A	M	J	J	A	S	O	N	D
	70%	63%	57%	49%	49%	48%	51%	49%	57%	63%	78%	81%

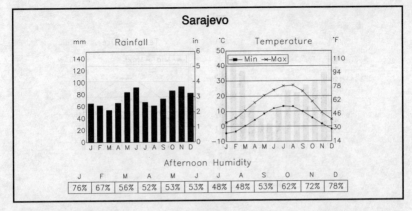

Sarajevo

Rainfall

Temperature

Min Max

Afternoon Humidity

J	F	M	A	M	J	J	A	S	O	N	D
76%	67%	56%	52%	53%	53%	48%	48%	53%	62%	72%	78%

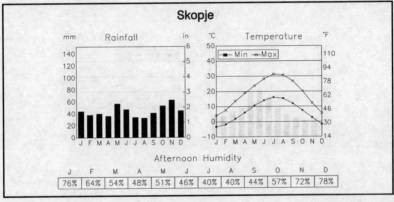

Skopje

Rainfall

Temperature

Min Max

Afternoon Humidity

J	F	M	A	M	J	J	A	S	O	N	D
76%	64%	54%	48%	51%	46%	40%	40%	44%	57%	72%	78%

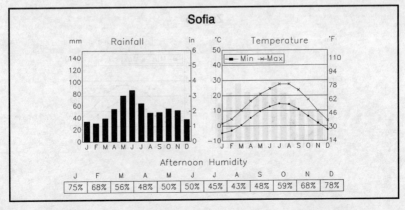

Sofia

Rainfall

Temperature

Min Max

Afternoon Humidity

J	F	M	A	M	J	J	A	S	O	N	D
75%	68%	56%	48%	50%	50%	45%	43%	48%	59%	68%	78%

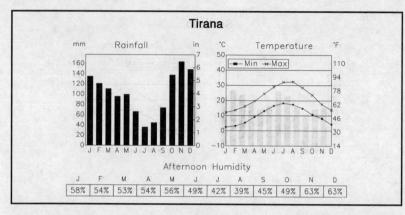

Tirana

J	F	M	A	M	J	J	A	S	O	N	D
58%	54%	53%	54%	56%	49%	42%	39%	45%	49%	63%	63%

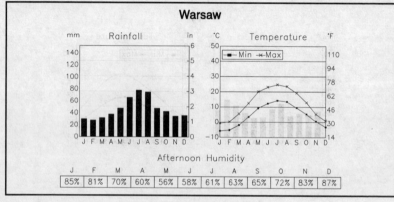

Warsaw

J	F	M	A	M	J	J	A	S	O	N	D
85%	81%	70%	60%	56%	58%	61%	63%	65%	72%	83%	87%

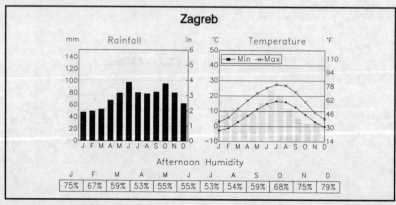

Zagreb

J	F	M	A	M	J	J	A	S	O	N	D
75%	67%	59%	53%	55%	55%	53%	54%	59%	68%	75%	79%

Index

TEXT

Map references are in **bold** type.

914

Thanks

Thanks to all these travellers who wrote in with their comments on the previous edition:

Joanne Abelson (USA), A'arif F Abdulkareem (Bahrain), Geert Acke (B), John M Arndorfer (USA), Mark Awbery (GB), Larry Bailey (USA), Sara Banaszak (USA), Justin Barr (AUS), Ludwig Bauer (A), Lena Berglöw (S), Gerald Berstell (USA), Ian Birbeck (GB), William Blatt (USA), Robert B Boardman (USA), Caroline Bock (D), Martin Bohnstedt (A), Alessandro Bonelli (I), Michael Brant (USA), Peter & Judith Brenchley (GB), Colleen Brewis (ZA), G Brown (GB), Timothy Bunge (AUS), Bruce Burger (USA) Neil Calow (GB), Anne Campbell (CDN), Bob Cariffe (USA), C William Carson (USA), Robert Carter (USA), Vic Carter (AUS), Clark Cartwright (GB), Marie-Christine Chalmers (CDN), Elaine Chang (USA), Ben Chaston (GB), Miles Clayton (GB), Fred Clements (NZ), Kevin Collins (USA), Steve Cook (USA), Simon Cookson (GB), J E Côté (CDN), Steve Coyle (USA), Leah Cutter (USA), Mark A Czerkawski (CDN), Charles Daniels (CDN), Claire Dannenbaum (USA), Deni Dante (AUS), Richard Davis (GB), Anne Deakin (GB), Gilbert Dingle (AUS), Martin Dinn (CDN), G Dixon (GB), Paul J Doran (AUS), Jennifer DuBois (A), Nick Duncan (CDN), Sue E Easton (GB), Alberta R Edwards (USA), Robert Egg (D), Derek Ellis (GB), Derek Emson (GB), Tony English (GB), Gerhard & Annet Eshuis (NL), Miklós Farkas (H), William W Farner (USA), Christopher Feierabend (USA), Wlodzimierz Fenrych (PL), Beverly J Ferrucci (USA), Wendy Fletcher (CDN), Lilian Forrest (GB), Richard Fox (GB), Shawn Fuller (USA), Polly Ghilchik (GB), Jan Giddings (USA), Stacy Gilbert (USA), Suzanne M Ginger (USA), David L Glatstein (USA), Jonathan Goldstein (USA), George Gose (USA), Kathi Goss (GB), Paul de Graaf (AUS), Betsy Green (USA), Eleanor Griffiths (GB), Sian Griffiths (GB), Todd Gunner (USA) Ron Haering (AUS), Yvonne Halloran (GB), P Hamilton (GB), Clare Hanna (GB), Steve Hanson (GB), Mary Hassell (AUS), Douglas Havens (USA), Paul Hemmings (GB), Richard Henke (USA), Peter Hide (GB), Julian Hopkins (B), Philip Howell (GB), Jessica Hyman (AUS), John Jackson (DK), Wanda Jastrzembski (USA), Peter R. Johnson (GB), Ian Jonas USA), Scott & Tina Jones (AUS), Gregers JoVrgensen (S), Maureen Kane (USA), Donald Kellough (CDN), Ann Kernodle (USA), Drew & Ruth Klee (USA), Fred R Kogen (USA), André Koppe (NL), Zachari Krystev (BG), Piotr & Jane Kumelowski (USA), Barbara Kurch (USA) Simon Lane (GB), Jan W A Lanzing (NL), Rhea & Gary Lazar (CDN), Marco de Leeuw (NL), Brian Lence (GB), A Leigh (GB), Keith A. Liker (USA), Eva Lihovay (H), Tom Lowe (GB), Hugh Macindoe (AUS), Gerald Marlow (NZ), Norm F Mathews (AUS), Dennis McConnell (USA), Barrie McCormick (GB), Patrick J McCormick (USA), Ross McGibbon (GB), Sara Meaker (USA), Federico Medici (I), Rachelle Meiner (USA), Peter Milne (CDN), Antonio Minevi (BG), Wendy Mitchell (GB), Brian Moore (GB), Geoffrey Morant (GB), Chris Morey (GB), Dr Alison J Mowbray (CDN), Judith L Nathanson (USA), Camilla Nes, Roger Newton (AUS), Beryl Nicholson (GB), Anne-Marie Nicoara (USA), Wanda Nieckarz (PL), John Nobles (GB), Lenart Nolle (D) Lily O'Connor (GB), Philip J Offer (GB), Mick Ogrizek (AUS), Milton Owen (USA), George Petros (AUS), D Phillips (GB), Jim Pitketry (CDN), Lubomir Popyordanov (BG), Chris Powers (USA), Dr Zdzisław Preisner (PL), Don Prince (USA), Johan Ragnerad (S), Soren Rasmussen (DK), Potashnik Raz (IL), William Redgrave (GB), Bill Reifsnider (USA), Cathy Reid (AUS), Neil Richardson (GB), Andreas Rogall (D), Caroline Rowlatt (AUS), Susan Rsala (GB), Sue Rutherford (USA), Brendan Ryan (AUS), Deborah Ryan (PL), Peter Rynders (NL) Gabriella Safran (AUS), Heather Santora (GB), Harijs J. Saukants (USA), E B Seemann (GB), Lee Sharrocks (GB), Caroline Silk (GB), Attila Sipos (H), Janneke Slager (NL), Anne Small (NZ), A Smith (AUS), Dominic Snivalsen (GB), Femi Sobo (GB), F Sporon-Fiedler (DK), Carl Stitjer (USA), Julia Stone (AUS), Matthew Sutcliffe (GB), Gerry Sutherland (GB), Krisztina Szendi-Horvath (H), Andrew Taylor (GB), Neil Taylor (GB), Mike Terrell (B), Dean Travers (AUS), Julle Tuuliainen (SF) Patricia Vazquez (E), Harold van Voornveld (NL), Alice Weekers (GB), Lucas van Wees (NL), George Von der Muhll (USA), Kazunati Wada (J), Alex Wade (GB), Henry Walls (IRL), Mark Walshe (GB), Tony Walter (CDN), Michael Weiner (A), Anne Westover (USA), Alison White (GB), Welby Whiting (USA), Larry Wiggins (GB), Darren Williams (GB), John Williams (GB), Tim Wilson (AUS), David Wookey (GB) and William L Wright (GB)

All it costs to have your name included here in the next edition is one postage stamp.

PLANET TALK
Lonely Planet's FREE quarterly newsletter

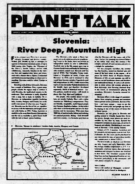

We love hearing from you and think you'd like to hear from us.

When...is the right time to see reindeer in Finland?
Where...can you hear the best palm-wine music in Ghana?
How...do you get from Asunción to Areguá by steam train?
What...is the best way to see India?

For the answer to these and many other questions read PLANET TALK.

Every issue is packed with up-to-date travel news and advice including:

- *a letter from Lonely Planet founders Tony and Maureen Wheeler*
- *travel diary from a Lonely Planet author - find out what it's really like out on the road*
- *feature article on an important and topical travel issue*
- *a selection of recent letters from our readers*
- *the latest travel news from all over the world*
- *details on Lonely Planet's new and forthcoming releases*

To join our mailing list contact any Lonely Planet office (address below).

LONELY PLANET PUBLICATIONS
Australia: PO Box 617, Hawthorn 3122, Victoria (tel: 03-9819 1877)
USA: Embarcadero West, 155 Filbert St, Suite 251, Oakland, CA 94607 (tel: 510-893 8555)
TOLL FREE: (800) 275-8555
UK: 10 Barley Mow Passage, Chiswick, London W4 4PH (tel: 0181-742 3161)
France: 71 bis rue du Cardinal Lemoine – 75005 Paris (tel: 1-46 34 00 58)

Also available: Lonely Planet T-shirts. 100% heavyweight cotton (S, M, L, XL)

Lonely Planet guides to Europe

Central Europe on a shoestring
From the snow-capped peaks of the Austrian Alps, the medieval castles of Hungary and the vast forests of Poland to the festivals of Germany, the arty scene in Prague and picturesque lakes of Switzerland, this guide is packed with practical travel advice to help you make the most of your visit. This new shoestring guide covers travel in Austria, Czech Republic, Germany, Hungary, Liechtenstein, Poland, Slovakia and Switzerland.

Mediterranean Europe on a shoestring
Details on hundreds of galleries, museums and architectural masterpieces and information on outdoor activities including hiking, sailing and skiing. Information on travelling in Albania, Andorra, Cyprus, France, Greece, Italy, Malta, Morocco, Portugal, Spain, Tunisia, Turkey and the former republics of Yugoslavia.

Scandinavian & Baltic Europe on a shoestring
A comprehensive guide to travelling in this region including details on galleries, festivals and museums, as well as outdoor activities, national parks and wildlife. Countries featured are Denmark, Estonia, the Faroe Islands, Finland, Iceland, Latvia, Lithuania, Norway and Sweden.

Western Europe on a shoestring
This long-awaited guide covers all of Western Europe's well-loved sights and provides routes for cycling and driving tours, plus details on hiking, climbing and skiing. All the travel facts on Andorra, Austria, Belgium, Britain, France, Germany, Greece, Ireland, Italy, Liechtenstein, Luxembourg, Netherlands, Portugal, Spain and Switzerland.

Baltic States & Kaliningrad – travel survival kit
The Baltic States burst on to the world scene almost from nowhere in the late 1980s. Now that travellers are free to move around the region they will discover nations with a rich and colourful history and culture, and a welcoming attitude to all travellers.

Britain – travel survival kit
Britain remains one of the most beautiful islands in the world. All the words, paintings and pictures that you have read and seen are not just romantic exaggerations. This comprehensive guide will help you to discover and enjoy this ever-popular destination.

Czech & Slovak Republics – travel survival kit
The Czech and Slovak Republics are two of the most exciting travel destinations in Europe. This guide is the essential resource for independent travellers. It's full of down-to-earth information and reliable advice for every budget – from five stars to five dollars a day.

Finland – travel survival kit
Finland is an intriguing blend of Swedish and Russian influences. With its medieval stone castles, picturesque wooden houses, vast forest and lake district, and interesting wildlife, it is a wonderland to delight any traveller.

France – travel survival kit
Stylish, diverse, celebrated by romantics and revolutionaries alike, France is a destination that's always in fashion. A comprehensive guide packed with invaluable advice.

Greece – travel survival kit
Famous ruins, secluded beaches, sumptuous food, sun-drenched islands, ancient pathways and much more are covered in this comprehensive guide to this ever-popular destination.

Hungary – travel survival kit
Formerly seen as the gateway to eastern Europe, Hungary is a romantic country of music, wine and folklore. This guide contains detailed background information on Hungary's cultural and historical past as well as practical advice on the many activities available to travellers.

Ireland – travel survival kit

Ireland is one of Europe's least 'spoilt' countries. Green, relaxed and welcoming, it does not take travellers long before they feel at ease. An entertaining and comprehensive guide to this troubled country.

Italy – travel survival kit

Italy is art – not just in the galleries and museums. You'll discover its charm on the streets and in the markets, in rustic hill-top villages and in the glamorous city boutiques. A thorough guide to the thousands of attractions of this ever-popular destination.

Poland – travel survival kit

With the collapse of communism, Poland has opened up to travellers, revealing a rich cultural heritage. This guide will help you make the most of this safe and friendly country.

Prague – city guide

Since the 'Velvet Revolution' in 1989, Prague and its residents have grasped their freedom with a youthful exuberance, even frenzy. This thoroughly comprehensive guide will show you the sights and hidden delights of this vivacious city.

Switzerland – travel survival kit

Ski enthusiasts and chocolate addicts know two excellent reasons for heading to Switzerland. This travel survival kit gives travellers many more: jazz, cafés, boating trips...and the Alps of course!

USSR – travel survival kit

Invaluable advice on getting around and beating red tape for individual and group travellers alike. This comprehensive guide includes an unsanitised historical background and complete information on art and culture. Over 130 reliable maps, and all place names are given in Cyrillic script. Includes the independent states.

Vienna – city guide

There's so much to see and do in Vienna and this guide is the best way to ensure you enjoy it all.

Trekking in Greece

Mountainous landscape, the solitude of ancient pathways and secluded beaches await those who dare to extend their horizons beyond Athens and the antiquities. Covers the main trekking regions and includes contoured maps of trekking routes.

Also available:
Central Europe phrasebook

Languages in this book cover travel in Austria, the Czech Republic, France, Germany, Hungary, Italy, Liechtenstein, Slovakia and Switzerland.

Eastern Europe phrasebook

Discover the most enjoyable way to get around and make friends in Bulgarian, Czech, Hungarian, Polish, Romanian and Slovak.

Mediterranean Europe phrasebook

Ask for directions to the galleries and museums in Albanian, Greek, Italian, Macedonian, Maltese, Serbian & Croatian and Slovene.

Scandinavian Europe phrasebook

Find your way around the ski trails and enjoy the local festivals in Danish, Finnish, Icelandic, Norwegian and Swedish.

Western Europe phrasebook

Show your appreciation for the great masters in Basque, Catalan, Dutch, French, German, Irish, Portuguese and Spanish (Castilian).

Russian phrasebook

This indispensable phrasebook will help you get information, read signs and menus, and make friends along the way. Includes phonetic transcriptions and Cyrillic script.

Lonely Planet Guidebooks

Lonely Planet guidebooks cover every accessible part of Asia as well as Australia, the Pacific, South America, Africa, the Middle East, Europe and parts of North America. There are five series: *travel survival kits*, covering a country for a range of budgets; *shoestring guides* with compact information for low-budget travel in a major region; *walking guides*; *city guides* and *phrasebooks*.

Australia & the Pacific
Australia
Australian phrasebook
Bushwalking in Australia
Islands of Australia's Great Barrier Reef
Outback Australia
Fiji
Fijian phrasebook
Melbourne city guide
Micronesia
New Caledonia
New South Wales
New Zealand
Tramping in New Zealand
Papua New Guinea
Bushwalking in Papua New Guinea
Papua New Guinea phrasebook
Rarotonga & the Cook Islands
Samoa
Solomon Islands
Sydney city guide
Tahiti & French Polynesia
Tonga
Vanuatu
Victoria
Western Australia

North-East Asia
Beijing city guide
China
Cantonese phrasebook
Mandarin Chinese phrasebook
Hong Kong, Macau & Canton
Japan
Japanese phrasebook
Korea
Korean phrasebook
Mongolia
North-East Asia on a shoestring
Seoul city guide
Taiwan
Tibet
Tibet phrasebook
Tokyo city guide

South-East Asia
Bali & Lombok
Bangkok city guide
Cambodia
Indonesia
Indonesian phrasebook
Jakarta city guide
Laos
Malaysia, Singapore & Brunei
Myanmar (Burma)
Burmese phrasebook
Philippines
Pilipino phrasebook
Singapore city guide
South-East Asia on a shoestring
Thailand
Thai phrasebook
Thai Hill Tribes phrasebook
Vietnam
Vietnamese phrasebook

Middle East
Arab Gulf States
Egypt & the Sudan
Arabic (Egyptian) phrasebook
Iran
Israel
Jordan & Syria
Middle East
Turkey
Turkish phrasebook
Trekking in Turkey
Yemen

Indian Ocean
Madagascar & Comoros
Maldives & Islands of the East Indian Ocean
Mauritius, Réunion & Seychelles

Mail Order

Lonely Planet guidebooks are distributed worldwide. They are also available by mail order from Lonely Planet, so if you have difficulty finding a title please write to us. US and Canadian residents should write to Embarcadero West, 155 Filbert St, Suite 251, Oakland CA 94607, USA; European residents should write to 10 Barley Mow Passage, Chiswick, London W4 4PH; and residents of other countries to PO Box 617, Hawthorn, Victoria 3122, Australia.

The Lonely Planet Story

Lonely Planet published its first book in 1973 in response to the numerous 'How did you do it?' questions Maureen and Tony Wheeler were asked after driving, bussing, hitching, sailing and railing their way from England to Australia.

Written at a kitchen table and hand collated, trimmed and stapled, *Across Asia on the Cheap* became an instant local bestseller, inspiring thoughts of another book.

Eighteen months in South-East Asia resulted in their second guide, *South-East Asia on a shoestring*, which they put together in a backstreet Chinese hotel in Singapore in 1975. The 'yellow bible' as it quickly became known to backpackers around the world, soon became *the* guide to the region. It has sold well over half a million copies and is now in its 8th edition, still retaining its familiar yellow cover.

Today there are over 140 Lonely Planet titles in print – books that have that same adventurous approach to travel as those early guides; books that 'assume you know how to get your luggage off the carousel' as one reviewer put it.

Although Lonely Planet initially specialised in guides to Asia, they now cover most regions of the world, including the Pacific, South America, Africa, the Middle East and Europe. The list of *walking guides* and *phrasebooks* (for 'unusual' languages such as Quechua, Swahili, Nepali and Egyptian Arabic) is also growing rapidly.

The emphasis continues to be on travel for independent travellers. Tony and Maureen still travel for several months of each year and play an active part in the writing, updating and quality control of Lonely Planet's guides.

They have been joined by over 50 authors, 110 staff – mainly editors, cartographers & designers – at our office in Melbourne, Australia, at our US office in Oakland, California and at our European office in Paris; another five at our office in London handle sales for Britain, Europe and Africa. Travellers themselves also make a valuable contribution to the guides through the feedback we receive in thousands of letters each year.

The people at Lonely Planet strongly believe that travellers can make a positive contribution to the countries they visit, both through their appreciation of the countries' culture, wildlife and natural features, and through the money they spend. In addition, the company makes a direct contribution to the countries and regions it covers. Since 1986 a percentage of the income from each book has been donated to ventures such as famine relief in Africa; aid projects in India; agricultural projects in Central America; Greenpeace's efforts to halt French nuclear testing in the Pacific; and Amnesty International.

Lonely Planet's basic travel philosophy is summed up in Tony Wheeler's comment, 'Don't worry about whether your trip will work out. Just go!'